DEDICATION

To my wife, Therese J. Libby, and my children, Julie, Andrew, Eric, and Rachel, my grandchildren, Jack, Kayla, and Brooke, and my sons-in-law Jason Macy and Patrick Stephens.
    —L.J.S.

To my wife, Jennifer, and our son, Ryan
    —B.C.W.

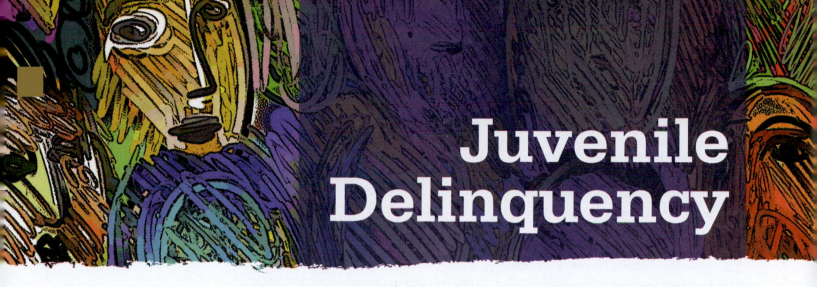

Juvenile Delinquency

THEORY, PRACTICE, AND LAW

THIRTEENTH EDITION

LARRY J. SIEGEL
University of Massachusetts, Lowell

BRANDON C. WELSH
Northeastern University

CENGAGE
Learning·

Australia • Brazil • Mexico • Singapore • United Kingdom • United States

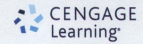

Juvenile Delinquency: Theory, Practice, and Law, Thirteenth Edition

Larry J. Siegel and Brandon C. Welsh

Senior Product Director: Marta Lee-Perriard

Senior Product Manager:
Carolyn Henderson Meier

Senior Content Developer: Shelley Murphy

Senior Marketing Manager: Mark Linton

Senior Content Project Manager:
Christy Frame

Senior Art Director: Helen Bruno

Senior Manufacturing Planner: Judy Inouye

Production Service and Compositor:
Lori Hazzard, MPS Limited

Photo Development Editor: Kim Adams Fox

Photo Researcher: Thirupathiraja Inbaraj,
Lumina Datamatics, Inc.

Text Researcher: Rashmi Manoharan,
Lumina Datamatics, Inc.

Copy Editor: Lunaea Weatherstone

Text Designer: Debbie Dutton

Cover Designer: Irene Morris Design

Cover Image: Diana Ong/Getty Images

For product information and technology assistance, contact us at
Cengage Customer & Sales Support, 1-800-354-9706

For permission to use material from this text or product,
submit all requests online at **www.cengage.com/permissions**
Further permissions questions can be e-mailed to
permissionrequest@cengage.com

Library of Congress Control Number: 2016955270

Student Edition:
ISBN: 978-1-337-09183-1

Loose-leaf Edition:
ISBN: 978-1-337-09247-0

Cengage
20 Channel Center Street
Boston, MA 02210
USA

Cengage is a leading provider of customized learning solutions with employees residing in nearly 40 different countries and sales in more than 125 countries around the world. Find your local representative at **www.cengage.com**

Cengage products are represented in Canada by Nelson Education, Ltd.

To learn more about Cengage Solutions, visit **www.cengage.com**

Purchase any of our products at your local college store or at our preferred online store **www.cengagebrain.com**

Printed in the United States of America
Print Number: 01   Print Year: 2017

About the Authors

Larry J. Siegel

Larry J. Siegel was born in the Bronx, New York. While living on Jerome Avenue and attending City College of New York in the 1960s, he was swept up in the social and political currents of the time. He became intrigued with the influence contemporary culture had on individual behavior. Did people shape society or did society shape people? He applied his interest in social forces and human behavior to the study of crime and justice. After graduating from CCNY, he attended the newly opened program in criminal justice at the State University of New York at Albany, earning both his MA and PhD degrees there. After completing his graduate work, Dr. Siegel spent nine years at Northeastern University and also held teaching positions at the University of Nebraska–Omaha and Saint Anselm College in New Hampshire before joining the faculty at the University of Massachusetts–Lowell, where he now serves as Professor Emeritus. Dr. Siegel has written extensively in the area of crime and justice, including books on juvenile law, delinquency, criminology, criminal justice, and criminal procedure. He teaches courses in criminal justice, criminology, and delinquency at both the undergrad and grad level. He is a court-certified expert on police conduct and has testified in numerous legal cases. The parents of four and grandparents of three, Larry and his wife, Terry, reside in Naples, Florida.

Larry J. Siegel

Brandon C. Welsh

Brandon C. Welsh is a Professor of Criminology at Northeastern University and Senior Research Fellow at the Netherlands Institute for the Study of Crime and Law Enforcement in Amsterdam. He received his undergraduate and MA degrees at the University of Ottawa and his PhD from Cambridge University in England. His research interests focus on the prevention of crime and delinquency and evidence-based crime policy. Dr. Welsh has published extensively in these areas and is an author or editor of 10 books.

Brandon C. Welsh

Brief Contents

Contents

part two
Theories of Delinquency   77

part three
Social, Community, and Environmental Influences on Delinquency 251

Preface

"I'm not a monster," claims teenager Ashlee Martinson, now in prison for shooting her stepfather, Thomas Ayers, 37, and fatally stabbing her mother, Jennifer Ayers, 40, more than 30 times.[1] For her crimes, Martinson pleaded guilty to second-degree homicide and received a sentence of 23 years in prison. Does she regret her decision to kill? "I'm happy," she has told people. "I know that sounds crazy, because I'm in prison, but I feel like I'm free. I can wake up every day and know that I am safe. I was just a girl, an abused girl, who was forced to make a really bad decision. I'm not the monster that they portrayed me to be."

She claims that after years of alleged abuse, she suffered from severe depression and post-traumatic stress disorder. Poetry on her webpage shows a darker side:

I clean the dry blood off my tools from a previous session.

The last body has been disposed of just hours before, yet I have not been satisfied with the pain, agony and blood.

I bend down as they start to wake.

"Welcome to hell." I whisper in her ear. "Never again will you see the light of day."

What sparked the killing? On March 7, 2015, a day after her 17th birthday, Martinson got into an argument with her parents, who had discovered that the teenager had a 22-year-old boyfriend and sent him a Facebook message telling him to stay away from their daughter, threatening to press charges. Martinson snapped, grabbing a shotgun and killing her stepfather before stabbing her mother. She later claimed that her mother's boyfriends had been abusing her since she was a young child and one of them raped her when she was 9 years old. Although Thomas Ayers did not hurt her physically, he would abuse her mother and sisters to punish her. Court documents support her story: Thomas Ayers had been accused of assault, kidnapping, child enticement, and being party to the crime of sexual assault of a child younger than 15; he had numerous prior arrests and convictions.

Ashlee Martinson is not alone nor unique. It has become routine to see cases of teens engaging in violent crimes at school, on the street, and at home. What should be done with these violent young offenders? Should they be given special treatment because of their age? Should someone like Ashlee be sent to an adult prison or can she be treated in the community? Can even the most violent juveniles be successfully treated and rehabilitated? Or should they be tried as adults and given long prison sentences, even if it means life behind bars?

---

[1] Lindsey Bever, "I'm Not a Monster': A Teen Horror Blogger Explains Why She Killed Her Parents," *Washington Post*, November 2, 2016, https://www.washingtonpost.com/news/true-crime/wp/2016/11/02/im-not-a-monster-a-teen-horror-blogger-explains-why-she-killed-her-parents/; Adam Carlson, "Teen Horror Blogger Ashlee Martinson Sentenced to 23 Years in Prison in Slayings of Mother and Stepfather," *People*, June, 11, 2016, http://people.com/crime/ashlee-martinson-sentenced-to-23-years-for-killing-mother-and-stepfather/.

JUVENILE DELINQUENCY: Theory, Practice, and Law

Issues such as youth violence have sparked interest in the study of juvenile delinquency not only in the United States but also around the world. Inexplicable incidents of violence occur all too frequently in schools, homes, and public places. Teen gangs can be found in most major cities. Hundreds of thousands of youths are known to be the victims of serious neglect and sexual and physical abuse each year; many more cases may be unreported or hidden. It is not surprising, considering the concern with the problems of youth, that courses on juvenile delinquency have become popular offerings on the nation's college campuses. We have written *Juvenile Delinquency: Theory, Practice, and Law* to help students understand the nature of juvenile delinquency, its cause and correlates, as well as the current strategies being used to control or eliminate its occurrence. Our book also reviews the legal rules that have been set down either to protect innocent minors or control adolescent misconduct: Can children be required to submit to drug testing in school? Can teachers legally search suspicious students or use corporal punishment as a method of discipline? Should children be allowed to testify on closed-circuit TV in child abuse cases?

Our primary goals in writing this 13th edition remain the same as in the previous editions:

1. To be as objective as possible, presenting the many diverse views and perspectives that characterize the study of juvenile delinquency and reflect its interdisciplinary nature. We take no single position nor espouse a particular viewpoint or philosophy.

2. To maintain a balance of research, theory, law, policy, and practice. It is essential that a textbook on delinquency not be solely a theory book without presenting the juvenile justice system or contain sections on current policies without examining legal issues and cases.

3. To be as thorough and up-to-date as possible. As always, we have attempted to include the most current data and information available.

4. To make the study of delinquency interesting as well as informative. We want to encourage readers' interest in the study of delinquency so they will pursue it on an undergraduate or graduate level.

We have tried to provide a textbook that is both scholarly and informative, comprehensive yet interesting, well organized and objective yet provocative.

Organization of the Text

The 13th edition of *Juvenile Delinquency: Theory, Practice, and Law* has 17 chapters:

- Chapter 1, Childhood and Delinquency, contains extensive material on the history of childhood and the legal concept of delinquency and status offending. This material enables the reader to understand how the concept of adolescence evolved over time and how that evolution influenced the development of the juvenile court and the special status of delinquency.

- Chapter 2, The Nature and Extent of Delinquency, covers the measurement of delinquent behavior, trends, and patterns in teen crime and victimization, and also discusses the correlates of delinquency, including race, gender, class, and age, and chronic offending.

- Chapter 3, Individual Views of Delinquency, covers individual-level views of the cause of delinquency, which include choice, biological, and psychological theories.

- Chapter 4, Structure, Process, Culture, and Delinquency, looks at theories that hold that culture and socialization control delinquent behavior.

- Chapter 5, Social Reaction, Social Conflict, and Delinquency, reviews theories that state that delinquency is a product of human interaction as well as the economic and political forces that control the way people interact.

- Chapter 6, Developmental Theories of Delinquency: Life-Course, Propensity, and Trajectory, covers developmental theories of delinquency, including such issues as the onset, continuity, paths, and termination of a delinquent career.

- Chapter 7, Gender and Delinquency, explores the sex-based differences that are thought to account for the gender patterns in the delinquency rate.

- Chapter 8, The Family and Delinquency, covers the influence of families on children and delinquency. The concept of child abuse is covered in detail, and the steps in the child protection system are reviewed.

- Chapter 9, Peers and Delinquency: Juvenile Gangs and Groups, reviews the effect peers have on delinquency and the topic of teen gangs.

- Chapter 10, Schools and Delinquency, looks at the influence of schools and the education process, delinquency within the school setting, and the efforts by schools to prevent delinquency.

- Chapter 11, Drug Use and Delinquency, reviews the influence drugs and substance abuse have on delinquent behavior and what is being done to reduce teenage drug use.

- Chapter 12, Delinquency Prevention: Social and Developmental Perspectives, covers delinquency prevention and efforts being made to help kids avoid a life of crime.

- Chapter 13, Juvenile Justice: Then and Now, gives extensive coverage to the emergence of state control over children in need and the development of the juvenile justice system. It also covers the contemporary juvenile justice system, the major stages in the justice process, the role of the federal government in the juvenile justice system, an analysis of the differences between the adult and juvenile justice systems, and extensive coverage of the legal rights of children.

- Chapter 14, Police Work with Juveniles, discusses the role of police in delinquency prevention. It covers legal issues such as major court decisions on searches and *Miranda* rights of juveniles. It also contains material on how race and gender affect police discretion as well as efforts by police departments to control delinquent behavior.

- Chapter 15, Juvenile Court Process: Pretrial, Trial, and Sentencing, contains information on plea bargaining in juvenile court, the use of detention, and transfer to adult jails. It contains an analysis of the critical factors that influence the waiver decision, the juvenile trial, and sentencing.

- Chapter 16, Juvenile Corrections: Probation, Community Treatment, and Institutionalization, covers material on probation and other community dispositions, including restorative justice programs and secure juvenile corrections, with emphasis on legal issues such as right to treatment and unusual programs such as boot camps.

- Chapter 17, Delinquency and Juvenile Justice Abroad, looks at delinquency around the world and examines efforts to control antisocial youth in other nations.

What's New in This Edition

Since the study of juvenile delinquency is a dynamic, ever-changing field of scientific inquiry and because the theories, concepts, and processes of this area of study are constantly evolving, we have updated *Juvenile Delinquency: Theory, Practice, and Law* to reflect the changes that have taken place in the study of delinquent behavior during the past few years.

Like its predecessors, the 13th edition includes a review of recent legal cases, research studies, and policy initiatives. It aims to provide a groundwork for the study of juvenile delinquency by analyzing and describing the nature and extent of delinquency, the suspected causes of delinquent behavior, and the environmental influences on youthful misbehavior. It also covers what most experts believe are the critical issues in juvenile delinquency and analyzes crucial policy issues, including the use of pretrial detention, waiver to adult court, and restorative justice programs. While these principles remain the backbone of the text, we have also incorporated into the 13th edition the following:

- **Chapter 1** opens with an update on the Keaira Brown case, a girl who was just 13 years old when she was found guilty of first-degree murder and attempted aggravated robbery. There are new data on teen problems such as health care, diet, and suicide rates are presented. A new Cyber Delinquency feature looks at "sextortion," sexual extortion on the Net. There is a new Evidence-Based Juvenile Justice feature that looks at the Family Key programs, designed to provide highly effective case management services that prevent at-risk youth from repeat violations that could result in juvenile probation or detention.

- **Chapter 2** begins with a vignette on the prosecution of two violent street gangs—2Fly and BMB—that wreaked havoc on the streets of the Northern Bronx for years by committing countless acts of violence against rival gang members and citizens. A new Focus on Delinquency, "Co-offending and Delinquency," examines whether delinquency tends to be a group activity and whether many adolescents join gangs and groups in order to facilitate their illegal activities. A Youth Stories feature, "*Room*: Kids Held Captive," looks at cases that inspired the 2015 film *Room* for which Brie Larson won an Oscar. The data on juvenile offending patterns and victim patterns have been updated.

- **Chapter 3** begins with an update on the story of Adam Lanza, a boy with sensory processing disorder (SPD), which made him over-respond to stimuli, who later committed the Sandy Hook Elementary School massacre. There is new research by Bruce Jacobs and Michael Cherbonneau on car theft that shows how teen offenders must figure out a way to make their behavior seem normal to observers, to hide their intentions from prying eyes, and to neutralize the desire of car owners to take action to protect their property. Other new works cover such topics as the safety of gated communities and whether the installation of closed-circuit television (CCTV) surveillance cameras and improved street lighting, techniques can deter would-be delinquents. There is a new section on "pulling levers policing" or focused deterrence, which is about activating or pulling every deterrent "lever" available to reduce the targeted problem. Research on juvenile burglars finds that they like to target residences close to where they live so they know the territory and have access to escape routes.

- **Chapter 4** begins with the tale of what happened when three teenagers from Seattle's Down with the Crew gang—a violent affiliate of the Black Gangster Disciples gang—broke into the home of a 66-year-old man with the intention of committing an easy robbery. We update the data on economic disadvantage that show that many millions of Americans still live below the poverty line: there are now about 43 million Americans living in poverty, defined as a family of four earning about $24,000 per year. There are new data on race-based social and economic disparity. New research shows that more cohesive communities, where residents have a stake in the community and know and trust one another, have much lower delinquency rates than less less-unified areas.

  A Youth Stories feature looks at Ethan Couch, a 16-year-old Texas boy who killed four people while driving drunk and then claimed he suffers from affluenza—being too rich and spoiled to understand the consequences of his actions. A new section, "Variations on Neutralization Theory," shows how the theory has evolved since it was first formulated. An Evidence-Based Juvenile Justice feature looks at Families and Schools Together (FAST), a multifamily group intervention program designed to build protective factors for children, empower parents to be the primary prevention agents for their own children, and build supportive parent-to-parent groups.

- **Chapter 5** now begins with a vignette about 14-year-old Ahmed Mohamed, who made national headlines when he brought a disassembled clock to school, an act that caused his teachers to worry about a terrorist device and the principal to call the police. There is a Youth Stories feature entitled "Was It Rape?" which analyzes the sexual assault at prestigious St. Paul's prep school in New Hampshire. A new Focus on Delinquency box entitled "The Consequences of Labeling" reviews the 2016 report by the Centers for Disease Control and Prevention on the risks faced by approximately 1.3 million lesbian, gay, and bisexual (LGB) high school students in the United States. A Cyber Delinquency feature, "Recruiting Young Terrorists," discusses how the Net is being used to convince American teens to join ISIS and other radical groups. An Evidence-Based Juvenile Justice box looks at Family Group Conferencing in New Zealand.

- **Chapter 6** begins with a vignette about 35-year-old Rebecca Falcon, who is serving a life sentence for a crime she committed when she was a 15-year-old girl. In 2015, the Florida Supreme Court ruled that Falcon and other juvenile criminals should be eligible for parole. A Focus on Delinquency box covers research on the important topic of persistence versus desistance. There is material on social schematic theory (SST) that suggests that people develop schemas or cognitive shortcuts to organize and interpret information.

- **Chapter 7** has an opening vignette on 12-year-old Morgan Geyser and Anissa Weier who lured a friend into the woods and stabbed her, in what is now known as the "Slender Man" case. The Focus on Delinquency covering the trafficking in children has been updated. An Evidence-Based Juvenile Justice box looks at the Practical Academic Cultural Educational (PACE) Center, whose mission is to provide girls and young women an opportunity for a better future through education, counseling, training, and advocacy.

  Another Evidence-Based Juvenile Justice feature describes the Keep Safe program, a multicomponent intervention program aimed at building prosocial skills and promoting placement stability for girls in foster care who are transitioning from elementary school to middle school. A new Focus on Delinquency box looks at abused girls in the juvenile justice system. Data on gender differences in official and self-report delinquency have been updated and new research on gender differences on personality and cognition provided.

- **Chapter 8** starts with the story of two teenage brothers, Robert and Michael Bever, who planned and executed the murder of five members of their family. A Youth Stories feature on the Nevil family murders covers the trial of a teenager who was just 13 when he shot and killed his 12-year-old girlfriend's parents. A Focus on Delinquency box looks at the concept of trauma; traumatic experiences have been linked to a wide range of problems, including addiction, depression, anxiety, and risk-taking behavior. Data on the nature and extent of child abuse and neglect have been updated.

- **Chapter 9** has a new chapter opening vignette about the case of Michael, an 18-year-old gang member who was referred to a gang intervention service when he was 15 years old. There is a new section on deviancy training, in which close friends reinforce deviant behavior through talk and interaction. A new exhibit entitled "Words or Deeds?" looks at research showing how peer pressure works. Data on gangs have been updated, including new information on migration trends. A new section on gang cooperation shows that collaboration among street gangs has increased; gangs have merged or formed hybrid gangs to counter enforcement control efforts. The most recent gang surveys are reviewed; data now show that street gang activity continues to be oriented toward violent crimes, such as assault, street level and large scale drug trafficking, home invasions, homicide, robbery, intimidation, threats, weapons trafficking, and sex trafficking. A Youth Stories feature entitled "Lisa's Story" looks at the life of a young girl in Los Angeles who by the time she was 13 was heavily into drugs and "hitting up and shooting up" with a local gang. We show how a growing number of law enforcement agencies are incorporating social media into their gang investigations, specifically to identify gang members and monitor their criminal activity via the Net. An Evidence-Based Juvenile Justice feature covers the Newport News STEP Program. This 10-week program serves young people between the ages of 16 and 24 and provides paid work training experience, enrichment activities, workshops, financial literacy training, and GED preparation classes.

■ **Chapter 10** begins with an important 2016 case in which a federal appeals court ruled that Gavin Grimm, a transgender high school student who was born as a female, can sue his school board on discrimination grounds because it barred him from using the boys' bathroom. There are data from the most recent international student testing that shows the United States ranked 27th out of 62 nations tested in mathematics. Data collected by the National Center for Education Statistics show few if any improvements in educational achievement. A Focus on Delinquency box, "Race and School Discipline," looks at whether minority youth are subject to harsh disciplinary practices in public school and what effect this has on their academic achievement. We now cover the detracking movement that has helped alleviate some of the tracking system's most significant problems. The latest data from the National Center for Educational Statistics cover school crime, showing that were about 850,100 nonfatal victimizations at school in the past year. We also include a new study by the Centers for Disease Control and Prevention (CDC) on school shootings. A Cyber Delinquency feaure, "Free Speech in Cyberspace," looks at whether schools can control personal websites, Twitter messages, texts, and emails that are quickly spread among the student body, or YouTube postings that show secretly made recordings of teachers in unflattering poses.

■ **Chapter 11** opens with the death of a Florida teen, Helen Marie Witty, caused by another teen who was driving while under the influence of alcohol and other drugs. As part of her sentence, the driver is required to speak to high school students about the dangers of drinking and driving. The chapter updates recent trends and patterns in juvenile drug use with data based on three national surveys, including the large-scale Monitoring the Future (MTF) survey. The chapter covers the latest research on the effects of medical marijuana laws on juvenile drug use. It updates research on the major explanations for why youths take drugs, including peer pressure and rational choice, and updates research on why juveniles sell drugs. We also added new material reviewing the most up-to-date research on what works to reduce juvenile drug use, including an Evidence-Based Juvenile Justice feature on multisystemic therapy.

■ **Chapter 12** opens with a milestone program by the British government to provide home visitation services to new young mothers and their babies, modeled after the Nurse-Family Partnership program in the United States. A Focus on Delinquency feature has been updated with new material on public support for delinquency prevention programs. The chapter also substantially updates material on what works in delinquency prevention, with new evaluations and reviews on the effectiveness of programs that take place in early childhood and the teenage years. One example is afterschool programs. Some new studies have been added on the financial costs of delinquency, as the high costs of juvenile crime are sometimes used to justify more spending on prevention programs. An Evidence-Based Juvenile Justice feature has been updated to present the latest research findings on the Blueprints for Healthy Youth Development initiative.

- **Chapter 13** opens with the case of Florida teen Michael Hernandez, who took the life of his classmate Jaime Gough and was sentenced to life in prison without the possibility of parole. Owing in part to a recent Supreme Court ruling that life sentences cannot be imposed automatically, Hernandez will be eligible for a "judicial review" for parole eligibility after serving 25 years. We profile the latest information on the oldest age for juvenile court jurisdiction in delinquency cases. The chapter updates the section on a comprehensive juvenile justice strategy, which combines elements of delinquency prevention and intervention and justice approaches. For the Evidence-Based Juvenile Justice feature, the latest research findings on teen courts are presented, and we highlight the new Department of Justice findings on juvenile drug courts.

- **Chapter 14** begins with a story about the intersection of inner-city gang violence, a gunshot injury to 7-year-old Tajahnique Lee, and the growing concern of the police about witness intimidation. The chapter presents new research on juveniles' attitudes toward police and updates statistics on the handling of juvenile offenders by police, which show that 6 in 10 juveniles (62 percent) who are arrested are referred to juvenile court. The chapter includes new research on training police in procedural justice and reviews the latest developments following the shooting of Michael Brown in Ferguson, Missouri, including the President's Task Force on 21st Century Policing. It also brings together the latest findings on what works when it comes to police efforts to prevent juvenile crime, including an updated Evidence-Based Juvenile Justice feature on "pulling levers" policing and the national evaluation of the G.R.E.A.T. program.

- **Chapter 15** opens with a violent case involving a group of teens who beat to death a homeless man, drawing attention to the debate on transfers of juveniles to adult court. The chapter includes up-to-date statistics on juvenile court case flow, from the decision to release or detain, to waivers to adult court, to juvenile court dispositions, and presents new research on plea bargaining. In the Evidence-Based Juvenile Justice feature, updated information is provided on the effectiveness of transfers to adult court. The chapter also includes the latest Supreme Court rulings on life without parole for juvenile offenders.

- **Chapter 16** begins with long-standing concerns about the safety of juvenile offenders and their need for treatment while in correctional facilities, profiling the case of Joseph Daniel Maldonado in California. The chapter reports on the latest trends in juvenile probation and incarceration, showing that juvenile incarceration rates are at an all-time low. It examines new research on restorative justice and economic sanctions for juvenile offenders. It also revisits the gender gap in correctional treatment for juvenile offenders and reports on the latest findings of the Juvenile Residential Facility Census. The latest research findings on what works in treating juvenile offenders are reviewed, and material on juvenile aftercare and reentry services is updated.

- **Chapter 17** begins with some of the growing crime problems facing China, a product of social and economic shifts that are also impacting other countries. The chapter presents new material on delinquency and juvenile justice systems around the world. It updates international statistics on juvenile violent and property crime, and reports on the latest European School Survey Project on Alcohol and other Drugs. The Focus on Delinquency feature provides an updated profile of juvenile violence in Japan, showing that violence is on the decline after years of substantial increases.

Learning Tools

To access additional course materials, including CourseMate, please visit www.cengagebrain.com. At the CengageBrain.com home page, search for the ISBN of your title (from the back cover of your book) using the search box at the top of the page. This will take you to the product page where these resources can be found.

The text contains the following features designed to help students learn and comprehend the material:

- **Chapter Outline and Learning Objectives** Each chapter begins with an outline and a list of chapter objectives. The summary is keyed to and corresponds with the learning objectives.

- **Concept Summary** This feature is used throughout the text to help students review material in an organized fashion.

- **Professional Spotlights** These boxed features provide students with a look at what professional career opportunities are available in the area of delinquency treatment, prevention, and intervention. For example, Chapter 13 spotlights juvenile probation officer Carla Stalnaker.

- **Cyber Delinquency** This feature highlights contemporary problems faced by today's youth: delinquency and victimization in the cyber age. Chapter 14, for example, discusses policing juveniles in cyberspace.

- **Focus on Delinquency** As in previous editions, these boxed inserts focus attention on topics of special importance and concern. For example, in Chapter 16, "Mental Health Needs of Juvenile Inmates" discusses that as many as two out of three incarcerated juveniles suffer from mental health problems, but many states are cutting back on funding for mental health programs.

- **Case Profile** This feature discusses real-life situations in which at-risk youths worked their way out of delinquency. These stories are then tied to the material in the chapter with thought-provoking critical thinking boxes.

- **Youth Stories** This interesting feature focuses on current cases and incidents that have made the news and illustrate the trials and tribulations of youths in contemporary society.

- **Evidence-Based Juvenile Justice** These thought-provoking boxes discuss major initiatives and programs. For example, in Chapter 17, "Precourt Diversion Programs Around the World" tells how keeping youths who have become involved in minor delinquent acts from being formally processed through the juvenile justice system has become a top priority of many countries.

- **Weblinks** In the margins of every chapter are links to websites that can be used to help students enrich their understanding of important issues and concepts found in the text.

- **Viewpoint and Doing Research on the Web** Each chapter ends with a feature called Viewpoint that presents a hypothetical case for the student to analyze. The Doing Research on the Web feature presents material found in articles on the Web to lead students to research ideas contained in the chapter.

- **Key Terms** Key terms are defined throughout the text when they appear in a chapter.

- **Questions for Discussion** Each chapter includes thought-provoking discussion questions.

- **Running Glossary** A glossary sets out and defines key terms used in the text. The definitions appear in the text margin where the concept is introduced, as well as in the comprehensive glossary at the end of the book.

Ancillary Materials

MindTap® for Criminal Justice The most applied learning experience available, MindTap is dedicated to preparing students to make the kinds of reasoned decisions they will have to as criminal justice professionals faced with real-world challenges. Available for virtually every criminal justice course, MindTap offers customizable content, course analytics, an e-reader, and more—all within your current learning management system. With its rich array of assets—video cases, interactive visual summaries, decision-making scenarios, quizzes, and writing skill builders—MindTap is perfectly suited to today's criminal justice students, engaging them, guiding them toward mastery of basic concepts, and advancing their critical thinking abilities.

Instructor's Manual with Lesson Plans The manual includes learning objectives, key terms, a detailed chapter outline, a chapter summary, lesson plans, discussion topics, student activities, "What If" scenarios, media tools, and sample syllabi. The learning objectives are correlated with the discussion topics, student activities, and media tools.

Downloadable Word Test Bank The enhanced test bank includes a variety of questions per chapter—a combination of multiple-choice, true/false, completion, essay, and critical thinking formats, with a full answer key. The test bank is coded to the learning objectives that appear in the main text, and identifies where in the text (by section) the answer appears. Finally, each question in the test bank has been carefully reviewed by experienced criminal justice instructors for quality, accuracy, and content coverage so instructors can be sure they are working with an assessment and grading resource of the highest caliber.

Cengage Learning Testing Powered by Cognero, the accompanying assessment tool is a flexible, online system that allows you to:

- Import, edit, and manipulate test bank content from the text's test bank or elsewhere, including your own favorite test questions
- Create ideal assessments with your choice of 15 question types (including true/false, multiple choice, opinion scale/likert, and essay)
- Create multiple test versions in an instant using drop-down menus and familiar, intuitive tools that take you through content creation and management with ease
- Deliver tests from your LMS, your classroom, or wherever you want—plus, import and export content into other systems as needed

Online PowerPoint Lectures Helping you make your lectures more engaging while effectively reaching your visually oriented students, these handy Microsoft PowerPoint® slides outline the chapters of the main text in a classroom-ready presentation. The PowerPoint® slides reflect the content and organization of the new edition of the text and feature some additional examples and real-world cases for application and discussion.

Acknowledgments

We would like to give special thanks to our terrific and supportive senior project manager, Carolyn Henderson Meier, and our superb senior content developer, Shelley Murphy. This text would not have been possible to complete without their help and TLC. We love working with the incomparable senior content project manager Christy Frame, and production editor Lori Hazzard as always produced a marvelous book. Copy editor supreme Lunaea Weatherstone did a thorough job, and it is always a pleasure to work with her. Mark Linton, marketing manager, is another fabulous member of the Cengage team. Kim Adams Fox deserves a lot of praise for her photo choices.

The preparation of this text would not have been possible without the aid of our colleagues who helped by reviewing the previous editions and giving us important suggestions for improvement. Reviewers for the 12th edition were:

Amy Pinero, Baton Rouge Community College

Lisa Nored, University of Southern Mississippi

Lynn Tankersley, Mercer University

Scott Belshaw, University of North Texas

Many thanks to all.

Larry Siegel
Brandon Welsh

part one

The Concept of Delinquency

the field of juvenile delinquency has been an important area of study since the turn of the twentieth century. Academicians, practitioners, policy makers, and legal scholars have devoted their attention to basic questions about the nature of youth crime: How should the concept of juvenile delinquency be defined? Who commits delinquent acts? How much delinquency occurs each year? Is the rate of delinquent activity increasing or decreasing? What can we do to prevent delinquency?

Part One reviews these basic questions in detail. Chapter 1 discusses the current state of American youth and the challenges they face. It covers the origins of society's concern for children and the development of the concept of delinquency. It shows how the definition of delinquency was developed and how the legal definition has evolved. While society has chosen to treat adult and juvenile law violators separately, it has also expanded the definition of youthful misbehaviors eligible for social control; these are referred to as *status offenses*. Status offenses include such behaviors as truancy, running away, and incorrigibility. Critics suggest that juveniles' noncriminal behavior is probably not a proper area of concern for law enforcement agencies and that these cases are better handled by social service organizations.

Chapter 2 examines the nature and extent of delinquent behavior. It covers how social scientists gather information on juvenile delinquency and provides an overview of some major trends in juvenile crime. Chapter 2 also contains information on some of the critical factors related to delinquency, such as race, gender, class, and age. It discusses the concept of the chronic delinquent, those who continually commit delinquent acts in their youth and continue to offend as adults.

CHAPTER 1
Childhood and Delinquency

Learning Objectives

1. Discuss the problems of youth in American culture
2. Distinguish between ego identity and role diffusion
3. Discuss the specific issues facing American youth
4. Examine the recent social improvements enjoyed by American youth
5. Discuss why the study of delinquency is so important and what this study entails
6. Describe the life of children during feudal times
7. Articulate the treatment of children in the seventeenth and eighteenth centuries
8. Discuss childhood in the American colonies
9. Evaluate the child savers and the creation of delinquency
10. Identify the elements of juvenile delinquency today
11. Define what is meant by the term *status offender*

Chapter Outline

The Adolescent Dilemma
Adolescent Problems
Problems in Cyberspace
Teen Suicide
Are Things Improving?

The Study of Juvenile Delinquency

The Development of Childhood
Childhood in the Middle Ages
Development of Concern for Children
Childhood in America

The Concept of Delinquency
Delinquency and *Parens Patriae*
The Legal Status of Delinquency
Legal Responsibility of Youth

Status Offenders
How Common Is Status Offending?
The History of Status Offenses
The Status Offender in the Juvenile
   Justice System
Reforming Status Offense Laws
Are They Really Different?
Increasing Social Control over Youth

Chapter Features

Cyber Delinquency: Sextortion: Sexual Extortion on the Net

Evidence-Based Juvenile Justice—Intervention: Southwest Key Programs

Case Profile: Akeema's Story

KEAIRA BROWN WAS JUST 13 YEARS OLD when she was charged with murder and became the youngest person in Wyandotte County, Kansas, ever to be tried as an adult. Her family life was close but troubled. Her mother, Cheryl Brown, had three other children, two enrolled in local colleges. Keaira was involved in after-school activities, including playing the violin. But when her mom went to prison on a drug charge, things began to spiral downhill for Keaira, and when she was only 10 she attempted suicide. On July 23, 2008, at about 4:00 PM, Keaira was supposed to be at a summer program at the Boys and Girls Club in Kansas City. Instead, she was involved in the carjacking of Scott Sappington, Jr., a junior at Sumner Academy, who had just dropped his siblings off at their grandmother's house. When he returned to his car, neighbors heard him yell, "Hey, hey," then there was a struggle inside the car, and he was shot in the head. An investigation led to a 6-year-old who told police that a young girl told a group of children to get rid of her bloody clothes. Police distributed pictures of the bloody clothes to the media, and soon after, the clothes were traced back to Keaira Brown.

Kansas State Corrections

Prosecutors thought the murder was a result of a carjacking that went wrong, while Keaira's family claimed she was an innocent pawn for area gang members who thought she would not be prosecuted because of her age. They were incorrect. In April, almost a year after the crime, a Wyandotte County judge ruled that Keaira should face trial as an adult. On November 9, 2010, Keaira Brown was found guilty of first-degree murder and attempted aggravated robbery and received a life sentence with parole eligibility after 20 years.

Since the *Brown* decision, courts have taken a hard look at putting juveniles in prison for life, expressing the fact that teens do not have the maturity of an adult and should not be punished in the same manner. Nonetheless, when Keaira Brown appealed her sentence in 2014, the Kansas Supreme Court upheld her conviction and sentence, ruling that the district court was justified in prosecuting her as an adult for felony murder and attempted aggravated robbery.

S tories such as that of Keaira Brown are certainly not unique. While the Supreme Court ruled in *Roper v. Simmons* that juveniles cannot be sentenced to the death penalty, it is quite legal to incarcerate them in adult prison for life if they commit a capital crime, as long as the judge takes their age into account before sentencing takes place (*Miller v. Alabama*).[1] And even though Keaira will be eligible for parole after spending 20 years in prison, there is no guarantee she will earn early release; she may in fact spend the rest of her life behind bars.

The problems of youth in contemporary society can be staggering. Because of trouble and conflict occurring in their families, schools, and communities, adolescents experience stress, confusion, and depression. There are approximately 75 million children in the United States, a number that is projected to increase to about 80 million by 2030.[2]

Since the mid-1960s, children have been decreasing as a proportion of the total US population. Today 23 percent of the population are 18 and under, down from a peak of 36 percent in the 1990s, at the end of the so-called baby boom. Children are projected to remain a fairly stable percentage, about 22 percent, of the total population through 2050. Though the number of children is projected to remain stable, the population is projected to become even more diverse in the

Roper v. Simmons
A juvenile under 18 years of age who commits a capital crime cannot face the death penalty.

Miller v. Alabama
In this case, the Supreme Court held that mandatory life sentences, without the possibility of parole, are unconstitutional for juvenile offenders.

exhibit 1.1

Six Generations of Americans

The Greatest Generation: Born after World War I and raised during the Depression, they overcame hardships, fought in World War II, and went on to build America into the world's greatest superpower. They were willing to put off personal gain for the common good.

Baby Boomers: Born between the end of World War II and the Kennedy-Johnson years, and now approaching retirement age, "boomers" are considered the generation that has benefited the most from the American Dream and post-war leadership. Their parents, who grew up during the Great Depression, made sure their children had the best of everything. Baby boomers benefited from affordable college and post-graduate education, relatively low housing costs, and plentiful job opportunities. Though they experienced some significant setbacks, such as the war in Vietnam, they are a privileged generation that has been accused of being self-absorbed and materialistic.

Generation X: Born between 1963 and 1980 and now approaching 50, gen-Xers are often accused of being unfocused and uncommitted—the "why me?" generation. Coming of age between 1980 and 1990, when divorce was rampant and greed was good, they are not attached to careers or families. They lived through the 1990s, a time with significant social problems, including teen suicide, homelessness, the AIDS epidemic, a downsizing of the workforce, and overseas conflict. Generation X is described as pessimistic, suspicious, and frustrated slackers who wear grunge clothing while listening to alternative music after they move back home with their parents.

They do not want to change the world, just make their way in it and through it without complications.

Generation Y (Millennials): Born between 1980 and 2000, gen-Y kids, otherwise known as millennials, were deeply influenced by the 9/11 attacks and as a result are more patriotic than their older peers. They were weaned on reality TV and are sometimes called the *MTV generation*. Compared to their elders, millennials are incredibly sophisticated technologically and have mastered the art of social media. Gen-Y members live in a world that is much more racially and ethnically diverse than their parents, and most are willing to accept diversity. Their worldview is aided by the rapid expansion in cable TV channels, satellite radio, the Internet, e-zines, etc. They may have lived in families with either a single caretaker or two working parents. Millennials are often accused of being self-centered, irresponsible, and having a lack of understanding of how the work world functions. They are also open-minded, liberal, upbeat, and overtly passionate about racial and gender equality.

Generation Z: Born between 2000 and 2012, they are the first generation to have grown up in a world dominated by the Internet and instant communication; iPads, group video games, texting, and tweeting are their milieu. Will this next generation have the same opportunities as their grandparents in a global economy in which the United States is competing with other powerful nations for dominance?

Generation Alpha: Born after 2012, it's just too early to tell.

The mission of the **Children's Defense Fund** (http://www.childrensdefense.org/) is to "leave no child behind" and to ensure every child "a healthy start, a head start, a fair start, a safe start, and a moral start in life," as well as a successful passage to adulthood with the help of caring families and communities. The CDF works to provide a strong, effective voice for kids who cannot vote, lobby, or speak for themselves.

decades to come. By 2023, fewer than half of all children are projected to be white, non-Hispanic; by 2050, 38 percent of children are projected to be white, non-Hispanic, down from 55 percent today.[3] By that time the US population is expected to reach 450 million people.

During the baby boom (1946–1964), the number of children grew rapidly (see Exhibit 1.1). Now as the baby boomers enter their senior years, their needs for support and medical care will increase. At the same time, a significant number of kids who are poor and at risk for delinquency and antisocial behavior will need both private and public assistance and aid. While the number of poor kids and the elderly will be rising, the 30- to 50-year-old population (generation X) who will be expected to care and pay for these groups will constitute a much smaller share of the population. Meanwhile, globalization means that generations Y and Z will be facing increasing economic competition from workers abroad and automation at home. The stress placed on young people is sure to increase in the future.

The Adolescent Dilemma

As they go through their tumultuous teenage years, the problems of American society and the daily stress of modern life have a significant effect on our nation's youth. Adolescence is unquestionably a time of transition. During this period, the self, or basic personality, is still undergoing a metamorphosis and is vulnerable to a host of external determinants as well as internal physiological changes. Many youths become extremely vulnerable to emotional turmoil and experience anxiety, humiliation, and mood swings. Adolescents also undergo a period of biological development that proceeds at a far faster pace than at any other time in their lives except infancy. Over a period of a few years, their height, weight, and sexual characteristics change dramatically. The average age at which girls reach puberty today is 12.5 years; 150 years ago, girls matured sexually at age 16. Although they may become biologically mature and capable of having children as early as 14, many youngsters remain emotionally and intellectually immature. By the time they reach 15, a significant number of teenagers are unable to adequately meet the requirements and responsibilities of the workplace, family, and neighborhood. Many suffer from health problems, are educational under-achievers, and are already skeptical about their ability to enter the American mainstream.

In later adolescence (ages 16 to 18), youths may experience a life crisis that famed psychologist Erik Erikson labeled the struggle between **ego identity** and **role diffusion**. Ego identity is formed when youths develop a full sense of the self, combining how they see themselves and how they fit in with others. Role diffusion occurs when they experience personal uncertainty, spread themselves too thin, and place themselves at the mercy of people who promise to give them a sense of identity they cannot mold for themselves.[4] Psychologists also find that late adolescence is a period dominated by the yearning for independence from parental domination.[5] Given this explosive mixture of biological change and desire for autonomy, it isn't surprising that the teenage years are a time of rebelliousness and conflict with authority at home, at school, and in the community.

Adolescent Problems

American youths face countless social, economic, and psychological problems that have been linked to delinquency and antisocial behaviors. Considering the problems they face, it may not be surprising to some that this latest generation of adolescents has been described as cynical and preoccupied with material acquisitions. By age 18, American youths have spent more time in front of a television than in the classroom; each year they may see thousands of rapes, murders, and assaults on TV. Today's teens routinely watch programming with violent and sexually explicit content on cable TV and the Net. They listen to hip-hop music with explicit lyrics that routinely describe sexuality and promiscuity. How will this exposure affect them? Should we be concerned? Maybe we should. Research shows that kids

ego identity
According to Erik Erikson, ego identity is formed when youths develop a full sense of the self, combining how they see themselves and how they fit in with others.

role diffusion
According to Erik Erikson, role diffusion occurs when people spread themselves too thin, experience personal uncertainty, and place themselves at the mercy of people who promise to give them a sense of identity they cannot develop for themselves.

Adolescent poverty has been linked to delinquency. Michell and Alex, who are homeless, sit with their daughter Alexis outside the Pan Am Shelter in Queens in New York City. The facility, a former hotel which currently houses dozens of homeless families, has been denounced by area residents who fear higher crime rates and lower property values if homeless people stay there. Organizers held a rally at the shelter to stress that the real problem is a lack of affordable housing for working-class and middle-class families.

Spencer Platt/Getty Images

who listen to music with a sexual content are much more likely to engage in precocious sex than adolescents whose musical tastes run to Taylor Swift or Adele; in contrast, there is also evidence that listening to any music, even angry heavy metal, can help calm anger and hostile emotions.[6]

Troubles in the home, the school, and the neighborhood, coupled with health and developmental hazards, have placed a significant portion of American youth **at risk**. Youths considered at risk are those dabbling in various forms of dangerous conduct such as drug abuse, alcohol use, and precocious sexuality. They are living in families that, because of economic, health, or social problems, are unable to provide adequate care and discipline.[7]

at-risk youth
Young people who are extremely vulnerable to the negative consequences of school failure, substance abuse, and early sexuality.

Data on population characteristics can be found at the website of the US Census Bureau (http://www.census.gov).

Adolescent Poverty   According to the US Census Bureau, the nation's official poverty rate is now about 15 percent, a figure that has persisted and even risen despite government efforts to help the poor. This means that about 47 million Americans, or one in seven residents, are living on $24,000 a year for a family of four. Millions of others—the so-called working poor—live just above the poverty line, struggling to make ends meet.[8] Real incomes are falling, and poverty in the United States is more prevalent now than in the 1960s when a War on Poverty was declared by the Johnson administration. Working hard and playing by the rules is not enough to lift families out of poverty: even if parents work full time at the federal minimum wage, the family still lives in poverty.

While poverty problems have risen for nearly every age, gender, and racial/ethnic group, the increases in poverty have been most severe among the nation's youngest families (adults under 30), especially those with one or more children present in the home. Kids are particularly hard hit by poverty: more than 20 percent of children under 18 (15.5 million) live in poverty, as compared to about 14 percent of people 18 to 64, and 10 percent of people 65 and older (see Figure 1.1).[9] About 7 million children live in extreme poverty, which means half of the poverty level or about $12,000 per year for a family of four.[10]

Which kids live in poverty? Those living in a single-parent, female-headed household are significantly more likely to suffer poverty than those in two-parent families.

Child poverty can have long-lasting negative effects on children's cognitive achievement, educational attainment, nutrition, physical and mental health, and social behavior. Educational achievement scores between children in affluent and low-income families have been widening over the years, and the incomes and wealth of families have become increasingly important determinants of adolescents' high school graduation, college attendance, and college persistence and graduation. The chances of an adolescent from a poor family with weak academic skills obtaining a bachelor's degree by his or her mid-20s is now close to zero.[11]

figure 1.1

Poverty Rates by Age

SOURCE: US Census Bureau, "Income, Poverty and Health Insurance Coverage in the United States: 2014," September 16, 2015, http://census.gov/newsroom/press-releases/2015/cb15-157.html (accessed August 2016).

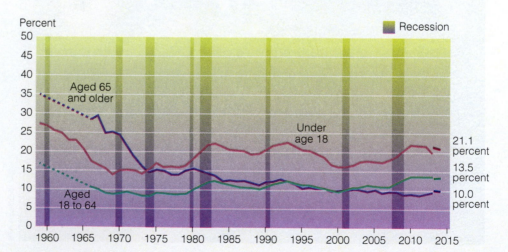

Diet and Health Problems   Receiving adequate food and health care is another significant concern for American youth. It may be hard to believe, but there are still millions of children in the United States who do not have access to the nutrition needed for an active, healthy life. Many still do not get enough food, while others suffer reduced food intake and diet quality, as well as anxiety about an adequate food supply. In the most extreme cases, children are going hungry, skipping meals, or have not eaten for a whole day because the household could not afford enough food. How many kids fall into the "food insecure group"? About 16 million children (21 percent of all children) live in households that are classified as food insecure. About 765,000 of these children (1 percent of all children) live in households classified as having very low food security. The children most vulnerable to food insecurity are minority children living in single-parent households with incomes below the federal poverty threshold. Recent national estimates indicate that only about 20 percent of adolescents eat five or more servings of fruits and vegetables per day, and less than 20 percent meet current physical activity recommendations of one hour of exercise a day.[12]

Kids with health problems may only be helped if they have insurance. And while most kids now have health care coverage of some sort, about 7 percent or 6 million youth do not.[13] As might be expected, children who are not healthy, especially those who live in lower-income families and children from minority backgrounds, are subject to illness and early mortality. The infant mortality rate in the United States is now 6 per 1,000 births, ranking 38th in the world out of 175 nations—better than many third-world nations but far below many industrialized nations, including Germany, Croatia, and Great Britain. It remains to be seen whether the new national health care policy, created by the Health Care and Education Reconciliation Act of 2010 (aka Obamacare), will eventually reduce or eliminate inadequate health care for America's children.

Mental Health Problems   Mental health concerns, such as childhood depression, can have a significant impact on adolescent development and well-being that adversely affects school work, peer and family relationships, and aggravates preexisting health conditions such as asthma and obesity. Youths who have had a **major depressive episode (MDE)** (about 11 percent of all teens) in the past year are at greater risk for suicide and are more likely than other youths to initiate alcohol and other drug use, experience concurrent substance use disorders, and smoke daily. As Figure 1.2 shows, depression is rising among all age groups; girls experience depression significantly more often than boys.

Racial Inequality   Despite years of effort to reduce or eliminate its occurrence, racial inequality still exists. Minority kids are much more likely than white,

major depressive episode (MDE)
A period of at least two weeks when a person experienced a depressed mood or loss of interest or pleasure in daily activities plus at least four additional symptoms of depression (such as problems with sleep, eating, energy, concentration, and feelings of self-worth).

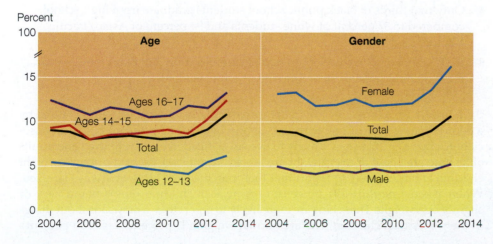

figure 1.2

Percentage of Youth Ages 12–17 Who Experienced A Major Depressive Episode (MDE) in the Past Year by Age And Gender

SOURCE: Federal Interagency Forum on Child and Family Statistics, http://www.childstats.gov/americaschildren/health4.asp (accessed August 2016).

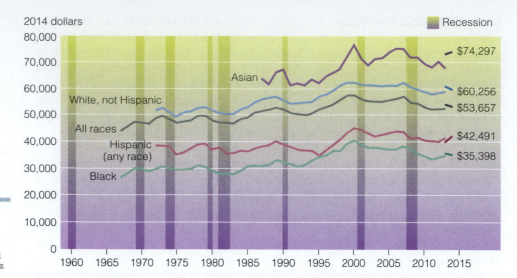

figure 1.3

Real Median Household Income by Race and Hispanic Origin

SOURCE: US Census Bureau, *Current Population Survey, 1968 to 2015 Annual Social and Economic Supplements.*

non-Hispanic children to experience poverty; proportionately, Hispanic and black children are about three times as likely to be poor than their white peers.[14] As Figure 1.3 shows, African American median income is significantly below that of white and Asian families.

Inequality can also be found in other elements of social life. Educational problems are more likely to hit minority kids the hardest. African American children are half as likely as white children to be placed in a gifted and talented class and more than one and a half times as likely to be placed in a class for students with emotional disturbances. They are also more likely to face disciplinary problems, including being two and a half times as likely to be held back or retained in school, almost three times as likely to be suspended from school, and more than four times as likely to be expelled. The Children's Defense Fund, a leading child advocacy group, finds:

- Black students fall behind early on and do not catch up. Without an education children are dead on arrival in America's economy.

- Black children arrive in kindergarten with lower levels of school readiness than white children.

- Black children make up 18 percent of preschool enrollment but 48 percent of preschool children receiving more than one out-of-school suspension.

- More than 80 percent of fourth and eighth grade black public school students cannot read or compute at grade level, compared to less than 57 percent of white students.

- Only two-thirds of black public school students graduate from high school, compared to 83 percent of white students and 94 percent of Asian/Pacific Islander students.

- Each school day, 763 black high school students drop out. Black students are more than twice as likely to drop out as white students.[15]

Self-Image Problems Adolescents are particularly vulnerable to stress caused by a poor self-image. According to recent surveys by the American Psychological Association, citizens of all ages are likely to live stress-filled lives, but children and adults alike who are obese or overweight are more likely to feel stressed out; overweight children are more likely to report that their parents were often or always stressed. When asked, one-third (31 percent) of American children report being very or slightly overweight. These kids are more likely to report they worry a lot about things in their lives than children who are normal weight (31 percent versus 14 percent).

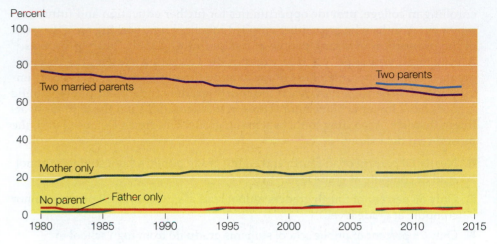

figure 1.4

Percentage of Children Ages 0–17 by Presence of Parents in Household

SOURCE: US Census Bureau, *Current Population Survey, Annual Social and Economic Supplement.*

Overweight children are also significantly more likely than normal-weight children to report they worry about the way they look or about their weight (36 percent versus 11 percent). Children, regardless of weight or age, say they can tell that their parents are stressed when they argue and complain, which many children say makes them feel sad and worried.[16]

Family Problems   Divorce strikes about half of all new marriages, and many intact families sacrifice time with each other to afford more affluent lifestyles. Today, as Figure 1.4 shows, about 64 percent of children ages 0–17 live with two married parents, down from 77 percent in 1980. Of these, 24 percent live with only their mother, 4 percent live with only their father, and 4 percent live with neither of their parents. The majority of children who live with neither of their parents are living with grandparents or other relatives. Others who live with neither parent live with foster parents or other nonrelatives.

Kids who live with only one parent are much more likely to experience poverty than those living in two-parent families. Because of family problems, children are being polarized into two distinct economic groups: those in affluent, two-earner, married-couple households and those in poor, single-parent households.

Substandard Living Conditions   Millions of children live in substandard housing—high-rise, multiple-family dwellings—which can have a negative influence on their long-term psychological health.[17] Adolescents living in deteriorated urban areas are prevented from having productive and happy lives. Many die from random bullets and drive-by shootings. Some are homeless and living on the street, where they are at risk of drug addiction and sexually transmitted diseases (STDs), including AIDS. Today about one-third of US households with children have one or more of the following three housing problems: physically inadequate housing, crowded housing, or housing that costs more than 30 percent of the household income.[18] Despite the fact that the minimum wage has increased, the poor can barely afford to live in even the lowest-cost neighborhoods of metro areas such as Chicago, New York, and Washington, DC.[19]

Formed in 1985, the **Children's Rights Council (CRC)** is a national nonprofit organization based in Washington, DC, that works to ensure children have meaningful and continuing contact with both their parents and extended family regardless of the parents' marital status. http://www.crckids.org/.

Inadequate Educational Opportunity   Education shapes the personal growth and life chances of children. Early educational experiences of young children, such as being read to daily, encourage the development of essential skills and prepare children for success in school. Later aspects of academic performance, such as mastering academic subjects, completing high school, and enrolling in college, provide opportunities for further education and future employment. Youths who are neither enrolled in school nor working are a measure of the proportion of young people at risk of limiting their future prospects.[20] Although all young people face stress in the education system, the risks are greatest for the poor, members of racial and ethnic minorities, and recent immigrants. By the time they reach the fourth grade, students in poorer public schools have lower achievement scores in mathematics than those in more affluent districts. According to the watchdog group Children's Defense Fund, the most recent data show:

- Nearly 60 percent of all fourth and eighth grade public school students cannot read or compute at grade level.
- Only 66 percent of fourth graders cannot read at grade level, 59 percent cannot compute at grade level.
- Only 78 percent of public school students graduate from high school in four years.
- Although 75 percent of high school students who took the ACT college entrance exam took a core curriculum in high school, only 25 percent were ready for college-level English, math, science, and reading.
- Poor children and children of color fare worse in our educational system: 75 percent or more of lower income fourth and eighth grade public school students cannot read or compute at grade level, compared to 52 percent or fewer of higher income students.
- Almost 75 percent of fourth and eighth grade black and Hispanic public school students cannot read or compute at grade level. One in three black students and three in ten Hispanic and American Indian/Alaska Native students do not graduate from high school in four years.[21]

The problems faced by kids who drop out of school do not end in adolescence. Adults 25 years of age and older without a high school diploma earn 30 percent less than those who have earned a diploma. High school graduation is the single most effective preventive strategy against adult poverty.

At home, poor children receive less academic support from their harried parents. Take for instance having parents who read to their children at home, a key to future academic success. Although most children ages 3 to 5 who are not yet in kindergarten are read to daily by a family member, the likelihood of having heard a story at home is stratified by class. The higher the parents' income, the more likely they are to read to their young children.[22]

Problems in Cyberspace

Kids today are forced to deal with problems and issues their parents could not even dream about. While the Internet and other technological advances have opened a new world of information gathering and sharing, they have also brought a basketful of new problems ranging from sexting to cyberstalking.

Cyberbullying Experts define bullying among children as repeated, negative acts committed by one or more children against another.[23] These negative acts may be physical or verbal in nature—for example, hitting or kicking, teasing or taunting—or they may involve indirect actions such as manipulating friendships or purposely excluding other children from activities.

While in the past bullies were found in the school yard, they can now use the Internet to harass their victims through texts or instant messages. Physical distance is no longer a barrier to the frequency and depth of harm doled out by a bully to his or her victim.[24] Obscene, insulting, and slanderous messages can be posted to social media sites or sent directly to the victim via cell phones; bullying has now morphed from the physical to the virtual.

Cyberbullying is the willful and repeated harm inflicted through Internet social media sites such as Facebook, blogs, or microblogging applications such as Twitter. Like their real-world counterparts, cyberbullies are malicious aggressors who seek implicit or explicit pleasure or profit through the mistreatment of other individuals. Although power in traditional bullying might be physical (stature) or social (competency or popularity), online power may simply stem from Net proficiency.

It is difficult to get an accurate count of the number of teens who have experienced cyberbullying. A recent study by Justin Patchin and Sameer Hinduja, who run the Cyberbullying Research Center, reviewed the existing literature on cyberbullying, more than 70 published research articles.[25] They found:

- About 21 percent of teens have been cyberbullied and about 15 percent admitted to cyberbullying others at some point in their lifetimes. This means that about one out of every four teens has experienced cyberbullying, and about one out of every six teens has done it to others.
- Adolescent girls are just as likely, if not more likely, than boys to experience cyberbullying (as a victim and/or offender).
- Cyberbullying is related to low self-esteem, suicidal ideation, anger, frustration, and a variety of other emotional and psychological problems.
- Cyberbullying is related to other issues in the real world, including school problems, antisocial behavior, substance use, and delinquency.
- Traditional bullying is still more common than cyberbullying.
- Traditional bullying and cyberbullying are closely related: those who are bullied at school are bullied online, and those who bully at school bully online.

Cyberstalking Cyberstalking refers to the use of the Internet, social media, or other electronic communication to stalk another person. Some predatory adults pursue minors through online chat rooms, establish a relationship with the child, and later make contact. Today, Internet predators are more likely to meet and develop relationships with at-risk adolescents, and beguile underage teenagers, rather than use coercion and violence.[26]

Catfishing Catfishing refers to the practice of setting up a fictitious online profile, most often for the purpose of luring another into a fraudulent romantic relationship. According to *The Urban Dictionary*, a catfish is "someone who pretends to be someone they're not using Facebook or other social media." So, to "catfish someone" is to set up a fake social media profile with the goal of duping that person into falling for the false persona. In a case that got national attention, 13-year-old Megan Meier began an online relationship with a boy she knew as Josh Evans. For almost a month, Megan corresponded with this boy, exclusively online because he said he didn't have a phone and was homeschooled. One day Megan received a message from Josh on her MySpace profile saying, "I don't know if I want to be friends with you any longer because I hear you're not nice to your friends." This was followed by bulletins being posted through MySpace calling Megan "fat" and a "slut." After seeing the messages, Megan became distraught and ran up to her room. A few minutes later, Megan's mother Tina found her hanging in her bedroom closet. Though Tina rushed her daughter to the hospital, Megan died the next day.

Six weeks after their daughter's death, the Meier family learned that the boy with whom Megan had been corresponding never existed. Josh Evans (and his online profile) was created by Lori Drew, a neighbor and the mother of one of Megan's friends. She created the profile as a way to spy on what Megan was saying about her daughter. Drew was eventually acquitted in federal court for her role in Megan's death.[27]

cyberbullying
Willful and repeated harm inflicted through Internet social media sites or electronic communication methods such as Twitter.

Sextortion: Sexual Extortion on the Net

Eighteen-year-old Anthony Stancl impersonated two girls ("Kayla" and "Emily") on Facebook. He befriended and formed online romantic relationships with a number of boys in his high school (again, while posing and interacting as these two girls). He then convinced at least 31 of those boys to send him nude pictures or videos of themselves. As if that weren't bad enough, Stancl—still posing as a girl and still communicating through Facebook—tried to convince more than half to meet with a male friend and let him perform sexual acts. If they refused, "she" told them that the pictures and videos would be released for all to see. Seven boys actually submitted to this horrific request and were coerced into engaging in sex acts with Stancl. He took numerous pictures of these encounters with his cell phone, and the police eventually found more than 300 nude images of male teens on his computer. He was charged with five counts of child enticement, two counts of second-degree sexual assault of a child, two counts of third-degree sexual assault, possession of child pornography, and repeated sexual assault of the same child, and received a 15-year prison sentence.

Stancl's actions have become so common that the word *sextortion* has been coined to refer to sexual exploitation in which a victim is coerced or threatened into engaging in sexual acts, and then exploited by means of threats of the release of sexual images or information to parents or the public.

In some instances sextortion is the work of a lone operator such as Stancl, while in others it is perpetrated by a group of exploiters who conspire to victimize numerous children. In 2016, Brian K. Hendrix was sentenced to 21 years in prison on child pornography charges. Before his arrest and conviction, Hendrix operated two websites designed to trick children into engaging in sexually explicit activity that he was secretly recording. More 300 American children—some as young as 8 years old—and an estimated 1,600 other youths from around the world were victims.

Hendrix and co-conspirators tricked their young victims by creating fake profiles on social networking sites, where they posed as teenagers to lure children to their websites. Once there, the conspirators—still masquerading as teens—showed the children videos of prior victims to make the new victims think that they were chatting with another minor. Using these videos, Hendrix and his co-conspirators coerced and enticed children to engage in sexually explicit activity on their own web cameras, which the website automatically recorded. Conspirators earned points based on their contribution to the success of website objectives, which allowed them access to the sexually exploitative videos of children.

AP Images/Tom Lynn

Anthony Stancl leaves the Waukesha County Court House after being charged with five counts of child enticement, two counts of second-degree sexual assault of a child, two counts of third-degree sexual assault, possession of child pornography, and repeated sexual assault of the same child. After trial, Stancl received a 15-year prison sentence.

The majority of the victims were American, but victims were also located in Canada and several other countries. Most of the children had no idea they had been victimized, and their parents were in shock. The victims and their families came from all social and economic backgrounds, from both single-parent and two-parent families. An investigation into Hendrix's activities resulted in the conviction of nine online predators, including Hendrix, with prison sentences ranging between 18 and 21 years.

The Hendrix case shows a new level of sophistication for cyber attacks on children. These predators had the technical proficiency to give their website the ability to record the criminal activity—along with psychological knowledge and preparation designed to break down all the child's barriers.

CRITICAL THINKING

The punishment for sextortion can be severe: the coercion of a child by an adult to produce what is considered child pornography carries heavy penalties, which can include up to life sentences for the offender. Should people like Stancl and Hendrix be punished in the same manner as a rapist or murderer, or is that too severe for sextortion?

SOURCES: Department of Justice, Office of Public Affairs, "Member of International Child Exploitation Conspiracy Sentenced to 21 Years in Prison," April 8, 2016, https://www.justice.gov/opa/pr/member-international-child-exploitation-conspiracy-sentenced-21-years-prison; Laurel Walker, "Stancl Gets 15 Years in Prison in Facebook Coercion Case," *Milwaukee Journal Sentinel*, February 24, 2010, http://www.jsonline.com/news/waukesha/85252392.html. (accessed September 2016.)

Sexting Adolescents now have to worry that the compromising photos they send their boyfriends or girlfriends—a practice called sexting—can have terrible repercussions. Jesse Logan, an 18-year-old Ohio high school girl, sent nude pictures of herself to her boyfriend. When they broke up, he betrayed her trust by sending them over the Net to friends and schoolmates. As soon as the photos got into the hands of her classmates, they began harassing her, calling her names and destroying her reputation. Jesse became depressed and reclusive, afraid to go to school, and in a final act of desperation she hanged herself in her bedroom.[28]

There is some question of how often sexting occurs. Justin Patchin and Sameer Hinduja of the Cyberbullying Research Center reviewed existing surveys and found the percentage of students who reported sending a sext ranged from 2.5 percent to 28 percent. Much of these differences in rates can likely be attributed to the different ways the studies were set up and how the terms were defined. There were more positive responses if students were asked about "sexually suggestive images" than if they were asked about sending "naked images." Similarly, since older teens were more likely to participate in sexting, including 18- and 19-year-olds in the surveys showed higher levels of sexting. Patchin and Hinduja's own research found that 8 percent of teens had sent a "naked or semi-naked image" of themselves to others, including middle and high school students between the ages of 11 and 18.[29]

Teen Suicide

During the teen years, feelings of stress, anxiety, and depression can overwhelm young people and lead them to consider suicide as a "solution." Though most kids do not take their own lives, millions remain troubled and disturbed and at risk for delinquency, drug use, and other forms of antisocial behavior. Acting out or externalized behavior that begins in early adolescence may then persist into adulthood.[30]

In the United States, the teen suicide rate remains unacceptably high: suicide is the third leading cause of death among young people ages 15 to 24, averaging about 4,600 per year. Though teens commit suicide at a lower rate than adults and the elderly, the incidence of suicide, especially among young girls, is growing more rapidly: young girls ages 10–14 tripled their suicide rate between 1999 and 2014 (Figure 1.5).

Among students in grades 9 through 12 in the United States about 17 percent seriously considered attempting suicide in the previous 12 months (22 percent of females and 11 percent of males). Almost 14 percent of students made a plan about how they would attempt suicide; about 8 percent attempted suicide; about 3 percent made a suicide attempt that resulted in an injury that required medical attention. The top three methods used in suicides of young people include firearm (45 percent), suffocation (40 percent), and poisoning (8 percent).[31]

Are Things Improving?

Though American youth do face many hazards, there are some bright spots on the horizon. Teenage birthrates nationwide have declined substantially during the past decade, with the sharpest declines among African American girls. In the same period, the teen abortion rate has also declined. These data indicate that more teens are using birth control and practicing safe sex.

Fewer children are being born with health risks today than in 1990. This probably means that fewer women are drinking or smoking during pregnancy and that fewer are receiving late or no prenatal care. In addition, since 1990 the number of children immunized against disease has increased.

Youths are also drinking less alcohol and taking fewer dangerous drugs. The most recent national survey shows that use of both alcohol and cigarettes reached their lowest points since 1975. Use of several particularly dangerous illicit drugs—including MDMA (ecstasy, Molly), heroin, amphetamines, and synthetic marijuana—are also in decline.[32]

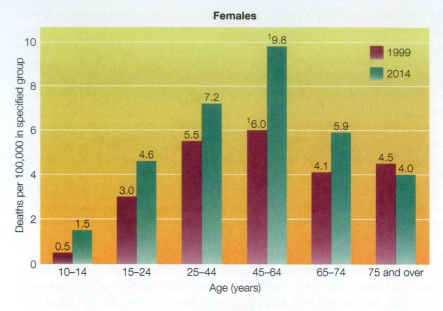

figure 1.5

Suicide Rates for Females and Males, by Age: The United States, 1999 and 2014

SOURCE: Centers for Disease Control and Prevention, "Suicide Prevention: Youth Suicide," http://www.cdc.gov/violenceprevention/suicide/youth_suicide.html (accessed September 2016).

College enrollment, now at more than 20 million, is expected to set new records from fall 2018 through fall 2024, increasing by 14 percent.[33] About 30 percent of the adult population in the United States now have college degrees. Although these are encouraging signs, the improvement of adolescent life continues to be a national goal.

The Study of Juvenile Delinquency

juvenile delinquency
Participation in illegal behavior by a minor who falls under a statutory age limit.

The problems of youth in modern society are a major national concern especially when they are linked to **juvenile delinquency**, or criminal behavior committed by minors.

About 750,000 youths are now arrested each year for crimes ranging in seriousness from loitering to murder. While this number seems high, juvenile arrests have actually been in decline; more than a million youths were being arrested annually just a few years ago.[34] Though most juvenile law violations are minor, some young offenders are extremely dangerous and violent. About 850,000 youths belong to more than 30,000 gangs in the United States.[35] Violent street gangs and groups can put fear into an entire city (see Chapter 9 for more on gangs).

Youths involved in multiple serious criminal acts—referred to as lifestyle, repeat, or **chronic delinquent offenders**—are now recognized as a serious social problem. State juvenile authorities must deal with these offenders, along with responding to a range of other social problems, including child abuse and neglect, school crime and vandalism, family crises, and drug abuse. In a series of studies, Mark Cohen, Alex Piquero, and Wesley Jennings examined the costs to society of various groups of juvenile offenders, including high-rate chronic offenders who kept on committing serious crimes as adults.[36] They found that the average cost for each of these offenders was over $1.5 million, and their cost to society increased as they grew older. The "worst of the worst" of these offenders, who committed 53 known crimes, cost society $1,696,000 by the time he reached his mid-20s. In all, the high-rate offenders studied had an annual cost to society of over half a billion dollars.

Given the diversity and gravity of these problems, there is an urgent need for strategies to combat such a complex social phenomenon as juvenile delinquency. But formulating effective strategies demands a solid understanding of delinquency's causes and prevention. Is delinquency a function of psychological abnormality? A collective reaction by youths against destructive social conditions? The product of a disturbed home life and disrupted socialization? Does serious delinquent behavior occur only in large urban areas among lower-class youths? Or is it spread throughout the entire social structure? What impact do family life, substance abuse, school experiences, and peer relations have on youth and their law-violating behaviors? We know that most youthful law violators do not go on to become adult criminals (what is known as the **aging-out process**). Yet we do not know why some youths become chronic delinquents whose careers begin early and persist into their adulthood. Why does the onset of delinquency begin so early in some children? Why does the severity of their offenses escalate? What factors predict the **persistence**, or continuation, of delinquency, and conversely, what are the factors associated with its desistance, or termination? Unless the factors that control the onset and termination of a delinquent career are studied in an orderly and scientific manner, developing effective prevention and control efforts will be difficult.

The study of delinquency also involves analysis of the law enforcement, court, and correctional agencies designed to treat youthful offenders who fall into the arms of the law—known collectively as the **juvenile justice system**. How should police deal with minors who violate the law? What are the legal rights of children? Should minors who commit murder receive the death penalty? What kind of correctional programs are most effective with delinquent youths? How useful are educational, community, counseling, and vocational development programs? Is it true, as some critics claim, that most efforts to rehabilitate young offenders are doomed to failure? Should we adopt a punishment or a treatment orientation to combat delinquency, or something in between?

In sum, the scientific study of delinquency requires understanding the nature, extent, and cause of youthful law violations and the methods devised for their control. We also need to study important environmental and social issues associated with delinquent behavior, including substance abuse, child abuse and neglect, education, and peer relations. This text investigates these aspects of juvenile delinquency along with the efforts being made to treat problem youths and prevent the spread of delinquent behavior. Our study begins with a look back to the development of the concept of childhood and how children were first identified as a unique group with its own special needs and behaviors.

The Development of Childhood

The treatment of children as a distinct social group with special needs and behaviors is, in historical terms, a relatively new concept. It is only for the past 350 years or so that any mechanism existed to care for even the neediest children, including those left orphaned and destitute. How did this concept of concern for children develop?

chronic delinquent offenders (also known as chronic juvenile offenders, chronic delinquents, or chronic recidivists)
Youths who have been arrested four or more times during their minority and perpetuate a striking majority of serious criminal acts. This small group is believed to engage in a significant portion of all delinquent behavior; these youths do not age out of crime but continue their criminal behavior into adulthood.

aging-out process (also known as desistance or spontaneous remission)
The tendency for youths to reduce the frequency of their offending behavior as they age; aging-out is thought to occur among all groups of offenders.

persistence
The process by which juvenile offenders persist in their delinquent careers rather than aging out of crime.

juvenile justice system
The segment of the justice system, including law enforcement officers, the courts, and correctional agencies, designed to treat youthful offenders.

Childhood in the Middle Ages

In Europe, during the Middle Ages (roughly 500–1500 CE), the concept of childhood as we know it today did not exist. In the **paternalistic family** of the time, the father was the final authority on all family matters and exercised complete control over the social, economic, and physical well-being of his wife and children.[37] Children who did not obey were subject to severe physical punishment, even death.

The Lower Classes For peasant children, the passage into adulthood was abrupt. As soon as they were physically capable, children of all classes were expected to engage in adult roles. Among the working classes, males engaged in farming and/or learning a skilled trade, such as masonry or metal-working; females aided in food preparation or household maintenance.[38] Some peasant youths went into domestic or agricultural service on the estate of a powerful landowner or into trades or crafts, perhaps as a blacksmith or farrier (horseshoer).

This view of medieval childhood was shaped by Philippe Aries, whose influential book *Centuries of Childhood* is considered a classic of historical scholarship. Aries argued that most young people were apprenticed, became agricultural or factory workers, and generally entered adult society at a very early age.[39] According to Aries, high infant mortality rates kept parents emotionally detached from their children. Paintings of the time depict children as mini-adults who were sent off to work as soon as they were capable. Western culture did not have a sense of childhood as a distinct period of life until the very late nineteenth and early twentieth centuries.

Though Aries's view that children in the Middle Ages were treated as "miniature adults" has become the standard view, in a more recent book, historian Nicholas Orme puts forth evidence that medieval children may have been valued by their parents and did experience a prolonged period of childhood. In his *Medieval Children*, Orme finds that the medieval mother began to care for her children even before their delivery. Royal ladies borrowed relics of the Virgin Mary from the church to protect their unborn children, while poorer women used jasper stones or drawings of the cross, which were placed across their stomachs to ensure a healthy and uneventful birth. Parents associated their children's birthdays with a saint's feast day. Medieval children devised songs, rhymes, and games. Some simple games made use of cherry pits or hazelnuts, but children also had toys, which included dolls and even mechanical toys made for royalty.[40]

Children of the Nobility Though their lives were quite different, children of the affluent, landholding classes also assumed adult roles at an early age. Girls born into aristocratic families were educated at home and married in their early teens. A few were taught to read, write, and do sufficient mathematics to handle household accounts in addition to typical female duties such as supervising servants and ensuring the food supply of the manor.

The Pierpont Morgan Library/Art Resource, NY

As soon as they were physically capable, children of the Middle Ages were expected to engage in adult roles. Young girls worked as maids and housekeepers and at such tasks as food preparation, clothes washing, and household maintenance. Boys worked on farms and performed such tasks as blacksmith or farrier (horseshoer).

paternalistic family
A family style wherein the father is the final authority on all family matters and exercises complete control over his wife and children.

At age 7 or 8, boys born to landholding families were either sent to a monastery or cathedral school to be trained for lives in the church or selected to be a member of the warrior class and sent to serve a term as a squire—an apprentice and assistant to an experienced knight. At age 21, young men of the knightly classes completed their term as squire, received their own knighthood, and returned home to live with their parents. Most remained single because it was widely believed there should be only one married couple residing in a manor or castle. To pass the time and maintain their fighting edge, many young knights entered the tournament circuit, engaging in melees and jousts to win fame and fortune. Upon the death of their fathers, young nobles assumed their inherited titles, married, and began their own families.

The customs and practices of the time helped shape the lives of children and, in some instances, greatly amplified their hardships and suffering. **Primogeniture** required that the oldest surviving male child inherit family lands and titles. He could then distribute them as he saw fit to younger siblings. There was no absolute requirement, however, that portions of the estate be distributed equally; many youths who received no lands were forced to enter religious orders, become soldiers, or seek wealthy patrons. Primogeniture often caused intense family rivalry that led to blood feuds and tragedy.

primogeniture
During the Middle Ages, the right of firstborn sons to inherit lands and titles, leaving their brothers the option of a military or religious career.

Dower The dower system mandated that a woman's family bestow money, land, or other wealth (called a dowry) on a potential husband or his family in exchange for his marriage to her. In return, the young woman received a promise of financial assistance, called a jointure, from the groom's family. Jointure provided a lifetime income if a wife outlived her mate. The dower system had a significant impact on the role of women in medieval society and consequently on the role of children. Within this system, a father or male guardian had the final say in his daughter's choice of marital partner, as he could threaten to withhold her dowry.

Some women were denied access to marriage simply because of their position in the family. A father with many daughters and few sons might find himself financially unable to obtain suitable marriages for them. Consequently, the youngest girls in many families were forced either to enter convents or stay at home, with few prospects for marriage and family.

The dower system had far-reaching effects on the position of women in society, forcing them into the role of second-class citizens dependent upon their fathers, brothers, and guardians. It established a pattern in which females who did not conform to what males considered to be acceptable standards of feminine behavior could receive harsh sanctions; it established a sexual double standard that in part still exists today.

Childrearing The harshness of medieval life influenced childrearing practices during the fifteenth and sixteenth centuries. For instance, newborns were almost immediately handed over to wet nurses, who fed and cared for them during the first two years of their life. These women often lived away from the family so that parents had little contact with their children. Even the wealthiest families employed wet nurses, because it was considered demeaning for a noblewoman to nurse. Wrapping a newborn entirely in bandages, or **swaddling**, was a common practice. The bandages prevented any movement and enabled the wet nurse to manage the child easily. This practice was thought to protect the child, but it most likely contributed to high infant mortality rates because the child could not be kept clean.

swaddling
The practice during the Middle Ages of completely wrapping newborns in long bandage-like cloths in order to restrict their movements and make them easier to manage.

Discipline was severe during this period. Young children of all classes, both peasant and wealthy, were subjected to stringent rules and regulations. They were beaten severely for any sign of disobedience or ill temper. Many children of this time would be considered abused by today's standards. The relationship between parent and child was remote. Children were expected to enter the world of adults and to undertake responsibilities early in their lives, sharing in the work of siblings and parents. Children thought to be suffering from disease or retardation were often abandoned to churches, orphanages, or foundling homes.[41]

The roots of the impersonal relationship between parent and child can be traced to high mortality rates, which made sentimental and affectionate relationships risky. Parents were reluctant to invest emotional effort in relationships that could so easily be terminated by violence, accidents, or disease. Many believed that children must be toughened to ensure their survival in a hostile world. Close family relationships were viewed as detrimental to this process. Also, because the oldest male child was viewed as the essential player in a family's well-being, younger male and female siblings were considered economic and social liabilities.

Development of Concern for Children

Throughout the seventeenth and eighteenth centuries, a number of developments in England heralded the march toward the recognition of children's rights. Some of these events eventually affected the juvenile legal system as it emerged in America. They include (a) changes in family style and child care, (b) the English Poor Laws, (c) the apprenticeship movement, and (d) the role of the chancery court.[42]

Changes in Family Structure   Family structure and the role of children began to change after the Middle Ages. Extended families, which were created over centuries, gave way to the nuclear family structure with which we are familiar today. It became more common for marriage to be based on love and mutual attraction between men and women rather than on parental consent and paternal dominance. The changing concept of marriage—from an economic arrangement to an emotional commitment—also began to influence the way children were treated within the family structure. Though parents still rigidly disciplined their children, they formed closer parental ties and developed greater concern for their offspring's well-being.

To provide more control over children, grammar and boarding schools were established and began to flourish in many large cities during this time.[43] Young boys studied grammar, Latin, law, and logic, often beginning at a young age. Teachers in these institutions regularly ruled by fear, and flogging was their main method of discipline. Students were beaten for academic mistakes as well as moral lapses. Such brutal treatment fell on both the rich and the poor throughout all levels of educational life, including universities. This treatment abated in Europe with the rise of the Enlightenment, but it remained in full force in Great Britain until late in the nineteenth century. Although this brutal approach to children may be difficult to understand now, the child in that society was a second-class citizen.

Toward the close of the eighteenth century, the work of such philosophers as Voltaire, Rousseau, and Locke launched a new age for childhood and the family.[44] Their vision produced a period known as the Enlightenment, which stressed a humanistic view of life, freedom, family, reason, and law. The ideal person was sympathetic to others and receptive to new ideas. These new beliefs influenced both the structure and lifestyle of the family. The father's authority was tempered, discipline in the home became more relaxed, and the expression of love and affection became more commonplace among family members. Upper- and middle-class families began to devote attention to childrearing, and the status of children was advanced.

As a result of these changes, in the nineteenth century children began to emerge as a readily distinguishable group with independent needs and interests. Parents often took greater interest in their upbringing. In addition, serious questions arose over the treatment of children in school. Public outcries led to a decrease in excessive physical discipline. Restrictions were placed on the use of the whip, and in some schools, the imposition of academic assignments or the loss of privileges replaced corporal punishment. Despite such reforms, many children still led harsh lives. Girls were still undereducated, punishment was still primarily physical, and schools continued to mistreat children.

Poor Laws   Government action to care for needy children can be traced to the **Poor Laws** of Britain. As early as 1535, England passed statutes allowing for the appointment of overseers to place destitute or neglected children as servants in the homes of the affluent.[45] The Poor Laws forced children to serve during their minority in the care of families who trained them in agricultural, trade, or domestic services. The Elizabethan Poor Laws of 1601 were a model for dealing with poor children for more than 200 years. These laws created a system of church wardens and overseers who, with the consent of justices of the peace, identified vagrant, delinquent, and neglected children and took measures to put them to work. Often this meant placing them in poorhouses or workhouses, or apprenticing them to masters.

The Apprenticeship Movement   Under the apprenticeship system, children were placed in the care of adults who trained them to discharge various duties and obtain skills. Voluntary apprentices were bound out by parents or guardians who wished to secure training for their children. Involuntary apprentices were compelled by the authorities to serve until they were 21 or older. The master–apprentice relationship was similar to the parent–child relationship in that the master had complete responsibility for and authority over the apprentice. If an apprentice was unruly, a complaint could be made and the apprentice could be punished. Incarcerated apprentices were often placed in rooms or workshops apart from other prisoners and were generally treated differently from those charged with a criminal offense. Even at this early stage, the conviction was growing that the criminal law and its enforcement should be applied differently to children.

Chancery Court   After the fifteenth century, a system of **chancery courts** became a significant arm of the British legal system. They were originally established as "courts of equity" to handle matters falling outside traditional legal actions. These early courts were based on the traditional English system in which a chancellor acted as the "king's conscience" and had the ability to modify the application of legal rules and provide relief considering the circumstances of individual cases. The courts were not concerned with technical legal issues; rather, they focused on rendering decisions or orders that were fair or equitable. With respect to children, the chancery courts dealt with issues of guardianship of children who were orphaned, their property and inheritance rights, and the appointment of guardians to protect them until they reached the age of majority and could care for themselves. For example, if a wealthy father died before his heir's majority, or if there were some dispute as to the identity (or legitimacy) of his heir, the crown might ask the case to be decided by the chancery court in an effort to ensure that inheritance rights were protected (and taxes collected!).

Chancery court decision making rested on the proposition that children and other incompetents were under the protective control of the king; thus, the Latin phrase *parens patriae* was used, referring to the role of the king as the father of his country. The concept was first used by English kings to establish their right to intervene in the lives of the children of their vassals—children whose position and property were of direct concern to the monarch.[46] The concept of *parens patriae* became the theoretical basis for the protective jurisdiction of the chancery courts acting as part of the crown's power. As time passed, the monarchy used *parens patriae* more and more to justify its intervention in the lives of families and children by its interest in their general welfare.[47]

The chancery courts dealt with the property and custody problems of the wealthier classes. They did not have jurisdiction over children charged with criminal conduct. Juveniles who violated the law were handled within the framework of the regular criminal court system. Nonetheless, the concept of *parens patriae* grew to refer primarily to the responsibility of the courts and the state to act in the best interests of the child.

Childhood in America

While England was using its chancery courts and Poor Laws to care for children in need, the American colonies were developing similar concepts. The colonies were a haven for poor and unfortunate people looking for religious and economic opportunities denied them in England and Europe. Along with early settlers, many children came not as citizens but as indentured servants, apprentices, or agricultural workers. They were recruited from the various English workhouses, orphanages, prisons, and asylums that housed vagrant and delinquent youths during the sixteenth and seventeenth centuries.[48]

At the same time, the colonies themselves produced illegitimate, neglected, abandoned, and delinquent children. The colonies' initial response to caring for such unfortunate children was to adopt court and Poor Laws systems similar to those in England. Involuntary apprenticeship, indenture, and binding out of children became integral parts of colonization in America. For example, Poor Laws legislation requiring poor and dependent children to serve apprenticeships was passed in Virginia in 1646 and in Massachusetts and Connecticut in 1673.[49]

The master in colonial America acted as a surrogate parent, and in certain instances, apprentices would actually become part of the nuclear family structure. If they disobeyed their masters, apprentices were punished by local tribunals. If masters abused apprentices, courts would make them pay damages, return the children to the parents, or find new guardians. Maryland and Virginia developed an orphan's court that supervised the treatment of youths placed with guardians and ensured that they were not mistreated or taken advantage of by their masters. These courts did not supervise children living with their natural parents, leaving intact the parents' right to care for their children.[50]

By the beginning of the nineteenth century, as the agrarian economy began to be replaced by industry, the apprenticeship system gave way to the factory system. Yet the problems of how to deal effectively with growing numbers of dependent youths increased. Early American settlers believed that hard work, strict discipline, and rigorous education were the only reliable means to salvation. A child's life was marked by work alongside parents, some schooling, prayer, more work, and further study. Work in the factories, however, often taxed young laborers by placing demands on them that they were too young to endure. To alleviate a rapidly developing problem, the Factory Act of the early nineteenth century limited the hours children were permitted to work and the age at which they could begin to work. It also prescribed a minimum amount of schooling to be provided by factory owners.[51] This and related statutes were often violated, and conditions of work and school remained troublesome issues well into the twentieth century. Nevertheless, the statutes were a step in the direction of reform.

Controlling Children   In America, as in England, moral discipline was rigidly enforced. "Stubborn child" laws were passed that required children to obey their parents.[52] It was not uncommon in the colonies for children who were disobedient or disrespectful to their families to be whipped or otherwise physically chastised. Children were often required to attend public whippings and executions because these events were thought to be important forms of moral instruction. Parents often referred their children to published works and writings on behavior and discipline and expected them to follow their precepts carefully. Because community and church leaders frowned on harsh punishments, child protection laws were passed as early as 1639 (in New Haven, Connecticut). Nonetheless, these laws were generally symbolic and rarely enforced. They expressed the community's commitment to God to oppose sin; offenders who abused their children usually received lenient sentences.[53]

Although most colonies adopted a protectionist stance, few cases of child abuse were actually brought before the courts. There are several explanations for this neglect. The absence of child abuse cases may reflect the nature of life in what were extremely religious households. Children were productive laborers and respected as such by their parents. In addition, large families provided many siblings and kinfolk who could care for children and relieve stress-producing burdens on parents.[54] Another view is that though many children were harshly punished in early American families, the acceptable limits of discipline were so high that few parents were charged with assault. Any punishment that fell short of maiming or permanently harming a child was considered within the sphere of parental rights.[55]

The Concept of Delinquency

Considering the rough treatment handed out to children who misbehaved at home or at school, it should come as no surprise that children who actually broke the law and committed serious criminal acts were dealt with harshly. Before the twentieth century, little distinction was made between adult and juvenile offenders. Although judges considered the age of an offender when deciding punishments, both adults and children were often eligible for the same forms of punishment—prison, corporal punishment, and even the death penalty. In fact, children were treated with extreme cruelty at home, at school, and by the law.[56]

Over the years, this treatment changed as society became sensitive to the special needs of children. Beginning in the mid-nineteenth century, as immigrant youth poured into America, there was official recognition that children formed a separate group with its own separate needs. Around the nation, in cities such as New York, Boston, and Chicago, groups known as **child savers** formed to assist children in need. They created community programs to serve needy children and lobbied for a separate legal status for children, which ultimately led to the development of a formal juvenile justice system. The child saving movement and the history of the development of the juvenile justice system will be discussed in more detail in Chapter 13.

child savers
Nineteenth-century reformers who developed programs for troubled youth and influenced legislation creating the juvenile justice system; today some critics view them as being more concerned with control of the poor than with their welfare.

In 1920, parents accompany their 8-year-old son to a court appearance before a juvenile court judge. The boy was charged with stealing a bicycle.

Lewis W. Hine/George Eastman House/Getty Images

Delinquency and *Parens Patriae*

The current treatment of juvenile delinquents is a by-product of the developing national consciousness during the nineteenth century. The designation "delinquent" became popular at the onset of the twentieth century when the first separate juvenile courts were instituted. The child savers believed that treating minors and adults equivalently violated the humanitarian ideals of American society. Consequently, the newly emerging juvenile justice system operated under the *parens patriae* philosophy. Minors who engaged in illegal behavior were viewed as victims of improper care, custody, and treatment at home. Dishonest behavior was a sign that the state should step in and take control of the youths before they committed more serious crimes. The state, through its juvenile authorities, should act in the **best interests of the child**. This means that children should not be punished for their misdeeds but instead should be given the care and custody necessary to remedy and control wayward behavior. It makes no sense to find children guilty of specific crimes, such as burglary or petty larceny, because that stigmatizes them and labels them as thieves or burglars. Instead, the catchall term *juvenile delinquency* should be used, as it indicates that the child needs the care, custody, and treatment of the state.

best interests of the child
A philosophical viewpoint that encourages the state to take control of wayward children and provide care, custody, and treatment to remedy delinquent behavior.

The Legal Status of Delinquency

Though the child savers fought hard for a separate legal status of "juvenile delinquent" early in the twentieth century, the concept that children could be treated differently before the law can actually be traced back much farther to its roots in the British legal tradition. Early English jurisprudence held that children under the age of 7 were legally incapable of committing crimes. Children between the ages of 7 and 14 were responsible for their actions, but their age might be used to excuse or lighten their punishment. Our legal system still recognizes that many young people are incapable of making mature judgments and that responsibility for their acts should be limited. Children can intentionally steal cars and know full well that the act is illegal, but they may be incapable of fully understanding the consequences of their behavior and the harm it may cause. Therefore, the law does not punish a youth as it would an adult, and it sees youthful misconduct as evidence of unreasoned or impaired judgment.

Today, the legal status of "juvenile delinquent" refers to a minor child who has been found to have violated the penal code. Most states define "minor child" as an individual who falls under a statutory age limit, most commonly 17 or 18 years of age. Because of their minority status, juveniles are usually kept separate from adults and receive different consideration and treatment under the law. For example, most large police departments employ officers whose sole responsibility is youth crime and delinquency. Every state has some form of separate juvenile court with its own judges, probation department, and other facilities. Terminology is also different: Adults are tried in court; children are adjudicated. Adults can be punished; children are treated. If treatment is mandated, children can be sent to secure detention facilities; they cannot normally be committed to adult prisons.

Children also have their own unique legal status. Minors apprehended for a criminal act are usually charged with being a juvenile delinquent regardless of the crime they commit. These charges are usually confidential, trial records are kept secret, and the name, behavior, and background of delinquent offenders are sealed. Eliminating specific crime categories and maintaining secrecy are efforts to shield children from the stigma of a criminal conviction and to prevent youthful misdeeds from becoming a lifelong burden. Each state defines juvenile delinquency differently, setting its own age limits and boundaries. The federal government also has a delinquency category for youngsters who violate federal laws, but typically allows the states to handle delinquency matters.

Legal Responsibility of Youth

In our society, the actions of adults are controlled by two types of law: criminal and civil. Criminal laws prohibit activities that are injurious to the well-being of society and threaten the social order, such as drug use, theft, and rape; they are legal actions brought by state authorities against private citizens. Civil laws, on the other hand, control interpersonal or private activities and are usually initiated by individual citizens. The ownership and transfer of property, contractual relationships, and personal conflicts (torts) are the subject of the civil law. Also covered under the civil law are provisions for the care and custody of those people who cannot care for themselves—the mentally ill, incompetent, or infirm.

Today, the juvenile delinquency concept occupies a legal status falling somewhere between criminal and civil law. Under *parens patriae*, delinquent acts are not considered criminal violations nor are delinquents considered criminals. Children cannot be found guilty of a crime and punished like adult criminals. The legal action against them is considered more similar (though not identical) to a civil action that determines their "need for treatment." This legal theory recognizes that children who violate the law are in need of the same care and treatment as law-abiding citizens who cannot care for themselves and require state intervention into their lives.

Delinquent behavior is sanctioned less heavily than criminality because the law considers juveniles as being less responsible for their behavior than adults. As a class, adolescents are believed to (a) have a stronger preference for risk and novelty, (b) assess the potentially negative consequences of risky conduct less unfavorably than adults, (c) have a tendency to be impulsive and more concerned with short-term than long-term consequences, (d) have a different appreciation of time and self-control, and (e) be more susceptible to peer pressure.[57] Although many adolescents may be more responsible and calculating than adults, under normal circumstances the law is willing to recognize age as a barrier to having full responsibility over one's actions. The limited moral reasoning ability of very young offenders is taken into consideration when assessing their legal culpability. In *Timothy J. v. Superior Court of Sacramento County*, a California appellate court made it clear that some juvenile defendants may simply be too young to stand trial. The case involved an 11-year-old defendant prosecuted for stealing candy bars. The court ruled that the child was so immature that he could not understand the legal proceedings or assist in his own defense. In doing so, the justices overruled prior case law that held that children must have either a mental disorder or a developmental disability to be deemed incompetent to stand trial. In the words of the court:

> As a matter of law and logic, an adult's incompetence to stand trial must arise from a mental disorder or developmental disability that limits his or her ability to understand the nature of the proceedings and to assist counsel . . . The same may not be said of a young child whose developmental immaturity may result in trial incompetence despite the absence of any underlying mental or developmental abnormality.[58]

The upper age of jurisdiction is defined as the oldest age at which a juvenile court has original jurisdiction over an individual for law violating behavior. Today, 42 states and the District of Columbia set the upper limit of juvenile court jurisdiction at age 18; after his or her 18th birthday someone who commits crime is sent to adult court. In another 7 states, the cutoff is 17; New York and North Carolina set the juvenile age limit at 16.[59] In recent years the trend has been to expand juvenile court jurisdiction over teens in trouble with the law. Five states have raised the age of juvenile jurisdiction to cover all ages under 18: Connecticut started the trend in 2009, and Mississippi, Massachusetts, Illinois, and New Hampshire followed in 2010, 2012, 2013, and 2014, respectively.[60]

Juvenile vs. Adult Although youths share a lesser degree of legal responsibility than adults, the line between juvenile and adult offenders is often blurred. Both juveniles and adults are subject to arrest, trial, and incarceration. Appeal courts, recognizing this overlap, have granted juveniles many of the same legal protections granted to adults accused of criminal offenses. These legal protections include the right to consult an attorney, to be free from self-incrimination, and to be protected from illegal searches and seizures.

Although appreciation of the criminal nature of the delinquency concept has helped increase the legal rights of minors, it has also allowed state authorities to declare that some offenders are "beyond control" and cannot be treated as children. This recognition has prompted the policy of **waiver**, or transferring legal jurisdiction over the most serious and experienced juvenile offenders to the adult court for criminal prosecution. To the dismay of reformers, waived youth may find themselves serving time in adult prisons. And while punishment is no more certain or swift once they are tried as adults, kids transferred to adult courts are often punished more severely than they would have been if treated as the minors they really are.[61] It is possible that thousands of youths under age 18 have their cases processed in adult criminal court each year as a result of prosecutorial or judicial waiver, statutory exclusion, or because they reside in states with a lower age of criminal jurisdiction. (Waiver will be discussed in detail in Chapter 15.) On a more positive note, the number of juveniles being treated as adults has been in decline. On any given day, an estimated 4,600 youths under the age of 18 are inmates in adult jails; of these, 75 percent are being held as adults. The number of youths in adult jail has been in significant decline since 2000, when more than 7,500 were locked in adult jails.[62]

So though the *parens patriae* concept is still applied to children whose law violations are not considered serious, the more serious juvenile offenders can be declared "legal adults" and placed outside the jurisdiction of the juvenile court.

waiver (also known as bindover or removal)
Transferring legal jurisdiction over the most serious and experienced juvenile offenders to the adult court for criminal prosecution.

Status Offenders

status offense
Conduct that is illegal only because the child is underage.

A child also becomes subject to state authority for committing **status offenses**—actions that would not be considered illegal if perpetrated by an adult; such conduct is illegal only because the child is underage. For example, more than 40 states now have some form of law prohibiting minors from purchasing, using, or possessing tobacco products. The Massachusetts statue is contained in Exhibit 1.2.

These statutes also impose a variety of sanctions on juveniles who smoke, including a monetary fine, suspension from school, and denial of a driver's license. In Florida, it is unlawful for any person under 18 years of age to knowingly possess any tobacco product. For a first violation, the punishment is 16 hours

---

exhibit 1.2

Massachusetts Crimes Against Public Health, Chapter 270, Section 6

Whoever sells a cigarette, chewing tobacco, snuff or any tobacco in any of its forms to any person under the age of eighteen or, not being his parent or guardian, gives a cigarette, chewing tobacco, snuff or tobacco in any of its forms to any person under the age of eighteen shall be punished by a fine of not less than one hundred dollars for the first offense, not less than two hundred dollars for a second offense and not less than three hundred dollars for any third or subsequent offense.

SOURCE: The 189th General Court of the Commonwealth of Massachusetts, https://malegislature.gov/Laws/GeneralLaws/PartIV/TitleI/Chapter270/Section6 (accessed September 2016).

of community service or a \$25 fine. In addition, the underage purchaser must attend a school-approved anti-tobacco program. A second violation within 12 weeks of the first violation gets a \$25 fine; for a third or subsequent violation within 12 weeks of the first violation, the teen can have his or her driver's license withheld, suspended, or revoked by the court.[63] Exhibit 1.3 describes some typical status offense statutes.

How Common Is Status Offending?

It is extremely difficult to evaluate the annual number of status offenses, as most cases escape police detection and those that do not are often handled informally by social service agencies. Yet according to data compiled by the Federal Bureau

---

exhibit 1.3

Status Offense Laws: Kentucky and Wisconsin

Kentucky

The court shall have exclusive jurisdiction in proceedings concerning any child living, or found within the district, who allegedly:

(1) Has been an habitual runaway from his parent or person exercising custodial control or supervision of the child;

(2) Is beyond the control of the school or beyond the control of parents;

(3) Has been an habitual truant from school;

(4) Has committed a tobacco offense under;

(5) Has committed an alcohol offense under;

Wisconsin

The court has exclusive original jurisdiction over a child alleged to be in need of protection or services which can be ordered by the court, and:

(1) Who is without a parent or guardian;

(2) Who has been abandoned;

(2m) Whose parent has relinquished custody of the child;

(3) Who has been the victim of abuse, including injury that is self-inflicted or inflicted by another;

(3m) Who is at substantial risk of becoming the victim of abuse, including injury that is self-inflicted or inflicted by another, based on reliable and credible information that another child in the home has been the victim of such abuse;

(4) Whose parent or guardian signs the petition requesting jurisdiction under this subsection and is unable or needs assistance to care for or provide necessary special treatment or care for the child;

(4m) Whose guardian is unable or needs assistance to care for or provide necessary special treatment or care for the child, but is unwilling or unable to sign the petition requesting jurisdiction under this subsection;

(5) Who has been placed for care or adoption in violation of law;

(8) Who is receiving inadequate care during the period of time a parent is missing, incarcerated, hospitalized or institutionalized;

(9) Who is at least age 12, signs the petition requesting jurisdiction under this subsection and is in need of special treatment or care which the parent, guardian or legal custodian is unwilling, neglecting, unable or needs assistance to provide;

(10) Whose parent, guardian or legal custodian neglects, refuses or is unable for reasons other than poverty to provide necessary care, food, clothing, medical or dental care or shelter so as to seriously endanger the physical health of the child;

(10m) Whose parent, guardian or legal custodian is at substantial risk of neglecting, refusing or being unable for reasons other than poverty to provide necessary care, food, clothing, medical or dental care or shelter so as to endanger seriously the physical health of the child, based on reliable and credible information that the child's parent, guardian or legal custodian has neglected, refused or been unable for reasons other than poverty to provide necessary care, food, clothing, medical or dental care or shelter so as to endanger seriously the physical health of another child in the home;

(11) Who is suffering emotional damage for which the parent, guardian or legal custodian has neglected, refused or been unable and is neglecting, refusing or unable, for reasons other than poverty, to obtain necessary treatment or to take necessary steps to ameliorate the symptoms;

(11m) Who is suffering from an alcohol and other drug abuse impairment, exhibited to a severe degree, for which the parent, guardian or legal custodian is neglecting, refusing or unable to provide treatment; or

(13) Who has not been immunized.

SOURCES: Kentucky Statutes, "Status Offenders: 630.020, Jurisdiction of Court," https://docjt.ky.gov/legal/documents/JuvenileLawbooklet.pdf; Wisconsin Statutes, Children's Code § 48.13, http://legis.wisconsin.gov/statutes/Stat0048.pdf (accessed September 2016).

of Investigation, about 150,000 juveniles are arrested each year for status-type offenses such as disorderly conduct, breaking curfew, and violating liquor laws.[64] About 109,000 of these status offenders are petitioned to juvenile court each year.[65] As Figure 1.6 shows, the number of status offenders petitioned to juvenile court has plunged in recent years, declining about 50 percent since 2000. Petitions for such acts as running away, curfew and liquor law violations, and ungovernability have had the greatest declines.

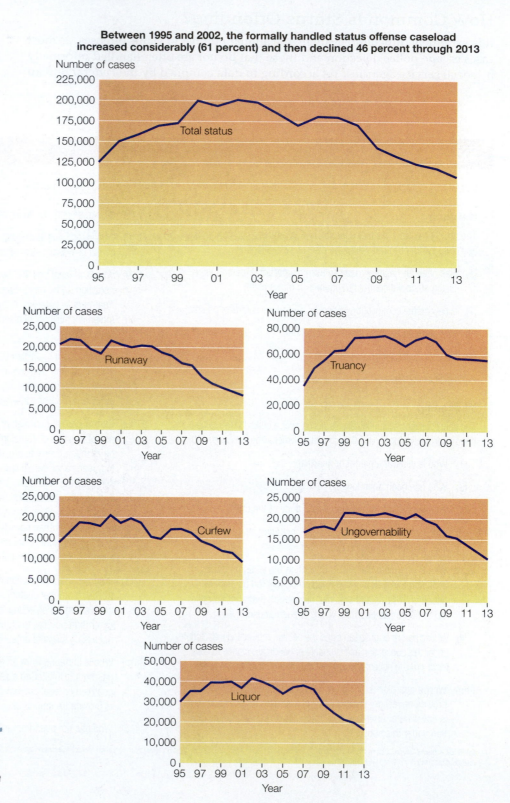

Between 1995 and 2002, the formally handled status offense caseload increased considerably (61 percent) and then declined 46 percent through 2013

figure 1.6

Status Offense Trends

SOURCE: Office of Juvenile Justice and Delinquency Prevention and National Center for Juvenile Justice, *Juvenile Court Statistics, 2013*, http://www.ojjdp.gov/ojstatbb/njcda/pdf /jcs2013.pdf (accessed September 2016).

The History of Status Offenses

A historical basis exists for status offense statutes. It was common practice early in the nation's history to place disobedient or runaway youths in orphan asylums, residential homes, or houses of refuge.[66] In 1646, the Massachusetts Stubborn Child Law was enacted, which provided, "If any man have a stubborne and rebellious sonne of sufficient years and understanding, which will not obey the voice of his father or the voice of his mother, and that when they have chastened him will not harken unto them" they could bring him before the court and testify that he would not obey. If the magistrate then found the child to be unrepentant and incapable of control, such a child could be put to death.[67]

When the first juvenile courts were established in Illinois, the Chicago Bar Association described part of their purpose as follows:

> The whole trend and spirit of the [1899 Juvenile Court Act] is that the State, acting through the Juvenile Court, exercises that tender solicitude and care over its neglected, dependent wards that a wise and loving parent would exercise with reference to his own children under similar circumstances.[68]

State control over a child's noncriminal behavior is believed to support and extend the *parens patriae* philosophy because it is assumed to be in the best interests of the child. Typically, status offenders are petitioned to the juvenile court when it is determined that their parents are unable or unwilling to care for or control them and that the offender's behavior is self-destructive or harmful to society. Young teenage girls are much more likely to engage in precocious sex while under the influence of alcohol if they are involved with older teens. Parents may petition their underage daughter to juvenile court if they feel her sexual behavior is getting out of control and they are powerless to stop its occurrence.[69] The case then falls within the jurisdiction of state legal authorities, and failure to heed a judicial command might result in detention in the juvenile correctional system.

At first, juvenile codes referred to status offenders as **wayward minors**, sometimes failing to distinguish them in any significant way from juvenile delinquents. Both classes of children could be detained in the same detention centers and placed in the same youth correctional facilities. A trend begun in the 1960s has resulted in the creation of separate status offense categories—children, minors, persons, youths, or juveniles in need of supervision (CHINS, MINS, PINS, YINS, or JINS)—which vary from state to state. The purpose of creating separate status offender categories was to shield noncriminal youths from the stigma attached to the label "juvenile delinquent" and to signify that they were troubled youths who had special needs and problems. Most states now have separate categories for juvenile conduct that would not be considered criminal if committed by an adult; these sometimes pertain to neglected or dependent children as well.

wayward minors
Early legal designation of youths who violate the law because of their minority status; now referred to as status offenders.

Legally, delinquents and status offenders are considered independent concepts, but the distinction between them has become blurred. Some noncriminal conduct may be included in the definition of delinquency, and some less serious criminal offenses occasionally may be included within the status offender definition. Replacing a juvenile delinquency charge with a status offense charge can be used as a bargaining chip to encourage youths to admit to the charges against them in return for a promise of being treated as a (less stigmatized) status offender receiving less punitive treatment. Concept Summary 1.1 summarizes the differences among delinquents, adult criminals, and status offenders.

The Status Offender in the Juvenile Justice System

Separate status offense categories may avoid some of the stigma associated with the delinquency label, but they can have relatively little practical effect on the child's treatment. Youths in either category can be picked up by the police and

Treatment Differences Among Juvenile Delinquents, Status Offenders, and Adults

	Juvenile Delinquent	Status Offender	Adult
Act	Delinquent	Behavior forbidden to minors	Criminal
Enforcement	Police	Police	Police
Detention	Secure detention	Nonsecure shelter care	Jail
Adjudication	Juvenile court	Juvenile court	Criminal court
Correctional Alternative	State training school	Community treatment facility	Prison

brought to a police station. They can be petitioned to the same juvenile court, where they have a hearing before the same judge and come under the supervision of the probation department, the court clinic, and the treatment staff. At a hearing, status offenders may see little difference between the treatment they receive and the treatment of the delinquent offenders sitting across the room. Although status offenders are usually not detained or incarcerated with delinquents, they can be transferred to secure facilities if they are repeatedly unruly and considered uncontrollable; about 5 percent of all status offenders are placed in pretrial detention of some sort. Some states are more likely to petition status offenses formally to the juvenile court, while others handle most cases informally. Within individual states, some courts make a habit of prosecuting status offenders, and others will divert most cases to treatment institutions.[70] Some states process status offenders to the social service system while others keep them within the jurisdiction of the juvenile court. The Evidence-Based Juvenile Justice feature reviews a program that has been successful in helping status offenders.

Efforts have been ongoing to reduce the penalties and stigma borne by status offenders and help kids avoid becoming status offenders. The Case Profile entitled "Akeema's Story" shows how one young status offender was able to overcome her problems.

Office of Juvenile Justice and Delinquency Prevention (OJJDP)
Branch of the US Justice Department charged with shaping national juvenile justice policy through disbursement of federal aid and research funds.

The federal government's **Office of Juvenile Justice and Delinquency Prevention (OJJDP)**, an agency created to identify the needs of youths and fund policy initiatives in the juvenile justice system, has made it a top priority to encourage the removal of status offenders from secure lockups, detention centers, and post-disposition treatment facilities that also house delinquent offenders. States in violation of the initiative are ineligible to receive any of the millions of dollars in direct grants for local juvenile justice annually awarded by the federal government.[71] This initiative has been responsible for significantly lowering the number of status offenders kept in secure confinement.

Despite this mandate, juvenile court judges in many states can still detain status offenders in secure lockups if the youths are found in contempt of court. The act that created the OJJDP was amended in 1987 to allow status offenders to be detained and incarcerated for violations of valid court orders.[72] Children have been detained for misbehaving in court or not dressing appropriately for their court appearance.[73] There is also some question whether the "valid court order" exception disproportionately affects girls, who are much more likely to be arrested for status offenses than boys and receive more severe punishment than boys. Because girls are more likely to be status offenders, criminalization of status offenses through the "violation of court order" exception may contribute to the increasing numbers of girls in the juvenile justice system.[74]

Southwest Key Programs

Key programs focus on unlocking the potential of youth and families through a variety of residential and nonresidential program models and settings. Headquartered in Austin, Texas, Southwest Key Programs provides direct services through child welfare, mental health, juvenile justice, and educational systems. The success of their Austin Family Keys program prompted other applications around the United States; the program is now being used in Texas, California, New York, Georgia, Arizona, and Wisconsin.

Southwest Key's Alternatives to Out-of-Home Placement model provides case management services that help prevent at-risk youth from repeat violations that could result in juvenile probation or detention. Youth and families are provided with a unique combination of support services designed to address the needs of their specific circumstances, discourage future acts of delinquent behavior, and promote positive youth development. The level of service provided is tailored to the individualized need of the particular youth and family referred to the program.

The model addresses the multiple contributing factors to a youth's potential detention, including but not limited to multiple violations, failure to attend school, and curfew violations. Casework staff work in partnership with the youth and family to address and overcome these factors, ultimately supporting their efforts to lead law-abiding and productive lives.

Family Keys Runaway Program

The Family Keys Runaway Program serves young people and their families involved with family court as a result of a runaway emergency PINS (Person in Need of Supervision) petition. The goal is to decrease the number of runaway youth placed in out-of-home care and to keep the child in the home. The program provides families with intensive, short-term crisis intervention services coupled with service referrals and linkages. It also provides families who have filed a runaway petition an immediate home-based intervention service in which a workable plan is developed to address the needs of the runaway youth and the family as a whole.

Immediately upon filing a runaway petition, a caseworker is available to talk through concerns with the family and begin discussion about needed/available services and supports. The family is given information regarding the court process and what will take place when the child is picked up. While the child remains missing, regular intervention focuses on the family's concerns for their child, as well as anger issues and family conflict. Once the child is found or returns home, the caseworker is immediately available to attend court with the family and provide recommendations to the court based on the predetermined plan and family assessment. The family support caseworker continues to work with the family to assist in implementing the plan and/or recommendations made by family court. During this time the caseworker also works to develop a relationship with the youth and assess his or her concerns. In addition, the caseworker ensures that support services are put into place as quickly as possible, utilizing community resources as needed. If the child is placed for short-term evaluation, the caseworker works closely with the placement agency to ensure meaningful family involvement and to see that the youth returns to his or her community as soon as possible.

Family Keys staff continues working with the family in the development and implementation of a long-term plan that includes needed services and support. Families receive services for a four- to eight-week period during which crises can be calmed, service needs identified, and service referrals and linkages put into place. The family support caseworkers work in partnership with families, adults, and youths to deescalate family conflicts, develop youth–adult contracts, and identify helpful services, prosocial activities, and supports available within the family network and the community.

CRITICAL THINKING

How would you answer a critic who argues that all social programs should be cut and that social programs are a waste of time? Does the Family Keys success story influence your thinking about intervening with troubled youth?

SOURCES: Southwest Key Programs, http://www.swkey.org/; Family Keys Runaway Program, http://www.swkey.org/programs/youth_justice/Family_Keys.pdf (accessed September 2016).

Several studies have found that as a result of deinstitutionalization, children who can no longer be detained are being recycled or relabeled as delinquent offenders so they can be housed in secure facilities. Juvenile court expert Barry Feld finds that juvenile court judges may relabel status offenders as delinquents in order to keep control over kids they feel are incorrigible. Evaluating data on assault charges leveled against adolescent girls, he found that increases in the number of girls being sent to juvenile institutions reflects policy changes rather than an actual increase in criminal activity. Ironically, a policy change designed to remove

case profile

Akeema's Story

AKEEMA PARKER ran away from home at the age of 17. She struggled with family issues and felt she could no longer live with her mother, stepfather, and younger siblings in their California home. Arriving in Colorado with no family support, no money, and no place to live, she joined other runaway adolescents, homeless on the streets. Akeema was using drugs and was eventually arrested and detained at a juvenile detention center for possession of methamphetamines and providing false information to a police officer. Five feet seven inches tall and weighing only 95 pounds, Akeema was an addict. Her health and quality of life were suffering greatly.

When Akeema entered the juvenile justice system she was a few months from turning 18. Due to issues of jurisdiction, budget concerns, and Akeema's age, system administrators encouraged the caseworker assigned to Akeema to make arrangements for her to return to her family in California. After interviewing her at length about her situation and need for treatment, the caseworker could see that Akeema had a strong desire to get her life back on track. She needed assistance, but the cost of her treatment would be more than $3,000 per month, and the county agency's budget was already stretched. Despite objections from administrators, the caseworker remained a strong advocate for Akeema, convincing them of the harsh reality she would face back at home without first receiving drug treatment. The caseworker's advocacy on her behalf, combined with Akeema's motivation to get her life together, compelled the department to agree to pay for her treatment program, but only until she turned 18. She was transported from the juvenile detention center to a 90-day drug and alcohol treatment program where she was able to detoxify her body and engage in intensive counseling. The program also provided family therapy through phone counseling for Akeema's mother, allowing the family to reconnect. Despite this renewed contact, returning home was not an option for Akeema.

Nearing the end of the 90-day program, Akeema was again faced with being homeless, but she was determined not to return to the streets. She needed an environment where she could make new friends who did not use and be supported in her sobriety. Due to her age, the county department of human services had to close the case and could no longer assist her with housing or an aftercare program. The caseworker provided Akeema with some places to call, but she would have to be her own advocate.

Akeema contacted a group home run by a local church that takes runaway adolescents through county placements and provides a variety of services for clients and their families. In Akeema's case, no funding was available, so she contacted the therapist at the group home and explained her situation. Initially, they indicated that they would not be able to assist her, but Akeema was persistent and determined to find a quality living environment for herself. She continued to contact professionals at the group home to plead her case and was eventually successful. Akeema entered the group home, was able to get her high school diploma, and eventually enrolled in an independent living program that helped her find a job and get her own apartment. Akeema has remained in contact with her juvenile caseworker. Though she has struggled with her sobriety on occasion, she has refrained from using methamphetamines and is now at a healthy weight. Her caseworker continues to encourage Akeema and has been an ongoing source of support, despite the fact that the client file was closed several years ago. Akeema's success can be credited to the initial advocacy of her caseworker, the effective interventions, and the strong determination demonstrated by this young woman.

CRITICAL THINKING

1. Housing is a major issue for many teens aging out of the justice system. Often, children placed in alternative care settings, such as foster homes or residential treatment centers, are not prepared to live on their own when they turn 18 or are released from juvenile custody. How can this issue be addressed?

2. Many juvenile delinquents commit crimes while under the influence of alcohol or drugs or because they are addicted and need to support their habit. If this is the case, should these juveniles be court-ordered into a treatment program? Why or why not? What can be done to prevent alcohol and drug abuse in the teen population?

3. Teens close to the age of 18, like Akeema, may be too old for the juvenile justice system, but too young for the adult system. What should be done with juveniles who are close to 18 when they receive a delinquency charge? Should something be done to bridge the gap between the juvenile justice system and the adult criminal justice system?

4. What should happen to teens who run away from home? This is considered a status offense, but many communities do not charge runaways or require them to be involved in the juvenile justice system. Do you agree with this? Should something more be done and, if so, what?

kids from secure confinement and protect them from stigma and labeling resulted in more negative labels and confinement in even more secure institutions.[75]

Even more troubling is the charge that some minors no longer subject to detention as status offenders are being committed involuntarily and inappropriately to in-patient drug treatment facilities and psychiatric hospitals.[76]

Change in the treatment of status offenders reflects the current attitude toward children who violate the law. On the one hand, there appears to be a national movement to severely sanction youths who commit serious, violent offenses. On the other hand, a great effort has been made to remove nonserious cases, such as those involving status offenders, from the official agencies of justice and place these youths in informal, community-based treatment programs. The quality of treatment on status offenders can be significant. Wesley Jennings found that the effect of formal processing on status offenders can increase the likelihood that they will get involved in subsequent delinquency. Half of the status offenders he studied in Florida, both males and females, accumulated delinquent arrests in adolescence following their initial referral for a status offense.[77]

Reforming Status Offense Laws

In 1976, the federal government's National Advisory Commission on Criminal Justice Standards and Goals, a task force created to develop a national crime policy, opted for the nonjudicial treatment of status offenders: "The only conduct that should warrant family court intervention is conduct that is clearly self-destructive or otherwise harmful to the child." To meet this standard, the commission suggested that the nation's juvenile courts confine themselves to controlling five status offenses: habitual truancy, repeated disregard for parental authority, repeated running away, repeated use of intoxicating beverages, and delinquent acts by youths under the age of 10.[78] Since this call to reform, a number of other prestigious institutions have joined in the call for status offense reform. The American Bar Association's National Juvenile Justice Standards Project, designed to promote significant improvements in the way children are treated by the police and the courts, called for the end of juvenile court jurisdiction over status offenders: "A juvenile's acts of misbehavior, ungovernability, or unruliness which do not violate the criminal law should not constitute a ground for asserting juvenile court jurisdiction over the juvenile committing them."[79] In 2006, the ABA issued this statement about reforming the juvenile status offender process:

> Many teens come before the courts because of behavior that would not otherwise subject them to judicial involvement if they were adults. Lawyers should examine how law,

Status offenses involve behaviors, such as drinking and smoking, that are forbidden to minors but legal for adults. Should a teen be placed in custody for underage smoking or running away or skipping school? Are such controls contrary to the ideals of freedom and liberty? Should any behaviors be prohibited youth because of their age, and if so, what are they?

Monkey Business Images/Getty Images

prosecutorial policy, and court practice address youth who are chronic runaways, persistent school truants, or continually out-of-control at home. They should also examine how these interventions differ between boys and girls, since there has been a significant increase in the number of girls entering the juvenile justice system. Special attention also needs to be given to the problem of and solutions to chronic truancy.[80]

These calls for reform prompted a number of states to experiment with replacing juvenile court jurisdiction over most status offenders with community-based treatment programs. Some states, such as Connecticut, have completely reorganized the treatment of status offenders and now refer all status offense cases involving children under 16 to the Department of Children and Family Services as a Family With Service Needs (FWSN). The troubled youths and their families are now directed to community resources for assistance and treatment, and those with specific treatment needs are referred to family support centers for individualized, group, and family therapy. The law provides for the coordinated utilization of a wide range of public and private social, educational, and court services at a local, regional, and statewide level. Kids cannot be placed in detention, though the juvenile court does retain authority over children who exhibit noncriminal behaviors, and although these children cannot be detained in a detention or correctional facility, they can be detained if they violate a court order because violation of a court order is a delinquent act.[81]

New York now requires that all alleged status offenders and their families be offered intervention and diversion services before status offense petitions may be filed. Only after intervention services have been offered and failed may the social service agency or juvenile justice agency designated to provide prevention services determine if it is appropriate to seek court involvement. New York has also increased the age limit for status offense jurisdiction from 16 to 18 so that thousands more needy kids fall under the jurisdiction of the New York family court each year.[82]

Other states have amended their laws to eliminate vague terms and language.[83] A few states have tried to amend status offense laws and offer help to families with neglected or dependent children, giving child protective services the primary responsibility for their care. However, juvenile court judges strongly resist the removal of status jurisdiction. They believe that reducing their authority over children leads to limiting juvenile court jurisdiction to only the most hardcore juvenile offenders and interferes with their ability to help youths before they commit serious antisocial acts.[84] Their concerns are fueled by research that shows that many status offenders, especially runaways living on the street, have serious emotional problems and engage in self-destructive behaviors ranging from substance abuse to self-mutilation and suicide.[85]

Are They Really Different?

Those who favor removing status offenders from juvenile court authority charge that their experience with the legal system further stigmatizes these already troubled youths, exposes them to the influence of "true" delinquents, and enmeshes them in a system that cannot really afford to help them.

Research shows that a majority of youth routinely engage in some form of status offenses and that those who refrain form an atypical minority.[86] "Illegal" acts such as teen sex and substance abuse have become normative and commonplace. It makes little sense to have the juvenile court intervene with kids who are caught in what has become routine teenage behavior.

In contrast, juvenile court jurisdiction over status offenders may be defended if in fact the youths' offending patterns are similar to those of delinquents. Is their current offense only the tip of an antisocial iceberg, or are they actually noncriminal youths who need only the loving hand of a substitute parent-figure interested in their welfare? Some studies show that many status offenders also had prior arrests for delinquent acts and that many delinquents exhibited behaviors that would define them as status offenders. One recent study that compared groups of status offenders and delinquents in New York found that the groups were very similar in terms of self-reported delinquency, histories of abuse and placement, peer influences, and psychiatric diagnosis. Males and those arrested by police were more likely to be petitioned as delinquents; females who had not yet been arrested were more likely to be treated as status offenders. Thus, the real difference between JDs and status offenders may be more indicative of how the system labels their behavior than actual offender behavior.[87]

These disparate findings may also be explained in part by the fact that there may be different types of status offenders, some similar to delinquents and others who are quite different.[88] It might be more realistic to divide status offenders into three groups: first-time status offenders, chronic status offenders, and those with both a delinquent record and a status offense record.[89] The fact that many young offenders have mixed delinquent/status offender records indicates that these legal categories are not entirely independent. It is also recognized that some "pure" first-time status offenders are quite different from delinquents and that a juvenile court experience can be harmful to them and escalate the frequency and seriousness of their law-violating behaviors, The removal of these status offenders from the juvenile court is an issue that continues to be debated. The predominant view today is that many status offenders and delinquents share similar social and developmental problems and that consequently both categories should fall under the jurisdiction of the juvenile court.

Increasing Social Control over Youth

Those in favor of retaining the status offense category point to society's responsibility to care for troubled youths. Some have suggested that the courts' failure to extend social control over wayward teens neglects the rights of concerned parents who are not able to care for and correct their children.[90] Others maintain that the status offense should remain a legal category so that juvenile courts can "force" a youth into receiving treatment.[91] Although it is recognized that a court appearance can produce negative stigma, the taint may be less important than the need for treatment.[92] In addition, concern over serious delinquency has resulted in laws that actually expand social control over juveniles.[93]

Curfews   One way jurisdictions have attempted to maintain greater control over wayward youth has been the implementation of curfew laws. The thought is that the opportunity to commit crimes will be reduced if troubled kids are given a curfew.

The first curfew law was created in Omaha, Nebraska, in 1880, and today about 500 US cities have youth curfews. Curfews typically prohibit children under 18 from being on the streets after 11:00 PM during the week and after midnight on weekends. About 100 cities also have daytime curfews designed to keep children off the streets and in school.[94]

Each year thousands of youth are arrested for curfew violations, and police favor curfews as an effective tool to control vandalism, graffiti, nighttime burglary, and auto theft. Nonetheless, so far there is little conclusive evidence that curfews have a significant impact on youth crime rates. There are a few research studies that show that curfews can reduce both theft and violent crime.[95] These are balanced by other empirical studies that find that juvenile crime and substance abuse levels are not affected by curfews.[96] Some research efforts have even found that after curfews were implemented victimizations increased significantly during noncurfew hours. This indicates that rather than suppressing delinquency, curfews merely shift the time of occurrence of the offenses. Some studies have found that strict enforcement of curfew laws actually increases juvenile crime rates.[97] The failure of curfews to control crime coupled with their infringement on civil rights prompted the American Civil Liberties Union to condemn the practice.[98] Other civil libertarians maintain that curfews are an overreaction to juvenile crime, that they are ineffective, and give the police too much power to control citizens who are being punished merely because of their age.[99]

There are a number of ongoing legal challenges to curfew laws. However, because the Supreme Court has not given guidance on this issue, some lower courts have upheld their constitutionality while others have struck them down. Typically, the legal issues challenged involve First Amendment rights. Curfew laws limiting the movement of juveniles impede their ability to engage in activities protected by the First Amendment, including free speech, assembly, and association.[100]

Other challenges have been based on discriminatory enforcement. A lawsuit against the city of Rochester, New York, found that the ordinance enabled police to arrest and interrogate a disproportionate percentage of minority youth; 94 percent of those picked up on curfew violations were black or Hispanic.[101] The Massachusetts Supreme Judicial Court struck down provisions of a local curfew law that made it a crime for youth under 17 to be on the street after 11:00 PM unless accompanied by a parent or a guardian. While they left in place civil penalties that allowed individuals convicted of violating the curfew to be fined up to $300, it is no longer permissible to charge curfew violators with a crime.[102] In 2016, the city of Los Angeles settled a lawsuit that accused the Los Angeles Police Department of enforcing curfew laws designed to prevent gang members from meeting, years after those laws were struck down as unconstitutional by the California court of appeals. The city is going to have to pay as much as $30 million to assist thousands of people who were subjected to unlawful curfews included in city gang injunctions.[103]

Disciplining Parents   So what happens if kids repeatedly break curfew and get into trouble and their parents refuse to do anything about it (or are incapable of doing anything)? Since the early twentieth century, there have been laws aimed at disciplining parents for contributing to the delinquency of a minor. The first of these was enacted in Colorado in 1903, and today all states have some form of statute requiring parents to take some responsibility for their children's misbehavior.[104] All states make it either mandatory or discretionary for the juvenile court to require a parent or guardian to pay at least part of the support costs for a child who is adjudicated delinquent and placed out of the home. Even when the payment is required, however, it is based on the parent's financial ability to make such payments. During the past decade, approximately one-half of the states enacted or strengthened existing parental liability statutes that make parents criminally liable for the actions of their delinquent children. These laws generally fall into one of three categories:

- *Civil liability.* An injured party may bring a case against the parents for property damage or personal injury caused by their child.
- *Criminal liability.* The guardian or other adult may be held criminally responsible for contributing to the delinquency of a minor. These laws apply when an adult does some action that encourages delinquent behavior by a child.
- *General involvement.* These statutes are based upon legislative efforts to make parents more involved in the juvenile court process and include such things as requiring the parents to pay for court costs, restitution, and treatment, and to participate in the juvenile's case. Failure to comply with the parental involvement requirements can lead to more punitive sanctions.[105]

exhibit 1.4

Parental Responsibility Laws

State	Auto	Property Damage	Personal Injury
Vermont	None	Liability up to $5,000 per child for willful or malicious damage to property. Vermont Statutes Title 15 Section 901.	Liability up to $5,000 per child for willful or malicious damage to person. Vermont Statutes Title 15 Section 901.
Virginia	None	Liability up to $2,500 for damage to public property by minor living with parents. Virginia Statutes Sec. 8.01-43. Same as to private property. Sec. 8.01-44.	None
Washington	None	Liability up to $5,000 for minor living with parents who willfully or maliciously defaces or destroys property. Revised Code of Washington Sec., 4.24.190.	None

Within this general framework there is a great deal of variation in responsibility laws. Some states (Florida, Idaho, Virginia) require parents to reimburse the government for the costs of detention or care of their children. Others (Maryland, Missouri, Oklahoma) demand that parents make restitution payments—for example, paying for damage caused by their children who vandalized a school. All states have incorporated parental liability laws in their statutes, although most recent legislation places limits on recovery; in some states, such as Texas, the upward boundary can be as much as $25,000. Exhibit 1.4 illustrates three such statutes.

Parents may also be held civilly liable, under the concept of *vicarious liability*, for the damages caused by their child. In some states, parents are responsible for up to $300,000 in damages; in others the liability cap is $3,500 (sometimes homeowner's insurance covers at least some of liability). Parents can also be charged with civil negligence if they should have known of the damage a child was about to inflict but did nothing to stop it—for example, when they give a weapon to an emotionally unstable youth. Juries have levied awards of up to $500,000 in such cases. Since 1990 there have been at least 18 cases in which parents have been ordered to serve time in jail because their children have been truant from school.

Some critics charge that these laws contravene the right to due process, because they are unfairly used only against lower-class and minority parents. As legal scholar Elena Laskin points out, imposing penalties on these parents may actually be detrimental.[106] Forcing a delinquent's mother to pay a fine removes money from someone who is already among society's poorest people. If a single mother is sent to jail, it leaves her children, including those who are not delinquent, with no parent to raise them; the kids may become depressed, and lose concentration and sleep. Even if punishment encourages the parent to take action it may be too late, because by the time a parent is charged with violating the statute, the child has already committed a crime, indicating that any damaging socialization by the parent has already occurred.[107] Finally, responsibility laws may not take the age of the child into account, leaving important questions unanswered: Are parents of older offenders equally responsible as those whose much younger children violate the law? Does an adolescent's personal share of responsibility increase with age? Despite these problems, surveys indicate that the public favors parental responsibility laws.[108]

SUMMARY

1 Discuss the problems of youth in American culture

- Young people are extremely vulnerable to the negative consequences of school failure, substance abuse, and early sexuality.
- Adolescents and young adults often experience stress, confusion, and depression because of trouble and conflict occurring in their families, schools, and communities.
- The problems of American society and the daily stress of modern life have had a significant effect on our nation's youth as they go through their tumultuous teenage years.

2 Distinguish between ego identity and role diffusion

- According to psychologist Erik Erikson, adolescence is a time of trial and uncertainty for many youths.
- According to Erikson, ego identity is formed when youths develop a full sense of the self, combining how they see themselves and how they fit in with others.
- Role diffusion occurs when people spread themselves too thin, experience personal uncertainty, and place themselves at the mercy of people who promise to give them a sense of identity they cannot develop for themselves.

3 Discuss the specific issues facing American youth

- Many children suffer from chronic health problems and receive inadequate health care.
- Children are living in substandard housing—high-rise, multiple-family dwellings—which can have a negative influence on their long-term psychological health.
- Although all young people face stress in the education system, the risks are greatest for the poor, members of racial and ethnic minorities, and recent immigrants.
- Minority kids usually attend the most underfunded schools, receive inadequate educational opportunities, and have the fewest opportunities to achieve conventional success.

4 Examine the recent social improvements enjoyed by American youth

- Teenage birthrates nationwide have declined substantially during the past decade.
- More children are being read to by their parents than ever before.
- Fewer children with health risks are being born today than in 1990.

5 Discuss why the study of delinquency is so important and what this study entails

- The problems of youth in modern society are both a major national concern and an important subject for academic study.
- Though most juvenile law violations are minor, some young offenders are extremely dangerous and violent.
- Some youths involved in multiple serious criminal acts are referred to as lifestyle, repeat, or chronic delinquent offenders.
- The scientific study of delinquency requires understanding the nature, extent, and cause of youthful law violations and the methods devised for their control. The study of delinquency also involves analysis of the law enforcement, court, and correctional agencies designed to treat youthful offenders who fall into the arms of the law—known collectively as the juvenile justice system.

6 Describe the life of children during feudal times

- In Europe during the Middle Ages (roughly 500 to 1500 CE), the concept of childhood as we know it today did not exist.
- In the paternalistic family of the time, the father was the final authority on all family matters and exercised complete control over the social, economic, and physical well-being of the family.
- Western culture did not have a sense of childhood as a distinct period of life until the very late nineteenth and early twentieth centuries.
- Discipline was severe during this period. Young children of all classes were subjected to stringent rules and regulations. They were beaten severely for any sign of disobedience or ill temper.
- The roots of the impersonal relationship between parent and child can be traced to high mortality rates, which made sentimental and affectionate relationships risky.

7 Articulate the treatment of children in the seventeenth and eighteenth centuries

- Extended families gave way to the nuclear family structure with which we are familiar today.
- To provide more control over children, grammar and boarding schools were established and began to flourish in many large cities during this time.
- The philosophy of the Enlightenment stressed a humanistic view of life, freedom, family, reason, and law. The ideal person was sympathetic to others and receptive to new ideas.

- Under the apprenticeship system, children were placed in the care of adults who trained them to discharge various duties and obtain skills.
- Chancery courts became a significant arm of the British legal system.
- The *parens patriae* concept gave the state the power to act on behalf of the child and provide care and protection equivalent to that of a parent.

8 Discuss childhood in the American colonies

- The colonies adopted Poor Laws systems similar to those in England.
- Apprenticeship, indenture, and binding out of children became integral parts of colonization in America.
- In America, as in England, moral discipline was rigidly enforced. "Stubborn child" laws were passed that required children to obey their parents.
- Although judges considered the age of an offender when deciding punishments, both adults and children were often eligible for the same forms of punishment—prison, corporal punishment, and even the death penalty.

9 Evaluate the child savers and the creation of delinquency

- Child savers were nineteenth-century reformers who developed programs for troubled youth and influenced legislation creating the juvenile justice system.
- The designation "delinquent" became popular at the onset of the twentieth century when the first separate juvenile courts were instituted.
- The state, through its juvenile authorities, was expected to act in the best interests of the child.
- This philosophical viewpoint encourages the state to take control of wayward children and provide care, custody, and treatment to remedy delinquent behavior.

10 Identify the elements of juvenile delinquency today

- Today, the legal status of "juvenile delinquent" refers to a minor child who has been found to have violated the penal code.
- Most states define "minor child" as an individual who falls under a statutory age limit, most commonly 17 or 18 years of age.
- Because of their minority status, juveniles are usually kept separate from adults and receive different consideration and treatment under the law.
- Under *parens patriae*, delinquent acts are not considered criminal violations nor are delinquents considered criminals. Children cannot be found guilty of a crime and punished like adult criminals.
- Although youths share a lesser degree of legal responsibility than adults, they are subject to arrest, trial, and incarceration.

11 Define what is meant by the term *status offender*

- A child also becomes subject to state authority for committing status offenses—actions that would not be considered illegal if perpetrated by an adult; such conduct includes running away, truancy, and disobedience.
- State control over a child's noncriminal behavior is believed to support and extend the *parens patriae* philosophy because it is assumed to be in the best interests of the child.
- Separate status offense categories may avoid some of the stigma associated with the delinquency label, but they can have relatively little practical effect on the child's treatment.
- Those in favor of retaining the status offense category point to society's responsibility to care for troubled youths.

KEY TERMS

Roper v. Simmons, p. 3
Miller v. Alabama, p. 3
ego identity, p. 5
role diffusion, p. 5
at-risk youth, p. 6
major depressive episode (MDE), p. 8
cyberbullying, p. 11
juvenile delinquency, p. 14

chronic delinquent offenders, p. 15
aging-out process, p. 15
persistence, p. 15
juvenile justice system, p. 15
paternalistic family, p. 16
primogeniture, p. 17
swaddling, p. 17
Poor Laws, p. 19

chancery courts, p. 19
parens patriae, p. 19
child savers, p. 22
best interests of the child, p. 22
waiver, p. 24
status offense, p. 24
wayward minors, p. 27
Office of Juvenile Justice and Delinquency Prevention (OJJDP), p. 28

QUESTIONS FOR DISCUSSION

1. Is it fair to have a separate legal category for youths? Considering how dangerous young people can be, does it make more sense to group offenders on the basis of what they have done and not on their age?

2. At what age are juveniles truly capable of understanding the seriousness of their actions?

3. Is it fair to institutionalize a minor simply for being truant or running away from home? Should the jurisdiction of status offenders be removed from juvenile court and placed with the state department of social services or some other welfare organization?

4. Should delinquency proceedings be secret? Does the public have the right to know who juvenile criminals are?

5. Can a get-tough policy help control juvenile misbehavior, or should *parens patriae* remain the standard?

6. Should juveniles who commit felonies such as rape or robbery be treated as adults?

VIEWPOINT

As the governor of a large southern state, you have been asked by a young man's family and friends to grant him a pardon. Nathaniel B. was convicted of second-degree murder and received a sentence of 28 years in the state penal system. Tried as an adult, he was found guilty of murder for intentionally killing Mr. Barry G., his English teacher, because he was angry over receiving a failing grade and being suspended for throwing water balloons. During trial, Nathaniel's attorney claimed that the gun Nathaniel brought to school had gone off accidentally after he pointed it at Mr. G. in an attempt to force him to let Nathaniel talk to two girls in the classroom.

"As he's holding the gun up, he's overwhelmed with tears," Nathaniel's lawyer told the jury. "His hand begins to shake, and the gun discharges. The gun discharged in the hands of an inexperienced 14-year-old with a junk gun." The prosecutor countered that Nathaniel's act was premeditated. He was frustrated because he was receiving an F in the class, and he was angry because he was being barred from talking to the girls. His victim "had no idea of the rage, hate, the anger, the frustration" filling the young man. There was also damaging information from police, who reported that Nathaniel told a classmate he was going to return to school and shoot the teacher; he said he'd be "all over the news."

At his sentencing hearing, Nathaniel read a statement: "Words cannot really explain how sorry I am, but they're all I have." His mother, Polly, blamed herself for her son's actions, claiming that he was surrounded by domestic abuse and alcoholism at home.

Now that he has served seven years in prison, Nathaniel's case has come to your attention. As governor, you recognize that his conviction and punishment raise a number of important issues. His mother claims that his actions were a product of abuse and violence in the home. You have read research showing that many habitually aggressive children have been raised in homes in which they were physically brutalized by their parents; this violence then persists into adulthood.

- Should troubled children, such as Nathaniel, be punished again by the justice system?

- Should Nathaniel be held personally responsible for actions that may in fact have been caused by a home life beyond his control?

- Even though he was only 14 years old when he committed his crime, Nathaniel's case was heard in an adult court, and he received a long sentence to an adult prison. Should minor children who commit serious crimes, as Nathaniel did, be treated as adults, or should they be tried within an independent juvenile justice system oriented to treatment and rehabilitation?

- Would you pardon Nathaniel now that he has served more than seven years in prison?

DOING RESEARCH ON THE WEB

Before you make your decision in Nathaniel's case, you might want to look at the website of Children's Rights (http://www.childrensrights.org/), a group that fights to enshrine in the law of the land every child's right to be protected from abuse and neglect and to grow up in a safe, stable, permanent home. In addition, the Coalition for Juvenile Justice (CJJ) champions children and promotes community safety. The coalition's website (http://www.juvjustice.org/) provides information on judicial waiver.

NOTES

All URLs accessed September 2016.

1. *Miller v. Alabama*, 567 U.S. ___ (2012), http://www.scotusblog.com /miller-v-alabama/.
2. Child Trends Data Bank, "Appendix 1, Number of Children Under Age 18 in the United States, and as a Percentage of the Population: Selected Years, 1950–2014, and Projections, 2020–2050," November 2015, http://www.childtrends.org/wp-content/uploads/2012/07 /53_appendix1.pdf; *US Bureau of the Census, Age and Sex Composition in the United States: 2013*, Table 1, http://www.census.gov/population /age/data/2013comp.html.
3. Jennifer M. Ortman and Christine E. Guarneri, "United States Population Projections: 2000 to 2050," US Census Bureau, https://www .census.gov/population/projections/files/analytical-document09 .pdf.
4. Erik Erikson, *Childhood and Society* (New York: W. H. Norton, 1963).
5. Roger Gould, "Adult Life Stages: Growth Toward Self-Tolerance," *Psychology Today* 8:74–78 (1975).
6. Leah Sharman and Genevieve A. Dingle, "Extreme Metal Music and Anger Processing," *Frontiers of Human Neuroscience*, May 2015, http://journal.frontiersin.org/article/10.3389/fnhum.2015.00272 /full; Steven Martino, Rebecca Collins, Marc Elliott, Amy Strachman, David Kanouse, and Sandra Berry, "Exposure to Degrading versus Nondegrading Music Lyrics and Sexual Behavior Among Youth," *Pediatrics* 118:430–441 (2006).
7. Children's Defense Fund, "The State of America's Children, 2014," http://www.childrensdefense.org/library/state-of-americas -children/.
8. US Census Bureau, "Income, Poverty and Health Insurance Coverage in the United States: 2014," September 16, 2015, http://census.gov /newsroom/press-releases/2015/cb15-157.html.
9. Ibid.
10. Kids Count Data Center, Annie E. Casey Foundation, "Children in Extreme Poverty (50 Percent Poverty)," http://datacenter.kidscount .org/data/tables/45-children-in-extreme-poverty-50-percent-poverty.
11. Ibid.
12. Forum on Child and Family Statistics, *America's Children in Brief: Key National Indicators of Well-Being, 2015*, http://www.childstats.gov /americaschildren/.
13. Ibid.
14. Ibid.
15. Children's Defense Fund, "The State of Black Children in America: A Portrait of Continuing Inequality, 2014," http://www.childrensdefense .org/library/data/state-of-black-children-2014.pdf.
16. American Psychological Survey, "APA Survey Raises Concern about Health Impact of Stress on Children and Families," November 9, 2010, http://www.apa.org/news/press/releases/2010/11/stress-in -america.aspx.
17. Gary Evans, Nancy Wells, and Annie Moch, "Housing and Mental Health: A Review of the Evidence and a Methodological and Conceptual Critique," *Journal of Social Issues* 59:475–501 (2003).
18. Forum on Child and Family Statistics, *America's Children in Brief: Key National Indicators of Well-Being, 2015*.
19. US Department of Labor, "Wage and Hour Division (WHD), Minimum Wage Laws in the States – August 1, 2016," https://www.dol .gov/whd/minwage/america.htm.
20. Forum on Child and Family Statistics, *America's Children in Brief: Key National Indicators of Well-Being, 2015*, "Education," http://www .childstats.gov/americaschildren/edu.asp.
21. Children's Defense Fund, *The State of America's Children 2014*, "Education," http://www.childrensdefense.org/library/state-of-americas -children/documents/2014-SOAC_education.pdf.
22. Forum on Child and Family Statistics, *America's Children in Brief*.
23. Jane Ireland and Rachel Monaghan, "Behaviours Indicative of Bullying Among Young and Juvenile Male Offenders: A Study of Perpetrator and Victim Characteristics," *Aggressive Behavior* 32:172–180 (2006).
24. Justin Patchin and Sameer Hinduja, "Bullies Move Beyond the Schoolyard: A Preliminary Look at Cyberbullying" *Youth Violence and Juvenile Justice* 4:148–169 (2006).
25. Ibid.
26. Janis Wolak, David Finkelhor, Kimberly Mitchell, and Michele Ybarra, "Online 'Predators' and Their Victims: Myths, Realities, and Implications for Prevention and Treatment," *American Psychologist* 63:111–128 (2008).
27. Justin Patchin, "Catfishing as a Form of Cyberbullying," Cyberbullying Research Center, http://cyberbullying.org /catfishing-as-a-form-of-cyberbullying.
28. Mike Celizic, "Her Teen Committed Suicide over 'Sexting': Cynthia Logan's Daughter Was Taunted About Photo She Sent to Boyfriend," *Today*: Parenting, March 6, 2009, http://www.today.com/parents /her-teen-committed-suicide-over-sexting-2D80555048.
29. Justin Patchin and Sameer Hinduja, "New Teen Sexting Study," Cyberbullying Research Center, http://cyberbullying.org /new-teen-sexting-study.
30. Robin Malinosky-Rummell and David Hansen, "Long-Term Consequences of Childhood Physical Abuse," *Psychological Bulletin* 114:68–79 (1993).
31. Centers for Disease Control and Prevention, "Suicide Prevention: Youth Suicide," http://www.cdc.gov/violenceprevention/suicide /youth_suicide.html.
32. University of Michigan, Monitoring the Future, "Use of Ecstasy, Heroin, Synthetic Marijuana, Alcohol, Cigarettes Declined Among US Teens in 2015," http://www.monitoringthefuture.org /pressreleases/15drugpr_complete.pdf.
33. *Digest of Education Statistics 2014* (Washington, DC: National Center for Education Statistics, Institute of Education Sciences, US Department of Education, 2015), https://nces.ed.gov/programs/digest/d14/.
34. FBI, *Crime in the United States, 2014*, https://www.fbi.gov/about-us /cjis/ucr/crime-in-the-u.s/2014/crime-in-the-u.s.-2014/tables/.
35. Arlen Egley, Jr., James C. Howell, and Meena Harris, "Highlights of the 2012 National Youth Gang Survey," National Youth Gang Center, 2014.
36. Mark Cohen, Alex R. Piquero, and Wesley G. Jennings, "Studying the Costs of Crime Across Offender Trajectories," *Criminology and Public Policy* 9:279–305 (2010); Cohen, Piquero, and Jennings, "Monetary Costs of Gender and Ethnicity Disaggregated Group-Based Offending," *American Journal of Criminal Justice* 35:159–172 (2010).
37. See Lawrence Stone, *The Family, Sex, and Marriage in England: 1500–1800* (New York: Harper & Row, 1977).
38. This section relies on Jackson Spielvogel, *Western Civilization* (St. Paul, MN: West, 1991), pp. 279–286.
39. Philippe Aries, *Centuries of Childhood: A Social History of Family Life* (New York: Knopf, 1962).
40. Nicholas Orme, *Medieval Children* (New Haven, CT: Yale University Press, 2003).
41. Aries, *Centuries of Childhood*.
42. See Douglas R. Rendleman, "*Parens Patriae*: From Chancery to the Juvenile Court," *South Carolina Law Review* 23:205 (1971).
43. See Stone, *The Family, Sex, and Marriage in England*, and Lawrence Stone, ed., *Schooling and Society: Studies in the History of Education* (Baltimore: Johns Hopkins University Press, 1970).
44. Ibid.
45. See Wiley B. Sanders, "Some Early Beginnings of the Children's Court Movement in England," *National Probation Association Yearbook* (New York: National Council on Crime and Delinquency, 1945).
46. Douglas Besharov, *Juvenile Justice Advocacy—Practice in a Unique Court* (New York: Practicing Law Institute, 1974), p. 2.
47. Rendleman, "*Parens Patriae*."
48. See Anthony Platt, "The Rise of the Child Saving Movement: A Study in Social Policy and Correctional Reform," *Annals of the American Academy of Political and Social Science* 381:21–38 (1969).
49. Robert H. Bremner, ed., and John Barnard, Tamara K. Hareven, and Robert M. Mennel, asst. eds., *Children and Youth in America* (Cambridge, MA: Harvard University Press, 1970), p. 64.
50. Elizabeth Pleck, "Criminal Approaches to Family Violence, 1640–1980," in Lloyd Ohlin and Michael Tonry, eds., *Family Violence* (Chicago: University of Chicago Press, 1989), pp. 19–58.
51. Ibid.
52. John R. Sutton, *Stubborn Children: Controlling Delinquency in the United States, 1640–1981* (Berkeley: University of California Press, 1988).
53. Pleck, "Criminal Approaches to Family Violence," p. 29.
54. John Demos, *Past, Present and Personal* (New York: Oxford University Press, 1986), pp. 80–88.

55. Elizabeth Pleck, *Domestic Tyranny: The Making of Social Policy Against Family Violence from Colonial Times to the Present* (New York: Oxford University Press, 1987), pp. 28–30.

56. Graeme Newman, *The Punishment Response* (Philadelphia: J. B. Lippincott, 1978), pp. 53–79.

57. Stephen J. Morse, "Immaturity and Irresponsibility," *Journal of Criminal Law and Criminology* 88:15–67 (1997).

58. *Timothy J. v. Superior Court of Sacramento* County, 58 Cal.Rptr.3d 746 (2007).

59. *OJJDP Statistical Briefing Book 2015*, Jurisdictional Boundaries, http://www.ojjdp.gov/ojstatbb/structure_process/qa04102.asp.

60. Campaign for Youth Justice, Raise the Age, 2016, http://cfyj.org/news/blog/tag/Raise%20the%20Age.

61. Kareem Jordan and David Myers, "Juvenile Transfer and Deterrence: Reexamining the Effectiveness of a 'Get-Tough' Policy," *Crime and Delinquency* 57:247–270 (2011).

62. Todd D. Minton and Daniela Golinelli, "Jail Inmates at Midyear 2013 – Statistical Tables," Bureau of Justice Statistics, 2014.

63. State of Florida, Title XXXIV, Alcoholic Beverages and Tobacco, Chapter 569 Section 11, https://www.flsenate.gov/Laws/Statutes/2011/569.11.

64. FBI, *Crime in the United States, 2014*, Table 28.

65. Office of Juvenile Justice and Delinquency Prevention and National Center for Juvenile Justice, *Juvenile Court Statistics, 2013*, http://www.ojjdp.gov/ojstatbb/njcda/pdf/jcs2013.pdf.

66. See David Rothman, *The Discovery of the Asylum* (Boston: Little, Brown, 1971).

67. Quote from Jerry Tyler, Thomas Segady, and Stephen Austin, "Parental Liability Laws: Rationale, Theory, and Effectiveness," *Social Science Journal* 37:79–97 (2000).

68. Reports of the Chicago Bar Association Committee, 1899, cited in Anthony Platt, *The Child Savers* (Chicago: University of Chicago Press, 1969), p. 119.

69. L. Kris Gowen, S. Shirley Feldman, Rafael Diaz, and Donnovan Somera Yisrael, "A Comparison of the Sexual Behaviors and Attitudes of Adolescent Girls with Older vs. Similar-Aged Boyfriends," *Journal of Youth and Adolescence* 33:167–176 (2004).

70. David J. Steinharthe, *Status Offenses: The Future of Children* (David and Lucile Packard Foundation, Winter 1996).

71. To read more about the Office of Juvenile Justice and Delinquency Prevention programs and priorities, go to http://www.ojjdp.gov.

72. 42 U.S.C.A. 5601–5751 (1983 and Supp. 1987).

73. Claudia Wright, "Contempt No Excuse for Locking Up Status Offenders, Says Florida Supreme Court," *Youth Law News* 13:1–3 (1992).

74. Susanna Zawacki, "Girls' Involvement in Pennsylvania's Juvenile Justice System," *Pennsylvania Juvenile Justice Statistical Bulletin*, October 2005, http://www.ncjj.org/Publication/Girls-Involvement-in-Pennsylvanias-Juvenile-Justice-System.aspx.

75. Barry Feld, "Violent Girls or Relabeled Status Offenders? An Alternative Interpretation of the Data," *Crime and Delinquency* 55:241–265 (2009).

76. Steinharthe, *Status Offenses*, p. 5.

77. Wesley Jennings, "Sex Disaggregated Trajectories of Status Offenders: Does CINS/FINS Status Prevent Male and Female Youth from Becoming Labeled Delinquent?" *American Journal of Criminal Justice* 36:177–187 (2011).

78. National Advisory Commission on Criminal Justice Standards and Goals, *Juvenile Justice and Delinquency Prevention* (Washington, DC: Government Printing Office, 1977), p. 311.

79. American Bar Association Joint Commission on Juvenile Justice Standards, *Summary and Analysis* (Cambridge, MA: Ballinger, 1977), sect. 1.1.

80. "Recommendations from the ABA Youth at Risk Initiative Planning Conference," *Family Court Review*, http://onlinelibrary.wiley.com/doi/10.1111/j.1744-1617.2007.00152.x/full.

81. Connecticut Superior Court for Juvenile Matters, 46-3-31, Families with Service Needs (FWSN), http://www.dir.ct.gov/dcf/policy/court46/46-3-31.htm.

82. New York State Office of Children and Family Services, "Chapter 57 of the Laws of 2005, PINS Reform."

83. Gail Robinson and Tim Arnold, "Changes in Laws Impacting Juveniles—An Overview," *The Advocate* 22:14–15 (2000).

84. Barry Feld, "Criminalizing the American Juvenile Court," in Michael Tonry, ed., *Crime and Justice: A Review of Research* (Chicago: University of Chicago Press, 1993), p. 232.

85. Sean Kidd, "Factors Precipitating Suicidality Among Homeless Youth: A Quantitative Follow-up," *Youth and Society* 37:393–422 (2006); Kimberly Tyler et al., "Self-Mutilation and Homeless Youth: The Role of Family Abuse, Street Experiences, and Mental Disorders," *Journal of Research on Adolescence* 13:457–474 (2003).

86. Carolyn Smith, "Factors Associated with Early Sexual Activity Among Urban Adolescents," *Social Work* 42:334–346 (1997).

87. Camela M. Steinke and Elisa M. Martin, "Status Offenders and Delinquent Youth: Actual or Artificial Taxonomy," *Child Welfare* 93:71–90 (2014).

88. Randall Shelden, John Horvath, and Sharon Tracy, "Do Status Offenders Get Worse? Some Clarifications on the Question of Escalation," *Crime and Delinquency* 35:202–216 (1989).

89. Solomon Kobrin, Frank Hellum, and John Peterson, "Offense Patterns of Status Offenders," in D. Shichor and D. Kelly, eds., *Critical Issues in Juvenile Delinquency* (Lexington, MA: Lexington Books, 1980), pp. 203–235.

90. Lawrence Martin and Phyllis Snyder, "Jurisdiction over Status Offenses Should Not Be Removed from the Juvenile Court," *Crime and Delinquency* 22:44–47 (1976).

91. Lindsay Arthur, "Status Offenders Need a Court of Last Resort," *Boston University Law Review* 57:631–644 (1977).

92. Martin and Snyder, "Jurisdiction over Status Offenses Should Not Be Removed from the Juvenile Court," p. 47.

93. David McDowall and Colin Loftin, "The Impact of Youth Curfew Laws on Juvenile Crime Rates," *Crime and Delinquency* 46:76–92 (2000).

94. Tony Favro, "Youth Curfews Popular with American Cities, but Effectiveness and Legality Are Questioned," City Mayors Society, July 21, 2009, http://www.citymayors.com/society/usa-youth-curfews.html.

95. Patrick Kline, "The Impact of Juvenile Curfew Laws on Arrest of Youth and Adults," *American Law and Economic Review* 14:44–67 (2012).

96. Elyse Grossman, David Jernigan, and Nancy Miller, "Do Juvenile Curfew Laws Reduce Underage Drinking?" *Journal of Studies on Alcohol and Drugs* 77:589–595 (2016); Danny Cole, "The Effect of a Curfew Law on Juvenile Crime in Washington, D.C.," *American Journal of Criminal Justice* 27:217–232 (2003).

97. Kenneth Adams, "The Effectiveness of Juvenile Curfews at Crime Prevention," *Annals of the American Academy of Political and Social Science* 587:136–159 (2003).

98. Michael Luke, "ACLU, Others Take Aim at Expanding Teen Curfew Citywide," WWLTV Eyewitness News, January 18, 2012.

99. Margaret Anne Cleek, John Youril, Michael Youril, and Richard Guarino, "Don't Worry, It's Just a Tool: Enacting Selectively Enforced Laws Such as Curfew Laws Targeting Only the Bad Guys," *Justice Policy Journal* 7:1–23 (2010).

100. Cody Stoddard, Benjamin Steiner, Jacqueline Rohrbach, Craig Hemmens, and Katherine Bennett, "All the Way Home: Assessing the Constitutionality of Juvenile Curfew Laws," *American Journal of Criminal Law* 42:177–211 (2015).

101. *Anonymous v. City of Rochester* (2009), http://www.law.cornell.edu/nyctap/I09_0095.htm.

102. Jonathan Saltzman, "SJC Sharply Limits Youth Curfew Law: Bars Criminal Charge, Allows Civil Penalty," *Boston Globe*, September 26, 2009.

103. Joel Rubin and Emily Alpert Reyes, "L.A. to Pay Up to $30 Million in Curfew Lawsuit Settlement to Provide Job Training for Gang Members," *Los Angeles Times*, March 16, 2016, http://www.latimes.com/local/lanow/la-me-ln-gang-injunction-deal-20160316-story.html.

104. Gilbert Geis and Arnold Binder, "Sins of Their Children: Parental Responsibility for Juvenile Delinquency," *Notre Dame Journal of Law, Ethics, and Public Policy* 5:303–322 (1991).

105. Eve Brank, Edie Greene, and Katherine Hochevar, "Holding Parents Responsible: Is Vicarious Responsibility the Public's Answer to Juvenile Crime?" *Psychology, Public Policy, and Law* 17:507–529 (2011).

106. Elena Laskin, "How Parental Liability Statutes Criminalize and Stigmatize Minority Mothers," *American Criminal Law Review* 37:1195–1217 (2000).

107. Brank, Greene, and Hochevar, "Holding Parents Responsible: Is Vicarious Responsibility the Public's Answer to Juvenile Crime?"

108. Eve Brank and Victoria Weisz, "Paying for the Crimes of Their Children: Public Support of Parental Responsibility" *Journal of Criminal Justice* 32:465–475 (2004).

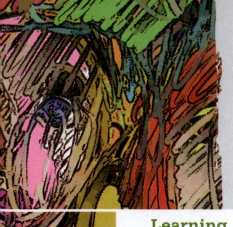

CHAPTER 2

The Nature and Extent of Delinquency

Learning Objectives

1. Explain how the Uniform Crime Report (UCR) data are gathered and used
2. Discuss the concept of self-reported delinquency
3. Evaluate the utility of the National Crime Victimization Survey
4. List alternative measures of delinquent activity and behavior
5. Analyze recent trends in juvenile delinquency
6. Recognize the factors that affect the juvenile crime rate
7. Interpret the social and personal correlates of delinquency
8. Discuss the concept of the chronic offender
9. Identify the causes of chronic offending
10. Summarize the factors that predict teen victimization

Chapter Outline

Chapter Features

Focus on Delinquency: Shaping Delinquency Trends

Focus on Delinquency: Co-offending and Delinquency

Case Profile: Naomi's Story

Youth Stories: *Room*: Kids Held Captive

Cyber Delinquency: Christopher Gunn

IN APRIL 2015, the US Attorney for the Southern District of New York issued a statement to the press:

> Today, we seek to eviscerate two violent street gangs—2Fly and BMB—that have allegedly wreaked havoc on the streets of the Northern Bronx for years by committing countless acts of violence against rival gang members and innocents alike. The gangs' alleged victims include not only a 15-year-old child stabbed and left to die in the street, as well as a 92-year-old woman shot by a stray bullet in her own home, but also extend to the thousands of residents of Eastchester Gardens and its surrounding neighborhoods terrorized for years by the gangs' open-air drug dealing and senseless violence. We bring these charges today so that all New Yorkers, including those in or near NYCHA public housing, can live their lives as they deserve: free of drugs, free of guns, and free of gang violence . . .

The indictments arose from a joint investigation by numerous law enforcement agencies into the years-long gang war between two rival gangs, 2Fly and BMB, that terrorized the Northern Bronx with shootings, stabbings, slashings, beatings, and robberies.

2Fly is a subset of the Young Gunnaz or YG street gang, which operates throughout New York City. 2Fly is based in the Bronx, within and around the Eastchester Gardens housing development (ECG) and in an area called the Valley or the V. Members and associates of 2Fly control the narcotics trade at ECG, which takes place in the open air at the playground and in apartments. 2Fly members and associates store guns at the playground or in nearby apartments and cars in order to protect the narcotics business and for protection against rival gangs.

Their rivals are BMB, a subset of the Young Bosses or YBz street gang, which operates throughout New York City. BMB members sometimes refer to themselves as the Money Making

A sign for the Eastchester Gardens NYCHA housing complex stands in the Bronx, New York, April 27, 2016.

Shannon Stapleton/Reuters

Mafia or Triple M. BMB members and associates store guns in abandoned homes and other places near their drug spots.

The primary narcotics trafficking activity for both gangs is marijuana and crack cocaine, but they also sell powder cocaine and prescription pills such as oxycodone. The rivalry between the 2Fly and BMB gangs has led to the following murders, among others:

- Sadie Mitchell, 92, killed in her own home by a stray bullet fired by an associate of BMB
- Jeffrey Delmore, 15, stabbed to death by members of BMB
- Alexander "A.J." Walters, 17, stabbed to death by members of 2Fly
- Donville Simpson, 17, shot to death by members of 2Fly
- Keshon Potterfield, 18, shot to death by a member of BMB

During the arrests and searches, agents seized quantities of marijuana, crack cocaine, and oxycodone, as well as firearms, ammunition, scalpels, and knives.[1]

While many people believe that when adolescents commit crime they stick to petty offenses—shoplifting, smoking pot, spray painting their school—the activities of violent street gangs show that the opposite is often true. Kids today engage in serious crimes such as robbery, rape, and—as the members of 2Fly and BMB were so willing to do—even murder. Who commits these serious acts, and where are they most likely to occur? News stories about gang crime convince the public that juvenile crime is rampant, but does the media paint an accurate picture of what is really going on in the United States? Is the juvenile crime rate increasing or decreasing? Are juveniles more likely than adults to become the victims of crime? To understand the causes of delinquent behavior and to devise effective means to reduce its occurrence, we must seek answers to these questions using accepted scientific methods of data collection and analysis.

Most Americans rely on lurid news stories to form their impression of crime and delinquency. Considering the violent content of news programming, it's not surprising that more than one-third of Americans say they are afraid to walk alone in their neighborhood at night.[2] Even though the crime rate has dropped considerably for more than a decade, about 70 percent of Americans still believe it is more dangerous today than a year ago.[3]

When experts want to find out more about the nature and extent of crime and delinquency, they do not rely on hearsay but instead use valid and reliable tools of crime measurement. Today, they typically rely on three primary sources of data: official records, victim surveys, and self-report surveys. It is important to understand how these data sets are collected to gain insight into how delinquency is measured and what the data sources tell us about youth crime and victimization. Each issue is discussed in detail in this chapter.

Official Records of Delinquency: The Uniform Crime Report

Federal Bureau of Investigation (FBI)
Arm of the US Department of Justice that investigates violations of federal law, gathers crime statistics, runs a comprehensive crime laboratory, and helps train local law enforcement officers.

Uniform Crime Report (UCR)
Compiled by the FBI, the UCR is the most widely used source of national crime and delinquency statistics.

Part I crimes
Offenses including homicide and non-negligent manslaughter, forcible rape, robbery, aggravated assault, burglary, larceny, arson, and motor vehicle theft. Recorded by local law enforcement officers, these crimes are tallied quarterly and sent to the FBI for inclusion in the UCR.

Part II crimes
All crimes other than Part I crimes; recorded by local law enforcement officers, arrests for these crimes are tallied quarterly and sent to the FBI for inclusion in the UCR.

Some of the most valuable information about delinquent behavior comes from data collected from local law enforcement agencies by the **Federal Bureau of Investigation (FBI)** and published yearly in their **Uniform Crime Report (UCR)**.[4]

The UCR includes both criminal acts reported to local law enforcement departments and the number of arrests made by police agencies. The FBI receives and compiles records from more than 17,000 police departments serving a majority of the US population. The FBI tallies and annually publishes the number of reported offenses by city, county, standard metropolitan statistical area, and geographical divisions of the United States for the most serious crimes, referred to as **Part I crimes**: murder and non-negligent manslaughter, forcible rape, robbery, aggravated assault, burglary, larceny, arson, and motor vehicle theft.

In addition to these statistics, the UCR gathers data on the number and characteristics (age, race, and gender) of individuals who have been arrested for these and all other crimes, referred to as **Part II crimes**). This is particularly important for delinquency research because it shows how many minors are arrested each year.

Compiling the Uniform Crime Report

The methods used to compile the UCR are quite complex. Each month, law enforcement agencies report the number of crimes known to them. These data are collected from records of all crime complaints that victims, officers who discovered the infractions, or other sources reported to these agencies.

Whenever crime complaints are found through investigation to be unfounded or false, they are eliminated from the actual count. However, the number of actual offenses known is reported to the FBI whether or not anyone is arrested for the crime, the stolen property is recovered, or prosecution ensues.

In addition, each month, law enforcement agencies also report how many crimes were cleared. Crimes are cleared in two ways: (1) when at least one person is arrested, charged, and turned over to the court for prosecution, or (2) by exceptional means, when some element beyond police control precludes the physical arrest of an offender (such as when the offender leaves the country). Data on the number of clearances involving the arrest of only juvenile offenders, data on the value of property stolen and recovered in connection with Part I offenses, and detailed information pertaining to criminal homicide are also reported. Traditionally, slightly more than 20 percent of all reported Part I crimes are cleared by arrest each year (see Figure 2.1).

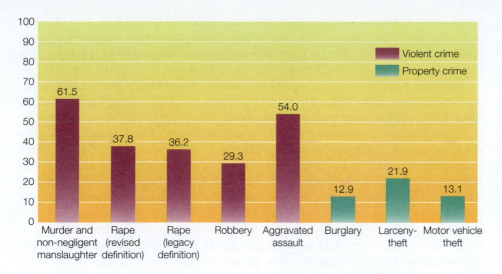

figure 2.1

Percent of Crimes Cleared by Arrest or Exceptional Means, 2015

SOURCE: FBI, *Crime in the United States, 2015*, https://ucr.fbi.gov/crime-in-the-u.s/2015/crime-in-the-u.s.-2015/offenses-known-to-law-enforcement/clearances/clearances (accessed September 2016).

Violent crimes are more likely to be solved than property crimes because police devote additional resources to these more serious acts. For these types of crime, witnesses (including the victim) are frequently available to identify offenders, and in many instances the victim and offender were previously acquainted.

The UCR uses three methods to express crime data. First, the number of crimes reported to the police is expressed as raw figures. In 2015, an estimated 1,197,704 violent crimes occurred nationwide. Second, crime rates per 100,000 people are computed: in 2015, an estimated 372 violent crimes took place per 100,000 inhabitants. This is the equation used:

$$\frac{\text{Number of Reported Crimes}}{\text{Total US Population}} \times 100,000 = \text{Rate per } 100,000$$

Third, the FBI computes changes in rate of crime and the number of crimes over time. The 2015 data show that the number of murders rose sharply from the previous year: the number of murders committed in 2015 rose almost 11 percent from the 2014 estimate.[5]

Is the UCR Valid?

Though the UCR is the primary source of official crime data, experts have long questioned its accuracy. Less than half of all violent crimes and only one-third of property crimes are reported to the police.[6] One reason is lack of confidence in law enforcement; some victims do not trust the police or have faith in their ability to solve crimes. Cities in which people believe the police can help them are more likely to report crime.[7] Victims without property insurance believe it is useless to report theft. Some victims fail to report because they fear reprisals from an offender's friends or family or, in the case of family violence, from their spouse, boyfriend, or girlfriend.[8]

The more serious the crime and the greater the loss, the more likely citizens will report crime to police.[9] If they are injured, especially if a weapon was involved, they are more likely to consider the incident serious and report it to the police. If the crime was completed, and the criminal got away with their wallet, purse, car, or package, reporting is more likely to occur. Crimes involving multiple offenders are also more likely to come to the attention of police than those with a single perpetrator.[10] Some victims believe that the incident was "a private matter," that "nothing could be done," or that the victimization was "not important enough."

People who are themselves involved in criminal activities and have "dirty hands" are less likely to report crime than those whose "hands are clean." The dirty hands may not be related to criminal activity: people who cheat on their spouse, drink excessively, or have other skeletons in the closet are less likely to call the police than their less deviant peers. Some crimes that directly influence children, such as child abuse, may be underreported considering the age of the victims and their ability to contact police authorities.

Another problem: local law enforcement agencies may make intentional and/or unintentional errors in their reporting practices. John Eterno and Eli Silverman studied reporting practices in New York City and found that police commanders, under intense pressure to reduce crime by hard-charging police commissioners, manipulated crime statistics in order to show success.[11] Some police departments may alter record keeping to show they are effective at fighting crime and their methods are providing positive results.[12] Others may define crimes loosely—for example, reporting any assault on a woman as an attempted rape—whereas others pay strict attention to FBI guidelines.[13] And ironically, as the tech revolution has taken hold, police departments are getting better at recording and reporting crime. In some local jurisdictions, what appears to be a rising crime rate may simply be an artifact of improved police record-keeping ability!

The complex scoring procedure used by the FBI means that many serious crimes are not counted. According to the "Hierarchy Rule," in a multiple-offense incident, only the most serious crime is counted. Thus if an armed bank robber commits a robbery, assaults a patron as he flees, steals a car to get away, and damages property during a police chase, only the robbery is reported because it is the most serious offense. Consequently, many lesser crimes go unreported.

Crime reporting practices can have a significant influence on the crime rate and can shape the crime trends reported in the UCR.[14] What may be viewed as a significant decline in crime may in fact represent a change in victims' behavior more than in criminals' behavior.

Although these questions are troubling, the problems associated with collecting and verifying the official UCR data are consistent and stable over time. This means that although the absolute accuracy of the data can be questioned, the trends and patterns they show are probably reliable. In other words, we cannot be absolutely sure about the actual number of adolescents who commit crimes, but it is likely that the teen crime rate has been in a significant decline.

The National Incident-Based Reporting System (NIBRS)

National Incident-Based Reporting System (NIBRS)
Program that collects data on each reported crime incident and requires local police to provide at least a brief account of each incident and arrest.

The FBI is currently instituting a program called the **National Incident-Based Reporting System (NIBRS)** that collects data on each reported crime incident. Instead of submitting statements of the kinds of crime that individual citizens reported to the police and summary statements of resulting arrests, when fully implemented NIBRS will require local police agencies to provide at least a brief account of each incident and arrest, including the incident, victim, and offender information. Under NIBRS, law enforcement authorities provide information to the FBI on each criminal incident involving 46 specific offenses, including the eight Part I crimes, which occur in their jurisdiction; arrest information on the 46 offenses plus 11 lesser offenses is also provided in NIBRS. These expanded crime categories include numerous additional crimes, such as blackmail, embezzlement, drug offenses, and bribery; this allows a national database on the nature of crime, victims, and criminals to be developed. Today, 6,520 law enforcement agencies, representing coverage of more than 93 million US inhabitants, submit NIBRS data. While not yet nationally representative, this coverage represents 35 percent of all law enforcement agencies that participate in the UCR program.[15] When fully implemented and adopted across the nation, NIBRS should bring about greater uniformity in cross-jurisdictional reporting and improve the accuracy of official crime data.

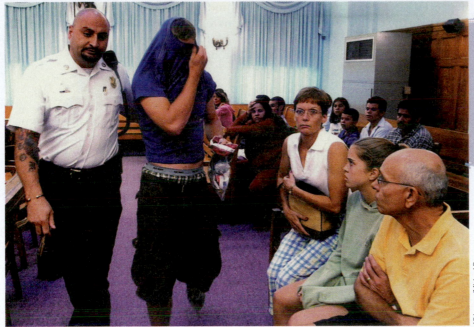

Measuring the full extent of delinquency is difficult because many acts are not included in the UCR. Here, a young man is escorted past his family after a court appearance on a charge of making a false bomb threat while boarding a flight. Would this act be reported to the FBI's program?

AP Images/Michael Dwyer

While official data are used quite often in delinquency research, the data only represent the number of kids arrested and not how many are actually committing delinquent acts. To remedy this flaw, researchers often rely on self-report data in their research.

Self-Report Surveys

One of the most important tools to measure delinquency and youthful misconduct is the **self-report survey**. These surveys ask kids to describe, in detail, their recent and lifetime participation in antisocial activity—for example, "How many times in the past year did you take something worth more than $50?" In many instances, but not always, self-reports are given in groups, and the respondents are promised anonymity in order to ensure the validity and honesty of the responses.[16] But even when the reports are given on an individual basis, respondents are guaranteed that their answers will remain confidential.

In addition to questions about delinquent behavior, most self-report surveys contain questions about attitudes, values, and behaviors. There may be questions about a participant's substance abuse history (e.g., how many times have you used marijuana?) and the participant's family history (e.g., did your parents ever strike you with a stick or a belt?). By correlating the responses, delinquency experts are able to analyze the relationships among values, attitudes, personal factors, and delinquent behaviors. Statistical analysis of the responses can be used to determine such issues as whether people who report being abused as children are also more likely to use drugs as adults or if school failure leads to delinquency.[17]

Some self-report surveys are carried out on an annual basis and employ national samples so that delinquency trends can be recorded and analyzed. An indispensable source of self-report data is the Monitoring the Future (MTF) study, which researchers at the University of Michigan Institute for Social Research (ISR) have been conducting surveys annually since 1978. This national survey typically involves more than 2,500 high school seniors.[18] The MTF is considered the national standard to measure substance abuse trends among American teens.

The MTF data indicate that the number of people who break the law is far greater than the number projected by official statistics. Almost everyone questioned is found to have violated a law at some time, including truancy, alcohol

self-report survey
Questionnaire or survey technique that asks subjects to reveal their own participation in delinquent or criminal acts.

abuse, false ID use, shoplifting or larceny under $50, fighting, marijuana use, and damage to the property of others. Furthermore, self-reports dispute the notion that criminals and delinquents specialize in one type of crime or another; offenders seem to engage in a mixed bag of crime and deviance.

Are Self-Reports Valid?

Critics of self-report studies frequently suggest that it is unreasonable to expect kids to candidly admit illegal acts. Some surveys contain an overabundance of trivial offenses, such as shoplifting small items or using false identification to obtain alcohol, often lumped together with serious crimes to form a total crime index. Consequently, comparisons between groups can be highly misleading. Responses may be embellished by some subjects who wish to exaggerate the extent of their deviant activities, and understated by others who want to shield themselves from possible exposure.

The "missing cases" phenomenon is also a concern. Even if 90 percent of a school population voluntarily participate in a self-report study, researchers can never be sure whether the few who refuse to participate or are absent that day make up a significant portion of the school's population of persistent high-rate offenders. Research indicates that offenders with the most extensive prior criminality are the most likely "to be poor historians of their own crime commission rates."[19] It is also unlikely that the most serious chronic offenders in the teenage population are willing to cooperate with researchers administering self-report tests.[20] Institutionalized youths, who are not generally represented in the self-report surveys, are not only more delinquent than the general youth population but are also considerably more misbehaving than the most delinquent youths identified in the typical self-report survey. Consequently, self-reports may measure only nonserious, occasional delinquents while ignoring hard-core chronic offenders who may be institutionalized and unavailable for self-reports.

Reporting practices may differ among racial, ethnic, and gender groups. One study found that while girls are generally more willing to report drug use than boys, Hispanic girls tend to underreport substance abuse. Such gender/cultural differences in self-reporting can skew data and provide misleading results.[21]

There is also concern that the way self-reports are administered may change their outcomes. In one recent study, researchers compared the responses of two groups: one told to be "honest and thoughtful" and a control group that was not instructed to be truthful. There were important differences between the two groups: those who were told to tell the truth reported more offenses and less perceived risk.

To address these criticisms, various techniques have been used to verify self-report data. The "known group" method compares people known to be offenders with those who are not, to see whether the former report more crime, which they should. Research shows that when people are asked whether they have ever been arrested or sent to court, their responses accurately reflect their true-life experiences.[22] In addition, responses to self-reports are consistent over time: people who either exaggerate or understate their criminal activities in youth also do so as adults, indicating that self-reports are stable and consistent over time.[23]

Self-report data must be interpreted with some caution. Asking subjects about their past behavior may capture more serious crimes but miss minor criminal acts; that is, people remember armed robberies and rapes better than they do minor assaults and altercations.[24] Some kids fabricate their criminal histories, while others (e.g., substance abusers) may have a tough time accounting for their prior misbehavior.[25] Other factors that influence self-report validity are age, criminal history, currency of the reported event, IQ, education level, and variety of criminal acts. Despite these caveats, some of the most recent research supports the validity of the self-report method with both occasional and committed (e.g., gang members) delinquents.[26] They therefore remain a fixture in delinquency research methodology.

National Crime Victimization Survey (NCVS)

An issue of interest for delinquency scholars is juvenile victimization. How many kids are victims each year, and who are the adolescents most likely to become crime victims? To address this issue, the federal government sponsors the **National Crime Victimization Survey (NCVS)**, a comprehensive, nationwide survey of victimization in the United States.[27]

The NCVS is administered to persons age 12 or older from a nationally representative sample of households, defined as a group of members who all reside at a sampled address. Persons are considered household members when the sampled address is their usual place of residence at the time of the interview and when they have no usual place of residence elsewhere. Once selected, households remain in the sample for three years, and eligible persons in these households are interviewed every six months either in person or over the phone for a total of seven interviews. In the most recent survey, about 90,000 households were selected and more than 158,000 persons age 12 or older were interviewed for the NCVS. Each household was interviewed twice during the year. The response rate was 87 percent for households and 87 percent for eligible persons.[28] Since the NCVS relies on a sample rather than a census of the entire US population, the data are weighted to reflect population totals and to compensate for survey nonresponse and other aspects of the sample design.

Since its inception, the survey has undergone a number of significant modifications. In 1993, it was redesigned to provide detailed information on the frequency and nature of the crimes of rape, sexual assault, personal robbery, aggravated and simple assault, household burglary, theft, and motor vehicle theft. In 2006, significant methodological changes were made, including a new sampling method, a change in the method of handling first-time interviews with households, and a change in the method of interviewing. Some selected areas were dropped from the sample while others were added. Finally, computer-assisted personal interviewing (CAPI) replaced paper and pencil interviewing (PAPI).

The NCVS finds that fewer than half of violent crimes, fewer than one-third of personal theft crimes (such as pocket picking), and fewer than half of household thefts are reported to police. Victims seem to report to the police only crimes that involve considerable loss or injury. If we are to believe NCVS findings, the official UCR statistics do not provide an accurate picture of the crime problem because many crimes go unreported to the police.

While it contains many underreported incidents, the NCVS may also suffer from some methodological problems. As a result, its findings must be interpreted with caution. Among the potential problems are the following:

- Overreporting due to victims' misinterpretation of events. A lost wallet may be reported as stolen, or an open door may be viewed as a burglary attempt.

- Underreporting due to the embarrassment of reporting crime to interviewers, fear of getting in trouble, or simply forgetting an incident.

- Inability to record the personal criminal activity of those interviewed, such as drug use or gambling; murder is also not included, for obvious reasons.

- Sampling errors, which produce a group of respondents who do not represent the nation as a whole.

- Inadequate question format that invalidates responses. Some groups, such as adolescents, may be particularly susceptible to error because of question format and wording.[29]

National Crime Victimization Survey (NCVS)
The ongoing victimization study conducted jointly by the Justice Department and the US Census Bureau that surveys victims about their experiences with law violation.

exhibit 2.1

Secondary Sources of Delinquency Data

In addition to the primary sources of crime data—UCR, NCVS, and self-report surveys—criminologists use several other methods to acquire data. Although this list is not exhaustive, the methods described here are routinely used in criminological research and data collection.

Cohort Research Data

Collecting cohort data involves observing over time a group of people who share certain characteristics. Researchers might select all girls born in Boston in 1990 and then follow their behavior patterns for 20 years. The research data might include their school experiences, arrests, and hospitalizations, along with information about their family life (marriages, divorces, parental relations, for example). If the cohort is carefully drawn, it may be possible to accumulate a complex array of data that can be used to determine which life experiences are associated with criminal careers.

Experimental Data

Sometimes criminologists conduct controlled experiments to collect data on the cause of crime. To carry out experimental research, criminologists manipulate, or intervene in, the lives of their subjects to see the outcome or the effect of the intervention. True experiments usually have three elements: (1) random selection of subjects, (2) a control or comparison group, and (3) an experimental condition.

Observational and Interview Research

Sometimes criminologists focus their research on relatively few subjects, interviewing them in depth or observing them as they go about their activities. This research often results in the kind of in-depth data that large-scale surveys do not yield.

Meta-analysis and Systematic Review

Meta-analysis involves gathering data from a number of previous studies. Compatible information and data are extracted and pooled together. When analyzed, the grouped data from several different studies provide a more powerful and valid indicator of relationships than the results provided by a single study. Similar to meta-analysis, a systematic review involves collecting the findings from previously conducted scientific studies that address a particular problem, appraising and synthesizing the evidence, and using the collective evidence to address a particular scientific question.

Data Mining

A relatively new criminological technique, data mining uses multiple advanced computational methods, including artificial intelligence (the use of computers to perform logical functions), to analyze large data sets that usually involve one or more data sources. The goal is to identify significant and recognizable patterns, trends, and relationships that are not easily detected through traditional analytical techniques.

Crime Mapping

Criminologists now use crime mapping to create graphical representations of the spatial geography of crime. Computerized crime maps enable criminologists to analyze and correlate a wide array of data to create immediate, detailed visuals of crime patterns.

In addition to these primary sources of crime data, criminologists use other data in their studies. These are set out in Exhibit 2.1.

Trends in Crime and Delinquency

Crime and delinquency rates trended upward between 1960 and 1992, when about 14.6 million crimes were recorded. Since then, the number of crimes has been in decline; in 2015, about 9 million crimes were reported to the police, a drop of almost 5 million recorded crimes from the peak despite a boost of more than 50 million in the general population.

What the UCR Tells Us About Delinquency

disaggregated
Analyzing the relationship between two or more independent variables (such as murder convictions and death sentence) while controlling for the influence of a dependent variable (such as race).

Because the UCR arrest statistics are **disaggregated** (broken down) by suspect's age, they can be used to estimate adolescent delinquency. Juvenile arrest data must be interpreted with caution, however. First, the number of teenagers arrested does not represent the actual number of youths who have committed delinquent acts. Some offenders are never counted because they are never caught. Others are counted more than once because multiple arrests of the same individual for different crimes are counted separately in the UCR. Consequently, the total number of arrests does not equal the number of people who have been arrested. Put another way, if 1 million arrests of youths under 18 years of age were made in a given year, we could not be sure if 1 million individuals had been arrested once or if 250,000 chronic offenders had been arrested four times each.

When an arrested offender commits multiple crimes, only the most serious one is recorded. In addition, we know that only 20 percent of crimes are cleared by arrest. If this ratio applies to juveniles, it is possible that the 2 million arrested juveniles committed 10 million crimes before they were apprehended. If 1 million juveniles are arrested, the number of crimes committed is at least 1 million, but it may be much higher.

Despite these limitations, the nature of arrest data remains constant over time. Consequently, arrest data can provide some indication of the nature and trends in juvenile crime. What does the UCR tell us about the nature and extent of delinquency?

Juvenile Arrest Trends

The latest data available show a total of about 11 million arrests in 2015. Of these arrests, about 500,000 were for serious Part I violent crimes and 1.5 million for serious Part I property crimes. Considering all crimes, both serious and minor, the highest number of arrests (more than a million each) were for drug abuse violations, larceny-theft, and driving under the influence.

Juveniles were responsible for about 8 percent of all arrests, including about 10 percent of the Part I violent crime arrests and about 14 percent of the property crime arrests for the most serious property crimes such as burglary, larceny, and car theft (see Table 2.1). Because kids ages 14 to 18, who account for almost all underage arrests, constitute about 6 percent of the population, these data show that teens account for a disproportionate share of all arrests for serious crime.

About 500,000 juvenile arrests were made in 2015 for Part II offenses. Included in this total were status violations: 33,000 arrests for liquor law violations, 55,000 for disorderly conduct, and 33,000 for curfew violations.[30]

Despite the fact that teens are arrested more often than their older brothers and sisters, the two groups are both committing less crime: recent trends in juvenile delinquency arrests reflect the general crime rate. The juvenile arrest rate began to climb in the 1980s, peaked during the mid-1990s, and then began to fall; it has since been in decline. The number of juveniles arrested is now 50 percent lower than in 2005.

Even the teen murder rate, which had remained stubbornly high, has undergone a decline during the past few years.[31] In 1997, 1,700 youths were arrested for murder, a number that by 2015 had declined by almost two-thirds (605 arrests for murder). Similarly, 3,800 juveniles were arrested for rape in 1997, falling to fewer than 2,745 in 2015.

So despite a continuing media barrage covering the havoc caused by violent youth gangs roaming the streets, arrests of juveniles actually decreased significantly in the past decade. And while juveniles account for a disproportionate number of arrests, the recent decline in the juvenile arrest rate has been significant, far outstripping that experienced by adults.

What factors account for change in the crime and delinquency rates? This is the topic of the Focus on Delinquency box entitled "Shaping Delinquency Trends."

table 2.1

Persons Arrested for Serious Crimes, by Age

	Under 15	Under 18	Over 18
Serious violent crime	3%	10%	90%
Serious property crime	4%	14%	86%
Total all crimes	2%	8%	92%

Source: FBI, *Crime in the United States, 2015.*

Shaping Delinquency Trends

Delinquency experts have identified a variety of social, economic, personal, and demographic factors that influence juvenile crime rate trends. The most important influences on delinquency rates are discussed here.

Age

Because teenagers have relatively high crime rates, crime experts view changes in the population age distribution as having the greatest influence on crime trends: As a general rule, the crime rate follows the proportion of young males in the population. Kids who commit a lot of crime early in childhood are also likely to continue to commit crime in their adolescence and into adulthood. The more teens in the population, the higher the crime rate. However, the number of senior citizens is also expanding, and their presence in the population may have a moderating effect on crime rates (seniors do not commit much crime), offsetting the effect of teens.

Economy/Jobs

There is debate over the effect the economy has on crime rates. It seems logical that when the economy turns down, people (especially those who are unemployed) will become more motivated to commit theft crimes. Kids who find it hard to get after-school jobs or find employment after they leave school may be motivated to seek other forms of income such as theft and drug dealing. As the economy heats up, delinquency rates should decline because people can secure good jobs—why risk breaking the law when there are legitimate opportunities?

However, this issue is far from settled. A poor economy may actually help lower delinquency rates because it limits the opportunity kids have to commit crime. Unemployed parents are at home to supervise children and guard their possessions, and because there is less money to spend, people have fewer valuables worth stealing. Law-abiding kids do not suddenly begin to violate the law just because there is an economic downturn.

Although the effect of the economy on delinquency rates is still in question, it is possible that over the long haul a strong economy will help lower delinquency rates, while long periods of sustained economic weakness and unemployment may eventually lead to increased rates. Crime skyrocketed in the 1930s during the Great Depression; crime rates fell when the economy surged for almost a decade during the 1990s. Also, economic effects may be very localized: people in one area of the city are doing well, but people living in another part of town may be suffering unemployment. The economic effect on the delinquency rates may vary by neighborhood or even by street.

Immigration

Immigration has become one of the most controversial issues in American society. One reason given by those who want to tighten immigration laws is that immigrants have high crime rates and should be prevented from entering the country. However, the most empirically sound research indicates that immigrants are actually less violent and criminal than the general population. Mexican immigrants, for example, experience lower rates of violence compared to their native-born counterparts. Immigration has a *negative* effect on overall levels of homicides and drug-related homicides specifically. In sum, as the number of immigrants in the population increases, the overall delinquency may decline.

Social Problems

As the level of social problems increases—such as single-parent families, dropout rates, racial conflict, and teen pregnancies—so do delinquency rates. Delinquency rates are correlated with the number of unwed mothers in the population. It is possible that children of unwed mothers need more social services than children in two-parent families. As the number of kids born to single mothers increases, the child welfare system is taxed and services depleted. The teenage birthrate has trended downward in recent years, and so have delinquency rates.

Racial conflict may also increase delinquency rates. Areas undergoing racial change, especially those experiencing a migration of minorities into predominantly white neighborhoods, seem prone to significant increases in their delinquency rate. Whites in these areas may be using violence to protect what they view as their home turf. Racially motivated crimes actually diminish as neighborhoods become more integrated and power struggles are resolved.

Abortion

It is possible that the link between delinquency rates and abortion is the result of three mechanisms: (1) selective abortion on the part of women most at risk to have children who would engage in delinquent activity, (2) improved childrearing or environmental circumstances because women are having fewer children, and (3) absence of unwanted children who stand the greatest risk of delinquency. If abortion were illegal, Donohue and Levitt find, delinquency rates might be 10 to 20 percent higher than they currently are with legal abortion.

Recently, Gary Shoesmith reanalyzed the data on abortion and crime while disaggregating the data by age, education, and state of

Self-Reported Findings

When self-report studies were first created and used, delinquency experts found that the number of children who break the law was far greater than official statistics had led them to believe.[32] In fact, when truancy, alcohol consumption, petty theft, and recreational drug use are included in self-report scales, delinquency appears to be almost universal. The most common offenses are truancy, drinking alcohol, using a false ID, shoplifting or larceny under five dollars, fighting, using marijuana, and damaging the property of others. In Chapter 11, self-report data will be used to gauge trends in adolescent drug abuse.

residence. His findings question Donohue and Levitt's conclusion that "unwantedness leads to high crime." Shoesmith concludes that the association between abortion and crime only applies to teen mothers and not older women, who now account for more 80 percent of abortions. The odds of a child from an unwanted pregnancy becoming a criminal decline rapidly as the mother's age and education increase; consequently, half of all abortions have virtually no effect on crime. Because the teen birth rate is in sharp decline, so too is the crime rate. So it's not abortion per se that has an effect on crime, it's abortion among teenage mothers only.

The abortion–crime association is still being debated. And due to its controversial nature it will most likely be a research topic for quite some time.

Guns

The availability of firearms may influence the delinquency rate, especially the proliferation of weapons in the hands of teens. Surveys of high school students indicate that between 6 and 10 percent carry guns at least some of the time. Guns also cause escalation in the seriousness of delinquency. As the number of gun-toting students increases, so does the seriousness of violent delinquency: A school yard fight may well turn into murder.

Gangs

Another factor that affects delinquency rates is the explosive growth in teenage gangs. Surveys indicate that there are more than 800,000 gang members in the United States. Boys who are members of gangs are far more likely to possess guns than nongang members; criminal activity increases when kids join gangs.

Drug Use

Some experts tie increases in the violent delinquency rate between 1980 and 1990 to the crack epidemic, which swept the nation's largest cities, and to drug-trafficking gangs that fought over drug turf. These well-armed gangs did not hesitate to use violence to control territory, intimidate rivals, and increase market share. As the crack epidemic has subsided, so has the violence in New York City and other metropolitan areas where crack use was rampant. A sudden increase in drug use, on the other hand, may be a harbinger of future increases in the delinquency rate.

Media

Some experts argue that violent media can influence the direction of delinquency rates. The introduction of home video players, DVDs, cable TV, computers, and video games coincided with increasing teen violence rates. Perhaps the increased availability of media violence on these platforms produced more aggressive teens? Watching violence on TV may be correlated with aggressive behaviors, especially when viewers have a pre-existing tendency toward delinquency and violence. Research shows that the more kids watch TV, the more often they get into violent encounters.

Juvenile Justice Policy

Some law enforcement experts have suggested that a reduction in delinquency rates may be attributed to adding large numbers of police officers and using them in aggressive police practices aimed at reducing gang membership, gun possession, and substance abuse. It is also possible that tough laws such as waiving juveniles to adult courts or sending them to adult prisons can affect crime rates. The fear of punishment may inhibit some would-be delinquents, and tough laws place a significant number of chronic juvenile offenders behind bars, lowering delinquency rates.

CRITICAL THINKING

Although juvenile delinquency rates have been declining in the United States, they have been increasing in Europe. Is it possible that factors that correlate with delinquency rate changes in the United States have little utility in predicting changes in other cultures? What other factors may increase or reduce delinquency rates?

SOURCES: Richard B. Felson and Jeremy Staff, "Committing Economic Crime for Drug Money," *Crime and Delinquency*, first published online June 26, 2015; Gary L. Shoesmith, "Crime, Teenage Abortion, and Unwantedness," *Crime and Delinquency*, first published online November 18, 2015; Graham Ousey and Charis Kubrin, "Immigration and the Changing Nature of Homicide in US Cities, 1980–2010," *Journal of Quantitative Criminology* 30:453–483 (2014); Bianca Bersani, "A Game of Catch-Up? The Offending Experience of Second-Generation Immigrants," *Crime and Delinquency* 60:60–84 (2014); David Weisburd, Cody Telep, and Brian Lawton, "Could Innovations in Policing Have Contributed to the New York City Crime Drop Even in a Period of Declining Police Strength? The Case of Stop, Question and Frisk as a Hot Spots Policing Strategy," *Justice Quarterly* 31:129–153 (2014); Richard Rosenfeld and Robert Fornango, "The Impact of Police Stops on Precinct Robbery and Burglary Rates in New York City, 2003–2010," *Justice Quarterly* 31:96–122 (2014); Jeremy Staff, D. Wayne Osgood, John Schulenberg, Jerald Bachman, and Emily Messersmith, "Explaining the Relationship Between Employment and Juvenile Delinquency," *Criminology* 48:1101–1131 (2010); Tim Wadsworth, "Is Immigration Responsible for the Crime Drop? An Assessment of the Influence of Immigration on Changes in Violent Crime Between 1990 and 2000," *Social Science Quarterly* 91:531–553 (2010); Brad Bushman and Craig Anderson, "Media Violence and the American Public," *American Psychologist* 56:477–489 (2001); John J. Donohue III and Steven D. Levitt, "The Impact of Legalized Abortion on Crime," *Quarterly Journal of Economics* 116:379–420 (2001).

As you may recall, the University of Michigan's Institute for Social Research's Monitoring the Future (MTF) survey is considered one of the most important ongoing self-report studies. In its current form, approximately 50,000 8th, 10th, and 12th grade students are surveyed each year. In addition, annual follow-up questionnaires are mailed to a sample of each graduating class for a number of years after their initial participation.

When the results of the most recent MTF surveys are compared with various studies conducted over a 20-year period, a uniform pattern emerges. The use of drugs and alcohol increased markedly in the 1970s, leveled off in the 1980s,

Self-report surveys can assess the occurrence of crimes that are rarely reported to police and enable researchers to gauge the motives kids may have to commit these acts. Here, a surveillance video provided by Anne Arundel County police shows vandals inside the Chesapeake High School in Pasadena, Maryland. Roughly 12 hours after the senior class graduated, vandals returned to the school and caused significant property damage. Crimes such as vandalism are rarely reported to police and are best measured by self-report surveys.

increased until the mid-1990s, and has been in decline ever since. Theft, violence, and damage-related crimes are more stable.

Findings from the most recent MTF survey are contained in Table 2.2.[33] As Table 2.2 shows, a surprising number of teenagers report involvement in serious criminal behavior. About 13 percent reported hurting someone badly enough that the victim needed medical care (6 percent said they did it more than once); about 25 percent reported stealing something worth less than $50, and another 9 percent stole something worth more than $50; 24 percent reported shoplifting one or more times; 11 percent damaged school property, 5 percent more than once.

If the MTF data are accurate, the crime problem is much greater than official statistics would lead us to believe. There are approximately 41 million youths between the ages of 10 and 18. Extrapolating from the MTF findings, this group

table 2.2

Monitoring the Future Survey of Criminal Activity of High School Seniors

Type of Delinquency	Percentage Engaging in Offenses	
	Committed Once	Committed Two or More Times
Set fire on purpose	1	2
Damaged school property	6	5
Damaged work property	2	2
Auto theft	2	2
Auto part theft	2	2
Break and enter	11	13
Theft, less than $50	11	14
Theft, more than $50	4	5
Shoplift	10	14
Gang or group fight	9	8
Hurt someone badly enough to require medical care	7	6
Used force or a weapon to steal	1	2
Hit teacher or supervisor	1	2
Participated in serious fight	7	5

SOURCE: Data provided by *Monitoring the Future* (Ann Arbor, MI: Institute for Social Research, 2015).

accounts for more than 100 percent of all the theft offenses reported in the UCR. About 3 percent of high school students said they had used force to steal (which is the legal definition of a robbery). Two-thirds of them said they committed this crime more than once in a year. At this rate, high school students alone commit more than 1.56 million robberies per year. In comparison, the UCR now tallies about 325,000 robberies for all age groups yearly. While official data show that the overall crime rate is in decline, the MTF surveys indicate that, with a few exceptions, self-reported participation in theft, violence, and damage-related crimes seems to be more stable than the trends reported in the UCR arrest data.

Are the Data Sources Compatible?

Each source of crime data has strengths and weaknesses. The FBI survey contains data on the number and characteristics of people arrested, information that the other data sources lack. It is also the source of information on particular crimes such as murder, which no other data source can provide.[34] While used extensively, the UCR omits the many crimes that victims choose not to report to police, and relies on the reporting accuracy of individual police departments.

The NCVS includes unreported crime missed by the UCR and also contains important information on the personal characteristics of victims. However, the data consist of estimates made from relatively limited samples of the total US population, so that even narrow fluctuations in the rates of some crimes can have a major impact on findings. The NCVS also relies on personal recollections that may be inaccurate. It does not include data on important crime patterns, including murder and drug abuse.

Self-report surveys provide useful information because questions on delinquent activity are often supplemented with items measuring the personal characteristics of offenders, such as their attitudes, values, beliefs, and psychological profiles. Self-reports can also be used to measure drug and alcohol abuse; these data are not included in the UCR and NCVS. Yet, at their core, self-reports rely on the honesty of criminal offenders and drug abusers, a population not generally known for accuracy and integrity.

Although their tallies of delinquency are certainly not in synch, the patterns and trends measured by various data sources are often quite similar: When the UCR shows a drop in illegal activity, so too does the NCVS. They all generally agree about the personal characteristics of serious delinquents (i.e., age and gender) and where and when delinquency occurs (i.e., urban areas, nighttime, and summer months). Because the measurement problems inherent in each source are consistent over time, the sources are reliable indicators of changes and fluctuations in delinquency rates.

What the Future Holds

Today, there are about 320 million people in the United States, about 75 million of whom are 18 and under. Although many come from supportive homes, others lack stable families and adequate supervision; these are some of the children who will soon enter their prime crime years. Though teen violence may increase, it is unlikely that this will translate into skyrocketing crime rate increases, because the effect of teenage crime is offset by the growing number of relatively crime-free senior citizens.[35]

Of course, prognostications, predictions, and forecasts are based on contemporary conditions that can change at any time due to the sudden emergence of war, terrorism, social unrest, economic meltdown, and the like.[36] Technological developments such as e-commerce on the Internet have created new classes of crime that are not recorded by any of the traditional methods of crime measurement. It's possible that some crimes such as fraud, larceny, prostitution, obscenity, vandalism, stalking, and harassment have increased over the Internet while falling under the radar of official crime data. The sharp increase in the 2015 violent crime rate, especially a surprise spike in the murder rate, is another ominous sign. Whether this is a single-year phenomenon or a long-term trend remains to be seen.

Correlates of Delinquency

Measurement of the personal traits and social characteristics associated with adolescent misbehavior is a crucial aspect of delinquency research. If, for example, a strong association exists between delinquent behavior and family income, then poverty and economic deprivation must be considered in any explanation of the onset of adolescent criminality. If the delinquency–income association is not present, then other forces may be responsible for producing antisocial behavior. It would be fruitless to concentrate delinquency control efforts in areas such as job creation and vocational training if social status were found to be unrelated to delinquent behavior. Similarly, if only a handful of delinquents are responsible for most serious crimes, then crime control policies might be made more effective by identifying and treating these offenders. The next sections discuss where and when delinquent acts take place, as well as the relationship between delinquency and the characteristics of gender, race, social class, and age.

Time, Place, and Nature of Delinquency

Most delinquent acts occur during the warm summer months of July and August. Weather may affect delinquent behavior in a number of different ways. During the summer, teenagers are out of school and have greater opportunity to commit crime. Homes are left vacant more often during the summer, making them more vulnerable to property crimes. Weather may also have a direct effect on behavior: As it gets warmer, kids get more violent.[37] However, some experts believe if it gets too hot—over 85 degrees—the frequency of some violent acts such as sexual assault begins to decline.[38]

There are also geographic differences in the incidence of delinquent behaviors.[39] Metropolitan areas are more delinquency prone than suburban or rural areas. But even in urban areas there are stable block-by-block and neighborhood-by-neighborhood differences in the delinquency rate.[40]

There are also regional differences: typically, the western and southern states have had consistently higher delinquency rates than the Midwest and Northeast, which have been linked to differences in cultural values, population makeup, gun ownership, and economic differences.

Some delinquent acts are committed alone while others are group efforts. The Focus on Delinquency feature looks at this issue in greater depth.

Gender and Delinquency

Males are significantly more delinquent than females. The teenage gender arrest ratio for all crimes is about 3:1, male to female. For serious violent crime, it's approximately 4:1, and for property crime approximately 2:1. The only exception to this pattern is that girls are more likely than boys to be arrested as runaways. There are two possible explanations: Girls could be more likely than boys to run away from home; police may view the female runaway as the more serious problem and therefore are more likely to process girls through official justice channels. This may reflect paternalistic attitudes toward girls, who are viewed as likely to "get in trouble" if they are on the street.

While males still commit more crimes than females, the arrest rate for both sexes has declined in the past decade. Ten years ago about 270,000 girls were being arrested each year; today that number has declined to about 207,000; the number of teen girls arrested annually for murder dropped from 70 to 39.[41]

Co-offending and Delinquency

It is generally believed that violent delinquency tends to be a group activity and that many adolescents join gangs and groups in order to facilitate their illegal activities. How true is this version of delinquent behavior? Is most violent delinquency a group activity?

According to the most recent data, violent delinquent acts are more likely committed by adolescents who acted alone (64 percent) than those who acted with co-offenders (36 percent). Nonetheless, adolescents were much more likely to co-offend than adults.

When adolescents did co-offend, they most commonly did so with other adolescents (59 percent) or young adults (28 percent). Kids tended to choose members of their own racial group: co-offenders were all white or all black in nearly 75 percent of violent victimizations committed by adolescents and in more than 70 percent of victimizations committed by adolescents who acted with young adults.

Victims were adolescents in 66 percent of serious violent victimizations committed by adolescents who acted alone and in 69 percent of those committed by adolescents who co-offended with other adolescents.

Why do kids co-offend? Peer support encourages offending in adolescence. Rather than being shunned by their peers, antisocial adolescents enjoy increased social status among peers who admire their risk-taking behaviors. Because co-offending requires offenders to cooperate with one another in a risky endeavor, it is more likely to occur in communities that contain a supply of appropriate delinquent associates who can keep their mouth shut and never cooperate with police. Co-offending is more prevalent in neighborhoods that are less disadvantaged, more stable, and contain more teens who can be trusted. Ironically, this means that efforts to improve neighborhood stability and cohesiveness may also help produce an environment that encourages group offending.

Does it pay to offend in groups or are you better off as a lone wolf? Recent research by Marie Skubak Tillyer and Rob Tillyer found that co-offending results in significantly less property value stolen per offender, while increasing the likelihood of an incident resulting in an arrest. One reason for the greater apprehension risk: the more robbers, the more likely the victim will recognize someone they know. Why do robbers commit crime in groups if co-offending produces lower gain and greater pain?

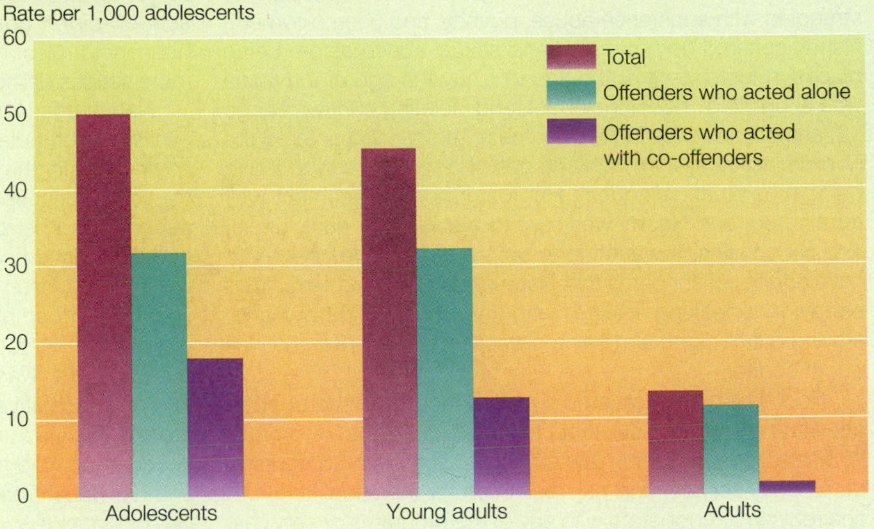

figure 2.2A

Violent Victimizing Rates, by Offender Age Group and Co-Offending Status, 2004–2013

SOURCE: US Department of Justice, Bureau of Justice Statistics, "Co-Offending Among Adolescents in Violent Victimizations, 2004–13," July 2016.

Committing crime in groups helps to control offender fear during the incident while increasing peer group respect. Working in a group also may facilitate opportunities for more frequent offending, thus leading to higher overall profits for the offender. So in the final tally, working in a group may produce higher overall profit even if it does require more "work."

CRITICAL THINKING

The data presented here are for violent offenses only. Do you think that kids are more likely to co-offend in property crimes such as car theft and burglary?

SOURCES: Barbara A. Oudokork and Rachel E. Morgan, "Co-Offending Among Adolescents in Violent Victimizations, 2004–13," Bureau of Justice Statistics, July 2016, http://www.bjs.gov/content/pub/pdf/caavv0413.pdf; Franklin Zimring and Hannah Laqueur, "Kids, Groups, and Crime: In Defense of Conventional Wisdom," *Journal of Research in Crime and Delinquency* 52:403–413 (2015); Derek Kreager, "When It's Good to Be 'Bad': Violence and Adolescent Peer Acceptance," *Criminology* 45:893–923 (2007); Lisa Stolzenberg and Stewart D'Alessio, "Co-offending and the Age-Crime Curve," *Journal of Research in Crime and Delinquency* 45:65–86 (2008); David R. Schaefer, Nancy Rodriguez, and Scott H. Decker, "The Role of Neighborhood Context in Youth Co-offending," *Criminology* 52:117–139 (2014); Marie Skubak Tillyer and Rob Tillyer, "Maybe I Should Do This Alone: A Comparison of Solo and Co-offending Robbery Outcomes," *Justice Quarterly* 32:1064–1088 (2015).

Official arrest data may significantly underreport the total amount of female delinquency. Self-report data also seem to show that the incidence of female delinquency is much higher than believed earlier, and that the most common crimes committed by males are also the ones most female offenders commit. Because the relationship between gender and delinquency rate is so important, this topic will be discussed further in Chapter 7.

The Case Profile tells the true story of how one young girl overcame the adversities that made her at risk for delinquency.

case profile

Naomi's Story

NAOMI was born in a poor, urban neighborhood. As her parents struggled with substance abuse, poverty, and unemployment, Naomi suffered both physical and sexual abuse before being placed in foster care at the age of 5. By the age of 9, Naomi was shoplifting, skipping school, and violating curfew. At age 13, she physically assaulted her foster mother and entered the juvenile justice system with charges of disorderly conduct and being a habitual delinquent. Her foster home placement was terminated, and Naomi was sent to live with her aunt, uncle, and six cousins. It wasn't long before her relatives began to have additional concerns that Naomi was exhibiting sexualized behavior, "sneaking around" with her 17-year-old boyfriend, staying out all night, and being disrespectful. They felt she was out of control.

Naomi had been ordered by the juvenile court to cooperate with her family's household rules, attend school on a regular basis, have no further law violations, complete 25 hours of community service, and pay restitution for the shoplifting, but she refused to cooperate with any of the programs or services, continuing to come and go as she pleased. The family was receiving support from Naomi's intensive supervision program counselor, as well as a family therapist, but during the second month of placement with her relatives, at the age of 14, Naomi disclosed that she was pregnant and planning to keep her baby. The program counselor and other professionals involved in Naomi's case had to work with her and her family to reevaluate their plan.

Naomi was enrolled in a school specifically designed to support teens who are pregnant or already parenting, where in addition to her academic studies to complete high school, she would receive help from parenting classes, independent living courses, and relationship counseling. Naomi also received services from a neighborhood intervention program that focused on providing structure and accountability for her through counselors and daily group meetings to encourage her. Even with these additional supports and interventions, Naomi continued to get involved in some minor status offenses: She skipped school, didn't come home on time, and would not follow household rules. Nonetheless, she had no involvement with more serious delinquent activities.

Naomi continued to live with her aunt and uncle, and did eventually complete her community service and restitution payment. After the baby was born Naomi began to understand the consequences of her actions. With continued services and support from her counselors, she started following the rules and expectations of her family. Upon taking responsibility to find the necessary medical and child care for her daughter, Naomi found employment—a position in retail—and started planning for her future. Despite being at high risk for dropping out of school, Naomi completed her high school education and had a positive view of her future. The team of involved professionals continued to provide the needed supports and encouraged Naomi to make good decisions for both herself and her baby. She still struggles at times, but has remained free of further law violations.

CRITICAL THINKING

1. Naomi received a number of interventions to address her issues, but it still took a long time for her to reduce her delinquent behavior. How long should the juvenile justice system give a young person to change? How many chances should a teen get? Do you think she would have likely been removed from her aunt and uncle's home if her criminal behavior had continued?

2. As Naomi grew older, she was less involved in criminal activity. Discuss the reasons for the "aging-out" process and apply them to this case example.

3. What childhood risk factors did Naomi have regarding the possibility of becoming a persistent delinquent? How was this avoided? What can be done to reduce chronic offending among at-risk youth?

Race and Delinquency

There are approximately 40 million white and 12 million African American youths 19 and under in the United States, a ratio of a little more than three to one. The official statistics show that minority youths are arrested for serious criminal behavior at a rate that is disproportionate to their representation in the population. About 60 percent of teens arrested for murder are African American and 69 percent of those arrested for robbery; African American teens are involved in more than half of all arrests for serious violent crimes and almost 40 percent of serious property crimes. Self-report studies using large samples show that about 30 percent of black males have experienced at least one arrest by age 18 (versus about 22 percent for white males), and by age 23 almost half of all black males have been arrested (versus about 38 percent for white males).[42]

According to the concept of institutional racism, African American delinquency rates are influenced by differential enforcement and treatment of black teens by police. Here, police arrest a protester in Ferguson, Missouri, on November 25, 2014, during demonstrations a day after violent protests and looting broke out following a grand jury's decision not to prosecute a white police officer for shooting Michael Brown, an unarmed black teenager.

Jewel Samad/Getty Images

While it is possible that African American teens are arrested more often because they commit more crime, it is also possible this pattern reflects institutional bias in the juvenile justice system. In other words, African American youths are more likely to be formally arrested by the police, who, in contrast, will treat white youths informally.

One way to examine this issue is to compare the racial differences in self-reported data with those found in the official delinquency records. Given the disproportionate numbers of African Americans arrested, charges of racial discrimination would be supported if we found little difference between the number of self-reported minority and white crimes.

Early researchers found that the relationship between race and self-reported delinquency was virtually nonexistent.[43] These findings supported the conclusion that racial differences in the official crime data may reflect the fact that African American youths have a much greater chance of being arrested and officially processed.[44]

More recent studies present a mixed bag of results. While some recent self-report surveys show that offending differences between African American and white youths are marginal and not significant, others do find that African American youth are more likely to self-report delinquent acts at a more frequent rate.[45]

Institutional Racism and Delinquency   How can the disproportionate number of African American youngsters arrested for serious crimes be explained? One view blames disproportionate minority involvement in arrest as a function of institutional bias. As the Black Lives Matter movement suggests, race-based differences in the delinquency rate can be explained in part as an effect of unequal or biased treatment by the juvenile justice system. Police are more likely to stop, search, and arrest racial minorities than they are members of the white majority. Institutional bias creates a vicious cycle because they are targeted more frequently, African American teens are more likely to possess a criminal record; having a criminal record is associated with repeat stops and searches.[46]

To make matters worse, according to the **racial threat theory**, as the percentage of minorities in the population increases, so too does the amount of social control imposed on minority citizens at every stage of the justice system, from arrest to final release.[47]

racial threat theory
As the size of the black population increases, the perceived threat to the white population increases, resulting in a greater amount of social control imposed against African Americans by police.

As pressure grows to contain "the racial threat," police will then routinely search, question, and detain all African American males in an area if a violent criminal has been described as "looking or sounding black"; this is called **racial profiling**. A recent meta-analysis of numerous studies that estimates the effect of race on the police decision to arrest found significant evidence that minority suspects are more likely to be arrested than white suspects when stopped by police for the same behaviors.[48] Racial profiling may be more common in communities where there are relatively few racial minorities (i.e., "white neighborhoods"). In racially segregated communities, police may be especially suspicious of people based on their race if it is inconsistent with the neighborhood racial composition.[49]

The Effects of Profiling   Racial profiling takes a particular toll on younger African American males, who often see their experience with police as unfair or degrading. They approach future encounters with preexisting hostility; police take this as a sign that young black men pose a special danger. They respond with harsh treatment, and a never-ending cycle of mutual mistrust is created.[50]

In the event they are picked up again and sent back to juvenile court, their earlier record makes them eligible for harsher treatment.[51] Racial discrimination at the onset of the justice system ensures that minorities receive greater punishments at its conclusion.[52]

Juvenile court judges may see the offenses committed by minority youths as more serious than those committed by white offenders. Consequently, they are more likely to keep minority juveniles in detention pending trial in juvenile court than they are white youths with similar backgrounds.[53] White juveniles are more likely to receive lenient sentences or have their cases dismissed.[54] As a result, African American youths, suspected by police, are more likely to accumulate an adult criminal record and face a bleak future in a jobless economy in which those with a criminal record are less likely to receive job offers.[55]

In sum, according to the institutional racism view, the disproportionate number of minority youth who are arrested is less a function of their involvement in serious crime and more the result of the race-based decision making in the juvenile justice system.[56] Institutional racism by police and the courts is still an element of daily life in the African American community, a factor that undermines faith in social and political institutions and weakens confidence in the justice system.[57]

Structural Racism and Delinquency   Another view of race differences in the delinquency rate holds that although evidence of some racial bias does exist in the justice system, there is enough correspondence between official and self-report data to conclude that racial differences in the crime rate are real. If African American youths are arrested at a disproportionately high rate for crimes such as robbery and assault, it is a result of actual offending rates rather than bias on the part of the criminal justice system.[58]

According to the structural racism view, racial differentials are tied to the social and economic disparity suffered by African American youths. Too many are forced to live in the nation's poorest areas that suffer high crime rates.[59] Many black youths are forced to attend essentially segregated schools that are underfunded and deteriorated, a condition that increases the likelihood of their being incarcerated in adulthood.[60] The burden of social and economic marginalization has weakened the African American family structure. When families are weakened or disrupted, their ability to act as social control agents is compromised.[61]

Even during times of economic growth, lower-class African Americans are left out of the economic mainstream, causing a growing sense of frustration and failure.[62] As a result of being shut out of educational and economic opportunities enjoyed by the rest of society, this population may be prone, some believe, to the lure of illegitimate gain and criminality.

This vision is not entirely bleak. Even among at-risk African American kids growing up in communities characterized by poverty, high unemployment levels, and single-parent households, those who do live in stable families with reasonable incomes and educational achievement are much less likely to engage in violent behaviors than those lacking family support.[63] Consequently, racial differences in the delinquency rate would evaporate if the social and economic characteristics of racial minorities were improved to levels currently enjoyed by whites, and African American kids could enjoy the same social, economic, and educational privileges.[64]

For more information about **race-related issues in America**, visit the University of Pittsburgh's Center on Race and Social Problems (http://www.crsp.pitt.edu/).

Socioeconomic Status (SES) and Delinquency

There is a significant association between economic status and delinquent involvement. Teens of all races and ethnicities living on the lowest rungs of the social structure have the greatest incentive to engage in antisocial activity.[65] It seems logical that kids who are unable to obtain desired goods and services legally will resort to illegal activities—such as selling narcotics—to obtain a share of the American Dream: if you can't afford a car, steal it; if you can't afford designer clothes, become a drug dealer.

Instrumental crimes are those committed by indigent people to compensate for the lack of legitimate economic opportunity. Kids living in poverty also engage in disproportionate amounts of **expressive crimes** such as rape and assault, as a result of their frustration with what they believe to be an unfair and unjust society. Boiling with anger over social issues as **income inequality**, they express their rage with irrational crimes that bring them no economic gain.[66] While it is true that middle- and upper-class youth also engage in delinquent acts, they are less likely to join gangs or commit serious felony offenses.

While the association between socioeconomic status and delinquency may be apparent, experts differ on the manner in which these two factors are related:

instrumental crimes
Offenses designed to improve the financial or social position of the criminal.

expressive crimes
Crimes that have no purpose except to accomplish the behavior at hand, such as shooting someone.

income inequality
The unequal distribution of household or individual income across the various participants in an economy.

- Youths who lack wealth or social standing are the ones who use illegal means to achieve their goals and compensate for their lack of economic resources.

- Kids living in communities that lack economic and social opportunities have more incentive to engage in illegal acts.

- Kids who live in these areas believe that they can never compete socially or economically with adolescents being raised in more affluent areas. They may turn to illegal behavior for monetary gain and psychological satisfaction.[67]

- Family life is most likely to be frayed and disrupted in low-income areas. As a consequence, gangs and law-violating youth groups thrive in a climate that undermines and neutralizes the adult supervision that families provide.[68]

- Kids who live in poor families within poor communities are doubly at risk for delinquency and find it hard to resist the lure of the streets.[69]

- Neighborhoods experiencing income inequality and resource deprivation have crime rates significantly higher than those that can provide equal or more economic opportunities to their citizens.[70]

- Police devote more resources to less affluent areas, and consequently apprehension rates may be higher there. Police may also be more likely to formally arrest and prosecute lower-class youths, especially racial and ethnic minorities, while giving those in the middle and upper classes more lenient treatment, such as handling their law violations with a warning.

Age and Delinquency

It is generally accepted that age is inversely related to criminality: Crime is a young person's game. Adolescents, especially those who are destined to become high rate offenders, begin committing crime in their childhood, rapidly increase their offending activities in late adolescence, and then begin a slowdown in adulthood.[71]

Andrea Mohin/The New York Times/Redux

Jonathan Rosario, born to a drug-addicted mother, spent the first seven years of his life in a housing project in the Mott Haven section of the Bronx. As a young man, feeling rebellious, he began cutting classes and getting involved in trouble. He was arrested after he was caught smoking marijuana on the street. Then a friend asked him to hold on to three guns for safekeeping. Without giving it much thought, Rosario agreed to do so, storing them in the apartment he shared with a girlfriend. One day, the police showed up; there was an outstanding warrant for his arrest. He had failed to appear in court a second time on the marijuana charges because he had not realized he had to. The police searched the apartment, found the guns, and charged him with possession of guns and ammunition. After a few days on Rikers Island, he was sentenced to three years of probation. Why does someone like Rosario continually get involved in offending? Later he was able to turn his life around, with the help of a settlement house program. Does his story mean that even chronic offenders can one day leave a life of crime?

Crime is attractive to young people because it brings social benefits. Deviance in adolescence is fueled by the need for money and sex and reinforced by a teen culture whose informal rules stress defying conventional morality. It is not a coincidence that kids get piercings and tattoos as soon as the law allows. Kids who assume an outlaw persona find that their antisocial acts bring them increased social status among peers who admire their risk-taking behaviors. Young criminals may be looking for an avenue of behavior that improves their peer group standing.[72]

At the same time, teenagers are becoming independent from parents and other adults who enforce conventional standards of morality and behavior. They have a new sense of energy and strength and are involved with peers who are similarly vigorous and frustrated.

It is not surprising, then, that regardless of race, sex, social class, intelligence, or any other social variable, people commit less crime as they age. This phenomenon, referred to as the *aging-out process*, is also sometimes called *desistance from crime* or *spontaneous remission*.[73] Aging out of crime may be a function of the natural history of the human life cycle, and no one is immune.[74] Even the most chronic juvenile offenders commit less crime as they age. Though high-rate offenders will commit more crime as adults than their nondelinquent peers, even these committed and persistent delinquents will slow down as they age; few people get into as much trouble when they are 51 as they did when they were 15.[75]

Age also impacts delinquency because the earlier kids commit crime in their life cycle, the more serious and aggressive their criminal involvement. **Age of onset** is an important determinant of the length and seriousness of a delinquent

age of onset
Age at which youths begin their delinquent careers; early onset is believed to be linked with chronic offending patterns.

career. Kids who are persistent offenders begin committing crime early in their childhood, rapidly increase their offending activities in late adolescence, and only begin to slow down in adulthood.[76] Those kids who demonstrate antisocial tendencies at a very early age are also more likely to commit more crimes and for a longer period of time.

In sum, youths who get involved with delinquency at a very early age are most likely to become career criminals; age is a key determinant of delinquency.[77]

Why Does Crime Decline with Age?   Delinquency experts have developed a number of reasons for the aging-out process:

■ *Growing older means having to face the future.* Young people, especially the indigent and antisocial, tend to "discount the future."[78] Why should they delay gratification when faced with an uncertain future? As they mature, troubled youths are able to develop a long-term life view and resist the need for immediate gratification.[79]

■ *With maturity comes the ability to resist the "quick fix" to their problems.* Research shows that some kids may turn to crime as a way to solve the problems of adolescence, loneliness, frustration, and fear of peer rejection. As they mature, conventional means of problem solving become available. Life experience helps former delinquents seek nondestructive solutions to their personal problems.[80]

■ *Maturation coincides with increased levels of responsibility.* Petty crimes are risky and exciting social activities that provide adventure in an otherwise boring world. As youths grow older, they take on new responsibilities that are inconsistent with criminality.[81] For example, young people who marry, enlist in the armed services, or enroll in vocational training courses are less likely to pursue criminal activities.[82]

■ *Personalities can change with age.* As they mature, rebellious youngsters may develop increased self-control and be able to resist antisocial behavior.[83] In adulthood, people strengthen their ability to delay gratification and forgo the immediate gains that law violations bring. They also start wanting to take responsibility for their behavior and to adhere to conventional mores, such as establishing long-term relationships and starting a family.[84] Getting married, raising a family, and creating long-term family ties provide the stability that helps people desist from crime.[85]

■ *Young adults become more aware of the risks that accompany crime.* As adults, they are no longer protected by the relatively kindly arms of the juvenile justice system.[86]

Of course, not all juvenile criminals desist as they age; some go on to become chronic adult offenders. Yet even they slow down as they age. Crime is too dangerous, physically taxing, and unrewarding, and punishments too harsh and long lasting, to become a way of life for most people.[87]

Chronic Offending: Careers in Delinquency

Although most adolescents age out of crime, a relatively small number of youths begin to violate the law early in their lives (early onset) and continue at a high rate well into adulthood (persistence). The association between early onset and high-rate persistent offending has been demonstrated in samples drawn from a variety of cultures, time periods, and offender types. These offenders are resistant to change and seem immune to the effects of punishment. Arrest, prosecution, and conviction do little to slow down their offending careers.

These chronic offenders are responsible for a significant amount of all delinquent and criminal activity. Because almost everyone commits less crime as they age, it is difficult to predict or identify in advance the relatively few offenders who will continue to commit crime as they travel through their life course.[88]

Current interest in the delinquent life cycle was prompted in part by the "discovery" in the 1970s of the chronic juvenile (or delinquent) offender. According to this view, a relatively small number of youthful offenders commit a significant percentage of all serious crimes, and many of these same offenders grow up to become chronic adult criminals.

Chronic offenders can be distinguished from other delinquent youths. Many youthful law violators are apprehended for a single instance of criminal behavior, such as shoplifting or joyriding. Chronic offenders begin their delinquent careers at a young age (under 10 years), have serious and persistent brushes with the law, and may be excessively violent and destructive. They do not age out of crime but continue their law-violating behavior into adulthood.[89] Most research shows that early, repeated delinquent activity is the best predictor of future adult criminality.

A number of research efforts have set out to chronicle the careers of serious delinquent offenders. The next sections describe these initiatives.

Delinquency in a Birth Cohort

The concept of the chronic career offender is most closely associated with the research efforts of Marvin Wolfgang.[90] In 1972, Wolfgang, Robert Figlio, and Thorsten Sellin published a landmark study, *Delinquency in a Birth Cohort*. They followed the delinquent careers of a cohort of 9,945 boys born in Philadelphia from birth until they reached age 18. Data were obtained from police files and school records. Socioeconomic status was determined by locating the residence of each member of the cohort and assigning him the median family income for that area. About one-third of the boys (3,475) had some police contact. The remaining two-thirds (6,470) had none. Those boys who had at least one contact with the police committed a total of 10,214 offenses.

The most significant discovery of Wolfgang and his associates was that of the so-called chronic offender. The data indicated that 54 percent (1,862) of the sample's delinquent youths were repeat offenders. The repeaters could be further categorized as nonchronic recidivists and chronic recidivists. Nonchronic recidivists had been arrested more than once but fewer than five times. In contrast, the 627 boys labeled chronic recidivists had been arrested five times or more. Although these offenders accounted for only 18 percent of the delinquent population (6 percent of the total sample), they were responsible for 52 percent of all offenses. Known today as the "chronic 6 percent," this group perpetrated 71 percent of the homicides, 82 percent of the robberies, and 64 percent of the aggravated assaults (see Figure 2.2).

Arrest and juvenile court experience did little to deter chronic offenders. In fact, the greater the punishment, the more likely they were to engage in repeat delinquent behavior. Strict punishment also increased the probability that further court action would be taken. Two factors stood out as encouraging recidivism: the seriousness of the original offense and the severity of the punishment. The researchers concluded that efforts of the juvenile justice system to eliminate delinquent behavior may be futile.

Wolfgang and his colleagues conducted a second cohort study with children born in 1958 and substantiated the finding that a relatively few chronic offenders are responsible for a significant portion of all delinquent acts.[91] Wolfgang's results have been duplicated in a number of research studies conducted in locales across the United States and also in Great Britain.[92] Some have used the records of court-processed youths, and others have employed self-report data. One study that followed a 10 percent sample of the original Pennsylvania cohort (974 subjects) to age 30 found that 70 percent of the persistent adult offenders had also been chronic juvenile offenders. Chronic juvenile offenders had an 80 percent chance of becoming adult offenders and a 50 percent chance of being arrested four or more times as adults.[93] Paul Tracy and Kimberly Kempf-Leonard conducted a follow-up study of all the subjects in the second 1958 cohort. By age 26, Cohort II subjects were displaying the same behavior patterns as their older peers. Kids who started their delinquent careers early, committed a violent crime, and continued offending throughout adolescence were most likely to persist in criminal behavior as adults.

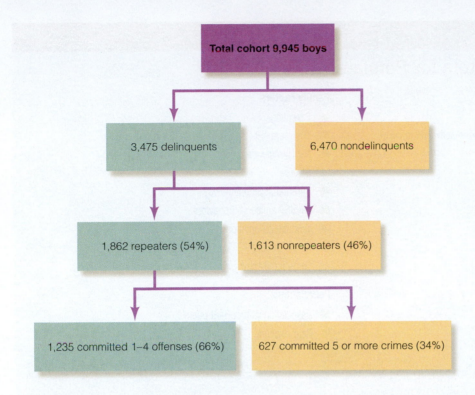

figure 2.2

Distribution of Offenses in the Philadelphia Cohort

© Cengage Learning 2015

Delinquents who began their offending careers with serious offenses or who quickly increased the severity of their offending early in life were most likely to persist in their criminal behavior into adulthood. Severity of offending rather than frequency of criminal behavior had the greatest impact on later adult criminality.[94]

These studies indicate that chronic juvenile offenders continue their law-violating careers as adults, a concept referred to as the **continuity of crime**. Kids who are disruptive as early as age 5 or 6 are most likely to exhibit disruptive behavior throughout adolescence.[95]

continuity of crime
The idea that chronic juvenile offenders are likely to continue violating the law as adults.

What Causes Chronic Offending?

Research indicates that chronic offenders suffer from a number of personal, environmental, social, and developmental deficits, as shown in Exhibit 2.2. Other research studies have found that early involvement in criminal activity (for example, getting arrested before age 15), relatively low intellectual development, and parental drug involvement were key predictive factors for future chronic offending.[96] Measurable problems in learning and motor skills, cognitive abilities, family relations, and other areas also predict chronicity.[97] Youthful offenders who persist are more likely to abuse alcohol, become economically dependent, have lower aspirations, and have a weak employment record.[98] Apprehension and punishment seem to have little effect on their offending behavior. Youths who have long juvenile records will most likely continue their offending careers into adulthood.

Policy Implications

Efforts to chart the life cycle of crime and delinquency will have a major influence on both theory and policy. Rather than simply asking why youths become delinquent or commit antisocial acts, theorists are charting the onset, escalation, frequency, and cessation of delinquent behavior. Research on delinquent careers has also influenced policy. If relatively few offenders commit a great proportion of all delinquent acts and then persist as adult criminals, it follows that steps should be taken to limit their criminal opportunities.[99] One approach is to identify persistent offenders at the beginning of their offending careers and provide early treatment.[100]

exhibit 2.2

Childhood Risk Factors for Persistent Delinquency

Individual Factors

- Early antisocial behavior
- Emotional factors such as high behavioral activation and low behavioral inhibition
- Poor cognitive development
- Low intelligence
- Hyperactivity

School and Community Factors

- Failure to bond to school
- Poor academic performance
- Low academic aspirations
- Living in a poor family
- Neighborhood disadvantage
- Disorganized neighborhoods
- Concentration of delinquent peer groups
- Access to weapons

Family Factors

- Parenting
- Maltreatment
- Family violence
- Divorce
- Parental psychopathology
- Familial antisocial behaviors
- Teenage parenthood
- Family structure
- Large family size

Peer Factors

- Association with deviant peers
- Peer rejection

SOURCE: Gail Wasserman, Kate Keenan, Richard Tremblay, John Coie, Todd Herrenkohl, Rolf Loeber, and David Petechuk, "Risk and Protective Factors of Child Delinquency," *Child Delinquency Bulletin Series* (Washington, DC: Office of Juvenile Justice and Delinquency Prevention, 2003).

This might be facilitated by research aimed at identifying traits (for example, impulsive personalities) that can be used to classify high-risk offenders.[101] Because many of these youths suffer from a variety of problems, treatment must be aimed at a broad range of educational, family, vocational, and psychological problems. Focusing on a single problem, such as a lack of employment, may be ineffective.[102]

Juvenile Victimization

Richard and Maureen Kanka thought their daughter Megan was safe in their quiet, suburban neighborhood in Hamilton Township, New Jersey. On July 29, 1994, their lives were shattered when 7-year-old Megan went missing. Maureen Kanka searched the neighborhood and met 33-year-old Jesse Timmendequas, who lived across the street. Timmendequas told her that he had seen Megan earlier that evening while he was working on his car. The police were called in and soon focused their attention on Timmendequas's house when they learned that he and two other residents were convicted sex offenders who had met at a treatment center and decided to live together upon their release. Timmendequas soon confessed to luring Megan into his home by telling her she could see his puppy and then raping and strangling her to death. Jesse Timmendequas was sentenced to death on June 20, 1997, and remained on New Jersey's death row until December 17, 2007, when the state's death penalty was abolished and his sentence was commuted to life in prison without the possibility of parole.

Megan's death led to a national crusade to develop laws that require sex offenders to register with local police when they move into a neighborhood and require local authorities to provide community notification of the sex offender's presence. On the federal level, the Jacob Wetterling Crimes Against Children Law passed in May 1996, which requires states to pass some version of "Megan's Law" or lose federal aid. All 50 states plus the District of Columbia have complied. Eleven-year-old Jacob Wetterling was abducted in 1989 from near his home in

Sheila Pott poses with a portrait of her daughter Audrie in Los Altos, California, on May 23, 2013. Audrie Pott committed suicide in September 2012 after being sexually assaulted by three boys during a house party in Saratoga, California. Photos of the incident were circulated around Pott's high school, prompting the teenager to hang herself in a bathroom at home. There has been a spate of such cyber victimizations that have resulted in young women taking their own lives.

AP Images/Marcio Jose Sanchez

St. Joseph, Minnesota. On September 1, 2016, the FBI recovered Jacob's remains from a nearby pasture. The location was revealed by Danny Heinrich, a known sex offender who confessed to kidnapping and murdering Jacob 27 years earlier.[103]

As the Megan Kanka and Jacob Wetterling cases sadly tell us, juveniles are also victims of crime. The difference is particularly striking when we compare teens with people over age 65: teens are 15 times more likely to become victims than their grandparents. The data also indicate that male teenagers have a significantly higher chance than females of becoming victims of most violent crime, and that African American youth have a greater chance of becoming victims of violent crimes than whites of the same age. Young girls are much more likely to be the victim of sexual assaults, while boys are much more likely to be the victims of robbery. In either event, the likelihood of victimization for both crimes declines after the teenage years.

In the Youth Stories feature, notorious cases of juvenile victimization are discussed in some detail.

Juvenile Victimization Trends

Delinquency rates have been in decline for the past two decades, so it comes as no surprise that rates of adolescent victimization for serious violent crime—rape or sexual assault, robbery, and aggravated assault—have undergone similar declines. As Table 2.3 shows, the percent of juveniles who have suffered violent

table 2.3

Rate of violent victimization, by victim demographic characteristics, 2005, 2013, and 2014

Victim Demographic Characteristics	Violent Crime[a]			Serious Violent Crime		
	2005	2013	2014	2005	2013	2014
Age						
12–17	59.8	52.1	30.1	14.9	10.8	8.8
18–24	61.0	33.8	26.8	23.5	10.7	13.6
25–34	29.7	29.6	28.5	11.5	10.2	8.6
35–49	24.9	20.3	21.6	7.1	7.1	8.9
50–64	15.0	18.7	17.9	4.4	6.9	7.0
65 or older	3.6	3.1	3.1	2.0	1.1	1.3

[a]Includes rape or sexual assault, robbery, aggravated assault, and simple assault. Excludes homicide because the NCVS is based on interviews with victims and therefore cannot measure murder.
SOURCE: Jennifer L. Truman and Lynn Langton, "Criminal Victimization, 2014," Bureau of Justice Statistics, September 2015, http://www.bjs.gov/content/pub/pdf/cv14.pdf (accessed September 2016).

Room: Kids Held Captive

The 2015 film *Room* for which Brie Larson won an Oscar is loosely based on a number of incidents in which young girls are kidnapped and held captive for long periods of time; some had children by their captors.

■ Elizabeth Smart, a 14-year-old Salt Lake City girl, was kidnapped from her home on June 5, 2002. She was taken in the middle of the night from a room she shared with her 9-year-old sister, Mary Katherine, who pretended to be asleep. A massive search failed to find Elizabeth, and many felt the girl was gone forever. Months later, Mary Katherine suddenly remembered that she had heard the kidnapper's voice before

Melissa Baum, whose 10-year-old daughter Lindsey disappeared in June 2009, wipes a tear from her eye after being introduced in 2013 to kidnap survivor Elizabeth Smart at a speaking engagement. Smart told Baum and the rest of her audience about her harrowing abduction at age 14 and her nine-month ordeal at the hands of her kidnapper.

and that it belonged to a man named Emmanuel, whom the Smarts had hired to work around the house. The police did not consider this information reliable, so the family turned to a sketch artist to draw a rendering that was released to the media and given media attention on TV shows such as *Larry King Live* and *America's Most Wanted*. Family members of Brian David Mitchell, the real name of Emmanuel, recognized him in the drawing and provided photos. Now wanted by police around the nation, Mitchell was spotted in Sandy, Utah, on March 12, 2003, nine months after the abduction. Mitchell and his wife, Wanda Barzee, were taken into custody and Elizabeth Smart reunited with her family. During Mitchell's 2010 trial, Elizabeth Smart, now 23 years old, testified about her horrific experiences during the nine months she was held captive. She was raped every day and constantly threatened that she would be killed if she tried to escape. Mitchell was eventually found guilty of kidnapping and sexual assault, charges that brought him a life sentence in prison. Barzee had earlier pleaded guilty and was sentenced to 15 years in prison.

■ Eleven-year-old Jaycee Lee Dugard was abducted on June 10, 1991, at a school bus stop within sight of her home in South Lake Tahoe, California. After being

grabbed off the street by Phillip Garrido, she was held captive for 18 years, living in a tent in a walled-off compound on land Garrido owned in Antioch, California. Raped repeatedly, Dugard bore two daughters, in 1994 and 1998. Law enforcement officers had visited the residence at least twice but failed to detect Jaycee or her children. Garrido and his wife were indicted on charges including kidnapping, rape, and false imprisonment. In 2011, Garrido received a sentence of 431 years to life and his wife Nancy was sentenced to 36 years to life.

■ Amanda Berry, Gina DeJesus, and Michelle Knight were all held captive in a home in Cleveland owned by a local musician and bus driver named Ariel Castro. Amanda Berry was kidnapped when she was 17 years old. She left her part-time job at a Burger King on April 21, 2003, and was not heard from again. Her family never gave up hope and sought public support on TV shows like *America's Most Wanted*. Gina DeJesus was 14, in seventh grade, when she vanished while walking home from school on April 2, 2004. Michelle Knight was 21 when she disappeared. She was last seen at a cousin's house on August 22, 2002, not far from where Berry and DeJesus were last seen.

victimizations has been lowered by almost 50 percent just in the past decade. Some notable trends have taken place. There has been a significant convergence of male and female teen victimization rates. Today male and female youth are equally likely to experience serious violent crime; 20 years ago males were twice as likely to be victims. Rates of serious violent crime victimization among white and Hispanic youth have been in sharp decline, while rates have remained the same among black youth.[104]

The three women were chained up in the basement of Castro's home and repeatedly beaten and raped. Berry gave birth in captivity and her child was 6 years old at the time of their rescue in 2013. After they were rescued when neighbors heard them screaming, the women told police that Castro's beatings had resulted in their having numerous miscarriages. Michelle Knight told her rescuers that Castro had impregnated her multiple times and forced her to abort each time. Castro would starve Knight for weeks and then repeatedly punch her in the stomach until she miscarried. Ariel Castro was sentenced to life plus 1,000 years in prison. He hanged himself in his prison cell one month after sentencing.

Gina DeJesus (left) and Amanda Berry (center) are honored at the National Center for Missing and Exploited Children's Hope Awards dinner in Washington, D.C.

AP Images/Cliff Owen

■ Elisabeth Fritzl, an Austrian girl, was held captive by her own father for 24 years. In 1984, when she was 18, Elisabeth was forced into a basement dungeon by her father, Josef Fritzl. He told her mother and police that the girl had run away to join a cult, and he would periodically force her to write letters saying as much, which he would have postmarked from distant locations for legitimacy. Over the years, Josef raped Elisabeth regularly and fathered seven children. Elisabeth finally made it out of her horrible imprisonment in 2008, when her daughter Kerstin, a member of the dungeon, fell unconscious due to kidney failure and was taken to the hospital. When authorities became aware of the situation, Elisabeth was finally freed by police along with her children, and Josef was sentenced to life behind bars.

All the women were survivors despite their brutal treatment. Elizabeth Smart has become a journalist and advocate for missing and abused children. In July 2010, the State of California approved a $20 million settlement with Jaycee Dugard to compensate her for "various lapses by the Corrections Department [which contributed to] Dugard's continued captivity, ongoing sexual assault, and mental and/or physical abuse." Amanda Berry, Michelle Knight, and Gina DeJesus have reunited with their families. Elisabeth Fritzl lives in an undisclosed Austrian village with her children; she is 44, but the only photographs of her ever published show her aged 16 and under.

These abductions are tragically not unique. Nearly 30,000 children are taken and sexually assaulted by strangers each year. While cases involving long-term abduction and sexual exploitation are relatively rare, briefer detention and rape of children is all too common.

CRITICAL THINKING

How much punishment does a kidnapper deserve? Should a person such as Ariel Castro, who abducts a young woman, impregnates her, and then causes her to miscarry, be charged with murder?

SOURCES: Eesha Pandit, "In the Cleveland Kidnapping Case, Bystander Intervention Worked. What Happens When It Doesn't?" The Nation, May 13, 2013, http://www.thenation.com/article /174302/cleveland-kidnapping-case-bystander-intervention-worked-what-happens-when-it -doesnt; Russell Goldman, "Elizabeth Smart Tells Court Brian David Mitchell Would Pray for Sex," ABC News, November 10, 2010, http://abcnews.go.com/US/elizabeth-smart-tells-court-brian -david-mitchell-pray/story?id=12110773; Netter and Sabina Ghebremedhin, "Jaycee Dugard Found After 18 Years, Kidnap Suspect Allegedly Fathered Her Kids," ABC News, August 27, 2009, http:// abcnews.go.com/US/jaycee-lee-dugard-found-family-missing-girl-located/story?id=8426124; Allan Hall, Monster (London: Penguin, 2008). (All URLs accessed September 2016.)

Reporting Victimizations   How often do kids report their victimizations to police, school, and medical authorities? Results from the most recent National Survey of Children's Exposure to Violence (NatSCEV) found that compared with a similar study in the early 1990s, authorities were more likely to know about incidents of violence, which may reflect an ongoing effort by school authorities, criminal justice and child protection agencies, and advocates to promote disclosure.[105] The survey found that school, police, and medical

Christopher Gunn

In 2011, 31-year-old Christopher Gunn pleaded guilty to producing child pornography in connection with an online sextortion scheme that spanned the globe. Over a period of more than two years, Gunn repeatedly used chat rooms and other social media outlets to threaten hundreds of young girls ages 9 to 16 located throughout the United States and internationally and coerce them into sending him sexually suggestive photos. The first scheme—dubbed "the New Kid Ruse"—involved contacting the victims over Facebook and pretending to be a new kid in town looking for friends. Once he had gained their trust through chatting, Gunn would ask the girls a series of personal questions, such as their sexual histories, intimate details about their bodies, and so on. If they divulged that personal information, Gunn would then ask the girls to send him a topless photo. If they refused, he would threaten to e-mail their intimate conversation to the school principal or post it on Facebook for everyone to see. The second scheme—dubbed "the Justin Bieber Ruse"—involved pretending to be pop star Justin Bieber, contacting young girls via video chat services, such as Omegle and Skype, and offering them free concert tickets, backstage passes, or some other fan-related benefits if they would agree to send him a webcam transmission or a photo of themselves with their breasts exposed.

For those who complied, Gunn continued sending further demands and more threatening communications. If any of his demands were not met, Gunn would threaten to withhold the benefits he had promised the girls and/or to injure the girls' reputations by publishing their compromising images and videos over the Internet. More than 10 girls were forced to send him sexually suggestive photos. At the sentencing hearing, the prosecutor read a transcript of a conversation between Gunn and a 13-year-old victim. In the transcript, the victim told Gunn that she did not want to take her shirt off in front the webcam. Gunn replied that if she didn't, he would push Send, meaning send the prior pictures to the victim's friends and family. The victim responded that she was only 13 years old and that she had "a life, please do not ruin it." Gunn responded, "I am sending it now since u won't do what I want." The victim then told Gunn that if he pushed Send, she would kill herself. Gunn completely disregarded her cry for help and demanded that she take off her top. The victim complied. Gunn was sentenced to 30 years in prison for his crimes against children.

CRITICAL THINKING

In order to deter predators like Christopher Gunn, what's more effective—to educate kids about the dangers of online involvement with strangers or to harshly punish adults who prey upon children?

SOURCE: US Attorney's Office, Middle District of Alabama, "Montgomery Man Pleads Guilty to Massive Online Sextortion Plot," August 23, 2012, http://www.fbi.gov/mobile/press-releases/2012/montgomery -man-pleads-guilty-to-massive-online-sextortion-plot (accessed September 2016).

authorities knew about half of all child victimizations; school authorities (e.g., teachers, principals, and counselors) were the most likely to know of the victimizations. Police, however, were the ones most likely to know about the most serious victimizations, including sexual abuse by an adult, kidnapping, and gang or group assaults.

So while disclosure is increasing, child victimizations are decreasing.[106] It is possible that an increase in reporting has produced sufficient action by authorities to help limit juvenile victimization.

Teen Victims

NCVS data can also tell us something about the relationship between victims and offenders. This information is available because victims of violent personal crimes, such as assault and robbery, can identify the age, sex, and race of their attackers.

In general, teens tend to be victimized by their peers, whereas victims age 20 and over identified their attackers as being 21 or older. However, people in almost all age groups who are victimized by *groups* of offenders identify their attackers as teenagers or young adults.

The data also tell us that victimization is intraracial (within race). White teenagers tend to be victimized by white teens, and African American teenagers tend to be victimized by African American teens. Young people are more often victimized by strangers than adults and the likelihood of stranger victimization declines with age. As the Cyber Delinquency feature shows, the Internet has created a new source of victimization threat. In the cyber age, teens may now be victimized by adults posing as teens whose victims can span the globe.

SUMMARY

1 Explain how the UCR data are gathered and used

- Official data on delinquent behavior are gathered in the Uniform Crime Report (UCR).

- The UCR gathers data on the number and characteristics (age, race, and gender) of individuals who have been arrested. This is particularly important for delinquency research because it shows how many underage minors are arrested each year.

- The accuracy of the UCR is somewhat suspect because surveys indicate that fewer than half of all crime victims report incidents to police.

2 Discuss the concept of self-reported delinquency

- These surveys ask kids to describe, in detail, their recent and lifetime participation in antisocial activity.

- Self-reports are given in groups, and the respondents are promised anonymity in order to ensure the validity and honesty of the responses.

- In addition to questions about delinquent behavior, most self-report surveys contain questions about attitudes, values, and behaviors.

3 Evaluate the utility of the National Crime Victimization Survey

- The National Crime Victimization Survey (NCVS) is a comprehensive, nationwide survey of victimization in the United States.

- Each year data are obtained from a large nationally representative sample who are asked to report their experiences with crimes.

- Due to the care with which the samples are drawn and the high completion rate, NCVS data are considered a relatively unbiased, valid estimate of all victimizations for the target crimes included in the survey.

4 List alternative measures of delinquent activity and behavior

- Delinquency experts routinely use a number of other methods to acquire data on youth crime and delinquency.

- Collecting cohort data involves observing over time a group of kids who share a like characteristic.

- Sometimes researchers are able to conduct controlled experiments to collect data on the causes of delinquency.

- Meta-analysis involves gathering data from a number of previous studies.

- Data mining uses multiple advanced computational methods, including artificial intelligence (the use of computers to perform logical functions), to analyze large data sets usually involving one or more data sources.

5 Analyze recent trends in juvenile delinquency

- Crime and delinquency rates trended upward between 1960 and 1991 when police recorded about 15 million crimes. Since then the number of crimes has been in steep decline.

- The number of juvenile arrests has declined significantly during the past decade.

- Juveniles were responsible for about 8 percent of all arrests, including about 10 percent of the Part I violent crime arrests and about 14 percent of arrests for the most serious property crimes, such as burglary, larceny, and car theft.

- Because kids ages 14 to 18, who account for almost all underage arrests, constitute about 6 percent of the population, teens account for a disproportionate share of all arrests for serious crime.

6 Recognize the factors that affect the juvenile crime rate

- Because teenagers have extremely high crime rates, crime experts view changes in the population age distribution as having the greatest influence on crime trends.

- As a general rule, the crime rate follows the proportion of young males in the population.

- There is debate over the effect the economy has on crime rates. A drop in the delinquency rate has been linked to a strong economy. Some believe that a poor economy may actually help lower delinquency rates because it limits the opportunity kids have to commit crime.

- As the level of social problems increases—such as single-parent families, dropout rates, racial conflict, and teen pregnancies—so do delinquency rates.

- Racial conflict may also increase delinquency rates.

- There is evidence that the decade-long drop in the delinquency rate can be attributed to the availability of legalized abortion. The effect of abortion on the delinquency rate may be a factor of fewer teenage girls having babies.

- The availability of firearms may influence the delinquency rate, especially the proliferation of weapons in the hands of teens.

- Another factor that affects delinquency rates is the explosive growth in teenage gangs.

- Some experts argue that violent media can influence the direction of delinquency rates.

7 Interpret the social and personal correlates of delinquency

- Delinquents are disproportionately male, although female delinquency rates are rising faster than those for males.

- Minority youth are overrepresented in the delinquency arrest rate, especially for violent crime.

- Most experts believe that adolescent crime as a lower-class phenomenon. Official statistics indicate that lower-class youths are responsible for the most serious delinquent acts.

- There is general agreement that delinquency rates decline with age.

8 Discuss the concept of the chronic offender

- Some experts believe this phenomenon is universal, whereas others believe a small group of offenders persist in crime at a high rate.

- The age–crime relationship has spurred research on the nature of delinquency over the life course.

- Delinquency data show the existence of a chronic persistent offender who begins his or her offending career early in life and persists as an adult.

- Marvin Wolfgang and his colleagues identified chronic offenders in a series of cohort studies conducted in Philadelphia.

9 Identify the causes of chronic offending

- Ongoing research has identified the characteristics of persistent offenders as they mature, and both personality and social factors help us predict long-term offending patterns.

- Early involvement in criminal activity, relatively low intellectual development, and parental drug involvement have been linked to later chronic offending.

- Measurable problems in learning and motor skills, cognitive abilities, family relations, and other areas also predict chronicity.

- Apprehension and punishment seem to have little effect on offending behavior. Youths who have long juvenile records will most likely continue their offending careers into adulthood.

10 Summarize the factors that predict teen victimization

- Teenagers are more likely to become victims of crime than are people in other age groups.

- The teen victimization rate has been in steep decline.

- Teens tend to be victimized by their peers.

- A majority of teens have been victimized by other teens, whereas victims ages 20 and over identified their attackers as being 21 or older.

KEY TERMS

QUESTIONS FOR DISCUSSION

1. What factors contribute to the aging-out process?

2. Why are males more delinquent than females? Is it a matter of lifestyle, culture, or physical properties?

3. Discuss the racial differences found in the crime rate. What factors account for differences in the African American and white crime rates?

4. Should kids who have been arrested more than three times be given mandatory incarceration sentences?

5. Do you believe that self-reports are an accurate method of gauging the nature and extent of delinquent behavior?

VIEWPOINT

As a juvenile court judge you are forced to make a tough decision during a hearing: whether a juvenile should be waived to the adult court. It seems that gang activity has become a way of life for residents living in local public housing projects. The Bloods sell crack, and the Wolfpack controls the drug market. When the rivalry between the two gangs exploded, 16-year-old Shatiek Johnson, a Wolfpack member, shot and killed a member of the Bloods; in retaliation, the Bloods put out a contract on his life. While in hiding, Shatiek was confronted by two undercover detectives who recognized the young fugitive. Fearing for his life, Shatiek pulled a pistol and began firing, fatally wounding one of the officers. During the hearing, you learn that Shatiek's story is not dissimilar from that of many other children raised in tough housing projects. With an absent father and a single mother who could not control her five sons, Shatiek lived in a world of drugs, gangs, and shootouts long before he was old enough to vote. By age 13, Shatiek had been involved in the gang-beating death of a homeless man in a dispute over $10, for which he was given a one-year sentence at a youth detention center and released after six months. Now charged with a crime that could be considered first-degree murder if committed by an adult, Shatiek could—if waived to the adult court—be sentenced to life in prison or even face the death penalty.

At the hearing, Shatiek seems like a lost soul. He claims he thought the police officers were killers out to collect the bounty put on his life by the Bloods. He says that killing the rival gang boy was an act of self-defense. The district attorney confirms that the victim was, in fact, a known gang assassin with numerous criminal convictions. Shatiek's mother begs you to consider the fact that her son is only 16 years old, that he has had a very difficult childhood, and that he is a victim of society's indifference to the poor.

- Would you treat Shatiek as a juvenile and see if a prolonged stay in a youth facility could help this troubled young man, or would you transfer (waive) him to the adult justice system?
- Does a 16-year-old like Shatiek deserve a second chance?
- Is Shatiek's behavior common among adolescent boys or unusual and disturbing?

DOING RESEARCH ON THE WEB

To help you answer these questions and to learn more about gang membership, go to the Gang Resistance Education And Training (G.R.E.A.T.) program website (http://www.great-online.org/). The G.R.E.A.T. program is a school-based, law enforcement officer–instructed classroom curriculum. With prevention as its primary objective, the program is intended as an immunization against delinquency, youth violence, and gang membership.

Another valuable site is Youth.gov (http://youth.gov/), a collaborative web-based resource supported by various federal agencies focused on general youth-related issues. Youth.gov is the US government website that helps users create, maintain, and strengthen effective youth programs. Included are youth facts, funding information, and tools to help users assess community assets, generate maps of local and federal resources, search for evidence-based youth programs, and keep up to date on the latest youth-related news.

NOTES

All URLs accessed September 2016.

1. US Attorneys Office, Southern District of New York, "120 Members and Associates of Two Rival Street Gangs in the Bronx Charged in Federal Court with Racketeering, Narcotics, and Firearms Offenses; Believed to be Largest Gang Takedown in New York City History," April 27, 2016, https://www.justice.gov/usao-sdny/pr/120-members-and-associates-two-rival-street-gangs-bronx-charged-federal-court.
2. Andrew Dugan, "In U.S., 37% Do Not Feel Safe Walking at Night Near Home," http://www.gallup.com/poll/179558/not-feel-safe-walking-night-near-home.aspx.
3. Gallup Poll, "Crime, 2015," http://www.gallup.com/poll/1603/Crime.aspx.
4. Official data in this chapter come from FBI, *Crime in the United States, 2015*, https://ucr.fbi.gov/crime-in-the-u.s/2015/crime-in-the-u.s.-2015.
5. FBI, *Preliminary Semiannual Uniform Crime Report*, January–June 2015, https://www.fbi.gov/about-us/cjis/ucr/crime-in-the-u.s/2015/preliminary-semiannual-uniform-crime-report-januaryjune-2015/tables/table-1.

6. Jennifer Truman and Lynn Langton, *Criminal Victimization, 2014*, Bureau of Justice Statistics, http://www.bjs.gov/content/pub/pdf/cv14.pdf. Victim data in this chapter come from this source.

7. Min Xie, "Area Differences and Time Trends in Crime Reporting: Comparing New York with Other Metropolitan Areas" *Justice Quarterly* 31:43–73 (2014).

8. Richard Felson, Steven Messner, Anthony Hoskin, and Glenn Deane, "Reasons for Reporting and Not Reporting Domestic Violence to the Police," *Criminology* 40:617–648 (2002).

9. Bradford W. Reyns and Ryan Randa, "Victim Reporting Behaviors Following Identity Theft Victimization: Results from the National Crime Victimization Survey," *Crime and Delinquency*, first published online December 18, 2015.

10. Heather Zaykowski, "Reconceptualizing Victimization and Victimization Responses," *Crime and Delinquency* 61:271–296 (2015).

11. John Eterno and Eli B. Silverman, *The Crime Numbers Game: Management by Manipulation* (Boca Raton, FL: CRC Press, 2012).

12. William K. Rashbaum, "Retired Officers Raise Questions on Crime Data," *New York Times*, February 6, 2010, http://www.nytimes.com/2010/02/07/nyregion/07crime.html.

13. Duncan Chappell, Gilbert Geis, Stephen Schafer, and Larry Siegel, "Forcible Rape: A Comparative Study of Offenses Known to the Police in Boston and Los Angeles," in James Henslin, ed., *Studies in the Sociology of Sex* (New York: Appleton Century Crofts, 1971), pp. 169–193.

14. Eric P. Baumer and Janet L. Lauritsen, "Reporting Crime to the Police, 1973–2005: A Multivariate Analysis of Long-Term Trends in the National Crime Survey (NCS) and National Crime Victimization Survey (NCVS)," *Criminology* 48:131–185 (2010).

15. "FBI Releases 2014 Crime Statistics from the National Incident-Based Reporting System," December 14, 2015, https://www.fbi.gov/about-us/cjis/ucr/nibrs/2014/resource-pages/summary-of-nibrs-2014_final.pdf.

16. A pioneering effort in self-report research is A. L. Porterfield, *Youth in Trouble* (Fort Worth, TX: Leo Potishman Foundation, 1946); for a review, see Robert Hardt and George Bodine, *Development of Self-Report Instruments in Delinquency Research: A Conference Report* (Syracuse, NY: Syracuse University Youth Development Center, 1965). See also Fred Murphy, Mary Shirley, and Helen Witner, "The Incidence of Hidden Delinquency," *American Journal of Orthopsychology* 16:686–696 (1946).

17. Christiane Brems, Mark Johnson, David Neal, and Melinda Freemon, "Childhood Abuse History and Substance Use Among Men and Women Receiving Detoxification Services," *American Journal of Drug and Alcohol Abuse* 30:799–821 (2004).

18. Lloyd Johnston, Patrick O'Malley, Richard Miech, Jerald Bachman, and John Schulenberg, *Monitoring the Future National Survey Results on Drug Use, 1975–2015*, Institute for Social Research, University of Michigan, 2016, http://www.monitoringthefuture.org/pubs/monographs/mtf-overview2015.pdf.

19. Leonore Simon, "Validity and Reliability of Violent Juveniles: A Comparison of Juvenile Self-Reports with Adult Self-Reports Incarcerated in Adult Prisons," paper presented at the annual meeting of the American Society of Criminology, Boston, November 1995, p. 26.

20. Stephen Cernkovich, Peggy Giordano, and Meredith Pugh, "Chronic Offenders: The Missing Cases in Self-Report Delinquency Research," *Journal of Criminal Law and Criminology* 76:705–732 (1985).

21. Julia Yun Soo Kim, Michael Fendrich, and Joseph S. Wislar, "The Validity of Juvenile Arrestees' Drug Use Reporting: A Gender Comparison," *Journal of Research in Crime and Delinquency* 37:419–432 (2000).

22. Alex Piquero, Carol Schubert, and Robert Brame, "Comparing Official and Self-Report Records of Offending Across Gender and Race/Ethnicity in a Longitudinal Study of Serious Youthful Offenders," *Journal of Research in Crime and Delinquency* 51:526–556 (2014).

23. Amanda. Emmert, Arna Carlock, Alan Lizotte, and Marvin Krohn, "Predicting Adult Under- and Over-Reporting of Self-Reported Arrests from Discrepancies in Adolescent Self-Reports of Arrests: A Research Note," *Crime and Delinquency*, first published online March 12, 2015.

24. Jennifer Roberts, Edward Mulvey, Julie Horney, John Lewis, and Michael Arter, "A Test of Two Methods of Recall for Violent Events," *Journal of Quantitative Criminology* 21:175–193 (2005).

25. Lila Kazemian and David Farrington, "Comparing the Validity of Prospective, Retrospective, and Official Onset for Different Offending Categories," *Journal of Quantitative Criminology* 21:127–147 (2005).

26. Vincent Webb, Charles Katz, and Scott Decker, "Assessing the Validity of Self-Reports by Gang Members: Results from the Arrestee Drug Abuse Monitoring Program," *Crime and Delinquency* 52:232–252 (2006).

27. Truman and Langton, *Criminal Victimization, 2014*.

28. Ibid.

29. L. Edward Wells and Joseph Rankin, "Juvenile Victimization: Convergent Validation of Alternative Measurements," *Journal of Research in Crime and Delinquency* 32:287–307 (1995).

30. FBI, *Crime in the United States, 2015, Table 38*, https://ucr.fbi.gov/crime-in-the-u.s/2015/crime-in-the-u.s.-2015/tables/table-38.

31. Thomas Bernard, "Juvenile Crime and the Transformation of Juvenile Justice: Is There a Juvenile Crime Wave?" *Justice Quarterly* 16:336–356 (1999).

32. The following are classic studies comparing self-report and official data: Maynard Erickson and LaMar Empey, "Court Records, Undetected Delinquency, and Decision Making," *Journal of Criminal Law, Criminology, and Police Science* 54:456–469 (1963); Martin Gold, "Undetected Delinquent Behavior," *Journal of Research in Crime and Delinquency* 3:27–46 (1966); James Short and F. Ivan Nye, "Extent of Unrecorded Delinquency, Tentative Conclusions," *Journal of Criminal Law, Criminology, and Police Science* 49:296–302 (1958).

33. Lloyd Johnston, Patrick O'Malley, and Jerald Bachman, *Monitoring the Future, 8* (Ann Arbor, MI: Institute for Social Research, 2011), http://www.monitoringthefuture.org/.

34. Barbara Warner and Brandi Wilson Coomer, "Neighborhood Drug Arrest Rates: Are They a Meaningful Indicator of Drug Activity? A Research Note," *Journal of Research in Crime and Delinquency* 40:123–139 (2003).

35. Steven Levitt, "The Limited Role of Changing Age Structure in Explaining Aggregate Crime Rates," *Criminology* 37:581–599 (1999).

36. Julie Phillips, "The Relationship Between Age Structure and Homicide Rates in the United States, 1970 to 1999," *Journal of Research in Crime and Delinquency* 43:230–260 (2006).

37. Brad Bushman, Morgan Wang, and Craig Anderson, "Is the Curve Relating Temperature to Aggression Linear or Curvilinear? Assaults and Temperature in Minneapolis Reexamined," *Journal of Personality and Social Psychology* 89:62–66 (2005).

38. Paul Bell, "Reanalysis and Perspective in the Heat-Aggression Debate," *Journal of Personality and Social Psychology* 89:71–73 (2005); Ellen Cohn, "The Prediction of Police Calls for Service: The Influence of Weather and Temporal Variables on Rape and Domestic Violence," *Journal of Environmental Psychology* 13:71–83 (1993).

39. Timothy Hart and Terance Miethe, "Configural Behavior Settings of Crime Event Locations: Toward an Alternative Conceptualization of Criminogenic Microenvironments," *Journal of Research in Crime and Delinquency* 52:373–402 (2015).

40. David Weisburd, "The Law of Crime Concentration and the Criminology of Place," *Criminology* 53:133–157 (2015).

41. FBI, *Crime in the United States, 2015, Table 40*, https://ucr.fbi.gov/crime-in-the-u.s/2015/crime-in-the-u.s.-2015/tables/table-40.

42. Robert Brame, Shawn Bushway, Ray Paternoster, and Michael G. Turner, "Demographic Patterns of Cumulative Arrest Prevalence by Ages 18 and 23," *Crime and Delinquency* 60:471–486 (2014).

43. Leroy Gould, "Who Defines Delinquency? A Comparison of Self-Report and Officially Reported Indices of Delinquency for Three Racial Groups," *Social Problems* 16:325–336 (1969); Harwin Voss, "Ethnic Differentials in Delinquency in Honolulu," *Journal of Criminal Law, Criminology, and Police Science* 54:322–327 (1963); Ronald Akers, Marvin Krohn, Marcia Radosevich, and Lonn Lanza-Kaduce, "Social Characteristics and Self-Reported Delinquency," in Gary Jensen, ed., *Sociology of Delinquency* (Beverly Hills, CA: Sage, 1981), pp. 48–62.

44. David Huizinga and Delbert Elliott, "Juvenile Offenders: Prevalence, Offender Incidence, and Arrest Rates by Race," *Crime and Delinquency* 33:206–223 (1987); see also Dale Dannefer and Russell Schutt, "Race and Juvenile Justice Processing in Court and Police Agencies," *American Journal of Sociology* 87:1113–1132 (1982).

45. Rolf Loeber, David P. Farrington, Alison E. Hipwell, Stephanie D. Stepp, and Lia Ahonen, "Constancy and Change in the Prevalence and Frequency of Offending When Based on Longitudinal Self-Reports or Official Records: Comparisons by Gender, Race, and Crime Type," *Journal of Developmental and Life-Course Criminology* 1:150–168 (2015); *Monitoring the Future, 2014*.

46. Rob Tillyer, "Opening the Black Box of Officer Decision-Making: An Examination of Race, Criminal History, and Discretionary Searches," *Justice Quarterly* 31:961–986 (2014).

47. Andres F. Rengifo and Don Stemen, "The Unintended Effects of Penal Reform: African American Presence, Incarceration, and the Abolition of Discretionary Parole in the United States," *Crime and Delinquency*, first published online May 25, 2012; David Eitle and Susanne Monahan, "Revisiting the Racial Threat Thesis: The Role of Police Organizational Characteristics in Predicting Race-Specific Drug Arrest Rates," *Justice Quarterly* 26:528–561 (2009).

48. Tammy Rinehart Kochel, David B. Wilson, and Stephen D. Mastrofski, "Effect of Suspect Race on Officers' Arrest Decisions," *Criminology* 49:473–512 (2011).

49. Kenneth Novak and Mitchell Chamlin, "Racial Threat, Suspicion, and Police Behavior: The Impact of Race and Place in Traffic Enforcement," *Crime and Delinquency* 58:275–300 (2012).

50. Richard Rosenfeld, Jeff Rojek, and Scott Decker, "Age Matters: Race Differences in Police Searches of Young and Older Male Drivers," *Journal of Research in Crime and Delinquency* 49:31–55 (2011).

51. Rodney Engen, Sara Steen, and George Bridges, "Racial Disparities in the Punishment of Youth: A Theoretical and Empirical Assessment of the Literature," *Social Problems* 49:194–221 (2002).

52. Karen Parker, Brian Stults, and Stephen Rice, "Racial Threat, Concentrated Disadvantage and Social Control: Considering the Macro-Level Sources of Variation in Arrests," *Criminology* 43:1111–1134 (2005); Lisa Stolzenberg, Stewart J. D'Alessio, and David Eitle, "A Multilevel Test of Racial Threat Theory," *Criminology* 42:673–698 (2004).

53. Michael Leiber and Kristan Fox, "Race and the Impact of Detention on Juvenile Justice Decision Making," *Crime and Delinquency* 51:470–497 (2005); Traci Schlesinger, "Racial and Ethnic Disparity in Pretrial Criminal Processing," *Justice Quarterly* 22:170–192 (2005).

54. Christina DeJong and Kenneth Jackson, "Putting Race into Context: Race, Juvenile Justice Processing, and Urbanization," *Justice Quarterly* 15:487–504 (1998).

55. Michael Hallett, "Reentry to What? Theorizing Prisoner Reentry in the Jobless Future," *Critical Criminology* 20:213–228 (2012).

56. Engen, Steen, and Bridges, "Racial Disparities in the Punishment of Youth."

57. Nicole Gonzalez Van Cleve and Lauren Mayes, "Criminal Justice Through 'Colorblind' Lenses: A Call to Examine the Mutual Constitution of Race and Criminal Justice," *Law and Social Inquiry* 40:406–432 (2015); David Eitle, Stewart D'Alessio, and Lisa Stolzenberg, "Racial Threat and Social Control: A Test of the Political, Economic, and Threat of Black Crime Hypotheses," *Social Forces* 81:557–576 (2002); Michael Leiber and Jayne Stairs, "Race, Contexts, and the Use of Intake Diversion," *Journal of Research in Crime and Delinquency* 36:56–86 (1999); Darrell Steffensmeier, Jeffery Ulmer, and John Kramer, "The Interaction of Race, Gender, and Age in Criminal Sentencing: The Punishment Cost of Being Young, Black, and Male," *Criminology* 36:763–798 (1998.

58. Samuel Walker, Cassia Spohn, and Miriam DeLone, *The Color of Justice: Race, Ethnicity, and Crime in America* (Belmont, CA: Brooks/Cole, 1992), pp. 46–47.

59. Mallie Paschall, Robert Flewelling, and Susan Ennett, "Racial Differences in Violent Behavior Among Young Adults: Moderating and Confounding Effects," *Journal of Research in Crime and Delinquency* 35:148–165 (1998).

60. Gary LaFree and Richard Arum, "The Impact of Racially Inclusive Schooling on Adult Incarceration Rates Among U.S. Cohorts of African Americans and Whites Since 1930," *Criminology* 44:73–103 (2006).

61. Julie Phillips, "Variation in African-American Homicide Rates: An Assessment of Potential Explanations," *Criminology* 35:527–559 (1997).

62. Melvin Thomas, "Race, Class, and Personal Income: An Empirical Test of the Declining Significance of Race Thesis, 1968–1988," *Social Problems* 40:328–339 (1993).

63. Thomas McNulty and Paul Bellair, "Explaining Racial and Ethnic Differences in Adolescent Violence: Structural Disadvantage, Family Well-Being, and Social Capital," *Justice Quarterly* 20:1–32 (2003).

64. Julie Phillips, "White, Black, and Latino Homicide Rates: Why the Difference?" *Social Problems* 49:349–374 (2002).

65. Felipe Estrada and Anders Nilsson, "Segregation and Victimization: Neighbourhood Resources, Individual Risk Factors and Exposure to Property Crime," *European Journal of Criminology* 5:193–216 (2008).

66. Aki Roberts and Dale Willits, "Income Inequality and Homicide in the United States: Consistency Across Different Income Inequality Measures and Disaggregated Homicide Types," *Homicide Studies* 19:28–57 (2015).

67. Robert Agnew, "A General Strain Theory of Community Differences in Crime Rates," *Journal of Research in Crime and Delinquency* 36:123–155 (1999).

68. Bonita Vesey and Steven Messner, "Further Testing of Social Disorganization Theory: An Elaboration of Sampson and Groves's 'Community Structure and Crime,'" *Journal of Research in Crime and Delinquency* 36:156–174 (1999).

69. Carter Hay, Edward Fortson, Dusten Hollist, Irshad Altheimer, and Lonnie Schaible, "Compounded Risk: The Implications for Delinquency of Coming from a Poor Family that Lives in a Poor Community," *Journal of Youth and Adolescence* 36:593–605 (2007).

70. John R. Hipp and Adam Boessen, "Egohoods as Waves Washing Across the City: A New Measure of Neighborhoods," *Criminology* 51:287–327 (2013); Ramiro Martinez, Jacob Stowell, and Jeffrey Cancino, "A Tale of Two Border Cities: Community Context, Ethnicity, and Homicide," *Social Science Quarterly* 89:1–16 (2008).

71. Misaki Natsuaki, Xiaojia Ge, and Ernst Wenk, "Continuity and Changes in the Developmental Trajectories of Criminal Career: Examining the Roles of Timing of First Arrest and High School Graduation," *Journal of Youth and Adolescence* 37:431–444 (2008).

72. Derek Kreager, "When It's Good to Be 'Bad': Violence and Adolescent Peer Acceptance," *Criminology* 45:893–923 (2007).

73. See, generally, David Farrington, "Age and Crime," in Michael Tonry and Norval Morris, eds., *Crime and Justice: An Annual Review*, vol. 7 (Chicago: University of Chicago Press, 1986), pp. 189–250; Travis Hirschi and Michael Gottfredson, "Age and the Explanation of Crime," *American Journal of Sociology* 89:552–584 (1983).

74. James Q. Wilson and Richard Herrnstein, *Crime and Human Nature* (New York: Simon & Schuster, 1985), pp. 126–147.

75. Michael Gottfredson and Travis Hirschi, "The True Value of Lambda Would Appear to Be Zero: An Essay on Career Criminals, Criminal Careers, Selective Incapacitation, Cohort Studies, and Related Topics," *Criminology* 24:213–234 (1986); further support for their position can be found in Lawrence Cohen and Kenneth Land, "Age Structure and Crime," *American Sociological Review* 52:170–183 (1987).

76. Misaki Natsuaki, Xiaojia Ge, and Ernst Wenk, "Continuity and Changes in the Developmental Trajectories of Criminal Career: Examining the Roles of Timing of First Arrest and High School Graduation," *Journal of Youth and Adolescence* 37:431–444 (2008).

77. Marvin Wolfgang, Robert Figlio, and Thorsten Sellin, *Delinquency in a Birth Cohort* (Chicago: University of Chicago Press, 1972); Lyle Shannon, *Assessing the Relationship of Adult Criminal Careers to Juvenile Careers: A Summary* (Washington, DC: US Department of Justice, 1982); D. J. West and David P. Farrington, *The Delinquent Way of Life* (London: Heinemann, 1977); Donna Hamparian, Richard Schuster, Simon Dinitz, and John Conrad, *The Violent Few* (Lexington, MA: Lexington Books, 1978).

78. Margo Wilson and Martin Daly, "Life Expectancy, Economic Inequality, Homicide, and Reproductive Timing in Chicago Neighbourhoods," *British Journal of Medicine* 31:1271–1274 (1997).

79. Edward Mulvey and John LaRosa, "Delinquency Cessation and Adolescent Development: Preliminary Data," *American Journal of Orthopsychiatry* 56:212–224 (1986).

80. Timothy Brezina, "Delinquent Problem-Solving: An Interpretive Framework for Criminological Theory and Research," *Journal of Research in Crime and Delinquency* 37:3–30 (2000).

81. Gordon Trasler, "Cautions for a Biological Approach to Crime," in Sarnoff Mednick, Terrie Moffitt, and Susan Stack, eds., *The Causes of Crime, New Biological Approaches* (Cambridge: Cambridge University Press, 1987), pp. 7–25.

82. Alicia Rand, "Transitional Life Events and Desistance from Delinquency and Crime," in Marvin Wolfgang, Terrence Thornberry, and Robert Figlio, eds., *From Boy to Man, from Delinquency to Crime* (Chicago: University of Chicago Press, 1987), pp. 134–163.

83. Marc LeBlanc, "Late Adolescence Deceleration of Criminal Activity and Development of Self- and Social-Control," *Studies on Crime and Crime Prevention* 2:51–68 (1993).

84. *Ibid.*

85. Ryan King, Michael Massoglia, and Ross MacMillan, "The Context of Marriage and Crime: Gender, the Propensity to Marry, and Offending in Early Adulthood," *Criminology* 45:33–65 (2007).

86. Barry Glassner, Margaret Ksander, Bruce Berg, and Bruce Johnson, "Note on the Deterrent Effect of Juvenile vs. Adult Jurisdiction," *Social Problems* 31:219–221 (1983).

87. Neal Shover and Carol Thompson, "Age, Differential Expectations, and Crime Desistance," *Criminology* 30:89–104 (1992).

88. Lila Kazemian and David Farrington, "Exploring Residual Career Length and Residual Number of Offenses for Two Generations of Repeat Offenders," *Journal of Research in Crime and Delinquency* 43:89–113 (2006).

89. Arnold Barnett, Alfred Blumstein, and David Farrington, "A Prospective Test of a Criminal Career Model," *Criminology* 27:373–388 (1989).

90. Wolfgang, Figlio, and Sellin, *Delinquency in a Birth Cohort*.

91. Paul Tracy, Marvin Wolfgang, and Robert Figlio, *Delinquency in Two Birth Cohorts, Executive Summary* (Washington, DC: US Department of Justice, 1985).

92. Shannon, *Assessing the Relationship of Adult Criminal Careers to Juvenile Careers*; Howard Snyder, *Court Careers of Juvenile Offenders* (Washington, DC: Office of Juvenile Justice and Delinquency Prevention, 1988); Donald J. West and David P. Farrington, *The Delinquent Way of Life* (London: Heinemann, 1977); Donna Hamparian, Richard Schuster, Simon Dinitz, and John Conrad, *The Violent Few* (Lexington, MA: Lexington Books, 1978).

93. See, generally, Wolfgang, Thornberry, and Figlio, *From Boy to Man*.

94. Paul Tracy and Kimberly Kempf-Leonard, *Continuity and Discontinuity in Criminal Careers* (New York: Plenum, 1996).

95. R. Tremblay, R. Loeber, C. Gagnon, P. Charlebois, S. Larivee, and M. LeBlanc, "Disruptive Boys with Stable and Unstable High Fighting Behavior Patterns During Junior Elementary School," *Journal of Abnormal Child Psychology* 19:285–300 (1991).

96. Peter Jones, Philip Harris, James Fader, and Lori Grubstein, "Identifying Chronic Juvenile Offenders," *Justice Quarterly* 18:478–507 (2001).

97. Jennifer White, Terrie Moffitt, Felton Earls, Lee Robins, and Phil Silva, "How Early Can We Tell? Predictors of Childhood Conduct Disorder and Adolescent Delinquency," *Criminology* 28:507–535 (1990).

98. Kimberly Kempf-Leonard, Paul Tracy, and James Howell, "Serious, Violent, and Chronic Juvenile Offenders: The Relationship of Delinquency Career Types to Adult Criminality," *Justice Quarterly* 18:449–478 (2001).

99. Kimberly Kempf, "Crime Severity and Criminal Career Progression," *Journal of Criminal Law and Criminology* 79:524–540 (1988).

100. Jeffrey Fagan, "Social and Legal Policy Dimensions of Violent Juvenile Crime," *Criminal Justice and Behavior* 17:93–133 (1990).

101. Peter Greenwood, *Selective Incapacitation* (Santa Monica, CA: Rand, 1982).

102. Terence Thornberry, David Huizinga, and Rolf Loeber, "*The Prevention of Serious Delinquency and Violence*," in James Howell, Barry Krisberg, J. David Hawkins, and John Wilson, eds., *Sourcebook on Serious, Violent, and Chronic Juvenile Offenders* (Thousand Oaks, CA: Sage, 1995).

103. Pam Louwagie and Jennifer Brooks, "Danny Heinrich Confesses to Abducting and Killing Jacob Wetterling," *Star Tribune, September 7, 2016*, http://www.startribune.com/danny-heinrich-confesses-to-abducting-and-killing-jacob-wetterling/392438361/.

104. Nicole White and Janet Lauritsen, *Violent Crime Against Youth, 1994–2010*, US Department of Justice, Office of Justice Programs, Bureau of Justice Statistics 2012, http://bjs.ojp.usdoj.gov/content/pub/pdf/vcay9410.pdf.

105. David Finkelhor, Heather Turner, Anne Shattuck, Sherry Hamby, and Kristen Kracke, "Children's Exposure to Violence, Crime, and Abuse: An Update," Office of Juvenile Justice and Delinquency Prevention, 2015, http://www.ojjdp.gov/pubs/248547.pdf.

106. David Finkelhor, Richard Ormrod, Heather Turner, and Sherry Hamby, *Child and Youth Victimization Known to Police, School, and Medical Authorities*, OJJDP National Survey of Children's Exposure to Violence Series, 2012, http://www.ojjdp.gov/pubs/235394.pdf.

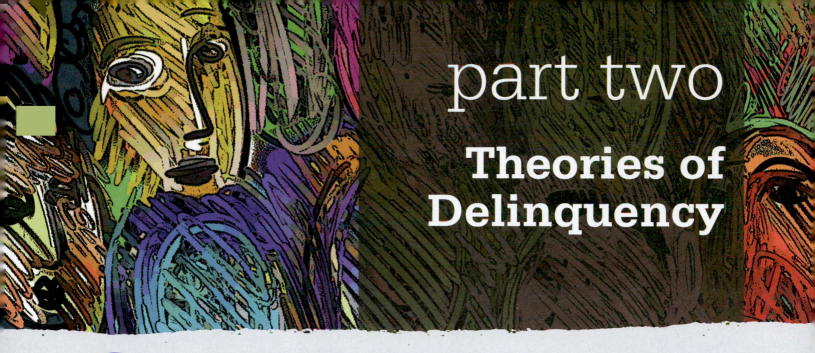

part two
Theories of Delinquency

a theory can be defined as an abstract statement that explains why certain phenomena or things do (or do not) happen. A valid theory must (a) be able to predict future occurrences of the phenomenon in question and (b) be verifiable by testing through experiment or some other form of empirical observation. So a theory stating that kids who watch excessive amounts of violent TV shows will also engage in aggressive behavior can only be considered valid if:

- Empirically sound testing can verify the association is valid: watching violent TV is a direct cause of violence and not influenced by other factors.

- The more children watch violent TV shows in the present, the more likely they will engage in personal violence in the future.

By developing empirically verifiable statements, or hypotheses, and organizing them into theories of delinquency causation, social scientists hope to identify the causes of delinquency and propose methods to curtail or eliminate its occurrence. These are some of the questions they ask: What causes delinquent behavior? Why do some youths enter a life of crime that persists into their adulthood? Are people products of their environment, or is the likelihood of their becoming a delinquent determined at birth?

Since the study of delinquency is essentially interdisciplinary, it is not surprising that a variety of theoretical models have been formulated to explain juvenile misbehavior. Each reflects the training and orientation of its creator. Consequently, theories of delinquency reflect many different avenues of inquiry, including biology, psychology, sociology, political science, and economics. Chapter 3 reviews theories that hold that delinquency is essentially caused by individual-level factors, such as personal choices and decision making, or by psychological and biological factors. Chapter 4 reviews social theories of delinquency that hold that youthful misbehavior is caused by children's place in the social structure, their relationships with social institutions and processes, or their reaction to the effects of social conflict. The social reaction and social conflict theories covered in Chapter 5 hold that the decision to label behavior as deviant or delinquent is subjective, and people become immoral when labeled as such. Chapter 6 discusses those theories of delinquency that regard it as a developmental process, reflecting the changes that occur in young people's lives as they evolve during their life.

CHAPTER 3
Individual Views of Delinquency

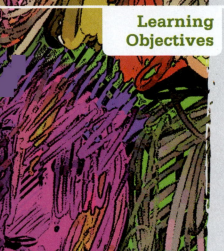

FROM THE TIME HE WAS LITTLE, Adam Lanza couldn't bear to be touched. By middle school, the commotion in his classroom upset him and kept him apart from other kids. At age 6, he was diagnosed with "sensory integration disorder"— now known as sensory processing disorder (SPD), which made him over-respond to stimuli and find clothing, physical contact, light, sound, and food unendurable. Those with SPD may also under-respond and feel little or no reaction to pain or extreme hot and cold. There may be sensory motor problems that can cause weakness and clumsiness or delay in developing motor skills. His mother, Nancy, warned people about him. One of her friends told reporters, "Adam was a quiet kid. He never said a word. There was a weirdness about him, and Nancy warned me once at one of the Scout meetings . . . 'Don't touch Adam.' She said he just can't stand that. He'd become teary-eyed and I think he would run to his mother."[1]

When Adam was in the ninth grade, his mother brought him to Yale University's Child Study Center for a psychiatric consult.[2] The doctors' recommendation was for "extensive special education supports, ongoing expert consultation, and rigorous therapeutic supports," a diagnosis that went largely unheeded. Adam was also probably suffering from untreated anxiety and obsessive-compulsive disorder, autism spectrum disorder, and Asperger syndrome. He was 6 feet tall and weighed only 112 pounds, and, needless to say, probably suffered from anorexia as well.[3]

Adam Lanza, 13 years old

Kateleen Foy/Getty Images

Despite these problems, Lanza resisted taking medication, a decision that was apparently supported by his mother. He began to be disconnected from other people and most likely from his own body. He joined an online community for mass-murder enthusiasts.

Could these psychological conditions be the reason why on December 14, 2012, the withdrawn Lanza shot his mother four times in her own bed, then went to Sandy Hook Elementary School in Newtown, Connecticut, and killed six female teachers and administrators and massacred 20 first-graders before taking his own life?[4] Most people would concur.

Some experts suggest that it was not mental illness per se that caused Lanza to commit mass murder but the lack of treatment for his mental condition. Backing up this claim is research on the trend in mass shootings that finds a link between these incidents and a decline in mental health treatment. In the 1980s, there were 18 mass shooting episodes during the entire decade; in the 1990s, there were 54. Since 2000, there has been an average of 16 per year or almost 10 times as many as the 1980s.[5] At the same time, the availability of mental health treatment has been reduced by budget cuts, and as a result the number of state hospital beds per capita has dropped to 1850 levels, or 14 beds per 100,000 people.[6] If more treatment were available for troubled kids like Lanza, might the Sandy Hook massacre have been prevented?

Some delinquency experts believe that the decision to commit an illegal act is a product of an individual-level decision-making process shaped by the personal characteristics and traits of the decision maker. Delinquents are not in fact a "product of their environment," but instead, individual actors, sometimes directed by some inner trait—selfish temperament, impulsive personality, abnormal hormones, mental illness—in their choice of antisocial over conventional behaviors.

If delinquency, the argument goes, reflects social and economic factors, how is it that many youths residing in the most dangerous and deteriorated neighborhoods are law-abiding citizens? According to the most recent US Census Bureau data, more than 48 million Americans now live in poverty, including millions of children, yet the vast majority of poor people do not become delinquents and criminals or join law-violating youth gangs.[7] Research indicates that relatively few youths in any population, even the most economically disadvantaged, actually become hard-core, chronic delinquents.[8] If poverty and environment were solely responsible for antisocial behaviors, there would be many more delinquent youths, and delinquency rates would be increasing rather than in decline.

If social factors are not responsible for the onset of delinquency, what is? To some experts the locus of delinquency is rooted in the *individual*: how the individual makes decisions, the quality of his or her biological makeup, and his or her personality and psychological profile.

Individual-level explanations of delinquency can be divided into two distinct categories. One position, referred to as **choice theory**, suggests that young offenders *choose* to engage in antisocial activity because they believe their actions will be beneficial and profitable. Whether they join a gang, steal cars, or sell drugs, their delinquent acts are motivated by the reasoned belief that illegal acts can be profitable and relatively risk free. They have little fear of getting caught and, if they are apprehended, discount the legal consequences. Some are motivated by fantasies of riches, whereas others may simply enjoy the excitement and short-term gratification produced by delinquent acts such as beating up an opponent or stealing a car.

Even hard-core choice theorists do not believe that *all* youthful misbehavior can be traced to rational decision making and calculated thought processes. At least some delinquent acts, especially violent ones, such as Adam Lanza's mass shooting, seem irrational, selfish, or hedonistic. How can these irrational acts be explained? The answer may be found in the offender's aberrant physical and/or psychological makeup. Some youths may be driven more by biological or psychological abnormalities, such as hyperactivity, low intelligence, biochemical imbalance, or genetic defects, than they are by a conscious and rational desire. This view of delinquency is referred to here generally as **trait theory** because it links delinquency to biological and psychological traits that control human development.

Choice and trait theories, though independent, are linked here because they share some common ground:

- Both focus on mental and behavioral processes at the individual level.
- Both consider delinquency as an individual-level problem, not a social problem.
- Both recognize that because all people are different, each person reacts to the same set of environmental and social conditions in a unique way.
- Because the root cause of delinquency is located at the individual level, delinquency prevention and control efforts must be directed at the individual offender. We must change people rather than society.

This chapter first covers those theoretical models that focus on individual choice. Then we discuss the view that biological and psychological development controls youngsters' ability to make choices, rendering some of them violent, aggressive, and antisocial.

Rational Choice Theory

The first formal explanations of crime and delinquency held that human behavior was a matter of choice. Because it was assumed that people had **free will** to choose their behavior, those who violated the law were motivated by personal needs such as greed, revenge, survival, and hedonism. Over 250 years ago, Cesare Beccaria argued that people weigh the benefits and consequences of their future actions before deciding on a course of behavior.[9] His writings formed the core of what is referred to today as **classical criminology**.

According to this classical view, the decision to violate the law comes after a careful weighing of the benefits and costs of criminal behaviors. Most potential

choice theory
Holds that youths will engage in delinquent and criminal behavior after weighing the consequences and benefits of their actions; delinquent behavior is a rational choice made by a motivated offender who perceives that the chances of gain outweigh any possible punishment or loss.

trait theory
Holds that youths engage in delinquent or criminal behavior due to aberrant physical or psychological traits that govern behavioral choices; delinquent actions are impulsive or instinctual rather than rational choices.

free will
View that people are in charge of their own destinies and are free to make personal behavior choices unencumbered by environmental factors.

classical criminology
Holds that decisions to violate the law are weighed against possible punishments, and to deter crime, the pain of punishment must outweigh the benefit of illegal gain; led to graduated punishments based on seriousness of the crime (let the punishment fit the crime).

law violators would cease their actions if the potential pain associated with a behavior outweighed its anticipated gain; conversely, law-violating behavior seems attractive if the future rewards seem far greater than the potential punishment.[10]

Classical criminologists argued that punishment should be only severe enough to deter a particular offense and that punishments should be graded according to the seriousness of particular crimes: "Let the punishment fit the crime." In his famous analysis, Beccaria stated that to be effective, punishment must be sufficiently severe, certain, and swift to control crime. If rapists and murderers were punished in a similar fashion—put to death—it might encourage a rapist to kill his victims in order to prevent them from calling the police or testifying in court.[11]

Get more information on **Cesare Beccaria** via the Constitution Society (http://www.constitution.org/cb/beccaria_bio.htm) and the Internet Encyclopedia of Philosophy (http://www.iep.utm.edu/beccaria/).

The Rational Delinquent

According to the rational choice view, delinquents are careful and logical decision makers. Before they decide to violate the law and commit a delinquent act, they weigh the possible benefits or profits, such as cash to buy cars, clothes, and other luxury items, with the potential costs or penalties, such as arrest followed by a long stay in a juvenile facility. If, for instance, they believe that drug dealers are rarely caught and even then usually avoid severe punishments, the youths will more likely choose to become dealers than if they believe that dealers are almost always caught and punished by lengthy prison terms. Some kids may know people or hear about criminals who make a significant income from illegal activities and want to follow in their footsteps.[12] Same with sexually aggressive behavior: males are more likely to be sexually aggressive if they (a) believe they can get away with it and (b) believe their friends do it too; peer approval means they will not be stigmatized by their close friends.[13]

Once involved in antisocial activities, many delinquent kids take a reasoned approach to their criminal enterprises. Juvenile burglars like to target residences close to where they live so they know the territory and have access to escape routes. While adults are willing to travel to commit crimes, juveniles stay close to home (unless they happen to have a car and driver's license!).[14] Young street robbers are likely to choose victims who are vulnerable and do not pose any threat.[15] Robbers are more likely to use physical force against a victim who resists; compliant victims are treated with greater restraint.[16]

Betty, 14 (right), with her friend, Christian, 14, are shown hanging out in a city park. Betty, the newcomer in the park, decided to run away after getting involved in numerous family conflicts. "I'm just tired of it all, and I don't want to be in my house anymore," she said, explaining why she had run away. "One month there is money, and the next month there is none. One day, she [her mother] is taking it out on me and hitting me, and the next day she is ignoring me. It's more stable out here. . . . I can survive fine out here," Betty said as she brandished a switchblade she pulled from her dirty sweatshirt pocket. At a nearby picnic table was part of the world she and the others were trying to avoid: a man with swastikas tattooed on his neck and an older homeless woman with rotted teeth, holding a pit bull named Diablo. Was Betty's decision to run away truly rational?

Monica Almeida/The New York Times/Redux

Even joining a gang takes rational choice. Potential gang members must send out signals that they are quality individuals who are worthy of membership and deserve to be selected. Being willing to commit crime, having the right background, and "correct" ethnic and gender identity are all "signals" that demonstrate a good potential for gang membership.[17] After they join gangs, members demonstrate a reasoned analysis of market conditions, interests, and risks. When James Densley studied gangs in London, he found that they evolved from nonviolent, noncriminal adolescent peer groups into organized criminal enterprises.[18] Nothing was left to chance, one gang member, street name Wolverine, explained to Densley:

We was committing crimes so we sat down together, it was like a meeting, I suppose, and we just gave each other names and it started like that. Because it was not like socializing, it was actually going out to commit crime and do stuff. We was premeditating what we was doing before it happened. Planning it up.

Densley found that gang boys learn special skills—how to seize territory, how to use violence, how to maintain secrecy, how to obtain intelligence—that enable them to successfully regulate and control the production and distribution of illegal drugs while maximizing their profits.

Shaping Delinquent Choices

Choice theorists believe that law-violating behavior occurs when a reasoning offender decides to take the chance of violating the law after considering his or her personal situation (need for money, learning experiences, opportunities for conventional success), values (conscience, moral values, need for peer approval), and situation (overcoming some immediate problem). What are some of the most important social developments that produce or influence delinquent decision making?

Personal Problems   Kids may be forced to choose delinquent behavior to help them solve problems.[19] Adolescents may find themselves feeling "out of control" because society limits their opportunities and resources. By engaging in antisocial behaviors, some adolescents are able to exert control over their own lives and destinies. When they cut school they are avoiding a situation they find uncomfortable; when they run away from home they may be fleeing from physical or sexual abuse. Delinquency may also enable them to deal with rivals or adversaries by getting a gun for self-protection from a local gang.

Financial Needs/Rewards   The choice of delinquency may be shaped by economic needs. Kids may obtain things they desire by stealing or sell drugs to buy stylish outfits. Those who use drugs may increase their delinquent activities in proportion to the costs of their habit. As the cost of their drug habit increases, the lure of illegal profits becomes overwhelmingly attractive.[20]

Kids may also choose delinquency because they believe they have little chance of becoming successful in the conventional world. In the long run, they view drug dealing and car thefts as their ticket to a better life; in the short run, delinquency can provide them with the cash for better tech devices or flashy jewelry. When Steven Levitt and Sudhir Alladi Venkatesh studied the financial rewards of being in a drug gang, they found that despite enormous risks to health, life, and freedom, the average gang member earned only slightly more than what they could in the legitimate labor market (about $6–11 per hour).[21] Why did they stay in the gang? Gang members believed that there was a strong potential for future riches if they stayed in the drug business and achieved a "management" position as a gang leader who earned quite a bit more than the rank-and-file members.[22] In reality, the likelihood of becoming a well-off gang leader was pretty remote, but kids based their behavior on what they believed would happen in the future and not upon what was really likely to occur—for example, the likelihood that they would get shot, go to jail, and never actually become a gang leader.

Parental Controls and Supervision   Parental supervision is a key determinant of violent and aggressive behaviors. Adolescents whose parents are poor supervisors have the freedom to socialize with their peers, an opportunity that enables them to engage in deviant behaviors.[23]

Teenage boys may have the highest crime rates because they, rather than their sisters, are given autonomy and unsupervised socialization.[24] When does girls' behavior coincide with that of boys? Physically mature girls have a lifestyle more similar to boys, and without parental supervision they are the ones most likely to engage in antisocial acts.[25]

Lack of supervision can neutralize any positive benefits accrued from after-school or summer jobs. Though gainful employment sounds like a healthy choice, an adolescent's work experience may actually increase delinquency rather than limit its occurrence. Rather than saving for college, as their parents might hope, kids who get jobs use their cash to buy drugs and alcohol; after-school jobs may attract teens who are more impulsive than ambitious.[26] At work, they have the opportunity for unsupervised socialization with their peers; lack of parental supervision increases criminal motivation.[27] Though some adults may think that providing teens with a job will reduce criminal activity—under the theory that "idle hands are the devil's workshop"—some aspects of the work experience, such as autonomy, increased social status among peers, and increased income, may neutralize the positive effects of working. The after-school job effect is most pronounced on novice delinquents who may be experiencing unsupervised freedom for the first time. In contrast, experienced offenders may actually benefit from an after-school job.[28]

Revenge, Deterrence, and Vengeance   Some adolescents may choose crime in order to retaliate against a hated rival or seek vengeance for an actual or perceived wrong. Psychologist Richard Felson argues that violence can be used to achieve a number of specific goals:

- *Control*. The violent person may want to control his victim's behavior and life.
- *Retribution*. Violence may be used to punish someone without calling the police or using the justice system to address grievances. Kids will take the law into their own hands if they do not trust the law.
- *Deterrence*. The attacker may want to stop or deter someone from repeating acts that he considers hostile or provocative.
- *Reputation*. An attack may be motivated by the need to enhance reputation and create self-importance in the eyes of others. Kids with a tough rep shield themselves from revenge and retribution if they choose to victimize other adolescents.[29]

Compulsion   Some adolescents act compulsively. We know that a relatively small group of chronic offenders commits a significant percentage of all serious crimes. Some psychologists believe this select group suffers from an innate or inherited emotional state that renders them both incapable of fearing punishment and less likely to appreciate the consequences of crime. Their compulsive behavior and heightened emotional state negate the deterrent effect of the law; they are unlikely to be deterred by the future threat of punishment.

Take for instance sex offenders, whose compulsive behavior is difficult to control. The evidence showing that public sex offender registration can control crime has been spotty. Research shows that registration lists and similar mechanisms have little effectiveness on delinquent sex offenders.[30]

Creating Scripts   As they gain experience, some kids create *scripts* that guide their interactions with victims. If they follow the script, they can commit their crimes and avoid detection. Before committing their crimes, young sex offenders will go through a series of steps, first locating their victims in institutional, domestic, or public locations, then gaining their victims' trust, and then formulating strategies to proceed to the best location for sexual contact. For that purpose, offenders will usually promise rewards or give inducements such as money to the victim; if that does not work, they may threaten or use violence to get their way.[31]

Auto thieves try to avoid confrontation at all costs. They rely on speed and stealth and not physical force. Auto thieves are deterred by the threat of confrontation with car owners. They know that making a mistake in planning can produce severe reactions for even minor violations. Consequently, they calculate how long the car's owner will be absent, the likelihood of their return, and the potential for retaliation. Offenders must figure out a way to make their behavior seem normal to observers, to hide their intentions from prying eyes, and to neutralize the desire of car owners to take action to protect their property. Most develop techniques not only to steal the car but to avoid detection and to escape if detected.[32]

Routine Activities

routine activities theory
View that crime is a "normal" function of the routine activities of modern living; offenses can be expected if there is a motivated offender and a suitable target that is not protected by capable guardians.

predatory crime
Violent crimes against people, and crimes in which an offender attempts to steal an object directly from its holder.

Given the fact that youthful behavior may be shaped by life experiences, why do some kids choose to commit crimes while others are resigned to a conventional lifestyle? And are there structural factors that influence delinquent decision making? According to **routine activities theory**, originally developed by Lawrence Cohen and Marcus Felson, the volume and distribution of **predatory crime** (violent crimes against the person and crimes in which an offender attempts to steal an object directly from its holder) are influenced by the interaction of three variables that reflect the routine activities found in everyday American life: the *lack of capable guardians* (such as homeowners and their neighbors, friends, and relatives), the availability of *suitable targets* (such as homes containing easily salable goods), and the presence of *motivated offenders* (such as unemployed teenagers). If each of these components is present, there is greater likelihood that a predatory crime will take place (see Figure 3.1).[33]

Capable Guardians   The presence of capable guardians who can protect homes and possessions can reduce the motivation to commit delinquent acts. Even the most motivated offenders may ignore valuable targets if they are well guarded. Private homes and/or public businesses may be considered off-limits if they are well protected by capable guardians and efficient security systems.[34]

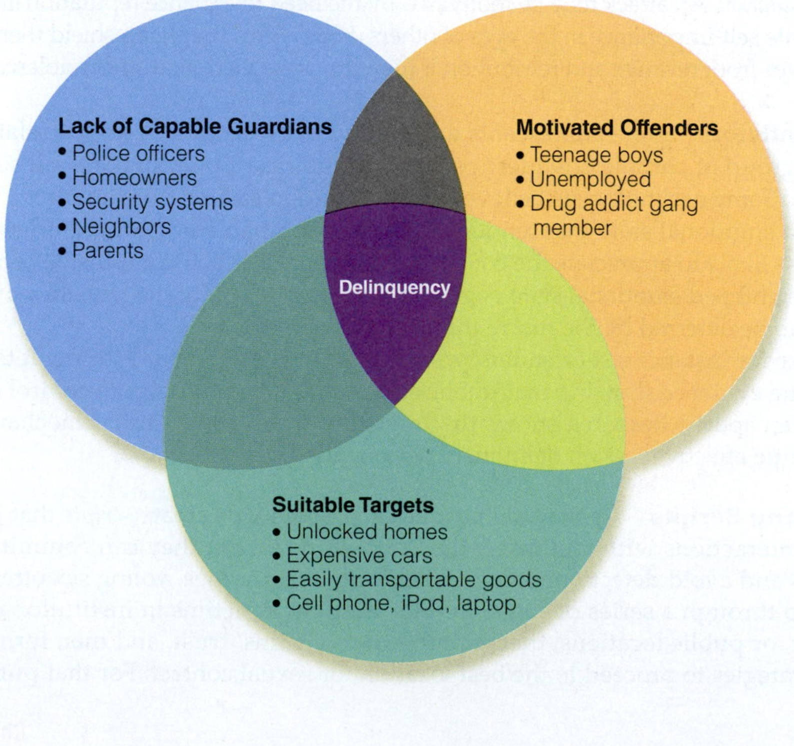

figure 3.1

Routine Activities Theory Posits the Interaction of Three Factors Helps Explain Fluctuations in the Delinquency Rate

© Cengage Learning 2015

Lack of Capable Guardians
• Police officers
• Homeowners
• Security systems
• Neighbors
• Parents

Motivated Offenders
• Teenage boys
• Unemployed
• Drug addict gang member

Delinquency

Suitable Targets
• Unlocked homes
• Expensive cars
• Easily transportable goods
• Cell phone, iPod, laptop

Since 1970, the number of adult caretakers at home during the day has decreased because more women have entered the workforce. Because mothers are at work and children are in daycare, homes are left unguarded and become suitable targets. Similarly, with the growth of suburbia and the decline of the traditional neighborhood, the number of such familiar guardians as family, neighbors, and friends has diminished.[35] One way to reduce target attraction is to create formal and/or informal social control mechanisms. Living in a gated community with security guards and coded gates reduces the risk of being targeted by burglars.[36] Delinquency levels are relatively low in neighborhoods where residents keep a watchful eye on their neighbors' property.[37]

Parents who monitor their children's activities serve as guardians. The more time kids spend with their parents and the less time with their friends, the more limited their opportunity to commit delinquent activities.[38]

Delinquent youth are also wary of police guardianship. Proactive, aggressive law enforcement officers who quickly get to the scene of the crime help deter would-be delinquents by reducing their criminal motivation.[39] And having police around also convinces youths that committing crime is just too dangerous: the more crimes that result in arrest, the lower the subsequent delinquency rate.[40]

Suitable Targets   Routine activities theory suggests that the availability of suitable targets such as easily transportable commodities will increase delinquency rates.[41] Research has generally supported the fact that the more wealth a home contains, the more likely it will become a target.[42] As iPads and other small high-tech devices have become more commonplace, burglary rates have risen. The more high-priced, easily transported, and easily resold goods are made available, the more offenders will be motivated to profit from their theft.[43]

Motivated Offenders   As the number and motivation of offenders increase, so too do delinquency rates. What increases delinquent motivation? One possible source is scarcity of resources. Delinquency rates may increase if there is a surplus of youths of the same age category competing for a limited number of jobs and educational opportunities.

Motivated offenders, suitable targets, and the lack of guardianship have an interactive effect. Delinquency rates will increase if these motivated offenders are placed in close proximity to unguarded, suitable targets. Take after-school programs, for example. Although many adults believe that such programs can reduce delinquency levels, after-school programs designed to reduce criminal activity may produce higher crime rates because they lump together motivated offenders—teen boys—with vulnerable victims, other teen boys.[44]

Controlling Delinquency

If delinquency is a rational choice, as some believe, then delinquency prevention is a matter of three general strategies: (1) It stands to reason that it can be prevented by convincing potential delinquents that they will be severely punished for committing delinquent acts; then (2) they must be punished so severely that they never again commit crimes; or (3) it must be so difficult to commit crimes that the potential gain is not worth the risk. This vision has generated four strategies of control: general deterrence, specific deterrence, incapacitation, and situational crime prevention. Each is discussed below.

General Deterrence

The **general deterrence** concept holds that the choice to commit delinquent acts is structured by the threat of punishment. If kids believe they will get away with illegal behavior, they may choose to commit crime.[45] If, on the other hand, kids

general deterrence
Crime control policies that depend on the fear of criminal penalties, such as long prison sentences for violent crimes; the aim is to convince law violators that the pain outweighs the benefit of criminal activity.

Boston police gang unit officers John Burrows, left, and Andrew Hunter try to calm a group of bystanders after they arrested a juvenile gang member. The gang unit stresses ties to the community and cooperation to reduce gang violence in Boston.

Boston Globe/Getty Images

believe that their illegal behavior will result in apprehension and severe punishment, only the truly irrational would commit crime; they would be *deterred*.[46]

One of the guiding principles of deterrence theory is that the more severe, certain, and swift the punishment, the greater its deterrent effect will be.[47] Even if a particular crime carries a severe punishment, there will be relatively little deterrent effect if most people do not believe they will be caught.[48] Conversely, even a mild sanction may deter delinquency if kids believe punishment is certain.[49] So if the juvenile justice system can convince would-be delinquents that they will be caught—for example, by putting more police officers on the street—they may decide that delinquency simply does not pay.[50] In other words, kids will more likely be deterred from delinquency if they believe that they will get caught; what happens to them after apprehension seems to have less impact.[51]

Perception and Deterrence According to deterrence theory, not only the actual chance of punishment but also the *perception that punishment will be forthcoming* influence the decision to engage in delinquency.[52] A central theme of deterrence theory is that people who believe or imagine that they will be punished for crimes in the present will avoid doing those crimes in the future.[53] Even the most committed young offenders (e.g., gang members) who fear legal punishments will forego delinquent activities.[54] Conversely, the likelihood of being arrested and punished will have little effect on kids if they believe that they have only a small chance of suffering apprehension and punishment in the future. If kids can be convinced that illegal activities will lead to serious punishment, they will be deterred regardless of the actual or real chance of their being caught and punished.

While logical, the association between perception and deterrence is not a simple one nor does it appear to be linear—that is, the greater the perception of punishment, the less kids are willing to commit crime. Perception of punishment appears to change and evolve over time, shaped by a delinquent's experience and personality. Some kids are more *deterrable* than others, their perceptions shaped by their own personal experiences. It comes as no surprise that when delinquent offenders are separated into two groups—high-rate offenders who constantly break the law and low-rate offenders who occasionally are involved in antisocial behaviors—the former group's members perceive less risk and more reward from delinquent acts; low-rate offenders tend to view it as less rewarding.[55]

Actual Deterrence and Delinquency   Not only are people deterred from the perceived threat of punishment, but they will also avoid crime if the threat of punishment is real. The more cops are likely to make arrests, the courts to convict, and the correctional system to punish, the less likely it is that kids will engage in delinquency. This approach may work with youth because, unlike adults who do a poor job of estimating their chances of being punished, kids actually are more aware of the threat of punishment and the likelihood it will be applied if they get caught.[56]

How have actual deterrence measures been operationalized? If kids choose delinquency because "it pays," then it stands to reason that they will forgo illegal behavior if they can be convinced that "crime does not pay."[57] One method is to raise the risk of delinquency by creating mechanical devices that increase the likelihood that an offender will be observed and captured. The installation of closed-circuit television (CCTV) surveillance cameras and improved street lighting can deter would-be delinquents who fear detection and apprehension.[58]

Such measures as adding police officers and having them aggressively patrol the streets, adding school resource officers, and creating antigang units are all measures designed to convince would-be delinquents that the chances of apprehension are too great to risk crime. Another approach is to threaten harsh punishments such as waiver to adult court and a sentence to prison. Many kids know that as they age they will no longer be treated as a juvenile, and that an adult prison sentence is much more serious than a stay in a juvenile correctional center. Soon they may begin to realize that the risks of crime are greater than the potential profits and decide to go straight.

Cities that increase the size of their patrol force are the ones most likely to experience a reduction in crime and delinquency.[59] Proactive, aggressive law enforcement officers who quickly get to the scene of the crime may help deter delinquent activities.[60] Increasing the visibility of the police, hiring more officers, and allocating them in ways that increase the perceived risk of apprehension does produce significant deterrent effects. Deterring potential offenders is a more economical crime control mechanism than incapacitating people in prison after they have committed a criminal offense.[61]

Focusing police activity on particular problems seems to work best.[62] Police are now more willing to use aggressive tactics, such as gang-busting units, to deter membership in drug-trafficking gangs. Youthful-looking officers have been sent undercover into high schools in order to identify, contact, and arrest student drug dealers.[63]

Traditionally the juvenile court relied on the *parens patriae* philosophy, which mandates that children be treated and not punished. This limits the power of the law to deter juvenile crime. Kids know that the sanctions given out in juvenile court are far more lenient than those given adults, and that knowledge negates the application of get-tough measures. However, the juvenile courts have also attempted to initiate a deterrence strategy. Juvenile court judges have been willing to waive youths to adult courts.[64] In sum, actual deterrence policies may work and their application seems to have had a significant influence on the declining delinquency rate.

Shame and Humiliation   One aspect of deterrence that seems to have an impact on juveniles is shame, embarrassment, and social disgrace. If kids fear being rejected by family and peers, they will be reluctant to engage in deviant behavior.[65] Kids who say they would be ashamed if their involvement in crime becomes public are less likely to offend than those not so easily embarrassed.[66]

While shame can be a powerful deterrent, young offenders also seem to be influenced by forgiveness and acceptance. They are less likely to repeat their delinquent acts if victims are willing to grant them forgiveness.[67]

The fear of exposure and consequent shaming may vary according to the cohesiveness of community structure and the type of crime. Informal sanctions may be most effective in highly unified areas where everyone knows one another and the crime cannot be hidden from public view. The threat of informal sanctions seems to have the greatest influence on instrumental crimes, which involve planning, and not on impulsive or expressive criminal behaviors or those associated with substance abuse.[68]

Focused Deterrence   Under some circumstances a targeted strategy that directs a surge of law enforcement activity against a few repeat offenders may help reduce delinquency rates.[69] One well-known approach, known as "pulling levers policing" or **focused deterrence** is about activating or pulling every deterrent "lever" available to reduce the targeted problem. If it is juvenile gang violence, responses may include shutting down drug markets, serving warrants, enforcing probation restrictions, and making disorder arrests. A major component of this approach is communicating direct and explicit messages to offenders about the responses they can expect if this behavior is not stopped. One of the most successful examples of this strategy is Boston's Operation Ceasefire, which employs a variety of law enforcement and social agencies, including probation and parole, the Bureau of Alcohol, Tobacco, Firearms, and Explosives (ATF), gang outreach and prevention street workers, local police, and the Drug Enforcement Administration (DEA).

The Ceasefire group delivers its message clearly to gang members: "We're ready, we're watching, we're waiting. Who wants to be next?" Careful evaluations using sophisticated matching group comparisons found that the program was an effective deterrent to gang crime.[70] There is more on this program in Chapter 9.

Do General Deterrence Strategies Work?   Punishment is up, millions of people are behind bars, and the crime rate is down. So it seems like deterrence strategies do work! Or do they? While the general deterrence concept makes logical sense, there is actually little conclusive evidence that the threat of apprehension and punishment alone can deter delinquency.[71] There are a number of reasons why strategies that attempt to frighten teens may not work:

- Deterrence strategies are based on the idea of a rational, calculating offender; they may not be effective when applied to immature young people. Many offenders are under the influence of drugs when they commit crimes, others suffer from mental illness, while many bear the burden of both mental illness and drug abuse.[72] They may be impulsive and imprudent rather than reasoning and calculating. Minors tend to be less capable of making mature judgments about their behavior choices when under the influence of drugs and alcohol. In sum, even the harshest deterrence strategies may have little effect on psychologically or drug-impaired youth.[73]

- The deterrent threat of punishment may have little influence among high-risk offenders, such as teens living in economically depressed neighborhoods who actually commit most of the crimes in the United States. Even if they truly fear the consequences of the law, they must commit crime to survive in a hostile environment.[74] Young people in these areas have less to lose if arrested; they have a limited stake in society and are not worried about their future. They also may not make connections between delinquent behavior and punishment because they see many people in their neighborhood commit crimes and not get caught or punished.[75]

- It is also possible that experience with the law and punishment actually defuses fear of punishment, thus neutralizing its deterrent effect. Greg Pogarsky and his associates found that getting arrested had little deterrent effect on youth and that kids who experienced punishment were the ones most likely to continue committing crime. One reason may be that crime-prone youth, the ones who have a long history of delinquency, know that crime provides immediate gratification, whereas the threat of punishment remains far in the future.[76]

focused deterrence
A policy that relies on pulling every deterrent "lever" available to reduce crime in the targeted problem.

- Kids may learn to adapt to deterrent measures. Police crackdowns and gang sweeps may convince them that it's too dangerous for them to commit crime at the moment, but that does not mean they are willing to forgo future delinquent activities. They find ways to adapt to this perceived threat:
  - They reduce the number of crimes they are willing to commit during a particular period of time.
  - They commit less-serious crimes, assuming that even if they are apprehended, the punishment will not be as severe for a "minor" infraction. They are unlikely to be placed in a juvenile facility or waived to adult court for shoplifting, but robbery is another matter entirely.
  - They take action to reduce the chance that they will be caught and to reduce the risk of detection (e.g., stop wearing their gang colors or tagging walls).
  - They relocate to more favorable terrain.[77]

Deterring delinquency through the fear of punishment may have value under some but not all circumstances and for some offenders and some crimes, but right now the jury is still out on whether it can be an effective delinquency control policy.

Specific Deterrence

The theory of **specific deterrence** holds that the more severely young offenders are punished, the less likely they are to repeat their illegal acts. General deterrence focuses on potential offenders; specific deterrence targets offenders who have already been apprehended. For example, juveniles are sent to secure incarceration facilities with the understanding that their ordeal will deter future misbehavior.

specific deterrence
Sending convicted offenders to secure incarceration facilities so that punishment is severe enough to convince offenders not to repeat their criminal activity.

Specific deterrence strategies suppose that people can "learn from their mistakes" and that kids who are caught and punished will perceive greater risk than those who have escaped detection.[78] As the perceived benefits of crime decline, desistance escalates.[79] Specific deterrence strategies may actually work better with young, inexperienced juvenile offenders than adult miscreants. Research shows that punishment has less of an effect on the experienced offender than it does on the novice.[80] Therefore, punishing an inexperienced juvenile offender may convince them that crime does not pay, while punishing a more experienced offender is simply business as usual.

While novice delinquents may be scared off by an arrest, the more experienced offender will not, and these experienced delinquents, who after multiple arrests are placed in a juvenile justice facility, may actually be more likely to persist in their delinquent behaviors.[81] In fact, a history of prior arrests, convictions, and punishments has proven to be the best predictor of rearrest among young offenders released from correctional institutions.[82] Once involved in the system, the threat of punishment seems to have little deterrent effect. Why is this so?

- Offenders may believe that though they were caught and punished, the experience was actually beneficial: they have learned from their experiences, now know how to beat the system, and can get away with crime.[83]

- Kids who have already been severely punished by being placed in a juvenile facility may represent the "worst of the worst," who will offend again no matter what punishments they experience.[84]

- Punishment may bring defiance rather than deterrence. Adolescents who are harshly treated may want to show that they cannot be broken by the system.

- Punishment might be perceived to be capricious, unjust, or unfair, causing some kids to want to lash out and retaliate against what they consider to be unfair treatment. Deterrence strategies cannot work because interaction with agents of the justice system (e.g., police) creates labeling and stigma that are powerful delinquency producing forces. Research shows that rather than reduce delinquency, kids who have been stopped and arrested are more likely to commit future crimes and hold antisocial attitudes than those who avoid stigmatizing police contacts.[85]

Incapacitation

It stands to reason that delinquents' ability to commit illegal acts will be eliminated or at least curtailed by putting them behind bars. About 70,000 young people are now housed in juvenile correctional facilities, and others, because their case has been waived to the adult court, are incarcerated in adult prisons; there are about 25,000 teenagers serving time in adult prisons.

While it seems logical that incarcerating the most dangerous repeat juvenile offenders will reduce their ability to commit delinquent acts, a strict incapacitation policy does not always produce the desired effect:

- Incarceration, especially in an adult prison, exposes younger offenders to higher-risk, more experienced inmates who can influence their lifestyle and help shape their attitudes. These prisons are "schools for crime." The short-term delinquency reduction effect of incapacitating offenders is negated if the experience has the long-term effect of escalating the frequency and severity of their future criminality upon release.

- If crime and delinquency are functions of rational choice, the profits of illegal activity are sure to convince kids that crime pays. Therefore, there will always be someone ready to take the place of the incarcerated offenders and replace them in the gang, group, or clique. New delinquents will be recruited and trained, offsetting any benefit accrued by incarceration.

- Imprisoning established offenders may open new opportunities for competitors who were suppressed by more experienced delinquents or controlled by their tougher rivals. Incarcerating gang members may open illegal markets to new groups and gangs who are even hungrier and more aggressive than the ones they replaced.

- Teens are unlikely to be incarcerated in a juvenile facility or sent to prison until well into their offending career. By the time they are arrested, waived, and sent to an adult prison they are already past the age when they are likely to commit crime. As a result, a strict incarceration policy may keep people in prison beyond the time they are a threat to society while a new cohort of high-risk adolescents is on the street.[86]

- An incapacitation strategy is also terribly expensive. The prison system costs billions of dollars each year, and incarcerating a juvenile costs substantially more than an adult. Kids must be provided with both adequate treatment and education. Even if incarceration could reduce the crime rate, the costs would be enormous.

- Even if incarceration can have a short-term effect, almost all delinquents eventually return to society. Because many of these kids are drug- and gang-involved, most come from comparatively few urban inner-city areas. Their return may contribute to family disruption, undermine social institutions, and create community disorganization. Rather than acting as a crime suppressant, incarceration may have the long-term effect of accelerating crime rates.[87]

So while it is logically correct that a stay in a secure facility can reduce the length of a criminal career, there is some question whether increasing the size of the prison population reduces crime rates.[88]

Situational Crime Prevention

situational crime prevention
Crime prevention method that relies on reducing the opportunity to commit criminal acts by (a) making them more difficult to perform, (b) reducing their reward, and (c) increasing their risks.

According to the concept of **situational crime prevention**, in order to reduce delinquent activity, planners must be aware of the characteristics of sites and situations that are at risk to crime; the things that draw or push kids toward these sites and situations; what equips potential delinquents to take advantage of illegal opportunities offered by these sites and situations; and what constitutes the immediate triggers for delinquent actions.[89] Delinquency can be neutralized if (a) potential targets are carefully guarded, (b) the means to commit crime are controlled, and

(c) potential offenders are carefully monitored. Desperate people may contemplate crime, but only the truly irrational will attack a well-defended, inaccessible target and risk strict punishment.

Rather than deterring or punishing individuals in order to reduce delinquency rates, situational crime prevention strategies aim to reduce the opportunities people have to commit particular crimes. The idea is to make it so difficult to commit specific criminal acts that would-be delinquent offenders will be convinced that the risks of crime are greater than the rewards.[90] Controlling the situation of crime can be accomplished by increasing the effort, increasing the risks, and/or reducing the rewards attached to delinquent acts.

Typically, situational crime prevention programs are divided into six categories:

- Increasing the effort to commit delinquent acts
- Increasing the risks of delinquent activity
- Reducing the rewards attached to delinquent acts
- Increasing the shame of committing a delinquent act
- Reducing provocations that produce delinquent acts
- Removing excuses for committing a delinquent act

Increasing the effort required to commit delinquency can involve **target-hardening techniques** such as placing steering locks on cars, putting unbreakable glass on storefronts, or installing a locking device on cars that prevents drunken drivers from starting the vehicle (breath-analyzed ignition interlock device).[91] Access control can be maintained by locking gates and fencing yards.[92] The facilitators of crime can be controlled by such measures as banning the sale of spray paint to adolescents in an effort to cut down on graffiti, or having photos put on credit cards to reduce their value if stolen.

Increasing the risks of delinquency might involve such measures as improving surveillance lighting, using CCTV monitoring, creating neighborhood watch programs, controlling building entrances and exits, installing burglar alarms and security systems, and increasing the number of private security officers and police patrols. Research conducted in the United States and England indicates that installation of streetlights may convince would-be burglars that their entries will be seen and reported.[93] Closed-circuit TV cameras have been shown to reduce the amount of car theft from parking lots while reducing the need for higher-cost security personnel.[94] Delinquency rate reductions seem to be maximized when CCTV and improved street lighting are used in tandem.[95]

Reducing the rewards of delinquency includes strategies such as marking property so it is more difficult to sell when stolen and using caller ID to discourage obscene phone calls. Tracking systems, such as those made by the LoJack Corporation, help police locate and return stolen vehicles.

Because delinquent acts are sometimes the result of extreme provocation, it might be possible to reduce delinquency rates by creating programs that reduce conflict. Posting guards outside schools at closing time might prevent childish taunts from escalating into full-blown brawls. Anti-bullying programs that have been implemented in schools are another method of reducing provocation. Because alcohol is a significant factor in various kinds of crime, including rape and assaults, increasing the drinking age, introducing non-alterable photo IDs, or raising the price of beer, wine, and hard liquor so that they are beyond the typical teenager's budget might help reduce the incidence of violent crime. And there would be significant fringe benefits, including fewer auto accidents and more money for state treasuries.[96]

Some delinquents neutralize their responsibility for their acts by learning to excuse their behavior. They say things like "I didn't know that was illegal" or "I had no choice." It might be possible to reduce delinquency by eliminating excuses. For example, teenage vandalism may be reduced by posting wall signs warning that anyone spraying graffiti will be severely punished, eliminating the excuse "I didn't know that was illegal."

target-hardening technique
Crime prevention technique that makes it more difficult for a would-be delinquent to carry out the illegal act—for example, by installing a security device in a home.

Indirect Benefits and Deficits Increasing the risk to commit one type of delinquent act may also help prevent others, a phenomenon known as **diffusion of benefits**.[97] Video cameras set up in a mall to convince teens not to shoplift can also reduce property damage because young graffiti artists fear they are being caught on camera. Police surveillance set up to control drug zones may reduce the incidence of prostitution and other public order crimes by scaring off would-be clients.[98] Intensive police patrols designed to target teen gangs may help reduce crime in neighboring areas as well.[99]

If they are effective, situational efforts may also discourage potential criminals. Discouragement may cause potential delinquents to either leave the area or seek other methods of gaining financial rewards.

While there are hidden benefits to situational prevention, there may also be costs that limit their effectiveness. A program that seems successful may simply be redirecting young offenders to alternative targets. This is known as **displacement**; delinquency is not prevented but deflected or displaced. To suppress gang activity, police patrols may be beefed in a vulnerable area, only to have gang boys shift their drug dealing to a "safer" neighborhood.[100]

Another problem is that some situational crime prevention programs only have a short-term effect. Would-be delinquents soon learn how to avoid police patrols; they may try new offenses they had previously avoided, shifting from burglary to car theft. Others begin to see that the threat is not as bad as they first thought. They soon realize they can avoid police patrols and resume illegal activities.[101] See Concept Summary 3.1 for a summary of delinquency prevention strategies.

Why Do Delinquents Choose Delinquency?

All the delinquency control methods based on choice theory assume the delinquent to be a motivated offender who breaks the law because he or she perceives an abundance of benefits and an absence of threat. Increase the threat and reduce the benefits, and the delinquency rate should decline.

CONCEPT SUMMARY 3.1

Delinquency Control Strategies Based on Rational Choice

Situational Crime Prevention

- This strategy is aimed at convincing would-be delinquents to avoid specific targets. It relies on the doctrine that crime can be avoided if motivated offenders are denied access to suitable targets.
- Applications of this strategy are home security systems or guards, which broadcast the message that guardianship is great here, stay away; the potential reward is not worth the risk of apprehension.
- Problems with the strategy are the extinction of the effect and displacement of crime.

General Deterrence Strategies

- These strategies are aimed at making potential delinquents fear the consequences of their acts. The threat of punishment is meant to convince rational delinquents that crime does not pay.
- Applications of these strategies are mandatory sentences, waiver to adult court, and aggressive policing.
- Problems with these strategies are that delinquents are immature and may not fear punishment, and the certainty of arrest and punishment is low.

Specific Deterrence Strategy

- This strategy refers to punishing known delinquents so severely that they will never be tempted to repeat their offenses. If delinquency is rational, then painful punishment should reduce its future allure.
- An application of this strategy is placement in a punitive juvenile detention facility or secure institution.
- A problem with this strategy is that punishment may increase reoffending rates rather than deter future delinquency.

Incapacitation Strategies

- These strategies attempt to reduce crime rates by denying motivated offenders the opportunity to commit crime. If, despite the threat of law and punishment, some people still find crime attractive, the only way to control their behavior is to incarcerate them for extended periods.
- An application of these strategies is long, tough, mandatory sentences, putting more kids behind bars.
- A problem with these strategies is that people are kept in prison beyond the years they may commit crime. Minor, nondangerous offenders are locked up, and this is a very costly strategy.

This logic is hard to refute. The two-decade-long crime drop seems to be linked to deterrence and incapacitation strategies and the use of situational crime prevention to reduce the opportunity to commit crime. Yet several questions still remain unanswered. First, why do some people continually choose to break the law, even after suffering its consequences? Why are some kids law abiding even though they are indigent and have little chance of gaining economic success? Conversely, why do some affluent youths break the law when they have everything to lose and little more to gain?

Choice theorists also have problems explaining seemingly irrational crimes, such as vandalism, arson, and even drug abuse. To say a teenager who painted swastikas on a synagogue or attacked a gay couple was making a "rational choice" seems inadequate to explain such a destructive, purposeless act.

The relationships observed by rational choice theorists can also be explained in other ways. For example, though the high victimization rates in lower-class neighborhoods can be explained by an oversupply of motivated offenders, they may also be due to other factors, such as social conflict and disorganization.[102]

In sum, although choice theories can contribute to understanding criminal events and victim patterns, they leave a major question unanswered: Why do some people choose crime over legal activities?

Trait Theories: Biological and Psychological Views

A faithful and loyal choice theorist believes that selecting crime is usually part of an economic strategy, a function of carefully weighing the benefits of criminal over legal behavior. For example, youths decide to commit a robbery if they believe they will make a good profit, have a good chance of getting away with it, and, even if caught, stand little chance of being severely punished.

A number of delinquency experts believe that this model is incomplete. They consider it wrong to infer that all youths choose crime simply because they believe its advantages outweigh its risks. If that were the case, how could senseless and profitless crimes such as vandalism and random violence be explained? Is it possible that killers like Adam Lanza, profiled in the opening vignette, are mentally stable, rational decision makers?

Incidents such as the Sandy Hook shooting convince some experts that violent or deviant behavioral choices are a function of an individual's mental and/or physical makeup. Most law-abiding youths have personal traits that keep them within the mainstream of conventional society. In contrast, youths who choose to engage in repeated aggressive, antisocial, or conflict-oriented behavior manifest abnormal traits that influence their behavior choices.[103] Uncontrollable, impulsive behavior patterns place some youths at odds with society, and they soon find themselves in trouble with the law. Although delinquents may choose their actions, the decision is a product of all but uncontrollable mental and physical properties and traits.

The view that delinquents are somehow "abnormal" is not a new one. Some of the earliest theories of criminal and delinquent behavior stressed that crime was a product of personal traits and that measurable physical and mental conditions, such as IQ and body build, determined behavior. This view is generally referred to today as positivism. Positivists believe that the scientific method can be used to measure the causes of human behavior and that behavior is a function of often uncontrollable factors, such as mental illness.

The source of behavioral control is one significant difference between trait and choice theories. Although the former reasons that behavior is controlled by personal traits, the latter views behavior as purely a product of human reasoning. To a choice theorist, reducing the benefits of crime by increasing the likelihood and severity of punishment will eventually lower the crime rate. Trait theorists question the utility of punishment because those who commit crimes lack the capacity to understand their consequences. In the following sections, the history and primary components of trait theory are reviewed.

Origins of Trait Theory

The first attempts to discover why criminal tendencies develop focused on the physical makeup of offenders. Biological traits present at birth were thought to predetermine whether people would live a life of crime.

The origin of this school of thought is generally credited to the Italian physician Cesare Lombroso (1835–1909).[104] Known as the father of criminology, Lombroso put his many years of medical research to use in his theory of **criminal atavism**.[105] Lombroso found that delinquents manifest physical anomalies that make them biologically and physiologically similar to our primitive ancestors. These atavistic individuals are savage throwbacks to an earlier stage of human evolution. Because of this link, the "born criminal" has such physical traits as enormous jaws, strong canines, a flattened nose, supernumerary teeth (double rows, as in snakes), handle-shaped ears, hawk-like noses, or fleshy lips. Lombroso made such statements as, "It was easy to understand why the span of the arms in criminals so often exceeds the height, for this is a characteristic of apes, whose forelimbs are used in walking and climbing."[106]

Contemporaries of Lombroso refined the notion of a physical basis of crime. Rafaele Garofalo (1851–1934) shared Lombroso's belief that certain physical characteristics indicate a criminal or delinquent nature.[107] Enrico Ferri (1856–1929), a student of Lombroso, believed that a number of biological, social, and organic factors caused delinquency and crime.[108]

These early views portrayed delinquent behavior as a function of a single factor or trait, such as body build or defective intelligence. They had a significant impact on early American criminology, which relied heavily on developing a science of "criminal anthropology."[109] Eventually, these views evoked criticism for their unsound methodology and lack of proper scientific controls. Some researchers used captive offender populations and failed to compare experimental subjects with control groups of nondelinquents or undetected delinquents. These methodological flaws made it impossible to determine whether biological traits produce delinquency. It is equally plausible that police were more likely to arrest, and courts convict, the mentally and physically abnormal. By the middle of the twentieth century, biological theories had fallen out of favor as an explanation of delinquency.

Contemporary Biosocial Theory

For most of the twentieth century, delinquency experts scoffed at the notion that a youth's behavior was controlled by physical conditions present at birth. During this period, the majority of delinquency research focused on social factors, such as poverty and family life, which were believed to be responsible for law-violating behavior. However, there is growing evidence that environmental conditions interact with human traits and conditions to influence behavior. Research studies that considered both biological and social factors in the production of delinquent behavior became more common and acceptable, and the term **biosocial theory** was coined to reflect the assumed links between physical and mental traits, the social environment, and behavior.[110]

As John Paul Wright and Francis Cullen put it:

> . . . the ideological dam preventing the development of biosocial perspectives is weakening and has sprung some leaks. The reality that humans are biological creatures who vary in biological traits is becoming too obvious to ignore.[111]

criminal atavism
The idea that delinquents manifest physical anomalies that make them biologically and physiologically similar to our primitive ancestors, savage throwbacks to an earlier stage of human evolution.

For more on Lombroso and the **crime-producing physical traits** identified by Lombroso, visit http://www.newworldencyclopedia .org/entry/Cesare_Lombroso.

biosocial theory
A theory of delinquency causation that integrates biologically determined traits and environmental stimuli.

Biosocial theorists argue that no two people (except for identical twins) are alike, and therefore each will react to environmental stimuli in a distinct way. They assume that a combination of personal traits and the environment produces individual behavior patterns. People with pathological traits such as brain damage, an abnormal personality, or a low IQ may have a heightened risk for crime. This risk is elevated by environmental stresses such as poor family life, educational failure, substance abuse, and exposure to delinquent peers. For example, studies examining gene–environment interaction find that genetic makeup has a greater influence on violent behavior when an individual is exposed to neighborhood disadvantage and lives in a community with high violent-crime rates.[112]

Vulnerability vs. Differential Susceptibility

Trait theorists today recognize that delinquency-producing interactions involve both personal traits (such as defective intelligence, impulsive personality, and abnormal brain chemistry) and environmental factors (such as family life, educational attainment, socioeconomic status, and neighborhood conditions). However, there are actually two views on how this interaction unfolds. The **vulnerability model** supposes a direct link between traits and crime. Some people develop physical or mental traits at birth, or soon thereafter, that affect their social functioning and put them in danger of poor behavior choices. They suffer from biological or psychological problems that render them defenseless to social pressures and vulnerable to developing behavior problems.[113]

In contrast, the **differential susceptibility model** suggests that some people possess physical or mental traits that make them more susceptible to environmental influences.[114] Given their makeup, they are at risk when they encounter unfavorable social environments, but they can also benefit more than others from a favorable and supportive environment. When the social environment is adverse, individuals with this particular set of traits manifest more aggression; when the environment is supportive, those with the same makeup demonstrate less aggression than the average person. Their makeup makes them more susceptible to the environment, whether it be good or bad.[115]

The individual-level factors that have been linked to antisocial behavior cluster into three distinct areas: biochemical factors, neurological dysfunction, and genetic influences. These three views are discussed in some detail below.

vulnerability model
Assumes there is a direct link between traits and crime; some people are vulnerable to crime from birth.

differential susceptibility model
The view that some people are predisposed to environmental influences.

Biochemical Factors

There is a suspected relationship between antisocial behavior and biochemical makeup.[116] One view is that body chemistry can govern behavior and personality, including levels of aggression and depression.[117] Adolescents may be exposed to damaging chemical contaminants in utero if their mothers ingest harmful substances during pregnancy.[118] The influence of damaging chemical and biological contaminants may also occur if the mother's diet either lacks or has an excess of important nutrients, such as manganese, which may later cause developmental problems in their offspring.[119] In sum, exposure to harmful chemicals and poor diet in utero, at birth, and beyond may affect people throughout their life course.

Another view is that abnormal body chemistry is an indirect cause of antisocial behavior through its association with abnormal psychological and mental conditions. Research conducted over the past decade shows that an over- or undersupply of certain chemicals and minerals, including sodium, mercury, potassium, calcium, amino acids, and/or iron, can lead to depression, hyperactivity, cognitive problems, intelligence deficits, memory loss, or abnormal sexual activity; these conditions have been associated with crime and delinquency.[120] Attention deficit hyperactivity disorder (ADHD), believed to be a precursor of delinquent behaviors, has been linked to the presence of excessive iron.[121]

Smoking and Drinking   Maternal alcohol abuse and smoking during gestation have long been linked to prenatal damage and subsequent antisocial behavior in adolescence. Exposure to secondhand cigarette smoke during pregnancy predicts later conduct disorder; exposure to smoke in childhood has been associated with increased psychopathology in adolescence.[122] Having a parent who smokes may have a greater effect on behavior than low birthweight and poor parenting practices.

Research now shows that people who start drinking by the age of 14 are five times more likely to become alcoholics than people who hold off on drinking until the age of 21. It is possible that early exposure of the brain to alcohol may short-circuit the growth of brain cells, impairing the learning and memory processes that protect against addiction. Thus, early ingestion of alcohol will have a direct influence on behavior.[123]

Environmental Contaminants   One area of concern is that overexposure to particular environmental contaminants, including metals and minerals such as iron and manganese, may produce effects that put kids at risk for antisocial behavior.[124] Exposure to the now-banned PCB (polychlorinated biphenyls), a chemical once used in insulation materials, has been shown to influence brain functioning and intelligence levels.[125] Pesticides such as chlorpyrifos, once used heavily in inner-city neighborhoods, have also been linked to behaviors associated with delinquency. Children exposed to large amounts of chlorpyrifos before birth are at elevated risk for developmental delays and symptoms of ADHD.[126] Another suspected cause of dysfunctional behavior is phthalates, industrial chemicals widely used as solvents and ingredients in plastics. Thousands of household items, from shampoos to flooring products, contain phthalates, and research shows that exposure is related to childhood misbehavior and improper functioning.[127]

Lead Contamination   In 2014, Flint, Michigan's drinking water became contaminated with lead. How did this happen? As a cost-cutting move, the city began drawing its water from the Flint River and treating it at the city water treatment plant while a new water pipeline to Lake Huron was being completed. Until then, Flint had used Lake Huron water treated by the Detroit Water and Sewerage Department. As a result of this change, lead leached from pipes and fixtures into the drinking water and more than 8,000 of the city's children were exposed to toxic lead.[128]

Of all environmental contaminants, exposure to lead is the one that has been linked most often to antisocial behaviors on both the individual and group levels.[129] Recent research shows that almost any elevated level of lead ingestion is related to lower IQ scores, a factor linked to aggressive behavior.[130] There is also evidence linking lead exposure to mental illnesses, such as schizophrenia, which have been linked to antisocial behaviors.[131] Young children with high levels of lead in their blood later display antisocial behavioral symptoms such as externalizing (acting-out) behaviors and school problems.[132]

Research also shows that lead effects may actually begin in the womb due to the mother's dietary consumption of foods, such as seafood, that are high in lead content.[133] Improved prenatal care may help mothers avoid the danger of lead exposure and reduce long-term crime rates.

Scientists at the Centers for Disease Control and Prevention (CDC) have issued strong warnings about the presence of lead in the environment. They estimate that at least 4 million households have children who are being exposed to high levels of lead. There are approximately half a million US children ages 1 to 5 with blood-lead levels above the reference level at which the CDC recommends public health actions be initiated (5 micrograms per deciliter (μg/dL).[134]

Diet and Delinquency   There is also evidence that diet may influence behavior through its impact on body chemistry. Of particular concern is an unusually high intake of such items as artificial food coloring, milk, and sweets. Some scientists believe that chronic under- or oversupply of vitamins, such as C, B3, and B6, may be related to restlessness and antisocial behavior in youths. Evidence also exists that allergies to foods can influence mood and behavior, resulting in personality swings between hyperactivity and depression.[135]

Research conducted in the United States and abroad has linked youth violence and misbehavior to dietary intake. A number of specific food products have been linked to antisocial behaviors, such as the omega-6 fats found in corn, safflower, soybean, cottonseed, and sunflower oils. National Institutes of Health scientists have found that the murder rate is 20 times higher in countries with the highest omega-6 intake, compared with those with the lowest.

Not only does diet affect kids during their lifetime, but their mother's prenatal diet may also be equally influential. Take for instance the consumption of seafood, a major source of omega-3 fatty acids, which are essential for early brain development. It has been suspected that because contemporary Western diets often contain too little of these nutrients, this flaw in maternal diet during pregnancy may impede child development later in life.[136]

Biochemical research has linked diet to behavior. Excessive intake of certain substances, such as sugar, and the lack of proper vitamins and proteins have been tied to aggression and antisocial behaviors. Considering this connection, should teen diets be closely monitored?

Are the effects of diet on delinquent behavior long lasting? To find out, Adrian Raine and his colleagues charted the long-term effects of a two-year diet enrichment program for 3-year-olds in the African nation of Mauritania. One hundred randomly selected children were placed in a program providing them with nutritious lunches, physical exercise, and enhanced education. They were then compared with a control group made up of children who did not participate in the program. By age 17, kids who had been malnourished before they entered the nutrition program had higher scores on physical and psychological well-being than malnourished kids who had not been in the program. By age 23, the malnourished kids who had been in the program 20 years earlier still did better on personality tests and had lower levels of self-reported crimes than the malnourished children who had not been placed in the program. Overall, the results showed that providing children with nutritious diets and enriched environments is associated with greater mental health and reduced antisocial activities later in life.[137]

Though more research is needed before the scientific community reaches a consensus on the specific association between diet and crime, there is mounting evidence that vitamins, minerals, chemicals, and other nutrients from a diet rich in fruits, vegetables, and whole grains can improve brain function, basic intelligence, and academic performance. In contrast, those lacking in proper diet seem at greatest risk to crime and delinquency.

It is also possible that a poor diet is indirectly related to antisocial activity. For example, **attention deficit hyperactivity disorder (ADHD)** has been linked to delinquency and its cause may be diet driven. Specific foods linked to a higher rate of ADHD included fast foods, processed meats, red meat, high-fat dairy products, and candy.[138]

attention deficit hyperactivity disorder (ADHD)
A disorder in which a child shows a developmentally inappropriate lack of attention, impulsivity, and hyperactivity.

Hormonal Levels   Another area of biochemical research is concerned with hormonal levels. Antisocial behavior allegedly peaks in the teenage years because hormonal activity is at its highest level during this period. Research suggests that increased levels of the male androgen testosterone are responsible for excessive levels of violence among teenage boys.[139]

Adolescents who experience more intense moods, mood swings, anxiety, and restlessness than people at other points in development also have the highest crime rates.[140] These mood and behavior changes have been associated with family conflict and antisocial behavior.

A number of biosocial theorists are now evaluating the association between criminal activities ranging from fraud to violent behavior episodes and hormone levels.[141] An association between hormonal activity and antisocial behavior is suggested because rates of both factors peak in adolescence.[142] Hormonal sensitivity may begin at the very early stages of life when the fetus can be exposed to abnormally high levels of testosterone while in the uterus. This may trigger a heightened response to the release of testosterone when an adolescent male reaches puberty. Although testosterone levels appear normal, the young male is at risk for overaggressive behavior responses.

Hormonal activity as an explanation of gender differences in the delinquency crime rate will be discussed further in Chapter 7.

Neurological Dysfunction

neurological
Pertaining to the brain and nervous system structure.

minimal brain dysfunction (MBD)
Damage to the brain itself that causes antisocial behavior injurious to the individual's lifestyle and social adjustment.

Another focus of biosocial theory is the **neurological**—or brain and nervous system—structure of offenders. It has been suggested that children who manifest behavioral disturbances may have neurological deficits, such as damage to the hemispheres of the brain; this is sometimes referred to as **minimal brain dysfunction (MBD)**.[143] Impairment in brain functioning may be present at birth, produced by factors such as low birthweight, brain injury during pregnancy, birth complications, and inherited abnormalities. Brain injuries can also occur later in life as a result of brutal beatings or sexual abuse by a parent and can actually cause adverse physical changes in the brain. These deformities can lead to depression, anxiety, and other serious emotional conditions.[144] Regardless of its cause, the association between crime and neurological impairment is quite striking: about 20 percent of known offenders report some type of traumatic brain injury and suffer from a number of antisocial traits throughout their life course.[145]

Teenage Brains Is there something about teenage brains that make their owners crime prone? There is evidence that aggressive teen behavior may be linked to the amygdala, an area of the brain that processes information regarding threats and fear, and to a lessening of activity in the frontal lobe, a brain region associated with decision making and impulse control.

Research psychiatrist Guido Frank investigated why some teenagers are more prone than others to "reactive" aggression—that is, unpremeditated aggression in response to a trigger (for instance, an accidental bump from a passerby). He found that reactively aggressive adolescents—most commonly boys—frequently misinterpret their surroundings, feel threatened, and act inappropriately aggressive. They tend to strike back when being teased, blame others when getting into a fight, and overreact to accidents. Their behavior is emotionally "hot," defensive, and impulsive; teens with this behavior are at high risk for lifelong social, career, or legal problems.

Frank's research helps explain what goes on in the brains of some teenage boys who respond with inappropriate anger and aggression to perceived threats. It is possible that rather than having a social or environmental basis, such behavior is associated with brain functioning and not environment, socialization, personality, or other social and psychological functions.[146]

Another research study examining the relationship between brain structure and delinquency was conducted by Graeme Fairchild and colleagues with 25 girls between the ages of 14 and 18 who exhibited antisocial and/or violent behavior.[147] The study compared them with 30 girls with no history of violent behavior. Fairchild found that participants with a history of violence had major difficulties controlling their temper, lashing out and breaking things around their homes when they got angry, and had often been involved in serious fights. Fairchild and his team evaluated the girls' ability to recognize six facial expressions: anger, disgust, sadness, fear, surprise, and happiness. They found that the violent or antisocial girls were significantly impaired in identifying anger and disgust. Fairchild's findings suggest that antisocial behavior or violence may not simply reflect bad choices but that, at some level, the brains of individuals with antisocial behavior may work differently. This might make it harder for them to read emotions in others—particularly to realize that someone is angry with them—and to learn from punishment. Fairchild notes that the facial recognition deficits of the violent girls resemble the deficits seen in boys with childhood-onset conduct disorder. However, the girls' violent behavior began in their teenage years rather than in childhood, suggesting differences in antisocial behavior between girls and boys, with girls being protected from showing antisocial behavior until their teenage years.

The Long-Term Effects of Neurological Trauma   Children who suffer from measurable neurological deficits at birth also may experience a number of antisocial traits throughout their life course. Such damage can lead to reduction in executive functioning (EF), a condition that refers to impairment of the cognitive processes that facilitate the planning and regulation of goal-oriented behavior. An extensive meta-analysis conducted by James Ogilvie and his associates found that antisocial groups performed significantly worse on measures of EF compared with controls.[148] Impairments in EF have been implicated in a range of developmental disorders, including ADHD, conduct disorder (CD), autism, and Tourette syndrome. EF impairments also have been implicated in a range of neuropsychiatric and medical disorders, including schizophrenia, major depression, alcoholism, and structural brain disease; research has even linked this type of deficit to becoming a habitual liar.[149]

There is also a suspected link between brain dysfunction and **conduct disorder (CD)**, considered a precursor of long-term chronic offending. Children with CD lie, steal, bully other children, frequently get into fights, and break schools' and parents' rules; many are callous and lack empathy and/or guilt.[150] Children suffering from one form of CD, antisocial substance disorder (ASD), have been found to repeatedly engage in risky antisocial and drug-using behaviors. Research has linked this behavior with misfiring in particular areas of the brain and suppressed neural activity.[151] Conduct disorder will be discussed more fully later in the chapter.

Supporting Research   A number of research efforts have attempted to substantiate a link between neurological impairment and crime. There is evidence that this relationship can be detected quite early and that children who suffer from measurable neurological deficits at birth are more likely to become criminals later in life.[152] Measurement of the brain activity of antisocial youths has revealed impairments that might cause them to experience otherwise unexplainable outbursts of anger, hostility, and aggression. Evidence has been found linking brain damage to mental disorders such as schizophrenia and depression.[153] Cross-national studies also support a link between neurological dysfunction and antisocial behavior.[154]

Clinical analysis of convicted murderers has found that a significant number had suffered head injuries as children, and this resulted in neurological impairment.[155] Not surprisingly, studies of death row inmates found that a significant number had suffered head injuries as children, resulting in damage to their central nervous system and neurological impairment.[156]

Researchers have used the electroencephalogram to measure the brain waves and activity of delinquents and then compared them with those of law-abiding adolescents. Behaviors believed to be highly correlated with abnormal EEG functions include poor impulse control, inadequate social ability, hostility, temper tantrums, destructiveness, and hyperactivity.[157]

conduct disorder (CD)
A disorder of childhood and adolescence that involves chronic behavior problems, such as defiant, impulsive, or antisocial behavior and substance abuse.

Learning Disabilities   One specific type of MBD that has generated considerable interest is **learning disability (LD)**, a term that has been defined by the National Advisory Committee on Handicapped Children:

Children with special learning disabilities exhibit a disorder in one or more of the basic psychological processes involved in understanding or using spoken or written languages. They may be manifested in disorders of listening, thinking, talking, reading, writing, or arithmetic. They include conditions which have been referred to as perceptual handicaps, brain injury, minimal brain dysfunction, dyslexia, developmental aphasia, etc. They do not include learning problems which are due to visual, hearing, or motor handicaps, to mental retardation, emotional disturbance, or to environmental disadvantages.[158]

Learning-disabled kids usually exhibit poor motor coordination (such as problems with poor hand/eye coordination, trouble climbing stairs, clumsiness), have behavior problems (lack of emotional control, hostility, cannot stay on task), and have improper auditory and vocal responses (do not seem to hear, cannot differentiate sounds and noises).

The relationship between learning disabilities and delinquency has been highlighted by studies showing that arrested and incarcerated children have a far higher LD rate than children in the general population.[159]

Typically, there are two possible explanations of the link between learning disabilities and delinquency.[160] One view, known as the *susceptibility rationale*, argues that the link is caused by certain side effects of learning disabilities, such as impulsiveness, ADHD, poor ability to learn from experience, and inability to take social cues. As a result, LD kids may be more aggressive and more likely to engage in violent episodes than non-LD youth.[161] In contrast, the *school failure rationale* assumes that the frustration caused by the LD child's poor school performance will lead to a negative self-image and acting-out behavior.

Because of social bias, LD kids are more likely to get arrested, and if petitioned to juvenile court, their poor school record can influence the outcome of the case. LD youths bring with them to court a record of school problems and low grades and a history of frustrating efforts by agents of the educational system to provide meaningful assistance. Adolescents becoming formally involved with the juvenile justice system because of school-related behavior and discipline problems is referred to as the "school-to-prison pipeline." In his study of the pipeline, Christopher Mallett found that adolescents with learning disabilities are disproportionately represented within this pipeline. Youthful offenders with learning disabilities, when compared with nondisabled youthful offenders, were more likely to be suspended from school, were adjudicated delinquent at younger ages, and were more frequently held in detention centers. These outcomes are all risk factors for ongoing delinquent behaviors and aptly illustrate the school-to-prison pipeline.[162]

Attention Deficit Hyperactivity Disorder (ADHD)   Many parents have noticed that their children do not pay attention to them—they run around and do things in their own way. Sometimes this inattention is a function of age; in other instances, it is a symptom of attention deficit hyperactivity disorder (ADHD), in which a child shows a developmentally inappropriate lack of attention, impulsivity, and hyperactivity. ADHD has various symptoms:

- Lack of attention
  - Frequently fails to finish projects
  - Does not seem to pay attention
  - Does not sustain interest in play activities
  - Cannot sustain concentration on schoolwork or related tasks
  - Is easily distracted
- Impulsivity
  - Frequently acts without thinking
  - Often calls out in class

- Does not want to wait his or her turn
- Shifts from activity to activity
- Cannot organize tasks or work
- Requires constant supervision in line or games

■ Hyperactivity

- Constantly runs around and climbs on things
- Shows excessive motor activity while asleep
- Cannot sit still; is constantly fidgeting
- Does not remain in his or her seat in class
- Is constantly on the go like a "motor"
- Has difficulty regulating emotions
- Has difficulty getting started
- Has difficulty staying on track
- Has difficulty adjusting to social demands

About 14 percent of US boys and 6 percent of girls have been diagnosed with this disorder, and it is the most common reason children are referred to mental health clinics.[163] The accompanying Case Profile focuses on the problems associated with ADHD.

ADHD has been associated with poor school performance, grade retention, placement in special needs classes, bullying, stubbornness, and lack of response to discipline. Although the origin of ADHD is still unknown, suspected causes include neurological damage, prenatal stress, and even reactions to food additives and chemical allergies. Some psychologists believe that the syndrome is essentially a chemical problem—specifically, an impairment in the chemical system that supports rapid and efficient communication in the brain's management system.[164]

There are also ties to family turmoil: parents of ADHD children are more likely to be divorced or separated, and ADHD children are much more likely to move to new locales than non-ADHD children.[165] It may be possible that emotional turmoil either produces symptoms of ADHD or, if they already exist, causes them to intensify.

A series of research studies now links ADHD to the onset and sustenance of a delinquent career.[166] One analysis of data on nearly 14,000 individuals participating in the National Longitudinal Study of Adolescent Health found that children with ADHD are at a heightened risk for criminality as adults. The data showed that participants with the inattentive type of ADHD were 6.5 percent more likely to commit a crime than their non-ADHD peers, while those with impulsive symptoms were 11 percent more likely, and those with a combination of inattention and hyperactivity were 5 percent more likely to report participating in criminal activities as young adults.[167] It is not surprising, then, that children with ADHD are more likely than non-ADHD youths to use illicit drugs, alcohol, and cigarettes in adolescence, be arrested, be charged with a felony, have multiple arrests, and be sent to prison.[168]

In addition to adolescent misbehavior, hyperactive ADHD children are at greater risk for antisocial activity and drug use/abuse that persists into adulthood.[169] Many ADHD children also suffer from CD and continually engage in aggressive and antisocial behavior in early childhood. The disorders are sustained over the life course: children diagnosed as ADHD are more likely to be suspended from school and engage in criminal behavior as adults.[170]

While the association between ADHD and delinquent behavior has been empirically shown, the actual path has been debated. One view is that the association is direct and that hyperactivity leads to aggressive antisocial behaviors.[171] Others view the association as being more indirect: hyperactivity results in poor school achievement; school failure leads to substance abuse and depression, conditions that have long been associated with the onset of antisocial behaviors.[172]

case profile

Timothy's Story

TIMOTHY was a 13-year-old biracial male residing with his mother and younger sister. His biological father was not involved in his life, and there was a history of domestic violence with his mother's subsequent partners. There was also a family history of mental illness, criminal activity, child abuse, and poverty. Despite living in multiple homes and his family experiencing homelessness for periods of time, Timothy had attended the same school for the past three years due to an agreement with his school district; consequently, school staff knew him well. Although his teachers reported that Timothy was a bright child, his grades were poor and attendance was inconsistent. His school records indicated that, historically, he was a very good student with minimal behavioral problems. It was noted that other children picked on Timothy and viewed him as a "nerdy" child. Subsequently, Timothy was referred to his school social worker during his eighth-grade school year for emerging behaviors related to his bullying of other youths. He had harassed other students by texting and using social media websites to spread rumors. There was significant concern that he was at risk for increased police contact and possible delinquency charges, although none had been filed.

After identifying Timothy as a student at risk, school staff worked with him to find a program that would meet his needs. A comprehensive mental health assessment determined that he was struggling with some issues related to an undiagnosed attention deficit hyperactivity disorder. Despite this diagnosis, Timothy's mother was against the use of medications. Given her own history, she was also very uncomfortable with any type of mental health involvement. She reported that she had been treated poorly and did not trust any professional assistance.

The community social worker worked diligently to establish a strong and trusting relationship with both Timothy and his mother. The social worker helped the family find more permanent housing and provided opportunities for the mother to better meet the children's basic needs. Eventually Timothy's mother agreed to the medication and service recommendations, and Timothy was able to focus on school and gain a better understanding of his behavioral consequences.

Timothy was accepted into a community program that had a strong focus on working with young people who have the potential to go to college and may need additional supports. He began a four-year pre-college technology access and training program for talented students of color and economically disadvantaged students. The program's mission was to prepare students for technical, academic, and personal excellence. Timothy was provided with training, mentoring, leadership development, community service, and internship opportunities.

Timothy thrived in the program and today is a successful member of his community. He is employed and attending college. Timothy had no further issues related to bullying and was never involved in the juvenile justice system. He remains in contact with the program and the social worker who assisted him and his family.

CRITICAL THINKING

Should a disorder such as ADHD excuse people from responsibility if they get involved with delinquent behavior? Should they be treated rather than punished?

The **National Center for Learning Disabilities** (http://www.ncld.org/) provides national leadership in support of children and adults with learning disabilities.

How is ADHD treated? Behavior therapy techniques are routinely used (see Exhibit 3.1). Another typical treatment is doses of stimulants, such as Adderall and Ritalin, which, ironically, help control emotional and behavioral outbursts. Other therapies, such as altering diet and food intake, are being investigated.[173] However, treatment is not always effective. Though some treated children with ADHD improve, many do not and continue to show a greater occurrence of externalizing (acting-out) behaviors and significant deficits in areas such as social skills, peer relations, and academic performance over the life course. They are more likely to require social services such as special education, tutoring, or psychotherapy.[174]

Arousal Theory   It has long been suspected that obtaining "thrills" is a motivator of crime. Adolescents may engage in such crimes as shoplifting and vandalism simply because they offer the attraction of getting away with it; delinquency is a thrilling demonstration of personal competence.[175] Is it possible that thrill seekers are people who have some form of abnormal brain functioning that directs their behavior?

arousal theorists
Delinquency experts who believe that aggression is a function of the level of an individual's need for stimulation or arousal from the environment. Those who require more stimulation may act in an aggressive manner to meet their needs.

Arousal theorists believe that, for a variety of genetic and environmental reasons, some people's brains function differently in response to environmental stimuli. All of us seek to maintain a preferred or optimal level of arousal: too much

How Behavior Therapy Is Used to Treat ADHD

Research shows that behavior therapy is an important part of treatment for children with ADHD. ADHD affects not only a child's ability to pay attention or sit still at school, but it also affects relationships with family and other children. Children with ADHD often show behaviors that can be very disruptive to others. Behavior therapy is a treatment option that can help reduce these behaviors. It is often helpful to start behavior therapy as soon as a diagnosis is made.

The goals of behavior therapy are to learn or strengthen positive behaviors and eliminate unwanted or problem behaviors. Behavior therapy can include behavior therapy training for parents, behavior therapy with children, or a combination. Teachers can also use behavior therapy to help reduce problem behaviors in the classroom.

In parent training in behavior therapy, parents learn new skills or strengthen their existing skills to teach and guide their children and to manage their behavior. Parent training in behavior therapy has been shown to strengthen the relationship between the parent and child, and to decrease children's negative or problem behaviors. Parent training in behavior therapy is also known as behavior management training for parents, parent behavior therapy, behavioral parent training, or just parent training.

In behavior therapy with children, the therapist works with the child to learn new behaviors to replace behaviors that don't work or cause problems. The therapist may also help the child learn to express feelings in ways that do not create problems for the child or other people.

SOURCE: Division of Human Development and Disability, National Center on Birth Defects and Developmental Disabilities, Centers for Disease Control and Prevention, August 11, 2016, http://www.cdc.gov/ncbddd/adhd /treatment.html (accessed September 2016).

stimulation leaves us anxious and stressed out; too little makes us feel bored and weary. There is, however, variation in the way children's brains process sensory input. Some nearly always feel comfortable with little stimulation, while others require a high degree of environmental input to feel comfortable. The latter group become "sensation seekers" who seek stimulating activities that may include aggressive, violent behavior patterns.[176] Youths seeking arousal may be impulsive and lacking in self-control, traits that have been identified with high levels of delinquent and criminal behaviors.[177]

The factors that determine a person's level of arousal have not been fully explained. Suspected sources include brain chemistry (for example, serotonin levels) and brain structure.[178] The number of nerve cells with receptor sites for neurotransmitters in the brain differs among people; some have many more than others. Another view is that adolescents with low heart rates are more likely to commit crimes because they seek stimulation to increase their arousal levels to normal.[179]

Some people need the excitement of crime to feel good and normal. Alyssa Bustamante is shown with her attorney, Gary Brotherton, at the Cole County Circuit Court in Jefferson City, Missouri. Bustamante pleaded guilty to second-degree murder charges in the death of 9-year-old Elizabeth Olten. Just 15 at the time of the murder, she wrote in her diary, "I just f***ing killed someone. I strangled them and slit their throat and stabbed them now they're dead. I don't know how to feel atm [at the moment], was ahmazing. As soon as you get over the 'ohmygawd I can't do this' feeling, it's pretty enjoyable. I'm kinda nervous and shaky though right now. Kay, I gotta go to church now…lol." Bustamante was given a life sentence with the possibility of parole.

AP Images/Julie Smith

Genetic Influences

Individuals who share genes are alike in personality regardless of how they are reared, whereas rearing environment induces little or no personality resemblance.[180]

Biosocial theorists also study the genetic makeup of delinquents.[181] The genes–crime association may be either direct or indirect. According to the direct view, (1) antisocial behavior is inherited, (2) the genetic makeup of parents is passed on to children, and (3) genetic abnormality is directly linked to a variety of antisocial behaviors.[182] For example, Ronald Simons and his associates found that adolescent genetic makeup is directly linked to an aggressive response to provocation.[183] It is also possible that the association is indirect: genes are related to some personality or physical traits that are also linked to antisocial behavior.[184] For example, genetic makeup may shape friendship patterns and orient people toward deviant peer associations; interacting with delinquent peers has been linked to antisocial behaviors.[185] Adolescent attachment to parents may be controlled by their genetic makeup; attachment that is weak and attenuated has been linked to criminality.[186]

It has been hypothesized that youths, both males and females, maintain a heritable genetic configuration that predisposes them to delinquent behaviors.[187] Biosocial theorists believe that in the same way that genes for height and eye color are inherited, antisocial behavior characteristics and mental disorders may be passed down from one generation to the next.

Parent–Child Similarities   If antisocial tendencies are inherited, the children of criminal parents should be more likely to become law violators than the offspring of conventional parents. A number of studies have found that parental criminality and deviance do, in fact, powerfully influence delinquent behavior.[188] For example, there is a significant relationship between parent and child suicide attempts.[189] Some of the most important data on parental deviance were gathered by Donald J. West and David P. Farrington as part of the long-term Cambridge Youth Survey. These cohort data indicate that a significant number of delinquent youths have criminal fathers.[190] However, 8 percent of the sons of noncriminal fathers eventually became chronic offenders, about 37 percent of youths with criminal fathers were multiple offenders.[191] In another analysis, Farrington found that one type of parental deviance, school yard aggression or bullying, may be both inter- and intragenerational. Bullies have children who bully others, and these second-generation bullies grow up to father children who are also bullies, in a never-ending cycle.[192]

Farrington's findings are supported by research data from the Rochester Youth Development Study (RYDS), a longitudinal analysis that has been monitoring the behavior of 1,000 area youths since 1988. RYDS researchers have also found an intergenerational continuity in antisocial behavior: criminal fathers produce delinquent sons who grow up to have delinquent children themselves.[193] It is possible that at least part of the association is genetic.[194]

Sibling Similarities   It stands to reason that if the cause of crime is in part genetic, the behavior of siblings should be similar because they share genetic material. Research does show that if one sibling engages in antisocial behavior, so do his/her brothers and sisters; the effect is greatest among same-sex siblings.[195] Sibling pairs who report warm, mutual relationships and share friends are the most likely to behave in a similar fashion, including drug abuse and delinquency.[196]

While the similarity of siblings' behavior seems striking, what appears to be a genetic effect may also be explained by other factors:

- Siblings who live in the same environment are influenced by similar social and economic factors.

- Deviant siblings may grow closer because of shared interests.

- Younger siblings who admire their older siblings may imitate the elders' behavior.

- The deviant sibling forces or threatens the brother or sister into committing delinquent acts.

- Siblings living in a similar environment may develop similar types of friends; it is peer behavior that is the critical influence.[197]

While these limitations need to be further explored, the research evidence seems to show a concordance of behavior in siblings that cannot be explained by environmental factors, that delinquency and crime runs in families, and that a few families with shared genetic traits account for a significant amount of all criminal and delinquent behaviors.[198]

Twin Similarities To control for environmental effects, biosocial theorists have compared the behavior of twins and non-twin siblings and found that the twins, who share more genetic material, are also more similar in their behavior. This indicates that it is heredity and not environment that controls behavior.[199] Recent twin studies have found a highly significant association in childhood antisocial and aggressive behaviors, including conduct disorder, ratings of aggression, delinquency, and psychopathic traits, a finding that supports a genetic basis to antisocial behavior.[200]

An even more rigorous test of genetic theory involves comparison of the behavior of identical monozygotic (MZ) twins with same-sex fraternal dizygotic (DZ) twins; although the former have an identical genetic makeup, the latter share only about 50 percent of their genetic combinations. Research has shown that MZ twins are significantly closer in their personal characteristics, such as intelligence, than are DZ twins.[201] Other relevant findings include:

- There is a significantly higher risk for suicidal behavior among MZ twin pairs than DZ twin pairs.[202]

- Differences between MZ and DZ twins have been found in tests measuring psychological dysfunctions, such as conduct disorders, impulsivity, and antisocial behavior.[203]

- MZ twins are closer than DZ twins in level of aggression and verbal skills.[204]

- Both members of MZ twin pairs who suffer child abuse are more likely to engage in later antisocial activity than DZ pairs.[205]

- Callous, unemotional traits in very young children can be a warning sign for future psychopathy and antisocial behavior. MZ twin pairs are more likely to be similar in levels of callous, unemotional behavior than DZ pairs.[206]

One famous study of twin behavior still under way is the Minnesota Study of Twins Reared Apart (also called the Minnesota Twin Family Study). This research compares the behavior of MZ and DZ twin pairs who were raised together with the behavior of twins who were separated at birth and in some cases did not even know of each other's existence. The study shows some striking similarities in behavior and ability for twin pairs raised apart. An MZ twin reared away from a co-twin has about as good a chance of being similar to the co-twin in terms of personality, interests, and attitudes as one who has been reared with his or her co-twin. The conclusion: Similarities between twins are due to genes, not the environment. Because twins reared apart are so similar, the environment, if it influences them at all, makes them different (see Exhibit 3.2).[207]

Adoption Studies Another way to determine whether delinquency is an inherited trait is to compare the behavior of adopted children with that of their biological parents. If the criminal behavior of children is more like that of their biological parents (whom they have never met) than that of their adoptive parents (who brought them up), it would indicate that the tendency toward delinquency is inherited, rather than shaped by the environment.

Studies of this kind have generally supported the hypothesis that there is a link between genetics and behavior.[208] Adoptees share many of the behavioral

exhibit 3.2

Findings from the Minnesota Study of Twins Reared Apart

■ MZ (identical) twins become more similar with respect to abilities such as vocabularies and arithmetic scores as they age. As DZ (fraternal) twins get older they become less similar with respect to vocabularies and arithmetic scores.

■ MZ twin children have very similar brain wave patterns. By comparison, DZ twins do not show as much similarity. These results indicate that the way the brain processes information may be greatly influenced by genes.

■ An EEG is a measure of brain activity or brain waves that can be used to monitor a person's state of arousal. MZ twins tend to produce strikingly similar EEG spectra; DZ twins show far less similarity.

■ MZ twins tend to have more similar ages at the time of death than DZ twins do. That is, MZ twins are more likely to die at about the same age, and DZ twins are more likely to die at different ages.

SOURCE: Used by permission of the Minnesota Center for Twin and Family Research.

and intellectual characteristics of their biological parents despite the social and environmental conditions found in their adoptive homes. For example, biological parents of adopted hyperactive children are more likely to show symptoms of hyperactivity than are the adoptive parents; although not all hyperactive children become delinquent, a link has long been suspected.[209] Adoptees have been found to be more likely to get involved in criminality if their biological parent has also displayed a history of antisocial behaviors; the behavior of the biological parent may have a greater influence than that of the adoptive parent.[210]

The Association Between Inherited Traits and Delinquency

Even if an association between inherited traits and delinquency can be demonstrated, its direction remains somewhat hazy. The relationship between inherited traits and delinquency may be either direct or indirect.

Direct Association   Possessing a particular genetic structure makes a person prone to aggression, violence, and antisocial behavior.[211] Regardless of environmental influences, kids with a particular genetic code are the ones most likely to get involved in antisocial behaviors. This explains antisocial behavior among upper-class youth, some of whom may be the product of a damaged genetic package. It also accounts for the fact that the majority of the poor and desperate are still neither violent nor delinquency prone. Since the environment plays only a secondary role in the production of deviant behaviors, it is heredity and not social forces that produces delinquency.

Indirect Association   Some kids possess inherited traits that make them prone to antisocial behavior. For example, psychopathy, impulsivity, and neuroticism have been found to be heritable; these conditions are also associated with delinquency.[212] Genetics may also shape family relationships, and the quality of parent–child relationships is related to antisocial behaviors.[213]

Connecting delinquent behavior to heredity is quite controversial because it implies that the cause of delinquency is (a) present at birth, (b) "transmitted" from one generation to the next, and (c) cannot be easily changed (because genes cannot be altered). Nor does it help that existing research has been inconclusive. Even the most methodologically sophisticated research using identical twin pairs must be interpreted with caution. If the behavior similarities between MZ twins are greater than those between DZ twins, the association may be explained by environmental rather than genetic factors: MZ twins are more likely to look alike and to share physical traits than DZ twins, and they are more likely to be treated similarly, so any correspondence in behavior may be a function of socialization and/or environment and not heredity.[214]

Is There a Genetic Basis for Delinquency?

There are few more controversial topics than the assertion that delinquency is caused by some inherited traits. There would be little point to spending on educational or vocational treatment if delinquency is caused by some genetic anomaly that is immune to such measures. Critics of genetic theory believe that even if there is some evidence that delinquency is inherited, the social environment plays a more critical role in shaping behavior than genes and heredity, especially during the critical periods of childhood and adolescence. One take on the association is that the environment shapes biological processes; as environmental conditions change, so do the brain and nervous system. Adverse, dangerous, and negative environments sculpt or change an individual's brain functioning, causing them to respond to environmental events with aggression, violence, and coercion.[215] Thus, if antisocial behavior is shaped at the genetic level, it's because environmental factors influence biological functioning and not because delinquent and antisocial tendencies are inherited.[216] Of course, not all genetic advocates are willing to abandon their view that behavior is inherited.

It is also possible that what appears to be a genetic connection can be explained by what is referred to as the **contagion effect**: kids copy both conventional and antisocial behavior of siblings.[217] Because the relationship between identical twins is extremely close, the contagion effect may be stronger than with other sibling pairs. And because the relationship is enduring, if one twin is antisocial, it legitimizes and supports the criminal behavior of his or her co-twin into adulthood.[218] Needless to say, the debate over the heritability of delinquent tendencies remains an open issue.

contagion effect
Delinquency spreads when kids copy the behavior of peers and siblings.

Evolutionary Theory

Some theorists have speculated that the human traits producing violence and aggression have been nurtured and produced through the long process of human evolution.[219] According to this **evolutionary theory**, the competition for scarce resources has influenced and shaped the human species.[220] Over the course of human existence, people have been shaped to engage in actions that promote their well-being and ensure the survival and reproduction of their genetic line. Males who are impulsive risk takers may be able to father more children; impulsive behavior is inherited and becomes intergenerational. It is not surprising that human history has been marked by war, violence, and aggression.

Crime rate differences between the genders, then, are less a matter of socialization than inherent differences in the mating patterns that have developed between the sexes over time.[221] Among young men, reckless, life-threatening "risk-proneness" is especially likely to evolve in societies where choosing not to compete means the inability to find suitable mates and to reproduce.[222] Aggressive males have had the greatest impact on the gene pool. The descendants of these aggressive males now account for the disproportionate amount of male aggression and violence.[223]

This evolutionary model suggests that a subpopulation of men has evolved with genes that incline them toward extremely low parental involvement. Sexually aggressive, they use their cunning to gain sexual conquests with as many females as possible. Because females would not willingly choose them as mates, they use stealth to gain sexual access—cheating—including such tactics as mimicking the behavior of more stable males.[224] Psychologist Byron Roth notes that these flamboyant, sexually aggressive males are especially attractive to younger, less intelligent women who begin having children at a very early age.[225] Their fleeting courtship process produces children with low IQs, aggressive personalities, and little chance of proper socialization in father-absent families. Because the criminal justice system treats them leniently, argues Roth, sexually irresponsible men are free to prey upon young girls. Over time, their offspring will yield an ever-expanding supply of offspring who are both antisocial and sexually aggressive.

Concept Summary 3.2 offers a summary of the major biosocial theories of delinquency.

evolutionary theory
Explaining the existence of aggression and violent behavior as positive adaptive behaviors in human evolution; these traits allowed their bearers to reproduce disproportionately, which has had an effect on the human gene pool.

Biosocial Theories

Biochemical	**Premise**	Crime, especially violence, is a function of diet, vitamin intake, hormonal imbalance, and/or food allergies.
	Strengths	Explains irrational violence. Shows how the environment interacts with personal traits to influence behavior.
Neurological	**Premise**	Criminals and delinquents often suffer brain impairment, as measured by the EEG. Learning disabilities such as attention deficit hyperactivity disorder and minimum brain dysfunction are related to antisocial behavior.
	Strengths	Helps explain relationship between child abuse and crime, and why there is a relationship between victimization and violence (e.g., people who suffer head trauma may become violent).
Genetic	**Premise**	Delinquent traits and predispositions are inherited. Criminality of parents can predict the delinquency of children.
	Strengths	Explains why only a small percentage of youths in a high-crime area become chronic offenders.
Evolutionary	**Premise**	Behavior patterns and reproductive traits, developed over the millennia, control behavior.
	Strengths	Explains male aggressiveness. Helps us understand why violence is so common.

Psychological Theories of Delinquency

Some experts view the cause of delinquency as essentially psychological.[226] After all, most behaviors labeled delinquent—violence, theft, sexual misconduct—seem to be symptomatic of some underlying psychological problem. Psychologists point out that many delinquent youths have poor home lives, destructive relationships with neighbors, friends, and teachers, and conflicts with authority figures in general. These relationships seem to indicate a disturbed personality structure. Furthermore, numerous studies of incarcerated youths indicate that the youths' personalities are marked by negative, antisocial behavior characteristics. And because delinquent behavior occurs among youths in every racial, ethnic, and socioeconomic group, psychologists view it as a function of emotional and mental disturbance, rather than purely a result of social factors, such as racism, poverty, and class conflict. Although many delinquents do not manifest significant psychological problems, enough do to give clinicians a powerful influence on delinquency theory.

Because psychology is a complex and diversified discipline, more than one psychological perspective on crime exists. Three prominent psychological perspectives on delinquency are the psychodynamic, the behavioral, and the cognitive.[227]

Psychodynamic Theory

psychodynamic theory
Branch of psychology that holds that the human personality is controlled by unconscious mental processes developed early in childhood.

According to **psychodynamic theory**, whose basis is the pioneering work of the Austrian physician Sigmund Freud (1856–1939), law violations are a product of an abnormal personality structure formed early in life and which thereafter controls human behavior choices.[228] In extreme cases, mental torment drives people into violence and aggression. The basis of psychodynamic theory is the assumption that human behavior is controlled by unconscious mental processes developed early in childhood.

According to Freud, the human personality contains three major components. The *id* is the unrestrained, primitive, pleasure-seeking component with which each child is born. The *ego* develops through the reality of living in the world and helps manage and restrain the id's need for immediate gratification. The *superego* develops through interactions with parents and other significant people and represents the development of conscience and the moral rules shared by most adults.

Unconscious motivations for behavior come from the id's action in response to two primal needs—sex and aggression. Human behavior is often marked by symbolic actions that reflect hidden feelings about these needs. For example, stealing a car may reflect a person's unconscious need for shelter and mobility to escape from hostile enemies (aggression) or perhaps an urge to enter a closed, dark, womblike structure that reflects the earliest memories (sex).

All three segments of the personality operate simultaneously. The id dictates needs and desires, the superego counteracts the id by fostering feelings of morality and righteousness, and the ego evaluates the reality of a position between these two extremes. If these components are properly balanced, the individual can lead a normal life. If one aspect of the personality becomes dominant at the expense of the others, the individual exhibits abnormal personality traits (see Figure 3.2).

A number of psychologists and psychiatrists expanded upon Freud's original model to explain the onset of antisocial behaviors. Erik Erikson speculated that many adolescents experience a life crisis in which they feel emotional, impulsive, and uncertain of their role and purpose.[229] He coined the phrase **identity crisis** to denote this period of inner turmoil and confusion. Erikson's approach might characterize the behavior of youthful drug abusers as an expression of confusion over their place in society, their inability to direct behavior toward useful outlets, and perhaps their dependency on others to offer them solutions to their problems.

In his classic work, psychoanalyst August Aichorn found that social stress alone could not produce such an emotional state. He identifies **latent delinquents**—youths whose troubled family life leads them to seek immediate gratification without consideration of right and wrong or the feelings of others.[230] In its most extreme form, delinquency may be viewed as a form of psychosis that prevents delinquent youths from appreciating the feelings of their victims or controlling their own impulsive needs for gratification.

Psychodynamics of Delinquency Applying these concepts, psychodynamic theory holds that youth crime is a result of unresolved mental anguish and internal conflict. Some children, especially those who have been abused or mistreated, may experience unconscious feelings associated with resentment, fear, and hatred. If this conflict cannot be reconciled, the children may regress to a state in which they become id-dominated. This regression may be considered responsible for a great number of mental diseases, and in many cases it may be related to criminal behavior.[231]

Delinquents are id-dominated people who suffer from the inability to control impulsive drives. Perhaps because they suffered unhappy experiences in childhood or had families who could not provide proper love and care, delinquents suffer from weak or damaged egos that make them unable to cope with conventional society.[232] Adolescent antisocial behavior is a consequence of feeling unable to cope with feelings of oppression. Criminality, in fact, allows youths to strive by producing positive psychic results: helping them to feel free and independent; giving them the possibility of excitement and the chance to use their skills and imagination; providing the promise of positive gain; allowing them to blame others

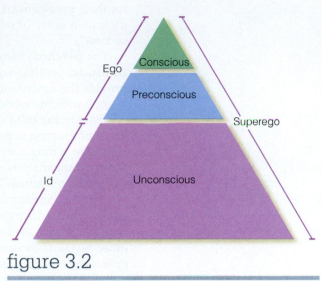

figure 3.2

Structure of the Id, Ego, and Superego

© Cengage Learning 2015

identity crisis
Psychological state, identified by Erikson, in which youth face inner turmoil and uncertainty about life roles.

latent delinquents
Youths whose troubled family life leads them to seek immediate gratification without consideration of right and wrong or the feelings of others.

For biographical material related to **Sigmund Freud and his works**, go to http://www.iep.utm.edu/freud/.

for their predicament (e.g., the police); and giving them a chance to rationalize their own sense of failure ("If I hadn't gotten into trouble, I could have been a success").[233]

The psychodynamic approach places heavy emphasis on the family's role. Antisocial youths frequently come from families in which parents are unable to provide the controls that allow children to develop the personal tools they need to cope with the world.[234] If neglectful parents fail to develop a child's superego adequately, the child's id may become the predominant personality force; the absence of a strong superego results in an inability to distinguish clearly between right and wrong. Destructive behavior may actually be a call for help. In fact, some psychoanalysts view delinquent behaviors as motivated by an unconscious urge to be punished. These children, who feel unloved, assume the reason must be their own inadequacy; hence, they deserve punishment. Later, the youth may demand immediate gratification, lack compassion and sensitivity for the needs of others, disassociate feelings, act aggressively and impulsively, and demonstrate other psychotic symptoms. Antisocial behavior, then, may be the result of conflict or trauma occurring early in a child's development, and delinquent activity may become an outlet for violent and antisocial feelings.

Attachment Theory

attachment theory
A form of psychodynamic tradition that holds that the ability to form attachments—emotional bonds to another person—has important lasting psychological implications that follow adolescents across the life span.

A view most closely associated with psychologist John Bowlby, **attachment theory** is a form of psychodynamic tradition that holds that the ability to form attachments—emotional bonds to another person—has important lasting psychological implications that follow adolescents across the life span. Attachments are formed soon after birth, when infants bond with their mothers. They will become frantic, crying and clinging, to prevent separation or to reestablish contact to a missing parent. Bowlby noted that this behavior is not restricted to humans and occurs in all mammals, indicating that separation anxiety may be instinctual or evolutionary. After all, attachment figures, especially the mother, provide support and care, and without attachment an infant would be helpless and could not survive.[235] Bowlby's most important finding was that to grow up mentally healthy, "the infant and young child should experience a warm, intimate, and continuous relationship with his mother (or permanent mother substitute) in which both find satisfaction and enjoyment."[236]

According to this view, failing to develop proper attachment may cause people to fall prey to a number of psychological disorders. Psychologists believe that children with attachment problems lack trust and respect for others. They often display many psychological symptoms, some that resemble ADHD. They may be impulsive and have difficulty concentrating and consequently experience difficulty in school. As adults, they often have difficulty initiating and sustaining relationships with others and find it difficult to sustain romantic relationships. Psychologists have linked people having detachment problems with a variety of antisocial behaviors, including sexual assault and child abuse.[237] It has been suggested that boys disproportionately experience disrupted attachment and that these disruptions are causally related to disproportionate rates of male offending.[238] Those who are not attached to parents and get little parental support are at risk of engaging in risky sexual behavior and sexual assaults when they hit their teens.[239] There is also evidence that disrupted parental attachment is related to the onset and persistence of substance abuse and misuse.[240]

Mental Disorders and Delinquency

The view that violent delinquent behaviors can be linked to mental disorders seems plausible to most Americans. An entire generation has grown up on films and TV shows that portray violent criminals as mentally deranged and physically abnormal.[241] They are believed to suffer from psychosis, a serious mental disorder characterized by thinking and emotions that indicate that the person has lost contact with reality. Psychotic behavior involves both hallucinations and inappropriate responses. Psychosis takes many forms, the most common being *schizophrenia*, a condition marked by illogical thought processes, distorted perceptions, and abnormal emotional expression. The most serious types of violence and antisocial behavior might be motivated by psychosis.[242]

Of a less serious nature are a variety of mood and/or behavior disorders that render people histrionic, depressed, antisocial, or narcissistic.[243] These **mood disorders** are characterized by disturbance in expressed emotions.[244] Some suffer from **alexithymia**, a deficit in emotional cognition that prevents people from being aware of their feelings or being able to understand or talk about their thoughts and emotions; they seem robotic and emotionally dead.[245] Others may suffer from eating disorders and are likely to use fasting, vomiting, and drugs to lose weight or to keep from gaining weight.[246]

Mental illness dogs offenders across the life course, not surprising considering that many have long histories of trauma and dysfunctional family lives.[247] Those who suffer family stress, which includes having a parent who is mentally ill, are more likely to suffer mental illness themselves; they are also more likely to engage in repeat and serious delinquent behaviors.[248]

Delinquent adolescents have higher rates of clinical mental disorders than adolescents in the general population.[249] One study of incarcerated youth found that at least 88 percent of males and 92 percent of females had a psychiatric disorder of some kind and that for some disorders, such as anxiety disorder, females (55 percent) were more likely to manifest symptoms than males (26 percent).[250]

The effects of mental disorders can span the life course. People who suffer mental illness symptoms, who had a long history of social problems ranging from parental drug abuse to stressful life events and relationship strain across the life course, are the ones most likely to engage in violence in adulthood.[251] They are more likely to be arrested for multiple crimes.[252] There is evidence that mental disorders seem to be significantly related to involvement in some specific crimes, such as arson and assault.[253]

Disruptive Behavior Disorder   One mood disorder—**disruptive behavior disorder (DBD)**—is focused on as an important component of delinquency.[254] Most kids act out, especially when they are under stress. Younger children may become difficult when they are tired or hungry. They may defy parents and talk back to teachers. It would be unusual for a child not to go through the "terrible twos" or to be reasonable and mature when they are 3 years old! However, kids who are frequently uncooperative and hostile and who seem to be much more difficult than other children the same age may be suffering from a DBD.

This disorder has two components. The more mild condition is referred to as oppositional defiant disorder (ODD). Children suffering from ODD experience an ongoing pattern of uncooperative, defiant, and hostile behavior toward authority figures that seriously interferes with the youngster's day-to-day functioning. Symptoms of ODD may include frequent loss of temper; constant arguing with adults; defying adults or refusing adult requests or rules; deliberately annoying others; blaming others for mistakes or misbehavior; being angry and resentful; being spiteful or vindictive; or swearing or using obscene language.[255] The person with ODD is moody and easily frustrated, has a low opinion of himself or herself, and may abuse drugs as a form of self-medication.

Kids with ODD act out in many settings, but their behavior is more noticeable at home or at school. It is estimated that 5 to 15 percent of all school-age children have ODD. Though the causes of ODD are unknown, both biosocial and psychological sources are suspected.

The more serious DBD is conduct disorder (CD), which comprises a more acute group of behavioral and emotional problems in youngsters. As you may recall,

mood disorder
A condition in which the prevailing emotional mood is distorted or inappropriate to the circumstances.

alexithymia
A deficit in emotional cognition that prevents people from being aware of their feelings or being able to understand or talk about their thoughts and emotions; sufferers seem robotic and emotionally dead.

disruptive behavior disorder (DBD)
A consistent pattern of behaviors that continually breaks normal social rules and is extremely oppositional and defiant of authority.

children and adolescents with CD have great difficulty following rules and behaving in a socially acceptable way. They are often viewed by other children, adults, and social agencies as severely antisocial. Research shows that they are frequently involved in such activities as bullying, fighting, and cruelty to animals. Kids suffering from CD are more likely to carry weapons than other kids. Sexual assault and arson are common activities. Children with CD have trouble being truthful and think nothing of lying to cover up their activities. When they defy their parents, their activities are more serious than the ODD child: they cut school, stay out all night, or run away from home.

What causes CD? Numerous biosocial and psychological factors are suspected. There is evidence that interconnections between the frontal lobes and other brain regions may influence CD. Research also shows that levels of serotonin can influence the onset of CD. CD has been shown to aggregate in families, suggesting a genetic basis of the disorder.

It is generally assumed that ODD is more treatable than CD. Treatment might include parent training programs to help manage the child's behavior, individual psychotherapy, anger management, family psychotherapy, and cognitive behavioral therapy to assist problem solving.[256]

Is the Link Valid? There is a great deal of empirical evidence showing that kids who suffer from psychological deficits are prone to violence and antisocial behavior.[257] Violent youths have been clinically diagnosed as "overtly hostile," "explosive or volatile," "anxious," and "depressed."[258] Many delinquents exhibit indications of such psychological abnormalities as schizophrenia, paranoia, and obsessive behaviors; female offenders seem to have more serious mental health symptoms and psychological disturbances than male offenders.[259] Antisocial youths frequently come from families in which parents are unable to give love, set consistent limits, and provide the controls that allow children to develop the necessary personal tools to cope with the world in which they live.[260]

Although this evidence is persuasive, the association between mental disturbance and delinquency is unresolved. It is possible that any link is caused by some intervening variable or factor:

- Psychologically troubled youth do poorly in school, and school failure leads to delinquency.[261]

- Psychologically troubled youth have conflict-ridden social relationships that make them prone to commit delinquent acts.[262]

- While good parenting is considered a barrier against delinquency, youth who maintain abnormal psychological characteristics such as low self-control, a hostile view of relationships, and acceptance of deviant norms may neutralize the influence of positive parenting on controlling their conduct.[263]

- Kids who suffer child abuse are more likely to have mental anguish and commit violent acts; child abuse is the actual cause of both problems.[264]

- Living in a stress-filled urban environment may produce symptoms of both mental illness and crime.[265]

- Kids who are delinquent have reduced life chances. They do poorly in school and as adults are relegated to lower-class economic status. Educational failure and status deprivation are related to depression and other psychological deficits.[266]

- Adolescents with severe mental illness are more at risk to violent victimization than the mentally healthy.[267] Violent victimization has been linked to increased delinquency rates. Efforts to deinstitutionalize the mentally ill and treat them in more humane community settings may expose them to higher rates of both victimization and criminality.[268]

It is also possible that the link is spurious and caused by the treatment of the mentally ill. The police may be more likely to arrest the mentally ill, giving the

Nehemiah Griego

On January 19, 2013, five people were found dead in their home in South Valley, New Mexico. Police found two rifles that were used to shoot five members of the Griego family, including three children. Nehemiah Griego, 15, was soon arrested in connection with the murders. He told police that he killed his sleeping mother, Sarah, around midnight and then killed his 9-year-old brother Zephaniah with the same .22-caliber rifle. Hearing his sisters, 5-year-old Jael and 2-year-old Angelina, crying in their bedroom, Nehemiah shot both in the head.

Their father, Greg Griego, was a former pastor at the local Calvary Church and a chaplain for the Albuquerque Fire Department. When he returned home around dawn from working a shift at a homeless shelter, Nehemiah shot him multiple times with a semi-automatic rifle.

Nehemiah later claimed that he had been having suicidal and homicidal thoughts, that he had obtained the guns from his parents' closet, and had planned to go on a shooting rampage, killing many others. Police uncovered text messages between Nehemiah and his 12-year-old girlfriend before the murders indicating that both youths had planned to kill their parents, but she backed out. In the texts, Nehemiah says that he is feeling insane. He sent the young girl a photo of his mother and brother after they were killed to prove he murdered his family, and then the two exchanged sexual texts.

Nehemiah said he killed his family because his parents were abusive. However, psychological profiling indicated that he suffered from mental health issues, including schizoaffective disorder and post-traumatic stress disorder, coupled with learning disabilities.

AP Images/Bernalillo County Sheriff's Deptartment

On October 16, 2015, Griego pleaded guilty to two counts of second-degree murder and three counts of child abuse resulting in death. On February 11, 2016, Judge John J. Romero from the New Mexico Children's Court ruled that Nehemiah Griego is "amenable to treatment" and would be sentenced as a juvenile. Griego, now 19, will most likely be released from a youth detention facility when he turns 21, pending an appeal by the district attorney.

CRITICAL THINKING

Do you feel comfortable that a boy who killed five members of his family could be released after only five years in custody? Should he have been tried as an adult and sentenced to life in prison?

SOURCES: Haley Rush and Lysee Mitri, "Testimony Reveals Why Teen Says He Killed Family, Judge to Decide on Sentencing Teen as an Adult in the Murder of 5," KRQE News 14, January 11, 2016, http://krqe .com/2016/01/11/judge-to-decide-on-sentencing-teen-who-killed-5-as-an-adult/; AP, "New Mexico Teen Who Killed Entire Family, Including Pastor-Dad, Cleared by Judge for Early Release from State Custody," *New York Daily News*, February 12, 2016, http://www.nydailynews.com/news/crime/n-m-teen-killed-family -cleared-early-release-article-1.2529537. (Accessed September 2016.)

---

illusion that they are crime prone.[269] However, research by Paul Hirschfield and his associates gives only mixed support to this view: while some mental health problems increase the risk of arrest, others bring out more cautious or compassionate police responses.[270] The Youth Stories feature reviews a famous crime linked to a teen's mental illness.

Behavioral Theory

Not all psychologists agree that behavior is controlled by unconscious mental processes determined by parental relationships developed early in childhood. Behavioral psychologists argue that a person's personality is learned throughout life during interaction with others. Based primarily on the works of the American psychologist John B. Watson (1878–1958) and popularized by Harvard professor

FOCUS ON DELINQUENCY

The Media and Delinquency

One aspect of social learning theory that has received a great deal of attention is the belief that children will model their behavior after characters they observe on TV or see in movies. Not surprising considering that children ages 6 and under spend an average of two hours a day using screen media such as TV and computers, about the same amount of time they spend playing outside, and significantly more than the amount they spend reading or being read to (about 39 minutes per day). Marketing research indicates that adolescents ages 11 to 14 watch violent horror movies at a higher rate than any other age group; kids this age use older peers and siblings and apathetic parents to gain access to R-rated films. Violent video games are also a problem: Americans now spend twice as much money on video games as they spend going to the movies. Eighty percent of the games produced are violent, with realistic graphics that include blood, decapitation, guns, knives, mutilation, and death. Video games may have a greater impact on their audience than TV and movies because they immerse the players visually, auditorily, and physically rather than have them remain passive observers. There is evidence that violent video game exposure decreases helpful behaviors and increases aggressive thoughts, angry feelings, physiological arousal, and aggressive behaviors. One reason may be because exposure to violence in the virtual world desensitizes kids to violence in the real world, making it appear less threatening and foreboding. Matt DeLisi and his associates found that violent video game playing is correlated with aggression, even among the most disturbed delinquent offenders. Based on data from a sample of institutionalized juvenile delinquents, violent video games were associated with antisocial behavior even in a sample whose members are suffering from psychopathy.

Colorado theater shooter James Holmes is led out of the courtroom after being formally sentenced in Centennial, Colorado. Holmes killed 12 people in a rampage that some believe was linked to his obsession with violent video games.

TV and Violence

A number of research methods have been used to measure the effect of adolescent TV viewing on violent behavior. One method is to expose groups of subjects to violent TV shows in a laboratory setting and then compare their behavior to that of control groups who viewed nonviolent programming; observations have also been made in playgrounds, athletic fields, and residences. Other experiments require subjects to answer attitude surveys after watching violent TV shows. Still another approach is to use aggregate measures of TV viewing; for example, the number of violent TV shows on the air during a given time period is compared to crime rates during the same period.

Most evaluations of experimental data gathered using these techniques indicate that watching violence on TV is correlated with aggressive behaviors. Subjects who view violent TV shows are likely to commence aggressive behavior almost immediately. Children exposed to violent programming at a young age have a higher tendency for violent and aggressive behavior later in life than children who are not so exposed.

---

behaviorism
Branch of psychology concerned with the study of observable behavior rather than unconscious processes; focuses on particular stimuli and responses to them.

B. F. Skinner (1904–1990), **behaviorism** concerns itself solely with measurable events and not the unobservable psychic phenomena described by psychoanalysts.

Behaviorists suggest that individuals learn by observing how people react to their behavior. Behavior is triggered initially by a stimulus or change in the environment. If a particular behavior is reinforced by some positive reaction or event, that behavior will be continued and eventually learned. However, behaviors that are not reinforced or are punished will be extinguished or become extinct. For example, if children are given a reward (ice cream for dessert) for eating their entire dinner, eventually they will learn to eat properly as a matter of habit. Conversely, if children are punished for some misbehavior, they will eventually learn to associate disapproval with that act and avoid it.

Viewing media violence has been related to both short- and long-term increases in aggressive attitudes, values, and behaviors. Teens who watch violent media are the ones most likely to engage in dating violence, especially if they do not hold strong antiviolence attitudes. Kids, especially young women, who observe "mean girls" harassing someone on TV are more likely to later engage in that behavior themselves.

Even relatively brief exposure to violent movie clips increased anxiety among late adolescents, indicating that media can create personality change. This change may account for the long-term effects of violent media: adolescents exposed to violent media are more likely to persist in aggressive behavior as adults. Children who watch more than an hour of TV each day show an increase in assaults, fights, robberies, and other acts of aggression later in life and into adulthood.

How Is Media Connected to Violence?

There are a number of views that explain the link between watching violence and acting in a violent fashion. These include:

- Television violence allows aggressive youths to rationalize their behavior as a socially acceptable and common activity.

- Television violence may disinhibit aggressive behavior. Disinhibition takes place when people are seen being rewarded for violence and when violence is seen as socially acceptable.

- Watching violent media may create changes in personality and cognition, which in the long term produces negative behavioral changes.

- Viewing violence can lead to emotional desensitization toward violence in real life.

- Children exposed to violence are more likely to assume that acts of violence are socially acceptable behavior.

- Viewing violence increases fear of becoming a victim of violence, with a resultant increase in self-protective behaviors and a mistrust of others.

- Exposure to violent TV shows, movies, and video games has been found to desensitize parts of the brain that have been related to violence. .

Is the Connection Valid?

The association between violent media and violent behavior is still being studied. There are social scientists who question the claim that TV viewing is related to antisocial behavior, and claim that experimental results are inconclusive and short-lived. Kids may have an immediate reaction to viewing violence on TV, but aggression is quickly extinguished once the viewing ends. Experiments showing that kids act aggressively in a laboratory setting after watching violent TV shows fail to link aggression to actual delinquent behaviors, such as rape or assault. Aggregate data are also inconclusive. Little evidence exists that areas with the highest levels of violent TV viewing also have rates of violent crime that are above the norm. Millions of children watch violence every night yet fail to become violent criminals. And even if a violent behavior–TV link could be established, it would be difficult to show that antisocial people develop aggressive traits merely from watching TV. Aggressive youths may simply enjoy watching TV shows that conform to and support their behavioral orientation. In other words, a personal inclination toward violence may lead to viewing violent media, and not vice versa. Further research is needed to clarify this important issue.

SOURCES: Sarah Coyne, "Effects of Viewing Relational Aggression on Television on Aggressive Behavior in Adolescents: A Three-Year Longitudinal Study," *Developmental Psychology* 52:284–295 (2016); Sarah Coyne, Mark Callister, Laura Stockdale, Holly Coutts, and Kevin Collier, "Just How Graphic Are Graphic Novels? An Examination of Aggression Portrayals in Manga and Associations with Aggressive Behavior in Adolescents," *Violence and Victims* 30:208–224 (2015); Sukkyung You, Euikyung Kim, and Unkyung No, "Impact of Violent Video Games on the Social Behaviors of Adolescents: The Mediating Role of Emotional Competence," *School Psychology International* 36:94–111 (2015); Morgan Tear and Mark Nielsen, "Video Games and Prosocial Behavior: A Study of the Effects of Non-Violent, Violent, and Ultra-Violent Gameplay," *Computers in Human Behavior* 41:8–13 (2014); Matt DeLisi, Michael Vaughn, Douglas Gentile, Craig Anderson, and Jeffrey Shook, "Violent Video Games, Delinquency, and Youth Violence: New Evidence," *Youth Violence and Juvenile Justice* 11:132–142 (2013).

Social Learning Theory Not all behaviorists strictly follow the teachings of Watson and Skinner. Some hold that a person's learning and social experiences, coupled with his or her values and expectations, determine behavior. This is known as the **social learning theory** approach. The most widely read social learning theorists are Albert Bandura, Walter Mischel, and Richard Walters.[271] In general, they hold that children will model their behavior according to the reactions they receive from others, either positive or negative; the behavior of those adults they are in close contact with, especially parents; and the behavior they view on television and in movies (see the Focus on Delinquency feature "The Media and Delinquency"). If children observe aggression and see that the aggressive behavior, such as an adult slapping or punching someone during an argument, is approved

social learning theory (psychological)
The view that behavior is modeled through observation, either directly through intimate contact with others or indirectly through media; interactions that are rewarded are copied, whereas those that are punished are avoided.

or rewarded, they will likely react violently during a similar incident. Eventually, the children will master the techniques of aggression and become more confident that their behavior will bring tangible rewards.[272]

By implication, social learning suggests that children who grow up in a home where violence is a way of life may learn to believe that such behavior is acceptable and rewarding. Even if parents tell children not to be violent and punish them if they are, the children will still model their behavior on the observed parental violence.

Thus, children are more likely to heed what parents *do* than what they *say*. By mid-childhood, some children have already acquired an association between their use of aggression against others and the physical punishment they receive at home. Often their aggressive responses are directed at other family members and siblings. The family may serve as a training ground for violence because the child perceives physical punishment as the norm during conflict situations with others.[273]

Adolescent aggression is a result of disrupted dependency relations with parents. This refers to the frustration and anger a child feels when parents provide poor role models and hold back affection and nurturing. Children who lack close dependent ties to their parents may have little opportunity or desire to model themselves after them or to internalize their standards of behavior. In the absence of such internalized controls, the child's aggression is likely to be expressed in an immediate, direct, and socially unacceptable fashion such as violence and aggression.[274]

Cognitive Theory

cognitive theory
The branch of psychology that studies the perception of reality and the mental processes required to understand the world we live in.

A third area of psychology that has received increasing recognition in recent years is **cognitive theory**. Psychologists with a cognitive perspective focus on mental processes—the way people perceive and mentally represent the world around them, and how they solve problems. The pioneers of this school were Wilhelm Wundt (1832–1920), Edward Titchener (1867–1927), and William James (1842–1910). The cognitive perspective contains several subgroups. Perhaps the most important for criminological theory is the moral and intellectual development branch, which is concerned with how people morally represent and reason about the world.

Jean Piaget (1896–1980), the founder of this approach, hypothesized that a child's reasoning processes develop in an orderly fashion, beginning at birth and continuing until age 12 and older.[275] At first, during the *sensorimotor stage*, children respond to the environment in a simple manner, seeking interesting objects and developing their reflexes. By the fourth and final stage, the *formal operational stage*, they have developed into mature adults who can use logic and abstract thought.

Lawrence Kohlberg (1927–1987) applied the concept of developmental stages to issues in criminology.[276] He suggested that people travel through stages of moral development, during which the basis for moral and ethical decision making changes. It is possible that serious offenders have a moral orientation that differs from that of law-abiding citizens. Kohlberg's stages of development are as follows:

Stage 1. Right is obedience to power and avoidance of punishment.

Stage 2. Right is taking responsibility for oneself, meeting one's own needs, and leaving to others the responsibility for themselves.

Stage 3. Right is being good in the sense of having good motives, having concern for others, and "putting yourself in the other person's shoes."

Stage 4. Right is maintaining the rules of a society and serving the welfare of the group or society.

Stage 5. Right is based on recognized individual rights within a society with agreed-upon rules—a social contract.

Stage 6. Right is an assumed obligation to principles applying to all humankind—principles of justice, equality, and respect for human personality.

Kohlberg classified people according to the stage on this continuum at which their moral development had ceased to grow. In studies conducted by Kohlberg and his associates, criminals were found to be significantly lower in their moral judgment development than noncriminals of the same social background.[277] The majority of noncriminals were classified in stages 3 and 4, whereas a majority of criminals were in stages 1 and 2. Moral development theory, then, suggests that people who obey the law simply to avoid punishment or who have outlooks mainly characterized by self-interest are more likely to commit crimes than those who view the law as something that benefits all of society and who honor the rights of others. Subsequent research with delinquent youths has found that a significant number were in the first two moral development categories, whereas non-delinquents were ranked higher.[278] In addition, higher stages of moral reasoning are associated with such behaviors as honesty, generosity, and nonviolence, which are considered incompatible with delinquency.[279]

Information Processing Cognitive theorists who study information processing try to explain antisocial behavior in terms of perception and analysis of data. When people make decisions, they engage in a sequence of cognitive thought processes. They first encode information so that it can be interpreted. They then search for a proper response and decide upon the most appropriate action; finally, they act on their decision.[280]

According to this approach, adolescents who use information properly, who are better conditioned to make reasoned judgments, and who can make quick and reasoned decisions when facing emotion-laden events are the ones best able to avoid antisocial behavior choices.[281] In contrast, delinquency-prone adolescents may have cognitive deficits and use information incorrectly when they make decisions.[282] They have difficulty making the "right decision" while under stress. One reason is that they may be relying on mental "scripts" learned in their early childhood that tell them how to interpret events, what to expect, how they should react, and what the outcome of the interaction should be.[283] Hostile children may have learned improper scripts by observing how others react to events; their own parents' aggressive and inappropriate behavior would have considerable impact. Some children may have had early and prolonged exposure to violence, such as child abuse, which increases their sensitivity to teasing and maltreatment. They may misperceive behavioral cues because their decision making was shaped by traumatic life events.[284]

Oversensitivity to rejection by their peers is a continuation of sensitivity to rejection by parents.[285] Violence becomes a stable behavior because the scripts that emphasize aggressive responses are repeatedly rehearsed as the child matures. They view crime as an appropriate means to satisfy their immediate personal needs, which take precedence over more distant social needs such as obedience to the law.[286]

Violence-prone kids see the world around them as filled with aggressive people. They are overly sensitive and tend to overreact to provocation. As these children mature, they use fewer cues than most people to process information. Some use violence in a calculating fashion as a means of getting what they want; others react in an overly volatile fashion to the slightest provocation. When they attack victims, they may believe they are defending themselves, even though they are misreading the situation.[287] Adolescents who use violence as a coping technique with others are also more likely to exhibit other social problems, such as drug and alcohol abuse.[288]

There is also evidence that delinquent boys who engage in theft are more likely to exhibit cognitive deficits than nondelinquent youth. For example, they have a poor sense of time, leaving them incapable of dealing with or solving social problems in an effective manner.[289]

The Evidence-Based Juvenile Justice feature looks at a treatment program that used a cognitive approach to treat sexually abused children.

Therapeutic Approaches for Sexually Abused Children

Sexual abuse of children is a significant social problem. Estimates suggest that between 20 and 32 percent of females experience sexual abuse, and 4 to 8 percent of males are victims. Therapeutic approaches for sexually abused children and adolescents are designed to reduce the effects of sexual abuse that can manifest in various ways, such as posttraumatic stress disorder (PTSD), fear, and anxiety; 37 to 53 percent of sexually abused children develop PTSD. Traumatic reactions may include re-experiencing the abuse through memories or dreams, or actively attempting to avoid situations or stimuli that remind the child of the abuse. Victims may engage in externalizing behaviors such as sexual behavioral problems, hyperactivity, and aggression. Alternatively, the effects of sexual abuse can cause children to exhibit internalizing behaviors such as depression and anxiety.

Sexual abuse can be a single occurrence or can occur over a period of time, sometimes even years. The duration of exposure depends on a range of factors, such as the perpetrator's access to the child or young person and the steps taken to secure the victim's silence, such as threats. Child sexual abuse can be perpetrated within the family, by those known to the children outside of the home, or by strangers. The majority of sexual abuse is committed by people known to the victim, although most are not members of their family; around one third of perpetrators are family members. Therapeutic approaches for sexually abused children and adolescents aim to reduce the developmental consequences that result from this distinct form of maltreatment.

Using Cognitive Behavioral Therapy

There are a variety of therapeutic approaches that are designed to treat the negative impacts of child sexual abuse, such as cognitive behavioral therapy (CBT), cognitive behavioral therapy for sexually abused preschoolers, trauma-focused cognitive behavioral therapy, child-centered therapy, eye movement desensitization and reprocessing, imagery rehearsal therapy, a recovering from abuse program, supportive counseling, and stress inoculation training.

CBT is a well-known treatment approach that can be delivered individually to the victim or in a group setting. For child victims of sexual abuse, CBT focuses on the meaning of the events for children and their nonoffending parents, addressing the maladaptive cognitions (e.g., being "soiled"), misattributions (e.g., feelings of blame), and low self-esteem. Interventions may also try to address overt behaviors such as sexualized behavior, externalizing behaviors, or internalizing behaviors.

CBT is designed to address symptoms such as emotional distress, anxiety, and behavior problems. CBT helps children cope effectively with their emotional distress by teaching relaxation techniques and various other skills such as emotional

expression skills and cognitive coping skills. Further, children and their parents are taught how to label feelings and communicate them to others. To reduce anxiety, CBT teaches children and adolescents to recognize the signs of anxiety and the stimuli that trigger it so that they can gradually replace their maladaptive responses with adaptive ones. Finally, to reduce behavior problems, CBT teaches parents how behavior is triggered, shaped, and possibly maintained by consequences. CBT also teaches parents how to improve their child's behavior, and about the impact that the sexual abuse had so that they are better able to understand their child's behavior.

Alternative Approaches

As a type of cognitive behavioral treatment, imagery rehearsal therapy (IRT) can also be used as a therapeutic approach to child sexual abuse. Given that approximately 70 percent of individuals with PTSD experience chronic nightmares, which most often include reliving their traumatic experiences, IRT is used to help alleviate the posttraumatic nightmares With IRT, children and adolescents are asked to recall their nightmares and, in time, rewrite the nightmares into less threatening content.

Another therapeutic approach that can be used to treat victims of child sexual abuse is eye movement desensitization and reprocessing (EMDR). The goal of EMDR treatment is to help individuals who have experienced traumatic stress to reprocess and adaptively store traumatic memories. Treatment sessions focus on the past experiences that may have caused PTSD or other psychological disorders; the current circumstances that trigger dysfunctional emotions, beliefs, and sensations; and the positive experiences that can improve future adaptive behaviors and mental health.

Therapeutic approaches to child and adolescent sexual abuse have been found to have statistically significant impacts on symptoms of PTSD/trauma. Research shows that participants in treatment groups had lower PTSD/trauma symptoms than comparison group participants. Meta-analysis of treatment programs indicates groups experienced greater decreases in PTSD/trauma symptoms as a result of therapy, compared with the comparison groups.

CRITICAL THINKING

Do you believe that a treatment program such as cognitive behavioral therapy can work with sexually abused children, or are their problems beyond the scope of a program based on psychological counseling? If you do not believe such a program would work, how would you deal with kids who have suffered such abuse? Would anti-anxiety medications work better?

SOURCE: Shane Harvey, "Therapeutic Approaches for Sexually Abused Children and Adolescents," National Institute of Justice, http://www.crimesolutions.gov/PracticeDetails.aspx?ID=45 (accessed September 2016).

Personality and Delinquency

Personality can be defined as the reasonably stable patterns of behavior, including thoughts and emotions, that distinguish one person from another.[290] An individual's personality reflects characteristic ways of adapting to life's demands and problems. The way we behave is a function of how our personality enables us to interpret life events and make appropriate behavioral choices.

Can the cause of delinquency be linked to personality? There has been a great deal of research on this subject and an equal amount of controversy and debate over the findings.[291] In their early work, Sheldon Glueck and Eleanor Glueck identified a number of personality traits that characterize delinquents:

self-assertiveness	suspicion
extroversion	poor personal skills
defiance	destructiveness
ambivalence	mental instability
impulsiveness	sadism
feeling unappreciated	hostility
narcissism	lack of concern for others
distrust of authority	resentment[292]

The Gluecks' research is representative of the view that delinquents maintain a distinct personality whose characteristics increase the probability that (a) they will be aggressive and antisocial and (b) their actions will involve them with agents of social control, ranging from teachers to police.

Personality and Antisocial Behaviors   Since the Gluecks' findings were published, other research efforts have attempted to identify personality traits that would increase the chances for a delinquent career.[293] A common theme is that delinquents are hyperactive, impulsive individuals with short attention spans (attention deficit disorder), who frequently manifest conduct disorders, anxiety disorders, and depression.[294] These traits make them prone to problems ranging from psychopathology to drug abuse, sexual promiscuity, and violence.[295] Suspected traits include impulsivity, hostility, and aggressiveness.[296] The psychologist Hans Eysenck identified two important personality traits that he associated with antisocial behavior: extraversion and neuroticism. Eysenck defines **extraverts** as impulsive individuals who lack the ability to examine their own motives and behaviors; **neuroticism** produces anxiety, tension, and emotional instability.[297] Youths who lack self-insight and are impulsive and emotionally unstable are likely to interpret events differently than youths who give reasoned judgments to life events. Though the former may act destructively, for example, by using drugs, the latter will be able to reason that such behavior is ultimately self-defeating and life threatening. Youths who are both neurotic and extraverted often lack insight, are highly impulsive, and more likely than other delinquents to become chronic offenders.[298]

extravert
A person who behaves impulsively and doesn't have the ability to examine motives and behavior.

neuroticism
A personality trait marked by unfounded anxiety, tension, and emotional instability.

Antisocial Personality Disorder   It has also been suggested that chronic delinquency may result from a syndrome commonly referred to as **antisocial personality disorder (ASPD)** (though the more archaic and outmoded terms psychopathic or sociopathic personality are still used).[299] Though no more than 3 percent of the male offending population may be classified as antisocial, it is possible that a large segment of persistent chronic offenders share this trait.[300]

Antisocial youths typically start out by showing symptoms of ODD and then CD in youth. They are callous and unemotional.[301] As they mature they exhibit a low level of guilt and anxiety and persistently violate the rights of others.[302] In their late teens they exhibit superficial charm and above-average intelligence; these often mask a disturbed personality that makes them incapable of forming enduring relationships with others.[303] Frequently involved in such deviant behaviors as truancy, running away, lying, substance abuse, and impulsivity, people

antisocial personality disorder (ASPD)
A person lacking in warmth and affection, exhibiting inappropriate behavior responses, and unable to learn from experience.

AP Images/Steve Yeater

Dr. Heather Bowlds, who is in charge of the sex offender treatment program, and youth correctional counselor Joseph Bruns (right) listen as Tony (center) talks during a group counseling session at the O.H. Close Youth Correctional facility in Stockton, California. Courts have seen the number of sex offense cases involving juvenile offenders rise dramatically in recent years.

with ASPD lack the ability to empathize with others. From an early age, their home life is filled with frustration, bitterness, and quarreling. Consequently, throughout life, the person suffering from ASPD is unreliable, unstable, demanding, and egocentric. Hervey Cleckley, a leading authority on this type of offender, uses this definition:

> [they are] chronically antisocial individuals who are always in trouble, profiting neither from experience nor punishment, and maintaining no real loyalties to any person, group, or code. They are frequently callous and hedonistic, showing marked emotional immaturity, with lack of responsibility, lack of judgment, and an ability to rationalize their behavior so that it appears warranted, reasonable, and justified.[304]

Those considered antisocial are believed to be thrill seekers who engage in violent, destructive behavior.[305] They may constantly engage in risky behaviors such as car theft and joyriding.[306]

What Causes Antisocial Personalities to Develop? A number of factors have been found to contribute to the development of ASPD: having an emotionally disturbed parent, a lack of love, parental rejection during childhood, and inconsistent discipline. Children who lack the opportunity to form an attachment to a mother figure in the first three years of life, who suffer sudden separation from the mother figure, or who see changes in the mother figure are most likely to develop psychopathic personalities. According to this view, the path runs from antisocial parenting to ASPD to criminality.[307]

Another view is that antisocial personality is heritable and passed down genetically from one generation to the next.[308] Inherited genetic makeup may cause antisocial children to suffer from lower than normal levels of arousal.[309] While most youth may become anxious and afraid when facing the prospect of committing a delinquent act, antisocial kids may need that excitement to bring them up to comfortable arousal levels so they feel "normal."[310]

Intelligence and Delinquency

Psychologists have long been concerned with the development of intelligence and its subsequent relationship to behavior. It has been charged that children with low IQs are responsible for a disproportionate share of delinquency.

Early criminologists believed that low intelligence was a major cause of delinquency. They thought that if it could be determined which individuals were less intelligent, it might be possible to identify potential delinquents before they committed socially harmful acts.[311] Because social scientists had a captive group of subjects in training schools and penal institutions, studies began to appear that measured the correlation between IQ and crime by testing adjudicated juvenile delinquents. Delinquent juveniles were believed to be inherently substandard in intelligence and naturally inclined to commit more crimes than more intelligent people. Thus, juvenile delinquents were used as a test group around which numerous theories about intelligence were built.

Nature Theory When the newly developed IQ tests were administered to inmates of prisons and juvenile training schools in the first decades of the twentieth century, a large proportion of the inmates scored low on the tests. Henry Goddard found in his studies in 1920 that many institutionalized people were what he considered "feebleminded" and thus concluded that at least half of all juvenile delinquents were mental defectives.[312]

Similarly, in 1926, William Healy and Augusta Bronner tested a group of delinquents in Chicago and Boston and found that 37 percent were subnormal in intelligence.[313] They concluded that delinquents were 5 to 10 times more likely to be mentally deficient than nondelinquent boys.

These and other early studies were embraced as proof that low IQ scores indicated potentially delinquent children and that a correlation existed between innate low intelligence and deviant behavior. IQ tests were believed to measure the inborn genetic makeup of individuals, and many criminologists accepted the predisposition of substandard individuals toward delinquency. This view is referred to as **nature theory** of intelligence.

Nurture Theory Development of culturally sensitive explanations of human behavior in the 1930s led to the **nurture theory** of intelligence. This school of thought holds that intelligence must be viewed as partly biological but primarily sociological. Nurture theory argues that intelligence is not inherited and that low-IQ parents do not necessarily produce low-IQ children.[314] It discredits the notion that people commit crimes because they have low IQ scores. Instead, it holds that environmental stimulation from parents, relatives, schools, peer groups, and innumerable others creates a child's IQ level and that low IQs result from an environment that also encourages delinquent and criminal behavior.[315] For example, if educational environments could be improved, the result might be both an elevation in IQ scores and a decrease in delinquency.[316] Studies challenging the assumption that people automatically committed delinquent acts because they had below-average IQs began to appear as early as the 1920s. John Slawson's study of 1,543 delinquent boys in New York institutions found that although 80 percent of the delinquents achieved lower scores in abstract verbal intelligence than the general population, delinquents were about normal in mechanical aptitude and nonverbal intelligence. Slawson found no relationship between the number of arrests, the types of offenses, and IQ.[317] In 1931, Edwin Sutherland also evaluated IQ studies of criminals and delinquents and found evidence disputing the association between intelligence and criminality.[318] These findings did much to discredit the notion that a strong relationship existed between IQ and criminality, and for many years the IQ–delinquency link was ignored.

IQ and Delinquency Today A study published by Travis Hirschi and Michael Hindelang revived interest in the association between IQ and delinquency.[319] After conducting a thorough statistical analysis of IQ and delinquency data sets, Hirschi and Hindelang concluded both that IQ tests are a valid predictor of intelligence and that "the weight of evidence is that IQ is more important than race and social class" for predicting delinquent involvement. They argued that a low IQ increases the likelihood of delinquent behavior through its effect on school performance: youths with low IQs do poorly in school, and school failure and academic incompetence are highly related to delinquency.

The Hirschi–Hindelang findings have been supported by a number of research efforts.[320] In their widely read *Crime and Human Nature*, James Q. Wilson and Richard Herrnstein came to this conclusion:

> . . . there appears to be a clear and consistent link between criminality and low intelligence. That is, taking all offenders as a group, and ignoring differences among kinds of crime, criminals seem, on the average, to be a bit less bright and to have a different set of intellectual strengths and weaknesses than do noncriminals as a group.[321]

Contemporary research efforts have continued to uncover an association between low IQ scores and antisocial behavior. Scores on intelligence tests have been used to predict violent behavior and to distinguish between groups of violent and nonviolent offenders.[322] On an individual level, there is evidence linking low IQ scores with violent crimes, including murder.[323] In addition to these micro-level studies, others using macro-level state and county data found that IQ and

nature theory
Holds that low intelligence is genetically determined and inherited.

nurture theory
Holds that intelligence is partly biological but mostly sociological; negative environmental factors encourage delinquent behavior and depress intelligence scores for many youths.

delinquency rates are associated. A number of research projects have found evidence that states and counties whose residents have higher IQs experience lower crime rates than those with less-intelligent kids.[324]

Those experts who believe that IQ may have a direct influence on the onset of delinquent involvement argue that the key linkage between IQ and delinquency is the ability to manipulate abstract concepts. Low intelligence limits adolescents' ability to "foresee the consequences of their offending and to appreciate the feelings of victims."[325] Therefore, youths with limited intelligence are more likely to misinterpret events and gestures, act foolishly, take risks, and engage in harmful behavior.

IQ and Delinquency Controversy The relationship between IQ and delinquency is extremely controversial. It implies there is a condition present at birth that accounts for a child's delinquent behavior throughout the life cycle and that this condition is not easily changed or improved. By implication, if delinquency is not spread evenly through the social structure, neither is intelligence. The controversy has been fueled by charges that IQ tests are culturally biased and invalid, which makes any existing evidence at best inconclusive. Kids who live in disadvantaged neighborhoods find their verbal ability is stunted and this deficit makes them prone to delinquency. Environment then mediates the association between verbal ability and delinquency.[326]

There is also evidence that delinquency is a reflection of poor school performance and educational failure, and that if there is an IQ–delinquency link it's because kids with low IQ do poorly in the classroom.[327] As Wilson and Herrnstein put it, "A child who chronically loses standing in the competition of the classroom may feel justified in settling the score outside, by violence, theft, and other forms of defiant illegality."[328] Because the relationship runs from low IQ to poor school performance to frustration to delinquency, school officials need to recognize the problem and plan programs to help underachievers perform better in school. As the hypothesized relationship between IQ and delinquency, even if proved to be valid, is an indirect one, educational enrichment programs can help counteract any influence intellectual impairment has on the predilection of young people to commit crime.

Critiquing Individual-Level Theories

Individual-level studies have been criticized on a number of grounds. One view is that the research methodologies they employ are weak and invalid. Most research efforts use adjudicated or incarcerated offenders. It is often difficult to determine whether findings represent the delinquent population or merely those most likely to be arrested and adjudicated by officials of the justice system. For example, some critics have described the methods used in heredity studies as "poorly designed, ambiguously reported and exceedingly inadequate in addressing the relevant issues."[329]

Some critics also fear that individual-level research can be socially and politically damaging. If an above-average number of indigent youth become delinquent offenders, can it be assumed that the less affluent are impulsive, greedy, have low IQs, or are genetically inferior? To many social scientists, the implications of this conclusion are unacceptable in light of what is known about race, gender, and class bias.

Critics also suggest that individual-level theory is limited as a generalized explanation of delinquent behavior because it fails to account for the known patterns of criminal behavior. Delinquent behavior trends seem to conform to certain patterns linked to social-ecological rather than individual factors—social class, seasonality, population density, and gender roles. Social forces that appear to be influencing the onset and maintenance of delinquent behavior are not accounted for by explanations of delinquency that focus on the individual. If, as is often the case, the delinquent rate is higher in one neighborhood than another, are we to conclude that youths in the high-crime area are more likely to be watching violent TV shows or eating more sugar-coated cereals than those in low-crime neighborhoods? How can individual traits explain the fact that crime rates vary between cities and between regions?

Defending Individual-Level Theory The legitimization of social-psychological, psychiatric, and biosocial approaches to explaining deviant behavior may prove to be an important and productive paradigm shift in the decades ahead.[330]

Theorists who focus on individual behavior contend that critics overlook the fact that their research often gives equal weight to environmental and social as well as mental and physical factors.[331] For example, some people may have particular developmental problems that place them at a disadvantage in society, limit their chances of conventional success, and heighten their feelings of anger, frustration, and rage. Though the incidence of these personal traits may be spread evenly across the social structure, families in one segment of the population have the financial wherewithal to help treat the problem, whereas families in another segment may lack the economic means and the institutional support needed to help their children. Delinquency rate differences may be a result of differential access to opportunities either to commit crime or receive the care and treatment needed to correct and compensate for developmental problems.

In addition, individual-level theorists believe that, like it or not, youths are in fact different and may have differing potentials for antisocial acts. For example, gender differences in the violence rate may be explained by the fact that after centuries of aggressive mating behavior, males have become naturally more violent than females.[332] Male aggression may be more a matter of genetic transfer than socialization or cultural patterns.

Trait Theory and Delinquency Prevention

Because many individual-oriented theorists are also practitioners and clinicians, it is not surprising that a great deal of delinquency prevention efforts are based in psychological and biosocial theory. As a group, individual perspectives on delinquency suggest that prevention efforts should be directed at strengthening a youth's home life and personal relationships. Almost all of these theoretical efforts point to the child's home life as a key factor in delinquent behavior. If parents cannot supply proper nurturing, love, care, discipline, nutrition, and so on, the child cannot develop properly. Whether one believes that delinquency has a biosocial basis, a psychological basis, or a combination of both, it is evident that delinquency prevention efforts should be oriented to reach children early in their development.

It is, therefore, not surprising that county welfare agencies and privately funded treatment centers have offered counseling and other mental health services to families referred by schools, welfare agents, and juvenile court authorities. In some instances, intervention focuses on a particular family problem that has the potential for producing delinquent behavior, such as alcohol and drug problems, child abuse, or sexual abuse. In other situations, intervention is more generalized and oriented toward developing the self-image of parents and children or improving discipline in the family.

In addition, individual approaches have been used to prevent court-adjudicated youths from engaging in further criminal activities. It has become almost universal practice for incarcerated and court-adjudicated youths to be given some form of mental and physical evaluation before they begin their term of correctional treatment. Such rehabilitation methods as psychological counseling and psychotropic medication (involving such drugs as Valium or Ritalin) are often prescribed. In some instances, rehabilitation programs are provided through drop-in centers that service youths who are able to remain in their homes, while more intensive programs require residential care and treatment. The creation of such programs illustrates how agents of the juvenile justice system believe that many delinquent youths and status offenders have psychological or physical problems and that their successful treatment can help reduce repeat criminal behavior. Faith in this treatment approach suggests widespread agreement among juvenile justice system professionals that the cause of delinquency can be traced to individual pathology; if not, why bother treating them?

Some questions remain about the effectiveness of individual treatment as a delinquency prevention technique. Little hard evidence exists that clinical treatment alone can prevent delinquency or rehabilitate known delinquents. It is possible that programs designed to help youths may actually stigmatize and label them, hindering their efforts to live conventional lives.[333] Because this issue is so critical, it will be discussed further in Chapter 5.

SUMMARY

1 Distinguish between the two branches of individual-level theories of delinquency

- Some delinquency experts, referred to as choice theorists, believe that delinquency is a product of an individual decision-making process.

- Other experts believe that delinquency is the product of some individual trait such as temperament, personality, or hormones.

- Choice theory suggests that young offenders choose to engage in antisocial activity because they believe their actions will be beneficial and profitable.

- Trait theory suggests that youthful misbehavior is driven by biological or psychological abnormalities, such as hyperactivity, low intelligence, biochemical imbalance, or genetic defects.

- Both theories focus on mental and behavioral processes at the individual level and on delinquency as an individual problem, not a social problem.

2 Explain the principles of choice theory

- Choice theory assumes that people have free will to choose their behavior.

- Those who violate the law are motivated by personal needs such as greed, revenge, survival, and hedonism.

- The classical view of crime and delinquency holds that the decision to violate the law is based on a careful weighing of the benefits and costs of criminal behaviors.

- Punishment should be only severe enough to deter a particular offense.

- Delinquents are rational decision makers who choose to violate the law.

- Choice theorists believe that law-violating behavior occurs when a reasoning offender decides to take the chance of violating the law after considering his or her personal situation, values, and situation.

3 Discuss the routine activities theory of delinquency

- Routine activities theory holds that delinquency is a function of the activities of capable guardians, the availability of suitable targets, and the presence of motivated offenders (such as unemployed teenagers).

- The presence of capable guardians who can protect homes and possessions can reduce the motivation to commit delinquent acts.

- Routine activities theory suggests that the availability of suitable targets such as easily transportable commodities will increase delinquency rates.

- As the number and motivation of offenders increase, so too do delinquency rates.

4 Critique the principles of general deterrence theory

- The general deterrence concept holds that the choice to commit delinquent acts is structured by the threat of punishment.

- One of the guiding principles of deterrence theory is that the more severe, certain, and swift the punishment, the greater its deterrent effect will be.

- Deterrence strategies are based on the idea of a rational, calculating offender; they may not be effective when applied to immature young people.

- The deterrent threat of punishment may have little influence on the highest-risk group of young offenders—teens living in economically depressed neighborhoods.

5 Examine the concept of specific deterrence

- The concept of specific deterrence holds that if offenders are punished severely, the experience will convince them not to repeat their illegal acts.

- Some research studies show that arrest and conviction may under some circumstances lower the frequency of reoffending.

- Punishment, especially in an adult prison, can backfire by exposing younger offenders to higher-risk, more experienced inmates who can influence their lifestyle and help shape their attitudes.

6 Discuss the concept of situational crime prevention

- According to the concept of situational crime prevention, delinquency can be neutralized if (a) potential targets are carefully guarded, (b) the means to commit crime are controlled, and (c) potential offenders are carefully monitored.

- Situational crime prevention strategies aim to reduce the opportunities people have to commit particular crimes.

- Increasing the effort required to commit delinquency can involve target-hardening techniques such as putting unbreakable glass on storefronts.

- Increasing the risks of delinquency might involve such measures as improving surveillance lighting, using closed-circuit TV monitoring, and creating neighborhood watch programs.

- Reducing the rewards of delinquency includes strategies such as marking property so it is more difficult to sell when stolen.

7 Trace the history and development of trait theory

- The first attempts to discover why criminal tendencies develop focused on the physical makeup of offenders.

- The origin of this school of thought is generally credited to the Italian physician Cesare Lombroso.

- Early views portrayed delinquent behavior as a function of a single biological factor or trait, such as body build or defective intelligence.

8 Evaluate the branches and substance of biological trait theory

- Trait theorists argue that no two people (with rare exceptions, such as identical twins) are alike, and therefore each will react to environmental stimuli in a distinct way.

- One view is that body chemistry can govern behavior and personality, including levels of aggression and depression.

- One area of concern is that overexposure to particular environmental contaminants, including metals and minerals such as iron and manganese, may produce effects that put kids at risk for antisocial behavior.

- There is also evidence that diet may influence behavior through its impact on body chemistry.

- Hormonal levels are another area of biochemical research. Antisocial behavior allegedly peaks in the teenage years because hormonal activity is at its highest level during this period.

- Another focus of biosocial theory is the neurological (brain and nervous system) structure of offenders.

- Biosocial theorists also study the genetic makeup of delinquents. Studies of this kind have generally supported the hypothesis that there is a link between genetics and behavior.

9 Compare the various psychological theories of delinquency

- According to psychodynamic theory, law violations are a product of an abnormal personality structure formed early in life and which thereafter controls human behavior choices. The basis of psychodynamic theory is the assumption that human behavior is controlled by unconscious mental processes developed early in childhood.

- Behavioral psychologists argue that a person's personality is learned throughout life during interaction with others. Behaviorists suggest that individuals learn by observing how people react to their behavior.

- Cognitive theorists who study information processing try to explain antisocial behavior in terms of perception and analysis of data. When people make decisions, they engage in a sequence of cognitive thought processes. Delinquency-prone adolescents may have cognitive deficits and use information incorrectly when they make decisions.

10 Examine the psychological traits that have been linked to delinquency

- Delinquents are hyperactive, impulsive individuals with short attention spans (attention deficit disorder), who frequently manifest conduct disorders, anxiety disorders, and depression.

- Antisocial youths exhibit a low level of guilt and anxiety and persistently violate the rights of others.

- Psychologists have long been concerned with the development of intelligence and its subsequent relationship to behavior. It has been charged that children with low IQs are responsible for a disproportionate share of delinquency.

KEY TERMS

QUESTIONS FOR DISCUSSION

1. Is there such a thing as the "born criminal"? Are some people programmed at birth to commit crimes?

2. Is crime psychologically abnormal? Can there be "normal" crimes?

3. How would psychodynamic theory explain such delinquent acts as shoplifting or breaking and entering a house?

4. Can delinquent behavior be deterred by the threat of punishment? If not, how can it be controlled?

5. Should we incarcerate violent juvenile offenders for long periods of time—10 years or more?

6. Does watching violent TV and films encourage youth to be aggressive and antisocial? Do advertisements for beer featuring attractive, provocatively dressed young men and women encourage drinking and precocious sex? If not, why bother advertising?

7. Discuss the characteristics of antisocial youths. Do you know anyone who fits the description?

8. Is it fair, just, and moral to experiment with a control group of children who are not given a proper diet in order to test the effect of nutrition on delinquency?

VIEWPOINT

You are a state legislator who is a member of the subcommittee on juvenile justice. Your committee has been asked to redesign the state's juvenile code because of public outrage over serious juvenile crime. At an open hearing, a professor from the local university testifies that she has devised a surefire test to predict violence-prone delinquents. The procedure involves brain scans, DNA testing, and blood analysis. Used with samples of incarcerated adolescents, her procedure has been able to distinguish with 70 percent accuracy between youths with a history of violence and those who are exclusively property offenders. The professor testifies that if each juvenile offender were tested with her techniques, the violence-prone career offender could easily be identified and given special treatment.

Opponents argue that this type of testing is unconstitutional because it violates the Fifth Amendment protection against self-incrimination and can unjustly label nonviolent offenders. Any attempt to base policy on biosocial makeup seems inherently wrong and unfair.

Those who favor the professor's approach maintain that it is not uncommon to single out the insane or mentally incompetent for special treatment and that these conditions often have a biological basis. It is better that a few delinquents be unfairly labeled than seriously violent offenders be ignored until it is too late.

- Is it possible that some kids are born to be delinquents? Or do kids "choose" crime?
- Is it fair to test kids to see if they have biological traits related to crime, even if they have never committed a single offense?

- Should special laws be created to deal with the potentially dangerous offender?
- Should offenders be typed on the basis of their biological characteristics?

DOING RESEARCH ON THE WEB

Before you address this issue, you may want to research the literature on predicting delinquent behavior. Start with this article on Adrian Raine: https://penncurrent.upenn.edu/2011-03-24/research/can -science-predict-criminal-behavior. This one covers the use of brain scans: http://www.crimetraveller .org/2016/03/brain-scans-criminal-behavior/.

NOTES

All URLs accessed September 2016.

1. Susan Donaldson James, "Newtown Shooter Lanza Had Sensory Processing Disorder," ABC News, February 20, 2013, http://abcnews.go.com/Health/newtown-shooter -adam-lanza-sensory-processing-disorder-controversial /story?id=18532645.
2. Alison Leigh Cowan, "Adam Lanza's Mental Problems 'Completely Untreated' Before Newtown Shootings, Report Says," *New York Times*, November 21, 2014, http://www.nytimes.com/2014/11 /22/nyregion/before-newtown-shootings-adam-lanzas-mental -problems-completely-untreated-report-says.html.
3. Office of the Child Advocate, State of Connecticut, *Shooting at Sandy Hook Elementary School*, November 21, 2014, http://www.cbsnews .com/htdocs/pdf/00_2014/11-2014/Office-of-the-Child-Advocate -Report-PDF.pdf.
4. James, "Newtown Shooter Lanza Had Sensory Processing Disorder."
5. Pete Blair and Katherine Schweit, *A Study of Active Shooter Incidents, 2000–2013*, Texas State University and Federal Bureau of Investigation, https://www.fbi.gov/news/stories/2014/september /fbi-releases-study-on-active-shooter-incidents/pdfs/a-study -of-active-shooter-incidents-in-the-u.s.-between-2000-and-2013.
6. Adam Lankford, *The Myth of Martyrdom: What Really Drives Suicide Bombers, Rampage Shooters, and Other Self-Destructive Killers* (New York: Palgrave Macmillan, 2013).
7. US Census Bureau, *Income, Poverty and Health Insurance Coverage in the United States: 2014*, September 16, 2015, http://census.gov /newsroom/press-releases/2015/cb15-157.html.
8. Marvin Wolfgang, Robert Figlio, and Thorsten Sellin, *Delinquency in a Birth Cohort* (Chicago: University of Chicago Press, 1972).
9. Cesare Beccaria, *On Crimes and Punishments*, 6th ed., Henry Paolucci, trans. (Indianapolis: Bobbs-Merrill, 1977).
10. See Ernest Van den Haag, *Punishing Criminals* (New York: Basic Books, 1975).
11. Beccaria, *On Crimes and Punishments*, p. 43.
12. Pierre Tremblay and Carlo Morselli, "Patterns in Criminal Achievement: Wilson and Abrahamsen Revisited," *Criminology* 38:633–660 (2000).
13. Emily Strang and Zoë Peterson, "The Relationships Among Perceived Peer Acceptance of Sexual Aggression, Punishment Certainty, and Sexually Aggressive Behavior," *Journal of Interpersonal Violence* 28:3369–3385 (2013).
14. Michael Townsley, Daniel Birks, Wim Bernasco, Stijn Ruiter, Shane D. Johnson, and Gentry White, "Burglar Target Selection: A Cross-National Comparison," *Journal of Research in Crime and Delinquency* 52:3–31 (2015).

15. Richard Felson and Steven Messner, "To Kill or Not to Kill? Lethal Outcomes in Injurious Attacks," *Criminology* 34:519–545 (1996).
16. Marie Rosenkrantz Lindegaard, Wim Bernasco, and Scott Jacques, "Consequences of Expected and Observed Victim Resistance for Offender Violence During Robbery Events," *Journal of Research in Crime and Delinquency* 52:32–61 (2015).
17. David C. Pyrooz and James A. Densley, "Selection into Street Gangs, Signaling Theory, Gang Membership, and Criminal Offending" *Journal of Research in Crime and Delinquency* 53:447–481 (2016).
18. James Densley, "It's Gang Life, but Not As We Know It: The Evolution of Gang Business," *Crime and Delinquency* 60:517–546 (2014).
19. Timothy Brezina, "Delinquent Problem-Solving: An Interpretive Framework for Criminological Theory and Research," *Journal of Research in Crime and Delinquency* 37:3–30 (2000).
20. Christopher Uggen and Melissa Thompson, "The Socioeconomic Determinants of Ill-Gotten Gains: Within-Person Changes in Drug Use and Illegal Earnings," *American Journal of Sociology* 109:146–185 (2003).
21. Steven Levitt and Sudhir Alladi Venkatesh, "An Economic Analysis of a Drug-Selling Gang's Finances," *NBER Working Papers 6592* (Cambridge, MA: National Bureau of Economic Research, Inc., 1998).
22. Bill McCarthy, "New Economics of Sociological Criminology," *Annual Review of Sociology* 28:417–442 (2002).
23. Nathalie Fontaine, Mara Brendgen, Frank Vitaro, and Richard Tremblay, "Compensatory and Protective Factors Against Violent Delinquency in Late Adolescence: Results from the Montreal Longitudinal and Experimental Study," *Journal of Criminal Justice* 45:54–62 (2016).
24. Brenda Sims Blackwell, "Perceived Sanction Threats, Gender, and Crime: A Test and Elaboration of Power-Control Theory," *Criminology* 38:439–488 (2000).
25. Dana Haynie, "Contexts of Risk: Explaining the Link Between Girls' Pubertal Development and Their Delinquency Involvement," *Social Forces* 82:355–397 (2003).
26. Raymond Paternoster, Shawn Bushway, Robert Brame, and Robert Apel, "The Effect of Teenage Employment on Delinquency and Problem Behaviors," *Social Forces* 82:297–336 (2003).
27. Matthew Ploeger, "Youth Employment and Delinquency: Reconsidering a Problematic Relationship," *Criminology* 35:659–675 (1997).
28. Robert Apel, Shawn Bushway, Robert Brame, Amelia Haviland, Daniel Nagin, and Ray Paternoster, "Unpacking the Relationship Between Adolescent Employment and Antisocial Behavior: A Matched Samples Comparison," *Criminology* 45:67–97 (2007).
29. Richard B. Felson, *Violence and Gender Reexamined* (Washington, DC: American Psychological Association, 2002).
30. Cynthia Najdowski, Hayley Cleary, and Margaret Stevenson, "Adolescent Sex Offender Registration Policy: Perspectives on General

Deterrence Potential from Criminology and Developmental Psychology," *Psychology, Public Policy, and Law* 22:114–125 (2016).

31. Benoit Leclerc, Richard Wortley, and Stephen Smallbone, "Getting into the Script of Adult Child Sex Offenders and Mapping out Situational Prevention Measures," *Journal of Research in Crime and Delinquency* 48:209–237 (2011).

32. Bruce Jacobs and Michael Cherbonneau, "Managing Victim Confrontation: Auto Theft and Informal Sanction Threats," *Justice Quarterly* 33:21–44 (2016).

33. Lawrence Cohen and Marcus Felson, "Social Change and Crime Rate Trends: A Routine Activities Approach," *American Sociological Review* 44:588–608 (1979).

34. Brandon Welsh and David Farrington, "Surveillance for Crime Prevention in Public Space: Results and Policy Choices in Britain and America," *Criminology and Public Policy* 3:701–730 (2004).

35. Denise Osborn, Alan Trickett, and Rob Elder, "Area Characteristics and Regional Variates as Determinants of Area Property Crime Levels," *Journal of Quantitative Criminology* 8:265–282 (1992).

36. Lynn A. Addington and Callie Marie Rennison, "Keeping the Barbarians Outside the Gate? Comparing Burglary Victimization in Gated and Non-Gated Communities," *Justice Quarterly* 32:168–192 (2015).

37. Paul Bellair, "Informal Surveillance and Street Crime: A Complex Relationship," *Criminology* 38:137–167 (2000).

38. Grace Barnes, Joseph Hoffman, John Welte, Michael Farrell, and Barbara Dintcheff, "Adolescents' Time Use: Effects on Substance Use, Delinquency and Sexual Activity," *Journal of Youth and Adolescence* 36:697–710 (2007).

39. Richard Timothy Coupe and Laurence Blake, "The Effects of Patrol Workloads and Response Strength on Arrests at Burglary Emergencies," *Journal of Criminal Justice* 33:239–255 (2005).

40. Hope Corman and Naci Mocan, "Alcohol Consumption, Deterrence and Crime in New York City," *Journal of Labor Research* 36:103–128 (2015).

41. William Smith, Sharon Glave Frazee, and Elizabeth Davison, "Furthering the Integration of Routine Activity and Social Disorganization Theories: Small Units of Analysis and the Study of Street Robbery as a Diffusion Process," *Criminology* 38:489–521 (2000).

42. James Massey, Marvin Krohn, and Lisa Bonati, "Property Crime and Routine Activities of Individuals," *Journal of Research in Crime and Delinquency* 26:397–429 (1989).

43. Lawrence Cohen, Marcus Felson, and Kenneth Land, "Property Crime Rates in the United States: A Macrodynamic Analysis, 1947–1977, with Ex-Ante Forecasts for the Mid-1980s," *American Journal of Sociology* 86:90–118 (1980).

44. Denise Gottfredson and David Soulé, "The Timing of Property Crime, Violent Crime, and Substance Use Among Juveniles," *Journal of Research in Crime and Delinquency* 42:110–120 (2005).

45. Rolf Becker and Guido Mehlkop, "Social Class and Delinquency: An Empirical Utilization of Rational Choice Theory with Cross-Sectional Data of the 1990 and 2000 German General Population Surveys (Allbus)," *Rationality and Society* 18:193–235 (2006); Daniel Nagin and Greg Pogarsky, "Integrating Celerity, Impulsivity, and Extralegal Sanction Threats into a Model of General Deterrence: Theory and Evidence," *Criminology* 39:865–892 (2001).

46. Nagin and Pogarsky, "Integrating Celerity, Impulsivity, and Extralegal Sanction Threats into a Model of General Deterrence."

47. Beccaria, *On Crimes and Punishments*.

48. For the classic analysis on the subject, see Johannes Andenaes, *Punishment and Deterrence* (Ann Arbor: University of Michigan Press, 1974).

49. Daniel Nagin and Greg Pogarsky, "An Experimental Investigation of Deterrence: Cheating, Self-Serving Bias and Impulsivity," *Criminology* 41:167–195 (2003).

50. Tomislav V. Kovandzic and John J. Sloan, "Police Levels and Crime Rates Revisited: A County-Level Analysis from Florida (1980–1998)," *Journal of Criminal Justice* 30:65–76 (2002).

51. Nagin and Pogarsky, "An Experimental Investigation of Deterrence."

52. Robert Apel, Greg Pogarsky, and Leigh Bates, "The Sanctions–Perceptions Link in a Model of School-Based Deterrence," *Journal of Quantitative Criminology* 25:201–226 (2009).

53. Nagin and Pogarsky, "Integrating Celerity, Impulsivity, and Extralegal Sanction Threats into a Model of General Deterrence."

54. Cheryl L. Maxson, Kristy N. Matsuda, and Karen Hennigan, "Deterrability Among Gang and Nongang Juvenile Offenders: Are Gang Members More (or Less) Deterrable than Other Juvenile Offenders?" *Crime and Delinquency* 57:516–543 (2011).

55. Thomas Loughran, Alex Piquero, Jeffrey Fagan, and Edward Mulvey, "Differential Deterrence: Studying Heterogeneity and Changes in Perceptual Deterrence Among Serious Youthful Offenders," *Crime and Delinquency* 58:3–27 (2012).

56. Robert Apel, "Sanctions, Perceptions, and Crime: Implications for Criminal Deterrence," *Journal of Quantitative Criminology* 29:67–101 (2013).

57. James Q. Wilson and Richard Herrnstein, *Crime and Human Nature* (New York: Simon and Schuster, 1985), p. 396.

58. Brandon Welsh, David Farrington, and Sema Taheri, "Effectiveness and Social Costs of Public Area Surveillance for Crime Prevention," *Annual Review of Law and Social Science* 11:111–130 (2015).

59. John Worrall and Tomislav Kovandzic, "Police Levels and Crime Rates: An Instrumental Variables Approach," *Social Science Research* 39:506–516 (2010).

60. Coupe and Blake, "The Effects of Patrol Workloads and Response Strength on Arrests at Burglary Emergencies."

61. Steven Durlauf and Daniel Nagin, "Imprisonment and Crime: Can Both Be Reduced?" *Criminology and Public Policy* 10:13–54 (2011).

62. Michael White, James Fyfe, Suzanne Campbell, and John Goldkamp, "The Police Role in Preventing Homicide: Considering the Impact of Problem-Oriented Policing on the Prevalence of Murder," *Journal of Research in Crime and Delinquency* 40:194–226 (2003).

63. 64 Tony Newman, "Stop Sending Undercover Cops into Our Schools to Entrap Our Kids on Drug Charges," Drug Policy Alliance, December 13, 2013, http://www.drugpolicy.org/blog/stop-sending-undercover-cops-our-schools-entrap-our-kids-drug-charges.

64. Leona Lee, "Factors Determining Waiver in a Juvenile Court," *Journal of Criminal Justice* 22:329–339 (1994).

65. Donald Green, "Past Behavior as a Measure of Actual Future Behavior: An Unresolved Issue in Perceptual Deterrence Research," *Journal of Criminal Law and Criminology* 80:781–804, at 803 (1989); Matthew Silberman, "Toward a Theory of Criminal Deterrence," *American Sociological Review* 41:442–461 (1976); Linda Anderson, Theodore Chiricos, and Gordon Waldo, "Formal and Informal Sanctions: A Comparison of Deterrent Effects," *Social Problems* 25:103–114 (1977). See also Maynard Erickson and Jack Gibbs, "Objective and Perceptual Properties of Legal Punishment and Deterrence Doctrine," *Social Problems* 25:253–264 (1978); and Daniel Nagin and Raymond Paternoster," Enduring Individual Differences and Rational Choice Theories of Crime," *Law and Society Review* 27:467–485 (1993).

66. Robert Svensson, Frank Weerman, Lieven Pauwels, Gerben Bruinsma, and Wim Bernasco, "Moral Emotions and Offending: Do Feelings of Anticipated Shame and Guilt Mediate the Effect of Socialization on Offending?" *European Journal of Criminology* 10:22–39 (2013).

67. Harry Wallace, Julie Juola Exline, and Roy Baumeister, "Interpersonal Consequences of Forgiveness: Does Forgiveness Deter or Encourage Repeat Offenses?" *Journal of Experimental Social Psychology* 44:453–460 (2008).

68. Thomas Peete, Trudie Milner, and Michael Welch, "Levels of Social Integration in Group Contexts and the Effects of Informal Sanction Threat on Deviance," *Criminology* 32:85–105 (1994).

69. Anthony Braga, "Pulling Levers: Focused Deterrence Strategies and the Prevention of Gun Homicide," *Journal of Criminal Justice* 36:332–343 (2008).

70. Anthony Braga, David Hureau, and Andrew Papachristos, "Deterring Gang-Involved Gun Violence: Measuring the Impact of Boston's Operation Ceasefire on Street Gang Behavior," *Journal of Quantitative Criminology* 30:113–139 (2014).

71. Doris MacKenzie and David Farrington, "Preventing Future Offending of Delinquents and Offenders: What Have We Learned from Experiments and Meta-analyses?" *Journal of Experimental Criminology* 11:565–595 (2015).

72. James A. Swartz and Arthur J. Lurigio, "Serious Mental Illness and Arrest: The Generalized Mediating Effect of Substance Use," *Crime and Delinquency* 53:581–604 (2007).

73. Eric Jensen and Linda Metsger, "A Test of the Deterrent Effect of Legislative Waiver on Violent Juvenile Crime," *Crime and Delinquency* 40:96–104 (1994).

74. Nagin and Pogarsky, "Integrating Celerity, Impulsivity, and Extralegal Sanction Threats into a Model of General Deterrence."

75. Ibid.

76. Greg Pogarsky, Ki Deuk Kim, and Ray Paternoster, "Perceptual Change in the National Youth Survey: Lessons for Deterrence Theory and Offender Decision-Making," *Justice Quarterly* 22:1–29 (2005).

77. Bruce Jacobs, "Deterrence and Deterrability," *Criminology* 48:417–442 (2010).

78. Shamena Anwar and Thomas Loughran, "Testing a Bayesian Learning Theory of Deterrence Among Serious Juvenile Offenders," *Criminology* 49:667–698 (2011).

79. Ibid.; Rudy Haapanen, Lee Britton, and Tim Croisdale, "Persistent Criminality and Career Length," *Crime and Delinquency* 53:133–155 (2007).

80. Christina Dejong, "Survival Analysis and Specific Deterrence: Integrating Theoretical and Empirical Models of Recidivism," *Criminology* 35:561–576 (1997).

81. Paul Tracy and Kimberly Kempf-Leonard, *Continuity and Discontinuity in Criminal Careers* (New York: Plenum, 1996).

82. Pamela Lattimore, Christy Visher, and Richard Linster, "Predicting Rearrest for Violence Among Serious Youthful Offenders," *Journal of Research in Crime and Delinquency* 32:54–83 (1995).

83. Peter Wood, "Exploring the Positive Punishment Effect Among Incarcerated Adult Offenders," *American Journal of Criminal Justice* 31:8–22 (2007).

84. Jacobs, "Deterrence and Deterrability."

85. Stephanie Wiley and Finn-Aage Esbensen, "The Effect of Police Contact: Does Official Intervention Result in Deviance Amplification?" *Crime and Delinquency* 62:283–307 (2016).

86. Jose Canela-Cacho, Alfred Blumstein, and Jacqueline Cohen, "Relationship Between the Offending Frequency of Imprisoned and Free Offenders," *Criminology* 35:133–171 (1997).

87. James Lynch and William Sabol, "Prisoner Reentry in Perspective," Urban Institute, http://www.urban.org/UploadedPDF/410213_reentry.PDF.

88. Rudy Haapanen, Lee Britton, and Tim Croisdale, "Persistent Criminality and Career Length," *Crime and Delinquency* 53:133–155 (2007).

89. Patricia Brantingham, Paul Brantingham, and Wendy Taylor, "Situational Crime Prevention as a Key Component in Embedded Crime Prevention," *Canadian Journal of Criminology and Criminal Justice* 47:271–292 (2005).

90. Marcus Felson, "Routine Activities and Crime Prevention," in National Council for Crime Prevention, *Studies on Crime and Crime Prevention, Annual Review*, vol. 1 (Stockholm: Scandinavian University Press, 1992), pp. 30–34.

91. Andrew Fulkerson, "Blow and Go: The Breath-Analyzed Ignition Interlock Device as a Technological Response to DWI," *American Journal of Drug and Alcohol Abuse* 29:219–235 (2003).

92. Barry Webb, "Steering Column Locks and Motor Vehicle Theft: Evaluations for Three Countries," in Ronald Clarke, ed., *Crime Prevention Studies* (Monsey, NY: Criminal Justice Press, 1994), pp. 71–89.

93. David Farrington and Brandon Welsh, "Improved Street Lighting and Crime Prevention," *Justice Quarterly* 19:313–343 (2002).

94. Brandon Welsh and David Farrington, "Effects of Closed-Circuit Television on Crime," *Annals of the American Academy of Political and Social Science* 587:110–136 (2003).

95. Brandon Welsh and David Farrington, "Crime Prevention and Hard Technology: The Case of CCTV and Improved Street Lighting," in James Byrne and Donald Rebovich, eds., *The New Technology of Crime, Law, and Social Control* (Monsey, NY: Criminal Justice Press, 2007).

96. Philip Cook and Jens Ludwig, "The Economist's Guide to Crime Busting," *NIJ Journal* 270 (2012), http://nij.gov/nij/journals/270/economists-guide.htm.

97. Ronald Clarke and David Weisburd, "Diffusion of Crime Control Benefits: Observations of the Reverse of Displacement," in Ronald Clarke, ed., *Crime Prevention Studies*, vol. 2 (New York: Criminal Justice Press, 1994).

98. David Weisburd and Lorraine Green, "Policing Drug Hot Spots: The Jersey City Drug Market Analysis Experiment," *Justice Quarterly* 12:711–734 (1995).

99. Anthony A. Braga, Andrew V. Papachristos, and David M. Hureau, "The Effects of Hot Spots Policing on Crime: An Updated Systematic Review and Meta-Analysis," *Justice Quarterly*, first published online May 16, 2012.

100. Bruce Taylor, Christopher Koper, and Daniel Woods, "A Randomized Control Trial of Different Policing Strategies at Hot Spots of Violent Crime," *Journal of Experimental Criminology* 7:149–181 (2011).

101. Evan Sorg, Cory Haberman, Jerry Ratcliffe, and Elizabeth Groff, "Foot Patrol in Violent Crime Hot Spots: The Longitudinal Impact of Deterrence and Posttreatment Effects of Displacement," *Criminology* 51:65–101 (2013).

102. Massey, Krohn, and Bonati, "Property Crime and the Routine Activities of Individuals."

103. David Shantz, "Conflict, Aggression, and Peer Status: An Observational Study," *Child Development* 57:1322–1332 (1986).

104. For an excellent review of Lombroso's work, as well as that of other well-known theorists, see Randy Martin, Robert Mutchnick, and W. Timothy Austin, *Criminological Thought, Pioneers Past and Present* (New York: Macmillan, 1990).

105. Marvin Wolfgang, "Cesare Lombroso," in Herman Mannheim, ed., *Pioneers in Criminology* (Montclair, NJ: Patterson Smith, 1970), pp. 232–271.

106. Gina Lombroso-Ferrero, *Criminal Man According to the Classification of Cesare Lombroso* (1911), reprint edition (Montclair, NJ: Patterson Smith, 1972), p. 7.

107. Rafaele Garofalo, *Criminology* (1914), reprint edition (Glenridge, NJ: Patterson Smith, 1968).

108. See Thorsten Sellin, "Enrico Ferri," in Mannheim, ed., *Pioneers in Criminology*, pp. 361–384.

109. Nicole Hahn Rafter, "Criminal Anthropology in the United States," *Criminology* 30:525–547 (1992).

110. For a general review, see J. C. Barnes and Brian Boutwell, "Biosocial Criminology: The Emergence of a New and Diverse Perspective," *Criminal Justice Studies* 28:1–5 (2015).

111. John Paul Wright and Francis T. Cullen, "The Future of Biosocial Criminology: Beyond Scholars' Professional Ideology," *Journal of Contemporary Criminal Justice* 28:237–253 (2012), at 244.

112. J. C. Barnes and Bruce Jacobs, "Genetic Risk for Violent Behavior and Environmental Exposure to Disadvantage and Violent Crime: The Case for Gene–Environment Interaction," *Journal of Interpersonal Violence* 28:92–120 (2013).

113. Anthony Walsh, "Behavior Genetics and Anomie/Strain Theory," *Criminology* 38:1075–1108 (2000).

114. Jay Belsky, "Variation in Susceptibility to Rearing Influences: An Evolutionary Argument," *Psychological Inquiry* 8:182–186 (1997).

115. Ronald Simons, Man Kit Lei, Steven Beach, Gene Brody, Robert Philibert, and Frederick Gibbons, "Social Environmental Variation, Plasticity Genes, and Aggression: Evidence for the Differential Susceptibility Hypothesis," *American Sociological Review* 76:833–912 (2011).

116. See Adrian Raine, *The Psychopathology of Crime* (San Diego: Academic Press, 1993).

117. Paul Marshall, "Allergy and Depression: A Neurochemical Threshold Model of the Relation Between the Illnesses," *Psychological Bulletin* 113:23–43 (1993).

118. "Diet and the Unborn Child: The Omega Point," *The Economist*, January 19, 2006.

119. Jonathon Ericson, Francis Crinella, K. Alison Clarke-Stewart, Virginia Allhusen, Tony Chan, and Richard T. Robertson, "Prenatal Manganese Levels Linked to Childhood Behavioral Disinhibition," *Neurotoxicology and Teratology* 29:181–187 (2007); Joseph Hibbeln, John Davis, Colin Steer, Pauline Emmett, Imogen Rogers, Cathy Williams, and Jean Golding, "Maternal Seafood Consumption in Pregnancy and Neurodevelopmental Outcomes in Childhood (ALSPAC Study): An Observational Cohort Study," *The Lancet* 369:578–585 (2007).

120. K. Murata, P. Weihe, E. Budtz-Jorgensen, P. J. Jorgensen, and P. Grandjean, "Delayed Brainstem Auditory Evoked Potential Latencies in 14-Year-Old Children Exposed to Methylmercury," *Journal of Pediatrics* 144:177–183 (2004); Eric Konofal, Samuele Cortese, Michel Lecendreux, Isabelle Arnulf, and Marie Christine Mouren, "Effectiveness of Iron Supplementation in a Young Child with Attention-Deficit/Hyperactivity Disorder," *Pediatrics* 116:732–734 (2005).

121. Eric Konofal, Michel Lecendreux, Isabelle Arnulf, and Marie-Christine Mouren, "Iron Deficiency in Children with Attention-Deficit/Hyperactivity Disorder," *Archives of Pediatric and Adolescent Medicine* 158:1113–1115 (2004).

122. Lisa M. Gatzke-Kopp and Theodore Beauchaine, "Direct and Passive Prenatal Nicotine Exposure and the Development of Externalizing Psychopathology," *Child Psychiatry and Human Development* 38:255–269 (2007).

123. F. T. Crews, A. Mdzinarishvili, D. Kim, J. He, and K. Nixon, "Neurogenesis in Adolescent Brain Is Potently Inhibited by Ethanol," *Neuroscience* 137:437–445 (2006).

124. Gail Wasserman, Xinhua Liu, Faruque Parvez, Habibul Ahsan, Diane Levy, Pam Factor-Litvak, Jennie Kline, Alexander van Geen, Vesna Slavkovich, Nancy J. Lolacono, Zhongqi Cheng, Yan Zheng, and Joseph Graziano, "Water Manganese Exposure and Children's Intellectual Function in Araihazar, Bangladesh," *Environmental Health Perspectives* 114:124–129 (2006).

125. Jens Walkowiak, Jörg-A. Wiener, Annemarie Fastabend, Birger Heinzow, Ursula Krämer, Eberhard Schmidt, Hans-J. Steingürber, Sabine Wundram, and Gerhard Winneke, "Environmental Exposure to Polychlorinated Biphenyls and Quality of the Home Environment: Effects on Psychodevelopment in Early Childhood," *The Lancet* 358:92–93 (2001).

126. Virginia Rauh, Robin Garfinkel, Frederica Perera, Howard Andrews, Lori Hoepner, Dana B. Barr, Ralph Whitehead, Deliang Tang, and Robin W. Whyatt, "Impact of Prenatal Chlorpyrifos Exposure on Neurodevelopment in the First 3 Years of Life Among Inner-City Children," *Pediatrics* 118:1845–1859 (2006).

127. Stephanie M. Engel, Amir Miodovnik, Richard Canfield, Chenbo Zhu, Manori Silva, Antonia Calafat, and Mary Wolff, "Prenatal Phthalate Exposure Is Associated with Childhood Behavior and Executive Functioning," *Environmental Health Perspectives* 118:565–571 (2010).

128. Jessica Durando, "How Water Crisis in Flint, Mich., Became Federal State of Emergency," *USA Today*, January 20, 2015.

129. David Bellinger, "Lead," *Pediatrics* 113:1016–1022 (2004); Jeff Evans, "Asymptomatic, High Lead Levels Tied to Delinquency," *Pediatric News* 37:13 (2003); Herbert Needleman, Christine McFarland, Roberta Ness, Stephen Fienberg, and Michael Tobin, "Bone Lead Levels in Adjudicated Delinquents: A Case Control Study," *Neurotoxicology and Teratology* 24:711–717 (2002).

130. Todd Jusko, Charles Henderson Jr., Bruce Lanphear, Deborah Cory-Slechta, Patrick J. Parsons, and Richard Canfield, "Blood Lead Concentrations < 10 µg/dL and Child Intelligence at 6 Years of Age," *Environmental Health Perspectives* 116:243–248 (2008); Bruce P. Lanphear, Richard Hornung, Jane Khoury, Kimberly Yolton, Peter Baghurst, David C. Bellinger, Richard L. Canfield, Kim N. Dietrich, Robert Bornschein, Tom Greene, Stephen J. Rothenberg, Herbert L. Needleman, Lourdes Schnaas, Gail Wasserman, Joseph Graziano, and Russell Roberts, "Low-Level Environmental Lead Exposure and Children's Intellectual Function: An International Pooled Analysis," *Environmental Health Perspectives* 113:894–899 (2005).

131. Mark Opler, Alan Brown, Joseph Graziano, Manisha Desai, Wei Zheng, Catherine Schaefer, Pamela Factor-Litvak, and Ezra S. Susser, "Prenatal Lead Exposure, [Delta]-Aminolevulinic Acid, and Schizophrenia," *Environmental Health Perspectives* 112:548–553 (2004).

132. Aimin Chen, Bo Cai, Kim Dietrich, Jerilynn Radcliffe, and Walter Rogan, "Lead Exposure, IQ, and Behavior in Urban 5- to 7-Year-Olds: Does Lead Affect Behavior Only by Lowering IQ?" *Pediatrics* 119:650–658 (2007).

133. Emily Oken, Robert O. Wright, Ken P. Kleinman, David Bellinger, Chitra J. Amarasiriwardena, Howard Hu, Janet W. Rich-Edwards, and Matthew W. Gillman, "Maternal Fish Consumption, Hair Mercury, and Infant Cognition in a U.S. Cohort," *Environmental Health Perspectives* 113:1376–1380 (2005).

134. Centers for Disease Control and Prevention, http://www.cdc.gov/nceh/lead/.

135. Emily Oken, Marie Louise Østerdal, Matthew W. Gillman, Vibeke K. Knudsen, Thorhallur I. Halldorsson, Marin Strøm, David C. Bellinger, Mijna Hadders-Algra, Kim Fleischer Michaelsen, and Sjurdur F. Olsen, "Associations of Maternal Fish Intake during Pregnancy and Breastfeeding Duration with Attainment of Developmental Milestones in Early Childhood: A Study from the Danish National Birth Cohort," *American Journal of Clinical Nutrition* 88:789–796 (2008).

136. Marshall, "Allergy and Depression," pp. 23–29.

137. Adrian Raine, Kjetil Mellingen, Jianghong Liu, Peter Venables, and Sarnoff Mednick, "Effects of Environmental Enrichment at Age Three to Five Years on Schizotypal Personality and Antisocial Behavior at Ages Seventeen and Twenty-Three Years," *American Journal of Psychiatry* 160:1–9 (2003).

138. Wendy Oddy, Monique Robinson, Gina Ambrosini, Therese O'Sullivan, Nicholas de Klerk, Lawrence Beilin, Sven Silburn, Stephen Zubrick, and Fiona Stanley, "The Association Between Dietary Patterns and Mental Health in Early Adolescence," *Preventive Medicine* 49:39–44 (2009).

139. A. Maras, M. Laucht, D. Gerdes, C. Wilhelm, S. Lewicka, D. Haack, L. Malisova, and M. H. Schmidt, "Association of Testosterone and Dihydrotestosterone with Externalizing Behavior in Adolescent Boys and Girls," *Psychoneuroendocrinology* 28:932–940 (2003).

140. Christy Miller Buchanan, Jacquelynne Eccles, and Jill Becker, "Are Adolescents the Victims of Raging Hormones? Evidence for Activational Effects of Hormones on Moods and Behavior at Adolescence," *Psychological Bulletin* 111:62–107 (1992).

141. Jooa Julia Lee, Francesca Gino, Ellie Shuo Jin, Leslie Rice, and Robert Josephs, "Hormones and Ethics: Understanding the Biological Basis

of Unethical Conduct," *Journal of Experimental Psychology* 144:891–897 (2015); Cave Sinai, Tatja Hirvikoski, Anna-Lena Nordström, Peter Nordström, Åsa Nilsonne, Alexander Wilczek, Marie Åsberg, and Jussi Jokinen, "Thyroid Hormones and Adult Interpersonal Violence Among Women with Borderline Personality Disorder," *Psychiatry Research* 227:253–257 (2015).

142. Alex Piquero and Timothy Brezina, "Testing Moffitt's Account of Adolescent-Limited Delinquency," *Criminology* 39:353–370 (2001).

143. Laurence Tancredi, *Hardwired Behavior: What Neuroscience Reveals About Morality* (London: Cambridge University Press, 2005).

144. "McLean Researchers Document Brain Damage Linked to Child Abuse and Neglect," newsletter of McLean's Hospital, Belmont, MA, December 14, 2000.

145. Brian Perron and Matthew Howard, "Prevalence and Correlates of Traumatic Brain Injury Among Delinquent Youths," *Criminal Behaviour and Mental Health* 18:243–255 (2008).

146. Society for Neuroscience News Release, "Studies Identify Brain Areas and Chemicals Involved in Aggression; May Speed Development of Better Treatment," http://www.sfn.org/Press-Room/News-Release-Archives/2007/studies-identify-brain.

147. Physorg.com, "Violent Teenage Girls Fail to Spot Anger or Disgust in Others' Faces," http://www.physorg.com/news192377654.html.

148. James Ogilvie, Anna Stewart, Raymond Chan, and David Shum, "Neuropsychological Measures of Executive Function and Antisocial Behavior: A Meta-Analysis," *Criminology* 49:1063–1107 (2011).

149. Ibid.; Yaling Yang, Adrian Raine, Todd Lencz, Susan Bihrle, Lori Lacasse, and Patrick Colletti, "Prefrontal White Matter in Pathological Liars," *British Journal of Psychiatry* 187:320–325 (2005).

150. Alice Jones, Kristin Laurens, Catherine Herba, Gareth Barker, and Essi Viding, "Amygdala Hypoactivity to Fearful Faces in Boys with Conduct Problems and Callous-Unemotional Traits," *American Journal of Psychiatry* 166:95–102 (2009).

151. Thomas Crowley, Manish S. Dalwani, Susan K. Mikulich-Gilbertson, Yiping P. Du, Carl W. Lejuez, Kristen M. Raymond, and Marie T. Banich, "Risky Decisions and Their Consequences: Neural Processing by Boys with Antisocial Substance Disorder," *PLOS One* 5 (2010), published online, http://www.ncbi.nlm.nih.gov/pmc/articles/PMC2943904/.

152. Adrian Raine, Patricia Brennan, Birgitte Mednick, and Sarnoff A. Mednick, "High Rates of Violence, Crime, Academic Problems, and Behavioral Problems in Males with Both Early Neuromotor Deficits and Unstable Family Environments," *Archives of General Psychiatry* 53:544–549 (1996).

153. Adrian Raine et al., "Interhemispheric Transfer in Schizophrenics, Depressives and Normals with Schizoid Tendencies," *Journal of Abnormal Psychology* 98:35–41 (1989).

154. Jean Seguin, Robert Pihl, Philip Harden, Richard Tremblay, and Bernard Boulerice, "Cognitive and Neuropsychological Characteristics of Physically Aggressive Boys," *Journal of Abnormal Psychology* 104:614–624 (1995).

155. Peer Briken, Niels Habermann, Wolfgang Berner, and Andreas Hill, "The Influence of Brain Abnormalities on Psychosocial Development, Criminal History and Paraphilias in Sexual Murderers," *Journal of Forensic Sciences* 50:1–5 (2005).

156. Dorothy Otnow Lewis, Jonathan Pincus, Marilyn Feldman, Lori Jackson, and Barbara Bard, "Psychiatric, Neurological, and Psychoeducational Characteristics of 15 Death Row Inmates in the United States," *American Journal of Psychiatry* 143:838–845 (1986).

157. Charlotte Johnson and William Pelham, "Teacher Ratings Predict Peer Ratings of Aggression at 3-Year Follow-Up in Boys with Attention Deficit Disorder with Hyperactivity," *Journal of Consulting and Clinical Psychology* 54:571–572 (1987).

158. Cited in Charles Post, "The Link Between Learning Disabilities and Juvenile Delinquency: Cause, Effect, and 'Present Solutions,'" *Juvenile and Family Court Journal* 31:59 (1981).

159. Christopher A. Mallett, "Youthful Offending and Delinquency: The Comorbid Impact of Maltreatment, Mental Health Problems, and Learning Disabilities," *Child and Adolescent Social Work Journal* 31:369–392 (2014).

160. Charles Murray, *The Link Between Learning Disabilities and Juvenile Delinquency: A Current Theory and Knowledge* (Washington, DC: Government Printing Office, 1976).

161. Mary K. Evans, Samantha S. Clinkinbeard, and Pete Simi, "Learning Disabilities and Delinquent Behaviors Among Adolescents: A Comparison of Those With and Without Comorbidity," *Deviant Behavior* 36:200–220 (2015); Xin Wei, Jennifer W. Yu, and Debra Shaver, "Longitudinal Effects of ADHD in Children with Learning

Disabilities or Emotional Disturbances," *Exceptional Children* 80:205–219 (2014).

162. Christopher Mallett, "The 'Learning Disabilities to Juvenile Detention' Pipeline: A Case Study," *Children and Schools* 36:147–162 (2014).

163. Centers for Disease Control and Prevention, http://www.cdc.gov/nchs/fastats/adhd.htm.

164. Thomas Brown, *Attention Deficit Disorder: The Unfocused Mind in Children and Adults* (New Haven, CT: Yale University Press, 2005).

165. Leonore Simon, "Does Criminal Offender Treatment Work?" *Applied and Preventive Psychology* 7:137–159 (1998).

166. Terrie Moffitt and Phil Silva, "Self-Reported Delinquency, Neuropsychological Deficit, and History of Attention Deficit Disorder," *Journal of Abnormal Child Psychology* 16:553–569 (1988).

167. Jason Fletcher and Barbara Wolfe, "Long-Term Consequences of Childhood ADHD on Criminal Activities," *Journal of Mental Health Policy and Economics* 12:119–138 (2009).

168. Patricia Westmoreland, Tracy Gunter, Peggy Loveless, Jeff Allen, Bruce Sieleni, and Donald Black, "Attention Deficit Hyperactivity Disorder in Men and Women Newly Committed to Prison," *International Journal of Offender Therapy and Comparative Criminology* 54:361–377 (2010).

169. Russell Barkley, Mariellen Fischer, Lori Smallish, and Kenneth Fletcher, "Young Adult Follow-Up of Hyperactive Children: Antisocial Activities and Drug Use," *Journal of Child Psychology and Psychiatry* 45:195–211 (2004); Molina Pelham Jr., "Childhood Predictors of Adolescent Substance Use in a Longitudinal Study of Children with ADHD," *Journal of Abnormal Psychology* 112:497–507 (2003); Peter Muris and Cor Meesters, "The Validity of Attention Deficit Hyperactivity and Hyperkinetic Disorder Symptom Domains in Nonclinical Dutch Children," *Journal of Clinical Child and Adolescent Psychology* 32:460–466 (2003).

170. Elizabeth Hart et al., "Criterion Validity of Informants in the Diagnosis of Disruptive Behavior Disorders in Children: A Preliminary Study," *Journal of Consulting and Clinical Psychology* 62:410–414 (1994).

171. Joseph Biederman, Michael Monuteaux, Eric Mick, Thomas Spencer, Timothy Wilens, Julie Silva, Lindsey Snyder, and Stephen Faraone, "Young Adult Outcome of Attention Deficit Hyperactivity Disorder: A Controlled 10-Year Follow-Up Study," *Psychological Medicine* 36:167–179 (2006).

172. Jukka Savolainen, Alex Mason, Jonathan Bolen, Mary Chmelka, Tuula Hurtig, Hann Ebeling, Tanja Nordström, and Anja Taanila, "The Path from Childhood Behavioural Disorders to Felony Offending: Investigating the Role of Adolescent Drinking, Peer Marginalisation and School Failure," *Criminal Behaviour and Mental Health* 25:375–388 (2015); Ivy Defoe, David Farrington, and Rolf Loeber, "Disentangling the Relationship Between Delinquency and Hyperactivity, Low Achievement, Depression, and Low Socioeconomic Status: Analysis of Repeated Longitudinal Data," *Journal of Criminal Justice* 41:100–107 (2013).

173. Karen Harding, Richard Judah, and Charles Gant, "Outcome-Based Comparison of Ritalin[R] versus Food-Supplement Treated Children with AD/HD," *Alternative Medicine Review* 8:319–330 (2003).

174. Stephen Hinshaw, Elizabeth Owens, Nilofar Sami, and Samantha Fargeon, "Prospective Follow-Up of Girls with Attention-Deficit/Hyperactivity Disorder into Adolescence: Evidence for Continuing Cross-Domain Impairment," *Journal of Consulting and Clinical Psychology* 74:489–499 (2006).

175. Jack Katz, *Seductions of Crime* (New York: Basic Books, 1988), pp. 12–15.

176. Lee Ellis, "Arousal Theory and the Religiosity-Criminality Relationship," in Peter Cordella and Larry Siegel, eds., *Contemporary Criminological Theory* (Boston: Northeastern University, 1996), pp. 65–84.

177. Olivia Choy, Adrian Raine, Jill Portnoy, Anna Rudo-Hutt, Yu Gao, and Liana Soyfer, "The Mediating Role of Heart Rate on the Social Adversity-Antisocial Behavior Relationship: A Social Neurocriminology Perspective," *Journal of Research in Crime and Delinquency* 52:303–341 (2015).

178. Lee Ellis and Anthony Hoskin, "Criminality and the 2D:4D Ratio: Testing the Prenatal Androgen Hypothesis," *International Journal of Offender Therapy and Comparative Criminology* 59:295–312 (2015).

179. Adrian Raine, Peter Venables, and Sarnoff Mednick, "Low Resting Heart Rate at Age 3 Years Predisposes to Aggression at Age 11 Years: Evidence from the Mauritius Child Health Project," *Journal of the American Academy of Adolescent Psychiatry* 36:1457–1464 (1997).

180. David Rowe, *The Limits of Family Influence: Genes, Experiences and Behavior* (New York: Guilford Press, 1995), p. 64.

181. For a review, see Lisabeth Fisher DiLalla and Irving Gottesman, "Biological and Genetic Contributors to Violence—Widom's Untold Tale," *Psychological Bulletin* 109:125–129 (1991).

182. Anita Thapar, Kate Langley, Tom Fowler, Frances Rice, Darko Turic, Naureen Whittinger, John Aggleton, Marianne Van den Bree, Michael Owen, and Michael O'Donovan, "Catechol O-methyltransferase Gene Variant and Birth Weight Predict Early-Onset Antisocial Behavior in Children with Attention-Deficit/Hyperactivity Disorder," *Archives of General Psychiatry* 62:1275–1278 (2005).

183. Ronald L. Simons, Man Kit Lei, Eric A. Stewart, Steven R. H. Beach, Gene H. Brody, Robert A. Philibert, and Frederick X. Gibbons, "Social Adversity, Genetic Variation, Street Code, and Aggression: A Genetically Informed Model of Violent Behavior," *Youth Violence and Juvenile Justice* 10:3–24 (2012).

184. Kevin Beaver, John Paul Wright, and Matt DeLisi, "Delinquent Peer Group Formation: Evidence of a Gene X Environment Correlation," *Journal of Genetic Psychology* 169:227–244 (2008).

185. Kevin Beaver, Chris Gibson, Michael Turner, Matt DeLisi, Michael Vaughn, and Ashleigh Holand, "Stability of Delinquent Peer Associations: A Biosocial Test of Warr's Sticky-Friends Hypothesis," *Crime and Delinquency* 57:907–927 (2011).

186. Kevin M. Beaver, "The Effects of Genetics, the Environment, and Low Self-Control on Perceived Maternal and Paternal Socialization: Results from a Longitudinal Sample of Twins," *Journal of Quantitative Criminology* 27:85–105 (2011).

187. Carol Van Hulle, Brian D'Onfrio, Joseph Rodgers, Irwin Waldman, and Benjamin Lahey, "Sex Differences in the Causes of Self-Reported Adolescent Delinquency," *Journal of Abnormal Psychology* 116:236–248 (2007).

188. K. Dean, P. B. Mortensen, H. Stevens, R. M. Murray, E. Walsh, and E. Agerbo, "Criminal Conviction Among Offspring with Parental History of Mental Disorder," *Psychological Medicine* 42:571–581 (2012).

189. Ping Qin, "The Relationship of Suicide Risk to Family History of Suicide and Psychiatric Disorders," *Psychiatric Times* 20:62–63 (2003).

190. D. J. West and D. P. Farrington, "Who Becomes Delinquent?" in D. J. West and D. P. Farrington, eds., *The Delinquent Way of Life* (London: Heinemann, 1977), pp. 1–28; D. J. West, *Delinquency: Its Roots, Careers, and Prospects* (Cambridge, MA: Harvard University Press, 1982).

191. West, *Delinquency*, p. 114.

192. David Farrington, "Understanding and Preventing Bullying," in Michael Tonry, ed., *Crime and Justice*, vol. 17 (Chicago: University of Chicago Press, 1993), pp. 381–457.

193. Terence Thornberry, Adrienne Freeman-Gallant, Alan Lizotte, Marvin Krohn, and Carolyn Smith, "Linked Lives: The Intergenerational Transmission of Antisocial Behavior," *Journal of Abnormal Child Psychology* 31:171–185 (2003).

194. David Rowe and David Farrington, "The Familial Transmission of Criminal Convictions," *Criminology* 35:177–201 (1997).

195. Abigail Fagan and Jake Najman, "Sibling Influences on Adolescent Delinquent Behaviour: An Australian Longitudinal Study," *Journal of Adolescence* 26:547–559 (2003).

196. David Rowe and Bill Gulley, "Sibling Effects on Substance Use and Delinquency," *Criminology* 30:217–232 (1992); see also David Rowe, Joseph Rogers, and Sylvia Meseck-Bushey, "Sibling Delinquency and the Family Environment: Shared and Unshared Influences," *Child Development* 63:59–67 (1992).

197. Dana Haynie and Suzanne McHugh, "Sibling Deviance: In the Shadows of Mutual and Unique Friendship Effects?" *Criminology* 41:355–393 (2003).

198. Kevin Beaver, "The Familial Concentration and Transmission of Crime," *Criminal Justice and Behavior* 40:139–155 (2013).

199. Louise Arseneault, Terrie Moffitt, Avshalom Caspi, Alan Taylor, Fruhling Rijsdijk, Sara Jaffee, Jennifer Ablow, and Jeffrey Measelle, "Strong Genetic Effects on Cross-situational Antisocial Behaviour Among 5-year-old Children According to Mothers, Teachers, Examiner-Observers, and Twins' Self-Reports," *Journal of Child Psychology and Psychiatry* 44:832–848 (2003).

200. Laura Baker, Kristen Jacobson, Adrian Raine, Dora Isabel Lozano, and Serena Bezdjian, "Genetic and Environmental Bases of Childhood Antisocial Behavior: A Multi-Informant Twin Study," *Journal of Abnormal Psychology* 116:219–235 (2007).

201. For a general review, see Nancy Segal, *Entwined Lives: Twins and What They Tell Us about Human Behavior* (New York: Dutton, 2000); David Rowe, "Sibling Interaction and Self-Reported Delinquent Behavior: A Study of 265 Twin Pairs," *Criminology* 23:223–240 (1985); Nancy Segal, "Monozygotic and Dizygotic Twins: A Comparative Analysis of Mental Ability Profiles," *Child Development* 56:1051–1058 (1985).

202. Qin, "The Relationship of Suicide Risk to Family History of Suicide and Psychiatric Disorders."

203. Jane Scourfield, Marianne Van den Bree, Neilson Martin, and Peter McGuffin, "Conduct Problems in Children and Adolescents: A Twin Study," *Archives of General Psychiatry* 61:489–496 (2004); Jeanette Taylor, Bryan Loney, Leonardo Bobadilla, William Iacono, and Matt McGue, "Genetic and Environmental Influences on Psychopathy Trait Dimensions in a Community Sample of Male Twins," *Journal of Abnormal Child Psychology* 31:633–645 (2003).

204. Ginette Dionne, Richard Tremblay, Michel Boivin, David Laplante, and Daniel Perusse, "Physical Aggression and Expressive Vocabulary in 19-Month-Old Twins," *Developmental Psychology* 39:261–273 (2003).

205. Sara R. Jaffee, Avshalom Caspi, Terrie Moffitt, Kenneth Dodge, Michael Rutter, Alan Taylor, and Lucy Tully, "Nature X Nurture: Genetic Vulnerabilities Interact with Physical Maltreatment to Promote Conduct Problems," *Development and Psychopathology* 17:67–84 (2005).

206. Essi Viding, James Blair, Terrie Moffitt, and Robert Plomin, "Evidence for Substantial Genetic Risk for Psychopathy in 7-Year-Olds," *Journal of Child Psychology and Psychiatry* 46:592–597 (2005).

207. Thomas Bouchard, "Genetic and Environmental Influences on Intelligence and Special Mental Abilities," *American Journal of Human Biology* 70:253–275 (1998); some findings from the Minnesota study can be viewed at https://mctfr.psych.umn.edu/.

208. Remi Cadoret, Colleen Cain, and Raymond Crowe, "Evidence for a Gene-Environment Interaction in the Development of Adolescent Antisocial Behavior," *Behavior Genetics* 13:301–310 (1983).

209. Jody Alberts-Corush, Philip Firestone, and John Goodman, "Attention and Impulsivity Characteristics of the Biological and Adoptive Parents of Hyperactive and Normal Control Children," *American Journal of Orthopsychiatry* 56:413–423 (1986).

210. For similar findings, see William Gabrielli and Sarnoff Mednick, "Urban Environment, Genetics, and Crime," *Criminology* 22:645–653 (1984).

211. Brian Boutwell and Kevin Beaver, "A Biosocial Explanation of Delinquency Abstention," *Criminal Behaviour and Mental Health* 18:59–74 (2008).

212. Gregory Carey and David DiLalla, "Personality and Psychopathology: Genetic Perspectives," *Journal of Abnormal Psychology* 103:32–43 (1994).

213. Kevin M. Beaver, "The Effects of Genetics, the Environment, and Low Self-Control on Perceived Maternal and Paternal Socialization: Results from a Longitudinal Sample of Twins," *Journal of Quantitative Criminology*, published online July 9, 2010, http://www.springerlink.com/content/1579675h65435717/.

214. Alice Gregory, Thalia Eley, and Robert Plomin, "Exploring the Association Between Anxiety and Conduct Problems in a Large Sample of Twins Aged 2–4," *Journal of Abnormal Child Psychology* 32:111–123 (2004).

215. Callie Burt and Ronald Simons, "Pulling Back the Curtain on Heritability Studies: Biosocial Criminology in the Postgenomic Era," *Criminology* 52:223–262 (2014).

216. J. C. Barnes, John Paul Wright, Brian B. Boutwell, Joseph A. Schwartz, Eric J. Connolly, Joseph L. Nedelec, and Kevin M. Beaver, "Demonstrating the Validity of Twin Research in Criminology," *Criminology* 52:588–626 (2014).

217. Marshall Jones and Donald Jones, "The Contagious Nature of Antisocial Behavior," *Criminology* 38:25–46 (2000).

218. Ibid., p. 31.

219. Lawrence Cohen and Richard Machalek, "A General Theory of Expropriative Crime: An Evolutionary Ecological Approach," *American Journal of Sociology* 94:465–501 (1988).

220. For a general review, see Martin Daly and Margo Wilson, "Crime and Conflict: Homicide in Evolutionary Psychological Theory," in Michael Tonry, ed., *Crime and Justice, An Annual Edition* (Chicago: University of Chicago Press, 1997), pp. 51–100.

221. David Rowe, Alexander Vazsonyi, and Aurelio Jose Figuerdo, "Mating-Effort in Adolescence: A Conditional of Alternative Strategy," *Personal Individual Differences* 23:105–115 (1997).

222. Ibid.

223. Lee Ellis, "The Evolution of Violent Criminal Behavior and Its Nonlegal Equivalent," in Harry Hoffman, ed., *Crime in Biological, Social, and Moral Contexts* (New York: Praeger, 1990), pp. 61–81.

224. Lee Ellis and Anthony Walsh, "Gene-Based Evolutionary Theories of Criminology," *Criminology* 35:229–276 (1997).

225. Byron Roth, "Crime and Child Rearing," *Society* 34:39–45 (1996).

226. For a thorough review of this issue, see David Brandt and S. Jack Zlotnick, *The Psychology and Treatment of the Youthful Offender* (Springfield, IL: Charles C Thomas, 1988).

227. Spencer Rathus, *Psychology* (New York: Holt, Rinehart and Winston, 1996), pp. 11–21.

228. See Sigmund Freud, *An Outline of Psychoanalysis*, James Strachey, trans. (New York: Norton, 1963).

229. See Erik Erikson, *Identity, Youth, and Crisis* (New York: Norton, 1968).

230. August Aichorn, *Wayward Youth* (New York: Viking Press, 1935).

231. David Abrahamsen, *Crime and Human Mind* (New York: Columbia University Press, 1944), p. 137.

232. See Fritz Redl and Hans Toch, "The Psychoanalytic Perspective," in Hans Toch, ed., *Psychology of Crime and Criminal Justice* (New York: Holt, Rinehart and Winston, 1979), pp. 193–195.

233. Seymour Halleck, *Psychiatry and the Dilemmas of Crime* (Berkeley: University of California Press, 1971).

234. Brandt and Zlotnick, *The Psychology and Treatment of the Youthful Offender*, pp. 72–73.

235. John Bowlby, "Maternal Care and Mental Health," *World Health Organization Monograph* (WHO Monographs Series No. 2) (Geneva: World Health Organization, 1951), p. 53.

236. Ibid., p. 13.

237. Eric Wood and Shelley Riggs, "Predictors of Child Molestation: Adult Attachment, Cognitive Distortions, and Empathy," *Journal of Interpersonal Violence* 23:259–275 (2008).

238. Karen L. Hayslett-McCall and Thomas J. Bernard, "Attachment, Masculinity, and Self-control: A Theory of Male Crime Rates," *Theoretical Criminology* 6:5–33 (2002).

239. Leslie Gordon Simons, Tara Sutton, Ronald Simons, Frederick Gibbons, and Velma McBride Murry, "Mechanisms that Link Parenting Practices to Adolescents' Risky Sexual Behavior: A Test of Six Competing Theories," *Journal of Youth and Adolescence* 45:255–270 (2016); Melissa D. Grady, Jill Levenson, and Tess Bolder, "Linking Adverse Childhood Effects and Attachment: A Theory of Etiology for Sexual Offending," *Trauma Violence Abuse*, published online January 25, 2016.

240. Kara Fletcher, Jennifer Nutton, and Denise Brend, "Attachment, a Matter of Substance: The Potential of Attachment Theory in the Treatment of Addictions," *Clinical Social Work Journal* 43:109–117 (2015).

241. Scott Parrott and Caroline Parrott, "Law and Disorder: The Portrayal of Mental Illness in U.S. Crime Dramas," *Journal of Broadcasting and Electronic Media* 59:640–657 (2015).

242. Halleck, *Psychiatry and the Dilemmas of Crime*.

243. Paige Crosby Ouimette, "Psychopathology and Sexual Aggression in Nonincarcerated Men," *Violence and Victimization* 12:389–397 (1997).

244. Minna Ritakallio, Riittakerttu Kaltiala-Heino, Janne Kivivuori, Tiina Luukkaala, and Matti Rimpelä, "Delinquency and the Profile of Offences Among Depressed and Non-Depressed Adolescents," *Criminal Behaviour and Mental Health* 16:100–110 (2006); Ellen Kjelsberg, "Gender and Disorder Specific Criminal Career Profiles in Former Adolescent Psychiatric In-Patients," *Journal of Youth and Adolescence* 33:261–270 (2004).

245. Grégoire Zimmermann, "Delinquency in Male Adolescents: The Role of Alexithymia and Family Structure," *Journal of Adolescence* 29:321–332 (2006).

246. Ching-hua Ho, J. B. Kingree, and Martie P. Thompson, "Associations Between Juvenile Delinquency and Weight-Related Variables: Analyses from a National Sample of High School Students," *International Journal of Eating Disorders* 39:477–483 (2006).

247. Patricia Kerig, Karin Vanderzee, Stephen Becker, and Rose Marie Ward, *Journal of Child and Adolescent Trauma* 5:129–144 (2012).

248. Dexter Voisin, Caitlin Elsaesser, Dong Kim, Sadiq Patel, and Annie Cantara, "The Relationship Between Family Stress and Behavioral Health Among African American Adolescents," *Journal of Child and Family Studies* 25:2201–2210 (2016).

249. Robert Vermeiren, "Psychopathology and Delinquency in Adolescents: A Descriptive and Developmental Perspective," *Clinical Psychology Review* 23:277–318 (2003).

250. Niranjan Karnik, Marie Soller, Allison Redlich, Melissa Silverman, Helena Kraemer, Rudy Haapanen, and Hans Steiner, "Prevalence of and Gender Differences in Psychiatric Disorders Among Juvenile Delinquents Incarcerated for Nine Months," *Psychiatric Services* 60:838–841 (2009).

251. Nathan Link, Francis Cullen, Robert Agnew, and Bruce Link "Can General Strain Theory Help Us Understand Violent Behaviors Among People with Mental Illnesses?' *Justice Quarterly* 33:729–754 (2016).

252. David Vinkers, Edwin de Beurs, and Marko Barendregt, "Psychiatric Disorders and Repeat Offending," *American Journal of Psychiatry* 166:489 (2009).

253. David Vinkers, Edwin Beurs, Marko Barendregt, Thomas Rinne, and Hans Hoek, "The Relationship Between Mental Disorders and Different Types of Crime," *Criminal Behaviour and Mental Health* 21:307–320 (2011).

254. Jeffrey Burke, Rolf Loeber, and Boris Birmaher, "Oppositional Defiant Disorder and Conduct Disorder: A Review of the Past 10 Years, Part II," *Journal of the American Academy of Child and Adolescent Psychiatry* 41:1275–1294 (2002).

255. Kjelsberg, "Gender and Disorder Specific Criminal Career Profiles in Former Adolescent Psychiatric In-Patients"; Barbara Maughan, Richard Rowe, Julie Messer, Robert Goodman, and Howard Meltzer, "Conduct Disorder and Oppositional Defiant Disorder in a National Sample: Developmental Epidemiology," *Journal of Child Psychology and Psychiatry and Allied Disciplines* 45:609–621 (2004).

256. Paul Rohde, Gregory N. Clarke, David E. Mace, Jenel S. Jorgensen, and John R. Seeley, "An Efficacy/Effectiveness Study of Cognitive-Behavioral Treatment for Adolescents with Comorbid Major Depression and Conduct Disorder," *Journal of the American Academy of Child and Adolescent Psychiatry* 43:660–669 (2004).

257. Joyce Akse, Bill Hale, Rutger Engels, Quinten Raaijmakers, and Wim Meeus, "Co-occurrence of Depression and Delinquency in Personality Types," *European Journal of Personality* 21:235–256 (2007).

258. Jennifer Beyers and Rolf Loeber, "Untangling Developmental Relations Between Depressed Mood and Delinquency in Male Adolescents," *Journal of Abnormal Child Psychology* 31:247–267 (2003).

259. Dorothy Espelage, Elizabeth Cauffman, Lisa Broidy, Alex Piquero, Paul Mazerolle, and Hans Steiner, "A Cluster-Analytic Investigation of MMPI Profiles of Serious Male and Female Juvenile Offenders," *Journal of the American Academy of Child and Adolescent Psychiatry* 42:770–777 (2003).

260. Brandt and Zlotnick, *The Psychology and Treatment of the Youthful Offender*, pp. 72–73.

261. Eric Silver, "Mental Disorder and Violent Victimization: The Mediating Role of Involvement in Conflicted Social Relationships," *Criminology* 40:191–212 (2002).

262. Ibid.

263. Ronald Simons, Leslie Gordon Simons, Yi-Fu Chen, Gene Brody, and Kuei-Hsiu Lin, "Identifying the Psychological Factors that Mediate the Association Between Parenting Practices and Delinquency," *Criminology* 45:481–517 (2007).

264. Stacy De Coster and Karen Heimer, "The Relationship Between Law Violation and Depression: An Interactionist Analysis," *Criminology* 39:799–836 (2001).

265. B. Lögdberg, L.-L. Nilsson, M. T. Levander, and S. Levander, "Schizophrenia, Neighbourhood, and Crime," *Acta Psychiatrica Scandinavica* 110:92–97 (2004); Stacy DeCoster and Karen Heimer, "The Relationship Between Law Violation and Depression: An Interactionist Analysis," *Criminology* 39:799–837 (2001).

266. Sonja Siennick, "The Timing and Mechanisms of the Offending-Depression Link," *Criminology* 45:583–615 (2007).

267. H. Khalifeh, S. Johnson, L. M. Howard, R. Borschmann, D. Osborn, K. Dean, C. Hart, J. Hogg, and P. Moran, "Violent and Non-violent Crime Against Adults with Severe Mental Illness," *British Journal of Psychiatry* 206:275–282 (2015).

268. Tamsin B. R. Short, Stuart Thomas, Stefan Luebbers, Paul Mullen, and James Ogloff, "A Case-Linkage Study of Crime Victimisation in Schizophrenia-Spectrum Disorders over a Period of Deinstitutionalization," *BMC Psychiatry* 13:1–9 (2013).

269. Courtenay Sellers, Christopher Sullivan, Bonita Veysey, and Jon Shane, "Responding to Persons with Mental Illnesses: Police Perspectives on Specialized and Traditional Practices," *Behavioral Sciences and the Law* 23:647–657 (2005).

270. Paul Hirschfield, Tina Maschi, Helene Raskin White, Leah Goldman Traub, and Rolf Loeber, "Mental Health and Juvenile Arrests: Criminality, Criminalization, or Compassion?" *Criminology* 44:593–630 (2006).

271. See Albert Bandura and Frances Menlove, "Factors Determining Vicarious Extinction of Avoidance Behavior Through Symbolic Modeling," *Journal of Personality and Social Psychology* 8:99–108 (1965); Albert Bandura and Richard Walters, *Social Learning and Personality Development* (New York: Holt, Rinehart and Winston, 1963).

272. David Perry, Louise Perry, and Paul Rasmussen, "Cognitive Social Learning Mediators of Aggression," *Child Development* 57:700–711 (1986).

273. Bonnie Carlson, "Children's Beliefs about Punishment," *American Journal of Orthopsychiatry* 56:308–312 (1986).

274. Albert Bandura and Richard Walters, *Adolescent Aggression* (New York: Ronald Press, 1959), p. 32.

275. See Jean Piaget, *The Moral Judgment of the Child* (London: Keagan Paul, 1932).

276. Lawrence Kohlberg, *Stages in the Development of Moral Thought and Action* (New York: Holt, Rinehart and Winston, 1969).

277. L. Kohlberg, K. Kauffman, P. Scharf, and J. Hickey, *The Just Community Approach in Corrections: A Manual* (Niantic, CT: Connecticut Department of Corrections, 1973).

278. Scott Henggeler, *Delinquency in Adolescence* (Newbury Park, CA: Sage Publications, 1989), p. 26.

279. Ibid.

280. K. A. Dodge, "A Social Information Processing Model of Social Competence in Children," in M. Perlmutter, ed., *Minnesota Symposium in Child Psychology*, vol. 18 (Hillsdale, NJ: Erlbaum, 1986), pp. 77–125.

281. Adrian Raine, Peter Venables, and Mark Williams, "Better Autonomic Conditioning and Faster Electrodermal Half-Recovery Time at Age 15 Years as Possible Protective Factors Against Crime at Age 29 Years," *Developmental Psychology* 32:624–630 (1996).

282. Jean Marie McGloin and Travis Pratt, "Cognitive Ability and Delinquent Behavior Among Inner-City Youth: A Life-Course Analysis of Main, Mediating, and Interaction Effects," *International Journal of Offender Therapy and Comparative Criminology* 47:253–271 (2003).

283. L. Huesman and L. Eron, "Individual Differences and the Trait of Aggression," *European Journal of Personality* 3:95–106 (1989).

284. Judith Baer and Tina Maschi, "Random Acts of Delinquency: Trauma and Self-Destructiveness in Juvenile Offenders," *Child and Adolescent Social Work Journal* 20:85–99 (2003).

285. Rolf Loeber and Dale Hay, "Key Issues in the Development of Aggression and Violence from Childhood to Early Adulthood," *Annual Review of Psychology* 48:371–410 (1997).

286. Tony Ward and Claire Stewart, "The Relationship Between Human Needs and Criminogenic Needs," *Crime and Law* 9:219–225 (2003).

287. J. E. Lochman, "Self and Peer Perceptions and Attributional Biases of Aggressive and Nonaggressive Boys in Dyadic Interactions," *Journal of Consulting and Clinical Psychology* 55:404–410 (1987).

288. Kathleen Cirillo et al., "School Violence: Prevalence and Intervention Strategies for At-Risk Adolescents," *Adolescence* 33:319–331 (1998).

289. Leilani Greening, "Adolescent Stealers' and Nonstealers' Social Problem-Solving Skills," *Adolescence* 32:51–56 (1997).

290. See Walter Mischel, *Introduction to Personality*, 4th ed. (New York: Holt, Rinehart and Winston, 1986).

291. D. A. Andrews and J. Stephen Wormith, "Personality and Crime: Knowledge and Construction in Criminology," *Justice Quarterly* 6:289–310 (1989); Donald Gibbons, "Comment—Personality and Crime: Non-Issues, Real Issues, and a Theory and Research Agenda," *Justice Quarterly* 6:311–324 (1989).

292. Sheldon Glueck and Eleanor Glueck, *Unraveling Juvenile Delinquency* (Cambridge, MA: Harvard University Press, 1950).

293. See Hans Eysenck, *Personality and Crime* (London: Routledge and Kegan Paul, 1977).

294. David Farrington, "*Psychobiological Factors in the Explanation and Reduction of Delinquency*," *Today's Delinquent* 7:37–51 (1988).

295. Laurie Frost, Terrie Moffitt, and Rob McGee, "Neuropsychological Correlates of Psychopathology in an Unselected Cohort of Young Adolescents," *Journal of Abnormal Psychology* 98:307–313 (1989).

296. Edelyn Verona and Joyce Carbonell, "Female Violence and Personality," *Criminal Justice and Behavior* 27:176–195 (2000).

297. Hans Eysenck and M. W. Eysenck, *Personality and Individual Differences* (New York: Plenum, 1985).

298. Catrien Bijleveld and Jan Hendriks, "Juvenile Sex Offenders: Differences Between Group and Solo Offenders," *Psychology, Crime and Law* 9:237–246 (2003).

299. For a review of this concept, see Ronald Blackburn, "Personality Disorder and Psychopathy: Conceptual and Empirical Integration," *Psychology, Crime and Law* 13:7–18 (2007).

300. Linda Mealey, "The Sociobiology of Sociopathy: An Integrated Evolutionary Model," *Behavioral and Brain Sciences* 18:523–540 (1995).

301. Jamie L. Flexon, "Evaluating Variant Callous-Unemotional Traits Among Noninstitutionalized Youth, Implications for Violence Research and Policy," *Youth Violence and Juvenile Justice* 13:18–40 (2015).

302. Gisli Gudjonsson, Emil Einarsson, Ólafur Örn Bragason, and Jon Fridrik Sigurdsson, "Personality Predictors of Self-Reported

Offending in Icelandic Students," *Psychology, Crime and Law* 12:383–393 (2006).

303. Peter Johansson and Margaret Kerr, "Psychopathy and Intelligence: A Second Look," *Journal of Personality Disorders* 19:357–369 (2005).

304. Hervey Cleckley, "Psychopathic States," in S. Aneti, ed., *American Handbook of Psychiatry* (New York: Basic Books, 1959), pp. 567–569.

305. Lewis Yablonsky, *The Violent Gang* (Baltimore: Penguin, 1971), pp. 195–205.

306. Sue Kellett and Harriet Gross, "Addicted to Joyriding? An Exploration of Young Offenders' Accounts of Their Car Crime," *Psychology, Crime and Law* 12:39–59 (2006).

307. Sonja Krstic, Raymond A. Knight, and Carrie A. Robertson, "Developmental Antecedents of the Facets of Psychopathy: The Role of Multiple Abuse Experiences," *Journal of Personality Disorders* 19:1–17 (2015).

308. Kevin Beaver, Meghan Rowland, Joseph Schwartz, and Joseph Nedelec, "The Genetic Origins of Psychopathic Traits in Adult Males and Females: Results from an Adoption-Based Study," *Journal of Criminal Justice* 39:426–432 (2011).

309. Rolf Holmqvist, "Psychopathy and Affect Consciousness in Young Criminal Offenders," *Journal of Interpersonal Violence* 23:209–224 (2008).

310. James Blair, Derek Mitchell, and Karina Blair, *The Psychopath: Emotion and the Brain* (New York: Blackwell Publishing, 2005).

311. L. M. Terman, "Research on the Diagnosis of Predelinquent Tendencies," *Journal of Delinquency* 9:124–130 (1925); Terman, *Measurement of Intelligence* (Boston: Houghton Mifflin, 1916). For example, see M. G. Caldwell, "The Intelligence of Delinquent Boys Committed to Wisconsin Industrial School," *Journal of Criminal Law and Criminology* 20:421–428 (1929); and C. Murcheson, *Criminal Intelligence* (Worcester, MA: Clark University, 1926), pp. 41–44.

312. Henry Goddard, *Efficiency and Levels of Intelligence* (Princeton, NJ: Princeton University Press, 1920).

313. William Healy and Augusta Bronner, *Delinquency and Criminals: Their Making and Unmaking* (New York: Macmillan, 1926).

314. Joseph Lee Rogers, H. Harrington Cleveland, Edwin van den Oord, and David Rowe, "Resolving the Debate over Birth Order, Family Size, and Intelligence," *American Psychologist* 55:599–612 (2000).

315. Kenneth Eels, *Intelligence and Cultural Differences* (Chicago: University of Chicago Press, 1951), p. 181.

316. Sorel Cahahn and Nora Cohen, "Age versus Schooling Effects on Intelligence Development," *Child Development* 60:1239–1249 (1989).

317. John Slawson, *The Delinquent Boys* (Boston: Budget Press, 1926).

318. Edwin Sutherland, "Mental Deficiency and Crime," in Kimball Young, ed., *Social Attitudes* (New York: Henry Holt, 1973).

319. Travis Hirschi and Michael Hindelang, "Intelligence and Delinquency: A Revisionist Review," *American Sociological Review* 42:471–586 (1977).

320. Terrie Moffitt and Phil Silva, "IQ and Delinquency: A Direct Test of the Differential Detection Hypothesis," *Journal of Abnormal Psychology* 97:1–4 (1988); E. Kandel et al., "IQ as a Protective Factor for Subjects at a High Risk for Antisocial Behavior," *Journal of Consulting and Clinical Psychology* 56:224–226 (1988); Christine Ward and Richard McFall, "Further Validation of the Problem Inventory for Adolescent Girls: Comparing Caucasian and Black Delinquents and Nondelinquents," *Journal of Consulting and Clinical Psychology* 54:732–733 (1986).

321. Wilson and Herrnstein, *Crime and Human Nature*, p. 148.

322. Alex Piquero, "Frequency, Specialization, and Violence in Offending Careers," *Journal of Research in Crime and Delinquency* 37:392–418 (2000).

323. Matt DeLisi, Alex Piquero, and Stephanie Cardwell, "The Unpredictability of Murder," *Youth Violence and Juvenile Justice* 14:26–42 (2016).

324. Kevin Beaver and John Paul Wright, "The Association Between County-Level IQ and County-Level Crime Rates," *Intelligence* 39:22–26 (2011); Jared Bartels, Joseph Ryan, Lynn Urban, and Laura Glass, "Correlations Between Estimates of State IQ and FBI Crime Statistics," *Personality and Individual Differences* 48:579–583 (2010).

325. David Farrington, "Juvenile Delinquency," in John C. Coleman, ed., *The School Years* (London: Routledge, 1992), p. 137.

326. Thomas McNulty, Paul Bellair, and Stephen Watts, "Neighborhood Disadvantage and Verbal Ability as Explanations of the Black–White Difference in Adolescent Violence: Toward an Integrated Model," *Crime and Delinquency* 59:140–160 (2013).

327. Jean McGloin, Travis Pratt, and Jeff Maahs, "Rethinking the IQ-Delinquency Relationship: A Longitudinal Analysis of Multiple Theoretical Models," *Justice Quarterly* 21:603–635 (2004).

328. Wilson and Herrnstein, p. 171.

329. Glenn Walters and Thomas White, "Heredity and Crime: Bad Genes or Bad Research," *Justice Quarterly* 27:455–485, at 478 (1989).

330. John Cochran, Peter Wood, and Bruce Arneklev, "Is the Religiosity-Delinquency Relationship Spurious? A Test of Arousal and Social Control Theories," *Journal of Research in Crime and Delinquency* 31:92–113 (1994).

331. Lee Ellis, "Genetics and Criminal Behavior," *Criminology* 10:43–66, at 58 (1982).

332. Lee Ellis, "The Evolution of the Nonlegal Equivalent of Aggressive Criminal Behavior," *Aggressive Behavior* 12:57–71 (1986).

333. Edwin Schur, *Radical Nonintervention: Rethinking the Delinquency Problem* (Englewood Cliffs, NJ: Prentice Hall, 1973).

CHAPTER 4

Structure, Process, Culture, and Delinquency

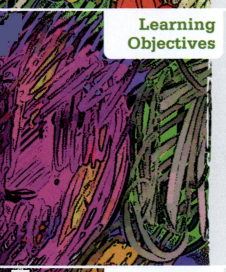

Learning Objectives

1 Explain the association between social conditions and crime
2 Summarize the association between social structure and delinquency
3 Categorize the principles of social disorganization theory
4 Express how social ecologists view the cause of delinquency
5 Analyze the concept of anomie and how it impacts delinquent behavior
6 Give examples of the recent developments in strain theory
7 Define the term *cultural deviance* and analyze theories of cultural deviance
8 Describe the concept of social process and socialization
9 Paraphrase the concept of social learning and social learning theories
10 Give examples of the elements of social control theory

Chapter Outline

Social Factors and Delinquency

Social Structure and Delinquency
Child Poverty

Social Structure Theories

Social Disorganization Theory
The Legacy of Shaw and McKay
Social Ecology Theory
The Effect of Collective Efficacy

Strain Theory
Merton's Theory of Anomie
Institutional Anomie Theory
General Strain Theory

Cultural Deviance Theories
Gang Culture
Lower-Class Values and Focal Concerns

Theory of Delinquent Subculture
Theory of Differential Opportunity
Social Structure Theory and
Public Policy

Social Process Theories
Elements of Socialization
The Effects of Socialization on
Delinquency

Social Learning Theory
Differential Association Theory
Neutralization Theory
Variations on Neutralization Theory

Social Control Theory
Self-Concept and Delinquency
Hirschi's Social Bond Theory

Chapter Features

Focus on Delinquency: The Code of the Streets

Youth Stories: Ethan Couch

Evidence-Based Juvenile Justice—Prevention: Families and Schools Together (FAST)

Case Profile: Steph's Story

IN NOVEMBER 2014, three teenagers from Seattle's Down with the Crew gang—a violent affiliate of the Black Gangster Disciples—set out from Seattle for a 50-mile drive south to the community of Lakewood. Their intention was to rob a large-scale drug house they had received information about.

Around 9:30 PM, a 66-year-old Lakewood man answered a knock at his door and was confronted by the three teens, who forced their way into the home. Though the gang boys soon realized they had busted into the wrong house, they decided to make the best of a bad situation. They pistol-whipped the owner until he was unconscious, tied his hands, and covered him with a blanket. After he was subdued, the gang boys broke down a bathroom door and dragged out his 61-year-old wife, stabbed her, tied her hands, and placed her under the same blanket. After brutalizing the couple, they began to systematically loot the house, carrying stolen items to their car. When the husband regained consciousness, he was able to free himself and his wife, and with all three gang boys outside, he locked the front door, hid in the bedroom, called 911, and retrieved his handgun. When the gangbangers forced their way back inside and kicked down the locked bedroom door, the man fired two shots, hitting teen gang member Taijon Vorhees both times. At that point, all three robbers fled and drove away. The two uninjured gang members—Duprea Wilson and Qiuordai Taylor—threw

Gangster Disciple Gang logo

© Cengage Learning

the dying Vorhees out of the car. The two bumbling gangsters were quickly captured and tried as adults on a variety of felony charges. In March 2016, a jury found Wilson and Taylor guilty on all counts, and the judge sentenced them each to 56 years in prison.[1]

A violent crime committed by three gang members is certainly not a unique event, even in a suburb of Seattle, Washington, not usually known as a hotbed of gang activity. Gangs have become a fixture of the American urban experience. The most recent national survey finds that gangs exist in all levels of the social strata, from rural counties to metropolitan areas. There are now an estimated 30,000 gangs and about 800,000 gang members located in 3,300 cities and towns throughout America. Gang homicides seem to be on an upswing; there are almost 2,000 gang-related killings each year.[2]

To delinquency experts it comes as no surprise that most large gangs develop in poor, deteriorated urban neighborhoods. Many kids in these areas grow up hopeless and alienated, believing that they have little chance of being part of the American Dream.[3] Joining a gang holds the promise of economic rewards and status enhancements, which the conventional world simply cannot provide.

There are numerous reasons why kids join gangs, but certainly many are motivated by a dysfunctional life, inadequate education, and peer pressure, all factors tied to elements of socialization: family, peers, school, and community. When these forces are frayed and damaged, so too is the path a teen travels into adulthood. In essence, understanding delinquent behavior requires us to account for the destructive influence that social forces have on human behavior rather than individual characteristics and traits.

Why are social views of delinquency so popular? One reason is the consistent social patterns found in the delinquency rate. We know that youths are more likely to commit crimes if they live in the poorest neighborhoods within large urban areas. It seems unlikely that most kids with physical or mental problems live in a particular section of town that also happens to be disorganized and deteriorated. Or that teens in one neighborhood watch violent TV shows and films while those in another spend their time on the History Channel. The fact that delinquency rates are highest in the poorest neighborhoods seems more than just a coincidence.

To some delinquency experts, these facts can only mean one thing: the cause of delinquency rests within the dynamics of the social world. They point to cultural norms, social processes, and social institutions as the key elements that shape human behavior. When these elements are strained, delinquency rates increase.[4]

Social Factors and Delinquency

What are the critical social factors believed to cause or affect delinquent behaviors?

- *Interpersonal interactions*. Social relationships with families, peers, schools, jobs, criminal justice agencies, and the like may play an important role in shaping behavioral choices.[5] Inappropriate and disrupted social relations have been linked to crime and delinquency.[6]

- *Community conditions*. Crime and delinquency rates are highest in deteriorated inner-city areas. These communities, wracked by poverty, decay, fear, and despair, also maintain high rates of criminal victimization.[7]

- *Exposure to violence*. Kids living in poor neighborhoods are exposed to a constant stream of antisocial behaviors.[8] Even when neighborhood disadvantage and poverty are taken into account, the more often children are exposed to violence within their residential community, the more likely they are to become violent themselves.[9] One Chicago area study of racial differences in exposure to violence found that the odds of being subjected to violence were 74 percent and 112 percent higher for Hispanic and black kids, respectively, than for white adolescents.[10] Exposure to violence may help explain racial and ethnic differences in the delinquency rate.

- *Social change*. Political unrest and mistrust, economic stress, and family disintegration are social changes that have been found to precede sharp increases in delinquency rates.[11]

- *Low socioeconomic status*. Millions of people have scant, if any, resources and suffer socially and economically as a result.[12] People who live in poverty may have the greatest incentive to commit delinquency.

- *Racial disparity*. The consequences of racial disparity can be significant, especially when it translates into income inequality. The poverty rate among minority groups is still significantly higher than that of whites.[13]

All of these social problems and conditions take a toll on American youth and may help turn them toward antisocial behaviors. In this chapter we will review the most prominent social theories of delinquency that are based on the effects of social problems and social relations. They are divided here into two distinct groups:

- *Social structure theories* hold that delinquency is a function of a person's place in the economic structure.

- *Social process theories* view delinquency as the result of a person's interaction with critical elements of socialization.

Social Structure and Delinquency

stratified society
Grouping society into classes based on the unequal distribution of scarce resources.

People in the United States live in a **stratified society**. Social strata are created by the unequal distribution of wealth, power, and prestige. Social classes are segments of the population whose members have a relatively similar portion of desirable things and who share attitudes, values, norms, and an identifiable lifestyle.

In US society, it is common to identify people as upper-, middle-, and lower-class citizens, with a broad range of economic variations existing within each group. The top 1 percent of households have an annual income of about $400,000 and/or about $1.5 million in liquid assets.[14]

In contrast, though there has been a recent decline in the number of people living below the poverty line, there are still more than 40 million impoverished Americans, defined as a family of four earning $24,000 per year; this amounts to more than 13 percent of the US population.[15] Those living below the poverty line are often forced to live in inadequate housing, have poor health care, and suffer from disrupted family lives, underemployment, and despair.

Income inequality has become a national concern. There is growing fear that the balance of economic and social power is shifting further toward the already affluent, driving the relatively poor to choose illegal, albeit life-enhancing behaviors.[16] There is already data showing a strong positive association between income inequality and violent crime.[17]

Those living in poverty are forced to reside in neighborhoods that experience inadequate housing and health care, disrupted family lives, underemployment, and despair. Living in poor areas magnifies the effect of personal social and economic problems. When kids whose families are poor reside in a poverty-stricken area, they are more likely to engage in antisocial behavior than kids from poor families growing up in more affluent areas. The combination of having a poor family living in a disorganized area may be devastating.[18]

Members of the lower class also suffer in other ways. They are more prone to depression, less likely to have achievement motivation, and less likely to put off immediate gratification for future gain. For example, they may be less willing to stay in school because the rewards for educational achievement are in the distant future.

Sociologist Oscar Lewis coined the phrase **culture of poverty** to describe this condition.[19] Apathy, cynicism, helplessness, and mistrust of social institutions such as schools, government agencies, and the police mark the culture of poverty. This mistrust prevents members of the lower class from taking advantage of the meager opportunities available to them. Lewis's work was the first of a group that described the plight of at-risk children and adults.

Economic disparity will continually haunt members of the **underclass** and their children over the course of their life span. Even if they value education and other middle-class norms, their desperate life circumstances (e.g., high unemployment and nontraditional family structures) may prevent them from developing the skills, habits, and lifestyles that lead first to educational success and later to success in the workplace.[20] Their ability to maintain social ties in the neighborhood become weak and attenuated, further weakening a neighborhood's cohesiveness and its ability to regulate the behavior of its citizens.[21]

culture of poverty
View that lower-class people form a separate culture with their own values and norms, which are sometimes in conflict with conventional society.

underclass
Group of urban poor whose members have little chance of upward mobility or improvement.

Child Poverty

In Chapter 1, we noted that economic disadvantage and poverty can be especially devastating to younger children. Despite this devastation, more than 20 percent of all youth now live in families with incomes below the poverty line, and another 20 percent escape poverty but live in families considered "poor."[22] Not only are they poor, but the number of homeless children in the United States has surged in recent years to an all-time high, amounting to one child in every 30. The National Center on Family Homelessness calculates that nearly 2.5 million American children are now currently homeless.[23]

Chapter 1 also told how poverty takes an even greater toll on minority kids. According to the US Census Bureau, the median family income of Latinos and African Americans is two-thirds that of whites, and the percentage of racial and ethnic minorities living in poverty is double that of European Americans.[24] African American household median income is about $35,000 compared to $54,000 for non-Hispanic white households and almost $75,000 for Asian homes. About

28 percent of African Americans were living at the poverty level, compared to 11 percent of non-Hispanic whites. The unemployment rate for blacks is twice that for non-Hispanic whites (about 10 percent versus about 5 percent), a finding consistent for both men and women.[25] There are also race-based differences in high school completion; white and Asian rates are higher than those of minorities.[26]

These economic and social disparities have haunted members of the minority underclass and their children despite efforts to erase race-based inequality.[27] Though most minority group members value education and other middle-class norms, their desperate life circumstances, such as high unemployment and nontraditional family structures, prevent them from developing the skills and habits that lead first to educational success and later to success in the workplace; these deficits have been linked to crime and drug abuse.[28]

Race-based social and economic disparity can take a terrific toll. Many urban European Americans use their economic, social, and political advantages (i.e., white privilege) to live in sheltered gated communities patrolled by security guards and police.[29] In contrast, a significant proportion of minority group members are relegated to living in segregated inner-city areas, where they are hit hard by race-based disparity such as income inequality and institutional racism.[30] While fewer than 10 percent of so-called white neighborhoods can be considered as poverty zones, residents in 75 percent of minority communities live below the poverty level.[31]

These social factors have been explored in depth by Harvard sociologist William Julius Wilson, who coined the term "the truly disadvantaged" to describe the plight of poor inner-city minority families.[32] Today, Wilson notes, the ability of black men to be family providers has declined, increasing stress for the African American family.[33]

Social Structure Theories

The effects of income inequality, poverty, racism, and despair are viewed by many delinquency experts as key causes of youth crime and drug abuse. Kids growing up poor and living in households that lack economic resources are much more likely to get involved in serious crime than their wealthier peers.[34] To explain this phenomenon, social structure theories suggest that the social forces present in deteriorated lower-class areas are the key determinant of delinquent behavior patterns. Social forces begin to affect people while they are relatively young and continue to influence them throughout their lives. Though not all youthful offenders become adult criminals, many who reside in poverty-stricken lower-class areas become enculturated into the values of inner-city neighborhoods and are the ones most likely to persist in delinquency. Logically, because delinquency rates are consistently higher in lower-class urban centers than in middle-class suburbs, social forces must be operating in blighted urban areas that influence or control behavior.[35]

How can this association between poverty and delinquency be precisely explained? What are the connections that lead from being poor to becoming a delinquent? There are actually three independent yet overlapping theories that reside within the social structure perspective—social disorganization theory, strain theory, and cultural deviance theory.

■ *Social disorganization theory* focuses on the conditions within the urban environment that affect delinquency rates. A disorganized area is one in which institutions of social control—such as the family, commercial establishments, and schools—have broken down and can no longer carry out their expected or stated functions. Indicators of social disorganization include high unemployment, school dropout rates, deteriorated housing, low income levels, and large numbers of single-parent households. Residents in these areas experience conflict and despair, and as a result, antisocial behavior flourishes.

■ *Strain theory* holds that delinquency is a function of the disconnect between the goals people have and the means they can use to obtain them legally. Most

social structure theories
Explain delinquency using socioeconomic conditions and cultural values.

enculturated
The process by which an established culture teaches an individual its norms and values, so that the individual can become an accepted member of the society. Through enculturation, the individual learns what is accepted behavior within that society and his or her particular status within the culture.

social disorganization theory
The inability of a community to exert social control allows youths the freedom to engage in illegal behavior.

strain theory
Links delinquency to the strain of being locked out of the economic mainstream, which creates the anger and frustration that lead to delinquent acts.

cultural deviance theory
A unique lower-class culture develops in disorganized neighborhoods whose set of values and beliefs puts residents in conflict with conventional social norms.

people in the United States desire wealth, material possessions, power, prestige, and other life comforts. And although these social and economic goals are common to people in all economic strata, strain theorists insist that the ability to obtain these goals is class dependent. Members of the lower class are unable to achieve these symbols of success through conventional means. Consequently, they feel anger, frustration, and resentment, which is referred to as "strain." Lower-class citizens can either accept their condition and live out their days as socially responsible, if unrewarded, citizens, or they can choose an alternative means of achieving success, such as theft, violence, or drug trafficking.

■ *Cultural deviance theory*, the third variation of structural theory, combines elements of both strain and social disorganization. According to this view, because of strain and social isolation, a unique lower-class culture develops in disorganized neighborhoods. These independent subcultures maintain a unique set of values and beliefs that are in conflict with conventional social norms. Criminal behavior is an expression of conformity to lower-class subcultural values and traditions and not a rebellion from conventional society. Subcultural values are handed down from one generation to the next in a process called **cultural transmission**.

cultural transmission
Cultural norms and values are passed down from one generation to the next.

Although each of these theories is distinct in crucial aspects, each approach has at its core the view that socially isolated people, living in disorganized neighborhoods, are the ones most likely to experience delinquency-producing social forces. Each branch of social structure theory will now be discussed in some detail.

Social Disorganization Theory

Social disorganization theory ties delinquency rates to socioeconomic conditions:

■ Long-term, unremitting poverty undermines the basic stabilizing forces of the community—family, school, peers, and neighbors—rendering them weakened, attenuated, and ineffective.

■ Poverty undermines the ability of the community to control its inhabitants—to assert informal **social control**—is damaged and frayed.

social control
Ability of social institutions to influence human behavior; the justice system is the primary agency of formal social control.

■ The community becomes "socially disorganized" and its residents surrender to the lure of antisocial behavior. Without social controls, kids are free to join gangs, violate the law, and engage in uncivil and destructive behaviors.

■ Residents develop a sense of hopelessness and mistrust of conventional society. They are frustrated by their inability to become part of the American Dream. Neighborhood kids are constantly exposed to disruption, violence, and incivility.

■ Kids growing up in these disadvantaged areas are at risk for recruitment into gangs and law-violating youth groups.

■ Neighborhood disintegration and the corresponding erosion of social control are the primary causes of delinquent behavior. Community values, norms, and cohesiveness control behavior choices, not personal decision making and individual traits.

Social disorganization theory was first formulated early in the twentieth century by sociologists Clifford Shaw and Henry McKay. These Chicago-based scholars found that delinquency rates were high in what they called **transitional neighborhoods**—areas that had changed from affluence to decay. Here, factories and commercial establishments were interspersed with private residences. In such environments, teenage gangs developed as a means of survival, defense, and friendship. Gang leaders recruited younger members, passing on delinquent traditions and ensuring survival of the gang from one generation to the next (cultural transmission).

transitional neighborhood
Area undergoing a shift in population and structure, usually from middle-class residential to lower-class mixed use.

While mapping delinquency rates in Chicago, Shaw and McKay noted that distinct ecological areas had developed that could be visualized as a series of concentric zones, each with a stable delinquency rate (see Figure 4.1).[36]

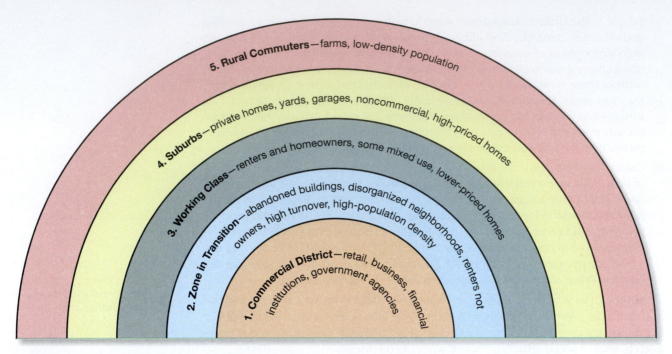

figure 4.1

The Concentric Zone Model

SOURCE: http://www.umsl.edu/~keelr/200/socdisor.html (accessed July 2013).

The areas of heaviest delinquency concentration appeared to be the poverty-stricken, transitional, inner-city zones. The zones farthest from the city's center were the least prone to delinquency. Analysis of these data indicated a stable pattern of delinquent activity in the ecological zones over a 65-year period.[37] These patterns persisted as different ethnic or racial groups moved into the zone. Shaw and McKay found that delinquency was tied to neighborhood characteristics rather than the personal characteristics or culture of the residents.

According to their social disorganization view, a healthy, organized community has the ability to regulate itself so that common goals may be achieved.[38] Those neighborhoods that become disorganized are incapable of social control because they are wracked by deterioration and economic failure.[39] Shaw and McKay claimed that areas continually hurt by poverty and long-term unemployment also experience social disorganization.[40]

The Legacy of Shaw and McKay

Social disorganization concepts articulated by Shaw and McKay have remained a prominent fixture of criminological scholarship and thinking for more than 75 years. Although cultural and social conditions have changed and American society today is much more heterogeneous and mobile than during Shaw and McKay's time, the most important elements of their findings still hold up.[41]

The concept of social disorganization provides a valuable contribution to our understanding of the causes of delinquent behavior. Because they introduced new variables such as social control and the ecology of the city to the study of delinquency, Shaw and McKay's pioneering efforts have had a lasting influence on our understanding of human behaviors.

Social Ecology Theory

social ecologists
Theorists who focus attention on the influence social institutions have on individual behavior and who suggest that law-violating behavior is a response to social rather than individual forces operating in an urban environment.

Shaw and McKay's social disorganization views have been updated by contemporary **social ecologists**, whose work emphasizes the association of community deterioration and economic decline with delinquency, but places less emphasis on values and norms and more on community characteristics and their influence on interpersonal relations. According to this more contemporary view, living in deteriorated, crime-ridden neighborhoods exerts a powerful influence over behavior that is strong enough to neutralize the positive effects of a supportive family and close social ties.[42] In the following sections, some of the more recent social ecological research is discussed in detail.

Community Disorder   Social ecologists have found an association between delinquency rates and community deterioration: disorder, poverty, alienation, disassociation, and fear of delinquency.[43] The presence of disruptive institutions, such as taverns and bars, destabilize neighborhoods and increase the rate of violent crimes.[44]

Areas in which houses are in poor repair, boarded up and burned out, and whose owners are best described as "slumlords" are also the location of the highest violence rates and gun crime.[45] These are neighborhoods in which retail establishments often go bankrupt, are abandoned, and deteriorate physically.[46]

Neighborhood decay serves as a magnet for delinquents and delinquency.[47] The most impulsive kids who lack both social and self-control are free to engage in antisocial activities without fear of restraint or disapproval.[48] When community social control efforts are blunted, delinquency rates increase, further weakening neighborhood cohesiveness.[49]

The concept of **community deterioration and crime** was the subject of a famous *Atlantic* magazine article titled "Broken Windows" http://www .theatlantic.com/magazine/archive /1982/03/broken-windows /304465/.

Poverty Concentration   Inner-city poverty becomes concentrated when working- and middle-class families, both black and white, flee to the suburbs.[50] As the working and middle classes relocate, they take with them their financial and institutional resources and support, undermining the community's level of informal social control.[51] People left behind are socially isolated and have a tough time managing urban decay and controlling youth gangs—after all, the most successful people in the community have left for greener pastures.[52] Young men growing up in such a neighborhood are the most likely to engage in risk taking and delinquency, especially those who perceive few opportunities for legitimate success.[53]

Social problems accumulate in areas that experience poverty concentration. Businesses are disinclined to locate in these concentrated poverty areas; banks become reluctant to lend money for new housing or businesses.[54] Unemployment rates skyrocket, destabilizing households, and producing unstable families who produce children who use violence and aggression to deal with limited opportunity. Because gang violence becomes normative, impressionable youth are led to adopt criminal lifestyles.[55]

Poverty concentration can become quite damaging as large groups or cohorts of people of the same age are forced to compete for relatively scant resources.[56] The result is income and wealth disparities, nonexistent employment opportunities, inferior housing patterns, and unequal access to health care.[57] Limited employment opportunities reduce the stabilizing influence of parents and other adults, who may once have counteracted the allure of youth gangs. Urban areas marked by concentrated poverty become isolated and insulated from the social mainstream and more prone to gang activity, violence, and homicide.[58]

Community Fear   People feel safe in neighborhoods that are orderly and in repair.[59] When people feel distant from one another, disconnected from others in the community, they are more likely to view their environment as a dangerous place.[60] Those living in neighborhoods that suffer social and physical incivilities—rowdy youth, trash and litter, graffiti, abandoned storefronts, burned-out buildings, strangers, drunks, vagabonds, loiterers, prostitutes, noise, congestion, angry words, dirt, and stench—are much more likely to be fearful. Put another way, disorder breeds fear.[61]

Fear is based on experience.[62] Gangs flourish in deteriorated neighborhoods with high levels of poverty, lack of investment, high unemployment rates, and population turnover.[63] Unlike any other crime, however, gang activity is frequently undertaken out in the open, on the public ways, and in full view of the rest

When fear grips a neighborhood, people may seek to flee to safer environments, undermining the area's human capital. Here, a woman walks past graffiti in an alley where residents say gang members congregate in Irvington, New Jersey. State and local police swept through this block, arresting six people and painting over gang graffiti in what they promised would be a sustained crackdown on street gangs in one of New Jersey's deadliest cities.

of the community.[64] People become afraid when they are approached by neighborhood kids selling drugs or when they see gang members hanging out in community parks and playgrounds, undisturbed by the police.[65] They may fear that their children will also be approached and seduced by gang boys into the drug life.[66] Brazen criminal activity undermines community solidarity because it signals that the police must be either corrupt or inept. The fact that gangs are willing to engage openly in drug sales and other types of criminal activity shows their confidence that they have silenced or intimidated law-abiding people in their midst. The police and the community alike become hopeless about their ability to restore community stability, producing greater levels of community fear.

Fear can become contagious. People tell others when they have been victimized, spreading the word that the neighborhood is getting dangerous and that the chances of future victimization are high.[67] They dread leaving their homes at night and withdraw from community life. When people live in areas where the death rates are high and life expectancies are short, they may alter their behavior out of fear. They may feel, "Why plan for the future when there is a significant likelihood that I may never see it?" In such areas, young boys and girls may psychologically adjust by taking risks and discounting the future. Teenage birthrates soar and so do violence rates.[68] For these children, the inevitability of death skews their perspective of how they live their lives.

Siege Mentality The presence of community incivilities, especially when accompanied by relatively high delinquency rates and gang activity, convinces older residents that their neighborhood is dangerous; becoming a crime victim seems inevitable.[69] Eventually they become emotionally numb and indifferent to the suffering of others.[70] Some residents become so suspicious of authority that they develop a **siege mentality** in which the outside world is considered the enemy out to destroy the neighborhood. There is a common belief that police are violent and suspicious, ready to use force on residents. Considering this feeling of mistrust, when police ignore delinquency in poor areas or, conversely, when they are violent and corrupt, anger flares, and people take to the streets and react in violent ways.[71]

siege mentality
Residents become so suspicious of authority that they consider the outside world to be the enemy out to destroy the neighborhood.

Community Change In our postmodern society, urban areas are undergoing rapid structural changes in racial and economic composition. Some may become multiracial, while others become racially homogeneous. Some areas become stable and family oriented, while in others, mobile, never-married people predominate.[72] While changing neighborhoods experience higher delinquency rates, stable neighborhoods have the strength to restrict substance abuse and criminal activity.[73]

As areas decline, residents flee to safer, more stable localities. Flight has become racialized: affluent whites are able to leave communities in decline, and their place is taken by less affluent minority group families who suffer the pains associated with living with concentrated poverty.[74] Those who cannot leave because they are unable to live in more affluent communities face an increased risk of victimization. Some, of course, adapt to neighborhood change. They may create new friendship networks, which help create more stability in their lives.[75]

But not all minority families get "left behind." Those who can move to more affluent neighborhoods do so and soon find that their lifestyles and life chances improve immediately and continue to do so over their life span.[76] Take for instance the Gautreaux Project, a court-ordered initiative begun in 1976, designed to provide a metropolitan-wide remedy for racial discrimination in Chicago's public housing program by helping inner-city families relocate to more affluent white suburbs. Research on the effects of the Gautreaux Project shows that most families who moved to Chicago's suburbs were still living in those suburbs 10 and even 20 years later, and that their children's attitudes toward school improved along with their grades. As Gautreaux children grew up and left home, they moved to neighborhoods that were far safer and more affluent than the inner-city neighborhoods their families had left behind.[77] When sociologists Patrick Sharkey and Robert Sampson examined data on the Gautreaux Project, they found it had benefits that went beyond moving families out of crime-prone areas. Families who were moved to other neighborhoods within the city of Chicago actually experienced an increased risk of violence. In contrast, those families who went to areas outside the city experienced a reduction in exposure to violence and violent offending. Moving outside the city not only brought these families into contact with better schools and higher-income neighbors, but also reduced their levels of fear and increased perceptions of control over their new environment.[78]

Collective Efficacy   Community efforts at social control are weak and attenuated in socially disorganized neighborhoods, where the population is transient, and interpersonal relationships remain superficial and nonsupportive.[79] In these unstable neighborhoods, residents find that the social support they need to live a conventional life is absent or lacking. The resulting lack of social cohesion produces an atmosphere where antisocial behavior becomes normative.[80]

One element of collective efficacy involves the association between social control agencies and the community they serve. Here, in 2013, Douglas County Sheriff Department Lt. Brian Murphy spends some time on the playground with kids during recess at Buffalo Ridge Elementary School in Castle Pines, Colorado, part of a new cooperative effort between law enforcement and schools for more routine police presence at local primary schools. Local police have begun a practice of completing their paperwork from their cruisers in school parking lots and are encouraged to spend more time inside schools.

collective efficacy
The ability of communities to regulate the behavior of their residents through the influence of community institutions, such as the family and school. Residents in these communities share mutual trust and a willingness to intervene in the supervision of children and the maintenance of public order.

In contrast, more cohesive communities, where residents have a stake in the community and know and trust one another, have much lower delinquency rates than less unified areas.[81] These cohesive communities, in which people develop strong interpersonal ties, develop what is known as **collective efficacy**: mutual trust, a willingness to intervene in the supervision of children, and the maintenance of public order.[82] Residents in these areas enjoy a better life because the fruits of cohesiveness are better neighborhood-level education, health care, and housing opportunities.[83]

There are actually three forms of collective efficacy: informal, institutional, and public social control. Informal social control provided by these community-level institutions is a key determinant of neighborhood delinquency rates.[84]

■ *Informal social control.* Some elements of collective efficacy operate on the primary or private level and involve peers, families, and relatives. These sources exert informal control by either awarding or withholding approval, respect, and admiration. Informal control mechanisms include direct criticism, ridicule, ostracism, desertion, or physical punishment.[85]

The most important wielder of informal social control is the family, which may keep at-risk kids in check through such mechanisms as corporal punishment, withholding privileges, or ridiculing lazy or disrespectful behavior. The family's ability to apply informal social control takes on greater importance in neighborhoods with few social ties among adults and limited collective efficacy. In these areas parents cannot call upon neighborhood resources to take up the burden of controlling children and face the burden of providing adequate supervision.[86]

The family is not the only force of informal social control. In some neighborhoods, people are committed to preserving their immediate environment by confronting destabilizing forces such as teen gangs.[87] By helping neighbors become more resilient and self-confident, adults in these areas provide the external support systems that enable youth to desist from delinquency.[88] Residents teach one another that they have moral and social obligations to their fellow citizens; children learn to be sensitive to the rights of others and to respect differences.

■ *Institutional social control.* Community organizations such as the justice system, church, schools, and community centers provide institutional social control. Children are at risk for recruitment into gangs and law-violating groups when these institutions are ineffective. For example, an effective police presence sends a message that the area will not tolerate delinquent behavior. Because they can respond vigorously to delinquency, the police prevent delinquent gangs from gaining a toehold in the neighborhood.[89] In contrast, delinquency rates are highest in areas where police are mistrusted or disliked.[90] Police can also help organize citizens in high-crime neighborhoods, and help them to become interested in what they can do about crime and delinquency in their neighborhood. Residents may join groups and attend meetings designed to reduce gang crime or drug use, thereby increasing community social control efforts.[91]

Neighborhood youth also respond positively to organized activities such as youth organizations and recreation centers for teens. These programs seem to have a positive effect on both the individual level (e.g., they improve participants' self-control) and institutional level (e.g., they encourage informal social control).[92]

■ *Public social control.* Stable neighborhoods are also able to arrange for external sources of social control. If they can draw on outside help and secure external resources—a process referred to as public social control—they are better able to reduce the effects of disorganization and maintain lower levels of delinquency and gang membership.[93]

In more disorganized areas, the absence of political powerbrokers limits access to external funding and protection.[94] Without outside funding, a neighborhood may lack the ability to "get back on its feet."[95] In these areas there are fewer police, and those that do patrol the area are less motivated and their resources are stretched tighter. These communities cannot mount an effective social control effort because as neighborhood disadvantage increases, its level of informal social control decreases.[96]

The Effect of Collective Efficacy

Adolescents who live in neighborhoods with concentrated disadvantage and low collective efficacy begin to lose confidence in their ability to avoid violence. They perceive, and rightly so, that the community cannot provide the level of social control needed to neutralize or make up for what individuals lack in personal self-control.[97] The lack of community controls may convince them to take matters into their own hands— some may cope by joining a gang or carrying a weapon for self-protection.

In contrast, more cohesive neighborhoods experience far less youthful misbehavior.[98] In areas where collective efficacy remains high, children are less likely to become involved with deviant peers and engage in problem behaviors. In these more stable areas, kids use their wits to avoid violent confrontations and to feel safe in their own neighborhood, a concept referred to as **street efficacy**.[99] Adolescents with high levels of street efficacy are less likely to resort to violence themselves or to associate with delinquent peers.[100] They instead can turn to community organizations and volunteer groups for support even when family influences are lacking.[101]

Collective efficacy has other benefits. When residents are satisfied that their neighborhoods are good places to live, they feel a sense of obligation to maintain order and are more willing to work hard to encourage informal social control. In areas where social institutions and processes—such as police protection—are working adequately, residents are willing to intervene personally to help control unruly children and uncivil adults.[102]

According to the social ecology school, then, the quality of community life, including levels of change, fear, incivility, poverty, and deterioration, has a direct influence on an area's delinquency rate. It is not some individual property or trait that causes people to commit delinquency but the quality and ambience of the community in which they reside. Delinquency rates are low in communities and neighborhoods that have high levels of formal and informal social control and have the ability to provide collective efficacy. The effect of these community-level influences seems strong both in the United States and abroad, no matter what the economic situation presents.[103]

street efficacy
Using one's wits to avoid violent confrontations and to feel safe.

To read an article showing the association between **collective efficacy and community health and well-being**, go to http://www.theatlantic.com/health/archive/2013/03/kind-neighbors-are-scarce-but-important/273375/

Strain Theory

Strain theory suggests that while most people share similar values and goals, such as a good education, a nice home, a great car, and stylish clothes, the ability to achieve these personal goals is stratified by socioeconomic class. While the affluent may live out the American Dream, the poor are shut out from achieving their goals. Because poor kids can't always get what they want, they begin to feel frustrated and angry, a condition referred to as strain.

As Robert Agnew points out, not all adolescents feel or succumb to strain.[104] Given the same set of circumstances, feelings of anomie or strain may vary, being a function of the individual's resistance or susceptibility to the events and conditions they encounter. Even in the face of highly stressful events, those with high resistance abilities are less likely to succumb to pressures for or attractions to delinquency, whereas those adolescents who are more susceptible to external strains are more likely to be negatively influenced. The question remains, why can some kids cope with strain while others succumb to anger and frustration? Having social supports at both the family and neighborhood levels seems to help. Some kids are more sensitive to the environment than others.

So while some kids can cope with feelings of strain, others, feeling economically and socially humiliated, want to humiliate others in turn.[105] Psychologists warn that under these circumstances kids who consider themselves "losers" begin to fear and envy "winners" who are doing very well at their expense. If they fail to take risky aggressive tactics, they are surely going to lose out in social competition and have little chance of future success.[106] Sharp divisions between the rich and poor create an atmosphere of envy and mistrust that may lead to violence and aggression.[107]

Merton's Theory of Anomie

anomie
Normlessness produced by rapidly shifting moral values; according to Merton, anomie occurs when personal goals cannot be achieved using available means.

French sociologist Émile Durkheim coined the term **anomie** (from the Greek *a nomos*, "without norms") to describe a society in which rules of behavior (i.e., values, customs, and norms) have broken down during periods of rapid social change or social crisis. Anomie undermines society's social control function. If a society becomes anomic, it can no longer establish and maintain control. Under these circumstances, the will to obey legal codes is strained, and alternatives, such as crime, become more attractive.

Durkheim's ideas were applied to the onset of crime and delinquency in contemporary society by sociologist Robert Merton in his theory of anomie.[108] Merton used a modified version of the concept of anomie to fit social, economic, and cultural conditions found in modern US society.[109] He found that two elements of culture interact to produce potentially anomic conditions: the clash of culturally defined goals and socially approved means. Contemporary society stresses the goals of acquiring wealth, success, and power. Socially permissible means include hard work, education, and thrift. If there is a dissonance between goals and means, anomie results.

In the United States, Merton argued, legitimate means to acquire wealth are stratified across class and status lines. Indigent lower-class kids, with insufficient formal education and few economic resources, soon find that they are denied the opportunity to get what they want: money, power, success. While everyone may want the same things, millions of people are simply unable to get them through legal or legitimate means. Consequently, they may develop criminal or delinquent solutions to the problem of attaining goals.

Social Adaptations Merton argued that each person has his or her own concept of the goals of society and the means at his or her disposal to attain them. Table 4.1 shows Merton's diagram of the hypothetical relationship between social goals, the means for getting them, and the individual actor. Here is a brief description of each of these modes of adaptation:

- *Conformity*. Conformity occurs when individuals both embrace conventional social goals and have the means at their disposal to attain them. The conformist desires wealth and success and can obtain them through education and a high-paying job. In a balanced, stable society, this is the most common social adaptation. If a majority of its people did not practice conformity, the society would cease to exist.

table **4.1**

Typology of Individual Modes of Adaptation

Modes of Adaptation	Cultural Goals	Institutionalized Means
Conformity	+	+
Innovation	+	−
Ritualism	−	+
Retreatism	−	−
Rebellion	±	±

Source: Adapted from Robert Merton, "Social Structure and Anomie," in *Social Theory and Social Structure* (Glencoe, IL: Free Press, 1957).

- *Innovation*. Innovation occurs when an individual accepts the goals of society but rejects or is incapable of attaining them through legitimate means. Many kids desire material goods and luxuries but lack the financial ability to attain them. The resulting conflict forces them to adopt innovative solutions to their dilemma: they steal, sell drugs, or extort money. Of the five adaptations, innovation is most closely associated with delinquent behavior.

- *Ritualism*. Ritualists are less concerned about accumulating wealth and instead gain pleasure from practicing traditional ceremonies regardless of whether they have a real purpose or goal. The strict set of manners and customs in religious orders, clubs, and college fraternities encourage and appeal to ritualists.

- *Retreatism*. Retreatists reject both the goals and the means of society. Merton suggests that people who adjust in this fashion are "in the society but not of it." Included in this category are "psychotics, psychoneurotics, chronic autists, pariahs, outcasts, vagrants, vagabonds, tramps, chronic drunkards, and drug addicts." Because such people are morally or otherwise incapable of using both legitimate and illegitimate means, they attempt to escape their lack of success by withdrawing—either mentally or physically.

- *Rebellion*. Rebellion involves substituting an alternative set of goals and means for conventional ones. Revolutionaries who wish to promote radical change in the existing social structure and who call for alternative lifestyles, goals, and beliefs are engaging in rebellion. Rebellion may be a reaction against a corrupt and hated government or an effort to create alternate opportunities and lifestyles within the existing system.

According to Merton, social inequality leads to perceptions of anomie. To resolve the goals/means conflict and relieve their sense of strain, some kids innovate by stealing or extorting money, others retreat into drugs and alcohol, others rebel by joining a gang or group, and still others get involved in ritualistic behavior by joining a religious cult.

Anomie and Immigration Considering the economic stratification of US society, and the general emphasis on economic success above all else, anomie predicts that crime and delinquency rates will be higher in lower-class culture. But there are some exceptions to this rule. You may recall that immigrants, especially those from Latin America, have lower delinquency rates than the general population. How can this finding be explained, considering that this group is one where feelings of anomie might be expected? In *Latino Homicide: Immigration, Violence, and Community*, sociologist Ramiro Martinez attempts to explain why the Latino homicide rate is relatively low despite the fact that many Latinos live in substandard communities. One reason is that Latino expectations for success and wealth are also relatively low, a worldview that helps shield them from the influence of residence in deteriorated communities. Moreover, many Latinos are immigrants who have fled conditions in their homelands that are considerably worse than they find in the United States. Since they are now relatively less deprived, the "strain" of living in poverty has less impact.[110] Martinez's conclusions are supported by research conducted by Grace Kao and Marta Tienda, who find that despite hardship and socioeconomic disadvantages, immigrants remain committed to their aspirations of conventional success. They believe they have more opportunities in the United States than were available in their countries of origin. Because immigrants often faced harsher environments in their home countries, they are more creative in inventing solutions to their current predicaments that do not involve criminal activities. Thus, because they are oriented toward conventional achievement, immigrants are less likely to seek innovative methods of dealing with anomie and more likely to embrace conformity.[111]

Institutional Anomie Theory

An important addition to the strain literature is the book *Crime and the American Dream*, by Steven Messner and Richard Rosenfeld. Their macro-level version of anomie theory views antisocial behavior as a function of cultural and institutional influences in US society, a model they refer to as "institutional anomie theory." Messner and Rosenfeld agree with Merton's view that the success goal is pervasive in American culture. They refer to this as the "American Dream," a term they employ as both a goal and a process. As a goal, the American Dream involves accumulating material goods and wealth via open individual competition. As a process, it involves both being socialized to pursue material success and believing that prosperity is an achievable goal in American culture. In the United States, the capitalist system encourages innovation in pursuit of monetary rewards. Businesspeople such as Bill Gates, Mark Zuckerberg, and Elon Musk are considered national heroes and leaders. Anomic conditions occur because the desire to succeed at any cost drives people apart, weakens the collective sense of community, fosters ambition, and restricts desires to achieve anything that is not material wealth. Achieving a "good name" and respect is not sufficient. Capitalist culture "exerts pressures toward delinquency by encouraging an anomic cultural environment, an environment in which people are encouraged to adopt an 'anything goes' mentality in the pursuit of personal goals . . . [and] the anomic pressures inherent in the American dream are nourished and sustained by an institutional balance of power dominated by the economy."[112]

What is distinct about American society, according to Messner and Rosenfeld, is that anomic conditions have been allowed to develop to such an extraordinary degree.[113] Because achieving financial status is the most significant element of American life, and trumps any other social value, it should come as no surprise that kids will commit crime to obtain symbols of wealth and power.

Impact of the American Dream Culture Why does anomie pervade American culture? According to Messner and Rosenfeld, it is because capitalist culture promotes intense pressures for economic success at the expense of the family, community, and religion. As a result, the value structure of society is dominated by economic realities that weaken institutional social control. In other words, people are so interested in making money that their behavior cannot be controlled by the needs of family or the restraints of morality.

There are three reasons social institutions have been undermined. First, noneconomic functions and roles have been devalued. Performance in other institutional settings—the family, school, or community—is assigned a lower priority than the goal of financial success. Few kids go to school to study the classics; most want a good job and to make money. Second, economic roles are now dominant. Workplace needs now take priority over those of the home, the school, the community, and other aspects of social life. A parent given the opportunity for a promotion thinks nothing of uprooting his family and moving them to another part of the country. Third, greed and materialism have developed cultlike status. According to Messner and Rosenfeld, delinquency rates remain high in the United States and gangs are ubiquitous because the American Dream mythology ensures that many kids will develop wishes and desires for material goods that cannot be satisfied by legitimate means. Kids will be willing to do anything to get ahead, from cheating on tests to get higher grades to selling drugs on campus.[114] Those who cannot succeed become willing to risk everything, including a prison sentence.

General Strain Theory

Sociologist Robert Agnew's **General Strain Theory (GST)** helps identify the micro-level, or individual, influences of strain. Agnew's theory explains why individuals who feel stress and strain are more likely to engage in delinquent acts.[115]

In some communities, strain is endemic and as a result antisocial behavior becomes a routine part of life. Here, in the Pine Ridge reservation, Everett Poor Thunder, a 55-year-old Native American Sioux with diabetes since 2004, stays with his grandson Noah, 8, at his trailer home in Red Shirts, where highly radioactive materials were found in its well water and the nearby Cheyenne River. Although the authorities deny it, in the village the diabetes rate is enormously high, and many of the residents, including Everett, believe it is accelerated by the contamination from uranium mines, in addition to the limited, unhealthy dietary options. On the reservation, Native American Sioux are the majority and most live in poverty due to nearly nonexistent job opportunities—the unemployment rate is said to be around 80 percent. Their life span used to be around 80 years but is now 57 years for men and 63 for women. In addition to rampant health problems—diabetes, heart attacks, cancer—the reservation also faces rising youth violence.

Multiple Sources of Stress   Agnew suggests that delinquency is the direct result of **negative affective states**—the anger, frustration, and adverse emotions that kids feel in the wake of negative and destructive social relationships. He finds that negative affective states are produced by a variety of sources of strain:

- *Failure to achieve positively valued goals.* This type of strain occurs when youths aspire to wealth and fame but lack the financial and educational resources to achieve their goals.[116]

- *Disjunction between expectations and achievements.* When kids compare themselves to peers who seem to be doing a lot better financially or socially, they will feel strain. For example, when a high school senior is accepted at a good college but not a "prestige school" like some of her friends, she will feel strain. She believes that she has not been treated fairly because the "playing field" is tilted against her or that "other kids have connections."

- *Removal of positively valued stimuli.* Strain may occur because of the actual or anticipated removal or loss of a positively valued stimulus from the individual.[117] The loss of a girlfriend or boyfriend can produce strain, as can the death of a loved one, moving to a new neighborhood or school, or the divorce or separation of parents.[118] The loss of positive stimuli may lead to delinquency as the adolescent tries to prevent the loss, retrieve what has been lost, obtain substitutes, or seek revenge against those responsible for the loss. A child who experiences parental separation or divorce early in his life may seek deviant peers to help fill his emotional needs and in so doing increase his chances of criminality.[119] For example, recent research by Matthew Larson and Gary Sweeten

negative affective states
Anger, depression, disappointment, fear, and other adverse emotions that derive from strain.

shows that both males and females increase their involvement in antisocial activities after they suffer a romantic breakup.[120]

■ *Presentation of negative stimuli.* Negative experiences such child abuse and neglect, crime victimization, racism and discrimination, physical punishment, family and peer conflict, school failure, and interaction with stressful life events ranging from family breakup to dissatisfaction with friends can also produce feelings of strain.[121] Even such negative life experiences as poor health can bring on negative emotions and subsequent delinquent behaviors.[122]

The Effects of Strain   Each type of strain will increase the likelihood of experiencing such negative emotions as disappointment, depression, fear, and, most important, anger. Anger increases perceptions of being wronged and produces a desire for revenge, energizes individuals to take action, and lowers inhibitions. Violence and aggression seem justified if you have been wronged and are righteously angry. Being exposed to negative stimuli gets kids angry, and some react inappropriately: They assault their parents and/or teachers; they run away from home or drop out of school; they seek revenge (e.g., vandalize school property), or self-medicate by using drugs and alcohol.[123]

Kids who feel strain are the ones most likely to engage in antisocial behaviors.[124] Some seek out other angry kids and/or join gangs.[125] Peers may pressure them into even more forms of antisocial behavior, creating even more stress in their lives.[126]

Not all kids who feel strain succumb to deviant behaviors, but the ones who do, who can't seem to cope, have had a long history of experience with negative stimuli, including being crime victims themselves.[127] Juveniles who are impulsive, lack self-control, and have negative emotions are also likely to react to strain with delinquency and antisocial behaviors.[128] In contrast, those people who can call on others for help and have support from family, friends, and social institutions are better able to cope with strain.[129]

Sometimes delinquency can relieve these feelings of anger and rage. Although it may be socially disapproved, delinquency can provide relief and satisfaction for someone living an otherwise stress-filled life. Using violence for self-protection may increase feelings of self-worth among those who feel inadequate or intellectually insecure. Kids may lash out to mitigate the effects of strain. Research shows that children who report that they hit or strike their parents also report that they had been the target of parental violence (hitting, slapping). In this case, assaulting their parents may be viewed as a type of remedy for the strain caused by child abuse.[130]

Support for the GST   A number research studies have supported the validity of the GST. A few are set out below:

■ Experiments show that people who perceive strain because they are being treated unfairly report high levels of situational anger and high levels of theft.[131]

■ Living in strain-producing social conditions leads to negative emotions and involvement in antisocial acts.[132]

■ Kids who believe the path to success is blocked are more likely to perceive strain and engage in criminal activities.[133]

■ Research efforts conducted in foreign locales have found support for the basic premises of the GST. Agnew's vision does not seem culture bound.[134]

■ Kids who believe they have been treated fairly by friends and parents are less likely to develop negative emotionality and engage in delinquency.[135]

Cultural Deviance Theories

The third branch of social structure theory combines the effects of social disorganization and strain to explain how kids living in deteriorated neighborhoods react to social isolation and economic deprivation. Because their lifestyle is draining, frustrating, and dispiriting, members of the lower class create an independent subculture with its own set of rules and values. Middle-class culture stresses hard work, delayed gratification, formal education, and being cautious; the lower-class subculture stresses excitement, toughness, risk taking, fearlessness, immediate gratification, and "street smarts." The lower-class subculture is an attractive alternative because the urban poor find that it is impossible to meet the behavioral demands of middle-class society.

Unfortunately, subcultural norms often clash with conventional values. People who have close personal ties to the neighborhood, especially when they are to deviant networks such as gangs and delinquent groups, may find that community norms interfere with their personal desire for neighborhood improvement. So when the police are trying to solve a gang-related killing, neighbors may find that their loyalty to the gang boy and his family outweighs their desire to create a more stable crime-free community by giving information to the police.[136]

Gang Culture

The cultural deviance model assumes that kids will be drawn to the culture of the gang. Kids who feel alienated from the normative culture can find a home in the gang. In disorganized areas, gangs are a stable community feature rather than a force of disruption. Gang membership has appeal to adolescents who are alienated from their families as well as the mainstream of society. It is not surprising that kids who have had problems with the law and suffer juvenile justice processing are more likely to join gangs than nonstigmatized kids.[137]

Joining a gang is a type of "turning point" that changes the direction of people's lives. Gang membership portends a substantial change in emotions, attitudes, and social controls conducive to criminality.[138] The more embedded a boy becomes in the gang and its processes, the less likely he is to leave. When David Pyrooz and his research team interviewed gang members, they found that most of the less involved gang boys leave within six months of their first gang contact, while more involved kids stay at least two more years.[139]

Lower-Class Values and Focal Concerns

In his classic 1958 paper "Lower-Class Culture as a Generating Milieu of Gang Delinquency," Walter Miller identified the unique value system that defines lower-class culture.[140] Conformance to these **focal concerns** dominates life among the lower class. According to Miller, clinging to lower-class focal concerns promotes illegal or violent behavior. Toughness may mean displaying fighting prowess; street smarts may lead to drug deals; excitement may result in drinking, gambling, or drug abuse. Focal concerns do not necessarily represent a rebellion against middle-class values; rather, these values have evolved specifically to fit conditions in lower-class areas. The major lower-class focal concerns are set out in Exhibit 4.1.[141]

Kids who obey the cultural demands of their neighborhood and community find themselves at odds with middle-class society. They value toughness and want to show they are courageous in the face of provocation.[142] A reputation for toughness helps them acquire social power while insulating them from becoming victims. Violence is also seen as a means to acquire wealth (nice clothes, flashy cars, the latest smartphones), control or humiliate another person, defy authority, settle drug-related "business" disputes, attain retribution, satisfy the need for thrills or risk taking, and respond to challenges to one's manhood.[143]

The influence of lower-class focal concerns and culture seems as relevant today as when first identified more than 50 years ago. The Focus on Delinquency feature entitled "The Code of the Streets" discusses a recent version of the concept of cultural deviance.

focal concerns
The value orientation of lower-class culture that is characterized by a need for excitement, trouble, smartness, fate, and personal autonomy.

Miller's Lower-Class Focal Concerns

Trouble

In lower-class communities, people are evaluated by their actual or potential involvement in making trouble. Getting into trouble includes such behavior as fighting, drinking, and sexual misconduct. Dealing with trouble can confer prestige—for example, when a male establishes a reputation for being able to handle himself well in a fight. Not being able to handle trouble, and having to pay the consequences, can make a person look foolish and incompetent.

Toughness

Lower-class males want local recognition of their physical and spiritual toughness. They refuse to be sentimental or soft and instead value physical strength, fighting ability, and athletic skill. Those who cannot meet these standards risk getting a reputation for being weak, inept, and effeminate.

Smartness

Members of the lower-class culture want to maintain an image of being streetwise and savvy, using their street smarts, and having the

ability to outfox and out-con the opponent. Though formal education is not admired, knowing essential survival techniques, such as gambling, conning, and outsmarting the law, is a requirement.

Excitement

Members of the lower class search for fun and excitement to enliven an otherwise drab existence. The search for excitement may lead to gambling, fighting, getting drunk, and sexual adventures. In between, the lower-class citizen may simply "hang out" and "be cool."

Fate

Lower-class citizens believe their lives are in the hands of strong spiritual forces that guide their destinies. Getting lucky, finding good fortune, and hitting the jackpot are all slum dwellers' daily dreams.

Autonomy

Being independent of authority figures, such as the police, teachers, and parents, is required; losing control is an unacceptable weakness, incompatible with toughness.

SOURCE: From Walter Miller, "Lower-Class Culture as a Generating Milieu of Gang Delinquency," *Journal of Social Issues* 14:5–19. Copyright © 1958 by John Wiley and Sons. Reprinted by permission.

Theory of Delinquent Subculture

Albert Cohen first articulated the theory of delinquent subculture in his classic 1955 book *Delinquent Boys*.[144] Cohen's central position was that delinquent behavior of lower-class youths is actually a protest against the norms and values of middle-class US culture. Because social conditions make them incapable of achieving success legitimately, lower-class youths experience a form of culture conflict that Cohen labels **status frustration**.[145] As a result, many of them join together in gangs and engage in behavior that is "non-utilitarian, malicious, and negativistic."[146]

Cohen viewed the delinquent gang as a separate subculture, possessing a value system directly opposed to that of the larger society. He describes the subculture as one that "takes its norms from the larger culture, but turns them upside down. The delinquent's conduct is right by the standards of his subculture precisely because it is wrong by the norms of the larger cultures."[147]

According to Cohen, the development of the delinquent subculture is a consequence of socialization practices found in the ghetto or inner-city environment. These children lack the basic skills necessary to achieve social and economic success in the demanding US society. They also lack the proper education and therefore do not have the skills upon which to build a knowledge or socialization foundation. He suggests that lower-class parents are incapable of teaching children the necessary techniques for entering the dominant middle-class culture. The consequences of this deprivation include developmental handicaps, poor speech and communication skills, and inability to delay gratification.

Middle-Class Measuring Rods   One significant handicap that lower-class children face is the inability to positively impress authority figures, such as teachers, employers, or supervisors. Cohen calls the standards set by these authority figures **middle-class measuring rods**. The conflict and status frustration lower-class youths experience when they fail to meet these standards is a primary cause of delinquency. For example, the fact that a lower-class student is deemed by those in power to be substandard or below the average of what is expected can affect his or

status frustration
A form of culture conflict experienced by lower-class youths because social conditions prevent them from achieving success as defined by the larger society.

middle-class measuring rods
Standards by which teachers and other representatives of state authority evaluate students' behavior; when lower-class youths cannot meet these standards they are subject to failure, which brings on frustration and anger at conventional society.

The Code of the Streets

A widely cited view of the interrelationship of culture and behavior is Elijah Anderson's concept of the "code of the streets." He sees that life circumstances are tough for the "ghetto poor"—lack of jobs that pay a living wage, stigma of race, fallout from rampant drug use and drug trafficking, and alienation and lack of hope for the future. Living in such an environment places young people at special risk of delinquency and deviant behavior.

There are two cultural forces running through the neighborhood that shape their reactions: decent values and street values. *Decent values* are taught by families committed to middle-class values and representing mainstream goals and standards of behavior. Though they may be better off financially than some of their street-oriented neighbors, they are generally "working poor." They value hard work and self-reliance and are willing to sacrifice for their children; they harbor hopes for a better future for their children. Most go to church and take a strong interest in education. Some see their difficult situation as a test from God and derive great support from their faith and from the church community.

In opposition, *street values* are born in the despair of inner-city life and are in opposition to those of mainstream society. The street culture has developed what Anderson calls a code of the streets, a set of informal rules setting down both proper attitudes and ways to respond if challenged. If the rules are violated, there are penalties and sometimes violent retribution.

At the heart of the code is the issue of respect—loosely defined as being treated "right." The code demands that disrespect be punished or hard-won respect will be lost. With the right amount of respect, a person can avoid "being bothered" in public. If he is bothered, not only may he be in physical danger, but also he has been disgraced or "dissed" (disrespected). Some forms of dissing, such as maintaining eye contact for too long, may seem pretty mild. But to street kids who live by the code, these actions become serious indications of the other person's intentions and a warning of imminent physical confrontation.

These two orientations—decent and street—socially organize the community. Their coexistence means that kids who are brought up in decent homes must be able to successfully navigate the demands of the street culture. Even in decent families, parents recognize that the code must be obeyed or at the very least negotiated; it cannot simply be ignored.

The Respect Game

Young men in poor inner-city neighborhoods build their self-image on the foundation of respect. Having "juice" (as respect is sometimes called on the street) means that they can take care of themselves even if it means resorting to violence. For street youth, losing respect on the street can be damaging and dangerous. Once they have demonstrated that they can be insulted, beaten up, or stolen from, they become an easy target. Kids from decent families may be able to keep their self-respect by getting good grades or a scholarship. Street kids do not have that luxury. With nothing to fall back on, they cannot walk away from an insult. They must retaliate with violence.

One method of preventing attacks is to go on the offensive. Aggressive, violence-prone people are not seen as easy prey. Robbers do not get robbed, and street fighters are not the favorite targets of bullies. A youth who communicates an image of not being afraid to die and not being afraid to kill has given himself a sense of power on the street.

Anderson's work has been well received. A number of researchers have found that the code of the streets does exist and that Anderson's observations are valid. Those whose loyalty to the code of the streets is the greatest also experience the greatest frequency of violent offending. Adolescents with strong family ties are more likely to embrace decent values while those whose family is less influential are more likely to hold street code beliefs.

CRITICAL THINKING

1. Does the code of the street, as described by Anderson, apply in the neighborhood in which you were raised? Is it universal?

2. Is there a form of "respect game" being played out on college campuses? If so, what is the substitute for violence?

SOURCES: Elijah Anderson, *Code of the Street: Decency, Violence, and the Moral Life of the Inner City* (New York: Norton, 2000); Anderson, "The Code of the Streets," *Atlantic Monthly* 273:80–94 (1994); Richard Moule, Jr., Callie Burt, Eric Stewart, and Ronald Simons, "Developmental Trajectories of Individuals' Code of the Street Beliefs Through Emerging Adulthood," *Journal of Research in Crime and Delinquency* 52:342–372 (2015); Timothy Brezina, Robert Agnew, Francis T. Cullen, and John Paul Wright, "The Code of the Street: A Quantitative Assessment of Elijah Anderson's Subculture of Violence Thesis and Its Contribution to Youth Violence Research," *Youth Violence and Juvenile Justice* 2:303–328 (2004); Jeffrey Fagan, *Adolescent Violence: A View from the Street*, NIJ Research Preview (Washington, DC: National Institute of Justice, 1998).

---

her future life chances. A school record may be reviewed by juvenile court authorities and by the military. A military record, in turn, can influence whether or not someone is qualified for certain jobs.[148] Negative evaluations become part of a permanent file that follows an individual for the rest of his or her life. When he or she wants to improve, evidence of prior failures is used to discourage advancement.

The Formation of Deviant Subcultures   Cohen believes lower-class boys who suffer rejection by middle-class decision makers usually elect to join one of three existing subcultures: the corner boy, the college boy, or the delinquent boy. The *corner boy* role is the most common response to middle-class rejection. The *corner boy* is not a chronic delinquent but may be a truant who engages in petty or status offenses, such as precocious sex and recreational drug abuse. His main loyalty is to his peer group, on which he depends for support, motivation, and interest. His values, therefore, are those of the group with which he is in close personal contact. The corner boy, well aware of his failure to achieve the standards of the American Dream, retreats into the comforting world of his lower-class peers and eventually becomes a stable member of his neighborhood, holding a menial job, marrying, and remaining in the community.

The *college boy* embraces the cultural and social values of the middle class. Rather than scorning middle-class measuring rods, he actively strives to be successful by those standards. Cohen views this type of youth as one who is embarking on an almost hopeless path, since he is ill-equipped academically, socially, and linguistically to achieve the rewards of middle-class life.

The *delinquent boy* adopts a set of norms and principles in direct opposition to middle-class values. He engages in short-run hedonism, living for today and letting "tomorrow take care of itself."[149] Delinquent boys strive for group autonomy. They resist efforts by family, school, or other sources of authority to control their behavior. They may join a gang because it is perceived as autonomous, independent, and the focus of "attraction, loyalty, and solidarity."[150] Frustrated by their inability to succeed, these boys resort to a process Cohen calls reaction formation, taking middle-class values and turning them on their head. If the middle class respects hard work and sobriety, then the delinquent boy values leisure and substance abuse. Reaction formation can lead to irrational, malicious, and unaccountable hostility to the "enemy," which in this case, Cohen warns, is "the norms of respectable middle-class society."[151] Reaction formation causes delinquent boys to overreact to any perceived threat or slight. They sneer at the college boy's attempts at assimilation and scorn the corner boy's passivity. The delinquent boy is willing to take risks, violate the law, and flout middle-class conventions.

Cohen's work helps explain the factors that promote and sustain a delinquent subculture. By introducing the concepts of status frustration and middle-class measuring rods, Cohen makes it clear that social forces and not individual traits promote and sustain a delinquent career. By introducing the corner boy, college boy, delinquent boy triad, he helps explain why many lower-class youths do not become chronic offenders: there is more than one social path open to indigent youth.[152] His work is a skillful integration of strain and social disorganization theories and has become an enduring element of the criminological literature.

Theory of Differential Opportunity

In their classic work *Delinquency and Opportunity*, written more than 50 years ago, Richard Cloward and Lloyd Ohlin combined strain and social disorganization principles into a portrayal of a gang-sustaining delinquent subculture.[153] Cloward and Ohlin's view is that an independent delinquent subculture has formed within lower-class society.[154] Youth gangs are an important part of the delinquent subculture, and although not all illegal acts are committed by gang youth, they are the source of the most serious, sustained, and costly delinquent behaviors. Delinquent gangs spring up in disorganized areas where youths lack the opportunity to gain success through conventional means.

True to strain theory principles, Cloward and Ohlin portray inner-city kids as individuals who want to conform to middle-class values but lack the means to do so.[155]

Differential Opportunities The centerpiece of the Cloward and Ohlin theory is the concept of differential opportunity: The availability of both successful conventional and delinquent careers is limited. In stable areas, adolescents may be recruited by organized delinquent gangs, drug traffickers, or crime groups. Unstable areas, cannot support successful and profitable criminal opportunities. In these socially disorganized neighborhoods, adult role models are absent, and adolescents have few opportunities to join established gangs or to learn the fine points of professional crime. In other words, opportunities for success, both illegal and conventional, are closed for the most "truly disadvantaged" youth.

reaction formation
A psychological reaction that occurs when a person does or says something that is the opposite of what he or she really wants or what is socially expected and appropriate.

differential opportunity
The view that lower-class youths, whose legitimate opportunities are limited, join gangs and pursue criminal careers as alternative means to achieve universal success goals.

Because of differential opportunity, kids are likely to join one of three types of gangs:

- *Criminal gangs.* Criminal gangs exist in stable lower-class areas in which close connections among adolescent, young adult, and adult offenders create an environment for successful delinquent enterprise.[156] Youths are recruited into established criminal gangs that provide a training ground for a successful delinquent career.

- *Conflict gangs.* Conflict gangs develop in communities unable to provide either legitimate or illegitimate opportunities. These highly disorganized areas are marked by transient residents and physical deterioration. Delinquency in this area is "individualistic, unorganized, petty, poorly paid, and unprotected."[157] Conflict gang members fight to protect their own and their gang's integrity and honor. By doing so, they acquire a "rep," which provides them with a means for gaining admiration from their peers and consequently helps them develop their own self-image.[158]

- *Retreatist gangs.* Retreatists are double failures, unable to gain success through legitimate means and unwilling to do so through illegal ones. Some retreatists have tried crime or violence but are either too clumsy, weak, or scared to be accepted in delinquent or violent gangs. They then "retreat" into a role on the fringe of society. Members of the retreatist subculture constantly search for ways of getting high—alcohol, pot, heroin, unusual sexual experiences, music.

Social Structure Theory and Public Policy

Social structure theory has significantly influenced public policy. If the cause of delinquency is viewed as a function of poverty and lower-class status, alternatives to delinquency can be provided by giving inner-city youth opportunities to share in the rewards of conventional society.

One approach is to give indigent people direct financial aid through public assistance or welfare. Although welfare has been curtailed under the Federal Welfare Reform Act of 1996, research shows that crime rates decrease when families receive supplemental income through public assistance payments.[159]

Efforts have also been made to reduce delinquency by improving the community structure in inner-city high-crime areas. Crime prevention efforts based on social structure precepts can be traced back to the Chicago Area Project supervised by Clifford R. Shaw. This program attempted to organize existing community structures to develop social stability in otherwise disorganized slums. A contemporary version of this program, called the Weed and Seed Program, involved a two-pronged approach: law enforcement agencies and prosecutors cooperated in "weeding out" violent criminals and drug abusers, and public agencies and community-based private organizations collaborated to "seed" much-needed human services, including prevention, intervention, treatment, and neighborhood restoration programs. However, funding for this program ended in 2012 due to budget cutbacks.

Social Process Theories

To some sociological delinquency experts, an individual's relationship with critical elements of the social process is the key to understanding the onset and continuation of a delinquent career. *How you live*, they believe, is more important than *where you live*. According to this view, delinquency is a function of **socialization**, the interactions people have with various organizations, institutions, and processes of society. Most kids are influenced by their family relationships, peer group associations, educational experiences, and interactions with authority figures, including teachers, employers, and agents of the justice system. If these relationships are positive and supportive, kids can succeed within the rules of society; if these

socialization
The process by which human beings learn to adopt the behavior patterns of the community in which they live, which requires them to develop the skills and knowledge necessary to function within their culture and environment.

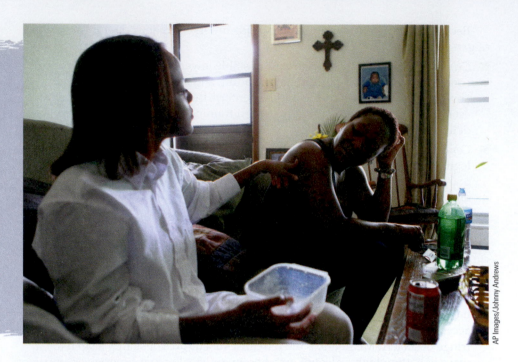

According to social process theories, kids can overcome childhood difficulties if they have strong ties to family, peers, schools, and community. Here, Normandy High School senior Eboni talks with her mother about her day at school prior to heading to her job at a local restaurant in St. Louis. Eboni has spent a lot of time in homeless shelters, and her family has moved so often she can barely keep track of the schools she's attended. But that didn't stop the suburban St. Louis teenager from pursuing her dream of attending an Ivy League school. Despite a childhood with enough hardship to last several lifetimes, Eboni's hard work and perseverance are paying off and she will enter Columbia University on a full scholarship this fall.

AP Images/Johnny Andrews

relationships are dysfunctional and destructive, conventional success may be impossible, and delinquent solutions may become a feasible alternative. Taken together, this view is referred to as social process theory.

The influence of social process theories has endured because the relationship between social class and delinquency is still uncertain. Though millions of Americans live below the poverty line, relatively few commit serious crimes, and those who do later desist from delinquency despite the continuing pressure of poverty and social decay. Some other force, then, must be at work to explain why (a) the majority of poor at-risk kids living in the worst neighborhoods do not become persistent delinquent offenders and (b) why some who have no economic or social reason to commit delinquency do so anyway.

Elements of Socialization

Four elements of socialization stand out as having links to delinquency: family, school, peer relations, and religion and belief.

Family Influence   The primary influence on children is the family. When parenting is inadequate, a child's maturational processes will be interrupted and damaged. Youth who grow up in households characterized by conflict and tension, and where there is a lack of familial love and support, are susceptible to the crime-promoting forces in the environment.[160] Parents who are too controlling or too lenient create a condition that fosters delinquent behaviors; too much or too little can be a problem.[161] And parental deviance can influence a child's behavior: the likelihood of delinquent outcomes is enhanced if a parent gets in trouble with the law and suffers incarceration.[162] Adolescents who live in this type of environment develop poor emotional well-being, externalize problems, and engage in antisocial behavior.[163]

There is little question, then, that family relationships have a significant influence on behavior. Kids who grow up in homes where parents use severe discipline, yet lack warmth and are less involved in their children's lives, are prone to antisocial behavior.[164] The more often a child is physically disciplined and the harsher the discipline, the more likely they will engage in antisocial behaviors.[165] In contrast, parents who are supportive and effectively control their children in a noncoercive fashion—*parental efficacy*—are more likely to raise children who refrain from delinquency.[166] Delinquency will be reduced if parents provide the type of structure that integrates children into families while giving them the ability to assert their individuality and regulate their own behavior.[167]

School Effects   The educational process and adolescent achievement in school have been linked to delinquency. Children who do poorly in school, fail at their coursework, do not have a strong bond to the educational experience, lack educational motivation, and feel alienated are the most likely to engage in criminal acts.[168] Youths who feel that teachers do not care, who consider themselves failures, and who do poorly in school are more likely to become involved in a delinquent way of life than adolescents who are educationally successful. School dropouts, especially those who have been expelled, face a significant chance of entering a delinquent career.[169] In contrast, doing well in school and developing attachments to teachers have been linked to delinquency resistance.[170]

Peer Influence and Relations   Adolescents who engage in unsupervised socializing with peers are more likely to engage in delinquency and substance abuse, especially if the friends engage in antisocial activities themselves.[171] Those teens who have violent friends eventually become violent; those whose friends abuse substances will eventually specialize in substance abuse.[172]

Because the typical adolescent struggles to impress his closest friends and to preserve his social circle, peer relations can be a double-edged sword.[173] Popular kids socialize a lot and get to hang out with their friends without parental supervision; this freedom places them at risk mainly because they have more unsupervised opportunity to get into trouble.[174] Kids who maintain close relations with antisocial peers will sustain their own delinquent behavior into their adulthood.[175]

Effects of Religion and Belief   Logic would dictate that kids who hold high moral values and beliefs, who have learned to distinguish right from wrong, and who regularly attend religious services should also reject antisocial behaviors.[176] Religion binds people together and forces them to confront the consequences of their behavior. Committing delinquent acts would violate the principles of all organized religions.

With few exceptions, most research efforts do find that maintaining religious beliefs and attending religious services significantly helps reduce delinquency.[177] When Richard Petts used data from a national survey, he found that kids who are involved in religion are less likely to engage in delinquency. Religion enhances the effect of parental affection in two-parent homes and also helps kids living in single-parent homes resist the influence of deviant peers. Petts concludes that religious participation helps reduce deviant behavior involvement throughout the life course, from adolescence until marriage.[178]

The Effects of Socialization on Delinquency

To many delinquency experts, the elements of socialization described up to this point are the chief determinants of delinquent behavior. According to this view, adolescents living in even the most deteriorated urban areas can successfully resist inducements to delinquency if they have a positive self-image, learn moral values, and have the support of their parents, peers, teachers, and neighbors. The girl with a positive self-image who is chosen for a college scholarship has the warm, loving support of her parents and is viewed as someone "going places" by friends and neighbors. She is less likely to adopt a delinquent way of life than another adolescent who is abused at home, lives with criminal parents, and whose bond to her school and peer group is shattered because she is labeled a troublemaker.[179] The boy who has learned delinquent behavior from his parents and siblings and then joins a neighborhood gang is much more likely to become an adult criminal than his next-door neighbor who idolizes his hard-working, deeply religious parents.

youth STORIES

Ethan Couch

On June 15, 2013, Ethan Couch, a 16-year-old Texas boy, killed four people while driving drunk. It seems that Couch and seven friends had been drinking for hours before the crash, and some of them were caught on a surveillance video stealing two cases of beer from a nearby Walmart. At around 11:45 PM, the intoxicated teens were in a Ford F350 pickup going 70 mph (30 over the speed limit) when Couch swerved off the road and into a stalled SUV on the roadside, throwing the owner and three good Samaritans who were trying to help her get the car going 60 yards in the air. They were killed on impact; the kids riding with Couch were severely injured. Couch was three times over the legal alcohol limit when he slammed into the victims.

In a decision that received national attention, Couch was sentenced to probation even though prosecutors had sought a maximum sentence of 20 years. One reason for the light sentence was that during his trial, a defense psychologist testified that Couch suffered from "affluenza"—in other words, on the night of the crash he did not understand the consequences of his actions because of his privileged upbringing. His parents had taught him that wealth buys privilege and he could do anything he wanted without consequences because they were wealthy. If that were true, the state helped fuel those feelings further. Couch was supposed to go to a rehab clinic that would have cost his family approximately $500,000 annually. Instead, he was sent to a state facility which requires the family to only pay $1,100 per month for a $750 per day facility, leaving taxpayers to pay the remaining bill for his therapy. The six-acre facility offers a 90-day treatment program that includes horseback riding, mixed martial arts, massage, cookery classes, basketball, and a swimming pool.[180]

But that was not the end of the saga of Ethan Couch. On December 2, 2015, a video was found showing Couch at a party where alcohol was being served, a clear violation of his probation agreement. The next day Ethan was contacted by his probation officer and told to report for a drug test. Instead of complying, his mother, Tonya, withdrew $30,000 from her bank account and the two fled to Mexico. A directive to apprehend Couch for a probation violation was issued, and

Ethan Couch is accompanied by sheriff deputies after a juvenile court hearing in which a Texas judge ruled that Couch, who used an "affluenza" defense in a fatal drunk-driving wreck that killed four people, would be moved to adult court. On April 13, 2016, Couch was sentenced to serve four consecutive terms of 180 days in jail (one term for each of the 2013 car crash victims), equaling two years in jail.

Ethan and Tonya Couch were taken into custody in the Mexican resort city of Puerto Vallarta. Tonya was deported and jailed in Texas on a charge of hindering the apprehension of a felon. After fighting deportation, Ethan was flown back to the United States and his case was transferred to the adult court system. On April 13, 2016, the court sentenced Ethan Couch to serve four consecutive terms of 180 days in prison, one term for each of the 2013 car crash victims; his lawyers are currently fighting to get him out of jail on a technicality.

CRITICAL THINKING

If some people get the judge to lower their sentence because they had a tough childhood and had to overcome adversity, is it that strange to have someone argue that their privileged childhood impeded their judgment and consequently their ability to know right from wrong?

SOURCES: Hunter Stuart, "Ethan Couch, 'Affluenza' Teen, Facing 5 Lawsuits," *Huffington Post*, December 12, 2013, http://www.huffingtonpost.com/2013/12/18/ethan-couch-affluenza-lawsuits-car-crash-texas_n_4461585.html; Ramit Plushnick-Masti, "'Affluenza' Isn't a Recognized Diagnosis, Experts Say After 'Brat' Spared from Jail in Drunk Driving Case," *National Post*, December 12, 2013, http://news.nationalpost.com/2013/12/12/affluenza-defence-used-to-protect-teen-driver-who-killed-four-was-never-meant-to-be-used-in-court-expert-says/; Jim Douglas, "'Affluenza' Teen Ethan Couch Transferred to Adult Jail," *USA Today*, http://www.usatoday.com/story/news/nation-now/2016/02/06/affluenza-teen-ethan-couch-jail-time-adult/79920884/. (URLs accessed September 2016.)

It is socialization, not the social structure, that determines life chances. The more social problems encountered during the socialization process, the greater the likelihood that youths will encounter difficulties and obstacles as they mature, such as being unemployed or becoming a teenage mother.

Theorists who believe that an individual's socialization determines the likelihood of delinquency adopt the social process approach to human behavior. The social process approach has two independent branches:

- *Social learning theory* suggests that adolescents learn the techniques and attitudes of crime from close and intimate relationships with delinquent peers; delinquency is a learned behavior.

- *Social control theory* maintains that everyone has the potential to become a delinquent but that most adolescents are controlled by their bonds to society. Delinquency occurs when the forces that bind adolescents to society are weakened or broken.

Put another way, **social learning theory** assumes adolescents are born good and learn to be bad; **social control theory** assumes adolescents are born bad and must be controlled in order to be good. Each of these independent branches will be discussed separately. The Youth Stories feature shows how socialization can influence behavior.

social learning theory
Hypothesizes that delinquency is learned through close relationships with others; asserts that children are born good and learn to be bad from others.

social control theory
Posits that delinquency results from a weakened commitment to the major social institutions (family, peers, and school); lack of such commitment allows youths to exercise antisocial behavioral choices.

Social Learning Theory

Social learning theorists believe delinquency is a product of learning the norms, values, and behaviors associated with delinquent activity. Social learning can involve the actual techniques of crime—how to hot-wire a car or roll a joint—as well as the psychological aspects of criminality—how to deal with the guilt or shame associated with illegal activities. Learning negative attitudes and beliefs can start early in life. Some kids develop a jaundiced, pessimistic, and cynical viewpoint in their adolescence. They learn to trust no one, take a dim view of their future, and figure out that the only way to get ahead in life is to break social rules. Ronald Simon and Callie Harbin Burt find that the path to a delinquent career involves learning to accept a unique cognitive framework that shapes both the way kids look at the world and their behavioral choices. As they try to cope with their environment, some develop a hostile, distrusting model and approach others with suspicion and aggression. They learn to believe such things as "When people are friendly, they usually want something from you" and "Some people oppose you for no good reason." They want everything right away and are willing to take risks to get what they want. Their life experiences teach them a cynical, contemptuous view of accepted social rules. Such a disparaging view of conventional norms increases the probability of engaging in antisocial behavior. Simon and Burt find that persistent exposure to antagonistic social circumstances and lack of exposure to positive conditions increase the chances of someone developing social schemas involving a hostile view of relationships. Embracing these schemas fosters situational definitions that lead to actions that are aggressive, opportunistic, and criminal. According to Simon and Burt, learning to distrust the world and the people in it, to embrace a here-and-now orientation, and to discount prohibitions against deviance is what drives people into a delinquent way of life.[181]

This section briefly reviews the three most prominent forms of social learning theory: differential association theory, differential reinforcement theory, and neutralization theory.

Differential Association Theory

One of the most prominent social learning theories is Edwin H. Sutherland's **differential association theory**. Often considered the preeminent US criminologist, Sutherland first put forth his theory in his 1939 text, *Principles of Criminology*.[182] The final version of the theory appeared in 1947. When Sutherland died in 1950, Donald Cressey, his longtime associate, continued his work. Cressey was so successful in explaining and popularizing his mentor's efforts that differential association remains one of the most enduring explanations of delinquent behavior.

differential association theory
Asserts that criminal behavior is learned primarily within interpersonal groups and that youths will become delinquent if definitions they have learned favorable to violating the law exceed definitions favorable to obeying the law within that group.

Sutherland's research on white-collar crime, professional theft, and intelligence led him to dispute the notion that delinquency was a function of the inadequacy of children in the lower classes.[183] To Sutherland, delinquency stemmed neither from individual traits nor from socioeconomic position; instead, he believed it to be a function of a learning process that could affect any individual in any culture. Acquiring a behavior is a social learning process, not a political or legal process. Skills and motives conducive to delinquency are learned as a result of contacts with pro-delinquency values, attitudes, and definitions and other patterns of delinquent behavior.

Principles of Differential Association   The basic principles of differential association are explained as follows:[184]

- *Delinquent behavior is learned.* Sutherland believed that the tools for crime and delinquency are acquired in the same manner as any other learned behavior, such as writing, painting, or reading.

- *Learning is a by-product of interaction.* Children actively participate in the learning process as they interact with other individuals, even their boyfriends or girlfriends.[185] Thus, delinquency cannot occur without the aid of others; it is a function of socialization.

- *Learning occurs within intimate groups.* Learning delinquent behavior occurs within intimate personal groups. Children's contacts with their most intimate social companions—family, friends, peers—have the greatest influence on their deviant behavior and attitude development. Research shows that children who grow up in homes where parents abuse alcohol are more likely to view drinking as being socially and physically beneficial.[186]

- *Criminal techniques are learned.* Some kids may meet and associate with older criminal "mentors" who teach them how to be successful criminals and gain the greatest benefits from their criminal activities.[187] They learn the proper way to pick a lock, shoplift, and obtain and use narcotics. In addition, novice delinquents learn to use the proper terminology for their acts and then acquire "proper" reactions to law violations. For example, getting high on marijuana and learning the proper way to smoke a joint are behavior patterns usually acquired from more experienced companions. Delinquents must learn how to react properly to their illegal acts, such as when to defend them, rationalize them, or show remorse for them.

- *Perceptions of legal code influence motives and drives.* The reaction to social rules and laws is not uniform across society, and children constantly come into contact with others who maintain different views on the utility of obeying the legal code. Some kids they admire may openly disdain or flout the law or ignore its substance. Kids experience what Sutherland calls "culture conflict" when they are exposed to different and opposing attitudes toward what is right and wrong, moral and immoral. The conflict of social attitudes and cultural norms is the basis for the concept of differential association.

- *Differential associations may vary in duration, frequency, priority, and intensity.* Whether a person learns to obey the law or to disregard it is influenced by the quality of social interactions. Those of lasting *duration* have greater influence than those that are brief. Similarly, *frequent* contacts have greater effect than rare and haphazard contacts. Sutherland did not specify what he meant by *priority*, but Cressey and others have interpreted the term to mean the age of children when they first encounter definitions of criminality. Contacts made early in life probably have a greater and more far-reaching influence than those developed later on. Finally, *intensity* is generally interpreted to mean the importance and prestige attributed to the individual or groups from whom the definitions are learned. The influence of a father, mother, or trusted friend far outweighs the effect of more socially distant figures.

- *Delinquent behavior is an expression of general needs and values, but it is not excused by those general needs and values because nondelinquent behavior is also an expression of those same needs and values.* What Sutherland means here is that delinquency and nondelinquency cannot have the same cause. For example, delinquency cannot be caused by economic needs because poor kids can also get jobs, save money, and so on. It is only the learning of deviant norms through contact with an excess of definitions favorable toward delinquency that produces illegal behavior.

According to Sutherland's theory, adolescents will learn to become law violators when they are in contact with kids, groups, or events that produce an excess of definitions favorable toward delinquency and are isolated from counteracting forces. A definition favorable toward delinquency occurs, for example, when a child is exposed to friends who sneak into a theater to avoid paying for a ticket or talk about the virtues of getting high on drugs. A definition unfavorable toward delinquency occurs when friends or parents demonstrate their disapproval of antisocial acts. Neutral behavior, such as reading a book, is neither positive nor negative with respect to law violation. Cressey argues that neutral behavior is important; for example, when a child is occupied doing something neutral, it prevents him or her from being in contact with those involved in delinquent behaviors.[188]

Testing Differential Theory There has been a long history of research efforts supportive of the core principles of differential association. The evidence does show a correlation between (a) having deviant parents and friends, (b) holding deviant attitudes, and (c) committing deviant acts.[189] Kids who report having attitudes that support deviant behavior are also likely to engage in deviant behavior.[190] This suggests that delinquents have learned deviant definitions and have incorporated them into their attitude structure. But who do they learn from?

One set of research studies tests the assumption that kids learn criminal attitudes and behaviors from their parents. The influence of parents is unmistakable; a number of studies have found that parental deviance has a powerful influence on delinquent behavior.[191] Kids whose parents are deviants and criminals are more likely to become criminals themselves and eventually to produce criminal children. The more that kids are involved with criminal parents, the more likely they are to commit crime, suggesting a pattern of learning rather than inheritance.[192]

Kids also learn from their peers.[193] As people mature, having delinquent friends who support criminal attitudes and behavior is strongly related to developing criminal careers.[194] Kids who engage in antisocial activities perceive and believe that their best friends and close associates engage in and approve of antisocial activities.[195] Kids who associate and presumably learn from popular, assertive, and aggressive peers are more likely to behave aggressively themselves.[196] Deviant peers interfere with the natural process of aging out of crime by helping provide the support that keeps kids in criminal careers.[197] Peer approval eases the path to chronic delinquency.

Romantic partners are another important influence. Kids involved with partners who engage in antisocial activities emulate their partner's behavior.[198] Adolescents with deviant romantic partners are more delinquent than those youths with more prosocial partners, regardless of friends' and parents' behavior.[199]

In sum, the more deviant an adolescent's social network and network of affiliations, including parents, peers, and romantic partners, the more likely they are to engage in antisocial behavior.[200] The association between crime and measures of differential association is "quite strong."[201]

Neutralization Theory

Neutralization theory is another type of social learning theory.[202] According to this view, the process of becoming a delinquent is a learning experience in which potential delinquents and criminals master techniques that enable them to counterbalance or neutralize conventional values and drift back and forth between

Handout/Alamy Stock Photo

Dylann Storm Roof murdered nine members of the Emanuel African Methodist Episcopal Church in a racially motivated killing on June 17, 2015 in Charleston, South Carolina. In a 2,400-word manifesto he posted on his website, Roof stated: "I have no choice. I am not in the position to, alone, go into the ghetto and fight. I chose Charleston because it is most historic city in my state, and at one time had the highest ratio of blacks to Whites in the country. We have no skinheads, no real KKK, no one doing anything but talking on the internet. Well someone has to have the bravery to take it to the real world, and I guess that has to be me." Does his statement indicate an effort to "neutralize" his murderous behavior?

subterranean values
The ability of youthful law violators to repress social norms.

drift
Idea that youths move in and out of delinquency and that their lifestyles can embrace both conventional and deviant values.

neutralization techniques
A set of attitudes or beliefs that allow would-be delinquents to negate any moral apprehension they may have about committing crime so that they may freely engage in antisocial behavior without regret.

illegitimate and conventional behavior. One reason this is possible is the subterranean value structure of American society. **Subterranean values** are morally tinged influences that have become entrenched in the culture but are publicly condemned. They exist side by side with conventional values and, while condemned in public, may be admired or practiced in private. Examples include viewing pornographic films, drinking alcohol to excess, and gambling on sporting events. In American culture, it is common to hold both subterranean and conventional values; few kids are "all good" or "all bad."

Even the most committed delinquents are not involved in delinquency all the time; they also attend school, family functions, and religious services. Their behavior can be conceived as falling along a continuum between total freedom and total restraint. This process, called **drift**, refers to the movement from one extreme of behavior to another, resulting in behavior that is sometimes unconventional, free, or deviant and at other times constrained and sober.[203]

Techniques of Neutralization   To neutralize moral constraints, kids learn a distinct set of justifications for their law-violating behavior. These **neutralization techniques** enable them to temporarily drift away from the rules of the normative society and participate in subterranean behaviors. These techniques of neutralization include the following patterns:[204]

■ *Deny responsibility*. Young offenders sometimes claim their unlawful acts were simply not their fault. Delinquents' acts resulted from forces beyond their control or were accidents.

■ *Deny injury*. By denying the wrongfulness of an act, delinquents are able to neutralize illegal behavior. For example, stealing is viewed as borrowing; vandalism is considered mischief that has gotten out of hand. Delinquents may find that their parents and friends support their denial of injury. In fact, they may claim that the behavior was merely a prank, helping affirm the offender's perception that delinquency can be socially acceptable.

■ *Deny the victim*. Delinquents sometimes neutralize wrongdoing by maintaining that the victim of crime "had it coming." Vandalism may be directed against a disliked teacher or neighbor, or homosexuals may be beaten up by a gang because their behavior is considered offensive. Denying the victim may also take the form of ignoring the rights of an absent or unknown victim: for example, stealing from the unseen owner of a department store. It becomes morally acceptable for the criminal to commit such crimes as vandalism when the victims, because of their absence, cannot be sympathized with or respected.

- *Condemn the condemners.* An offender views the world as a corrupt place with a dog-eat-dog code. Because police and judges are on the take, teachers show favoritism, and parents take out their frustrations on their kids, it is ironic and unfair for these authorities to condemn his or her misconduct. By shifting the blame to others, delinquents repress the feeling that their own acts are wrong.

- *Appeal to higher loyalties.* Novice delinquents often argue that they are caught in the dilemma of being loyal to their own peer group while attempting to abide by the rules of the larger society. The needs of the group take precedence over the rules of society because the demands of the former are immediate and localized.

In sum, the theory of neutralization presupposes a condition that allows people to neutralize unconventional norms and values by using such slogans as "I didn't mean to do it," "I didn't really hurt anybody," "They had it coming to them," "Everybody's picking on me," and "I didn't do it for myself." These excuses allow kids to drift into delinquent modes of behavior.

Variations on Neutralization Theory

Neutralization theory has been used to explain different behaviors and may be used in different ways than first conceived. Volkan Topalli argues that the theory may have to be revised because it ignores the influential street culture that exists in highly disadvantaged neighborhoods. Kids living in disorganized, gang-ridden neighborhoods disrespect authority and admire antisocial behavior, including substance abuse and violence. These adolescents place their own needs above those of all others. There is no need for them to neutralize conventional values in order to engage in delinquency since they are already "guilt free." Similarly, there is no need for them to "drift into delinquency, because their allegiance to nonconventional values and lack of guilt perpetually leave them in a state of openness to delinquency. Rather than being contrite or ashamed if they commit crimes, they take great pride in their criminal activities and abilities.[205]

If teens engaging in deviant behavior use neutralizations to reduce the moral burdens that accompany antisocial behaviors, what about those kids who engage in positive conventional behaviors that fall above the norm, in other words, those kids who are too good to be true? You probably know some of those people: the ones who answer every question in class; the ones who refuse to engage in underage drinking and partying; the kids to whom your parents make comparisons ("Why can't you be like David, he is so polite and well mannered?"). How do these overachievers deal with the potential fallout from being considered nerds and brownnosers?

Nicole Shoenberger, Alex Heckert, and Druann Heckert interviewed overachieving students and found that these students justified behavior by minimizing their own hard work, making it appear as if being a high achiever was not difficult; anyone could do it if they tried. They just did their best; they were no different from anyone else save for extra effort. As a response to being referred to as a "brownnoser" by fellow students, one explained that she was simply following instructions, doing what she had been told to by the teacher. Similarly high achievers denied injury to others: "No one is really hurt by what I did in class." If the other students look bad, then all they had to do was work harder and become overachievers themselves. One young woman named Lilly stated, "I never think if anyone gets hurt because of me being the smart kid. Why or how would that affect others? It's like, why would I even know that?" Others appealed to higher loyalties: they had to get a good job, earn recommendations, or meet their parents' expectations. High achievers often felt they had to distinguish themselves from other students for their future goals. In sum, to feel comfortable in their roles, high-achieving students must create strategies for navigating and neutralizing the youth subculture that deemphasizes high academic achievement and embraces partying.[206]

Testing Neutralization Theory   Attempts have been made to verify the assumptions of neutralization theory empirically.[207] A number of studies have found that kids do in fact neutralize before engaging in a wide range of deviant behavior, ranging from committing crimes to cheating on tests.[208] Neutralizations tend to be used for some crimes more than others and by some offenders more than others.

One area of research has been directed at determining whether there really is a need for law violators to neutralize moral constraints. The thinking behind this research is this: if delinquents hold values *in opposition* to accepted social norms, then there is really no need to neutralize. So far, the evidence is mixed. Some studies show that law violators approve of criminal behavior, such as theft and violence, and still others find evidence that even though they may be active participants themselves, delinquents voice disapproval of illegal behavior.[209]

Social Control Theory

Social control theories maintain that all people have the potential to violate the law and that modern society presents many opportunities for illegal activity. Criminal activities, such as drug abuse and car theft, are often exciting pastimes that hold the promise of immediate reward and gratification.

Considering the attractions of delinquency, the question control theorists pose is, why do people obey the rules of society? A choice theorist would respond that it is the fear of punishment; structural theorists would say that obedience is a function of having access to legitimate opportunities; learning theorists would explain that obedience is acquired through contact with law-abiding parents and peers. In contrast, social control theorists argue that people obey the law because behavior and passions are being controlled by internal and external forces. Because they have been properly socialized, most people have developed a strong moral sense, which renders them incapable of hurting others and violating social norms.[210] Properly socialized people believe that getting caught at criminal activity will hurt a dearly loved parent or jeopardize their chance at a college scholarship, or perhaps they feel that their job will be forfeited if they get in trouble with the law. In other words, people's behavior, including criminal activity, is controlled by their attachment and commitment to conventional institutions, individuals, and processes. On the other hand, those who have not been properly socialized, who lack a commitment to others or themselves, are free to violate the law and engage in deviant behavior. Those who are uncommitted are not deterred by the threat of legal punishments because they have little to lose.[211]

Self-Concept and Delinquency

Early versions of control theory speculated that control was a product of social interactions. Maladaptive social relations produced weak self-concept and poor self-esteem, rendering kids at risk to delinquency. In contrast, youths who felt good about themselves and maintained a positive attitude were able to resist the temptations of the streets. As early as 1951, sociologist Albert Reiss described how delinquents had weak egos.[212] Scott Briar and Irving Piliavin noted that youths who believe criminal activity will damage their self-image and their relationships with others will be most likely to conform to social rules; they have a commitment to conformity. In contrast, those less concerned about their social standing are free to violate the law.[213] In his *containment theory*, pioneering control theorist Walter Reckless argued that a strong self-image insulates a youth from the pressures and pulls of criminogenic influences in the environment.[214] In a series of studies conducted within the school setting, Reckless and his colleagues found that nondelinquent youths are able to maintain a positive self-image in the face of environmental pressures toward delinquency.[215]

While these early works are valuable, Travis Hirschi's vision of social control, articulated in his highly influential 1969 book *Causes of Delinquency*, is now the dominant version of the theory.[216]

Hirschi's Social Bond Theory

In his insightful work, Hirschi links the onset of delinquency to the weakening of the ties that bind people to society. All kids are potential law violators, but they are kept under control by their relationships with friends, parents, neighbors, teachers, and employers. Without these social ties or bonds, and in the absence of sensitivity to and interest in others, they would be free to commit criminal acts. Hirschi does not view society as containing competing subcultures with unique value systems. Most people are aware of the prevailing moral and legal code. He suggests, however, that in all elements of society people vary in how they respond to conventional social rules and values. Among all ethnic, religious, racial, and social groups, people whose bond to society is weak may fall prey to criminogenic behavior patterns.

Elements of the Social Bond   Hirschi argues that the **social bond** a person maintains with society is divided into four main elements: attachment, commitment, involvement, and belief.

> **social bond**
> Ties a person to the institutions and processes of society; elements of the bond include attachment, commitment, involvement, and belief.

- *Attachment.* Attachment refers to a person's sensitivity to and interest in others.[217] Psychologists believe that without a sense of attachment a person becomes a psychopath and loses the ability to relate coherently to the world. The acceptance of social norms and the development of a social conscience depend on attachment to and caring for other human beings. Attachment to parents is the most important. Even if a family is shattered by divorce or separation, a child must retain a strong attachment to one or both parents.[218] Without this attachment, it is unlikely that feelings of respect for others in authority will develop.

- *Commitment.* Commitment involves the time, energy, and effort expended in conventional lines of action, such as getting an education and saving money for the future. If people build a strong commitment to conventional society, they will be less likely to engage in acts that will jeopardize their hard-won position. A lack of commitment to conventional values may foreshadow a condition in which risk-taking behavior, such as delinquency, becomes a reasonable behavior alternative. The association may be reciprocal. Kids who drink and engage in deviant behavior are more likely to fail in school; kids who fail in school are more likely to later drink and engage in deviant behavior.[219]

- *Involvement.* Heavy involvement in conventional activities leaves little time or opportunity for illegal behavior. Kids' involvement in school, recreation, and family insulates them from the potential lure of delinquent behavior, whereas idleness enhances misbehavior.[220]

■ *Belief.* People who live in the same social setting often share common moral beliefs; they may adhere to such values as sharing, sensitivity to the rights of others, and admiration for the legal code. If these beliefs are absent or weakened, an adolescent is more likely to participate in antisocial or illegal acts.

Hirschi further suggests that the interrelationship of social bond elements controls subsequent behavior. Kids who feel kinship and sensitivity to parents and friends should be more likely to adopt and work toward legitimate goals. Those who reject social relationships are more likely to lack commitment to conventional goals. Similarly, youths who are highly committed to conventional acts and beliefs are more likely to be involved in conventional activities. The Evidence-Based Juvenile Justice feature looks at a program that can help kids build bonds to schools and parents.

Testing Social Bond Theory   One of Hirschi's most significant contributions was his attempt to test the principal hypotheses of social bond theory. He administered a detailed self-report survey to a sample of more than 4,000 junior and senior high school students in Contra Costa County, California.[221] In a detailed analysis of the data, Hirschi found considerable evidence to support the control theory model. Among Hirschi's more important findings are the following:

■ Youths who were strongly attached to their parents were less likely to commit criminal acts.

■ Commitment to conventional values, such as striving to get a good education and refusing to drink alcohol and "cruise around," was indicative of conventional behavior.

■ Youths involved in conventional activity, such as homework, were less likely to engage in criminal behavior.

■ Youths involved in unconventional behavior, such as smoking and drinking, were more delinquency prone.

■ Youths who maintained weak and distant relationships with people tended toward delinquency.

■ Those who shunned unconventional acts were attached to their peers.

■ Delinquents and nondelinquents shared similar beliefs about society.

In addition to Hirschi's own testing, social bond theory has been corroborated by numerous research studies conducted not only in the United States but also in different countries and cultures.[222] Taken in sum, the research indicates that as Hirschi predicts, kids who are attached to their families, friends, and school are less likely to get involved in a deviant peer group and consequently less likely to engage in criminal activities.[223] Kids who feel attached to their parents, especially if they are authoritative and respected, are the ones less likely to engage in antisocial behaviors.[224] Attachment to education is equally important. Youths who are detached from the educational experience are at risk of criminality; those who are committed to school are less likely to engage in delinquent acts.[225] Detachment and alienation from school may be even more predictive of delinquency than school failure and/or educational underachievement.[226]

Attachment is not the only element of the social bond that has been related to the onset of delinquency. As predicted by Hirschi, researchers have found that kids who are committed to school and educational achievement are less likely to become involved in delinquent behaviors than those who lack such commitment.[227] Similarly, youths who are involved in conventional leisure activities, such as supervised social activities and noncompetitive sports, are less likely to engage in delinquency than those who are involved in unconventional leisure activities

Families and Schools Together (FAST)

Families and Schools Together (FAST) is a multifamily group intervention program designed to build protective factors for children, to empower parents to be the primary prevention agents for their own children, and to build supportive parent-to-parent groups. The overall goal of the FAST program is to intervene early to help at-risk youth succeed in the community, at home, and in school and thus avoid problems such as adolescent delinquency, violence, addiction, and dropping out of school. The FAST program achieves its goals by respecting and supporting parents and by using the existing strengths of families, schools, and communities in creative partnerships. The program is geared to at-risk children ages 4 to 12 and their families.

Program Theory

Developed more than 25 years ago, FAST has been implemented in more than 800 schools in 45 states and five countries. It is based on several disciplines, including social ecology of child development, child psychiatry, family stress, family systems, social support, family therapy, parent-led play therapy, group work, adult education, and community development. FAST offers youth structured opportunities for involvement in repeated relationship-building interactions with the primary caretaking parent, other family members, other families, peers, school representatives, and community representatives.

The program begins when a teacher or other school professional identifies a child with problem behaviors who is at risk for serious future academic and social problems. The professional refers the family for participation in the program, and trained recruiters—often FAST graduates—visit the parents at home to discuss the school's concerns and invite them to participate in the program. The family then gathers with 8 to 12 other families for eight weekly meetings, usually held in the school. The meetings, which typically last two and a half hours, include planned opening and closing routines, a family meal, structured family activities and communications, parent mutual-support time, and parent–child play therapy. These group activities support parents to help teach their child to connect to the cultures of work and school. Families participate in a graduation ceremony at the end of eight weeks and then continue to participate in monthly follow-up meetings, run by the families, for two years.

At the local level, FAST is run by trained four- to eight-person FAST teams comprising parents, teachers, other school representatives, and community-based professionals; at the middle school and high school levels, youth are also provided with leadership opportunities within the team. Each FAST team is representative of the population served—that is,

consistent with the gender, ethnicity, and culture of the participating families.

Each FAST team includes:

- For the first FAST cycle, one parent partner whose child is currently in the school grade participating in FAST. For FAST programs that have completed one or more FAST cycles, two to three FAST graduate parents.

- One school partner, ideally a school teacher for the targeted student population.

- Two community partners who are knowledgeable about local community resources, often with expertise in substance abuse prevention or mental health and emotional well-being.

- One recreation coordinator who organizes child or youth activities and exercises.

- At the middle school level, one youth advocate (a school employee) and one graduate youth partner (a high school aged youth) are part of the team.

- At the high school level, three youth partners are included.

Evaluations indicate that the program is quite successful. Among the findings of various projects:

- When compared to control students, FAST students have lower scores on an aggressive behavior scale and lower scores on the withdrawn scale.

- FAST students were rated higher on academic achievement than control students.

- FAST participants had significantly lower teacher-reported externalizing behavior than comparison participants.

- FAST students have significantly higher social skills than the students in the comparison group.

- Two years after intervention, teachers rate FAST students significantly higher than comparison students on the academic scale of the Child Behavior Checklist (CBCL).

- When compared to the control group, participants in the FAST group had significantly improved family adaptability.

CRITICAL THINKING

At what age do you feel intervention is most effective? Would a preschool program work better than one aimed at middle school and high school students?

SOURCES: Families and Schools Together, https://www.familiesandschools.org/; National Institute of Justice, "Crime Solutions, Program Profile: Families and Schools Together (FAST)," 2011, http://www.crimesolutions.gov /ProgramDetails.aspx?ID=185; Rashelle Musci, Catherine Bradshaw, Brion Maher, George R. Uhl, Sheppard Kellam, and Nicholas Ialongo, "Reducing Aggression and Impulsivity Through School-Based Prevention Programs: A Gene by Intervention Interaction," *Prevention Science* 15:831–840 (2014). (URLs accessed September 2016.)

and unsupervised, peer-oriented social pursuits.[228] Likewise, children who are involved in religious activities and hold conventional religious beliefs are less likely to become involved in substance abuse.[229]

Cross-national surveys have also supported the general findings of Hirschi's control theory, finding that the social bond influences delinquency in other countries and cultures.[230]

The elements of the social bond seem to be both interrelated and cumulative—that is, kids who feel detached are more likely to be uncommitted, and those who are uninvolved are also more likely to lack belief in conventional values. Kids who suffer more than one tear in their social bond are more likely to engage in antisocial activities than adolescents who maintain some elements of their bond to society. People who feel kinship and sensitivity to parents and friends should be more likely to adopt and work toward legitimate goals or gain skills that help them avoid antisocial or dangerous behaviors. Girls, for example, who have higher levels of bonding to parents and develop good social skills in adolescence are less likely to experience dating violence as young adults. The reason: a close bond to parents reduces early adolescent alcohol use, a factor that shields girls from victimization.[231]

Critiquing Social Bond Theory Hirschi's view of delinquency is considered one of the most important theoretical contributions of the twentieth century. Nonetheless, questions are still raised about some of its elements. For example, there is still uncertainty about Hirschi's contention that delinquents are detached loners whose bond to their family and friends has been broken. A number of research efforts have shown that, in contradistinction to Hirschi, delinquents maintain relationships with their peers and their friendship patterns seem quite similar to conventional youth.[232] Hirschi would counter that what appears to be a close friendship is really a relationship of convenience and that "birds of a feather flock together" only when it suits their criminal activities. His view is supported by recent research conducted by criminologists Lisa Stolzenberg and Stewart D'Alessio, who found that more often than not, juvenile offenses are committed by individuals acting alone, and that group offending, when it does occur, is incidental and of little importance to explaining the onset of delinquency.[233]

One of the most important elements in Hirschi's theory is that involvement in conventional activities such as sports should reduce the opportunity for delinquency. However, research now shows that kids who are involved in activities outside the home without parental supervision actually engage in more delinquent activity than their uninvolved peers.[234] How is this possible? Did Hirschi get it wrong? Not really. Kids who spend a lot of time hanging out with their friends, unsupervised by parents and/or other authority figures, are in fact the ones most likely to get involved in antisocial acts such as drinking and taking drugs.[235] This is especially true of kids who date a lot and own or have access to cars.[236] So, some involvements may help kids, while those that are unsupervised with friends may actually hurt them.

Finally, social bond theory projects that a weakened bond leads to delinquency, but it is possible the chain of events may flow in the opposite direction: kids who break the law find that their bond to parents, schools, and society eventually becomes weak and attenuated.[237] For example, recent research by Martha Gault-Sherman shows that attachment to parents weakens *after* kids get involved in delinquency.[238]

Although these criticisms need to be addressed with further research, the weight of existing empirical evidence supports control theory, and it has emerged as one of the preeminent theories in criminology. For many delinquency experts, it is perhaps the most important way of understanding the onset of youthful misbehavior. Concept Summary 4.1 sets out the theories discussed in this chapter. The Case Profile feature addresses the issue of social process and delinquent behavior.

Theories of Structure, Process, Culture

Theory	Major Premise	Strengths	Research Focus
Social Disorganization Theories			
Shaw and McKay's concentric zones theory	Delinquency is a product of transitional neighborhoods that display social disorganization and value conflict.	Identifies why delinquency rates are highest in lower-class areas. Points out the factors that produce delinquency. Suggests programs to help reduce delinquency.	Poverty; disorganization
Social ecology theory	The conflicts and problems of urban social life and communities (including fear, unemployment, deterioration) influence delinquency rates.	Accounts for urban delinquency rates and trends.	Social control; fear; collective efficacy; unemployment
Cultural Deviance Theories			
Miller's focal concerns theory	Citizens who obey the street rules of lower-class life (focal concerns) find themselves in conflict with the dominant culture.	Identifies the core values of lower-class culture and shows their association to delinquency.	Cultural norms; focal concerns
Cohen's theory of delinquent subculture	Status frustration of lower-class boys, created by their failure to achieve middle-class success, causes them to join gangs.	Shows how the conditions of lower-class life produce delinquency. Explains violence and destructive acts. Identifies conflict of lower class with middle class.	Gangs; culture conflict; middle-class measuring rods; reaction formation
Cloward and Ohlin's theory of opportunity	Blockage of conventional opportunities causes lower-class youths to join criminal, conflict, or retreatist gangs.	Shows that even illegal opportunities are structured in society. Indicates why kids become involved in a particular type of delinquent activity. Presents a way of preventing delinquency.	Gangs; cultural norms; culture conflict; effects of blocked opportunity
Social Learning Theories			
Differential association theory	People learn to commit delinquency from exposure to antisocial definitions.	Explains onset of criminality. Explains the presence of delinquency in all elements of social structure. Explains why some people in high-delinquency areas refrain from criminality. Can apply to adults and juveniles.	Measuring definitions toward delinquency; influence of deviant peers and parents
Neutralization theory	Youths learn ways of neutralizing moral restraints and periodically drift in and out of delinquent behavior patterns.	Explains why many delinquents do not become adult criminals. Explains why youthful law violators can participate in conventional behavior.	Whether kids who use neutralizations commit more delinquency; beliefs, values, and delinquency
Social Control Theory			
Hirschi's social bond theory	A person's bond to society prevents him or her from violating social rules. If the bond weakens, the person is free to commit delinquency.	Explains the onset of delinquency. Can apply to both middle- and lower-class delinquency. Explains its theoretical constructs adequately so they can be measured. Has been empirically tested.	The associations among commitment, attachment, involvement, belief, and delinquency

case profile

Steph's Story

STEPH is a 14-year-old European American female with no history of delinquent activity. She resides with both parents and three siblings in a middle-class neighborhood. Her family has been recently impacted by the economic downturn, and her parents were forced to move out of their home after a foreclosure. Steph attends her local high school and has a number of friends. Reports indicated that she may have been a victim of sexual abuse as a child, but nothing had been substantiated. She is reported to be sexually active and sexually inappropriate with peers at times.

Steph was referred to the local county human services juvenile delinquency program due to her involvement with buying and selling prescription drugs. It was also reported that Steph stole prescription medications from family and friends and was using on a regular basis. Steph was caught at school selling Adderall. She reported that she had stolen the pills from a sibling diagnosed with attention deficit hyperactivity disorder and was selling them for $20 per pill. Steph reported that her friends and other students at school wanted the drug because they believed it helped them lose weight, focus better, enhance their libido, and increase their confidence. She also stated that she had been using it, as well as other prescription drugs that she found in her home. Steph reported that she had been taking her grandfather's heart medication on occasion.

As a result of her behavior, Steph was arrested for selling prescription drugs and was expelled from school. The delinquency social worker reported that Steph was very fortunate that the district attorney did not formally charge her but had instead asked the social worker to assess the situation and make recommendations related to treatment and education. Upon further assessment it was revealed that Steph had very little knowledge of the dangerous side effects related to her use or regarding the potential dangers for others. An alcohol and drug evaluation recommended that Steph cooperate with a mandatory drug abuse program and abstain from any further use. She was also required to receive education related to the use and sale of the prescription drugs, and this was provided through groups at the treatment program. In addition, the delinquency social worker had Steph complete a research paper on the dangers of abusing prescription drugs.

After completing the above recommendations, the social worker had Steph visit an emergency room and talk with medical staff regarding their experiences with patients abusing prescription drugs. Overall, this experience had the greatest impact on Steph. In particular, she connected with a nurse and doctor team who discussed their firsthand case examples relating to young people abusing prescription drugs. Many of the patients had little or no knowledge of what was in their systems and suffered significant medical complications and consequences. Steph also had an opportunity to share her story with the medical team and get direct information related to the potential dangers of her own use and the risks to others due to her behavior. Steph continues with aftercare services and indicates she has learned some very painful lessons.

CRITICAL THINKING

Discuss the implications of Steph's experience for your view of the social basis of delinquency. Does her story suggest that it is process and not structure that shapes people's lives and behavior? Do kids turn to drug use because of who they are, where they live, or because of their life experiences?

SUMMARY

1 Explain the association between social conditions and crime

- Crime and delinquency rates are highest in deteriorated inner-city areas.
- Kids living in poor neighborhoods are exposed to a constant stream of antisocial behaviors.
- Political unrest and mistrust, economic stress, and family disintegration are social changes that have been found to precede sharp increases in delinquency rates.

- Millions of people have scant, if any, resources and suffer socially and economically as a result.
- The consequences of racial disparity take a toll on youth. The poverty rate among minority groups is still significantly higher than that of whites.

2 Summarize the association between social structure and delinquency

- People in the United States live in a stratified society.

- Social classes are segments of the population whose members have a relatively similar portion of desirable things and who share attitudes, values, norms, and an identifiable lifestyle.

- Those living in poverty are forced to live in neighborhoods that experience inadequate housing and health care, disrupted family lives, underemployment, and despair.

- Children are hit especially hard by poverty, and being poor during early childhood may have a more severe impact on behavior than it does during adolescence and adulthood.

- Besides their increased chance of physical illness, poor children are much more likely than wealthy children to suffer various social and physical ills, ranging from low birth weight to a limited chance of earning a college degree.

3 Categorize the principles of social disorganization theory

- Social disorganization theory focuses on the conditions within the urban environment that affect delinquency rates.

- Social disorganization theory ties delinquency rates to socioeconomic conditions.

- Long-term, unremitting poverty undermines a community and its residents. Delinquency rates are sensitive to the destructive social forces operating in lower-class urban neighborhoods.

- Residents develop a sense of hopelessness and mistrust of conventional society. Residents of such areas are frustrated by their inability to become part of the American Dream.

- Poverty undermines the basic stabilizing forces of the community—family, school, peers, and neighbors—rendering them weakened, attenuated, and ineffective.

- The ability of the community to control its inhabitants—to assert informal social control—is damaged and frayed.

4 Express how social ecologists view the cause of delinquency

- Social ecologists have found an association between delinquency rates and community deterioration: disorder, poverty, alienation, disassociation, and fear of delinquency.

- Poverty becomes "concentrated" in deteriorated areas. As working- and middle-class families flee, elements of the most disadvantaged population are consolidated within inner-city poverty areas.

- People feel safe in neighborhoods that are orderly and in repair. In contrast, those living in neighborhoods that suffer social and physical incivilities are much more likely to be fearful. Put another way, disorder breeds fear.

- The presence of community incivilities, especially when accompanied by relatively high delinquency rates and gang activity, convinces older residents that their neighborhood is dangerous; becoming a crime victim seems inevitable.

5 Analyze the concept of anomie and how it impacts delinquent behavior

- French sociologist Émile Durkheim coined the term "anomie" to describe a society in which rules of behavior have broken down during periods of rapid social change or social crisis.

- Robert Merton in his theory of anomie used a modified version of the concept of anomie to fit social, economic, and cultural conditions found in modern US society.

- According to anomie theory, social inequality leads to perceptions of anomie.

6 Give examples of the recent developments in strain theory

- Strain theory suggests that while most people share similar values and goals, the ability to achieve these personal goals is stratified by socioeconomic class.

- Steven Messner and Richard Rosenfeld view antisocial behavior as a function of cultural and institutional influences in US society; a model they refer to as the American Dream involves accumulating material goods and wealth via open individual competition.

- Sociologist Robert Agnew's General Strain Theory helps identify the micro-level, or individual, influences of strain. Agnew's theory explains why individuals who feel stress and strain are more likely to engage in delinquent acts.

- Agnew suggests that delinquency is the direct result of negative affective states—the anger, frustration, and adverse emotions that kids feel in the wake of negative and destructive social relationships.

7 Define the term *cultural deviance* and analyze theories of cultural deviance

- Because their lifestyle is draining, frustrating, and dispiriting, members of the lower class create an independent subculture with its own set of rules and values.

- Walter Miller identified the unique value system that defines lower-class culture. Conformance to these focal concerns dominates life within the lower class.

- Because social conditions make them incapable of achieving success legitimately, lower-class youths experience a form of culture conflict.

- Youth gangs are an important part of the delinquent subculture, and although not all illegal acts are committed by gang youth, they are the source of the most serious, sustained, and costly delinquent behaviors.

- Delinquent gangs spring up in disorganized areas where youths lack the opportunity to gain success through conventional means.

8 Describe the concept of social process and socialization

- According to the social process view, how you were raised (i.e., socialized) is more important than where you live.

- Delinquency is a function of socialization, the interactions people have with various organizations, institutions, and processes of society.

- Most kids are influenced by their family relationships, peer group associations, educational experiences, and interactions with authority figures, including teachers, employers, and agents of the justice system.

- If these relationships are positive and supportive, kids can succeed within the rules of society; if these relationships are dysfunctional and destructive, conventional success may be impossible, and delinquent solutions may become a feasible alternative.

9 Paraphrase the concept of social learning and social learning theories

- Social learning theories suggest that delinquent behavior is learned in a process that is similar to learning any other human behavior.

- One of the most prominent social learning theories is Edwin H. Sutherland's differential association theory, which asserts that criminal behavior is learned primarily within interpersonal groups and that youths will become delinquent if definitions they have learned favorable to violating the law exceed definitions favorable to obeying the law within that group.

- A delinquent career develops if learned antisocial values and behaviors are not at least matched or exceeded by conventional attitudes and behaviors.

10 Give examples of the elements of social control theory

- Social control theories maintain that all people have the potential to violate the law and that modern society presents many opportunities for illegal activity.

- Social control theorists argue that people obey the law because behavior and passions are being controlled by internal and external forces.

- Travis Hirschi links the onset of delinquency to the weakening of the ties that bind people to society.

- Hirschi argues that the social bond a person maintains with society is divided into four main elements: attachment, commitment, involvement, and belief.

- Youths who are strongly attached to their parents are less likely to commit criminal acts.

- Youths involved in conventional activity, such as homework, are less likely to engage in criminal behavior.

- Youths who maintain weak and distant relationships with people tend toward delinquency.

KEY TERMS

stratified society, p. 138

culture of poverty, p. 139

underclass, p. 139

social structure theories, p. 140

enculturated, p. 140

social disorganization theory, p. 140

strain theory, p. 140

cultural deviance theory, p. 140

cultural transmission, p. 141

social control, p. 141

transitional neighborhood, p. 141

social ecologists, p. 142

siege mentality, p. 144

collective efficacy, p. 146

street efficacy, p. 147

anomie, p. 148

General Strain Theory (GST), p. 150

negative affective states, p. 151

focal concerns, p. 153

status frustration, p. 154

middle-class measuring rods, p. 154

reaction formation, p. 156

differential opportunity, p. 156

socialization, p. 157

social learning theory, p. 160

social control theory, p. 160

differential association theory, p. 160

subterranean values, p. 164

drift, p. 164

neutralization techniques, p. 164

social bond, p. 167

QUESTIONS FOR DISCUSSION

1. Is there a transitional neighborhood in your town or city?

2. Is it possible that a distinct lower-class culture exists? Are lower-class values different from those of the middle class?

3. Have you ever perceived anomie? What causes anomie? Is there more than one cause of strain?

4. How does poverty cause delinquency?

5. Do middle-class youths become delinquent for the same reasons as lower-class youths?

VIEWPOINT

You have just been appointed as a presidential adviser on urban problems. The president informs you that she wants to initiate a demonstration project in a major city aimed at showing that government can do something to reduce poverty, crime, and drug abuse. The area she has chosen for development is a large inner-city neighborhood with more than 100,000 residents. The neighborhood suffers from disorganized community structure, poverty, and hopelessness. Predatory delinquent gangs run free and terrorize local merchants and citizens. The school system has failed to provide opportunities and education experiences sufficient to dampen enthusiasm for gang recruitment. Stores, homes, and public buildings are deteriorated and decayed. Commercial enterprise has fled the area, and civil servants are reluctant to enter the neighborhood. There is an uneasy truce among the various ethnic and racial groups that populate the area. Residents feel that little can be done to bring the neighborhood back to life.

You are faced with suggesting an urban redevelopment program that can revitalize the area and eventually lower the crime rate. You can bring any element of the public and private sector to bear on this rather overwhelming problem—including the military! You can also ask private industry to help in the struggle, promising them tax breaks for their participation.

■ Do you believe that living in such an area contributes to high delinquency rates? Or is poverty merely an excuse and delinquency a matter of personal choice?

■ What programs do you feel could break the cycle of urban poverty?

■ Would reducing the poverty rate produce a lowered delinquency rate?

■ What role does the family play in creating delinquent behaviors?

DOING RESEARCH ON THE WEB

The National Center for Children in Poverty (http://www.nccp.org/) has a great deal of information that can help formulate an answer to these questions. CARE (http://www.care.org/) is a leading humanitarian organization fighting global poverty. Its site also has a lot of useful information on child poverty. The Children's Defense Fund (http://www.childrensdefense.org/policy-priorities/ending-child-poverty/) is also active in drawing attention to the effects of child poverty.

NOTES

All URLs accessed September 2016.

1. Pierce County, Washington, "Pair Sentenced to 56 Years in Deadly Lakewood Home-Invasion Robbery," March 25, 2016, https://www.co.pierce.wa.us/CivicAlerts.aspx?AID=2749.

2. Arlen Egley, Jr., James Howell, and Meena Harris, *Highlights of the 2012 National Youth Gang Survey* (Washington, DC: Office of Juvenile Justice and Delinquency Prevention, 2014), http://www.ojjdp.gov/pubs/248025.pdf.

3. Steven Messner and Richard Rosenfeld, *Crime and the American Dream* (Belmont, CA: Wadsworth, 1994), p. 11.

4. Gary LaFree, *Losing Legitimacy: Street Crime and the Decline of Social Institutions in America* (Boulder, CO: Westview, 1998).

5. Edwin M. Lemert, *Human Deviance, Social Problems, and Social Control* (Englewood Cliffs, NJ: Prentice Hall, 1967).

6. See, generally, Stephen Cernkovich and Peggy Giordano, "Family Relationships and Delinquency," *Criminology* 25:295–321 (1987); Paul Howes and Howard Markman, "Marital Quality and Child

Functioning: A Longitudinal Investigation," *Child Development* 60:1044–1051 (1989).

7. Lance Hannon, "Extremely Poor Neighborhoods and Homicide," *Social Science Quarterly* 86:1418–1434 (2005); Geetanjali Dabral Datta, S. V. Subramanian, Graham Colditz, Ichiro Kawachi, Julie Palmer, and Lynn Rosenberg, "Individual, Neighborhood, and State-Level Predictors of Smoking Among U.S. Black Women: A Multilevel Analysis," *Social Science and Medicine* 63:1034–1044 (2006).

8. Stacey Nofziger and Don Kurtz, "Violent Lives: A Lifestyle Model Linking Exposure to Violence to Juvenile Violent Offending," *Journal of Research in Crime and Delinquency* 42:3–26 (2005); Joanne Kaufman, "Explaining the Race/Ethnicity–Violence Relationship: Neighborhood Context and Social Psychological Processes," *Justice Quarterly* 22:224–251 (2005).

9. Justin Patchin, Beth Huebner, John McCluskey, Sean Varano, and Timothy Bynum, "Exposure to Community Violence and Childhood Delinquency," *Crime and Delinquency* 52:307–332 (2006).

10. Gregory Zimmerman and Steven Messner, "Individual, Family Background, and Contextual Explanations of Racial and Ethnic Disparities in Youths' Exposure to Violence," *American Journal of Public Health* 103:435–442 (2013).

11. LaFree, *Losing Legitimacy*.

12. Sam Roberts, *Who We Are Now: The Changing Face of America in the Twenty-First Century* (New York: Times Books, Henry Holt, 2004).

13. US Department of Census Data, "Income, Poverty, and Health Insurance Coverage in the United States, 2005," http://www.census.gov /prod/2006pubs/p60-231.pdf.

14. Drew DeSilver, "High-Income Americans Pay Most Income Taxes, but Enough to Be 'Fair'?" March 24, 2015, http://www.pewresearch .org/fact-tank/2015/03/24/high-income-americans-pay-most -income-taxes-but-enough-to-be-fair/; Phil DeMuth, "Are You Rich Enough? The Terrible Tragedy of Income Inequality Among the 1%," *Forbes Magazine*, November 25, 2013, http://www.forbes.com/sites /phildemuth/2013/11/25/are-you-rich-enough-the-terrible-tragedy -of-income-inequality-among-the-1/.

15. US Census Bureau, *Income and Poverty in the United States, 2015*, https://www.census.gov/library/publications/2016/demo /p60-256.html.

16. Tomislav Kovandzic, Lynne Vieraitis, and Mark Yeisley, "The Structural Covariates of Urban Homicide: Reassessing the Impact of Income Inequality and Poverty in the Post-Reagan Era," *Criminology* 36:569–600 (1998).

17. Aki Roberts and Dale Willits, "Income Inequality and Homicide in the United States: Consistency Across Different Income Inequality Measures and Disaggregated Homicide Types," *Homicide Studies* 19:28–57 (2015).

18. Carter Hay, Edward Fortson, Dusten Hollist, Irshad Altheimer, and Lonnie Schaible, "Compounded Risk: The Implications for Delinquency of Coming from a Poor Family that Lives in a Poor Community," *Journal of Youth and Adolescence* 36:593–605 (2007).

19. Oscar Lewis, "The Culture of Poverty," *Scientific American* 215:19–25 (1966).

20. James Ainsworth-Darnell and Douglas Downey, "Assessing the Oppositional Culture Explanation for Racial/Ethnic Differences in School Performances," *American Sociological Review* 63:536–553 (1998).

21. Barbara Warner, "The Role of Attenuated Culture in Social Disorganization Theory," *Criminology* 41:73–97 (2003).

22. National Center for Children in Poverty (NCCP), *Child Poverty, 2015*, http://www.nccp.org/publications/childpoverty_pubs.html.

23. National Center on Family Homelessness, "America's Youngest Outcasts," http://www.air.org/sites/default/files/downloads/report /Americas-Youngest-Outcasts-Child-Homelessness-Nov2014.pdf.

24. US Department of Census Data, "Poverty Main," http://www .census.gov/hhes/www/poverty/.

25. US Department of Health and Human Services, "African Americans," http://minorityhealth.hhs.gov/omh/browse.aspx?lvl=3&lvlid=61.

26. National Center for Education Statistics, *The Condition of Education 2014* (NCES 2014-083), Status Dropout Rates, http://nces.edu.gov /fastfacts/display.asp?id=16.

27. Deirdre Bloome, "Racial Inequality Trends and the Intergenerational Persistence of Income and Family Structure," *American Sociological Review* 79:1196–1225 (2014).

28. James Ainsworth-Darnell and Douglas Downey, "Assessing the Oppositional Culture Explanation for Racial/Ethnic Differences in School Performances," *American Sociological Review* 63:536–553 (1998).

29. Bruce Jacobs and Lynn Addington, "Gating and Residential Robbery," *Prevention and Community Safety 18:19–37 (2016)*; Lynn

Addington and Callie Marie Rennison, "Keeping the Barbarians Outside the Gate? Comparing Burglary Victimization in Gated and Non-Gated Communities," *Justice Quarterly* 32:168–192 (2015); Maria Velez, Lauren Krivo, and Ruth Peterson, "Structural Inequality and Homicide: An Assessment of the Black-White Gap in Killings," *Criminology* 41:645–672 (2003).

30. Karen Parker and Matthew Pruitt, "Poverty, Poverty Concentration, and Homicide," *Social Science Quarterly* 81:555–582 (2000).

31. Ruth Peterson and Lauren Krivo, *Divergent Social Worlds: Neighborhood Crime and the Racial-Spatial Divide* (New York: Russell Sage, 2012).

32. William Julius Wilson, *The Truly Disadvantaged* (Chicago: University of Chicago Press, 1987).

33. William Julius Wilson, *More than Just Race: Being Black and Poor in the Inner City* (New York: Norton, 2009).

34. David Bjerk, "Measuring the Relationship Between Youth Criminal Participation and Household Economic Resources," *Journal of Quantitative Criminology* 23:23–39 (2007).

35. See Charles Tittle and Robert Meier, "Specifying the SES/Delinquency Relationship," *Criminology* 28:271–295, at 293 (1990).

36. Clifford R. Shaw and Henry D. McKay, *Juvenile Delinquency and Urban Areas*, rev. ed. (Chicago: University of Chicago Press, 1972), p. 355.

37. Frederick Thrasher, *The Gang* (Chicago: University of Chicago Press, 1927).

38. Robert Bursik and Harold Grasmick, "Longitudinal Neighborhood Profiles in Delinquency: The Decomposition of Change," *Journal of Quantitative Criminology* 8:247–256 (1992).

39. Steven Messner, Lawrence Raffalovich, and Richard McMillan, "Economic Deprivation and Changes in Homicide Arrest Rates for White and Black Youths, 1967–1998: A National Time Series—Analysis," *Criminology* 39:591–614 (2001).

40. Shaw and McKay, *Juvenile Delinquency and Urban Areas*, rev. ed.

41. Claire Valier, "Foreigners, Crime and Changing Mobilities," *British Journal of Criminology* 43:1–21 (2003).

42. Stacy De Coster, Karen Heimer, and Stacy Wittrock, "Neighborhood Disadvantage, Social Capital, Street Context, and Youth Violence," *Sociological Quarterly* 47:723–753 (2006).

43. See, generally, Bursik, "Social Disorganization and Theories of Crime and Delinquency," pp. 519–551.

44. Ruth Peterson, Lauren Krivo, and Mark Harris, "Disadvantage and Neighborhood Violent Crime: Do Local Institutions Matter?" *Journal of Research in Crime and Delinquency 37:31–63 (2000)*.

45. Keith Harries and Andrea Powell, "Juvenile Gun Crime and Social Stress: Baltimore, 1980–1990," *Urban Geography* 15:45–63 (1994).

46. Ellen Kurtz, Barbara Koons, and Ralph Taylor, "Land Use, Physical Deterioration, Resident-Based Control, and Calls for Service on Urban Streetblocks," *Justice Quarterly* 15:121–149 (1998).

47. William Spelman, "Abandoned Buildings: Magnets for Crime?" *Journal of Criminal Justice* 21:481–493 (1993).

48. Shayne Jones and Donald R. Lynam, "In the Eye of the Impulsive Beholder: The Interaction Between Impulsivity and Perceived Informal Social Control on Offending," *Criminal Justice and Behavior* 36:307–321 (2009).

49. Robert Sampson, Jeffrey Morenoff, and Felton Earls, "Beyond Social Capital: Spatial Dynamics of Collective Efficacy for Children," *American Sociological Review* 64:633–660 (1999).

50. Kyle Crowder and Scott South, "Spatial Dynamics of White Flight: The Effects of Local and Extralocal Racial Conditions on Neighborhood Out-Migration," *American Sociological Review* 73:792–812 (2008).

51. Paul Jargowsky and Yoonhwan Park, "Cause or Consequence? Suburbanization and Crime in U.S. Metropolitan Areas," *Crime and Delinquency* 55:28–50 (2009).

52. Edward Shihadeh, "Race, Class, and Crime: Reconsidering the Spatial Effects of Social Isolation on Rates of Urban Offending," *Deviant Behavior* 30:349–378 (2009).

53. Corina Graif, "Delinquency and Gender Moderation in the Moving to Opportunity Intervention: The Role of Extended Neighborhoods," *Criminology 53:366–398 (2015)*.

54. Jeffrey Morenoff, Robert Sampson, and Stephen Raudenbush, "Neighborhood Inequality, Collective Efficacy, and the Spatial Dynamics of Urban Violence," *Criminology* 39:517–560 (2001).

55. Jargowsky and Park, "Cause or Consequence?"

56. Adam Boessen and John Hipp, "Close-Ups and the Scale of Ecology: Land Uses and the Geography of Social Context and Crime," *Criminology 53:399–426 (2015)*.

57. Gregory Squires and Charis Kubrin, "Privileged Places: Race, Uneven Development and the Geography of Opportunity in Urban

America," *Urban Studies* 42:47–68 (2005); Matthew Lee, Michael Maume, and Graham Ousey, "Social Isolation and Lethal Violence Across the Metro/Nonmetro Divide: The Effects of Socioeconomic Disadvantage and Poverty Concentration on Homicide," *Rural Sociology* 68:107–131 (2003).

58. Lee, Maume, and Ousey, "Social Isolation and Lethal Violence Across the Metro/Nonmetro Divide"; Charis E. Kubrin, "Structural Covariates of Homicide Rates: Does Type of Homicide Matter?" *Journal of Research in Crime and Delinquency* 40:139–170 (2003); Darrell Steffensmeier and Dana Haynie, "Gender, Structural Disadvantage, and Urban Crime: Do Macrosocial Variables Also Explain Female Offending Rates?" *Criminology* 38:403–438 (2000).

59. Joseph Schafer, Beth Huebner, and Timothy Bynum, "Fear of Crime and Criminal Victimization: Gender-Based Contrasts," *Journal of Criminal Justice* 34:285–301 (2006).

60. John Hipp, "Micro-structure in Micro-neighborhoods: A New Social Distance Measure, and Its Effect on Individual and Aggregated Perceptions of Crime and Disorder," *Social Networks* 32:148–159 (2010).

61. Xu Yili, Mora Fiedler, and Karl Flaming, "Discovering the Impact of Community Policing: The Broken Windows Thesis, Collective Efficacy, and Citizens' Judgment," *Journal of Research in Crime and Delinquency* 42:147–186 (2005).

62. Matthew Lee and Terri Earnest, "Perceived Community Cohesion and Perceived Risk of Victimization: A Cross-National Analysis," *Justice Quarterly* 20:131–158 (2003); Stephanie Greenberg, "Fear and Its Relationship to Crime, Neighborhood Deterioration, and Informal Social Control," in James Byrne and Robert Sampson, eds., *The Social Ecology of Crime* (New York: Springer Verlag, 1985), pp. 47–62.

63. G. David Curry and Irving Spergel, "Gang Homicide, Delinquency, and Community," *Criminology* 26:381–407 (1988).

64. Lawrence Rosenthal, "Gang Loitering and Race," *Journal of Criminal Law and Criminology* 91:99–160 (2000).

65. Pamela Wilcox, Neil Quisenberry, and Shayne Jones, "The Built Environment and Community Crime Risk Interpretation," *Journal of Research in Crime and Delinquency* 40:322–345 (2003).

66. C. L. Storr, C.-Y. Chen, and J. C. Anthony, "'Unequal Opportunity': Neighborhood Disadvantage and the Chance to Buy Illegal Drugs," *Journal of Epidemiology and Community Health* 58:231–238 (2004).

67. Wesley Skogan, "Fear of Crime and Neighborhood Change," in Albert Reiss and Michael Tonry, eds., *Communities and Crime* (Chicago: University of Chicago Press, 1986), pp. 191–232.

68. Margo Wilson and Martin Daly, "Life Expectancy, Economic Inequality, Homicide, and Reproductive Timing in Chicago Neighborhoods," *British Journal of Medicine* 314:1271–1274 (1997).

69. Pamela Wilcox Rountree and Kenneth Land, "Burglary Victimization, Perceptions of Crime Risk, and Routine Activities: A Multilevel Analysis Across Seattle Neighborhoods and Census Tracts," *Journal of Research in Crime and Delinquency* 33:147–180 (1996).

70. Tim Phillips and Philip Smith, "Emotional and Behavioural Responses to Everyday Incivility," *Journal of Sociology* 40:378–399 (2004); Catherine E. Ross, John Mirowsky, and Shana Pribesh, "Powerlessness and the Amplification of Threat: Neighborhood Disadvantage, Disorder, and Mistrust," *American Sociological Review* 66:568–580 (2001).

71. William Terrill and Michael Reisig, "Neighborhood Context and Police Use of Force," *Journal of Research in Crime and Delinquency* 40:291–321 (2003).

72. Finn-Aage Esbensen and David Huizinga, "Community Structure and Drug Use: From a Social Disorganization Perspective," *Justice Quarterly* 7:691–709 (1990).

73. Bridget Freisthler, Elizabeth Lascala, Paul Gruenewald, and Andrew Treno, "An Examination of Drug Activity: Effects of Neighborhood Social Organization on the Development of Drug Distribution Systems," *Substance Use and Misuse* 40:671–686 (2005).

74. John Hipp, "The Role of Crime in Housing Unit Racial/Ethnic Transition," *Criminology* 48:683–725 (2010).

75. Barbara Warner, Kristin Swartz, Shila René Hawk, "Racially Homophilous Social Ties and Informal Social Control," *Criminology* 53:204–230 (2015).

76. Micere Keels, Greg Duncan, Stefanie Deluca, Ruby Mendenhall, and James Rosenbaum, "Fifteen Years Later: Can Residential Mobility Programs Provide a Long-Term Escape from Neighborhood Segregation, Crime, and Poverty?" *Demography* 42:51–72 (2005).

77. Northwestern University, Institute for Policy Research, Gautreaux at 40 Conference, http://www.ipr.northwestern.edu/events/other-events/gautreaux-at-40-conference.html.

78. Patrick Sharkey and Robert Sampson, "Destination Effects: Residential Mobility and Trajectories of Adolescent Violence in a Stratified Metropolis," *Criminology* 48.639–681 (2010).

79. Kelly Socia and Janet Stamatel, "Neighborhood Characteristics and the Social Control of Registered Sex Offenders," *Crime and Delinquency* 58:565–587 (2012).

80. Todd A. Armstrong, Charles M. Katz, and Stephen M. Schnebly, "The Relationship Between Citizen Perceptions of Collective Efficacy and Neighborhood Violent Crime" *Crime and Delinquency* 61:121–142 (2015); Paul Bellair and Christopher Browning, "Contemporary Disorganization Research: An Assessment and Further Test of the Systemic Model of Neighborhood Crime," *Journal of Research in Crime and Delinquency* 47:496–521 (2010).

81. Justin Medina, "Neighborhood Firearm Victimization Rates and Social Capital Over Time," *Violence and Victims* 30:81–96 (2015); M. R. Lindblad, K. R. Manturuk, and R. G. Quercia, "Sense of Community and Informal Social Control Among Lower Income Households: The Role of Homeownership and Collective Efficacy in Reducing Subjective Neighborhood Crime and Disorder," *American Journal of Community Psychology* 51:123–139 (2013); Rebecca Wickes, John Hipp, Renee Zahnow, and Lorraine Mazerolle, "'Seeing' Minorities and Perceptions of Disorder: Explicating the Mediating and Moderating Mechanisms of Social Cohesion," *Criminology* 51:519–560 (2013).

82. Jeffrey Michael Cancino, "The Utility of Social Capital and Collective Efficacy: Social Control Policy in Nonmetropolitan Settings," *Criminal Justice Policy Review* 16:287–318 (2005); Chris Gibson, Jihong Zhao, Nicholas Lovrich, and Michael Gaffney, "Social Integration, Individual Perceptions of Collective Efficacy, and Fear of Crime in Three Cities," *Justice Quarterly* 19:537–564 (2002).

83. Andrea Altschuler, Carol Somkin, and Nancy Adler, "Local Services and Amenities, Neighborhood Social Capital, and Health," *Social Science and Medicine* 59:1219–1230 (2004).

84. Paul Bellair and Christopher Browning, "Contemporary Disorganization Research: An Assessment and Further Test of the Systemic Model of Neighborhood Crime," *Journal of Research in Crime and Delinquency* 47:496–521 (2010).

85. Donald Black, "Social Control as a Dependent Variable," in D. Black, ed., *Toward a General Theory of Social Control* (Orlando, FL: Academic Press, 1990).

86. Jennifer Beyers, John Bates, Gregory Pettit, and Kenneth Dodge, "Neighborhood Structure, Parenting Processes, and the Development of Youths' Externalizing Behaviors: A Multilevel Analysis," *American Journal of Community Psychology* 31:35–53 (2003).

87. Ralph Taylor, "Social Order and Disorder of Street Blocks and Neighborhoods: Ecology, Microecology, and the Systemic Model of Social Disorganization," *Journal of Research in Crime and Delinquency* 34:113–155 (1997).

88. Suzanna Fay-Ramirez, "The Comparative Context of Collective Efficacy: Understanding Neighbourhood Disorganisation and Willingness to Intervene in Seattle and Brisbane," *Australian and New Zealand Journal of Criminology* 48:513–542 (2015).

89. David Klinger, "Negotiating Order in Patrol Work: An Ecological Theory of Police Response to Deviance," *Criminology* 35:277–306 (1997).

90. Robert Kane, "Compromised Police Legitimacy as a Predictor of Violent Crime in Structurally Disadvantaged Communities," *Criminology* 43:469–498 (2005).

91. Bellair and Browning, "Contemporary Disorganization Research."

92. Gregory Zimmerman, Brandon Welsh, Brandon, and Chad Posick, "Investigating the Role of Neighborhood Youth Organizations in Preventing Adolescent Violent Offending: Evidence from Chicago," *Journal of Quantitative Criminology* 31:565–593 (2015).

93. Maria Velez, "The Role of Public Social Control in Urban Neighborhoods: A Multi-Level Analysis of Victimization Risk," *Criminology* 39:837–864 (2001).

94. Robert Sampson, "Neighborhood and Community," *New Economy* 11:106–113 (2004).

95. Robert Bursik and Harold Grasmick, "Economic Deprivation and Neighborhood Crime Rates, 1960–1980," *Law and Society Review* 27:263–278 (1993).

96. Delbert Elliott, William Julius Wilson, David Huizinga, Robert Sampson, Amanda Elliott, and Bruce Rankin, "The Effects of Neighborhood Disadvantage on Adolescent Development," *Journal of Research in Crime and Delinquency* 33:389–426 (1996).

97. Per-Olof H. Wikström and Kyle Treiber, "The Role of Self-Control in Crime Causation," *European Journal of Criminology* 4:237–264 (2007).

98. John R. Hipp and Wouter Steenbeek, "Types of Crime and Types of Mechanisms: What Are the Consequences for Neighborhoods over Time?" *Crime and Delinquency*, first published online September 9, 2015.

99. Patrick Sharkey, "Navigating Dangerous Streets: The Sources and Consequences of Street Efficacy," *American Sociological Review* 71:826–846 (2006).

100. Ibid.

101. James Wo, John Hipp, and Adam Boessen, "Voluntary Organizations and Neighborhood Crime: A Dynamic Perspective," *Criminology* 54:212–241 (2016).

102. Eric Silver and Lisa Miller, "Sources of Informal Social Control in Chicago Neighborhoods," *Criminology* 42:551–585 (2004).

103. Lorraine Mazerolle, Rebecca Wickes, and James McBroom, "Community Variations in Violence: The Role of Social Ties and Collective Efficacy in Comparative Context," *Journal of Research in Crime and Delinquency* 47:3–30 (2010).

104. Robert Agnew, "A Theory of Crime Resistance and Susceptibility," *Criminology* 54:181–211 (2016).

105. John Braithwaite, "Poverty Power, White-Collar Crime, and the Paradoxes of Criminological Theory," *Australian and New Zealand Journal of Criminology* 24:40–58 (1991).

106. Wilson and Daly, "Life Expectancy, Economic Inequality, Homicide, and Reproductive Timing in Chicago Neighborhoods."

107. P. M. Krueger, S. A. Bond Huie, R. G. Rogers, and R. A. Hummer, "Neighborhoods and Homicide Mortality: An Analysis of Race/Ethnic Differences," *Journal of Epidemiology and Community Health* 58:223–230 (2004).

108. Robert Merton, *Social Theory and Social Structure*, enlarged ed. (New York: Free Press, 1968).

109. For an analysis, see Richard Hilbert, "Durkheim and Merton on Anomie: An Unexplored Contrast in Its Derivatives," *Social Problems* 36:242–256 (1989).

110. Ramiro Martinez Jr., *Latino Homicide: Immigration, Violence, and Community* (New York: Routledge, 2002).

111. Grace Kao and Marta Tienda, "Optimism and Achievement: The Educational Performance of Immigrant Youth," *Social Science Quarterly* 76:1–19 (1995).

112. Steven Messner and Richard Rosenfeld, *Crime and the American Dream* (Belmont, CA: Wadsworth Publishing, 1997), p. 61.

113. Ibid.

114. Lisa Muftic, "Advancing Institutional Anomie Theory," *International Journal of Offender Therapy and Comparative Criminology* 50:630–653 (2006).

115. Robert Agnew, "Foundation for a General Strain Theory of Crime and Delinquency," *Criminology* 30:47–87 (1992).

116. Stephen Baron, "Street Youth, Strain Theory, and Crime," *Journal of Criminal Justice* 34:209–223 (2006).

117. Agnew, "Foundation for a General Strain Theory of Crime and Delinquency," p. 57.

118. Tami Videon, "The Effects of Parent–Adolescent Relationships and Parental Separation on Adolescent Well-Being," *Journal of Marriage and the Family* 64:489–504 (2002).

119. Cesar Rebellon, "Reconsidering the Broken Homes/Delinquency Relationship and Exploring Its Mediating Mechanism(s)," *Criminology* 40:103–135 (2002).

120. Matthew Larson and Gary Sweeten, "Breaking Up Is Hard to Do: Romantic Dissolution, Offending, and Substance Use During the Transition to Adulthood," *Criminology* 50:605–636 (2012).

121. Ronald Simons, Yi Fu Chen, and Eric Stewart, "Incidents of Discrimination and Risk for Delinquency: A Longitudinal Test of Strain Theory with an African American Sample," *Justice Quarterly* 20:827–854 (2003); Robert Agnew and Helene Raskin White, "An Empirical Test of General Strain Theory," *Criminology* 30:475–499 (1992).

122. John Stogner and Chris Gibson, "Wealthy and Wise: Incorporating Health Issues as a Source of Strain in Agnew's General Strain Theory," *Journal of Criminal Justice* 38:1150–1159 (2010).

123. Sherod Thaxton and Robert Agnew, "The Nonlinear Effects of Parental and Teacher Attachment on Delinquency: Disentangling Strain from Social Control Explanations," *Justice Quarterly* 21:763–791 (2004).

124. Stacy De Coster and Lisa Kort-Butler, "How General Is General Strain Theory?" *Journal of Research in Crime and Delinquency* 43:297–325 (2006).

125. Paul Mazerolle, Velmer Burton, Francis Cullen, T. David Evans, and Gary Payne, "Strain, Anger, and Delinquent Adaptations Specifying General Strain Theory," *Journal of Criminal Justice* 28:89–101 (2000);

Paul Mazerolle and Alex Piquero, "Violent Responses to Strain: An Examination of Conditioning Influences," *Violence and Victimization* 12:323–345 (1997).

126. George E. Capowich, Paul Mazerolle, and Alex Piquero, "General Strain Theory, Situational Anger, and Social Networks: An Assessment of Conditioning Influences," *Journal of Criminal Justice* 29:445–461 (2001).

127. Carter Hay and Michelle Evans, "Violent Victimization and Involvement in Delinquency: Examining Predictions from General Strain Theory," *Journal of Criminal Justice* 34:261–274 (2006).

128. Robert Agnew, Timothy Brezina, John Paul Wright, and Francis T. Cullen, "Strain, Personality Traits, and Delinquency: Extending General Strain Theory," *Criminology* 40:43–71 (2002).

129. Wan-Ning Bao, Ain Haas, and Yijun Pi, "Life Strain, Coping, and Delinquency in the People's Republic of China," *International Journal of Offender Therapy and Comparative Criminology* 51:9–24 (2007).

130. Timothy Brezina, "Teenage Violence Toward Parents as an Adaptation to Family Strain: Evidence from a National Survey of Male Adolescents," *Youth and Society* 30:416–444 (1999).

131. Cesar Rebellon, Nicole Leeper Piquero, Alex Piquero, and Sherod Thaxton, "Do Frustrated Economic Expectations and Objective Economic Inequity Promote Crime? A Randomized Experiment Testing Agnew's General Strain Theory" *European Journal of Criminology* 6:47–71 (2009).

132. Joanne Kaufman, Cesar Rebellon, Sherod Thaxton, and Robert Agnew, "A General Strain Theory of Racial Differences in Criminal Offending," *Australian and New Zealand Journal of Criminology* 41:421–437 (2008).

133. Stephen Cernkovich, Peggy Giordano, and Jennifer Rudolph, "Race, Crime and the American Dream," *Journal of Research in Crime and Delinquency* 37:131–170 (2000).

134. Ruth Liu, *Sociological Inquiry* 82:578–600 (2012); Wen-Hsu Lin and Thomas Mieczkowski, "Subjective Strains, Conditioning Factors, and Juvenile Delinquency: General Strain Theory in Taiwan," *Asian Journal of Criminology* 6:69–87 (2011); Byongook Moon, Merry Morash, Cynthia Perez McCluskey, and Hye-Won Hwang, "A Comprehensive Test of General Strain Theory: Key Strains, Situational- and Trait-Based Negative Emotions, Conditioning Factors, and Delinquency," *Journal of Research in Crime and Delinquency* 46:182–212 (2009); Giacinto Froggio, Nereo Zamaro, and Massimo Lori, "Exploring the Relationship Between Strain and Some Neutralization Techniques," *European Journal of Criminology* 6:73–88 (2009).

135. Cesar Rebellon, Michelle Manasse, Karen Van Gundy, and Ellen Cohn, "Perceived Injustice and Delinquency: A Test of General Strain Theory," *Journal of Criminal Justice* 40:230–237 (2012).

136. Christopher Browning, Seth Feinberg, and Robert D. Dietz, "The Paradox of Social Organization: Networks, Collective Efficacy, and Violent Crime in Urban Neighborhoods," *Social Forces* 83:503–534 (2004).

137. Jon Gunnar Bernburg, Marvin Krohn, and Craig Rivera, "Official Labeling, Criminal Embeddedness, and Subsequent Delinquency: A Longitudinal Test of Labeling Theory," *Journal of Research in Crime and Delinquency* 43:67–88 (2006).

138. Chris Melde and Finn-Aage Esbensen, "Gang Membership as a Turning Point in the Life Course," *Criminology* 49:513–552 (2011).

139. David C. Pyrooz, Gary Sweeten, and Alex R. Piquero, "Continuity and Change in Gang Membership and Gang Embeddedness," *Journal of Research in Crime and Delinquency*, online publication February 7, 2012.

140. Walter Miller, "Lower-Class Culture as a Generating Milieu of Gang Delinquency," *Journal of Social Issues* 14:5–19 (1958).

141. Ibid., pp. 14–17.

142. Fred Markowitz and Richard Felson, "Social-Demographic Attitudes and Violence," *Criminology* 36:117–138 (1998).

143. Jeffrey Fagan, *Adolescent Violence: A View from the Street*, NIJ Research Preview (Washington, DC: National Institute of Justice, 1998).

144. Albert Cohen, *Delinquent Boys* (New York: Free Press, 1955).

145. Ibid., p. 25.

146. Ibid., p. 28.

147. Ibid.

148. Clarence Schrag, *Crime and Justice American Style* (Washington, DC: US Government Printing Office, 1971), p. 74.

149. Cohen, *Delinquent Boys*, p. 30.

150. Ibid., p. 31.

151. Ibid., p. 133.

152. J. Johnstone, "Social Class, Social Areas, and Delinquency," *Sociology and Social Research* 63:49–72 (1978); Joseph Harry, "Social Class

and Delinquency: One More Time," *Sociological Quarterly* 15:294–301 (1974).

153. Richard Cloward and Lloyd Ohlin, *Delinquency and Opportunity* (New York: Free Press, 1960).

154. Ibid., p. 7.

155. Ibid., p. 85.

156. Ibid., p. 171.

157. Ibid., p. 73.

158. Ibid., p. 24.

159. James DeFronzo, "Welfare and Burglary," *Crime and Delinquency* 42:223–230 (1996).

160. Diana Formoso, Nancy Gonzales, and Leona Aiken, "Family Conflict and Children's Internalizing and Externalizing Behavior: Protective Factors," *American Journal of Community Psychology* 28:175–199 (2000).

161. DeAnna Harris-McKoy, "Adolescent Delinquency: Is Too Much or Too Little Parental Control a Problem?" *Journal of Child and Family Studies* 25:2079–2088 (2016).

162. Lauren Porter and Ryan King, "Absent Fathers or Absent Variables? A New Look at Paternal Incarceration and Delinquency," *Journal of Research in Crime and Delinquency* 52:414–443 (2015).

163. Ming Cui and Rand D. Conger, "Parenting Behavior as Mediator and Moderator of the Association Between Marital Problems and Adolescent Maladjustment," *Journal of Research on Adolescence* 18:261–284 (2008).

164. Joshua Mersky, James Topitzes, and Arthur J. Reynolds, "Unsafe at Any Age: Linking Childhood and Adolescent Maltreatment to Delinquency and Crime," *Journal of Research in Crime and Delinquency*, first published August 1, 2011.

165. Jennifer Lansford, Laura Wager, John Bates, Gregory Pettit, and Kenneth Dodge, "Forms of Spanking and Children's Externalizing Behaviors," *Family Relations* 6:224–236 (2012).

166. John Paul Wright and Francis Cullen, "Parental Efficacy and Delinquent Behavior: Do Control and Support Matter?" *Criminology* 39:677–706 (2001).

167. Karol Kumpfer and Rose Alvarado, "Strengthening Approaches for the Prevention of Youth Problem Behaviors," *American Psychologist* 58:457–465 (2003); Carter Hay, "Parenting, Self-Control, and Delinquency: A Test of Self-Control Theory," *Criminology* 39:707–736 (2001).

168. Daniel Seddig, "Crime-Inhibiting, Interactional and Co-Developmental Patterns of School Bonds and the Acceptance of Legal Norms," *Crime and Delinquency*, first published April 1, 2015.

169. G. Roger Jarjoura, "Does Dropping Out of School Enhance Delinquent Involvement? Results from a Large-Scale National Probability Sample," *Criminology* 31:149–172 (1993); Terence Thornberry, Melanie Moore, and R. L. Christenson, "The Effect of Dropping Out of High School on Subsequent Criminal Behavior," *Criminology* 23:3–18 (1985).

170. Carolyn Smith, Alan Lizotte, Terence Thornberry, and Marvin Krohn, *Resilient Youth: Identifying Factors that Prevent High-Risk Youth from Engaging in Delinquency and Drug Use* (Albany, NY: Rochester Youth Development Study, 1994), pp. 19–21.

171. Evelien Hoeben and Frank Weerman, "Why Is Involvement in Unstructured Socializing Related to Adolescent Delinquency?" *Criminology* 54:242–281 (2016).

172. Kyle Thomas, "Delinquent Peer Influence on Offending Versatility: Can Peers Promote Specialized Delinquency?" *Criminology* 5:280–308 (2015).

173. Danielle Payne and Benjamin Cornwell, "Reconsidering Peer Influences on Delinquency: Do Less Proximate Contacts Matter?" *Journal of Quantitative Criminology* 23:127–149 (2007).

174. Amy Anderson and Lorine Hughes, "Exposure to Situations Conducive to Delinquent Behavior: The Effects of Time Use, Income, and Transportation," *Journal of Research in Crime and Delinquency* 46:5–34 (2009).

175. Isabela Granic and Thomas Dishion, "Deviant Talk in Adolescent Friendships: A Step Toward Measuring a Pathogenic Attractor Process," *Social Development* 12:314–334 (2003).

176. T. David Evans, Francis Cullen, R. Gregory Dunaway, and Velmer Burton Jr., "Religion and Crime Reexamined: The Impact of Religion, Secular Controls, and Social Ecology on Adult Criminality," *Criminology* 33:195–224 (1995).

177. Colin Baier and Bradley Wright, "If You Love Me, Keep My Commandments: A Meta-Analysis of the Effect of Religion on Crime," *Journal of Research in Crime and Delinquency* 38:3–21 (2001); Byron Johnson, Sung Joon Jang, David Larson, and Spencer De Li, "Does Adolescent Religious Commitment Matter? A Reexamination of the Effects of Religiosity on Delinquency," *Journal of Research in Crime*

and Delinquency 38:22–44 (2001); Sung Joon Jang and Byron Johnson, "Neighborhood Disorder, Individual Religiosity, and Adolescent Use of Illicit Drugs. A Test of Multilevel Hypothesis," *Criminology* 39:109–144 (2001).

178. Richard Petts, "Family and Religious Characteristics' Influence on Delinquency Trajectories from Adolescence to Young Adulthood," *American Sociological Review* 74:465–483 (2009).

179. Walter Miller, *Violence by Youth Gangs and Youth Groups as a Crime Problem in Major American Cities* (Washington, DC: US Government Printing Office, 1975).

180. Hunter Stuart, "Ethan Couch, 'Affluenza' Teen, Facing 5 Lawsuits," *Huffington Post*, December 12, 2013, http://www.huffingtonpost.com/2013/12/18/ethan-couch-affluenza-lawsuits-car-crash-texas_n_4461585.html; Ramit Plushnick-Masti, "'Affluenza' Isn't a Recognized Diagnosis, Experts Say After 'Brat' Spared from Jail in Drunk Driving Case," *National Post*, December 12, 2013, http://news.nationalpost.com/2013/12/12/affluenza-defence-used-to-protect-teen-driver-who-killed-four-was-never-meant-to-be-used-in-court-expert-says/.

181. Ronald L. Simons and Callie Harbin Burt, "Learning to Be Bad: Adverse Social Conditions, Social Schemas, and Crime," *Criminology* 49:553–598 (2011).

182. Edwin H. Sutherland, *Principles of Criminology* (Philadelphia: Lippincott, 1939).

183. See, for example, Edwin Sutherland, "White-Collar Criminality," *American Sociological Review* 5:2–10 (1940).

184. See Edwin Sutherland and Donald Cressey, *Criminology*, 8th ed. (Philadelphia: Lippincott, 1970), pp. 77–79.

185. Dana Haynie, Peggy Giordano, Wendy Manning, and Monica Longmore, "Adolescent Romantic Relationships and Delinquency Involvement," *Criminology* 43:177–210 (2005).

186. Sandra Brown, Vicki Creamer, and Barbara Stetson, "Adolescent Alcohol Expectancies in Relation to Personal and Parental Drinking Patterns," *Journal of Abnormal Psychology* 96:117–121 (1987).

187. Carlo Morselli, Pierre Tremblay, and Bill McCarthy, "Mentors and Criminal Achievement," *Criminology* 44:17–43 (2006).

188. Ibid.

189. Matthew Ploeger, "Youth Employment and Delinquency: Reconsidering a Problematic Relationship," *Criminology* 35:659–675 (1997).

190. Paul Vowell and Jieming Chen, "Predicting Academic Misconduct: A Comparative Test of Four Sociological Explanations," *Sociological Inquiry* 74:226–249 (2004).

191. For an early review, see Barbara Wooton, *Social Science and Social Pathology* (London: Allen and Unwin, 1959).

192. Terence P. Thornberry, "The Apple Doesn't Fall Far from the Tree (or Does It?): Intergenerational Patterns of Antisocial Behavior—The American Society of Criminology 2008 Sutherland Address," *Criminology* 47:297–325 (2009); Terence Thornberry, Adrienne Freeman-Gallant, Alan Lizotte, Marvin Krohn, and Carolyn Smith, "Linked Lives: The Intergenerational Transmission of Antisocial Behavior," *Journal of Abnormal Child Psychology* 31:171–184 (2003).

193. Andy Hochstetler, Heith Copes, and Matt DeLisi, "Differential Association in Group and Solo Offending," *Journal of Criminal Justice* 30:559–566 (2002).

194. Glenn Walters, "Proactive Criminal Thinking and the Transmission of Differential Association: A Cross-Lagged Multi-Wave Path Analysis," *Criminal Justice and Behavior* 42:1128–1144 (2015).

195. Ryan Meldrum and Jamie Flexon, "Is Peer Delinquency in the Eye of the Beholder? Assessing Alternative Operationalizations of Perceptual Peer Delinquency," *Criminal Justice and Behavior* 42:938–951 (2015).

196. Joel Hektner, Gerald August, and George Realmuto, "Effects of Pairing Aggressive and Nonaggressive Children in Strategic Peer Affiliation," *Journal of Abnormal Child Psychology* 31:399–412 (2003); Matthew Ploeger, "Youth Employment and Delinquency: Reconsidering a Problematic Relationship," *Criminology* 35:659–675 (1997); William Skinner and Anne Fream, "A Social Learning Theory Analysis of Computer Crime Among College Students," *Journal of Research in Crime and Delinquency* 34:495–518 (1997); Denise Kandel and Mark Davies, "Friendship Networks, Intimacy, and Illicit Drug Use in Young Adulthood: A Comparison of Two Competing Theories," *Criminology* 29:441–467 (1991).

197. Mark Warr, "Age, Peers, and Delinquency," *Criminology* 31:17–40 (1993).

198. Dana Haynie, Peggy Giordano, Wendy Manning, and Monica Longmore, "Adolescent Romantic Relationships and Delinquency Involvement," *Criminology* 43:177–210 (2005).

199. Robert Lonardo, Peggy Giordano, Monica Longmore, and Wendy Manning, "Parents, Friends, and Romantic Partners: Enmeshment in Deviant Networks and Adolescent Delinquency Involvement," *Journal of Youth and Adolescence* 38:367–383 (2009).

200. Ibid.

201. Travis C. Pratt, Francis T. Cullen, Christine S. Sellers, L. Thomas Winfree Jr., Tamara D. Madensen, Leah E. Daigle, Noelle E. Fearn, and Jacinta M. Gau, "The Empirical Status of Social Learning Theory: A Meta-Analysis," *Justice Quarterly*, November 2009.

202. Gresham Sykes and David Matza, "Techniques of Neutralization: A Theory of Delinquency," *American Sociological Review* 22:664–670 (1957); David Matza, *Delinquency and Drift* (New York: Wiley, 1964).

203. Matza, *Delinquency and Drift*, p. 51.

204. Sykes and Matza, "Techniques of Neutralization," pp. 664–670; see also David Matza, "Subterranean Traditions of Youths," *Annals of the American Academy of Political and Social Science* 378:116 (1961).

205. Volkan Topalli, "When Being Good Is Bad: An Expansion of Neutralization Theory," *Criminology* 43:797–836 (2005).

206. Nicole Shoenberger, Alex Heckert, and Druann Heckert, "Techniques of Neutralization Theory and Positive Deviance," *Deviant Behavior* 33:774–791 (2012).

207. Ian Shields and George Whitehall, "Neutralization and Delinquency Among Teenagers," *Criminal Justice and Behavior* 21:223–235 (1994); Robert A. Ball, "An Empirical Exploration of Neutralization Theory," *Criminologica* 4:22–32 (1966). See also M. William Minor, "The Neutralization of Criminal Offense,"*Criminology* 18:103–120 (1980); Robert Gordon, James Short, Desmond Cartwright, and Fred Strodtbeck, "Values and Gang Delinquency: A Study of Street Corner Groups," *American Journal of Sociology* 69:109–128 (1963).

208. Robert Morris and Heith Copes, *Criminal Justice Review* 37:442–460 (2012); Edward Brent and Curtis Atkisson, *Research in Higher Education* 52:640–658 (2011).

209. Robert Agnew, "The Techniques of Neutralization and Violence," *Criminology* 32:555–580 (1994); Michael Hindelang, "The Commitment of Delinquents to Their Misdeeds: Do Delinquents Drift?" *Social Problems* 17:500–509 (1970); Robert Regoli and Eric Poole, "The Commitment of Delinquents to Their Misdeeds: A Reexamination," *Journal of Criminal Justice* 6:261–269 (1978).

210. Scott Briar and Irving Piliavin, "Delinquency: Situational Inducements and Commitment to Conformity," *Social Problems* 13:35–45 (1965–1966).

211. Lawrence Sherman and Douglas Smith, with Janell Schmidt and Dennis Rogan, "Crime, Punishment, and Stake in Conformity: Legal and Informal Control of Domestic Violence," *American Sociological Review* 57:680–690 (1992).

212. Albert Reiss, "Delinquency as the Failure of Personal and Social Controls," *American Sociological Review* 16:196–207 (1951).

213. Briar and Piliavin, "Delinquency: Situational Inducements and Commitment to Conformity."

214. Walter Reckless, *The Crime Problem* (New York: Appleton-Century-Crofts, 1967), pp. 469–483.

215. Among the many research reports by Reckless and his colleagues are Frank Scarpitti, Ellen Murray, Simon Dinitz, and Walter Reckless, "The Good Boy in a High Delinquency Area: Four Years Later," *American Sociological Review* 23:555–558 (1960); Walter Reckless, Simon Dinitz, and Ellen Murray, "The Good Boy in a High Delinquency Area," *Journal of Criminal Law, Criminology, and Police Science* 48:12–26 (1957); Reckless, Dinitz, and Murray, "Self-Concept as an Insulator Against Delinquency," *American Sociological Review* 21:744–746 (1956); Walter Reckless and Simon Dinitz, "Pioneering with Self-Concept as a Vulnerability Factor in Delinquency," *Journal of Criminal Law, Criminology, and Police Science* 58:515–523 (1967); Walter Reckless, Simon Dinitz, and Barbara Kay, "The Self-Component in Potential Delinquency and Potential Non-Delinquency," *American Sociological Review* 22:566–570 (1957).

216. Travis Hirschi, *Causes of Delinquency* (Berkeley: University of California Press, 1969).

217. Ibid., p. 231.

218. Tiffiney Barfield-Cottledge, "The Triangulation Effects of Family Structure and Attachment on Adolescent Substance Use," *Crime and Delinquency* 61:297–320 (2015).

219. Robert Crosnoe, "The Connection Between Academic Failure and Adolescent Drinking in Secondary School," *Sociology of Education* 79:44–60 (2006).

220. Lisa Kort-Butler and David Martin, "The Influence of High School Activity Portfolios on Risky Behaviors in Emerging Adulthood," *Justice Quarterly* 32:381–409 (2015).

221. Hirschi, Causes of Delinquency, pp. 66–74.

222. Yoonsun Han, Heejoo Kim, and Dong Hun Lee, "Application of Social Control Theory to Examine Parent, Teacher, and Close Friend Attachment and Substance Use Initiation Among Korean Youth," *School Psychology International* 37:340–358 (2016); Özden Özbay and Yusuf Ziya Özcan, "A Test of Hirschi's Social Bonding Theory," *International Journal of Offender Therapy and Comparative Criminology* 50:711–726 (2006).

223. Helen Garnier and Judith Stein, "An 18-Year Model of Family and Peer Effects on Adolescent Drug Use and Delinquency," *Journal of Youth and Adolescence* 31:45–56 (2002).

224. Rick Trinkner, Ellen S. Cohn, Cesar J. Rebellon, and Karen Van Gundy, "Don't Trust Anyone over 30: Parental Legitimacy as a Mediator Between Parenting Style and Changes in Delinquent Behavior over Time," *Journal of Adolescence* 35:119–132 (2012).

225. Allison Ann Payne, "A Multilevel Analysis of the Relationships Among Communal School Organization, Student Bonding, and Delinquency," *Journal of Research in Crime and Delinquency* 45:429–455 (2008).

226. Norman White and Rolf Loeber, "Bullying and Special Education as Predictors of Serious Delinquency," *Journal of Research in Crime and Delinquency* 45:380–397 (2008).

227. Michael Cretacci, "Religion and Social Control: An Application of a Modified Social Bond of Violence," *Criminal Justice Review* 28:254–277 (2003).

228. Jonathan Zaff, Kristin Moore, Angela Romano Papillo, and Stephanie Williams, "Implications of Extracurricular Activity Participation During Adolescence on Positive Outcomes," *Journal of Adolescent Research* 18:599–631 (2003).

229. Mark Regnerus and Glen Elder, "Religion and Vulnerability Among Low-Risk Adolescents," *Social Science Research* 32:633–658 (2003); Mark Regnerus, "Moral Communities and Adolescent Delinquency: Religious Contexts and Community Social Control," *Sociological Quarterly* 44:523–554 (2003).

230. Marianne Junger and Ineke Haen Marshall, "The Interethnic Generalizability of Social Control Theory: An Empirical Test," *Journal of Research in Crime and Delinquency* 34:79–112 (1997); Josine Junger-Tas, "An Empirical Test of Social Control Theory," *Journal of Quantitative Criminology* 8:18–29 (1992).

231. Carl Maas, Charles Fleming, Todd Herrenkohl, and Richard Catalano, "Childhood Predictors of Teen Dating Violence Victimization," *Violence and Victims* 25:131–149 (2010).

232. Peggy Giordano, Stephen Cernkovich, and M. D. Pugh, "Friendships and Delinquency," *American Journal of Sociology* 91:1170–1202 (1986).

233. Lisa Stolzenberg and Stewart D'Alessio, "Co-offending and the Age–Crime Curve," *Journal of Research in Crime and Delinquency* 45:65–86 (2008).

234. Velmer Burton, Francis Cullen, T. David Evans, R. Gregory Dunaway, Sesha Kethineni, and Gary Payne, "The Impact of Parental Controls on Delinquency," *Journal of Criminal Justice* 23:111–126 (1995).

235. Anderson and Hughes, "Exposure to Situations Conducive to Delinquent Behavior."

236. Patrick Seffrin, Peggy Giordano, Wendy Manning, and Monica Longmore, "The Influence of Dating Relationships on Friendship Networks, Identity Development, and Delinquency," *Justice Quarterly* 26:238–267 (2009).

237. Allen E. Liska and M. D. Reed, "Ties to Conventional Institutions and Delinquency: Estimating Reciprocal Effects," *American Sociological Review* 50:547–560 (1985).

238. Martha Gault-Sherman, "It's a Two-Way Street: The Bidirectional Relationship Between Parenting and Delinquency," *Journal of Youth and Adolescence* 41:121–145 (2012).

CHAPTER 5

Social Reaction, Social Conflict, and Delinquency

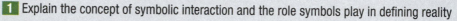

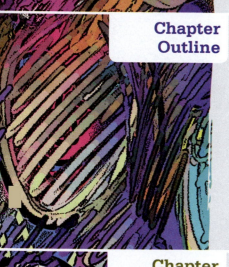

Chapter Features

Youth Stories: Was It Rape?

Focus on Delinquency: The Consequences of Labeling

Cyber Delinquency: Recruiting Young Terrorists

Case Profile: Jay's Story

Evidence-Based Juvenile Justice—Intervention: Family Group Conferencing (FGC): The New Zealand Model

YOU MAY REMEMBER when 14-year-old Ahmed Mohamed made national headlines as the "clock boy," who brought a disassembled clock to MacArthur High School in Irving, Texas. The contraption had wires and gears connected to a circuit board with a digital display, all contained in a small metal case decorated with a tiger hologram. Ahmed's engineering teacher admired the clock, but advised him to keep it out of sight. When the alarm accidentally went off in English class, the clock was confiscated because the teacher thought it looked like a bomb; the principal called the police. Five police officers interrogated the boy for an hour and a half, asking his intentions for bringing the clock to school. Though Ahmed repeated that he just wanted to show his teachers what he could make, the police still suspected that he was trying to make a bomb. He was taken out of school in handcuffs and brought to a juvenile detention center, where he was fingerprinted, required to take a mug shot, and further questioned before being released to his parents. He was suspended from school for three days.

Ahmed quickly became a national celebrity and a symbol of anti-Muslim sentiment and suspicion. He was invited to the White House where he met with President Barack Obama. Then given a scholarship, he and his family moved to Qatar where Ahmed attended school before returning to the United States, hiring an attorney, and filing suit against the school district. The suit cited a pattern of disproportionate disciplinary actions for black students and

AP Images/LM Otero

a history of anti-Muslim bias. The lawsuit alleged that Ahmed was discriminated against based on his race and religion. It also claimed that his Fourth Amendment rights were violated when he was interrogated by police and principal Daniel Cummings for over an hour without the presence of his parents before he was arrested.[1]

Was Ahmed unfairly targeted and stigmatized because he was a Muslim? Or were the teacher and principal being understandably cautious in a world where bombings and terror attacks have become routine? The lawsuit assumes that if a white Christian boy had brought the same device into the school he would have been praised for ingenuity. Ahmed, the lawsuit charges, was interrogated and arrested solely because of his appearance and beliefs. Do you agree?

Two theories of delinquency are discussed in this chapter—social reaction theory and social conflict theory. **Social reaction theory**, which is also commonly called **labeling theory** (the two terms are used interchangeably here), holds that the decision to label behavior as deviant or delinquent is subjective, based on the attitudes, values, and morals of the decision maker. People are bad, evil, or delinquent only when they are viewed that way by others. Even such crimes as murder, rape, and assault are bad or evil only because people label them as such. The difference between a forcible rape and a consensual sexual encounter often rests on what the members of a jury or judge believe and how they interpret the events that took place. It depends on your viewpoint and the view of those who are in a position to judge their acts.

Social conflict theory (also called conflict theory) also focuses more on the role of decision makers but adds a political twist: the law serves the interests of the powerful, and people are arrested, adjudicated, and punished based on whether their actions are viewed as a threat to the existing economic and social order. Social reaction theory and social conflict theory differ, however, on the motivation for labeling and social control. While social reaction theory focuses on the beliefs, attitudes, and moral values of those in power, social conflict theory is oriented toward their economic and political interests. These two views will be examined in detail below.

social reaction theory (also called labeling theory)
Posits that society creates deviance through a system of social control agencies that designate (or label) certain individuals as delinquent, thereby stigmatizing youths and encouraging them to accept this negative personal identity.

social conflict theory (also called conflict theory)
Asserts that society is in a state of constant internal conflict, and focuses on the role of social and governmental institutions as mechanisms for social control.

Social Reaction Theory

Social reaction, or labeling, theory explains how sustained delinquent behavior stems from destructive social interactions and encounters. According to this theory, illegal acts, including delinquent behaviors, are defined by the social audience's reaction and not the moral content of the illegal act itself.[2] Even the crime of murder is socially constructed. Though most people would agree that killing someone is wrong and evil, there are circumstances where taking a life is excusable: in self-defense; in time of war; if it is the product of a mental disease; if it is legally mandated (capital punishment); if it is the result of an accident. And there are gray areas that are subject to debate. Some people consider shooting someone who is trying to steal your car justified, whereas others consider it murder; some people are opposed to abortion, whereas others fight to preserve its legality. The roots of this vision can be found in a branch of sociology known as **symbolic interaction**.[3]

symbolic interaction
Holds that people communicate via symbols—gestures, signs, words, or images—that stand for or represent something else.

The Concept of Symbolic Interaction

Symbolic interaction theory holds that people communicate via symbols—gestures, signs, words, or images—that stand for or represent something else. For example, when you see a person with a gold ring on the fourth finger of his left hand you know he is married. The ring is not merely a piece of jewelry but a representation or symbol of the wearer's status. It tells you that he lives a conventional lifestyle, is most likely emotionally stable, ready for commitment, and so on. Similarly, wearing an expensive watch such as a Rolex symbolizes that the owner is successful, wealthy, and confident; this is referred to as a **status symbol**. Sometimes symbols take the form of a gesture. If a guy asks a girl out on a date and she rolls her eyes, shakes her head, and turns her back, he quickly gets the message: this is not going to work.

status symbol
Something, such as a possession, rank, or activity, by which one's social or economic prestige is measured.

As you can imagine, symbols are subjective. A Rolex may keep no better time than a Timex, yet one conveys an image of wealth and success and the other of thrift and frugality. Similarly, body language is open to interpretation and can be easily misread.

People often interpret symbolic gestures from others and incorporate them in their self-image. When a teacher puts an A on your paper, it tells you that you are an excellent student, and the symbol pumps up your self-image. Symbols are also used by people to let others know how well they are doing and whether they are liked or appreciated. How people view reality depends on the content of the messages and situations they encounter, the subjective interpretation of these interactions, and how they shape future behavior. There is no objective reality. People interpret the reactions of others, and this interpretation assigns meaning. Because interpretation changes over time, so do the meanings of concepts and symbols.

Interpreting Deviance

Because the definitions of crime and delinquency are purely subjective, they can change from place to place and from year to year. Acts such as abortion, marijuana use, possession of a handgun, and gambling have been legal at some time in history and illegal at others. In some jurisdictions, driving at 35 miles an hour is illegal, while in others, 70 is just fine!

Definitions of crime and delinquency may vary between legal jurisdictions, so what is outlawed in one state is perfectly legal in another. Take for instance the crime of rape, which often involves a great deal of interpretation. In some states it is considered rape if, after the sex act begins, a man continues after his partner tells him to stop; in other states the same act is considered legal and justified.[4] Sometimes definitions change because of an incident that is shocking and controversial.

In 2016, a California judge gave Brock Turner, a former swimmer convicted in the sexual assault of an unconscious woman at Stanford University, a six-month sentence. The public outcry was so widespread that the California legislature quickly passed bills toughening rape laws. One bill makes any sexual assault a rape, including penetration with a foreign object. State law had previously defined rape more narrowly, as nonconsensual sexual intercourse.[5]

States define the age limit for consent differently: in most states, the age of consent is 16; however, in a number of states, including California, Florida, and Wisconsin, the age is 18. Consequently, what is defined as the crime of statutory rape in one state is legal in another.

Two famous statements sum up this position. In one, sociologist Kai Erickson argued, "Deviance is not a property inherent in certain forms of behavior, it is a property conferred upon those forms by the audience which directly or indirectly witnesses them."[6] In another, sociologist Howard S. Becker stated,

> Social groups create deviance by making rules whose infractions constitute deviance, and by applying those rules to particular people and labeling them as outsiders. From this point of view, deviance is not a quality of the act a person commits, but rather a consequence of the application by others of rules and sanctions to an "offender." The deviant is one to whom the label has successfully been applied; deviant behavior is behavior that people so label.[7]

Becker refers to people who create rules as "moral entrepreneurs." An example of a moral entrepreneur today might be members of an ultra-orthodox religious group who target the gay community and mount a campaign to prevent gays from adopting children.[8] The Youth Stories feature looks at a case that illustrates the subjectivity of the definition of crime and deviance.

Jason Connolly/Getty Images

The concept of deviance is often fluid. What may be considered deviant at one time is normative at another. Here, people light up during the Denver 420 Rally, the world's largest celebration of both the legalization of cannabis and cannabis culture. Colorado is one of four US states along with the District of Columbia that have legalized the use of recreational marijuana.

Becoming Labeled

Social reaction theory picks up on these concepts of *interaction* and *interpretation*.[9] Throughout their lives, people are given a variety of symbolic labels, some positive ("she's a real go-getter"), others negative ("he is an accident waiting to happen"). People can also be labeled because of groups they belong to or because of their status, such as mental patient or special ed student.[10] These labels help define not just one trait but the whole person; they rob people of social opportunities. Kids labeled as "at risk" are also assumed to be dangerous, dishonest, unstable, violent, strange, and otherwise unsound. In contrast, an "honor student" is also assumed to be smart, honest, hard working, and competent. Labels can improve self-image and social standing. Research shows that people who are labeled with one positive trait, such as being physically attractive, are assumed to maintain other traits, such as being intelligent and competent.[11] In contrast, negative labels—troublemaker, mentally ill, stupid—help **stigmatize** the recipients of these labels and reduce their self-image. Those who have accepted these labels are more prone to engage in delinquent behaviors than those whose self-image has not been so tarnished.[12]

Both positive and negative labels involve subjective interpretation of behavior: a troublemaker is merely a kid who people label as troublesome. There need not be any objective proof or measure indicating that the person is actually a troublemaker. Just as we assume that a Rolex is a terrific timepiece, we assume that someone labeled a troublemaker is a bad apple. Though a label may be a function of rumor, innuendo, or unfounded suspicion, its adverse impact can be immense.

stigmatize
To mark someone with disgrace or reproach; to characterize or brand someone as disgraceful or disreputable.

Was It Rape?

In 2015, a 15-year-old freshman girl was flattered to be contacted by one of the most popular seniors at the exclusive St. Paul's School in Concord, New Hampshire. Owen Labrie, 18, used email to convince the girl to meet him as part of the "senior salute" ritual in which graduating seniors seduce younger students and gain points for each girl with whom they had sex. The victim's names are put on a chalkboard so the seniors can keep score.

The victim, later identified as Francesca "Chessy" Prout, claimed that she had intended merely to kiss or make out with Labrie but not go any further. She testified that she helped him partially undress her, and she freely engaged in some intimate sexual contact. But when she drew the line and told him to stop, he failed to listen, forcing her into three unwanted sex acts.

A complaint was filed and Labrie put on trial. Labrie, who had already been accepted on a scholarship to Harvard, testified that the young woman consented to his advances and that actual sexual intercourse had not taken place.

In the end, a jury found Labrie not guilty of the most serious charge of forcible rape but convicted him of several lesser charges, including endangering the welfare of a child, and using a computer and the Internet to "seduce, solicit, lure, or entice a child" in order to commit a sexual assault. He was also found guilty of three counts of misdemeanor sexual assault.

Why was he found not guilty of the most serious charge even though the jury believed he did have sex with the young woman, who was still a minor? The reason is that under New Hampshire law, an individual can be found guilty of aggravated felonious sexual assault only if the victim clearly indicates that she doesn't "freely consent," or before she has "an adequate chance to flee and/or resist." The jury concluded that there was no real proof that she resisted. Also, under New Hampshire's "Romeo and Juliet" law, if a person has penetrative consensual sex with a minor between the ages 13 and 16 but is within four years of that age, they are guilty of *misdemeanor* sexual assault. If the age difference is more than four years, they are guilty of *felony* sexual assault. Since Labrie was 18 and the young woman 15, he could only be convicted of a misdemeanor.

The judge sentenced Labrie to a year in a county jail and he was forced to register as a sex offender. Meanwhile, the victim's parents filed suit against St. Paul's School, alleging that the school turned a blind eye to a "warped culture of sexual misconduct" by "fostering, permitting, and condoning a tradition of ritualized statutory rape." The lawsuit alleges that the concept of "scoring"—with older students "tracking their sexual conquests of young girls—has long been part of [St. Paul's] ethos" and that the school failed to put a halt to it. Lawyers said that St. Paul's "had children boarding with them and as such, they assume the role of parents. They

Owen Labrie is escorted out of the Merrimack County, New Hampshire, Superior Court, where he was convicted of sexually assaulting a 15-year-old girl as part of a game of sexual conquest called Senior Salute.

knew that the children under their care were threatened by this senior salute, by pervasive games of sexual conquest, and they did nothing to stop it. The family is not asking for money but merely that the rape culture be ended.

The St. Paul's case is a good illustration of how subjective judgments and decision-making control how crime is defined and whom is to be a considered a criminal. If the jury believed the victim, Labrie's actions constituted rape and he would have been sent to prison for 15 years; if they believed Labrie, he should have been set free. But they sought a middle ground, labeling the act as both consensual yet forbidden (because of the victim's age). If the decision stands (it's on appeal), Labrie's greatest punishment will be carrying a sex offender label for the rest of his life.

CRITICAL THINKING

1. The victim returned to school but because of taunts and harassment transferred to another institution. Knowing the scrutiny she would be placed under, what could possibly motivate someone like her to bring false charges in this case? What would she gain by lying?
2. Let's say a teenager climbs through a window, enters a dwelling, and leaves via the front door with some valuable sporting goods and other items. Would you label this a burglary? What other circumstances might explain the teen's behavior

SOURCES: Jess Bidgood, "Owen Labrie of St. Paul's School Is Found Not Guilty of Main Rape Charge," *New York Times*, August 28, 2015, http://www.nytimes.com/2015/08/29/us/st-pauls-school-rape-trial-owen-labrie .html; Andy Rosen and Peter Schworm, "Labrie Acquitted of Felony Rape in St. Paul's School Trial," *Boston Globe*, August 28, 2015; Jennifer Levitz, "Parents Sue St. Paul's School After 'Senior Salute' Sexual-Assault Case," *Wall Street Journal*, June 1, 2016, http://www.wsj.com/articles/parents-sue-st-pauls-school-after -senior-salute-sexual-assault-case-1464830358. (URLs accessed September 2016.)

The Source of Labels

Labels can be formal or informal and come from parents, peers, and the justice system. Kids who perceive that they have been negatively labeled by significant others such as peers and teachers are more likely to self-report delinquent behavior and to adopt a deviant self-concept.[13] They are likely to seek deviant friends and join gangs, associations that escalate their involvement in criminal activities.[14] Parental labeling is extremely damaging because it may cause adolescents to seek deviant peers whose behavior amplifies the effect of the labeling.[15] Children negatively labeled by their parents routinely suffer a variety of problems, including antisocial behavior and school failure.[16] This process has been observed in the United States and abroad, indicating that the labeling process is universal.[17] In contrast, when parents stick by kids, the effect of negative labels bestowed by others can be neutralized.[18]

In addition to these informal labels, official labels from the juvenile justice system can also have a devastating effect. An official label increases the risk of youths later dropping out of high school, for example. Rather than deterring crime, court intervention increases the likelihood of future criminality.[19] The younger the adolescent, the more powerful influence the negative label can have on his or her self-image.[20]

Differential Labeling

An important principle of social reaction theory is that the law is differentially applied, benefiting those who hold economic and social power and penalizing the powerless. The probability of being brought under the control of legal authority is a function of a person's race, wealth, gender, and social standing. While wealthy white delinquents are frequently let off with a warning, poor kids and children of color who commit similar acts are much more likely to face arrest and incarceration.[21] Nowhere is this dynamic more visible than in the so-called War on Drugs. African American drug offenders have a significantly higher likelihood of suffering drug arrests, an imbalance that increases with age. Before age 17, whites and blacks have similar likelihoods of drug arrest. In early adulthood, race disparities in drug arrest grow substantially; by age 22, African Americans have 83 percent greater odds of a drug arrest than whites, and at age 27 this disparity is 235 percent. These disparities exist while controlling for differences in both the nature and extent of drug offending.[22] Clearly, this evidence supports the labeling theory assertion that personal characteristics and social interactions are more important variables in developing criminal identities than merely violating the law.

Why is this differential labeling allowed to take place? Although substantive and procedural laws govern almost every aspect of the American justice system, discretionary decision making controls its operation at every level. From the police officer's decision on whom to arrest to the prosecutor's decisions on whom to charge and for how many and what kind of charges or whether to treat the offender as a juvenile or prosecute in adult court, to the judge's decision on the length of the sentence, discretion works to the detriment of minorities, including African Americans, Latinos, Asian Americans, and Native Americans.[23] When Tammy Rinehart Kochel, David Wilson, and Stephen Mastrofski reviewed the existing literature on police arrest practices, screening more than 4,500 published and unpublished research studies, they found that minority suspects stopped by police are significantly more likely to be arrested than white suspects. The chances of a white suspect being arrested was 20 percent, whereas the average probability for a nonwhite suspect was calculated at 26 percent. These findings are clear evidence of differential labeling practices.[24] Once a case reaches the court system, racial bias influences the application of punishment. Surveys show that as the

The Consequences of Labeling

It has long been suspected that Lesbian, Gay, Bisexual, Trans, and Queer (LGBTQ) students who suffer stigma, labeling, and bullying are at risk of depression and suicidal ideation. To determine the extent of the problem, in 2016 the Centers for Disease Control and Prevention (CDC) conducted the first nationally representative study on the risks faced by approximately 1.3 million lesbian, gay, and bisexual (LGB) high school students in the United States. The CDC analyzed data from surveys of more than 15,000 students in grades 9 through 12 as well as data from 25 state surveys and 19 large urban school district surveys.

In the report, sexual minority students were defined as:

- Those who identified themselves as gay, lesbian, or bisexual
- Those who had had sexual contact with only persons of the same sex
- Those who had had sexual contact with persons of both sexes

The data show that LGB students experience substantially higher levels of physical and sexual violence and bullying than other students. Specifically, this report found that compared to their heterosexual peers, LGB students are significantly more likely to report:

- Being physically forced to have sex (18 percent LGB versus 5 percent heterosexual)

- Experiencing physical dating violence (18 percent LGB versus 8 percent heterosexual)
- Experiencing sexual dating violence (23 percent LGB versus 9 percent heterosexual)
- Being bullied at school or online (at school: 34 percent LGB versus 19 percent heterosexual; online: 28 percent LGB versus 14 percent heterosexual)

While physical and sexual violence and bullying are serious health dangers on their own, a combination of complex factors can place young people at high risk for suicide, depression, addiction, poor academic performance, and other severe consequences. The data demonstrate that LGB students may be at substantial risk for these serious outcomes:

- More than 40 percent of LGB students have seriously considered suicide, and 29 percent reported having attempted suicide during the past 12 months.
- Sixty percent of LGB students reported having been so sad or hopeless they stopped doing some of their usual activities.

numbers of racial and ethnic minorities in the population increase, so do calls for harsher punishments.[25]

Not only does differential labeling take place in the justice system, but it also infects the educational system. Research shows that African American children receive more disciplinary infractions than children from other racial categories, even when their behavior is quite similar. Having a higher percentage of black students in a school translates into a greater use of disciplinary tactics, a factor that may explain why minority students fare less well and are more likely to disengage from schools at a younger age than whites.[26] In disadvantaged, urban schools in minority areas, administrators and teachers are more likely to respond to misbehavior in a punitive manner and less likely to respond in a restorative manner as they do in suburban, mostly white schools.[27] One reason for differential labeling: decision makers may want to help kids from "good families" avoid a negative label, a luxury not granted to poor and minority group members.[28]

In sum, a major premise of social reaction theory is that racial, age, income, and gender differences in the delinquency rate reflect the fact that the law is differentially constructed and applied. It favors the powerful members of society who direct its content and penalizes people whose actions represent a threat to those in control, such as minority group members and the poor who demand equal rights.[29] If the law was totally unbiased, official data would reflect self-report studies, which show that delinquency is spread equally among racial and class groups.

The Consequences of Labeling

If a devalued status is conferred by a significant other—teacher, police officer, elder, parent, or valued peer—the negative label and resulting stigma may cause permanent harm. Labeled kids may consider themselves social outcasts.

- LGB students are up to five times more likely than other students to report using illegal drugs.

- More than 10 percent of LGB students reported missing school during the past 30 days due to safety concerns. While not a direct measure of school performance, absenteeism has been linked to low graduation rates, which can have lifelong consequences.

The CDC report documents that LGB students have a higher prevalence of many health risk behaviors compared with heterosexual students. It is evident that labeling and stigma can have a significant negative effect on these youth.

Although there are no simple solutions to address the health risks LGB students face, research demonstrates the importance of school, community, and family support for LGB youth.

- Focused public health and school-based actions and policies that support safe and supportive environments for LGBTQ students are key.

- Youth-serving agencies and organizations can help facilitate access to education and information, health care services, and evidence-based programs and interventions designed to address the health-related behaviors that impact LGBTQ youth.

- Outreach efforts and educational programs can provide parents and families with the information and skills they need to support LGBTQ youth.

Because many health-related behaviors initiated during adolescence often extend into adulthood, they can potentially have a lifelong negative effect on health outcomes, educational attainment, employment, housing, and overall quality of life. Many LGBTQ students, therefore, need coordinated action to meet their needs and improve their health and well-being.

CRITICAL THINKING

1. Do you think that attitudes toward LGBTQ students are changing? Is there greater acceptance of LGBTQ students? Is the risk of negative labeling reduced?

2. If there is greater acceptance, how can you explain the fact LGBTQ students face far greater health and safety risks than heterosexual students?

SOURCE: Centers for Disease Control and Prevention, *Sexual Identity, Sex of Sexual Contacts, and Health-Related Behaviors Among Students in Grades 9–12—United States and Selected Sites, 2015*, August 12, 2016, http://www.cdc.gov/mmwr/volumes/65/ss/pdfs/ss6509.pdf (accessed September 2016).

The degree to which a person is perceived as a social outcast may affect his or her treatment at home, at work, at school, and in other social situations. Labels carry stigma and exclusion that can bring harmful consequences. The Focus on Delinquency feature reviews a recent study on the burdens suffered by LGB students.

Children may find that their parents consider them a bad influence on younger brothers and sisters; they routinely suffer a variety of problems, including antisocial behavior and school failure.[30] Labeling alienates parents from their children, and negative labels reduce children's self-image and increase delinquency; this process is referred to as **reflected appraisals**.[31] Parental labeling is extremely damaging because it may cause adolescents to seek deviant peers whose behavior amplifies the effect of the labeling.[32] In contrast, when parents stick by kids, the effect of negative labels bestowed by others can be neutralized.[33]

School officials may suspend, expel, or limit students who acquire negative labels to classes reserved for people with behavioral problems. And once stigmatized while in school, the negative label follows them into adulthood. David Ramey found that students who were punished for behavioral problems by being suspended or expelled from school are more likely to be involved in the criminal justice system later in life. In contrast, those viewed as being in need of therapy and/or medication during childhood are more likely to be involved in the mental health system as adults.[34]

If they are labeled as a delinquent or druggie, they may find their eligibility for employment severely restricted. Furthermore, if the label is bestowed as the result of adjudication for a delinquent act, the labeled person may be subjected to official sanctions ranging from a mild reprimand to incarceration. For example, a judge may be asked to decide whether a deviant act is the product of willful deliberation or a mental disease or defect.

reflected appraisal
The process in which a person's awareness of how other people see them becomes the basis for self-perception.

Beyond these immediate results, social reaction theory maintains that, depending on the visibility of the label and the manner and severity with which it is applied, a person who has been negatively labeled will have an increasing commitment to a deviant career.[35] Labeled kids may find themselves turning to others similarly stigmatized for support and companionship. Isolated from conventional society, they may identify themselves as members of an outcast group and become locked into a deviant career.

These effects can plague people over the life course. Giza Lopes and her associates found kids who get involved with the police in adolescence suffer long-term effects of this negative labeling experience well into their 30s; early police intervention is indirectly related to adult social problems such as substance abuse, unemployment, and welfare dependence.[36] Getting arrested during adolescence is associated with future offending; rather than deterring crime, formal labels increase its occurrence. [37] Official labels also increase financial hardship during young adulthood, which, in turn, decreases the odds of entering into a stable and sustaining marriage. Because marriage is viewed as a barrier to a criminal career, this means that even minimally invasive contact with the criminal justice system during adolescence has long-lasting consequences for success as an adult. [38]

Once they attain a criminal record, young adults are shut out of many occupations and have limited employment opportunities, factors that increase the likelihood of being locked into a delinquent and criminal career. The impact of having a criminal record is most often felt among African Americans, who may already experience racial discrimination in the labor market. Research shows that a criminal record reduces the likelihood of a job callback or offer by approximately 50 percent.[39]

Damaged Identity   One consequence of labeling is personal reassessment. Stigmatized as "troublemakers," adolescents may begin to incorporate the label into their own self-image, "If everyone says I am a troublemaker, it must be true."[40] Although labels may not have caused adolescents to initiate delinquent behaviors, once applied they increase the likelihood of persistent offending because kids now have a "damaged identity."[41] Recent research by Emily Restivo and Mark Lanier found that official labeling may lead to an increased delinquent self-identity, decreased prosocial expectations, and an increased association with delinquent peers. Restivo and Lanier conclude that the labeling process creates a new damaged identity for the individual that places them in the company of other damaged people. The result is they are expected to fail, and association with delinquent peers solidifies that outcome.[42]

Damaged identities follow kids around and may never go away. Their bad behavior may be captured by cell phone cameras and show up on the Net almost instantly. A damaged identity provokes some adolescents into repeating their antisocial behaviors, creating new labels and amplifying old ones.[43] Rather than deter future offending, being repeatedly arrested, processed, punished, and labeled may actually increase the probability that a person will get involved in subsequent antisocial behavior.

Bearing a negative label limits conventional opportunities, such as educational attainment and employment. Kids who are labeled in adolescence are much more likely to engage in crime in early adulthood unless they are able to overcome labels and do well in school and obtain meaningful employment opportunities.[44]

Joining Deviant Cliques   Another outcome of the stigma-generating process is the formation of deviant cliques and groups. When kids are labeled as troublemakers or social problems, they may join with similarly outcast delinquent peers in a clique or group that facilitates their antisocial behavior.[45] Eventually, antisocial behavior becomes habitual and automatic.[46] The desire to join deviant cliques and groups may stem from a self-rejecting attitude ("At times, I think I am no good at all"), which eventually results in a weakened commitment to conventional values and behaviors.

In turn, these children may acquire motives to deviate from social norms. Facilitating this attitude and value transformation is the bond social outcasts form with similarly labeled peers in the form of a deviant subculture.[47] Delinquent peers then may help labeled youths "reject their rejectors." Teachers are "stupid"; cops are "dishonest"; parents "just don't understand."[48] Group identity enables outcast youths to show contempt for the sources of the labels and to distance themselves. These actions help solidify both the grip of deviant peers and the impact of the labels.[49] Those who have accepted these labels are more prone to engage in delinquent behaviors than those whose self-image has not been so tarnished.[50]

Membership in a deviant subculture often involves conforming to group norms that conflict with those of conventional society. Deviant behaviors that defy conventional values can serve a number of different purposes. Some acts are defiant, designed to show contempt for the source of the negative labels. Other acts are planned to distance the transgressor from further contact with the source of criticism (for example, joining a gang gives kids the social support lacking from absent or overly critical parents).[51]

Important Labeling Concepts

Social reaction theorists have derived a number of important concepts to better understand the labeling process and its consequences. These contributions are set out in some detail in the following sections.

Primary and Secondary Deviance   Edwin Lemert's concept of primary deviance and secondary deviance has become a standard view of the labeling process.[52] According to Lemert, **primary deviance** involves norm violations or crimes that have very little influence on the actor and can be quickly forgotten. For example, a college student takes a "five-finger discount" at the campus bookstore. He successfully steals a textbook, uses it to get an A in a course, goes on to graduate, is admitted into law school, and later becomes a famous judge. Because his shoplifting goes unnoticed, it is a relatively unimportant event that has little bearing on his future life.

In contrast, **secondary deviance** occurs when a deviant event comes to the attention of significant others or social control agents who apply a negative label. The newly labeled offender then reorganizes his or her behavior and personality around the consequences of the deviant act. The shoplifting student is caught by a security guard and expelled from college. With his law school dreams dashed and his future cloudy, his options are limited; people who know him say he "lacks character," and he begins to share their opinion. He eventually becomes a drug dealer and winds up in prison.

Secondary deviance involves resocialization into a deviant role. The labeled person is transformed into one who, according to Lemert, "employs his behavior or a role based upon it as a means of defense, attack, or adjustment to the overt and covert problems created by the consequent social reaction to him."[53] Secondary deviance produces a deviance amplification effect. Offenders feel isolated from the mainstream of society and become firmly locked within their deviant role. They may seek others similarly labeled to form deviant subcultures or groups. Ever more firmly enmeshed in their deviant role, they are locked into an escalating cycle of deviance, apprehension, more powerful labels, and identity transformation. Lemert's concept of secondary deviance expresses the core of social reaction theory: Deviance is a process in which one's identity is transformed. Efforts to control the offenders, whether by treatment or punishment, simply help lock them in their deviant role.

The Secret Deviant and the Falsely Accused   In one of the most well-known social reaction concepts, Howard S. Becker recognized that four possible outcomes develop in the relationship between labeling and delinquent or other deviant behaviors.[54] (See Exhibit 5.1.)

primary deviance
Norm violations that have very little influence on the actor and can be quickly forgotten and/or overlooked.

secondary deviance
Deviant acts that define the actor and create a new identity.

To read articles and other musings from the great **Howard S. Becker**, go to his website at http://howardsbecker.com/.

Those kids who engage in delinquency and also get caught and labeled are called *pure deviants*; their opposite number, *conformists*, are both rule-abiding and free of negative labels. Some kids are *falsely accused*, or blamed for something they did not do, while some who continually break rules avoid labeling; these are called *secret deviants*. Pure deviants are the kids most likely to repeat their antisocial activities, while conformists are the ones most likely to stay straight and never engage in antisocial behaviors. While this outcome is a key to the validity of social reaction theory, what happens to the kids who fall in the other two categories is even more critical. If labeling theory is valid, the falsely accused will be more likely to become secondary deviants (i.e., chronic offenders) than the secret deviants. While the latter may be more troubled, because they have escaped the labeling process they are not affected by negative stigma. And, according to social reaction theory, negative labels, even false ones, are the critical element that creates secondary deviance and results in a delinquent career. In other words, it is more damaging in the long run to be falsely accused than to be a secret deviant. This is one of the key concepts in labeling theory.

Retrospective Reading   An attempt to connect present behavior with past characteristics is referred to as a **retrospective reading**. After someone is labeled because of some unusual or inexplicable act, people begin to reconstruct the person's identity so that the act and the label are correlated. Neighbors say, "We always knew there was something wrong with that boy!" It is not unusual for the media to lead the way and interview boyhood friends of an assassin or serial killer. The media will soon report that the suspect was withdrawn, suspicious, and negativistic as a youth, expressing violent thoughts and ideation, a loner, troubled, and so on. Yet, until now no one was suspicious and nothing was done. Once the label is bestowed, all the prior evidence suddenly makes sense. By conducting a retrospective reading, we can now understand what prompted his current behavior; therefore, the label must be accurate.[55]

retrospective reading
An attempt to explain present misbehavior with behavior from the past.

Dramatization of Evil   Labels become the basis of personal identity. As the negative feedback of law enforcement agencies, parents, friends, teachers, and other figures amplifies the force of the original label, stigmatized offenders may begin to reevaluate their own identities. If they are not really evil or bad, they may ask themselves, why is everyone making such a fuss? Frank Tannenbaum, a social reaction theory pioneer, referred to this process as the **dramatization of evil**. With respect to the consequences of labeling delinquent behavior, Tannenbaum stated:

dramatization of evil
The process of social typing that transforms an offender's identity from a doer of evil to an evil person.

The process of making the criminal, therefore, is a process of tagging, defining, identifying, making conscious and self-conscious; it becomes a way of stimulating, suggesting and evoking the very traits that are complained of. If the theory of relation of response to stimulus has any meaning, the entire process of dealing with the young delinquent is mischievous insofar as it identifies him to himself or to the environment as a delinquent person. The person becomes the thing he is described as being.[56]

Self-Fulfilling Prophecy   The labeling process helps create a **self-fulfilling prophecy**.[57] If children continually receive negative feedback from parents, teachers, and others whose opinion they take to heart, they will interpret this rejection as accurate. Their behavior will begin to conform to the negative expectations; they will become the person others perceive them to be ("Teachers already think I'm stupid, so why should I bother to study?"). The self-fulfilling prophecy leads to a damaged self-image and an increase in antisocial behaviors.[58] Research shows that adolescents who perceive labels from significant others also report more frequent delinquent involvement; perceptions of negative labels are significant predictors of serious delinquent behaviors.[59]

self-fulfilling prophecy
Deviant behavior patterns that are a response to an earlier labeling experience; youths act out these social roles even if they were falsely bestowed.

Degradation Ceremonies   To drive home the point that the youthful suspect is an outcast who should be shunned by society, the justice system relies on what sociologist Harold Garfinkel called a **degradation ceremony**. During this ritual the public identity of an offender is transformed in a solemn process in which the targeted person is thrust outside the social mainstream.[60] This process may be seen when a youngster goes before the juvenile court, is scolded by a judge, has charges read, and is officially labeled a delinquent; this process contains all the conditions for "successful degradation.

degradation ceremony
Going to court, being scolded by a judge, or being found delinquent after a trial are examples of public ceremonies that can transform youthful offenders by degrading their self-image.

The Juvenile Justice Process and Labeling

Processing through the juvenile justice system seems to unleash the labeling process and create secondary deviant identities. Here offenders find (perhaps for the first time) that authority figures consider them incorrigible outcasts who must be separated from the right-thinking members of society. To reach that decision, the judge relies on the testimony of witnesses—parents, teachers, police officers, social workers, and psychologists—who may testify that the offender is unfit to be part of conventional society. As the label "juvenile delinquent" is conferred on offenders, their identities may be transformed from "kids who have done something bad" to "bad kids."[61]

There is little question that being stigmatized by the juvenile justice system with a degradation ceremony may be a life-transforming event. Children who get involved with official labeling agencies such as the police are the ones most likely to engage in future deviant and criminal behaviors, especially if they are the most vulnerable, at-risk adolescents.[62] When adolescents with no prior police contact are compared to those who were stopped and/or arrested by police, only the latter group reported higher levels of future delinquency.[63] Arrest may amplify a juvenile's "cumulative disadvantage" and trigger exclusionary processes that limit conventional opportunities, such as educational attainment and employment.[64]

Kids enter the system as people in trouble with the law, but emerge as bearers of criminal histories, which are likely to reinvolve them in criminal activity. Authority figures anticipate that these troublemakers will continue their life of crime, and they become perennial suspects.[65] If they are institutionalized, the effect is even more damaging. A study by Nadine Lanctôt and her colleagues found that having been institutionalized as an adolescent is predictive of precarious, premature, unstable, and unsatisfied life conditions in adulthood. Formerly institutionalized males and females experienced more socioeconomic difficulties, earlier and premature transitions to adulthood, difficulties at work, instability in romantic relationships, and less emotional well-being. Being institutionalized as a juvenile will hit girls particularly hard. As adults, young women who had been sent away as juveniles had significant difficulty coping with adulthood, were dependent on government assistance, were significantly more likely to have become teen mothers, and suffered from low self-esteem and depression.[66] Because it creates stigma and a damaged self-image, the system designed to reduce delinquency may help produce young criminals.

Is Labeling Theory Valid?

Labeling theory has been the subject of much academic debate. Those who criticize it point to its inability to specify the conditions that must exist before an act or individual is labeled deviant—that is, why some people are labeled and others remain "secret deviants."[67] Some critics argue that the deterrent effect of punishment offsets the crime-producing effects of stigma. In *Beyond Probation*, Charles Murray and Louis Cox found that youths assigned to a program designed to reduce labels were more likely later to commit delinquent acts than a comparison group who were placed in a more punitive state training school. The implication was that the threat of punishment was deterrent and that the crime-producing influence of labels was minimal.[68]

There is also some question about the real cost of being labeled. Some question whether negative social reactions and stigma produce delinquency.[69] Many delinquent careers exist without labeling, and it is possible that negative labeling often comes after, rather than before, chronic offending. Getting labeled by the justice system and having an enduring delinquent record may have relatively little effect on kids who have been burdened with social and emotional problems since birth.[70]

While these criticisms are telling, there are a number of reasons why social reaction may play an important role in understanding the ebb and flow of a delinquent career:[71]

- The labeling perspective identifies the role played by social control agents in the process of delinquency causation. Delinquent behavior cannot be fully understood if the agencies and individuals empowered to control and treat it are neglected.

- Labeling theory recognizes that delinquency is not a disease or pathological behavior. It focuses attention on the social interactions and reactions that shape individual behavior.

- Labeling theory distinguishes between delinquent acts (primary deviance) and delinquent careers (secondary deviance) and shows that these concepts must be interpreted and treated differently.

Social reaction is also important because of its focus on interaction as well as the situations surrounding the crime. Rather than viewing the delinquent as a robot-like creature whose actions are predetermined, it recognizes that crime is often the result of complex interactions and processes. The decision to commit crime involves actions of a variety of people, including peers, the victim, the police, and other key characters. Labels may expedite crime because they guide the actions of all parties involved in these delinquent interactions. Actions deemed innocent when performed by one person are considered provocative when someone who has been labeled as deviant engages in them. Similarly, labeled people may be quick to judge, take offense, or misinterpret behavior of others because of past experience.

Labeling theory is also supported by research showing that offenders who are placed in treatment programs aimed at reconfiguring their self-image may be able to develop revamped identities and desist from crime. Some are able to go through "redemption rituals" in which they can cast off their damaged identities and develop new ones. As a result, they develop an improved self-concept, which reflects the positive reinforcement they receive while in treatment.[72]

Labeling and Delinquent Careers   As interest in delinquent careers has escalated, labeling theory has taken on new relevance.[73] Labeling theory may help explain why some youths continue down the path of antisocial behaviors (they are labeled), whereas most are able to desist from crime (they are free of stigma). People who experience the impact of negative labeling may develop a deviant identity such as drug addict. As with differential association, the acceptance of labels is influenced by the frequency, duration, priority, and intensity of the labeling process. The more intense and prolonged the labeling process, the greater its effect and the more likely it is the target will be locked into a deviant career path.[74]

Kids who are labeled may find themselves shut out of educational and employment opportunities. Those who have been suspended from school or labeled as troublemakers may find that these experiences haunt them a decade later when they seek employment as adults.[75] As a result, these labeled youths are more likely to sustain delinquent careers and persist in their behavior into adulthood.[76] Recent research by Margit Wiesner and her colleagues found that kids who were in trouble and arrested at an early age were more likely to lose their jobs and have spotty employment records when they became adults. Having problems and getting labeled had a greater impact on adult employment performance than getting involved in early misbehavior; that is, labeling may have a more important influence on adult behavior than early onset of delinquency or other indicators of adolescent crisis.[77]

In addition to explaining the continuity of crime, labeling theory may also help us understand why many hard-core offenders desist. Those who receive sufficient positive feedback may be able to transform their self-image and create a new self, helping them to go straight.[78]

Social Reaction Theory and Social Policy

As the dangers of labeling became known, a massive effort was made to limit the interface of youths with the juvenile justice system. One approach was to divert youths from official processing at the time of their initial contact with police. The usual practice was to have police refer children to treatment facilities rather than to the juvenile court. In a similar vein, children who were petitioned to juvenile court might be eligible for alternative programs rather than traditional juvenile justice processing. For example, restitution allowed children to pay back the victims of their crimes for the damage (or inconvenience) they caused instead of receiving an official delinquency label.

If a youth was found delinquent, efforts were made to reduce stigma by using alternative programs such as boot camp or intensive probation monitoring. Alternative community-based sanctions substituted for state training schools, a policy known as **deinstitutionalization**. Whenever possible, anything producing stigma was to be avoided, a philosophy referred to as nonintervention.

deinstitutionalization
Removing juveniles from adult jails and placing them in community-based programs to avoid the stigma attached to these facilities.

While these programs were initially popular, critics claimed that the nonintervention movement created a new class of juvenile offenders who heretofore might have avoided prolonged contact with juvenile justice agencies; they referred to this phenomenon as "widening the net."[79] Evaluation of existing programs did not indicate that they could reduce the recidivism rate of clients.[80] While these criticisms proved damaging, many nonintervention programs still operate.

Social Conflict Theory

The world is beset by conflict, and American teens are not immune to its lure. According to social conflict theory (or critical theory—the two terms are interchangeable), those who hold power in contemporary society get to set the rules, control the law, and decide who is a deviant, delinquent, and/or criminal. Their motives are not moral but financial and economic. They care little about the moral content of the law as long as it protects the interests of those who hold social and economic power.

According to this view, society is in a constant state of internal and external conflict, as different groups strive to impose their will on others. Those with money and power succeed in shaping the law to meet their needs and maintain their interests. They want to make sure that manipulating the system to make enormous profits is legal while shoplifting, pilferage, and theft are severely punished. The law must protect the wealth of those in power while controlling people whose behavior does not conform to the needs of the power elite. Those who violate their rules are defined as criminals, delinquents, and status offenders and punished accordingly.

Those in power use the justice system to maintain their status while keeping others subservient. Men use their economic power to subjugate women; members of the majority want to stave off the economic advancement of minorities; capitalists want to reduce the power of workers to ensure they are willing to accept low wages. Conflict theory centers around a view of society in which an elite class uses the law as a means of meeting threats to its status. The ruling class is a self-interested collective whose primary interest is self-gain. Conflict theorists observe that while spending has been cut on social programs during the past few years, spending on the prison system has skyrocketed. They fear that draconian criminal laws designed to curb terrorism, such as the USA Patriot Act, may be turned against political dissenters. Critical thinkers believe that they are responsible for informing the public about the dangers of these developments and applaud the actions of whistle-blowers such as Edward Snowden.

Law and Justice

Social conflict theorists view the law and the justice system as vehicles for controlling the have-not members of society. Legal institutions help the powerful and rich to impose their standards of good behavior on the entire society. The law protects the property and physical safety of the haves from attack by the have-nots, and helps control the behavior of those who might otherwise threaten the status quo. The ruling elite draws the lower-middle class into this pattern of control, leading it to believe it has a stake in maintaining the status quo. The poor may or may not commit more crimes than the rich, but they certainly are arrested more often.[81] It is not surprising to conflict theorists that complaints of police brutality are highest in minority neighborhoods, especially those that experience relative deprivation. (African American residents earn significantly less money than the majority and therefore have less political and social power.[82]) Police misbehavior, which is routine in minority neighborhoods, would never be tolerated in affluent white areas. Consequently, a deep-rooted hostility is generated among members of the lower class toward a social order they may neither shape nor share.[83]

Conflict theorists suggest that rather than inhibiting delinquent behavior, the justice system may help sustain such behavior. They claim that the capitalist state fails to control delinquents because it is in the state's interest to maintain a large number of outcast deviant youths. These youths can be employed as marginal workers, willing to work for minimum wage in jobs no one else wants. Thus, labeling by the justice system fits within the capitalist managers' need to maintain an underclass of cheap labor.

Globalization

The new global economy is a particular vexing development for social conflict theory. **Globalization**, which refers to the process of creating transnational markets and political and legal systems, has shifted the focus of critical inquiry to a world perspective.

globalization
The process of creating a global economy through transnational markets and political and legal systems.

Globalization began when large companies decided to establish themselves in foreign markets by adapting their products or services to the local culture. The process took off with the fall of the Soviet Union, which opened new European markets. The development of China into a super-industrial power encouraged foreign investors to take advantage of China's huge supply of workers. As the Internet and communication revolution unfolded, companies were able to establish instant communications with their far-flung corporate empires, a technological breakthrough that further aided trade and foreign investments. A series of transnational corporate mergers produced ever-larger transnational corporations.

Some experts believe globalization can improve the standard of living in third-world nations by providing jobs and training, but critical theorists question the altruism of multinational corporations. Their motives are exploiting natural resources, avoiding regulation, and taking advantage of desperate workers. When

Globalization has had an impact on local economies, but there are consequences. In Bangladesh, aluminum factories make pots and jars for export. Around 30 to 50 percent of the workers are children, many of them under age 15. The reason: child labor is cheap labor. Current economic conditions in Bangladesh make it impossible to ban child labor completely. The children's families are in need, and they have no other options.

these giant corporations set up factories in a developing nation, it is not to help the local population but to get around environmental laws and take advantage of needy workers who may be forced to labor in substandard conditions. Globalization has replaced imperialism and colonization as a new form of economic domination and oppression.

Conflict Theory and Delinquency

In our advanced technological society, those with economic and political power control the legal definition of delinquency and the manner in which the law is enforced.[84] Consequently, the only crimes available to poor kids are the severely sanctioned "street crimes": rape, murder, theft, and mugging. Members of the middle class may engage in petty delinquent acts such as smoking marijuana or shoplifting, acts that generate social disapproval but are rarely punished severely. At the top of the social pyramid are the power elite, extremely wealthy people whose fortunes were created and are now maintained on the backs of the working class. They make millions while paying desperate workers subsistence wages. Moreover, the power elite are involved in acts that should be described as crimes but are not, such as racism, sexism, and profiteering. Although regulatory laws control illegal business activities, these are rarely enforced, and violations are lightly punished. Figure 5.1 illustrates how social conflict theorists view the system.

Conflict theorists view delinquency as a normal response to the conditions created by capitalism.[85] In fact, the creation of a legal category, delinquency, is a function of the class consciousness that occurred around the

Control of Law and Society
Those who hold economic power control the law and the agencies that administer it.

Application of the Law
The law is differentially administered to favor the rich and powerful and control the "have-not" members of society.

Delinquent Behavior
The rebellious behavior of lower-class youths is defined and controlled by state authorities.

Criminal Careers
Youths who will not conform and fulfill the roles of menial laborers are defined as criminals.

figure 5.1

Social Conflict Theory

turn of the twentieth century.[86] In *The Child Savers*, Anthony Platt documented the creation of the delinquency concept and the role played by wealthy child savers in forming the philosophy of the juvenile court. Platt believed the child-saving movement's real goal was to maintain order and control while preserving the existing class system.[87] He and others have concluded that the child savers were powerful citizens who aimed to control the behavior of disenfranchised youths.

Conflict thinkers still view delinquent behavior as a function of the capitalist system's inherent inequity. They argue that capitalism accelerates the trend toward replacing human labor with machines so that youths are removed from the labor force. From early childhood, the values of capitalism are reinforced. Social control agencies such as schools prepare youths for placement in the capitalist system by presenting them with behavior models that will help them conform to later job expectations. Rewards for good schoolwork correspond to the rewards a manager uses with employees. In fact, most schools are set up to reward youths who show promise in self-discipline and motivation and are therefore judged likely to perform well in the capitalist system. Youths who are judged inferior as potential work prospects become known as losers and punks and wind up in delinquent roles.

Class and Delinquency   The capitalist system affects youths differently at each level of the class structure. In the lowest classes, youths form gangs, which can be found in the most desolated ghetto areas. These gangs serve as a means of survival in a system that offers no reasonable alternative. Lower-class youths who live in more stable areas are on the fringe of delinquent activity because the economic system excludes them from meaningful opportunity.

Conflict theory also acknowledges middle-class delinquency. The alienation of individuals from one another, the competitive struggle, and the absence of human feeling—all qualities of capitalism—contribute to middle-class delinquency. Because capitalism is dehumanizing, it is not surprising that even middle-class youths turn to drugs, gambling, and illicit sex to find escape.

Globalization and Delinquency   According to conflict theory, globalization will have a profound influence on the future of indigent youth. Technological advances such as efficient and widespread commercial airline traffic, improvements

According to social conflict theory, income inequality that results from the highly competitive capitalist system is a major cause of delinquency. Here, the family of 15-year-old Tyquan Jamison, who was shot in the chest while playing basketball on the streets of Brownsville in Brooklyn, New York City, say a prayer next to his casket. Brownsville for decades has been one of the city's most dangerous neighborhoods, and gun violence is up nearly 50 percent from a historic low in 2009. Passed over in the gentrification of Brooklyn, Brownsville's people cram into low-cost public housing projects, trapped in a world of unemployment, teen pregnancy, and extreme tension with the police—decades-old problems that the world's wealthiest nation has not figured out how to solve.

Shannon Stapleton/Reuters

CYBER DELINQUENCY

Recruiting Young Terrorists

The Islamic State of Iraq and the Levant (ISIL, also known as ISIS and Daesh) is now actively using the Internet to recruit Westerners. ISIL has used the Web and social media to recruit at least 30,000 foreign fighters from more than 100 countries to fight in Syria and Iraq. In almost every American case, social media played some part in recruitment and/or radicalization. One web video tells potential recruits, "I am your brother in Islam here in Syria. We have safety here for your family and children." ISIL has its own multilingual media arm, Al-Hayat, which produces videos using American-made GoPro action cameras. Al-Hayat has released videos featuring foreign fighters who speak Western languages and who encourage young people to come to Syria to wage violent jihad or help the caliphate in some other way.

There are numerous instances of young people, both immigrant and native born, attempting to travel to the Middle East to join ISIL. One case involved Hoda Muthana, a young Yemeni-American woman from Hoover, Alabama, who grew up a in a conservative household. At age 17 she began to immerse herself in online Islamic fundamentalist literature. She created an alter ego on Twitter, gaining thousands of followers around the globe. Telling people she was going to Atlanta for a college field trip, Muthana boarded a flight to Turkey. Within a month of her arrival in Syria she married an Australian foreign fighter named Suhan Rahman, who was later killed in an airstrike. From her home in Raqqa, Muthana continues to issue ISIL propaganda messages online.

In another incident, Mohammed Hamzah Khan, a Chicago area teen, was recruited to join ISIS with his two younger siblings. The three were arrested as they were about to board an aircraft bound for Vienna and then Istanbul, Turkey. In a letter left for his parents, Khan wrote, "An Islamic State has been established, and it is thus obligatory upon every able-bodied male and female to migrate, I cannot live under a law in which I am afraid to speak my beliefs. I simply cannot sit here and let my brothers and sisters get killed with my own hard-earned money." His younger brother also wrote a letter stating, "This nation is openly against Islam and Muslims. The evil of this country makes me sick." When Khan's younger sister was interviewed after her arrest, she told FBI agents her attempt to join ISIS was fueled by the killing of innocent children in places like Syria and Afghanistan. It was unfair, she said, that these killings were excused, when crimes by Muslims who were merely defending themselves were denounced.

After pleading guilty to one felony count of attempting to provide material support to a terrorist organization, Mohammed Hamzah Khan will spend at least five years behind bars and then remain under court supervision for 15 years while undergoing "psychological and violent-extremism counseling," performing at least 120 hours of community service each year, and allowing court personnel to search his cell phone, email, and computer four times a month.

These cases are not unique. In the past few years:

- A 17-year-old high school student from Virginia pleaded guilty to supporting ISIL by acting as a travel agent to help a friend from school join the group in Syria.

- A 16-year-old in South Carolina "lured by the ideology of ISIS" was convicted on gun charges.

- Three teenagers from Denver were stopped in transit to Turkey en route to ISIL in Syria. If not for a last-minute intervention of US and German officials, who scrambled to act after frantic calls from one of the girls' fathers, the teenagers likely would have joined the wave of minors drawn to terrorist organizations.

ISIL typically recruits Western youth who are isolated, uncertain, disillusioned, and who believe they have no purpose. Like other gangs, they offer a sense of family and belonging that appeals to teens and gives them an opportunity to join a group with a passionate purpose and direction.

CRITICAL THINKING

How can we stop youth from joining ISIL when we cannot seem to stop them from joining a neighborhood gang? Is the lure of joining a local gang similar to the appeal of joining ISIL?

SOURCES: Lorenzo Vidino and Seamus Hughes, *Isis in America: From Retweets to Raqqa*, George Washington University, December 2015, https://cchs.gwu.edu/isis-in-america; CBS News, "ISIS Recruits Fighters Through Powerful Online Campaign," August 29, 2014, http://www.cbsnews.com/news/isis-uses-social-media-to-recruit-western-allies/; Jason Meisner, "Bolingbrook Man Pleads Guilty to Terrorism Charge," *Chicago Tribune*, October 29, 2015, http://www.chicagotribune.com/news/local/breaking/ct-terror-case-bolingbrook-man-plea-20151029-story.html; Lorenzo Vidino and Seamus Hughes, "How to Stop ISIS from Recruiting American Teens," *Washington Post*, June 17, 2015, https://www.washingtonpost.com/blogs/monkey-cage/wp/2015/06/17/how-to-stop-isis-from-recruiting-american-teens/. (URLs accessed September 2016.)

---

in telecommunications (ranging from global cell phone connectivity to the Internet), and the growth of international trade have all aided the growth in illicit transnational activities. These changes have facilitated the cross-border movement of goods and people, conditions exploited by criminals who now use Internet chat rooms to plan their activities. Gangs can now cross unpatrolled borders to expand their activities to new regions of the world. Transnational crime groups exploit this new freedom to travel to regions where they cannot be extradited, base their operations in countries with ineffective or corrupt law enforcement, and launder their money in countries with bank secrecy or few effective controls. Globalization has allowed both individual offenders and criminal gangs to gain tremendous operational benefits while reducing risks of apprehension and punishment. This extends to international terrorist groups such as ISIL, as the Cyber Delinquency feature illustrates.

The Economy and Delinquency in Contemporary Society

All of these social and economic changes are bound to have a serious effect on American society and the way it treats children. Workers in the United States in high-paying manufacturing jobs may be replaced not by machines but by foreign workers in overseas factories. Instant communication via the Internet and global communications will speed the effect immeasurably. Government policies that are designed to increase corporate profits tend to aggravate rather than ease the financial stress being placed on ordinary families. Contemporary monetary policy, trade policy, and tax policy are harmful to working-class families. While affluent whites fear corporate downsizing, poor minorities in central cities are shut out of any economic revival. The modern marketplace, with its reliance on sophisticated computer technologies, is continually decreasing demand for low-skilled workers, which impacts African Americans more negatively than other better-educated and more affluent groups.[88]

Minority youth are hit the hardest by the effects of globalization. Sociologist William Julius Wilson has written of the plight of the African American community. He suggests that as difficult as life was in the 1940s and 1950s for African Americans, they at least had a reasonable hope of steady work. Now, because of the globalization of the economy, those opportunities have evaporated. Though in the past racial segregation limited opportunity, growth in the manufacturing sector fueled upward mobility and provided the foundation of today's African American middle class. Those opportunities no longer exist as manufacturing plants have moved to inaccessible rural and overseas locations where the cost of doing business is lower. With manufacturing opportunities all but obsolete in the United States, service and retail establishments that depended on blue-collar spending have similarly disappeared, leaving behind an economy based on welfare and government support. In less than 20 years, formerly active African American communities have become crime-infested inner-city neighborhoods.

Beyond sustaining inner-city poverty, the absence of employment opportunities has torn at the social fabric of the nation's poorest communities. Work helps socialize young people into the wider society, instilling in them such desirable values as discipline, caring, and respect for others. When work becomes scarce, the discipline and structure it provides are absent. Community-wide underemployment destroys social cohesion, increasing the presence of neighborhood social problems ranging from drug use to educational failure. Schools in these areas do not teach basic skills, and because desirable employment is lacking, there are few adults to serve as role models. In contrast to more affluent suburban households where daily life is organized around job and career demands, children in inner-city areas are not socialized in the workings of the mainstream economy. If anything, globalization increases the attractiveness of gangs, and gang membership may provide inner-city youth with a substitute for the now-vanished high-paid manufacturing jobs that are located overseas.[89]

Some critical theorists believe that if conflict is the cause of delinquency, then removing or reducing economic and personal conflict is the key to its control. For some, this goal can only be accomplished by thoroughly reordering society so that capitalism is destroyed and a socialist state is created. Others call for a more "practical" application of conflict principles. Nowhere has this been more successful than in what is known as the **restorative justice** movement.

restorative justice
Using humanistic, nonpunitive strategies to right wrongs and restore social harmony.

There has been an ongoing effort to reduce the conflict created by the application of harsh punishments to offenders, many of whom are powerless social outcasts. Conflict theorists argue that the "old methods" of punishment are a failure and scoff at claims that the crime rate has dropped because we have toughened laws and increased penalties.[90] Rather than casting troubled kids aside, restorative justice is a method of restoring them back into the community.[91] The next sections discuss the foundation and principles of restorative justice.

The restorative justice approach to delinquency prevention would have police officers talk to youngsters about the potential social harm caused by delinquent acts rather than acting as social control agents who rely on punishment and deterrence to control crime.

The Concept of Restorative Justice

The term *restorative justice* is often hard to define because it encompasses a variety of programs and practices that address victims' harms and needs, hold kids accountable for the harm they cause, and involve victims, offenders, and communities in the process of healing. The core value of the restoration process can be translated into respect for all, including those who are different from us and even those who seem to be our enemies. Restorative justice is a set of principles, a philosophy, an alternate set of guiding questions that provide an alternative framework for thinking about wrongdoing.[92] Restorative justice would reject concepts such as "punishment," "deterrence," and "incarceration" and embrace "apology," "rehabilitation," "reparation," "healing," "restoration," and "reintegration."

Restorative justice has grown out of a belief that the traditional justice system has done little to involve the community in the process of dealing with crime and wrongdoing. What has developed is a system of coercive punishments administered by bureaucrats that are inherently harmful to offenders and reduce the likelihood that offenders will ever become productive members of society. This system relies on punishment, stigma, and disgrace. Advocates of restorative justice argue that rather than today's punitive mentality, what is needed is a justice policy that repairs the harm caused by delinquency and that includes all parties who have suffered from that harm: the victim, the community, and the offender.

Reintegrative Shaming   One of the key foundations of the restoration movement is contained in John Braithwaite's influential book *Crime, Shame, and Reintegration*.[93] Braithwaite's vision rests on the concept of **shame**: the feeling we get when we don't meet the standards we have set for ourselves or that significant others have set for us. Shame can lead people to believe that they are defective, that there is something wrong with them. Braithwaite notes that countries such as Japan, in which conviction for crimes brings an inordinate amount of shame, have extremely low crime and delinquency rates. In Japan, criminal prosecution proceeds only when the normal process of public apology, compensation, and the victim's forgiveness breaks down.

Shame is a powerful tool of informal social control. Citizens in cultures in which crime is not shameful, such as the United States, do not internalize an abhorrence for crime because when they are punished, they view themselves as mere victims of the justice system. Their punishment comes at the hands of neutral

shame
The feeling we get when we don't meet the standards we have set for ourselves or that significant others have set for us.

strangers, like police and judges, who are being paid to act. In contrast, shaming relies on the victim's participation.[94]

Braithwaite divides the concept of shame into two distinct types. The most common form of shaming typically involves stigmatization, an ongoing process of degradation in which the offender is branded as an evil person and cast out of society. Shaming can occur at a school disciplinary hearing or a juvenile court trial. Bestowing stigma and degradation may have a general deterrent effect: it makes people afraid of social rejection and public humiliation. As a specific deterrent, stigma is doomed to failure; kids who suffer humiliation at the hands of the juvenile justice system "reject their rejectors" by joining a deviant subculture of like-minded people, such as a juvenile gang, that collectively resists social control. Despite these dangers, there has been an ongoing effort to brand offenders and make their shame both public and permanent. Many states have passed sex offender registry and notification laws that make public the names of those convicted of sex offenses and warn neighbors of their presence in the community.[95]

But the fear of shame can backfire or be neutralized. When shame is managed well, people acknowledge they made mistakes and suffered disappointments, and try to work out what can be done to make things right; this is referred to as shame management. However, in some cases, to avoid the pain of shaming, people engage in improper shame management, a psychological process in which they deny shame by shifting the blame of their actions to their target or to others.[96] They may blame others, get angry, and take out their frustrations on those whom they can dominate. Improper shame management of this sort has been linked to antisocial acts, including schoolyard bullying.[97]

Braithwaite argues that crime control can be better achieved through a policy of **reintegrative shaming**. Here disapproval is extended to the offenders' evil deeds, while at the same time they are cast as respected people who can be reaccepted by society. A critical element of reintegrative shaming occurs when the offenders begin to understand and recognize their wrongdoing and shame themselves. To be reintegrative, shaming must be brief and controlled and then followed by ceremonies of forgiveness, apology, and repentance.

To prevent delinquency, Braithwaite charges, society must encourage reintegrative shaming. Similarly, parents who use reintegrative shaming techniques in their childrearing practices may improve parent–child relationships and ultimately reduce the delinquent involvement of their children.[98] Because informal social controls may have a greater impact than legal or formal ones, it may not be surprising that the fear of personal shame can have a greater deterrent effect than the fear of legal sanctions. It may also be applied to produce specific deterrence. Offenders can meet with victims so that delinquents can experience shame. Family members and peers can be present to help the offender reintegrate. Such efforts can humanize a system of justice that today relies on repression rather than forgiveness as the basis of specific deterrence. The Case Profile entitled "Jay's Story" shows how one young offender was restored to society.

The Process of Restoration

The restoration process begins by redefining antisocial behavior in terms of a conflict among the offender, the victim, and affected constituencies (families, schools, workplaces, and so forth). Therefore, it is vitally important that the resolution take place within the context in which the conflict originally occurred rather than being transferred to a specialized institution that has no social connection to the community or group from which the conflict originated. In other words, most conflicts are better settled in the community than in a court.

By maintaining "ownership" or jurisdiction over the conflict, the community is able to express its shared outrage about the offense. Shared community outrage is directly communicated to the offender. The victim is also given a chance to voice his or her story, and the offender can directly communicate his or her need for

reintegrative shaming
Techniques used to allow offenders to understand and recognize their wrongdoing and shame themselves. To be reintegrative, shaming must be brief and controlled and then followed by ceremonies of forgiveness, apology, and repentance.

case profile

Jay's Story

JAY SIMMONS, the youngest of six children, was living with his family in an impoverished community when he entered the juvenile justice system. Growing up in a tough urban neighborhood took an early toll on Jay and his family. Around the age of 11, his problems were becoming more evident at home and school. He was absent from school on a regular basis, often stayed out all night with friends, and was eventually arrested on retail theft charges. Jay's parents were struggling to find permanent housing and faced being homeless, so Jay was voluntarily placed in foster care. A teacher at his school took a strong interest in Jay and offered to care for him until his parents could again meet his needs. The family continued to have contact with Jay and hoped to have him return home when their situation improved.

A smart young man with many positive attributes, Jay was an engaging person and a talented athlete who excelled in school sports. Many adults could see great potential in him, but Jay's criminal activity continued. His foster parents became increasingly concerned that they could not provide the care and treatment Jay needed. In a short period of time Jay was arrested on two more violations for disorderly conduct and battery while becoming involved in fights at school. He was at risk for being placed in a more secure living environment. In juvenile court for his delinquent behavior, Jay was sentenced to community supervision and probation. After an initial assessment, Jay's probation officer made formal dispositional recommendations to the court.

Although his foster parents had established clear rules for him, Jay felt torn between his old way of life and the new possibilities. Because of his family's issues of poverty, health concerns, unemployment, and homelessness, he had been very independent prior to his involvement with the juvenile justice system, doing what he wanted, staying in different places with different people much of the time. Jay now struggled with the new rules and expectations. He missed some of his initial appointments with his probation officer and continued to skip school. There were also concerns that Jay was drinking alcohol and becoming involved in gang activities.

Jay's probation officer, family, and foster parents encouraged him to follow the court-ordered recommendations and understand the consequences of his behavior. He developed a very strong relationship with his foster parents, who were direct and honest with Jay about their concerns, often confronting him and contacting his coach, social workers, and parents about his behavior. The Substitute Care Unit at the local human services agency provided valuable support to Jay, his family, and foster parents during these difficult times, making home and school visits, trying to help maintain his placement in the foster home, and encouraging him to make good decisions. The team of professionals, coaches, and parents remained in close contact regarding Jay's behavior, as well as his academic progress. This level of parental involvement and teamwork made a huge impact on Jay and held him more accountable for his choices. He began to see his own potential and the need to make changes in his life.

Accountability was a key ingredient to Jay's success. He attended a retail theft group to address his criminal behavior and to encourage him to take responsibility for his actions. The program brought 8 to 10 teenagers who had been involved in retail thefts together with volunteers from the community, store security personnel, and a program leader. With fellow group members Jay could discuss the nature of his crimes, why they were wrong, the impact on victims, and how to prevent future delinquent acts by making better choices. The group participants and family members also met with a group facilitator to discuss the juvenile court process and what parents can expect if their children have further delinquencies, providing valuable information to the parents and a forum to ask questions and learn about other resources. Jay was also held accountable by being required to complete a period of community service. He worked with the Youth Restitution Program and was assigned a counselor who would help him locate volunteer opportunities and verify his participation.

Jay's involvement with a variety of programs and the many caring adults in his life made a significant difference for him. He continued to excel in sports and began to work harder in school. Although Jay never returned to his parental home, with the support of his foster parents he did remain in close contact with his family and they regularly attended activities together. With a new vision for his life, Jay started thinking seriously about going to college. He successfully completed his court-ordered programs, stayed out of trouble, eventually graduating from high school and receiving a full athletic scholarship to attend college.

CRITICAL THINKING

Is there a danger that efforts to involve kids in restorative programs may backfire and instead label them as troubled youth who need to be monitored? What can be done to limit stigma and labeling?

social reintegration and treatment. All restoration programs involve an understanding among all the parties involved in a criminal act: the victim, the offender, and community. Although processes differ in structure and style, they generally include these elements:

- The offender is asked to recognize that he or she caused injury to personal and social relations along with a determination and acceptance of responsibility (ideally accompanied by a statement of remorse). Only then can the offender be restored as a productive member of the community.

- Restoration involves turning the justice system into a "healing" process rather than being a distributor of retribution and revenge.

- Reconciliation is a big part of the restorative approach. Most people involved in offender–victim relationships actually know one another or were related in some way before the criminal incident took place. Instead of treating one of the involved parties as a victim deserving of sympathy and the other as a criminal deserving of punishment, it is more productive to address the issues that produced conflict between these people.[99]

- The effectiveness of justice ultimately depends on the stake a person has in the community (or a particular social group). If a person does not value his or her membership in the group, the person will be unlikely to accept responsibility, show remorse, or repair the injuries caused by his or her actions. In contrast, people who have a stake in the community and its principal institutions, such as work, home, and school, find that their involvement enhances their personal and familial well-being.[100]

- There must be a commitment to the victim to make both material (monetary) restitution and symbolic reparation (an apology).

- A determination must be made of community support and assistance for both victim and offender.

The intended result of the process is to repair injuries suffered by the victim and the community while assuring reintegration of the offender. The basic principles of restorative justice are set out in Exhibit 5.2.

Restoration Programs

Negotiation, mediation, consensus-building, and peacemaking have been part of the dispute resolution process in European and Asian communities for centuries.[101] Native American and First Nations (native Canadian) people have long used the type of community participation in the adjudication process (for example, sentencing circles, sentencing panels, elders panels) that restorative justice advocates are now embracing.[102]

Based on Native American practices, in some communities kids accused of breaking the law meet with community members, victims (if any), community leaders, and agents of the justice system in a **sentencing circle**. Each member of

sentencing circle
A peacemaking technique in which offenders, victims, and other community members are brought together in an effort to formulate a sanction that addresses the needs of all.

---

exhibit 5.2

Basic Principles of Restorative Justice

- Crime is an offense against human relationships.
- Victims and the community are central to justice processes.
- The first priority of justice processes is to assist victims.
- The second priority is to restore the community, to the degree possible.

- The offender has personal responsibility to victims and to the community for crimes committed.
- The offender will develop improved competency and understanding as a result of the restorative justice experience.
- Stakeholders share responsibilities for restorative justice through partnerships for action.

SOURCE: Anne Seymour, "Restorative Justice/Community Justice," in *National Victim Assistance Academy Textbook* (Washington, DC: National Victim Assistance Academy, 2001).

the circle expresses his or her feelings about the act that was committed and raises questions or concerns. The accused can express regret about his or her actions and a desire to change the harmful behavior. People may suggest ways the offender can make things up to the community and those he or she harmed. A treatment program, such as Alcoholics Anonymous, can be suggested, if appropriate.

Restorative justice is now being embraced on many levels within our society and the justice system:

■ *Community.* Communities that isolate people and have few mechanisms for interpersonal interaction encourage and sustain delinquency. Those that implement forms of community dialogue to identify problems and plan tactics for their elimination, guided by restorative justice practices and principles, may create a climate in which violent crime is less likely to occur.[103]

■ *Schools.* Some schools have embraced restorative justice practices to deal with students involved in drug and alcohol abuse without resorting to more punitive measures such as expulsion. Schools in Minnesota, Colorado, and elsewhere involve students in "relational rehabilitation" programs that strive to improve individuals' relationships with key figures in the community who may have been harmed by their actions.[104]

■ *Police.* Restorative justice has also been implemented by police when crime is first encountered. The community policing models are an attempt to bring restorative concepts into law enforcement. Restorative justice relies on the fact that policy makers need to listen and respond to the needs of those who will be affected by their actions, and community policing relies on policies established with input and exchanges between officers and citizens.[105]

■ *Courts.* Restorative programs in the courts typically involve diverting the formal court process. These programs encourage meeting and reconciling the conflicts between offenders and victims via victim advocacy, mediation programs, and sentencing circles, in which crime victims and their families are brought together with offenders and their families in an effort to formulate a sanction that addresses the needs of each party. Victims are given a chance to voice their stories, and offenders can help compensate them financially or provide some service (such as fixing damaged property).[106] The goal is to enable offenders to appreciate the damage they have caused, to make amends, and to be reintegrated into society.

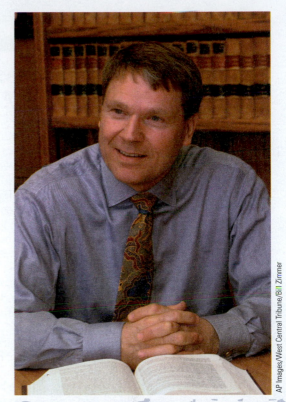

AP Images/West Central Tribune/Bill Zimmer

Willmar, Minnesota, Judge Donald Spilseth is an advocate of sentencing circles. He believes that this approach to sentencing gives youths time and attention the traditional court system never could. Circle sentencing is a court-approved option for some juvenile offenders, an alternative to the traditional route through the system that often involves a quick session in court, probation, and sometimes time spent at a detention facility. Circle sentencing focuses on restoring justice among offenders, the victims they harmed, and the community.

Balanced and Restorative Justice (BARJ) Gordon Bazemore has argued that restoration programs should focus on the concept of balance.[107] According to this approach, the juvenile justice system should give equal weight to these elements:

■ *Holding offenders accountable to victims.* "Offender accountability" refers specifically to the requirement that offenders make amends for the harm resulting from their crimes by repaying or restoring losses to victims and the community.

■ *Providing competency development for offenders in the system so they can pursue legitimate endeavors after release.* Competency development, the rehabilitative goal for intervention, requires that people who enter the justice system should exit the system more capable of being productive and responsible in the community.

■ *Ensuring community safety.* The community protection goal explicitly acknowledges and endorses a longtime public expectation—a safe and secure community.

Family Group Conferencing (FGC): The New Zealand Model

One popular restorative justice initiative, Family Group Conferencing (FGC), involves the group of people most affected by crime and delinquency—the victim and the offender, and the family, friends, and key supporters of both—in deciding the resolution of the delinquent/criminal act. FGC begins when a facilitator contacts the victim and offender to explain the process and invites them to the conference; the facilitator also asks them to identify and invite key members of their support system. Participation is voluntary. In order to participate in the FGC, the offending youth must be willing to admit his or her responsibility for the delinquent act. The parties affected are brought together by a trained facilitator to discuss how they and others have been harmed by the offense and how that harm might be repaired.

The conference typically begins with the offender describing the incident, followed by each participant describing the impact of the incident on his or her life. Through these narrations, the youthful offender is faced with the human impact of his or her behavior on the victim, on those close to the victim, and on the offender's own family and friends. The victim has the opportunity to express feelings and ask questions about the offense. After a thorough discussion of the impact of the offense on those present, the victim is asked to identify desired outcomes from the conference and thus helps shape the obligations that will be placed on the offender. All participants may contribute to the process of determining how the offender might best repair the harm he or she has caused. The session ends with participants signing an agreement outlining their expectations and commitments.

The New Zealand Model

Family group conferencing is used extensively in New Zealand. Their model is set out in detail below.

People who can go to the family group conference:

- Young person
- Young person's family
- Victim and support people
- Youth justice coordinator
- Police
- Young person's lawyer, called a youth advocate
- A social worker
- Other professionals, for example health and education

An interpreter can attend the meeting if needed.

Who organizes the family group conference?
The FGC is arranged by the youth justice coordinator from Child, Youth and Family. The youth justice coordinator is the key person for the young person and their family. They are there to help everyone get the most out of the meeting and to answer any worries or questions.

Preparing for the family group conference
Getting as many family members as possible to the FGC is the main thing that will help create a positive change for the young person. If you are attending an FGC for a young person in your family, you might want to think about:

- Who is in your extended family or whānau [extended family in Maori society]?
- Where do you want the FGC to be held?
- What special customs would you like to be part of the FGC?
- Who is a leader in your family who could help with the meeting?
- Who do you know that could help your young person with school, getting a job, learning new skills, or be a role model?

What happens at a family group conference?
Each family group conference is unique because the young person and their family help decide how the meeting will be

The balanced approach means that justice policies and priorities should seek to address each of the three goals in each case and that system balance should be pursued. The goal of achieving balance suggests that no one objective can take precedence over any other without creating a system that is out of balance and implies that efforts to achieve one goal (e.g., offender accountability) should not hinder efforts to achieve other goals.

BARJ is founded on the belief that justice is best served when the victim, community, and offender are viewed as equal clients of the justice system who will receive fair and balanced attention, be actively involved in the justice process, and gain tangible benefits from their interactions with the justice system.

Research efforts generally show that BARJ programs can effectively reduce offender recidivism rates. In addition to recidivism reduction, desired outcomes run. But generally there are three parts to a family group conference: Getting the facts, talking, and making a plan.

1. Getting the facts

Everyone will hear what the police say happened. If the young person agrees with what the police say happened, the next step will be to talk about how the young person can make things right. If the young person does not agree with what the police say happened, the conference will end, and the police or the court will decide what to do next.

2. Time to talk

Everyone talks about what the young person did wrong (the offences), and how it made other people feel, like the victim and the young person's family. The victim will talk about how the crime affected them and what they think should happen, what the young person can do to make things right.

3. The plan

The young person and their family talk about a plan to put things right. The plan should be fair to the victim and help the young person learn from their mistakes. Once the family has thought about a plan, they report their ideas back to the meeting. Everyone talks about it and decides if they agree on the plan. If agreement can't be reached, a judge will decide the plan.

A good plan will help a young person:

- Face up to it and admit to what they have done wrong
- Put it right with the victim as much as possible and accept consequences
- Move on by supporting the young person to make positive choices from now on
- Be strong as part of their family and whānau

The plan will also include:

- Who in the family will support the young person
- A clear timeframe for when the tasks need to be done
- Who will monitor each of the tasks

After the family group conference:
The young person will need help from their family to make the plan work. Once the plan has been made, it is legally binding and has to be completed. The plan will be reviewed by Child, Youth and Family to make sure all the tasks are done.

If the plan isn't being carried out as agreed, the youth justice coordinator will talk to the family about getting things back on track.

Do FGC Programs Work?

Edmund McGarrell and Natalie Kroovand Hipple used a randomized design to test an FGC program in Indianapolis, Indiana. More than 800 first-time-offending youths were randomly assigned to either a family group conference or one of a number of more traditional court-ordered programs. The cases were tracked for 24 months following the initial arrest, and the results indicated a significant difference between the two groups. Kids in the traditional programs experienced much higher failure rates and committed more offenses after arrest than those assigned to FGC. Because this study was so carefully constructed, the findings are an important indicator of the utility of restorative justice measures with delinquent youth.

CRITICAL THINKING

Do you believe that family group conferencing can make a difference in a young offender's life? Or do you think a more punishment-oriented response would produce better results? Explain your beliefs.

SOURCES: New Zealand Ministry of Social Development, Family Group Conferencing, 2016, http://www.cyf .govt.nz/youth-justice/family-group-conferences.html; Mark Umbreit, *Family Group Conferencing, Implications for Crime Victims* (Washington, DC. Office for Victims of Crime, 2000), http://www.ncjrs.gov/ovc _archives/reports/family_group/welcome.html; Edmund McGarrell and Natalie Kroovand Hipple, "Family Group Conferencing and Re-offending Among First-Time Juvenile Offenders: The Indianapolis Experiment," *Justice Quarterly* 24:221–246 (2007). (URLs accessed September 2016.)

commonly include restoration, victim and offender satisfaction with the process, and program completion. Research indicates the following circumstances affect the likelihood of program completion:

- When there is a strong focus on restoration, program completion is higher.
- The likelihood of completion, particularly for restitution and community service, may be related to level of supervision and time for program completion.[108]

Program satisfaction for the victim and offender may be affected by a number of issues:

- Perceived fairness of the process and outcome increases satisfaction.
- Satisfaction with mediation activities is related to the attitude of the mediator, and it increases when activities are conducted in person.

- Voluntary participation by the victim affects satisfaction with the program. Though victims' desire to participate in BARJ programs is widespread, a small but substantial proportion prefer that the offender be processed through traditional juvenile justice means. Victim satisfaction with the program decreases when participation is mandatory.[109]

Another popular restorative justice model is described in the Evidence-Based Juvenile Justice feature.

SUMMARY

1 Explain the concept of symbolic interaction and the role symbols play in defining reality

- Social reaction, or labeling, theory holds that criminality is promoted by becoming negatively labeled by significant others.
- Social reaction theory is based on the concept of symbolic interaction.
- People communicate through symbols that can be gestures, words, or physical products.
- According to this view, those in power—moral entrepreneurs—wish to shape the law and justice process according to their own sense of morality.
- People are labeled deviant if they fall outside this subjective definition of good.

2 Analyze the impact of the labeling process

- Labels such as "delinquent" isolate kids from society and lock them into lives of antisocial behaviors.
- Labels create expectations that the labeled person will act in a certain way; labeled people are always watched and suspected.
- Eventually these people begin to accept their labels as personal identities, locking them further into lives of crime and deviance.

3 Compare the terms *primary deviant* and *secondary deviant*

- According to Lemert, primary deviants are people who do bad acts but are not defined as deviants by others.
- Secondary deviants are people who consider themselves deviants and are viewed by others as deviants.
- Secondary deviants accept a deviant identity as a personal role.
- Lemert suggests that people who accept labels are involved in secondary deviance, while primary deviants are able to maintain an undamaged identity.

4 Identify the four quadrants of Becker's table of deviance and reaction

- Kids who engage in delinquency and also get caught and labeled are called *pure deviants*.
- *Conformists* are both rule abiding and free of negative labels.
- Some kids are *falsely accused* or blamed for something they did not do.
- Some kids who continually break rules are able to avoid labeling; these are called *secret deviants*.

5 Summarize the unequal application of delinquent labels

- An important principle of social reaction theory is that the law is differentially applied, benefiting those who hold economic and social power and penalizing the powerless.
- The probability of being brought under the control of legal authority is a function of a person's race, wealth, gender, and social standing.
- The labeling process favors the powerful members of society who direct its content and penalizes people whose actions represent a threat to those in control, such as minority group members and the poor who demand equal rights.

6 Demonstrate the long-term effects of labels

- If a devalued status is conferred by a significant other—teacher, police officer, elder, parent, or valued peer—the negative label and resulting stigma may cause permanent harm.
- Labeled kids may consider themselves social outcasts.
- When kids are labeled as troublemakers or social problems, they may join with similarly outcast delinquent peers in a clique or group that facilitates their antisocial behavior.

7 Explain the strengths of the social reaction perspective

- Social reaction identifies the role played by social control agents in the process of delinquency causation. Delinquent behavior cannot be fully understood if the agencies and individuals empowered to control and treat it are neglected.

- Social reaction recognizes that delinquency is not a disease or pathological behavior. It focuses attention on the social interactions and reactions that shape individual behavior.

- Social reaction theory distinguishes between delinquent acts (primary deviance) and delinquent careers (secondary deviance) and shows that these concepts must be interpreted and treated differently.

8 Apply the core elements of social conflict theory

- According to social conflict theory, those who hold power in contemporary society get to set the rules, control the law, and decide who is a deviant, delinquent, or criminal.

- Social conflict theory asserts that society is in a state of constant internal conflict, and focuses on the role of social and governmental institutions as mechanisms for social control.

- Globalization, which usually refers to the process of creating transnational markets and political and legal systems, has shifted the focus of critical inquiry to a world perspective.

- Globalization may have a profound influence on the future of indigent youth. Workers in the United States may be replaced in high-paying manufacturing jobs, not by machines but by foreign workers in overseas factories.

9 Define the basic principles of restorative justice

- Restorative justice uses humanistic, nonpunitive strategies to right wrongs and restore social harmony.

- Restorative justice has grown out of a belief that the traditional justice system has done little to involve the community in the process of dealing with crime and wrongdoing.

- Reintegrative shaming techniques are used to allow offenders to understand and recognize their wrongdoing and shame themselves. To be reintegrative, shaming must be brief and controlled and then followed by ceremonies of forgiveness, apology, and repentance.

- The restoration process redefines antisocial behavior in terms of a conflict among the offender, the victim, and affected constituencies.

10 Illustrate how restoration can be used to reduce delinquent behaviors

- Restoration techniques include negotiation, mediation, consensus-building, sentencing circles, sentencing panels, and elders panels.

- According to restorative justice, rather than punishing, shaming, and excluding those who violate the law, efforts should be made to use humanistic techniques that reintegrate people into society.

- Restorative programs rely on victims, relatives, neighbors, and community institutions rather than courts and prisons.

- Two well-known restorative programs are Family Group Conferencing (FGC) and the Balanced and Restorative Justice (BARJ) approach.

KEY TERMS

QUESTIONS FOR DISCUSSION

1. How would a restorative justice advocate respond to a proposed policy easing the waiver of youth to adult court?

2. Considering recent changes in American culture, how would a critical theorist explain an increase in the juvenile gang population?

3. Is conflict inevitable in all cultures? If not, what can be done to reduce the level of conflict in our own society?

4. One way to reduce stigma and labeling would be to legalize acts that are now considered illegal. If you have the power, what would you legalize and what might be the consequences?

5. Are you familiar with any instances of "retrospective reading" in your home town? Have you ever engaged in it yourself, saying, "I always knew he had problems"?

VIEWPOINT

As an expert on juvenile justice, you have been asked to review and revise a proposed court-based restorative justice program. The administrator sends you the following proposal:

- In cases where an offender has admitted to the act, the judge can, at his or her discretion, offer the adolescent the choice of either the normal course of justice or participation in the community reparation project.

- At this point the court adjourns for approximately 30 minutes while the probation officer explains the project to the offender. If the offender decides to participate in the project, a meeting will be called in the near future.

- This meeting is always attended by the youth, two panel members representing the community, the police officers involved in the case, and the probation officer. If the delinquent acts involve victims, they are also invited to attend the meeting, although their participation is not mandatory.

- At the meeting, offenders are asked to explain the circumstances of the offense, why it happened, how they felt about it then, and how they feel about their actions now. Together, the group decides how the offender might make reparation to the victim and/or the community for the damage caused by the offense.

- Once agreement is reached about the form of the reparation, a contract is drawn up that sets out treatment courses the offender will be expected to take (e.g., treatment for alcoholism, substance abuse, anger management). Reparation may include letters of apology to the victim, restitution, and other proportionate and appropriate activities.

- Contracts generally cover a period of approximately six months and are monitored by the probation officer. If the terms of the contract are successfully completed, the record of the offense will be dropped. If the terms are not met, the case will go back to the juvenile court and proceed in the normal manner.

As a delinquency expert, what is your take on the proposed program? How do you think the program should handle kids who fail to complete the restoration bargain? Are there any other approaches you would try with these kids?

DOING RESEARCH ON THE WEB

There are numerous restorative justice sites on the Web that can help you formulate an answer. Many are internationally based. You might want to look at one or more of these:

- The Victim–Offender Reconciliation Program (VORP) Information and Resource Center (http://www.vorp.com/)

- Restorative Justice Online (http://www.restorativejustice.org/)
- Australian Institute of Criminology (http://www.aic.gov.au/)

NOTES

All URLs accessed September 2016.

1. Andrew Buncombe, "Ahmed Mohamed Demands $15m Compensation and Written Apology After Homemade Clock Arrest," *Independent*, November 25, 2015, http://www.independent.co.uk /news/people/ahmed-mohamed-demands-15m-compensation-for -homemade-clock-arrest-a6745706.html; Avi Selk, "Irving 9th-Grader Arrested After Taking Homemade Clock to School: 'So You Tried to Make a Bomb?'" *Dallas Morning News*, September 16, 2015, http:// www.dallasnews.com/news/dallas-county/2015/09/15/ahmed -mohamed-swept-up-hoax-bomb-charges-swept-away-as-irving -teen-s-story-floods-social-media.

2. Edwin Schur, *Labeling Deviant Behavior* (New York: Harper & Row, 1972), p. 21.

3. George Herbert Mead, *Mind, Self and Society* (Chicago: University of Chicago Press, 1934); Mead, *The Philosophy of the Act* (Chicago: University of Chicago Press, 1938); Charles Horton Cooley, *Human Nature and the Social Order* (New York: Schocken, 1964), originally published in 1902; Herbert Blumer, *Symbolic Interactionism: Perspective and Method* (Englewood Cliffs, NJ: Prentice Hall, 1969).

4. Ernesto Londoño, "Court Says Consensual Sex Can't Become Rape," *Washington Post*, November 2, 2006, http://www.washingtonpost .com/wp-dyn/content/article/2006/11/01/AR2006110103225.html.

5. Alex Dobuzinskis, "California Toughens Rape Laws After Stanford Case Uproar," Reuters, September 30, 2016, http://www.reuters .com/article/us-california-rape-idUSKCN1202H2.

6. Kai Erickson, "Notes on the Sociology of Deviance," *Social Problems* 9:397–414 (1962).

7. Howard Becker, *Outsiders, Studies in the Sociology of Deviance* (New York: Macmillan, 1963), p. 9.

8. Laurie Goodstein, "The Architect of the 'Gay Conversion' Campaign," *New York Times*, August 13, 1998, p. A10.

9. Bruce Link, Elmer Streuning, Francis Cullen, Patrick Shrout, and Bruce Dohrenwend, "A Modified Labeling Theory Approach to Mental Disorders: An Empirical Assessment," *American Sociological Review* 54:400–423 (1989).

10. Patrick Corrigan, "How Stigma Interferes with Mental Health Care," *American Psychologist* 59:614–625 at 614 (2004).

11. Linda Jackson, John Hunter, and Carole Hodge, "Physical Attractiveness and Intellectual Competence: A Meta-Analytic Review," *Social Psychology Quarterly* 58:108–122 (1995).

12. Mike Adams, Craig Robertson, Phyllis Gray-Ray, and Melvin Ray, "Labeling and Delinquency," *Adolescence* 38:171–186 (2003).

13. Ibid.

14. Jón Gunnar Bernburg, Marvin Krohn, and Craig Rivera, "Official Labeling, Criminal Embeddedness, and Subsequent Delinquency: A Longitudinal Test of Labeling Theory," *Journal of Research in Crime and Delinquency* 43:67–88 (2006).

15. Xiaoru Liu, "The Conditional Effect of Peer Groups on the Relationship Between Parental Labeling and Youth Delinquency," *Sociological Perspectives* 43:499–515 (2000).

16. Ruth Triplett, "The Conflict Perspective, Symbolic Interactionism, and the Status Characteristics Hypothesis," *Justice Quarterly* 10:540–558 (1993).

17. Lening Zhang, "Official Offense Status and Self-Esteem Among Chinese Youths," *Journal of Criminal Justice* 31:99–105 (2003).

18. Dylan B. Jackson and Carter Hay, "The Conditional Impact of Official Labeling on Subsequent Delinquency: Considering the Attenuating Role of Family Attachment," *Journal of Research in Crime and Delinquency*, first published online July 20, 2012.

19. Lee Michael Johnson, Ronald Simons, and Rand Conger, "Criminal Justice System Involvement and Continuity of Youth Crime," *Youth and Society* 36:3–29 (2004).

20. Gary Sweeten, "Who Will Graduate? Disruption of High School Education by Arrest and Court Involvement," *Justice Quarterly* 23:462–480 (2006).

21. Roland Chilton and Jim Galvin, "Race, Crime and Criminal Justice," *Crime and Delinquency* 31:3–14 (1985).

22. Ojmarrh Mitchell and Michael S. Caudy, "Examining Racial Disparities in Drug Arrests," *Justice Quarterly* 32:288–313 (2015).

23. National Minority Advisory Council on Criminal Justice, *The Inequality of Justice* (Washington, DC: author, 1981), p. 200.

24. Tammy Rinehart Kochel, David Wilson, and Stephen Mastrofski, "Effect of Suspect Race on Officers' Arrest Decisions," *Criminology* 49:473–512 (2011).

25. Brian Johnson, Eric Stewart, Justin Pickett, and Marc Gertz, "Ethnic Threat and Social Control: Examining Public Support for Judicial Use of Ethnicity in Punishment," *Criminology* 49:401–441 (2011).

26. Michael Rocques and Raymond Paternoster, "Understanding the Antecedents of the 'School-to-Jail' Link: The Relationship Between Race and School Discipline," *Journal of Criminal Law and Criminology* 101:633–665 (2011).

27. Allison Ann Payne and Kelly Welch, "Modeling the Effects of Racial Threat on Punitive and Restorative School Discipline Practices," *Criminology* 48:1019–1062 (2010).

28. Christina DeJong and Kenneth Jackson, "Putting Race into Context: Race, Juvenile Justice Processing, and Urbanization," *Justice Quarterly* 15:487–504 (1998).

29. Joan Petersilia, "Racial Disparities in the Criminal Justice System: A Summary," *Crime and Delinquency* 31:15–34 (1985).

30. Ruth Triplett, "The Conflict Perspective, Symbolic Interactionism, and the Status Characteristics Hypothesis," *Justice Quarterly* 10:540–558 (1993).

31. Ross Matsueda, "Reflected Appraisals, Parental Labeling, and Delinquency: Specifying a Symbolic Interactionist Theory," *American Journal of Sociology* 97:1577–1611 (1992).

32. Xiaoru Liu, "The Conditional Effect of Peer Groups on the Relationship Between Parental Labeling and Youth Delinquency," *Sociological Perspectives* 43:499–515 (2000).

33. Dylan B. Jackson and Carter Hay, "The Conditional Impact of Official Labeling on Subsequent Delinquency: Considering the Attenuating Role of Family Attachment," *Journal of Research in Crime and Delinquency*, first published online July 20, 2012.

34. David Ramey, "The Influence of Early School Punishment and Therapy/Medication on Social Control Experiences During Young Adulthood," *Criminology* 54 (2016).

35. *President's Commission on Law Enforcement and the Administration of Justice, Task Force Report: Juvenile Delinquency and Youth* (Washington, DC: US Government Printing Office, 1967), p. 43.

36. Giza Lopes, Marvin Krohn, Alan Lizotte, Nicole Schmidt, Bob Edward Vásquez, and Jón Gunnar Bernburg, "Labeling and Cumulative Disadvantage: The Impact of Formal Police Intervention on Life Chances and Crime During Emerging Adulthood," *Crime and Delinquency* 58:456–488 (2012).

37. Daniel Ryan Kavish, Christopher Mullins, and Danielle Soto, "Interactionist Labeling: Formal and Informal Labeling's Effects on Juvenile Delinquency," *Crime and Delinquency*, first published online July 15, 2014.

38. Nicole Schmidt, Giza Lopes, Marvin Krohn, and Alan Lizotte, "Getting Caught and Getting Hitched: An Assessment of the Relationship Between Police Intervention, Life Chances, and Romantic Unions," *Justice Quarterly* 32:976–1005 (2015).

39. Amy Solomon, "In Search of a Job: Criminal Records as Barriers to Employment," *NIJ Journal 270* (2012), http://www.nij.gov/nij/journals/270/criminal-records.htm.

40. Suzanne Ageton and Delbert Elliott, *The Effect of Legal Processing on Self-Concept* (Boulder, CO: Institute of Behavioral Science, 1973).

41. Robert Sampson and John Laub, "A Life-Course Theory of Cumulative Disadvantage and the Stability of Delinquency," in Terence Thornberry, ed., *Developmental Theories of Crime and Delinquency* (New Brunswick, NJ: Transaction Press, 1997), pp. 133–161; Douglas Smith and Robert Brame, "On the Initiation and Continuation of Delinquency," *Criminology* 4:607–630 (1994).

42. Emily Restivo and Mark Lanier, "Measuring the Contextual Effects and Mitigating Factors of Labeling Theory," *Justice Quarterly* 32:116–141 (2015).

43. Sampson and Laub, "A Life-Course Theory of Cumulative Disadvantage and the Stability of Delinquency."

44. Jón Gunnar Bernburg and Marvin Krohn, "Labeling, Life Chances, and Adult Crime: The Direct and Indirect Effects of Official Intervention in Adolescence on Crime in Early Adulthood," *Criminology* 41:1287–1319 (2003).

45. Bernburg, Krohn, and Rivera, "Official Labeling, Criminal Embeddedness, and Subsequent Delinquency."

46. Karen Heimer and Ross Matsueda, "Role-Taking, Role-Commitment, and Delinquency," *American Sociological Review* 59:365–390 (1994).

47. Howard Kaplan and Robert Johnson, "Negative Social Sanctions and Juvenile Delinquency: Effects of Labeling in a Model of Deviant Behavior," *Social Science Quarterly* 72:98–122 (1991).

48. Howard Kaplan, Robert Johnson, and Carol Bailey, "Deviant Peers and Deviant Behavior: Further Elaboration of a Model," *Social Psychology Quarterly* 30:277–284 (1987).

49. Ibid.

50. Adams, Robertson, Gray-Ray, and Ray, "Labeling and Delinquency."

51. Kaplan, Johnson, and Bailey, "Deviant Peers and Deviant Behavior: Further Elaboration of a Model."

52. Edwin Lemert, *Social Pathology* (New York: McGraw-Hill, 1951).

53. Ibid., p. 75.

54. Becker, *Outsiders*.

55. Ronald Farrell, "Deviance Imputations, Early Recollections and the Reconstruction of Self," *International Journal of Social Psychiatry* 30:189–199 (1984).

56. Frank Tannenbaum, *Crime and the Community* (New York: Columbia University Press, 1938), pp. 19–20.

57. Charles H. Cooley, *Human Nature and the Social Order* (New York: Scribner's, 1902).

58. Ross Matsueda, "Reflected Appraisals, Parental Labeling, and Delinquency: Specifying a Symbolic Interactionist Theory," *American Journal of Sociology* 97:1577–1611 (1992).

59. Adams, Robertson, Gray-Ray, and Ray, "Labeling and Delinquency."

60. Harold Garfinkel, "Conditions of Successful Degradation Ceremonies," *American Journal of Sociology* 5:420–424 (1956).

61. Tannenbaum, *Crime and the Community*.

62. Robert Morris and Alex Piquero, "For Whom Do Sanctions Deter and Label?" *Justice Quarterly* 30:837–868 (2013).

63. Stephanie Ann Wiley, Lee Ann Slocum, and Finn-Aage Esbensen, "The Unintended Consequences of Being Stopped or Arrested: An Exploration of the Labeling Mechanisms Through Which Police Contact Leads to Subsequent Delinquency," *Criminology* 51:927–966 (2013).

64. Bernburg and Krohn, "Labeling, Life Chances, and Adult Crime."

65. Adams, Robertson, Gray-Ray, and Ray, "Labeling and Delinquency," p. 178.

66. Nadine Lanctôt, Stephen Cernkovich, and Peggy Giordano, "Delinquent Behavior, Official Delinquency, and Gender: Consequences for Adulthood Functioning and Well-Being," *Criminology* 45:131–157 (2007).

67. Jack Gibbs, "Conceptions of Deviant Behavior: The Old and the New," *Pacific Sociological Review* 9:11–13 (1966).

68. Charles A. Murray and Louis Cox, *Beyond Probation* (Beverly Hills: Sage Publications, 1979).

69. Charles Tittle, "Labeling and Crime: An Empirical Evaluation," in Walter Gove, ed., *The Labeling of Deviance: Evaluating a Perspective* (New York: Wiley, 1975), pp. 157–179.

70. Megan Kurlychek, Robert Brame, and Shawn Bushway, "Enduring Risk? Old Criminal Records and Predictions of Future Criminal Involvement," *Crime and Delinquency* 53:64–83 (2007).

71. Raymond Paternoster and Leeann Iovanni, "The Labeling Perspective and Delinquency: An Elaboration of the Theory and an Assessment of the Evidence," *Justice Quarterly* 6:358–394 (1989).

72. Shadd Maruna, Thomas Lebel, Nick Mitchell, and Michelle Maples, "Pygmalion in the Reintegration Process: Desistance from Crime Through the Looking Glass," *Psychology, Crime, and Law* 10:271–281 (2004).

73. Nathaniel Ascani, "Labeling Theory and the Effects of Sanctioning on Delinquent Peer Association: A New Approach to Sentencing Juveniles," *Perspectives* (Spring 2012):80–84.

74. Alex Heckert and Druann Heckert, "Differential Labeling Theory," *Sociological Imagination* 46:24–40 (2010).

75. Scott Davies and Julian Tanner, "The Long Arm of the Law: Effects of Labeling on Employment," *Sociological Quarterly* 44:385–404 (2003).

76. Bernburg and Krohn, "Labeling, Life Chances, and Adult Crime."

77. Margit Wiesner, Hyoun K. Kim, and Deborah M. Capaldi, "History of Juvenile Arrests and Vocational Career Outcomes for At-Risk Young Men," *Journal of Research in Crime and Delinquency* 47:91–117 (2010).

78. Maruna, Lebel, Mitchell, and Maples, "Pygmalion in the Reintegration Process."

79. James Austin and Barry Krisberg, "The Unmet Promise of Alternatives to Incarceration," *Crime and Delinquency* 28:3–19 (1982).

80. William Selke, "Diversion and Crime Prevention," *Criminology* 20:395–406 (1982).

81. Matthew Petrocelli, Alex Piquero, and Michael Smith, "Conflict Theory and Racial Profiling: An Empirical Analysis of Police Traffic Stop Data," *Journal of Criminal Justice* 31:1–10 (2003).

82. Malcolm Homes, "Minority Threat and Police Brutality: Determinants of Civil Rights Criminal Complaints in U.S. Municipalities," *Criminology* 38:343–368 (2000).

83. Ibid.

84. Jeffery Reiman, *The Rich Get Richer and the Poor Get Prison* (New York: Wiley, 1984), pp. 43–44.

85. Robert Gordon, "Capitalism, Class, and Crime in America," *Crime and Delinquency* 19:174 (1973).

86. Richard Quinney, *Class, State, and Crime* (New York: Longman, 1977), p. 52.

87. Anthony Platt, "The Triumph of Benevolence: The Origins of the Juvenile Justice System in the United States," in Richard Quinney, ed., *Criminal Justice in America: A Critical Understanding* (Boston: Little, Brown, 1974), p. 367; see also Anthony Platt, *The Child Savers* (Chicago: University of Chicago Press, 1969).

88. William Julius Wilson, *The Truly Disadvantaged* (Chicago: University of Chicago Press, 1987); *When Work Disappears, The World of the Urban Poor* (New York: Alfred Knopf, 1996); *The Bridge over the Racial Divide: Rising Inequality and Coalition Politics*, Wildavsky Forum Series, 2 (Berkeley: University of California Press, 1999).

89. To read about Wilson's views, go to William Julius Wilson and Richard Taub, *There Goes the Neighborhood: Racial, Ethnic, and Class Tensions in Four Chicago Neighborhoods and Their Meaning for America* (New York: Knopf, 2006); Wilson, *The Truly Disadvantaged; When Work Disappears, The World of the Urban Poor; The Bridge over the Racial Divide.*

90. Robert DeFina and Thomas Arvanites, "The Weak Effect of Imprisonment on Crime: 1971–1998," *Social Science Quarterly* 83:635–654 (2002).

91. Kathleen Daly and Russ Immarigeon, "The Past, Present and Future of Restorative Justice: Some Critical Reflections," *Contemporary Justice Review* 1:21–45 (1998).

92. Howard Zehr, *The Little Book of Restorative Justice* (Intercourse, PA: Good Books, 2002), pp. 1–10.

93. John Braithwaite, *Crime, Shame, and Reintegration* (Melbourne, Australia: Cambridge University Press, 1989).

94. Ibid., p. 81.

95. Anthony Petrosino and Carolyn Petrosino, "The Public Safety Potential of Megan's Law in Massachusetts: An Assessment from a Sample of Criminal Sexual Psychopaths," *Crime and Delinquency* 45:140–158 (1999).

96. Eliza Ahmed, Nathan Harris, John Braithwaite, and Valerie Braithwaite, *Shame Management Through Reintegration* (Cambridge: Cambridge University Press, 2001).

97. Eliza Ahmed, "What, Me Ashamed? Shame Management and School Bullying," *Journal of Research in Crime and Delinquency* 41:269–294 (2004).

98. Carter Hay, "An Exploratory Test of Braithwaite's Reintegrative Shaming Theory," *Journal of Research in Crime and Delinquency* 38:132–153 (2001).

99. Gene Stephens, "The Future of Policing: From a War Model to a Peace Model," in Brendan Maguire and Polly Radosh, eds., *The Past, Present and Future of American Criminal Justice* (Dix Hills, NY: General Hall, 1996), pp. 77–93.

100. Rick Shifley, "The Organization of Work as a Factor in Social Well-Being," *Contemporary Justice Review* 6:105–126 (2003).

101. Kay Pranis, "Peacemaking Circles: Restorative Justice in Practice Allows Victims and Offenders to Begin Repairing the Harm," *Corrections Today* 59:74–78 (1997).

102. Carol LaPrairie, "The 'New' Justice: Some Implications for Aboriginal Communities," *Canadian Journal of Criminology* 40:61–79 (1998).

103. Diane Schaefer, "A Disembodied Community Collaborates in a Homicide: Can Empathy Transform a Failing Justice System?" *Contemporary Justice Review* 6:133–143 (2003).

104. David R. Karp and Beau Breslin, "Restorative Justice in School Communities," *Youth and Society* 33:249–272 (2001).

105. Paul Jesilow and Deborah Parsons, "Community Policing as Peacemaking," *Policing and Society* 10:163–183 (2000).

106. Gordon Bazemore and Curt Taylor Griffiths, "Conferences, Circles, Boards, and Mediations: The 'New Wave' of Community Justice Decision Making," *Federal Probation* 61:25–37 (1997).

107. This section is based on Gordon Bazemore and Mara Schiff, "Paradigm Muddle or Paradigm Paralysis? The Wide and Narrow Roads to Restorative Justice Reform (or, a Little Confusion May Be a Good Thing),"*Contemporary Justice Review* 7:37–57 (2004).

108. Juvenile Justice Evaluation Center Publications, http://www.jrsa.org/pubs/juv-justice/.

109. Ibid.

CHAPTER 6

Developmental Theories of Delinquency:
Life-Course, Propensity, and Trajectory

Learning Objectives

1 Compare and contrast the three forms of developmental theory

2 Trace the history of and influences on developmental theory

3 Describe the principles of the life-course approach to developmental theory

4 Explain the concept of problem behavior syndrome

5 Articulate the principles of Sampson and Laub's age-graded life-course theory

6 Define the concept of a latent trait

7 Outline the principles and assumptions of the General Theory of Crime (GTC)

8 Discuss both the strengths and weaknesses of the GTC

9 Identify the different trajectories delinquency takes

10 Distinguish between adolescent-limited and life-course persistent offenders

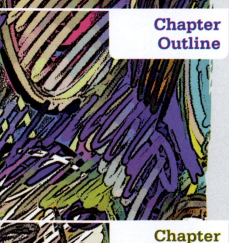

Chapter Outline

The Creation of a Developmental View of Delinquency

Life-Course Theory
  Negative Life Events
  Life-Course Concepts
  Persistence and Desistance

Theories of the Delinquent Life Course
  Age-Graded Theory

Propensity Theories
  State Dependence

Propensity and Opportunity
General Theory of Crime

Trajectory Theory
  Late Bloomers and Nonstarters
  Pathways to Delinquency
  Adolescent-Limited and Life-Course
    Persistent Offenders

Evaluating Developmental Theories

Public Policy Implications of Developmental Theory

Chapter Features

Focus on Delinquency: Persistence vs. Desistence

Focus on Delinquency: Shared Beginnings, Divergent Lives

Youth Stories: Craig Price

Evidence-Based Juvenile Justice— Prevention: Across Ages

FROM THE BEGINNING, Rebecca Falcon was troubled. Her home life in Kansas was no bargain. When she was 6, her mother's fiancé began to molest her. She was having sex with boys by age 12; at 13, she was assaulted by schoolmates; at 14, boys were bragging that she would do whatever they asked. Falcon never dared to say no, even when she didn't want to have sex, because she craved love and was willing to do whatever it took to feel wanted. She began to cut herself and drink and take pills by the time she was 15; she even attempted suicide. Her mother and stepfather could not find any other solution to her problems, so they shipped her off to live with her grandmother in Florida. Alone and afraid, Falcon started to hang out with a group of older boys again. She later told an interviewer, "I didn't want to injure myself and that's why I became hard and harder."

In November 1997, she hailed a cab with an 18-year-old friend named Clifton Gilchrist. She was drunk, he had his gun, and they carried out a spontaneous and unplanned robbery of the driver, Richard Todd Phillips, 25, who was shot in the head and died several days later. Each of the teenagers later said the other had done the shooting.[1]

While it was never clear who fired the death shot or precisely what happened that night, the jury found Rebecca guilty of murder. The foreman, Steven Sharp, said later that it was enough that she was there during the robbery. "It broke my heart," said Sharp. "As tough as it is, based on the crime, I think it's appropriate. It's terrible to put a 15-year-old behind bars forever." Both teenagers were convicted and sentenced to life without parole.

Now 35 years old, Rebecca Falcon is in contact with the cab driver's widow, who agrees that a life sentence was too harsh a penalty for a 15-year-old girl. In 2015, the Florida Supreme Court seemed to agree, ruling that Falcon and other juvenile criminals should be eligible for parole. The justices relied on the 2012 US Supreme Court case *Miller v. Alabama*, which held that a mandatory life sentence without parole for juveniles is unconstitutional.[2] In 2016, in *Montgomery v. Louisiana*, the Court made it mandatory on all states that the *Miller* doctrine be applied retroactively, allowing juveniles convicted of murder to be considered for parole.[3]

Should someone like Rebecca Falcon be eligible for parole? The person she is today may have little resemblance to the troubled person she was when she committed her crime. She has written letters to the victim's family apologizing for her crimes. And because mandatory life sentences for teens convicted of murder are no longer constitutional, Falcon is currently preparing for a new sentencing hearing, during which a judge will take into account factors such as her emotional maturity at the time of the crime.[4]

Rebecca Falcon's story is typical of many kids who face significant social and emotional problems as children, then as adolescents, later as teens, and then into their adulthood. This pattern is not lost on those delinquency experts who see delinquency as an ongoing, evolving process that can be traced back to an adolescent's earliest childhood. Many young offenders, like Falcon, have a long history of problem behaviors. Yet the majority are able to transition out of delinquency as they mature into adulthood.

Because serious juvenile offending is rarely a "one-shot deal," delinquency experts now recognize that it is important to chart the natural history of a delinquent career. We know that most but not all young offenders do not become adult criminals; as people mature they significantly reduce their participation in crime and the frequency of their antisocial activities.[5]

Why is it, then, that some kids abandon the delinquent way of life as they mature, whereas others persist in antisocial behavior into their adulthood? Why do some offenders escalate their delinquent activities while others decrease or limit their law violations? Why do some specialize in particular delinquent acts while others become generalists who shoplift, take drugs, engage in violence, steal cars, and so on? Why do some delinquents reduce their criminal activity for a brief period only to resume it later in life? Research shows that some offenders begin their delinquent careers at a very early age, whereas others begin later. How can early- and late-onset delinquency be explained?

Focusing attention on these questions has produced what is known as the **developmental theory** of delinquency, a view that looks at the onset, continuity, and termination of a delinquent career. In this chapter, we look at these theories that recognize that delinquent and criminal behavior is not an unchanging human characteristic, but one that ebbs and flows over the life course. While antisocial behavior is relatively uncommon during early childhood, even preadolescents may engage in crime if the conditions are right. While most delinquent offenders reduce their offending behavior by their mid-twenties, a few persist unabated into adulthood. Traditional theories of crime and delinquency neither distinguish among different phases of criminal careers nor explain these differences in offending trajectories. In this chapter, we will review developmental theories of delinquency and the various forms they take.

developmental theory
The view that delinquency is a dynamic process influenced by social experiences as well as individual characteristics.

The Creation of a Developmental View of Delinquency

The foundation of developmental theory can be traced to the pioneering work of Sheldon Glueck and Eleanor Glueck. While at Harvard University in the 1930s, the Gluecks popularized research on the life cycle of delinquent careers. In a series of longitudinal research studies, they followed the careers of known delinquents to determine the social, biological, and psychological characteristics that predicted persistent offending.[6] The Gluecks made extensive use of interviews and records in their elaborate comparisons of delinquents and nondelinquents.[7]

The Gluecks' research focused on early onset of delinquency as a harbinger of a delinquent career: "The deeper the roots of childhood maladjustment, the smaller the chance of adult adjustment."[8] They also noted the stability of offending careers: children who are antisocial early in life are the most likely to continue their offending careers into adulthood.

The Gluecks identified a number of personal and social factors related to persistent offending. The most important of these factors was family relations, considered in terms of quality of discipline and emotional ties with parents. The adolescent raised in a large, single-parent family of limited economic means and educational achievement was the most vulnerable to delinquency.

The Gluecks did not restrict their analysis to social variables. When they measured such biological and psychological traits as body type, intelligence, and personality, they found that physical and mental factors also played a role in determining behavior. Children with low intelligence, a background of mental disease, and a powerful (mesomorph) physique were the most likely to become persistent offenders.

The Philadelphia cohort research by Marvin Wolfgang and his associates was another milestone prompting interest in explaining delinquent career development.[9] As you may recall (Chapter 2), Wolfgang found that while many offenders commit a single delinquent act and desist from crime, a small group of chronic offenders engage in frequent and repeated delinquent activity and continue to do so across their life span. Wolfgang's research focused attention on delinquent

Find information about the **life and work of Sheldon and Eleanor Glueck** in the "Papers of Eleanor T. and Sheldon Glueck, 1911–1972," at the Harvard Law School library (http://oasis.lib.harvard.edu/oasis /deliver/~law00108) and read this article in the *Harvard Crimson*: http://www .thecrimson.com/article/1952/4 /11/gluecks-study-of-500 -juvenile-delinquents/.

careers and chronic criminality. Delinquency experts were now forced to ask this fundamental question: What prompts one adolescent to engage in persistent delinquent activity while another, who on the surface suffers the same life circumstances, finds a way to steer clear of delinquency and travel along a more conventional path?

From these roots a developmental theory of delinquency has developed. Today, there are actually three independent yet interrelated developmental views. The first, referred to as the life-course theory, suggests that delinquent behavior is a dynamic process, influenced by individual characteristics as well as social experiences, and that the factors that cause antisocial behaviors change dramatically over a person's life span.

The life-course theory is challenged by another group of scholars who suggest that human development is controlled by a hidden master trait that remains stable and unchanging throughout a person's lifetime. As people travel through their life course this latent trait or propensity is always there, directing their behavior. Because this underlying characteristic is enduring, an individual's involvement in antisocial behavior is shaped less by personal change and attributes and more by external forces such as opportunity, need, and circumstance. Delinquency may increase when an adolescent joins a gang, which provides him with more opportunities to commit crime and the support he needs to carry out criminal acts. In other words, the propensity to commit delinquent acts is constant, but the opportunity to commit them is constantly fluctuating.

A third developmental view suggests there are multiple trajectories in a delinquent career. According to this approach, there are subgroups within a population that follow distinctively different developmental trajectories toward and away from a delinquent career. Some kids may begin early in antisocial activities and demonstrate a propensity for crime, while others begin later and are influenced by life circumstances. Trajectory theory suggests that there is no single delinquent pathway and that there are different types and classes of offenders.[10]

The main points, similarities, and differences of these positions are set out in Concept Summary 6.1.

life-course theory
Focuses on changes in criminality over the life course; developmental theory.

latent trait
A stable feature, characteristic, property, or condition, such as defective intelligence or impulsive personality, that makes some people delinquency prone over the life course.

propensity
An innate inclination, preference, or tendency to act in a specific way.

trajectory theory
The view that there are multiple independent paths to a delinquent career and that there are different types and classes of offenders.

CONCEPT SUMMARY 6.1

Developmental Theories

Propensity Theory
- People have a master trait: personality, intelligence, genetic makeup.
- People do not change; delinquent opportunities change; maturity brings fewer opportunities.
- Early social control and proper parenting can reduce delinquent propensity.

Life-Course Theory
- People change over the life course.
- The factors that influence antisocial behavior evolve as a person matures.
- Evolving informal social controls help at-risk kids avoid criminal careers.

Trajectory Theory
- There is more than one path to a delinquent career.
- There are different types of offenders and offending patterns.

- Some kids start their offending careers while they are quite young, another group begins when they are older, while others are able to avoid any form of antisocial activities.

Similarities Within the Three Developmental Views
- Focus on delinquent careers.
- Delinquency must be viewed as a path rather than an event.
- Delinquent careers are the focus.
- Integration of multiple factors.

Differences Among the Three Developmental Views
- Propensity: An unseen and unchanging latent trait controls antisocial behavior.
- Life course: People are constantly evolving.
- Trajectory: The focus is on the different paths people take from delinquency to crime.

Life-Course Theory

According to life-course theory, delinquency is constantly evolving and the factors that produce antisocial behaviors at one point in the life cycle may not be relevant at another. While some people show a propensity to offend early in their lives, the nature and frequency of their activities are often affected by external forces that shape their personal development.[11]

Even as toddlers, people begin relationships and behaviors that will determine their adult life course. At first they must learn to conform to social rules and function effectively in society. Later they are expected to begin to think about careers, leave their parental homes, find permanent relationships, and eventually marry and begin their own families.[12] These transitions are expected to take place in order—beginning with completing school, then entering the workforce, getting married, and having children.

Some individuals, however, are incapable of maturing in a reasonable and timely fashion because of family, environmental, or personal problems.[13] In some cases, transitions can occur too early—an adolescent girl who engages in precocious sex gets pregnant and is forced to drop out of high school. In other cases, transitions may occur too late—a teenage male falls in with the wrong crowd, goes to prison, and subsequently finds it difficult to break into the job market; he puts off getting married because of his diminished economic circumstances. Sometimes interruption of one transition can harm another. A teenager who has family problems may find that her educational and career development is upset or that she suffers from psychological impairments.[14] Because a transition from one stage of life to another can be a bumpy ride, the propensity to commit crimes is neither stable nor constant: it is a developmental process.

Kids who get in trouble early may find it difficult to shake the criminal way of life as they mature. Those who join gangs are more likely to get involved in antisocial behavior after they leave the gang than before they joined; gang membership creates long-term disruptions.[15] One reason is that joining a gang can lead to educational underachievement, a factor routinely associated with career criminality.[16] Youths who join gangs are 30 percent less likely to graduate from high school and 58 percent less likely to earn a four-year degree than youths of similar background who do not become gang members.[17] But even those who have been in trouble throughout their adolescence may manage to find stable work and maintain intact marriages as adults; these life events help them desist from crime. In contrast, less fortunate adolescents who develop arrest records and get involved with the wrong crowd may find themselves at risk for delinquency and later adult criminal careers.[18]

Negative Life Events

Regardless of the cause of their early externalizing behaviors, as children mature they go through cognitive changes and their thinking patterns change. While some may persist in their illegal conduct, personal maturity may help others reduce the attraction of antisocial activities. Teens who want to drink, take drugs, and get in trouble may go through a positive transformation in their thinking in early adulthood, helping them to desist from crime.[19]

In contrast, disruptions in life's major transitions can be destructive and ultimately can promote long-term criminal careers. Those who are already at risk because of socioeconomic problems or family dysfunction are the most susceptible to these awkward transitions. Delinquency, according to this view, cannot be attributed to a single cause nor does it represent a single underlying tendency.[20] A social or personal factor that may have an important influence at one stage of life (such as delinquent peers) may have little influence later on.[21] These negative life events can become cumulative: as people acquire more personal deficits, the chances of acquiring additional ones increase.[22] The cumulative impact of these disruptions sustains antisocial behaviors from childhood into adulthood.[23]

Life-course theories also recognize that as people mature, the factors that influence their behavior change.[24] As people make important life transitions—from child to adolescent, from adolescent to adult, from unwed to married—the nature of social interactions changes.[25] At first, family relations may be most influential; it comes as no shock to life-course theorists when research shows that antisocial behavior runs in families and that having criminal relatives is a significant predictor of future misbehaviors.[26] In later adolescence, school and peer relations predominate; in adulthood, vocational achievement and marital relations may be the most critical influences. Some antisocial children who are in trouble throughout their adolescence may manage to find stable work and maintain intact marriages as adults; these life events help them desist from crime. In contrast, less fortunate adolescents who develop arrest records and get involved with the wrong crowd may find themselves at risk for delinquency and later adult criminal careers.[27]

Life-Course Concepts

In the following sections, some of the more important concepts associated with this newly emerging developmental perspective of delinquency are discussed in some detail.

Problem Behavior Syndrome Delinquency may best be understood as one of many social problems faced by at-risk youth, a view called **problem behavior syndrome (PBS)**. Those who suffer from PBS are prone to more personal difficulties than the general population.[28] They find themselves with a range of personal dilemmas, from drug abuse to being accident prone, to requiring more health care and hospitalization, to becoming teenage parents, to having mental health problems.[29] PBS has also been linked to individual-level personality problems (such as impulsiveness, rebelliousness, and low ego), family problems (such as intrafamily conflict and parental mental disorder), substance abuse, poor health, and educational failure.[30]

According to this view, delinquency is one among a group of these interrelated social problems that seem to cluster together.[31] People who suffer from one of these conditions typically exhibit symptoms of the rest.[32] All varieties of delinquent behavior, including violence, theft, and drug offenses, may be part of a generalized PBS, indicating that all forms of antisocial behavior have similar developmental patterns.[33] Take these patterns, for example:

- Adolescents with a history of gang involvement are more likely to have been expelled from school, be a binge drinker, test positively for marijuana, have been in three or more fights in the past six months, and test positive for sexually transmitted diseases.[34]

problem behavior syndrome (PBS)
A cluster of antisocial behaviors that may include family dysfunction, substance abuse, smoking, precocious sexuality and early pregnancy, educational underachievement, suicide attempts, sensation seeking, and unemployment, as well as delinquency.

Brian Shumway/Redux

Social and personal problems are cumulative. Pam found herself homeless in Orange County, California. She was living with her boyfriend Rob in a tent in a small wooded area inside the I-405 off-ramp in Costa Mesa. She had followed Rob from Baltimore in an attempt to find his father. They got heavily into drugs, and Pam became pregnant. The search for Rob's father failed, along with their relationship. Rob was arrested on a warrant from the Midwest, and Pam moved in with a mother and daughter she had befriended, who lived at a motel. She continues to struggle with life, with a failed marriage and another pregnancy.

- Kids who gamble and take risks at an early age also take drugs and commit crimes.[35]
- People who suffer childhood trauma also commit crimes as adults, are sent to prison and are likely to attempt suicide.[36]

Teens who are chronic offenders are more likely to have greater than average mortality rates.[37] Delinquent and criminal conduct have been found to increase the chances of premature death due to a number of factors, including accidents, homicide, and suicide. The more serious, frequent, and long-lasting the delinquent career, the more likely the offender will suffer premature death.[38]

In sum, problem behavior syndrome portrays delinquency as a type of social problem rather than the product of other social problems.[39]

Offense Specialization/Generalization

Life-course theory recognizes that some offenders are specialists, limiting their delinquent activities to a cluster of acts such as theft offenses, including burglary and larceny, or violent offenses such as assault and rape.[40] However, most are generalists who engage in a garden variety of delinquent activity ranging from drug abuse, burglary, and/or rape, depending on the opportunity to commit crime and the likelihood of success.[41]

There is an ongoing debate over generalization/specialization. Some experts claim they have found evidence that more serious offenders soon begin to specialize in a narrower range of antisocial activities.[42] This means that there is only a single group of delinquents who start out generalizing but soon begin to specialize in a particular type of antisocial behavior.

It is also possible that the choice of crime is dictated by the offender's immediate circumstances. Some offenders may wish to specialize but are forced to engage in a wide variety of offenses because of limitations on the type of criminal acts that are their specialty.[43] For example, burglars may also commit robberies and auto theft when new burglar alarms and other security measures limit their access to homes.[44]

Age of Onset

Most life-course theories assume that the seeds of a delinquent career are planted early in life and that early onset of deviance strongly predicts later and more serious delinquency.[45] Children who will later become the most serious delinquents begin their deviant careers at a very early (preschool) age, and the earlier the onset of delinquency the more frequent, varied, and sustained the delinquent career.[46] If children are aggressive and antisocial during their public school years, they are much more likely to be troublesome and aggressive in adulthood.[47]

Early-onset delinquents seem to be more involved in aggressive acts ranging from cruelty to animals to peer-directed violence.[48] In contrast, late starters are more likely to be involved in nonviolent crimes such as theft.[49] Research by Daniel Nagin and Richard Tremblay shows that late-onset physical aggression is the exception, not the rule, and that the peak frequency of physical aggression occurs during early childhood and generally declines thereafter.[50]

What causes some kids to begin offending at an early age? Among the suspected root causes are poor parental discipline and monitoring, inadequate emotional support, distant peer relationships, and psychological issues and problems.[51] Research shows that poor parental discipline and monitoring seem to be keys to the early onset of delinquency and that these influences may follow kids into their adulthood, helping them shift from one form of deviant life style to another.[52]

Why is early onset so important? The earlier the onset of crime, the longer its duration.[53] The psychic scars of childhood are hard to erase.[54]

Starting early in delinquent behavior creates a downward spiral in a young person's life.[55] Thereafter, tension may begin to develop with parents and other family members, emotional bonds to conventional peers become weakened and frayed, and opportunities to pursue conventional activities, such as sports, dry up and wither away. Replacing them are closer involvement with more deviant peers and involvement in a delinquent way of life.[56] At an early age, children who are improperly socialized by unskilled parents are the most likely to rebel by wandering the streets with deviant peers.[57] In middle childhood, social rejection by conventional

Persistence vs. Desistance

One of the most important sources of data on this issue comes from the Cambridge Study in Delinquent Development, which has followed the offending careers of 411 London boys born in 1953. This cohort study, directed by David Farrington, is one of the most serious attempts to isolate the factors that predict lifelong continuity of delinquent behavior. The study uses self-report data as well as in-depth interviews and psychological testing. The boys were interviewed eight times over 24 years, beginning at age 8 and continuing to age 32.

Farrington has been able to identify factors that predict the discontinuity of delinquent offenses. He found that some kids who have backgrounds that put them at risk of becoming chronic delinquent offenders either remain nonoffenders or begin a delinquent career and then later desist. The factors that protected high-risk youths from beginning delinquent careers include having a somewhat shy personality, having few friends (at age 8), having nondeviant families, and being highly regarded by their mothers. Shy children with few friends avoided damaging relationships with other adolescents (members of a high-risk group) and were therefore able to avoid delinquency.

Personal abilities were found to counteract or neutralize delinquency promoting factors. Youths with high nonverbal intelligence, high verbal intelligence, and educational success while in high school were protected from the effects of poor childrearing practices. Similarly, at-risk youth who enjoyed higher than average family incomes were protected from the influence of deviant parents. In other words, the effects of living with a parent who was involved in crime was offset by the size of Mom and Dad's bank account.

Farrington suggests that life experiences shape the direction and flow of behavior choices. He finds that while there may be continuity in offending, the factors that predict delinquency at one point in the life course may not be the ones that predict delinquency at another. Although most adult delinquents begin their careers in childhood, life events may help some children forgo delinquency as they mature—for example, by finding a relatively good job. Conversely, unemployment seemed to be related to the escalation of theft offenses; violence and substance abuse were unaffected by unemployment. In a similar vein, getting married also helped diminish delinquent activity. However, choosing a spouse who was also involved in delinquent activity and had a delinquent record increased illegal activities and helped them to persist in crime.

Physical relocation also helped some offenders desist because they were forced to sever ties with co-offenders. For this reason, leaving the city for a rural or suburban area was linked to reduced delinquent activity.

CRITICAL THINKING

Although employment, marriage, and relocation helped potential offenders desist, not all desisters found success. At-risk youths who managed to avoid delinquent convictions were unlikely to avoid other social problems. Rather than becoming prosperous homeowners with flourishing careers, they tended to live in unkempt homes and have large debts and low-paying jobs. They were also more likely to remain single and live alone. Youths who experienced social isolation at age 8 were also found to experience it at age 32. Does this mean that efforts to help delinquents are doomed to fail? Even if they do not enter a delinquent way of life, are they fated to suffer other debilitating social problems?

SOURCES: David Farrington, Maria Ttofi, and Alex Piquero, "Risk, Promotive, and Protective Factors in Youth Offending: Results from the Cambridge Study in Delinquent Development," *Journal of Criminal Justice* 45:63–70 (2016); David Farrington, "Key Results from the First Forty Years of the Cambridge Study in Delinquent Development," in Terence Thornberry and Marvin Krohn, eds., *Taking Stock of Delinquency: An Overview of Findings from Contemporary Longitudinal Studies* (New York: Kluwer, 2002), pp. 137–185; David Farrington, "The Development of Offending and Anti-Social Behavior from Childhood: Key Findings from the Cambridge Study of Delinquent Development," *Journal of Child Psychology and Psychiatry* 36:2–36 (1995); David Farrington, *Understanding and Preventing Youth Crime* (London: Joseph Rowntree Foundation, 1996).

peers and academic failure sustain antisocial behavior; in later adolescence, commitment to a deviant peer group creates a training ground for crime. While others are able to age out of delinquency or desist, the youngest and most serious offenders may persist in their delinquent activity into late adolescence and even adulthood.

Persistence and Desistance

The best predictor of adult criminality is juvenile delinquency. Children who are repeatedly in trouble during early adolescence will generally still be antisocial in their middle teens; those who display conduct problems in youth are the ones most likely to commit crime as adults.[58] Delinquent activity is sustained because law violators and rule breakers seem to lack the social survival skills necessary to find work or to develop the interpersonal relationships they need to allow them to desist. As a result, antisocial behavior may be *contagious*: kids at risk for delinquency infect those around them, thereby creating an ever-widening circle of peers and acquaintances who support deviant behavior.[59]

If persistence is the norm, than why do some kids desist? Peggy Giordano and her associates found that desistance involves cognitive transformation.[60] Kids who desist must go through a constant learning process in order to discontinue their delinquent activity. They must begin to see the world differently and learn from experience in order to knife off from a delinquent way of life.

A classic study of delinquent persistence and desistence is reviewed in the Focus on Delinquency feature.

Theories of the Delinquent Life Course

A number of systematic theories have been formulated that account for onset, continuance, and desistance from crime. They typically interconnect *personal factors* such as personality and intelligence, *social factors* such as income and neighborhood, *socialization factors* such as marriage and military service, *cognitive factors* such as information processing and attention/perception, and *situational factors* such as delinquent opportunity, effective guardianship, and apprehension risk. In this sense they are **integrated theories** because they incorporate these social, personal, and developmental factors into complex explanations of human behavior. They do not focus on the relatively simple question—why do people commit crime?—but on more complex issues: Why do some offenders persist in delinquent careers while others desist from or alter their delinquent activity as they mature?[61] Why do some people continually escalate their delinquent involvement while others slow down and turn their lives around? Are all delinquents similar in their offending patterns, or are there different types of offenders and paths to offending? Life-course theorists want to know not only why people enter a delinquent way of life but why, once they do, they alter the trajectory of their delinquent involvement. In Exhibit 6.1, two of the more important life-course theories are briefly described, and in the next section, Sampson and Laub's age-graded theory is set out in detail.

integrated theories
Theories that incorporate social, personal, and developmental factors into complex explanations of human behavior.

---

exhibit 6.1

Principal Life-Course Theories

Social Development Model

Principal Theorists J. David Hawkins, Richard Catalano

Major Premise Community-level risk factors make some people susceptible to antisocial behaviors. Preexisting risk factors are either reinforced or neutralized by socialization. To control the risk of antisocial behavior, a child must maintain prosocial bonds. Over the life course, involvement in prosocial or antisocial behavior determines the quality of attachments. Commitment and attachment to conventional institutions, activities, and beliefs insulate youths from the criminogenic influences in their environment. The prosocial path inhibits deviance by strengthening bonds to prosocial others and activities. Without the proper level of bonding, adolescents can succumb to the influence of deviant others.

Interactional Theory

Principal Theorists Terence Thornberry and Marvin Krohn, Alan Lizotte, Margaret Farnworth

Major Premise The onset of crime can be traced to a deterioration of the social bond during adolescence, marked by weakened attachment to parents, commitment to school, and belief in conventional values. The cause of delinquency is bidirectional: Weak bonds lead kids to develop friendships with deviant peers and get involved in delinquency. Frequent delinquency involvement further weakens bonds and makes it difficult to reestablish conventional ones. Delinquency-promoting factors tend to reinforce one another and sustain a chronic criminal career. Kids who go through stressful life events such as a family financial crisis are more likely to later get involved in antisocial behaviors and vice versa. Delinquency is a developmental process that takes on different meaning and form as a person matures. During early adolescence, attachment to the family is critical; by mid-adolescence, the influence of the family is replaced by friends, school, and youth culture; by adulthood, a person's behavioral choices are shaped by his or her place in conventional society and his or her own nuclear family. Although delinquency is influenced by these social forces, it also influences these processes and associations. Therefore, delinquency and social processes are interactional.

Social Schematic Theory (SST)

Principal Theorists Ronald Simons and Callie Burt

Major Premise According to social schematic theory (SST), people develop schemas or cognitive shortcuts to organize and interpret information. In some instances schemas can exclude pertinent information and instead focus only on things that confirm preexisting beliefs and ideas. If a member of some group commits a notorious crime, we think "those people are all criminals," forgetting that the vast majority in any grouping are law-abiding citizens. Simons and Burt argue that seemingly unrelated family, peer, and community conditions—harsh parenting, racial discrimination, and community disadvantage—lead to crime because the lessons communicated by these events promote social schemas involving (a) a hostile view of people and relationships, (b) a preference for immediate rewards, and (c) a cynical view of conventional norms. When people encounter a stressful situation, these past experiences control responses. Negative life experiences allow some kids to legitimize their antisocial behavior: people abused me, so it's okay to abuse other people.

SOURCES: Terence Thornberry, "Toward an Interactional Theory of Delinquency," *Criminology* 25:863–891 (1987); Richard Catalano and J. David Hawkins, "The Social Development Model: A Theory of Antisocial Behavior," in J. David Hawkins, ed., *Delinquency and Crime: Current Theories* (New York: Cambridge University Press, 1996), pp. 149–197.] Ronald L. Simons and Callie Harbin Burt, "Learning to Be Bad: Adverse Social Conditions, Social Schemas, and Crime," *Criminology* 49:553–598 (2011); Ronald L. Simons, Callie H. Burt, Ashley B. Barr, Man-Kit Lei, and Eric A. Stewart, "Incorporating Routine Activities, Activity Spaces, and Situational Definitions into the Social Schematic Theory of Crime," *Criminology* 52:655–687 (2014).

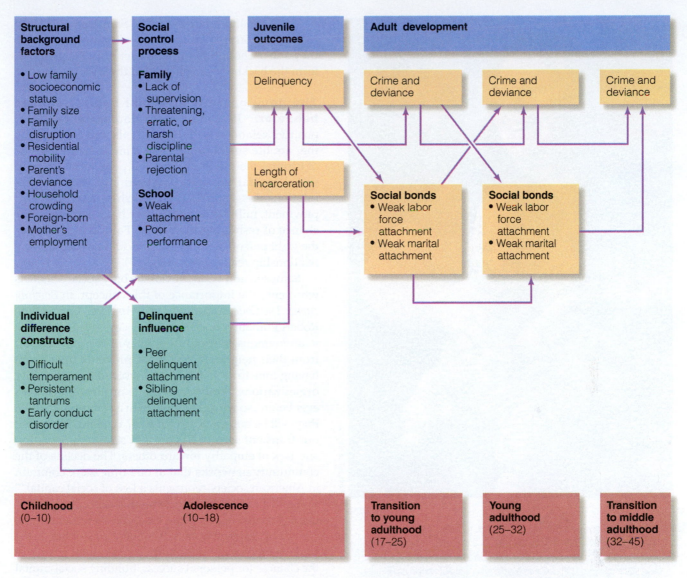

Structural background factors	Social control process	Juvenile outcomes	Adult development		

Structural background factors

- Low family socioeconomic status
- Family size
- Family disruption
- Residential mobility
- Parent's deviance
- Household crowding
- Foreign-born
- Mother's employment

Social control process

Family
- Lack of supervision
- Threatening, erratic, or harsh discipline
- Parental rejection

School
- Weak attachment
- Poor performance

Delinquency

Crime and deviance

Crime and deviance

Crime and deviance

Length of incarceration

Social bonds
- Weak labor force attachment
- Weak marital attachment

Social bonds
- Weak labor force attachment
- Weak marital attachment

Individual difference constructs

- Difficult temperament
- Persistent tantrums
- Early conduct disorder

Delinquent influence

- Peer delinquent attachment
- Sibling delinquent attachment

Childhood (0–10)	Adolescence (10–18)	Transition to young adulthood (17–25)	Young adulthood (25–32)	Transition to middle adulthood (32–45)

figure 6.1

Sampson and Laub's Age-Graded Theory

SOURCE: Adapted from Robert Sampson and John Laub, *Crime in the Making: Pathways and Turning Points Through Life* (Cambridge, MA: Harvard University Press, 1993), pp. 244–245.

Age-Graded Theory

In an influential 1993 work, *Crime in the Making*, Robert Sampson and John Laub formulated what they call the age-graded theory of informal social control (Figure 6.1). This theoretical model is considered the most widely accepted and researched life-course view.

In their pioneering research, Laub and Sampson reanalyzed the data originally collected by the Gluecks and found that while individual traits and childhood experiences are important in understanding the onset of delinquent and criminal behavior, they alone are not able to explain the continuity of crime from delinquency to adult criminality. [62]

How can the continuity of crime be explained? To answer this question, Laub and Sampson formulated what they call the age-graded theory of informal social control. Here they suggest that the strength of a person's bonds to social institutions (e.g., family, education, peers, jobs) will predict and explain first delinquent and then criminal involvement over the entire life course. Even children who have antisocial tendencies or propensities can stop or knife off from a delinquent way of life if they can form close ties with significant others and benefit from those ties. Over the life course, these social bonds will create a degree of informal social control that explains persistence in, or desistance from, crime.

According to age-graded theory, it is possible to knife off from a life of crime after a turning point in the life course. Erin Genther's heroin addiction brought her to dangerous lows, none more harrowing than the nights she spent sleeping in abandoned buildings on a street known as "Murder Drive." The turning point came with a positive pregnancy test. Genther's family and friends told her there was no way she could be a mother. But Genther's unborn baby provided powerful motivation to stay clean. She is shown here with her son, Owen.

Unlike many other theorists, Sampson and Laub focus more on why people stop offending than why they start. The following are a set of principles that form the backbone of age-graded theory.

The development of social capital shapes behavior.
People who develop social capital—positive relations with individuals and institutions that are life sustaining—have a much better chance of turning their lives around.[63] If people can develop social capital through personal and institutional relationships—marriage, friendship networks, employment, military service—they have a much better chance of reshaping their lives. Falling in love with the right person, getting married, and having a stable relationship really seems to help.

Sampson and Laub are not the only social scientists who sense the importance of this concept. In *Bowling Alone: The Collapse and Revival of American Community*, Robert Putnam argued that many Americans now live in anonymous communities where people are cut off from their neighbors and work prevents them from having time to socialize or get involved in community organizations. Americans move around more than ever before, so why get involved in a community when they will be gone in a year or two? Putnam claims that our transient society has created a sense of isolation and lack of empathy toward others. The decline of the community networks that at one time were common in American society represents a loss of social capital.[64]

Laub and Sampson seize on this concept by showing how social capital is an essential ingredient in the process of desisting from a delinquent way of life. In the same manner that building financial capital improves the chances for personal success, building social capital supports conventional behavior and inhibits deviant behavior. A successful marriage creates social capital when it improves a person's stature, creates feelings of self-worth, and encourages people to trust the individual. A successful career inhibits delinquency by creating a stake in conformity; why commit delinquency when you are doing well at school? The relationship is reciprocal. If kids are recognized by teachers for being a top student, they return the favor by doing the best job in class possible; if they are chosen as spouses, they blossom into devoted partners. In contrast, people who fail to accumulate social capital are more prone to commit delinquent acts.[65]

There are turning points in the life course that help people *knife off* from delinquency.
Problems in adolescence undermine life chances and reduce employability and social relations, increasing the likelihood of continued offending. In contrast, positive life experiences and relationships can be turning points that help people become reattached to society and allow them to knife off from a delinquent career path. Some turning points, such as gaining employment, create informal social control mechanisms that limit delinquent behavior opportunities. Adolescents who are at risk for delinquency can live conventional lives if they can achieve successful military careers or enter a successful marriage. Turning points may be serendipitous and unexpected: success may hinge on a lucky break—someone takes a chance on them, or they win the lottery.

social capital
Positive relations with individuals and institutions, as in a successful marriage or a successful career, that support conventional behavior and inhibit deviant behavior.

turning points
Positive life experiences, such as gaining employment, getting married, or joining the military, which create informal social control mechanisms that limit delinquent behavior opportunities.

Human agency is a key factor in a delinquent career. Human agency is the purposeful execution of choice and free will. Sampson and Laue recognize that desistance is a matter of choice: Former delinquents may choose to go straight and develop a new sense of self and an identity. They can choose to desist from delinquency and instead get real jobs, marry, have kids, and settle down.[66] While some kids persist in delinquency simply because they find it lucrative or perhaps because it serves as an outlet for their frustrations, others choose not to participate because as human beings they find other more conventional paths to be more beneficial and rewarding. Human choice cannot be left out of the equation.

Cumulative disadvantage takes a toll. Some kids not only fail to accumulate social capital but also experience social problems that weigh down their life chances. Kids who have one social deficit are more likely to suffer others. Nor do these social problems simply go away; they linger and vex people throughout their lives. Miscues accumulated in childhood continue to cause harm in adulthood. Take for instance the long-term effect of an early brush with the law. Teens who suffer arrest reduce their life chances for many years to come; a single arrest may make it hard to find a job when they become adults. [67]

People who acquire this **cumulative disadvantage** are more likely to commit delinquent acts and become crime victims.[68] When faced with personal crisis, they lack the social supports that can help them reject deviant solutions to their problems and instead maintain a conventional behavior trajectory. Joan Reid found that kids who were the victims of sex traffickers had limited social capital. Cumulative disadvantage led to them experience even more exploitation during young adulthood.[69]

Acquiring disadvantage begins at an early age. People who get in trouble early in life, especially those who are arrested and given an official criminal label, may find it difficult to shake the criminal way of life as they mature.[70] Racial disparity in the criminal justice system puts minority group members at a disadvantage, increasing the likelihood that they will become embedded in criminal careers.[71]

Not surprisingly, cumulative disadvantage appears to be intergenerational. Take for instance the effects of parental deviance. Having a parent behind bars reduces family income, gives kids the opportunity to gain antisocial peers, and subjects them to negative labels and stigma.[72] Children of incarcerated parents manifest mental health issues, are more prone to illegal drug use, have educational issues, earn less, and have problematic intimate relationships.[73] Not surprisingly, then, children whose fathers were incarcerated are more likely to suffer an arrest by age 25 than the offspring of conventional, law-abiding parents.[74] One exception to this pattern: girls who have been the victims of sexual abuse. Not surprisingly, female sex abuse victims seem to do better when their fathers are incarcerated.[75]

In sum, Sampson and Laub suggest that the motivation for delinquency and crime changes and varies over the life course as people gain and lose social capital. If they can gain capital and strengthen bonds, they can knife off from crime. For some, disadvantages accumulate and they lack the human agency to desist from a delinquent way of life.

Testing Age-Graded Theory Empirical research shows that, as predicted by Sampson and Laub, people change over the life course and the factors that predict antisocial behavior choices evolve over time.[76] Delinquency appears both to be (a) dynamic and (b) affected by levels of informal social control.

Evidence is also available that confirms Sampson and Laub's suspicion that delinquent career trajectories can be reversed if life conditions improve and individuals gain social capital.[77] Antisocial youths whose life circumstances improve have been shown to knife off from delinquent trajectories.[78] A number of research efforts have supported Sampson and Laub's position that accumulating social capital reduces delinquency rates.[79] Youths who accumulate social capital in childhood by doing well in school or having a tightly knit family are also the most

cumulative disadvantage
The tendency of prior social problems to produce future ones that accumulate and undermine success.

likely to maintain steady work as adults; employment may help insulate them from crime.[80] Delinquents who enter the military, serve overseas, and receive veterans' benefits enhance their occupational status (social capital) while reducing delinquent involvement.[81] Similarly, high-risk adults who are fortunate enough to obtain high-quality jobs are likely to reduce their delinquent activities even if they have a prior history of offending.[82]

Love, Marriage, and Delinquency   Age-graded theory places a lot of emphasis on the stability brought about by romantic relationships. Teens headed toward a life of crime can knife off that path if they meet the right mate, fall in love, and get married.[83] Falling in love and getting married reduces criminal activity; communities with high marriage rates have correspondingly low crime rates.[84] And it is marriage and not merely cohabitating that has a crime suppression effect.[85]

The marriage benefit is intergenerational: children who grow up in two-parent families are more likely to later have happy marriages themselves than children who are the product of divorced or never-married parents.

Of course, things don't always work out as planned and many relationships end in a breakup, a state of affairs that is associated with increases in delinquent behavior and drug use.[86] Even if their parents stay married, marital problems have a significant effect on kids. Parents who engage in intimate partner violence produce children who are similarly prone to physically and emotionally abusing their spouse.[87]

The question then remains: what prompts some youngsters to engage in loving relationships, while others are doomed to fall in and out of love without finding lasting happiness? Sociologist Rand Conger and his colleagues have discovered that the seeds of romantic success are planted early in childhood: kids who grow up with warm, nurturing parents are the ones most likely to have positive romantic relationships and later intact marriages. Well-nurtured kids develop into warm and supportive romantic partners who have relationships that are likely to endure.[88] It is the quality of parenting, not the observation of adult romantic relations, that socializes a young person to engage in behaviors likely to promote successful and lasting romantic unions as an adult.

What is it about love that prevents delinquency? Bill McCarthy and Teresa Casey examined the associations between love and delinquency among a sample of teens and found that adolescent romantic love can help fill the emotional void that occurs between the time when they break free of parental bonds and their acceptance of adult responsibilities.[89] But only meaningful relationships seem to work: love, not sex, is the key to success. Kids who get involved in sexual activity without the promise of love actually increase their involvement in delinquency and drug abuse; only true love reduces the likelihood of offending. Loveless sexual relations produce feelings of strain, which are correlated with antisocial activity. It is possible that kids who engage in sex without love or romance are willing to partake in other risky and/or self-indulgent behaviors. In contrast, romantic love discourages offending by strengthening the social bond.

Evaluating Age-Graded Theory   While a great deal of research supports age-graded theory, there are still questions left unanswered. To create their vision, Sampson and Laub used the Glueck data that were collected many years ago. Do the same social relations still exist, and do they have the same influence on delinquency? When the Gluecks collected their data, the effects of marriage and military service might have been much different. The divorce rate was much lower and marriages more stable. People had served in World War II and were part of the "Greatest Generation." Other influential elements of contemporary society had not yet been invented: computers, the Internet, TV, smart phones, and iPods. Though the Glueck boys and men drank alcohol, their drug use was minimal. Recent research by Ryan Schroeder and his colleagues find that drug use has unique effects and prevents people from desisting from crime. Drug use negates the influence of elements of social capital and is certainly an element of contemporary life that must be explored more fully.[90]

FOCUS ON DELINQUENCY

Shared Beginnings, Divergent Lives

Why are some delinquents destined to become persistent criminals as adults? John Laub and Robert Sampson conducted a follow-up to their reanalysis of Sheldon and Eleanor Glueck's study that matched 500 delinquent boys with 500 nondelinquents. The individuals in the original sample were reinterviewed by the Gluecks at ages 25 and 32. Now Sampson and Laub have located the survivors of the delinquent sample—the oldest 70 years old and the youngest 62—and reinterviewed this cohort.

Persistence and Desistance

Laub and Sampson find that delinquency and other forms of antisocial conduct in childhood are strongly related to adult delinquency and drug and alcohol abuse. Former delinquents also suffer consequences in other areas of social life, such as school, work, and family life. For example, delinquents are far less likely to finish high school than are nondelinquents and subsequently are more likely to be unemployed, receive welfare, and experience separation or divorce as adults.

In their research, Laub and Sampson address one of the key questions posed by life-course theories: is it possible for former delinquents to turn their lives around as adults? They find that most antisocial children do not remain antisocial as adults. For example, of men in the study cohort who survived to age 50, 24 percent had no arrests for delinquent acts of violence and property after age 17 (6 percent had no arrests for total delinquency); 48 percent had no arrests for predatory delinquency after age 25 (19 percent for total delinquency); 60 percent had no arrests for predatory delinquency after age 31 (33 percent for total delinquency); and 79 percent had no arrests for predatory delinquency after age 40 (57 percent for total delinquency). They conclude that desistance from delinquency is the norm and that most, if not all, serious delinquents desist from delinquency.

Why Do Delinquents Desist?

Laub and Sampson's earlier research indicated that building social capital through marriage and jobs was a key component of desistance from delinquency. However, in this new round of research, Laub and Sampson were able to find out more about long-term desistance by interviewing 52 men as they approached age 70. The follow-up showed a dramatic drop in criminal activity as the men aged. Between the ages of 17 and 24, 84 percent of the subjects had committed violent crimes; in their 30s and 40s, that number dropped to 14 percent; it fell to just 3 percent as the men reached their 60s and 70s. Property crimes and alcohol- and drug-related crimes showed significant decreases. They found that men who desisted from crime were rooted in structural routines and had strong social ties to family and community. Drawing on the men's own words, they found that one important element for "going straight" is the "knifing off" of individuals from their immediate environment and offering the men a new script for the future. Joining the military can provide this knifing-off effect, as does marriage or changing one's residence. One former delinquent (age 69) told them:

> I'd say the turning point was, number one, the Army. You get into an outfit, you had a sense of belonging, you made your friends. I think I became a pretty good judge of character. In the Army, you met some good ones, you met some foul balls. Then I met the wife. I'd say probably that would be the turning point. Got married, then naturally, kids come. So now you got to get a better job, you got to make more money. And that's how I got to the Navy Yard and tried to improve myself.

Former delinquents who "went straight" were able to put structure into their lives. Structure often led the men to disassociate from delinquent peers, reducing the opportunity to get into trouble. Getting married, for example, may limit the number of nights men can "hang with the guys." As one wife of a former delinquent said, "It is not how many beers you have, it's who you drink with." Even multiple offenders who did time in prison were able to desist with the help of a stabilizing marriage.

Former delinquents who can turn their lives around, who have acquired a degree of maturity by taking on family and work responsibilities, and who have forged new commitments are the ones most likely to make a fresh start and find new direction and meaning in life. It seems that men who desisted changed their identity as well, and this, in turn, affected their outlook and sense of maturity and responsibility. The ability to change did not reflect delinquency "specialty": violent offenders followed the same path as property offenders.

While many former delinquents desisted from delinquency, they still faced the risk of an early and untimely death. Thirteen percent of the delinquent as compared to only 6 percent of the nondelinquent subjects died unnatural deaths, such as violence, cirrhosis of the liver caused by alcoholism, poor self-care, suicide, and so on. By age 65, 29 percent of the delinquent and 21 percent of the nondelinquent subjects had died from natural causes. Frequent delinquent involvement in adolescence and alcohol abuse were the strongest predictors of an early and unnatural death. So while many troubled youths are able to reform, their early excesses may haunt them across their life span.

Policy Implications

Laub and Sampson find that youth problems—delinquency, substance abuse, violence, dropping out, teen pregnancy—often share common risk characteristics. Intervention strategies, therefore, should consider a broad array of antisocial, delinquent, and deviant behaviors and not limit the focus to just one subgroup or delinquency type. Because delinquency and other social problems are linked, early prevention efforts that reduce delinquency will probably also reduce alcohol abuse, drunk driving, drug abuse, sexual promiscuity, and family violence. The best way to achieve these goals is through four significant life-changing events: marriage, joining the military, getting a job, and changing one's environment or neighborhood. What appears to be important about these processes is that they all involve, to varying degrees, the following items: a knifing off of the past from the present; new situations that provide both supervision and monitoring as well as new opportunities of social support and growth; and new situations that provide the opportunity for transforming identity. Prevention of delinquency must be a policy at all times and at all stages of life.

CRITICAL THINKING

1. Do you believe that the factors that influenced the men in the original Glueck sample are still relevant for change—or example, a military career?
2. Would it be possible for men such as these to join the military today?
3. Do you believe that some sort of universal service program might be beneficial and help people turn their lives around?

SOURCES: John Laub and Robert Sampson, *Shared Beginnings, Divergent Lives: Delinquent Boys to Age 70* (Cambridge, MA: Harvard University Press, 2003); Laub and Sampson, "Understanding Desistance from Delinquency," in Michael Tonry, ed., *Delinquency and Justice: An Annual Review of Research*, vol. 28 (Chicago: University of Chicago Press, 2001), pp. 1–71; John Laub and George Vaillant, "Delinquency and Mortality: A 50-Year Follow-Up Study of 1,000 Delinquent and Nondelinquent Boys," *American Journal of Psychiatry* 157:96–102 (2000).

Another issue is the causal ordering assumed by Laub and Sampson: Are kids who desist from delinquency then able to find a suitable mate, get married, and find a good job? Or are people who find an appropriate mate and a good job then able to desist from law-violating behavior? Does desistance precede the accumulation of social capital or does the accumulation of social capital produce desistance? While Laub and Sampson believe the latter, there is also evidence that people who desist from crime and delinquency undergo a cognitive change; it is only after they quit a delinquent way of life that they are able to acquire mates, jobs, and other benefits that support their life change.[91] To test their theory further, Sampson and Laub have conducted a series of interviews with the survivors of the Glueck survey. Their findings are presented in the Focus on Delinquency feature "Shared Beginnings, Divergent Lives."

Propensity Theories

His friends described 17-year-old T. J. Lane as a very normal, unassuming teenage boy. So it was not surprising that many expressed shock after he was arrested for the February 27, 2012, shooting at Chardon High School in Chardon, Ohio, during which three students were killed and three others wounded, two seriously. What caused this seemingly normal boy to kill kids he hardly knew in a school he did not attend? Some said Lane had been teased at school, and afterwards put a wall around himself keeping him removed from other students. He attended the Lake Academy, described as a special school for kids "who need a different type of setting to succeed." Others claimed that Lane came from a troubled home that may have left him angry and withdrawn.

According to his records, T. J. Lane had a history of minor violence. He was arrested twice in December 2009, once for assaulting his uncle and once for hitting another boy in the face. While these seem like relatively minor scrapes, his father, Thomas M. Lane Jr., had a more serious criminal record. The elder Lane had been arrested on a wide range of offenses, including drug abuse and possession, violation of probation, public intoxication, and disorderly conduct. In 2002, he was incarcerated for one year for attempted murder. According to police reports, he physically and verbally assaulted a woman for nine hours while her three children were present.

Tried as an adult for the Chardon shooting, on March 19, 2013, T. J. Lane was sentenced to three life sentences in prison without parole. At his sentencing hearing, in a gesture that made headlines around the nation, he wore a white T-shirt with the word "Killer" handwritten across the front. He smiled and smirked during the hearing and loudly hurled profanities at the families of the victims who had gathered in the courtroom.[92]

Was T. J. Lane "born to kill"? Does he suffer from some trait or condition, that when switched on, produces a violent reaction? More than 25 years ago, in a groundbreaking paper, David Rowe, D. Wayne Osgood, and W. Alan Nicewander proposed the concept of latent traits to explain the flow of delinquency over the life cycle. Their model assumes that a number of people in the population have a personal attribute or characteristic that controls their inclination or propensity to commit crimes.[93] This disposition may be either present at birth or established early in life, and it then remains stable over the life course. Suspected latent traits include defective intelligence, damaged or impulsive personality, genetic abnormalities, the physical-chemical functioning of the brain, and environmental influences on brain function, such as drugs, chemicals, and injuries.[94]

Regardless of gender or environment, those who maintain one of these suspect traits may be at risk for delinquency and in danger of becoming career criminals; those who lack the traits have a much lower risk.[95] Thus, the propensity to commit delinquent and criminal acts is always there, a stable but unseen trait guiding behavior across the life course. The Youth Stories feature discusses the career of one persistent offender who may have had a propensity to commit violent acts.

youth STORIES

Craig Price

On September 4, 1989, in Warwick, Rhode Island, Joan Heaton, 39, and her two children, Jennifer, 10, and Melissa, 8, were found murdered, victims of an apparent burglary attempt gone awry. Suspicion swiftly fell on Craig Price, 15, a neighborhood kid with a long history of offenses, including breaking and entering, theft, peeping into houses, and using drugs. Craig was also known to have a violent temper, and police had been called to his house on more than one occasion to settle disputes. While investigating the case, they discovered quite a bit of similarity with the July 1987 death of Rebecca Spencer, who had been found in her living room, stabbed repeatedly with a packing knife.

Investigators obtained a warrant to search the Price home, where they found evidence incriminating Craig in the Heaton case. A trash bag full of incriminating evidence was also found in a shed behind the house. Placed under arrest, Craig gave a detailed account of the Heaton murders. He told police that he intended to burglarize the home, crawled in through a window, fell and broke a table. When Joan Heaton came downstairs to see what was going on and put on the kitchen light, Craig strangled her to death. Her screams woke the children, and when they attempted to call the police Craig restrained them, grabbed a knife, and began stabbing. When they fought back he bit them and smashed them over the head with a kitchen stool. The struggle was so intense that he accidentally stabbed himself in the hand. While telling his story, Craig also confessed to killing Rebecca Spencer under similar circumstances when he was just 13 years old.

Originally sentenced as a juvenile to serve a five-year term, Craig refused to submit to psychiatric examinations and therapy while in the juvenile institution. At a court hearing he was found in civil contempt and had a year added to his incarceration, to be served at the Adult Correctional Institution in Cranston, Rhode Island. He continued to have problems while in prison and had additional years added to his sentence, perhaps because authorities were simply afraid to have him released. In October 1998, seven more years were added to Craig's sentence for assaulting a correctional officer. In February 1999 and again in October 2001, Craig was sentenced to a total of four more years for again verbally and physically assaulting correctional officers. On July 29, 2009, he was involved in a prison fight with another inmate during which a correctional officer was stabbed in the finger. Consequently,

AP Images/Andrew Dickerman

Craig Price was transferred to another prison and his release date pushed up to 2020. He is now 42 years old.

CRITICAL THINKING

Can someone like Craig Price ever be truly rehabilitated? Would you advocate releasing someone who has killed multiple people if you knew he was going to move into your own neighborhood, even if correctional treatment specialists claim he has been rehabilitated?

SOURCES: Nancy Krause, "Denied: No Parole for Killer Craig Price," March 18, 2015, http://wpri.com/2015/03/16/denied-no-parole-for-killer-craig-price/ (accessed October 2016); Gregg McCrary and Katherine Ramsland, *The Unknown Darkness* (New York: William Morrow/Harper Collins, 2003).

State Dependence

Because latent traits are stable, people who are antisocial during adolescence are the most likely to persist in crime. The positive association between past and future criminality detected in the cohort studies of career criminals reflects the presence of this underlying stable criminal propensity. That is, if an impulsive personality contributes to delinquency in childhood, it should also cause the same

state dependence
The propensity to commit crime profoundly and permanently disrupts normal socialization over the life course.

people to offend as adults because personality traits remain stable over the life span. According to the concept of **state dependence**, kids who have the propensity to commit crime will find that this latent trait profoundly and permanently disrupts normal socialization. Disruptions in socialization thereafter increase the risk of prolonged antisocial behavior. In this view, early rule breaking increases the probability of future rule breaking because it weakens inhibitions to crime and strengthens criminal motivation. In other words, once kids get a taste of antisocial behavior, they like it and want to continue down a deviant path.[96]

Propensity and Opportunity

Although the propensity to commit delinquency is stable, the opportunity to commit delinquency fluctuates over time. People age out of crime. As they mature and develop, there are simply fewer opportunities to commit crimes and greater inducements to remain "straight." They may marry, have children, and obtain jobs. The former delinquents' newfound adult responsibilities leave them little time to hang with their friends, abuse substances, and get into scrapes with the law.

To understand this concept better, assume that intelligence as measured by IQ tests is a stable latent trait associated with crime. Intelligence remains stable and unchanging over the life course, but delinquency rates decline with age. How can latent trait theory explain this phenomenon? Teenagers have more opportunity to commit delinquency than adults, so at every level of intelligence, adolescent delinquency rates will be higher. As they mature, however, teens with both high and low IQs will commit less delinquency because their adult responsibilities provide them with fewer delinquent opportunities. They may get married and raise a family, get a job and buy a home. And as they age they lose strength and vigor, qualities necessary to commit crime. Though their IQ remains stable and their propensity to commit delinquency is unchanged, their living environment and biological condition have undergone radical change. Even if they wanted to engage in antisocial activities, the former delinquents may lack the opportunity and the energy to engage in illegal activities.

The most prominent propensity theory today is Gottfredson and Hirschi's **General Theory of Crime (GTC)**, which is discussed in detail next.

General Theory of Crime

General Theory of Crime (GTC)
A developmental theory that modifies social control theory by integrating concepts from biosocial, psychological, routine activities, and rational choice theories.

In their important work *A General Theory of Crime*, Michael Gottfredson and Travis Hirschi modified and redefined some of the principles articulated in Hirschi's original social control theory by adding elements of trait and rational choice theories and shifting the focus from social control to self-control, or the tendency to avoid acts whose long-term costs exceed their momentary advantages.[97]

According to Gottfredson and Hirschi, the propensity to commit antisocial acts is tied directly to a person's level of self-control. People with limited self-control tend to be impulsive; they are insensitive to other people's feelings, physical (rather than mental), risk takers, shortsighted, and nonverbal.[98] They have a here-and-now orientation and refuse to work for distant goals; they lack diligence, tenacity, and persistence. People lacking self-control tend to be adventuresome, active, physical, and self-centered. As they mature, they often have unstable marriages, jobs, and friendships.[99] They are less likely to feel shame if they engage in deviant acts and are more likely to find them pleasurable.[100] They are also more likely to engage in dangerous behaviors such as drinking, smoking, and reckless driving; all of these behaviors are associated with delinquency.[101]

Because those with low self-control enjoy risky, exciting, or thrilling behaviors with immediate gratification, they are more likely to enjoy delinquent acts, which require stealth, agility, speed, and power, than conventional acts, which demand long-term study and cognitive and verbal skills. As Gottfredson and Hirschi put it, they derive satisfaction from "money without work, sex without courtship, revenge without court delays."[102]

According to the General Theory of Crime, impulsive people who lack self-control are more likely to respond with violence to slight provocations. Here, James Austin Hancock, a teen charged in a school cafeteria shooting that took place on February 29, 2016, sits next to his attorney in Butler County Juvenile Court in Hamilton, Ohio. Hancock pleaded guilty to four counts of attempted murder and one count of inducing panic.

AP Images/Greg Lynch

Gottfredson and Hirschi suggest that delinquency is not the only outlet for people with an impulsive personality. Even if they do not engage in antisocial behaviors, impulsive people enjoy other risky behaviors such as smoking, drinking, gambling, and illicit sexuality.[103] Although these acts are not illegal, they provide immediate, short-term gratification. It is not surprising, considering their risky lifestyle, that impulsive people are more prone to be crime victims themselves than their less impulsive peers.[104]

Gottfredson and Hirschi claim that the principles of **self-control theory** can explain all varieties of delinquent misbehavior from teenage murder and suicide to texting while driving.[105] That is, such widely disparate crimes as burglary, robbery, embezzlement, drug dealing, murder, rape, and insider trading all stem from a deficiency of self-control. Likewise, gender, racial, and ecological differences in delinquency rates can be explained by discrepancies in self-control. Unlike other theoretical models that explain only narrow segments of delinquent behavior (such as theories of teenage gang formation), Gottfredson and Hirschi argue that self-control applies equally to all crimes, ranging from murder to corporate theft.

What Causes Low Self-Control/Impulsivity?

Gottfredson and Hirschi trace the root cause of poor self-control to inadequate childrearing practices that begin soon after birth. Parents who refuse or are unable to monitor a child's behavior, to recognize deviant behavior when it occurs, and to punish that behavior will produce children who lack self-control. Children who are not attached to their parents, who are poorly supervised, and whose parents are delinquent or deviant themselves are the most likely to develop poor self-control.

The low self-control children model may be intergenerational. Parents who themselves manifest low self-control are most likely to use damaging and inappropriate supervision and punishment mechanisms, such as corporal punishment; inappropriate discipline modes have been linked to lack of self-control in adolescence. These impulsive kids grow up to become poor parents, who use improper discipline, and produce another generation of impulsive kids.[106] Kids who have low self-control may strain parental attachments and the ability of parents to control children.

While Gottfredson and Hirschi believe that parenting and not heredity shapes self-control, some recent research efforts do show that the impulsive personality

self-control theory
The theory of delinquency that holds that antisocial behavior is caused by a lack of self-control stemming from an impulsive personality.

may have physical or social roots, or perhaps both. Children who suffer anoxia (oxygen starvation) during the birthing process are most likely to lack self-control later in life, suggesting that impulsivity may have a biological basis.[107] When Kevin Beaver and his associates examined impulsive personality and self-control in twin pairs they discovered evidence that these traits may be inherited rather than developed. That might explain the stability of these latent traits over the life course.[108]

Variations in Delinquency   If individual differences are stable over the life course, why do delinquency rates vary? Why do people commit less delinquency as they age? Why are some regions or groups more delinquency prone than others? Does that mean there are differences in self-control between groups? If male delinquency rates are higher than female rates, does that mean men are more impulsive and lacking in self-control? How does the GTC address these issues?

Gottfredson and Hirschi remind us that delinquent propensity and delinquent acts are separate concepts (Figure 6.2). On one hand, delinquent acts, such as robberies or burglaries, are illegal events or deeds that offenders engage in when they perceive them to be advantageous. Burglaries are typically committed by young males looking for cash, liquor, and entertainment; delinquency provides "easy, short-term gratification."[109] Delinquency is rational and predictable; kids engage in delinquency when it promises rewards with minimal threat of pain; the threat of punishment can deter crime. If targets are well guarded, delinquency rates diminish. Only the truly irrational offender would dare to strike under those circumstances.

On the other hand, delinquent offenders may be predisposed to commit crimes, but they are not robots who commit antisocial acts without restraint; their days are also filled with conventional behaviors, such as going to school, parties, concerts, and church. But given the same set of delinquent opportunities, such as having a lot of free time for mischief and living in a neighborhood with unguarded homes containing valuable merchandise, crime-prone people have a much higher probability of violating the law than do nondelinquents. The propensity to commit crimes remains stable throughout a person's life. Change in the frequency of delinquent activity is purely a function of change in delinquent opportunity.

If we accept this provision of the GTC, then both delinquent propensity and delinquent opportunity must be considered to explain delinquent participation. So if males and females are equally impulsive but their delinquency rates vary, the explanation is that males have more opportunity to commit crime. Young teenage girls may be more closely monitored by their parents and therefore lack the freedom to offend. Girls are also socialized to have more self-control than boys: although females get angry as often as males, many have been taught to blame themselves for such feelings. Females are socialized to fear that anger will harm relationships; males are encouraged to react with "moral outrage," blaming others for their discomfort.[110]

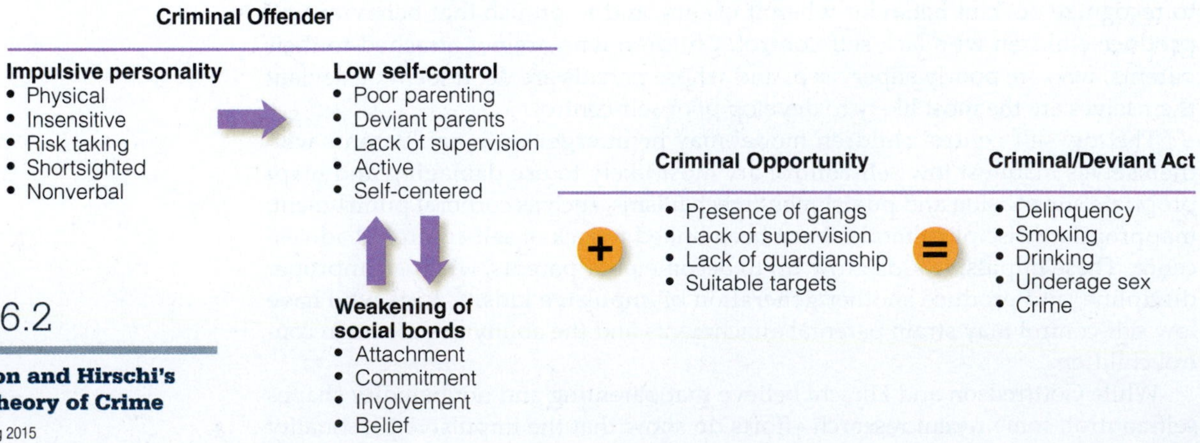

Criminal Offender

Impulsive personality
- Physical
- Insensitive
- Risk taking
- Shortsighted
- Nonverbal

Low self-control
- Poor parenting
- Deviant parents
- Lack of supervision
- Active
- Self-centered

Weakening of social bonds
- Attachment
- Commitment
- Involvement
- Belief

Criminal Opportunity

- Presence of gangs
- Lack of supervision
- Lack of guardianship
- Suitable targets

Criminal/Deviant Act
- Delinquency
- Smoking
- Drinking
- Underage sex
- Crime

figure 6.2

Gottfredson and Hirschi's General Theory of Crime

© Cengage Learning 2015

Opportunity can also be used to explain ecological variation in the delinquency rate. How does the GTC explain the fact that delinquency rates are higher in the summer than the winter? The number of impulsive people lacking in self-control is no higher in August than it is in December. Gottfredson and Hirschi would argue that seasonal differences are explained by opportunity: during the summer, kids are out of school and have more opportunity to commit crime. Similarly, if delinquency rates are higher in Los Angeles than Minneapolis, either there are more delinquent opportunities in the western city or the fast-paced life of Los Angeles attracts more impulsive people than the laid-back Midwest.

For an analysis of the **General Theory of Crime**, go to Bradley Wright's web page: http://www.everydaysociologyblog.com/2008/11/gottfredson-and.html.

Support for the GTC Since the publication of *A General Theory of Crime*, numerous researchers have attempted to test the validity of Gottfredson and Hirschi's theoretical views, and a great many research efforts using a variety of methodologies and subject groups have found empirical support for the basic assumptions of the GTC.[111] Gottfredson and Hirschi's view has become a cornerstone of contemporary delinquency theory.

Among the many principles of the General Theory that have been confirmed is linkage of low self-control with poor parenting. Regardless of community structure, kids with ineffective parents are more likely to exhibit low self-control than those who experience parental efficacy.[112]

There has also been research linking low self-control, impulsive personality, and delinquency.[113] As a group, researchers suggest that the lower a person's self-control, the more likely he is to engage in antisocial behaviors.[114] The lack of self-control may begin early in adolescence and be manifested in aggressive behavior that turns kids into school yard bullies. Aggressive bullies are rejected by other kids, marginalized, and prone to school failure, a path that winds up in a delinquent way of life.[115]

Recently, Matt DeLisi and Michael Vaughn examined the association between low self-control and criminal careers.[116] They found that compared to non–career offenders, career criminals had significantly lower levels of self-control and that the lower the level of self-control, the greater the chance of becoming a career criminal. Importantly, DeLisi and Vaughn discovered that low self-control was by far the strongest predictor of career criminality, exceeding the impact of age, race, ethnicity, gender, and other important social factors.

Not only has an association between impulsivity and crime been found, but levels of self-control can also help us understand the association between crime and other factors, including values, attitudes, and beliefs. For example, the fact that religious people commit less crime may be explained by the fact that people who attend services and believe in religion are less impulsive and have more self-control than nonbelievers.[117]

Analyzing the General Theory of Crime By integrating the concepts of opportunity and delinquency, Gottfredson and Hirschi help explain why some people who lack self-control can escape delinquency, and, conversely, why some people who have self-control might not escape delinquency. People who are at risk because they have impulsive personalities may forgo delinquent careers because there are no delinquent opportunities that satisfy their impulsive needs; instead, they may find other outlets for their impulsive personalities. In contrast, if the opportunity is strong enough, even people with relatively strong self-control may be tempted to violate the law; the incentives to commit delinquency may overwhelm self-control.

Integrating delinquent propensity and delinquent opportunity can explain why some children enter into chronic offending while others living in similar environments are able to resist delinquent activity. It can also help us understand why the honor student with a spotless record gets caught up in academic cheating. Even an honor roll student may find self-control inadequate if the potential for higher grades is present. The driven student, accustomed to both academic and social success, may find that the fear of failure can overwhelm self-control. Even the best, most respected student may be tempted to circumvent the rules to improve his or her grade point average.[118]

Although the General Theory seems persuasive, several questions and criticisms remain unanswered. Among the most important are the following:

- *The General Theory is tautological.* Some critics argue that the theory is tautological (involves circular reasoning): How do we know when people are impulsive? When they commit crimes! Are all delinquents impulsive? Of course, or else they would not have broken the law![119]

- *One of many personality traits correlated with crime.* Lack of self-control may in fact be associated with crime, but so are many other personality traits.[120] Personality traits such as low self-direction (the tendency not to act in one's long-term benefit) may be better predictors of delinquency than impulsivity.[121]

- *Ignores the environment.* Critics complain that Gottfredson and Hirschi discount the influence of environmental factors, despite evidence that the environment influences personality.[122] Environments may interact with personality to shape behaviors.[123] Take what criminologist Gregory Zimmerman found when he examined how environment and personality interact. In high-crime neighborhoods, impulsive adolescents were no more delinquent than their nonimpulsive peers. In contrast, in low-crime, safer areas, impulsive kids were much more likely to commit delinquent acts than their less reckless peers. How can this difference be explained? In disadvantaged neighborhoods, nearly everyone commits crime, so that having self-control means relatively little. In contrast, in low-crime areas, most kids conform and it's only the most impulsive who risk engaging in delinquent acts. In these higher-income neighborhoods, only those totally lacking in self-control are foolish enough to commit crime.[124] So neighborhood character may influence criminal decision making, an observation that contradicts the GTC.

- *Does not explain racial and gender differences.* Although distinct gender differences in the delinquency rate exist, there is little evidence that males are more impulsive than females (although females and males differ in many other personality traits).[125] Some research efforts have found gender differences in the association between self-control and crime; the theory predicts no such difference should occur.[126] Impulsivity alone may not be able to explain why males and females persist or desist.[127] Gottfredson and Hirschi explain racial differences in the delinquency rate as a failure of childrearing practices in the African American community.[128] In so doing, they overlook issues of institutional racism, poverty, and relative deprivation, which have been shown to have a significant impact on delinquency rate differentials.

- *Does not account for peer influence.* A number of research efforts show that the quality of peer relations either enhances or controls delinquent behavior and that these influences vary over time.[129] As children mature, peer influence continues to grow. Research shows that kids who lack self-control also have trouble maintaining relationships with law-abiding peers. They may choose (or be forced) to seek friends who are similarly limited in their ability to maintain self-control. Similarly, as they mature they may seek romantic relationships with law-violating boyfriends or girlfriends. These entanglements enhance the likelihood that they will get further involved in delinquency (girls seem more deeply influenced by their delinquent boyfriends than boys by their delinquent girlfriends).[130] This finding contradicts the GTC, which suggests the influence of friends is minimal and that a relationship established later in life (for example, making friends) should not influence delinquent propensity.

- *Self-control may not be stable.* The GTC assumes that self-control does not change over time and neither does delinquent propensity. However, there is evidence that changing life circumstances, such as starting and leaving school, abusing substances and then "getting straight," and starting or ending personal relationships, have a significant influence on personality.[131]

It is not surprising, therefore, that research efforts show that the stability in self-control predicted by Gottfredson and Hirschi may be an illusion. Some research efforts find stability in social control over the life course, while others find significant change and fluctuations.[132] As people mature, the focus of their lives likewise changes and they may be better able to control their impulsive behavior.[133] As Callie Burt and her associates recently found, adolescence is a period of dramatic biological, behavioral, and social changes; a young person's physical and neurological makeup is undergoing remodeling and restructuring. Environmental influences operate in concert with neurobiological changes to create a period of heightened change. During this period levels of impulsivity also change, a result that is not predicted by the GTC.[134]

■ *Many delinquents are rational and calculating, not impulsive.* Gottfredson and Hirschi assume that delinquents are impatient or "present-oriented." They choose to commit delinquency because the rewards can be enjoyed immediately while the costs or punishments come later or not at all. However, Steven Levitt and Sudhir Alladi Venkatesh found that many young gang boys are willing to wait years to "rise through the ranks" before earning high wages. Their stay in the gang is fueled by the promises of future compensation, a fact that contradicts the GTC. Levitt and Venkatesh conclude that the economic aspects of the decision to join the gang can be viewed as a tournament in which participants vie for large awards that only a small fraction will eventually obtain. Members of the gang accept low wages in the present in the hope that they will advance in the gang and earn well above market wages in the future.[135] Moreover, gang members seem acutely aware that they are making an investment in the future by forgoing present gains. As one noted:

> You think I want a be selling drugs on the street my whole life? No way, but I know these n— [above me] are making more money . . . So you know, I figure I got a chance to move up. But if not, s—, I get me a job doin' something else.[136]

Legal economist Yair Listokin notes that the expectation of future gains contradicts Gottfredson and Hirschi's vision of an impulsive delinquent who lives for today without worrying about tomorrow. In contrast, the young foot soldiers of the gang are sacrificing present wages for the hope of future gains. Listokin finds that the gang uses the same compensation structure as the one commonly used in law firms, where newly hired attorneys work long hours at low pay with the hope of becoming partners. The "foot soldiers," he concludes, are filling the role of law associates, a group not known for their impulsiveness.[137]

■ *Self-control may waver and change.* Gottfredson and Hirschi assume that impulsivity is a singular construct—one is either impulsive or not. However, (a) there may be more than one kind of impulsive personality, and (b) it may waver and change over time. [138]Some people may be impulsive because they are sensation seekers constantly looking for novel experiences, while others lack deliberation and rarely think through problems. Some may give up easily, while others act without thinking. Some people may have the ability to persist in self-control, while others "get tired" and eventually succumb to their impulses. Think of it this way: A dieter ogles the cheesecake in the fridge all day but has the self-control not to take a slice. Then he wakes hungry in the middle of the night and makes his way into the kitchen, thinking, "A little piece of cheesecake won't hurt me." His self-control slips, and his diet goes out the window. There is also evidence that self-control can be influenced by treatment programs aimed at doing just that. A recent meta-analysis by Alex Piquero, Wesley Jennings, and David Farrington found that a program aimed at improving a child/adolescent's self-control may actually work and also help reduce delinquency, regardless of the technique used or source (e.g., parents or teachers).[139]

Although questions like these remain, the strength of GTC lies in its simplicity and breadth. It attempts to explain all forms of crime and deviance, from lower-class gang delinquency to sexual harassment in the business community, with a single factor—low self-control. In fact, because they believe all forms of antisocial and deviant behavior may originate at the same source, Hirschi and Gottfredson have questioned the utility of the juvenile justice system and the practice of giving more lenient treatment to young delinquent offenders. Why separate youthful and adult offenders legally when the source of their antisocial behaviors (for example, impulsivity) is essentially the same?[140] Since its publication, the GTC remains one of the most important and heavily researched views of the onset and continuity of a delinquent career.

Trajectory Theory

Trajectory theory is a third developmental approach that combines elements of propensity and life-course theory. The basic premise is that there is more than one path to crime and more than one class of offender; there are different *trajectories* in an offending career as an offender progresses from delinquent to criminal. Sampson and Laub acknowledged that different delinquent-to-criminal trajectories exist when they recently (2016) stated:

> … we found that although child prognoses are relatively accurate in terms of predicting criminal behavior among individuals through their 20s, they do not yield distinct groupings that are prospectively valid over the entire life course—regardless of whether offenders are identified prospectively or ex post … there is variability among individual age–crime curves…. Given the heterogeneity in adult criminal trajectories that could not be predicted from childhood, we further argue that institutions play an important role in understanding crime over the life course.[141]

All kids are different, and one model cannot hope to describe every person's journey through life. Some are social and have a large peer group, while others are loners who make decisions on their own.[142] Factors that predict offending in males may have little influence on females.[143] While both sexes maintain different offending trajectories (for example, chronic offender, desister, nonstarter), males are more likely to become persistent offenders and have higher rates of offending within each trajectory.[144] There are also different offending trajectories: delinquents who commit violent crimes may be different from nonviolent property and drug offenders and maintain a unique set of personality traits and problem behaviors.[145] Some kids who begin committing violent crime at an early age later become adult violent offenders, but many do not, and some people begin their violent careers in adulthood, having escaped and/or avoided being violent as juveniles.[146]

Because propensity theories disregard social influences during the life span, and life-course theories maintain that social events seem to affect all people equally, they both miss the fact that there are different classes and types of juvenile offenders. Adolescents offend at a different pace, commit different kinds of crimes, and are influenced by different external forces.[147] This view has become quite popular, and a recent meta-analysis by Wesley Jennings and his associates uncovered more than 100 recent research studies aimed at identifying different delinquent trajectories.[148]

Late Bloomers and Nonstarters

Not all persistent offenders begin at an early age. Some are precocious, beginning their delinquent careers early and persisting into adulthood.[149] Others stay out of trouble in adolescence and do not violate the law until their teenage years. Some offenders may peak at an early age and quickly desist, whereas others persist into adulthood. Some are high-rate offenders, whereas others offend at relatively low rates.[150] In sum, there are different paths to crime.

Take for instance the concept of *early onset*. Most developmental theorists maintain that persistent offenders are early starters, beginning their delinquent careers in their adolescence and persisting into adulthood. In contrast, trajectory theories recognize that some kids are *late bloomers* who stay out of trouble until their adulthood.[151] Researchers Sarah Bacon, Raymond Paternoster, and Robert Brame found that "late bloomers" are actually the people most likely to get involved in serious offending![152] Because the late bloomer combines psychopathology with risk-taking behavior and poor social skills, his behavior becomes increasingly violent over time.[153] So while these late starters may be late to the party, they eventually "catch up" in their late teens.

There is also a group of abstainers, or nonstarters. Despite the fact that self-report studies tell us most kids engage in a variety of antisocial activities and that teen drug use, theft, and general mischief are normative, there are those kids who never break the law; their conventional behavior makes them deviant in the teenage world where offending is the norm! Why do these nonstarters refrain from delinquency of any sort? This matter is still unsettled. According to social psychologist Terrie Moffitt, abstainers are social introverts as teens, whose unpopularity shields them from group pressure to commit delinquent acts.[154] Other experts, such as Xiaojin Chen and Michele Adam, disagree, suggesting that conformity may be related to close parental monitoring and involvement with pro-social peer groups more than it is to being unpopular.[155] Kids who do not learn delinquent behaviors from role models are the ones most likely to be abstainers.[156] Still another explanation may be biological: abstainers maintain a genetic code that insulates them from criminality-producing factors in the environment.[157] Not surprisingly, abstainers are more likely than other youth to become successful, well-adjusted adults.[158]

Pathways to Delinquency

Trajectory theorists recognize that career delinquents may travel more than a single road. Some may specialize in violence and extortion; others are solely involved in theft and fraud; a majority engage in a variety of delinquent acts.[159] Each type of specialist may be unique: kids who commit violent crimes may be different from nonviolent property and drug offenders.[160] But even among these violent offenders, there may be distinct career paths. Some start out as violent kids whose violent behavior declines with age and who eventually desist. Another group are *escalators* whose severity of violence increases over time. Escalators are more likely to live in racially mixed communities, experience racism, and have less parental involvement than people who avoid or decrease their violent behaviors.[161]

While most experts link early onset to long-term delinquent careers, another subset of young offenders that has been identified are those who start late but still persist in delinquency: late-onset escalators.[162] These youths began their violent careers relatively late in their adolescence after suffering a variety of psychological and social disturbances earlier in childhood, such as stress and anxiety.[163]

Some of the most important research on delinquent paths or trajectories has been conducted by Rolf Loeber and his associates. Using data from a longitudinal study of Pittsburgh youth, Loeber has identified three distinct paths to a delinquent career (Figure 6.3).[164]

- The **authority conflict pathway** begins at an early age with stubborn behavior. This leads to defiance (doing things one's own way, disobedience) and then to authority avoidance (staying out late, truancy, running away).

- The **covert pathway** begins with minor, underhanded behavior (lying, shoplifting) that leads to property damage (setting nuisance fires, damaging

authority conflict pathway
Pathway to delinquent deviance that begins at an early age with stubborn behavior and leads to defiance and then to authority avoidance.

covert pathway
Pathway to a delinquent career that begins with minor underhanded behavior, leads to property damage, and eventually escalates to more serious forms of theft and fraud.

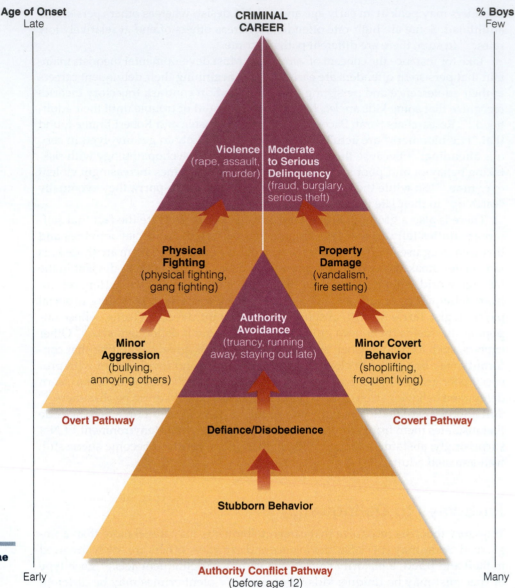

Age of Onset
Late

CRIMINAL
CAREER

% Boys
Few

Violence (rape, assault, murder)

Moderate to Serious Delinquency (fraud, burglary, serious theft)

Physical Fighting (physical fighting, gang fighting)

Property Damage (vandalism, fire setting)

Minor Aggression (bullying, annoying others)

Authority Avoidance (truancy, running away, staying out late)

Minor Covert Behavior (shoplifting, frequent lying)

Overt Pathway

Covert Pathway

Defiance/Disobedience

Stubborn Behavior

Early

Authority Conflict Pathway (before age 12)

Many

figure 6.3

Loeber's Pathways to Crime

SOURCE: Adapted from "Serious and Violent Juvenile Offenders," *Juvenile Justice Bulletin*, May 1998.

property). This behavior eventually escalates to more serious forms of delinquency, ranging from joyriding, pocket picking, larceny, and fencing to passing bad checks, using stolen credit cards, stealing cars, dealing drugs, and breaking and entering.

■ The **overt pathway** escalates to aggressive acts beginning with minor aggression (annoying others, bullying), leading to physical (and gang) fighting, and then to violence (attacking someone, forced theft).

The Loeber research indicates that each of these paths may lead to a sustained deviant career. Some people enter two and even three paths simultaneously: they are stubborn, lie to teachers and parents, are bullies, and commit petty thefts. These adolescents are the most likely to become persistent offenders as they mature.

overt pathway
Pathway to a delinquent career that begins with minor aggression, leads to physical fighting, and eventually escalates to violent delinquency.

Adolescent-Limited and Life-Course Persistent Offenders

adolescent-limited offenders
Kids who get into minor scrapes as youths but whose misbehavior ends when they enter adulthood.

According to psychologist Terrie Moffitt, most young offenders follow one of two paths. **Adolescent-limited offenders** may be considered "typical teenagers" who get into minor scrapes and engage in what might be considered rebellious teenage behavior with their friends.[165] As they reach their midteens, adolescent-limited delinquents begin to mimic the antisocial behavior of more troubled teens, only to reduce the frequency of their offending as they mature to around age 18.[166]

The second path is the one taken by a small group of **life-course persisters** who begin their offending career at a very early age and continue to offend well into adulthood.[167] Moffitt finds that life-course persisters combine family dysfunction with severe neurological problems that predispose them to antisocial behavior patterns. These afflictions can be the result of maternal drug abuse, poor nutrition, or exposure to toxic agents such as lead. There may also be a genetic basis to life-course persistence; some recent research links it to neurological deficiencies.[168] Life-course persisters may be aggressive as part of a strategy to increase their reproductive options, a view that jibes with sociobiology.[169]

It is not surprising, then, that life-course persisters display social and personal dysfunctions, including lower than average verbal ability, reasoning skills, learning ability, and school achievement, nor that they offend more frequently and engage in a greater variety of antisocial acts and manifest significantly more mental health problems, including psychiatric pathologies, than adolescent-limited offenders.[170] Persisters are more likely to manifest traits such as low verbal ability and hyperactivity; they display a negative or impulsive personality and seem particularly impaired on spatial and memory functions.[171] Individual traits rather than environment seem to have the greatest influence on life-course persistence.[172]

life-course persisters
Delinquents who begin their offending career at a very early age and continue to offend well into adulthood.

To find out what Terrie Moffitt and Avshalom Caspi are doing these days, go to their website: http://www .moffittcaspi.com/.

Evaluating Developmental Theories

Although the differences among the views presented in this chapter may seem irreconcilable, they in fact share some common ground. They indicate that a delinquent career must be understood as a passage along which people travel, that it has a beginning and an end, and that events and life circumstances influence the journey. The factors that affect a delinquent career may include structural factors, such as income and status; socialization factors, such as family and peer relations; biological factors, such as size and strength; psychological factors, including intelligence and personality; and opportunity factors, such as free time, inadequate police protection, and a supply of easily stolen merchandise.

Life-course theories emphasize the influence of changing interpersonal and structural factors (i.e., people change along with the world they live in). Propensity theories place more emphasis on the fact that behavior is linked less to personal change and more to changes in the surrounding world. Trajectory theories combine both perspectives and suggest that while some people are guided by a master trait, there may be more than one trait that influences delinquent behavior and more than one path that delinquents may take.

These perspectives differ in their view of human development. Do people constantly change, as life-course theories suggest, or are they stable, constant, and changeless, as the propensity view indicates? Are the factors that produce delinquency different for a variety of subsets of delinquent offenders, as the trajectory view suggests? Or does a master trait—for example, self-control—steer the course of human behavior and is it present in all offenders?

It is also possible that these positions are not mutually exclusive, and each may make a notable contribution to understanding the onset and continuity of a delinquent career. While more research is necessary, there is some indication that there may be an interaction between delinquent propensity and life-course changes. Life-impacting events—marriage, military service, jobs, and so on—may have greater or lesser impact on people depending on their level of self-control and impulsivity.[173] Bradley Entner Wright and his associates found evidence that low self-control in childhood predicts disrupted social bonds and delinquent offending later in life, a finding that supports latent trait theory.[174] They also found that maintaining positive social bonds helps reduce delinquency and that maintaining prosocial bonds could even counteract the effect of low self-control. Latent traits are an important influence on crime, but their findings indicate that social relationships that form later in life appear to influence delinquent behavior "above and beyond" individuals' preexisting characteristics.[175] This finding may reflect the fact that there are two classes of delinquents: a less serious group who are influenced by life events, and a more chronic group whose latent traits insulate them from any positive prosocial relationships, a finding that supports trajectory theory.[176]

Public Policy Implications of Developmental Theory

Developmental theory has served as the basis for a number of delinquency control and prevention efforts. These typically feature multisystemic treatment efforts designed to provide at-risk kids with personal, social, educational, and family services.[177]

Treatment programs based on developmental models now employ multidimensional strategies and target children in preschool through the early elementary grades in order to alter the direction of their life course. Many of the most successful programs are aimed at strengthening children's social-emotional competence and positive coping skills and suppressing the development of antisocial, aggressive behavior.[178] Research evaluations indicate that the most

On May 10, 2016, Sharon Bibbs, center, helps students, including Terrance Webster, Jr., with their math homework at the Kingman Boys and Girls Club in Washington DC's Logan Circle neighborhood. Gibbs has worked at the club for 27 years and now teaches the 4th grade after school program and helps with administrative duties. The club has been in Logan Circle for over 40 years. Developmental theorists would argue that programs such as the Boys and Girls Clubs may help kids knife off from a life of crime and enter more productive conventional trajectories. They reduce cumulative disadvantage, increase social capital and can be a positive turning point in the life course.

The Washington Post/Getty Images

promising multicomponent delinquency and substance abuse prevention programs for youths, especially those at high risk, are aimed at improving their developmental skills. They may include a school component, an after-school component, and a parent-involvement component. All of these components have the common goal of increasing protective factors and decreasing risk factors in the areas of the family, the community, the school, and the individual.[179] The Boys and Girls Clubs and School Collaborations' Substance Abuse Prevention Program includes a school component called SMART (Skills Mastery and Resistance Training), an after-school component called SMART Kids, and a parent-involvement component called SMART Parents. Each component is designed to reduce specific risk factors in the children's school, family, community, and personal environments.[180]

Another successful program, Fast Track, is designed to prevent serious antisocial behavior and related adolescent problems in high-risk children entering first grade. The intervention is guided by a developmental approach that suggests that antisocial behavior is the product of the interaction of multiple social and psychological influences:

- Residence in low-income, high-delinquency communities places stressors and influences on children and families that increase their risk levels. In these areas, families characterized by marital conflict and instability make consistent and effective parenting difficult to achieve, particularly with children who are impulsive and of difficult temperament.

- Children of high-risk families usually enter the education process poorly prepared for its social, emotional, and cognitive demands. Their parents often are unprepared to relate effectively with school staff, and a poor home–school bond often aggravates the child's adjustment problems. They may be grouped with other children who are similarly unprepared. This peer group may be negatively influenced by disruptive classroom contexts and punitive teachers.

- Over time, aggressive and disruptive children are rejected by families and peers and tend to receive less support from teachers beginning in elementary school and lasting throughout adolescence. During this period, peer influences, academic difficulties, and dysfunctional personal identity development can contribute to serious conduct problems and related risky behaviors.[181]

Compared with children in the control group, children in the intervention group displayed significantly less aggressive behavior at home, in the classroom, and on the playground. By the end of third grade, 37 percent of the intervention group had become free of conduct problems, compared with 27 percent of the control group. By the end of elementary school, 33 percent of the intervention group had a developmental trajectory of decreasing conduct problems, compared with 27 percent of the control group. Furthermore, placement in special education by the end of elementary school was about one-fourth lower in the intervention group than in the control group.

Group differences continued through adolescence. Court records indicate that by eighth grade, 38 percent of the intervention group boys had been arrested, in contrast with 42 percent of the control group. Finally, psychiatric interviews after ninth grade indicate that the Fast Track intervention reduced serious conduct disorder by over a third, from 27 percent to 17 percent. These effects generalized across gender and ethnic groups and across the wide range of child and family characteristics measured by Fast Track. The Evidence-Based Juvenile Justice feature describes another developmental-based program, Across Ages.

Across Ages

Across Ages is a drug prevention program for youths ages 9 to 13. The program's goal is to strengthen the bonds between adults and children to provide opportunities for positive community involvement. It is unique and highly effective in its pairing of older adult mentors (age 55 and above) with young adolescents, mainly those entering middle school.

Designed as a school- and community-based demonstration research project, Across Ages was founded in 1991 by the Substance Abuse and Mental Health Services Administration's Center for Substance Abuse Prevention and was replicated in Philadelphia and West Springfield, Massachusetts. Today, there are more than 30 replication sites in 17 states. Specifically, the program aims to:

- Increase knowledge of health and substance abuse and foster healthy attitudes, intentions, and behavior toward drug use among targeted youth.

- Improve school bonding, academic performance, school attendance, and behavior and attitudes toward school.

- Strengthen relationships with adults and peers.

- Enhance problem-solving and decision-making skills.

Target Population

The project was designed for and tested on African American, Hispanic/Latino, white, and Asian American middle school students living in a large urban setting. The goal was to assess many risk factors faced by urban youth, including no opportunity for positive free-time activities, few positive role models, and stresses caused by living in extended families when parents are incarcerated or substance abusers.

How It Works

Program materials are offered in English or Spanish so they can be used cross-culturally. A child is matched with an older adult and participates in the following activities and interventions:

- Mentoring for a minimum of two hours each week in one-on-one contact

- Community service for one to two hours per week

- Social competence training, which involves the "Social Problem-Solving Module," composed of 26 weekly lessons at 45 minutes each

- Activities for the youth and family members and mentors

Benefits and Outcomes

Participating youths learn positive coping skills and have an opportunity to be of service to their community. The program aims to increase prosocial interactions and protective factors and decrease negative ones.

Protective Factors to Increase

- *Individual*. Relationship with significant adult; engagement in positive free-time activities; problem-solving/conflict resolution skills; bonding to school.

- *Peer*. Association with peers engaged in positive behavior and activities.

- *Family*. Engagement in positive family activities; improved communication between parents and children.

- *School*. Improved school attendance, behavior, and performance.

- *Community*. Useful role in the community; positive feedback from community members.

Risk Factors to Decrease

- *Individual*. School failure; identified behavior problems in school; lack of adult role models; poor decision-making and problem-solving skills.

- *Peer*. Engagement in risky behavior.

- *Family*. Substance-abusing parents and siblings; incarcerated family members; little positive interaction between parents and children.

- *School*. Lack of bonding to school.

- *Community*. Residence in communities lacking opportunities for positive recreational activities and with high incidence of drug-related delinquency.

Applying Across Ages in Maryland

A notable Across Ages program is now being run by Interages, a nonprofit agency whose goal is to address community needs through caring and supportive partnerships between older adults and children and youth. Since 1986, Interages has operated the Montgomery County Intergenerational Resource Center, through which it assists professionals and organizations in developing intergenerational programs for their communities. They have run an Across Ages program since 2003 that focuses on helping children develop strong decision-making skills, problem-solving abilities, and community awareness, and on building a strong relationship between mentors and children. Mentoring is the cornerstone of the program. The key concepts taught to the children are reinforced by the relationship they have with their mentors. Mentors act as advocates, challengers, nurturers, role models, and—most of all—friends.

Through these relationships, the children begin to develop awareness, self-confidence, and the skills needed to overcome overwhelming obstacles. The following are among the most popular activities:

- Problem-solving "talk time"
- Creating problem-solving skits
- Group community service activities at local nursing homes
- "Social Problem-Solving Skills" academic lessons
- Self-esteem and team-building activities
- Group discussions
- Family day field trips
- Tree planting and stream cleanup
- Yearly donation of snacks and gifts benefiting local homeless children
- Individual mentor/mentee activities

Over the last 25 years, Interages programs have involved over 30,000 children and older adults in over 100 schools and 50 senior facilities. Interages has worked very hard to develop and implement relevant intergenerational programs that meet community needs. As the years have progressed some programs have run their natural course and concluded and some continue to this day. The Intergenerational Bridges, Project SHARE, and Dialogues Across the Ages programs are still active today. Programs implemented over the last decade that are part of the solid base of Interages intergenerational programs include Grandreaders, Intergenerational Bridges: High School Service Learning Program, Makeover Madness, Mature Mentors, Grandbuddies, Head Start Read-Aloud, LEAP (Leadership and Empowerment Action Program), and Math Club. In 2016, Interages celebrated 30 years of service to Montgomery County residents as a leader in intergenerational programming.

Evaluations of the Across Ages Program

Using a classic experimental design in which control and experimental groups were chosen, evaluation of the Across Ages approach showed the following:

Outcomes for Youth

- Significant improvement in knowledge about and reactions to drug use
- Significant decrease in substance use (e.g., alcohol and tobacco)
- Significant improvement in school-related behavior as measured by increased school attendance, decreased suspensions from school, and improved grades
- Significant improvement in attitudes toward school and the future
- Significant improvement in attitudes toward adults in general and older adults in particular
- Improvement in well-being

The level of mentor involvement was positively related to improvement on various outcome measures.

Outcomes for Families

- Increased participation in school-related activities
- More positive communication with children
- Engaged in more activities (positive) as a family
- Gained access to community resources
- Expanded support networks

Participation in the project leads to increased knowledge about the negative effects of drug abuse and decreased use of alcohol and tobacco. Participants improve school attendance, improve grades, and get fewer suspensions. Another positive outcome from the project is seen in the youths' attitudes toward older adults. At the same time, the project helps the older volunteers feel more productive, experience a greater sense of purpose, and regain a central role in their communities. Evaluations of similar programs find that participants who were retained in the program were more likely to report higher levels of family supervision, lower family conflict, and fewer family relocations during the past year than those who left the program.

CRITICAL THINKING

1. Should such issues as early onset and problem behavior syndrome be considered when choosing participants for prevention programs such as Across Ages?
2. Could participation in such programs label or stigmatize participants and thereafter lock them into a deviant role?

SOURCES: JCA Heyman Interages Center, https://www.accessjca.org/programs/interages/; Debra Zand, Nicole Renick Thomson, Mary Dugan, James A. Braun, Pat Holterman-Hommes, and Patricia L. Hunter, "Predictors of Retention in an Alcohol, Tobacco, and Other Drug Prevention Study," *Evaluation Review* 30:209–222 (2006); Across Ages, http://acrossages.org/evaluations. (URLs accessed October 2016.)

SUMMARY

1 Compare and contrast the three forms of developmental theory

- Developmental theory of delinquency looks at the onset, continuity, and termination of a delinquent career.

- Life-course theory suggests that delinquent behavior is a dynamic process, influenced by individual characteristics as well as social experiences, and the factors that cause antisocial behaviors change dramatically over a person's life span.

- Propensity theory suggests that a stable feature, characteristic, property, or condition, such as defective intelligence or impulsive personality, makes some people delinquency prone over the life course.

- Trajectory theory suggests that there is more than one path to a delinquent career.

2 Trace the history of and influences on developmental theory

- The Gluecks followed the careers of known delinquents to determine the social, biological, and psychological characteristics that predicted persistent offending.

- The most important of these factors was family relations, considered in terms of quality of discipline and emotional ties with parents.

- The Philadelphia cohort research by Marvin Wolfgang and his associates was another milestone in explaining delinquent career development.

3 Describe the principles of the life-course approach to developmental theory

- According to the life-course view, even as toddlers people begin relationships and behaviors that will determine their adult life course.

- Some individuals are incapable of maturing in a reasonable and timely fashion because of family, environmental, or personal problems.

- A positive life experience may help some kids desist from delinquency for a while, whereas a negative one may cause them to resume their activities.

- Disruptions in life's major transitions can be destructive and ultimately can promote delinquency.

- As people make important life transitions—from child to adolescent, from adolescent to adult, from unwed to married—the nature of social interactions changes.

4 Explain the concept of problem behavior syndrome

- The developmental view is that delinquency may best be understood as one of many social problems faced by at-risk youth, a view called problem behavior syndrome (PBS).

- According to this view, delinquency is one among a group of interrelated antisocial behaviors that cluster together.

- PBS typically involves family dysfunction, sexual and physical abuse, substance abuse, smoking, precocious sexuality and early pregnancy, educational underachievement, suicide attempts, sensation seeking, and unemployment.

5 Articulate the principles of Sampson and Laub's age-graded life-course theory

- Repeat negative experiences create a condition called cumulative disadvantage. Serious problems in adolescence undermine life chances and reduce employability and social relations. People who increase their cumulative disadvantage risk continued offending.

- Positive life experiences and relationships can help people become reattached to society and allow them to knife off from a delinquent career path. Two critical turning points are marriage and career.

- Informal social control is a key element that helps at-risk kids avoid a life of crime.

- Another vital feature that helps people desist from delinquency is human agency, or the purposeful execution of choice and free will.

6 Define the concept of a latent trait

- A number of people in the population have a personal attribute, or latent trait, that may be either present at birth or established early in life, and it can remain stable over time.

- Suspected latent traits include defective intelligence, damaged or impulsive personality, genetic abnormalities, the physical-chemical functioning of the brain, and environmental influences on brain function such as drugs, chemicals, and injuries.

- Because latent traits are stable, people who are antisocial during adolescence are the most likely to persist in crime.

7 Outline the principles and assumptions of the General Theory of Crime

- People with limited self-control tend to be impulsive; they are insensitive to other people's feelings, physical (rather than mental), risk takers, shortsighted, and nonverbal.

- Because those with low self-control enjoy risky, exciting, or thrilling behaviors with immediate gratification, they are more likely to enjoy delinquent acts, which require stealth, agility, speed, and power, than conventional acts, which demand long-term study and cognitive and verbal skills.

- Low self-control develops early in life and remains stable into and through adulthood.
- Gottfredson and Hirschi trace the root cause of poor self-control to inadequate childrearing practices that begin soon after birth and can influence neural development.
- Gottfredson and Hirschi claim that the principles of self-control theory can explain all varieties of delinquent behavior and all the social and behavioral correlates of crime.

8 Discuss both the strengths and weaknesses of the GTC

- By integrating the concepts of socialization and delinquency, Gottfredson and Hirschi help explain why some people who lack self-control can escape delinquency and, conversely, why some people who have self-control might not escape delinquency.
- Some critics argue that the theory is tautological (involves circular reasoning): How do we know when people are impulsive? When they commit crimes! Are all delinquents impulsive? Of course, or else they would not have broken the law!

9 Identify the different trajectories delinquency takes

- Career delinquents may travel more than a single road. Some may specialize in violence and extortion;

some may be involved in theft and fraud; others may engage in a variety of delinquent acts.

- Some offenders may begin their careers early in life, whereas others are late bloomers who begin committing delinquency when most people desist. Some are frequent offenders, while others travel a more moderate path.
- Some offenders are violent and aggressive, others are stubborn and defiant, while another path begins with being underhanded and sneaky.

10 Distinguish between adolescent-limited and life-course persistent offenders

- According to psychologist Terrie Moffitt, adolescent-limited offenders may be considered "typical teenagers" who get into minor scrapes and engage in what might be considered rebellious teenage behavior with their friends.
- They reduce the frequency of their offending as they mature to around age 18.
- In contrast, life-course persisters begin their offending career at a very early age and continue to offend well into adulthood.
- Moffitt finds that life-course persisters combine family dysfunction with severe neurological problems that predispose them to antisocial behavior patterns.

KEY TERMS

QUESTIONS FOR DISCUSSION

1. Do you consider yourself to have social capital? If so, what form does it take?

2. Someone you know gets a perfect score on the SAT. What personal, family, and social characteristics do you think this individual has? Another person becomes a serial killer. Without knowing this person, what personal, family, and social characteristics do you think this individual has? If "bad behavior" is explained by multiple problems, is "good behavior" explained by multiple strengths?

3. Do you believe it is a latent trait that makes a kid delinquency prone, or is delinquency a function of environment and socialization?

4. Do you agree with the multiple pathways model? Do you know people who have traveled down those paths?

5. Do people really change, or do they stay the same but appear to be different because their life circumstances have changed?

VIEWPOINT

In 2000, Michael was a 17-year-old popular high school football player. One evening Michael offered a lift to a 16-year-old girl he met at a party. During the ride home, Michael, who had been drinking, wanted to have sex with the girl. When she refused his advances, he punched her in the face, held her down, and forced her to have sex despite her protestations. Charged with rape, Michael was released on $250,000 bail, which was put up by his affluent parents. While out on bail, Michael fled the jurisdiction, crossing the border into Canada and eventually finding his way to Europe (police believe he was aided by his parents in securing tickets and a fake identity). Once there, being already fluent in French, Michael was able to establish himself with a false identity in a small town outside Paris where he found work to support himself. Over the years he established a small business and became successful. A respected community member, Michael married a local woman and had two children. Known in France as "Paul," Michael was involved in community affairs and even served on the town council. At age 32, Michael got into a minor traffic accident and the subsequent investigation revealed his true identity. He was taken into custody and extradited to the United States. Rather than face trial, he has pleaded guilty and throws himself on the mercy of the court.

At a sentencing hearing, Michael asks that he be released on probation so he can return to his home. He argues that at the time of the incident he was young, foolish, and inebriated. He is a changed person and no longer would even think of such risky and aggressive behavior. He is truly repentant. He has not broken the law or committed another crime since the incident. He claims that now his family needs him, he poses no danger to society, and he has lived an exemplary life for the last 17 years. He would be willing to make financial restitution if needed. When contacted, the victim is ambivalent; she is now married with two children and has no interest in the matter.

Should Michael be allowed to remain in his French community or be sent to prison? Is it possible that people change over the life course? What allows someone like Michael to knife off from a delinquent career? Should someone be punished in adulthood for a crime committed as a teen? Are the factors that led Michael to commit his crime unchanging and stable over the life course?

DOING RESEARCH ON THE WEB

The Seattle Social Development Project (http://www.promisingpractices.net/program.asp?programid=64) uses the social development model as a cornerstone for their treatment programs. The Life History Studies Program at the University of Pittsburgh (http://www.wpic.pitt.edu/research/famhist/) is a longitudinal study designed to test the principles of life-course theory. You might also want to read some of the highlights of the Rochester Youth Study (http://www.albany.edu/hindelang/youth_study.html), another longitudinal study of the delinquent life course.

NOTES

All URLs accessed September 2016.

1. Adam Liptak, "Jailed for Life After Crimes as Teenagers," New York Times, October 3, 2005, http://www.nytimes.com/2005/10/03/national/03lifers.html.
2. *Miller v. Alabama*, 567 U.S. ___ (2012)
3. *Montgomery v. Louisiana*, 577 U.S. ___ (2016)
4. Associated Press, Florida Supreme Court Orders New Sentences in Juvenile Cases, WCTV, March 19, 2015, http://www.wctv.tv/home/headlines/Florida-Supreme-Court-Orders-New-Sentences-in-Juvenile-Cases-296911291.html.
5. Hanno Petras, Paul Nieuwbeerta, and Alex R. Piquero, "Participation and Frequency During Criminal Careers Across the Life Span," *Criminology* 48:607–638 (2010).
6. See, generally, Sheldon Glueck and Eleanor Glueck, *500 Criminal Careers* (New York: Knopf, 1930); Glueck and Glueck, *One Thousand Juvenile Delinquents* (Cambridge, MA: Harvard University Press, 1934); Glueck and Glueck, *Predicting Delinquency and Crime* (Cambridge, MA: Harvard University Press, 1967), pp. 82–83; Glueck and Glueck, *Unraveling Juvenile Delinquency* (Cambridge, MA: Harvard University Press, 1950).
7. Glueck and Glueck, *Unraveling Juvenile Delinquency*.
8. Ibid., p. 48.
9. Marvin Wolfgang, Robert Figlio, and Thorsten Sellin, *Delinquency in a Birth Cohort* (Chicago: University of Chicago Press, 1972).
10. Alex Piquero, "Taking Stock of Developmental Trajectories of Criminal Activity Over the Life Course," in Akiva Liberman, ed., *The Long View of Crime: A Synthesis of Longitudinal Research* (New York: Springer, 2008), pp. 23–78.
11. Raymond Paternoster, Charles Dean, Alex Piquero, Paul Mazerolle, and Robert Brame, "Generality, Continuity, and Change in Offending," *Journal of Quantitative Criminology* 13:231–266 (1997).
12. Marvin Krohn, Alan Lizotte, and Cynthia Perez, "The Interrelationship Between Substance Use and Precocious Transitions to Adult Sexuality," *Journal of Health and Social Behavior* 38:87–103 (1997), at 88.

13. Jennifer M. Beyers and Rolf Loeber, "Untangling Developmental Relations Between Depressed Mood and Delinquency in Male Adolescents," *Journal of Abnormal Child Psychology* 31:247–266 (2003).

14. Stephanie Milan and Ellen Pinderhughes, "Family Instability and Child Maladjustment Trajectories During Elementary School," *Journal of Abnormal Child Psychology* 34:43–56 (2006).

15. Chris Melde and Finn-Aage Esbensen, "The Relative Impact of Gang Status Transitions: Identifying the Mechanisms of Change in Delinquency," *Journal of Research in Crime and Delinquency*, first published online October 30, 2013.

16. Allison Ann Payne and Kelly Welch, "The Centrality of Schools in the Lifecourse: The Case for Focusing on School-Related Influences in Developmental Theory and Research," *Deviant Behavior* 37:748–760 (2016).

17. David Pyrooz, "From Colors and Guns to Caps and Gowns? The Effects of Gang Membership on Educational Attainment," *Journal of Research in Crime and Delinquency* 51:56–87 (2014).

18. Lara DePadilla, Molly Perkins, Kirk Elifson, and Claire Sterk, "Adult Criminal Involvement: A Cross-Sectional Inquiry into Correlates and Mechanisms over the Life Course," *Criminal Justice Review* 37:110–126 (2012).

19. Deirdre Healy, "Betwixt and Between: The Role of Psychosocial Factors in the Early Stages of Desistance," *Journal of Research in Crime and Delinquency* 47:419–443 (2010).

20. Joan McCord, "Family Relationships, Juvenile Delinquency, and Adult Criminality," *Criminology* 29:397–417 (1991).

21. Paul Mazerolle, "Delinquent Definitions and Participation Age: Assessing the Invariance Hypothesis," *Studies on Crime and Crime Prevention* 6:151–168 (1997).

22. Peggy Giordano, Stephen Cernkovich, and Jennifer Rudolph, "Gender, Delinquency, and Desistance: Toward a Theory of Cognitive Transformation?" *American Journal of Sociology* 107:990–1064 (2002).

23. John Hagan and Holly Foster, "S/He's a Rebel: Toward a Sequential Stress Theory of Delinquency and Gendered Pathways to Disadvantage in Emerging Adulthood," *Social Forces* 82:53–86 (2003).

24. G. R. Patterson, Barbara DeBaryshe, and Elizabeth Ramsey, "A Developmental Perspective on Antisocial Behavior," *American Psychologist* 44:329–335 (1989).

25. Robert Sampson and John Laub, "Crime and Deviance in the Life Course," *American Review of Sociology* 18:63–84 (1992).

26. David Farrington, Darrick Jolliffe, Rolf Loeber, Madga Stouthamer-Loeber, and Larry Kalb, "The Concentration of Offenders in Families, and Family Criminality in the Prediction of Boys' Delinquency," *Journal of Adolescence* 24:579–596 (2001).

27. DePadilla et al., "Adult Criminal Involvement: A Cross-Sectional Inquiry into Correlates and Mechanisms over the Life Course."

28. Terence Thornberry, Carolyn Smith, and Gregory Howard, "Risk Factors for Teenage Fatherhood," *Journal of Marriage and the Family* 59:505–522 (1997); Todd Miller, Timothy Smith, Charles Turner, Margarita Guijarro, and Amanda Hallet, "A Meta-analytic Review of Research on Hostility and Physical Health," *Psychological Bulletin* 119:322–348 (1996); Marianne Junger, "Accidents and Crime," in T. Hirschi and M. Gottfredson, eds., *The Generality of Deviance* (New Brunswick, NJ: Transaction Books, 1993).

29. Krysia Mossakowski, "Dissecting the Influence of Race, Ethnicity, and Socioeconomic Status on Mental Health in Young Adulthood," *Research on Aging* 30:649–671 (2008); James Marquart, Victoria Brewer, Patricia Simon, and Edward Morse, "Lifestyle Factors Among Female Prisoners with Histories of Psychiatric Treatment," *Journal of Criminal Justice* 29:319–328 (2001); Rolf Loeber, David Farrington, Magda Stouthamer-Loeber, Terrie Moffitt, Avshalom Caspi, and Don Lynam, "Male Mental Health Problems, Psychopathy, and Personality Traits: Key Findings from the First 14 Years of the Pittsburgh Youth Study," *Clinical Child and Family Psychology Review* 4:273–297 (2002).

30. John Stogner, Chris Gibson, and J. Mitchell Miller, "Examining the Reciprocal Nature of the Health–Violence Relationship: Results from a Nationally Representative Sample," *Justice Quarterly* 31:473–499 (2014).

31. Magda Stouthamer-Loeber and Evelyn Wei, "The Precursors of Young Fatherhood and Its Effect on Delinquency of Teenage Males," *Journal of Adolescent Health* 22:56–65 (1998); Richard Jessor, John Donovan, and Francis Costa, *Beyond Adolescence: Problem Behavior and Young Adult Development* (New York: Cambridge University Press, 1991); Xavier Coll, Fergus Law, Aurelio Tobias, Keith Hawton, and Joseph Tomas, "Abuse and Deliberate Self-Poisoning in Women: A Matched Case-Control Study," *Child Abuse and Neglect* 25:1291–1293 (2001).

32. Richard Miech, Avshalom Caspi, Terrie Moffitt, Bradley Entner Wright, and Phil Silva, "Low Socioeconomic Status and Mental Disorders: A Longitudinal Study of Selection and Causation During Young Adulthood," *American Journal of Sociology* 104:1096–1131 (1999); Krohn, Lizotte, and Perez, "The Interrelationship Between Substance Use and Precocious Transitions to Adult Sexuality," p. 88; Richard Jessor, "Risk Behavior in Adolescence: A Psychosocial Framework for Understanding and Action," in D. E. Rogers and E. Ginzburg, eds., *Adolescents at Risk: Medical and Social Perspectives* (Boulder, CO: Westview Press, 1992).

33. Deborah Capaldi and Gerald Patterson, "Can Violent Offenders Be Distinguished from Frequent Offenders? Prediction from Childhood to Adolescence," *Journal of Research in Crime and Delinquency* 33:206–231 (1996).

34. Gina Wingood, Ralph DiClemente, Rick Crosby, Kathy Harrington, Susan Davies, and Edward Hook III, "Gang Involvement and the Health of African American Female Adolescents," *Pediatrics* 110:57 (2002).

35. David Husted, Nathan Shapira, and Martin Lazoritz, "Adolescent Gambling, Substance Use, and Other Delinquent Behavior," *Psychiatric Times* 20:52–55 (2003).

36. Hayden Smith and Jenelle Power, "Applying the Dual-Taxonomy of Offending to Self-Injury: Do Offenders Exhibit Life-Course-Persistent Self-Injurious Behavior?" *Victims and Offenders* 10:179–213 (2015).

37. Alex Piquero, David Farrington, Jonathan Shepherd, and Katherine Auty, "Offending and Early Death in the Cambridge Study in Delinquent Development," *Justice Quarterly* 31:445–472.

38. Paul Nieuwbeerta and Alex Piquero, "Mortality Rates and Causes of Death of Convicted Dutch Criminals 25 Years Later," *Journal of Research in Crime and Delinquency* 45:256–286 (2008).

39. David Fergusson, L. John Horwood, and Elizabeth Ridder, "Show Me the Child at Seven II: Childhood Intelligence and Later Outcomes in Adolescence and Young Adulthood," *Journal of Child Psychology and Psychiatry and Allied Disciplines* 46:850–859 (2005).

40. Jacqueline Schneider, "The Link Between Shoplifting and Burglary: The Booster Burglar," *British Journal of Criminology* 45:395–401 (2005).

41. Glenn Deane, Richard Felson, and David Armstrong, "An Examination of Offense Specialization Using Marginal Logit Models," *Criminology* 43:955–988 (2005).

42. Christopher Sullivan, Jean Marie McGloin, Travis Pratt, and Alex Piquero, "Rethinking the 'Norm' of Offender Generality: Investigating Specialization in the Short-Term," *Criminology* 44:199–233 (2006).

43. Christopher Sullivan, Jean Marie McGloin, James Ray, and Michael Caudy, "Detecting Specialization in Offending: Comparing Analytic Approaches," *Journal of Quantitative Criminology* 25:419–441 (2009).

44. Jean Marie McGloin, Christopher J. Sullivan, and Alex R. Piquero, "Aggregating to Versatility? Transitions Among Offender Types in the Short Term," *British Journal of Criminology* 49:243–264 (2009).

45. Alex R. Piquero and He Len Chung, "On the Relationships Between Gender, Early Onset, and the Seriousness of Offending," *Journal of Criminal Justice* 29:189–206 (2001).

46. David Nurco, Timothy Kinlock, and Mitchell Balter, "The Severity of Preaddiction Criminal Behavior Among Urban, Male Narcotic Addicts and Two Nonaddicted Control Groups," *Journal of Research in Crime and Delinquency* 30:293–316 (1993).

47. Hanno Petras, Nicholas Ialongo, Sharon Lambert, Sandra Barrueco, Cindy Schaeffer, Howard Chilcoat, and Sheppard Kellam, "The Utility of Elementary School TOCA-R Scores in Identifying Later Criminal Court Violence Among Adolescent Females," *Journal of the American Academy of Child and Adolescent Psychiatry* 44:790–797 (2005); Hanno Petras, Howard Chilcoat, Philip Leaf, Nicholas Ialongo, and Sheppard Kellam, "Utility of TOCA-R Scores During the Elementary School Years in Identifying Later Violence Among Adolescent Males," *Journal of the American Academy of Child and Adolescent Psychiatry* 43:88–96 (2004).

48. W. Alex Mason, Rick Kosterman, J. David Hawkins, Todd Herrenkohl, Liliana Lengua, and Elizabeth McCauley, "Predicting Depression, Social Phobia, and Violence in Early Adulthood from Childhood Behavior Problems," *Journal of the American Academy of Child and Adolescent Psychiatry* 43:307–315 (2004); Rolf Loeber and David Farrington, "Young Children Who Commit Crime: Epidemiology, Developmental Origins, Risk Factors, Early Interventions, and Policy Implications," *Development and Psychopathology* 12:737–762 (2000); Patrick Lussier, Jean Proulx, and Marc Leblanc, "Criminal Propensity, Deviant Sexual Interests and Criminal Activity of Sexual Aggressors Against Women: A Comparison of Explanatory Models," *Criminology* 43:249–281 (2005).

49. Dawn Jeglum Bartusch, Donald Lynam, Terrie Moffitt, and Phil Silva, "Is Age Important? Testing a General versus a Developmental Theory of Antisocial Behavior," *Criminology* 35:13–48 (1997).

50. Daniel Nagin and Richard Tremblay, "What Has Been Learned from Group-Based Trajectory Modeling? Examples from Physical Aggression and Other Problem Behaviors," *Annals of the American Academy of Political and Social Science* 602:82–117 (2005).

51. Mary Campa, Catherine Bradshaw, John Eckenrode, and David Zielinski, "Patterns of Problem Behavior in Relation to Thriving and Precocious Behavior in Late Adolescence," *Journal of Youth and Adolescence* 37:627–640 (2008); Mason, Kosterman, Hawkins, Herrenkohl, Lengua, and McCauley, "Predicting Depression, Social Phobia, and Violence in Early Adulthood from Childhood Behavior Problems"; Loeber and Farrington, "Young Children Who Commit Crime."

52. Kristin Carbone-Lopez and Jody Miller, "Precocious Role Entry as a Mediating Factor in Women's Methamphetamine Use: Implications for Life-Course and Pathways Research," *Criminology* 50:187–220 (2012).

53. Mason at al., "Predicting Depression, Social Phobia, and Violence in Early Adulthood from Childhood Behavior Problems"; Ronald Prinz and Suzanne Kerns, "Early Substance Use by Juvenile Offenders," *Child Psychiatry and Human Development* 33:263–268 (2003).

54. David Gadd and Stephen Farrall, "Criminal Careers, Desistance and Subjectivity: Interpreting Men's Narratives of Change," *Theoretical Criminology* 8:123–156 (2004).

55. Mason et al., "Predicting Depression, Social Phobia, and Violence in Early Adulthood from Childhood Behavior Problems"; Prinz and Kerns, "Early Substance Use by Juvenile Offenders."

56. Sarah Bacon, Raymond Paternoster, and Robert Brame, "Understanding the Relationship Between Onset Age and Subsequent Offending During Adolescence," *Journal of Youth and Adolescence* 38:301–311 (2009).

57. G. R. Patterson, L. Crosby, and S. Vuchinich, "Predicting Risk for Early Police Arrest," *Journal of Quantitative Criminology* 8:335–355 (1992).

58. Glenn Walters, "Criminal and Substance Involvement from Adolescence to Adulthood: Precursors, Mediators, and Long-term Effects," *Justice Quarterly* 32:729–747 (2015); Nicole Leeper Piquero and Terrie Moffitt, "Can Childhood Factors Predict Workplace Deviance?" *Justice Quarterly* 31:664–693 (2014); Margit Wiesner and Michael Windle, "Young Adult Substance Use and Depression as a Consequence of Criminality Trajectories During Middle Adolescence," *Journal of Research on Adolescence* 16:239–264 (2006).

59. Marshall Jones and Donald Jones, "The Contagious Nature of Antisocial Behavior," *Criminology* 38:25–46 (2000).

60. Peggy Giordano, Wendi Johnson, Wendy Manning, Monica Longmore, and Mallory Minter, "Intimate Partner Violence in Young Adulthood: Narratives of Persistence and Desistance," *Criminology* 53:330–365 (2015).

61. Stephen Farrall and Benjamin Bowling, "Structuration, Human Development, and Desistance from Crime," *British Journal of Criminology* 39:253–268 (1999).

62. Robert Sampson and John Laub, *Crime in the Making: Pathways and Turning Points Through Life* (Cambridge, MA: Harvard University Press, 1993).

63. James Coleman, "Social Capital in the Creation of Human Capital," *American Journal of Sociology* 94:S95–S120 (1988).

64. Robert Putnam, *Bowling Alone: The Collapse and Revival of American Community* (New York: Touchstone Books by Simon & Schuster, 2001).

65. Daniel Nagin and Raymond Paternoster, "Personal Capital and Social Control: The Deterrence Implications of a Theory of Criminal Offending," *Criminology* 32:581–606 (1994).

66. Robert Sampson and John Laub, "A Life-Course View of the Development of Crime," *Annals of the American Academy of Political and Social Science* 602:12–45 (2005).

67. Amy L. Solomon, "In Search of a Job: Criminal Records as Barriers to Employment," *NIJ Journal* 270:42–51 (2012).

68. Daniel Nagin and Raymond Paternoster, "Personal Capital and Social Control: The Deterrence Implications of a Theory of Criminal Offending," *Criminology* 32:581–606 (1994).

69. Joan Reid, "Exploratory Review of Route-Specific, Gendered, and Age-Graded Dynamics of Exploitation: Applying Life Course Theory to Victimization in Sex Trafficking in North America," *Aggression and Violent Behavior* 17:257–271 (2012).

70. DePadilla, Perkins, Elifson, and Sterk, "Adult Criminal Involvement: A Cross-Sectional Inquiry into Correlates and Mechanisms over the Life Course."

71. Besiki Kutateladze, Nancy Andiloro, Brian Johnson, and Cassia Spohn, "Cumulative Disadvantage: Examining Racial and Ethnic Disparity in Prosecution and Sentencing," *Criminology* 52:514–551 (2014).

72. Joseph Murray, Rolf Loeber, and Dustin Pardini, "Parental Involvement in the Criminal Justice System and the Development of Youth Theft, Marijuana Use, Depression, and Poor Academic Performance," *Criminology* 50:255–302 (2012).

73. Daniel Mears and Sonja Siennick, "Young Adult Outcomes and the Life-Course Penalties of Parental Incarceration," *Journal of Research in Crime and Delinquency* 53:3–35 (2016).

74. Michael Roettger, and Raymond Swisher, "Associations of Fathers' History of Incarceration with Sons' Criminality and Arrest Among Black, White, and Hispanic Males in the United States," *Criminology* 49:1109–1148 (2011).

75. Raymond Swisher and Unique Shaw-Smith, "Paternal Incarceration and Adolescent Well-Being: Life Course Contingencies and Other Moderators," *Journal of Criminal Law and Criminology* 104:929–959 (2015).

76. Leonore M. J. Simon, "Social Bond and Criminal Record History of Acquaintance and Stranger Violent Offenders," *Journal of Crime and Justice* 22:131–146 (1999).

77. Robert Hoge, D. A. Andrews, and Alan Leschied, "An Investigation of Risk and Protective Factors in a Sample of Youthful Offenders," *Journal of Child Psychology and Psychiatry* 37:419–424 (1996).

78. David S. Kirk, "Residential Change as a Turning Point in the Life Course of Crime: Desistance or Temporary Cessation?" *Criminology* 50:329–358 (2012).

79. Ross Macmillan, Barbara J. McMorris, and Candace Kruttschnitt, "Linked Lives: Stability and Change in Maternal Circumstances and Trajectories of Antisocial Behavior in Children," *Child Development* 75:205–220 (2004).

80. Avshalom Caspi, Terrie Moffitt, Bradley Entner Wright, and Phil Silva, "Early Failure in the Labor Market: Childhood and Adolescent Predictors of Unemployment in the Transition to Adulthood," *American Sociological Review* 63:424–451 (1998).

81. Robert Sampson and John Laub, "Socioeconomic Achievement in the Life Course of Disadvantaged Men: Military Service as a Turning Point, circa 1940–1965," *American Sociological Review* 61:347–367 (1996).

82. Christopher Uggen, "Ex-Offenders and the Conformist Alternative: A Job Quality Model of Work and Crime," *Social Problems* 46:127–151 (1999).

83. Elaine Eggleston Doherty and Margaret E. Ensminger, "Marriage and Offending Among a Cohort of Disadvantaged African Americans," *Journal of Research in Crime and Delinquency* 50:104–131 (2013); Ronald L. Simons and Ashley B. Barr, "Shifting Perspectives: Cognitive Changes Mediate the Impact of Romantic Relationships on Desistance from Crime," *Justice Quarterly*, first published online July 20, 2012.

84. Michael Rocque, Chad Posick, Steven E. Barkan, and Ray Paternoster, "Marriage and County-Level Crime Rates: A Research Note," *Journal of Research in Crime and Delinquency* 52:130–145 (2015); Simons and Barr, "Shifting Perspectives: Cognitive Changes Mediate the Impact of Romantic Relationships on Desistance from Crime."

85. Sonja Siennick, Jeremy Staff, D. Wayne Osgood, John Schulenberg, Jerald Bachman, and Matthew VanEseltine, "Partnership Transitions and Antisocial Behavior in Young Adulthood: A Within-Person, Multi-Cohort Analysis," *Journal of Research in Crime and Delinquency* 51:735–758 (2014).

86. Matthew Larson, Gary Sweeten, and Alex Piquero "With or Without You? Contextualizing the Impact of Romantic Relationship Breakup on Crime Among Serious Adolescent Offenders," *Journal of Youth and Adolescence* 45:54–72 (2016); Matthew Larson and Gary Sweeten, "Breaking Up Is Hard to Do: Romantic Dissolution, Offending, and Substance Use During the Transition to Adulthood," *Criminology* 50:605–636 (2012).

87. Kelly Knight, Scott Menard, Sara Simmons, Leana Bouffard, and Rebecca Orsi, "Life Course and Intergenerational Continuity of Intimate Partner Aggression and Physical Injury: A 20-Year Study," *Violence and Victims* 31:381–401 (2016).

88. Rand Conger, Institute for Social and Behavioral Research, 2013.

89. Bill McCarthy and Teresa Casey, "Love, Sex, and Crime: Adolescent Romantic Relationships and Offending," *American Sociological Review* 73:944–969 (2008).

90. Ryan Schroeder, Peggy Giordano, and Stephen Cernkovich, "Drug Use and Desistance Processes," *Criminology* 45:191–222 (2007).

91. Torbjørn Skardhamar and Jukka Savolainen, "Changes in Criminal Offending Around the Time of Job Entry: A Study of Employment and Desistance," *Criminology* 52:263–291 (2014).

92. Christina Ng, "How Ohio School Killer T. J. Lane Snuck 'Killer' T-Shirt Past Authorities," *ABC News*, March 20, 2013, http://abcnews.go.com/US/ohio-school-killer-tj-lane-snuck-killer-shirt/story?id=18774193; David S. Glasier, "T. J. Lane's History in Focus: Records Indicate Chardon Shooting Suspect Has Troubled Past," *News Herald*, March 11, 2012, http://news-herald.com/articles/2012/03/11/news/nh5209273.txt.

93. David Rowe, D. Wayne Osgood, and W. Alan Nicewander, "A Latent Trait Approach to Unifying Criminal Careers," *Criminology* 28:237–270 (1990).

94. Lee Ellis, "Neurohormonal Bases of Varying Tendencies to Learn Delinquent and Criminal Behavior," in E. Morris and C. Braukmann, eds., *Behavioral Approaches to Crime and Delinquency* (New York: Plenum, 1988), pp. 499–518.

95. David Rowe, Alexander Vazsonyi, and Daniel Flannery, "Sex Differences in Crime: Do Means and Within-Sex Variation Have Similar Causes?" *Journal of Research in Crime and Delinquency* 32:84–100 (1995).

96. Bacon, Paternoster, and Brame, "Understanding the Relationship Between Onset Age and Subsequent Offending During Adolescence."

97. Travis Hirschi and Michael Gottfredson, eds., *The Generality of Deviance* (New Brunswick, NJ: Transaction, 1994), p. 3; Michael Gottfredson and Travis Hirschi, *A General Theory of Crime* (Stanford, CA: Stanford University Press, 1990).

98. Gottfredson and Hirschi, *A General Theory of Crime*, p. 90.

99. Ibid., p. 89.

100. Alex Piquero and Stephen Tibbetts, "Specifying the Direct and Indirect Effects of Low Self-Control and Situational Factors in Offenders' Decision Making: Toward a More Complete Model of Rational Offending," *Justice Quarterly* 13:481–508 (1996).

101. David Forde and Leslie Kennedy, "Risky Lifestyles, Routine Activities, and the General Theory of Crime," *Justice Quarterly* 14:265–294 (1997).

102. Gottfredson and Hirschi, *A General Theory of Crime*, p. 112.

103. Ibid.

104. Christopher Schreck, Eric Stewart, and Bonnie Fisher, "Self-Control, Victimization, and Their Influence on Risky Lifestyles: A Longitudinal Analysis Using Panel Data," *Journal of Quantitative Criminology* 22:319–340 (2006).

105. Phillip Quisenberry, "Texting and Driving: Can It Be Explained by the General Theory of Crime?" *American Journal of Criminal Justice* 40:303–316 (2015); Stacey Nofziger and Valerie Callanan, "Predicting Suicidal Tendencies Among High Risk Youth with the General Theory of Crime," *Deviant Behavior* 37:167–183 (2016).

106. Ryan Meldrum, Jacob Young, Carter Hay, and Jamie Flexon, "Does Self-Control Influence Maternal Attachment? A Reciprocal Effects Analysis from Early Childhood Through Middle Adolescence," *Journal of Quantitative Criminology*, first published online March 24, 2012; Stacey Nofziger, "The 'Cause' of Low Self-Control: The Influence of Maternal Self-Control," *Journal of Research in Crime and Delinquency* 45:191–224 (2008).

107. Kevin M. Beaver and John Paul Wright, "Evaluating the Effects of Birth Complications on Low Self-Control in a Sample of Twins," *International Journal of Offender Therapy and Comparative Criminology* 49:450–472 (2005).

108. Kevin M. Beaver, J. Eagle Shutt, Brian Boutwell, Marie Ratchford, Kathleen Roberts, and J. C. Barnes, "Genetic and Environmental Influences on Levels of Self-Control and Delinquent Peer Affiliation: Results from a Longitudinal Sample of Adolescent Twins," *Criminal Justice and Behavior* 36:41–60 (2009).

109. Gottfredson and Hirschi, *A General Theory of Delinquency*, p. 27.

110. For a review of this issue, see Anne Campbell, *Men, Women, and Aggression* (New York: Basic Books, 1993).

111. David Brownfield and Ann Marie Sorenson, "Self-Control and Juvenile Delinquency: Theoretical Issues and an Empirical Assessment of Selected Elements of a General Theory of Crime," *Deviant Behavior* 14:243–264 (1993); Harold Grasmick, Charles Tittle, Robert Bursik, and Bruce Arneklev, "Testing the Core Empirical Implications of Gottfredson and Hirschi's General Theory of Crime," *Journal of Research in Crime and Delinquency* 30:5–29 (1993); John Cochran, Peter Wood, and Bruce Arneklev, "Is the Religiosity–Delinquency Relationship Spurious? A Test of Arousal and Social Control Theories," *Journal of Research in Crime and Delinquency* 31:92–123 (1994); Marc LeBlanc, Marc Ouimet, and Richard Tremblay, "An Integrative Control Theory of Delinquent Behavior: A Validation 1976–1985," *Psychiatry* 51:164–176 (1988).

112. Chris Gibson, Christopher Sullivan, Shayne Jones, and Alex Piquero, "Does It Take a Village? Assessing Neighborhood Influences on Children's Self-Control," *Journal of Research in Crime and Delinquency* 47:31–62 (2010).

113. Brownfield and Sorenson, "Self-Control and Juvenile Delinquency"; Grasmick, Tittle, Bursik, and Arneklev, "Testing the Core Empirical Implications of Gottfredson and Hirschi's General Theory of Crime"; Cochran, Wood, and Arneklev, "Is the Religiosity–Delinquency Relationship Spurious?"; LeBlanc, Ouimet, and Tremblay, "An Integrative Control Theory of Delinquent Behavior."

114. Sullivan, McGloin, Pratt, and Piquero, "Rethinking the 'Norm' of Offender Generality"; Daniel Nagin and Greg Pogarsky, "Time and Punishment: Delayed Consequences and Criminal Behavior," *Journal of Quantitative Criminology* 20:295–317 (2004).

115. Norman White and Rolf Loeber, "Bullying and Special Education as Predictors of Serious Delinquency," *Journal of Research in Crime and Delinquency* 45:380–397 (2008).

116. Matt Delisi and Michael Vaughn, "The Gottfredson-Hirschi Critiques Revisited: Reconciling Self-Control Theory, Criminal Careers, and Career Criminals," *International Journal of Offender Therapy and Comparative Criminology* 52:520–537 (2008).

117. Michael Reisig, Scott Wolfe, and Travis Pratt, "Low Self-Control and the Religiosity-Crime Relationship," *Criminal Justice and Behavior* 39:1172–1191 (2012); Michael Reisig, Scott Wolfe, and Kristy Holtfreter, "Legal Cynicism, Legitimacy, and Criminal Offending: The Non-Confounding Effect of Low Self-Control," *Criminal Justice and Behavior* 38:1170–1184 (2011); Daniel Nagin and Greg Pogarsky, "Time and Punishment: Delayed Consequences and Criminal Behavior," *Journal of Quantitative Criminology* 20:295–317 (2004).

118. Michael Benson and Elizabeth Moore, "Are White-Collar and Common Offenders the Same? An Empirical and Theoretical Critique of a Recently Proposed General Theory of Crime," *Journal of Research in Crime and Delinquency* 29:251–272 (1992).

119. Ronald Akers, "Self-Control as a General Theory of Crime," *Journal of Quantitative Criminology* 7:201–211 (1991).

120. Jean-Louis Van Gelder and Reinout E. De Vries, "Traits and States: Integrating Personality and Affect into a Model of Criminal Decision Making," *Criminology* 50:637–371 (2012).

121. Richard Wiebe, "Reconciling Psychopathy and Low Self-Control," *Justice Quarterly* 20:297–336 (2003).

122. Alex Piquero, John MacDonald, Adam Dobrin, Leah Daigle, and Francis Cullen, "Self-Control, Violent Offending, and Homicide Victimization: Assessing the General Theory of Crime," *Journal of Quantitative Criminology* 21:55–71 (2005).

123. Chris Gibson, "An Investigation of Neighborhood Disadvantage, Low Self-Control, and Violent Victimization Among Youth," *Youth Violence and Juvenile Justice* 10:41–63 (2012).

124. Gregory Zimmerman, "Impulsivity, Offending, and the Neighborhood: Investigating the Person–Context Nexus," *Journal of Quantitative Criminology* 26:301–332 (2010).

125. Alan Feingold, "Gender Differences in Personality: A Meta Analysis," *Psychological Bulletin* 116:429–456 (1994).

126. Charles Tittle, David Ward, and Harold Grasmick, "Gender, Age, and Crime/Deviance: A Challenge to Self-Control Theory," *Journal of Research in Crime and Delinquency* 40:426–453 (2003).

127. Brent Benda, "Gender Differences in Life-Course Theory of Recidivism: A Survival Analysis," *International Journal of Offender Therapy and Comparative Criminology* 49:325–342 (2005).

128. Gottfredson and Hirschi, *A General Theory of Crime*, p. 153.

129. Delbert Elliott and Scott Menard, "Delinquent Friends and Delinquent Behavior: Temporal and Developmental Patterns," in J. David Hawkins, ed., *Crime and Delinquency: Current Theories* (Cambridge: Cambridge University Press, 1996).

130. Dana Haynie, Peggy Giordano, Wendy Manning, and Monica Longmore, "Adolescent Romantic Relationships and Delinquency Involvement," *Criminology* 43:177–210 (2005).

131. Brie Diamond, "Assessing the Determinants and Stability of Self-Control into Adulthood," *Criminal Justice and Behavior* 43:951–968 (2016); Dustin Pardini, Jelena Obradovic, and Rolf Loeber, "Interpersonal Callousness, Hyperactivity/Impulsivity, Inattention, and Conduct Problems as Precursors to Criminality Persistence in Boys: A Comparison of Three Grade-Based Cohorts," *Journal of Clinical Child and Adolescent Psychology* 35:46–59 (2006).

132. Brie Diamond, Robert Morris, and Alex Piquero, "Stability in the Underlying Constructs of Self-Control," *Crime and Delinquency*, first published online September 9, 2015; Ojmarrh Mitchell and Doris Layton MacKenzie, "The Stability and Resiliency of Self-Control in a Sample of Incarcerated Offenders," *Crime and Criminality* 52:432–449 (2006).

133. Charles R. Tittle and Harold G. Grasmick, "Delinquent Behavior and Age: A Test of Three Provocative Hypotheses," *Journal of Criminal Law and Criminology* 88:309–342 (1997).

134. Callie Burt, Gary Sweeten, and Ronald Simons, "Self-Control Through Emerging Adulthood: Instability, Multidimensionality, and Criminological Significance," *Criminology* 52:450–487 (2014).

135. Steven Levitt and Sudhir Alladi Venkatesh, "An Economic Analysis of a Drug-Selling Gang's Finances," *Quarterly Journal of Economics* 13:755–789 (2000).

136. Ibid., p. 773.

137. Yair Listokin, "Future-Oriented Gang Members? Gang Finances and the Theory of Present-Oriented Criminals," *American Journal of Economics and Sociology* 64:1073–1083 (2005).

138. Travis Pratt, "A Self-Control/Life-Course Theory of Criminal Behavior," *European Journal of Criminology* 13:129–146 (2016).

139. Alex Piquero, Wesley Jennings, and David Farrington, "On the Malleability of Self-Control: Theoretical and Policy Implications Regarding a General Theory of Crime," *Justice Quarterly* 27:803–834 (2010).

140. Travis Hirschi and Michael Gottfredson, "Rethinking the Juvenile Justice System," *Crime and Delinquency* 39:262–271 (1993).

141. Robert Sampson and John Laub, "Turning Points and the Future of Life-Course Criminology," *Journal of Research in Crime and Delinquency* 53:321–335 (2016).

142. George E. Higgins, Melissa L. Ricketts, Catherine D. Marcum, and Margaret Mahoney, "Primary Socialization Theory: An Exploratory Study of Delinquent Trajectories," *Criminal Justice Studies* 23:133–146 (2010).

143. Nicole Leeper Piquero and Terrie E. Moffitt, "Can Childhood Factors Predict Workplace Deviance?" *Justice Quarterly*, published online February 21, 2012.

144. Yao Zheng and Harrington Cleveland, "Identifying Gender-Specific Developmental Trajectories of Nonviolent and Violent Delinquency from Adolescence to Young Adulthood," *Journal of Adolescence* 36:371–381 (2013).

145. Donald Lynam, Alex Piquero, and Terrie Moffitt, "Specialization and the Propensity to Violence: Support from Self-Reports but Not Official Records," *Journal of Contemporary Criminal Justice* 20:215–228 (2004).

146. Stacy Tzoumakis, Patrick Lussier, Marc Le Blanc, and Garth Davies, "Onset, Offending Trajectories, and Crime Specialization in Violence," *Youth Violence and Juvenile Justice* 11:143–164 (2013).

147. Alex Piquero, Robert Brame, Paul Mazerolle, and Rudy Haapanen, "Crime in Emerging Adulthood," *Criminology* 40:137–170 (2002).

148. Wesley Jennings and Jennifer Reingle, "On the Number and Shape of Developmental/Life-Course Violence, Aggression, and Delinquency Trajectories: A State-of-the-Art Review," *Journal of Criminal Justice* 40:472–489 (2012).

149. Ick-Joong Chung, Karl G. Hill, J. David Hawkins, Lewayne Gilchrist, and Daniel Nagin, "Childhood Predictors of Offense Trajectories," *Journal of Research in Crime and Delinquency* 39:60–91 (2002).

150. Amy D'Unger, Kenneth Land, Patricia McCall, and Daniel Nagin, "How Many Latent Classes of Delinquent/Criminal Careers? Results from Mixed Poisson Regression Analyses," *American Journal of Sociology* 103:1593–1630 (1998).

151. Chung, Hill, Hawkins, Gilchrist, and Nagin, "Childhood Predictors of Offense Trajectories."

152. Bacon, Paternoster, and Brame, "Understanding the Relationship Between Onset Age and Subsequent Offending During Adolescence."

153. Victor van der Geest, Arjan Blokland, and Catrien Bijleveld, "Delinquent Development in a Sample of High-Risk Youth: Shape, Content, and Predictors of Delinquent Trajectories from Age 12 to 32," *Journal of Research in Crime and Delinquency* 46:111–143 (2009).

154. Terrie Moffitt, "A Review of Research on the Taxonomy of Life-Course Persistent versus Adolescence-Limited Antisocial Behavior," in F. T. Cullen, J. P. Wright, and K. R. Blevins, eds., *Taking Stock: The Status of Criminological Theory*, vol. 15 (New Brunswick, NJ: Transaction Publications, 2006), pp. 277–311.

155. Xiaojin Chen and Michele Adam, "Are Teen Delinquency Abstainers Social Introverts? A Test of Moffitt's Theory," *Journal of Research in Crime and Delinquency* 47:439–468 (2010).

156. Matthew Johnson and Scott Menard, "A Longitudinal Study of Delinquency Abstention: Differences Between Life-Course Abstainers and Offenders from Adolescence into Adulthood," *Youth Violence and Juvenile Justice* 10:278–291 (2012).

157. J. C. Barnes, Kevin Beaver, and Brian Boutwell, "Examining the Genetic Underpinnings to Moffitt's Developmental Taxonomy: A Behavioral Genetic Analysis," *Criminology* 49:923–954 (2011).

158. Jennifer Gatewood Owens and Lee Ann Slocum, "Abstainers in Adolescence and Adulthood: Exploring the Correlates of Abstention Using Moffitt's Developmental Taxonomy," *Crime and Delinquency*, published online February 7, 2012.

159. Margit Wiesner and Ranier Silbereisen, "Trajectories of Delinquent Behaviour in Adolescence and Their Covariates: Relations with Initial and Time-Averaged Factors," *Journal of Adolescence* 26:753–771 (2003).

160. Lynam, Piquero, and Moffitt, "Specialization and the Propensity to Violence."

161. Jennifer Reingle, Wesley Jennings, and Mildred Maldonado-Molina, "Risk and Protective Factors for Trajectories of Violent Criminality Among a Nationally Representative Sample of Early Adolescents," *Youth Violence and Juvenile Justice*, published online February 16, 2012.

162. Sarah El Sayed, Daniel Pacheco, and Robert Morris, "The Link Between Onset Age and Adult Offending: The Role of Developmental Profiles," *Deviant Behavior* 37:989–1002 (2016).

163. Georgia Zara and David Farrington, "Childhood and Adolescent Predictors of Late Onset Criminal Careers," *Journal of Youth and Adolescence* 38:287–300 (2009).

164. Rolf Loeber, Phen Wung, Kate Keenan, Bruce Giroux, Magda Stouthamer-Loeber, Wemoet Van Kammen, and Barbara Maughan, "Developmental Pathways in Disruptive Behavior," *Development and Psychopathology* 23:12–48 (1993).

165. Alex Piquero and Timothy Brezina, "Testing Moffitt's Account of Adolescent-Limited Delinquency," *Criminology* 39:353–370 (2001).

166. Terrie Moffitt, "Adolescence-Limited and Life-Course Persistent Antisocial Behavior: A Developmental Taxonomy," *Psychological Review* 100:674–701 (1993).

167. Terrie Moffitt, "Natural Histories of Delinquency," in Elmar Weitekamp and Hans-Jurgen Kerner, eds., *Cross-National Longitudinal Research on Human Development and Criminal Behavior* (Dordrecht, Netherlands: Kluwer, 1994), pp. 3–65.

168. Barnes, Beaver, and Boutwell, "Examining the Genetic Underpinnings to Moffitt's Developmental Taxonomy."

169. Brian Boutwell, J. C. Barnes, Raelynn Deaton, and Kevin Beaver, "On the Evolutionary Origins of Life-Course Persistent Offending: A Theoretical Scaffold for Moffitt's Developmental Taxonomy," *Journal of Theoretical Biology* 322:72–80 (2013).

170. Robert Vermeiren, "Psychopathology and Criminality in Adolescents: A Descriptive and Developmental Perspective," *Clinical Psychology Review* 23:277–318 (2003); Paul Mazerolle, Robert Brame, Ray Paternoster, Alex Piquero, and Charles Dean, "Onset Age, Persistence, and Offending Versatility: Comparisons Across Sex," *Criminology* 38:1143–1172 (2000).

171. Adrian Raine, Rolf Loeber, Magda Stouthamer-Loeber, Terrie Moffitt, Avshalom Caspi, and Don Lynam, "Neurocognitive Impairments in Boys on the Life-Course Persistent Antisocial Path," *Journal of Abnormal Psychology* 114:38–49 (2005).

172. Per-Olof Wikstrom and Rolf Loeber, "Do Disadvantaged Neighborhoods Cause Well-Adjusted Children to Become Adolescent Delinquents? A Study of Male Juvenile Serious Offending, Individual Risk and Protective Factors, and Neighborhood Context," *Criminology* 38:1109–1142 (2000).

173. Graham Ousey and Pamela Wilcox, "The Interaction of Antisocial Propensity and Life-Course Varying Predictors of Delinquent Behavior: Differences by Method of Estimation and Implications for Theory," *Criminology* 45:313–354 (2007).

174. Bradley Entner Wright, Avshalom Caspi, Terrie Moffitt, and Phil Silva, "Low Self-Control, Social Bonds, and Crime: Social Causation, Social Selection, or Both?" *Criminology* 37:479–514 (1999).

175. Ibid., p. 504.

176. Stephen Cernkovich and Peggy Giordano, "Stability and Change in Antisocial Behavior: The Transition from Adolescence to Early Adulthood," *Criminology* 39:371–410 (2001).

177. Heather Lonczk, Robert Abbott, J. David Hawkins, Rick Kosterman, and Richard Catalano, "Effects of the Seattle Social Development Project on Sexual Behavior, Pregnancy, Birth, and Sexually Transmitted Disease Outcomes by Age 21 Years," *Archive of Pediatrics and Adolescent Medicine* 156:438–447 (2002).

178. Kathleen Bodisch Lynch, Susan Rose Geller, and Melinda G. Schmidt, "Multi-Year Evaluation of the Effectiveness of a Resilience-Based Prevention Program for Young Children," *Journal of Primary Prevention* 24:335–353 (2004).

179. This section leans on Thomas Tatchell, Phillip Waite, Renny Tatchell, Lynne Durrant, and Dale Bond, "Substance Abuse Prevention in Sixth Grade: The Effect of a Prevention Program on Adolescents' Risk and Protective Factors," *American Journal of Health Studies* 19:54–61 (2004).

180. Nancy Tobler and Howard Stratton, "Effectiveness of School-Based Drug Prevention Programs: A Meta-Analysis of the Research," *Journal of Primary Prevention* 18:71–128 (1997).

181. Fast Track Project, Data Center, http://fasttrackproject.org/datacenter.php.

part three

Social, Community, and Environmental Influences on Delinquency

Social, community, and environmental relations are thought to exert a powerful influence on an adolescent's involvement in delinquent activities. Kids who fail at home, at school, and in the neighborhood are considered in danger of developing and/or sustaining delinquent careers. Research indicates that chronic, persistent offenders are quite likely to experience educational failure, poor home life, substance abuse, and unsatisfactory peer relations.

Social, community, and environmental relations can also have a positive influence and shield at-risk children from involvement in a delinquent way of life. Consequently, many delinquency prevention efforts focus on improving family relations, supporting educational achievement, and utilizing community resources. Some begin early in childhood, others during the teen years, while a third type of prevention effort is designed to help those who have been involved in antisocial behavior to desist from further activities.

Part Three contains six chapters devoted to the influences critical social and environmental forces have on delinquency. Chapter 7 explores gender relations and their relationship to delinquency. Chapter 8 is devoted to the family, and Chapter 9 looks at peer relations, including juvenile groups and gangs. Chapter 10 examines the relationship between education and delinquency, and Chapter 11 concerns substance abuse. Finally, Chapter 12 looks at how the community environment is being used to help youths avoid involvement in delinquent behaviors.

CHAPTER 7
Gender and Delinquency

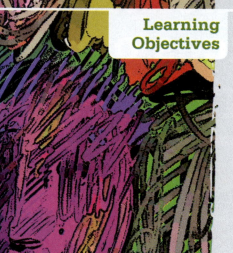

IN LATE MAY 2014, in the Milwaukee suburb of Waukesha, Wisconsin, two 12-year-old girls, Morgan Geyser and Anissa Weier, lured their friend Payton Leutner, 11, into the woods behind Geyser's home in the middle of the night. There, Geyser and Weier allegedly stabbed Leutner 19 times and left her for dead. Leutner was able crawl to a road, where she lay bleeding in a ditch with stab wounds in her arms, legs, and torso until a bicyclist found her and called 911. Luckily the quick attention saved her life, though she was hospitalized for six days.

Why would two young girls try to kill a best friend? Geyser and Weier had discovered the legend of the Slender Man on the Creepypasta Wiki, a website that hosts Internet horror stories. They told investigators that they believed this paranormal predator was real and that they wanted to become his "proxies" to prove their loyalty to him, prove his existence, and prevent him from harming their families. The only way they could become the Slender Man's proxies was to murder someone. After they carried out the attack, they would become servants of the Slender Man and be allowed to live in his mansion, which they believed was in Nicolet National Forest.

On July 27, 2016, the Second District Appeals Court for Wisconsin upheld the Circuit Court judge's decision to try the girls as adults. The attorneys for the perpetrators claim that the girls suffer from emotional and psychological problems, ranging from oppositional defiant disorder to schizophrenia, thus rendering adult court unnecessary. The court, however, ruled that

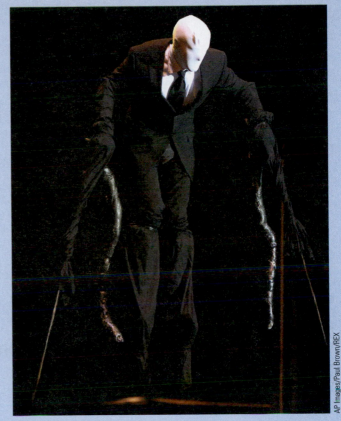

AP Images/Paul Brown/REX

An image of the Slender Man, the fictional character that drove two young women to stab a friend.

the stabbing was not accidental or impulsive but premeditated and extremely violent.[1] Both girls offered insanity pleas, and their mental state is still being considered.

W hile the Slender Man story is admittedly bizarre, the fact that young girls are now engaging in violent crime is certainly not unique or unusual. In the past, experts considered female delinquency an aberration, a function of emotional or family-related problems, and as such not an important subject of study. In fact, the few "true" female delinquents were oddities whose criminal activity was a function of having masculine traits and characteristics, a concept referred to today as the **masculinity hypothesis**.[2]

Contemporary interest in female delinquency has surged, fueled by observations of the struggles young women now face and the fact that they are committing more frequent and serious delinquent acts. Although females still commit fewer serious violent crimes than males, the illegal acts that young women engage in today are quite similar to those of young men. Larceny and aggravated assault, the crimes for which most young men are arrested, are also the most common offenses for which females are arrested; there is also evidence that girls are getting more heavily involved in gangs and gang violence.

Young women soon find that antisocial behaviors bring with them consequences that can be both long term and devastating. Early onset female offenders face higher rates of premature mortality, substantial rates of psychiatric problems, dysfunctional and often violent interpersonal relationships, not to mention

masculinity hypothesis
View that women who commit crimes have biological and psychological traits similar to those of men.

significantly higher risks of remaining involved in antisocial activities across the life course.[3] Another collateral risk of teen misbehavior is early motherhood: one recent study of more than 70,000 teen girls involved in adolescent misbehavior found the strongest association between childhood risk and teen pregnancy involved juvenile delinquency. Girls who had been referred to the state juvenile justice department were three-and-a-half times more likely to have a baby while still a teenager than girls who had not been arrested.[4]

This chapter provides an overview of gender factors in delinquency. We first discuss some of the gender differences in development and how they may relate to offending rates. Then we turn to some theoretical explanations of the causes of female delinquency: (1) the trait view, (2) the socialization view, (3) the liberal feminist view, and (4) the critical feminist view.

The website of the **Commonwealth Fund** (http://www.commonwealthfund.org/) provides information on the state of adolescent girls and the risks they face.

Gender Differences in Development

Do gender differences in development, including socialization, cognition, and personality, pave the way for future differences in misbehaving?[5] It is possible that the gender-based traits that produce delinquency may exist as early as infancy, when infant girls show greater control over their emotions, whereas boys are more easily angered and depend more on input from their mothers.[6]

Socialization Differences

Psychologists believe that differences in the way females and males are socialized affect their development. Parents may treat boys and girls differently, encouraging what they consider to be appropriate male and female behavior, respectively. It is not surprising that fathers are more likely to teach their sons about using and maintaining weapons while not sharing this knowledge with their daughters; self-report studies show that boys are three times more likely than girls to report hunting or shooting with a family member.[7]

Males learn to value independence, whereas females are taught that their self-worth depends on their ability to sustain relationships. Girls, therefore, run the risk of losing themselves in their relationships with others and, because so many relationships go sour, also run the risk of feeling alienated, because of the failure to achieve relational success.[8] It is not surprising that research shows, given a similar set of provocations such as lack of social support from families and peers, that girls react by getting depressed while boys are more likely to engage in delinquent behaviors.[9]

Socialization also influences aggressive behaviors. Although there are few gender differences in aggression during the first few years of life, girls are socialized to be less aggressive than boys and are supervised more closely.[10] Boys are exposed to more risk factors in their development and are given fewer protections. The combination of greater risk and less protection may manifest itself in levels of antisocial behaviors and aggression.[11] Differences in aggression become noticeable between ages 3 and 6, when children are socialized into organized groups, such as the daycare center. Males are more likely to display physical aggression, whereas females display relational aggression—for example, by excluding disliked peers from play groups.[12]

Cognitive Differences

There are also cognitive differences between males and females, starting in childhood. The more replicated findings about gender difference in cognitive performance suggest female superiority on visual-motor speed and language ability and male superiority on mechanical and visual-spatial tasks.[13] Put another way, males excel in tasks that assess the ability to manipulate visual images in working memory, whereas females do better in tasks that require retrieval from long-term memory and the acquisition and use of verbal information.[14] Gender group strengths found in the early school years become more established at adolescence and remain stable through adulthood.[15]

Girls learn to speak earlier and faster, and with better pronunciation, most likely because parents talk more to their infant daughters than to their infant sons. A girl's verbal proficiency enables her to develop a skill that may later help her deal with conflict without resorting to violence.[16] When faced with conflict, women might be more likely to attempt to negotiate, rather than to respond passively or resist physically, especially when they perceive increased threat of harm or death.[17]

When girls are aggressive, they are more likely than boys to hide their behavior from adults; girls who bully others are less likely than boys to admit their behavior.[18] Girls are shielded by their moral sense, which directs them to avoid harming others. Their moral sensitivity may counterbalance the effects of family problems.[19] Females display more self-control than males, a factor that has been related to criminality.[20]

In most cases cognitive differences are small, narrowing, and usually attributed to cultural expectations. When given training, girls can increase their visual-spatial skills. However, differences still exert a penalty on young girls.

Personality Differences

Adolescent females use different knowledge than males and have different ways of interpreting their interactions with others. Girls are often stereotyped as talkative, but research shows that in many situations boys spend more time talking than girls. Females are more willing to reveal their feelings and more likely to express concern and empathy for others.[21] Males are more likely to introduce new topics and to interrupt conversations. Girls score higher on scales measuring agreeableness, while boys are more open to experience.[22]

These gender differences may have an impact on self-esteem and self-concept. One reason is that girls are more likely to worry about their weight and be more dissatisfied with the size and shape of their bodies.[23] Young girls are regularly confronted with unrealistically high standards of slimness that make them extremely unhappy with their own bodies; it is not surprising that the incidence of eating disorders, such as anorexia and bulimia, has increased markedly in recent years. In a classic 1982 study, psychologist Carol Gilligan uncovered an alternative explanation for this decline in female self-esteem: as girls move into adolescence, they become aware of the conflict between the positive way they see themselves and the negative way society views females. Many girls respond by "losing their voices"—that is, submerging their own feelings and accepting the negative view of women conveyed by adult authorities.[24]

The fact that males and females display different personality traits is significant considering the association between personality and delinquency. Each presents a different set of problems for agents of the juvenile justice system: males who have trouble dealing with disturbing interactions turn to violence and aggression; females turn to status offending.[25]

Emotional Differences

There are differences in the way boys and girls regulate their emotions and feelings.[26] Girls are often stereotyped as being more emotional than boys, but research shows that in many situations gender difference in emotionality is narrow.[27] Nonetheless, research shows that females are more willing to reveal their feelings and more likely to express concern for others. A recent review of the literature on emotional development found that girls are more willing to display more positive emotions and internalizing emotions—sadness, anxiety, and sympathy—than

Adolescence can be a trying time for young women, and because of the stresses of socialization, many become the victim of psychological problems and disorders. Shown here at Denver's Children's Hospital for eating disorder patients, two 15-year-old girls work on their art therapy books during a session at the Ponzio Creative Arts Therapy Program. The program offers art, dance/movement, music, and yoga therapies that help children identify, explore, and transform emotional and psychological difficulties.

Andy Cross/Denver Post/Getty Images

boys; in contrast, males display more externalizing emotions—such as anger— than girls. The gender gap in emotion increases with age: girls exhibit more positive emotions as they reach maturity while boys lag behind.[28]

This change in emotional maturity may help explain gender differences in teen delinquency rates. Males may have higher levels of delinquency than females because they cannot handle the strain of the teenage years as well as females.[29] Males are more likely to cope with strain through crime, due to their inability to develop the self-control needed to manage their emotions.[30] Concept Summary 7.1 discusses these various gender differences.

What Causes Gender Differences—Biology or Socialization?

Why do these gender differences occur? Some experts suggest that gender differences may have a biological origin: males and females are essentially different.

CONCEPT SUMMARY 7.1

Gender Differences

	Females	Males
Socialization	Sustain relationships	Are independent
	Are less aggressive	Are aggressive
	Blame self	Externalize anger
Cognitive	Have superior verbal ability	Have superior visual-spatial ability
	Speak earlier	Are better at math
	Have better pronunciation	
	Read better	
Personality	Have lower self-esteem	Have higher self-esteem
	Are self-aware	Are materialistic
	Have better attention span	Have lower attention span
Emotional	Internalize emotions	Externalize emotions
	Express sadness, anxiety	Express anger

They have somewhat different brain organizations; females are more left brain–oriented and males more right brain–oriented. (The left brain is believed to control language; the right, spatial relations.)[31] Others point to the hormonal differences between the sexes as the key to understanding their behavior.

A second view is that gender differences are developed over the life course and reflect different treatment of males and females. In her book *The Two Sexes: Growing Up Apart, Coming Together*, psychologist Eleanor Maccoby argues that gender differences are not a matter of individual personality or biological difference but the way kids socialize and how their relationships are structured.[32] Despite the best efforts of parents who want to break down gender boundaries, kids still segregate themselves by gender in their playgroups. Thus, a "boy culture" and a "girl culture" develop side by side. Kids also take on different roles depending on whom they are with and who is being exposed to the behavior. A boy will be all macho bravado when he is with his peers but may be a tender, loving big brother with his little sister.

Little girls aren't "passive" as a result of some ingrained quality; they have learned to be passive only when boys are present. According to Maccoby, gender separation has partly biological and partly social causes. Though biological and cognitive differences do impact behavior, Maccoby claims that gender distinctions arise mainly in social interactions and that peer groups are highly influential in enhancing gender. Take for instance the macho male jock culture, which encourages its members to become risk takers and engage in status-type offenses such as drinking.[33] Nonetheless, biological and social factors are so intertwined that it is erroneous to think of gender differences as having an independent social or physical origin.

Another view is that gender differences are a result of the interaction of socialization, learning, and enculturation. Boys and girls may behave differently because they have been exposed to different styles of socialization, learned different values, and had different cultural experiences.[34] According to psychologist Sandra Bem's **gender-schema theory**, our culture polarizes males and females by forcing them to obey mutually exclusive gender roles, or "scripts." Girls are expected to be "feminine," exhibiting sympathetic and gentle traits. In contrast, boys are expected to be "masculine," exhibiting assertiveness and dominance.

Children internalize these scripts and accept gender polarization as normal. Children's self-esteem becomes wrapped up in how closely their behavior conforms to the proper sex role stereotype. When children begin to perceive themselves as either boys or girls (which occurs at about age 3), they search for information to help them define their role; they begin to learn what behavior is appropriate for their sex.[35] Girls are expected to behave according to the appropriate script and to seek approval of their behavior: Are they acting as girls should at that age? Masculine behavior is to be avoided. In contrast, males look for cues from their peers to define their masculinity; aggressive behavior may be rewarded with peer approval, whereas sensitivity is viewed as unmasculine.[36] Girls are less affected by peer influence and more by the bond they may share with parents and significant others.[37]

gender-schema theory
A theory of development that holds that children internalize gender scripts reflecting the gender-related social practices of the culture. Once internalized, these gender scripts predispose the kids to construct a self-identity that is consistent with the scripts.

Not So Different After All Not every social scientist agrees that there are significant differences between the genders. In an important meta-analysis of studies examining gender differences in such traits as personality, cognition, communication skills, and leadership ability, psychologist Janet Shibley Hyde found that men and women are basically more alike than different on these critical psychological variables; she refers to her finding as the **gender similarities hypothesis**. Hyde found that gender differences had either no effect or a very small effect on most of the psychological variables examined, with only a few exceptions: compared with women, men were more physically aggressive, and they approved of sex without commitment. Hyde also found that gender differences fluctuate with age, growing smaller or larger at different times in the life span, indicating that differences are not stable and change over the life course. One significant myth she claims to have debunked: boys do better at math. According to her findings, boys and girls perform equally well in math until high school, at which point boys do become more

gender similarities hypothesis
The belief that gender differences in personality, cognition, intelligence, etc., are much smaller than previously believed.

proficient. It is possible that girls avoid advanced classes believing erroneously that they are doomed to failure, thereby creating a self-fulfilling prophecy.[38]

Hyde's work is not without its critics.[39] Yet, she may be addressing an important contemporary phenomenon: even if gender differences existed before, they may now be eroding. If so, this phenomenon may be impacting gender differences in delinquency.

Gender Differences and Delinquency

Research conducted in the United States and abroad has found that the factors that direct the trajectories of male delinquency are quite different from those that influence female delinquency. Males are more aggressive and less likely to form attachments to others, factors that might help them maintain their crime rates over their life span. Males view aggression as an appropriate means to gain status. Boys are also more likely than girls to socialize with deviant peers, and when they do, they display personality traits that make them more susceptible to delinquency. They are more often exposed to delinquency-producing strains in the environment, such as crime victimization, and are more likely to react to conflict with aggressive responses rather than empathy and understanding.[40]

This pattern fits within the two cultures view, which suggests that girls and boys differ in their social behavior largely because their sex-segregated peer groups demand behaviors, such as aggression, that may not be characteristic of them in other social situations.[41] What is typically assumed to be an inherent difference in antisocial behavior tendencies may actually be a function of peer socialization differences. The fact that young boys perceive their roles as being more dominant than young girls may be a function of peer pressure. Male perceptions of power, their ability to have freedom and hang with their friends, help explain gender differences in personality.[42] It follows, then, that if members of both sexes were equally exposed to the factors that produce delinquency, their delinquency rates would be equivalent. While socialization may be a strong force, inherent gender differences in cognition, personality, and biology still seem to play a role in shaping interpersonal interactions, including aggression, and cannot be totally discounted.[43] Cognitive and personality differences are magnified when children internalize gender-specific behaviors. Boys who aren't tough may appear weak, cowardly, and effeminate. Girls, in contrast, are expected to form closer bonds with their friends and to share feelings.

The mission of the **International Council for Research on Women** (http://www.icrw.org/) is to enhance the connections among research, policy analysis, advocacy, and innovative programming on behalf of women and girls.

Gender Patterns in Delinquency

Within all social and economic strata, males still commit more delinquency than females.[44] However, the gender gap in crime and delinquency arrests has been closing. In 1995, the male:female delinquency arrest ratio was 3:1; today it's closer to 2:1 (the violent crime arrest ratio is still more than 5:1 male).

Similarly, self-report studies (see Table 7.1) indicate that the rank-ordering of male and female delinquent behaviors is more similar than ever. That is, the illegal acts most common for boys—petty larceny, using a false ID, and smoking marijuana—are also the ones most frequently committed by girls.[45]

In addition, the factors that explain the onset of male delinquency, such as the influence of delinquent peers, are similar to the ones that explain female delinquency. In other words, the pathways of offending appear to be similar across genders.[46]

Several policy shifts may have escalated girls' arrest-proneness:

- The definition of violent crime may have expanded so that minor incidents that girls are more likely to commit are now included in the arrest data.

- Police are more likely to make arrests in private settings (e.g., home and school) where girls' violence is more likely to occur

- Family and societal attitudes toward juvenile females are less tolerant now.

table 7.1

Percentage of High School Seniors Admitting to at Least One Offense During the Past 12 Months, by Gender

Delinquent Acts	Males	Females
Serious fight	11	7
Gang fight	13	11
Hurt someone badly	11	4
Used a weapon to steal	4	1
Theft, more than $50	8	5
Theft, less than $50	23	22
Shoplift	31	17
Breaking and entering	25	19
Arson	3	2
Damaged school property	8	9
Car theft	4	3
Car part theft	8	4

Source: *Monitoring the Future, 2015* (Ann Arbor, MI: Institute for Social Research, 2015).

These developments reflect both a growing intolerance of violence in the law and among the citizenry and an expanded application of preventive punishment and risk management strategies that emphasize early identification and enhanced formal control of problem individuals or groups, particularly problem youth.[47]

While the gender gap has narrowed, gender differences are still significant for the most serious violent crime. Arrest for murder is typically 10:1 in favor of males; fewer than 50 girls ages 18 and under are typically arrested on murder charges each year, as compared to more than 500 boys.

One reason for the gender disparity in lethal violence is that males and females display differences in the victims they target and the weapons they use. The typical male juvenile kills a friend or acquaintance with a handgun during an argument. In contrast, the typical female is as likely to kill a family member as an acquaintance and is more likely to use a knife. Both males and females tend to kill males—generally their brothers, fathers, or friends.

Police and the Gender Gap   How can the narrowing of the gender gap in delinquency be explained? One possibility is that police are changing the manner in which they handle cases involving adolescent females, showing them less favoritism, resulting in a greater likelihood of girls getting arrested. Research using self-report data shows that girls' violence or drug use has remained rather stable.[48] Therefore, any gender convergence in the delinquency arrest rate may be due to changing police procedures and not actual change in delinquent activity.

One reason for police intervention is due to heightened sensitivity to domestic violence. Many state and local police agencies have implemented mandatory arrest policies in response to domestic disturbances, including those between parents and children. Behaviors once considered "ungovernable" (a status offense) may, in a domestic situation, result instead in an arrest for simple assault. Policies of mandatory arrest for domestic violence, initially adopted to protect victims from further attacks, also provide parents with a method for attempting to control their "unruly" daughters. Girls fight with family members or siblings more frequently than boys, who more often fight with friends or strangers. This dynamic makes girls more vulnerable to arrest under changing domestic violence laws, and therefore increases their presence in the arrest statistics.[49]

A number of institutes at major universities are devoted to the **study of women's issues.** You can visit the website of the one at the University of California–Los Angeles (UCLA) at http://www.csw.ucla.edu/.

On September 9, 2016, Anissa Weier, accused of trying to kill a classmate to please horror character the Slender Man, listens to her attorney, Joseph Smith, during a hearing at Waukesha (Wisconsin) County Circuit Court. Weier entered a plea of not guilty by reason of mental disease or defect to the attempted homicide charge.

AP Images/Michael Sears

Female Violence While notion of a female "crime wave," may be overstated, some girls are violent, and female violence has taken on distinct patterns and trends:

- *Peer violence.* The majority of girls' violence is directed at same-sex peers. Girls fight with peers to gain status, to defend their sexual reputation, and in self-defense against sexual harassment.

- *Family violence.* Girls fight more frequently at home with parents than do boys, who engage more frequently in violence outside the household. Some incidents represent striking back against what they view as an overly controlling structure. Other girls attack family members as a defense against or an expression of anger stemming from being sexually and/or physically abused by members of the household.

- *Violence at school.* When girls fight at school, they may do so as a result of teacher labeling, in self-defense, or out of a general sense of hopelessness.

- *Violence within disadvantaged neighborhoods.* Girls in disadvantaged neighborhoods are more likely to perpetrate violence against others because of the increased risk of victimization, parental inability to protect them from community predators, and lack of opportunities for success.

- *Girls in gangs.* Girls associated with primarily male gangs exhibit more violence than those in all-female gangs. Girls in gangs are more violent than other girls but less violent than boys in gangs.[50]

In the sections below, we will explore the theoretical basis of female delinquency.

Trait Theory and Female Delinquency

There is a long tradition of tracing gender differences in delinquency to traits that are uniquely male or female. The argument that biological and psychological differences between males and females can explain differences in crime rates is not a new one. The earliest criminologists focused on physical characteristics believed to be precursors of crime.

Early Biological Explanations

With the publication in 1895 of *The Female Offender*, Cesare Lombroso (with William Ferrero) extended his work on criminality to females.[51] Lombroso maintained that

Morgan Geyser, along with Anissa Weier, was accused of trying to kill a 12-year-old classmate to please the Slender Man. She is shown as she pleaded not guilty by reason of insanity.

AP Images/Michael Sears

women were lower on the evolutionary scale than men, more childlike and less intelligent.[52] Women who committed crimes could be distinguished from "normal" women by physical characteristics—excessive body hair, wrinkles, and an abnormal cranium, for example.[53] In appearance, delinquent females appeared closer to men than to other women. The masculinity hypothesis suggested that delinquent girls had excessive male characteristics.[54]

Lombrosian thought had a significant influence for much of the twentieth century. Delinquency rate differentials were explained in terms of gender-based differences. In 1925, Cyril Burt linked female delinquency to menstruation.[55] Similarly, William Healy and Augusta Bronner suggested that males' physical superiority enhanced their criminality. Their research showed that about 70 percent of the delinquent girls they studied had abnormal weight and size, a finding that supported the masculinity hypothesis.[56] At this time, so-called experts suggested that female delinquency goes unrecorded because the female is the instigator rather than the perpetrator.[57] Females first use their sexual charms to instigate crime and then beguile males in the justice system to obtain deferential treatment. The fact that female criminality is overlooked or forgiven by male agents of the justice system is referred to as the **chivalry hypothesis**. Those who believe in the chivalry hypothesis point to data showing that females make up a far greater percentage of the arrestee population than they do the prison inmate cohort, a finding that suggests that women and girls are treated more leniently than men and boys even after they are arrested, tried, and convicted.[58]

chivalry hypothesis (also known as paternalism hypothesis)
The view that low female crime and delinquency rates are a reflection of the leniency with which police treat female offenders.

Early Psychological Explanations

Psychologists also viewed the physical differences between males and females as a basis for their behavior differentials. Sigmund Freud maintained that girls interpret their lack of a penis as a sign that they have been punished. Boys fear that they can be punished by having their penises cut off, and thus learn to fear women. From this conflict comes *penis envy*, which often produces an inferiority complex in girls, forcing them to make an effort to compensate for their "defect." One way to compensate is to identify with their mothers and accept a maternal role. Also, girls may attempt to compensate for their lack of a penis by dressing well and beautifying themselves.[59] Freud also claimed that "if a little girl persists in her first wish—to grow into a boy—in extreme cases she will end as a manifest homosexual, and otherwise she will exhibit markedly masculine traits in the conduct of her later life, will choose a masculine vocation, and so on."[60]

In the mid-twentieth century, psychodynamic theorists suggested that girls are socialized to be passive, which helps explain their low crime rate. However, this condition also makes some females susceptible to being manipulated by men—hence, their participation in sex-related crimes, such as prostitution. A girl's wayward behavior, psychoanalysts suggested, was restricted to neurotic theft (kleptomania) and overt sexual acts, which were symptoms of personality maladaption.[61]

According to these early versions of the psychoanalytic approach, gender differences in the delinquency rate can be traced to differences in psychological orientation. Male delinquency reflects aggressive traits, whereas female delinquency is a function of repressed sexuality, gender conflict, and abnormal socialization.

Contemporary Trait Views

Contemporary biosocial and psychological theorists have continued the tradition of attributing gender differences in delinquency to physical and emotional traits. These theorists recognize that it is the interaction of biological and psychological traits with the social environment that produces delinquency.

Early Puberty/Precocious Sexuality Early theorists linked female delinquency to early puberty and **precocious sexuality**. According to this view, girls

precocious sexuality
Sexual experimentation in early adolescence.

who experience an early onset of physical maturity are most likely to engage in antisocial behavior.[62] Female delinquents were believed to be promiscuous and more sophisticated than male delinquents.[63] Linking female delinquency to sexuality was responsible, in part, for the view that female delinquency is symptomatic of maladjustment.[64]

Equating female delinquency purely with sexual activity is no longer taken seriously, but early sexual maturity has been linked to other problems, such as a higher risk of teen pregnancy and sexually transmitted diseases.[65] It also produces increased conflict between parents and teens.[66] It is not unusual to see intrafamily conflicts brewing up around issues such as dating, selecting friends, and changing behavioral expectations.[67]

One reason for this *Sturm und Drang* is that "early bloomers" may be more attractive to older adolescent boys, and increased contact with this high-risk group places the girls in jeopardy for antisocial behavior. Research shows that young girls who date boys three or more years older are more likely to engage in precocious sex, feel pressured into having sex, and engage in sex while under the influence of drugs and/or alcohol than girls who date more age-appropriate boys.[68] And all too often these factors are interrelated: adolescent females who use recreational drugs and drink alcohol are more likely to hang out with male friends. Their peer experience will enhance their delinquency and heighten their risk of sexual victimization.[69]

Early puberty is most likely to encourage delinquent activities that occur in the context of socializing with peers and having romantic relationships with boys.[70] Girls who are romantically attached to older boys who encourage antisocial behavior are more likely to engage in delinquency than those who lack such "encouraging" partners.[71] The delinquency gap between early and late bloomers narrows when the latter group reaches sexual maturity and increases in girls' exposure to boys.[72]

Girls who are more sexually developed relative to their peers are more likely to socialize at an early age and to get involved in deviant behaviors, especially "party deviance," such as drinking, smoking, and substance abuse. Such behavior can have long-term consequences. The association is often reciprocal: precocious sexuality increases a young woman's involvement in antisocial activities; engaging in antisocial activities increases the likelihood of risky sexual behaviors.[73]

Sociologist Sampson Lee Blair examined the long-term consequences of adolescent delinquency and substance use on the marital choices of young adults. Using a nationally representative sample of more than 10,000 people, his analyses found that both substance use and delinquent behavior in the adolescent years significantly affect the likelihood of marriage and the age at first marriage of young adults. Delinquent behaviors appear to increase the likelihood of marriage and lower the age at first marriage for both sexes, while higher levels of substance use (alcohol and marijuana) substantially lower females' likelihood of marriage. The results suggest that a gender difference exists in how risk-taking behaviors in adolescence impact marital outcomes in adulthood.[74]

Early Puberty and Victimization If reaching puberty at an early age increases the likelihood of delinquent behavior, does it also increase victimization risk? Research by Dana Haynie and Alex Piquero found that both boys and girls who reached puberty at an early age increase their chances of victimization. The association was gendered: boys were less likely to become victims if their friendship network contained girls; in contrast, girls' victimization was not moderated by the sexual makeup of their peer group.[75]

Why does peer group makeup influence boys' victimization more than girls'? It is possible that females are much less likely to be involved in serious, violent delinquency, and therefore having a higher concentration of them in a male's peer network reduces his exposure to more violent boys. In contrast, boys who associate mostly with male peers may feel compelled to engage in risky behaviors—in order to keep up with their friends they have to drink, drive fast, and get involved in brawls. Girls may feel less peer pressure to engage in risky behavior; their male friends may protect them rather than put them in danger.

In sum, although early puberty and sexual development may put girls at risk for juvenile delinquency and substance abuse, they may also help shield them from victimization risk.

Why Do Girls Mature Early?   Why do some girls mature early and place themselves at risk for delinquency? Psychologist Jay Belsky proposed an explanation for the finding that girls whose fathers abandon them tend to reach puberty early and to exhibit increased promiscuity. Belsky suggested that some girls exposed to high levels of stress, particularly due to paternal absence in early childhood, may often respond by becoming depressed and insecure, gaining weight and then experiencing accelerated puberty as a result of hormonal changes precipitated by the weight gain, and becoming sexually active with multiple partners and unstable relationships, often resulting in early childbearing.[76]

New research, however, suggests a different explanation for the link between paternal absence and both early puberty and promiscuity in girls. David Comings and colleagues tested male and female subjects and found a particular gene pattern with a short AR allele was associated with assaultive behavior, impulsiveness, sexual compulsiveness and increased number of sexual partners, and feelings of reduced internal control in the male subjects. In females, the presence of the short AR pattern was associated with parental divorce, paternal absence during childhood, and early puberty. Their conclusion: the link between paternal abandonment and early puberty in girls is genetic. Fathers who have the suspect gene pattern engage in marital conflict and abandonment. Their daughters, who inherit the gene, are more likely to reach puberty at an early age and engage in risky behaviors such as precocious sexual activity, childbearing, and disruptive personal relationships. The cause of these mutually dysfunctional behaviors is not stress or learning, but shared genes passed from the fathers to their daughters. Their findings also explain why girls whose fathers die do not experience the same changes in behavior and timing of puberty onset as girls whose fathers abandon them. Fathers who die early would be no more likely to carry the short AR gene than fathers in the general population.[77]

Hormonal Effects   As you may recall from Chapter 3, some biosocial theorists link antisocial behavior to hormonal influences.[78] One view is that hormonal imbalance may influence aggressive behavior in young girls. Cortisol, responsible for controlling inflammation and suppressing the immune response, is the primary hormone released during long periods of stress or physical trauma. It has also been linked to aggressive behavior in young women. When Kathleen Pajer and her colleagues studied 47 adolescent girls with conduct disorder (CD) and 37 control girls, taking three separate measurements of cortisol, they found that girls with conduct disorder had significantly lower cortisol levels than girls in the normal control group at all three sampling times. They conclude that antisocial girls may suffer from "dysregulation of the hypothalamic-pituitary-adrenal axis," which regulates cortisol levels.[79]

Another view is that excessive amounts of male hormones (androgens) are related to delinquency. The androgen most often related to antisocial behavior is testosterone.[80] In general, females who test higher for testosterone are more likely to engage in stereotypical male behaviors.[81] Females who have low androgen levels are less aggressive than males, whereas those who have elevated levels will take on characteristically male traits, including aggression.[82]

Some females who are overexposed to male hormones in utero may become "constitutionally masculinized." They may develop abnormal hair growth, large musculature, low voice, irregular menstrual cycle, and hyperaggressive behavior. Females exposed to male hormones in utero are more likely to engage in aggressive behavior later in life.[83]

Premenstrual Syndrome   Early biotheorists suspected that premenstrual syndrome (PMS) was a direct cause of the relatively rare instances of female violence: "For several days prior to and during menstruation, the stereotype has been that 'raging hormones' doom women to irritability and poor judgment—two facets of premenstrual syndrome."[84] The link between PMS and delinquency was popularized by Katharina Dalton, whose studies of English women led her to conclude that females are more likely to commit suicide and be aggressive and otherwise antisocial before or during menstruation.[85]

Today there is conflicting evidence on the relationship between PMS and female delinquency. Research shows that a significant number of incarcerated females committed their crimes during the premenstrual phase, and also that a small percentage of women appear vulnerable to cyclical hormonal changes that make them more prone to anxiety and hostility.[86] Nonetheless, it is possible that any association is spurious because the stress of antisocial behavior produces early menstruation.

Aggression   According to some biosocial theorists, gender differences in the delinquency rate can be explained by inborn differences in aggression.[87] Some psychologists believe that males are inherently more aggressive, a condition that appears very early in life, before socialization can influence behavior.

Gender-based differences in aggression have been developing for millions of years and reflect the dissimilarities in the male and female reproductive systems. Males are more aggressive because they wish to possess as many sex partners as possible to increase their chances of producing offspring. Females have learned to control their aggressive impulses because having multiple mates does not increase their chances of conception. Instead, females concentrate on acquiring things that will help them rear their offspring, such as a reliable mate who will supply material resources.[88]

Contemporary Psychological Views

Because girls are socialized to be less aggressive than boys, it is possible that the young women who get involved in antisocial and violent behavior suffer from some form of mental anguish or abnormality. Girls are also more likely than boys to be involved in status offenses such as running away and truancy, behaviors that suggest underlying psychological distress.

Research indicates that antisocial adolescent girls do suffer a wide variety of psychiatric problems, including PTSD, and have dysfunctional and violent relationships at home and with their romantic partners.[89] Incarcerated adolescent female offenders have more acute mental health symptoms and psychological disturbances than male offenders.[90] Female delinquents score high on psychological tests measuring such traits as psychopathic deviation, schizophrenia, paranoia, and psychasthenia (a psychological disorder characterized by phobias, obsessions, compulsions, or excessive anxiety).[91] Clinical interviews indicate that female delinquents are significantly more likely than males to suffer from **callous and unemotional traits (CU)** and mood disorders, including any disruptive disorder, major depressive disorder, and separation anxiety disorder.[92]

Females seem to be more susceptible to the psychological damage produced from living in a dysfunctional household than males.[93] One study of female arsonists found that they were often from profoundly unstable homes, experienced difficulty with school attendance and behavior, had little or no contact with at least one parent, and were in a crisis at the time of the arson offence. In addition to an unstable home life, solo female juveniles often felt upset, angry, and expressed suicidal thoughts.[94] In sum, there are experts who believe that female delinquents suffer from psychological deficits ranging from lack of self-control to serious impairments.[95]

callous and unemotional traits (CU)
A persistent pattern of behavior that reflects a disregard for others, and also a lack of empathy and generally deficient affect.

Socialization Views

Socialization views are based on the idea that a child's social development may be the key to understanding delinquent behavior. If a child experiences impairment, family disruption, and so on, the child will be more susceptible to delinquent associations and criminality.

Linking crime rate variations to gender differences in socialization is not a recent phenomenon. In a 1928 work, *The Unadjusted Girl*, W. I. Thomas suggested that some girls who have not been socialized under middle-class family controls can become impulsive thrill seekers. According to Thomas, female delinquency is linked to the wish for luxury and excitement.[96] Inequities in social class condemn poor girls from demoralized families to using sex as a means to gain amusement, pretty clothes, and other luxuries. Precocious sexuality makes these girls vulnerable to older men, who lead them down the path to decadence.[97]

Socialization and Delinquency

Scholars concerned with gender differences in crime are interested in the distinction between the lifestyles of males and females. Girls are supervised more closely than boys, and if they behave in a socially disapproved fashion, their parents may be more likely to notice. Adults may be more tolerant of deviant behavior in boys and expect boys to act tough and take risks. Closer supervision restricts the opportunity for crime and the time available to mingle with delinquent peers. Girls who are supervised closely may be less likely to engage in deviant behavior in adolescence and later go on to live more conventional adult lifestyles (i.e., marry and raise a family).[98] It follows, then, that the adolescent girl who is growing up in a troubled home and lacks supervision may be more prone to delinquency.[99]

Focus on Socialization In the 1950s, a number of researchers began to focus on gender-specific socialization patterns. They made three assumptions about gender differences in socialization:

- Families exert a more powerful influence on girls than on boys.
- Parents are stricter with girls because they perceive them as needing control.
- Girls rarely form close relationships with female peers, because they view them as rivals for males who would make eligible marriage partners.[100]

According to early socialization views, a child's social development may be the key to understanding delinquent behavior. Children will be more susceptible to delinquent associations if they experience impairment or family disruption. Improper socialization is likely to have an even more damaging effect on females than on males because girls are less likely than boys to have close-knit peer associations and are therefore in need of close parental relationships to retain emotional stability. In fact, girls may become sexually involved with boys to receive support from them, a practice that tends to magnify their problems.

PhotosIndia.com LLC/Alamy Stock Photo

Because of these associations, in some families adolescent girls rebel against strict parental controls, turning to the streets for companionship. Those girls who lack reasonable parental guidance are at risk for entering into affairs with older men who exploit them, involve them in sexual deviance (i.e., pimp them on the street), and father their illegitimate children.[101] The result is prostitution, drug abuse, and marginal lives. Their daughters, also lacking in supportive family relationships, are doomed to repeat this pattern in a never-ending cycle of exploitation.

Broken Homes/Fallen Women   A number of experts share emphasis on the family as a primary influence on delinquent behavior. Male delinquents were portrayed as rebels who esteemed toughness, excitement, and other lower-class values. Males succumbed to the lure of delinquency when they perceived few legitimate opportunities. In contrast, female delinquents were portrayed as troubled adolescents who suffered inadequate home lives and, more often than not, were victims of sexual and physical abuse. Ruth Morris described delinquent girls as unattractive youths who reside in homes marked by family tensions.[102] In *The Delinquent Girl* (published in 1970), Clyde Vedder and Dora Somerville suggested that female delinquency is usually a problem of adjustment to family pressure.[103] They also suggested that girls have serious problems in a male-dominated culture with rigid and sometimes unfair social practices.

Other early efforts linked rebellious behavior to sexual conflicts in the home.[104] Broken or disrupted homes were found to predict female delinquency.[105] Females petitioned to juvenile court were more likely than males to be charged with ungovernable behavior and sex offenses. They also were more likely to reside in single-parent homes.[106] Studies of incarcerated juveniles found that most of the male delinquents were incarcerated for burglary and other theft-related offenses, but female delinquents tended to be involved in incorrigibility and sex offenses. The conclusion: boys became delinquent to demonstrate their masculinity; girls were delinquent as a result of hostility toward parents and a consequent need to obtain attention from others.[107]

Contemporary Socialization Views

Contemporary socialization views still hold that family interaction is the key to understanding female delinquency. If a girl grows up in an atmosphere of family tension, where hostility exists between her parents, or where her parents are absent or law violators themselves, she is likely to turn to a delinquent way of life. Girls whose parents are convicted of crimes and incarcerated are themselves significantly likely to get involved in drug abuse and delinquency.[108]

Gender Differences   Because girls are less likely than boys to have close-knit peer associations, they are more likely to need close parental relationships to retain emotional stability.[109] In conventional families, girls tend to be closely monitored while boys are permitted greater latitude to stay out late, drive around with friends, or get involved in other unstructured behaviors linked to delinquency. A strong bond to parents may help insulate girls from social forces that produce delinquency.[110]

The gender gap narrows when girls engage in the same routine activities as boys (staying out late, partying, and riding around with friends); they run the risk of engaging in similar types of delinquent behavior.[111] The more unsupervised activities girls participate in, the more likely they are to engage in deviant activities such as substance abuse.[112]

The socialization approach holds that a poor home life is likely to have an even more damaging effect on females than on males.[113] In fact, girls may become sexually involved with boys to receive support from them, a practice that tends to magnify their problems if their boyfriends encourage them to engage in antisocial behaviors.[114] The Case Profile "Kaitlin's Story" illustrates the problems faced by a young woman whose home life could not provide the support she so desperately needed.

case profile

Kaitlin's Story

KAITLIN is a 15-year-old high school sophomore. She attends school on a regular basis and is a member of the school band. Her mother has recently split from her long-term partner and has a new girlfriend. Kaitlin is an only child and has sporadic contact with her biological father, who lives out of state. Recently, Kaitlin has reported feeling depressed and somewhat isolated. She has also begun talking with her school social worker on a regular basis to address a decline in her grades and troubles at school. Kaitlin was recently caught purchasing prescription drugs in a school bathroom. She was referred to a first offenders program and ordered to attend counseling.

Before services could be set up for Kaitlin, the police and rescue workers were called to the family home. Kaitlin had overdosed on a pain medication that her mother had in the medicine cabinet. She was rushed to a local hospital where she received medical care and spent the night. Kaitlin reported to the hospital psychiatrist that she was not currently suicidal, and hospital social workers assisted in creating a community plan for her to be discharged home.

Upon her arrival home, the school social worker and a therapist in the community met with Kaitlin and her mother. They arranged for Kaitlin to meet with the school social worker on a daily basis to check in and for Kaitlin to attend therapy two or three times a week. The therapist specialized in working with adolescents and had a small office at the local community center that was a block from Kaitlin's home. This proximity allowed for frequent contact with providers as well as the ongoing support Kaitlin needed. It also reduced issues related to a lack of transportation and barriers that often impact compliance. The social worker and therapist initially suspected that Kaitlin was having significant issues with her mother's sexuality. What they learned rather quickly was that Kaitlin had no concerns regarding this issue. Kaitlin reported feeling her mother was a healthy and happy person and that she supported her mother. The main challenges for Kaitlin were the loss of the relationship with her mother's long-term partner and the fact that her mother was spending large portions of time with her new girlfriend. Kaitlin reported feeling lonely, sad, and depressed. She wanted to visit with her mother's ex-partner and also to have more time alone with her mother. Kaitlin longed for the days when she and her mother went bike riding and did other family activities together.

With the assistance of the therapist and school social worker, Kaitlin was able to better understand her deep feelings of sadness and her suicide attempt. They also began to participate in family therapy, which allowed Kaitlin to talk with her mother about her need to spend time with her mother's ex-partner, as well as with her mother. The family was able to arrange for these visits, and Kaitlin and her mother began doing more planned activities together. Kaitlin continued receiving the support at school and within the community center from the therapist and others. She successfully completed the requirements for the first offenders program and did not receive any additional delinquency referrals.

CRITICAL THINKING

1. Kaitlin was disturbed by the loss of her mother's long-term partner and the fact that her mother was spending a lot of time with her new girlfriend. Did Kaitlin's home life and socialization lead to her problems? Do you believe a more traditional home produces more traditional offspring?

2. Kaitlin and her counselor visited with each other often, and they seem to have had a supportive interaction. Do you believe that therapists can have a significant influence on patient development?

Delinquency and Abuse

One focus of socialization theory is the effects of abuse on behavior. Girls seem to be more deeply affected than boys by child abuse, and the link between abuse and female delinquency seems stronger than it is for male delinquency.[115]

These experiences take a toll on their behavior choices. Research shows that girls who are the victims of child sexual abuse and physical abuse are the ones most likely to engage in violent and nonviolent criminal behavior.[116] Those with exposure to significant levels of violence are also the ones most likely to become crime victims and the target of relationship violence.[117]

Girls may be forced into a life of sexual promiscuity because their sexual desirability makes them a valuable commodity for families living on the edge. There are cases of youths being "lent out" to drug dealers so their parents or partners can get high. Girls on the streets are encouraged to sell their bodies because they have little else of value to trade.[118] Meda Chesney-Lind, a prominent feminist scholar, has described this association: "Young women on the run from homes characterized by sexual abuse and parental neglect are forced, by the very statutes designed to protect them, into the life of an escaped convict."[119] Many of these girls may find themselves pregnant at a very young age. Physical and sexual abuse and the toll it takes on young girls are not unique to any one culture.

Chesney-Lind's warning is substantiated by recent research conducted by Pernilla Johansson and Kimberly Kempf-Leonard. Using data from a large sample of 10,000 youths petitioned to juvenile court, the researchers found that for girls with at least one prior runaway, the risk of chronic offending (as compared to occasional offending) was five times higher than the risk for females without a prior runaway; the effect of running away was greater on girls than boys. Girls in the sample were also much more likely than boys to have been subject to abuse. Nearly 25 percent of females but only 7 percent of males had been subject to suspected abuse or maltreatment, including sexual abuse, physical abuse, emotional abuse, and child protective services involvement. Not surprisingly, 30 percent of the females and 15 percent of the males had some form of mental health problems.[120] This research highlights the association between socialization and delinquency and shows that many young girls bear a heavy load of emotional problems that lead them to a delinquent way of life. For example when compared to males, female juvenile homicide offenders have higher rates of reported childhood abuse, more serious substance abuse, and mental health problems, findings which suggest that the home life of females has an extremely strong impact on their mental health and law-violating behaviors.[121]

Trauma, Victimization, and Delinquent Paths   The prevailing research shows that young girls are more likely to be the target of victimization and abuse than any other group. Kristin Carbone-Lopez and Jody Miller found that early victimization—including sexual abuse—may help produce a precocious maturity that facilitates a young woman's path into drug use and offending.[122] Their research, involving in-depth interviews with methamphetamine users, also found that the onset of deviance is likely to occur when young women are prematurely thrust into adult roles and responsibilities. The women described their troubled childhoods: more than one-third reported childhood sexual abuse; three-quarters described other family dysfunction, including domestic violence, substance abuse, neglect, and mental illness; one in six came from homes deeply embedded in methamphetamine markets. All of them described precocious movements into adult roles and responsibilities, whether early independent living, differential association with older deviant peers and romantic partners, responsibilities for sibling care, early motherhood, or—most often—some combination of these early transitions.

Protective Measures   Not all abused girls become delinquent offenders; many do not, and they are able to go on and lead productive lives. What protects them from delinquency? Stephanie Hawkins, Phillip Graham, Jason Williams, and Margaret Zahn found that the most consistent protective effect was the extent to which a girl felt she had caring adults in her life. The presence of caring adults reduced the likelihood that girls would engage in several forms of delinquent behaviors. An exception to this pattern were those girls who suffered physical assault, who generally had less trust for any adult as they matured into adulthood. If these victimized young women were connected to their schools, they were less likely to report committing aggressive or antisocial acts. School may provide a refuge from an unsafe home environment. Because the majority of their day was spent at school, becoming connected with this institution and the resources available there seems to serve as a protection against delinquency.

Religiosity also helped protect girls at high risk for delinquency from violent behavior. Girls from disadvantaged neighborhoods and those who had been sexually abused were less likely to engage in violent forms of delinquency if they were religious. However, girls who had been neglected or physically assaulted were more likely to engage in aggravated assault if they were religious. It is possible that when girls are neglected and experience repeated physical assaults early in life, their belief systems become skewed to support the idea that violence is an acceptable and normal behavior. Additionally, if girls who are physically abused live in homes where religious beliefs are promoted, religion could function as a belief system that supports violence.[123]

This research illustrates the path from early adversity to precocious adult role taking and to adult criminality. Girls who are raised in troubled homes, who may be victims of sexual and physical abuse, are the ones who grow up too fast, accumulate social deficits, and find themselves enmeshed in a delinquent way of life. In contrast, girls who are raised with supportive families and with positive school and community influences may avoid this fate.

Socialization and Gangs   Males are more likely to join gangs than females, but those girls who do engage with a delinquent peer group are more likely to pursue antisocial behavior, a finding that is not unexpected. Girls who join gangs begin by associating with delinquent peers, a pursuit that strains their relationships with parents and teachers.[124] Joan Moore's analysis of gang girls in East Los Angeles found that many came from troubled homes. Sixty-eight percent of the girls she interviewed were afraid of their fathers, and 55 percent reported fear of their mothers.[125] Many of the girls reported that their parents were overly strict and controlling, despite the fact that they engaged in criminality themselves. Moore also details accounts of sexual abuse; about 30 percent of the girls reported that family members had made sexual advances.[126] Emily Gaarder and Joanne Belknap's interviews with young women sent to adult prisons indicated that most had endured prolonged sexual abuse and violence. One of their subjects, Lisa, a young European American woman, was serving time for attempted murder. Lisa had used drugs and alcohol, and joined gangs to escape the pain and troubles of her home life. Her mother was an alcoholic and her father a convicted rapist. She had been sexually and physically abused by her stepfather from the ages of 9 to 11. Soon after, Lisa began skipping school, started using alcohol, and took acid. She joined a gang when she was 12. "They were like a family to me," she told Gaarder and Belknap. "But I became involved in a lot of stuff. . . . I got high a lot, I robbed people, burglarized homes, stabbed people, and was involved in drive-bys." At age 15, she stabbed a woman in a fight. She is serving 7 to 15 years for the crime. Lisa made this statement:

> I had just gotten out of this group home. The lady I stabbed had been messing with my sister's fiancé. This woman [had] a bunch of my sister's stuff, like her stereo and VCR, so me, my sister, her fiancé, and my boyfriend went over to pick up the stuff. We were all getting high beforehand. When we got to the house, my sister and I went in . . . . They [her sister and the victim] started fighting over him, and I started stabbing her with a knife. I always carried a knife with me because I was in a gang.[127]

In summary, the socialization approach holds that family interaction is the key to understanding female delinquency. If a girl grows up in an atmosphere of sexual tension, where hostility exists between her parents, or where her parents are absent, she is likely to turn to outside sources for support. In contrast, a strong bond to parents may help insulate girls from social forces that produce delinquency.[128]

In order to help girls through this often painful transition from child to adult, a number of community programs have focused on socialization. The Evidence-Based Juvenile Justice feature shows how helping girls overcome age-related problems can also enable them to avoid involvement in the juvenile justice system.

Practical Academic Cultural Educational (PACE) Center

Established in 1985, the Practical Academic Cultural Educational (PACE) Center for Girls introduced a gender-responsive, school-based program as an alternative to incarceration or institutionalization for at-risk adolescent girls in Jacksonville, Florida. The success of the Jacksonville program led to replication in other Florida cities. PACE currently operates 19 direct care centers, outreach programs, and preteen centers, and provides social and educational services to 2,000 Florida girls and their families each year. The PACE mission is to provide girls and young women an opportunity for a better future through education, counseling, training, and advocacy.

PACE's direct care and outreach programs serve girls ages 11 to 18 who have been identified as dependent (i.e., in need of protective services), truant, runaway, ungovernable, delinquent, pregnant, or in need of academic skills. Girls may be referred by a variety of sources, including the juvenile justice system, the Florida Department of Children and Family Services, school personnel, community service agencies, and parents. PACE aims to decrease risk factors in four domains: school, family, behavior, and substance abuse. A fundamental emphasis of the program is intervention in and prevention of school withdrawal, juvenile delinquency, teen pregnancy, substance abuse, and welfare dependency. Specific program components include academic education, individualized attention, gender-specific life management skills enhancement (through PACE's Spirited Girls! curriculum), case management, parental involvement, community volunteer services, career enhancement and awareness, and transition services. Girls attend PACE daily to work toward their individualized educational and social goals. Participants are supported by a teacher/adviser, who provides academic case management, and a social services staff member, who oversees all other case management needs, including social, emotional, and physical needs. Once a girl completes the goals on her individualized treatment plan, she transitions from the day program into transitional services. PACE provides three years of transitional services to all girls who are enrolled for 30 days or longer and three months of transitional services to girls who are enrolled for fewer than 30 days. Throughout the transitional service period, case management, counseling, support, and follow-up are provided to each girl and her family.

CRITICAL THINKING

What theoretical perspectives would support the PACE approach? In other words, which theories of delinquency are at work here?

SOURCE: Office of Juvenile Justice and Delinquency Prevention, Practical Academic Cultural Educational (PACE) Center for Girls, Inc., http://www.pacecenter.org/ (accessed October 2016).

Developmental Views

Developmental theorists have begun to use the life-course and other developmental approaches to characterize the ebb and flow of girls' delinquent careers. Research shows that the trajectories of girls' delinquency vary: there are groups that can be characterized as nonoffenders, low-rate offenders, and high-rate offenders. Lia Ahonen and her colleagues found there were differences in the versatility of girls' offending, with high-rate delinquents being more versatile, engaging in both violence and theft. They found a small group of high-rate, versatile offending girls who resemble the male group of life-course persistent offenders first identified by Terrie Moffitt (see Chapter 6).[129]

Recently, the Girls Study Group evaluated the developmental trajectory of female delinquency. They found that girls did not start offending at a specific age or become involved in delinquency by committing any one offense. Girls' first reported offending varied across all offense types and was committed at different ages. For example, girls who sold drugs did not begin offending until their late teens. The largest proportion of girls whose first offense was a status offense began their offending at the age of 13 or 14. The largest proportion of girls whose first offense was minor theft, minor assault, public disorder, property damage, or use of alcohol began these offenses during childhood, ages 7 to 10.

The study group found that girls' delinquency had other familiar developmental patterns. Most began to engage in some form of delinquency in childhood.

Keep Safe

Keep Safe is a multicomponent intervention program aimed at building prosocial skills and promoting placement stability with girls in foster care transitioning from elementary school to middle school. The objective is to prevent delinquency and substance abuse. The design and content of the program are shaped by developmental theories that suggest that building early prosocial skills for youths in foster care can influence their susceptibility to emotional and behavioral difficulties over the life course.

Keep Safe contains two components: one concentrates on the caregivers and one on the girls. The first component consists of six sessions of group-based caregiver training. The sessions for the caregivers concentrate on developing a behavioral reinforcement system—which encourages adaptive behaviors in the home, school, and community—and on improving parenting skills as a means of increasing child placement stability. Follow-up intervention services (i.e., ongoing training and support) are provided to the caregivers once a week with two-hour foster-parent group meetings during the first year of middle school.

The second component consists of six group-based skills training sessions for the girls. During the summer, the girls complete a curriculum designed to increase their social skills for positive peer relationships, increase their self-confidence, and decrease their susceptibility to negative peer influence. All of the sessions are highly structured and include specific content and directions for each activity. The sessions include an introduction to the session topic, role plays, and a game or activity to practice the new skill. The girls receive weekly individual coaching sessions during their first year of middle school. The coaching sessions serve to provide ongoing social support and training.

Evaluation of Keep Safe has found that those in the program report significantly less tobacco use, marijuana use, and overall substance use compared with the control group; the program's effect on alcohol use and association with delinquent peers was not significant. Girls in the treatment group reported committing less delinquent behavior in the past year than girls in the control group.

CRITICAL THINKING

What kind of role-playing games would you suggest for this group? Have you ever engaged in such an activity? If so, what was your experience like?

SOURCE: National Institute of Justice, "Program Profile: Keep Safe," http://www.crimesolutions.gov/Program Details.aspx?ID=372 (accessed October 2016).

They could be divided into offending patterns that were similar to those exhibited by boys:

- *Persisters*, who were continually involved in delinquent behavior over several years
- *Desisters*, who stopped offending after a period of delinquent behavior
- *Intermittent offenders*, girls who were sporadically involved in delinquent behavior over several years
- *Late bloomers*, who did not engage in delinquent behavior until late adolescence

The largest proportion of delinquent youth showed persistent patterns of delinquency. However, there were also intergroup differences within these categories. For example, within the persister group, the age of onset varied; girls reported their first delinquent activity anywhere from middle childhood through adolescence.[130]

The view that female delinquency is a developmental process has not been lost on treatment providers, who have begun to shape program models to address girls' developmental needs. The Evidence-Based Juvenile Justice feature "Keep Safe" discusses one such program.

Liberal Feminist Views

The feminist movement has, from its origins, fought to help women break away from their traditional roles and gain economic, educational, and social advancement. There is little question that the women's movement has revised the way women perceive their roles in society, and it has altered the relationships of women to many social institutions.

Liberal feminism has influenced thinking about delinquency. According to liberal feminists, females are less delinquent than males because their social roles provide fewer opportunities to commit crime. As the roles of women become more similar to those of men, so will their crime patterns. Female criminality is motivated by the same influences as male criminality. According to Freda Adler's *Sisters in Crime* (published in 1975), by striving for independence, women have begun to alter the institutions that had protected males in their traditional positions of power.[131] Adler argued that female delinquency would be affected by the changing role of women. As females entered new occupations and participated in sports, politics, and other traditionally male endeavors, they would also become involved in crimes that had heretofore been male-oriented; delinquency rates would then converge. She noted that girls were becoming increasingly involved in traditionally masculine crimes such as gang activity and fighting.[132]

Support for Liberal Feminism

A number of studies support the feminist view of gender differences in delinquency.[133] More than 30 years ago, Rita James Simon explained how the increase in female criminality is a function of the changing role of women. She claimed that as women were empowered economically and socially, they would be less likely to feel dependent and oppressed. Consequently, they would be less likely to attack their traditional targets: their husbands, their lovers, or even their own children.[134] Instead, their new role as breadwinner might encourage women to engage in traditional male crimes, such as larceny and car theft.

Simon's view has been supported in part by research showing a significant correlation between the women's rights movement and the female crime rate.[135] If 1966 is used as a jumping-off point (because the National Organization for Women was founded in that year), there are indications that patterns of serious female crime (robbery and auto theft) correlate with indicators of female emancipation (the divorce rate and participation in the labor force). Although this research does not prove that female crime is related to social change, it identifies behavior patterns that support that hypothesis.

In addition to these efforts, self-report studies support the liberal feminist view by showing that gender differences in delinquency are fading—that is, the delinquent acts committed most and least often by girls are nearly identical to those reported most and least often by boys.[136] The pattern of female delinquency, if not the extent, is now similar to that of male delinquency, and with few exceptions the factors that seem to motivate both male and female criminality are similar.[137]

As the sex roles of males and females have become less distinct, their offending patterns have become more similar. Girls may be committing crimes to gain economic advancement and not because they lack parental support. Both of these patterns were predicted by liberal feminists.

Critical Feminist Views

A number of feminist writers have attempted to explain the cause of crime, gender differences in crime rates, and the exploitation of female victims from a critical perspective. According to the critical feminist view, many girls who are labeled delinquent are actually victims, forced to be on the streets or in gangs to escape abuse they have suffered at home.[138] Those who are on the street, who are homeless, have experienced significant social problems, including childhood abuse and sexual molestation.[139] When they come before the juvenile court they are more likely to lose their freedom than boys because judges are paternalistic and closed minded. They want to protect girls by housing them in state institutions.

Critical feminism views gender inequality as stemming from the unequal power of men and women in a capitalist society, which leads to the exploitation

AP Images/Danielle Guerra

of women by fathers and husbands. Under this system, women are considered a commodity worth possessing, like land or money.[140] As the Focus on Delinquency feature "Trafficking in Children" shows, many girls in developing nations are the victims of one particularly vile form of exploitation.

Patriarchy and Delinquency

According to critical thinkers, the origin of the exploitation and victimization of women can be traced to the development of private property and male domination of the laws of inheritance, which led to male control over property and power.[141] A **patriarchal** system developed in which men's work was valued and women's work was devalued. As capitalism prevailed, the division of labor by gender made women responsible for the unpaid maintenance and reproduction of the current and future labor force, work that was derisively called "domestic work." Although this unpaid work done by women is crucial and profitable for capitalists, who reap these free benefits, such labor is exploitative and oppressive for women.[142] Even when women gained the right to work for pay, they were exploited as cheap labor. The dual exploitation of women within the household and in the labor market means that women produce far greater surplus value for capitalists than men.

Patriarchy, or male supremacy, has been and continues to be supported by capitalists. This system sustains female oppression at home and in the workplace.[143] Although the number of traditional patriarchal families is in steep decline, in those that still exist, a wife's economic dependence ties men more securely to wage-earning jobs, further serving the interests of capitalists by undermining potential rebellion against the system.

patriarchal
A social system in which men are dominant in family, government, and business matters.

Gender Conflict

Critical feminists link delinquent behavior patterns to the gender conflict created by paternalism and gender-based economic inequality. Because male domination renders lower-class women powerless, they are forced to commit less serious,

Trafficking in Children

Every year, scores of women and children—primarily from Southeast Asia and Eastern Europe—are lured by the promise of good jobs and then end up in the sex trade in industrialized countries. The data are notoriously unreliable, but estimates of the number of people trafficked internationally each year range between 600,000 and 1 million from 124 different countries around the world. The United States is not immune: an estimated 45,000 to 50,000 individuals are trafficked into the United States annually. While these numbers are vast, relatively few cases are known to legal authorities and far fewer are prosecuted and convicted. However, by all indications the numbers of trafficked child victims has been increasing. For example, the number of child victims of human trafficking helped by the International Organization of Migration (IOM) increased to 2,040 in 2011, up 27 percent from 1,565 in 2008. While the number of female victims remained stable, the number of male victims rose 27 percent, reflecting growing public recognition of the trafficking of men and boys. While the IOM numbers only reflect a small part of the problem, they indicate an ongoing increase in the number of victims.

Most victims are foreigners in the country where they have been abused and victimized, though most are from the region, often from neighboring countries (e.g., eastern European girls trafficked to western Europe). Domestic trafficking is also widely practiced, and for one in three trafficking cases, the exploitation takes place in the victim's country of citizenship.

Many forms of trafficking exist. Young girls and women are common targets of commercial sexual exploitation. They may be forced into prostitution and other sexual activities such as the production of pornography. There are accounts of women being forced to service 30 men a day and of children trapped in pornography rings. Others become human containers in the transportation of drugs through forced ingestion of condoms or other containers of illegal substances. Labor servitude can be found in nearly every area of industry. Young girls have been forced to work in sweatshops, factories, agricultural fields, and fisheries. Victims may work long hours in unpleasant, unsanitary, or dangerous conditions for low wages, sometimes unable to take breaks or leave the facility. In some instances, debts may be passed on to other family members or even entire villages from generation to generation, creating a constant supply of indentured servants for traffickers.

Victim Stories

Vietnam

When Ping was 12 years old, an acquaintance offered her and a friend jobs in a different city in Vietnam. Ping and her friend accepted the offer. The recruiter took them to a local bus station and placed them on a bus with their "caretaker." When they disembarked, the caretaker revealed they were in China and had been sold into prostitution with 20 other girls. When one of the girls refused to do as she was told, the owners beat her severely. Ping suffered in the brothel for almost a year before authorities raided the establishment, rescued the girls, and returned them to Vietnam. Although Ping still suffers from headaches and poor

Orlando Sierra/Getty Images

Stopping the trafficking of children has become an international endeavor. Two members of a gang that traffics people to the United States as shown as they are being taken to court in Tegucigalpa, Mexico, on June 9, 2016. At least seven people were arrested in an operation against human trafficking, four of whom were found with 82 Central American migrants on the border with Guatemala.

vision—including moments of blindness—as a result of her exploitation, she is training for a career in hairdressing.

Mexico

Maria Elena was 13 years old when a family acquaintance told her she could make ten times as much money waiting tables in the United States than she could in her small village. She and several other girls were driven across the border and then continued the rest of the way on foot. They traveled four days and nights through the desert, making their way into Texas, then crossing east toward Florida. Finally, Maria Elena and the other girls arrived at their destination, a rundown trailer where they were forced into prostitution. Maria Elena was gang-raped and locked in the trailer until she agreed to do what she was told. She lived under 24-hour watch and was forced to have sex with up to 30 men a day. When she got pregnant, she was forced to have an abortion and sent back to work the next day. Maria Elena finally made her escape only to be arrested along with her traffickers.

Nepal/India

At a carpet factory in Nepal, Nayantara met a labor broker who promised her a good job as a domestic worker in Lebanon. The broker convinced her to take the job opportunity, assuring her that she did not have to pay anything. He instead took Nayantara to India, confiscated her passport, and sold her to a brothel where she was forced to have sex with at least 35 men each day with only five hours of sleep. When she tried to refuse, the brothel owner would beat Nayantara with an iron pole until she gave in. She was not allowed to contact her family or anyone else outside of the brothel, and her freedom of movement was constantly controlled. After six months, the police raided the brothel and imprisoned all the women and girls. The owner was arrested with them but was released five months earlier than her victims because she bribed the police. When Nayantara was released from jail after 17 months, she was returned to the brothel and sold to another owner within a month. Coming to the realization that she would never be able to pay off her debts, she ran away and eventually found her way back to Nepal. She has found refuge in a shelter.

United States

When Ashley was 12 years old, she got into a fight with her mother and ran away from home. She ended up staying with a friend's older brother at his house and intended to go home the next day, but when she tried to leave he told her that he was a pimp and she was now his property. He locked her in a room, beat her daily, and advertised her for sex on websites. Once she looked out a window and saw her mother on the street, crying and posting flyers with Ashley's photo. When Ashley tried to shout her mother's name from the window, her pimp grabbed her by the hair and yanked her back, threatening, "If you shout, I'll kill you." Ashley eventually escaped her confinement and is now at a treatment center for girls who have been sexually trafficked.

Why Global Trafficking?

Human trafficking is facilitated by the global economy and relaxation of corporate boundaries. The young female victims are often poor and aspire to a better life. They may be forced, coerced, deceived, and psychologically manipulated into industrial or agricultural work, marriage, domestic servitude, organ donation, or sexual exploitation. Although victims often come from poorer countries, the market for labor and sex is found in wealthier countries or in countries that, while economically poor, cater to the needs of citizens from wealthy countries, of corporations, or of tourists.

While some individuals are trafficked directly for purposes of prostitution or commercial sexual exploitation, even those trafficked for legitimate work may become victims of interpersonal violence. Women trafficked for domestic work in wealthy countries or laborers trafficked for construction, logging, factory, or farm work are vulnerable to exploitation by their employers. Individuals trafficked for labor purposes are usually unfamiliar with their new location and the language spoken there. They often lack formal education and do not know about the human and legal resources that could help them.

Afghanistan is typical of a third-world country where trafficking is a significant social problem. It is a source, transit, and destination country for men, women, and children subjected to trafficking in persons, specifically forced labor and forced prostitution. Afghan boys and girls are trafficked within the country for forced prostitution and forced labor in brick kilns, carpet-making factories, and domestic service. Afghan women and girls are subjected to forced prostitution, forced marriages—including marriages in which husbands force their wives into prostitution—and involuntary domestic servitude in Pakistan and Iran, and possibly India. Some families knowingly sell their children for forced prostitution, including for *bacha baazi*—in which wealthy men use harems of young boys for social and sexual entertainment. Other families send their children with brokers to gain employment. Many of these children end up in forced labor, particularly in Pakistani carpet factories. Families sometimes make cost-benefit analyses regarding how much debt they can incur based on their tradable family members. Women and girls from Iran, Tajikistan, and possibly Uganda and China are forced into prostitution in Afghanistan. Some international security

contractors may have been involved in the sex trafficking of these women. Brothels and prostitution rings are sometimes run by foreigners, sometimes with links to larger criminal networks. Tajik women are also believed to be trafficked through Afghanistan to other countries for prostitution. Trafficked Iranian women transit Afghanistan en route to Pakistan.

Can Sex Trafficking Be Controlled?

Controlling human trafficking and sex tourism has proven to be difficult. Some countries have recently written laws to prevent their citizens from engaging in sexual activities with minors while traveling outside their own country. These laws try to deter sex tourism, making travelers reconsider their actions in light of the consequences. However, enforcement of these laws may prove challenging due to jurisdiction and proof, so the practice continues unabated in many parts of the world. The United States passed the Trafficking Victims Protection Act of 2003 and then strengthened it with a 2005 revision. Included in the bill was the Operation Innocence Lost program, a nationwide initiative that helps law enforcement agents pursue sex traffickers and child prostitution rings.

The federal laws created several new crimes, including human trafficking, sex trafficking, forced labor, and document servitude, which involves the withholding or destruction of identity or travel documents as a means of controlling young victims. They outlawed psychological manipulation, which means that traffickers can be prosecuted if they cause victims to believe that they would be harmed if they resist. Provisions of the 2005 act provide state and local law enforcement with new tools to target demand and investigate and prosecute sex trafficking. Whether or not these measures will prove sufficient to reduce the sexual exploitation of children remains to be seen.

Other nations have tried a number of approaches to reduce trafficking. In India, the focus has been minority and marginalized communities because they are most vulnerable to traffickers. One organization trains journalists on how to better report cases of human trafficking. These efforts aim to better inform people in remote communities who may only get news in their local language and may not often see reporting on human trafficking. Reporters uncovered human trafficking cases within their own communities and increased attention on the role of state government and police in prevention efforts. In the Loreto region of Peru, an area known for human trafficking, a campaign was conducted to raise awareness among tourists, mass media, tourism operators, and the general public about the criminal penalties for those who sexually exploit children. Thousands of such efforts, many depending on multinational cooperation, are now in operation around the globe.

CRITICAL THINKING

1. How would you reduce the incidence of human trafficking? Would you punish the sex tourists as felons? Can anything be done to protect young girls from sexual predators?

2. Does pornography on the Internet increase interest in sex with underage females, and should greater controls be placed on Internet viewing?

SOURCES: US Department of State, *Trafficking in Persons Report*, 2016, http://www.state.gov/documents /organization/258876.pdf; Michael Pittaro and Anthony Normore, "International Efforts by Police Leadership to Combat Human Trafficking," FBI Law Enforcement Bulletin, June 2016, https://leb.fbi.gov/2016/june /international-efforts-by-police-leadership-to-combat-human-trafficking; US Department of State, *Trafficking in Persons Report*, 2015, https://www.state.gov/documents/organization/245365.pdf; United Nations Office on Drugs and Crime, *Global Report on Trafficking in Persons*, 2014, http://www.unodc.org/documents /data-and-analysis/glotip/GLOTIP_2014_full_report.pdf. (URLs accessed October 2016.)

nonviolent, self-destructive crimes, such as abusing drugs. Recent efforts of the capitalist classes to undermine the social support of the poor has hit women, especially women of color, particularly hard. The reduction of welfare support, concentration on welfare fraud, and cutbacks to social services have all directly and uniquely affected women.[144]

Powerlessness also increases the likelihood that women will become targets of violent acts.[145] When lower-class males are shut out of the economic opportunity structure, they try to build their self-image through acts of machismo; such acts may involve violent abuse of women. This type of reaction accounts for a significant percentage of female victims who are attacked by a spouse or intimate partner. According to this view, female victimization should decline as women's place in society is elevated and they are able to obtain more power at home, in the workplace, and in government. Empirical research seems to support this view. Cross-national data show that in nations where the status of women is generally high, sexual violence rates are significantly lower than in nations where women do not enjoy similar educational and occupational opportunities.[146] Women's victimization rates decline as they are empowered socially, economically, and legally.[147]

Masculinities and Delinquency   In *Masculinities and Crime*, James Messerschmidt suggests that in every culture males try to emulate "ideal" masculine behaviors.[148] In Western culture, this means being authoritative, in charge, combative, and controlling. Failure to adopt these roles leaves men feeling effeminate and unmanly. Their struggle to dominate women in order to prove their manliness is called "doing gender." Crime is a vehicle for men to "do gender" because it separates them from the weak and allows them to demonstrate physical bravery. Violence directed toward women is an especially economical way to demonstrate manhood. Would a weak, effeminate male ever attack a woman?

Feminist writers have supported this view by maintaining that in contemporary society men achieve masculinity at the expense of women. In the best-case scenario, men must convince others that in no way are they feminine or have female qualities. As they are typically portrayed in the media, men are sloppy and don't cook or do housework because these are "female" activities. To show their manhood, they work at excluding, hurting, denigrating, exploiting, or otherwise abusing women. The worst insult within male peer groups is to call someone woman-like (i.e., "you throw like a girl") and abuse him accordingly. Men need to defend themselves at all costs from being contaminated with femininity, and these efforts begin in children's playgroups and continue into adulthood and marriage.[149]

Relationship Conflict   The interplay of gender, conflict, and power relationships shapes the direction and content of adolescent personal relationships. When Jody Miller and Norman White conducted in-depth interviews with African American adolescents in St. Louis, Missouri, they found significant differences in dating violence structured by gender relationships.[150] To gain status among their friends, boys must take the role of being a "playa" (player)—guys who use girls for sex and have multiple sexual partners and conquests. Playas have little emotional attachment to their sexual partners, and adopt a detached, uninvolved "cool" attitude and demeanor. They are much more likely to cheat on their girlfriends, whereas girls are more likely to be loyal to their boyfriends. In addition, boys are more willing to share sexual details with their peers, mistreat their girlfriends openly in front of friends, and downplay the meaningfulness of their relationships. This dynamic shapes the nature of dating violence: girls' violence is related to emotionality, especially the anger they experience when they suspect their boyfriend is cheating. Some girls attack their boyfriends to get an emotional response from them, to drive them out of their cool state, even if it means being struck back harder in return. Some are willing to interpret the violent response as an indicator that the boy actually likes them; any response is favorable, even if it is violent.

Exploitation and Delinquency

Critical feminists also focus on the social forces that shape women's lives and experiences to explain female delinquency.[151] They attempt to show how the sexual victimization of girls is a function of male socialization because so many young males learn to be aggressive and to exploit women. Males seek same-sex peer groups for social support; these groups encourage members to exploit and sexually abuse women. On college campuses, peers encourage sexual violence against women who are considered "sluts" or "slags." These derogatory labels allow the males to justify their actions; a code of secrecy then protects the aggressors from retribution.[152]

According to the critical feminist view, exploitation triggers the onset of female delinquent and deviant behavior. When female victims run away and abuse substances, they may be reacting to abuse they have suffered at home or at school. Their attempts at survival are labeled as deviant or delinquent behavior.[153] When the exploited girl finds herself in the arms of the justice system, her problems may just be beginning. While boys who get in trouble may be considered overzealous youth or kids who just went too far, girls who get in trouble are seen as in opposition and a threat to acceptable images of femininity; their behavior is considered even more unusual and dangerous than male delinquency.[154] Girls are overrepresented as status offenders and are more likely to be detained or incarcerated for status offending than boys, indications that juvenile judges are paternalistic and anxious to take control of young women who do not measure up to traditional visions of female morality.[155]

Power-Control Theory

John Hagan and his associates have speculated that gender differences in delinquency are a function of class differences that influence family life. Hagan, who calls his view **power-control theory**, suggests that class influences delinquency by controlling the quality of family life.[156] In paternalistic families, fathers assume the role of breadwinners, and mothers have menial jobs or remain at home. Mothers are expected to control the behavior of their daughters while granting greater freedom to sons. The parent–daughter relationship can be viewed as a preparation for the "cult of domesticity," which makes daughters' involvement in delinquency unlikely. Hence, males exhibit a higher degree of delinquent behavior than their sisters.

power-control theory
Holds that gender differences in the delinquency rate are a function of class differences and economic conditions that influence the structure of family life.

According to power-control theory, as more families become egalitarian, with both parents sharing equal roles and having equal authority, children's roles will become more homogenous. Because sons and daughters are treated equally, their behavior will take on similar patterns. Some, like Alice Blair, shown here listening to coach Russ Wilson during a huddle in Paint Creek, Texas, will take on what has been considered a traditional male role. Blair plays defense on the school's six-person football team.

AP Images/Matt Slocum

In **egalitarian families**—in which the husband and wife share similar positions of power at home and in the workplace—daughters gain a kind of freedom that reflects reduced parental control. These families produce daughters whose law-violating behaviors mirror those of their brothers. Ironically, these kinds of relationships also occur in households with absent fathers. Similarly, Hagan and his associates found that when both fathers and mothers hold equally valued managerial positions, the similarity between the rates of their daughters' and sons' delinquency is greatest. Therefore, middle-class girls are most likely to violate the law because they are less closely controlled than lower-class girls.

Research conducted by Hagan and his colleagues has tended to support the core relationship between family structure and gender differences in delinquency.[157] Other social scientists have produced tests of the theory, which have generally supported its hypothesis. Brenda Sims Blackwell and Mark Reed found that the gap between brother-sister delinquency is greatest in patriarchal families and least in egalitarian families, a finding consistent with the core premise of power-control theory.[158]

Gender and the Juvenile Justice System

Gender differences not only have an effect on crime patterns but also may have a significant impact on the way children are treated by the juvenile justice system. Girls who wind up in the arms of the law are more likely than boys to come from abusive households. While some are helped, others are reabused, being punished for behavior that may be no fault of their own.[159] They display elevated levels of substance abuse and PTSD-like symptoms.[160] Not surprisingly, considering this background, girls in the juvenile justice system are more nonconforming, oppositional, and likely to exhibit borderline personality traits. They are prone to substance abuse, impulsive actions, and suicide ideation, signs that there are distinct personality differences between offending and nonoffending adolescent females.[161]

While on the surface it seems like males are treated more harshly than females and that boys are more likely to be incarcerated than girls, the truth is that in many ways girls receive more punitive treatment than boys, especially in cases involving sexual matters or offenses (see the Focus on Delinquency feature "Abused Girls in the Juvenile Justice System"). This is not a recent phenomenon. Throughout the history of the juvenile justice system, girls were more likely to be punished for immoral behavior than actual delinquency. Meda Chesney-Lind's now classic research first identified the fact that police are more likely to arrest female adolescents for sexual activity and to ignore the same behavior among male delinquents. Girls are more likely than boys to be picked up by police for status offenses and are more likely to be kept in detention for such offenses.[162]

Some critics believe that girls, more than boys, are still disadvantaged if their behavior is viewed as morally incorrect by government officials or if they are considered beyond parental control.[163] Girls may still be subject to harsh punishments if they are considered dangerously immoral.[164] Even though girls are still less likely to be arrested than boys, those who fail to measure up to stereotypes of proper female behavior are more likely to be sanctioned than male offenders.[165] Recent research by Tia Stevens and her associates found that over the past decades, regardless of racial/ethnic group, the girls who are involved in behavior considered inappropriate for females are more likely to be formally charged and involved in the juvenile justice system. It may be that tolerance for misbehavior significantly decreases when girls violate gender norms, and the punishment can sometimes be very harsh.[166]

FOCUS ON DELINQUENCY

Abused Girls in the Juvenile Justice System

A recent review of the problems faced by abused girls in the juvenile justice system was conducted by researchers at the Georgetown Law Center on Poverty and Inequality. They found that officials and policy makers still show a lack of concern about girls' victimization. Juvenile justice administrators seem to be more concerned with controlling girls' behavior than addressing the factors that brought them to the attention of the juvenile justice system in the first place. In many jurisdictions the majority of girls who process through the system are victims of physical and sexual abuse. Running away, engaging in precocious sexual behavior, taking drugs, and other behaviors that bring them in contact with agents of the juvenile justice system may be a result of abuse and neglect. Nonetheless, the juvenile justice system rarely meets medical needs related to sexual abuse that girls have experienced, including gynecological and obstetric care, despite the fact that a significant percentage of girls in the juvenile justice system are or have been pregnant—a risk that is enhanced because of childhood trauma and sexual abuse. The Georgetown team also found that most juvenile justice facilities are unaccredited and do not offer specialized services for pregnant girls who have been sexually abused. Nor are they in compliance with accepted standards of pediatric or reproductive health care. Some pregnant girls in juvenile justice facilities report being shackled, hungry, and without access to prenatal and parenting education.

The Georgetown team found that conditions in juvenile justice facilities risk re-traumatizing girls. Routine procedures such as restraints and strip searches, as well as the isolating, punitive environment itself, can be particularly harmful to victims of trauma by triggering their traumatic stress symptoms. Girls in such conditions tend to respond by internalizing their negative experiences, entering into depression or engaging in self-harm. These reactions can increase the risk of additional harm, including suicide attempts and self-mutilation. To make matters worse, some girls experience new incidents of sexual victimization while in the system. Taken together, lack of appropriate care and re-triggering conditions can lead to a harmful cycle of trauma that often turns inward.

The Georgetown team asserts that arresting and detaining abused girls effectively punishes them for being victims, and it fails to provide the services necessary to heal and recover. It is simply an unacceptable response to child sexual abuse. Some of the many recommendations they make to alleviate this problem include:

- Implement accountability mechanisms to ensure that states comply with standards and guidelines for gender-specific services, including issuing annual public reports on progress toward compliance with standards and guidelines

- Increase funds available to incentivize states to create gender-specific, trauma-informed prevention and treatment programs and services

- Require at least one state advisory group member to have expertise in gender-specific issues, such as sexual abuse and domestic child sex trafficking, as well as knowledge of effective interventions

- Require states to employ validated, comprehensive screening and assessments to evaluate all children entering the juvenile justice system for trauma and to develop appropriate treatment plans and programming in response to identified needs

- Require states to screen children at intake for commercial sexual exploitation and divert identified victims away from the juvenile justice system whenever possible

CRITICAL THINKING

Considering the *parens patriae* model that shapes juvenile justice, should abused girls who engage in status offenses fall under juvenile court jurisdiction or would they better be handled within other treatment dispensing agencies?

SOURCE: Malika Saada Saar, Rebecca Epstein, Lindsay Rosenthal, and Yasmin Vaf, Human Rights Project for Girls, "The Sexual Abuse to Prison Pipeline: The Girls' Story," Georgetown Law Center on Poverty and Inequality, 2013, https://www.law.georgetown.edu/academics/centers-institutes/poverty-inequality/upload/2015_COP_sexual-abuse_layout_web-2.pdf (accessed October 2016).

Lisa Pasko's research confirms that the focus of the juvenile justice system continues to be on girls' sexual behavior. She notes that in the early eras, courts blamed the cause of girls' sexually immoral behavior on bad families, alcohol or drug use, poverty, and immigrant status. Girls may have been incarcerated for immorality, incorrigibility, and truancy, but underlying the recorded charge was usually some form of sexual offense. Girls are not directly arrested and adjudicated for sexual immorality, but the focus remains on their "bad" choices; they are still told to take responsibility for their sexual decisions. In the contemporary era, the correctional focus remains on the control and micromanagement of girls' bodies and sexuality.[167]

The justice system also seems biased against LGBT (lesbian, gay, bisexual, or transgender) people, who are disproportionately incarcerated. Though they make up approximately 6 percent of the youth population, it is now estimated that LGBT youth comprise 13 to 15 percent of youth involved in the juvenile justice system.[168]

SUMMARY

1 Evaluate the development of interest in female delinquency

- Early delinquency experts often ignored female offenders, assuming that girls rarely violated the law, or if they did, that their illegal acts were status offenses.

- Contemporary interest in the association between gender and delinquency has surged because girls are now getting involved in serious delinquent acts that are quite similar to those of young men.

- Another reason for the interest in gender studies is that conceptions of gender differences have changed.

2 Discuss the gender differences in development

- Gender differences in development include socialization, cognition, and personality.

- Psychologists believe that differences in the way females and males are socialized affect their development.

- Although there are few gender differences in aggression during the first few years of life, girls are socialized to be less aggressive than boys and are supervised more closely.

- There are also cognitive differences between males and females starting in childhood.

- In most cases cognitive differences are small and gradually narrowing.

3 Compare and contrast gender differences in personality and socialization

- Some experts suggest that gender differences may have a biological origin: males and females are essentially different.

- Females are more left brain–oriented and males more right brain–oriented.

- A second view is that gender differences are developed over the life course and reflect different treatment of males and females.

- Another view is that gender differences are a result of the interaction of socialization, learning, and enculturation.

4 Interpret recent trends in gender differences in the delinquency rate

- Gender differences in the delinquency rates have narrowed.

- Boys still account for more serious violent crime arrests.

- According to self-report data, gender patterns in delinquency have become similar.

5 Give an example of the early biological explanations of female delinquency

- Lombroso maintained that women were lower on the evolutionary scale than men, more childlike, and less intelligent.

- Women who committed crimes could be distinguished from "normal" women by physical characteristics—excessive body hair, wrinkles, and an abnormal cranium, for example.

- In appearance, delinquent females appeared closer to men than to other women. The masculinity hypothesis suggested that delinquent girls had excessive male characteristics.

- So-called experts suggested that female delinquency goes unrecorded because the female is the instigator rather than the perpetrator.

6 Compare contemporary trait views of female delinquency

- Empirical evidence suggests that girls who reach puberty at an early age are at the highest risk for delinquency.

- One reason is that early bloomers may be more attractive to older adolescent boys, and increased contact with this high-risk group places the girls in jeopardy for antisocial behavior.

- One view is that hormonal imbalance may influence aggressive behavior in young girls.

- Another view is that excessive amounts of male hormones (androgens) are related to delinquency.

- Because girls are socialized to be less aggressive than boys, it is possible that the young women who get involved in antisocial and violent behavior are suffering from some form of mental anguish or abnormality.

- Clinical interviews indicate that female delinquents are significantly more likely than males to suffer from mood disorders.

7 Discuss the association between socialization and female delinquency

- Girls may be supervised more closely than boys. If girls behave in a socially disapproved fashion, their parents may be more likely to notice.

- Girls seem to be more deeply affected than boys by child abuse, and the link between abuse and female delinquency seems stronger than it is for male delinquency.

- A significant body of literature links abusive home lives to gang participation and crime.
- The socialization approach holds that family interaction is the key to understanding female delinquency.
- Girls are expected to follow narrowly defined behavioral patterns.

8 Evaluate the feminist view of female delinquency

- Liberal feminism has influenced thinking about delinquency.
- According to liberal feminists, females are less delinquent than males because their social roles provide fewer opportunities to commit crime.
- Critical feminists hold that gender inequality stems from the unequal power of men and women and the subsequent exploitation of women by men.
- Critical feminists focus on the social forces that shape girls' lives. They attempt to show how the sexual victimization of girls is often a function of male socialization and that young males learn to be exploitive of women.

9 Critique Hagan's power-control theory

- John Hagan and his associates have speculated that gender differences in delinquency are a function of class differences that influence family life.
- His power-control theory suggests that class influences delinquency by controlling the quality of family life.

- In paternalistic families, fathers assume the role of breadwinners, and mothers have menial jobs or remain at home.
- In egalitarian families—in which the husband and wife share similar positions of power at home and in the workplace—daughters gain a kind of freedom that reflects reduced parental control.
- Power-control theory helps explain the relative increase in female delinquency by stressing the significance of changing feminine roles.

10 Analyze the treatment of girls in the juvenile justice system

- Gender differences not only have an effect on crime patterns but also may have a significant impact on the way children are treated by the juvenile justice system.
- As a general rule, males who are involved in the justice system are sanctioned more severely than females.
- Girls are more likely than boys to receive harsh punishment if their behavior is viewed as morally incorrect by government officials or if they are considered beyond parental control.
- Girls may still be subject to harsh punishments if they are considered dangerously immoral.

KEY TERMS

QUESTIONS FOR DISCUSSION

1. Are girls delinquent for different reasons than boys? Do girls have a unique set of problems?

2. As sex roles become more homogenous, do you believe female delinquency will become identical to male delinquency in rate and type?

3. Does the sexual double standard still exist?

4. Are lower-class girls more strictly supervised than upper- and middle-class girls? Is control stratified across class lines?

5. Are girls the victims of unfairness at the hands of the justice system, or do they benefit from "chivalry"?

VIEWPOINT

As the principal of a northeastern middle school, you get a call from a parent who is disturbed because he heard a rumor that the student literary digest plans to publish a story with a sexual theme. The work is written by a middle school girl who became pregnant during the year and underwent an abortion. You ask for and receive a copy of the narrative.

The girl's story is actually a cautionary tale of young love that results in an unwanted pregnancy. The author details the abusive home life that led her to engage in an intimate relationship with another student, her pregnancy, her conflict with her parents, her decision to abort, and the emotional turmoil that the incident created. She tells students to use contraception if they are sexually active and recommends appropriate types of birth control. There is nothing provocative or sexually explicit in the work.

Some teachers argue that girls should not be allowed to read this material because it has sexual content from which they must be protected, and that in a sense it advocates defiance of parents. Also, some parents may object to a story about precocious sexuality because they fear it may encourage their children to "experiment." Such behavior is linked to delinquency and drug abuse. Those who advocate publication believe that girls have a right to read about such important issues and decide on their own course of action.

- Should you force the story's deletion, because its theme is essentially sexual and controversial?
- Should you allow publication, because it deals with the subject matter in a mature fashion?
- Do you think reading and learning about sexual matters encourages or discourages experimentation in sexuality?
- Should young girls be protected from such material? Would it cause them damage?
- Inequalities still exist in the way boys and girls are socialized by their parents and treated by social institutions. Do these gender differences also manifest themselves in the delinquency rate? What effect do gender roles have on behavior choices?

DOING RESEARCH ON THE WEB

To help you answer these questions and to find more information on the issue of school censorship, read the case of *Hazelwood School District et al. v. Kuhlmeier et al.* at http://www.bc.edu/bc_org/avp/cas/comm /free_speech/hazelwood.html. Go to the National Scholastic Press Association journalism website (http://www.studentpress.org/nspa/) to read more about school news and censorship issues.

NOTES

All URLs accessed September 2016.

1. Kelley Robinson, "'Slender Man' Stabbing Survivor Returns to School." ABC News, September 3, 2014, http://abcnews.go.com /US/slender-man-stabbing-survivor-returns-school/story? id=25230582.
2. Cesare Lombroso and William Ferrero, *The Female Offender* (New York: Philosophical Library, 1895).
3. Kathleen Pajer, "What Happens to 'Bad' Girls? A Review of the Adult Outcomes of Antisocial Adolescent Girls," *American Journal of Psychiatry* 155:862–870 (1998).
4. David Barrett, Antonis Katsiyannis, Dalun Zhang, and J. Kingree, "Predictors of Teen Childbearing Among Delinquent and Non-Delinquent Females," *Journal of Child and Family Studies* 24:970–978 (2015).
5. Darcy Miller, Catherine Trapani, Kathy Fejes-Mendoza, Carolyn Eggleston, and Donna Dwiggins, "Adolescent Female Offenders: Unique Considerations," *Adolescence* 30:429–435 (1995).
6. Rolf Loeber and Dale Hay, "Key Issues in the Development of Aggression and Violence from Childhood to Early Adulthood," *Annual Review of Psychology* 48:371–410 (1997).
7. Philip Cook and Susan Sorenson, "The Gender Gap Among Teen Survey Respondents: Why Are Boys More Likely to Report a Gun in the Home than Girls?" *Journal of Quantitative Criminology* 22:61–76 (2006).
8. Allison Morris, *Women, Crime, and Criminal Justice* (Oxford: Basil Blackwell, 1987).
9. Sarah Meadows, "Evidence of Parallel Pathways: Gender Similarity in the Impact of Social Support on Adolescent Depression and Delinquency," *Social Forces* 85:1143–1167 (2007).
10. Dennis Giever, "An Empirical Assessment of the Core Elements of Gottfredson and Hirschi's General Theory of Crime," paper presented at the annual meeting of the American Society of Criminology, Boston, November 1995.
11. Abigail Fagan, M. Van Horn, J. Hawkins, and Michael Arthur, "Gender Similarities and Differences in the Association Between Risk and Protective Factors and Self-Reported Serious Delinquency," *Prevention Science* 8:115–124 (2007).
12. Loeber and Hay, "Key Issues in the Development of Aggression and Violence," p. 378.
13. Thomas Parsons, Albert Rizzo, Cheryl Van Der Zaag, Jocelyn McGee, and J. Galen Buckwalter, "Gender Differences and Cognition Among Older Adults," *Aging, Neuropsychology and Cognition* 12:78–88 (2005).

14. Diane Halpern and Mary LaMay, "The Smarter Sex: A Critical Review of Sex Differences in Intelligence," *Educational Psychology Review* 12:229–246 (2000).

15. Parsons, Rizzo, Van Der Zaag, McGee, and Buckwalter, " Gender Differences and Cognition Among Older Adults."

16. James Messerschmidt, *Masculinities and Crime: Critique and Reconceptualization of Theory* (Lanham, MD: Rowman & Littlefield, 1993).

17. Debra Kaysen, Miranda Morris, Shireen Rizvi, and Patricia Resick, "Peritraumatic Responses and Their Relationship to Perceptions of Threat in Female Crime Victims," *Violence Against Women* 11:1515–1535 (2005).

18. D. J. Pepler and W. M. Craig, "A Peek Behind the Fence: Naturalistic Observations of Aggressive Children with Remote Audiovisual Recording," *Developmental Psychology* 31:548–553 (1995).

19. Daniel Mears, Matthew Ploeger, and Mark Warr, "Explaining the Gender Gap in Delinquency: Peer Influence and Moral Evaluations of Behavior," *Journal of Research in Crime and Delinquency* 35:251–266 (1998).

20. John Gibbs, Dennis Giever, and Jamie Martin, "Parental Management and Self-Control: An Empirical Test of Gottfredson and Hirschi's General Theory," *Journal of Research in Crime and Delinquency* 35:40–70 (1998); Velmer Burton, Francis Cullen, T. David Evans, Leanne Fiftal Alarid, and R. Gregory Dunaway, "Gender, Self-Control, and Crime," *Journal of Research in Crime and Delinquency* 35:123–147 (1998).

21. Jolien Van der Graaff, Susan Branje, Minet De Wied, Skyler Hawk, Pol Van Lier, and Wim Meeus, "Perspective Taking and Empathic Concern in Adolescence: Gender Differences in Developmental Changes," *Developmental Psychology* 50:881–888 (2014).

22. Regula Lehmann, Jaap Denissen, J. Mathias Allemand, and Lars Penke, "Age and Gender Differences in Motivational Manifestations of the Big Five from Age 16 to 60," *Developmental Psychology* 49:365–383 (2013).

23. Spencer Rathus, *Voyages in Childhood* (Belmont, CA: Wadsworth, 2004).

24. Carol Gilligan, *In a Different Voice* (Cambridge, MA: Harvard University Press, 1982).

25. Byongook Moon and Merry Morash, "Gender and General Strain Theory: A Comparison of Strains, Mediating, and Moderating Effects Explaining Three Types of Delinquency," *Youth and Society*, published online July 16, 2014.

26. Peter Zimmermann and Alexandra Iwanski, "Emotion Regulation from Early Adolescence to Emerging Adulthood and Middle Adulthood: Age Differences, Gender Differences, and Emotion-Specific Developmental Variations," *International Journal of Behavioral Development* 38:182–194 (2014).

27. Nicole M. Else-Quest, Ashley Higgins, Carlie Allison, and Lindsay Morton, "Gender Differences in Self-Conscious Emotional Experience: A Meta-Analysis," *Psychological Bulletin* 138:947–981 (2012).

28. Tara Chaplin and Amelia Aldao, "Gender Differences in Emotion Expression in Children: A Meta-Analytic Review," *Psychological Bulletin* 138:1–31 (2012).

29. Robert Agnew, "Reflection on 'A Revised Strain Theory of Delinquency,'" *Social Forces* 91:33–38 (2012).

30. Lisa Broidy and Robert Agnew, "Gender and Crime: A General Strain Theory Perspective," *Journal of Research in Crime and Delinquency* 34:275–306 (1997).

31. David Roalf, Natasha Lowery, and Bruce Turetsky, "Behavioral and Physiological Findings of Gender Differences in Global-Local Visual Processing," *Brain and Cognition* 60:32–42 (2006).

32. Eleanor Maccoby, *The Two Sexes: Growing Up Apart, Coming Together* (Cambridge, MA: Belknap Press, 1999).

33. Kathleen Miller, Merrill Melnick, Grace Barnes, Don Sabo, and Michael Farrell, "Athletic Involvement and Adolescent Delinquency," *Journal of Youth and Adolescence* 36:711–723 (2007).

34. David Rowe, Alexander Vazsonyi, and Daniel Flannery, "Sex Differences in Crime: Do Means and Within-Sex Variation Have Similar Causes?" *Journal of Research in Crime and Delinquency* 32:84–100 (1995).

35. Sandra Bem, *The Lenses of Gender* (New Haven, CT: Yale University Press, 1993).

36. Walter DeKeseredy and Martin Schwartz, "Male Peer Support and Woman Abuse," *Sociological Spectrum* 13:393–413 (1993).

37. Kenneth Sanchagrin, Karen Heimer, and Anthony Paik, "Adolescent Delinquency, Drinking, and Smoking: Does the Gender of Friends Matter?" *Youth and Society*, first published online December 18, 2014.

38. Janet Shibley Hyde, "The Gender Similarities Hypothesis," *American Psychologist* 60:581–592 (2005).

39. John Archer, "The Importance of Theory for Evaluating Evidence on Sex Differences," *American Psychologist* 61:638–639 (2006); Richard Lippa, "The Gender Reality Hypothesis," *American Psychologist* 61:639–640 (2006).

40. Agnew, "Reflection on 'A Revised Strain Theory of Delinquency.'"

41. Eleanor Maccoby, "Gender and Group Process: A Developmental Perspective," *Current Directions in Psychological Science* 11:54–58 (2002).

42. Jean Bottcher, "Social Practices of Gender: How Gender Relates to Delinquency in the Everyday Lives of High-Risk Youths," *Criminology* 39:893–932 (2001).

43. Audrey Zakriski, Jack Wright, and Marion Underwood, "Gender Similarities and Differences in Children's Social Behavior: Finding Personality in Contextualized Patterns of Adaptation," *Journal of Personality and Social Psychology* 88:844–855 (2005).

44. Yao Zheng and Harrington Cleveland, "Identifying Gender-Specific Developmental Trajectories of Nonviolent and Violent Delinquency from Adolescence to Young Adulthood," *Journal of Adolescence* 36:371–381 (2013).

45. Data from *Monitoring the Future, 2011* (Ann Arbor, MI: Institute for Social Research, 2013).

46. Wesley Jennings, Mildred Maldonado-Molina, and Kelli Komro, "Sex Similarities/Differences in Trajectories of Delinquency Among Urban Chicago Youth: The Role of Delinquent Peers," *American Journal of Criminal Justice* 35:56–75 (2010).

47. Darrell Steffensmeier, Jennifer Schwartz, Hua Zhong, and Jeff Ackerman, "An Assessment of Recent Trends in Girls' Violence Using Diverse Longitudinal Sources: Is the Gender Gap Closing?" *Criminology* 43:355–406 (2005).

48. Sara Goodkind, John Wallace, Jeffrey Shook, Jerald Bachman, and Patrick O'Malley, "Are Girls Really Becoming More Delinquent? Testing the Gender Convergence Hypothesis by Race and Ethnicity, 1976–2005," *Children and Youth Services Review* 31:885–895 (2009).

49. Margaret Zahn, Susan Brumbaugh, Darrell Steffensmeier, Barry Feld, Merry Morash, Meda Chesney-Lind, Jody Miller, Allison Ann Payne, Denise C. Gottfredson, and Candace Kruttschnitt, *Violence by Teenage Girls: Trends and Context* (Washington, DC: Office of Juvenile Justice and Delinquency Prevention, 2008), http://www.ncjrs.gov/pdffiles1/ojjdp/218905.pdf.

50. Ibid.

51. Lombroso and Ferrero, *The Female Offender*.

52. Ibid., p. 122.

53. Ibid., pp. 51–52.

54. For a review, see Anne Campbell, *Girl Delinquents* (Oxford: Basil Blackwell, 1981), pp. 41–48.

55. Cyril Burt, *The Young Delinquent* (New York: Appleton, 1925); see also Warren Middleton, "Is There a Relation Between Kleptomania and Female Periodicity in Neurotic Individuals?" *Psychology Clinic* (December 1933), pp. 232–247.

56. William Healy and Augusta Bronner, *Delinquents and Criminals: Their Making and Unmaking* (New York: Macmillan, 1926).

57. Ibid., p. 10.

58. Lauren Glaze and Danielle Kaeble, *Correctional Populations in the United States, 2013* (Washington, DC: Bureau of Justice Statistics, 2014).

59. Sigmund Freud, *An Outline of Psychoanalysis*, trans. James Strachey (New York: Norton, 1949), p. 278.

60. Sigmund Freud, *Three Essays of the Theory of Sexuality* (New York: Avon Books, 1962), p. 27. (Original work published 1905.)

61. Peter Blos, "Pre-Oedipal Factors in the Etiology of Female Delinquency," *Psychoanalytic Studies of the Child* 12:229–242 (1957).

62. Sheldon Glueck and Eleanor Glueck, *Five Hundred Delinquent Women* (New York: Knopf, 1934).

63. J. Cowie, V. Cowie, and E. Slater, *Delinquency in Girls* (London: Heinemann, 1968).

64. Anne Campbell, "On the Invisibility of the Female Delinquent Peer Group," *Women and Criminal Justice* 2:41–62 (1990).

65. Carolyn Smith, "Factors Associated with Early Sexual Activity Among Urban Adolescents," *Social Work* 42:334–346 (1997).

66. Margaret A. Zahn, Robert Agnew, Diana Fishbein, Shari Miller, Donna-Marie Winn, Gayle Dakoff, Candace Kruttschnitt, Peggy Giordano, Denise C. Gottfredson, Allison A. Payne, Barry C. Feld, and Meda Chesney-Lind, "Causes and Correlates of Girls' Delinquency Justice and Delinquency Prevention," OJJDP, April 2010, http://www.ncjrs.gov/pdffiles1/ojjdp/226358.pdf.

67. Tom A. McAdams, Randall Salekin, C. Nathan Marti, Whitney S. Lester, and Edward D. Barker, "Co-occurrence of Antisocial Behavior

and Substance Use: Testing for Sex Differences in the Impact of Older Male Friends, Low Parental Knowledge and Friends' Delinquency," *Journal of Adolescence* 37:247–256 (2014).

68. L. Kris Gowen, S. Shirley Feldman, Rafael Diaz, and Donnovan Somera Yisrael, "A Comparison of the Sexual Behaviors and Attitudes of Adolescent Girls with Older vs. Similar-Aged Boyfriends," *Journal of Youth and Adolescence* 33:167–176 (2004).

69. John Stogner, J. Mitchell Miller, Bonnie S. Fisher, Eric A. Stewart, and Christopher J. Schreck, "Peer Group Delinquency and Sexual Victimization: Does Popularity Matter?" *Women and Criminal Justice* 24:62–81 (2014).

70. Dana Haynie, "Contexts of Risk? Explaining the Link Between Girls' Pubertal Development and Their Delinquency Involvement," *Social Forces* 82:355–397 (2003).

71. Elizabeth Cauffman, Susan Farruggia, and Asha Goldweber, "Bad Boys or Poor Parents: Relations to Female Juvenile Delinquency," *Journal of Research on Adolescence* 18:699–712 (2008).

72. Avshalom Caspi, Donald Lynam, Terrie Moffitt, and Phil Silva, "Unraveling Girls' Delinquency: Biological, Dispositional, and Contextual Contributions to Adolescent Misbehavior," *Developmental Psychology* 29:283–289 (1993).

73. Jennifer Lansford, Kenneth Dodge, Reid Griffith Fontaine, John Bates, and Gregory Pettit, "Peer Rejection, Affiliation with Deviant Peers, Delinquency, and Risky Sexual Behavior," *Journal of Youth and Adolescence* 43:1742–1751 (2014).

74. Sampson Lee Blair, "The Influence of Risk-Taking Behaviors on the Transition into Marriage: An Examination of the Long-Term Consequences of Adolescent Behavior," *Marriage and Family Review* 46:126–146 (2010).

75. Dana Haynie and Alex Piquero, "Pubertal Development and Physical Victimization in Adolescence," *Journal of Research in Crime and Delinquency* 43:3–35 (2006).

76. Jay Belsky, "Early Child Care and Early Child Development: Major Findings from the NICHD Study of Early Child Care," *European Journal of Developmental Psychology* 3:95–110 (2006).

77. David Comings, Donn Muhleman, James Johnson, and James MacMurray, "Parent-Daughter Transmission of the Androgen Receptor Gene as an Explanation of the Effect of Father Absence on Age of Menarche," *Child Development* 73:1046–1051 (2002).

78. Eleanor Maccoby and Carol Jacklin, *The Psychology of Sex Differences* (Stanford, CA: Stanford University Press, 1974).

79. Kathleen Pajer, William Gardner, Robert Rubin, James Perel, and Stephen Neal, "Decreased Cortisol Levels in Adolescent Girls with Conduct Disorder," *Archives of General Psychiatry* 58:297–302 (2001).

80. Alan Booth and D. Wayne Osgood, "The Influence of Testosterone on Deviance in Adulthood: Assessing and Explaining the Relationship," *Criminology* 31:93–118 (1993).

81. D. H. Baucom, P. K. Besch, and S. Callahan, "Relationship Between Testosterone Concentration, Sex Role Identity, and Personality Among Females," *Journal of Personality and Social Psychology* 48:1218–1226 (1985).

82. Lee Ellis, "Evidence of Neuroandrogenic Etiology of Sex Roles from a Combined Analysis of Human, Nonhuman Primate, and Nonprimate Mammalian Studies," *Personality and Individual Differences* 7:519–552 (1986).

83. Diana Fishbein, "The Psychobiology of Female Aggression," *Criminal Justice and Behavior* 19:99–126 (1992).

84. Spencer Rathus, *Psychology*, 3rd ed. (New York: Holt, Rinehart & Winston, 1987), p. 88.

85. See, generally, Katharina Dalton, *The Premenstrual Syndrome* (Springfield, IL: Charles C Thomas, 1971).

86. Diana Fishbein, "Selected Studies on the Biology of Antisocial Behavior," in John Conklin, ed., *New Perspectives in Criminology* (Needham Heights, MA: Allyn & Bacon, 1996), pp. 26–38.

87. Lee Ellis, "The Victimful-Victimless Crime Distinction and Seven Universal Demographic Correlates of Victimful Criminal Behavior," *Personality and Individual Differences* 9:525–548 (1988).

88. Lee Ellis, "Evolutionary and Neurochemical Causes of Sex Differences in Victimizing Behavior: Toward a Unified Theory of Criminal Behavior and Social Stratification," *Social Science Information* 28:605–636 (1989).

89. David Foy, Iya Ritchie, and Alison Conway, "Trauma Exposure, Posttraumatic Stress, and Comorbidities in Female Adolescent Offenders: Findings and Implications from Recent Studies," *European Journal of Psychotraumatology* 3:1–13 (2012).

90. Jan ter Laak, Martijn de Goede, Liesbeth Aleva, Gerard Brugman, Miranda van Leuven, and Judith Hussmann, "Incarcerated

Adolescent Girls: Personality, Social Competence, and Delinquency," *Adolescence* 38:251–265 (2003).

91. Dorothy Espelage, Elizabeth Cauffman, Lisa Broidy, Alex Piquero, Paul Mazerolle, and Hans Steiner, "A Cluster-Analytic Investigation of MMPI Profiles of Serious Male and Female Juvenile Offenders," *Journal of the American Academy of Child and Adolescent Psychiatry* 42:770–777 (2003).

92. Kristen McCabe, Amy Lansing, Ann Garland, and Richard Hough, "Gender Differences in Psychopathology, Functional Impairment, and Familial Risk Factors Among Adjudicated Delinquents," *Journal of the American Academy of Child and Adolescent Psychiatry* 41:860–867 (2002).

93. Majone Steketee, Marianne Junger, and Josine Junger-Tas, "Sex Differences in the Predictors of Juvenile Delinquency: Females Are More Susceptible to Poor Environments; Males Are Influenced More by Low Self-Control," *Journal of Contemporary Criminal Justice* 29:88–105 (2013).

94. Kristine Hickle and Dominique Roe-Sepowitz, "Female Juvenile Arsonists: An Exploratory Look at Characteristics and Solo and Group Arson Offences," *Legal and Criminological Psychology* 15:385–399 (2010).

95. Alex Mason and Michael Windle, "Gender, Self-Control, and Informal Social Control in Adolescence: A Test of Three Models of the Continuity of Delinquent Behavior," *Youth and Society* 33:479–514 (2002).

96. William I. Thomas, *The Unadjusted Girl with Cases and Standpoint for Behavior Analysis* (Boston: Little, Brown, 1923)

97. Ibid., p. 109.

98. Elaine Eggleston Doherty, Kerry Green, and Margaret Ensminger, "The Impact of Adolescent Deviance on Marital Trajectories," *Deviant Behavior* 33:185–206 (2012).

99. Ibid.

100. Ruth Morris, "Female Delinquents and Relational Problems," *Social Forces* 43:82–89 (1964).

101. Cowie, Cowie, and Slater, *Delinquency in Girls*, p. 27.

102. Morris, "Female Delinquents and Relational Problems."

103. Clyde Vedder and Dora Somerville, *The Delinquent Girl* (Springfield, IL: Charles C Thomas, 1970).

104. Ames Robey, Richard Rosenwal, John Small, and Ruth Lee, "The Runaway Girl: A Reaction to Family Stress," *American Journal of Orthopsychiatry* 34:763–767 (1964).

105. William Wattenberg and Frank Saunders, "Sex Differences Among Juvenile Court Offenders," *Sociology and Social Research* 39:24–31 (1954).

106. Don Gibbons and Manzer Griswold, "Sex Differences Among Juvenile Court Referrals," *Sociology and Social Research* 42:106–110 (1957).

107. Gordon Barker and William Adams, "Comparison of the Delinquencies of Boys and Girls," *Journal of Criminal Law, Criminology, and Police Science* 53:470–475 (1962).

108. Erin Kathleen Midgley and Celia Lo, "The Role of a Parent's Incarceration in the Emotional Health and Problem Behaviors of At-Risk Adolescents," *Journal of Child and Adolescent Substance Abuse* 22:85–103 (2013).

109. Stacy Tzoumakis, Patrick Lussier, and Raymond Corrado, "Female Juvenile Delinquency, Motherhood, and the Intergenerational Transmission of Aggression and Antisocial Behavior," *Behavioral Sciences and the Law* 30:211–237 (2012).

110. Meredith Worthen, "Gender Differences in Parent-Child Bonding: Implications for Understanding the Gender Gap in Delinquency," *Journal of Crime and Justice* 34:3–23 (2011).

111. D. Wayne Osgood, Janet Wilson, Patrick O'Malley, Jerald Bachman, and Lloyd Johnston, "Routine Activities and Individual Deviant Behaviors," *American Sociological Review* 61:635–655 (1996).

112. Megan Bears Augustyn and Jean Marie McGloin, "The Risk of Informal Socializing with Peers: Considering Gender Differences Across Predatory Delinquency and Substance Use," *Justice Quarterly* 30:117–143 (2013).

113. Steketee, Junger, and Junger-Tas, "Sex Differences in the Predictors of Juvenile Delinquency," 88–105.

114. Cauffman, Farruggia, and Goldweber, "Bad Boys or Poor Parents."

115. Angela Dixon, Pauline Howie, and Jean Starling, "Trauma Exposure, Posttraumatic Stress, and Psychiatric Comorbidity in Female Juvenile Offenders," *Journal of the American Academy of Child and Adolescent Psychiatry* 44:798–806 (2005).

116. Hyeouk Chris Hahm, Yoona Lee, Al Ozonoff, and Michael Wert, "The Impact of Multiple Types of Child Maltreatment on Subsequent Risk Behaviors Among Women During the Transition from Adolescence to

Young Adulthood," *Journal of Youth and Adolescence* 39:528–540 (2010); Veronica Herrera and Laura Ann McCloskey, "Sexual Abuse, Family Violence, and Female Delinquency: Findings from a Longitudinal Study," *Violence and Victims* 18:319–334 (2003).

117. Sherry Hamby, David Finkelhor, and Heather Turner, "Teen Dating Violence: Co-occurrence with Other Victimizations in the National Survey of Children's Exposure to Violence (NatSCEV)," *Psychology of Violence* 2:111–124 (2012).

118. Emily Gaarder and Joanne Belknap, "Tenuous Borders: Girls Transferred to Adult Court," *Criminology* 40:481–518 (2002).

119. Meda Chesney-Lind, "Girls' Crime and Woman's Place: Toward a Feminist Model of Female Delinquency," *Crime and Delinquency* 35:5–29, at 20 (1989).

120. Pernilla Johansson and Kimberly Kempf-Leonard, "A Gender-Specific Pathway to Serious, Violent, and Chronic Offending? Exploring Howell's Risk Factors for Serious Delinquency," *Crime and Delinquency* 55:216–240 (2009).

121. Dominique Eve Roe-Sepowitz, "Comparing Male and Female Juveniles Charged with Homicide: Child Maltreatment, Substance Abuse, and Crime Details," *Journal of Interpersonal Violence* 24:601–617 (2009).

122. Kristin Carbone-Lopez and Jody Miller, "Precocious Role Entry as a Mediating Factor in Women's Methamphetamine Use: Implications for Life-Course and Pathways Research," *Criminology* 50:187–220 (2012).

123. Stephanie R. Hawkins, Phillip W. Graham, Jason Williams, and Margaret A. Zahn, "Resilient Girls—Factors that Protect Against Delinquency," OJJDP, 2009, http://www.ncjrs.gov/pdffiles1/ojjdp/220124.pdf.

124. David Brownfield, "Gender and Gang Membership: Testing Theories to Account for Different Rates of Participation," *Journal of Gang Research* 19:25–32 (2012).

125. Joan Moore, *Going Down to the Barrio: Homeboys and Homegirls in Change* (Philadelphia: Temple University Press, 1991), p. 93.

126. Ibid., p. 101.

127. Gaarder and Belknap, "Tenuous Borders."

128. Jennifer Kerpelman and Sondra Smith-Adcock, "Female Adolescents' Delinquent Activity: The Intersection of Bonds to Parents and Reputation Enhancement," *Youth and Society* 37:176–200 (2005).

129. Lia Ahonen, Wesley G. Jennings, Rolf Loeber, and David P. Farrington, "The Relationship Between Developmental Trajectories of Girls' Offending and Police Charges: Results from the Pittsburgh Girls Study," *Journal of Developmental and Life-Course Criminology*, published online July 2016.

130. David Huizinga, Shari Miller, and the Conduct Problems Prevention Research Group, "Developmental Sequences of Girls' Delinquent Behavior," OJJDP, 2013, http://www.ojjdp.gov/pubs/238276.pdf.

131. Freda Adler, *Sisters in Crime* (New York: McGraw-Hill, 1975).

132. Ibid., pp. 10–11.

133. Rita James Simon, "Women and Crime Revisited," *Social Science Quarterly* 56:658–663 (1976).

134. Ibid., pp. 660–661.

135. Roy Austin, "Women's Liberation and Increase in Minor, Major, and Occupational Offenses," *Criminology* 20:407–430 (1982).

136. Michael Hindelang, "Age, Sex, and the Versatility of 'Delinquency Involvements,'" *Social Forces* 14:525–534 (1971).

137. Darrell Steffensmeier and Dana Haynie, "Gender, Structural Disadvantage, and Urban Crime: Do Macrosocial Variables Also Explain Female Offending Rates?" *Criminology* 38:403–438 (2000); Beth Bjerregaard and Carolyn Smith, "Gender Differences in Gang Participation and Delinquency," *Journal of Quantitative Criminology* 9:329–350 (1993).

138. See, generally, Meda Chesney-Lind and Lisa Pasko, *The Female Offender: Girls, Women, and Crime* (Thousand Oaks, CA: Sage, 2012).

139. Kia Asberg and Kimberly Renk, "Safer in Jail? A Comparison of Victimization History and Psychological Adjustment Between Previously Homeless and Non-homeless Incarcerated Women," *Feminist Criminology* 10:165–187 (2015).

140. Herman Schwendinger and Julia Schwendinger, *Rape and Inequality* (Newbury Park, CA: Sage, 1983).

141. Kathleen Daly and Meda Chesney-Lind, "Feminism and Criminology," *Justice Quarterly* 5:497–538 (1988).

142. Janet Saltzman Chafetz, "Feminist Theory and Sociology: Underutilized Contributions for Mainstream Theory," *Annual Review of Sociology* 23:97–121 (1997).

143. Ibid.

144. Gillian Balfour, "Re-imagining a Feminist Criminology," *Canadian Journal of Criminology and Criminal Justice* 48:735–752 (2006).

145. Jane Roberts Chapman, "Violence Against Women as a Violation of Human Rights," *Social Justice* 17:54–71 (1990).

146. Carrie Yodanis, "Gender Inequality, Violence against Women, and Fear," *Journal of Interpersonal Violence* 19:655–675 (2004).

147. Victoria Titterington, "A Retrospective Investigation of Gender Inequality and Female Homicide Victimization," *Sociological Spectrum* 26:205–236 (2006).

148. James Messerschmidt, *Masculinities and Crime: Critique and Reconceptualization of Theory* (Lanham, MD: Rowman & Littlefield, 1993).

149. Angela P. Harris, "Gender, Violence, Race, and Criminal Justice," *Stanford Law Review* 52:777–810 (2000).

150. Jody Miller and Norman White, "Gender and Adolescent Relationship Violence: A Contextual Examination," *Criminology* 41:1207–1248 (2003).

151. Suzie Dod Thomas and Nancy Stein, "Criminality, Imprisonment, and Women's Rights in the 1990s," *Social Justice* 17:1–5 (1990).

152. Walter DeKeseredy and Martin Schwartz, "Male Peer Support and Woman Abuse: An Expansion of DeKeseredy's Model," *Sociological Spectrum* 13:393–413 (1993).

153. Daly and Chesney-Lind, "Feminism and Criminology." See also Drew Humphries and Susan Caringella-MacDonald, "Murdered Mothers, Missing Wives: Reconsidering Female Victimization," *Social Justice* 17:71–78 (1990).

154. Kjersti Ericsson and Nina Jon, "Gendered Social Control: 'A Virtuous Girl' and 'a Proper Boy,'" *Journal of Scandinavian Studies in Criminology and Crime Prevention* 9:126–141 (2006).

155. Andrew L. Spivak, Brooke M. Wagner, Jennifer M. Whitmer, and Courtney L. Charish, "Gender and Status Offending: Judicial Paternalism in Juvenile Justice Processing," *Feminist Criminology* 9:224–248 (2014).

156. John Hagan, A. R. Gillis, and John Simpson, "The Class Structure and Delinquency: Toward a Power-Control Theory of Common Delinquent Behavior," *American Journal of Sociology* 90:1151–1178 (1985); John Hagan, John Simpson, and A. R. Gillis, "Class in the Household: A Power-Control Theory of Gender and Delinquency," *American Journal of Sociology* 92:788–816 (1987).

157. John Hagan, A. R. Gillis, and John Simpson, "Clarifying and Extending Power-Control Theory," *American Journal of Sociology* 95:1024–1037 (1990).

158. Brenda Sims Blackwell and Mark Reed, "Power-Control as a Between and Within-Family Model: Reconsidering the Unit of Analysis," *Journal of Youth and Adolescence* 32:385–400 (2003).

159. Merry Morash, "The Nature of Co-Occurring Exposure to Violence and of Court Responses to Girls in the Juvenile Justice System," *Violence Against Women* 22:923–942 (2016).

160. Dana Smith and Lisa Saldana, "Trauma, Delinquency, and Substance Use: Co-occurring Problems for Adolescent Girls in the Juvenile Justice System," *Journal of Child and Adolescent Substance Abuse* 22:450–465 (2013).

161. Patrick Kennedy, Thomas Kelly, Joanne Grigor, Ellen Vale, Claire Mason, and Roberta Caiazza, "Personality Features of an Adolescent Female Offending Population," *Journal of Forensic Psychiatry and Psychology* 26:297–308 (2015).

162. Thomas J. Gamble, Sherrie Sonnenberg, John Haltigan, and Amy Cuzzola-Kern, "Detention Screening: Prospects for Population Management and the Examination of Disproportionality by Race, Age, and Gender," *Criminal Justice Policy Review* 13:380–395 (2002); Kimberly Kempf-Leonard and Lisa Sample, "Disparity Based on Sex: Is Gender-Specific Treatment Warranted?" *Justice Quarterly* 17:89–128 (2000).

163. Meda Chesney-Lind and Randall Shelden, *Girls, Delinquency, and Juvenile Justice* (Belmont, CA: West/Wadsworth, 1998).

164. Holly Hartwig and Jane Myers, "A Different Approach: Applying a Wellness Paradigm to Adolescent Female Delinquents and Offenders," *Journal of Mental Health Counseling* 25:57–75 (2003).

165. Miriam Sealock and Sally Simpson, "Unraveling Bias in Arrest Decisions: The Role of Juvenile Offender Typescripts," *Justice Quarterly* 15:427–457 (1998).

166. Tia Stevens, Merry Morash, and Meda Chesney-Lind, "Are Girls Getting Tougher, or Are We Tougher on Girls? Probability of Arrest and Juvenile Court Oversight in 1980 and 2000," *Justice Quarterly* 28:719–744 (2011).

167. Lisa Pasko, "Damaged Daughters: The History of Girls' Sexuality and the Juvenile Justice System," *Journal of Criminal Law and Criminology* 100:1099–1130 (2010).

168. Kristi Holsinger and Jessica P. Hodge, "The Experiences of Lesbian, Gay, Bisexual, and Transgender Girls in Juvenile Justice Systems," *Feminist Criminology*, first published online February 2014.

CHAPTER 8

The Family and Delinquency

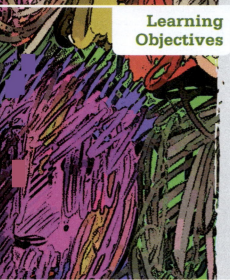

ON JULY 22, 2015, five members of the Bever family were murdered in Broken Arrow, Oklahoma. Police quickly determined that Robert Bever, 19, and his brother Michael, 17, were the perpetrators. They had planned out the murder of their family for at least a year in advance. Two of their sisters, ages 13 and 2, survived the attack. The 13-year-old later told authorities that her two oldest brothers knifed the family to death. She said that her brothers were both physically and psychologically abused by their father and had started to stockpile weapons in advance of the attack. The brothers told police that the killings were part of a plot to carry out further mass killings. Robert expressed a desire for notoriety as a serial killer. The teens told of their plan to kill their family, cut up the bodies, and store them in bins in the attic before taking the family vehicle as well as guns and ammunition to randomly attack other locations and kill 10 people at each place.[1]

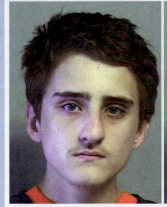

Tulsa County Sheriff's Office/EPA/Redux

Michael Bever (L) and Robert Bever (R) who were arrested in connection with the deaths of five family members, including young children.

While the Bever brothers story is extreme, in fact, most delinquency experts agree that interactions between parents and children, between siblings, and across genders, provide opportunities for children to acquire or inhibit antisocial behavior patterns.[2] Even kids who are predisposed toward delinquency because of abnormal personality traits or mood disorders may find their life circumstances improved and their involvement with antisocial behavior diminished if they are exposed to positive and effective parenting.[3]

Families may be more important than peer groups as an influence on adolescent misbehavior.[4] It comes as no surprise that research shows that young adults who maintain positive lifestyles report having had warm relationships with their parents, while those who perceived a lack of parental warmth and support were later much more likely to get involved in antisocial behaviors.[5] Families that lack the resources to support at-risk youth simply may be unable to prevent their offspring from entering a delinquent way of life.[6]

Good parenting lowers the risk of delinquency for children living in high-crime areas. Research shows kids resist the temptation of the streets if they receive fair discipline and support from parents who provide them with positive role models.[7]

Warm and supportive relationships with parents provide an environment for adolescents in which they are able to adapt to environmentally derived stress and strain in a healthy manner. Families that bond and that have dinner together on a regular basis seem to be most able to shield children from damaging social and cultural influences.[8] Positive relationships with parents promote prosocial behavior even among adolescents who are exposed to damaging life events or chronic environmental strains.[9]

Because these issues are critical for understanding delinquency, this chapter is devoted to an analysis of the family's role in producing or inhibiting delinquency. We first cover the changing face of the American family. We will review the way family structure and function influence delinquent behavior. The relationships among child abuse, neglect, and delinquency are covered in some depth.

The Changing American Family

The assumed relationship between delinquency and family life is critical today, because the American family is changing. Extended families, once common, are now for the most part anachronisms. In their place is the **nuclear family**, described as a

For a great deal of information on programs for families and children, visit the **David and Lucile Packard Foundation** website: http://www.packard.org/what-we-fund/children-families-and-communities/.

nuclear family
A family unit composed of parents and their children; this smaller family structure is subject to great stress due to the intense, close contact between parents and children.

"dangerous hothouse of emotions," because of the close contact between parents and children; in these families, problems are unrelieved by contact with other kin living nearby.[10]

Family life in America is rapidly changing. Two-parent households are on the decline because divorce, remarriage, and cohabitation are on the rise. Another recent trend: families are getting smaller due to the increase in single-parent households and a drop in fertility. Today 4 in 10 births occur to women who are single or living with a nonmarital partner.

The declining share of children living in what is often deemed a "traditional" family has been largely supplanted by the rising shares of children living with single or cohabiting parents. While in the past a child born to a married couple was very likely to grow up in a home with those two parents, this is much less common today, and about 30 percent of children younger than 6 experience a major change in their family or household structure, in the form of parental divorce, separation, marriage, cohabitation, or death. As a result of these changes, there is no longer one normative family form. Among baby boomer families, 73 percent of all children were living in a family with two married parents in their first marriage. By 1980, only 61 percent of children were living with two married parents, and today that number has declined to about 50 percent. In contrast, about 15 percent of American children are living with parents in a remarriage and 7 percent are living with parents who are cohabiting without marriage. About 26 percent of American children live with one parent, up from 22 percent in 2000 and just 9 percent in 1960.

These changes may be attributed to the fact that Americans are bailing out of marriage at higher rates than in the past. About two-thirds (67 percent) of married people younger than 50 are still in their first marriage; that share was 83 percent in 1960.

Fragile Families

Nonmarital childbearing increased dramatically in the United States during the latter half of the twentieth century, changing the context in which American children are raised and giving rise to a new family form—*fragile families*, defined as unmarried couples with children. Some analysts see these changes as a positive sign of greater individual freedom and women's economic independence; others argue that they contribute to poverty and income inequality.[11] Given the importance of families to children's health and development, researchers and policy makers have become increasingly interested in the nature of parental relationships in fragile families and their implications for children's future life chances, especially children's access to resources and the stability and quality of these resources. Parents living in cooperative, stable unions tend to pool their incomes and work together to raise their child. By contrast, those living apart in uncooperative relationships can jeopardize their child's resources, both financial and social. Such living arrangements can also impact on a child's well-being: research indicates that child abuse is more likely to occur in two-parent families in which one caretaker is a live-in boyfriend or stepfather.[12]

In sum, at the time their child is born, unmarried parents have high hopes for a future together. About half of these parents are living together, and another 30 percent are romantically involved. Relationship quality and father involvement are high. Underlying this optimism, however, are signs of problems, including distrust of the opposite sex and a belief that a single mother can raise a child as well as a married mother. Five years later, the picture is more mixed. On the positive side, about a third of parents are living together, about half of non-cohabiting fathers see their child on a regular basis, and co-parenting relationships are positive. On the negative side, a third of fathers have virtually disappeared from their children's lives, and new partnerships and new children are common, leading to high instability and growing complexity in these families.

Teen Moms/Single Moms Living in a single-parent home, especially one headed by an unmarried teenage mother, has long been associated with difficulties for both the mother and her child. As you may recall (Chapter 1), kids born into single-parent homes are more likely to live in poverty and to experience long-term physical and social difficulties.[13] One reason is that more than 90 percent of teens who give birth are unmarried, compared with 62 percent in 1980, and young single moms may have a tough time earning a decent living in a tough economy.[14]

Very often these conditions are interactive: teen moms suffer social problems, which in turn have a negative effect on their children. Research shows that by age 14, when compared to the children of older moms, the offspring of teen mothers were more likely to have disturbed psychological behavior, poorer school performance, poorer reading ability, were involved with the criminal justice system, and were more likely to smoke and drink on a regular basis. However, the connection between teen moms and troubled children flows through their economic circumstances—those without economic means were much more likely to produce troubled kids than those who enjoyed support, financial and otherwise, from their families.[15]

While teenage moms still experience difficulties, there are significantly fewer of them in the population than there were 20 years ago. Availability of birth control and the legalization of abortion have helped reduce the number of pregnant teens. According to the most recent data available (2014), a total of 249,078 babies were born to women and girls aged 15 to 19 years, for a birth rate of 24.2 per 1,000 women in this age group, a drop of 9 percent from the prior year. As Figure 8.1 shows, there has been a dramatic decline in teen birth rates over the past 15 years. Why have teen birth rates fallen so dramatically? More teens are delaying or reducing sexual activity; more of the teens who are sexually active are using birth control than in previous years; availability of legal abortions has also reduced the rate of teen births.[16]

Teen girls most likely to get pregnant are those with less favorable socioeconomic conditions, such as poor education and low family income levels. Teens in child welfare systems are at higher risk of teen pregnancy and birth than other groups: young women living in foster care are more than twice as likely to become pregnant than those not in foster care.

Child Care

Charged with caring for children is a daycare system whose workers are often paid minimum wage. Of special concern are "family daycare homes," in which a single provider takes care of three to nine children. Today about 50 percent of all

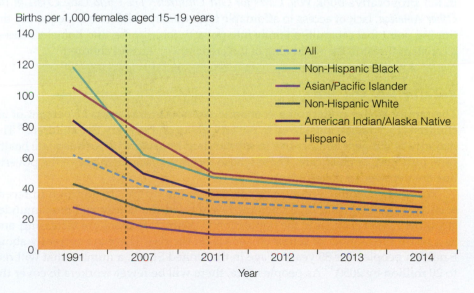

Births per 1,000 females aged 15–19 years

figure 8.1

Birthrates for Females Ages 15–19 by Race and Ethnicity Origin

SOURCE: National Vital Statistics Reports, http://www.cdc.gov/nchs/data/nvsr/nvsr65/nvsr65_03.pdf (accessed October 2016).

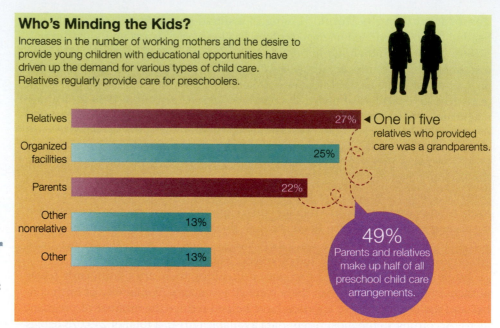

figure 8.2

Child Care: Who's Minding the Kids?

SOURCE: US Census Department, Child Care, An Important Part of American Life, https://www.census.gov/library /visualizations/2013/comm/child_care.html (accessed October 2016).

young children, about 12 million, are in some form of child care, either before or after they begin their formal education. Children living in poverty are much more likely to be in non-parental care than more affluent kids. Several states neither license nor monitor these private providers. Even in states that mandate registration and inspection of daycare providers, it is estimated that 90 percent or more of the facilities operate "underground." It is not uncommon for one adult to care for eight infants, an impossible task regardless of training or feelings of concern. During times of economic downturn, unlicensed child care provides a more reasonable alternative to state-regulated and therefore more costly licensed centers. Because punishments are typically a small fine, prosecutors rarely go after unlicensed child care operators unless tragedy strikes. It has become routine for children to die in these unlicensed facilities due to lack of care or outright neglect.

Children from working poor families are most likely to suffer from inadequate child care; these children often spend time in makeshift arrangements that allow their parents to work but lack the stimulating environment children need to thrive (see Figure 8.2). Unlike many other Western countries, the United States does not provide universal daycare to working mothers. As a result, writes Valerie Polakow in her provocative book *Who Cares for Our Children? The Child Care Crisis in the Other America*, lack of access to affordable high-quality child care is frequently the tipping point that catapults a family into poverty, joblessness, and homelessness—a constant threat to the well-being of lower-class women and children.[17]

Economic Stress

The family is also undergoing economic stress. At last count, 21 percent of all children (15.5 million kids) lived in poverty, about one in every five children.[18] The majority of indigent families live in substandard housing without adequate health care, nutrition, or child care. Those whose incomes place them above the poverty line are deprived of government assistance.

Will this economic pressure be reduced in the future? In addition to recent economic upheaval and high unemployment rates, the family will remain under stress because of changes in the population makeup. Life spans are increasing, and as a result the number of senior citizens is on the rise. There are currently about 6 million people over 85 years of age in the United States, a number that will rise to 20 million by 2050.[19] As people retire, there will be fewer workers to cover the

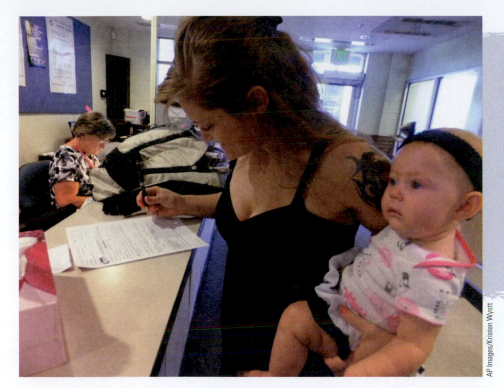

Economic stress can influence family functioning. Here, Laura, 27, with her daughter, fills out a form at the Jefferson Action Center, an assistance center in the Denver suburb of Lakewood. Laura grew up in a solidly middle-class family, but she and her boyfriend, who has struggled to find work, are now relying on government assistance to cover food and $650 rent for their family. More than 40 million Americans now live below the poverty line, a number unseen in nearly half a century, erasing gains from the war on poverty in the 1960s amid a weak economy and a fraying government safety net. Will economic hardship eventually produce increases in the delinquency rate?

AP Images/Kristen Wyatt

costs of Social Security, medical care, and nursing home care. Because the elderly will require a greater percentage of the nation's income for their care, less money will be available to care for needy children. These costs will put greater economic stress on families. Voter sentiment has an impact on the allocation of public funds, and there is concern that an older generation, worried about health care costs, may be reluctant to spend tax dollars on at-risk kids.

Rand Conger, one of the nation's leading experts on family life, has found that economic stress appears to have a harmful effect on parents and children. According to his "family stress model" of economic hardship, such factors as low income and income loss increase parents' sadness, pessimism about the future, anger, despair, and withdrawal from other family members. Economic stress has this impact on parents' social-emotional functioning through the daily pressures it creates for them, such as being unable to pay bills or acquire basic necessities (adequate food, housing, clothing, and medical care). As parents become more emotionally distressed, they tend to interact with one another and their children in a more irritable and less supportive fashion. These patterns of behavior increase instability in the marriage and also disrupt effective parenting practices, such as monitoring children's activities and using consistent and appropriate disciplinary strategies. Marital instability and disrupted parenting, in turn, increase children's risk of suffering developmental problems, such as depression, substance abuse, and engaging in delinquent behaviors. These economic stress processes also decrease children's ability to function in a competent manner in school and with peers.[20]

The Family's Influence on Delinquency

The effect of these family stressors can have a significant impact on children's behavior. The family is the primary unit in which children learn the values and attitudes that guide their actions throughout their lives. Family disruption or change can have a long-lasting impact on children. In contrast, effective parenting can help neutralize the effect of both individual (e.g., emotional problems) and social (e.g., delinquent peers) forces, which promote delinquent behaviors.[21]

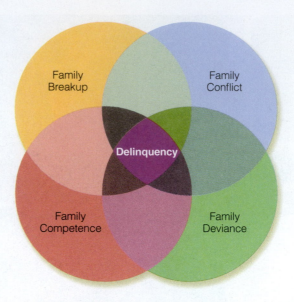

figure 8.3

Family Influences on Behavior

Each of these four factors has been linked to antisocial behavior and delinquency. Interaction between these factors may escalate delinquent activity.

© Cengage Learning

Four categories of family dysfunction seem to promote delinquent behavior: families disrupted by separation and divorce, families involved in interpersonal conflict, ineffective parents who lack proper parenting skills, and families that contain deviant parents who may transmit their behavior to their children (see Figure 8.3).[22] These factors may interact with one another: drug-abusing parents may be more likely to experience family conflict, child neglect, and marital breakup. We now turn to the specific types of family problems that have been linked to delinquent behavior.

Family Breakup

One of the most enduring controversies in the study of delinquency is the relationship between a parent absent from the home and the onset of delinquent behavior. Parents or guardians act as the main source of informal social control. When a breakdown in the family occurs, the social control function is interrupted and children are free to get involved in antisocial behaviors.[23]

The association between family breakup and delinquency is particularly important since divorce and remarriage have become commonplace. Fewer people are getting married today than in the past: the share of all adults who have entered into marriage even once has fallen markedly, from 85 percent in 1960 to 70 percent today. Nonetheless, among those who get married, the chance of breakup is extremely high. According to the American Psychological Association, about 40 to 50 percent of married couples in the United States divorce. The divorce rate for subsequent marriages is even higher.[24]

Given that divorce is so prevalent, it comes as no surprise that almost 42 million adults in the United States have been married more than once, up from 22 million in 1980. The number of remarried adults has tripled since 1960, when there were 14 million.[25]

Research indicates that parents whose marriage is secure produce children who are self-confident and independent.[26] In contrast, research conducted in both the United States and abroad shows that children raised in homes with one or both parents absent may be prone to antisocial behavior.[27] A number of experts contend that a **broken home** is a strong determinant of a child's law-violating behavior. The connection seems self-evident, because a child is first socialized at home and therefore any disjunction in an orderly family structure could be expected to have a negative impact on the child.

The suspected broken home–delinquency relationship is important because, if current trends continue, less than half of all children born today will

broken home
Home in which one or both parents are absent due to divorce or separation; children in such an environment may be prone to antisocial behavior.

live continuously with their own mother and father throughout childhood. And because stepfamilies, also called **blended families**, are less stable than families consisting of two biological parents, an increasing number of children will experience family breakup two or even three times during childhood. Unfortunately, more than 60 percent of blended families are re-broken because of another divorce. This is stressful for everyone concerned, but especially for the children who are involved.[28]

Children who have experienced family breakup are more likely to demonstrate behavior problems across the life course.[29] Conversely, marriage seems to promote conventional behavior: the more married couples in a community, the lower the juvenile violence rate.[30]

The effects of divorce seem gender-specific:

- Boys seem to be more affected by the post-divorce absence of the father. In post-divorce situations, fathers seem less likely to be around to solve problems, to discuss standards of conduct, or to enforce discipline. A divorced father who remains actively involved in his child's life reduces his son's chances of delinquency.

- Girls are more affected by both the quality of the mother's parenting and post-divorce parental conflict. It is possible that extreme levels of parental conflict may serve as a model to young girls coping with the aftermath of their parents' separation.[31]

- There are distinct racial and ethnic differences in the impact of divorce/separation on youth. Some groups (e.g., Hispanics, Asians) have been raised in cultures where divorce is rare and parents have less experience in developing childrearing practices that buffer the effects of family breakup on adolescent problem behavior.[32]

Divorce and Delinquency   The relationship between broken homes and delinquency has been controversial, to say the least. It was first established in early research, which suggested that a significant association existed between parental absence and youthful misconduct.[33] For many years the link was clear: children growing up in broken homes were much more likely to fall prey to delinquency than those who lived in two-parent households.[34]

Beginning in the late 1950s, some researchers began to question the link between broken homes and delinquency. Early studies, they claimed, used the records of police, courts, and correctional institutions.[35] This research may have been tainted by sampling bias: youths from broken homes may get arrested more often than youths from intact families, but this does not necessarily mean they engage in more frequent and serious delinquent behavior. Official statistics may reflect the fact that agents of the justice system treat children from disrupted households more severely, because they cannot call on parents for support. The *parens patriae* philosophy of the juvenile courts calls for official intervention when parental supervision is considered inadequate.[36] A number of subsequent studies, using self-report data, have failed to establish any clear-cut relationship between broken homes and delinquent behavior.[37] Boys and girls from intact families seem as likely to self-report delinquency as those whose parents are divorced or separated. Researchers concluded that the absence of parents has a greater effect on agents of the justice system than it does on the behavior of children.[38]

The Link Between Divorce and Delinquency   The consensus is that family breakup is, in fact, traumatic and most likely does have a direct influence on adolescent misbehavior.[39] Research shows that the more often children are forced to go through family transitions, the more likely they are to engage in delinquent activity.[40] So the prevailing wisdom today is that divorce is related to delinquency and status offending, especially if a child had a close relationship with the parent who is forced to leave the home.[41]

blended families
Nuclear families that are the product of divorce and remarriage, blending one parent from each of two families and their combined children into one family unit.

Of course, not all kids growing up in homes in which parents are divorced or separated turn to delinquency. Most do not, and the majority grow up to live happy and fulfilled lives. One divorce situation is obviously different from another, and these differences may explain the effect of family dissolution on a child's misbehavior.

One factor may be how parents react to marital breakup. As you may recall (Chapter 6), developmental/life-course theorists, such as Robert Sampson and John Laub, believe that a good marriage helps men "knife off" from misbehavior. If conversely a divorce is hostile, anger and rage that may have precipitated the dissolution of the marriage may not be alleviated by separation. Domestic violence that may have been present in stress-filled marriages does not abate after separation but merely shifts to ex-partners who are targeted in the aftermath of divorce.[42] Parents who are in post-divorce turmoil may in turn influence their children to misbehave.

Another factor is how parental bonds are affected by marital breakup. The less time fathers lived with their children, the more conduct problems their children manifested. However, when fathers themselves engage in high levels of antisocial behavior, their leaving home may actually improve their children's behavior. Staying married may not be the answer to the problems faced by children living in single-parent families unless parents can refrain from deviant behaviors and become reliable sources of emotional and economic support.[43]

It is also possible that family breakup is not per se the cause of children's misbehavior, but rather, it's the aftermath of divorce that is to blame. After a divorce, some newly single parents may spend more time socializing outside of the home, looking for new romantic partners, at the expense of family time. Less supervision and a reduction of family attachments may be the real culprit and not the events leading up to divorce and separation associated with concurrent increases in offending.[44]

Long-Term Effects Not only does divorce hurt kids in the near term, it also has long-term consequences that harm their childhood and may last into adulthood. Children who grow up apart from their biological fathers typically do less well than children who grow up with both biological parents. They are less likely to finish high school and attend college, less likely to find and keep a steady job, and more likely to become teen parents. Although most children who grow up with a single parent do quite well, differences between children in one- and two-parent families are significant, and there is fairly good evidence that father absence per se is responsible for some social problems.[45]

In their classic book *The Unexpected Legacy of Divorce*, Judith Wallerstein, Julia Lewis, and Sandra Blakeslee reported on the findings of a longitudinal study with 131 children whose parents divorced during their adolescence.[46] They found that children of divorce develop lingering fears about their own ability to develop long-term relationships; these fears often impede their ability to marry and raise families. While most parents are able to reduce their emotional pain and get on with their lives a few years after they separate, this is not true of their children, whose emotional turmoil may last for decades. Wallerstein and her associates found that adolescents who experienced divorce are still struggling with the fear that their relationships will fail like those of their parents.

While divorce may take a heavy toll, it is true that many kids who experience family breakup are able to get through the ordeal in good shape. When E. Mavis Hetherington and John Kelly studied the children of divorce, they found that many do undergo some trauma, but for the most part they are much better off than those Wallerstein encountered.[47] While children in single-parent families and stepfamilies have more psychological problems than those in intact families, more than 75 percent ultimately do as well as children from intact families.

youth STORIES

The Nevil Family Murders

In 2016, Dallas Judge Andrea Martin ruled in juvenile court that a teenager who was just 13 when he shot and killed his 12-year-old girlfriend's parents, Alan and Darlene Nevil, will be released from prison on the condition that he spend six months to a year in super-intensive supervised parole and then remain on adult parole until August 2038, the end of his original 28-year sentence.

Why the early release? The teen, now 18, has completed a treatment program, and juvenile justice personnel believe that he has the ability to develop a successful transition plan. He excelled in work and school programs, earning a general equivalency diploma and both high school and college credits. He earned certification in carpentry and training in mobile air conditioning and landscaping, working with the grounds-keeping crew.

What prompted the double murder? The boy had moved from California to Texas at age 9 with his mom. His family history was troubled: two of his uncles had been murdered, one by a family member. He had been unable to protect his mother from domestic violence. He began drug use by age 10 and was soon introduced to gang activity. When he found a girlfriend, it changed his life—but in the wrong direction. It was the girl's idea to kill her mother and stepfather because they had grounded her and forbade her to see her young boyfriend. She later told police that the final straw was when they took away her coloring books. "I knew they had to die." The girl bragged that she was smarter than the boy and could get him to do anything she wanted. She told him she was pregnant and had been sexually abused by her stepfather. While the boy was first reluctant, upon hearing this news he went into a rage and agreed to carry out the murders.

The girl knew her parents' work schedules. When Darlene came home sometime after noon she was shot twice, in the back and the head. Then the teenagers waited for Alan, who was shot five times. He lived long enough to identify his killers.

Under the conditions of his parole, the boy will wear a monitor and not be able to leave a halfway house for anything other than work, treatment, or worship for the first six months to a year. He will also be required to find stable employment, attend anger management classes and counseling, and must refrain from communicating with gangs. His girlfriend remains in custody.

CRITICAL THINKING

Can a child of 13 realize the seriousness of his or her acts? Should age be considered when sentencing a teen who committed murder?

SOURCES: Ray Leszcynski, "Troubled History: Teen Gunman Who Will Be Paroled Had Been Pressured by Girlfriend to Kill Her Parents," *Dallas Morning News*, May 18, 2016, http://crimeblog.dallasnews.com/2016/05/teen-gunman-who-will-be-paroled-had-been-pressured-by-girlfriend-to-kill-her-parents.html/; Fox News, "Teen Who Murdered Girlfriend's Parents to Be Released on Parole," May 18, 2016, http://www.fox4news.com/news/142585993-story. (URLs accessed October 2016.)

Family Conflict

Not all unhappy marriages end in divorce; some continue in an atmosphere of conflict. Intrafamily conflict is a common experience in many American families. The link between parental conflict and delinquency was established more than 50 years ago when F. Ivan Nye found that a child's perception of his or her parents' marital happiness was a significant predictor of delinquency.[48] Contemporary studies support these early findings that children who grow up in maladapted homes and witness discord or violence later exhibit emotional disturbance and behavior problems.[49] There seems to be little difference between the behavior of children who merely witness **intrafamily violence** and those who are its victims.[50] Children who experience any form of family violence are more likely to act out than those who avoid relational conflict. However, children who experienced indirect types of family violence, such as exposure to the physical abuse of a sibling, are more likely to externalize behavior scores than children who experienced direct maltreatment and child physical abuse.[51] The Youth Stories feature discusses a family murder case that was the result of family conflict.

Which is worse, growing up in a home marked by conflict or growing up in a broken home? Research shows that children in both broken homes and high-conflict intact homes were worse off than children in low-conflict, intact families.[52] However, even when parents are divorced, kids who maintain attachments to their parents are less likely to engage in delinquency than those who are alienated and detached.[53] The influence of family conflict on delinquency is explored further in the Focus on Delinquency feature entitled "Bad Parents or Bad Kids?"

intrafamily violence
An environment of discord and conflict within the family; children who grow up in dysfunctional homes often exhibit delinquent behaviors, having learned at a young age that aggression pays off.

FOCUS ON DELINQUENCY

Bad Parents or Bad Kids?

Which comes first, bad parents or bad kids? Does parental conflict cause delinquency, or do delinquents create family conflict? Although damaged parent–child relationships are associated with delinquency, it is difficult to assess the relationship. It is often assumed that preexisting family problems cause delinquency, but it may also be true that children who act out put enormous stress on a family. Kids who are conflict prone may actually help destabilize households. To avoid escalation of a child's aggression, parents may give in to their children's demands. The children learn that aggression pays off. Parents may feel overwhelmed and shut their child out of their lives. Adolescent misbehavior may be a precursor of family conflict; strife leads to more adolescent misconduct, producing an endless cycle of family stress and delinquency.

David Huh and colleagues surveyed nearly 500 adolescent girls and found little evidence that poor parenting is a direct cause of children's misbehavior problems or that it escalates misbehavior. Rather, children's problem behaviors undermine parenting effectiveness. *Increases* in adolescent behavior problems, such as substance abuse, resulted in *decreases* in parental control and support. In contrast, parents' problems played only a small role in escalating their children's deviant or behavior problems. Huh suggests it is possible that parents whose children consistently act out may eventually become exasperated and give up on attempts at control.

Martha Gault-Sherman also found that family conflict may escalate *after* kids get involved in delinquency and that the parent–child relationship is interactional: while a lack of parental attachment has an effect on delinquency, an adolescent's delinquency helps decrease parental attachment. Lack of parental involvement with kids may influence delinquency, but involvement *declines* after kids get in trouble or engage in delinquency. Her findings regarding parental attachment provide strong evidence for the existence of a reciprocal relationship between parenting and delinquency.

Another take on the association between family conflict and children's delinquency comes from John Paul Wright and Kevin Beaver, who believe there is a genetic component to the relationship. Delinquent kids may reside in conflict-ridden families because they have inherited traits, such as low self-control. Wright and Beaver have found a large body of research showing that impulsivity and attention deficit hyperactivity disorder—both of which are aspects of low self-control—are inherited. Therefore, what appears to be the effect of bad parenting or family conflict is actually caused by "bad genes." Because of this genetic effect, the role of parenting may be more complicated than is typically assumed. Parents may help neutralize the effect of inherited traits, or the traits of parents may interact in unique ways with the traits of each of their children. It is possible the genetically determined traits of a child are likely to influence how a parent treats the child and not vice versa. So if family conflict is associated with delinquency, it may be because both parents and children have inherited a genetic disposition toward conflict and antisocial behavior.

CRITICAL THINKING

There may be a bright side to the association between family conflict and delinquency: Sonja Siennick recently found that young adult offenders receive more parental financial assistance than do their nonoffending peers and even their own nonoffending siblings. Offenders' life circumstances may trigger parental assistance even when kids have been involved in crime; parents do not give up on their troubled teens. Maybe it's because they feel guilty for causing their kids to engage in a delinquent way of life! What do you think?

SOURCES: Martha Gault-Sherman, "It's a Two-Way Street: The Bidirectional Relationship Between Parenting and Delinquency," *Journal of Youth and Adolescence* 41:121–145 (2012); Sonja Siennick, "Tough Love? Crime and Parental Assistance in Young Adulthood," *Criminology* 49:163–196 (2011); David Huh, Jennifer Tristan, Emily Wade, and Eric Stice, "Does Problem Behavior Elicit Poor Parenting? A Prospective Study of Adolescent Girls," *Journal of Adolescent Research* 21:185–204 (2006); John Paul Wright and Kevin Beaver, "Do Parents Matter in Creating Self-Control in Their Children? A Genetically Informed Test of Gottfredson and Hirschi's Theory of Low Self-Control," *Criminology* 43:1169–1202 (2005).

Family Competence

Children raised by parents who lack proper parenting skills are more at risk than those whose parents are supportive and effectively control their children in a noncoercive fashion.[54] Parents who are overly strict and controlling are more likely to produce children with behavioral problems.[55] Other parents are overly permissive and indulgent. They are warm and receptive to their children's needs, but place few boundaries and establish few rules; their kids are needy and lack self-control. Permissive yet disengaged parenting has been associated with negative behavioral outcomes.[56] In contrast, some parents who are overly authoritarian may lose legitimacy with their offspring despite their controlling efforts.[57]

The quality of parenting becomes more acute when kids lack other forms of social support. Research findings have shown that the impact of uninvolved and permissive parenting for problematic youth outcomes is greater in higher-risk neighborhoods. In other words, parental competence is required if a youngster hopes to escape the damage wrought by living in a disorganized lower-class neighborhood.[58] In contrast, children who are properly supervised, especially in disorganized areas, are less likely to succumb to the temptations of the streets.

Even children who appear to be at risk are better able to resist involvement in delinquent activity when they report that they can communicate with parents.[59]

Parents of beyond-control youngsters have been found to be inconsistent rule-setters, to be less likely to show interest in their children, and to display high levels of hostile detachment. Children who feel inhibited with their parents and refuse to discuss important issues with them are more likely to engage in deviant activities. Kids who report having troubled home lives also exhibit lower levels of self-esteem and are more prone to antisocial behaviors.[60]

Parental Efficacy   If bad or incompetent parenting can produce antisocial children, can competent parenting produce an opposite result? Studies show that delinquency will be reduced if both or at least one parent provides the type of structure that integrates children into families, while giving them the ability to assert their individuality and regulate their own behavior.[61] This phenomenon is referred to as **parental efficacy**.[62] In some cultures emotional support from the mother is critical, whereas in others the father's support remains the key factor.[63] Adolescents whose parents maintain close relationships with them report less delinquent behavior and substance use regardless of the type of family structure—that is, blended families, same-sex parents, and so on. Kids who reside in homes where parents are warm and giving are more likely to develop personality traits such as a positive self-image that helps them avoid the lure of delinquent behaviors.[64] This finding suggests that the quality of parent–adolescent relationships better predicts adolescent outcomes than family type.[65]

Inconsistent/Harsh Discipline   Parents of delinquent youths tend to be inconsistent disciplinarians, either overly harsh or extremely lenient. One debate concerns the efficacy of using physical discipline. National surveys find mixed views. Parents who advocate physical punishment believe that it is a necessary aspect of disciplining practices that produce well-behaved children; in contrast, opponents state that physical discipline harms children psychologically and interferes with their development.[66]

Opponents of physical punishment believe that it weakens the bond between parents and children, lowers the children's self-esteem, and undermines their faith in justice. It is possible that physical punishment encourages children to become more secretive and dishonest.[67] Overly strict discipline may have an even more insidious link to antisocial behaviors: abused children have a higher risk of neurological dysfunction than the nonabused, and brain abnormalities have been linked to violent crime.[68]

Despite public support for corporal punishment, there is growing evidence of a "violence begetting violence" cycle. Children who are subject to even minimal amounts of physical punishment may be more likely to use violence themselves.[69] Sociologist Murray Straus reviewed physical discipline in a series of surveys and found a powerful relationship between exposure to physical punishment and later aggression.[70]

Nonviolent societies are also ones in which parents rarely punish their children physically; there is a link between corporal punishment, delinquency, spousal abuse, and adult crime.[71] Research conducted in 10 European countries shows that the degree to which parents and teachers approve of corporal punishment is related to the homicide rate.[72]

Inconsistent Supervision   Evidence also exists that inconsistent supervision can promote delinquency. Early research by F. Ivan Nye found that mothers who threatened discipline but failed to carry it out were more likely to have delinquent children than those who were consistent in their discipline.[73]

Nye's early efforts have been supported by research showing a strong association between ineffective or negligent supervision and a child's involvement in delinquency.[74] The data show that youths who believe their parents care little about their activities are more likely to engage in criminal acts than those who believe their actions will be closely monitored.[75] Kids who are not closely supervised

parental efficacy
Families in which parents integrate their children into the household unit while helping them assert their individuality and regulate their own behavior.

Prepare Tomorrow's Parents
(http://www.preparetomorrowsparents.org/) is dedicated to addressing our nation's crises of child abuse, neglect and abandonment, teen pregnancy, and overall violence by bringing parenting, empathy, and nurturing skills to all school-age children and teens.

spend more time out in the community with their friends and are more likely to get into trouble. Poorly supervised kids may be more prone to acting impulsively and are therefore less able to employ self-control to restrain their activities.[76]

Mothers' Employment   Parents who closely supervise their children and have close ties with them help reduce the likelihood of adolescent delinquent behavior.[77] When life circumstances prevent or interfere with adequate supervision, delinquent opportunities may increase. Some critics have suggested that even in intact homes, a working mother who is unable to adequately supervise her children provides the opportunity for delinquency.

The association between mothers' employment and delinquency may be a function of preexisting conditions: mothers may work because they lack financial resources to be stay-at-home caretakers. Environmental conditions may also play a role. In poor neighborhoods that lack collective efficacy, parents cannot call upon neighborhood resources to take up the burden of controlling children.[78]

Though there is some evidence that the children of working moms are more prone to delinquency, the issue is far from settled.[79] There are also research efforts that have found a mother's employment may have little effect on youthful misbehavior, especially when the children are adequately supervised.[80] Stacy De Coster found that both the children of mothers who are employed and who hold nontraditional values and those whose mothers are homemakers and hold traditional values are less likely than others to be delinquent if the mothers do not exhibit distress and are able to have emotional bonds with their children. Emotional bonds ultimately protect youths from delinquent peer associations regardless of whether they have working or stay-at-home moms.[81]

Resource Dilution   Parents may find it hard to control their children because they have such large families that their resources, such as time, are spread too thin (**resource dilution**). It is also possible that the relationship is indirect, caused by the connection of family size to some external factor; resource dilution has been linked to educational underachievement, long considered a correlate of delinquency.[82] Middle children may suffer because they are most likely to be home when large numbers of siblings are also at home and economic resources are most stretched. Large families are more likely to produce delinquents than small ones, and middle children are more likely to engage in delinquent acts than first- or last-born children.

resource dilution
A condition that occurs when parents have such large families that their resources, such as time and money, are spread too thin, causing lack of familial support and control.

Family Deviance

A number of studies have found that parental deviance has a powerful influence on delinquent behavior.[83] Children who are socialized in homes where parents drink, take drugs, or commit crimes are more likely to engage in those behaviors themselves.[84] Fathers with a long history of criminality have been found to produce sons who are also likely to get arrested for crimes.[85] The effects can be both devastating and long term: the children of deviant parents produce delinquent children themselves.[86] The Cambridge Youth Survey and the Cambridge Study in Delinquent Development (CSDD), a highly respected longitudinal cohort study conducted in England by David Farrington, has found that a significant number of delinquent youths have criminal fathers. About 8 percent of the sons of noncriminal fathers became chronic offenders, compared to 37 percent of youths with criminal fathers.[87] The CSDD also found that school yard bullying may be both inter- and intragenerational. Bullies have children who bully others, and these second-generation bullies grow up to become the fathers of children who are also bullies (see Chapter 10 for more on bullying in the school yard).[88] Thus, one family may have a grandfather, father, and son who are or were school yard bullies.[89]

Parental Involvement in the Justice System   The negative effect of having deviant parents is enhanced if they suffer arrest, conviction, and incarceration.[90] Parental incarceration seems to take the worst toll: children whose parents go to prison are much more likely to be at risk to delinquency and suffer an arrest by age 25 than children of nonincarcerated parents.[91] While it is possible that being separated from parents for any reason is related to delinquency, research shows that children who suffer parental separation due to illness, death, or divorce are less likely to become delinquents than those who are separated due to incarceration. Separation caused by parental imprisonment causes severe and long-term harm.[92]

While having an incarcerated parent may result in less supervision and family cohesion, it may be problems that preceded imprisonment—intrafamily conflict and abuse—that have the greatest influence on a child's subsequent delinquency.[93] When Peggy Giordano studied the lives of kids whose parents were incarcerated, she found that while family problems had preceded the arrest and incarceration, they continued and were exacerbated even after the parent was released. Economically disadvantaged women partnered up with highly antisocial men and were locked into a pattern of continued drug use and antisocial behaviors. They created a family climate of extreme unpredictability and stress for their children; family problems were intergenerational. Over time, many of these kids growing up in dysfunctional families find themselves in trouble with the law and are doomed to produce another generation of children who face the same sort and level of social problems.[94]

Deviant Siblings Some evidence also exists that having deviant siblings may influence behavior; research shows that if one sibling is a delinquent, there is a significant likelihood that his brother or sister will engage in delinquent behaviors.[95] Not surprisingly, siblings who maintain a warm relationship and feel close to one another are also likely to behave in a similar fashion. If one of these siblings takes drugs and engages in delinquent behavior, so too will his brother or sister.[96] A number of interpretations of these data are possible:

- Siblings who live in the same environment are influenced by similar social and economic factors; it is not surprising that their behavior is similar.

- Deviance is genetically determined, and the traits that cause one sibling to engage in delinquency are shared by his or her brother or sister.

- Deviant siblings grow closer because of shared interests. It is possible that the relationship is due to personal interactions: younger siblings imitate older siblings.

- One of the most common forms of child abuse involves siblings. It is possible that deviant siblings have shared experiences with abuse. Research shows that sibling experiences with violence is significantly related to substance use, delinquency, and aggression.[97]

Why Family Deviance Is Intergenerational Although the intergenerational transmission of deviance has been established, the link is still uncertain. A number of factors may play a role:

- *Inheritance/genetic factors.* The link between parental deviance and child misbehavior may be genetic.[98] Parents of delinquent youths have been found to suffer neurological conditions linked to antisocial behaviors, and these conditions may be inherited genetically.[99] It is possible that childhood misbehavior is strongly genetically influenced, with little or no environmental or experiential effect.[100] If children behave like their parents, it's because they share the same genes and not because they have learned to be bad or live in an environment that causes both parental and child misbehaviors.

- *Exposure to violence.* The children of criminal parents are more likely to have experienced more violence and injury than the norm. Exposure to violence has been linked to negative outcomes.[101]

- *Substance abuse.* Children of drug-abusing parents are more likely to get involved in drug abuse and delinquency than the children of nonabusers.[102] One possibility: parental substance abuse can produce children with neurological impairments that are related to delinquency.[103]

Helping deal with issues of teen pregnancy and other family issues, **Planned Parenthood** is the world's largest and oldest voluntary family planning organization. For more information about Planned Parenthood, visit their website: http://www.plannedparenthood.org/.

Delinquent behavior may run in families. Here, Jeremy Jarvis, 13 (left), and his brother Denver Jarvis, 15, appear in juvenile court in Ft. Lauderdale, Florida, at the Broward County Courthouse. The boys were charged with aggravated battery for participating in setting a 15-year-old boy on fire. Jeremy avoided incarceration, but Denver pleaded no contest in February 2012 to second-degree attempted murder and was sentenced to eight years in prison, a year of house arrest, and 21 years of probation. In 2013, his sentence was reduced to 10 years of probation. If deviance does run in families, do you think it's a product of the environment, socialization, or genetics?

■ *Parenting ability.* The link between parental deviance and child delinquency may be shaped by parenting ability. Deviant parents are less likely to have close relationships with their offspring. They are more likely to use overly harsh and inconsistent discipline, a parenting style that has consistently been linked to the onset of delinquent behavior.[104] Parents who themselves have been involved in crime exhibit lower levels of effective parenting and greater association with factors that can impede their parenting abilities (e.g., substance abuse and mental illness). Their children are more likely to have experienced negative effects of ineffective parenting such as abuse and out-of-home placement, factors highly associated with delinquency.[105]

■ *Stigma.* The association between parental deviance and children's delinquency may be related to labeling and stigma. Social control agents may be quick to fix a delinquent label on the children of known law violators, increasing the likelihood that they will pick up an "official" delinquent label.[106] The resulting stigma increases the chances they may fall into a delinquent career.

Child Abuse and Neglect

In one of New York City's most notorious child abuse cases, a 7-year-old Brooklyn girl named Nixmary Brown was horribly tortured and abused before being killed by a severe blow to the head.[107] The suspects in the case: Nixzaliz Santiago, her mother, and Cesar Rodriguez, her stepfather. At the time of her death, Nixmary weighed only 36 pounds and had been tied to a chair and forced to use a litter box for a toilet. According to her mother, Rodriguez, who beat the girl regularly, pushed her head under the bathtub faucet after stripping her naked, beat her, and tied her to a stool. Then he listened to music in another room. Some time later, the mother got up the nerve to go to her daughter and found that the little girl's body was cold. Law enforcement agents said that the abuse the 7-year-old experienced was among the worst they had ever witnessed. Autopsy reports revealed she had cuts and bruises all over her body, two black eyes, and a skull that was hit so hard her brain bled. Both Nixmary's mother and stepfather got long prison sentences for their crimes.

In the aftermath of this terrible crime, New York Mayor Michael Bloomberg told the press, "How can anybody fathom what these parents did to this young, 7-year-old girl? It sort of defies description." Tragically, Nixmary's situation was known to authorities for some time before her death. The city's Administration

Some famous celebrities have been associated with child abuse and neglect. Here, NFL player Adrian Peterson of the Minnesota Vikings chats with his attorney, Rusty Hardin, during a court appearance in Conroe, Texas. Peterson pleaded no contest to the misdemeanor charge of recklessly assaulting his 4-year-old son. He avoided a jail sentence and was put on probation and fined $4,000. He was also ordered to perform 80 hours of community service.

for Children's Services had received two complaints about the family. The first, in 2004, was found to be unsubstantiated, and the second occurred on December 1, 2005, when the young girl showed up at school with a black eye. Yet little was done to help her or remove her from her brutal home. When asked why they did not get a court order, child welfare authorities blamed the parents for being uncooperative, ignoring repeated phone calls from caseworkers and turning them away at the door. Still, the head of New York's welfare system couldn't explain why caseworkers didn't get a warrant to enter the house, nor did they attempt to take Nixzmary from home and place her in foster care. After her death, New York passed Nixzmary's Law, which increased the sentence for an adult convicted of torturing a child, changing the maximum sentence to life in prison.[108]

Nixzmary's horrible death is tragically not unique. Thousands of children are physically abused or neglected by their parents or other adults each year and this treatment has serious consequences for their behavior over the life course. Because of this topic's importance, the remainder of this chapter is devoted to the issues of child abuse and neglect and their relationship with delinquent behavior.

Historical Foundation

Parental abuse and neglect are not modern phenomena. Maltreatment of children has occurred throughout history. Some concern for the negative effects of such maltreatment was voiced in the eighteenth century in the United States, but concerted efforts to deal with the problem did not begin until 1874.

In that year, residents of a New York City apartment building reported to public health nurse Etta Wheeler that a child in one of the apartments was being abused by her stepmother. The nurse found a young child named Mary Ellen Wilson who had been repeatedly beaten and was malnourished from a diet of bread and water. Even though the child was seriously ill, the police agreed that the law entitled the parents to raise Mary Ellen as they saw fit. The New York City Department of Charities claimed it had no custody rights over Mary Ellen.

According to legend, Mary Ellen's removal from her parents had to be arranged through the Society for the Prevention of Cruelty to Animals (SPCA) on the grounds that she was a member of the animal kingdom. The truth, however, is less sensational: Mary Ellen's case was heard by a judge. Because the child needed protection, she was placed in an orphanage.[109] The SPCA was actually founded the following year.[110]

Little research into the problems of maltreated children occurred before that of C. Henry Kempe, of the University of Colorado. In 1962, Kempe reported the results of a survey of medical and law-enforcement agencies that indicated the child abuse rate was much higher than had been thought. He coined a term, **battered child syndrome**, which he applied to cases of nonaccidental injury of children by their parents or guardians.[111]

battered child syndrome
Nonaccidental physical injury of children by their parents or guardians.

Defining Abuse and Neglect

Kempe's pioneering work has been expanded in a more generic expression of **child abuse** that includes neglect as well as physical abuse. Specifically, it describes any physical or emotional trauma to a child for which no reasonable explanation, such as an accident, can be found. Child abuse is generally seen as a pattern of behavior rather than a single act. The effects of a pattern of behavior are cumulative. That is, the longer the abuse continues, the more severe the effect will be.[112]

child abuse
Any physical, emotional, or sexual trauma to a child, including neglecting to give proper care and attention, for which no reasonable explanation can be found.

Although the terms *child abuse* and *neglect* are sometimes used interchangeably, they represent different forms of maltreatment. **Neglect** refers to deprivations children suffer at the hands of their parents (lack of food, shelter, health care, love). Abuse is a more overt form of aggression against the child, one that often requires medical attention. The distinction between the terms is often unclear because, in many cases, both abuse and neglect occur simultaneously. What are the forms that abuse and neglect may take?

neglect
Passive neglect by a parent or guardian, depriving children of food, shelter, health care, and love.

- *Physical abuse* includes throwing, shooting, stabbing, burning, drowning, suffocating, biting, or deliberately disfiguring a child. Included within this category is shaken baby syndrome (SBS), a form of child abuse affecting between 1,200 and 1,600 children every year. SBS is a collection of signs and symptoms resulting from violently shaking an infant or child.[113]

- *Physical neglect* results from parents' failure to provide adequate food, shelter, or medical care for their children, as well as failure to protect them from physical danger.

- *Emotional abuse* or neglect is manifested by constant criticism and rejection of the child.[114] Those who suffer emotional abuse have significantly lower self-esteem as adults.[115]

- *Emotional neglect* includes inadequate nurturing, inattention to a child's emotional development, and lack of concern about maladaptive behavior.

- *Abandonment* refers to the situation in which parents leave their children with the intention of severing the parent–child relationship.[116]

abandonment
Parents physically leave their children with the intention of completely severing the parent–child relationship.

- *Sexual abuse* refers to the exploitation of children through rape, incest, and molestation by parents, family members, friends, or legal guardians. Sexual abuse can vary from rewarding children for sexual behavior that is inappropriate for their level of development to using force or the threat of force for the purposes of sex. It can involve children who are aware of the sexual content of their actions and others too young to have any idea what their actions mean.

The Effects of Abuse

Regardless of how abuse is defined, the effects can be devastating. Mental health and delinquency experts have found that abused kids experience mental and social problems across their life span, ranging from substance abuse to possession of a damaged personality.[117] Children who have experienced some form of maltreatment suffer devalued sense of self, mistrust of others, a tendency to perceive hostility in others in situations where the intentions of others are ambiguous, and a tendency to generate antagonistic solutions to social conflicts. Victims of abuse are prone to suffer mental illness, such as dissociative identity disorder (DID) (sometimes known as multiple personality disorder [MPD]); research shows that child abuse is present in the histories of the vast majority of DID subjects.[118] Children who experience maltreatment are at increased risk for adverse health effects and

Trauma and Its Effects

According to the Substance Abuse and Mental Health Services Administration (SAMHSA), "Individual trauma results from an event, series of events, or set of circumstances that is experienced by an individual as physically or emotionally harmful or life threatening and that has lasting adverse effects on the individual's functioning and mental, physical, social, emotional, or spiritual well-being." If trauma follows a single event that is limited in time (such as a car accident, shooting, or earthquake), it is called *acute trauma*.

When children are exposed to multiple traumatic events over time that are severe, pervasive, and interpersonal in nature (such as repeated abuse and neglect), and they experience long-term consequences from these experiences, this is called *complex trauma*. Complex trauma may interfere with a child's ability to form secure attachments to caregivers and many other aspects of healthy physical and mental development.

Historical trauma affects populations that have experienced cumulative and collective trauma over multiple generations. Affected groups in the United States include Native Americans, African Americans, immigrant groups, and families experiencing intergenerational poverty. Children in these families may exhibit signs and symptoms of trauma—such as depression, grief, guilt, and anxiety—even if they have not personally experienced traumatic events.

Traumatic experiences overwhelm children's natural ability to cope. They cause a "fight, flight, or freeze" response that affects children's bodies and brains. Chronic or repeated trauma may result in toxic stress that interferes with normal child development and causes long-term harm to children's physical, social, emotional, or spiritual well-being. These adverse effects can include changes in a child's emotional responses, impulse control, self-image, attachments to caregivers, relationships with others, and ability to think, learn, and concentrate.

Across the life span, traumatic experiences have been linked to a wide range of problems, including addiction, depression, anxiety, and risk-taking behavior. These in turn can lead to a greater likelihood of chronic ill health: obesity, diabetes, heart disease, cancer, and even early death.

Not all children will experience all of these effects. Children's responses to traumatic events are unique and affected by many factors, including their age at the time of the event, the frequency and perceived severity of trauma, and the child's innate sensitivity, as well as protective factors such as the presence of positive relationships with healthy caregivers, physical health, and natural coping skills. Trauma of all kinds is extremely common among children involved with child welfare. Studies show that as many as 9 out of 10 children in foster care have been exposed to some form of violence. Entry into the child welfare system causes additional trauma due to separation from family, school, neighborhood, and community, as well as fear and uncertainty about the future. In addition, children who enter the child welfare system are more likely than others to have experienced multiple traumatic events and to exhibit more complex symptoms. For example, one study showed that nearly half of youth who were subjects of maltreatment reports had emotional or behavioral problems that were clinically significant. Professionals who work within child-serving systems must be aware of a child's trauma history and its effects, or their actions and responses to the child may inadvertently trigger trauma memories, worsen symptoms, or further traumatize the child. When child welfare professionals are mindful of a child's history of trauma, they are better positioned to connect that child to appropriate, trauma-informed, evidence-based services for support. With awareness and knowledge of how to address and treat children's trauma histories, the child welfare system can become a place of healing.

CRITICAL THINKING

Studies consistently show that children involved with child welfare are prescribed psychotropic medications at higher rates than the general population. Should such medications be routinely used to control the affects of trauma?

SOURCE: Children's Bureau, "Developing a Trauma-Informed Child Welfare System," May 2015, https://www.childwelfare.gov/pubPDFs/trauma_informed.pdf (accessed October 2016).

---

behaviors across the life course, including smoking, alcoholism, drug abuse, eating disorders, severe obesity, depression, suicide, sexual promiscuity, and certain chronic diseases.[119] Maltreatment during infancy or early childhood can cause brain impairment, leading to physical, mental, and emotional problems such as sleep disturbances, panic disorder, and attention deficit hyperactivity disorder. Brain dysfunction is particularly common among victims of shaken baby syndrome. About 25 to 30 percent of infant victims with SBS die from their injuries; nonfatal consequences of SBS include varying degrees of visual impairment (e.g., blindness), motor impairment (e.g., cerebral palsy), and cognitive impairments.[120]

Psychologists suggest that maltreatment encourages children to use aggression as a means of solving problems and prevents them from feeling empathy for others. It diminishes their ability to cope with stress and makes them vulnerable to the violence in the culture. Abused children have fewer positive interactions with peers, are less well liked, and are more likely to have disturbed social interactions.[121] Not surprisingly, recent research has found that juvenile female prostitutes more often than not came from homes in which abuse, both physical and substance, was present.[122] The Focus on Delinquency feature reviews the effect of childhood trauma on behavior.

The Extent of Child Abuse

Estimating the extent of child abuse is almost impossible. Many victims are so young that they have not learned to communicate. Some are too embarrassed or afraid to do so. Many incidents occur behind closed doors, and even when another adult witnesses inappropriate or criminal behavior, the adult may not want to get involved in a "family matter." Indications of the severity of the problem came from a groundbreaking 1980 survey conducted by sociologists Richard Gelles and Murray Straus.[123] Gelles and Straus estimated that between 1.4 and 1.9 million children in the United States were subject to physical abuse from their parents. This abuse was rarely a one-time act: the average number of assaults per year was 10.5, and the median was 4.5. Gelles and Straus also found that 16 percent of the couples in their sample reported spousal abuse; 50 percent of the multichild families reported attacks between siblings; 20 percent of the families reported incidents in which children attacked parents.[124]

The Gelles and Straus survey was a milestone in identifying child abuse as a national phenomenon. Subsequent surveys conducted in 1985 and 1992 indicated that the incidence of severe violence toward children had declined.[125] One reason was that parental approval of corporal punishment, which stood at 94 percent in 1968, decreased to 68 percent by 1994.[126] Recognition of the problem may have helped moderate cultural values and awakened parents to the dangers of physically disciplining children. Nonetheless, more than 1 million children were still being subjected to severe violence annually. If the definition of "severe abuse" used in the survey had included hitting with objects such as a stick or a belt, the number of child victims would have been closer to 7 million per year.

Monitoring Abuse   Since the pioneering efforts by Gelles and Straus, the Department of Health and Human Services has been monitoring the extent of child maltreatment through its annual survey of child protective services (CPS).[127] The DHHS survey counts victims in two ways:

- The duplicate count of child victims counts a child each time he or she was found to be a victim.

- The unique count of child victims counts a child only once regardless of the number of times he or she was found to be a victim during the reporting year.

The last data available (2014) indicate that approximately 3.2 million children were the subjects of at least one report. Of these, approximately one-fifth of the children were found to be victims with dispositions of substantiated abuse, while the remaining four-fifths of the children were determined not to be victims of maltreatment. Victim demographics include:

- Victims in their first year of life had the highest rate of victimization, at 24 per 1,000 children.

- More than 90 percent of victims were found to be victims in a single report, and less than 7 percent of victims were found to be victims in more than one report. The latest data on child abuse and neglect are summarized in Figure 8.4.

Though these figures seem staggering, the number and rate of abuse has actually been in decline. Fifteen years ago, more than 1 million children were identified as victims of abuse or neglect nationwide, and the rate of victimization of children was approximately 15 per 1,000 children; today the 700,000 substantiated cases of child neglect/abuse amount to a rate of about 9 per 1,000 children under 18. While these results are encouraging, trends in reported child maltreatment may be more reflective of the effect budgetary cutbacks have on CPS's ability to monitor, record, and investigate reports of abuse than an actual decline in child abuse rates.

The Nature of Abuse

What do the data tell us about the nature of abuse? There is a direct association between age and abuse: victimization rates are higher for younger children than

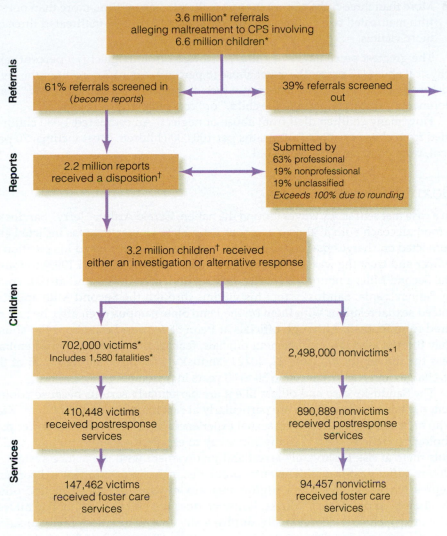

Referrals

3.6 million* referrals alleging maltreatment to CPS involving 6.6 million children*

61% referrals screened in (*become reports*)

39% referrals screened out

Reports

2.2 million reports received a disposition†

Submitted by
63% professional
19% nonprofessional
19% unclassified
Exceeds 100% due to rounding

Children

3.2 million children† received either an investigation or alternative response

702,000 victims*
Includes 1,580 fatalities*

2,498,000 nonvictims*[1]

Services

410,448 victims received postresponse services

890,889 nonvictims received postresponse services

147,462 victims received foster care services

94,457 nonvictims received foster care services

*Indicates a nationally estimated number.

†*Please refer to the report* Child Maltreatment 2014 *http://www.acf.hhs.gov/programs/cb/research-data-technology /statistics-research/child-maltreatment for information regarding how the estimates were calculated.*

Average 1.83 children per referral.

[1]*The estimated number of unique nonvictims was calculated by subtracting the unique count of estimated victims from the unique count of estimated children.*

figure 8.4

Child Abuse and Neglect Data

US Department of Health and Human Services, *Child Maltreatment, 2014*, http://www.acf.hhs.gov/sites/default /files/cb/cm2014.pdf.

for their older brothers and sisters. The youngest children are the most vulnerable to maltreatment. About half of all victims are 5 and under; about two-thirds of all abuse victims are under 7 years old. In general, the rate and percentage of victimization decrease with age.

While boys and girls have an almost equal chance of being victimized, there are racial differences in the abuse rate. African American children, Pacific Islander children, and American Indian or Alaska Native children suffer child abuse rates (per 1,000 children) far higher than European American children, Hispanic children, and Asian American children.

Who abused these children?

■ Four-fifths of perpetrators were between the ages of 18 and 44 years.

■ More than one-half of perpetrators were women.

■ The three largest percentages of perpetrators were white (49 percent), African American (20 percent), and Hispanic (20 percent).

■ Fewer than 8 percent of perpetrators were involved in more than one report.

■ More than three-fifths of perpetrators maltreated one victim, more than one-fifth maltreated two victims, and the remaining 16 percent maltreated three or more victims.

The greatest percentages of children suffered from neglect (75 percent) and physical abuse (17 percent), sexual abuse (8 percent). About 7 percent of the child victims fall into the "other" category, which consists of such conditions as "abandonment," "threats of harm to the child," or "congenital drug addiction."

How many children died from abuse or neglect? An estimated 1,580 children died from abuse or about 2.13 deaths per 100,000 children. Most victims, 70 percent, were younger than 3 years old.

Sexual Abuse

In a case that sent shock waves around the nation, Gerald Arthur "Jerry" Sandusky, a football coach with a 30-year career at Penn State University, was indicted and convicted on charges that he was a serial molester. Sandusky used his position of power and trust (he was Assistant Coach of the Year in 1986 and 1999) to found the Second Mile, a nonprofit charity serving underprivileged and at-risk youth in Pennsylvania. Sandusky met his victims through the Second Mile and had forced sexual relations with them on the Penn State campus even after he had retired from football. Although officials at Penn State found out about the abuse, they did not alert law enforcement officials, fearing the publicity would embarrass the university. On June 22, 2012, Sandusky was found guilty on 45 of the 48 charges and was sentenced to 30 to 60 years in prison.[128]

The Sandusky case and others like it are particularly serious because adolescent victims of sexual abuse are particularly at risk for stress and anxiety.[129] Kids who have undergone traumatic sexual experiences have been found to suffer psychological deficits later.[130] Many run away to escape their environment, which puts them at risk for juvenile arrest and involvement with the justice system.[131] Others suffer post-traumatic mental problems, including acute stress disorders, depression, eating disorders, nightmares, anxiety, suicidal ideation, and other psychological problems.[132] Stress, however, does not end in childhood. Children who are psychologically, sexually, or physically abused are more likely to suffer low self-esteem and be more suicidal as adults.[133] They are also placed at greater risk to be reabused as adults than those who escaped childhood victimization.[134]

Child abuse has been linked to violence and delinquency. There have been a number of tragic cases of abuse, none more notorious than the one involving former Penn State University assistant football coach Jerry Sandusky, shown here being taken from the Centre County Courthouse in Bellefonte, Pennsylvania. Sandusky was sentenced to at least 30 years in prison for molesting scores of young boys in the child sexual abuse scandal that brought shame to Penn State and led to coach Joe Paterno's downfall.

AP Images/Matt Rourke

The reabused carry higher risks for psychological and physical problems, ranging from sexual promiscuity to increased HIV infection rates.[135] Abuse as a child may lead to despair, depression, and even homelessness as adults. One study of homeless women found that they were much more likely than other women to report childhood physical abuse, childhood sexual abuse, adult physical assault, previous sexual assault in adulthood, and a history of mental health problems.[136]

Extent of Sexual Abuse   Attempts to determine the extent of sexual abuse indicate that perhaps one in four girls and one in six boys will be sexually abused before they turn 18 years old.[137] More than 58,000 children are sexually abused each year; 8.3 percent of reported child abuse cases are sexual abuse, the majority by family members.

Although sexual abuse is still quite prevalent, the number of reported cases has been in significant decline since 2001, when an estimated 325,000 incidents of sexual abuse occurred in the United States.[138] These data may either mean that the actual number of cases is truly in decline or that social service professionals are failing to recognize abuse cases because of overwork and understaffing.

Causes of Child Abuse and Neglect

Why do people abuse and hurt children? Maltreatment of children is a complex problem with neither a single cause nor a single solution. It cuts across racial, ethnic, religious, and socioeconomic lines. Abusive parents cannot be categorized by sex, age, or educational level.

Of all factors associated with child abuse, three are discussed most often: (1) parents who themselves suffered abuse tend to abuse their own children; (2) the presence of an unrelated adult increases the risk of abuse; and (3) isolated and alienated families tend to become abusive. A cyclical pattern of violence seems to be perpetuated from one generation to another. Evidence indicates that a large number of abused and neglected children grow into adulthood with a tendency to engage in violent behavior. The behavior of abusive parents can often be traced to negative experiences in their own childhood—physical abuse, emotional neglect, and incest. These parents become unable to separate their own childhood traumas from their relationships with their children. Abusive parents often have unrealistic perceptions of normal development. When their children are unable to act appropriately—when they cry or strike their parents—the parents may react in an abusive manner.[139]

Parents may also become abusive if they are isolated from friends, neighbors, or relatives. Many abusive parents describe themselves as alienated from their extended families, and they lack close relationships with persons who could provide help in stressful situations.[140] The relationship between alienation and abuse may be particularly acute in homes where there has been divorce or separation, or in which parents have never actually married; abusive punishment in single-parent homes has been found to be twice that of two-parent families.[141] Parents who are unable to cope with stressful events—divorce, financial stress, recurring mental illness, drug addiction—are most at risk.[142]

Substance Abuse and Child Abuse   Abusive families suffer from severe stress, and it is therefore not surprising that they frequently harbor members who turn to drugs and alcohol.[143] Among confirmed cases of child maltreatment, 40 percent involve the use of alcohol or other drugs. Alcohol and other substances may act as disinhibitors, lessening impulse control and allowing parents to behave abusively. Children in this environment often demonstrate behavioral problems and are diagnosed as having conduct disorders. This may result in provocative behavior. Increased stress resulting from a parent's preoccupation with drugs combined with behavioral problems exhibited by the child increases the likelihood of maltreatment. Frequently, these parents suffer from depression, anxiety, and low self-esteem. They live in an atmosphere of stress and family conflict. Children raised in such households are themselves more likely to have problems with alcohol and other drugs.[144]

Stepparents and Abuse   Research indicates that stepchildren share a greater risk for abuse than do biological offspring.[145] Stepparents may have less emotional attachment to the children of another. Often the biological parent has to choose between the new mate and the child, sometimes even becoming an accomplice in the abuse.[146]

Stepchildren are overrepresented in cases of **familicide**, mass murders in which a spouse and one or more children are slain. It is also more common for fathers who kill their biological children to commit suicide than those who kill stepchildren, an indication that the latter act is motivated by hostility and not despair.[147]

Social Class and Abuse   Surveys indicate a high rate of reported abuse and neglect among people in lower economic classes. Children from families with a household income of less than $15,000 per year experience more abuse than children living in more affluent homes. Child care workers indicate that most of their clients either live in poverty or face increased financial stress because of unemployment and economic recession. These findings suggest that parental maltreatment of children is predominantly a lower-class problem. Is this conclusion valid?

One view is that low-income families, especially those headed by a single parent, are often subject to greater environmental stress and have fewer resources to deal with such stress than families with higher incomes.[148] A relationship seems to exist between the burdens of raising a child without adequate resources and the use of excessive force. Self-report surveys do show that indigent parents are more likely than affluent parents to hold attitudes that condone physical chastisement of children.[149]

Higher rates of maltreatment in low-income families reflect the stress caused by the limited resources that lower-class parents have to help them raise their children; in contrast, middle-class parents devote a smaller percentage of their total resources to raising a family.[150] This burden becomes especially onerous in families with emotionally and physically handicapped children. Stressed-out parents may consider special-needs children a drain on finances with little potential for future success; research finds that children with disabilities are maltreated at a rate almost double that of other children.[151]

The Child Protection System: Philosophy and Practice

For most of our nation's history, courts have assumed that parents have the right to bring up their children as they see fit. In the 2000 case *Troxel v. Granville*, the Supreme Court ruled that the due process clause of the Constitution protects against government interference with certain fundamental rights and liberty interests, including parents' fundamental right to make decisions concerning the care, custody, and control of their children.[152] If the care a child receives falls below reasonable standards, the state may take action to remove a child from the home and place her or him in a less threatening environment. In these extreme circumstances, the rights of both parents and children are constitutionally protected. In the cases of *Lassiter v. Department of Social Services* and *Santosky v. Kramer*, the Supreme Court recognized the child's right to be free from parental abuse and set down guidelines for a termination-of-custody hearing, including the right to legal representation.[153] States provide a guardian *ad litem* (a lawyer appointed by the court to look after the interests of those who do not have the capacity to assert their own rights). States also ensure confidentiality of reporting.[154]

Although child protection agencies have been dealing with abuse and neglect since the late nineteenth century, recent awareness of the problem has prompted judicial authorities to take increasingly bold steps to ensure the safety of children.[155] The assumption that the parent–child relationship is inviolate has been challenged. In 1974, Congress passed the Child Abuse Prevention and Treatment Act (CAPTA), which provides funds to states to bolster their services for maltreated children and their parents.[156] The act provides federal funding to states

familicide
Mass murders in which a spouse and one or more children are slain.

Troxel v. Granville
The Supreme Court ruled that the due process clause of the Constitution protects against government interference with certain fundamental rights and liberty interests, including parents' fundamental right to make decisions concerning the care, custody, and control of their children.

Santosky v. Kramer
The US Supreme Court recognized the child's right to be free from parental abuse and set down guidelines for a termination-of-custody hearing, including the right to legal representation.

in support of prevention, investigation, and treatment. It also provides grants to public agencies and nonprofit organizations for demonstration programs.

The Child Abuse Prevention and Treatment Act has been the impetus for the states to improve the legal frameworks of their child protection systems. Abusive parents are subject to prosecution under statutes against assault, battery, and homicide.

Investigating and Reporting Abuse

Maltreatment of children can easily be hidden from public view because the victims may be too young for school or because their parents do not take them to a doctor or a hospital. Parents abuse their children in private and, even when confronted, often accuse their children of lying or blame the children's medical problems on accidents.

To help protect children, every state has some form of law requiring citizens to report suspected cases of abuse. New Jersey and Wyoming are the only two states that do not require specific professional groups to report abuse but instead require all persons to report abuse. In another 16 states and Puerto Rico, any person who suspects child abuse or neglect is required to report; these states also specify certain professionals who must report.[157] Individuals designated as mandatory reporters typically have frequent contact with children. They include:

- Social workers
- Teachers, principals, and other school personnel
- Physicians, nurses, and other health care workers
- Counselors, therapists, and other mental health professionals
- Child care providers
- Medical examiners or coroners
- Law enforcement officers

Once reported to a child protection agency, the case is screened by an intake worker and then turned over to an investigative caseworker. In some jurisdictions, if CPS substantiates a report, the case will likely be referred to a law enforcement agency that will be responsible for investigating the case, collecting evidence that can later be used in court proceedings. If the caseworker determines that the child is in imminent danger of severe harm, the caseworker may immediately remove the child from the home. A court hearing must be held shortly after to approve custody. Stories abound of children erroneously taken from their homes, but it is much more likely that these "gatekeepers" will consider cases unfounded and take no action. Among the most common reasons for screening out cases is that the reporting party is involved in a child custody case, despite the research showing that the risk of abuse increases significantly in the aftermath of divorce.[158] One of the success stories is discussed in the Case Profile "Patrick's Story."

Even when there is compelling evidence of abuse, most social service agencies will try to involve the family in voluntary treatment. Postinvestigation services are offered on a voluntary basis by child welfare agencies to ensure the safety of children. These services address the safety of the child and are usually based on an assessment of the family's strengths, weaknesses, and needs. Examples of postinvestigation services include individual counseling, case management, family-based services (services provided to the entire family, such as counseling or family support), in-home services, foster care services, and court services. Each year more than 60 percent of victims receive postinvestigation services.

Case managers do periodic follow-ups to determine if treatment plans are being followed. If parents are uncooperative, or if the danger to the child is so great that he or she must be removed from the home, a complaint will be filed in the criminal, family, or juvenile court system. To protect the child, the court could then issue temporary orders for placing the child in shelter care during investigation, providing services, or prohibiting suspected abusers from having contact with the child.

The oldest federal agency for children, the **Children's Bureau** is part of the Administration on Children, Youth and Families, a section of the Administration for Children and Families, under the Department of Health and Human Services. It is responsible for assisting states in the delivery of child welfare services, services designed to protect children and strengthen families. For more information about these subjects, visit their website at http://www.acf.hhs.gov/cb.

case profile

Patrick's Story

PATRICK is a 15-year-old male referred to the county juvenile justice system for disorderly conduct in the family home and possession of marijuana. Patrick and his family had been evicted from their apartment after the last of many police calls, and the family was staying at a local homeless shelter. There was a history of domestic violence in the home as well as other contacts with law enforcement, generally related to family discord.

Patrick's father and mother both had histories of significant alcohol abuse, and Patrick had spent part of his childhood in and out of foster homes due to chronic neglect issues. The local child protection agency had assessed the home on a number of occasions, and records indicated that the living conditions in the home were often found to be deplorable. Patrick and his siblings would be removed from the home while it was being cleaned up—but would then return home again. Patrick's school records indicated that teachers had been concerned about his hygiene as well as a lack of regular attendance. His grades were poor overall and he appeared unmotivated academically. His teachers reported that he was pleasant in the classroom and did not demonstrate any behavioral concerns at school.

Patrick's parents reported to the juvenile justice social worker that Patrick was defiant and belligerent toward them. They described him as "angry all the time" and "unwilling to follow any rules." Although the family was staying at the local homeless shelter, the parents reported that Patrick's whereabouts were unknown to them. They suspected that he was staying with friends but were not really sure. They stated that Patrick was "almost an adult" and "at this point he can do what he wants." They both denied their long-term issue was alcohol and appeared to have very little insight regarding the family system and issues.

Patrick was indeed staying with friends as well as continuing to attend school. The social worker made contact with Patrick at school and began to help him open up about his personal and family situation. Upon further discussion with Patrick, he disclosed a history of physical abuse by both his parents as well as the neglect. Patrick acknowledged his frustration toward his parents and indicated willingness for treatment related to his anger management and drug use concerns. Due to the new child maltreatment reports as well as the delinquency petition, Patrick was placed in a treatment foster home where he received a number of needed services and interventions. The treatment foster parents who were chosen for Patrick had successfully worked with many young men with similar backgrounds and delinquent behavior. The foster parents and Patrick also received additional weekly support in the home, which included addressing behavioral issues, school concerns, family relationships, substance abuse, and anger management.

Within six months of placement, Patrick's grades were improving and he was doing well in his outpatient treatment programs for anger management and substance use. He reported feeling more stable and less focused on his parent's chronic alcohol issues. He also reported feeling relieved that he lived in a home with significantly less chaos. To date, Patrick has not had any further referrals for delinquent behavior. Patrick's parents were repeatedly offered a number of services but to date have refused to engage with Patrick's treatment or participate in their own.

CRITICAL THINKING

After reading Patrick's story, what changes would you advocate for the foster care system to improve outcomes?

The Process of State Intervention

Although procedures vary from state to state, most follow a similar legal process once a social service agency files a court petition alleging abuse or neglect.[159] Figure 8.5 diagrams this process.

If the allegation of abuse is confirmed, the child may be placed in protective custody. Most state statutes require that the court be notified "promptly" or "immediately" if the child is removed; some states, including Arkansas, North Carolina, and Pennsylvania, have gone as far as requiring that no more than 12 hours elapse before official action is taken. If the child has not been removed from the home, state authorities are given more time to notify the court of suspected abuse. Some states set a limit of 30 days to take action, whereas others mandate that state action take no more than 20 days once the case has been investigated.

When an abuse or neglect petition is prosecuted, an **advisement hearing** (also called a preliminary protective hearing or emergency custody hearing) is held.

advisement hearing
A preliminary protective or temporary custody hearing in which the court will review the facts, determine whether removal of the child is justified, and notify parents of the charges against them.

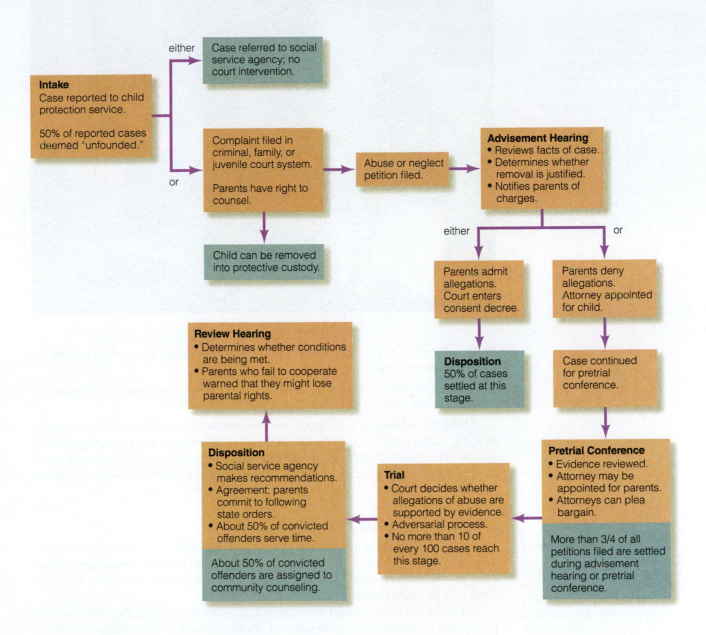

The court will review the facts of the case, determine whether permanent removal of the child is justified, and notify the parents of existing charges. Parents have the right to counsel in all the cases of abuse and neglect, and many states require the court to appoint an attorney for the child as well. If the parents admit the allegations, the court enters a consent decree, and the case is continued for disposition. Approximately half of all cases are settled by admission at the advisement hearing. If the parents deny the petition, an attorney is appointed for the child and the case is continued for a **pretrial conference**.

At the pretrial conference, the attorney for the social service agency presents an overview of the case and the evidence. Such matters as admissibility of photos and written reports are settled. At this point the attorneys can negotiate a settlement of the case, in which the parents accept a treatment plan detailing:

■ The types of services that the child and the child's family will receive, such as parenting classes, mental health or substance abuse treatment, and family counseling

figure 8.5

The Process of State Intervention in Cases of Abuse and Neglect

© Cengage Learning

pretrial conference
The attorney for the social services agency presents an overview of the case, and a plea bargain or negotiated settlement can be agreed to in a consent decree.

Even when the state intervenes, neglected and abused children can face a long road. Mackenzie Teo was just 5 months old the first time she and her siblings were taken from a mother struggling with addiction and placed in the care of the state. At times, she was separated from her brothers and sisters. She received neither the glasses she needed nor the orthopedic shoes, leaving her with a limp. Before being legally adopted, she had lived in 20 foster care homes, changing schools each time.

Nick Cote/The New York Times/Redux

- Reunification goals, including visitation schedules and a target date for the child's return home
- Concurrent plans for alternative permanent placement options should reunification goals not be met

About 85 out of every 100 petitions filed are settled at either the advisement hearing or the pretrial conference. Of the 15 remaining cases, five are generally settled before trial. Usually no more than 10 cases out of every 100 actually reach the trial stage of the process. This trial is an adversarial hearing designed to prove the state's allegations.

Disposition and Review

The most crucial part of an abuse or neglect proceeding is the **disposition hearing**. The social service agency presents its case plan, which includes recommendations such as conditions for returning the child to the parents or a visitation plan if the child is to be taken permanently from the parents.

If a child has been abused or neglected, the course of action depends on state policy, the severity of the maltreatment, an assessment of the child's immediate safety, the risk of continued or future maltreatment, the services available to address the family's needs, and whether the child was removed from the home and a court action to protect the child was initiated. The following options are available:

- *No or low risk.* The family's case may be closed with no services if the maltreatment was a one-time incident, the child is considered to be safe, there is no or low risk of future incidents, and any services the family needs will not be provided through the child welfare agency but through other community-based resources and service systems.
- *Low to moderate risk.* Referrals may be made to community-based or voluntary in-home child welfare services if the CPS worker believes the family would benefit from these services and the child's present and future safety would be enhanced. This may happen even when no abuse or neglect is found if the family needs and is willing to participate in services.
- *Moderate to high risk.* The family is offered voluntary in-home services to address safety concerns and help reduce the risks. If these are refused, the agency may seek intervention by the juvenile dependency court. Once there is

a judicial determination that abuse or neglect occurred, juvenile dependency court may require the family to cooperate with in-home services if it is believed that the child can remain safely at home while the family addresses the issues contributing to the risk of future maltreatment. If the child has been seriously harmed, is considered to be at high risk of serious harm, or the child's safety is threatened, the court may order the child's removal from the home or affirm the agency's prior removal of the child. The child may be placed with a relative or in foster care.

In making their decisions, courts are guided by three interests: the role of the parents, protection for the child, and the responsibility of the state. Frequently, these interests conflict. In fact, at times even the interests of the two parents are not in harmony. The state attempts to balance the parents' natural right to control their child's upbringing with the child's right to grow into adulthood free from harm. This is referred to as the **balancing-of-the-interests approach**.

Periodically, **review hearings** are held to determine if the conditions of the case plan are being met. Parents who fail to cooperate are warned that they may lose their parental rights. Most abuse and neglect cases are concluded within a year. Either the parents lose their rights and the child is given a permanent foster care or other type of placement, or the child is returned to the parents and the court's jurisdiction ends.

Criminal Charges

In many states, certain types of abuse, such as sexual abuse and serious physical abuse, are routinely referred to law enforcement authorities with the intent of a criminal complaint being filed in a district or county court. If charges are filed, parents will be tried on charges ranging from child endangerment to felony assault or even to homicide. Typically during trial, the social service agency presents its case plan and recommendations for care of the child and treatment of the parents, including incarceration and counseling or other treatment.

About half of all convicted parents will be required to serve time in incarceration; about half will be assigned to a form of treatment. At that point some children may be placed in temporary care; in other cases, parental rights are terminated and the child is placed in the custody of the child protective service. Legal custody can then be assigned to a relative or some other person.

Even if criminal charges are not filed, the perpetrator's name may be placed on a state child maltreatment registry if abuse or neglect is confirmed. A registry is a central database that collects information about maltreated children and individuals who are found to have abused or neglected those children. These registries are usually confidential and used for internal child protective purposes only. However, they may be used in background checks for certain professions that involve working to protect children from contact with individuals who are abusers.[160]

Foster Care

Every year, hundreds of thousands of children are removed from their homes due to parental absence, deviance, conflict, or incompetence. Federal law requires the court to hold a permanency hearing, which determines the permanent plan for the child, within 12 months after the child enters **foster care** and every 12 months thereafter.

Foster care quality has been a problem. Many of these kids have already experienced multiple threats to their healthy development and safety. And to make matters worse, these vulnerable children then enter a fragmented foster care system that lacks the necessary resources, technical proficiency, and interagency coordination to provide families with needed services and supports. Various aspects of the current foster care population are noteworthy:

■ African American children make up the largest proportion of children in care.

■ Over one-quarter of all children in care are under age 5.

balancing-of-the-interests approach
Efforts of the courts to balance the parents' natural right to raise a child with the child's right to grow into adulthood free from physical abuse or emotional harm.

review hearings
Periodic meetings to determine whether the conditions of the case plan for an abused child are being met by the parents or guardians of the child.

foster care
Placing a child in the temporary care of a family other than its own as a result of state intervention into problems within the birth family; can be used as a temporary shelter while a permanent adoption effort is being completed.

Sometimes foster care can lead to adoption. Here, Judge Daniel Swords of Hampden Juvenile Court in Springfield, Massachusetts, holds Alexandra Rubio after adoption proceedings in his courtroom. The family waited almost two years for the adoption to go through. Angel and Sandra Rubio laugh as Alexandra gives her dad a high-five. "It's great to have a day like this. I wish we had more," says Judge Swords.

- Most children are placed in nonrelative foster homes, but substantial numbers are also placed with relatives or in group homes or institutions.

- Of those children exiting care, most are reunited with their birth parents or primary caretakers, or are adopted.

- A child is more likely to enter care due to neglect than due to physical, sexual, and psychological abuse combined.[161]

Living within the foster care system can be a trying and emotionally traumatic experience for children. It is estimated that somewhere between 30 and 80 percent of children in foster care exhibit emotional and/or behavioral problems. Many are traumatized by their experiences before entering foster care, while others are troubled by the foster care experience itself. Within three months of placement, many children exhibit signs of depression, aggression, or withdrawal. Children in foster care are often forced to change schools, placing them at risk educationally. It comes as no surprise that many youths leaving foster care end up in jail or on public assistance.[162]

Are kids better off being taken from a conflict-ridden or otherwise troubled home care situation and placed in foster care? A recent study using the advanced analytic tools of applied economics shows that children faced with two options—being allowed to stay at home or being placed into foster care—have generally better life outcomes when they remain with their families. Economist Joseph Doyle used a randomized design and found that children on the margin of foster care placement have better employment, delinquency, and teen motherhood outcomes when they remain at home. Among the findings:[163]

- Only 14 percent of young adults were arrested at least once when staying at home, and 44 percent were arrested when going to foster care.

- Only 33 percent became teen mothers when staying at home and 56 percent became mothers when going to foster care.

- At least 33 percent held a job for at least three months when staying at home and only 20 percent held a job for at least three months when going to foster care.

These outcomes are significant considering the number of kids in foster care today. Doyle's research suggests that keeping families intact will produce better results, and therefore a greater portion of the social welfare budget should be spent on family preservation.

Preventing Child Abuse

The child protection system should be a last resort, and the key to solving the abuse problem is through early prevention. There have been a number of successful efforts to prevent child maltreatment.[164] The first step is to identify kids who are at risk for abuse in order to target interventions as early as possible. Researchers have identified five factors that are consistently correlated with maltreatment—child age, race, poverty, parental drug involvement, and single parenting. These factors interact in complex ways, but children who are characterized by all five are at higher risk than children who have only one. Once identified, a number of strategies have been tried:

- *Communitywide interventions.* Some programs focus on communitywide solutions to abuse. For example, the Triple P—Positive Parenting Program has proven quite successful. This program consists of several levels of intervention: a media-based campaign targeting the entire community, intensive treatments for progressively smaller groups of families that are at progressively greater risk for maltreatment, and individual family treatment.

- *Home visiting programs.* In these family-based interventions, trained professionals visit parents in their homes and administer a standard program that can range in intensity from one visit to multiple visits over months or even years. Some home visiting programs have been shown to have positive effects in areas of family life related to child abuse risk.

- *Helping families with drug or alcohol abuse.* Some programs require drug-addicted parents with reports of maltreatment to enroll in drug treatment within a few months and allow them up to 18 months to show progress in all problem areas, including addiction. Only if there is no measurable progress on every front are children removed and placed with relatives or an adoptive home.

- *Sexual abuse education.* Schools, religious groups, and youth organizations are now operating programs that teach children what to do in situations of potential abuse, how to stop potential offenders, and how to find help. Such programs also teach children not to blame themselves if they are victimized, a prevention strategy designed to head off emotional problems often triggered by abuse. There is reason to believe that these programs produce benefits such as increased disclosure and less self-blame following abuse.

The Abused Child in Court

One of the most significant problems associated with abuse cases is the trauma a child must go through in a court hearing. Children get confused and frightened and may change their testimony. Much controversy has arisen over the accuracy of children's reports of physical and sexual abuse, resulting in hung juries. Prosecutors and experts have been accused of misleading children or eliciting incriminating testimony. In what probably is the best-known case, the McMartin Day Care case in California, children told not only of being sexually abused but also of being forced to participate in bizarre satanic rituals during which the McMartins mutilated animals and forced the children to touch corpses in hidden underground passageways. Prosecutors decided not to press forward after two trials ended in deadlock. Some jurors, when interviewed after the verdict, said that although they believed that children had been abused, the interviewing techniques used by prosecutors had been so suggestive that they had not been able to discern what really happened.[165]

State jurisdictions have instituted procedures to minimize the trauma to the child. Most have enacted legislation allowing videotaped statements or interviews with child witnesses taken at a preliminary hearing or at a formal deposition to be admissible in court. Videotaped testimony spares child witnesses the trauma of testifying in open court. States that allow videotaped testimony usually put some restrictions on its use. Some prohibit the government from calling the child to testify at trial if the videotape is used; some states require a finding that the child is "medically unavailable" because of the trauma of the case before videotaping can be used; some require that the defendant be present during the videotaping; a few specify that the child not be able to see or hear the defendant.

Most states now allow a child's testimony to be given on closed-circuit television (CCTV). The child can view the judge and attorneys, and the courtroom participants can observe the child. The standards for CCTV testimony vary widely. Some states, such as New Hampshire, assume that any child witness under age 12 would benefit from not having to appear in court. Others require an independent examination by a mental health professional to determine whether there is a "compelling need" for CCTV testimony.

In addition to innovative methods of testimony, children in sexual abuse cases have been allowed to use anatomically correct dolls to demonstrate happenings that they cannot describe verbally. The Victims of Child Abuse Act of 1990 allows children to use these dolls when testifying in federal courts; 10 states have passed similar legislation.[166] Similarly, states have relaxed their laws of evidence to allow out-of-court statements by the child to a social worker, teacher, or police officer to be used as evidence (such statements would otherwise be considered **hearsay**). Typically, corroboration is required to support these statements if the child does not also testify.

hearsay
Out-of-court statements made by one person and recounted in court by another; such statements are generally not allowed as evidence except in child abuse cases in which a child's statements to social workers, teachers, or police may be admissible.

The prevalence of sexual abuse cases has created new problems for the justice system. Often accusations are made in conjunction with marital disputes. The fear is growing that children may become pawns in custody battles; the mere suggestion of sexual abuse is enough to affect the outcome of a divorce action. The justice system must develop techniques that can get at the truth without creating a lifelong scar on the child's psyche.

Legal Issues   A number of cases have been brought before the Supreme Court testing the right of children to present evidence at trial using nontraditional methods. Two issues stand out. One is the ability of physicians and mental health professionals to testify about statements made to them by children, especially when the children are incapable of testifying. The second concerns the way children testify in court.

White v. Illinois
The Supreme Court ruled that the state's attorney is not required to produce young victims at trial or to demonstrate the reason why they were unavailable to serve as witnesses.

In a 1992 case, *White v. Illinois*, the Supreme Court ruled that the state's attorney is not required to produce young victims at trial or to demonstrate the reason why they were unavailable to serve as witnesses.[167] *White* involved statements given by the child to the child's babysitter and mother, a doctor, a nurse, and a police officer concerning the alleged assailant in a sexual assault case. The prosecutor twice tried to call the child to testify, but both times the 4-year-old experienced emotional difficulty and could not appear in court. The outcome hinged solely on the testimony of the five witnesses.

By allowing others to testify as to what the child said, *White* removed the requirement that prosecutors produce child victims in court. This facilitates the prosecution of child abusers in cases where a court appearance by a victim would prove too disturbing or where the victim is too young to understand the court process.[168] The Court noted that statements made to doctors during medical examinations or those made when a victim is upset carry more weight than ones made after careful reflection. The Court ruled that such statements can be repeated during trial, because the circumstances in which they were made could not be duplicated simply by having the child testify to them in court.

In-Court Statements   Children who are victims of sexual or physical abuse often make poor witnesses. Yet their testimony may be crucial. In a 1988 case, *Coy v. Iowa*, the Supreme Court placed limitations on efforts to protect child witnesses in court. During a sexual assault case, a one-way glass screen was set up so that the child victims would not be able to view the defendant (the defendant, however, could view the witnesses).[169] The Iowa statute that allowed the protective screen assumed that children would be traumatized by their courtroom experience. The Court ruled that unless there is a finding that the child witness needs special protection, the Sixth Amendment of the Constitution grants defendants face-to-face confrontation with their accusers. In her dissenting opinion, Justice Sandra Day O'Connor suggested that if courts found it necessary, it would be appropriate to allow children to testify via CCTV or videotape.

Justice O'Connor's views became law in *Maryland v. Craig*.[170] In this case a daycare operator was convicted of sexually abusing a 6-year-old child; one-way CCTV testimony was used during the trial. The decision was overturned in the Maryland Court of Appeals on the grounds that the procedures used were insufficient to show that the child could only testify in this manner because a trial appearance would be too traumatic. On appeal, the Court ruled that the Maryland statute that allows CCTV testimony is sufficient because it requires a determination that the child will suffer distress if forced to testify. The Court noted that CCTV could serve as the equivalent of in-court testimony and would not interfere with the defendant's right to confront witnesses.

Maryland v. Craig
A state statute that allows closed-circuit television (CCTV) testimony in child abuse cases is legal because it requires a determination that the child will suffer distress if forced to testify in court. CCTV can serve as the equivalent of in-court testimony and does not interfere with the defendant's right to confront witnesses.

Abuse, Neglect, and Delinquency

A significant amount of research suggests that being the target of abuse is associated with subsequent episodes of delinquency and violence (see Exhibit 8.1).[171] The more often a child is physically disciplined and the harsher the discipline, the more likely they will later engage in antisocial behaviors.[172] Kids who were neglected have been shown to be at greater risk to be arrested for later juvenile drug and alcohol offenses than non-neglected children.[173] The effects of abuse appear to be long term: exposure to abuse in early life provides a foundation for violent and antisocial behavior in late adolescence and adulthood.[174] Kids who are abused are likely to grow up to be abusers themselves.[175] They are most likely to become the victim of violent crimes.[176]

Clinical histories of known juvenile offenders support the abuse–delinquency link. These have confirmed that between 70 and 80 percent of juvenile offenders have abusive backgrounds, and many report serious injury, including bruises, lacerations, fractures, and being knocked unconscious by a parent or guardian.[177]

Another approach is to use survey data. When Janet Currie and Erdal Tekin used highly sophisticated statistical tests to evaluate data from a large national survey of youth, they found that maltreatment doubles the probability of engaging in many types of delinquency and crime. There were distinct patterns in the

---

exhibit 8.1

Consequences of Child Abuse and Neglect

- 14 percent of all men in prison in the United States were abused as children.

- 36 percent of all women in prison were abused as children.

- Children who experience child abuse and neglect are 59 percent more likely to be arrested as a juvenile, 28 percent more likely to be arrested as an adult, and 30 percent more likely to commit violent crime.

- As many as two-thirds of the people in treatment for drug abuse reported being abused or neglected as children.

- Abused children are 25 percent more likely to experience teen pregnancy.

- Abused teens are less likely to practice safe sex, putting them at greater risk for STDs.

- About 30 percent of abused and neglected children will later abuse their own children, continuing the horrible cycle of abuse.

- About 80 percent of 21-year-olds who were abused as children met criteria for at least one psychological disorder.

- More than five children die every day as a result of child abuse.

- Approximately 80 percent of children who die from abuse are under the age of 4.

- Children who experience child abuse and neglect are about nine times more likely to become involved in criminal activity.

SOURCE: Reprinted by permission from Childhelp, "Child Abuse Statistics and Facts," https://www.childhelp.org/child-abuse-statistics/ (accessed October 2016).

abuse–crime association. Lower-class children are more likely to be mistreated and suffer more damaging effects from their abuse than those in the upper and middle classes; abused boys are at greater risk to commit crime than are girls; children suffering sexual abuse have a greater chance of getting involved in delinquency and substance abuse than those who are physically abused; the more often and severe the abuse, the more likely a child will later engage in crime.[178] Ironically, cases that come to the attention of child protection agencies are also the ones most likely to violate the law; state intervention seems to do little to reduce the abuse–offending link.

Recently Cathy Widom reviewed results from four research investigations in the Midwest, Rochester (New York), Mecklenburg (North Carolina), and the Northwest and concluded that despite differences in geographic region, time period, youths' ages, definition of child maltreatment, and assessment technique, there is convincing evidence that a link exists between child maltreatment and subsequent crime and delinquency. In addition, the findings indicate that children who experience violence in childhood are at an increased risk to become perpetrators of violence later in life. These children are also at an increased risk for mental health problems, suicide attempts, greater alcohol problems in women, lower rates of employment, and decreased levels of cognitive and intellectual functioning.[179]

Is There an Abuse–Delinquency Link?

While the Widom review is quite convincing, many questions remain to be answered about the abuse–delinquency link. Even though an association has been found, it does not necessarily mean that most abused children become delinquent. Many do not, and many delinquent youths come from what appear to be model homes. And, although many studies have found an abuse–delinquency link, others find the association is either insignificant or inconsistent (e.g., applying to girls and not to boys).[180] Widom herself finds that the majority of both abused and nonabused kids do not engage in antisocial behavior.[181]

Beyond the difficulty of showing a clear-cut link between abuse and delinquency, it is also difficult to assess the temporal order of the linkage: Does early abuse lead to later delinquency? Or conversely, are antisocial kids subject to overly harsh parental discipline and abuse? It is also possible that a third explanation exists: some external factor, such as environmental deprivation, causes both abuse and delinquency. That is, kids in lower-class areas are the ones most likely to be abused and kids living in lower-class areas are also more likely to become delinquent.[182] It is possible that environmental deprivation causes both abuse and delinquency.

Research also shows that the timing and extent of abuse may shape its impact. Kids who are maltreated solely during early childhood may be less likely to engage in chronic delinquency than those whose abuse is lasting and persists into later adolescence.[183] Persistent maltreatment also gives the victims little opportunity to cope or deal with their ongoing victimization.[184] In sum, while the evidence shows a clear link between abuse and subsequent delinquent behavior, the true nature of the association has yet to be determined.

The Family and Delinquency Control Policy

Since the family is believed to play such an important role in the production of youth crime, it follows that improving family functioning can help prevent delinquency. Counselors commonly work with the families of antisocial youths as part of a court-ordered treatment strategy. Family counseling and therapy are almost mandatory when the child's acting-out behavior is suspected to be the result of family-related problems such as child abuse or neglect.[185] Some jurisdictions have integrated family counseling services into the juvenile court.[186]

Homebuilders

Homebuilders is an in-home, intensive family preservation service (IFPS) and reunification program for families with children (newborn to 17 years old) returning from or at risk of placement into foster care, group or residential treatment, psychiatric hospitals, or juvenile justice facilities. The Homebuilders model is designed to improve parental skills, parental capabilities, family interactions, children's behavior, and family safety. The goals are to prevent the unnecessary out-of-home placement of children through an intensive, onsite intervention and to teach families new problem-solving skills to improve family functioning.

Homebuilders therapists work with youths and families involved in the child welfare, juvenile justice, and mental health systems. For high-risk families involved with the child protective services system, the goal of the program is to remove the risk of harm to the child instead of removing the child. Therapists work with families to teach them new behaviors and help them make better choices for their children, while ensuring child safety. In addition, Homebuilders works with youths and their families to address issues that lead to delinquency, while allowing youths to remain in the community. Program staff ensure that kids attend classes regularly, adhere to curfews, comply with the courts, and learn anger management and conflict-resolution skills to avoid getting into more trouble. Youths are helped to avoid the trauma and stigma of psychiatric hospitalization or residential treatment for mental health-related issues by providing crisis intervention and skill building, involving the families in the youths' treatment, and broadening the continuum of care.

The primary intervention components of the Homebuilders model are engaging and motivating family members; conducting holistic, behavioral assessments of strengths and problems; developing outcome-based goals; using evidence-based cognitive-behavioral interventions; teaching skills to facilitate behavior change; and developing and enhancing ongoing supports and resources.

The core program strategies are:

- *Intervention at crisis point*. Homebuilders therapists work with families when they are in crisis. Families are seen within 24 hours of referral to the program.

- *Accessibility*. Services are provided in the family's home and community (e.g., school) at times convenient to families, including evenings, weekends, and holidays. Therapists are available 24 hours a day, 7 days a week, for crisis intervention. This accessibility allows close monitoring of potentially dangerous situations.

- *Flexibility*. Intervention strategies and methods are tailored to meet the needs, values, and lifestyles of each family. Services are provided when and where the families wish. Therapists also provide a wide range of services, such as helping families meet the basic needs of food, clothing, and shelter; using public transportation; budgeting; and, when necessary, dealing with the social services system.

- *Time limited and low caseload*. Families receive four to six weeks of intensive intervention, with up to two "booster sessions." Therapists typically serve two families at a time and provide 80 to 100 hours of service, with an average of 45 hours of face-to-face contact with the family.

- *Strengths-based*. Therapists help clients identify and prioritize goals, strengths, and values and help them use and enhance strengths and resources to achieve their goals.

- *Ecological/holistic assessment and individualized treatment planning*. Assessments of family strengths, problems, and barriers to service/treatment and outcome-based goals and treatment plans are completed collaboratively with each family.

- *Research-based treatment practices*. Therapists use evidence-based treatment practices, including motivational interviewing, behavioral parent training, cognitive-behavior therapy strategies, and relapse prevention. Therapists teach family members a variety of skills, including child behavior management, effective discipline, positive behavioral support, communication skills, problem-solving skills, resisting peer pressure, mood management skills, safety planning, and establishing daily routines.

- *Support and resource building*. Therapists help families assess their formal and informal support systems and develop and enhance ongoing supports and resources for maintaining and facilitating changes.

Systematic research shows the program can be a cost-effective intervention method. A cost-benefit analysis found that, for each dollar invested in the Homebuilders program, the total benefit-to-cost ratio per participant was $2.54. The total benefits minus the costs was $4,775, a positive result indicating that money is saved by investing in the program. The California Evidence-Based Clearinghouse for Child Welfare includes the Institute's Homebuilders model as one of only five programs identified as being effective in reunifying families. The US Surgeon General has recognized Homebuilders as a model family strengthening program, the Office of Juvenile Justice Delinquency Prevention (OJJDP) and Center for Substance Abuse Prevention (CSAP) have designated Homebuilders as a model program for preventing juvenile delinquency, and the program has been accepted into the Substance Abuse and Mental Health Services Administration National Registry of Evidenced Based Programs and Practices to prevent or treat mental health or substance abuse disorders. Research consistently shows that 70 to 90 percent of referred families remain safely together six months to a year following services.

CRITICAL THINKING

Is it possible for a program like Homebuilders to work in the nation's most disorganized areas? Can an intervention program such as this overcome the effects of neighborhood dysfunction? Is this a Band-Aid approach to social problems?

SOURCE: Institute for Family Development, http://www.institutefamily.org/ (accessed October 2016).

There are a number of approaches to delinquency prevention based on improving family relations—or if that is not possible, offering an alternative. For example, mentoring programs involve nonprofessional volunteers who spend time with young people who have been targeted as having the potential for dropping out of school, school failure, and other social problems. They mentor in a supportive, nonjudgmental manner while also acting as role models. One of the most successful is the Quantum Opportunities Program (QOP), designed around the provision of three "quantum opportunities":

- Educational activities (peer tutoring, computer-based instruction, homework assistance)

- Service activities (volunteering with community projects)

- Development activities (curricula focused on life and family skills, and college and career planning)

Incentives in the form of cash and college scholarships have been offered to students for work carried out in these three areas. These incentives serve to provide short-run motivation for school completion and future academic and social achievement. In addition, staff receive cash incentives and bonuses for keeping youths involved in the program.[187] Another effective program, Homebuilders, is discussed in the Evidence-Based Juvenile Justice feature.

Another approach to involving the family in delinquency prevention is to attack the problem before it occurs. Early childhood prevention programs that target at-risk youths can relieve some of the symptoms associated with delinquency.[188] Frequent home visits by trained nurses and social service personnel help reduce child abuse and other injuries to infants.[189] Evidence suggests that early intervention may be the most effective method and that the later the intervention, the more difficult the change process.[190]

Because the family plays such a crucial role in delinquency prevention and control policies, it is one of the focus areas in Chapter 12's discussion of delinquency prevention strategies. Since it is suspected that child abuse leads to a cycle of violence, there are also programs designed to help abusive parents refrain from repeating their violent episodes.

SUMMARY

1 **Explain the link between family relationships and juvenile delinquency**

- There is little question that family dysfunction can lead to long-term social problems.

- Interactions between parents and children provide opportunities for children to acquire or inhibit antisocial behavior patterns.

- People who perceived a lack of parental warmth and support were later much more likely to get involved in antisocial behaviors.

- Good parenting lowers the risk of delinquency for children living in high-crime areas.

2 **Chart the changes American families are now undergoing**

- The nuclear family is showing signs of breakdown.

- The so-called traditional family—with a male breadwinner and a female who cares for the home—is a thing of the past.

- Children today live in a profusion of family living arrangements.

- Though there has been a sharp decline in teen pregnancies over the past decade, most kids born to unwed women have teen moms.

3 **Interpret the complex association between family breakup and delinquent behavior**

- About half of all marriages end in divorce.

- Research indicates that parents whose marriage is secure produce children who are secure and independent.

- Children who have experienced family breakup are more likely to demonstrate behavior problems and hyperactivity than children in intact families.

- There is a growing sentiment that family breakup is traumatic and most likely has a direct influence on factors related to adolescent misbehavior.

- Divorce may influence children's misbehavior through its effect on parental misbehavior.

- While family breakup is linked to delinquency, most kids whose parents are divorced or separated live happy and productive lives.

4 **Summarize why families in conflict produce more delinquents than those that function harmoniously**

- The link between parental conflict and delinquency is well established in the research literature.

- Children who grow up in dysfunctional homes often exhibit delinquent behaviors, having learned at a young age that aggression pays off.

- Kids who are conflict prone may actually help destabilize households.

5 **Compare and contrast the effects of good and bad parenting on delinquency**

- Children raised by parents who lack proper parenting skills are more at risk than those whose parents are supportive and effectively control their children.

- Parents of beyond-control youngsters have been found to be inconsistent rule-setters.

- Children who feel inhibited with their parents and refuse to discuss important issues with them are more likely to engage in deviant activities.

- Delinquency will be reduced if both or at least one parent can provide parental efficacy, or the type of structure that integrates children into families while giving them the ability to assert their individuality and regulate their own behavior.

6 **Discuss whether having deviant parents affects a child's behavioral choices**

- A number of studies have found that parental deviance has a powerful influence on delinquent behavior.

- A significant number of delinquent youths have criminal fathers.

- School yard bullying may be both inter- and intragenerational.

- The link between parental deviance and child misbehavior may be genetic.

- Children of drug-abusing parents are more likely to get involved in drug abuse and delinquency than the children of nonabusers.

- The link between parental deviance and child delinquency may be shaped by parenting ability, by learning deviant values, or it may even be related to labeling and stigma.

7 **Interpret sibling influence on delinquency**

- Some evidence shows that siblings may influence behavior.

- Siblings who live in the same environment are influenced by similar social and economic factors; it is not surprising that their behavior is similar.

- If deviance is genetically determined, the traits that cause one sibling to engage in delinquency are shared by his or her brother or sister.

- Deviant siblings grow closer because of shared interests. It is possible that the relationship is due to personal interactions: Younger siblings imitate older siblings.

8 **Discuss the nature and extent of child abuse**

- Parental abuse and neglect are not modern phenomena. Maltreatment of children has occurred throughout history.

- Child abuse includes neglect as well as physical and sexual abuse.

- Physical abuse includes throwing, shooting, stabbing, burning, drowning, suffocating, and biting.

- Physical neglect results from parents' failure to provide adequate food, shelter, or medical care for their children.

- Emotional abuse is manifested by constant criticism and rejection of the child.

- Emotional neglect includes inadequate nurturing and inattention to a child's emotional development.

- Abandonment refers to the situation in which parents leave their children with the intention of severing the parent–child relationship.

- Sexual abuse refers to the exploitation of children through rape, incest, and molestation by parents, other family members, friends, or legal guardians.

- Approximately 3 million allegations of child abuse and neglect involving 6 million children are made to child protective services agencies each year.

9 **List the assumed causes of child abuse**

- Abusive families suffer from severe stress.

- Substance abuse has been linked to child abuse.

- Parents who themselves suffered abuse tend to abuse their own children.

- The presence of an unrelated adult in the home increases the risk of abuse.

- Isolated and alienated families tend to become abusive.

- The behavior of abusive parents can often be traced to negative experiences in their own childhood—physical abuse, emotional neglect, and incest.

10 **Give examples of the child protection system and the stages in the child protection process**

- If the care a child receives falls below reasonable standards, the state may take action to remove the child from the home and place her or him in a less threatening environment.
- Child protection agencies have been dealing with abuse and neglect since the late nineteenth century.
- The Child Abuse Prevention and Treatment Act has been the impetus for the states to improve the legal frameworks of their child protection systems.
- All states have statutes requiring that persons suspected of child abuse and neglect be reported.
- Once reported to a child protection agency, the case is screened by an intake worker and then turned over to an investigative caseworker.
- In making their decisions, courts are guided by three interests: the role of the parents, protection for the child, and the responsibility of the state.

KEY TERMS

nuclear family, p. 287
broken home, p. 292
blended families, p. 293
intrafamily violence, p. 295
parental efficacy, p. 297
resource dilution, p. 298
battered child syndrome, p. 302
child abuse, p. 302

neglect, p. 302
abandonment, p. 302
familicide, p. 308
Troxel v. Granville, p. 308
Santosky v. Kramer, p. 308
advisement hearing, p. 310
pretrial conference, p. 311
disposition hearing, p. 312

balancing-of-the-interests approach, p. 313
review hearings, p. 313
foster care, p. 313
hearsay, p. 316
White v. Illinois, p. 316
Maryland v. Craig, p. 317

QUESTIONS FOR DISCUSSION

1. What are the meanings of the terms *child abuse* and *child neglect*?

2. Discuss the association between child abuse and delinquency. Give two different explanations for the positive relationship between abuse and antisocial behavior.

3. What causes parents to abuse their children?

4. What is meant by the child protection system? Do courts act in the best interest of the child when they allow an abused child to remain with the family?

5. Should children be allowed to testify in court via CCTV? Does this approach prevent defendants in child abuse cases from confronting their accusers?

6. Is corporal punishment ever permissible as a disciplinary method?

VIEWPOINT

You are an investigator with the county bureau of social services. A case has been referred to you by a middle school's head guidance counselor. It seems that a young girl, Emily, has been showing up to school in a dazed and listless condition. She has had a hard time concentrating in class and seems withdrawn and uncommunicative. The 13-year-old has missed more than her normal share of school days and has often been late to class. Last week, she seemed so lethargic that her homeroom teacher sent her to the school nurse. A physical examination revealed that she was malnourished and in poor physical health. She also had evidence of bruising that could only come from a severe beating. Emily told the nurse that she had been punished by her parents for doing poorly at school and failing to do her chores at home.

When her parents were called to school to meet with the principal and guidance counselor, they claimed to be members of a religious order that believes children should be punished severely for their misdeeds. Emily had been placed on a restricted diet as well as beaten with a belt to correct her misbehavior. When the guidance counselor asked them if they would be willing to go into family therapy, they were furious and told her to mind her own business. It's a sad day, they said, when "God-fearing American citizens cannot bring up their children according to their religious beliefs." The girl is in no immediate danger because her punishment has not been life threatening.

The case is then referred to your office. When you go to see the parents at home, they refuse to make any change in their behavior, claiming that they are in the right and you represent all that is wrong with society. The "lax" discipline you suggest leads to drugs, sex, and other teenage problems.

- Would you get a court order removing Emily from her house, placing her in foster care, and requiring the parents to go into counseling?
- Would you report the case to the district attorney's office so it could take criminal action against her parents under the state's child protection act?
- Would you take no further action, reasoning that Emily's parents have the right to discipline their child as they see fit?
- Would you talk with Emily and see what she wants to happen?

DOING RESEARCH ON THE WEB

To help you answer these questions and to find more information on child abuse, visit the website of the National Library of Medicine (http://www.nlm.nih.gov/). Their database provides both links and information on child abuse. Another useful site is Prevent Child Abuse America (http://preventchildabuse.org/), a group established in 1972 and dedicated to preventing all forms of child abuse.

NOTES

All URLs accessed September 2016.

1. CBS News, "Cops: Brothers Killed Family as Part of Mass Murder Plot; Wanted Fame," February 14, 2016, http://www.cbsnews.com/news/cops-brothers-who-killed-family-planned-mass-killings-wanted-fame/.
2. Abigail Fagan, M. Lee Van Horn, Susan Antaramian, and J. David Hawkins, "How Do Families Matter? Age and Gender Differences in Family Influences on Delinquency and Drug Use," *Youth Violence and Juvenile Justice* 9:50–170 (2011).
3. Callie Harbin Burt, Ronald Simons, and Leslie Simons, "A Longitudinal Test of the Effects of Parenting and the Stability of Self-Control: Negative Evidence for the General Theory of Crime," *Criminology* 44:353–396 (2006).
4. Dana Haynie and D. Wayne Osgood, "Reconsidering Peers and Delinquency: How Do Peers Matter?" *Social Forces* 84:1110–1130 (2005).
5. Emma Palmer and Kirsty Gough, "Childhood Experiences of Parenting and Causal Attributions for Criminal Behavior Among Young Offenders and Non-Offenders," *Journal of Applied Social Psychology* 37:790–806 (2007).
6. Karen Matta Oshima, Jin Huang, Melissa Jonson-Reid, and Brett Drake, "Children with Disabilities in Poor Households: Association with Juvenile and Adult Offending," *Social Work Research* 34:102–113 (2010).
7. Joan McCord, "Family Relationships, Juvenile Delinquency, and Adult Criminality," *Criminology* 29:397–417 (1991); Scott Henggeler, ed., *Delinquency and Adolescent Psychopathology: A Family Ecological Systems Approach* (Littleton, MA: Wright–PSG, 1982).
8. Bisakha Sen, "The Relationship Between Frequency of Family Dinner and Adolescent Problem Behaviors After Adjusting for Other Family Characteristics," *Journal of Adolescence* 33:187–196 (2010).
9. Sarah Meadows, "Evidence of Parallel Pathways: Gender Similarity in the Impact of Social Support on Adolescent Depression and Delinquency," *Social Forces* 85:1143–1167 (2007).
10. Ruth Inglis, *Sins of the Fathers: A Study of the Physical and Emotional Abuse of Children* (New York: St. Martin's Press, 1978), p. 131.
11. Sara McLanahan and Audrey N. Beck, "Parental Relationships in Fragile Families," *The Future of Children* 20 (2010), http://futureofchildren.org/futureofchildren/publications/journals/article/index.xml?journalid=73&articleid=529.
12. Ryan Spohn and Don Kurtz, "Family Structure as a Social Context for Family Conflict: Unjust Strain and Serious Delinquency," *Criminal Justice Review* 36:332–356 (2011).
13. William S. Comanor and Llad Phillips, "The Impact of Income and Family Structure on Delinquency," *Journal of Applied Economics* 5:209–232 (2002).
14. *America's Children: Key National Indicators of Well-Being, 2016,* http://childstats.gov/americaschildren/famsoc.asp.
15. Mary Shaw, Debbie Lawlor, and Jake Najman, "Teenage Children of Teenage Mothers: Psychological, Behavioural and Health Outcomes from an Australian Prospective Longitudinal Study," *Social Science and Medicine* 62:2526–2539 (2006).
16. Centers for Disease Control and Prevention, "Teen Pregnancy in the United States," 2016, http://www.cdc.gov/teenpregnancy/about/.
17. Valerie Polakow, *Who Cares for Our Children? The Child Care Crisis in the Other America* (New York: Teachers College Press, 2007).
18. US Census Bureau, "*Income, Poverty, and Health Insurance Coverage in the United States: 2014,*" http://www.census.gov/newsroom/press-releases/2015/cb15-157.html.
19. US Census Bureau, "Projected Population of the United States, by Age and Sex: 2000 to 2050," http://www.census.gov/population/projections/files/usinterimproj/natprojtab02a.pdf.
20. Rand Conger and Katherine Conger, "Understanding the Processes Through Which Economic Hardship Influences Families and Children," in D. Russell Crane and Tim B. Heaton, eds., *Handbook of Families and Poverty* (Thousand Oaks, CA: Sage Publications, 2008), pp. 64–81; Monica J. Martin, Rand D. Conger, Thomas J. Schofield, Shannon J. Dogan, Keith F. Widaman, M. Brent Donnellan, and Tricia K. Neppl, "Evaluation of the Interactionist Model of Socioeconomic Status and Problem Behavior: A Developmental Cascade Across Generations," Center for Poverty Research, University of California–Davis, http://poverty.ucdavis.edu/profile/rand-conger.
21. Christopher Sullivan, "Early Adolescent Delinquency: Assessing the Role of Childhood Problems, Family Environment, and Peer Pressure," *Youth Violence and Juvenile Justice* 4:291–313 (2006).
22. Rolf Loeber and Magda Stouthamer-Loeber, "Family Factors as Correlates and Predictors of Juvenile Conduct Problems and

Delinquency," in Michael Tonry and Norval Morris, eds., *Crime and Justice*, vol. 7 (Chicago: University of Chicago Press, 1986), pp. 39–41.

23. Carla Davis, "At-Risk Girls and Delinquency," *Crime and Delinquency* 53:408–435 (2007).

24. American Psychological Association, "Marriage and Divorce," 2016, http://www.apa.org/topics/divorce/.

25. Pew Research Center, "Four-in-Ten New Marriages Involve Remarriage," http://www.pewsocialtrends.org/2014/11/14/four-in-ten-couples-are-saying-i-do-again/st_2014-11-14_remarriage-01/.

26. Christopher Kierkus, Brian Johnson, and John Hewitt, "Cohabiting, Family and Community Stressors, Selection, and Juvenile Delinquency," *Criminal Justice Review* 35:393–411 (2010).

27. Andre Sourander, Henrik Elonheimo, Solja Niemelä, Art-Matti Nuutila, Hans Helenius, Lauri Sillanmäki, Jorma Piha, Tuulk Tamminen, Kirsti Kumpulkinen, Irma Moilanen, and Frederik Almovist, "Childhood Predictors of Male Criminality: A Prospective Population-Based Follow-up Study from Age 8 to Late Adolescence," *Journal of the American Academy of Child and Adolescent Psychiatry* 45:578–586 (2006).

28. Rae Simon, *Blended Families* (New York: Simon and Schuster, 2015); also see the classic article, Barbara Dafoe Whitehead, "Dan Quayle Was Right," *Atlantic Monthly* 271:47–84 (1993).

29. David M. Fergusson, Geraldine McLeod, and L. John Horwood, "Parental Separation/Divorce in Childhood and Partnership Outcomes at age 30," *Journal of Child Psychology and Psychiatry* 55:352–360 (2014).

30. Michael Rocque, Chad Posick, Steven E. Barkan, and Ray Paternoster, "Marriage and County-Level Crime Rates: A Research Note," *Journal of Research in Crime and Delinquency*, first published online August 19, 2014.

31. Ronald Simons, Kuei-Hsiu Lin, Leslie Gordon, Rand Conger, and Frederick Lorenz, "Explaining the Higher Incidence of Adjustment Problems Among Children of Divorce Compared with Those in Two-Parent Families," *Journal of Marriage and the Family* 61:131–148 (1999).

32. En-Ling Pan and Michael Farrell, "Ethnic Differences in the Effects of Intergenerational Relations on Adolescent Problem Behavior in U.S. Single-Mother Families," *Journal of Family Issues* 27:1137–1158 (2006).

33. Sheldon Glueck and Eleanor Glueck, *Unraveling Juvenile Delinquency* (Cambridge, MA: Harvard University Press, 1950); Ashley Weeks, "Predicting Juvenile Delinquency," *American Sociological Review* 8:40–46 (1943).

34. Jackson Toby, "The Differential Impact of Family Disorganization," *American Sociological Review* 22:505–512 (1957); Ruth Morris, "Female Delinquency and Relation Problems," *Social Forces* 43:82–89 (1964); Roland Chilton and Gerald Markle, "Family Disruption, Delinquent Conduct, and the Effects of Sub-classification," *American Sociological Review* 37:93–99 (1972).

35. For a review of these early studies, see Thomas Monahan, "Family Status and the Delinquent Child: A Reappraisal and Some New Findings," *Social Forces* 35:250–258 (1957).

36. Clifford Shaw and Henry McKay, *Report on the Causes of Crime: Social Factors in Juvenile Delinquency*, vol. 2 (Washington, DC: US Government Printing Office, 1931), p. 392.

37. John Laub and Robert Sampson, "Unraveling Families and Delinquency: A Reanalysis of the Gluecks' Data," *Criminology* 26:355–380 (1988); Lawrence Rosen, "The Broken Home and Male Delinquency," in M. Wolfgang, L. Savitz, and N. Johnston, eds., *The Sociology of Crime and Delinquency* (New York: Wiley, 1970), pp. 489–495.

38. Christina DeJong and Kenneth Jackson, "Putting Race into Context: Race, Juvenile Justice Processing, and Urbanization," *Justice Quarterly* 15:487–504 (1998).

39. Robert Johnson, John Hoffman, and Dean Gerstein, *The Relationship Between Family Structure and Adolescent Substance Abuse* (Washington, DC: Office of Applied Studies, Substance Abuse and Mental Health Services Administration, 1996).

40. Terence P. Thornberry, Carolyn A. Smith, Craig Rivera, David Huizinga, and Magda Stouthamer-Loeber, "*Family Disruption and Delinquency,*" *Juvenile Justice Bulletin* (Washington, DC: Office of Juvenile Justice and Delinquency Prevention, September 1999), https://www.ncjrs.gov/pdffiles1/ojjdp/178285.pdf.

41. Cesar Rebellon, "Reconsidering the Broken Homes/Delinquency Relationship and Exploring Its Mediating Mechanism(s)," *Criminology* 40:103–135 (2002).

42. Lisa Stolzenberg and Stewart D'Alessio, "The Effect of Divorce on Domestic Crime," *Crime and Delinquency* 53:281–302 (2007).

43. Sara Jaffee, Terrie Moffitt, Avshalom Caspi, and Alan Taylor, "Life with (or without) Father: The Benefits of Living with Two Biological Parents Depend on the Father's Antisocial Behavior," *Child Development* 74:109–117 (2003).

44. Ryan Schroeder, Aurea Osgood, and Michael Oghia, "Family Transitions and Juvenile Delinquency," *Sociological Inquiry* 80:579–604 (2010).

45. Sara McLanahan, "Father Absence and the Welfare of Children," working paper (Chicago: John D. and Catherine T. MacArthur Research Foundation, 1998).

46. Judith S. Wallerstein, Julia M. Lewis, and Sandra Blakeslee, *The Unexpected Legacy of Divorce* (New York: Hyperion, 2000).

47. E. Mavis Hetherington and John Kelly, *For Better or for Worse: Divorce Reconsidered* (New York: W. W. Norton, 2002).

48. F. Ivan Nye, "Child Adjustment in Broken and Unhappy Unbroken Homes," *Marriage and Family* 19:356–361 (1957); Nye, *Family Relationships and Delinquent Behavior* (New York: Wiley, 1958).

49. Diana Formoso, Nancy Gonzales, and Leona Aiken, "Family Conflict and Children's Internalizing and Externalizing Behavior: Protective Factors," *American Journal of Community Psychology* 28:175–199 (2000).

50. Peter Jaffe, David Wolfe, Susan Wilson, and Lydia Zak, "Similarities in Behavior and Social Maladjustment Among Child Victims and Witnesses to Family Violence," *American Journal of Orthopsychiatry* 56:142–146 (1986).

51. Lynette Renner, "Single Types of Family Violence Victimization and Externalizing Behaviors Among Children and Adolescents," *Journal of Family Violence* 27:177–186 (2012).

52. Paul Amato and Bruce Keith, "Parental Divorce and the Well-Being of Children: A Meta-Analysis," *Psychological Bulletin* 110:26–46 (1991).

53. Christopher Kierkus and Douglas Baer, "A Social Control Explanation of the Relationship Between Family Structure and Delinquent Behaviour," *Canadian Journal of Criminology* 44:425–458 (2002).

54. John Paul Wright and Francis Cullen, "Parental Efficacy and Delinquent Behavior: Do Control and Support Matter?" *Criminology* 39:677–706 (2001).

55. DeAnna Harris-McKoy, "Adolescent Delinquency: Is Too Much or Too Little Parental Control a Problem?" *Journal of Child and Family Studies* 25:2079–2088 (2016).

56. Kathleen Roche, Margaret Ensminger, and Andrew Cherlin, "Variations in Parenting and Adolescent Outcomes Among African American and Latino Families Living in Low-Income, Urban Areas," *Journal of Family Issues* 28:882–909 (2007).

57. Rick Trinkner, Ellen S. Cohn, Cesar J. Rebellon, and Karen Van Gundy, "Don't Trust Anyone over 30: Parental Legitimacy as a Mediator Between Parenting Style and Changes in Delinquent Behavior over Time," *Journal of Adolescence* 35:119–132 (2012).

58. Ibid.

59. Jennifer Wainright and Charlotte Patterson, "Delinquency, Victimization, and Substance Use Among Adolescents with Female Same-Sex Parents," *Journal of Family Psychology* 20:526–530 (2006).

60. Roslyn Caldwell, Jenna Silverman, Noelle Lefforge, and Clayton Silver, "Adjudicated Mexican-American Adolescents: The Effects of Familial Emotional Support on Self-Esteem, Emotional Well-Being, and Delinquency," *American Journal of Family Therapy* 32:55–69 (2004); Robert Vermeiren, Jef Bogaerts, Vladislav Ruchkin, Dirk Deboutte, and Mary Schwab-Stone," "Subtypes of Self-Esteem and Self-Concept in Adolescent Violent and Property Offenders," *Journal of Child Psychology and Psychiatry* 45:405–411 (2004).

61. Leslie Gordon Simons and Rand Conger, "Linking Mother-Father Differences in Parenting to a Typology of Family Parenting Styles and Adolescent Outcomes," *Journal of Family Issues* 28:212–241 (2007).

62. Carter Hay, "Parenting, Self-Control, and Delinquency: A Test of Self-Control Theory," *Criminology* 39:707–736 (2001).

63. Sonia Cota-Robles and Wendy Gamble, "Parent-Adolescent Processes and Reduced Risk for Delinquency: The Effect of Gender for Mexican American Adolescents," *Youth and Society* 37:375–392 (2006).

64. Wesley Church, Sara Tomek, Kathleen Bolland, Lisa Hooper, Jeremiah Jaggers, and John Bolland, "A Longitudinal Examination of Predictors of Delinquency: An Analysis of Data from the Mobile Youth Survey," *Children and Youth Services Review* 34:2400–2408 (2012).

65. Wainright and Patterson, "Delinquency, Victimization, and Substance Use Among Adolescents with Female Same-Sex Parents."

66. Stephanie Hicks-Pass, "Corporal Punishment in America Today: Spare the Rod, Spoil the Child? A Systematic Review of the Literature," *Best Practices in Mental Health* 5:71–88 (2009).

67. Loeber and Stouthamer-Loeber, "Development of Juvenile Aggression and Violence," p. 251.

68. Nathaniel Pallone and James Hennessy, "Brain Dysfunction and Criminal Violence," *Society* 35:21–27 (1998).

69. Eric Slade and Lawrence Wissow, "Spanking in Early Childhood and Later Behavior Problems: A Prospective Study of Infants and Young Toddlers," *Pediatrics* 113:1321–1330 (2004).

70. Murray Straus, "Discipline and Deviance: Physical Punishment of Children and Violence and Other Crime in Adulthood," *Social Problems* 38:101–123 (1991).

71. Murray A. Straus, "Spanking and the Making of a Violent Society: The Short- and Long-Term Consequences of Corporal Punishment," *Pediatrics* 98:837–843 (1996).

72. Ibid.

73. Nye, *Family Relationships and Delinquent Behavior*.

74. Laurence Steinberg, Ilana Blatt-Eisengart, and Elizabeth Cauffman, "Patterns of Competence and Adjustment Among Adolescents from Authoritative, Authoritarian, Indulgent, and Neglectful Homes: A Replication in a Sample of Serious Juvenile Offenders," *Journal of Research on Adolescence* 26:47–58 (2006).

75. Lisa Broidy, "Direct Supervision and Delinquency: Assessing the Adequacy of Structural Proxies," *Journal of Criminal Justice* 23:541–554 (1995).

76. James Unnever, Francis Cullen, and Robert Agnew, "Why Is 'Bad' Parenting Criminogenic? Implications from Rival Theories," *Youth Violence and Juvenile Justice* 4:3–33 (2006).

77. Sung Joon Jang and Carolyn A. Smith, "A Test of Reciprocal Causal Relationships Among Parental Supervision, Affective Ties, and Delinquency," *Journal of Research in Crime and Delinquency*, 34:307–336 (1997); Linda Waite and Lee Lillard, "Children and Marital Disruption," *American Journal of Sociology* 96:930–953 (1991).

78. Jennifer Beyers, John Bates, Gregory Pettit, and Kenneth Dodge, "Neighborhood Structure, Parenting Processes, and the Development of Youths' Externalizing Behaviors," *American Journal of Community Psychology* 31:35–53 (2003).

79. Joongyeup Lee, Hyunseok Jang, and Leana A. Bouffard, "Maternal Employment and Juvenile Delinquency: A Longitudinal Study of Korean Adolescents," *Crime and Delinquency*, first published online December 7, 2011.

80. Thomas Vander Ven and Francis Cullen, "The Impact of Maternal Employment on Serious Youth Crime: Does the Quality of Working Conditions Matter?" *Crime and Delinquency* 50:272–292 (2004); Thomas Vander Ven, Francis Cullen, Mark Carrozza, and John Paul Wright, "Home Alone: The Impact of Maternal Employment on Delinquency," *Social Problems* 48:236–257 (2001).

81. Stacy De Coster, "Mothers' Work and Family Roles, Gender Ideologies, Distress, and Parenting," *Sociological Quarterly* 53:585–609 (2012).

82. Douglas Downey, "Number of Siblings and Intellectual Development," *American Psychologist* 56:497–504 (2001).

83. For an early review, see Barbara Wooton, *Social Science and Social Pathology* (London: Allen and Unwin, 1959).

84. Stacy Tzoumakis, Patrick Lussier, and Raymond Corrado, "Female Juvenile Delinquency, Motherhood, and the Intergenerational Transmission of Aggression and Antisocial Behavior," *Behavioral Sciences and the Law* 30:211–237 (2012).

85. Marieke van de Rakt, Joseph Murray, and Paul Nieuwbeerta, "The Long-Term Effects of Paternal Imprisonment on Criminal Trajectories of Children," *Journal of Research in Crime and Delinquency* 49:81–108 (2012).

86. Daniel Shaw, "Advancing Our Understanding of Intergenerational Continuity in Antisocial Behavior," *Journal of Abnormal Child Psychology* 31:193–199 (2003).

87. Donald J. West and David P. Farrington, eds., "Who Becomes Delinquent?" in *The Delinquent Way of Life* (London: Heinemann, 1977); Donald J. West, *Delinquency: Its Roots, Careers, and Prospects* (Cambridge, MA: Harvard University Press, 1982).

88. David Farrington, "Understanding and Preventing Bullying," in Michael Tonry, ed., *Crime and Justice*, vol. 17 (Chicago: University of Chicago Press, 1993), pp. 381–457.

89. Carolyn Smith and David Farrington, "Continuities in Antisocial Behavior and Parenting Across Three Generations," *Journal of Child Psychology and Psychiatry* 45:230–247 (2004).

90. Joseph Murray, Rolf Loeber, and Dustin Pardini, "Parental Involvement in the Criminal Justice System and the Development of Youth Theft, Marijuana Use, Depression, and Poor Academic Performance," *Criminology* 50:255–312 (2012).

91. Erin Kathleen Midgley and Celia Lo, "The Role of a Parent's Incarceration in the Emotional Health and Problem Behaviors of At-Risk Adolescents," *Journal of Child and Adolescent Substance Abuse* 22:85–103 (2013); Michael Roettger and Raymond Swisher, "Associations of Fathers' History of Incarceration with Sons' Delinquency and Arrest among Black, White, and Hispanic Males in the United States," *Criminology* 49:1109–1148 (2011).

92. Joseph Murray and David Farrington, "Parental Imprisonment: Effects on Boys' Antisocial Behaviour and Delinquency Through the Life-Course," *Journal of Child Psychology and Psychiatry* 46:1269–1278 (2005).

93. Lauren Aaron and Danielle Dallaire, "Parental Incarceration and Multiple Risk Experiences: Effects on Family Dynamics and Children's Delinquency," *Journal of Youth and Adolescence* 39:1471–1484 (2010).

94. Peggy C. Giordano, *Legacies of Crime: A Follow-Up of the Children of Highly Delinquent Girls and Boys* (London: Cambridge University Press, 2010).

95. Abigail Fagan and Jake Najman, "Sibling Influences on Adolescent Delinquent Behaviour: An Australian Longitudinal Study," *Journal of Adolescence* 26:546–558 (2003).

96. David Rowe and Bill Gulley, "Sibling Effects on Substance Use and Delinquency," *Criminology* 30:217–232 (1992); see also David Rowe, Joseph Rogers, and Sylvia Meseck-Bushey, "Sibling Delinquency and the Family Environment: Shared and Unshared Influences," *Child Development* 63:59–67 (1992).

97. Deeanna Button and Roberta Gealt, "High Risk Behaviors Among Victims of Sibling Violence," *Journal of Family Violence* 25:131–140 (2010).

98. Matt DeLisi, Kevin Beaver, Michael Vaughn, and John Paul Wright, "All in the Family: Gene x Environment Interaction Between DRD2 and Criminal Father Is Associated with Five Antisocial Phenotypes," *Criminal Justice and Behavior* 36:1177–1187 (2009); John Paul Wright and Kevin Beaver, "Do Parents Matter in Creating Self-Control in Their Children? A Genetically Informed Test of Gottfredson and Hirschi's Theory of Low Self-Control," *Criminology* 43:1169–1202 (2005).

99. Leonore Simon, "Does Criminal Offender Treatment Work?" *Applied and Preventive Psychology* Summer:1–22 (1998).

100. Laura Baker, Kristen Jacobson, Adrian Raine, Dora Isabel Lozano, and Serena Bezdjian, "Genetic and Environmental Bases of Childhood Antisocial Behavior: A Multi-Informant Twin Study," *Journal of Abnormal Psychology* 116:219–235 (2007).

101. Dana DeHart and Sandra Altshuler, "Violence Exposure Among Children of Incarcerated Mothers," *Child and Adolescent Social Work Journal* 26:467–479 (2009).

102. Nancy Day, Lidush Goldschmidt, and Carrie Thomas, "Prenatal Marijuana Exposure Contributes to the Prediction of Marijuana Use at Age 14," *Addiction* 101:1313–1322 (2006).

103. Philip Harden and Robert Pihl, "Cognitive Function, Cardiovascular Reactivity, and Behavior in Boys at High Risk for Alcoholism," *Journal of Abnormal Psychology* 104:94–103 (1995).

104. Laub and Sampson, "Unraveling Families and Delinquency," p. 370.

105. Anne Dannerbeck, "Differences in Parenting Attributes, Experiences, and Behaviors of Delinquent Youth with and without a Parental History of Incarceration," *Youth Violence and Juvenile Justice* 3:199–213 (2005).

106. David P. Farrington, Gwen Gundry, and Donald J. West, "The Familial Transmission of Criminality," in Alan Lincoln and Murray Straus, eds., *Crime and the Family* (Springfield, IL: Charles C Thomas, 1985), pp. 193–206.

107. Kareem Fahim, "Mother Gets 43 Years in Death of Child, 7," *New York Times*, November 12, 2008, http://www.nytimes.com/2008/11/13/nyregion/13nixzmary.html.

108. Associated Press, "Gov Signs Nixzmary's Law," *New York Post*, October 10, 2009, http://www.nypost.com/p/news/local/item_6ilH907iltYusqmo4PogkO.

109. Richard Gelles and Claire Pedrick Cornell, *Intimate Violence in Families*, 2nd ed. (Newbury Park, CA: Sage, 1990), p. 33.

110. Lois Hochhauser, "Child Abuse and the Law: A Mandate for Change," *Harvard Law Journal* 18:200 (1973); see also Douglas J. Besharov, "The Legal Aspects of Reporting Known and Suspected Child Abuse and Neglect," *Villanova Law Review* 23:458 (1978).

111. C. Henry Kempe, F. N. Silverman, B. F. Steele, W. Droegemueller, and H. K. Silver, "The Battered-Child Syndrome," *Journal of the American Medical Association* 181:17–24 (1962).

112. Brian G. Fraser, "A Glance at the Past, a Gaze at the Present, a Glimpse at the Future: A Critical Analysis of the Development of Child Abuse Reporting Statutes," *Chicago-Kent Law Review* 54:643 (1977–1978).

113. Centers for Disease Prevention and Control, "Child Abuse and Neglect Prevention," http://www.cdc.gov/ViolencePrevention/childmaltreatment/.

114. See, especially, Inglis, *Sins of the Fathers*, ch. 8.

115. William Downs and Brenda Miller, "Relationships between Experiences of Parental Violence During Childhood and Women's Self-Esteem," *Violence and Victims* 13:63–78 (1998).

116. Ruth S. Kempe and C. Henry Kempe, *Child Abuse* (Cambridge, MA: Harvard University Press, 1978), pp. 6–7.

117. Fred Rogosch and Dante Cicchetti, "Child Maltreatment and Emergent Personality Organization: Perspectives from the Five-Factor Model," *Journal of Abnormal Child Psychology* 32:123–145 (2004).

118. Wendy Fisk, "Childhood Trauma and Dissociative Identity Disorder," *Child and Adolescent Psychiatric Clinics of North America* 5:431–447 (1996).

119. Centers for Disease Control and Prevention, "Child Abuse and Neglect Prevention."

120. National Center on Shaken Baby Syndrome, http://www.dontshake.org.

121. Mary Haskett and Janet Kistner, "Social Interactions and Peer Perceptions of Young Physically Abused Children," *Child Development* 62:679–690 (1991).

122. Kara Marie Brawn and Dominique Roe-Sepowitz, "Female Juvenile Prostitutes: Exploring the Relationship to Substance Use," *Children and Youth Services Review* 30:1395–1402 (2008).

123. Murray Straus, Richard Gelles, and Suzanne Steinmentz, *Behind Closed Doors: Violence in the American Family* (Garden City, NY: Anchor Books, 1980); Richard Gelles and Murray Straus, "Violence in the American Family," *Journal of Social Issues* 35:15–39 (1979).

124. Gelles and Straus, "Violence in the American Family," p. 24.

125. Richard Gelles and Murray Straus, *The Causes and Consequences of Abuse in the American Family* (New York: Simon & Schuster, 1988).

126. Murray A. Straus and Anita K. Mathur, "Social Change and Trends in Approval of Corporal Punishment by Parents from 1968 to 1994," in D. Frehsee, W. Horn, and K. Bussman, eds., *Violence Against Children* (New York: Aldine de Gruyter, 1996), pp. 91–105.

127. US Department of Health and Human Services, *Child Maltreatment, 2014*, http://www.acf.hhs.gov/sites/default/files/cb/cm2014.pdf.

128. Joe Drape, "Sandusky Guilty of Sexual Abuse of 10 Young Boys," *New York Times*, June 22, 2012, http://www.nytimes.com/2012/06/23/sports/ncaafootball/jerry-sandusky-convicted-of-sexually-abusing-boys.html.

129. Catherine Grus, "Child Abuse: Correlations with Hostile Attributions," *Journal of Developmental and Behavioral Pediatrics* 24:296–298 (2006).

130. Kim Logio, "Gender, Race, Childhood Abuse, and Body Image Among Adolescents," *Violence Against Women* 9:931–955 (2003).

131. Jeanne Kaufman and Cathy Spatz Widom, "Childhood Victimization, Running Away, and Delinquency," *Journal of Research in Crime and Delinquency* 36:347–370 (1999).

132. N. N. Sarkar and Rina Sarkar, "Sexual Assault on Woman: Its Impact on Her Life and Living in Society," *Sexual and Relationship Therapy* 20:407–419 (2005).

133. Michael Wiederman, Randy Sansone, and Lori Sansone, "History of Trauma and Attempted Suicide Among Women in a Primary Care Setting," *Violence and Victims* 13:3–11 (1998); Susan Leslie Bryant and Lillian Range, "Suicidality in College Women Who Were Sexually and Physically Abused and Physically Punished by Parents," *Violence and Victims* 10:195–215 (1995); Downs and Miller, "Relationships Between Experiences of Parental Violence During Childhood and Women's Self-Esteem"; Sally Davies-Netley, Michael Hurlburt, and Richard Hough, "Childhood Abuse as a Precursor to Homelessness for Homeless Women with Severe Mental Illness," *Violence and Victims* 11:129–142 (1996).

134. Jane Siegel and Linda Williams, "Risk Factors for Sexual Victimization of Women," *Violence Against Women* 9:902–930 (2003).

135. Michael Miner, Jill Klotz Flitter, and Beatrice Robinson, "Association of Sexual Revictimization with Sexuality and Psychological Function," *Journal of Interpersonal Violence* 21:503–524 (2006).

136. Lana Stermac and Emily Paradis, "Homeless Women and Victimization: Abuse and Mental Health History Among Homeless Rape Survivors," *Resources for Feminist Research* 28:65–81 (2001).

137. These data come from US Department of Health and Human Services, *Child Maltreatment, 2014*, http://www.acf.hhs.gov/sites/default/files/cb/cm2014.pdf.

138. Richard Estes and Neil Alan Weiner, *The Commercial Sexual Exploitation of Children in the U.S., Canada and Mexico* (Philadelphia: University of Pennsylvania, 2001); Lisa Jones and David Finkelhor, *The Decline in Child Sexual Abuse Cases* (Washington, DC: Office of Juvenile Justice and Delinquency Prevention, 2001).

139. Carolyn Webster-Stratton, "Comparison of Abusive and Nonabusive Families with Conduct-Disordered Children," *American Journal of Orthopsychiatry* 55:59–69 (1985); Brandt F. Steele and Carl B. Pollock, "A Psychiatric Study of Parents Who Abuse Infants and Small Children," in Ray Helfer and C. Henry Kempe, eds., *The Battered Child* (Chicago: University of Chicago Press, 1968), pp. 103–145.

140. Brandt F. Steele, "Violence Within the Family," in Ray E. Helfer and C. Henry Kempe, eds., *Child Abuse and Neglect: The Family and the Community* (Cambridge, MA: Ballinger, 1976), p. 13.

141. William Sack, Robert Mason, and James Higgins, "The Single-Parent Family and Abusive Punishment," *American Journal of Orthopsychiatry* 55:252–259 (1985).

142. Blair Justice and Rita Justice, *The Abusing Family* (New York: Human Sciences Press, 1976); Nanette Dembitz, "Preventing Youth Crime by Preventing Child Neglect," *American Bar Association Journal* 65:920–923 (1979).

143. Douglas Ruben, *Treating Adult Children of Alcoholics: A Behavioral Approach* (New York: Academic Press, 2000).

144. *The Relationship Between Parental Alcohol or Other Drug Problems and Child Maltreatment* (Chicago: Prevent Child Abuse America, 2000).

145. Martin Daly and Margo Wilson, "Violence Against Stepchildren," *Current Directions in Psychological Science* 5:77–81 (1996).

146. Ibid.

147. Margo Wilson, Martin Daly, and Antonietta Daniele, "Familicide: The Killing of Spouse and Children," *Aggressive Behavior* 21:275–291 (1995).

148. Richard Gelles, "Child Abuse and Violence in Single-Parent Families: Parent Absence and Economic Deprivation," *American Journal of Orthopsychiatry* 59:492–501 (1989).

149. Brett Drake and Melissa Jonson-Reid, "Poverty and Child Maltreatment," in Jill E. Korbin and Richard D. Krugman, eds., *Handbook of Child Maltreatment*, Vol. 2 (New York: Springer, 2014), pp. 131–148.

150. Robert Burgess and Patricia Draper, "The Explanation of Family Violence," in Lloyd Ohlin and Michael Tonry, eds., *Family Violence* (Chicago: University of Chicago Press, 1989), pp. 59–117.

151. Christopher Mallett, "Youthful Offending and Delinquency: The Comorbid Impact of Maltreatment, Mental Health Problems, and Learning Disabilities," *Child and Adolescent Social Work Journal* 31:369–392 (2014).

152. *Troxel et vir. v. Granville* No. 99-138 (June 5, 2000).

153. 452 U.S. 18, 101 S.Ct. 2153 (1981); 455 U.S. 745, 102 S.Ct. 1388 (1982).

154. For a survey of each state's reporting requirements, abuse and neglect legislation, and available programs and agencies, see Costa and Nelson, *Child Abuse and Neglect*.

155. Linda Gordon, "Incest and Resistance: Patterns of Father-Daughter Incest, 1880–1930," *Social Problems* 33:253–267 (1986).

156. P.L. 93B247 (1974); P.L. 104B235 (1996).

157. Children's Bureau, "Mandatory Reporters of Child Abuse and Neglect, 2015," https://www.childwelfare.gov/pubPDFs/manda.pdf.

158. Robin Fretwell Wilson, "Children at Risk: The Sexual Exploitation of Female Children After Divorce," *Cornell Law Review* 86:251–327 (2001).

159. Sue Badeau and Sarah Gesiriech, *A Child's Journey Through the Child Welfare System* (Washington, DC: The Pew Commission on Children in Foster Care, 2003).

160. Children's Bureau, "How the Child Welfare System Works."

161. Ibid.

162. Ibid.

163. Joseph Doyle, "Child Protection and Child Outcomes: Measuring the Effects of Foster Care," *American Economic Review* (2008), http://www.mit.edu/~jjdoyle/doyle_fosterlt_march07_aer.pdf.

164. "Preventing Child Maltreatment," Executive Summary, *The Future of Children* 19 (2009), http://futureofchildren.org/futureofchildren/publications/docs/19_02_ExecSummary.pdf.

165. PBS Frontline, "Innocence Lost the Plea," http://www.pbs.org/wgbh/pages/frontline/shows/innocence/. For an analysis of the accuracy of children's recollections of abuse, see Candace Kruttschnitt and Maude Dornfeld, "Will They Tell? Assessing Preadolescents' Reports of Family Violence," Journal of Research in Crime and Delinquency 29:136–147 (1992).

166. National District Attorneys Association, "Anatomical Dolls and Diagrams," November 2014, http://www.ndaa.org/pdf/Anatomical_Dolls_11_7_2014.pdf.

167. *White v. Illinois*, 502 U.S. 346; 112 S.Ct. 736 (1992).

168. Myrna Raeder, "*White*'s Effect on the Right to Confront One's Accuser," *Criminal Justice*, Winter 2–7 (1993).

169. *Coy v. Iowa*, 487 U.S. 1012 (1988).

170. *Maryland v. Craig*, 110 S.Ct. 3157 (1990).

171. See, for example, Cesar Rebellon and Karen Van Gundy, "Can Control Theory Explain the Link Between Parental Physical Abuse and Delinquency? A Longitudinal Analysis," *Journal of Research in Crime and Delinquency* 42:247–274 (2005).

172. Jennifer Lansford, Laura Wager, John Bates, Gregory Pettit, and Kenneth Dodge, "Forms of Spanking and Children's Externalizing Behaviors," *Family Relations* 6:224–236 (2012).

173. Wan-Yi Chen, Jennifer Propp, Ellen deLara, and Kenneth Corvo, "Child Neglect and Its Association with Subsequent Juvenile Drug and Alcohol Offense," *Child and Adolescent Social Work Journal* 28:273–290 (2011).

174. Sara Culhane and Heather Taussig, "The Structure of Problem Behavior in a Sample of Maltreated Youths," *Social Work Research* 33:70–78 (2009).

175. Egbert Zavala, "Testing the Link Between Child Maltreatment and Family Violence Among Police Officers," *Crime and Delinquency*, first published online November 22, 2010.

176. Marie Skubak Tillyer, "The Relationship Between Childhood Maltreatment and Adolescent Violent Victimization," *Crime and Delinquency* 61:973–995 (2015).

177. National Center on Child Abuse and Neglect, Department of Health, Education, and Welfare, *1977 Analysis of Child Abuse and Neglect Research* (Washington, DC: US Government Printing Office, 1978), p. 29.

178. Janet Currie and Erdal Tekin, "Does Child Abuse Cause Crime?" National Bureau of Economic Research, Working Paper No. 12171, 2006, http://www.nber.org/papers/w12171.

179. Cathy Widom, "Understanding Child Maltreatment and Juvenile Delinquency: The Research," Welfare League of America, 2010, http://66.227.70.18/programs/juvenilejustice/ucmjd03.pdf.

180. Bruce Rind, Philip Tromovitch, and Robert Bauserman, "A Meta-Analytic Examination of Assumed Properties of Child Sexual Abuse Using College Samples," *Psychological Bulletin* 124:22–53 (1998).

181. Widom, "Child Abuse, Neglect, and Violent Criminal Behavior," p. 267.

182. Matthew Zingraff, "Child Maltreatment and Youthful Problem Behavior," *Criminology* 31:173–202 (1993).

183. Timothy Ireland, Carolyn Smith, and Terence Thornberry, "Developmental Issues in the Impact of Child Maltreatment on Later Delinquency and Drug Use," *Criminology* 40:359–401 (2002).

184. Ibid.

185. Leonard Edwards and Inger Sagatun, "Dealing with Parent and Child in Serious Abuse Cases," *Juvenile and Family Court Journal* 34:9–14 (1983).

186. Susan McPherson, Lance McDonald, and Charles Ryer, "Intensive Counseling with Families of Juvenile Offenders," *Juvenile and Family Court Journal* 34:27–34 (1983).

187. US Department of Education, "The Quantum Opportunity Program," July 2, 2007.

188. The programs in this section are described in Edward Zigler, Cara Taussig, and Kathryn Black, "Early Childhood Intervention, a Promising Preventative for Juvenile Delinquency," *American Psychologist* 47:997–1006 (1992).

189. Lawrence W. Sherman, Denise C. Gottfredson, Doris L. MacKenzie, John Eck, Peter Reuter, and Shawn D. Bushway, *Preventing Crime: What Works, What Doesn't, What's Promising* (Washington, DC: National Institute of Justice, 1998).

190. Zigler, Taussig, and Black, "Early Childhood Intervention," pp. 1000–1004.

CHAPTER 9

Peers and Delinquency:
Juvenile Gangs and Groups

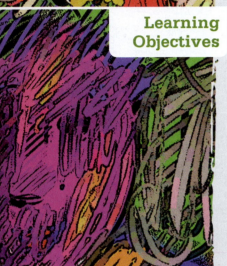

Learning Objectives

1 Give examples of the influence of peers on delinquency

2 Outline how romantic love influences delinquency

3 Analyze the various definitions used to describe gangs

4 Discuss the history of gangs

5 Identify the extent and location of the gang problem

6 List the various forms contemporary gangs take

7 Characterize the globalization of gangs

8 Describe female gangs and gang members

9 Compare the various theories of gang formation

10 Summarize the various forms of gang-control efforts in use today

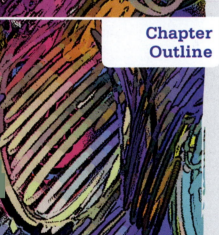

Chapter Outline

Adolescent Peer Relations
Peer Relations and Delinquency
Impact of Peer Relations
Youth Gangs
What Are Gangs?
How Did Gangs Develop?
Contemporary Gangs
Extent
Location
Migration
Collaboration
Globalization
Types
Cohesion
Age
Gender
Formation
Leadership

Communications
Ethnic and Racial Composition
Criminality and Violence
Why Do Youths Join Gangs?
The Anthropological View
The Social Disorganization/
Sociocultural View
The Anomie/Alienation View
The Family Tradition/
Learning View
The Psychological View
The Rational Choice View
Leaving the Gang
Controlling Gang Activity
Legal Controls
Law Enforcement Efforts
Community-Level Programs
Evaluating Gang-Control Efforts

Chapter Features

Focus on Delinquency: Birds of a Feather?

Cyber Delinquency: Gangs in Cyberspace

Case Profile: Luis's Story

Youth Stories: Lisa's Story

**Evidence-Based Juvenile Justice—
Intervention:** Newport News STEP Program

**Evidence-Based Juvenile Justice—
Intervention:** Cure Violence

WHILE GETTING INTO GANGS MAY BE EASY,

getting out can be a challenge. Sometimes kids can leave gangs if they are given proper intervention and treatment. Take the case of Michael, an 18-year-old gang member who was referred to a gang intervention service when he was 15 years old. After contact, Michael maintained a sporadic relationship with social service personnel over a two-year period while he rotated in and out of the juvenile justice system and struggled with his parents' substance addictions. Eventually, Michael moved in with his girlfriend's family, and her parents assumed guardianship. His girlfriend became pregnant and gave birth to a son. Michael successfully completed juvenile probation but could not maintain employment because of his limited educational achievement; he had literacy issues.

Michael sought to gain employment in the transportation industry so he could take care of his son and girlfriend. He also wished to rebuild his relationship with his parents, who were working to address their own substance addictions. Michael entered a local program that helped him obtain necessary identification documents and get enrolled in an online high school diploma program to address his literacy deficits and complete his GED. Social services also helped Michael access family counseling services so he could develop more effective skills to parent his young son.

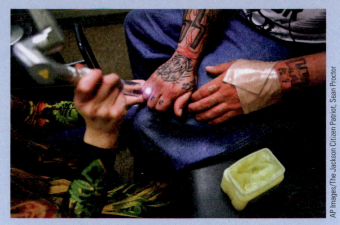

Removing tattoos is part of leaving the gang life behind.

AP Images/The Jackson Citizen Patriot, Sean Proctor

During repeated meetings, Michael shared that his biggest fear was having his son ask him about his gang-related tattoos. His social service contact helped him enroll in a tattoo removal program. During the tattoo removal process, word got out that his old gang was considering retaliation against Michael for his decision to leave the gang. Michael contacted the gang leaders and successfully explained that he was focusing on taking care of his family and accomplishing his career goals. Michael earned his high school diploma, received his transportation worker credentials, and obtained an entry-level position. He is currently working and taking care of his son and girlfriend.[1]

Despite Michael's success, the problem of gang control is a difficult one. Many gangs flourish in inner-city areas that offer lower-class youths few conventional opportunities, and members are resistant to offers of help that cannot deliver legitimate economic hope. Although gang members may be subject to arrest, prosecution, and incarceration, a new crop of young recruits is always ready to take the place of their fallen comrades. Those sent to prison find that, upon release, their former gangs are only too willing to have them return to action. There has been an outcry from politicians to increase punishment for the "little monsters" and to save the "fallen angels," or the victimized youths who are innocent.[2] While some antigang activity seems to work, the number of gang members has steadily increased and is now estimated to be more than 850,000!

Although some gangs are made up of only a few loosely organized neighborhood youths, others like the Crips, Bloods, and Latin Kings have thousands of members scattered around the United States and abroad. Take for instance the highly violent MS-13 gang. The latest available data indicate that along with some 10,000 members in the United States, MS-13 has an estimated 60,000 combined members in El Salvador, Honduras, and Guatemala.[3] A significant portion of all drug distribution in the nation's inner cities is believed to be gang controlled; gang violence accounts for more than 1,000 homicides each year.

We begin this chapter with a discussion of peer relations, showing how they influence delinquent behavior. A great deal of adolescent misbehavior is

The Federal Bureau of Investigation (FBI) website has quite a bit of information on **gangs and their control** (https://www.fbi.gov/investigate/violent-crime/gangs).

committed with peers in groups and cliques, groups that may morph into law-violating youth groups and gangs. Because of this connection and the seriousness of gang activity in the United States, we turn our attention to the definition, nature, and structure of delinquent gangs as well as efforts being made to control their criminal activities.

Adolescent Peer Relations

Although parents are the primary source of influence and attention in children's early years, between ages 8 and 14 children seek a stable peer group, and both the number and the variety of friendships increase as children go through adolescence. Friends soon begin to have a greater influence over decision making than parents.

As they go through adolescence, children form friendship *dyads*, an association with a single "best friend," then get into **cliques**, small groups of friends who share activities and confidences. They also belong to **crowds**, loosely organized groups of teens who share interests and activities such as sports, religion, or hobbies. Intimate friends play an important role in social development, but adolescents are also deeply influenced by this wider circle of friends. Adolescent self-image is in part formed by perceptions of one's place in the social world.[4] Kids not only are influenced by their close intimates but also model their behavior on that displayed by others they are less familiar with or do not associate with as long as it can impress their immediate group. In mid-adolescence, kids strive for peer approval and to impress their closest friends.[5]

In later adolescence, acceptance by peers continues to have a major impact on socialization. By their teens, children report that their friends give them emotional support when they are feeling bad and that they can confide intimate feelings to peers without worrying about their confidences being betrayed. Poor peer relations such as negative interactions with best friends have been found to be related to high social anxiety while, in contrast, close affiliation with a high-status peer crowd seems to afford protection against depression and other negative adolescent psychological symptoms.[6] Some kids seek others with similar fears and anxieties. They may feed off each other emotionally. Girls may seek peers with similar body image problems and together get involved in diet and extreme weight loss activities that can be physically and emotionally harmful.[7]

Popular youths do well in school and are socially astute. Kids who have lots of friends and a variety of peer group networks tend to be less delinquent than their less popular mates.[8] In contrast, children who are rejected by their peers are more likely to display aggressive behavior and to disrupt group activities by bickering or behaving antisocially. Kids choose friends who are similar in behavior and values, and the resemblance increases as the friendship develops; resemblance declines when friendship dissolves. In stable friendships, the more accepted popular partner exerts greater influence over the less accepted partner. If the more popular friend engages in delinquency and alcohol use, the less popular "follower" will be soon to follow.[9]

It is clear that peer status during childhood is an important contributor to a child's social and emotional development that follows children of both sexes over the life course. Girls who engage in aggressive behavior with childhood peers later have more conflict-ridden relationships with their romantic partners. Boys who are highly aggressive, and are therefore rejected by their peers in childhood are also more likely to engage in criminality and delinquency from adolescence into young adulthood.[10]

Peer influence may be more important than parental nurturance in the development of long-term behavior.[11] Peers guide each other and help each other learn to share and cooperate, to cope with aggressive impulses, and to discuss feelings they would not dare bring up at home. Youths can compare their own experiences

cliques
Small groups of friends who share intimate knowledge and confidences.

crowds
Loosely organized groups who share interests and activities.

with peers and learn that others have similar concerns and problems.[12] In fact, there is evidence that peers may actually outweigh the influence of parents in producing a delinquent way of life. Even children born into high-risk families—such as those with single teen mothers—can avoid delinquency if their friends are prosocial and refrain from drug use and criminality.[13] Conversely, negative peer influence can neutralize the positive effects of maternal monitoring and control on deviant behaviors.[14] Youths can compare their own experiences with peers and learn that others have similar concerns and problems.[15]

Peer Relations and Delinquency

Kids who hang out with delinquent friends, who spend time socializing with them without parental supervision, and who admire and want to emulate them are the ones most likely to increase involvement in antisocial behaviors.[16] Unstructured socializing is related to delinquency for at least three reasons: (1) adolescents are exposed to delinquent peers without parental controls, (2) exposure to delinquent peers affects the extent to which adolescents perceive temptations (opportunities) to engage in delinquency, and (3) exposure to delinquent peers affects adolescents' tolerance for substance use.[17] So peers encourage risk-taking behavior and drug use, two precursors to adolescent delinquency.

Deviancy Training   Research shows that peer group relationships are closely tied to delinquent behaviors. Delinquent acts tend to be committed in small groups rather than alone, a process referred to as *co-offending*.[18] Many kids are initiated into deviant activities such as smoking marijuana by their friends, and their friends' pro-deviant attitudes are then used to help support continued involvement in antisocial or illegal acts.[19] In a process called **deviancy training**, close friends reinforce deviant behavior through talk and interaction. They talk among themselves about what they have done, such as take drugs or have sex, and laugh and joke about what happened. Their laughter and support lead to more rule breaking. The more adolescents talk positively and reinforce deviant acts, the more likely their friends will engage in the antisocial behavior on a long-term basis.[20]

deviancy training
A process in which close friends reinforce deviant behavior choices through talk and interaction.

Peer relations, in all cultures, have been linked to adolescent behavior choices, including substance abuse and delinquency.

Janine Wiedel/Photolibrary/Alamy Stock Photo

Some kids are more susceptible to deviancy training than others.[21] Sensation seekers are more likely to be influenced by their friends than more passive teens.[22] Boys who mature early and reach puberty at a young age are also the ones most likely to develop strong attachments to delinquent, friends and to be influenced by deviancy training.[23] The earlier youngsters develop relationships with delinquent peers and the closer those relationships get, the more likely they will become delinquent.

Romantic Love   In his social bond theory, Travis Hirschi argued that delinquent youth were loners who did not form attachment to others. How then do they fare as romantic partners? When Peggy Giordano and her associates examined the romantic life of delinquents, they found that, surprisingly, they actually report more frequent contact with their romantic partners. However, as Hirschi may have predicted, Giordano found that delinquent youth argue more and report more verbal conflict with their romantic partners than their nondelinquent peers.[24]

Does this mean that delinquents are washouts as romantic partners? Not exactly. When sociologists Bill McCarthy and Teresa Casey examined the association between love, sex, and delinquency in a sample of teens, they found that the closeness offered by adolescent romantic love may fill an important void between the weakening of bonds with parents and the onset of adult attachments, and it may discourage an array of negative outcomes, including involvement in delinquency.[25] In contrast, adolescent sexual activity without the promise of love increases the likelihood of offending because it is associated with strain created by loveless relationships. McCarthy and Casey found that romantic love has a deterrent effect that actually encourages youths who have offended to decrease their involvement in crime. They speculate that romantic love discourages offending by strengthening the social bond. By contrast, the association between sex and crime is intensified in relationships short on love. It is possible that kids who engage in sex without love or romance are willing to partake in other risky and/or self-indulgent behaviors, including delinquency and drug usage.

Impact of Peer Relations

Does having antisocial peers cause delinquency, or are delinquents previously antisocial youths who seek out like-minded companions? While it is possible that delinquency is a product of peer influence, it is also possible that the relationship is spurious and produced by other factors. There are a number of views that provide alternative explanations for the peer–delinquency link:

- *Peer pressure can lead to delinquency.* The classic model is that a "good kid" is led astray by more deviant peers. Kids who use substances pressure their friends to do so also; shoplifters and car thieves convince their peers to go along for the ride (see Exhibit 9.1) [26]

- *Peer relations are controlled by flawed perceptions.* Kids may overestimate their friends' deviant behavior. It is this misperception, rather than actual peer behavior, that influences their delinquent choices. Kids think "all my friends drink, take drugs, and have sex, so I better do so too or I will not be part of the group." But their view is wrong; they are acting on false beliefs. Perception rather than actual peer behavior influences delinquent choices.[27]

- *Peer relations are controlled by selecting similar friends.* Antisocial youths join with like-minded friends; deviant peers sustain and amplify delinquent careers.[28] Deviant peers do not cause straight kids to go bad, but they amplify the likelihood of a troubled kid getting further involved in antisocial behaviors.[29] As children move through the life course, antisocial friends help them maintain delinquent careers and obstruct the aging-out process.[30]

Words or Deeds?

How does peer pressure work? Is it words or deeds? To find out, Owen Gallupe and his colleagues carried out two randomized experiments in which subjects were given a chance to steal a gift card worth about $15, which was placed in front of them on a table. Each experiment had (1) a control group, (2) a verbal prompting group in which the experimenters planted confederate(s) who then encouraged the subjects to steal the card, (3) a behavioral modeling group in which the experimenter's confederate(s) committed the theft themselves, and (4) a verbal prompting plus behavioral modeling group in which confederate(s) both encouraged theft and stole a gift card themselves. The first experiment used one confederate; the second experiment used two. The sample consisted of 335 undergraduate students.

Gallupe and his associates found that the experiment that involved both verbal prompting and behavioral modeling produced subjects who were most likely to steal; these were followed by the behavioral modeling group. There were no thefts in either the control or verbal prompting groups regardless of the number of confederates.

So while verbal peer pressure may have an effect on some teens, it appears that deeds rather than words may be more significant. Kids whose friends commit crime in their presence are more likely to be influenced than those who merely hear their peers bragging about their exploits.

SOURCE: Owen Gallupe, Holly Nguyen, Martin Bouchard, Jennifer Schulenberg, Allison Chenier, and Katie Cook, "An Experimental Test of Deviant Modeling," *Journal of Research in Crime and Delinquency* 53:482–505 (2016).

■ *Troubled kids choose delinquent peers out of necessity rather than desire.* Delinquent kids come from distressed homes, maintain emotional problems, and do poorly in school. These social factors, and not peer influence, are the true cause of their delinquent behaviors.[31] Why do delinquent kids have delinquent friends? The social baggage they cart around prevents them from developing associations with conventional peers. Because they are impulsive, they may choose friends who are of similar temperaments in order to sell drugs and commit crimes.[32]

■ *Labels and stigma control peer interaction.* Kids who display emotional or behavioral problems early in childhood are labeled "strange" or "weird" by other kids, labels that stick into mid-adolescence. Stigma leads to estrangement and feelings of isolation and loneliness. Alienated kids are susceptible to depression and psychological deficits that someday may lead to antisocial behavior and substance abuse.[33] Kids who are outsiders select delinquent friends who then have an important influence on their behavior. For example, kids who smoke may choose other smokers as their friends; hanging out with smokers supports and accelerates their smoking activity.[34]

Do They Really Flock Together? There is little question that the association between peer influence and delinquency is complex. While at first glance it seems that many crime-involved youth choose like-minded friends, many also hang out with kids who are not delinquent themselves, raising the question of whether birds of a feather really do flock together (see the Focus on Delinquency feature).

Having delinquent friends may actually turn out to have social benefits: having disreputable, sketchy friends can increase social standing and popularity among the teen population. No one wants to be considered a nerd or socially awkward. Teens may be afraid that if they *abstain* from rule-violating behaviors they will be socially isolated. Drinking, smoking pot, and partying are the norm in adolescent society; abstainers are disparaged, not admired.[35]

By ninth grade, kids who belong to the "party crowd" (a group that engages in underage drinking and precocious sex) gain rather than lose social capital. Participation in the party subculture has short-term costs (such as lower grades or detachment from school), but in the long term provides gains in the form of social capital and peer group popularity.[36] So while some kids may indeed seek out delinquent friends, they may do so to gain popularity, not to enter into a delinquent way of life.

Birds of a Feather?

It is ironic that even though the prevailing wisdom is that delinquency is strongly influenced by interaction and involvement with older and/or more experienced peers, most institutional treatment programs based in schools, community centers, and the juvenile justice system continue to organize deviant peers into groups and isolate them from conventional law-abiding kids. In their important book *Deviant Peer Influences in Programs for Youth: Problems and Solutions*, Kenneth A. Dodge, Thomas Dishion, and Jennifer Lansford find that public policy is often based on a misguided desire to remove deviant youths from the mainstream and segregate them, together, in groups.

Exclusion policy takes place on many different levels. Schools place children who display conduct problems in special education groups for diagnosis as "seriously emotionally disturbed" (SED) or "behaviorally or emotionally handicapped" (BEH). Once in these groups, students are treated in self-contained classrooms for almost the whole day. The effects of this aggregation include both the possibility of deviant peer influence and the loss of opportunities for positive influence from well-adjusted peers. Several studies indicate that students receiving special education services are more likely to suffer suspension and expulsion than their peers and that special education may actually increase problem behavior.

Problem kids are also lumped together in the juvenile justice system. Delinquents are placed in residential settings such as detention centers, training schools, reform schools, prisons, boot camps, and wilderness camps that are populated exclusively by other offending youth. In all of these settings, youths interact primarily with other deviant youths under circumstances of limited adult supervision.

Even community-based programs designed to keep at-risk youths off the streets offer little structure or adult supervision and simply provide a place for youths to hang out. These programs may have the unintended effect of increasing behavior problems by increasing the aggregation of at-risk youth.

In sum, while many experts believe that delinquent "birds of a feather flock together," school, community, and justice system policy has been to isolate at-risk kids, lumping them together and thereby magnifying negative effects of peer influence.

CRITICAL THINKING

If lumping problem youth together causes problems, is there a possible alternative solution? Is this an insurmountable problem?

SOURCE: Kenneth A. Dodge, Jennifer E. Lansford, and Thomas J. Dishion, "The Problem of Deviant Peer Influences in Intervention Programs," in Kenneth Dodge, Thomas Dishion, Jennifer Lansford, eds., *Deviant Peer Influences in Programs for Youth: Problems and Solutions* (New York: Guilford Press, 2006), pp. 3–13.

Youth Gangs

As youths move through adolescence, they gravitate toward cliques that provide them with support, assurance, protection, and direction. In some instances the peer group provides the social and emotional basis for antisocial activity. When this happens, the clique is transformed into a **gang**.

gang
Group of youths who collectively engage in delinquent behaviors.

Such a powerful mystique has grown up around gangs that mere mention of the word evokes images of black-jacketed youths roaming the streets in groups bearing such names as MS-13, Latin Kings, Crips, and Bloods. Films, television shows, novels, and even Broadway musicals (e.g., *West Side Story*, *Grease*) have popularized the youth gang.[37]

Considering the suspected role gangs play in violent crime and drug activity, it is not surprising that gangs have recently become the target of a great deal of research interest and government antigang activities. Important attempts have been made to gauge the size, location, makeup, and activities of gangs, and in the following sections this research will be discussed in some detail.

What Are Gangs?

Gangs are groups of youths who engage in delinquent behaviors. Yet gang delinquency differs from group delinquency. While the former involves long-lived institutions that have a distinct structure and organization, including identifiable leadership, division of labor, rules, rituals, and possessions, the latter consists of a short-lived alliance created to commit a particular crime or violent act.

Delinquency experts are often at odds over the precise definition of a gang. The term is sometimes used broadly to describe any congregation of youths who have joined together to engage in delinquent acts. However, police departments often use it only to refer to cohesive groups that hold and defend territory, or turf.[38]

Academic experts have also created a variety of definitions (see Exhibit 9.2). The core elements in the concept of the gang are that it is an **interstitial group**—one falling within the cracks and crevices of society—and that it maintains standard group processes, such as recruiting new members, setting goals, assigning roles, and developing status.[39]

Malcolm Klein argues that two factors stand out in all of these definitions:

■ Members have self-recognition of their gang status and use special vocabulary, clothing, signs, colors, graffiti, and names. Members set themselves apart from the community and are viewed as a separate entity by others. Once they get the label of "gang," members eventually accept and take pride in their status.

■ There is a commitment to criminal activity, although even the most criminal gang members spend the bulk of their time in noncriminal activities.[40]

interstitial group
Delinquent group that fills a crack in the social fabric and maintains standard group practices, such as setting goals, recruiting new members, developing status, and assigning roles.

---

exhibit 9.2

Definitions of Teen Gangs

Frederick Thrasher

An interstitial group originally formed spontaneously and then integrated through conflict. It is characterized by the following types of behavior: meeting face-to-face, milling, movement through space as a unit, conflict, and planning. The result of this collective behavior is the development of tradition, unreflective internal structure, esprit de corps, solidarity, morale, group awareness, and attachment to local territory.

Malcolm Klein

Any denotable adolescent group of youngsters who (a) are generally perceived as a distinct aggregation by others in their neighborhood, (b) recognize themselves as a denotable group (almost invariably with a group name), and (c) have been involved in a sufficient number of delinquent incidents to call forth a consistent negative response from neighborhood residents and/or law enforcement agencies.

Walter Miller

A self-formed association of peers, bound together by mutual interests, with identifiable leadership, well-developed lines of authority, and other organizational features, who act in concert to achieve a specific purpose or purposes, which generally include the conduct of illegal activity and control over a particular territory, facility, or type of enterprise.

G. David Curry and Irving Spergel

Groups containing law-violating juveniles and adults that are complexly organized, although sometimes diffuse, and sometimes cohesive, with established leadership and membership rules. The gang also engages in a range of crime (but with significantly more violence) within a framework of norms and values in respect to mutual support, conflict relations with other gangs, and a tradition of turf, colors, signs, and symbols. Subgroups of the gang may be deferentially committed to various delinquent or criminal patterns, such as drug trafficking, gang fighting, or burglary.

James Short

Groups of young people whose members meet together with some regularity, over time, on the basis of group-defined criteria of membership and group-defined organizational characteristics. In the simplest terms, gangs are unsupervised (by adults), self-determining groups that demonstrate continuity over time.

National Gang Center

A youth gang is commonly thought of as a self-formed association of peers having the following characteristics:

■ The group has three or more members, generally aged 12–24.

■ Members share an identity, typically linked to a name, and often other symbols.

■ Members view themselves as a gang, and they are recognized by others as a gang.

■ The group has some permanence and a degree of organization.

■ The group is involved in an elevated level of criminal activity.

United States Justice Department

(1) an association of three or more individuals; (2) whose members collectively identify themselves by adopting a group identity, which they use to create an atmosphere of fear or intimidation frequently by employing one or more of the following: a common name, slogan, identifying sign, symbol, tattoo or other physical marking, style or color of clothing, hairstyle, hand sign or graffiti; (3) the association's purpose, in part, is to engage in criminal activity and the association uses violence or intimidation to further its criminal objectives; (4) its members engage in criminal activity, or acts of juvenile delinquency that if committed by an adult would be crimes; (5) with the intent to enhance or preserve the association's power, reputation, or economic resources; (6) the association may also possess some of the following characteristics: (a) the members employ rules for joining and operating within the association; (b) the members meet on a recurring basis; (c) the association provides physical protection of its members from other criminals and gangs; (d) the association seeks to exercise control over a particular location or region, or it may simply defend its perceived interests against rivals; or (e) the association has an identifiable structure; (7) this definition is not intended to include traditional organized crime groups, such as La Cosa Nostra, groups that fall within the department's definition of "international organized crime," drug trafficking organizations or terrorist organizations.

SOURCES: Frederick Thrasher, *The Gang* (Chicago: University of Chicago Press, 1927), p. 57; Malcolm Klein, *Street Gangs and Street Workers* (Englewood Cliffs, NJ: Prentice Hall, 1971), p. 13; Walter Miller, "Gangs, Groups, and Serious Youth Crime," in David Schicor and Delos Kelly, eds., *Critical Issues in Juvenile Delinquency* (Lexington, MA: Lexington Books, 1980); James Short Jr. and Fred Strodtbeck, *Group Process and Gang Delinquency* (Chicago: University of Chicago Press, 1965); National Gang Intelligence Center, National Gang Report, 2015, https://www.fbi.gov/file-repository/national-gang-report-2015.pdf/. (URLs accessed October 2016.)

How Did Gangs Develop?

The youth gang is sometimes viewed as uniquely American, but gangs have also been reported in several other nations.[41] Nor are gangs a recent phenomenon. In the 1600s, London was terrorized by organized gangs that called themselves Hectors, Bugles, Dead Boys, and other colorful names. In the seventeenth and eighteenth centuries, English gang members wore distinctive belts and pins marked with serpents, animals, stars, and the like.[42] The first mention of youth gangs in America occurred in the late 1780s, when prison reformers noted the presence of gangs of young people hanging out on Philadelphia's street corners. By the 1820s, New York's Bowery and Five Points districts, Boston's North End and Fort Hill, and the outlying Southwark and Moyamensing sections of Philadelphia were the locales of youth gangs with colorful names like the Roach Guards, Chichesters, the Plug Uglies, and the Dead Rabbits.[43]

In the 1920s, Frederick Thrasher initiated the study of the modern gang in his analysis of more than 1,300 youth groups in Chicago.[44] He found that the social, economic, and ecological processes that affect the structure of cities create cracks in the normal fabric of society—weak family controls, poverty, and social disorganization—and referred to this as an *interstitial area*. According to Thrasher, groups of youths develop to meet such needs as play, fun, and adventure, activities that sometimes lead to delinquent acts. Impoverished areas present many opportunities for conflict between groups of youths and adult authority. If this conflict continues, the groups become more solidified and their activities become primarily illegal, and the groups develop into gangs.

According to Thrasher, adult society does not meet the needs of lower-class youths, and the gang solves the problem by offering excitement, fun, and opportunity. The gang is not a haven for disturbed youths but an alternative lifestyle for normal boys. Thrasher's work has had an important influence. Recent studies of delinquent gang behavior also view the gang as a means for lower-class boys to achieve advancement and opportunity as well as to defend themselves and to attack rivals.[45]

Gangs in the 1950s and 1960s   The threat of gangs and gang violence swept the public consciousness in the 1950s and early 1960s. Rarely did a week go by without a major city newspaper featuring a story on the violent behavior of fighting gangs and their colorful leaders and names—the Egyptian Kings, the Vice

In the late 1960s and into the 1970s, gangs began to reemerge in New York, Los Angeles, and other large cities. There are more than 800,000 gang members in the United States today. Here, members of the Chicago gang Blackstone Rangers exchange a power salute.

Art Shay/Getty Images

Lords, the Blackstone Rangers. Social service and law enforcement agencies directed major efforts to either rehabilitate or destroy the gangs. Movies, such as *The Wild Ones* and *Blackboard Jungle*, were made about gangs, and the Broadway musical *West Side Story* romanticized violent gangs.

In his classic 1967 work *Juvenile Gangs in Context*, Malcolm Klein summarized existing knowledge about gangs.[46] He concluded that gang membership was a way for individual boys to satisfy certain personal needs related to the development of youths caught up in the emotional turmoil typical of the period between adolescence and adulthood. A natural inclination to form gangs is reinforced by the perception that the gang represents a substitute for unattainable middle-class rewards.

The experience of being a member of a gang will dominate a youngster's perceptions, values, expectations, and behavior. Finally, the gang is self-reinforcing: it is within the gang more than anywhere else that a youngster may find forms of acceptance for delinquent behavior—rewards instead of negative sanctions. And as the gang strives for internal cohesion, the negative sanctions of the "outside world" become interpreted as threats to cohesion, thus providing secondary reinforcement for the values central to the legitimization of gang behavior.[47]

By the mid-1960s, the gang menace seemed to have disappeared. Some experts attribute the decline of gang activity to successful gang-control programs.[48] They believed that gangs were eliminated because police gang-control units infiltrated gangs, arrested leaders, and constantly harassed members.[49] Gang boys were more likely to be sanctioned by the juvenile justice system and receive more severe sentences than nongang youths.[50] Another explanation for the decline in gang activity was the increase in political awareness that developed during the 1960s. Many gang leaders became involved in the social or political activities of ethnic pride, civil rights, and antiwar groups. In addition, many gang members were drafted. Still another explanation is that gang activity diminished during the 1960s because many gang members became active users of heroin and other drugs, which curtailed their group-related criminal activity.[51]

Gangs Reemerge   Interest in gang activity began anew in the early 1970s. Bearing such names as Savage Skulls and Black Assassins, gangs began to form in New York's South Bronx neighborhoods in the spring of 1971 and quickly spread to other parts of the city. By 1975, there were 275 police-verified gangs, with 11,000 members.[52]

Gang activity also reemerged in other major cities, such as Chicago and Los Angeles. The Crips gang was created in Los Angeles in 1969 by teens Raymond Washington and Stanley "Tookie" Williams. Initially called the Baby Avenues, they evolved to Avenue Cribs, and then Cribs. According to legend, the gang name evolved into Crips because some of its members used canes to attack victims; it is also possible it was a simple spelling mistake in newspaper articles about the gang.

As the Crips gained power, other rival gangs feared their growing dominance. By late 1971, L.A. Brims, Piru Street Boys, the Bishops, Athens Park Boys, and other gang boys met to discuss how to combat Crip intimidation. The gangs merged and called themselves the Bloods, known for wearing a red bandana and slashing victims to draw their blood as part of the gang initiation rights. Eventually both these gangs sent representatives to organize chapters in distant areas or to take over existing gangs.

Why Did Gangs Reemerge?   One reason for the increase in gang activity may be involvement in the sale of illegal drugs.[53] Early gangs relied on group loyalty to encourage membership, but modern gang members are lured by the quest for drug profits. In some areas, gangs replaced organized crime families as the dominant suppliers of cocaine and crack. The traditional weapons of gangs—chains, knives, and homemade guns—were replaced by automatic weapons.

Gang formation was also the natural consequence of the economic and social dislocation that occurred when the economy shifted from a relatively high-paying manufacturing to low-wage service economy.[54] Some US cities that required a large population base for their manufacturing plants now face economic stress as these plants shut down. In this uneasy economic climate, gangs flourish, while the influence of successful adult role models and stable families declines. The presence of gangs in areas unaccustomed to delinquent group activity can have a devastating effect on community life.

While this social dislocation was occurring, the media fell in love with gang images, which appeared in films and music videos. Gangsta rap became a national phenomenon. Because there has been a diffusion of the gang culture through the popular media, in which gang boys are made to appear as successful heroes, urban kids may find the lure of gangs and law-violating peer groups irresistible.

Contemporary Gangs

The gang cannot be viewed as a uniform or homogeneous social concept. Gangs vary by activity, makeup, location, leadership style, and age. The next sections describe some of the most salient features of contemporary gangs.

Extent

There are a number of national indicators on the nature and trends in gang activity. According to the FBI's National Gang Report, which surveys law enforcement around the nation, street gang membership and gang-related crime increased in approximately 50 percent of reporting jurisdictions over the past two years.[55]

The National Youth Gang Survey (NYGS) measures gang activity around the United States.[56] The most recent survey involved 3,500 law enforcement jurisdictions that experience gang activities and included most larger cities and metropolitan areas. The NYGS found that, following a marked decline from the mid-1990s to the early 2000s, the prevalence rate of gang activity has significantly increased over the past decade. The most recent survey shows that there were an estimated 30,700 gangs (an increase from 29,900 in 2011) and 850,000 gang members (an increase from 782,500 in 2011) throughout 3,100 legal jurisdictions with gang problems. The number of reported gang-related homicides increased 20 percent from 1,824 in 2011 to 2,363 today.[57]

Location

A significant majority of urban areas report the presence of gangs, and gangs exist in all levels of the social strata, from rural counties to metropolitan areas. Traditionally, gangs have operated in large urban areas experiencing rapid population change. In these transitional neighborhoods, diverse ethnic and racial groups find themselves in competition with one another.[58] Intergang conflict and homicide rates are high in these areas, which house the urban "underclass."[59] However, these neighborhoods eventually evolve into permanently **disorganized neighborhoods**, where population shifts slow down, permitting patterns of behavior and traditions to develop over a number of years. Most typical are the poverty-stricken areas of Los Angeles and Chicago and the Mexican American **barrios** of the southwestern states and California. These areas contain large, structured gang clusters that are resistant to change or control by law enforcement agencies. Research by David Pyrooz confirms that cities with greater social and economic deprivation experience higher rates of gang homicide. Communities with fewer resources have limited capacities to regulate human behavior, and gangs are naturally occurring deviant social networks that engage in violence as a result of weakened social controls. It is not, he argues, that these communities are more tolerant of violent gang activities; rather, they lack the collective efficacy to control gangs.[60]

While some people think of gangs as a purely urban phenomenon, thousands of members are located in small cities, suburban counties, and even rural areas.

disorganized neighborhood
Inner-city areas of extreme poverty where the critical social control mechanisms have broken down.

barrio
A Spanish word meaning "neighborhood."

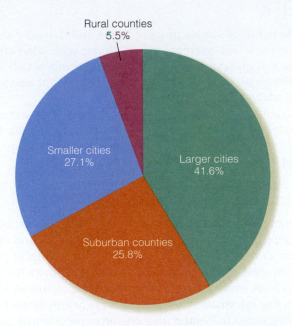

Rural counties
5.5%

Smaller cities
27.1%

Larger cities
41.6%

Suburban counties
25.8%

figure 9.1

Distribution of Gangs by Area Type

SOURCE: National Gang Center, National Youth Gang Survey, 2012.

However, the recent uptick in the number of gangs (and gang members) seems to be in the nation's largest cities, suggesting that gang activity is becoming even more concentrated in urban areas (see Figure 9.1).[61] The most recent findings do not support the popularly held notion that gang activity is migrating outward to less densely populated areas (see below for more on gang migration).

Migration

Because of redevelopment, gangs in some areas have relocated or migrated; gang members have organized new chapters when they relocate to new areas. Many jurisdictions have experienced gang migration, and in a few areas more than half of all gang members have come from other areas. Smaller areas, where gang problems are less common and/or chronic, were significantly less likely than larger areas to report gang-member migrants. About 9 percent of jurisdictions reported that more than half of the documented gang members in their jurisdictions had migrated from other areas.[62]

Why do gang members migrate? While the prevailing wisdom is that gang members move for criminal purposes (e.g., to sell drugs to new customers at higher prices), most do so for social reasons (e.g., members moving with families, pursuit of legitimate employment opportunities). Others seek new drug market opportunities or want to avoid law enforcement crackdowns in their hometowns. In all, less than 20 percent move to a new location solely in order to participate in illegal ventures in a new area that may have less gang competition. Most migrants are African American or Hispanic males who maintain close ties with members of their original gangs "back home." Some migrants join local gangs, shedding old ties and gaining new affiliations.

Although some experts fear the outcome of migration, it appears the number of migrants is relatively small in proportion to the overall gang population.[63] And, despite a widely held perception that larger proportions of gang-member migrants are positively associated with increases in local gang activities, such as violence, drugs, and conflict, the data show that the presence or the proportion of gang-member migrants has little effect on gang activities.

In sum, gang-member migration is far more the exception than the rule outside urban areas. Gang-member migrants are usually a small part of the total gang population, have likely moved to the area for legitimate social or family reasons, and have no prominent impact on local gang offenses.

Read more about **gang makeup** and other facts at the National Institute of Justice: http://www.nij.gov/topics /crime/gangs/pages/definitions .aspx.

Collaboration

While the media is full of stories of gang fights and drive-by shootings, some gangs are flexible organizations that form coalitions with other crews in order to attain as much money and power as possible. Gang members will feud with rivals when they interfere with its goals and objectives, but might also join forces in an alliance that will advance its objectives.

Collaboration among street gangs has increased; gangs have merged or formed hybrid gangs to counter enforcement control efforts. In San Diego, the Black MOB, Skanless, Neighborhood Crips, Lincoln Park, and West Coast Crips gangs are now working together to traffic females in 46 cities across 23 states.[64]

Globalization

The gang migration problem is not unique to the United States, and homegrown gangs and migrating transnational gangs have developed around the world.[65] One reason is that our global society has increased the percentage of people living in extreme poverty in some areas of the world.[66] As a result, there is a growing global urban underclass from which gang members are being recruited. In addition, globalization means that information and weapons are readily available anywhere in the world, allowing gangs to expand their resources for criminal enterprises.

The global criminal economy, especially the illegal distribution of drugs, involves gangs as both major and bit players. Numerous gangs operate in distressed areas such as the townships of South Africa where they rule politically and control the underground economy. Chinese triads operate all across the globe but are especially active in South Asia and the United States. In Eastern Europe, the turmoil caused by the move to a market economy and the loss of social safety nets has strengthened gangs and drug organizations. In Albania, one-quarter of all young males are involved in the drug economy.[67]

Gangs are now being exported from one nation to another. There are Jamaican posses in Kansas; San Diego's Calle Trente gang had a past relationship to Mexico's Arellano brothers cartel; the Russian "mafiya" now operates in Chicago; female Muslim gangs are active in Oslo, Norway; and L.A.'s MS-13 and 18th Street (Calle 18) gangs are now the largest gangs in Honduras and El Salvador (there is

Some gangs have a global reach, with branches in the United States and abroad. Mara Salvatrucha (MS-13), first emerged in the United States and migrated to El Salvador. Its leader, Borromeo Enrique Henríquez Solórzano, alias El Diablo, is shown during a press conference at La Esperanza jail, near San Salvador.

Roberto Escobar/EPA/Redux

more on these gangs below).[68] The changing social and economic conditions in our post-globalization world support the spread of gang activity:

- Worldwide urbanization and the concentration of population in crowded, poor, and disorganized cities has created fertile conditions for the growth of gangs, particularly in Latin America, Asia, and Africa.

- In the global era, the state has retreated from its role of providing social welfare and an economic safety net. Gangs and other groups of armed young men occupy the vacuum created by the retreat of the social welfare policies of the state.

- Kids who fear being marginalized in a technological economy that is growing more sophisticated by the day seek alternatives to conventional society. In some nations they may join fundamentalist religious groups or extremely nationalistic political parties. Others have embraced the hip-hop or gangsta culture that provides them with a new identity in opposition to the conventional mainstream culture from which they have been excluded.

- Globalization has created a flourishing underground economy that can be exploited by internationally connected enterprises run by gangs, cartels, and similar groups who can easily export black market items ranging from guns to pirated prerelease films.

- The wealth of the global economy has led to the redivision of space in cities across the globe. "Economic development," "making the city safe," and "ethnic cleansing" has meant clearing out undesirables from urban spaces coveted by dominant ethnic or religious majorities. In America, this often means displacing African American youth from city centers so these areas can be gentrified and rebuilt. This upheaval has increased the attractiveness of gangs for the displaced youths now living in ring-cities or nearby suburbs.

- Some gangs institutionalize and become permanent social actors in communities, cities, and nations rather than fading away after a generation. These gangs often replace or rival demoralized political groups and play important social, economic, and political roles in cities around the world.

Types

Gangs have been categorized by their dominant activity. Some are devoted to violence and to protecting neighborhood boundaries or turf; others are devoted to theft; some specialize in drug trafficking; still others are concerned with recreation rather than crime.[69] Jeffrey Fagan found that most gangs fall into one of these four categories:

- *Social gang.* Involved in few delinquent activities and little drug use other than alcohol and marijuana. Members are more interested in social activities.

- *Party gang.* Concentrates on drug use and sales but forgoes most delinquent behavior. Drug sales are designed to finance members' personal drug use.

- *Serious delinquent gang.* Engages in serious delinquent behavior while avoiding drug dealing and usage. Drugs are used only on social occasions.

- *Organized gang.* Heavily involved in criminality. Drug use and sales are related to other criminal acts. Gang violence is used to establish control over drug sale territories. This gang is on the verge of becoming a formal criminal organization.[70]

Cohesion

The standard definition of a gang implies that it is a cohesive group. However, some experts refer to gangs as **near-groups**, which have limited cohesion, impermanence, minimal consensus of norms, shifting membership, disturbed leadership, and limited definitions of membership expectations.[71] Gangs maintain a

near-groups
Clusters of youth who, outwardly, seem unified but actually have limited cohesion, impermanence, minimal consensus of norms, and shifting membership.

small core of committed members, who work constantly to keep the gang going, and a much larger group of affiliated youths who participate in gang activity only when the mood suits them.[72]

Current research indicates that although some gangs remain near-groups, others become quite organized and stable. These gangs resemble traditional organized crime families more than temporary youth groups. Some, such as Chicago's Latin Kings and Gangster Disciples, have members who pay regular dues, are expected to attend gang meetings regularly, and carry out political activities to further gang ambitions.

Age

The ages of gang members range widely, perhaps from as young as 8 to as old as 55.[73] Traditionally, most members of offending groups were usually no more than a few years apart in age, with a leader who may be a few years older than most other members.[74] However, because members are staying in gangs longer than in the past, the age spread between gang members has widened considerably.

Research indicates that youths first hear about gangs at around 9 years of age, get involved in violence at 10 or 11, and join their first gang at 12. By age 13, most members have (a) fired a pistol, (b) seen someone killed or seriously injured, (c) gotten a gang tattoo, and (d) been arrested.[75] Gang experts believe the average age of gang members has been increasing yearly, a phenomenon explained in part by the changing structure of the US economy: kids are staying in gangs longer because there are fewer jobs in the legitimate economy for untrained, uneducated workers.[76] Though gang members are aging, that does not mean very young kids are not being recruited into gangs in the United States and in other cultures.

Why Are Gang Members Aging? Gang members are getting older, and as Figure 9.2 shows, the majority are now legal adults. The relatively high-paid, low-skilled factory jobs that would entice older gang members to leave the gang have been lost to overseas competition. A transformed US economy now prioritizes information and services over heavy industry. This shift in emphasis undermines labor unions that might have attracted former gang boys. Equally damaging has been the embrace of social policies that stress security and the needs of the wealthy while weakening the economic safety net for the poor (e.g., reducing welfare eligibility). William Julius Wilson found that the inability of inner-city males to obtain

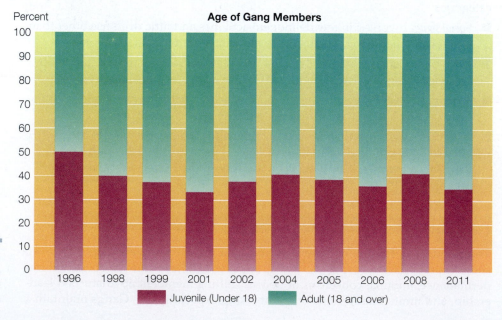

figure 9.2

Age of Gang Members

SOURCE: National Gang Center, National Youth Gang Survey Analysis, https://www.nationalgangcenter.gov /Survey-Analysis/Demographics#anchorage (accessed October 2016).

adequate jobs means that they cannot afford to marry and raise families. Criminal records acquired at an early age quickly lock these youths out of the job market so that remaining in a gang becomes an economic necessity.[77] In the wake of reduced opportunity for unskilled labor, gangs have become an important ghetto employer offering low-level drug-dealing opportunities that are certainly not available in the nongang world.[78]

Gender

Traditionally, gangs were considered a male-dominated enterprise. Of the more than 1,000 groups included in Thrasher's original survey, only half a dozen were female gangs. Females were involved in gangs in three ways: as auxiliaries (or branches) of male gangs, as part of sexually mixed gangs, or as autonomous gangs. Auxiliaries are a feminized version of the male gang name, such as the Lady Disciples rather than the Devil's Disciples.

It is difficult to accurately assess female gang representation. National data indicate that about 7 percent of gang members are female; smaller cities and rural counties report a higher percentage of female gang membership compared to urban areas.[79] As Figure 9.3 shows, the gender ratio of gang members has remained quite stable.

One reason for the gender gap is that females leave gangs at an earlier age than males, hence their smaller numbers. Gender-mixed gangs are also more commonly reported now than in the past, which is an important trend, since females in majority-male gangs exhibit the highest delinquency rates (including higher rates than males in all-male gangs). As Figure 9.4 shows, gangs that are mixed gender are typically located in smaller towns and in rural areas.

Girls in the Gang   Why do girls join gangs? There are a variety of reasons, including but not limited to financial opportunity, identity and status, peer pressure, family dysfunction, and protection.[80] Some admit that they join because they are bored and look to gangs for a social life; they are seeking fun and excitement and a means to find parties and meet boys. Still, others join simply because gangs are there in the neighborhood and are viewed as part of their way of life. And some children of gang members are just following in their parents' footsteps.[81]

What benefits does gang membership offer to females? According to the "liberation" view, ganging can provide girls with a sense of sisterhood, independence,

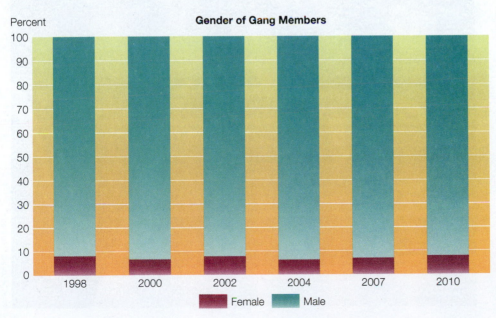

figure 9.3

Gender Ratio of Gang Members

SOURCE: National Gang Survey Analysis: Gender, https://www.nationalgangcenter.gov/Survey-Analysis /Demographics#anchorgender (accessed October 2016).

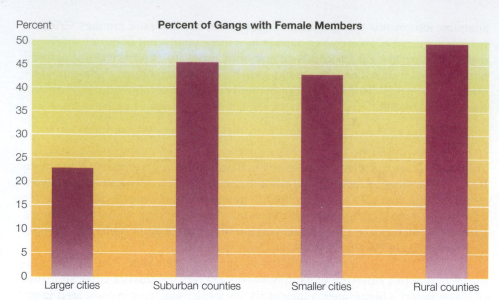

Percent of Gangs with Female Members

Percent

Larger cities | Suburban counties | Smaller cities | Rural counties

figure 9.4

Gangs with Female Members

SOURCE: National Gang Survey Analysis: Gender, https://www.nationalgangcenter.gov/Survey-Analysis /Demographics#anchorgender (accessed October 2016).

and solidarity, as well as a chance to earn profit through illegal activities. Research in Illinois found that girls from tough inner-city neighborhoods drift into gangs to escape the turmoil of their home lives, characterized by abuse, parental crime, and fatherless homes. Their affiliation begins when they hang around the street with gang boys, signaling their gang affiliation and symbolizing a lifestyle shift away from their home and school and into the street culture. The shift causes rifts with parents, leading to more time on the street and closer gang ties.[82] These young girls, typically ages 14 to 15, are targets for sexual and criminal exploitation.

Although initial female gang participation may be forged by links to male gang members, once in gangs, girls form close ties with other female members and engage in group criminal activity.[83] In contrast, the "social injury" view of female gang involvement suggests that young girls are still sexually exploited by male gang boys and are sometimes forced to exploit other females.

Girls who are members of male gang auxiliaries report that males control them by determining the arenas within which they can operate (e.g., the extent to which

Girls are used by gang members as a source of income. Here, a young woman is transported by Los Angeles police to the 77th Street Division station on a charge of prostitution. While the charge of soliciting or loitering with the intent to commit prostitution is a misdemeanor, the woman will be held for two to four days until she's formally charged. In South Central Los Angeles, prostitution flourishes and is often controlled by pimps who are current or former Bloods or Crips gang members.

Robert Nickelsberg/Getty Images

they may become involved in intergang violence). Males also play a divisive role in the girls' relationships with each other; this manipulation is absent for girls in independent gangs.[84] When criminologist Jody Miller studied female gangs in St. Louis, Missouri, and Columbus, Ohio, she found that girls in mixed gangs expressed little evidence of sisterhood and solidarity with other female gang members.[85] Rather, female gang members expressed hostility to other women in the gang, believing, for example, that those who suffered sexual assault by males in the same gang actually deserved what they got. Instead of trying to create a sense of sisterhood, female gang members tried to identify with males and view themselves as thereby becoming "one of the guys" in the gang.

Why do girls join gangs if they are exploitive and provide little opportunities for sisterhood? Miller found that even though being a gang member is not a walk in the park, most girls join gangs in an effort to cope with their turbulent personal lives, which may provide them with an even harsher reality; they see the gang as an institution that can increase their status and improve their lifestyle. The gang provides them with an alternative to a tough urban lifestyle filled with the risk of violence and victimization. Many of the girl gang members had early exposure to neighborhood violence, had encounters with girl gangs while growing up, had experienced severe family problems (violence or abuse), and had close family members who were gang involved.[86] Did they experience life benefits after they joined the gang? The evidence is mixed. Miller found that female gang members increased their delinquent activities and increased their risk of becoming a crime victim; they were more likely to suffer physical injury than girls who shunned gang membership. The risk of being sexually assaulted by male members of their own gang was also not insignificant nor is the risk of being in a violent domestic relationship.[87] However, female gang membership did have some benefits: it protected female gang members from sexual assault by nongang neighborhood men, which they viewed as a more dangerous and deadly risk.

Why do girls leave the gang? One not so surprising answer is that female gang members begin to drift away from gangs when they become young mothers. Fleisher and Krienert found that a majority of the Illinois gang girls they studied became inactive members soon after getting pregnant. Pregnancy leads to a disinterest in hanging around the streets and an interest in the safety of the fetus. Other girls became inactive after they decided to settle down and raise a family. But pregnancy seemed to be the primary motivating factor for leaving the gang life.[88] Some may reevaluate gang membership if they get in trouble with the law and do time in prison, though others may find that a prison experiences enmeshes them more in a criminal way of life.[89]

Formation

Gang formation involves a sense of territoriality. Most gang members live in close proximity to one another, and their sense of belonging extends only to their small area of the city. At first, a gang may form when members of an ethnic minority join together for self-preservation. As the group gains domination over an area, it may view the area as its own territory, or turf, which needs to be defended from outsiders.

Once formed, gangs grow when youths who admire the older gang members "apply" and are accepted for membership. Sometimes the new members will be given a special identity that reflects their apprenticeship status. Joan Moore and her associates found that *klikas*, or youth cliques, in Hispanic gangs remain together as unique groups with separate names, identities, and experiences; they also have more intimate relationships among themselves than among the general gang membership.[90] She likens *klikas* to a particular class in a university, such as the class of '19.

Moore also found that gangs can expand by including members' kin, even if they do not live in the neighborhood, and rival gang members who wish to join

klikas
Subgroups of same-aged youths in Hispanic gangs that remain together and have separate names and a unique identity in the gang.

because they admire the gang's way of doing things. Adding outsiders gives the gang the ability to take over new territory. However, it also brings with it new problems because it usually results in greater conflicts with rival gangs.

Leadership

Delinquent gangs tend to be small and transitory.[91] Youths often belong to more than a single group or clique and develop an extensive network of delinquent associates. Group roles can vary, and an adolescent who assumes a leadership role in one group may be a follower in another.

Those who assume leadership roles have earned their position by demonstrating fighting prowess, verbal quickness, or athletic distinction. They emphasize that leadership is held by one person and varies with particular activities, such as fighting, sex, and negotiations. In fact, in some gangs each age level has its own leaders. Older members are not necessarily considered leaders by younger members. In his analysis of Los Angeles gangs, Malcolm Klein observed that many gang leaders deny leadership. He overheard one gang boy claim, "We got no leaders, man. Everybody's a leader, and nobody can talk for nobody else."[92] The most plausible explanation of this ambivalence is the boy's fear that his decisions will conflict with those of other leaders.

There appear, then, to be diverse concepts of leadership, depending on the structure of the gang. Less organized gangs are marked by diffuse and shifting leadership. The more organized gangs have a clear chain of command and leaders who are supposed to plan activities and control members' behavior.[93]

Communications

Gangs seek recognition, both from their rivals and from the community. Image and reputation depend on the ability to communicate to the rest of the world. One major source of communication is **graffiti** (see Figure 9.5). Gang graffiti gives insights into gang rivalries, affiliation, and territory in a given community. Gang graffiti may include the elements, as described in Exhibit 9.3.

These wall writings are especially elaborate among Latino gangs, who call them *placasos* or *placa*, meaning "sign" or "plaque." Latino graffiti usually contains the writer's street name and the name of the gang. Strength or power is asserted through the terms *rifa*, which means to rule, and *controllo*, indicating that the gang controls the area. Another common inscription is "p/v," for *por vida*; this refers to the fact that the gang expects to control the area "for life." The numeral 13 signifies that the gang is *loco*, or wild. Crossed-out graffiti indicates that a territory is contested by a rival gang.

Gangs also communicate by means of a secret vocabulary. Members may refer to their crew, posse, troop, or tribe. Within larger gangs are "sets" who hang in particular neighborhoods, and "tips," small groups formed for particular purposes.

In some areas, gang members communicate their membership by wearing jackets with the name of their gang on the back. In Boston neighborhoods, certain articles of clothing (e.g., sneakers) are worn to identify gang membership. In Los Angeles, the Crips are identified with the color blue and will wear some article of blue clothing to communicate their allegiance; their rivals, the Bloods, identify with the color red.

graffiti
Inscriptions or drawings made on a wall or structure and used by delinquents for gang messages and turf definition.

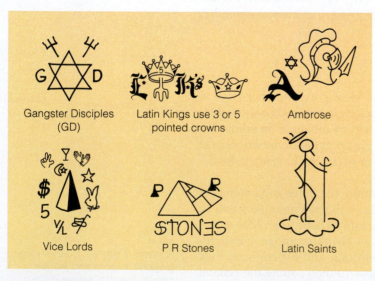

Gangster Disciples (GD)

Latin Kings use 3 or 5 pointed crowns

Ambrose

Vice Lords

P R Stones

Latin Saints

figure 9.5

Gang Symbols Used in Graffiti

SOURCE: Provided by Illinois State Police, http://www.isp.state.il.us/docs/5-572.pdf (accessed October 2016).

exhibit 9.3

Elements of Gang Graffiti

- *The name and/or initials of the gang* and, if relevant, its overall affiliation (Crips/Bloods/Sureños/Folks, etc.).

- *Threats or challenges to rivals.* These may include abbreviations such as BK for Blood Killer, CK for Crip Killer, or rival gang names with the word Killer or Killa. The number 187, common in gang graffiti around the United States, represents the California Penal Code for homicide. Rival gangs also may be threatened or "disrespected" by crossing their names out with an X or a line, or by writing insults or slurs next to their names.

- *Hints about the history of the gang*, such as telephone area codes, territorial markers, and street names from the gang's originating area.

- *A roll call or list of the gang members' nicknames.* Gang members often refer to one another by their nicknames and may not know the first and/or last names of fellow gang members. These nicknames often describe something about the gang members, such as physical appearance or personality. Names with the number 2 or higher behind them indicate there is more than one person in the gang with that nickname. When reading the graffiti, one can often easily determine that the scribe is either the first or the last moniker listed. As a matter of respect, a scribe may list monikers of his close associates first and his own last. However, if the same graffiti is done in a rival gang's turf, the scribe is likely to list his moniker first to let the rival gang know that it was he who initiated the insult and marked his territory.

- *Statements bragging about the gang's reputation.* These include words such as *loc/loco* ("crazy") and *rifamos* ("the best").

SOURCE: Michelle Arciaga, Wayne Sakamoto, and Errika Fearbry Jones, "Responding to Gangs in the School Setting," *National Gang Center Bulletin, 2010,* http://www.nationalgangcenter.gov/Content/Documents/Bulletin-5.pdf (accessed October 2016).

Hand Signs   Several years ago, a young woman was at a dance concert in Milwaukee, Wisconsin, when she was so carried away by the music that she jumped on stage and started to dance with the band. While dancing she used sign language to convey the message, "I love you," over and over. What she did not realize was that her gestures were almost identical to the Latin Kings hand sign, a turn of events that enraged several Latin Kings members on the dance floor; they perceived her hand signing as blatant disrespect to the Almighty Latin King and Queen Nation. Her innocent gestures cost the woman her life, as the FBI found out subsequently during a gang conspiracy investigation of the Latin Kings.[94]

Gang hand signs are quickly displayed with the fingers, hands, and body, and they have specific meanings to gang members. Hand signs are a powerful nonverbal form of communication because a quick flash of the hand can be used to announce gang affiliation or to issue a challenge or insult to a rival. They have been used by gangs for quite some time, beginning with Chinese triads. Some common hand signs are shown in Figure 9.6.

Similar to signing, **posting** is a system of positions, facial expressions, and body language to convey a message. Gang boys may hold their chin up to display their feeling of defiance and arrogance, or they may cross their arms and intently stare at someone to show their feeling of disapproval or as a challenge.

Flashing or tossing gang signs in the presence of rivals often escalates into a verbal or physical confrontation. Chicago gangs call this **representing**. Gang members will proclaim their affiliation and ask victims, "Who do you ride?" or "What do you be about?" An incorrect response will provoke an attack. False representing can be used to misinform witnesses and victims.

Tattoos   Gang tattoos are used to communicate an individual's membership in a gang. Many tattoos are messages, such as "outlaw," "thug life," "1%er," among others, and serve as expressions of gang mentality and do not specify any particular gang.

Though tattoos can be a sign of gang membership, they are also used by nonmembers.[95] The spider web is used by street and prison gangs, but it is also worn as a decorative tattoo by civilians. Worn by a gang member, the spider web indicates that the individual has served or is currently serving time in prison and is "caught in the web" of the justice system; it can also mean they are caught in the web of the gang lifestyle.

To view current examples of **gang graffiti** and learn to interpret what they mean, visit this website:

http://discovermagazine.com/2012/sep/25-the-graffiti-code-breaker.

posting
A system of positions, facial expressions, and body language used by gang members to convey a message.

representing
Tossing or flashing gang signs in the presence of rivals, often escalating into a verbal or physical confrontation.

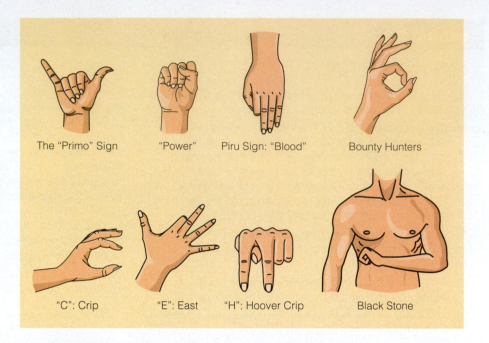

figure 9.6

Gang Hand Signs

SOURCE: Adapted from Gang Signs, http://zimmer
.csufresno.edu/~haralds/htmlfiles/gang-signs.html
(accessed October 2016).

The "Primo" Sign | "Power" | Piru Sign: "Blood" | Bounty Hunters

"C": Crip | "E": East | "H": Hoover Crip | Black Stone

Another universal tattoo, three dots, can be found anywhere on the body but often on the hand or near the eye, and means *mi vida loca*, or "my crazy life." It can also represent Christianity's holy trinity, or three places gang life will lead: hospital, cemetery, or prison.

Another of these commonly used tats, a theater-masks tattoo with "Smile Now, Cry Later" or "Laugh Now, Cry Later," symbolizes the philosophy of doing what you need to do to enjoy life now, because tomorrow you may be dead or in prison. It can also mean stay strong now and deal with whatever life brings later.

Though tattoos have played a major role in gang culture, they may be losing favor since they signal law enforcement that the bearer is a gang member. Many gang members are either avoiding tattoos or placing them inconspicuously on the body, such as inside the lip.

Digital and Cyber Communication   While tattoos and graffiti are the traditional methods of gang communications, gang boys now operate in the digital world as well. Street gangs typically use the voice and text messaging capabilities of cell phones to conduct drug transactions and arrange meetings with customers. Savvy to monitoring by law enforcement, members of street gangs use prepaid cell phones which they discard after conducting their drug-trafficking operations.

As the Cyber Delinquency feature indicates, gangs use social media to communicate along with the rest of American youth.

Ethnic and Racial Composition

According to the National Youth Gang Survey, African American and/or Hispanic youth predominate among documented gang members. Law enforcement agencies report a greater percentage of Hispanic and African American gang members compared with other races/ethnicities. Today about 49 percent of gang members are Hispanic, 35 percent African American, 9 percent white, and 7 percent other race/ethnicity, such as Asian. However, the racial composition of gangs varies considerably by locality. For example, white gang membership is lowest in larger cities (8 percent) but significantly higher in other area types, including rural counties (17 percent), where the rate is more than twice as high.[96]

The ethnic distribution of gangs corresponds to their geographic location; the racial/ethnic composition of gangs is an extension of the characteristics of the larger community.[97] In Philadelphia and Detroit, the overwhelming majority of

CYBER DELINQUENCY

Gangs in Cyberspace

Gang communications have entered the cyber age, and gang members often use social media to communicate and promote their illicit activities. Internet-based methods such as social networking sites, texting, and instant messaging are commonly used by gang members to communicate with one another and with drug customers. Gang members use social networking sites such as Instagram, YouTube, and Facebook as well as personal web pages to communicate and boast about their gang membership and related activities. Social media sites provide gangs with a platform to recruit new members, either through direct communication or indirectly through videos that spread the gang's brand and boast the benefits of the gang lifestyle.

Take these cases for instance:

- BMS, a combination of the Black MOB and Skanless gangs in California, used social media sites like Instagram, Facebook, YouTube, and Twitter to lure unwitting young girls into the gang lifestyle with rap videos and promises of a glamorous life. These girls were then forced into sex trafficking.

- A member of a neighborhood-based gang in the Bronx, New York, posted rap videos on YouTube espousing violence and the gang lifestyle. In response, he received text messages containing requests to join the gang. For example, he received a text message stating, "I'm from Queens but I watch all ya videos. Imma trying be down with the WTG Move." The rapper responded, "You can be WTG under me and b official" in exchange for $125.67.

- The BBE 900 gang in Cleveland invested illicit proceeds to create rap videos that were posted on social media sites and used to recruit new members, build the BBE 900 brand, and raise the intimidation factor.

Traditionally, gangs have demarcated their territory by spray painting their name, signs, and symbols on structures throughout their communities. Now they are using social media as "electronic graffiti walls." Messages and pictures posted on these electronic graffiti walls provide gangs with new avenues to mark their territory and communicate messages to rivals while spreading the gang's name.

According to open source reporting, as of February 2015, the Nike and Jordan gangs in Omaha, Nebraska, used YouTube to create and post rap videos that disrespected each other. Depicted in the videos, gang members used gang signs, counted drug money, and brandished guns. At the end of some videos, they encouraged viewers to add them as friends on Facebook and followers on Twitter.

Scott Decker and David Pyrooz conducted a survey of gang members, former members, and non-gang members in order to measure involvement in online criminal activities, and asked them about their participation in eight forms of online crime over the prior six months. The online crimes included:

- Illegally downloading movies, music, or software
- Selling stolen property online
- Conducting drug sales via the Internet
- Harassment
- Coordinating assaults online
- Searching online to find targets to rob or steal
- Uploading deviant videos (typically of fights)
- Assaults that took place in the street that were motivated by an online communication

A higher percentage of gang members reported participating in most of the offense types. The differences were most pronounced for illegal downloads, uploading deviant videos (typically fights and gang activities), and assaults on the street that were precipitated by online activities. In addition, they compared the overall prevalence of online offending across the three groups, and found that 43 percent of current gang members committed an offense online in the last six months, compared to less than one-third of former and non-gang members.

Decker and Pyrooz concluded that over the course of the past 10 years, Internet use has penetrated new groups, created new activities, and changed old ways of behavior. Gangs have been a part of these changes as well. In comparing gang members to non-gang members and former gang members, it is clear that the impact of gang membership on crime also holds for online criminal activities. Gang members were involved in all eight crime types at a higher level than the other groups. In addition, their overall involvement in these crime types was significantly higher than the other groups, nearly twice as high.

CRITICAL THINKING

There have been recent scandals over government monitoring of electronic communications, including the Net. Considering the expanding use of cyberspace by gangs to enhance their criminal activity, do you believe such monitoring by the government is justified?

SOURCES: Scott H. Decker and David Pyrooz, "Gang Offending and Online Behavior," *JRSA Journal* 30 (2012), http://www.jrsa.org/pubs/forum/sep2012_30-3/Gang_Offending_and_Online_Behavior.htm; National Gang Intelligence Center, *National Gang Threat Assessment, 2015*, https://www.fbi.gov/file-repository/stats-services-publications-national-gang-report-2015.pdf. (URLs accessed October 2016.)

---

gang members are African American. In New York and Los Angeles, Latino gangs predominate. Newly emerging immigrant groups are making their presence felt in gangs. Authorities in Buffalo, New York, estimate that 10 percent of their gang population is Jamaican. A significant portion of Honolulu's gangs is Filipino.

African American Gangs The first black youth gangs were organized in the early 1920s.[98] Since they had few rival organizations, they were able to concentrate on criminal activity rather than defending their turf. By the 1930s, the expanding number of rival gangs spawned inner-city gang warfare.

Gang signs and graffiti are important methods of communication among gang members. Flashing the wrong sign at the wrong time can lead to violent confrontations. Here, a Cambodian teen gang member, Boney, flashes a gang sign outside his home in Long Beach, California.

In Los Angeles, the first black youth gang formed in the 1920s was the Boozies. This gang virtually ran the inner city until the 1930s. In the next 20 years, a number of black gangs, including the Businessmen, Home Street, Slauson, and Neighborhood, emerged and met with varying degrees of criminal success. In the 1970s, the dominant Crips gang was formed. Other gangs merged into the Crips or affiliated with it by adding "Crips" to their name, so that the Main Street gang became the Main Street Crips. The dominance of the Crips has since been challenged by its archrivals, the Bloods. Both of these groups are heavily involved in drug trafficking.

In Chicago, the Blackstone Rangers dominated illicit activities for almost 25 years, beginning in the 1960s and lasting into the early 1990s, when its leader, Jeff Fort, and many of his associates were indicted and imprisoned.[99] The Rangers, who later evolved into the El Rukn gang, worked with "legitimate" businessmen to import and sell heroin. Earning millions in profits, they established businesses that helped them launder drug money. Though many of the convictions were later overturned, the power of El Rukn was ended.

One of the Rangers' chief rivals, the Black Gangster Disciples, morphed into the dominant gang in Chicago. They have a structure, activities, and relationships similar to traditional organized crime. Members are actively involved in politics through the formation of the "Growth and Development" movement. Gangster Disciples registered voters from the inner city and then "encouraged" the newly registered voters to vote for candidates loyal to their cause. While incarcerated, the Black Gangster Disciples will unite with allied gangs under the guise of the Brothers of Struggle (BOS). The gang continues to be involved in large-scale drug trafficking, murders, and white-collar crime.[100] They also have extensive ownership of "legitimate" private businesses. They offer protection against rival gangs and supply stolen merchandise to customers and employees.[101]

Today a number of African American gangs have a national presence across the United States; three of the largest are Black P. Stone Nation, Bloods, and Crips:

- *Black P. Stone Nation* consists of seven highly structured street gangs with a single leader and a common culture. Most of its estimated 6,000 to 8,000 members are African American males from the Chicago metropolitan area. The gang's main source of income is the street-level distribution of cocaine, heroin, marijuana, and, to a lesser extent, methamphetamine. Members also are involved in many other types of criminal activity, including assault, auto theft, burglary, carjacking, drive-by shootings, extortion, homicide, and robbery.

- *Bloods* is an association of structured and unstructured gangs that have adopted a single-gang culture. The original Bloods were formed in the early 1970s to provide protection from the Crips street gang in Los Angeles. Large, national-level Bloods gangs include Bounty Hunter Bloods and Crenshaw Mafia Gangsters. Bloods membership is estimated to be 7,000 to 30,000 nationwide; most members are African American males. Bloods gangs are active in 123 cities in 33 states. The main source of income for Bloods gangs is street-level distribution of cocaine and marijuana. Bloods members also are involved in transporting and distributing methamphetamine, heroin, and PCP (phencyclidine), but to a much lesser extent. The gangs also are involved in other criminal activity, including assault, auto theft, burglary, carjacking, drive-by shootings, extortion, homicide, identity fraud, and robbery.

A. Ramey/PhotoEdit Inc.

- *Crips* is a collection of structured and unstructured gangs that have adopted a common gang culture. Crips membership is estimated at 30,000 to 35,000; most members are African American males from the Los Angeles metropolitan area. Large, national-level Crips gangs include 107 Hoover Crips, Insane Gangster Crips, and Rolling 60s Crips. Crips gangs operate in 221 cities in 41 states. The main source of income for Crips gangs is the street-level distribution of powder cocaine, crack cocaine, marijuana, and PCP. The gangs also are involved in other criminal activity such as assault, auto theft, burglary, and homicide.[102]

African American gang members have some unique characteristics. They frequently use nicknames. In South Carolina, the personal moniker "Shotgun" would indicate the bearer's weapon of choice; a female gang member might call herself "Big Mama Blood" to show she is affiliated with the Bloods and that she means business.[103] The three most popular categories of black gang members' nicknames in Las Vegas are combinations of any single letter of the alphabet with a Loc, Mac, or Wak—for example, X-Loc, P-Mac, D-Wak. The next most popular nicknames are Dre or Baby with any letter following—Baby-X, for example.[104] In Baltimore, nicknames that were once benign, such as "Peanut King," have become more sinister: "Murder," "Killer," "Savage," and various forms of the word "bloody." Young gang members tattoo their names on their necks and arms, and ink teardrops under their eyes, one for each person they've killed.[105]

African and Caribbean Gangs   Immigrants from African nations such as the Sudan are also forming large gangs in the United States. Somali nationals—mostly refugees displaced by the wars in Somalia and surrounding countries—have migrated to low-income communities where Somali youth admire and emulate the local gangs, such as Bloods and Crips, as well as Ethiopian gangs. In 2010, 29 suspected Somalian gang members were indicted for a prostitution trafficking operation.[106] Over a 10-year period, Somalian gang members transported underage females from Minnesota to Ohio and Tennessee for prostitution. Other Somali gang members have been arrested for murdering drug dealers and engaging in home invasion robberies.

Along with Africa, youth from Caribbean nations have engaged in gang activity. According to the National Gang Intelligence Center (NGIC), Haitian gangs have proliferated in many states in recent years and are now present in Connecticut, Florida, Georgia, Indiana, Maryland, Massachusetts, New Jersey, New York, North Carolina, South Carolina, and Texas. The Zoe Pound gang, founded in Miami by Haitian immigrants, is involved in drug trafficking, robbery, and related violent crime. In February 2010, 22 suspected Zoe Pound members in Chicago were charged with possession of and conspiracy to traffic powder and crack cocaine from Illinois to Florida, according to FBI reporting.[107] The Haitian Boys Posse and Custer Street gang are involved in a myriad of criminal activities, including drug and weapons trafficking, robberies, shootings, and homicides along the East Coast.

Hispanic Gangs   The popularity of gangs and gang culture is relatively high among youth of Hispanic background, explaining in part their disproportionate participation in gang membership.[108] Take for instance the feared MS-13 gang, begun in Los Angeles by Salvadorans fleeing a civil war. When they first arrived in Los Angeles, they were preyed upon by preexisting Mexican gangs. The MS-13 gang was formed as a means of self-protection. The name refers to a *mara*, Spanish slang for "posse" or gang. *Salvatruchas* is local slang for being alert and ready to take action; 13 is a reference to their beginnings on 13th Street in Los Angeles.

Over time, the gang's ranks grew and members entered a variety of rackets, from extortion to drug trafficking. When law enforcement cracked down and deported members, the deportees quickly created outposts in El Salvador and throughout Central America. The Salvadoran government has responded by criminalizing gang membership and arresting thousands. But government efforts have not stemmed the tide of recruitment, and the gangs appear to be more popular than ever.[109]

Developing alongside MS-13 were their main rivals, the 18th Street gang. This group began as an offshoot of a preexisting Los Angeles gang, the Clanton 14 (named after a street in the gang's home neighborhood). The Clanton gang had been active in Los Angeles for decades and had also become quite choosy in its membership, rejecting recent Mexican immigrants and Chicanos. Those rejected formed their own gang and named it the 18th Street gang. Today, 18th Street gang members can be identified by their tattoos, most common the number 18, which is usually represented in Roman numerals (XVIII). Although 18th Street maintains a stronghold in several Southern California cities, members have migrated throughout the nation.[110]

Latino gangs such as MS-13 and the 18th Street gang have continued to grow and now constitute the largest number of gangs and gang memberships. Some experts believe that MS-13 is now the nation's most dangerous gang. Others claim that the 18th Street gang is the largest; membership estimates range from 8,000 to 15,000. Exhibit 9.4 describes another of the largest national Latino gangs.

Hispanic gangs are made up of youths whose ethnic ancestry can be traced to one of several Spanish-speaking cultures. They are known for their fierce loyalty to their "home" gang. Admission to the gang usually involves an initiation ritual in which boys are required to prove their *machismo*. The most common test requires novices to fight several established members or to commit some crime, such as a robbery. The code of conduct associated with membership means never ratting on a brother or even a rival.

In some areas, Hispanic gangs have a fixed leadership hierarchy. However, in Southern California, which has the largest concentration of Hispanic youth gangs, leadership is fluid. During times of crisis those with particular skills will assume command. One boy will lead in combat while another negotiates drug deals.

Hispanic gang members are known for their dress codes. Some wear dark caps pulled down over the ears with a small roll at the bottom. Others wear a folded bandana over the forehead and tied in back. Another popular headpiece is the "stingy brim" fedora or a baseball cap with the wearer's nickname and gang affiliation written on the bill. Members favor tank-style T-shirts that give them quick access to weapons.

Members mark off territory with colorful and intricate graffiti ("tagging"). Hispanic gang graffiti has very stylized lettering and frequently uses three-dimensional designs. Hispanic gangs have a strong sense of turf, and a great deal of gang violence is directed at warding off any threat to their control. Slights by rivals, including put-downs, stare-downs ("mad-dogging"), defacing gang insignia, and territorial intrusions, can set off a violent confrontation, often with high-powered automatic weapons. The Case Profile, "Luis's Story," examines one Latino gang member who was able to turn his life around.

exhibit 9.4

Almighty Latin King and Queen Nation

The Latin Kings street gang was formed in Chicago in the 1960s and consisted predominantly of Mexican and Puerto Rican males. Originally created with the philosophy of overcoming racial prejudice and creating an organization of "kings," the Latin Kings evolved into a criminal enterprise operating throughout the United States under two umbrella factions—Motherland, also known as KMC (King Motherland Chicago), and Bloodline (New York). All members of the gang refer to themselves as Latin Kings, and, currently, individuals of any nationality are allowed to become members. Latin Kings associating with the Motherland faction also identify themselves as the Almighty Latin King Nation (ALKN) and make up more than 160 structured chapters operating in 158 cities in 31 states. The membership of Latin Kings following KMC is estimated to be 35,000.

The Bloodline was founded by Luis Felipe in the New York State correctional system in 1986. Latin Kings associating with Bloodline also identify themselves as the Almighty Latin King and Queen Nation (ALKQN). Membership is estimated to be more than 7,000, divided among several dozen chapters operating in 15 cities in 5 states. Bloodline Latin Kings share a common culture and structure with KMC and respect them as the Motherland, but all chapters do not report to the Chicago leadership hierarchy. The gang's primary source of income is the street-level distribution of powder cocaine, crack cocaine, heroin, and marijuana. Latin Kings continue to portray themselves as a community organization while engaging in a wide variety of criminal activities, including assault, burglary, homicide, identity theft, and money laundering.

SOURCE: FBI, National Gang Threat Assessment, 2011, https://www.fbi.gov/stats-services/publications/2011-national-gang-threat-assessment/; National Gang Intelligence Center, National Gang Report, 2015.

case profile

Luis's Story

LUIS was a 16-year-old Latino male who identified himself as gang involved. After a fight at a party with a rival gang member, he was charged with substantial battery and resisting arrest. Luis already had a history of truancy and a police record for several thefts, vandalism, underage drinking, and curfew violations. He was smoking marijuana on a daily basis, not attending school, and had experienced little success in the educational environment outside of sports. Luis also exhibited significant anger management concerns and was viewed as a threat to the community.

His family was supportive but apprehensive about his behavior. Luis's mother was very involved in his life and was doing her best to raise her four children without any assistance or involvement from their father. Luis had felt like "the man of the family" from an early age. Within their family culture, Luis, being the oldest male, felt responsible for caring for his mother and younger siblings. He had joined a gang around the age of 11 in hopes that it would provide additional protection for his family. Despite numerous concerns from his family and the juvenile court, following his arrest Luis was allowed to return home until the next juvenile court proceeding. He was referred for electronic monitoring and an intensive home supervision program.

Luis arrived at his initial juvenile court plea hearing intoxicated and belligerent. His family was concerned that Luis was using drugs and alcohol and that he needed treatment, but the prosecuting attorney did not agree and petitioned for him to be sent directly to a juvenile correctional facility. While the next court hearing was pending, Luis participated in an alcohol and drug assessment, and it was recommended that he enter a residential treatment facility for his drug use and alcohol issues, anger management problems, and gang involvement issues. During the wait between court proceedings, he was involved in an intensive supervision program where he received individual counseling, group treatment, monitoring of his whereabouts and school activities, family and individual crisis intervention, and significant redirection regarding his choices. He was also referred to an alternative school program where his chances for success would be better. Luis's mother was hopeful that the services would assist him and that Luis would start to turn his life around.

At the dispositional hearing, there was disagreement regarding the best plan for Luis, and a contested hearing took place. The prosecuting attorney again wanted him sent directly to a juvenile correctional facility. The defense attorney argued that Luis needed alcohol and drug treatment, as well as other services, and that he should be sent to an inpatient treatment facility that had agreed to take him. Luis's probation officer and his family all advocated for him to get treatment rather than the correctional placement. He had been doing better in the community setting with the additional services and supports. The judge listened to all of the testimony and expressed concerns regarding Luis's juvenile court involvement record and the safety of the community. At the same time, she wanted to give him a chance to be successful in drug treatment. In the end, the judge ordered Luis to the juvenile correctional facility, but "stayed" the order, permitting Luis to enter treatment. This "stay" meant that if Luis left the treatment facility, or if he was terminated from the program, he would automatically go to juvenile corrections. If he was successful in treatment, he would most likely return to the community with the needed supports and services. If at any time Luis decided not to cooperate with the community aftercare plans, or if he had any further law violations, he could also be immediately sent to juvenile corrections. Luis and his family seemed to understand the seriousness of the situation and Luis agreed to treatment.

Luis entered the voluntary 90-day alcohol and drug treatment program and began to work on his sobriety, anger issues, gang involvement, and criminal thinking concerns. Luis's mother came to visit on a regular basis and participated in family sessions, though it was difficult to coordinate, given her work schedule and responsibility for the other children in the household. The involved professionals assisted with coordinating child care and arranging transportation so she could be there for Luis, who struggled at first and had a hard time adjusting to the rules of the facility. His mother and the team encouraged him to remain in treatment and try to focus on a positive future, and they reminded him of the "stayed" correctional order. Luis ultimately decided to engage in treatment and he completed the 90-day program.

The team of professionals, along with Luis and his mother, created an aftercare plan that initially included ongoing drug counseling and support, individual counseling, intensive supervision and monitoring, group supports, and placement in an alternative educational setting. Through the alternative school, Luis got involved in a program that offered troubled youth the experience of building homes for underprivileged families. Luis gained valuable work skills, as well as time to focus on positive activities. Though he still struggled with school, with his past gang involvement, and with making good choices, he was able to significantly decrease his police contacts and he had no further arrests as a juvenile. Luis remained living at home with his mother and siblings and was eventually released from the juvenile court–ordered services. The "stayed" correctional order was in place until the juvenile court closed the case upon Luis's 18th birthday.

CRITICAL THINKING

1. Unlike Luis, many kids are not helped and remain in gangs longer than ever before. Do you see a way, considering the global economy, to wean kids out of gangs? Are there any alternatives? What about easing the entry requirements for the military? As you may recall, Laub and Sampson's age-graded theory argues that a military career can help people "knife off" from crime (see Chapter 6).

2. Luis's mother was very involved in his life and says she was doing her best to raise her four children without any assistance or involvement from their father. Could this family situation have been a pivotal factor in Luis's decision to join a gang? What can be done to help kids in this situation?

Asian Gangs   Asian gangs are prominent in New York, Los Angeles, San Francisco, Seattle, and Houston. The earliest gangs, the Wah Ching, were formed in the nineteenth century by Chinese youths affiliated with adult crime groups (*tongs*). In the 1960s, two other gangs formed in San Francisco, the Joe Boys and Yu Li, and they now operate, along with the Wah Ching, in many major US cities. National attention focused on the activities of these Chinese gangs in 1977 when a shootout in the Golden Dragon restaurant in San Francisco left 5 dead and 11 wounded.

In addition to Chinese gangs, Samoan gangs have operated on the West Coast, as have Vietnamese gangs. The formation of Vietnamese gangs can be tied to external factors, including racism and economic problems, and to internal problems, including family stress and failure to achieve the success enjoyed by other Asians. Vietnamese gangs are formed when youths feel they need their *ahns*, or brothers, for protection.[111]

While most Asian gangs are local or regional, some now have a national presence. For example, the Tiny Rascal Gangsters is one of the largest and most violent Asian street gang associations in the United States. It is composed of at least 60 structured and unstructured gangs, commonly referred to as sets, with an estimated 5,000 to 10,000 members and associates who have adopted a common gang culture. They are most active in the Southwest, West Coast, and New England. The Rascals specialize in street-level distribution of powder cocaine, marijuana, ecstasy, and methamphetamine. Members also are involved in other criminal activity, including assault, drive-by shootings, extortion, home invasion, homicide, robbery, and theft.[112]

Asian gangs are unique and do not share many qualities with other ethnically centered groups. They tend to victimize members of their own ethnic group. They are more organized, have recognizable leaders, and are far more secretive than black or Hispanic groups. They tend to be far less territorial and less openly visible. Asian gangs are also known for the strict control gang elders have over younger members. Elders, some of whom may be in their 30s and 40s, are no longer engaged in street crime and violence but may instead be involved in other forms of illegal activities such as running gambling parlors, drug and human trafficking, and white-collar crime. In New England and California, Asian gangs maintain marijuana cultivation houses specifically for the manufacturing and distribution of high potency marijuana and pay members of the Asian community to reside in them—and not to talk.

They use the younger gang members to protect their business interests and to collect any unpaid gambling debts. In some jurisdictions, police can pressure the elders to control the violent tendencies of the younger members by threatening to crack down on their illegitimate business enterprises (i.e., having patrol cars parked in front of suspected gambling locations).[113]

Anglo Gangs   The first American youth gangs were made up of white ethnic youths of European ancestry. During the 1950s, they competed with African American and Hispanic gangs in the nation's largest cities. National surveys indicate that today less than 10 percent of gang members are white European Americans. Prevalence rates of white gang membership is lowest in larger cities (8 percent) but significantly higher in other area types, including rural counties, where the rate is more than twice as high. These gangs often organize around white supremacy and the **skinhead** culture.

skinhead
Member of a white supremacist gang, identified by a shaved skull and Nazi or Ku Klux Klan markings.

White gang boys are also being recruited by extremist groups, because recruiting gang members enables these groups to expand and spread their doctrine. Gangs then use these groups and their teachings for a number of reasons, including the ability to exploit Freedom of Religion rights; to increase membership and collaboration with other criminal organizations; and to respond to perceived injustices by attempting to enact social change, often by engaging in criminal activity.

The Internet has made it easy to recruit alienated white youth who are exposed to online message forums and social networking sites that are antigovernment and anti-immigration. Factors that contribute to growth of these gangs include the following:

- The white power music industry has experienced a substantial growth in on-line promotion and sales.

- Racist skinhead groups such as Hammerskin Nation and Blood & Honor have expanded globally, using the Internet to connect with chapters online.

- There is less competition from older white supremacist groups, whose activity has diminished due to the arrests or deaths of leaders.[114]

Hybrid Gangs Another recent phenomenon, hybrid gangs are devoted to making money through illegal activities such as drugs, robbery, and prostitution and are not territorial or homogenous in their makeup. Because criminal enterprise is their sole objective, hybrid gangs recruit from different racial/ethnic groups. They may even have openly gay members, something that would rarely be seen in traditional gangs.[115]

Hybrid gangs modify traditional gang culture with their personal interpretations and agendas and are more fluid in their rules and codes of behavior. Some members may belong to a variety of gangs and shift their allegiance when they believe a profitable criminal enterprise may be in the works. In sum, hybrid gangs involve:

- A mixture of racial/ethnic groups

- A mixture of symbols and graffiti associated with different gangs

- Wearing colors traditionally associated with a rival gang

- Less concern over turf or territory

- Members who sometimes switch from one gang to another[116]

Criminality and Violence

The most recent gang survey (2015) shows that street gang activity continues to be oriented toward violent crimes, such as assault, street-level and large-scale drug trafficking, home invasions, homicide, robbery, intimidation, threats, weapons trafficking, and sex trafficking. There are regional differences in gang crime: in the west, methamphetamine sales are common; in the north and south central states, gangs are more likely to traffic in cocaine; in the south and northeast, gangs are involved in dealing and trafficking heroin. The amounts generated by these crimes are substantial. One California-based gangs, the Hoover Crips, trafficked approximately $10 million of cocaine and marijuana that they bought from Mexican drug cartels and then distributed through Dallas, Oklahoma City, and Tulsa before going through Ohio to the northeastern United States.[117]

Regardless of their type, gang members typically commit more crimes than any other youths in the social environment.[118] Members self-report significantly more crime than nonmembers, and the more enmeshed a youth is in a gang, the more likely he is to report criminal behavior, to have an official record, and to get sent to juvenile court. The gang membership–crime relationship begins as early as middle school.[119]

While the association between gang membership and delinquency is unquestioned, there are actually three different explanations for the relationship:

- *Selection hypothesis*. Kids with a history of crime and violence join gangs and maintain their persistent delinquency once they become members.

- *Facilitation hypothesis*. Gang membership facilitates deviant behavior because it provides the structure and group support for antisocial activities.

- *Enhancement hypothesis*. Selection and facilitation work interactively, increasing the likelihood of enhanced criminality.[120]

Gang criminality has numerous patterns.[121] While it is commonly believed that gangs specialize in drug dealing, the major players in the drug importation and distribution business tend to be adults, not gang youths.[122] Nor does it appear that gang membership increases the personal use of drugs: kids who used drugs before they joined gangs continue to do so, but joining a gang does not encourage substance abuse. While gang boys may be dealers, they are not necessarily users.[123] Although gangs do not necessarily encourage drug use, it is still quite common. Geoffrey Hunt and his associates found that 82 percent of the female gang members they surveyed were multiple-drug users, using drugs such as cocaine, crack, LSD, PCP, methamphetamine, heroin, glue/inhalants, MDMA, and Quaaludes.[124]

Other gangs engage in a wide variety of criminal activity, ranging from felony assaults to drug dealing.[125] Gang members are most commonly involved in such crimes as larceny/theft, aggravated assault, and burglary/breaking and entering; a significant portion are involved in low-level street drug sales to generate profits for the gang.[126]

Do gang kids increase their involvement in criminal activity after they join gangs, or do gangs recruit kids who are already high-rate offenders? Data from the Rochester Youth Development Study (RYDS), a longitudinal cohort study of 1,000 youths in upstate New York, support the gang–crime association theory. Although only 30 percent of the youths in the sample report being gang members, they account for 65 percent of all reported delinquent acts. The RYDS data show that gang members account for 86 percent of all serious crimes, 63 percent of the alcohol use, and 61 percent of the drug abuse.[127] Gang members ratchet up their criminal activities. In the RYDS study, 66 percent of the chronic violent offenders were gang members.[128] So even among youth who have previously hung out with delinquent friends, joining a gang elevates their involvement in violent behaviors.[129]

Gang Violence   Research shows that gang members are more violent than nonmembers. Chris Melde and Finn-Aage Esbensen found that active gang members experienced a significant increase in violent behavior activities. After leaving the gang, their propensity for violence declined significantly, becoming no different from that of kids who had never been in a gang.[130] One reason is that kids who join gangs are also more likely to carry weapons than are nonmembers.[131] Terence Thornberry and his associates found that young gang members in Rochester, New York, were about 10 times more likely to carry handguns than nongang juvenile offenders, and gun-toting gang members committed about 10 times more violent crimes than nonmembers.[132] Richard Spano and John Bolland collected data on gang boys in Mobile, Alabama, and found that members who were exposed to violence and engaged in violent behavior themselves increased the likelihood of carrying a gun by 665 percent over kids who were neither exposed to violence nor engaged in violent acts themselves.[133]

It is not surprising, then, that youth gangs are responsible for a disproportionate number of homicides. About 2,000 gang-related homicides occur each year, about 13 percent of the total in the United States. In a typical year in the so-called "gang capitals" of Chicago and Los Angeles, around half of all homicides are gang-related; these two cities alone account for approximately one in four gang homicides.[134]

Research indicates that gang violence is impulsive and therefore comes in spurts. It usually involves defense of the gang and gang members' reputations.[135] Once the threat ends, the level of violence may recede, but it remains at a level higher than it was previously. Peaks in gang homicides tend to correspond to a series of escalating confrontations, usually over control of gang turf or a drug market.[136] The most dangerous areas are along disputed boundaries where a drug hot spot intersects with a turf hot spot. There are also "marauder" patterns in which members of rival gangs travel to their enemy's territory in search of victims.[137]

Violence is a core fact of gang formation and life.[138] Gang members feel threatened by other gangs and are wary of encroachments on their turf. It is not surprising that gangs try to recruit youths who are already gun owners; new members are likely to increase gun ownership and possession.[139] Gang members face a far greater chance of death at an early age than do nonmembers.[140]

Revenge, Honor, Courage, and Prestige While many boys are predisposed toward violence before joining a gang, research shows that once in gangs their violent behavior quickly escalates; after they leave, it significantly declines.[141] A recent study by Andrew Papachristos of gang homicide supports the association between cultural values and violence.[142] Papachristos finds that members do not kill because they are poor or young or live in a socially disadvantaged neighborhood, but rather because they live in a culture that maintains norms conducive to violent retaliation. When a gang boy kills a rival, murders spread through a process of social contagion as gangs are forced to respond in order to maintain their social status and honor through a display of solidarity. The culture that houses gangs associates honor with hypermasculinity and the use of violence to protect reputation. Because formal social control (i.e., the police) is absent in gang areas, violence is condoned or promoted as an acceptable form of social control. The need to conform to cultural values and to protect the gang's rep is more important than individual thoughts and feelings.

These motivations for gang violence were confirmed by criminologist Scott Decker during his interviews with gang boys who told him that violence is essential to the transformation of a peer group into a gang. When asked why he calls the group he belongs to a gang, one member replied, "There is more violence than a family. With a gang it's like fighting all the time, killing, shooting."[143]

When joining the gang, members may be forced to partake in violent rituals to prove their reliability. Gang members are ready to fight when others attack them or when they believe their territory or turf is being encroached upon. Violence may be directed against rival gang members accused of insults or against those involved in personal disputes. Gang members also expect to fight when they go to certain locations that are "off-limits" or attend events where violence is routine. A girl gang member may fight when she senses that a member of a rival gang is trying to hook up with her boyfriend. Gini Sykes spent two years hanging with girl gangs in New York City in order to develop an understanding of their lives and lifestyle. One girl, Tiny, told her how ferociousness made up for her lack of stature:

> Tiny fixed me with a cold stare that wiped away any earlier impression of childish cuteness. "See, we smaller girls, we go for your weak spot." Her gaze moved across my features. "Your face. Your throat. Your eyes, so we can blind you. I don't care if you have more weight on me. I'll still try to kill you because, you know, I have a bad temper."[144]

Tiny related the story of how she attacked a rival whom she caught in a sexual encounter with her boyfriend:

> "She was crying and begging, but she'd disrespected me in front of everybody. We started fighting and she pulled that blade out—." Tiny shrugged. "I just wasn't prepared. You can't tell when someone's got a razor in their mouth."

After she was cut, Tiny went into a defensive rage, and

> . . . frantically felt for the wound, blood seeping between her fingers. Suddenly, in self-preservation, she grabbed the girl's neck, and blinded by her own blood, began smashing her rival's head into the concrete until Isabel, hearing a siren, dragged her away. The girl had slashed Tiny's face eleven times.

Gang members are sensitive to any rivals who question their honor. Once an insult is perceived, the gang's honor cannot be restored until the "debt" is repaid. Police efforts to cool down gang disputes only delay the revenge, which can be a beating or a drive-by shooting. Random acts of revenge have become so common that physicians now consider them a significant health problem—a major contributor to early morbidity and mortality among adolescents and children in major gang cities.[145]

Violence is used to maintain the gang's internal discipline. If subordinates disobey orders, perhaps by using rather than selling drugs, they may be subject to disciplinary action by other gang members.

prestige crimes
Stealing or assaulting someone to gain
prestige in the neighborhood; often part of
gang initiation rites.

Another common gang crime is extortion, called "turf tax," which involves forcing people to pay the gang to be protected from dangerous neighborhood youths. **Prestige crimes** occur when a gang member steals or assaults someone to gain prestige in the gang. These crimes may be part of an initiation rite or an effort to establish a special reputation, a position of responsibility, or a leadership role; to prevail in an internal power struggle; or to respond to a challenge from a rival.

Organized Crime and Gangs   While the general public may associate gangs with violent acts such as drive-by shootings, some also equate gangs with organized crime such as large-scale drug dealing. There is no question that in particular communities in certain cities, youth gangs are very active in drug trafficking. However, the common stereotypes of the relationships between youth gangs, drug trafficking, and violence are often overblown. Youth gang expert Malcolm Klein finds distinctions between youth gangs and organized criminal cartels. To remain in business, he argues, organized crime groups must have strong leadership, codes of behavior enforced by the threat of severe sanctions, and a membership with a level of expertise and sophistication that enables them to accumulate and invest the proceeds of illegal activity. They can safely import narcotics and launder the proceeds of drug deals.[146] In contrast, his studies show that most street gangs are only loosely structured, with transient leadership and membership, easily transcended codes of loyalty, and informal rather than formal roles for the members.[147] As a result, very few youth gangs meet the essential criteria for classification as "organized crime." Youth gang involvement in the drug trade is mainly in street-level distribution rather than large-scale importation and distribution, activities that are managed by adult drug cartels or syndicates, traditional narcotic importers, and other adult criminal organizations. However, while they may not fit the classic definition of organized crime syndicates, youth gangs can become integrally involved in existing, adult-based distribution systems. Where drug-related violence occurs, it mainly stems from drug use and dealing by individual gang members and from gang member involvement in adult criminal drug distribution networks more than from drug-trafficking activities of the youth gang as an organized entity.

Why Do Youths Join Gangs?

Though gangs flourish in inner-city areas, gang membership cannot be assumed to be solely a function of lower-class identity. Many lower-class youths do not join gangs, and middle-class youths can be found joining gangs. Let's look at some of the suspected causes of gang delinquency.

The Anthropological View

In the 1950s, Herbert Block and Arthur Niederhoffer suggested that gangs appeal to adolescents' longing for the tribal process that sustained their ancestors.[148] They found that gang processes do seem similar to the puberty rites of some tribal cultures; gang rituals help the child bridge the gap between childhood and adulthood. For example, tattoos and other identifying marks are an integral part of gang culture. Gang initiation ceremonies are similar to the activities of young men in Pacific Island cultures. Many gangs put new members through a hazing to make sure they have "heart," a feature similar to tribal rites. In tribal societies, initiation into a cult is viewed as the death of childhood. By analogy, boys in lower-class urban areas yearn to join the gang and "really start to live." Membership in the gang "means the youth gives up his life as a child and assumes a new way of life."[149] Gang names are suggestive of "totemic ancestors" because they usually are symbolic (e.g., Cobras, Jaguars, and Kings).

The Gang Prevention and Intervention Survey found that fully two-thirds of gang members reported having members in their gang whose parents are also active members. These data indicate that ganging is passed on as a rite of passage from one generation to the next.[150] James Diego Vigil has described the rituals of gang initiation, which include pummeling to show that the boy is ready to leave his matricentric (mother-dominated) household; this is reminiscent of tribal initiation rites.[151] These rituals become an important part of gang activities. Hand signs and graffiti have a tribal flavor. Gang members adopt nicknames that reflect personality or physical traits: The more volatile are called "Crazy," "Loco," or "Psycho" and someone very thin might be called "Flaco."[152]

The Social Disorganization/Sociocultural View

Sociologists have commonly viewed the destructive sociocultural forces in poor inner-city areas as the major cause of gang formation. Thrasher introduced this concept, and it is found in the classic studies of Richard Cloward and Lloyd Ohlin and of Albert Cohen.[153] Irving Spergel's study *Racketville, Slumtown, and Haulburg* found that Slumtown—the area with the lowest income and the largest population—had the highest number of violent gangs.[154] According to Spergel, the gang gives lower-class youths a means of attaining status. Malcolm Klein's research of the late 1960s and 1970s also found that typical gang members came from dysfunctional and destitute families and lacked adequate role models.[155]

The social disorganization/sociocultural view retains its prominent position today. In their in-depth study of Rochester youth, Thornberry and his colleagues found that those who joined gangs suffered from a multitude of social problems, including early involvement in delinquency, violence, and drug abuse, dysfunctional family relations, educational deficits, and involvement with deviant peers.[156]

In *Barrio Gangs*, Vigil shows that gang members are pushed into membership because of poverty and minority status. Those who join gangs are the most marginal youths in their neighborhoods and families. Vigil finds that barrio dwellers experience psychological, economic, and social "stressors."[157] Gang members usually have more than one of these problems, causing them to suffer from "multiple marginality." Barrio youths join gangs seeking a sense of belonging.[158]

Overall, the sociocultural view assumes that gangs are a natural response to lower-class life and a status-generating medium for boys who cannot realize their aspirations by legitimate means. Youths who join gangs may hold conventional goals but are either unwilling or unable to accomplish them through conventional means.[159] Gangs are not made up solely of youths who seek deviant peers to compensate for parental brutality or incompetence. They recruit youths from many different kinds of families. The gang thus is a coalition of troubled youths who are socialized mainly by the streets rather than by conventional institutions.[160]

AP Images/Press Association

Gang violence can be experienced around the world. This gang in Manchester, England, included (top row, from left) Michael Lee, Liam Brogan, Lewis Tracy; (middle row, from left) Connor Browitt, Joshua Tracey, Katy Sharrock; (bottom row, from left) Callum Doran, Connah Doran, and Amanda Browitt. The gang, including boys and girls as young as 12, racially abused locals, vandalized property, and harassed, threatened, and intimidated anyone who stood up to them. One neighbor told police, "Some of these kids are so small, some might think it unbelievable for us to be terrified of them, but they were very menacing indeed. They would wander around the estate like a pack of wild dogs—they always seemed to be together. To us they were the wild runts."

The Anomie/Alienation View

According to this view, conditions of anomie/alienation encourage gang formation on both a cultural and individual level. On a cultural level, youths are encouraged to join gangs during periods of social, economic, and cultural turmoil.[161] Immigration or emigration, rapidly expanding or contracting populations, and the incursion of different racial/ethnic groups, or even different segments or generations of the same racial/ethnic population, can create fragmented communities and gang problems.[162]

On an individual level, gang membership appeals to adolescents who are alienated from the mainstream of society. It is not surprising that (a) kids who have had problems with the law and suffer juvenile justice processing are more likely to join gangs than nonstigmatized kids and (b) joining gangs further involves them in criminal activities.[163]

The Family Tradition/Learning View

Some youths join gangs because they are following in their parents' footsteps; they have learned the benefits of gang membership.[164] One recent study of Mexican American gang members found that almost three-quarters of gang boys were raised in households where relatives participated in illegal activities, and more than half had relatives who use drugs. Boys whose parents were in or had been in gangs were more likely to have prolonged rather than temporary gang membership.

While family tradition encourages kids to join gangs, the effect of neighborhood and community factors cannot be discounted. Gang families are more likely than not to live in areas with limited employment, and meager social and educational opportunity within the community shapes the experiences of these adolescents. These conditions necessitate that they maintain bonds with their families that oftentimes include drug use and criminally involved members.

The Psychological View

Some experts believe that gangs serve as an outlet for disturbed youths who experience a host of personal trials and tribulations. Some may have experienced childhood trauma, while others were seriously neglected, both precursors of psychological disturbance. It comes as no surprise, then, that gang members show signs of dissociation and emotional numbing (callous-unemotional traits) as well as post-traumatic stress disorder.[165]

In a classic study, Lewis Yablonsky found that violent gangs recruit their members from among the more sociopathic youths living in poverty-stricken communities.[166] Yablonsky views the sociopathic youth as one who "has not been trained to have human feelings or compassion or responsibility for another."[167]

Malcolm Klein's analysis of Los Angeles gang members also found that many suffer from a variety of personal deficits, including low self-concept, social deficits, poor impulse control, and limited life skills.[168]

The Rational Choice View

Some youths may make a rational choice to join a gang. They give out "signals"—doing poorly in school and getting suspended, willing to use violence in public places such as school, carrying a gun, having a family member in a gang, getting arrested, seriously injuring someone—behaviors that say to gang leaders that this would be a topflight recruit.[169]

Why does a potential member send out a signal? Some kids may turn to gangs as a method of obtaining desired goods and services, either directly, through theft and extortion, or indirectly, through drug dealing and weapons sales. In this case, joining a gang can be viewed as an "employment decision." Mercer Sullivan's study of Brooklyn gangs found that members call success at crime "getting paid." Gang boys also refer to the rewards of crime as "getting over," which refers to their pride at "beating the system," even though they are far from the economic mainstream.[170] According to this view, the gang boy has long been involved in criminal activity *prior* to his gang membership, and he joins the gang as a means of improving his illegal "productivity."[171]

Gang membership is *not* a necessary precondition for delinquency. Felix Padilla found this when he studied the Diamonds, a Latino gang in Chicago.[172] The decision to join the gang was made after an assessment of legitimate opportunities. The Diamonds made collective business decisions, and individuals who made their own deals were penalized. The gang maintained a distinct structure and carried out other functions similar to those of legitimate enterprises, including recruiting personnel and financing business ventures.

Drug use is a big part of the gang experience, and drug users may join gangs to enhance availability of drugs and support for their usage.[173] Terence Thornberry and his colleagues at the RYDS found that before youths join gangs, their substance abuse and delinquency rates are no higher than those of nongang members. When they are in the gang, their crime and drug abuse rates increase, only to decrease when they leave the gang. Thornberry concludes that gangs facilitate criminality rather than provide a haven for youths who are disturbed or already highly delinquent. This research is important because it lends support to the life-course model: events that take place during the life cycle, such as joining a gang, have a significant impact on criminal behavior and drug abuse.[174]

Personal Safety   Many gang boys are gun owners before they join, giving off a signal that they are worried about personal safety; they carry guns for defensive measures.[175] According to Irving Spergel, these adolescents may choose to join gangs from a "rational calculation" to achieve safety.[176] Youths who are new to a community may believe they will be harassed or attacked if they remain "unaffiliated." Girls also join gangs for protection. Though they may be exploited by male gang members, they are protected from assaults by nongang males in the neighborhood.[177]

Motivation may have its roots in inter-race or inter-ethnic rivalry; youths who reside in an area dominated by a different racial or ethnic group may be persuaded that gang membership is a means of protection. Ironically, gang members are more likely to be attacked than nonmembers.

Fun and Support   Some youths join gangs simply to have fun.[178] They enjoy hanging out with others like themselves and want to get involved in exciting experiences. There is evidence that youths learn pro-gang attitudes from their peers and that these attitudes direct them to join gangs.[179]

Some experts suggest that youths join gangs in an effort to obtain a family-like atmosphere. Many gang members report that they have limited contact with their parents, many of whom are unemployed and have substance abuse problems.[180] Those members who have strained family relations are also the ones most likely to be involved in the most serious and frequent criminal activity.[181] Kids may join gangs to compensate for the lack of a family life experienced at home.

The Thug Lifestyle   Some kids enter the gang life because they want to enhance a chosen "thug" lifestyle. They choose ganging because it celebrates deviance and criminality, values they have already embraced.[182] Where does the thug style come from? In some instances, kids see older boys in the neighborhood acting tough and getting respect. Sometimes, the thug style emulates the dress, swagger, and lingo of media gangsters such as Tony Montana from the cult movie *Scarface*. Set in 1980s Miami, the film's protagonist, Tony (played by Al Pacino), is a determined

Cuban immigrant who uses street smarts, toughness, and callous brutality to take over a drug empire, becoming enormously rich and powerful before succumbing to greed and his own psychological demons. Tony's analysis of how the American system works symbolizes the thug lifestyle:

> In this country, you gotta make the money first. Then when you get the money, you get the power. Then when you get the power, then you get the women.

Young gang boys want to embrace the movie gangster lifestyle and fatalism. They are ready to shoot it out with rival gang members and with the cops. In this "outlaw" world, gang boys can make their own rules, do what they want, and take what they wish without worrying about the consequences. It is a lifestyle where respect is demanded and power rules. Thugs enjoy their ability to use violence to gain vengeance against their enemies or to demonstrate their criminal skills. And like Tony Montana, their prowess is envied and rewarded with respect and financial gain. Just as a doctor, lawyer, or police officer identifies with his profession and gains self-worth from his professional calling and successes, self-esteem for many who choose to join a gang becomes dependent on their thug exploits. These views of why youths join gangs are summarized in Concept Summary 9.1.

Leaving the Gang

While there is quite a bit of speculation on why kids join gangs, less is known about why they leave. And most do leave in a relatively short time. Despite popular sayings such as "Blood in, Blood out," the majority of gang boys and girls remain in the gang for one year or less.

There seem to be two distinct patterns of gang desistance. Some gang members suddenly leave the gang.[183] One reason for the abrupt termination of gang activity may be exposure to violence long associated with ganging. The more kids are bound to their gang, the more likely they will become a crime victim.

The second pattern is a slow, gradual departure from gang membership precipitated by an ongoing change in lifestyle. This member leaves the gang because he gets married and begins spending more time with family and work than he does with the gang. Rather than an abrupt departure, desistance may be part of a slow maturation process in which the gang member turns emotionally from the

CONCEPT SUMMARY 9.1

Views of Gang Formation

View	Premise	Evidence
Anthropological	Gangs appeal to kids' tribal instincts	Use of totems, signs, secret languages, and symbols
Sociocultural	Gangs form because of destructive sociocultural forces in disorganized inner-city areas	Concentration of gangs in inner-city areas
Anomie/Alienation	Alienated kids join gangs; anomic social and economic conditions encourage gang activity	Upswing in gang activities after market force creates anomic situations Gang activity increases with globalization
Family tradition/Learning	Parents encourage children to follow them into the gang	Presence of fathers, sons, and brothers in the same gang
Psychological	Kids with personality problems form gangs and become leaders	Antisocial, destructive behavior patterns Increase in violence
Rational choice	Kids join gangs for protection, fun, survival, and to enhance their lifestyle	Presence of party gangs, gang members Protect one another

youth STORIES

Lisa's Story

Lisa started "kicking it with the homies" in her Los Angeles neighborhood when she was 13. By the time she was in high school, she was heavily into drugs and "hitting up and shooting up" with the gang. With her younger sister as her "crime partner," Lisa finally got the attention she was looking for. It wasn't long before she caught the eye of an older gang member. At 28, he was considered a shot-caller who commanded the respect of the younger gang members. Lisa assumed he made his money selling drugs, but she didn't ask, and he didn't talk about it. When Lisa got pregnant at 17, the couple married and moved to Chicago. As it turned out, Lisa's suspicions regarding her husband's income only hinted at a much more complicated reality: the Windy City was home base for an international drug cartel, and her new husband worked as a runner between Chicago and Mexico.

In her unexpected role as a mother of one and then two children, and wife to a drug lord, Lisa felt trapped. "I had all the glamour," she said, "but no friends or family. I practically had a double life. My husband had a different name, I couldn't talk to anybody, and he was never there." When her husband was killed in a drug feud, Lisa moved back to Los Angeles and shortly thereafter was incarcerated on charges of accessory to murder (in an unrelated case). She was a young widow separated from her children, with a long list of addictions and no hope for recovery.

After prison, Homeboy Industries was Lisa's off-ramp, as it is for other previously incarcerated and formerly gang-involved men and women who seek the agency's services. For more than 25 years and for thousands of clients, Homeboy has served as a beacon of hope in Los Angeles, illuminating an alternative route for those traumatized by the intergenerational cycle of gang violence. Lisa entered Homeboy's paid 18-month job training program, where she began working in maintenance and was quickly promoted to an administrative position.

During their time at Homeboy, clients are assigned case managers who help them chart an individualized course through therapy and additional services tailored to their needs. Classes include computer basics, bridge to college, building healthy relationships, parenting, domestic violence, and anger management. Clients participate in 12-step groups, have visible tattoos removed, obtain their GEDs, and work with mental health professionals to deal with the traumas they have experienced. Employment counselors assist clients with the creation of résumé's and guide them in setting career-oriented goals.

Lisa's words evoke what so many participants at Homeboy experience: "Because of the program, I'm finally getting the taste of a free world." In less than a year at Homeboy, Lisa has obtained her driver's license—an achievement a judge once deemed "impossible"—and is working to be granted visitation of her children. She has moved to a safer neighborhood and is saving money to pursue her longtime dream of becoming a makeup artist. The Homeboy model of therapeutic community served as a catalyst in changing both Lisa's thoughts and her behaviors regarding her future. "Before, I hated life. I felt like I was always a disappointment to everyone. Here, people look up to me as I transform my life."

A UCLA longitudinal, mixed-methods study of Homeboy Industries, currently being conducted by Todd Franke and Jorja Leap, has begun to document the shift in identity towards prosocial behaviors and the decrease in antisocial activities. In a subsample of 50 individuals followed over four years, 38 have expressed their belief that identity or the sense of self is a core issue, and that their involvement in the Homeboy program has allowed them to change. According to Leap, "Every sample member openly admitted to having belonged to a gang or neighborhood, but the majority invariably added, 'I have moved on,' or 'That's not part of me anymore.'" What the research has begun to demonstrate through both quantitative and qualitative measures is that effective reentry is achieved by replacing the conditional acceptance of gang membership with the unconditional love of a therapeutic community. Lisa's experience exemplifies this shift: "What makes us a family is that we try to help each other. We feel each other's pain."

CRITICAL THINKING

Should tax money be used to help get kids out of gangs by providing them with jobs or job training? Or should those resources just be used for law-abiding teens?

SOURCE: National Gang Center Newsletter, "Bonds of Compassion," Spring/Summer 2014, https://www.nationalgangcenter.gov/Content/Newsletters/NGC-Newsletter-2014-Spring-Summer.pdf (accessed October 2016).

---

gang toward conventional activity. For girls, motherhood and family may be the impetus for leaving the gang.[184] The Youth Stories feature focuses on one young woman who was able to change her life patterns and leave the gang life.

Regardless of the method of departure, leaving the gang reduces involvement in crime and delinquency, and also in violence and victimization. Not all members can leave; some are too enmeshed in the gang. But those who do significantly reduce their victimization risk.[185]

Controlling Gang Activity

The presence of gangs instills fear in community residents, and fear of gang intimidation, vandalism, graffiti, and drugs is very great in the most gang-infested communities. One study in Orange County, California, found that, not surprisingly, fear of crime and gangs was an "immediate" daily experience for people who lived in lower-income neighborhoods where gangs were most common. But there was also a spillover effect: fear of gangs and gang violence was present even if gangs were not an immediate danger or fixture in the neighborhood.[186] In the most gang-ridden areas, intimidation of other youths, adults, and business owners is not uncommon, and intimidation of witnesses or potential witnesses is particularly serious because it undermines the justice process.

Because gangs are now a national threat, there has been a concerted effort to control gang activity. In fact, the federal government has formed a National Gang Intelligence Center to acquire information on gangs and coordinate prevention efforts. A number of approaches have been tried, some involving efforts to control or deter gang activity through tough legal sanctions backed up by effective law enforcement. Another approach involves social service efforts designed to provide alternatives to gang membership. Both of these methods will be discussed in the next sections.

Legal Controls

A number of states have created laws specifically designed to control gang activity. One approach has been to create enhanced penalties for behaviors typically associated with gang members. Take for example drive-by shootings, a form of retaliation popular with gangs. A number of states have passed legislation increasing penalties for such behavior and adding sanctions to control its reoccurrence (e.g., the driver loses his license). Arizona's drive-by shooting law is set out in Exhibit 9.5.

Other jurisdictions have made it a crime to recruit gang members, to engage in organized gang activity, and to loiter for the purpose of carrying out gang business. Some cities have gone as far as passing anti-graffiti measures to curb the proliferation of written gang messages and threats. Exhibit 9.6 shows Denver's anti-graffiti statute.

Legal Injunctions   A civil gang injunction (CGI) is a preliminary or permanent court order issued in a civil case against a criminal street gang and its members to enjoin (prohibit) certain behavior within a defined safety zone, which may include associating together in public or violating trespass and curfew laws. The

---

exhibit 9.5

Drive-By Shooting Statute: Arizona

A. A person commits a drive-by shooting by intentionally discharging a weapon from a motor vehicle at a person, another occupied motor vehicle, or an occupied structure.

B. A motor vehicle from which a person commits a drive-by shooting is subject to seizure for forfeiture in the manner provided for in chapter 39 of this title.

C. Notwithstanding title 28, chapter 4, the judge shall order the surrender to the judge of any driver's license of the convicted person and, on surrender of the license, shall invalidate or destroy the license and forward the abstract of conviction to the department of transportation with an order of the court revoking the driving privilege of the person for a period of at least one year but not more than five years. On receipt of the abstract of conviction and order, the department of transportation shall revoke the driving privilege of the person for the period of time ordered by the judge.

D. Drive-by shooting is a class 2 felony.

SOURCE: Arizona State Legislature, "Arizona 13-1209. Drive-by shooting; driver's license revocation; classification; definitions."

exhibit 9.6

Anti-graffiti Statute: Denver, Colorado

Sec. 34-66. Possession of graffiti materials by minors prohibited

(a) It shall be unlawful for any person under the age of eighteen (18) years to possess any can of spray paint, broad tipped marker pen, glass cutting tool, or glass etching tool or instrument.

(b) A broad tipped marker pen is one with a tip that exceeds one-quarter (1/4) inch in width.

(c) It shall be an affirmative defense to charges under this section that the person possessing the materials was:

(1) Within their home;

(2) At their place of employment; or

(3) Upon real property with permission from the owner, occupant, or person having lawful control of such property, to possess such materials. (Ord. No. 424-95, § 1, 6-12-95)

SOURCE: City of Denver, https://www.denvergov.org/portals/712/documents/penalties.pdf (accessed October 2016).

goal is to abate a public nuisance caused by the conduct and activities of a gang. A public nuisance is an unreasonable interference with the comfortable enjoyment of life and property that affects an entire community. CGIs are most effective against a multigenerational turf-based criminal street gang with deep roots that openly commits criminal and nuisance activity in its own turf.[187]

The injunctions are aimed at disrupting gang activity before it can escalate into violence. Some jurisdictions, such as Fort Worth and San Francisco, have filed lawsuits against gangs and gang members, asking courts for injunctions barring them from hanging out together on street corners, in cars, or in particular areas. The injunctions can prohibit gang members from associating with each other, carrying weapons, possessing drugs, committing crimes, and displaying gang symbols in a safety zone—neighborhoods where suspected gang members live and are most active. Some injunctions set curfews for members and ban them from possessing alcohol in public areas, even if they're of legal drinking age. Those who disobey the order face a misdemeanor charge and up to a year in jail. In some cases, such injunctions don't allow gang members even to talk to people passing in cars or to carry spray paint.[188] Some libertarian organizations consider these restrictions as overreaching and violating civil rights.

Some appellate courts have restricted the scope of gang injunctions. In a 2001 case, *People v. Englebrecht*, the California Court of Appeal ruled that prosecutors must first prove through clear and convincing evidence that a person is a gang member before using an antigang injunction to restrict his or her right to engage in everyday activities. The case involved David Englebrecht, a 26-year-old father of three who despite not being a gang member was placed under a civil injunction designed to combat a local gang. Under the injunction, Englebrecht was prohibited from making loud noises, whistling, wearing certain clothing, using certain words or hand gestures, or being seen in public with other alleged gang members within an approximately one-square-mile area of Oceanside, California. Despite recognizing that the case involved a mistake of fact (i.e., Englebrecht was not a gang member), the court decided to render a decision that means that all nongang members will have greater protection against being wrongfully and arbitrarily subjected to court restrictions on their ordinary daily activities.[189]

If successful, these injunctions give police legal reasons to stop and question gang members, who often are found with drugs or weapons. When a CGI is issued, gang members with a history of committing felonies involving guns, narcotics, and intimidation abruptly quit associating in public with other gang members. Moreover, they obey the other provisions of the CGI, violation of which is a misdemeanor. The results of a CGI project are reduced criminal and nuisance gang activity, as well as a better quality of life for the people who live and work in the neighborhood.[190]

Law Enforcement Efforts

As gangs have spread from the central city to ring city, suburban, and even rural areas, police departments have responded by creating specialized gang-control units. Research shows that if gang members fear apprehension and punishment they will be as likely to be deterred as any other offender, hence police efforts to increase deterrence levels.[191] Knowing this outcome, police may be more likely to arrest known gang members than other misbehaving youth.[192]

Gang control takes three basic forms:

- *Youth services programs*, in which traditional police personnel, usually from the youth unit, are given responsibility for gang control
- *Gang details*, in which one or more police officers, usually from youth or detective units, are assigned exclusively to gang-control work
- *Gang units*, established solely to deal with gang problems, to which one or more officers are assigned exclusively to gang-control work

Today, about one in four law enforcement agencies with a gang problem operate a gang unit, including more than half of larger cities. According to the National Gang Center, across all area types, agencies with long-standing gang problems and/or higher numbers of documented gang members are more likely to report operating a gang unit. Some programs rely on intelligence gathering, aggressive enforcement, and "gang-breaking" activities. They attempt to arrest, prosecute, convict, and incarcerate gang leaders. The Chicago Police Department's gang crime section maintains intelligence on gang problems and trains its more than 400 officers to deal with gang problems. Officers identify street gang members and enter their names in a database that alerts the unit if the youths are picked up or arrested.

Gang Sweeps Many large police departments maintain gang units that engage in **gang sweeps**, a method of enforcement in which police, armed with arrest and search warrants, enter a neighborhood in force in an operation to make as many arrests as possible. Each department has its own method of sweeping up known gang members. In Las Vegas, gang-unit officers split into teams, each assigned to its own squad car. One pair of officers will patrol down a "hot street"—a street or area where gang members are known to hang out and conduct drug sales. Two other pairs in squad cars patrol the two streets immediately parallel to the hot street, keeping pace with the lead car. The fourth squad car remains out of sight at the end of the street, slowly patrolling toward the other three. This tactic squeezes gang members toward the center of the targeted area and allows easy pursuit if a suspect tries to flee. The Las Vegas police department has also formed a prevention section within the gang crimes bureau to integrate gang prevention and intervention efforts into policing and to strengthen the department's existing program efforts. The prevention section specializes in the development of gang prevention programs in coordination with other community and law enforcement partners and coalitions.[193]

gang sweep
A method of enforcement in which police, armed with arrest and search warrants, enter a neighborhood in force in an operation to make as many arrests as possible.

Technological Enforcement Gangs are now exploiting technology to shield their activities from law enforcement efforts. They seek the anonymity of instant messaging and the use of aliases on social media. Gang members are using video messaging applications to communicate that are difficult for law enforcement to monitor. They transmit via the Internet and leave no record of transmission on the device to be seized in police raids.[194]

To counteract gang efforts of technological concealment, Net-based technology is now frequently used in police antigang efforts. Most police agencies today maintain databases that allow sharing of gang intelligence and gang-related crime statistics with law enforcement agencies in other jurisdictions. A growing number of law enforcement agencies are incorporating social media into their gang investigations, specifically to identify gang members and monitor their criminal activity.

Police Intervention Strategies   Other departments take a more treatment-oriented intervention approach. Take for instance the Gang Intervention Through Curfew Enforcement program used in Akron, Ohio.[195] A small detail of gang-unit officers is assigned to conduct neighborhood sweeps in high-crime and gang neighborhoods to take the juveniles off the street who are at highest risk of gang membership, gang violence, or gang victimization. When juveniles are arrested for violation of the curfew ordinance, they are transported to a rehabilitative program center known as Oriana House. Here the juveniles receive counseling and are advised on how to stay out of street gangs. Parents or guardians are notified to pick up their child, and upon arrival at the program site, they are given educational materials designed to help them prevent their kids from becoming involved in gangs. A follow-up call is made by gang-unit officers to the parents or guardians of the suspected gang members to further reinforce the educational materials provided at Oriana House. Target sites are determined by locating gang parties, suspected gang fight locations, and known drug-trafficking spots used by gang members to "post up" and sell drugs.

Community-Policing Strategies   Some communities use community-policing strategies to combat gang activity, in which police officers are assigned to keep the peace in local neighborhoods (community policing will be discussed in more detail in Chapters 12 and 14). For example, Boston's Youth Violence Strike Force (YVSF) is one of the primary enforcement strategies that Boston is pursuing to combat youth gang violence. The YVSF is a multiagency coordinated task force made up of 45 to 50 full-time Boston police officers and others from Massachusetts State Police, the Department of Treasury's Bureau of Alcohol, Tobacco, Firearms, and Explosives (ATF), police departments from neighboring jurisdictions, Massachusetts Corrections, Probation, Parole, and Division of Youth Service (juvenile corrections) officers, and other agencies as appropriate. It works closely with the Suffolk County District Attorney's and state attorney general's offices, and participates in the Department of Justice's Anti-Violent Crime Initiative (AVCI) led locally by the US attorney. The YVSF investigates youth crimes, arrests those responsible, and breaks up the environment for crime. Drug dens have been closed through joint federal-state-local cooperation. Some former drug houses have been renovated to provide low-income elderly housing.

Another program, Operation Night Light, puts the YVSF together with concerned clergy members, youth outreach workers, and social service professionals to prevent youth and gang violence of probationers by regularly visiting their homes. Operation Night Light pairs one probation officer with two police officers to make surprise visits to the homes, schools, and worksites of high-risk youth probationers during the nontraditional hours of 7:00 PM to midnight.

Another gang reduction program begun in Boston is Operation Ceasefire, a problem-oriented policing approach that focuses police attention on specific places that are known for gang activity and gun violence. This program will be discussed in greater detail in Chapter 14; the Evidence-Based Juvenile Justice feature reviews the STEP program in Newport News, Virginia.

Community-Level Programs

During the late nineteenth century, social workers of the YMCA worked with youths in Chicago gangs.[196] During the 1950s, the **detached street worker** program was developed in major centers of gang activity. Social workers went into the community to work with gangs on their own turf. They participated in gang activities and tried to get to know their members. The purpose was to act as advocates for the youths, to provide them with positive role models, and to treat individual problems.

Detached street worker programs are sometimes credited with curbing gang activities in the 1950s and 1960s, although some critics claimed that they turned delinquent

detached street workers
Social workers who go out into the community and establish close relationships with juvenile gangs with the goal of modifying gang behavior to conform to conventional behaviors and help gang members get jobs and educational opportunities.

Newport News STEP Program

One way for businesses to work toward building stronger communities in gang-impacted areas is to provide employment experiences for youth who are at risk for gang involvement or for those who are members of a gang. Productive opportunities and access to work are among the best ways in which youth can realize their aspirations, utilize their potential, positively participate in society, and lead productive lives.

A recommended strategy in youth gang prevention and intervention initiatives is to help these youth gain practical and marketable skills through a comprehensive job-training program. These programs are commonly connected with intensive support services such as one-on-one mentoring, mental health counseling, anger management, substance abuse treatment, and other services that build job readiness skills. The ultimate goal of all these interventions is for youth to be adequately prepared for entry-level employment or internships in today's job market.

An exemplary job-training program is Virginia's Newport News Youth and Gang Violence Initiative's Summer Training and Enrichment Program (STEP). This 10-week program serves young people between the ages of 16 and 24 and provides paid work-training experience, enrichment activities, workshops, financial literacy training, and GED preparation classes. The program is designed to prepare youth for their futures by exposing them to various employment and career options. Young people learn valuable skills such as résumé preparation, job interview techniques, time management, financial management, professional work behavior, and networking. In addition to training, participants are given the opportunity to engage in field trips to various businesses and organizations to gain direct exposure to the business community.

Following an employment prescreening process, these youth are matched with employers, and all receive support and follow-up every step of the way. Youth outreach workers and job-training staff members monitor the youths' progress at their work sites and engage in ongoing communications with employers to ensure a positive experience for both youth and employers. The tremendous value of the partnership between job-training programs and business communities cannot be underestimated.

STEP participants are partnered with a worksite 25 to 30 hours a week to prepare them for the workforce. Through partnerships with city departments, nonprofit organizations, and for-profit businesses, the participants are given a hands-on work experience at their site placements and enrichment activities to expose them to different career options. Each participant in the program receives a biweekly stipend.

The program is considered highly successful. One youth who was living in a condemned house with her mother when she started STEP went on to secure a stable housing situation. Another participant went from believing that the world was against her and that no one was on her side to working well at her site and having faith in society.

Another success story is of two program participants known for always associating with the wrong crowd. Late one night, as their group was preparing to leave, the two STEP participants stated, "We're not going out tonight—we have to get up early for work tomorrow." STEP and the relationship with the employer had imparted a sense of responsibility and led them to make better decisions. Participants themselves reported that the program had kept them off the streets, provided an opportunity to gain good work experience, assisted them financially, and offered them an opportunity to make a difference.

CRITICAL THINKING

Do you think that the STEP program can be effective?

SOURCE: Newport News Youth and Gang Violence Prevention, https://www.nnva.gov/1907/Youth-Gang-Violence-Prevention.

groups into legitimate neighborhood organizations.[197] Others believe they helped maintain group solidarity, and as a result, new members were drawn to gangs.

Today, there are numerous community-level programs designed to limit gang activity. Some employ recreation areas open in the evening hours that provide supervised activities.[198] In some areas, citywide coordinating groups help orient gang-control efforts. In Los Angeles County, the Gang Alternative Prevention Program (GAPP) provides services to juveniles before they become entrenched in gangs, including individual and group counseling, bicultural and bilingual services to adolescents and their parents, and special programs such as tutoring, parent training, job development, and recreational and educational experiences.[199] Some police departments also sponsor prevention programs such as school-based lectures, police–school liaisons, recreation programs, and street worker programs that offer counseling, assistance to parents, and other services. The Stockton, California, police

Many kids who want to leave gangs and join conventional society lack the means to do so. One program designed to ease the way is Homeboy and Homegirl Industries, located in Los Angeles, California. The program was founded in 1992 by Father Gregory Boyle, a Jesuit priest, whose guiding principle was that when people are employed, they're much more likely to lead happy lives because they can be productive and constructive. Youths in the program not only receive access to numerous free services— tattoo removal, counseling, job referrals, and life-skills training—but are able to work (with pay) in the program's several businesses, which include silk-screening, maintenance, and food service, including its own cafe and bakery.

department sponsors a gang intervention called Operation Peacekeeper.[200] It puts outreach workers, who are former gang members themselves, on the street to support kids who want to leave gangs. The program includes monthly forums where known gang members are offered information about available programs as well as a warning that they are being watched. Operation Peacekeeper has been credited with a drop in gang-related homicides and has been praised because outreach workers are able to form bonds with youths unavailable to uniformed officers.

Still another approach has been to involve schools in gang-control programs. Some invite law enforcement agents to lecture students on the dangers of gang involvement and teach them gang-resistance techniques. Others provide resources that can help parents prevent their children from joining gangs, or if they are already members, get them out.

The Spergel Model   Sociologist Irving Spergel, a leading expert on gangs, has developed a model for helping communities deal with gang-involved youth that has become the basis for gang-control efforts around the nation. Spergel's model of gang prevention has been adopted by the Office of Juvenile Justice and Delinquency Prevention as a model called the Gang Reduction Program. The multimillion-dollar initiative was designed to reduce gang crime in targeted neighborhoods by incorporating research-based interventions to address individual, family, and community factors that contribute to juvenile delinquency and gang activity. The program secured local, state, and federal resources in support of community partnerships that implement progressive practices in the prevention, intervention, and suppression of gang activity.[201] The measures used in these programs have been carefully tested and appear to be valid and effective methods of gang control.

Evaluating Gang-Control Efforts

Because gang activity is so pervasive and sustained in some areas, police agencies view these gangs as organized criminal enterprises and deal with them as traditional organized crime families. The aim is to (a) develop informants through criminal prosecutions, payments, and witness protection programs; (b) rely heavily on electronic surveillance and long-term undercover investigations; and (c) use special statutes that create criminal liabilities for conspiracy, extortion, or engaging in criminal enterprises.[202]

While aggressive police tactics such as these may work, they also run the risk of becoming overzealous and alienating the community. Take for instance Los Angeles's antigang unit, Community Resources Against Street Hoodlums (CRASH), which at its peak contained 200 sworn officers. The unit conducted aggressive antigang actions, including Operation Hammer, which involved the unit moving through some of the city's toughest neighborhoods and arresting gang members for the slightest infractions, including wearing colors, flashing signs, jaywalking, and curfew violations. By making 25,000 arrests per year, the unit significantly reduced gang activity. But problems began to emerge. Unit members developed a warlike mentality, and CRASH officers began resisting supervision and flagrantly ignoring policies and procedures. This subculture eventually gave rise to the Rampart Scandal, in which Rampart CRASH unit officers in Los Angeles were found to be engaging in hard-core criminal activity. Officers admitted to attacking known gang members and falsely accusing them of crimes they had not committed. As a consequence, approximately 10 years after it had been fully staffed and promoted as the ideal in antigang enforcement, LAPD's gang unit was shut down because of corruption, the use of excessive force, and civil rights violations; the city paid out about $70 million to settle lawsuits related to the scandal.[203] The Rampart Scandal serves as a cautionary tale for police departments attempting to control gang activity, but the threat of racial profiling in gang-control efforts still remains an issue. Recent research shows that police are still more likely to target African American gang boys for arrest than they are members from other racial and ethnic groups.[204]

Ironically, these heavy-handed suppression tactics can increase gang cohesion while failing to reduce violence, and keep kids in gangs who would have quit if left to their own devices. In Chicago, a cycle of police suppression and incarceration combined to *sustain* unacceptably high levels of gang violence. Results from Dallas, Detroit, and St. Louis show no evidence of a positive impact on target neighborhoods. Most young people who enter gangs will leave the gang within a year. But law enforcement practices can target former gang members long after their active participation in the gang has ended, and may dissuade employers from offering jobs to former gang members or youth who merely look like gang members.

Because gangs represent only a small part of the crime rate, aggressive suppression tactics simply make the situation worse by alienating local residents and trapping youth in the criminal justice system. More often than not, minority youth are the target of antigang efforts, and their suppression gives people the impression that police are targeting minority kids.

In contrast to suppression tactics, cities that adopted treatment alternatives fared far better. New York City did not embrace the aggressive tactics used in Los Angeles even when gang crime was on the rise and has consequently experienced far less gang violence. When gang violence became a serious problem, the city established a system of well-trained street workers and gang intervention programs, grounded in effective social work practices and independent of law enforcement. Gang experts conclude that the city's serious problem with street gang violence had largely faded away by the 1980s.

The Problems of Reform   Social and economic solutions seem equally challenging. Experts suggest that to reduce the gang problem, hundreds of thousands of high-paying jobs are needed. This solution does not, however, seem practical. Many of the jobs for which undereducated gang boys can qualify are now being shipped overseas. Highly paid manufacturing jobs are particularly hard to obtain. It is unlikely that a boy who has five years as a Crip on his résumé will be in demand for legitimate work opportunities. The more embedded youths become in criminal enterprise, the less likely they are to find meaningful adult work. It is unlikely that gang members can suddenly be transformed into highly paid professionals. As discussed in the Evidence-Based Juvenile Justice feature, programs such as Cure Violence can be successful community-based gang-control programs.

Cure Violence

The Cure Violence (formerly Cease Fire) program has proven to be an effective broad community approach to preventing and reducing gang violence. Undergirded by the public health model, the program approaches violence as an infectious disease. The program tries to interrupt the next event, the next transmission, the next violent activity. Cure Violence targets a small population: members of the community with a high chance of "being shot or being shooters" in the near future. This model prevents violence through a three-pronged approach:

- *Detection and interruption*. Cure Violence is a data-driven model. Statistical information and street knowledge help identify where to concentrate efforts, focus resources, and intervene in violence. These data identify communities most impacted and provide a picture of those individuals at the highest risk for violence.

- *Behavior change*. Cure Violence intervenes in crises, mediates disputes between individuals, and intercedes in group disputes to prevent violent events. Outreach workers counsel clients and connect them with services; violence interrupters engage members of the target population on the street, mediating conflicts between gangs and working to prevent the cycle of retaliatory violence from starting after a violent incident. The core training for employees is related directly to the work and focuses on conflict mediation and response.

- *Changing community norms*. Cure Violence works to change the thinking on violence at the community level and for society at large through the use of public education, community-building activities, and motivational interviewing with the highest risk. For disproportionately impacted communities, violence has come to be accepted as an appropriate—even expected—way to solve conflict. At the street level, Cure Violence provides tools for those most likely to be involved in altercations to resolve conflicts in other ways.

Evaluations of Cure Violence

Multisite evaluations reveal that there were significant changes in gang homicide patterns (e.g., decreases in gang involvement in homicides and fewer retaliatory killings) that could be attributed to the program, but no individual site improved on all outcome measures.

The evaluation of Baltimore's Safe Streets program is the first rigorous evaluation of a replication of Cure Violence. Safe Streets outreach workers mediated 276 incidents. Safe Streets was fully implemented in four of Baltimore's most violent neighborhoods, engaging hundreds of high-risk youth and mediating more than 200 disputes with the potential to lead to a shooting. An evaluation showed statistically significant reductions in all four program sites, with reductions in killings of up to 56 percent and in shootings of up to 44 percent as well as strong evidence of norm change—rejecting the use of violence—in the program community. Reductions spread to surrounding communities. Norms on violence were changed: people in the program site were much less likely to accept the use of a gun to settle a dispute and four times more likely to show little or no support for gun use.

Another evaluation conducted in Chicago showed statistically significant results across all seven communities studied: reductions in shootings and killings of 41 percent to 73 percent, reductions in shooting hot spots of up to 40 percent, and the elimination of retaliation killings in five communities.

CRITICAL THINKING

Cure Violence works to change the culture of violence at the community level through the use of public education, community-building activities, motivational interviewing, and more. Do you believe that an external force, such as a treatment program, can change a street culture that has developed over many years? What else might be done to reduce violence at the community level?

SOURCES: National Gang Center, Cure Violence, http://www.nationalgangcenter.gov/SPT/Programs/139; Cure Violence, http://cureviolence.org/. (URLs accessed October 2016.)

Although social solutions to the gang problem seem elusive, the evidence shows that gang involvement is a socioecological phenomenon and must be treated as such. Youths who live in areas where their needs cannot be met by existing institutions join gangs when gang members are there to recruit them.[205] Social causes demand social solutions. Programs that enhance the lives of adolescents are the key to reducing gang delinquency. Another method is to devote more resources to the most deteriorated urban areas, even if it requires pulling funds from other groups that receive government aid, such as the elderly.[206] The national report of the Justice Policy Institute suggests the following changes be implemented:

- *Expand the use of evidence-based practices to reduce youth crime.* Instead of devoting more resources to the already heavily funded and ineffective gang enforcement tactics, policy makers should expand the use of evidence-based interventions that are scientifically proven to reduce juvenile recidivism.

- *Promote jobs, education, and healthy communities, and lower barriers to the reintegration into society of former gang members.* Gang researchers observe that employment and family formation help draw youth away from gangs. Creating positive opportunities through which gang members can leave their past, as opposed to ineffective policies that lock people into gangs or strengthen their attachments, can help improve public safety.

- *Redirect resources from failed gang enforcement efforts to proven public safety strategies.* Gang injunctions, gang sweeps, and various ineffective enforcement initiatives reinforce negative images of whole communities and run counter to best practices in youth development. The Justice Policy Institute suggests that, instead, localities should end practices that can make the youth violence problem worse, and refocus funds on effective public safety strategies.[207]

SUMMARY

1 Give examples of the influence of peers on delinquency

- In adolescence, friends begin to have a greater influence over decision making than parents.
- In mid-adolescence, kids strive for peer approval and to impress their closest friends.
- Acceptance by peers has a major impact on socialization.
- Peer status during childhood is an important contributor to a child's social and emotional development that follows them across the life course.
- Youths who report inadequate or strained peer relations are the ones most likely to become delinquent.

2 Outline how romantic love influences delinquency

- Delinquent youth actually report frequent contact with their romantic partners.
- Delinquent youth also fight more with their partners and report higher levels of verbal conflict.
- Adolescent sexual activity without the promise of love increases the likelihood of offending because it is associated with strain created by loveless relationships.
- Romantic love has a deterrent effect that actually encourages youth who have offended to decrease their involvement in crime.

3 Analyze the various definitions used to describe gangs

- Gangs are groups of youths who engage in delinquent behaviors.
- Gangs are an interstitial group—one falling within the cracks and crevices of society.

- Members have self-recognition of their gang status and use special vocabulary, clothing, signs, colors, graffiti, and names.
- There is a commitment to criminal activity, although even the most criminal gang members spend the bulk of their time in noncriminal activities.

4 Discuss the history of gangs

- In the 1600s, London was terrorized by organized gangs that called themselves Hectors, Bugles, Dead Boys, and other colorful names.
- In the 1920s, Frederick Thrasher initiated the study of the modern gang in his analysis of more than 1,300 youth groups in Chicago.
- According to Thrasher, gangs form because society does not meet the needs of lower-class youths.
- In the 1950s and early 1960s, the threat of gangs and gang violence swept the public consciousness.
- Interest in gang activity began anew in the early 1970s.
- One reason for the increase in gang activity may be involvement in the sale of illegal drugs.

5 Identify the extent and location of the gang problem

- At recent count, an estimated 850,000 gang members were active in the United States.
- Traditionally, gangs have operated in large urban areas experiencing rapid population change.
- While some people think of gangs as a purely urban phenomenon, thousands of gangs are located in small cities, suburban counties, and even rural areas.

- Because of redevelopment, gangs in some areas have relocated or migrated; gang members have organized new chapters when they relocate to new areas.

6 List the various forms contemporary gangs take

- There are different types of gangs, including the social gang, party gang, serious delinquent gang, and organized gang.
- Gangs are near-groups, which have limited cohesion, impermanence, minimal consensus of norms, shifting membership, disturbed leadership, and limited definitions of membership expectations.

7 Characterize the globalization of gangs

- Changing social and economic conditions in our post-globalization world support the spread of gang activity.
- One reason is that our global society has increased the percentage of people living in extreme poverty in some areas of the world.
- Globalization creates a class that benefits from expanding markets and a group of very poor who can be recruited by gangs.
- Globalization means that information and weapons are readily available anywhere in the world.
- Numerous gangs operate in distressed areas such as the townships of South Africa where they rule politically and control the underground economy.
- Gangs are now being exported from one nation to another.
- In the global era, the state has retreated from its role of providing social welfare and an economic safety net. Gangs and other groups of armed young men occupy the vacuum created by the retreat of the social welfare policies of the state.

8 Describe female gangs and gang members

- There are a variety of reasons why girls join gangs, including but not limited to financial opportunity, identity and status, peer pressure, family dysfunction, and protection.
- Ganging can provide girls with a sense of sisterhood, independence, and solidarity, as well as a chance to earn profit through illegal activities.

- Once in gangs, girls form close ties with other female members and engage in group criminal activity.
- Female gang members begin to drift away from gangs when they become young mothers.

9 Compare the various theories of gang formation

- The anthropological view is that gangs appeal to adolescents' longing for the tribal process that sustained their ancestors. Hand signs and graffiti have a tribal flavor.
- Sociologists have commonly viewed the destructive sociocultural forces in poor inner-city areas as the major cause of gang formation.
- Some believe that gangs serve as an outlet for disturbed youths who suffer a multitude of personal problems and deficits.
- Some youths may make a rational choice to join a gang.
- Some youths join gangs simply to have fun.

10 Summarize the various forms of gang-control efforts in use today

- A number of states have created laws specifically designed to control gang activity.
- One approach has been to create enhanced penalties for behaviors typically associated with gang members.
- Some jurisdictions have filed lawsuits against gangs and gang members, asking courts for injunctions barring them from hanging out together on street corners, in cars, or in particular areas.
- Today, about one in four law enforcement agencies with a gang problem operates a gang unit, including more than half of larger cities.
- Gang sweeps are a method of enforcement in which police, armed with arrest and search warrants, enter a neighborhood in force in an operation to make as many arrests as possible.
- Another approach is to provide jobs, counseling, education, and social opportunities for former gang members.

KEY TERMS

QUESTIONS FOR DISCUSSION

1. Does the emergence of hybrid gangs indicate that the juvenile gang is a form of organized crime?

2. What are the differences among violent, criminal, and drug-oriented gangs?

3. How do gangs in suburban areas differ from inner-city gangs?

4. Do delinquents have cold and brittle relationships with their peers?

5. Can gangs be controlled without changing the economic opportunity structure of society? Are there any truly meaningful alternatives to gangs today for lower-class youths?

6. Can you think of rituals in society that reflect an affinity or longing for more tribal times? (Hint: Have you ever pledged a fraternity or sorority, gone to a wedding, or attended a football game?) Do TV shows like *Survivor* show a longing for more tribal times? After all, they even use tribal names for the competing teams.

VIEWPOINT

After graduation you take a position with a local gang prevention program. One day you are approached by the director of the president's National Task Force on Gangs (NTFG). This group has been formed to pool resources from a variety of federal agencies, ranging from the FBI to Health and Human Services, in order to provide local jurisdictions with a comprehensive plan to fight gangs. The director claims that the gang problem is big and becoming bigger. Thousands of gangs are operating around the country, with hundreds of thousands of members. Government sources, he claims, indicate that there has been a significant growth in gang membership over the past 20 years. So far, the government has not been able to do anything at either a state or national level to stem this growing tide of organized criminal activity. The NTFG would like you to be part of the team that provides state and local jurisdictions with a gang-control activity model, which, if implemented, would provide a cost-effective means of reducing both gang membership and gang activity.

- Would you recommend that police employ antigang units that use tactics developed in the fight against organized crime families?

- Would you recommend the redevelopment of deteriorated neighborhoods in which gangs flourish?

- Would you try to educate kids about the dangers of gang membership?

- Would you recommend a treatment protocol to help gang members?

- Would you tell the director that gangs have always existed and there is probably not much the government can do to reduce their numbers?

DOING RESEARCH ON THE WEB

The National Gang Center (NGC) is a collaborative effort between the Office of Justice Programs' (OJP) Bureau of Justice Assistance (BJA) and the Office of Juvenile Justice and Delinquency Prevention (OJJDP). For more information about this topic, visit their website at http://www.nationalgangcenter.gov.

NOTES

All URLs accessed October 2016.

1. Michelle Arciaga Young and Victor Gonzalez, "Getting Out of Gangs, Staying Out of Gangs: Gang Intervention and Desistance Strategies," National Gang Center Bulletin, January 2013, http://www.nationalgangcenter.gov/Content/Documents/Getting-Out-Staying-Out.pdf.

2. Paul Perrone and Meda Chesney-Lind, "Representations of Gangs and Delinquency: Wild in the Streets?" *Social Justice* 24:96–117 (1997).

3. FBI, "Going Global on Gangs: New Partnership Targets MS-13," http://www.fbi.gov/news/stories/2007/october/ms13tag_101007.

4. Peggy Giordano, "The Wider Circle of Friends in Adolescence," *American Journal of Sociology* 101:661–697 (1995).

5. Danielle Payne and Benjamin Cornwell, "Reconsidering Peer Influences on Delinquency: Do Less Proximate Contacts Matter?" *Journal of Quantitative Criminology* 23:127–149 (2007).

6. Annette La Greca and Hannah Moore Harrison, "Adolescent Peer Relations, Friendships, and Romantic Relationships: Do They Predict Social Anxiety and Depression?" *Journal of Clinical Child and Adolescent Psychology* 34:49–61 (2005).

7. Delyse Hutchinson and Ronald Rapee, "Do Friends Share Similar Body Image and Eating Problems? The Role of Social Networks and Peer Influences in Early Adolescence," *Behaviour Research and Therapy* 45:1557–1577 (2007).

8. Caterina Gouvis Roman, Meagan Cahill, Pamela Lachman, Samantha Lowry, Carlena Orosco, and Christopher McCarty, with Megan Denver and Juan Pedroza, *Social Networks, Delinquency, and Gang Membership: Using a Neighborhood Framework to Examine the Influence of Network Composition and Structure in a Latino Community* (Washington, DC: Urban Institute, 2012), http://www.urban.org/research/publication/social-networks-delinquency-and-gang-membership.

9. Brett Laursen, Christopher Hafen, Margaret Kerr, and Hakin Stattin, "Friend Influence over Adolescent Problem Behaviors as a Function of Relative Peer Acceptance: To Be Liked Is to Be Emulated," *Journal of Abnormal Psychology* 121:88–94 (2012).

10. John Coie and Shari Miller-Johnson, "Peer Factors in Early Offending Behavior," in Rolf Loeber and David Farrington, eds., *Child Delinquents* (Thousand Oaks, CA: Sage, 2001), pp. 191–210.

11. Judith Rich Harris, *The Nurture Assumption: Why Children Turn Out the Way They Do* (New York: Free Press, 1998).

12. Ibid., p. 463.

13. J. C. Barnes and Robert Morris, "Young Mothers, Delinquent Children: Assessing Mediating Factors Among American Youth," *Youth Violence and Juvenile Justice* 10:172–189 (2012).

14. Marvella Bowman, Hazel Prelow, and Scott Weaver, "Parenting Behaviors, Association with Deviant Peers, and Delinquency in African American Adolescents: A Mediated-Moderation Model," *Journal of Youth and Adolescence* 36:517–527 (2007).

15. Harris, *The Nurture Assumption*, p. 463.

16. Jean Marie McGloin, "Delinquency Balance and Time Use: A Research Note," *Journal of Research in Crime and Delinquency* 49:109–121 (2012); Maury Nation and Craig Anne Heflinger, "Risk Factors for Serious Alcohol and Drug Use: The Role of Psychosocial Variables in Predicting the Frequency of Substance Use among Adolescents," *American Journal of Drug and Alcohol Abuse* 32:415–433 (2006).

17. Evelien Hoeben and Frank Weerman, "Why Is Involvement in Unstructured Socializing Related to Adolescent Delinquency?" *Criminology* 54:242–281 (2016).

18. Albert Reiss, "Co-Offending and Criminal Careers," in Michael Tonry and Norval Morris, eds., *Crime and Justice*, vol. 10 (Chicago: University of Chicago Press, 1988).

19. Arpana Agrawal, Michael Lynskey, Kathleen Bucholz, Pamela Madden, and Andrew Heath, "Correlates of Cannabis Initiation in a Longitudinal Sample of Young Women: The Importance of Peer Influences," *Preventive Medicine* 45:31–34 (2007).

20. Committee on the Science of Adolescence; Board on Children, Youth, and Families; Institute of Medicine and National Research Council, "The Science of Adolescent Risk-Taking: Workshop Report (2011)," https://www.nap.edu/catalog/12961/the-science-of-adolescent-risk-taking-workshop-report.

21. Glenn Walters, "Criminal Thought Content and Criminal Thought Process as Mediators of Peer Influence," *Criminal Justice Review* 41:318–334 (2016).

22. Fran Mann, Megan Patterson, Andrew Grotzinger, Jennifer Tackett, Natalie Kretsch, Elliot Tucker-Drob, and Paige Harden, "Sensation Seeking, Peer Deviance, and Genetic Influences on Adolescent Delinquency: Evidence for Person-Environment Correlation and Interaction," *Journal of Abnormal Psychology* 125:679–691 (2016).

23. Kevin Beaver and John Paul Wright, "Biosocial Development and Delinquent Involvement," *Youth Violence and Juvenile Justice* 3:168–192 (2005); Richard Felson and Dana Haynie, "Pubertal Development, Social Factors, and Delinquency Among Adolescent Boys," *Criminology* 40:967–989 (2002).

24. Peggy Giordano, Robert Lonardo, Wendy Manning, and Monica Longmore, "Adolescent Romance and Delinquency: A Further Exploration of Hirschi's 'Cold and Brittle' Relationships Hypothesis," *Criminology* 48:910–946 (2010).

25. Bill McCarthy and Teresa Casey, "Love, Sex, and Crime: Adolescent Romantic Relationships and Offending," *American Sociological Review* 73:944–969 (2008).

26. Meghan McDonough, Paul Jose, and Jaimee Stuart, "Bi-directional Effects of Peer Relationships and Adolescent Substance Use: A Longitudinal Study," *Journal of Youth and Adolescence* 45:1652–1663 (2016).

27. Jacob Young, J. C. Barnes, Ryan Meldrum, and Frank Weerman, "Assessing and Explaining Misperceptions of Peer Delinquency," *Criminology* 49:599–630 (2011).

28. Terence Thornberry and Marvin Krohn, "Peers, Drug Use, and Delinquency," in David Stoff, James Breiling, and Jack Maser, eds., *Handbook of Antisocial Behavior* (New York: Wiley, 1997), pp. 218–233; Thomas Dishion, Deborah Capaldi, Kathleen Spracklen, and Fuzhong Li, "Peer Ecology of Male Adolescent Drug Use," *Development and Psychopathology* 7:803–824 (1995).

29. Daneen Deptula and Robert Cohen, "Aggressive, Rejected, and Delinquent Children and Adolescents: A Comparison of Their Friendships," *Aggression and Violent Behavior* 9:75–104 (2004).

30. Mark Warr, "Age, Peers, and Delinquency," *Criminology* 31:17–40 (1993).

31. Dana Haynie and D. Wayne Osgood, "Reconsidering Peers and Delinquency: How Do Peers Matter?" *Social Forces* 84:1110–1130 (2005).

32. Stephen W. Baron, "Self-Control, Social Consequences, and Criminal Behavior: Street Youth and the General Theory of Crime," *Journal of Research in Crime and Delinquency* 40:403–425 (2003).

33. Sara Pedersen, Frank Vitaro, Edward Barker, and Anne Borge, "The Timing of Middle-Childhood Peer Rejection and Friendship: Linking Early Behavior to Early-Adolescent Adjustment," *Child Development* 78:1037–1051 (2007).

34. Beth Hoffman, Peter Monge, Chih-Ping Chou, and Thomas Valente, "Perceived Peer Influence and Peer Selection on Adolescent Smoking," *Addictive Behaviors* 32:1546–1554 (2007).

35. Timothy Brezina and Alex Piquero, "Moral Beliefs, Isolation from Peers, and Abstention from Delinquency," *Deviant Behavior* 28:433–465 (2007).

36. Frank Weerman, "Delinquent Peers in Context: A Longitudinal Network Analysis of Selection and Influence Effects," *Criminology* 49:253–286 (2011).

37. Well-known movie representations of gangs include *The Wild Ones* and *Hell's Angels on Wheels*, which depict motorcycle gangs, and *Saturday Night Fever*, which focuses on neighborhood street toughs; see also David Dawley, *A Nation of Lords* (Garden City, NY: Anchor, 1973).

38. Walter Miller, *Violence by Youth Gangs and Youth Groups as a Crime Problem in Major American Cities* (Washington, DC: US Government Printing Office, 1975).

39. Ibid., p. 20.

40. Malcolm Klein, *The American Street Gang: Its Nature, Prevalence, and Control* (New York: Oxford University Press, 1995), p. 30.

41. Irving Spergel, *The Youth Gang Problem: A Community Approach* (New York: Oxford University Press, 1995).

42. Ibid., p. 3.

43. Christopher Adamson, "Defensive Localism in White and Black: A Comparative History of European-American and African American Youth Gangs," *Ethnic and Racial Studies* 23:272–298 (2000).

44. Frederick Thrasher, *The Gang* (Chicago: University of Chicago Press, 1927).

45. National Youth Gang Center, http://www.nationalgangcenter.gov/About/FAQ.

46. Malcolm Klein, ed., *Juvenile Gangs in Context* (Englewood Cliffs, NJ: Prentice Hall, 1967), pp. 1–12.

47. Ibid., p. 6.

48. Irving Spergel, *Street Gang Work: Theory and Practice* (Reading, MA: Addison-Wesley, 1966).

49. Miller, *Violence by Youth Gangs*, p. 2.

50. Marjorie Zatz, "'Los Cholos': Legal Processing of Chicago Gang Members," *Social Problems* 33:13–30 (1985).

51. Miller, *Violence by Youth Gangs*, pp. 1–2.

52. Ibid.

53. Felix Padilla, *The Gang as an American Enterprise* (New Brunswick, NJ: Rutgers University Press, 1992), p. 3.

54. Pamela Irving Jackson, "Crime, Youth Gangs, and Urban Transition: The Social Dislocations of Postindustrial Economic Development," *Justice Quarterly* 8:379–897 (1991); Joan Moore, *Going Down to the Barrio: Homeboys and Homegirls in Change* (Philadelphia: Temple University Press, 1991), pp. 89–101.

55. National Gang Intelligence Center, National Gang Report, 2015, https://www.fbi.gov/file-repository/stats-services-publications-national-gang-report-2015.pdf.

56. Arlen Egley Jr., James C. Howell, and Meena Harris, "National Youth Gang Survey Analysis," https://www.nationalgangcenter.gov/Survey-Analysis.

57. Ibid.

58. William Julius Wilson, *The Truly Disadvantaged* (Chicago: University of Chicago Press, 1987).

59. Ibid.

60. David C. Pyrooz, "Structural Covariates of Gang Homicide in Large U.S. Cities," *Journal of Research in Crime and Delinquency*, first published August 17, 2011.

61. National Youth Gang Survey, 2012, https://www.nationalgangcenter .gov/Survey-Analysis/Measuring-the-Extent-of-Gang-Problems#dist ributionofgangmembers.

62. Ibid.

63. Ibid.

64. National Gang Intelligence Center, National Gang Report, 2015.

65. Jose Miguel Cruz, "Central American Maras: From Youth Street Gangs to Transnational Protection Rackets," *Global Crime* 11:379–398 (2010).

66. M. Michaux Parker, "Globalization and Gang Growth: The Four Phenomena Affect," *Journal of Gang Research* 19:33–49 (2012).

67. John Hagedorn, "Gangs," in Karen Christianson and David Levinson, eds., *The Encyclopedia of Community* (Thousand Oaks, CA: Sage, 2003), pp. 517–522.

68. John M. Hagedorn, "The Global Impact of Gangs," *Journal of Contemporary Criminal Justice* 21:153–169 (2005).

69. Jeffrey Fagan, "The Social Organization of Drug Use and Drug Dealing Among Urban Gangs," *Criminology* 27:633–669 (1989).

70. Ibid.

71. Lewis Yablonsky, *The Violent Gang* (Baltimore: Penguin, 1966), p. 109.

72. James Diego Vigil, *Barrio Gangs* (Austin: Texas University Press, 1988), pp. 11–19.

73. Mark Warr, "Organization and Instigation in Delinquent Groups," *Criminology* 34:11–37 (1996).

74. George W. Knox et al., *Gang Prevention and Intervention: Preliminary Results from the 1995 Gang Research Task Force* (Chicago: National Gang Crime Research Center, 1995), p. vii.

75. Ibid.

76. Wilson, *The Truly Disadvantaged*.

77. Ibid.

78. Hagedorn, "The Global Impact of Gangs."

79. National Youth Gang Survey, 2012.

80. Mars Eghigian and Katherine Kirby, "Girls in Gangs: On the Rise in America," *Corrections Today* 68:48–50 (2006).

81. Ibid.

82. Mark Fleisher and Jessie Krienert, "Life-Course Events, Social Networks, and the Emergence of Violence Among Female Gang Members," *Journal of Community Psychology* 32:607–622 (2004).

83. Karen Joe Laidler and Geoffrey Hunt, "Violence and Social Organization in Female Gangs," *Social Justice* 24:148–187 (1997); Joan Moore, *Going Down to the Barrio*; Anne Campbell, *The Girls in the Gang* (Cambridge, MA: Basil Blackwell, 1984).

84. Karen Joe Laidler and Meda Chesney-Lind, "'Just Every Mother's Angel': An Analysis of Gender and Ethnic Variations in Youth Gang Membership," *Gender and Society* 9:408–430 (1995).

85. Jody Miller, *One of the Guys: Girls, Gangs, and Gender* (New York: Oxford University Press, 2001).

86. Ibid.

87. Emilio Ulloa, Rachel Dyson, and Danita Wynes, "Inter-Partner Violence in the Context of Gangs: A Review," *Aggression and Violent Behavior* 17:397–404 (2012).

88. Fleisher and Krienert, "Life-Course Events, Social Networks, and the Emergence of Violence Among Female Gang Members."

89. David Pyrooz and Scott Decker, "Motives and Methods for Leaving the Gang: Understanding the Process of Gang Desistance," *Journal of Criminal Justice* 39:417–425 (2011).

90. Joan Moore, James Diego Vigil, and Robert Garcia, "Residence and Territoriality in Chicano Gangs," *Social Problems* 31:182–194 (1983).

91. Warr, "Organization and Instigation in Delinquent Groups."

92. Malcolm Klein, "Impressions of Juvenile Gang Members," *Adolescence* 3:59 (1968).

93. Scott Decker, Tim Bynum, and Deborah Weisel, "A Tale of Two Cities: Gangs and Organized Crime Groups," *Justice Quarterly* 15:395–425 (1998).

94. Donald Lyddane, "Understanding Gangs and Gang Mentality: Acquiring Evidence of the Gang Conspiracy," *United States Attorneys' Bulletin* 54:1–15 (2006), http://www.usdoj.gov/usao/eousa/foia _reading_room/usab5403.pdf.

95. National Gang Center Newsletter, Summer 2016, Gang Tattoos, https://www.nationalgangcenter.gov/Content/Newsletters /NGC-Newsletter-2016-Summer.pdf.

96. National Youth Gang Survey, 2012.

97. Ibid.

98. The following description of ethnic gangs leans heavily on the material developed in National School Safety Center, *Gangs in Schools: Breaking Up Is Hard to Do* (Malibu, CA: National School Safety Center, Pepperdine University, 1988), pp. 11–23.

99. Spergel, *The Youth Gang Problem*, pp. 136–137.

100. Southeast Connecticut Gang Activities Group, "Brotherhood of the Struggle," 2011, http://www.segag.org/ganginfo/frbrothdst.html.

101. Decker, Bynum, and Weisel, "A Tale of Two Cities."

102. National Gang Intelligence Center, National Gang Report, 2015.

103. US Attorney's Office, District of South Carolina, "Bloods Street Gang Members and Associates Arrested Following the Return of a 134-Count Federal RICO Indictment," July 11, 2012, http://www.fbi .gov/columbia/press-releases/2012/bloods-street-gang-members -and-associates-arrested-following-the-return-of-a-134-count-federal -rico-indictment.

104. Abigail Goldman, "What's in a Name? Police Guard Trove of Gangster Monikers, Often the Only Names by Which Suspects Are Known," *Las Vegas Sun*, April 7, 2008, http://www.lasvegassun .com/news/2008/apr/07/whats-name/.

105. Peter Hermann, "Nicknames Among Gang Members Become More Sinister: Criminals Often Don't Consider How a Nickname Will Sound in a Courtroom," *Baltimore Sun*, July 13, 2010, http://articles .baltimoresun.com/2010-07-13/news/bs-md-hermann-nicknames -crime-20100713_1_nicknames-gang-members-tattooed.

106. Amy Forliti, "Feds: Somali Gangs Ran Sex Ring in 3 States," NBC News, November 8, 2010, http://www.nbcnews.com/id/40073234 /ns/us_news-crime_and_courts/t/feds-somali-gangs-ran-sex -ring-states/.

107. FBI, 2011 National Gang Threat Assessment, https://www.fbi.gov /stats-services/publications/2011-national-gang-threat-assessment.

108. Thomas Winfree Jr., Frances Bernat, and Finn-Aage Esbensen, "Hispanic and Anglo Gang Membership in Two Southwestern Cities," *Social Science Journal* 38:105–118 (2001).

109. Arian Campo-Flores, "The Most Dangerous Gang in the United States," *Newsweek*, March 28, 2006; Ricardo Pollack, "Gang Life Tempts Salvador Teens," BBC News, http://news.bbc.co.uk/1/hi /world/americas/4201183.stm.

110. StreetGangs.com, "18th Street Gang in Los Angeles County," http://www.streetgangs.com/hispanic/18thstreet.

111. James Diego Vigil and Steve Chong Yun, "Vietnamese Youth Gangs in Southern California," in C. Ronald Huff, ed., *Gangs in America* (Newbury Park, CA: Sage, 1990), pp. 146–163.

112. FBI, "National Gang Threat Assessment—Emerging Trends," 2011, http://www.fbi.gov/stats-services/publications/2011-national -gang-threat-assessment/2011-national-gang-threat-assessment.

113. Anthony Braga, Jack McDevitt, and Glenn Pierce, "Understanding and Preventing Gang Violence: Problem Analysis and Response Development in Lowell, Massachusetts," *Police Quarterly* 9:20–46 (2006).

114. Anti-Defamation League press release (February 7, 2006), "ADL Reports Resurgence of Racist Skinheads in U.S. and Launches New Online Racist Skinhead Project," http://www.adl.org/presrele /neosk_82/4860_82.htm.

115. Mark Totten, "Gays in the Gang," *Journal of Gang Research* 19:1–24 (2012).

116. National Gang Center, "Are Today's Youth Gangs Different from Gangs in the Past?" http://www.nationalgangcenter.gov/About /FAQ.

117. National Gang Intelligence Center, National Gang Report, 2015.

118. Darlene Wright and Kevin Fitzpatrick, "Violence and Minority Youth: The Effects of Risk and Asset Factors on Fighting Among African American Children and Adolescents," *Adolescence* 41:251–262 (2006); Terence Thornberry and James H. Burch, *Gang Members and Delinquent Behavior* (Washington, DC: Office of Juvenile Justice and Delinquency Prevention, 1997).

119. G. David Curry, Scott Decker, and Arlen Egley Jr., "Gang Involvement and Delinquency in a Middle School Population," *Justice Quarterly* 19:275–292 (2002).

120. Uberto Gatti, Richard Tremblay, Frank Vitaro, and Pierre McDuff, "Youth Gangs, Delinquency and Drug Use: A Test of the Selection, Facilitation, and Enhancement Hypotheses," *Journal of Child Psychology and Psychiatry* 46:1178–1190 (2005).

121. Malcolm Klein, Cheryl Maxson, and Lea Cunningham, "Crack, Street Gangs, and Violence," *Criminology* 4:623–650 (1991).

122. Kevin Thompson, David Brownfield, and Ann Marie Sorenson, "Specialization Patterns of Gang and Nongang Offending: A Latent Structure Analysis," *Journal of Gang Research* 3:25–35 (1996).

123. Beth Bjerregaard, "Gang Membership and Drug Involvement: Untangling the Complex Relationship," *Crime and Delinquency* 56:3–34 (2010).

124. Geoffrey Hunt, Karen Joe Laidler, and Kristy Evans, "The Meaning and Gendered Culture of Getting High: Gang Girls and Drug Use Issues," *Contemporary Drug Problems* 29:375 (2002).

125. Sara Battin, Karl Hill, Robert Abbott, Richard Catalano, and J. David Hawkins, "The Contribution of Gang Membership to Delinquency Beyond Delinquent Friends," *Criminology* 36:93–116 (1998).

126. National Gang Intelligence Center, National Gang Report, 2015.

127. Terence P. Thornberry and James H. Burch, *Gang Members and Delinquent Behavior*; James C. Howell, "Youth Gang Drug Trafficking and Homicide: Policy and Program Implications," *Juvenile Justice Journal* 4:3–5 (1997).

128. Terence Thornberry, Marvin Krohn, Alan Lizotte, Carolyn Smith, and Kimberly Tobin, *Gangs and Delinquency in Developmental Perspective* (New York: Cambridge University Press, 2003).

129. Beidi Dong and Marvin Krohn, "Dual Trajectories of Gang Affiliation and Delinquent Peer Association During Adolescence: An Examination of Long-Term Offending Outcomes," *Journal of Youth and Adolescence* 45:746–762 (2016).

130. Chris Melde and Finn-Aage Esbensen, "Gangs and Violence: Disentangling the Impact of Gang Membership on the Level and Nature of Offending," *Journal of Quantitative Criminology*, first published online January 24, 2012.

131. Michael Vaughn, Matthew Howard, and Lisa Harper-Chang, "Do Prior Trauma and Victimization Predict Weapon Carrying Among Delinquent Youth?" *Youth Violence and Juvenile Justice* 4:314–327 (2006).

132. Thornberry, Krohn, Lizotte, Smith, and Tobin, *Gangs and Delinquency in Developmental Perspective.*

133. Richard Spano and John Bolland, "Is the Nexus of Gang Membership, Exposure to Violence, and Violent Behavior a Key Determinant of First Time Gun Carrying for Urban Minority Youth?" *Justice Quarterly* 28:838–862 (2011).

134. National Gang Intelligence Center, National Gang Report, 2015.

135. James C. Howell, "The Impact of Gangs on Communities," OJJDP, *NYGC Bulletin* 2:3 (August 2006).

136. Ibid.

137. James C. Howell, "Youth Gang Drug Trafficking and Homicide: Policy and Program Implications," *Juvenile Justice Journal* 4:3–5 (1997).

138. Beth Bjerregaard and Alan Lizotte, "Gun Ownership and Gang Membership," *Journal of Criminal Law and Criminology* 86:37–53 (1995).

139. Ibid.

140. Pamela Lattimore, Richard Linster, and John MacDonald, "Risk of Death Among Serious Young Offenders," *Journal of Research in Crime and Delinquency* 34:187–209 (1997).

141. Rachel Gordon, Benjamin Lahey, Eriko Kawai, Rolf Loeber, Magda Stouthamer-Loeber, and David Farrington, "Antisocial Behavior and Youth Gang Membership," *Criminology* 42:55–88 (2004).

142. Andrew Papachristos, "Murder by Structure: Dominance Relations and the Social Structure of Gang Homicide," *American Journal of Sociology* 115:74–128 (2009).

143. Scott Decker, "Collective and Normative Features of Gang Violence," *Justice Quarterly* 13:243–264 (1996).

144. Gini Sykes, *8 Ball Chicks: A Year in the Violent World of Girl Gangsters* (New York: Doubleday, 1998), pp. 2–11.

145. H. Range Hutson, Deirdre Anglin, and Michael Pratts Jr., "Adolescents and Children Injured or Killed in Drive-By Shootings in Los Angeles," *New England Journal of Medicine* 330:324–327 (1994); Miller, *Violence by Youth Gangs*, pp. 2–26.

146. Malcolm Klein, *Gang Cop: The Words and Ways of Officer Paco Domingo* (Walnut Creek, CA: Alta Mira Press, 2004).

147. Ibid., p. 59.

148. Herbert Block and Arthur Niederhoffer, *The Gang: A Study in Adolescent Behavior* (New York: Philosophical Library, 1958).

149. Ibid., p. 113.

150. Knox et al., *Gang Prevention and Intervention*, p. 44.

151. James Diego Vigil, "Group Processes and Street Identity: Adolescent Chicano Gang Members," *Ethos* 16:421–445 (1988).

152. James Diego Vigil and John Long, "Emic and Etic Perspectives on Gang Culture: The Chicano Case," in C. Ronald Huff, ed., *Gangs in America* (Newbury Park, CA: Sage, 1990), p. 66.

153. Albert Cohen, *Delinquent Boys* (New York: Free Press, 1955), pp. 1–19.

154. Irving Spergel, *Racketville, Slumtown, and Haulburg: An Exploratory Study of Delinquent Subcultures* (Chicago: University of Chicago Press, 1964).

155. Malcolm Klein, *Street Gangs and Street Workers* (Englewood Cliffs, NJ: Prentice Hall, 1971), pp. 12–15.

156. Thornberry, Krohn, Lizotte, Smith, and Tobin, *Gangs and Delinquency in Developmental Perspective.*

157. Vigil, *Barrio Gangs.*

158. Vigil and Long, "Emic and Etic Perspectives on Gang Culture," p. 61.

159. David Brownfield, Kevin Thompson, and Ann Marie Sorenson, "Correlates of Gang Membership: A Test of Strain, Social Learning, and Social Control," *Journal of Gang Research* 4:11–22 (1997).

160. John Hagedorn, Jose Torres, and Greg Giglio, "Cocaine, Kicks, and Strain: Patterns of Substance Use in Milwaukee Gangs," *Contemporary Drug Problems* 25:113–145 (1998).

161. Spergel, *The Youth Gang Problem*, pp. 4–5.

162. Ibid.

163. Jon Gunnar Bernburg, Marvin Krohn, and Craig Rivera, "Official Labeling, Criminal Embeddedness, and Subsequent Delinquency: A Longitudinal Test of Labeling Theory," *Journal of Research in Crime and Delinquency* 43:67–88 (2006).

164. Alice Cepeda, Jarron Saint Onge, Kathryn Nowotny, and Avelardo Valdez, "Associations Between Long-Term Gang Membership and Informal Social Control Processes, Drug Use, and Delinquent Behavior Among Mexican American Youth," *International Journal of Offender Therapy and Comparative Criminology* 60:1532–154 (2016).

165. Patricia Kerig, Shannon Chaplo, Diana Bennett, and Crosby Modrowski, "Harm as Harm," *Criminal Justice and Behavior* 43:635–652 (2016); Laura Thornton, Paul Frick, Elizabeth Shulman, James Ray, Lawrence Steinberg, and Elizabeth Cauffman, "Callous-Unemotional Traits and Adolescents' Role in Group Crime," *Law and Human Behavior* 39:368–377 (2015).

166. Yablonsky, *The Violent Gang*, p. 237.

167. Ibid., pp. 239–241.

168. Klein, *The American Street Gang.*

169. David Pyrooz and James Densley, "Selection into Street Gangs: Signaling Theory, Gang Membership, and Criminal Offending," *Journal of Research in Crime and Delinquency* 53:447–481 (2016).

170. Mercer Sullivan, *Getting Paid: Youth Crime and Work in the Inner City* (Ithaca, NY: Cornell University Press, 1989), pp. 244–245.

171. Finn-Aage Esbensen and David Huizinga, "Gangs, Drugs, and Delinquency in a Survey of Urban Youth," *Criminology* 31:565–587 (1993); G. David Curry and Irving Spergel, "Gang Involvement and Delinquency Among Hispanic and African American Adolescent Males," *Journal of Research in Crime and Delinquency* 29:273–291 (1992).

172. Padilla, *The Gang as an American Enterprise*, p. 103.

173. Kathleen MacKenzie, Geoffrey Hunt, and Karen Joe-Laidler, "Youth Gangs and Drugs: The Case of Marijuana," *Journal of Ethnicity in Substance Abuse* 4:99–134 (2005).

174. Terence Thornberry, Marvin Krohn, Alan Lizotte, and Deborah Chard-Wierschem, "The Role of Juvenile Gangs in Facilitating Delinquent Behavior," *Journal of Research in Crime and Delinquency* 30:55–87 (1993).

175. Henry Tigri, Shannon Reid, Michael Michael, and Jennifer Devinney, "Investigating the Relationship Between Gang Membership and Carrying a Firearm: Results from a National Sample," *American Journal of Criminal Justice* 41:168–184 (2016).

176. Spergel, *The Youth Gang Problem*, pp. 93–94.

177. Miller, *One of the Guys.*

178. Ibid., p. 93.

179. L. Thomas Winfree Jr., Teresa Vigil Backstrom, and G. Larry Mays, "Social Learning Theory, Self-Reported Delinquency, and Youth Gangs: A New Twist on a General Theory of Crime and Delinquency," *Youth and Society* 26:147–177 (1994).

180. Karen Joe Laidler and Geoffrey Hunt, "Violence and Social Organization in Female Gangs," *Social Justice* 24:148–187 (1997).

181. Chanequa Walker-Barnes and Craig A. Mason, "Delinquency and Substance Use Among Gang-Involved Youth: The Moderating Role of Parenting Practices," *American Journal of Community Psychology* 34:235–250 (2004).

182. Lyddane, "Understanding Gangs and Gang Mentality."

183. Scott Decker and Janet Lauritsen, "Leaving the Gangs," in C. Ronald Huff, ed., *Gangs in America*, 3rd ed. (Thousand Oaks, CA: Sage, 2002), pp. 51–67.

184. Eryn Nicolle O'Neal, Scott Decker, Richard Moule, and David Pyrooz, "Girls, Gangs, and Getting Out," *Youth Violence and Juvenile Justice* 14:43–60 (2016).

185. David C. Pyrooz, Scott Decker, and Vincent Webb, "The Ties that Bind: Desistance from Gangs," *Crime and Delinquency* 56 (2010).

186. Jodi Lane and James Meeker, "Subcultural Diversity and the Fear of Crime and Gangs," *Crime and Delinquency* 46:497–521 (2000).

187. Jim McDougal, "Civil Gang Injunctions," National Gang Center Newsletter, 2013, http://www.nationalgangcenter.gov/Content /Newsletters/NGC-Newsletter-2013-Winter.pdf.

188. Angela K. Brown, "Cities Sue Gangs in Bid to Stop Violence," *USA Today*, http://www.usatoday.com/news/topstories/2007-07-29 -3155555107_x.htm.

189. *People v. Englebrecht* (2001), May 09 CA1/4 D033527.

190. McDougal, "Civil Gang Injunctions."

191. Cheryl Maxson, Kristy Matsuda, and Karen Hennigan, "'Deterrability' Among Gang and Nongang Juvenile Offenders: Are Gang Members More (or Less) Deterrable than Other Juvenile Offenders?" *Crime and Delinquency* 57:516–543 (2011).

192. Mike Tapia, *Juvenile Arrest in America: Race, Social Class, and Gang Membership* (El Paso, TX: LFB Scholarly Publishing, 2012).

193. Las Vegas Metropolitan Police Department, Gang Prevention Program, 2016, http://www.lvmpd.com/CommunityPrograms /GangPreventionProgram/tabid/321/Default.aspx; Charles Katz and Vincent J. Webb, *Police Response to Gangs: A Multi-Site Study* (Washington, DC: US Department of Justice, 2004).

194. National Gang Intelligence Center, National Gang Report, 2015.

195. United States Conference of Mayors, *Best Practices of Community Policing in Gang Intervention and Gang Violence Prevention, 2006*, http://www.usmayors.org/bestpractices/community_policing _2006/gangbp_2006.pdf.

196. Barry Krisberg, "Preventing and Controlling Violent Youth Crime: The State of the Art," in Ira Schwartz, ed., *Violent Juvenile Crime* (Minneapolis: University of Minnesota, Hubert Humphrey Institute of Public Affairs, n.d.).

197. For a revisionist view of gang delinquency, see Hedy Bookin-Weiner and Ruth Horowitz, "The End of the Youth Gang," *Criminology* 21:585–602 (1983).

198. Quint Thurman, Andrew Giacomazzi, Michael Reisig, and David Mueller, "Community-Based Gang Prevention and Intervention: An Evaluation of the Neutral Zone," *Crime and Delinquency* 42:279–296 (1996).

199. Bureau of Justice Statistics, "Los Angeles County Gang Alternative Prevention Program: Evaluation Report," http://www.bjs.gov /index.cfm?ty=pbdetail&iid=3927.

200. Ellen Thompson, "Intervention Effective to Cut Gang Crime, Study Says," *Stockton Record*, July 19, 2007, http://www.recordnet .com/apps/pbcs.dll/article?AID=/20070719/A_NEWS/707190323 /-1/A_COMM01.

201. *Best Practices to Address Community Gang Problems: OJJDP's Comprehensive Gang Model* (Washington, DC: Office of Juvenile Delinquency Prevention, 2010), http://www.ncjrs.gov/pdffiles1/ojjdp/231200 .pdf.

202. Mark Moore and Mark A. R. Kleiman, *The Police and Drugs* (Washington, DC: National Institute of Justice, 1989), p. 8.

203. Charles Katz and Vincent Webb, *Policing Gangs in America* (New York: Cambridge University Press, 2006).

204. Michael Tapia, "Gang Membership and Race as Factors for Juvenile Arrest," *Journal of Research in Crime and Delinquency* 48:364–395 (2011).

205. Curry and Spergel, "Gang Involvement and Delinquency Among Hispanic and African American Adolescent Males."

206. Hagedorn, "Gangs, Neighborhoods, and Public Policy."

207. Judith Greene and Kevin Pranis, *Gang Wars: The Failure of Enforcement Tactics and the Need for Effective Public Safety Strategies* (Washington, DC: Justice Policy Institute, 2007), http://www.justicepolicy.org /images/upload/07-07_EXS_GangWars_GC-PS-AC-JJ.pdf.

CHAPTER 10
Schools and Delinquency

Learning Objectives

1. Discuss the role the educational experience plays in human development over the life course
2. Identify the problems facing the educational system in the United States
3. Give examples of the hazards faced by children if they are dropouts
4. Express the association between school failure and delinquency
5. Examine the personal and social factors that have been related to school failure
6. Calculate the extent of school crime
7. List the factors that contribute to delinquency in schools
8. Evaluate the efforts school systems are making to reduce crime on campus
9. Explain what is being done to improve school climate and increase educational standards
10. Summarize the legal rights of students

Chapter Outline

The School in Modern American Society
Socialization and Status
Educational Problems and Issues
Economic Disadvantage and Educational Achievement
Dropping Out
Academic Performance and Delinquency
The Direction of School Failure and Delinquency
Correlates of School Failure
Delinquency in the School
Extent of School Crime
Who Are the Victims of School Crime?

School Shootings
School Yard Bullying
The Causes of School Crime
Reducing School Crime
The Role of the School in Delinquency Prevention
School-Based Prevention Programs
Legal Rights in the School
The Right to Personal Privacy
Free Speech
School Prayer
School Discipline

Chapter Features

Focus on Delinquency: Race and School Discipline

Case Profile: Marie's Story

Evidence-Based Juvenile Justice—Prevention: Preventing School Yard Bullying

Professional Spotlight: Kevin Quinn, School Resource Officer

Cyber Delinquency: Free Speech in Cyberspace

IN 2016, A FEDERAL APPEALS court in Richmond, Virginia, ruled that Gavin Grimm, a transgender high school student who was born female, can sue his school board on discrimination grounds because it barred him from using the boys' bathroom. The court relied on the US Education Department's stated policy that transgender students should have full access to the bathrooms that match their gender identities rather than being forced to use bathrooms that correspond with his or her biological sex, a policy that would clash with Title IX of the Education Act, which prohibits sex discrimination at schools that receive federal funding. The Fourth Circuit is the highest court to decide on the question of whether bathroom restrictions constitute sex discrimination, and the decision could have widespread implications for the battle over LGBTQ (lesbian, gay, bisexual, transgender, questioning/queer) rights that is ongoing in several states. Why this issue is so important: Transgender students say that using the bathroom that corresponds with their gender identity is important for them—and others—to feel comfortable. A transgender boy who appears male may generally

Damon Winter/The New York Times/REDUX Pictures

raise alarms if he is forced to use the girls' bathroom. "Matters like identity and self-consciousness are something that most kids grapple with in this age range," Grimm said in an interview. "When you're a transgender teenager, these things are often very potent. I feel humiliated and dysphoric every time I'm forced to use a separate facility."[1]

I ssues such as the legal rights of LGBTQ students (The Supreme Court has decided to review the Grimm case) take on even greater importance because the school environment has been found to have a significant effect on both a child's emotional well-being and future achievement. Some research efforts suggest that its effect may be even greater than the home environment.[2] Because so much of an adolescent's time is spent in school, it would seem logical that some relationship exists between delinquent behavior and what is happening—or not happening—in classrooms. Yet while the school experience is so important, the nation's educational system has been rocked in recent years by scandals and problems ranging from school shootings to educational failures, from budget cuts to the embarrassing revelation that teachers are having sexual affairs with underage minors and, as a result, being sentenced to long prison terms.

Numerous studies have confirmed that delinquency is related to academic success: students who have trouble in school in adolescence will later become delinquents when they are teens.[3] Experts have concluded that many of the underlying problems of delinquency, as well as its prevention and control, are intimately connected with the nature and quality of the school experience. A positive educational experience solidifies legal and cultural norms while a negative one may encourage adolescents to disregard normative behaviors and beliefs.[4]

In this chapter, we first explore how educational achievement and delinquency are related and what factors in the school experience appear to contribute to delinquent behavior. Next, we turn to delinquency in the school setting—vandalism, theft, violence, and so on. Finally, we look at the attempts made by schools to prevent delinquency.

The School in Modern American Society

The school plays a significant role in shaping the values of children. In contrast to earlier periods, when formal education was a privilege of the upper classes, the US system of compulsory public education has made schooling a legal obligation.

Today, more than 90 percent of school-age children attend school, compared with only 7 percent in 1890.

In contrast to the earlier, agrarian days of US history, when most adolescents shared in the work of the family, today's young people spend most of their time in school. The school has become the primary instrument of socialization, the "basic conduit through which the community and adult influences enter into the lives of adolescents."[5]

Because young people spend a longer time in school, their adolescence is prolonged. As long as students are still dependent on their families and have not entered the work world, they are not considered adults. The responsibilities of adulthood come later to modern-day youths than to those in earlier generations, and some experts see this prolonged childhood as one factor contributing to the irresponsible and often irrational behavior of many juveniles who commit delinquent acts.

Socialization and Status

Another significant aspect of the educational experience is that children spend their school hours with their peers, and most of their activities after school take place with school friends. Young people rely increasingly on school friends and become less interested in adult role models. The norms of the peer culture are often at odds with those of adult society, and a pseudoculture with a distinct social system develops. Law-abiding behavior may not be among the values promoted in such an atmosphere. Kids enmeshed in this youth culture may admire bravery, defiance, and having fun much more than adults do.

The school has become a primary determinant of economic and social status. In this technological age, education is the key to a job that will mark its holder as "successful." No longer can parents ensure the status of their children through social class alone. Educational achievement has become of equal, if not greater, importance as a determinant of economic success. This emphasis on the value of education is fostered by parents, the media, and the schools themselves. Regardless of their social or economic background, most children grow up believing education is the key to success. However, many youths do not meet acceptable standards of school achievement. Whether failure is measured by test scores, not being promoted, or dropping out, the incidence of school failure continues to be a major problem for US society.

The school itself has become an engine of social change and improvement. School desegregation begun in the 1960s heralded a new age of racial inclusion that in the long run may help reduce crime rates. African American youth educated in states where a higher proportion of their classmates are white experience significantly lower incarceration rates later as adults. The constructive effects of racial inclusiveness in the school setting have grown stronger over time, highlighting the need for further educational integration.[6]

Educational Problems and Issues

In 2010, America woke up to some sobering educational news. It seems that for the first time, China participated in an international standardized testing curriculum known as the Program for International Student Assessment (PISA), sponsored by the Organization for Economic Cooperation and Development (OECD), a Paris-based group that includes the world's major industrial powers.

More than 5,000 15-year-old students in Shanghai took the PISA tests in math, reading, and science. The results were most startling: the Chinese students outscored their counterparts in dozens of other countries, including the United States. Nor were the test takers handpicked from the city's elite students to make China look good around the globe; they were in fact a representative cross-section of typical Shanghai students.[7]

Have things improved since then? The most recent PISA testing shows that that percentages of top performing 15-year-old students in mathematics literacy was 55 percent in China as compared to 9 percent in the United States; the United States ranked 27th out of 62 nations tested. While students in the United States did better than those in Lithuania, Romania, and Kazakhstan, they were significantly behind Slovenia, Vietnam, and Slovakia among others. Similar results could be found in science and reading scores where again China topped all other nations and the United States was in the middle of the pack.[8]

The results appeared to reflect the Chinese reverence for education. It is a culture that emphasizes teacher training and more time spent on studying than on extracurricular activities like sports. Chinese students spend less time than American students on athletics, music, and other activities not geared toward success in academic core subjects. Also, in recent years, teaching has become a valued occupation in China, and salaries have risen accordingly. In Shanghai, the authorities have undertaken important curricular reforms, and educators have been given more freedom to experiment. In contrast, budget cutbacks in the United States have resulted in teacher layoffs and reductions in special programs. It is difficult to convince students of the value of education when they see a ballplayer sign a $25 million annual contract, while teachers making $25,000 are considered "greedy" if they ask for a modest raise. Sadly, the PISA scores have remained stable or declined during the past decade.

Educational Achievement Trends The PISA results are reinforced by data collected by the National Center for Education Statistics that also show few if any improvements in educational achievement. As Figure 10.1 shows, in comparison to 2013, the national average mathematics scores for 12th-grade students are now lower and the average reading score is about the same; neither indicators show improvement.

Going back a decade or more does not show much improvement either: the average mathematics score in 2015 was not significantly different from those achieved in 2005 (Figure 10.1); reading scores are now lower than they were 25 years ago (Figure 10.2).[9]

Economic Disadvantage and Educational Achievement

It is a sad fact that economically disadvantaged children enter school lagging behind their more advantaged peers in terms of the knowledge and social competencies that are widely recognized as enabling children to perform at even the most basic level.[10] They face substantial gaps in measures of reading and mathematics proficiency, in prosocial behaviors and behavior problems, and in readiness to learn. Many

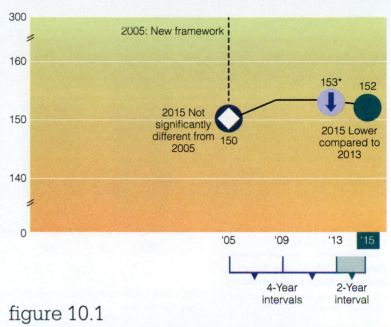

figure 10.1

Trends in Math Achievement Among Fourth Graders

SOURCE: National Center for Education Statistics, "The Nation's Report Card, 2015."

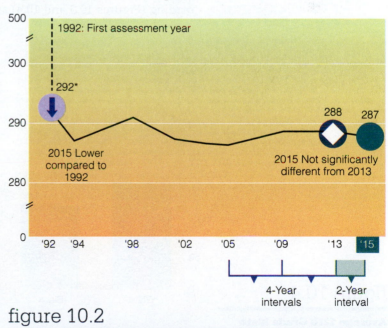

figure 10.2

Trends in Reading Achievement

SOURCE: National Center for Education Statistics, "The Nation's Report Card, 2015."

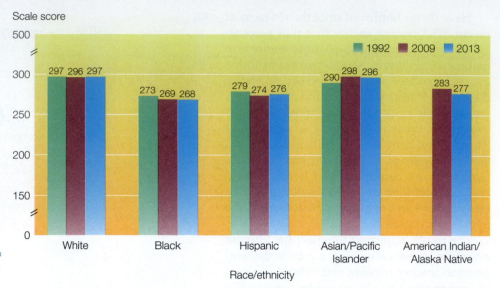

figure 10.3

Average 12th Grade Reading Score by Race and Ethnicity

SOURCE: National Center for Education Statistics, "The Nation's Report Card, 2015."

NOTE: Includes public and private schools. The National Assessment of Educational Progress (NAEP) reading scale ranges from 0 to 500.

children are not familiar with basic rules of print or writing (e.g., knowing that English is read from left to right and top to bottom, or where a story ends). About one-third of children whose mothers have less than a high school education suffer educational deficiencies compared to only 8 percent for children whose mothers have a college degree or higher. Many children from disadvantaged backgrounds fail to meet grade-level expectations on core subjects. As a consequence they face higher rates of special education placement and grade repetition.[11]

Minority Students   While minority students have made gains on many educational indicators over the past few decades, they still face greater obstacles than European American students. The most current data from the National Center for Education Statistics show that African American students still lag behind in reading (Figures 10.3 and 10.4) and math achievement and that there has been

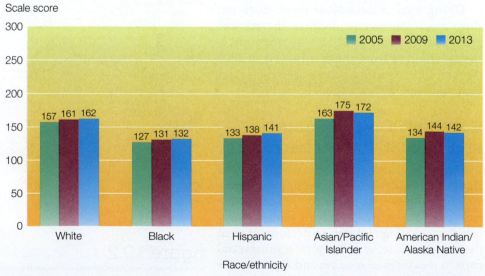

figure 10.4

Average 12th Grade Math Score by Race and Ethnicity

SOURCE: National Center for Education Statistics, "The Nation's Report Card, 2015."

NOTE: Includes public and private schools. At grade 12, the National Assessment of Educational Progress (NAEP) mathematics scale ranges from 0 to 300.

Race and School Discipline

Are minority youth subject to harsh disciplinary practices in public school and if so does that affect their academic achievement? To find out, the US Department of Education conducted a national survey of more than 72,000 schools serving 85 percent of the nation's students in public schools, showing that minority students, especially boys, face much harsher discipline in public schools than other students. One in five African American boys and more than one in ten African American girls received an out-of-school suspension, and in sum, black students were three and a half times as likely to be suspended or expelled as white students. Black students make up 18 percent of the students in the sample, but 35 percent of the students suspended once and 39 percent of the students expelled; over 70 percent of the students involved in school-related arrests or referred to law enforcement were Hispanic or black. Black and Hispanic students—particularly those with disabilities—are also disproportionately subject to seclusion or restraints. Students with disabilities make up 12 percent of the student body, but 70 percent of those subject to physical restraints. Black students with disabilities constituted 21 percent of the total, but 44 percent of those with disabilities subject to mechanical restraints, like being strapped down; Hispanic students were also overrepresented among those placed in seclusion. Many of the nation's largest districts had very different disciplinary rates for students of different races. In Los Angeles, for example, black students made up 9 percent of those enrolled, but 26 percent of those suspended; in Chicago, they made up 45 percent of the students, but 76 percent of the suspensions.

The DOE report is particularly vexing considering that nationally, blacks were 45 percent of girls suspended and 42 percent of girls expelled from K-12 public schools, blacks were 35 percent of boys suspended and 34 percent of boys expelled from K-12 public schools in the United States. The problem is more acute in southern states. A recent report by the Center for the Study of Race and Equity in Education at the University of Pennsylvania found significant disparity in school discipline in southern schools. Among the findings:

- *Disproportionality in suspensions.* In 132 southern school districts, blacks were disproportionately suspended at rates five times or higher than their representation in the student population. In 84 districts, blacks were 100 percent of the students suspended from public schools. In 346 districts, blacks were 75 percent or more of the students suspended from public schools.

- *Disproportionality in expulsions.* In 77 southern school districts, blacks were disproportionately expelled at rates five times or higher than their representation in the student population. In 181 districts, blacks were 100 percent of the students expelled from public schools. In 255 districts, blacks were 75 percent or more of the students expelled from public schools.

Any form of institutional racial disparity is of great concern, and the fact that race-based differences still exist illustrates one of the most significant problems facing the American school system.

CRITICAL THINKING

Considering the disproportionate application of disciplinary actions, would you advocate the use of peer review process in schools, allowing students to participate in the decision-making process? If not, why not?

SOURCES: Edward Smith and Shaun Harper, *Disproportionate Impact of K-12 School Suspension and Expulsion on Black Students in Southern States*, University of Pennsylvania, Center for the Study of Race and Equity in Education, 2015, https://www.gse.upenn.edu/equity/sites/gse.upenn.edu.equity/files/publications/Smith _Harper_Report.pdf; US Department of Education, "New Data from US Department of Education Highlights Educational Inequities Around Teacher Experience, Discipline and High School Rigor," March 6, 2012, http://www.ed.gov/news/press-releases/new-data-us-department-education-highlights-educational-inequities-around-teache. (URLs accessed October 2016.)

---

little if any improvement in scores for students of all races during the past two decades.[12] At grade 12, the white–black achievement gap in reading is larger today (30 points) than in 1992 (24 points), while the white–Hispanic reading achievement gap (22 points) is not measurably different from the gap in 1992; math scores have remained more stable.

One reason that minority students lag in educational achievement is that they are more likely to face student disciplinary actions than European Americans, a fact that is linked to multiple social problems, including dropping out and delinquency, and which may be responsible for what is known as the "school to jail link."[13] The Focus on Delinquency feature addresses this problem in some detail.

Dropping Out

Every day, hundreds of thousands of youths are absent from school; many are absent without an excuse and deemed **truant**. Some large cities report that unexcused absences can number in the thousands on certain days. Truancy can lead to school failure and **dropping out**.

truant
Being out of school without permission.

dropping out
Leaving school before completing the required program of education.

School systems have employed a number of different methods to reduce the dropout rate, and some seem to be succeeding. Fifth-grader Norman Bryant beams as he collects his prize, a backpack with school supplies, after winning the daily raffle at Simon Elementary School in Washington, D.C. The district has enormous truancy rates, even among young children. In the last year or two, the school system has made a big push to improve attendance. Simon Elementary is seen as a model, introducing incentives and games that are tied to attendance and meant to get kids excited about coming to school. They have also implemented systems to ensure that parents get a phone call whenever their kids are absent, weekly attendance meetings to talk about kids who are missing too much school, and partnership with a community-based organization that can make home visits and connect families with services.

Dropping out of high school has severe long-term financial and personal consequences. Dropouts are less likely to find jobs than their better educated peers, and they frequently experience considerably higher unemployment rates.[14]

Dropouts also face personal problems. They report being in worse health than adults who completed high school. Dropouts make up disproportionately higher percentages of the nation's prison and death row inmates. Among dropouts between the ages of 16 and 24, incarceration rates are 63 times higher than among college graduates. While there is no direct link between prison and the decision to leave high school early, dropouts are exposed to many of the same socioeconomic forces that are often linked to crime.[15] High school dropouts cost the economy hundreds of thousands of dollars over their lifetime in terms of lower tax contributions, higher reliance on Medicaid and Medicare, higher rates of criminal activity, and higher reliance on welfare.[16]

dropout factory
High schools in which the number of seniors is 60 percent (or less) of the number of ninth-graders.

In a few high schools—so-called **dropout factories**—mostly in inner-city neighborhoods, the high school completion rate is 40 percent or less. There are still more than one thousand of these failing schools in the United States. While they represent a small fraction of all public high schools in America, they account for about half of all high school dropouts each year.

status dropout rate
The percentage of an age group that is not enrolled in school and has not earned a high school diploma or equivalent.

The **status dropout rate** is the percentage of 16- to 24-year-olds who are not enrolled in school and have not earned a high school credential (either a diploma or an equivalency credential such as a GED certificate). While the status dropout rate remains a concern, there has been significant improvement since 1990: the high school status completion rate for Hispanic 18- to 24-year-olds increased from 59 percent to 85 percent, while the black and white status completion rates increased from 83 percent to 92 percent and from 90 percent to 94 percent, respectively (Figure 10.5).[17] The number of "dropout factory"

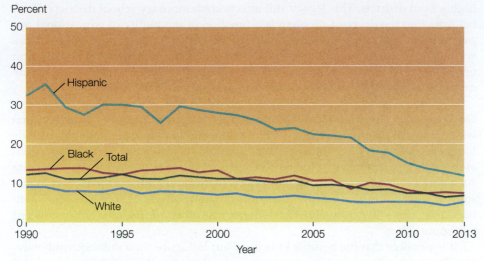

Percent

NOTE: The status dropout rate is the percentage of 16-to 24-year-olds who are not enrolled in school and have not earned a high school credential (either a diploma or an equivalency credential such as a GED certificate).

figure 10.5

Dropout Rate Trends by Race and Ethnicity

SOURCE: Lauren Musu-Gillette, Jennifer Robinson, Joel McFarland, Angelina KewalRamani, Anlan Zhang, Sidney Wilkinson-Flicker, et al., *Status and Trends in the Education of Racial and Ethnic Groups 2016, National Center for Education Statistics*, http://nces.ed.gov/pubs2016/2016007.pdf (accessed October 2016).

high schools has actually fallen in some cities such as Chicago and New York during the past decade.[18] There are still issues to confront: although white–Hispanic and white–black gaps in status completion rates for 18- to 24-year-olds narrowed between 1990 and 2013, the 2013 status completion rates for Hispanic and black individuals remained lower than the white rate.

Why Do Kids Drop Out? When surveyed, most dropouts say they left either because they did not like school or because they wanted to get a job. Kids who grow up fast, who are involved in drug abuse or other risky behaviors, may drop out of school in order to pursue an adult lifestyle.[19] Other risk factors include low academic achievement, poor problem-solving ability, low self-esteem, difficulty getting along with teachers, dissatisfaction with school, and being too old for their grade level.[20] Some dropouts could not get along with teachers, had been expelled, or were under suspension. Almost half of all female dropouts left school because they were pregnant or had already given birth.

Poverty and family dysfunction increase the chances of dropping out among all racial and ethnic groups. Dropouts are more likely than graduates to have lived in single-parent families headed by parents who were educational underachievers themselves. Wealthier kids residing with high-income parents have a much greater chance of completing high school than their indigent peers. Each year, students living in low-income families are more than four times more likely to drop out than their peers from high-income families.

Some youths have no choice but to drop out. They are pushed out of school because they lack attention or have poor attendance records. Teachers label them "troublemakers," and school administrators use suspensions, transfers, and other means to "convince" them that leaving school is their only option. Because minority students often come from circumstances that interfere with their attendance, they are more likely to be labeled "disobedient." Race-based disciplinary practices may help sustain high minority dropout rates. Although the African American dropout rate has declined faster than the white dropout rate over the past three decades, minority students still drop out at a higher rate than white students.[21]

In his thoughtful book *Creating the Dropout*, Sherman Dorn shows that graduation rates slowly but steadily rose during the twentieth century while regional, racial, and ethnic differences in graduation rates declined.[22] Nonetheless, Dorn argues that the relatively high dropout rate among minorities is the legacy of disciplinary policies instituted more than 40 years ago when educational administrators opposed to school desegregation employed a policy of race-based suspension and expulsion directed at convincing minority students to leave previously all-white high school districts. This legacy still affects contemporary school districts. Dorn believes that the dropout problem is a function of inequality of educational opportunity rather than the failure of individual students. The proportion of blacks who fail to graduate from high school remains high compared with the proportion of whites who fail to graduate because the educational system still fails to provide minority group members with the services and support they need.

Do Dropouts Commit More Crime After Leaving School?   Conventional wisdom is that dropouts commit a lot of crime and that dropping out causes kids to enter a delinquent way of life. After all, dropouts also make up disproportionately higher percentages of the nation's prison and death row inmates. Despite such notions, existing research on the effects of dropping out is a mixed bag. While some research findings indicate that dropping out of school enhances the likelihood that kids will get involved in delinquency, other efforts have not uncovered a dropout effect.[23]

It is possible that the reasons kids drop out influence their subsequent behavior. Those who drop out for economic or social reasons (e.g., they have a child) may be less likely to commit crimes than those who drop out because of behavioral problems. It's possible that the social problems that cause dropping out also produce antisocial activity. Gary Sweeten and his associates found that kids who leave school early tend to have a long history of academic failure and antisocial behaviors. Sweeten finds that the lifelong social problems that lead to dropping out also explain involvement in criminal activity after a student leaves school.[24]

Of course, not all kids drop out, and some defy the odds and stay in school, as attested to by the Case Profile "Marie's Story."

Academic Performance and Delinquency

Whether they drop out or not, kids who do poorly in school are at risk for delinquent behavior; students who are chronic underachievers in school are among the most likely to be delinquent. In fact, researchers find that school failure is a stronger predictor of delinquency than variables such as economic class membership, racial or ethnic background, or peer-group relations.[25]

Studies that compare the academic records of delinquents and nondelinquents—including their scores on standardized tests, failure rate, and other academic measures—have found that delinquents are often academically deficient, a condition that may lead to their leaving school and becoming involved in antisocial activities.[26] In addition to criminality, school failure is linked to other social problems ranging from needing social welfare to engaging in risky sexual activities.[27]

Children who report that they do not like school and do not do well in school are most likely to self-report delinquent acts.[28] In contrast, at-risk youths, even those with a history of abuse and mistreatment, who do well in school are often able to avoid delinquent involvement.[29]

An association between academic failure and delinquency is commonly found among chronic offenders. Those leaving school without a diploma were more likely to become involved in chronic delinquency than were high school graduates.[30] Only 9 percent of the chronic offenders in Marvin Wolfgang's Philadelphia *Delinquency in a Birth Cohort* study graduated from high school, compared with 74 percent of nonoffenders.[31] Chronic offenders also had more disciplinary actions than nonoffenders.[32]

The relationship between school achievement and persistent offending is supported by surveys that indicate that less than 40 percent of incarcerated felons had 12 or more years of education, compared with about 80 percent of the general population.[33] In sum, the school experience can be a significant factor in shaping the direction of an adolescent's life course.

case profile

Marie's Story

MARIE lives in the East Harlem borough of New York City with her mother and three siblings. Her father is not involved with the family, so they struggle to make ends meet and rely on Marie's grandmother to provide much of the children's care. From an early age Marie had problems in school, both behaviorally and academically. Significantly behind her grade level in reading, regularly challenging her teachers and other adults, and being disruptive in class, Marie was at great risk for dropping out of school and becoming involved in further delinquent behavior. The group of older troubled teens whom she considered to be her only friends set poor examples for behavior, causing more problems for Marie. The one area where she seemed confident and happy was on the basketball court, where Marie exhibited talent and a love for the game.

When her school started a mandatory after-school program, Marie began attending Drum Power, a youth leadership program that provides young people with an opportunity to learn the techniques and cultural/historical significance of West African traditional, Afro-Cuban, and Afro-Brazilian drumming. The goal of the program is to build self-esteem and self-confidence through discovering the rewards of discipline, teamwork, creativity, responsibility, and self-respect. Being of African descent, Marie was drawn to both the power of drums and the rhythms of African drumming. The process of learning traditional hand drumming requires discipline, commitment, and practice, and students learn that they can achieve their goals by employing their own positive energy and self-determination.

Marie thrived in the program. Although she still posed many challenges to school staff and was at risk due to her living and community environment, she showed great interest, motivation, and success in the Drum Power program. She loved the drums and music, and she connected with her youth counselors running the program. Because Drum Power was based at the school, the program counselors could communicate on a daily basis with Marie's teachers and the school staff regarding her progress, and they were able to discuss any ongoing concerns. This provided immediate resolution when there were problems and ongoing accountability for Marie. The program counselors also remained in close contact with her mother.

Participating in Drum Power for several years allowed Marie to establish excellent relationships with her program counselors, who in turn provided great encouragement to Marie, having a positive impact on her decisions and choices. Drumming was good for Marie, and her interest in African music grew, but it was her relationships with the program counselors that made the most difference for her. She started to understand how her behavior and bad choices were affecting her life. Marie learned the importance of self-control and setting priorities for herself daily. Seeing what a difference these things made for her, she could also begin to have a more positive vision for her life. Marie's mother became more involved with the school and also became involved with the Drum Power professionals when requested. The support of the professionals at school and at the Drum Power program was helpful to Marie's mother, who had been struggling with her own set of issues, and now she was better able to encourage her daughter to be successful.

CRITICAL THINKING

Marie eventually graduated from the program. She continued with her education and hopes to attend college upon graduation from high school. She stayed out of the juvenile justice system and was able to make significant changes in her life with the support of the counselors at Drum Power. Does this prove that the program is successful? Can you give other explanations for Marie's improved condition?

The Direction of School Failure and Delinquency

Although there is general agreement that school failure and delinquency are related, some questions remain concerning the nature and direction of this relationship. There are actually four independent views on the association:

- *Delinquency causes school failure*. Disruptive youth who lack self-control are aggressive and antisocial. These impulsive students are the ones most likely to face disciplinary problems and school failure.[34]

- *School failure is a direct cause of delinquent behavior*. Children who fail at school soon feel frustrated and rejected. Believing they will never achieve success through conventional means, they seek like-minded companions and together engage in antisocial behaviors. Educational failure evokes negative responses from important people in the child's life, including teachers, parents, and prospective employers. These reactions help solidify feelings of inadequacy and, in some cases, lead to a pattern of chronic delinquency.

■ *School failure leads to emotional and psychological problems that are the actual cause of antisocial behavior.* Academic failure reduces self-esteem, and reduced self-esteem is the actual cause of delinquency. Studies using a variety of measures of academic competence and self-esteem demonstrate that good students have a better attitude about themselves than poor students; low self-esteem has been found to contribute to delinquent behavior.[35] The association then runs from school failure to low self-concept to delinquency. Schools may mediate these effects by taking steps to improve the self-image of academically challenged children.

■ *School failure and delinquency share a common cause.* Both are caused by another outside condition, such as living in a poverty area or being socialized in a troubled family environment.

Correlates of School Failure

Despite disagreement over the direction the relationship takes, there is little argument that delinquent behavior is influenced by educational experiences. A number of factors have been linked to school failure; the most prominent are discussed in the next sections.

Personal Problems   Some kids have personal problems that they bring with them to school. Because of their deprived background and ragged socialization, some kids lack the verbal skills that are a prerequisite of educational success.[36] Others live in a dysfunctional family; a turbulent family life has been linked to academic underachievement.

Still others suffer psychological abnormality. The adolescent who both fails at school and engages in delinquency may be experiencing depression and other mental deficits that are associated both with their school failure and involvement in antisocial activities.[37] Personality structure may also be a key factor. Kids who have low self-control are more likely to engage in delinquent behavior *and* fail in school. An impulsive personality can cause both school failure and delinquency.[38]

School failure may also be linked to learning disabilities or reading disabilities that might actually be treatable if the proper resources were available.[39]

Social Class   During the 1950s, research by Albert Cohen indicated that delinquency was a phenomenon of working-class students who were poorly equipped

To get more educational data, go to the **National Center for Education Statistics** (NCES) website (http://nces.ed.gov/).

A young student visits the library with his class during the school day at Polaris High School in Orem, Utah. Polaris is an innovative new high school seeing early success with students most at risk of failing to graduate in the Alpine School District. Polaris was created after school officials tried to find a better way to help students who have fallen behind in earning credits, whether because of pregnancy, family trouble, legal problems, health issues, or drug abuse.

AP Images/Jim Mcauley

to function in middle-class schools. Cohen referred to this phenomenon as a failure to live up to "middle-class measuring rods."[40] Jackson Toby reinforced this concept, contending that the disadvantages lower-class children have in school (e.g., lack of verbal skills) are a result of their position in the social structure and that these disadvantages foster delinquency.[41] These views have been supported by the higher-than-average dropout rates among lower-class children.

One reason why lower-class children may do poorly in school is that economic problems require them to take part-time jobs. Working while in school seems to lower commitment to educational achievement and is associated with higher levels of delinquent behavior.[42]

Tracking   Most researchers have looked at academic **tracking**—dividing students into groups according to ability and achievement level—as a contributor to school failure. Placement in a non-college track means consignment to educational oblivion without apparent purpose. Studies indicate that non-college–track students experience greater academic failure and progressive deterioration of achievement, participate less in extracurricular activities, have an increased tendency to drop out, and commit more delinquent acts.

tracking
Dividing students into groups according to their ability and achievement levels.

In a classic study, Jennie Oakes found that school officials begin tracking students in the lowest grade levels. Educators separate youths into groups that have innocuous names ("special enrichment program"), but may carry the taint of academic incompetence. High school students may be tracked within individual subjects based on ability. Classes may be labeled in descending order: advanced placement, academically enriched, average, basic, and remedial. It is common for students to have all their courses in only one or two tracks.[43]

The effects of school labels accumulate over time. If students fail academically, they are often destined to fail again. Repeated instances of failure can help produce the career of the "misfit" or "dropout." Using a tracking system keeps certain students from having any hope of achieving academic success, thereby causing lack of motivation, which may foster delinquent behavior. Students may also conform their academic motivations according to their track. Research shows adolescents adapt their educational expectations to ability signals sent by schools. Those placed in honor tracks will experience elevated expectations while those relegated to lower tracks will behave accordingly; tracking produces a self-fulfilling prophecy.[44]

Detracking   In a follow-up study conducted 20 years later, Oakes found that research on the negative effects of tracking had spurred a detracking movement that had helped alleviate some of the tracking system's most significant problems, the creation of negative educational labels and stigma. The practice of placing students in tracking programs that placed students in higher and lower academic tracks with preset courses has given way to having students engage in self-tracking: the ability to choose classes that match educational comfort levels. Many schools have totally eliminated nonacademic lower tracks, allowing administrators and school boards to claim that all students are now in a college preparatory programs. While these changes are welcome, Oakes found that some administrators still believe in tracking and covertly maintain the system by steering students to classes that are structured according to the student's preordained ability. As a result, students taking AP English and math get a much different educational experience than those in the basic and remedial sections. Students guided toward more basic classes share many of the same problems as those who 20 years earlier were placed in lower tracks, such as reduced graduation rates and less likelihood of attending college. Oakes finds that minority students suffer as much under the new system of self-tracking as they did in the older method of tracking.[45]

Alienation   Student alienation has also been identified as a link between school failure and delinquency (see Exhibit 10.1). Students who report they neither like

exhibit 10.1

Sources of Student Alienation

- *School size.* Schools are getting larger because smaller school districts have been consolidated into multijurisdictional district schools. In 1900, there were 150,000 school districts; today there are approximately 13,500. Larger schools are often impersonal, and relatively few students can find avenues for meaningful participation. Teachers and other school personnel do not have the opportunity to deal with early indications of academic or behavior problems and thus act to prevent delinquency.

- *Irrelevant curriculum.* Some students may be unable to see the relevance or significance of what they are taught in school. The gap between their education and the real world leads them to feel that the school experience is little more than a waste of time.

- *Lack of payoff.* Many students, particularly those from low-income families, believe that school has no payoff in terms of their future. Because the legitimate channel of education appears to be meaningless, illegitimate alternatives become increasingly more attractive for students who did not plan to attend college or to use their high school educations directly in their careers.

- *Middle- and upper-class bias.* The preeminent role of the college preparatory curriculum and the second-class position of vocational and technical programs in many school systems alienate some lower-class students. Furthermore, methods of instruction as well as curriculum materials reflect middle-class mores, language, and customs and have little meaning for the disadvantaged child.

school nor care about their teachers' opinions are more likely to exhibit delinquent behaviors.[46] Alienation may be a function of students' inability to see the relevance of what they are taught. The gap between their education and the real world leads some students to feel that the school experience is a waste of time.[47]

In contrast, kids who form a bond to school also find that this commitment helps them resist delinquency-producing factors in the environment (e.g., antisocial peers).[48] Youths who report liking school and being involved in school activities are also less likely to engage in delinquent behaviors.[49] Involvement is especially beneficial in schools where students are treated fairly and where rules are laid out clearly.[50] Schools might lower delinquency rates if they can develop programs that counteract student alienation.

Delinquency in the School

In a pioneering study of school crime, *Violent Schools–Safe Schools* (published in 1977),[51] the federal government found that although teenagers spend only 25 percent of their time in school, 40 percent of the robberies and 36 percent of the physical attacks involving this age group occur there.

Since the Safe Schools study was published, crime has continued to be a significant problem in the nation's schools. Research still shows that a significant portion of all juvenile crime and victimization occurs during the school day. Though the most serious violent offenses do occur after school, the crimes that kids are most likely to get involved in, such as simple assault offenses, take place at school.[52]

Extent of School Crime

The latest data from the National Center for Educational Statistics (Figure 10.6) show that among students ages 12 to 18, there were about 850,100 nonfatal victimizations at school, which included 363,700 theft victimizations and 486,400 violent victimizations (simple assault and serious violent victimizations). In addition, there were 1.3 million reported discipline incidents during the school year, for reasons related to alcohol, drugs, violence, or weapons possession that resulted in a student being removed from the education setting for at least an entire school day. The latest data also show that about 50 students are killed in school each year.[53] In all, approximately 3 percent of students ages 12 to 18 report being victimized at school during the previous six months: 2 percent of students reported theft; 1 percent reported violent victimization; less than one-half of 1 percent reported serious

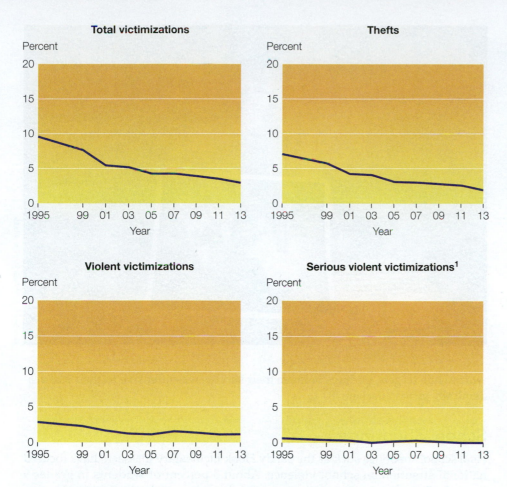

Total victimizations

Percent

Thefts

Percent

Violent victimizations

Percent

Serious violent victimizations[1]

Percent

figure 10.6

School Victimization Trends

SOURCE: US Department of Justice, Bureau of Justice Statistics, School Crime Supplement (SCS) to the National Crime Victimization Survey, 1995 through 2013. http://nces.ed.gov/programs/crimeindicators/ind_03.asp.

violent victimization. While these findings show that the scope of school delinquency is still significant, school crime rates have declined significantly in the past two decades, reflecting the general decrease in juvenile crime.

Teacher Attacks   Students are not the only victims of intimidation or violence in schools. Teachers are also subject to threats and physical attacks from students and school intruders. Surveys indicate that about 9 percent of teachers have been the victim of crimes. However, as with student victimization, teachers are much less likely to be attacked today than a decade ago. A school's location and makeup have a significant impact on the likelihood of teacher injury. Teachers in public schools in large cities are most at risk; those teaching in private schools in rural areas the least. Male teachers are attacked more often than female teachers.

Who Are the Victims of School Crime?

School crime is not a random event, and some kids are targeted because of their personal status and behavior. Students who take risks themselves and who associate with risk-taking peers are most likely to become victims. Engaging in risky behaviors increases students' exposure to motivated offenders. Being impulsive and lacking self-control adds to the mix; impulsive kids who lack self-control are the ones most often targeted by school crime. One reason: they may be viewed as suitable targets because of their often rash and thoughtless behaviors.[54]

Getting involved in after-school activities may increase victimization risk.[55] Anthony Peguero, Ann Marie Popp, and Dixie Koo found students involved in academic extracurricular activities were more likely to be selected as suitable targets for violent victimization, because they were viewed as weak and vulnerable by motivated offenders. Students viewed as upwardly mobile were seen as

Tammy Aaberg said that after her son Justin hanged himself at age 15, she learned he had been bullied by other students. To stop bullying, some students have gone as far as filing lawsuits against school districts alleging that school administrators failed to provide adequate protection for gay and lesbian students.

worthwhile targets, perhaps because their success was offensive to their less academically gifted attackers.[56]

School Shootings

Fatal school shootings such as the Sandy Hook Elementary massacre have focused national attention on school violence. About 5 percent of students in grades 9 through 12 report bringing weapons to school on a regular basis. Considering that there are about 15 million students in high school at the moment, this means that about 750,000 armed students enter school buildings on a routine basis. While troubling, the percentage of students who reported carrying a weapon on school property in the previous 30 days declined from 12 percent in 1993 to 5 percent today.[57]

To compound the tragedy, some school shootings are facilitated by parental neglect. On January 11, 2016, in Seattle, Raymond Lee Fryberg Jr. waits to enter a US District Court for his sentencing on gun charges. Fryberg, the father of a teenager who used his dad's gun to kill his classmates at a Washington high school, was charged with illegally possessing the firearm. He was found guilty of owning the gun used in the shooting despite being the subject of a domestic violence protection order.

Highly publicized incidents of school shootings such as Sandy Hook and Columbine have convinced the public that mass killings in school are a common occurrence. How true is that belief? According to the Centers for Disease Control and Prevention's study of school shootings:

- Between 14 and 34 school-age children are victims of homicide on school grounds on their way to and from school—each and every year.

- Most school-associated violent deaths occur during transition times—immediately before and after the school day and during lunch.

- Violent deaths are more likely to occur at the start of each semester.

- Nearly 50 percent of homicide perpetrators gave some type of warning signal, such as making a threat or leaving a note, prior to the event.

- Firearms used in school-associated homicides and suicides came primarily from the perpetrator's home or from friends or relatives.

- Homicide is the second leading cause of death among youth aged 5 to 18. Between 1 and 2 percent of these deaths happen on school grounds or on the way to or from school.

So while school shootings are tragic events, they are not as frequent as the media would have us believe.

Who Is the School Shooter?   Research finds a link between shootings and a history of being bullied by other students.[58] Many of these kids also perceive a lack of support from peers, parents, and teachers.[59] When Eric Harris and Dylan Klebold went on their murderous 1999 rampage at Columbine High School that left 12 students and one teacher dead, and 24 others wounded, one reason for their deadly action was feelings of being bullied and ostracized by more popular students. Harris and Klebold had spent more than a year planning the attack and building homemade bombs.[60]

Kids who have been the victims of crime themselves and who hang with peers who carry weapons are the ones most likely to bring guns to school.[61] A troubled kid who has little social support but carries deadly weapons makes for an explosive situation.

US Government Profile   The US Secret Service and the Federal Bureau of Investigation (FBI) have both developed a profile of school shootings and shooters.[62] Taken together, they found that most attacks were neither spontaneous nor impulsive. Shooters typically developed a plan of attack well in advance; more than half had considered the attack for at least two weeks and had a plan for at least two days.

Despite feelings of persecution, many school shooters were honor roll students from good communities and affluent two-parent homes and had not had serious problems at school. Shooters are almost exclusively male and most are white.

Like Adam Lanza, the school shooters' mental anguish was well known before the attack, and these kids had come to the attention of someone (school officials, police, fellow students) because of their bizarre and disturbing behavior. One student told more than 20 friends beforehand about his plans, which included killing students and planting bombs. Threats were communicated in more than three-fourths of the cases, and in more than half the incidents the attacker told more than one person. Some people knew detailed information, while others knew "something spectacular" was going to happen on a particular date. In less than one-fourth of the cases did the attacker make a direct threat to the target.

Shooters came from such a wide variety of backgrounds that no accurate or useful profile of at-risk kids could be developed. Some lived in intact families with strong ties to the community, while others were reared in foster homes with histories of neglect. Some had many friends and were considered popular. Drugs and alcohol seemed to have little involvement in school violence.

Many of the shooters had a history of feeling extremely depressed or desperate because they had been picked on or bullied. About three-fourths either threatened to kill themselves, made suicidal gestures, or tried to kill themselves before the attack; six of the shooters studied killed themselves during the incident. The most frequent motivation was revenge. More than three-fourths were known to hold a grievance, real or imagined, against the target or others. In most cases, this was the first violent act against the target. Two-thirds of the attackers described feeling persecuted, and in more than three-fourths of the incidents the attackers had difficulty coping with a major change in a significant relationship or a loss of status, such as a lost love or a humiliating failure. Not surprisingly, most shooters had experience with guns and weapons and had access to them at home. Exhibit 10.2 describes some of the most important factors linked to extreme incidents of school violence.

School Yard Bullying

bullying
Repeated, negative acts committed by one or more children against another; the acts may be physical or verbal.

The profile of the school shooter focused attention on school yard bullying because in many cases feelings of persecution and harassment is what set the shooter on his deadly rampage. Experts define **bullying** among children as repeated, negative acts committed by one or more children against another. These negative acts may be physical or verbal in nature—for example, hitting or kicking, teasing, or

---

exhibit 10.2

Factors Linked to School Violence

- *Social withdrawal.* In some situations, gradual and eventually complete withdrawal from social contacts occurs. The withdrawal often stems from feelings of depression, rejection, persecution, unworthiness, and lack of confidence.

- *Excessive feelings of isolation and being alone.* Research indicates that in some cases feelings of isolation and not having friends are associated with children who behave aggressively and violently.

- *Excessive feelings of rejection.* Children who are troubled often are isolated from their mentally healthy peers. Some aggressive children who are rejected by nonaggressive peers seek aggressive friends who, in turn, reinforce their violent tendencies.

- *Being a victim of violence.* Children who are victims of violence, including physical or sexual abuse in the community, at school, or at home, are sometimes at risk of becoming violent toward themselves or others.

- *Feelings of being picked on and persecuted.* The youth who feels constantly picked on, teased, bullied, singled out for ridicule, and humiliated at home or at school may initially withdraw socially.

- *Low school interest and poor academic performance.* In some situations—such as when the low achiever feels frustrated, unworthy, chastised, and denigrated—acting out and aggressive behaviors may occur.

- *Video games.* The diaries of the Columbine shooters, Dylan Klebold and Eric Harris, suggest addictive behavior with first-person-shooter video games. Although the level of their influence is controversial, violent video games can have a detrimental impact on vulnerable adolescents. While this does not mean that playing such games leads to homicidal acts, doing so can serve as a facilitator for impressionable adolescents who may not see any other outlet for their psychological pain.

- *Expression of violence in writings and drawings.* An overrepresentation of violence in writings and drawings that is consistently directed at specific individuals (family members, peers, other adults) over time may signal emotional problems and the potential for violence.

- *Uncontrolled anger.* Patterns of impulsive and chronic hitting, intimidating, and bullying behaviors, if left unattended, may later escalate into more serious behaviors.

- *History of discipline problems.* Chronic behavior and disciplinary problems, both in school and at home, may suggest that underlying emotional needs are not being met.

- *History of violent and aggressive behavior.* Unless provided with support and counseling, a youth who has a history of aggressive or violent behavior is likely to repeat those behaviors. Similarly, youths who engage in overt behaviors such as bullying, generalized aggression, and defiance, and covert behaviors such as stealing, vandalism, lying, cheating, and fire setting also are at risk for more serious aggressive behavior.

- *Membership in hate groups.* Belonging to a hate group and also the willingness to victimize individuals with disabilities or health problems are seen as precursors to violence.

- *Drug use and alcohol use.* Apart from being unhealthy behaviors, drug use and alcohol use reduce self-control and expose children and youth to violence, either as perpetrators or victims or both.

- *Inappropriate access to, possession of, and use of firearms.* Children and youth who inappropriately possess or have access to firearms can have an increased risk for violence or other emotional problems.

- *Serious threats of violence.* Recent incidents across the country clearly indicate that threats to commit violence against oneself or others should be taken very seriously. Steps must be taken to understand the nature of these threats and to prevent them from being carried out.

SOURCES: Centers for Disease Control and Prevention, "Understanding School Violence, 2016," http://www.cdc.gov/violenceprevention/pdf/school_violence_fact_sheet-a.pdf; Brandi Booth, Vincent Van Hasselt, and Gregory Vecchi, "Addressing School Violence," *FBI Law Enforcement Bulletin*, 2011, https://leb.fbi.gov/2011/may/addressing-school-violence. (URLs accessed October 2016.)

---

taunting—or they may involve indirect actions such as manipulating friendships or purposely excluding other children from activities. Implicit in this definition is an imbalance in real or perceived power between the bully and victim.[63]

National data indicate that in a single year about one-quarter of all public schools report that bullying occurred among students on a daily or weekly basis, and almost 10 percent reported widespread disorder in classrooms on a daily or weekly basis.[64] This means that more than 5 million students report being subject to some form of bullying, ranging from being called names to being assaulted or having their property destroyed. An additional 1.7 million say they are cyberbullied. Assuming that these are two different groups, it means that 7 million students out of a total of 25 million—more than 25 percent—are subject to some form of bullying each year (of course, it's possible that some students who are bullied in school are also being cyberbullied, reducing the total number of bullied youth). Girls are more likely to be bullied than boys; most bullying occurs in earlier grades, sixth through eighth, and trails off in high school. White students report more bullying than students of color; being poor increases a student's chances of being bullied.

The Effects of Bullying   Studies of bullying suggest that there are short- and long-term consequences for both the perpetrators and the victims of bullying.[65] Students who are chronic victims of bullying experience more physical and psychological problems than their peers who are not harassed by other children, and they tend not to grow out of the role of victim. Young people mistreated by peers may not want to be in school and may thereby miss out on the benefits of educational advancement and the social benefits of being connected to the school environment. On a more serious note, there is evidence linking bullying to suicide.[66]

Bullying is rarely a one-shot deal. Longitudinal studies have found that victims of bullying in early grades also reported being bullied several years later. Studies also suggest that chronically victimized students may, as adults, be at increased risk for depression, poor self-esteem, and other mental health problems, including schizophrenia.[67]

Who Become Bullies?   There are a number of views on this issue. Many bullies were victims themselves. Being bullied in early childhood is a critical risk factor in the development of future problems. Using data collected from a sample of 4,400 6th-grade through 12th-grade students from 33 schools, Sameer Hinduja and Justin Patchin found that bullies were influenced by their perceptions of peer behavior and adult supervision; bullies believe that their friends approve and engage in bullying themselves. At the same time, bullies did not believe that adults would punish them for their aggressive behavior.[68] This research indicates that bullying might be prevented if adults were willing to take a strong stand against the perpetrators rather than say things like "boys will be boys" or "let them work it out among themselves."

According to a recent book by sociologist Jessie Klein, boys who bully are motivated by a need to prove their masculinity. Terrorizing others is a contrivance that allows them to do so in the easiest way possible. Acting the bully allows them to express anger and rage—the only acceptable masculine emotions—while hiding emotions such as caring or sensitivity that they consider weak or feminine. Boys, and some girls for that matter, obtain social status by displaying aggression and a willingness to demonstrate power at another's expense. Some bullying is directed at the opposite sex. Klein claims that boys learn they can assert manhood not only by being popular with girls but also by wielding power over them physically, emotionally, and sexually. What develops is **gender policing**, pressure to conform to gender expectations. Students tend to become members of the "gender police," correcting their own and one another's behaviors, attitudes, and dress according to their perceived expectations for proper gender performance. By participating in gender policing, and targeting students they perceive to be failing in the task of meeting masculinity norms, bullies can elevate their social status.[69]

Not all experts agree with Klein. Research by Norman White and Rolf Loeber found that bullies have a long history of antisocial behaviors that precedes their

gender policing
Pressure to conform to gender expectations.

Preventing School Yard Bullying

A number of programs developed abroad have shown promise to prevent bullying. Two of the best known are the Olweus and KiVa models.

The Olweus Program

The first and best-known program to reduce bullying among schoolchildren was launched by Dan Olweus in Norway and Sweden in the early 1980s. Prompted by the suicides of several severely victimized children, Norway supported the development and implementation of a comprehensive program to address bullying among children in school. The program involved interventions at multiple levels:

■ *Schoolwide interventions.* A survey of bullying problems at each school, increased supervision, schoolwide assemblies, and teacher in-service training to raise the awareness of children and school staff regarding bullying.

■ *Classroom-level interventions.* The establishment of classroom rules against bullying, regular class meetings to discuss bullying at school, and meetings with all parents.

■ *Individual-level interventions.* Discussions with students to identify bullies and victims.

A number of research studies have found the program to be highly effective in reducing bullying and other antisocial behavior among students in primary and secondary schools. In some studies, within two years of implementation, both boys and girls report that bullying has decreased by half. These changes in behavior were more pronounced the longer the program was in effect. Moreover, students

reported significant decreases in rates of truancy, vandalism, and theft, and indicated that their school's climate was significantly more positive as a result of the program. Not surprisingly, those schools that had implemented more of the program's components experienced the most marked changes in behavior.

The core components of the Olweus antibullying program have been adapted for use in several other cultures, including Canada, England, and the United States, and the results have been similar: schools that were more active in implementing the program observed the most marked changes in reported behaviors. Maria Ttofi and her associates recently conducted a meta-analysis of 59 studies testing the effectiveness of bullying prevention programs around the world. They found that while many were successful, the Olweus system worked best.

The KiVa Antibullying Program

Created in Finland, KiVa is a school-based program that uses social-cognitive theory as a framework for understanding social behavior. KiVa predicts that changes in group behaviors can reduce bullying by reducing the rewards of bullying. The program is delivered to all students in grades 1, 4, and 7. It was designed for national use in the Finnish comprehensive schools, and the goal is to reduce school bullying and victimization. The central aims of the program are to:

■ Raise awareness of the role that a group plays in maintaining bullying

■ Increase empathy toward victims

school experiences.[70] Bullies rarely stop their antisocial behavior at the school yard gate, and bullying may be a critical risk factor in the development of future problems with violence and delinquency. Bullies are more likely to carry weapons in and out of school and get involved with substance abuse. And in addition to threatening other children, bullies are several times more likely than their nonbullying peers to commit antisocial acts, including vandalism, fighting, theft, drunkenness, and truancy, and to have an arrest by young adulthood. So whether bullying is a social phenomenon or a matter of general psychological malaise is still being debated.

Can Bullying Be Stopped? Recent research shows that a student's exposure to motivated bullies and the school's lack of guardianship efforts were associated with the student's risk of experiencing bullying victimization.[71] Consequently, experts suggest the following measures can help stop bullying:

■ Increase student engagement

■ Model caring behavior for students

Promote strategies to support the victim and to support children's self-efficacy to use those strategies

Increase children's skills in coping when they are victimized

The program is a whole-school intervention, meaning that it uses a multilayered approach to address individual-, classroom-, and school-level factors. The curriculum consists of 10 lessons that are delivered over 20 hours by classroom teachers. The students engage in discussions, group work, and role-playing exercises. They also watch short films about bullying. Each lesson is constructed around a central theme, and one rule is associated with that theme; after the lesson is delivered, the class adopts that rule as a class rule. At the end of the year, all the rules are combined into a contract, which all students then sign.

A program manual provides guidelines to the teachers on how much time should be devoted to each theme. Schools have the flexibility to decide how to organize the school year around the themes. Manuals and curricula are developmentally targeted, with versions available for grades 1–3, 4–6, and 7–9.

For primary school children, an antibullying computer game has been developed that students can play during and between the KiVa lessons. For secondary students, a virtual learning environment, "KiVa Street," has been developed; on KiVa Street, students can access information about bullying from a "library," or they can go to the "movie theater" to watch short films about bullying.

The program actively engages the school and parents. For recess, special vests are given to the playground helpers to enhance their visibility and remind students that the school takes bullying seriously. Materials are also posted around the school that promote antibullying messages. A PowerPoint presentation has been developed that schools can use to introduce the program to school staff and parents, and parents receive a guide that includes information about and advice on dealing with bullying.

In addition to prevention messages, teams are in place to deal with identified bullying cases. The three-person team meets with the classroom teacher to discuss the identified case. Then one or two team members meet with the victim (or victims) and the bully in a series of sessions.

CRITICAL THINKING

Should school yard bullies be expelled from school? Would such a measure make a bad situation worse? For example, might expelled bullies shift their aggressive behavior from the school yard to the community?

SOURCES: Dan Olweus, "A Useful Evaluation Design, and Effects of the Olweus Bullying Prevention Program," *Psychology, Crime and Law* 11:389–402 (2005); Dan Olweus, "Victimization by Peers: Antecedents and Long-Term Outcomes," in K. H. Rubin and J. B. Asendorf, eds., *Social Withdrawal, Inhibitions, and Shyness* (Hillsdale, NJ: Erlbaum, 1993), pp. 315–341; National Institute of Justice, "KiVa Antibullying Program," http://www.crimesolutions.gov/ProgramDetails.aspx?ID=100; Ken Seeley, Martin L. Tombari, Laurie J. Bennett, and Jason B. Dunkle, "Bullying in Schools: An Overview," *OJJDP Juvenile Justice Bulletin*, December 2011, http://www.ojjdp.gov/pubs/234205.pdf; Maria Ttofi, David Farrington, and Anna Baldry, "Effectiveness of Programmes to Reduce School Bullying," Swedish National Council for Crime Prevention, Stockholm, 2008, http://www.crim.cam.ac.uk/people/academic_research/maria_ttofi/pub1.pdf; Ann Marie Popp, "The Effects of Exposure, Proximity, and Capable Guardians on the Risk of Bullying Victimization," *Youth Violence and Juvenile Justice* 10:315–332 (2012). (URLs accessed October 2016.)

Offer mentoring programs

Provide students with opportunities for service learning as a means of improving school engagement

Address the difficult transition between elementary and middle school (from a single classroom teacher to teams of teachers with periods and class changes in a large school)

Start prevention programs early

Resist the temptation to use prefabricated curricula that are not aligned to local conditions[72]

Clearly, schools that make an effort to protect kids from their more aggressive classmates can help lower the incidence of school yard bullying. The Evidence-Based Juvenile Justice feature reviews two model programs that seem to help in reducing the bullying problem.

The Causes of School Crime

What are the suspected causes of school violence? Research indicates that they may be found at the individual, school, and community levels.

Individual-Level Causes   Kids who feel isolated and alone, with little parental attention, may be the most prone to alienation and substance abuse.[73] The level of student drinking and substance abuse may increase violent crime rates. As substance abuse increases among the student body, so too may school violence rates.[74] Because heavy drinking reduces cognitive ability, information processing skills, and the ability to process and react to verbal and nonverbal behavior, a student argument may quickly turn into a full-scale battle.[75]

School-Level Causes   Schools with high-achieving students, a drug-free environment, strong discipline, and involved parents have fewer behavioral problems in the student body.[76] Conversely, schools whose student body contains large numbers of students with emotional and psychological problems also have high rates of crime and violence.

Another factor related to delinquency is school climate—the quality and character of school life.[77] Schools with a high proportion of students below grade level in reading, with many students from families on welfare, and located in a community with high unemployment, crime, and poverty rates, are also at risk for delinquency.[78] Schools that have clear and firm disciplinary practices, such as expulsion for serious breaches of school rules, are more likely to be able to convince students that misbehavior will not be tolerated.[79]

In general, researchers find that several characteristics make schools more conducive to violent student behavior:

- Violence is more prevalent in large schools as compared to smaller ones. Eighty-nine percent of the large schools surveyed admitted to one or more criminal incidents in a year compared to only 38 percent of the smaller schools. Given a larger student population, exposure to violent acts on the school campus is greater, thereby leading to a larger number of incidents.

- Schools located in a city are more likely to experience criminal behaviors and violence than are rural schools.

- The physical condition of the school building can influence students' motivation, attitude, and behavior. Buildings that have uncomfortable temperatures, are polluted, have a large amount of graffiti, and are in need of repairs have higher incidences of fighting and other forms of violence. The physical learning atmosphere affects daily conduct.[80]

Community-Level Causes   Crime in schools reflects the patterns of antisocial behavior that exist in the surrounding neighborhood.[81] Schools in high-crime areas experience more crime than schools in safer areas. Students who report being afraid in school are actually more afraid of being in city parks, streets, or the subway. Because of this fear, students in high-crime areas may carry weapons for self-protection as they go from their homes to school.[82]

Schools experiencing crime and drug abuse are most likely to be found in socially disorganized neighborhoods with a high proportion of students below grade level in reading, with many students from families on welfare, and with high unemployment and poverty rates.[83] Neighborhoods with high population density and transient populations also have problem-prone schools.[84] In contrast, schools located in more stable areas, with high-achieving students, drug-free environments, and involved parents, have fewer behavioral problems within the student body.[85]

Community influences may undermine school stability and climate.[86] Poverty in a school's surrounding area influences the social characteristics of students. They may lack the readiness and interest to learn when compared with students from more affluent neighborhoods. Poor areas may find it difficult to hire and retain the most qualified faculty and/or provide students with the most up-to-date equipment and books. Because poor communities have lower tax bases, they are handcuffed when they want to provide remedial programs for students with learning issues or, conversely, enrichment programs for the gifted. Finally, parents and other students have neither the time nor the resources to become involved in school activities or participate in governance. These factors may eventually undermine school climate and destabilize the educational environment, which leads to school crime and disorder.

School or Community?   Does community violence influence school violence or vice versa? Research by Rod Brunson and Jody Miller found that school and community violence actually influence one another. When they interviewed male students in a disadvantaged urban community in St. Louis, Missouri, they found that most had been exposed to violence as perpetrators, victims, and/or witnesses. The more serious violence occurred in the neighborhood, as opposed to school contexts—punching and slapping occurred in school; getting shot or stabbed occurred in neighborhoods.

The youths interviewed by Brunson and Miller noted that violence often started with spontaneous conflicts begun in the community, which then migrated to the school. A great many of these problems revolved around gang membership, a factor that had a significant impact on violence in both the school and the community. Young men's gang affiliations, or even their neighborhoods' reputations, could carry over into school and cause conflicts. Tensions would escalate during school hours through further instigation, and then violent resolutions would play out just after school ended. The school experience amplified gang conflicts: while rival gang members could avoid each other in the community, they were forced to be in close proximity at school. Gang rivalry caused by a particular violent incident or long-standing feud would then fuel conflicts at school. Kids were bored at school; looking for excitement, they would spread rumors about one another, instigating conflicts and then "amping up" those conflicts in order to see fights. Once a fight began, bystanders tried to egg on the combatants and turn it into a full-scale brawl.

In sum, the factors that produced violence in the school and neighborhood were often intertwined. The fact that school brings together rival gang members and students from across neighborhoods, who would not interact normally, may contribute to violence. Conversely, some conflicts that begin at school are intentionally postponed until after school ends. So the most serious incidents of school-related violence may take place beyond the school grounds and immediately following school hours, yet are actually tied to the school setting and incidents that occur during the school day.[87]

Reducing School Crime

Schools around the country have mounted a campaign to reduce the incidence of delinquency on campus. Nearly all states have developed some sort of crime-free, weapon-free, or safe-school zone statute. Most have defined these zones to include school transportation and school-sponsored functions. Schools are also cooperating with court officials and probation officers to share information and monitor students who have criminal records. School districts are formulating crisis prevention and intervention policies and are directing individual schools to develop safe-school plans.

Some schools have instituted strict controls over student activity—for example, making locker searches, preventing students from having lunch off campus, and using patrols to monitor drug use. According to one national survey, a majority of schools have adopted a **zero tolerance policy** that mandates predetermined punishments for specific offenses, most often possession

zero tolerance policy
Mandating that action be taken for the slightest infraction of a school or criminal code violation.

Some schools now employ safety and/or school resource officers to patrol hallways in an effort to increase school security. In this image taken from a Greenwood (Mississippi) High School security video-tape, police officer Casey Wiggins, four months into his job, is seen holding a gun on an unarmed teen after the officer had been knocked to the ground.

of drugs, weapons, and tobacco, and also for engaging in violent behaviors. An extensive review of the literature found that, despite a 20-year history of implementation, there is little evidence that a zero tolerance approach to school discipline is effective.[88] Critics argue that these policies breed contempt for the rule of law, irreparably harm students' notions of fairness and justice, and contribute to the creation of the same divisions between students and teachers that exist between citizens and law enforcement; their weight falls disproportionately on minority students.[89]

School Security Efforts   Almost every school attempts to restrict entry of dangerous persons by having visitors sign in before entering, and most close the campus for lunch. Schools have attempted to ensure the physical safety of students and staff by using mechanical security devices such as surveillance cameras, metal detectors, and electronic barriers to keep out intruders, and have also employed roving security guards. Security measures include the following:

- *Access control.* Most schools control access to school buildings by locking or monitoring doors. About one-third of schools control access to school grounds with locked or monitored gates.

- *Lighting.* Some administrators keep buildings dark at night, believing that brightly illuminated schools give the buildings too high a profile and attract vandals who might not have bothered with the facility, or even noticed it, if the premises were not illuminated.

- *Picture IDs.* Many schools require faculty or staff to wear picture IDs; a few require students to wear similar identification.

- *Book bags.* Some schools require transparent book bags or ban book bags altogether.

- *Random checks.* Some schools use random metal detector checks, random dog sniffs, and random sweeps for contraband.

- *Security cameras.* About half of all schools use one or more security cameras to monitor the school.[90]

professional SPOTLIGHT

KEVIN QUINN works in the largest high school in the city and has found that a school resource officer (SRO) officer can make a difference in the lives of kids.

What does he find most rewarding about the job? Watching the kids grow up into young adults and then graduate, knowing that he had some small hand in helping them achieve that goal, whether they realize it or not. He has seen kids walk across the graduation stage whom he thought would never finish high school, even some whom he had to arrest. He is pleased when they thank him on graduation day, saying the arrest was the moment where they decided to turn their life around. He has also helped some students get out of abusive dating relationships. Quinn says the most interesting part of the job is seeing the educational system from the inside. Being a part of the administration team and attending their meetings has given him insight into what really goes on behind the scenes in schools and why school administrators do the things they do.

While Quinn does not follow a regular routine, there are some tasks that occur on a daily basis. Since he is the only police officer on the campus—and it spans more than 80 acres—he is the one responsible for taking care of any incidents that require law enforcement intervention. This ranges from petty thefts on campus to drug possession and any other incidents that are disclosed by students. He also assists the administration with keeping the school crisis plan updated and scheduling emergency response drills throughout the year.

Quinn believes that his biggest challenge is trying to get law enforcement officers and education professionals to work together to meet the same goals. Since the professions are inherently different, sometimes there is a conflict between the two, but at the end of the day they are trying to reach the same end result. This is where having trainings that cover SRO/administration relationships are critical to ensure both educators and police officers learn how to cooperate with each other for the good of the school community.

Kevin Quinn
School Resource Officer,
Chandler, Arizona, Police
Department

Employing Law Enforcement Some districts have gone so far as to infiltrate undercover detectives on school grounds. These detectives attend classes, mingle with students, contact drug dealers, make buys, and arrest campus dealers.[91] Other cities, like New York, maintain a significant uniformed police presence within the educational system. The NYPD School Safety Division is one of the largest law enforcement agencies in the United States, with approximately 5,000 school safety agents, whose stated mission is to provide a safe environment, conducive to learning, where students and faculty can be free from hostility and disruptions which can negatively impact the educational process.[92] Another approach is to assign a police officer known as a school resource officer to work on campus. The Professional Spotlight highlights the career of one such school-based police officer.

Improving the School Climate Some critics complain that even when security methods are effective, they reduce morale of the staff and students. Tighter security may reduce acts of crime and violence in school, only to displace them to the community. Similarly, expelling or suspending troublemakers puts them on the street with nothing to do, so that, in the end, lowering the level of crime in schools may not reduce the total amount of crime committed by young people.[93] A more realistic approach might involve early identification of at-risk students and exposing them to prosocial skills rather than threatening them with consequence-based punishments.[94] In addition to controlling gangs and drugs in the school, administrators who apply school rules evenly and increase the certainty of punishment for breaking school rules can create the multifaceted approach needed to provide a safer school environment.[95]

Another approach to improving the school climate is to increase educational standards. Programs have been designed to improve the standards of the teaching staff and administrators and the educational climate in the school, increase the relevance of the curriculum, and provide law-related education classes. Efforts to improve school climate should be encouraged. Recent research efforts have found preliminary support for the link between school climate and delinquency. Schools that encourage order, organization, and student bonding may also experience a decline in disorder and crime.[96]

Employing Social Programs   Controlling school crime is ultimately linked to the community and family conditions. When communities undergo such changes as increases in unemployment and the number of single-parent households, both school disruption and community crime rates may rise.[97] The school environment can be made safer only if community issues are addressed—for example, by taking steps to keep intruders out of school buildings, putting pressure on local police to develop community safety programs, increasing correctional services, strengthening laws on school safety, and making parents bear greater responsibility for their children's behavior. Schools must also use the resources of the community when controlling school crime. Most school districts refer problem students to social services outside the school, including outside referrals for students with substance abuse problems; most offer drug education within the school.

The Role of the School in Delinquency Prevention

Numerous organizations and groups have called for reforming the educational system to make it more responsive to the needs of students. Educational leaders now recognize that children undergo enormous pressures while in school that can lead to emotional and social problems. At one extreme are the pressures to succeed academically; at the other are the crime and substance abuse students face on school grounds. It is difficult to talk of achieving academic excellence in a deteriorated school dominated by gang members.

One way of improving schools and reducing delinquency is through sponsored educational reform. The cornerstone of the Bush administration's policy was the No Child Left Behind (NCLB) Act of 2001 (Public Law 107-110). This act authorizes federal programs aimed at improving America's primary and secondary schools by increasing the accountability for states, school districts, and schools and also providing parents more flexibility in choosing which schools their children will attend.[98] NCLB increases focus on reading and relies on outcome-based education or the belief that high expectations and setting of goals will result in success for all students.[99] Supplementing NCLB is Race to the Top, a US Department of Education program designed to spur reforms in state and local K–12 education. It provides incentives to states to implement large-scale reforms that result in improved student achievement, narrowed achievement gaps, and increased graduation and college enrollment rates.[100]

School-Based Prevention Programs

Education officials have instituted numerous programs to make schools more effective instruments of delinquency prevention.[101] Some of the most prevalent strategies are as follows:

- *Cognitive.* Increase students' awareness about the dangers of drug abuse and delinquency.
- *Affective.* Improve students' psychological assets and self-image to give them the resources to resist antisocial behavior.
- *Behavioral.* Train students in techniques to resist peer pressure.
- *Environmental.* Establish school management and disciplinary programs that deter crime, such as locker searches.
- *Therapeutic.* Treat youths who have already manifested problems.

More specific suggestions include creating special classes or schools with individualized programs that foster success for nonadjusting students. Efforts can be made to help students deal constructively with academic failure when it does occur.

More personalized student–teacher relationships have been recommended. This effort to provide young people with a caring, accepting adult role model will, it is hoped, strengthen the controls against delinquency. Counselors acting as liaisons between the family and the school might also be effective in preventing delinquency. These counselors try to ensure cooperation between the parents and the school and to secure needed services for troubled students. Some programs that help families and schools develop conflict-avoidance skills have proven effective in reducing violence levels and helping restrict disciplinary measures such as suspensions and expulsions.[102]

Experiments have been proposed to integrate job training and experience with classroom instruction, allowing students to see education as a relevant prelude to their careers. Job training programs emphasize public service, encouraging students to gain a sense of attachment to their communities.

Because three out of four mothers with school-age children are employed, and two-thirds of them work full time, there is a growing need for after-school programs. Today, after-school options include child care centers, tutoring programs at school, dance groups, basketball leagues, and drop-in clubs. State and federal budgets for education, public safety, crime prevention, and child care provide some funding for after-school programs. Research shows that younger children (ages 5 to 9) and those in low-income neighborhoods gain the most from after-school programs, showing improved work habits, behavior with peers and adults, and performance in school. Young teens who attend after-school activities achieve higher grades in school and engage in less risky behavior. These findings must be interpreted with caution. Because after-school programs are voluntary, participants may be the more motivated youngsters in a given population and the least likely to engage in antisocial behavior.[103] There is little evidence that attending after-school programs can have a measurable influence on delinquency.[104]

Legal Rights in the School

The actions of education officials often run into opposition from the courts, which are concerned with maintaining the legal rights of minors. The US Supreme Court has sought to balance the civil liberties of students with the school's mandate to provide a safe environment. Three of the main issues involved are privacy, free speech in school, and school discipline.

The Right to Personal Privacy

One major issue is the right of school officials to search students and their possessions on school grounds. Drug abuse, theft, assault and battery, and racial conflicts in schools have increased the need to take action against troublemakers. School administrators have questioned students about their illegal activities, conducted searches of students' persons and possessions, and reported suspicious behavior to the police.

In 1984, in *New Jersey v. T.L.O.*, the Supreme Court helped clarify a vexing problem: whether the Fourth Amendment's prohibition against unreasonable searches and seizures applies to school officials as well as to police officers.[105] In this case, the Court found that students are in fact constitutionally protected from illegal searches but that school officials are not bound by the same restrictions as law enforcement agents. In the world outside of school, police need "probable cause" before they can conduct a search, but educators can legally search students when there are reasonable grounds to believe the students have violated the law

New Jersey v. T.L.O.
The Fourth Amendment controls on search and seizure apply to school officials as well as police.

or broken school rules. In creating this distinction, the Court recognized the needs of school officials to preserve an environment conducive to education and to secure the safety of students.

Limiting Searches   But how far can school officials go in their student searches? Are there limits to the freedom they have to preserve a safe school environment? The Court clarified this issue in *Safford Unified School District v. Redding*, a 2009 case that drew national headlines. Savana Redding was a 13-year-old eighth-grade honors student at Safford Middle School, located about 127 miles from Tucson, Arizona, when on October 3, 2003, she was taken out of class by the school's vice principal. It seems that one of Redding's classmates had been caught possessing prescription-strength ibuprofen (400 mg—the strength of two Advils) and when asked where she got the pills she blamed Redding, who had no history of disciplinary issues or drug abuse.

Though Redding claimed she had no knowledge of the pills, she was subjected to a strip search by the school nurse and another female employee because the school has a zero tolerance policy for all over-the-counter medication (which students could not possess without prior written permission). During the search, Redding was forced to strip to her underwear, and her bra and underpants were pulled away from her body. No drugs were found. She later told authorities, "The strip search was the most humiliating experience I have ever had. I held my head down so that they could not see that I was about to cry."

After a trial court ruled that the search was legal, Redding sought help from the American Civil Liberties Union, whose attorneys brought an appeal before the Ninth Circuit Court. Here the judges ruled that the search was "traumatizing" and illegal, stating that "common sense informs us that directing a 13-year-old girl to remove her clothes, partially revealing her breasts and pelvic area, for allegedly possessing ibuprofen . . . was excessively intrusive." It further went on to say, "The overzealousness of school administrators in efforts to protect students has the tragic impact of traumatizing those they claim to serve. And all this to find prescription-strength ibuprofen."

Rather than let the appellate court decision stand, the school district appealed the case to the US Supreme Court, complaining that restrictions on conducting student searches would cast a "roadblock to the kind of swift and effective response that is too often needed to protect the very safety of students, particularly from the threats posed by drugs and weapons."[106] On June 25, 2009, the Supreme Court held that Redding's Fourth Amendment rights were indeed violated by the search.[107] With Justice David Souter writing for the majority, the Court agreed that search measures used by school officials to root out contraband must be "reasonably related to the objectives of the search and not excessively intrusive in light of the age and sex of the student and the nature of the infraction." In Redding's case, school officials did not have sufficient suspicion to extend the search to her underwear. In a separate opinion, Justice John Paul Stevens agreed that the strip search was unconstitutional and that the school administrators should be held personally liable for damages: "It does not require a constitutional scholar to conclude that a nude search of a 13-year-old child is an invasion of constitutional rights of some magnitude." (His opinion was in response to the majority's ruling that school officials could not be held personally liable because the law was unclear before the *Safford* decision.) The only justice to disagree with the main finding was Clarence Thomas, who concluded that the judiciary should not meddle with decisions of school administrators that are intended to be in the interest of school safety.

Limiting Interrogations   In addition to searches, the Supreme Court, in *J.D.B. v. North Carolina*, has also addressed the issue of questioning of students on school grounds. In this case, police stopped and questioned petitioner J.D.B., a 13-year-old seventh-grade student, upon seeing him near the site of two home break-ins. Five days later, after a digital camera matching one of the stolen items was found at J.D.B.'s school and seen in his possession, an investigator went to the

Safford Unified School District v. Redding
School searches must be reasonable and, considering the circumstances of the case, not overly intrusive.

J.D.B. v. North Carolina
A suspect's age must be considered in determining whether a confession was freely given and whether they believed they were in custody.

school and had J.D.B. taken from his classroom to a closed-door conference room. Police and school administrators questioned him for at least 30 minutes about the crime without first warning him about his right to remain silent (i.e., they did not give him a *Miranda* warning), nor did they give him the opportunity to call his grandmother, his legal guardian, or tell him he was free to leave the room. He confessed after officials urged him to tell the truth and told him about the prospect of juvenile detention. After he confessed, investigators advised him that he could refuse to answer questions and was free to leave. Asked whether he understood, J.D.B. nodded and provided further detail and wrote a statement. When later petitioned to juvenile court, his attorney pointed out that J.D.B. had been interrogated in a custodial setting without being afforded *Miranda* warnings and that his statements were involuntary. He was adjudicated delinquent, a finding affirmed by the North Carolina appellate courts, who found that he was not in custody when interrogated so *Miranda* need not apply. However, the Supreme Court reversed this finding, stating that a child's age must be considered during an interrogation. Unlike an adult, an underage student taken from a classroom and interrogated by police on school grounds might consider themselves in custody and feel coerced into confessing. Age, the Court ruled, must be considered when determining whether a person's statements to police were freely given or illegally induced.[108]

Drug Testing   Another critical issue involving privacy is the drug testing of students. In 1995, the Supreme Court extended schools' authority to search by legalizing a random drug-testing policy for student athletes. The Supreme Court's decision in *Vernonia School District 47J v. Acton* expanded the power of educators to ensure safe learning environments.[109] The testing was allowed because drugs are a serious threat to public safety and to the rights of children to receive a decent and safe education. In a subsequent case, *Board of Education of Independent School District No. 92 of Pottawatomie County et al. v. Earls et al.*, the court extended the right to test for drugs to all students, ruling that such a policy was a reasonable means of furthering the school district's important interest in preventing and deterring drug use among its schoolchildren and does not violate the students' rights to privacy or their due process rights. The Court concluded that the means used to enforce a drug search policy in both cases was not overly invasive or an intrusion on the students' privacy. Under the policy, a faculty monitor would wait outside a closed restroom stall for the student to produce a sample and must listen for the normal sounds of urination to guard against tampered specimens and ensure an accurate chain of custody. The policy requires that test results be kept in confidential files separate from a student's other records and released to school personnel only on a "need to know" basis. Moreover, the test results are not turned over to any law enforcement authority. Nor do the test results lead to the imposition of discipline or have any academic consequences. Rather, the only consequence of a failed drug test is to limit the student's privilege of participating in extracurricular activities.[110]

Board of Education of Independent School District No. 92 of Pottawatomie County et al. v. Earls et al.
Drug testing of students by school officials, if done in a reasonable fashion, is a legitimate exercise of school authority.

Academic Privacy   Students have the right to expect that their records will be kept private. Although state laws govern the disclosure of information from juvenile court records, a 1974 federal law—the Family Educational Rights and Privacy Act (FERPA)—restricts disclosure of information from a student's education records without parental consent.[111] The act defines an education record to include all records, files, and other materials, such as photographs, containing information related to a student that an education agency maintains. In 1994, Congress passed the Improving America's Schools Act, which allowed educational systems to disclose education records under these circumstances: (1) state law authorizes the disclosure, (2) the disclosure is to a juvenile justice agency, (3) the disclosure relates to the justice system's ability to provide preadjudication services to a student, and (4) state or local officials certify in writing that the institution or individual receiving the information has agreed not to disclose it to a third party other than another juvenile justice system agency.[112]

Free Speech

Freedom of speech is guaranteed in the First Amendment to the US Constitution. This right has been divided into two categories as it affects children in schools: passive and active speech. **Passive speech** is a form of expression not associated with actually speaking words; examples include wearing armbands or political protest buttons. In contrast, **active speech** involves actually speaking or taking some other physical action such as parading with a banner.

The most important Supreme Court decision concerning a student's right to passive speech was in 1969 in the case of *Tinker v. Des Moines Independent Community School District*.[113] This case involved the right to wear black armbands to protest the war in Vietnam. Three high school students, ages 16, 15, and 13, were suspended for wearing the armbands in school. The decision is significant because it recognizes the child's right to free speech in a public school system. Justice Abe Fortas stated in his majority opinion, "Young people do not shed their constitutional rights at the schoolhouse door."[114] *Tinker* established two things: (1) a child is entitled to free speech in school under the First Amendment of the US Constitution, and (2) the test used to determine whether the child has gone beyond proper speech is whether he or she materially and substantially interferes with the requirements of appropriate discipline in the operation of the school.

The concept of active speech was at issue again in the 1986 case *Bethel School District No. 403 v. Fraser*.[115] This case upheld a school system's right to suspend or otherwise discipline a student who uses obscene or profane language and gesture. Matthew Fraser, a Bethel high school student, used sexual metaphors in making a speech nominating a friend for student office. His statement included these remarks:

> I know a man who is firm—he's firm in his pants, he's firm in his shirt, his character is firm—but most . . . of all, his belief in you, the students of Bethel, is firm.
>
> Jeff Kuhlman is a man who takes his point and pounds it in. If necessary, he'll take an issue and nail it to the wall. He doesn't attack things in spurts—he drives hard, pushing and pushing until finally—he succeeds.
>
> Jeff is a man who will go to the very end—even the climax—for each and every one of you.
>
> So vote for Jeff for A.S.B. vice president—he'll never come between you and the best our high school can be.

The Court found that a school has the right to control lewd and offensive speech that undermines the educational mission. The Court drew a distinction between the sexual content of Fraser's remarks and the political nature of Tinker's armband. It ruled that the pervasive sexual innuendo of Fraser's speech interfered with the school's mission to implant "the shared values of a civilized social order" in the student body.

In a 1988 case, *Hazelwood School District v. Kuhlmeier*, the Court extended the right of school officials to censor "active speech" when it ruled that the principal could censor articles in a student publication.[116] In this case, students had written about their personal experiences with pregnancy and parental divorce. The majority ruled that censorship was justified in this case because school-sponsored publications, activities, and productions were part of the curriculum and therefore designed to impart knowledge. Control over such school-supported activities could be differentiated from the action the Tinkers initiated on their own accord. In a dissent, Justice William J. Brennan accused school officials of favoring "thought control."

Off-Campus Speech In addition to speech on campus, students have been disciplined for their off-campus activities, such as posting messages on their Internet web pages that school officials consider defamatory.[117] What rights do students have to express themselves away from school grounds? It depends on the

---

passive speech
A form of expression protected by the First Amendment but not associated with actually speaking words; examples include wearing symbols or protest messages on buttons or signs.

active speech
A form of expression that involves speaking or taking some other physical action such as parading with a banner.

Tinker v. Des Moines Independent Community School District
Students have freedom of speech unless it disrupts the operation of the school.

Bethel School District No. 403 v. Fraser
A school has the right to control lewd and offensive speech that undermines the educational mission.

Hazelwood School District v. Kuhlmeier
School officials have the right to censor "active speech"—for example, controlling the content of articles in a student publication.

circumstances. In what has come to be known as the "Bong Hits for Jesus" case, the Supreme Court in *Morse v. Frederick* ruled that school officials can control student speech at off-campus events. In 2002, Joseph Frederick unveiled a 14-foot paper sign on a public sidewalk outside his high school in Juneau, Alaska, that linked marijuana smoking and Jesus. The school principal confiscated it and suspended Frederick. He sued, and his case went all the way to the Supreme Court, where the justices concluded that Frederick's free speech rights were not violated because it was reasonable to conclude that the banner promoted illegal drug use, and had the principal failed to act it would send a powerful message to the students that the school condoned pro-drug messages.[118]

Morse v. Frederick
School officials can control student speech at off-campus events.

In a recent Oregon case, a federal circuit court extended the school's right to discipline students for inappropriate words and deeds to off-school locations. The action was brought by a middle school student suspended for harassing two younger students and making highly inappropriate sexual remarks. The student challenged his suspension under the First Amendment, arguing that because the harassment occurred off-campus, in a public park, the school lacked the authority to discipline his behavior. The appellate court ruled that (1) the school district had the authority to discipline plaintiff for his off-campus, sexually harassing speech; (2) the plaintiff's suspension was permissible under the First Amendment; (3) that the plaintiff was provided the informal procedures that the Constitution requires for a two-day, out-of-school suspension; and (4) the plaintiff failed to show that he has a substantive due process interest in maintaining a clean, nonstigmatizing school disciplinary record.[119]

The Supreme Court has yet to rule on the scope of the school's authority for off-campus behavior. However, as the Cyber Delinquency feature shows, there are limits to school censorship of off-campus speech, especially in the cyber age.

School Prayer

One of the most divisive issues involving free speech is school prayer. While some religious-minded administrators, parents, and students want to have prayer sessions in schools or have religious convocations, others view the practice both as a violation of the principle of separation of church and state and as an infringement on the First Amendment caution against creating a state-approved religion. The 2000 case of *Santa Fe Independent School District, Petitioner v. Jane Doe* helps clarify the issue.[120]

Santa Fe Independent School District, Petitioner v. Jane Doe
Student-led prayers at a school football game are inappropriate and are in violation of the First Amendment separation of church and state.

Before 1995, the Santa Fe High School student who occupied the school's elective office of student council chaplain delivered a prayer over the public address system before each varsity football game for the entire season. After the practice was challenged in federal district court, the school district adopted a different policy that permitted, but did not require, prayer initiated and led by a student at all home games. The district court entered an order modifying that policy to permit only nonsectarian, nonproselytizing prayer. However, a federal appellate court held that, even as modified, the football prayer policy was invalid. This decision was appealed to the US Supreme Court, which ruled that prayers led by an elected student undermine the protection of minority viewpoints. Such a system encourages divisiveness along religious lines and threatens the students not desiring to participate in a religious exercise.

Though the *Santa Fe* case severely limits school-sanctioned prayer at public events, the Court has not totally ruled out the role of religion in schools. In its ruling in *Good News Club v. Milford Central School* (2001), the Supreme Court required an upstate New York school district to provide space for an after-school Bible club for elementary students.[121] The Court ruled that it was a violation of the First Amendment's free speech clause to deny the club access to the school's space on the ground that the club was religious in nature; the school routinely let secular groups use its space. The Court reasoned that because the club's meetings were to be held after school hours, not sponsored by the school, and open

Free Speech in Cyberspace

Free speech has become a significant issue in the educational system because the cyber age provides numerous opportunities for students to test its limits, whether it be through personal websites, Twitter messages, texts and emails that are quickly spread among the student body, or YouTube postings that show secretly made recordings of teachers in unflattering poses. While the Supreme Court has not yet ruled on this issue, a number of cases have gone to state and federal courts. Some have favored students while other have upheld the right of schools to bring off campus disciplinary actions.

Pro-Student Decisions

■ High school senior Justin Layshock sued Mercer County's Hermitage School District after he was suspended for 10 days for creating what he called a "parody profile" of his school principal. The webpage largely consisted of jokes about the principal's size and weight. On appeal, the Third Circuit Court ruled the suspension violated Layshock's right to freedom of speech, finding that self-expression "that originated outside of the schoolhouse, did not disturb the school environment and was not related to any school-sponsored event" could not be punished.

■ J.S., an eighth-grader, sued the Blue Mountain School District after she was suspended for 10 days for creating a fake Internet profile of her school principal. Her profile did not list the principal's name but contained his picture and a narrative that stated he was a pedophile and a sex addict. The court noted that legal precedent has already been set that so long as the online content created by a student on their own time, using their own resources, is not disruptive to the learning environment, they cannot be disciplined. But if the content disrupts the learning environment, it becomes a "school issue" and is subject to disciplinary action. The court left the door open to controlling students who publish off-campus material that is disruptive, saying, "We decline to say that simply because the disruption to the learning environment originates from a computer located off campus, the school should be left powerless to discipline the student."

■ Katherine Evans, a Florida high school senior and honor student, repeatedly clashed with Sarah Phelps, her English teacher. To vent her frustration, she created a Facebook page titled "Ms. Sarah Phelps is the worst teacher I've ever had" and invited past and current students of Phelps to post their own comments. Two months later, Evans was suspended from school even though she had voluntarily taken down the Facebook page. She sued, supported by the Florida ACLU, claiming her First Amendment rights had been violated. Evans eventually reached a settlement with the school district in which her suspension was wiped from her school record, and $15,000 in attorneys' fees and $1 in damages were awarded. Her attorneys described the settlement as a victory for free-speech rights.

Pro-School Cases

■ In *Doninger v. Niehoff*, a federal appellate court reached an opposite conclusion. The case involved a student at Lewis S. Mills High School in Connecticut who was barred from the student government after she wrote that the superintendent and other school officials were "douchebags." The off-campus blog post also asked students to call an administrator and "piss her off more." The appeals court held that the trial judge's ruling that the student's speech "foreseeably create[d] a risk of substantial disruption within the school environment," which in that case allowed the school to regulate off-campus speech.

■ In *Wisniewski v. Board of Education of Weedsport Central School District*, an eighth-grade student's instant messages contained an icon depicting a pistol firing at a person's head with the words "Kill Mr. VanderMolen" underneath. The student used his parent's home computer when instant messaging with classmates. One classmate brought the icon to the attention of the teacher and supplied him with a copy. After an investigation, the school suspended the student for a semester. The student brought suit, alleging that he was improperly disciplined in violation of his First Amendment right to free speech. The Court of Appeals for the Second Circuit held that the fact that the "creation and transmission of the IM icon occurred away from school property [did] not necessarily insulate [the student] from school discipline." The court upheld the student's suspension for off-campus Internet speech by holding it was reasonably foreseeable that the messages would "materially and substantially disrupt the work and discipline of the school."

The clash between a student's right to free speech and the school's ability to maintain security and discipline has not been settled and will continue to grow as the cyber age provides new venues of expression.

CRITICAL THINKING

Considering the spate of cyberbullying and other online harassment incidents, would you advocate stricter controls of the Internet? Or does the First Amendment's right to free speech trump such regulation, even if the aim is to reduce social harm?

SOURCES: *Layshock v. Hermitage School District*, No. 07-4465 2008 (2010), http://www.ca3.uscourts.gov /opinarch/074465p1.pdf; Nathan Crabbe, "UF Student Settles Suit over Facebook Comments," *Gainesville Sun*, January 1, 2011, http://smartboard.blogs.gainesville.com/2011/01/uf-student-settles-facebook-sui/; *Doninger v. Niehoff*, 527 F.3d 41 (2d Cir. 2008); *Wisniewski v. Board of Education of Weedsport Central School District*, 494 F.3d 34, 35 (2007). (URLs accessed October 2016.)

to any student who obtained parental consent, it could not be perceived that the school was endorsing the club or that students might feel coerced to participate in its activities. In 2001, the Court let stand a Virginia statute that mandates that each school division in the state establish in its classrooms a "moment of silence" so that "each pupil may, in the exercise of his or her individual choice, meditate, pray, or engage in any other silent activity which does not interfere with, distract, or impede other pupils in the like exercise of individual choice."[122] The Court refused to hear an appeal filed by several Virginia students and their parents, which contended that a "moment of silence" establishes religion in violation of the First Amendment.[123] In its most recent statement on the separation of church and state, the Court refused to hear a case brought by a California father contesting the recital of the Pledge of Allegiance because it contains the phrase "under God."[124] Though the Court dismissed the case on a technical issue, some of the justices felt the issue should have been dealt with and dismissed. Chief Justice William Rehnquist wrote in his opinion:

> To give the parent of such a child a sort of "heckler's veto" over a patriotic ceremony willingly participated in by other students, simply because the Pledge of Allegiance contains the descriptive phrase "under God," is an unwarranted extension of the establishment clause, an extension which would have the unfortunate effect of prohibiting a commendable patriotic observance.[125]

School Discipline

Most states have statutes permitting teachers to use corporal punishment to discipline students in public school systems. Under the concept of *in loco parentis*, discipline is one of the assumed parental duties given to the school system. In two decisions, the Supreme Court upheld the school's right to use corporal punishment. In the 1975 case of *Baker v. Owen*, the Court stated:

in loco parentis
Latin for "in place of parents" or "instead of a parent." Used to signify that parents have given a person or institution all the rights to behave, act, and be and act as a parent.

> We hold that the Fourteenth Amendment embraces the right of parents generally to control the means and discipline of their children, but that the state has a countervailing interest in the maintenance of order in the schools . . . sufficient to sustain the right of teachers, and school officials must accord to students minimal due process in the course of inflicting such punishment.[126]

In 1977, the Supreme Court again spoke on the issue of corporal punishment in school systems in the case of *Ingraham v. Wright*, which upheld the right of teachers to use corporal punishment.[127] In this case, students James Ingraham and Roosevelt Andrews sustained injuries as a result of paddling at the Charles Drew Junior High School in Dade County, Florida. The legal problems raised in the case were (a) whether corporal punishment by teachers was a violation in this case of the Eighth Amendment against cruel and unusual punishment and (b) whether the due process clause of the Fourteenth Amendment required that the students

Ingraham v. Wright
Corporal punishment in schools is legally permissible.

AP Images/John Bazemore

Though it may be hard to believe, some school districts still use physical punishments to discipline students. Here, Kaley Zacher is shown with her mother, Kimberly, in Dublin, Georgia. Zacher gave permission for Kaley to be paddled twice at Southwest Laurents Elementary School. Although the use of corporal punishment in American schools has declined in recent decades, paddling is still on the books in 19 states, despite calls from the US Department of Education to curb punitive disciplinary measures. Such punishments have been shown to be disproportionately used on minority and disabled students.

receive proper notice and a hearing before receiving corporal punishment. The Court held that neither the Eighth Amendment nor the Fourteenth Amendment was violated in this case. Even though Ingraham suffered hematomas on his buttocks as a result of 20 blows with a wooden paddle and Andrews was hurt on the arm, the Supreme Court ruled that such punishment was not a constitutional violation. The Court established the standard that only reasonable discipline is allowed in school systems, but it accepted the degree of punishment administered in this case. The key principle in *Ingraham* is that the reasonableness standard that the Court articulated represents the judicial attitude that the scope of the school's right to discipline a child is by no means more restrictive than the rights of the child's own parents to impose corporal punishment.

Despite the *Ingraham* decision, the use of corporal punishment remains controversial but is still being used. A disproportionate number of the students who are physically punished suffer from mental or physical disabilities. One reason is that students were punished for conduct related to their disabilities: students with Tourette syndrome were paddled for exhibiting involuntary tics; students with autism were punished for repetitive behaviors such as rocking. Corporal punishment, opponents charge, may harm kids with disabilities, leading to a worsening of their conditions. For instance, some parents reported that students with autism became violent toward themselves or others following corporal punishment.[128] Today 21 states still allow physical punishment in schools and more than 100,000 students face physical punishment each year.[129]

SUMMARY

1 **Discuss the role the educational experience plays in human development over the life course**

- The school environment has been found to have a significant effect on a child's emotional well-being.
- The school has become a primary determinant of economic and social status.
- The school itself has become an engine of social change and improvement.

2 **Identify the problems facing the educational system in the United States**

- The role schools play in adolescent development is underscored by the problems faced by the US education system.
- Cross-national surveys that compare academic achievement show that the United States trails in critical academic areas.
- High school students in the United States are consistently outperformed by those from Asian and some European countries on international assessments of mathematics and science.
- Many children are at risk for educational problems, school failure, and delinquency.

3 **Give examples of the hazards faced by children if they are dropouts**

- Though dropout rates have been in decline, leaving school early is still a national problem.
- Minority students are at greater risk to drop out than white students. One reason is that they often face harsher disciplinary action from school officials.
- Dropouts are more likely than graduates to get involved in antisocial behavior.
- Dropouts earn significantly less than graduates over the life course.
- They have more health problems and cost society more than graduates.

4 **Express the association between school failure and delinquency**

- Kids who do poorly in school are at risk for delinquent behavior.
- School failure is a stronger predictor of delinquency than variables such as economic class membership, racial or ethnic background, or peer-group relations.
- An association between academic failure and delinquency is commonly found among chronic offenders.

5 Examine the personal and social factors that have been related to school failure

- School failure may also be linked to learning disabilities or reading disabilities that might be treatable if the proper resources were available.

- Most researchers have looked at academic tracking—dividing students into groups according to ability and achievement level—as a contributor to school failure.

- Student alienation has also been identified as a link between school failure and delinquency. Students who report they neither like school nor care about their teachers' opinions are more likely to exhibit delinquent behaviors.

- Many students, particularly those from low-income families, believe that school has no payoff in terms of their future.

6 Calculate the extent of school crime

- In its pioneering study of school crime, *Violent Schools–Safe Schools* (1977), the federal government found that there was a significant amount of delinquency in schools.

- Hundreds of thousands of delinquent acts occur at school each year.

- Kids are more likely to be victimized at school than in the community.

- Teachers are also subject to threats and physical attacks from students and school intruders.

7 List the factors that contribute to delinquency in schools

- Kids who feel isolated and alone with little parental attention may be the most prone to alienation and substance abuse.

- The level of student drinking and substance abuse may increase violent crime rates.

- Violence is more prevalent in large schools as compared to smaller ones.

- Schools located in a city are more likely to experience criminal behaviors and violence than rural schools.

- The physical condition of the school building can influence students' motivation, attitude, and behavior.

- There is also evidence that crime in schools reflects the patterns of antisocial behavior that exist in the surrounding neighborhood.

8 Evaluate the efforts school systems are making to reduce crime on campus

- Nearly all states have developed some sort of crime-free, weapon-free, or safe-school zone statute.

- Almost every school attempts to restrict entry of dangerous persons by having visitors sign in before entering, and most close the campus for lunch.

- Most schools control access to school buildings by locking or monitoring doors.

- Schools use random metal detector checks and one or more security cameras to monitor the school.

- Schools that have experienced behavioral problems are now employing uniformed police officers on school grounds, typically called school resource officers.

- Some districts have gone so far as to employ undercover detectives on school grounds.

9 Explain what is being done to improve school climate and increase educational standards

- Numerous organizations and groups have called for reforming the educational system to make it more responsive to the needs of students.

- The federal government has sponsored programs to get local schools to improve their standards and narrow racial gaps in achievement.

- Students' awareness about the dangers of drug abuse and delinquency is being improved.

- Students are being trained in techniques to resist peer pressure.

- School management and disciplinary programs are being set up that deter crime, such as locker search.

10 Summarize the legal rights of students

- The US Supreme Court has sought to balance the civil liberties of students with the school's mandate to provide a safe environment.

- Educators can legally search students when there are reasonable grounds to believe the students have violated the law or broken school rules.

- The Supreme Court has expanded the power of educators to ensure safe learning environments through drug testing of students.

- The Court has also established that a child is entitled to free speech in school under the First Amendment of the US Constitution. However, the Court ruled that a principal could censor articles in a student publication.

- School prayer is a controversial free speech issue; the Court has severely limited prayer but allows a moment of silence.

- Most states have statutes permitting teachers to use corporal punishment to discipline students in public school systems.

KEY TERMS

QUESTIONS FOR DISCUSSION

1. Was there a delinquency problem in your high school? If so, how was it dealt with?

2. Should disobedient youths be suspended from school? Does this solution hurt or help?

3. What can be done to improve the delinquency prevention capabilities of schools?

4. Is school failure responsible for delinquency, or are delinquents simply school failures?

5. Should teachers be allowed to physically punish unruly students?

VIEWPOINT

You are the principal of a suburban high school. It seems that one of your students, Steve Jones, has had a long-running feud with Mr. Metcalf, an English teacher whom he blames for unfairly giving him a low grade and for being too strict with other students. Steve set up a home-based website that posted insulting images of Metcalf and contained messages describing him in unflattering terms ("a slob who doesn't bathe often enough," for example). He posted a photo of the teacher with the caption "Public Enemy Number One." Word of the website has gotten around school, and although students think it's funny and cool, the faculty is outraged. You bring Steve into your office and ask him to take down the site, explaining that its existence has had a negative effect on school discipline and morale. He refuses, arguing that the site is home-based and you have no right to ask for its removal. Besides, he claims, it is just in fun and not really hurting anyone.

School administrators are asked to make these kinds of decisions every day, and the wrong choice can prove costly. You are aware that a case very similar to this one resulted in a $30,000 settlement in a damage claim against a school system when the principal suspended a student for posting an insulting website and the student later sued for violating his right to free speech.

- Would you suspend Steve if he refuses your request to take down the site?

- Would you allow him to leave it posted and try to placate Mr. Metcalf?

- What would you do if Mr. Metcalf had posted a site ridiculing students and making fun of their academic abilities?

DOING RESEARCH ON THE WEB

There are a number of important resources for educational law on the Internet. Check out the Education Law Association (https://educationlaw.org/), the Educational Resource Information Center (http://www.eric.ed.gov/), and the Education Law Center (http://www.edlawcenter.org/).

NOTES

All URLs accessed September 2016.

1. Moriah Balingit, "Federal Appeals Court Sides with Transgender Teen, Says Bathroom Case Can Go Forward," *Washington Post*, April 19, 2016, https://www.washingtonpost.com/local/education/federal-appeals-court-sides-with-transgender-teen-says-bathroom-case-can-go-forward/2016/04/19/6a873b88-f76b-11e5-9804-537defcc3cf6_story.html.

2. Roslyn Caldwell, Susan Sturges, and Clayton Silver, "Home versus School Environments and Their Influences on the Affective and Behavioral States of African American, Hispanic, and Caucasian Juvenile Offenders," *Journal of Child and Family Studies* 16:119–132 (2007).

3. Thomas Mowen and John Brent, "School Discipline as a Turning Point," *Journal of Research in Crime and Delinquency* 53:628–653 (2016).

4. Daniel Seddig, "Crime-Inhibiting, Interactional and Co-Developmental Patterns of School Bonds and the Acceptance of Legal Norms," *Crime and Delinquency* 62:1046–1071 (2016).

5. Kenneth Polk and Walter E. Schafer, eds., *Schools and Delinquency* (Englewood Cliffs, NJ: Prentice Hall, 1972), p. 13.

6. Gary LaFree and Richard Arum, "The Impact of Racially Inclusive Schooling on Adult Incarceration Rates Among U.S. Cohorts of African Americans and Whites Since 1930," *Criminology* 44:73–103 (2006).

7. Sam Dillon, "Top Test Scores from Shanghai Stun Educators," *New York Times*, December 7, 2010, http://www.nytimes.com/2010/12/07/education/07education.html.

8. Program for International Student Assessment (PISA), https://nces.ed.gov/pubs2014/2014024rev.pdf.

9. The National Assessment of Educational Progress (NAEP), http://nces.ed.gov/nationsreportcard/.

10. Lynn Karoly, M. Rebecca Kilburn, and Jill Cannon, *Early Childhood Interventions: Proven Results, Future Promise* (Santa Monica, CA: Rand Corporation, 2005).

11. Ibid.

12. Lauren Musu-Gillette, Jennifer Robinson, Joel McFarland, Angelina KewalRamani, Anlan Zhang, and Sidney Wilkinson-Flicker, *Status and Trends in the Education of Racial and Ethnic Groups 2016* (NCES 2016-007). US Department of Education, National Center for Education Statistics. Washington, DC, 2016, http://nces.ed.gov/pubs2016/2016007.pdf.

13. Michael Rocques and Raymond Paternoster, "Understanding the Antecedents of the 'School-to-Jail' Link: The Relationship Between Race and School Discipline," *Journal of Criminal Law and Criminology* 101:633–665 (2011).

14. Center for Labor Market Studies, Northeastern University and the Chicago Alternative Schools Network, "Left Behind in America: The Nation's Dropout Crisis," April 2009, http://iris.lib.neu.edu/cgi/viewcontent.cgi?article=1020.

15. Andrew Sum, Ishwar Khatiwada, and Joseph McLaughlin, with Sheila Palma, "The Consequences of Dropping Out of High School," Center for Labor Market Studies, Northeastern University, Boston, October 2009, https://repository.library.northeastern.edu/downloads/neu:376324.

16. Chris Chapman, Jennifer Laird, and Angelina KewalRamani, "Trends in High School Dropout and Completion Rates in the United States: 1972–2008 Compendium Report," National Center for Education Statistics, December 2010, http://nces.ed.gov/pubs2011/dropout08.

17. Lauren Musu-Gillette et al., *Status and Trends in the Education of Racial and Ethnic Groups 2016.*

18. US Department of Education, "Secretary Arne Duncan's Remarks at the Release of America's Promise Alliance Report, 'Building a Grad Nation,'" November 30, 2010, http://www.ed.gov/news/speeches/secretary-arne-duncans-remarks-release-america%E2%80%99s-promise-alliance-report-%E2%80%9Cbuilding-gra.

19. Joseph Gasper, *Drugs Use and Delinquency: Causes of Dropping Out of High School?* (El Paso, TX: LFB Scholarly Publishing, 2012).

20. Spencer Rathus, *Voyages in Childhood* (Belmont, CA: Wadsworth, 2004).

21. Heather Ann Thompson, "Criminalizing Kids: The Overlooked Reason for Failing Schools," *Dissent* 58:23–27 (2011).

22. Sherman Dorn, *Creating the Dropout* (New York: Praeger, 1996).

23. G. Roger Jarjoura, "Does Dropping Out of School Enhance Delinquent Involvement? Results from a Large-Scale National Probability Sample," *Criminology* 31:149–172 (1993).

24. Gary Sweeten, Shawn D. Bushway, and Raymond Paternoster, "Does Dropping Out of School Mean Dropping into Delinquency?" *Criminology* 47:47–91 (2009).

25. Wayne Welsh and Courtney Harding, "School Effects on Delinquency and School-Based Prevention," in Marvin D. Krohn and Jodi Lane, eds., *The Handbook of Juvenile Delinquency and Juvenile Justice* (Chichester, England: John Wiley, 2015).

26. Eugene Maguin and Rolf Loeber, "Academic Performance and Delinquency," in Michael Tonry, ed., *Crime and Justice: A Review of Research*, vol. 20 (Chicago: University of Chicago Press, 1995), pp. 145–264.

27. Matthew Makarios, Francis T. Cullen, and Alex R. Piquero, "Adolescent Criminal Behavior, Population Heterogeneity, and Cumulative Disadvantage: Untangling the Relationship Between Adolescent Delinquency and Negative Outcomes in Emerging Adulthood," *Crime and Delinquency*, published online February 26, 2015.

28. Terence Thornberry, Alan Lizotte, Marvin Krohn, Margaret Farnworth, and Sung Joon Jang, "Testing Interactional Theory: An Examination of Reciprocal Causal Relationships Among Family, School, and Delinquency," *Journal of Criminal Law and Criminology* 82:3–35 (1991).

29. Kimberly Bender, "The Mediating Effect of School Engagement in the Relationship Between Youth Maltreatment and Juvenile Delinquency," *Children and Schools* 34:37–48 (2012).

30. Lyle Shannon, *Assessing the Relationship of Adult Criminal Careers to Juvenile Careers: A Summary* (Washington, DC: US Government Printing Office, 1982).

31. Marvin Wolfgang, Robert Figlio, and Thorsten Sellin, *Delinquency in a Birth Cohort* (Chicago: University of Chicago Press, 1972).

32. Ibid., p. 94.

33. Caroline Wolf Harlow, *Education and Correctional Populations* (Washington, DC: Bureau of Justice Statistics, 2003).

34. Makarios, Cullen, and Piquero. "Adolescent Criminal Behavior, Population Heterogeneity, and Cumulative Disadvantage."

35. Brent Donnellan, Kali H. Trzesniewski, Richard W. Robins, Terrie E. Moffitt, and Avshalom Caspi, "Low Self-Esteem Is Related to Aggression, Antisocial Behavior, and Delinquency," *Psychological Science* 16:328–335 (2005); Martin Gold, "School Experiences, Self-Esteem, and Delinquent Behavior: A Theory for Alternative Schools," *Crime and Delinquency* 24:294–295 (1978).

36. Paul Bellair and Thomas McNulty, "Beyond the Bell Curve: Community Disadvantage and the Explanation of Black-White Differences in Adolescent Violence," *Criminology* 43:1135–1168 (2005).

37. Michael Gottfredson and Travis Hirschi, *A General Theory of Crime* (Stanford, CA: Stanford University Press, 1990).

38. Richard Felson and Jeremy Staff, "Explaining the Academic Performance–Delinquency Relationship," *Criminology* 44:299–320 (2006).

39. John Shelley-Tremblay, Natalie O'Brien, and Jennifer Langhinrichsen-Rohling, "Reading Disability in Adjudicated Youth: Prevalence Rates, Current Models, Traditional and Innovative Treatments," *Aggression and Violent Behavior* 12:376–392 (2007).

40. Albert K. Cohen, *Delinquent Boys* (New York: Free Press, 1955).

41. Jackson Toby, "Orientation to Education as a Factor in the School Maladjustment of Lower-Class Children," *Social Forces* 35:259–266 (1957).

42. John Paul Wright, Francis Cullen, and Nicolas Williams, "Working While in School and Delinquent Involvement: Implications for Social Policy," *Crime and Delinquency* 43:203–221 (1997).

43. Jeannie Oakes, *Keeping Track: How Schools Structure Inequality* (New Haven, CT: Yale University Press, 1985), p. 48.

44. Kristian Bernt Karlson, "Expectations on Track? High School Tracking and Adolescent Educational Expectations," *Social Forces*, first published online February 5, 2015.

45. Jeannie Oakes, *Keeping Track: How Schools Structure Inequality, 2nd edition* (New Haven, CT: Yale University Press, 2005).

46. Travis Hirschi, *Causes of Delinquency* (Berkeley: University of California Press, 1969), pp. 113–124, 132.

47. *Learning into the 21st Century, Report of Forum 5* (Washington, DC: White House Conference on Children, 1970).

48. Mikaela Dufur, John Hoffmann, David Braudt, Toby Parcel, and Karen Spence, Examining the Effects of Family and School Social Capital on Delinquent Behavior," *Deviant Behavior* 36:511–526 (2015); Jane Sprott, Jennifer Jenkins, and Anthony Doob, "The Importance of

School: Protecting At-Risk Youth from Early Offending," *Youth Violence and Juvenile Justice* 3:59–77 (2005).

49. Richard Lawrence, "Parents, Peers, School and Delinquency," paper presented at the annual meeting of the American Society of Criminology, Boston, November 1995.

50. Gary Gottfredson, Denise Gottfredson, Allison Payne, and Nisha Gottfredson, "School Climate Predictors of School Disorder: Results from a National Study of Delinquency Prevention in Schools," *Journal of Research in Crime and Delinquency* 42:412–444 (2005).

51. National Institute of Education, US Department of Health, Education and Welfare, *Violent Schools–Safe Schools: The Safe Schools Study Report to the Congress*, vol. 1 (Washington, DC: US Government Printing Office, 1977).

52. David A. Soule, Denise C. Gottfredson, and Erin Bauer, "It's 3 pm: Do You Know Where Your Child Is? A Study on the Timing of Juvenile Victimization and Delinquency," *Justice Quarterly* 25:623–646 (2008).

53. Data in the following sections come from National Center for Educational Statistics, *Indicators of School Crime and Safety: 2015*.

54. Marie Skubak Tillyer, Bonnie S. Fisher, and Pamela Wilcox, "The Effects of School Crime Prevention on Students' Violent Victimization, Risk Perception, and Fear of Crime: A Multilevel Opportunity Perspective," *Justice Quarterly* 28:249–277 (2011).

55. Philip Veliz and Sohaila Shakib, "Interscholastic Sports Participation and School Based Delinquency," *Sociological Spectrum* 32:558–580 (2012).

56. Anthony Peguero, Ann Marie Popp, and Dixie J. Koo, "Race, Ethnicity, and School-Based Adolescent Victimization," *Crime and Delinquency*, first published online February 28, 2011.

57. National Center for Education Statistics, *Indicators of School Crime and Safety: 2015*, "Students Carrying Weapons on School Property and Anywhere" and "Students' Access to Firearms."

58. Jessie Klein, *School Shootings and the Crisis of Bullying in America's Schools* (New York: New York University Press, 2012).

59. Christine Kerres Malecki and Michelle Kilpatrick Demaray, "Carrying a Weapon to School and Perceptions of Social Support in an Urban Middle School," *Journal of Emotional and Behavioral Disorders* 11:169–178 (2003).

60. CNN, "Columbine High School Shootings Fast Facts," http://www.cnn.com/2013/09/18/us/columbine-high-school-shootings-fast-facts/.

61. Pamela Wilcox and Richard Clayton, "A Multilevel Analysis of School-Based Weapon Possession," *Justice Quarterly* 18:509–542 (2001).

62. Bryan Vossekuil, Marisa Reddy, Robert Fein, Randy Borum, and William Modzeleski, *Safe School Initiative: An Interim Report on the Prevention of Targeted Violence in Schools* (Washington, DC: United States Secret Service, 2000); Mary Ellen O'Toole, "The School Shooter: A Threat Assessment Perspective, Federal Bureau of Investigation," https://www.fbi.gov/file-repository/stats-services-publications-school-shooter-school-shooter/view.

63. American Psychological Association, "Bullying," http://www.apa.org/topics/bullying/; American Educational Research Association (AERA), *Prevention of Bullying in Schools, Colleges, and Universities: Research Report and Recommendations* (Washington, DC: American Educational Research Association, 2013), http://www.aera.net/Portals/38/docs/News%20Release/Prevention%20of%20Bullying%20in%20Schools,%20Colleges%20and%20Universities.pdf.

64. National Center for Education Statistics, *Student Reports of Bullying and Cyber-Bullying: Results from the 2013 School Crime Supplement to the National Crime Victimization Survey*, April 2015, http://nces.ed.gov/pubs2015/2015056.pdf.

65. Jane Ireland and Rachel Monaghan, "Behaviors Indicative of Bullying Among Young and Juvenile Male Offenders: A Study of Perpetrator and Victim Characteristics," *Aggressive Behavior* 32:172–180 (2006).

66. Young Shin Kim and Bennett Leventhal, "Bullying and Suicide: A Review," *International Journal of Adolescent Medical Health* 20:133–154 (2008).

67. T. Joscelyne and S. Holttum, "Children's Explanations of Aggressive Incidents at School Within an Attribution Framework," *Child and Adolescent Mental Health* 11:104–110 (2006).

68. Sameer Hinduja and Justin W. Patchin, "Social Influences on Cyberbullying Behaviors Among Middle and High School Students," *Journal of Youth and Adolescence* 42:711–722 (2013).

69. Klein, *School Shootings and the Crisis of Bullying in America's Schools*.

70. Norman A. White and Rolf Loeber, "Bullying and Special Education as Predictors of Serious Delinquency," *Journal of Research in Crime and Delinquency* 45:380–397 (2008).

71. Ann Marie Popp, "The Effects of Exposure, Proximity, and Capable Guardians on the Risk of Bullying Victimization," *Youth Violence and Juvenile Justice*, first published online February 23, 2012.

72. Ken Seeley, Martin L. Tombari, Laurie J. Bennett, and Jason B. Dunkle, "Bullying in Schools: An Overview," *OJJDP Juvenile Justice Bulletin*, December 2011, http://www.ojjdp.gov/pubs/234205.pdf.

73. Lisa Hutchinson Wallace and David May, "The Impact of Parental Attachment and Feelings of Isolation on Adolescent Fear of Crime at School," *Adolescence* 40:457–474 (2005).

74. Robert Brewer and Monica Swahn, "Binge Drinking and Violence," *Journal of the American Medical Association* 294:16–20 (2005).

75. Tomika Stevens, Kenneth Ruggiero, Dean Kilpatrick, Heidi Resnick, and Benjamin Saunders, "Variables Differentiating Singly and Multiply Victimized Youth: Results from the National Survey of Adolescents and Implications for Secondary Prevention," *Child Maltreatment* 10:211–223 (2005); James Collins and Pamela Messerschmidt, "Epidemiology of Alcohol-Related Violence," *Alcohol Health and Research World* 17:93–100 (1993).

76. Nancy Weishew and Samuel Peng, "Variables Predicting Students' Problem Behaviors," *Journal of Educational Research* 87:5–17 (1993).

77. Celia Lo, Young Kim, Thomas Allen, Andrea Allen, Allison Minugh, and Nicoletta Lomuto, "The Impact of School Environment and Grade Level on Student Delinquency: A Multilevel Modeling Approach," *Crime and Delinquency* 5:622–657 (2011).

78. Rami Benbenishty and Ron Avi Astor, *School Violence in Context: Culture, Neighborhood, Family, School and Gender* (New York: Oxford University Press, 2005).

79. David Maimon, Olena Antonaccio, and Michael French, "Severe Sanctions, Easy Choice? Investigating the Role of School Sanctions in Preventing Adolescent Violent Offending," *Criminology* 50:495–524 (2012).

80. Kristin Eisenbraun, "Violence in Schools: Prevalence, Prediction, and Prevention," *Aggression and Violent Behavior* 12:459–469 (2007).

81. Richard Lawrence, *School Crime and Juvenile Justice* (New York: Oxford University Press, 1998).

82. Wayne Welsh, Robert Stokes, and Jack Greene, "A Macro-Level Model of School Disorder," *Journal of Research in Crime and Delinquency* 37:243–283 (2000).

83. Gary Gottfredson and Denise Gottfredson, *Victimization in Schools* (New York: Plenum Press, 1985), p. 18.

84. Daryl Hellman and Susan Beaton, "The Pattern of Violence in Urban Public Schools: The Influence of School and Community," *Journal of Research in Crime and Delinquency* 23:102–127 (1986).

85. Nancy Weishew and Samuel Peng, "Variables Predicting Students' Problem Behaviors," *Journal of Educational Research* 87:5–17 (1993).

86. Welsh, Stokes, and Greene, "A Macro-Level Model of School Disorder."

87. Rod Brunson and Jody Miller, "Schools, Neighborhoods, and Adolescent Conflicts: A Situational Examination of Reciprocal Dynamics," *Justice Quarterly* 26:1–27 (2009).

88. American Psychological Association Zero Tolerance Task Force, "Are Zero Tolerance Policies Effective in the Schools? An Evidentiary Review and Recommendations," *American Psychologist* 63:852–862 (2008).

89. S. David Mitchell, "Zero Tolerance Policies: Criminalizing Childhood and Disenfranchising the Next Generation of Citizens," June 24, 2014, University of Missouri School of Law Legal Studies Research Paper No. 2014-16, http://papers.ssrn.com/sol3/Papers.cfm?abstract_id=2458550.

90. National Center for Education Statistics, *Indicators of School Crime and Safety, 2012*.

91. Bruce Jacobs, "Anticipatory Undercover Targeting in High Schools," *Journal of Criminal Justice* 22:445–357 (1994).

92. New York City Police Department, School Safety Division, www.nyc.gov/html/nypd/html/school_safety/school_safety_overview.shtml.

93. Stuart Tremlow, "Preventing Violence in Schools," *Psychiatric Times* 21:61–65 (2004).

94. Allison Ann Payne, Denise Gottfredson, and Gary Gottfredson, "Schools as Communities: The Relationships Among Communal School Organization, Student Bonding, and School Disorder," *Criminology* 41:749–777 (2003).

95. Susan L. Wynne and Hee-Jong Joo, "Predictors of School Victimization: Individual, Familial, and School Factors," *Crime and Delinquency* 57:458–488 (2011).

96. Payne, Gottfredson, and Gottfredson, "Schools as Communities."

97. Hellman and Beaton, "The Pattern of Violence in Public Schools," pp. 122–123.

98. Glenn Cook, "Education Debates Return to the Headlines as Midterms Near," *American School Board Journal* 193:6–7 (2006).

99. Stuart Yeh, "Reforming Federal Testing Policy to Support Teaching and Learning," *Educational Policy* 20:495–524 (2006).

100. US Department of Education, "Race to the Top Program," http://www2.ed.gov/programs/racetothetop/.

101. Birch Bayh, "Challenge for the Third Century: Education in a Safe Environment—Final Report on the Nature and Prevention of School Violence and Vandalism," report of the Subcommittee to Investigate Juvenile Delinquency, 95th Congress, 1st Session, p. 95.

102. Douglas Breunlin, Rocco Cimmarusti, Joshua Hetherington, and Jayne Kinsman, "Making the Smart Choice: A Systemic Response to School-Based Violence," *Journal of Family Therapy* 28:246–266 (2006).

103. "When School Is Out," *The Future of Children*, vol. 9 (Los Altos, CA: David and Lucile Packard Foundation, Fall 1999).

104. Sema A. Taheri and Brandon C. Welsh, "After-School Programs for Delinquency Prevention, A Systematic Review and Meta-Analysis," *Youth Violence and Juvenile Justice*, published online January 20, 2015.

105. *New Jersey v. T.L.O.*, 469 U.S. 325, 105 S.Ct. 733 (1985).

106. *Safford United School District No. 1 v. Redding* [08-479].

107. *Safford v. Redding*, 557 U.S. ___ (2009).

108. *J.D.B. v. North Carolina*, No. 09–11121, June 16, 2011, http://www.supremecourt.gov/opinions/10pdf/09-11121.pdf.

109. *Vernonia School District 47J v. Acton*, 115 S.Ct. 2394 (1995); Bernard James and Jonathan Pyatt, "Supreme Court Extends School's Authority to Search," *National School Safety Center News Journal* 26:29 (1995).

110. *Board of Education of Independent School District No. 92 of Pottawatomie County et al. v. Earls et al.*, 01.332 (2002).

111. Michael Medaris, *A Guide to the Family Educational Rights and Privacy Act* (Washington, DC: Office of Juvenile Justice and Delinquency Prevention, 1998).

112. Ibid.

113. 393 U.S. 503, 89 S.Ct. 733 (1969).

114. Ibid., p. 741.

115. *Bethel School District No. 403 v. Fraser*, 478 U.S. 675, 106 S.Ct. 3159, 92 L.Ed.2d 549 (1986).

116. *Hazelwood School District v. Kuhlmeier*, 484 U.S. 260, 108 S.Ct. 562, 98 L.Ed.2d 592 (1988).

117. Terry McManus, "Home Web Sites Thrust Students into Censorship Disputes," *New York Times*, August 13, 1998, p. E9.

118. *Morse et al. v. Frederick*, 551 U.S. 393 (2007).

119. *C.R. v. Eugene Sch. Dist. 4J*, United States Ninth Circuit, D.C. No. CV 12-01042 TC (2016), http://cdn.ca9.uscourts.gov/datastore/opinions/2016/09/01/13-35856.pdf.

120. *Santa Fe Independent School District, Petitioner v. Jane Doe, individually and as next friend for her minor children, Jane and John Doe, et al.*, No. 99-62 (June 19, 2000).

121. *Good News Club et al. v. Milford Central School*, No. 99-2036 (2001).

122. Va. Code Ann. S 22.1-203 (Michie 2000).

123. *Brown v. Gilmore*, 01-384 (case heard on October 29, 2001).

124. *Elk Grove Unified School District v. Newdow*, No. 02-1624 (2004).

125. Ibid.

126. 423 U.S. 907, 96 S.Ct. 210, 46 L.Ed.2d 137 (1975).

127. 430 U.S. 651, 97 S.Ct. 1401 (1977).

128. ACLU and Human Rights Watch press release, "US: Students with Disabilities Face Corporal Punishment at Higher Rates," August 10, 2009, http://www.hrw.org/en/news/2009/08/07/us-students-disabilities-face-corporal-punishment-higher-rates.

129. Sarah D. Sparks and Alex Harwin, "Corporal Punishment Use Found in Schools in 21 States," *Education Week*, August 23, 2016, http://www.edweek.org/ew/articles/2016/08/23/corporal-punishment-use-found-in-schools-in.html.

CHAPTER 11
Drug Use and Delinquency

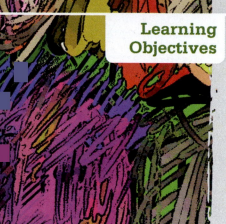

Learning Objectives

1 Identify which drugs are most frequently abused by American youth

2 Interpret the extent of the drug problem among American youth today

3 Discuss how teenage drug use in this country has changed over time

4 Appraise the main explanations for why youths take drugs

5 Identify the different behavior patterns of drug-involved youths

6 Examine the relationship between drug use and delinquency

7 Discuss the major drug control strategies

8 Assess the pros and cons of government use of different drug control strategies

Chapter Outline

Chapter Features

Youth Stories: Hope Turner

Case Profile: Fernando's Story

Focus on Delinquency: Does Drug Dealing Pay?

Focus on Delinquency: Drug Abuse Resistance Education (D.A.R.E.)

Evidence-Based Juvenile Justice— Treatment: Multisystemic Therapy

ON HER WAY HOME FROM high school, after celebrating the last day of classes by drinking alcohol and smoking marijuana with friends, Carla Wagner lost control of her car and hit Helen Marie Witty, age 16. Helen Marie was rollerblading on the sidewalk. The impact of the collision instantly killed the young victim. Wagner was convicted of manslaughter while driving under the influence and was sentenced to six years at a women's prison in Florida. As part of her sentence she is required to speak to high school students about the dangers of drinking and driving and the lifelong consequences that this criminal action can cause to victims and their families, as well as offenders. The victim's parents, Helen and John Witty, also speak to the same high school students to tell the story of their tragic loss. These educational campaigns have become more widespread in recent years, along with teen-focused antidrug workshops, which help youths learn more about what works and how they can play a role in preventing drug use in the community.

mylife photos/Alamy Stock Photo

There is little question that adolescent **substance abuse** and its association with delinquency are vexing problems. Almost every town, village, and city in the United States has confronted some type of teenage substance abuse problem. Self-report surveys indicate that just under half of high school seniors have tried drugs and almost two-thirds (64 percent) have used alcohol.[1]

Adolescents at high risk for drug abuse often come from the most impoverished communities and experience a multitude of problems, including school failure and family conflict.[2] Equally troubling is the association between drug use and crime.[3] Research indicates that between 5 and 8 percent of all juvenile male arrestees in some cities test positive for cocaine.[4] Self-report surveys show that drug abusers are more likely to become delinquents than are nonabusers.[5] The pattern of drug use and crime makes teenage substance abuse a key national concern.

This chapter addresses some important issues involving teenage substance abuse, beginning with a review of the kinds of drugs children and adolescents are using and how often they are using them. Then we discuss who uses drugs and what causes substance abuse. After describing the association between drug abuse and delinquent behavior, the chapter concludes with a review of efforts to prevent and control the use of drugs in the United States.

Frequently Abused Drugs

A wide variety of substances referred to as "drugs" are used by teenagers. Some are addicting, others not. Some create hallucinations, others cause a depressed stupor, and a few give an immediate uplift. This section identifies the most widely used substances and discusses their effects. All of these drugs can be abused, and because of the danger they present, many have been banned from private use. Others are available legally only under a physician's supervision, and a few are available to adults but prohibited for children.

Marijuana and Hashish

Commonly called "pot" or "weed," **marijuana** is produced from the leaves of *Cannabis sativa*. **Hashish** (hash) is a concentrated form of cannabis made from unadulterated resin from the female plant. The main active ingredient in both marijuana

substance abuse
Using drugs or alcohol in such a way as to cause physical, emotional, and/or psychological harm to yourself.

marijuana
The dried leaves of the cannabis plant.

hashish
A concentrated form of cannabis made from unadulterated resin from the female cannabis plant.

419

Marijuana is a drug commonly used by teenagers. Surveys indicate that marijuana use among high school students is much lower today than it was during its peak in the mid-1990s.

Malte Jaeger/laif/Redux

and hashish is tetrahydrocannabinol (THC), a mild hallucinogen. Marijuana is a drug commonly used by teenagers.

Smoking large amounts of pot or hash can cause distortions in auditory and visual perception, even producing hallucinatory effects. Small doses produce an early excitement ("high") that gives way to drowsiness. Pot use is also related to decreased activity, overestimation of time and space, and increased food consumption. When the user is alone, marijuana produces a dreamy state. In a group, users become giddy and lose perspective.

Marijuana is not physically addicting, but its long-term effects have been the subject of much debate. During the 1970s, it was reported that smoking pot caused a variety of physical and mental problems, including brain damage and mental illness. Although the dangers of pot and hash may have been overstated, use of these drugs does present some health risks, including an increased risk of lung cancer, chronic bronchitis, and other diseases. Marijuana smoking should be avoided by prospective parents because it lowers sperm count in male users, and females experience disrupted ovulation and a greater chance of miscarriage.[6]

synthetic marijuana
A mixture of chemicals derived from the cannibinoid family.

Like other drugs, marijuana can be refined or altered. One especially well known version is **synthetic marijuana**. Also known as Spice and K-2, this is an "herbal drug mixture" that most often combines designer chemicals derived from the cannibinoid family of drugs.[7] Only recently (in 2011) did the Drug Enforcement Administration add synthetic marijuana to its schedule of illegal drugs. Five percent of high school seniors report using this form of marijuana in the last year.[8]

While marijuana remains illegal for children and teenagers, in recent years some states have legalized the possession of marijuana for recreational use by adults. For example, in November 2012, both the states of Colorado and Washington legalized the possession of one ounce or less of marijuana by adults who are age 21 and older. In Oregon, marijuana became legal to use and grow as of July 2015 and legal to buy as of October 2015. Many other states have passed medical marijuana laws, which allow for the possession of marijuana by those with the expressed intent of use for medical purposes. These laws can be seen as one aspect of the legalization of drugs. A growing number of studies are examining the effects of these new laws on marijuana use in the general population and among youth.[9] Some studies have found that medical marijuana laws have increased adolescent marijuana use,[10] while the largest (using 24 years of the MTF survey) and most recent study found that medical marijuana laws do not increase adolescent use of marijuana.[11]

Cocaine

Cocaine is an alkaloid derivative of the coca plant. When first isolated in 1860, it was considered a medicinal breakthrough that could relieve fatigue, depression, and other symptoms, and it quickly became a staple of patent medicines. When its addictive qualities and dangerous side effects became apparent, its use was controlled by the Pure Food and Drug Act of 1906.

Cocaine is the most powerful natural stimulant. Its use produces euphoria, restlessness, and excitement. Overdoses can cause delirium, violent manic behavior, and possible respiratory failure. The drug can be sniffed, or "snorted," into the nostrils, or it can be injected. The immediate feeling of euphoria, or "rush," is short-lived, and heavy users may snort coke as often as every 10 minutes. Another dangerous practice is "speedballing"—injecting a mixture of cocaine and heroin.

Crack is processed street cocaine. Its manufacture involves using ammonia or baking soda (sodium bicarbonate) to remove the hydrochlorides and create a crystalline form of cocaine that can be smoked. In fact, crack gets its name from the fact that the sodium bicarbonate often emits a crackling sound when the substance is smoked. Also referred to as "rock," "gravel," and "roxanne," crack first gained popularity in the mid-1980s. It is relatively inexpensive, can provide a powerful high, and is highly addictive psychologically. Crack cocaine use has been in decline in recent years. Heavy criminal penalties, tight enforcement, and social disapproval have helped to lower crack use.

Heroin

Narcotic drugs produce insensibility to pain and free the mind of anxiety and emotion. Users experience relief from fear and apprehension, release of tension, and elevation of spirits. This short period of euphoria is followed by a period of apathy, during which users become drowsy and may nod off. **Heroin**, the most commonly used narcotic in the United States, is produced from opium, a drug derived from the opium poppy flower. Dealers cut the drug with neutral substances (sugar or lactose), and street heroin is often only 1 to 4 percent pure.

Heroin is probably the most dangerous commonly used drug. Users rapidly build up a tolerance for it, fueling the need for increased doses to obtain the desired effect. At first heroin is usually sniffed or snorted; as tolerance builds, it is "skin popped" (shot under the skin, but not into a vein), and finally it is injected into a vein, or "mainlined."[12] Through this progressive use, the user becomes an **addict**—a person with an overpowering physical and psychological need to continue taking a particular substance by any means possible. If addicts cannot get enough heroin to satisfy their habit, they suffer withdrawal symptoms, which include irritability, depression, extreme nervousness, and nausea. While still problematic, adolescent use of heroin has remained relatively stable over the last decade.[13]

Alcohol

The drug of choice for most teenagers continues to be **alcohol**. Almost six out of every ten (58 percent) high school seniors reported using alcohol in the past year, and almost two-thirds (64 percent) say they have tried it at some time during their lifetime; by the 12th grade, 47 percent of American youths report that they have been drunk.[14]

Just over 1.1 million drivers are arrested each year for driving under the influence (including 5,449 teen drivers), and about 736,000 more are arrested for other alcohol-related violations.[15] Drinking and driving by teenagers alone results in more than 800 deaths each year.[16] The economic cost is staggering. An estimated $185 billion is lost each year, including $36 billion from premature deaths, $88 billion in reduced work effort, and $19 billion arising from short- and long-term medical problems.[17]

---

cocaine
A powerful natural stimulant derived from the coca plant.

crack
A highly addictive crystalline form of cocaine containing remnants of hydrochloride and sodium bicarbonate, which emits a crackling sound when smoked.

heroin
A narcotic made from opium and then cut with sugar or some other neutral substance until it is only 1 to 4 percent pure.

addict
A person with an overpowering physical or psychological need to continue taking a particular substance or drug.

alcohol
Fermented or distilled liquids containing ethanol, an intoxicating substance.

What kind of people become addicts? View the **Schaffer Library of Drug Policy** website: http://www.druglibrary.org/schaffer/index.htm

Considering these problems, why do so many youths drink to excess? Youths who use alcohol report that it reduces tension, enhances pleasure, improves social skills, and transforms experiences for the better.[18] Although these reactions may result from limited use of alcohol, in higher doses alcohol acts as a depressant. Long-term use has been linked with depression and physical ailments ranging from heart disease to cirrhosis of the liver. Many teens also think drinking stirs their romantic urges, but scientific evidence indicates that alcohol decreases sexual response.[19]

Other Drug Categories

Other drug categories include anesthetic drugs, inhalants, sedatives and barbiturates, tranquilizers, hallucinogens, stimulants, steroids, designer drugs, and cigarettes.

anesthetic drugs
Central nervous system depressants.

Anesthetic Drugs   A variety of drugs called **anesthetic drugs** are central nervous system (CNS) depressants. Local anesthetics block nervous system transmissions; general anesthetics act on the brain to produce loss of sensation, stupor, or unconsciousness. The most widely abused anesthetic drug is phencyclidine (PCP), known as "angel dust." Angel dust can be sprayed on marijuana or other leaves and smoked, drunk, or injected. Originally developed as an animal tranquilizer, PCP creates hallucinations and a spaced-out feeling that causes heavy users to engage in violent acts. The effects of PCP can last up to two days, and the danger of overdose is high.

inhalants
Volatile liquids that give off a vapor, which is inhaled, producing short-term excitement and euphoria followed by a period of disorientation.

Inhalants   Some youths inhale vapors from lighter fluid, paint thinner, cleaning fluid, or model airplane glue to reach a drowsy, dizzy state that is sometimes accompanied by hallucinations. **Inhalants** produce a short-term euphoria followed by a period of disorientation, slurred speech, and drowsiness. Amyl nitrite ("poppers") is a commonly used volatile liquid packaged in capsule form, which is inhaled when the capsule is broken open.

sedatives
Drugs of the barbiturate family that depress the central nervous system into a sleeplike condition.

Sedatives and Barbiturates   The most commonly used drugs of the barbiturate family are **sedatives**, which depress the central nervous system into a sleeplike condition. On the illegal market, sedatives are called "goofballs" or "downers" and are often known by the color of the capsules: "reds" (Seconal), "blue devils" (Amytal), and "rainbows" (Tuinal).

Sedatives can be prescribed by doctors as sleeping pills. Illegal users employ them to create relaxed, sociable feelings; overdoses can cause irritability, repellent behavior, and unconsciousness. Barbiturates are the major cause of drug-overdose deaths.

tranquilizers
Drugs that reduce anxiety and promote relaxation.

Tranquilizers   Legally prescribed **tranquilizers**, such as Ampazine, Thorazine, Pacatal, and Sparine, were originally designed to control the behavior of people suffering from psychoses, aggressiveness, and agitation. Less powerful tranquilizers, such as Valium, Librium, Miltown, and Equanil, are used to combat anxiety, tension, fast heart rate, and headaches. The use of illegally obtained tranquilizers can lead to addiction, and withdrawal can be painful and hazardous.

hallucinogens
Natural or synthetic substances that produce vivid distortions of the senses without greatly disturbing consciousness.

Hallucinogens   Both natural and synthetic **hallucinogens** produce vivid distortions of the senses without greatly disturbing the viewer's consciousness. Some produce hallucinations, and others cause psychotic behavior in otherwise normal people.

One common hallucinogen is mescaline, named after the Mescalero Apaches, who first discovered its potent effect. Mescaline occurs naturally in peyote, a small cactus that grows in Mexico and the southwestern United States. After initial discomfort, mescaline produces vivid hallucinations and out-of-body sensations.

A second group of hallucinogens are synthetic alkaloid compounds. These can be transformed into lysergic acid diethylamide, commonly called LSD. This powerful substance stimulates cerebral sensory centers to produce visual hallucinations, intensify hearing, and increase sensitivity. Users often report a scrambling of sensations; they may "hear colors" and "smell music." Users also report feeling euphoric and mentally superior, although to an observer they appear disoriented. Anxiety and panic may occur, and overdoses can produce psychotic episodes, flashbacks, and even death.

Stimulants "Uppers," "speed," "pep pills," and "crystal" are **stimulants**— synthetic drugs that stimulate action in the central nervous system. They produce increased blood pressure, breathing rate, and bodily activity, and mood elevation. One widely used amphetamine produces psychological effects such as increased confidence, euphoria, impulsive behavior, and loss of appetite. Commonly used stimulants include Benzedrine ("bennies"), Dexedrine ("dex"), Dexamyl, Bephetamine ("whites"), and Methedrine ("meth," "speed," "crystal meth"). Methedrine is probably the most widely used and most dangerous amphetamine. Some people swallow it; heavy users inject it. Long-term heavy use can result in exhaustion, anxiety, prolonged depression, and hallucinations.

One form of methamphetamine is a crystallized substance with the street name of "ice" or "crystal." Ice methamphetamine looks similar to shards of ice or chunks of rock salt and is highly pure and extremely addictive.[20] Smoking this ice or crystal causes weight loss, kidney damage, heart and respiratory problems, and paranoia.[21]

Methamphetamines in general, whether in the three main forms of powder, ice, or tablets, have become an increasingly important priority of US law enforcement authorities. Although its use among secondary school students has shown a downward trend in the 17 years it has been investigated (1999–2015),[22] some states report much higher usage rates.[23] Authorities are also concerned because methamphetamine use in general has spread from its origins in the rural West to other parts of the country and into urban and suburban areas. According to the US Department of Justice's National Drug Intelligence Center, methamphetamine availability is highest in the Southeast region, followed by the Great Lakes, west Central, and Southwest regions.[24]

Other problems arise from the majority of it being produced domestically, either in "Mom and Pop" laboratories or super labs, which are mostly found in the Central Valley and southern areas of California. It can be made with many household products that are difficult or not feasible to regulate, and its production presents many dangers to people and the environment.[25] A number of states, including Oklahoma and Iowa, have banned over-the-counter cold medicines (such as Sudafed) that contain pseudoephedrine, an essential ingredient of methamphetamine, making them only available by prescription.[26] One study estimates that the economic cost of methamphetamine use in the United States exceeds $23 billion annually.[27] Because of this drug's popularity and deadly consequences, it is the subject of the accompanying Youth Stories feature.

Steroids Teenagers use highly dangerous **anabolic steroids** to gain muscle bulk and strength.[28] Black-market sales of these drugs approach $1 billion annually. Although not physically addicting, steroids can become an obsession among teens who desire athletic success. Long-term users may spend up to $400 a week on steroids and may support their habit by dealing the drug.

Steroids are dangerous because of the health problems associated with their long-term use: liver ailments, tumors, kidney problems, sexual dysfunction, hypertension, and mental problems such as depression. Steroid use runs in cycles, and other drugs—Clomid, Teslac, and Halotestin, for example—that carry their own dangerous side effects are often used to curb the need for high dosages of steroids. Finally, steroid users often share needles, which puts them at high risk for contracting HIV, the virus that causes AIDS.

stimulants
Synthetic substances that produce an intense physical reaction by stimulating the central nervous system.

anabolic steroids
Drugs used by athletes and bodybuilders to gain muscle bulk and strength.

Designer Drugs   Lab-created synthetics designed to get around existing drug laws, at least temporarily, are known as **designer drugs**. The most widely used designer drug is ecstasy, which is derived from speed and methamphetamine. After being swallowed, snorted, injected, or smoked, it acts simultaneously as a stimulant and a hallucinogen, producing mood swings, disturbing sleeping and eating habits, altering thinking processes, creating aggressive behavior, interfering with sexual function, and affecting sensitivity to pain. The drug can also increase blood pressure and heart rate. Teenage users taking ecstasy at raves have died from heat stroke because the drug can cause dehydration.

Cigarettes   Many countries around the world have established laws to prohibit the sale of cigarettes to minors. The reality, however, is that in many countries children and adolescents have easy access to tobacco products.[29] In the United States, the 1992 Synar Amendment requires states to enact and enforce laws restricting the sale of tobacco products to youths under the age of 18. States were required to reduce illegal sales rates to minors to no more than 20 percent. The Food and Drug Administration (FDA) rules require age verification for anyone under the age of 27 who is purchasing tobacco products. The FDA has also banned cigarette vending machines and self-service displays except in adult-only facilities. The signing of the Master Tobacco Settlement Agreement between 46 states and the tobacco industry in 1998 placed further restrictions on the advertising and marketing of cigarettes to young people and allocated substantial sums to antismoking campaigns.[30] Some efforts to enforce compliance with these restrictions and educate tobacco retailers about these laws have produced promising results.[31] Despite all of these measures, just under one out of every three high school seniors in America (31 percent) report having smoked cigarettes over their lifetime. However, in recent years cigarette use by high school students has been on a consistent decline.[32]

Some of this decline may be a result of the electronic alternative known as e-cigarettes. Popularized in the early 2000s, e-cigarettes entered the US market in 2007. An e-cigarette is a battery-charged device with a heating element at one end, which aerosolizes a liquid solution containing nicotine, and a mouthpiece at the other end used to inhale the vapor.[33] The process of inhaling vapor, whether it is nicotine, marijuana, or some other drug, is known as vaping. The use of e-cigarettes among teens has risen rather sharply in recent years. According to the Centers for Disease Control and Prevention's National Youth Tobacco Survey, the use of e-cigarettes (as measured in the last month) by high school students increased from 4.5 percent in 2013 to 13.4 percent in 2014. For middle school students, the increase in use of e-cigarettes was equally as large: from 1.1 percent in 2013 to 3.9 percent in 2014.[34]

Trends in Teenage Drug Use

Has America's decades-long War on Drugs paid off? Has drug use declined, or is it on the upswing? A number of national surveys conduct annual reviews of teen drug use by interviewing samples of teens around the nation. What do national surveys tell us about the extent of drug use, and what have been the recent trends in teen usage?

The Monitoring the Future (MTF) Survey

One of the most important and influential surveys of teen substance abuse is the annual Monitoring the Future survey conducted by the Institute for Social Research at the University of Michigan. In all, about 41,600 students located in 377 secondary schools participate in the study.

youth STORIES

Hope Turner

Hope Turner was just 5 years old when she was first exposed to methamphetamine. She didn't ingest it, but she just as easily could have. Her dad used methamphetamine on a regular basis and would leave the drug lying about the house. Called to the house on another matter one night in December 2005, Kansas City, Missouri, police discovered a gram of the drug and the implements used to smoke it. Hope was being watched by her dad that night, as was sometimes the case ever since her mom and dad had divorced.

The police charged Hope's dad with possession of an uncontrolled substance. But that was the extent of the case. Unlike some states, Missouri did not consider the use or possession of illicit drugs in the presence of a minor a form of child endangerment, a criminal offense punishable with a prison sentence.

The case made front page headlines and outraged the community and Dennine Turner, Hope's mom. Concerned for the safety of her own daughter and other children throughout the state, Dennine Turner lobbied the state legislature and the governor to take action. Methamphetamine use was especially problematic in the state. Its use by teenagers and adults was on the rise, and home "meth labs" were being uncovered by law enforcement at a rate of more than one a day, putting children at serious risk of exposure to the drug and injury from the toxic chemicals used in its manufacture.

A bill was eventually passed and signed into law by Missouri governor Jay Nixon on July 9, 2009. Known as "Hope's Law," after Hope Turner, it states, in part, "that anyone who possesses methamphetamine in the presence, or the home of, a person younger than 17, will be guilty of endangering the welfare of a child, in the first degree." In Missouri,

Hope Turner, now 9, watches Missouri Governor Jay Nixon sign "Hope's Law" at the Missouri State Highway Patrol Crime Laboratory in Jefferson City, MO, July 9, 2009.

child endangerment is a class-C felony, punishable by 5 to 15 years in prison. Hope's Law represents one way to help reduce the dangers that drugs present to children in the home. Could other states benefit from similar laws? What is the state of affairs across the country?

CRITICAL THINKING

Do you think laws like Hope's Law can make a difference in protecting children from the dangers of drugs? What are some other approaches that may prove helpful?

SOURCES: "Woman Pushes for Passage of Hope's Law," KMBC-Kansas City, Missouri, April 6, 2007; Lloyd Johnston, Patrick O'Malley, Richard A. Miech, Jerald Bachman, and John Schulenberg, *Monitoring the Future National Results on Drug Use, 1975–2015: Overview, Key Findings on Adolescent Drug Use* (Ann Arbor, MI: Institute for Social Research, University of Michigan, 2016), Table 5; National Drug Intelligence Center, *Methamphetamine Drug Threat Assessment*, p. 8; National Drug Intelligence Center, *Drug Availability in the United States* (Johnstown, PA: Author, 2010), Fig. 11; National Drug Intelligence Center, *Pseudoephedrine Smurfing Fuels Surge in Large-Scale Methamphetamine Production in California: Situation Report* (Johnstown, PA: Author, 2009); Dana Hunt, Sarah Kuck, and Linda Truitt, *Methamphetamine Use: Lessons Learned* (Cambridge, MA: Abt Associates, 2005), pp. iv, v; Fox Butterfield, "Fighting an Illegal Drug Through Its Legal Source," *New York Times*, January 30, 2005, p. A18; Kate Zernike, "Potent Mexican Meth Floods in as States Curb Domestic Variety," *New York Times*, January 23, 2006.

The most recent MTF survey (2015) indicates that, with a few exceptions, drug use among American adolescents continued to decline from the peak levels reached in 1996 and 1997. Annual drug use was down by more than one-third (37 percent) for 8th-graders during this period, while reductions have been somewhat lower for those in the 10th (28 percent) and 12th (9 percent) grades.[35] As Figure 11.1 shows, drug use peaked in the late 1970s and early 1980s and then began a decade-long decline until showing an uptick in the mid-1990s; usage for most drugs has been

figure 11.1

Trends in Annual Prevalence of Illicit Drug Use

SOURCE: Lloyd D. Johnston, Patrick M. O'Malley, Richard A. Miech, Jerald G. Bachman, and John E. Schulenberg, *Monitoring the Future National Survey Results on Drug Use, 1975–2015: Overview, Key Findings on Adolescent Drug Use* (Ann Arbor, MI: Institute for Social Research, University of Michigan, 2016), Table 6.

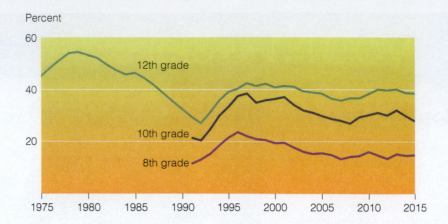

stable or in decline since then. Especially encouraging has been a significant drop in the use of alcohol by the youngest kids in the survey—a 22 percent drop in annual rates in the last five years (from 26.9 percent in 2011 to 21 percent in 2015) and a 38 percent drop in the last 10 years (from 33.6 percent in 2006). There has also been a continuing decline in cigarette smoking, as well as the use of smokeless tobacco products.

In recent years, a great deal of attention has been paid to the use of prescription-type drugs such as narcotics, tranquilizers, and sedatives among youths. This has involved both medical and nonmedical prescriptions of various stimulants.[36] From 2014 to 2015, annual use of OxyContin, a prescription painkiller narcotic, was slightly higher among 12th graders (3.3 percent to 3.7 percent) and slightly lower for 10th graders (3 percent to 2.6 percent) and 8th graders (1 percent to 0.8 percent). Annual use among all grades combined (2.3 percent in 2015) was substantially lower from the peak year of 2009, when it was 3.9 percent.[37]

The PRIDE Survey

A second source of information on teen drug and alcohol abuse is the national Parents' Resource Institute for Drug Education (PRIDE) survey.[38] Typically, findings from the PRIDE survey correlate highly with the MTF drug survey. The most recent PRIDE survey (for the 2013–2014 school year) indicates small to moderate reductions in drug activity over the previous school year, with larger decreases over the last 10 years. For example, less than 20 percent of students in grades 6 to 12 claimed to have used drugs during the past year, down from just over 22 percent in the 2004–2005 school year (Table 11.1). Any tobacco use and any alcohol use show much larger reductions over the 10-year period. The fact that two surveys generate roughly the same pattern in drug abuse helps bolster their validity and give support to a decline in teenage substance abuse.

table 11.1

Annual Drug Use, 2004–2005 vs. 2013–2014, Grades 6–12

	2004–05 (%)	2013–14 (%)	Rate of Decrease (%)
Any tobacco	29.1	16.6	43
Any alcohol	47.2	30.9	34.5
Any illicit drug	22.3	19.5	12.6

Source: *Pride Surveys Questionnaire for Grades 6 thru 12 Standard Report: 2013–14 Pride National Summary* (Bowling Green, KY: PRIDE Surveys, September 2014), Tables 1.12, 1.14, p. 26.

The National Survey on Drug Use and Health

Sponsored by the US Department of Health and Human Services' Substance Abuse and Mental Health Services Administration, the National Survey on Drug Use and Health (NSDUH, formerly called the National Household Survey on Drug Abuse) interviews approximately 70,000 people at home each year.[39] Like the MTF and PRIDE surveys, the latest NSDUH survey (2013) shows that drug and alcohol use, although still a problem, has stabilized or declined.

Although overall illicit drug use by youths ages 12 to 17 has shown impressive declines in recent years (a significant 13 percent reduction between 2009 and 2013),[40] it still remains a considerable problem. For example, *heavy drinking* (defined as having five or more alcoholic drinks on the same occasion on at least five different days in the past 30 days) was reported by more than 6 percent of the population ages 12 and older, or 16.5 million people.[41] Among youths ages 12 to 17, 1.2 percent were heavy drinkers and about 6 percent engaged in *binge drinking*, defined as having five or more alcoholic beverages on the same occasion at least once in the past 30 days.[42]

The latest NSDUH results show that rates of illicit drug use in the past month by adolescent males and females are somewhat different for overall illicit drug use (9.6 percent for males and 8 percent for females).[43] Previous surveys (2002–2004) found that adolescent females were closing the gap with their male counterparts in terms of usage of marijuana, alcohol, and cigarettes.[44] The most recent survey shows that current marijuana use is more common among male youths (7.9 percent) compared to their female counterparts (6.2 percent), while female youths are more likely to self-report nonmedical use of prescription psychotherapeutic drugs (2.4 percent compared to 2 percent for males).[45]

Are the Survey Results Accurate?

Student drug surveys must be interpreted with caution. First, it may be overly optimistic to expect that heavy users are going to cooperate with a drug-use survey, especially one conducted by a government agency. Even if willing, these students are likely to be absent from school during testing periods. Also, drug abusers are more likely to be forgetful and to give inaccurate accounts of their substance abuse.

Another problem is the likelihood that the most drug-dependent portion of the adolescent population is omitted from the sample. In some cities, almost half of all youths arrested dropped out of school before the 12th grade, and more than half of these arrestees are drug users.[46] Juvenile detainees (those arrested and held in a lockup) test positively for cocaine at a rate many times higher than those reporting recent use in the MTF and PRIDE surveys.[47] The inclusion of eighth-graders in the MTF sample is one way of getting around the dropout problem. Nonetheless, high school surveys may be excluding some of the most drug-prone young people in the population.

There is evidence that the accuracy of reporting may be affected by social and personal traits: girls are more willing than boys to admit taking drugs; kids from two-parent homes are less willing to admit taking drugs than kids growing up in single-parent homes. Julia Yun Soo Kim, Michael Fendrich, and Joseph Wislar speculate that it is culturally unacceptable for some subgroups in the population, such as Hispanic females, to use drugs, and therefore, in self-report surveys, they may underrepresent their involvement.[48]

Although these problems are serious, they are consistent over time and therefore do not hinder the *measurement of change* or trends in drug usage. That is, prior surveys also omitted dropouts and other high-risk individuals and were biased because of cultural issues. However, because these problems are built into every wave of the surveys, any change recorded in the annual substance abuse rate is probably genuine. So, although the validity of these surveys may be questioned, they are probably reliable indicators of trends in substance abuse.

Why Do Youths Take Drugs?

Why do youths engage in an activity that is sure to bring them overwhelming problems? It is hard to imagine that even the youngest drug users are unaware of the problems associated with substance abuse. Although it is easy to understand dealers' desires for quick profits, how can we explain users' disregard for long- and short-term consequences?

Self-report surveys are one source that can be drawn upon to elucidate some of the reasons or motives for why youths take drugs. Drawing upon 30 years of data collected from the Monitoring the Future survey (1976–2005), researchers identified a wide range of motives among high school seniors.[49] Social and recreational reasons were the most common responses, with more than half (57.2 percent) of all seniors saying they use drugs "to have a good time," "to experiment" (49.3 percent), and "to get high" (43 percent). Coping with negative affect was the next most common group of reasons for using drugs; for example, 38 percent of seniors reported using drugs "to relax," 19 percent "to get away from problems," and 15 percent "because of anger/frustration." Smaller percentages of students reported using drugs for other groups of reasons, including drug effect (e.g., "to increase drug effects"; 6.7 percent), compulsive use (e.g., "to get through the day"; 6.1 percent), cope with physical needs (e.g., "to sleep"; 7.1 percent), and miscellaneous (e.g., "because it tastes good"; 35.4 percent).[50] Concept Summary 11.1 reviews these and other most likely reasons why youths take drugs.

Social Disorganization

One explanation ties drug abuse to poverty, social disorganization, and hopelessness. Drug use by young minority group members has been tied to factors such as racial prejudice, low self-esteem, poor socioeconomic status, and the stress of living in a harsh urban environment.[51] The associations among drug use, race, and poverty have been linked to the high level of mistrust and defiance found in lower socioeconomic areas.[52] Despite the long-documented association between social disorganization and drug use, and even some specific drugs like methamphetamine,[53] the empirical data on the relationship between class and crime have been inconclusive.[54] For example, the National Youth Survey (NYS), a longitudinal

Young people take drugs for many reasons, including peer pressure, growing up in a rough neighborhood, poor family life, living with parents who abuse drugs, or to escape reality. Here, Misty Croslin, age 18, appears before Judge Charles Tinlin at the St. Johns County (Florida) Jail for her first appearance for felony drug trafficking charges. Distraught throughout her appearance, she told the judge about her parents' long-term abuse of drugs and alcohol, homelessness, and being left alone to care for her two younger brothers.

study of delinquent behavior conducted by Delbert Elliott and his associates, found little if any association between drug use and social class. The NYS found that drug use is higher among urban youths, but there was little evidence that minority youths or members of the lower class were more likely to abuse drugs than white youths and the more affluent.[55] Support for this finding also comes from research on youths' attitudes to drug use in high-risk communities.[56] Research by the RAND Corporation indicates that many drug-dealing youths had legitimate jobs at the time they were arrested for drug trafficking.[57] Therefore, it would be difficult to describe drug abusers simply as unemployed dropouts.

Peer Pressure

Research shows that adolescent drug abuse is highly correlated with the behavior of best friends, especially when parental supervision is weak.[58] Youths in inner-city areas where feelings of alienation run high often come in contact with drug users who teach them that drugs provide an answer to their feelings of inadequacy and stress.[59] Perhaps they join with peers to learn the techniques of drug use; their friendships with other drug-dependent youths give them social support for their habit. Empirical research efforts show that a youth's association with friends who are substance abusers increases the probability of drug use.[60] The relationship is reciprocal: adolescent substance abusers seek friends who engage in these behaviors, and associating with drug abusers leads to increased levels of drug abuse. Recent research by Gregory Zimmerman and Bob Edward Vásquez also finds that the peer effect on adolescent substance use may be nonlinear; that is, it decreases at higher levels of substance use, which suggests a "saturation" effect. The researchers also found that the peer influence on substance use is partially mediated by the perceptions of the health consequences of substance use and that neighborhood context plays a more important role than previously suggested.[61]

Peer networks may be the most significant influence on long-term substance abuse. Shared feelings and a sense of intimacy lead youths to become enmeshed in what has been described as the "drug-use subculture."[62] Research indicates that drug users do in fact have warm relationships with substance-abusing peers who help support their behaviors.[63] For example, some research points to the diminishing influence of friendship groups' drug use relative to schoolmates' (those not identified as friends, but attending the same school) drug use, but not when there is a high degree of social cohesion and connectedness among friends.[64] These behaviors can also be reinforced through adolescent peer networks brought about by dating and romantic relationships.[65] This lifestyle provides users with a clear role, activities they enjoy, and an opportunity for attaining status among their peers.[66] One reason it is so difficult to treat hard-core users is that quitting drugs means leaving the "fast life" of the streets.

Family Factors

Poor family life is also offered as an explanation for drug use. Studies have found that the majority of drug users have had an unhappy childhood, which included harsh punishment and parental neglect.[67] The drug abuse and family quality association may involve both racial and gender differences. Females and whites who were abused as children are more likely to have alcohol and drug arrests as adults; abuse is less likely to affect drug use in males and African Americans.[68] It is also common to find substance abusers within large families and where parents are divorced, separated, or absent.[69] Prenatal exposure to various illicit substances such as cocaine has also been found to be associated with adolescent drug use.[70]

Social psychologists suggest that drug abuse patterns may also result from observation of parental drug use.[71] Youths who learn that drugs provide pleasurable sensations may be most likely to experiment with illegal substances; a habit may develop if the user experiences lower anxiety and fear.[72] Research shows, for example, that gang members raised in families with a history of drug use were more likely than other gang members to use cocaine and to use it seriously. And even among gang members, parental abuse was found to be a key factor in the onset of adolescent drug use.[73] Observing drug abuse may be a more important cause of drug abuse than other family-related problems.

Other family factors associated with teen drug abuse include parental conflict over childrearing practices, failure to set rules, and unrealistic demands followed by harsh punishments. Low parental attachment, rejection, and excessive family conflict have all been linked to adolescent substance abuse.[74] The Case Profile entitled "Fernando's Story" tells how one young person worked to deal with family problems that contributed to his drug use and criminal activity.

Genetic Factors

The association between parental drug abuse and adolescent behavior may have a genetic basis.[75] Research has shown that biological children of alcoholics reared by nonalcoholic adoptive parents develop alcohol problems more often than the natural children of the adoptive parents.[76] A number of studies comparing alcoholism among identical and fraternal twins have found that the degree of concordance (both siblings behaving identically) is twice as high among the identical twin groups.[77]

A genetic basis for drug abuse is also supported by evidence showing that future substance abuse problems can be predicted by behavior exhibited as early as 6 years of age. The traits predicting future abuse are independent from peer relations and environmental influences.[78]

To read more about the **concept of addiction**, go to the Psychedelic Library: http://www.psychedelic-library .org/.

Emotional Problems

As we have seen, not all drug-abusing youths reside in lower-class urban areas. To explain drug abuse across social classes, some experts have linked drug use to emotional problems that can strike youths in any economic class. Psychodynamic explanations of substance abuse suggest that drugs help youths control or express unconscious needs. Some psychoanalysts believe adolescents who internalize their problems may use drugs to reduce their feelings of inadequacy. Introverted people may use drugs as an escape from real or imagined feelings of inferiority.[79] Another view is that adolescents who externalize their problems and blame others for their perceived failures are likely to engage in antisocial behaviors, including substance abuse. Research exists to support each of these positions.[80]

Drug abusers are also believed to exhibit psychopathic or sociopathic behavior characteristics, forming what is called an **addiction-prone personality**.[81] Drinking alcohol may reflect a teen's need to remain dependent on an overprotective mother or an effort to reduce the emotional turmoil of adolescence.[82]

addiction-prone personality
A personality that has a compulsion for mood-altering drugs, believed by some to be the cause of substance abuse.

case profile

Fernando's Story

FERNANDO ELLIS was a 15-year-old of Latino heritage who was referred to the local mental health/substance abuse agency after he attempted to jump out of his father's moving vehicle during a verbal argument. Fernando had been using and was high on drugs at the time. He was skipping school, using marijuana on a daily basis, and had numerous drug-related police contacts and charges. He was also on probation for selling drugs on school grounds.

Fernando's father worked long hours and drank to excess when he was at home. He introduced his son to alcohol and drugs at an early age, and offered little supervision or guidance. Fernando's mother was killed in an accident when Fernando was 12 years old, leaving his father to care for him and his three older siblings. In addition, Fernando was born with a birth defect that had often resulted in teasing by other children. At times, it was difficult to understand his speech, and he walked with a noticeable limp. It appeared Fernando was trying to fit in, "be cool," and gain acceptance by engaging in criminal activity.

At the juvenile court hearing, Fernando was ordered to complete community service and individual counseling, and was referred to the community mental health center for an alcohol and drug assessment, as well as a suicide risk assessment. He reluctantly cooperated with the order to avoid a more serious disposition.

Fernando's assessments indicated that although he did try to jump out of a moving car, he did not appear to be a suicide risk. He was under the influence at the time and in a very heated argument with his father. There was concern about his daily use of drugs and alcohol, and Fernando was referred to an outpatient drug treatment program at the center. In addition, Fernando met weekly with his counselor for individual counseling. They worked on his drug and alcohol issues, changing his behavior and habits, and on the grief and loss issues related to the sudden death of his mother. This loss was a major turning point for Fernando. Up to that time, he had been a good student who was not involved with drugs. Everything changed when his mother was killed.

Over the course of his work with his counselor, Fernando began to process this significant loss, as well as make positive changes in his life. A team of professionals including his teachers, probation officer, drug and alcohol counselor, and a mentor provided by the school all worked with Fernando to help him realize his goals. He began to attend school on a more regular basis, and worked to improve his relationships with his father and siblings and to reduce his criminal activity and drug and alcohol use. Fernando continued to occasionally use alcohol but eliminated his drug use. He also struggled with his home situation and sometimes ran away from home to stay with friends. Overall, Fernando dramatically reduced his criminal activity, although he remained on probation for the duration of the court order.

CRITICAL THINKING

1. Based on the information you read in this chapter, list the reasons why Fernando may have abused alcohol and drugs. What were the key family factors that may have played a role?

2. Although there was progress in the case, involved team members continued to have concerns for Fernando and his siblings. What could have been done to address these concerns? Do you think Fernando should have been removed from his parental home? How would this have impacted his situation?

3. If you were going to use a multisystemic treatment approach with Fernando, whom would you involve and what issues would you plan to address? Do you think this approach could be successful in the case? Why or why not?

Research on the psychological characteristics of narcotics abusers does, in fact, reveal the presence of a significant degree of pathology. Personality testing of users suggests that a significant percentage suffer from psychotic disorders. Studies have found that addicts suffer personality disorders characterized by a weak ego, a low frustration tolerance, and fantasies of omnipotence. Up to half of all drug abusers may also be diagnosed with antisocial personality disorder (ASPD), which is defined as a pervasive pattern of disregard for the rights of others.[83]

Problem Behavior Syndrome

For some adolescents, substance abuse is one of many problem behaviors that begin early in life and remain throughout the life course.[84] Longitudinal studies show that youths who abuse drugs are maladjusted, emotionally distressed, and have many social problems.[85] Having a deviant lifestyle means associating with delinquent peers, living in a family in which parents and siblings abuse drugs, being alienated from the dominant values of society, and engaging in delinquent behaviors at an early age.[86]

Youths who abuse drugs lack commitment to religious values, disdain education, and spend most of their time in peer activities.[87] Youths who take drugs do poorly in school, have high dropout rates, and maintain their drug use after they leave school.[88]

Rational Choice

Youths may choose to use drugs because they want to get high, relax, improve their creativity, escape reality, or increase their sexual responsiveness. Research indicates that adolescent alcohol abusers believe getting high will increase their sexual performance and facilitate their social behavior; they care little about negative consequences.[89] Substance abuse, then, may be a function of the rational, albeit mistaken, belief that substance abuse benefits the user.[90]

Pathways to Drug Abuse

gateway drug
A substance that leads to use of more serious drugs; alcohol use has long been thought to lead to more serious drug abuse.

There is no single path to becoming a drug abuser, but it is generally believed that most users start at a young age using alcohol as a gateway drug to harder substances. That is, drug involvement begins with drinking alcohol at an early age, which progresses to experimentation with marijuana, and finally, to using cocaine and even heroin.[91] Research on adolescent drug users in Miami found that youths who began their substance abuse careers early—by experimenting with alcohol at age 7, getting drunk at age 8, having alcohol with an adult present by age 9, and becoming regular drinkers by the time they were 11 years old—later became crack users.[92] Drinking with an adult present was a significant precursor of substance abuse and delinquency.[93] Recent medical research suggests that even nicotine can act as a gateway drug to the use of marijuana and cocaine, and that there is a molecular basis for this link.[94]

Although the gateway concept is still being debated, there is little disagreement that serious drug users begin their involvement with alcohol.[95] Though most recreational users do not progress to "hard stuff," most addicts first experiment with recreational alcohol and recreational drugs before progressing to narcotics. By implication, if teen drinking could be reduced, the gateway to hard drugs would be narrowed.

What are the patterns of teenage drug use? Are all abusers similar, or are there different types of drug involvement? Research indicates that drug-involved youths do take on different roles, lifestyles, and behavior patterns, some of which are described in the next sections.[96]

Adolescents Who Distribute Small Amounts of Drugs

Many adolescents who use and distribute small amounts of drugs do not commit any other serious delinquent acts. They occasionally sell marijuana, crystal, and PCP to support their own drug use. Their customers include friends, relatives, and acquaintances. Deals are arranged over the phone, in school, or at public meeting places; however, the actual distribution takes place in more private arenas, such as at home or in cars.

Petty dealers do not consider themselves "seriously" involved in drugs. One girl commented, "I don't consider it dealing. I'll sell hits of speed to my friends, and joints and nickel bags [of marijuana] to my friends, but that's not dealing." Petty dealers are insulated from the justice system because their activities rarely result in apprehension. In fact, few adults notice their activities because these adolescents maintain a relatively conventional lifestyle. In several jurisdictions, however, agents of the justice system are cooperating in the development of educational programs to provide nonusers with the skills to resist the "sales pitch" of petty dealers.

Adolescents Who Frequently Sell Drugs

A small number of adolescents are high-rate dealers who bridge the gap between adult drug distributors and the adolescent user. Though many are daily users, they take part in many normal activities, including going to school and socializing with friends.

Frequent dealers often have adults who "front" for them—that is, sell them drugs for cash. The teenagers then distribute the drugs to friends and acquaintances. They return most of the proceeds to the supplier, keeping a commission for themselves. They may also keep drugs for their personal use, and, in fact, some consider their drug dealing as a way of "getting high for free." One young user, Winston, age 17, told investigators, "I sell the cracks for money and for cracks. The man, he give me this *much*. I sell most of it and I get the rest for me. I like this much. Every day I do this."[97] James Inciardi and his associates found that about 80 percent of the youths who dealt crack regularly were daily users.[98]

Frequent dealers are more likely to sell drugs in parks, schools, or other public places. Deals occur irregularly, so the chance of apprehension is not significant. This irregularity combined with having to pay off others means the amount earned by drug dealers can be rather meager. Research on the earnings of drug dealers is discussed in the Focus on Delinquency feature entitled "Does Drug Dealing Pay?"

Teenage Drug Dealers Who Commit Other Delinquent Acts

A more serious type of drug-involved youth is the one who distributes multiple substances and commits both property and violent crimes; many are gang members.[99] These youngsters make up about 2 percent of the teenage population, but they may commit up to 40 percent of robberies and assaults and about 60 percent of all teenage felony thefts and drug sales. Few gender or racial differences exist among these youths. Girls are as likely as boys to become persistent drug-involved offenders, white youths as likely as black youths, and middle-class adolescents raised outside cities as likely as lower-class city children.[100]

In cities, these youths frequently are hired by older dealers to act as street-level drug runners. Each member of a crew of 3 to 12 youths will handle small quantities of drugs; the supplier receives 50 to 70 percent of the drug's street value. The crew members also act as lookouts, recruiters, and guards. Although they may be recreational drug users themselves, crew members refrain from using addictive drugs such as heroin. Between drug sales, the young dealers commit robberies, burglaries, and other thefts.

Most youngsters in the street drug trade either terminate their dealing or become drug dependent. A few, however, develop entrepreneurial skills. Those who are rarely apprehended by police advance in the drug business. They develop their own crews and may handle more than half a million dollars a year.

In many instances, these drug dealer–delinquents are members of teenage gangs. The gangs maintain "rock houses," or "stash houses," that receive drug shipments arranged by members who have the overseas connections and financial backing needed to wholesale drugs. The wholesalers pay the gang for permission to deal in their territory. Lower-echelon gang members help transport the drugs and work the houses, retailing cocaine and other drugs to neighborhood youths. Each member makes a profit for every ounce of rock sold. Police estimate that youths who work in rock houses will earn $700 and up for a 12-hour shift.[101]

Some experts question whether gangs are responsible for as much drug dealing as the media would have us believe. Some believe that the tightly organized "super" gangs are being replaced with loosely organized neighborhood groups. The turbulent environment of drug dealing is better handled by flexible organizations than by rigid, vertically organized gangs with a leader who is far removed from the action.[102]

FOCUS ON DELINQUENCY

Does Drug Dealing Pay?

In one of the first studies to investigate if drug dealing pays, economists Robert MacCoun and Peter Reuter found that drug dealers in Washington, DC, made about $30 per hour when they were working and cleared on average about $2,000 per month. These amounts are greater than most dealers could hope to have earned in legitimate jobs, but they are not enough to afford a steady stream of luxuries. It was also found that most small-time dealers also held conventional jobs.

Two more recent studies offer differing views on the economics of drug dealing. In an analysis of the financial activities of a drug-selling street gang in Chicago, economist Steven Levitt and sociologist Sudhir Venkatesh found that the average hourly wage of drug dealers or "foot soldiers" was between $2.50 and $7.10 (see Table 11.A). The results are based on a four-year period in which the gang was active. As an average wage per month, this comes to $140 to $470. In a typical month, drug dealers worked just over 50 hours. As shown in the table, the hourly wage of drug dealers is substantially lower than the average wage for all gang members and the gang leader. This finding suggests that, at least for drug dealers, factors other than income may explain participation in this activity.

In contrast, psychologists Michelle Little and Laurence Steinberg found that drug dealers derive a substantial income from selling drugs. Based on a large sample of serious male juvenile offenders in Philadelphia who reported incomes from drug sales, it was found that their average weekly wage was $1,693, or more than $6,700 per month.

Based on Levitt and Venkatesh's finding that drug dealers worked a little over 50 hours per month, the average hourly wage for this group of drug dealers comes to $135. Drug dealers who also held conventional jobs reported that their income from dealing was on average 41 times greater than what they made in the legal economy. It was also found that more than half the sample reported that they were involved in dealing drugs for more than a year. The authors speculated that income from drug sales served as an important incentive for continued involvement in illicit activities and may have acted as a disincentive for investment in conventional goals.

CRITICAL THINKING

Many are of the opinion that drug dealers make a great deal of money, which contributes to the public's view that dealers should be subject to more punitive dispositions. Does this research change your opinion of how society should treat drug dealers? How might this research be used to deter juveniles from dealing drugs?

SOURCES: Michelle Little and Laurence Steinberg, "Psychosocial Correlates of Adolescent Drug Dealing in the Inner City: Potential Roles of Opportunity, Conventional Commitments, and Maturity," *Journal of Research in Crime and Delinquency* 43:357–386 (2006); Steven D. Levitt and Sudhir A. Venkatesh, "An Economic Analysis of a Drug-Selling Gang's Finances," *Quarterly Journal of Economics* 115:755–789 (2000); Robert MacCoun and Peter Reuter, "Are the Wages of Sin $30 an Hour? Economic Aspects of Street-Level Drug Dealing," *Crime and Delinquency* 38:477–491 (1992).

TABLE 11.A: Estimated Hourly Wages of Members in a Drug-Selling Gang

	Drug Dealers	All Gang Members	Gang Leader
Year 1	$2.50	$5.90	$32.50
Year 2	$3.70	$7.40	$47.50
Year 3	$3.30	$7.10	$65.90
Year 4	$7.10	$11.10	$97.20

Note: Estimated hourly wages include both official and unofficial income sources. All wages are in 1995 dollars.

Source: Adapted from Levitt and Venkatesh, "An Economic Analysis of a Drug-Selling Gang's Finances," Table III.

Losers and Burnouts

Some drug-involved youths do not have the savvy to join gangs or groups and instead begin committing unplanned crimes that increase their chances of arrest. Their heavy drug use increases their risk of apprehension and decreases their value for organized drug distribution networks.

Drug-involved "losers" can earn a living by steering customers to a seller in a "copping" area, touting drug availability for a dealer, or acting as a lookout. However, they are not considered trustworthy or deft enough to handle drugs or money. Though these offenders get involved in drugs at an early age, they receive little attention from the justice system until they have developed an extensive arrest record. By then they are approaching the end of their minority and will either desist or become so entrapped in the drug-crime subculture that little can be done to deter their illegal activities.

Persistent Offenders

About two-thirds of substance-abusing youths continue to use drugs in adulthood, but about half desist from other criminal activities. Those who persist in both substance abuse and crime maintain these characteristics:

■ They come from poor families.

■ Other criminals are members of their families.

■ They do poorly in school.

■ They started using drugs and committing other delinquent acts at an early age.

■ They use multiple types of drugs and commit crimes frequently.

■ They have few opportunities in late adolescence to participate in legitimate and rewarding adult activities.[103]

Some evidence exists that these drug-using persisters have low nonverbal IQs and poor physical coordination. Nonetheless, there is little evidence to explain why some drug-abusing youths drop out of crime while others remain active.

Drug Use and Delinquency

An association between drug use and delinquency has been established, and this connection can take a number of forms.[104] Crime may be an instrument of the drug trade: violence erupts when rival gangs use weapons to settle differences and establish territorial monopolies. In New York City, authorities report that crack gangs will burn down their rivals' headquarters. In the 1990s, it was estimated that between 35 and 40 percent of New York's homicides were drug related.[105] This figure has come down somewhat since then.

Drug users may also commit crimes to pay for their habits.[106] One study conducted in Miami found that 573 narcotics users *annually* committed more than 200,000 crimes to obtain cash. Similar research with a sample of 356 addicts accounted for 118,000 crimes annually.[107]

Drug users may be more willing to take risks because their inhibitions are lowered by substance abuse. Cities with high rates of cocaine abuse are also more likely to experience higher levels of armed robbery. It is possible that crack and cocaine users are more willing to engage in a risky armed robbery to get immediate cash than a burglary, which requires more planning and effort.[108]

The relationship between alcohol and drug abuse and delinquency has been substantiated by a number of studies. Some have found that youths who abuse alcohol are most likely to engage in violence; as adults, those with long histories of drinking are more likely to report violent offending patterns.[109]

The National Institute of Justice's Arrestee Drug Abuse Monitoring (ADAM) program tracked trends in drug use among arrestees in urban areas. Some, but not all, of its 36 sites collected data on juveniles. Due to a lack of funding, the Department of Justice ended this program in 2004.[110] The most recent report (2002) found that among juvenile detainees almost 60 percent of juvenile males and 30 percent of juvenile females tested positive for marijuana, the most commonly used drug, and its prevalence was 10 and 6 times higher than cocaine use for juvenile males and females, respectively.[111] With the exception of methamphetamines, male detainees were more likely to test positive for the use of any drug than were female detainees. While males and minority-group members have somewhat higher positive test rates than females and Caucasians, drug use is prevalent among juvenile arrestees, reaffirming the close association between substance abuse and criminality.

Juvenile justice researchers Carl McCurley and Howard Snyder found that higher levels of youth problem behaviors and delinquency, ranging from school suspensions to major theft to gun carrying, are associated with drug use as well as

table 11.2

Drug Use, Problem Behaviors, and Delinquency

Behavior	Drank Alcohol (Past 30 days)		Used Marijuana (Past 30 days)		Sold Drugs (Ever)	
	No	Yes	No	Yes	No	Yes
Youth Ages 12–14						
Suspended from school	18%	31%	19%	46%	19%	55%
Vandalize property	13	37	14	50	14	56
Major theft	2	11	2	20	2	27
Attack/assault	8	28	9	36	9	53
Belong to a gang	1	7	1	16	1	18
Carry handgun	4	12	4	20	4	25
Arrested	2	8	3	15	2	22
Youth Ages 15–17						
Suspended from school	27%	38%	27%	52%	27%	63%
Vandalize property	10	23	11	33	11	40
Major theft	3	10	4	17	3	23
Attack/assault	8	21	10	29	9	37
Belong to a gang	1	5	1	9	1	12
Carry handgun	4	10	5	15	5	18
Arrested	5	12	5	21	5	26

Note: The time frame for "suspended from school" was ever; for the other items, it was the past 12 months. The value in the "yes" column differs significantly ($p < .05$) from the value in the "no" column for all column pairs within substance behavior and age groups.

Source: Carl McCurley and Howard Snyder, *Co-occurrence of Substance Use Behaviors in Youth* (Washington, DC: Office of Juvenile Justice and Delinquency Prevention, US Department of Justice, 2008), p. 3.

selling drugs.[112] This finding held up for younger and older teens (see Table 11.2). For example, among youths ages 12 to 14, 31 percent who reported drinking alcohol in the past month were suspended from school compared to 18 percent who did not drink alcohol. Similarly, for youths ages 15 to 17, school suspensions were significantly higher for those who drank alcohol compared to those who did not (38 percent versus 27 percent). These findings are based on data from the National Longitudinal Survey of Youth, a self-report survey administered to a nationally representative sample of youths ages 12 to 17. The researchers found that the difference in the prevalence of problem behaviors is even greater among youths, both younger and older, who used marijuana in the past month compared to their counterparts who did not: a twofold increase in school suspensions (19 percent versus 46 percent and 27 percent versus 52 percent), a threefold increase in vandalizing property (14 percent versus 50 percent and 11 percent versus 33 percent), and a five- and threefold increase in gun carrying (4 percent versus 20 percent and 5 percent versus 15 percent).

Drugs and Chronic Offending

It is possible that most delinquents are not drug users, but that police are more likely to apprehend muddle-headed substance abusers than clear-thinking abstainers. A second, more plausible interpretation of the existing data is that the drug abuse–crime connection is so powerful because many delinquents are in fact substance abusers.[113] Research by Bruce Johnson and his associates confirms this suspicion. Using data from a national self-report survey, these researchers found that less than 2 percent of the youths who responded to the survey (a) report using cocaine or heroin, and (b) commit two or more index crimes each year. However, these drug-abusing adolescents accounted for 40 to 60 percent of all the index crimes reported in the sample. Less than one-quarter of these delinquents committed crimes solely to support a drug habit. These data suggest that a small core of substance-abusing adolescents commit a significant proportion of all serious crimes. It is also evident that a behavior—drug abuse—that develops late in adolescence influences the extent of delinquent activity through the life course.[114]

The relationship between drug abuse and chronic offending is illustrated by Inciardi, Horowitz, and Pottieger's interviews with crack-involved youths in Miami. The 254 kids in their sample reported committing 223,439 criminal offenses during the 12 months prior to their interviews. It is not surprising that 87 percent of the sample had been arrested. The greater the involvement in the crack business, the greater the likelihood of committing violent crime. About 74 percent of the dealers committed robbery, and 17 percent engaged in assault. Only 12 percent of the nondealers committed robbery, and 4 percent engaged in assault.[115]

Explaining Drug Use and Delinquency

The association between delinquency and drug use has been established in a variety of cultures.[116] It is far from certain, however, whether (a) drug use *causes* delinquency, (b) delinquency *leads* youths to engage in substance abuse, or (c) both drug abuse and delinquency are *functions* of some other factor.[117]

Some of the most sophisticated research on this topic has been conducted by Delbert Elliott and his associates at the Institute of Behavioral Science at the University of Colorado.[118] Using data from the National Youth Survey, a longitudinal study of self-reported delinquency and drug use, Elliott and his colleagues David Huizinga and Scott Menard found a strong association between delinquency and drug use.[119] However, the direction of the relationship is unclear. As a general rule, drug abuse appears to be a *type* of delinquent behavior and not a *cause* of delinquency. Most youths become involved in delinquent acts *before* they are initiated into drugs; it is difficult therefore to conclude that drug use causes crime.

In other research involving the National Youth Survey, Jason Ford found that there is a reciprocal and ongoing relationship between alcohol use and delinquency during adolescence, and that part of the reason for this reciprocal relationship is that both behaviors have the effect of weakening youths' bonds with society, thereby promoting continued alcohol use and delinquency.[120]

According to the Elliott research, both drug use and delinquency seem to reflect developmental problems; they are both part of a disturbed lifestyle. This research reveals some important associations between substance abuse and delinquency:

- Alcohol abuse seems to be a cause of marijuana and other drug abuse, because most drug users started with alcohol, and youths who abstain from alcohol almost never take drugs.

- Marijuana use is a cause of multiple-drug use. About 95 percent of youths who use more serious drugs started on pot; only 5 percent of serious drug users never smoked pot.

- Youths who commit felonies started with minor delinquent acts. Few delinquents (1 percent) report committing only felonies.

Drug Control Strategies

Billions of dollars are being spent each year to reduce the importation of drugs, deter drug dealers, and treat users. Yet although the overall incidence of drug use has declined, drug use has concentrated in the nation's poorest neighborhoods, with a consequent association between substance abuse and crime.

A number of drug control strategies have been tried. Some are designed to deter drug use by stopping the flow of drugs into the country, apprehending dealers, and cracking down on street-level drug deals. Another approach is to prevent drug use by educating would-be users and convincing them to "say no" to drugs. A third approach is to treat users so that they can terminate their addictions. These and other drug control efforts are discussed in the following sections. Concept Summary 11.2 reviews the key strategies.

Key Drug Control Strategies

Law enforcement	Preventing drugs from entering the country Destroying crops used to make drugs Arresting members of drug cartels and street-level dealers
Education	Informing children about the dangers of drug use Teaching children to resist peer pressure
Community-based	Community organizations and residents taking action to deter drug dealing Engaging youth in prosocial activities
Treatment	Intervening with drug users, including counseling and experiential activities
Harm reduction	Minimizing the harmful effects caused by drug use and some of the more punitive responses to drug use

Law Enforcement Efforts

Law enforcement strategies are aimed at reducing the supply of drugs and, at the same time, deterring would-be users from drug abuse.

Source Control   One approach to drug control is to deter the sale of drugs through apprehension of large-volume drug dealers, coupled with enforcement of drug laws that carry heavy penalties. This approach is designed to punish known dealers and users and to deter those who are considering entering the drug trade.

A major effort has been made to cut off supplies of drugs by destroying overseas crops and arresting members of drug cartels; this approach is known as *source control*. The federal government has been encouraging exporting nations to step up efforts to destroy drug crops and to prosecute dealers. Other less aggressive source control approaches, such as crop substitution and alternative development programs for the largely poor farmers in other countries, have also been tried, and a review of international efforts suggests that "some success can be achieved in reduction of narcotic crop production."[121] Three South American nations—Peru, Bolivia, and Colombia—have agreed to coordinate control efforts with

Arresting large-volume drug dealers is an important strategy in reducing the supply of drugs. Here, St. Louis County police officer Justin Sparks arrests a man for having drug paraphernalia after the man allegedly attempted to purchase an over-the-counter cold medication containing pseudoephedrine in Fenton, Missouri. The man was denied the sale because he had already purchased the legal limit of pseudoephedrine for the month. Police use an electronic database to track pseudoephedrine sales in real time.

AP Images/Jeff Roberson

the United States. However, translating words into deeds is a formidable task. Drug lords fight back through intimidation, violence, and corruption. The United States was forced to invade Panama with 20,000 troops in 1989 to stop its leader, General Manuel Noriega, from trafficking in cocaine.

Even when efforts are successful in one area, they may result in a shift in production to another area or in the targeted crop being replaced by another. For example, enforcement efforts in Peru and Bolivia were so successful that they altered cocaine cultivation patterns. As a consequence, Colombia became the premier coca-cultivating country when the local drug cartels encouraged growers to cultivate coca plants. When the Colombian government mounted an effective eradication campaign in the traditional growing areas, the cartel linked up with rebel groups in remote parts of the country for their drug supply.[122] Leaders in neighboring countries expressed fear when the United States announced that they would provide billions in military aid—under the program known as "Plan Colombia"—to fight Colombia's rural drug dealers/rebels, assuming that success would drive traffickers over the border.[123] Another unintended effect of this campaign has been a recent shift by drug cartels to exploit new crops, from a traditional emphasis on coca to opium poppy, the plant used to make heroin.

On the other side of the world, Afghanistan has since reclaimed its position as the world leader in opium production, accounting for 92 percent of the global market.[124] This has come about after the fall of the Taliban government in 2001, which had banned poppy growing. Now, almost all of the heroin sold in Russia and three-quarters of that sold in Europe comes from Afghanistan. This has occurred despite new laws against poppy growing, law enforcement efforts, and crop substitution efforts on the part of agricultural aid organizations. Breaking with religious beliefs, Taliban forces are now promoting the growing of poppies—in some areas distributing leaflets that order farmers to grow the crop—and providing protection to drug smugglers, all in an effort to finance their operations against the US military and coalition forces in the country.[125] On the bright side, the United Nations estimates that in 2015 opium production in Afghanistan totaled 3,300 tons, a substantial decrease (48 percent) from the previous year.[126]

To find out more about the **federal government's drug control strategies**, go to the Office of National Drug Control Policy at the White House website (http://www.whitehouse.gov/ondcp/).

Border Control   Law enforcement efforts have also been directed at interdicting drug supplies as they enter the country. Border patrols and military personnel have been involved in massive interdiction efforts, and many billion-dollar seizures have been made. It is estimated that between one-quarter and one-third of the annual cocaine supply shipped to the United States is seized by drug enforcement agencies. Yet US borders are so vast and unprotected that meaningful interdiction is impossible. In 2014 (most recent data available), US federal law enforcement agencies seized untold thousands of pounds of cocaine and 11,000 pounds of heroin in the United States.[127] Global rates of interception of heroin and cocaine indicate that only 26 percent and 42 percent, respectively, of all imports are being seized by law enforcement.[128]

In recent years, another form of border control to interdict drugs entering the country has emerged: targeting Internet drug traffickers in foreign countries. With the increasing popularity of the Internet, some offenders are now turning to this source to obtain designer-type drugs. In Buffalo, New York, US customs agents discovered that a steady flow of packages containing the drug gamma-butyrolactone, or GBL, an ingredient of GBH (gamma hydroxybutyrate)—the date-rape drug—were entering the country from Canada; the drug was disguised as a cleaning product. Operation Webslinger, a joint investigation of federal law enforcement agencies in the United States and Canada, was put in place to track down the suppliers. Within a year, Operation Webslinger had shut down four Internet drug rings operating in the United States and Canada, made 115 arrests in 84 cities, and seized the equivalent of 25 million doses of GBH and other related drugs.[129] Shortly following this, another federal task force, known as Operation Gray Lord and involving the FDA and the Drug Enforcement Administration (DEA), was set up to combat illegal sales of narcotics on the Internet.[130]

If all importation were ended, homegrown marijuana and lab-made drugs such as ecstasy could become the drugs of choice. Even now, their easy availability and relatively low cost are increasing their popularity; they are a $10 billion business in the United States today. But there have been some signs of success. In 2014 (most recent data available), 5,935 illegal methamphetamine laboratories were seized by authorities across the United States. This is down considerably from the peak in 2003 when more than 10,000 labs were seized nationwide, and represents a 25 percent decrease from 2013. The DEA attributes this success to state restrictions on retail sales of ephedrine and pseudoephedrine products.[131] Many of these labs are operated out of homes, putting children—10,000 children were found in 8,000 of these labs over the years—at grave risk of being burned or injured, not to mention exposing them to illegal drugs.[132]

Targeting Dealers Law enforcement agencies have also made a concerted effort to focus on drug trafficking. Efforts have been made to bust large-scale drug rings. The long-term consequence has been to decentralize drug dealing and to encourage teenage gangs to become major suppliers. Ironically, it has proven easier for federal agents to infiltrate traditional organized crime groups than to take on drug-dealing gangs.

Police can also intimidate and arrest street-level dealers and users in an effort to make drug use so much of a hassle that consumption is cut back. Some street-level enforcement efforts have had success, but others are considered failures. A review of more than 300 international studies on police crackdowns on drug users and dealers found that this approach more often than not leads to increased violence; 87 percent of the studies reported an increase in violence due to these law enforcement practices.[133] "Drug sweeps" have also clogged correctional facilities with petty offenders while proving a drain on police resources. These sweeps are also suspected of creating a displacement effect: stepped-up efforts to curb drug dealing in one area or city may encourage dealers to seek friendlier territory.[134]

Education Strategies

Another approach to reducing teenage substance abuse relies on educational programs. Drug education now begins in kindergarten and extends through the 12th grade. An overwhelming majority of public school districts across the United States have implemented drug education programs with various components, including teaching students about the causes and effects of alcohol, drug, and tobacco use; teaching students to resist peer pressure; and referring students for counseling and treatment.[135] In a Texas survey of drug use among secondary school students that found drug use in rural school districts to be fast approaching usage rates in urban schools, the researchers speculate that funding cutbacks for drug education programs in the rural schools may be partly to blame.[136] Education programs, such as Project ALERT, which now operates in all 50 states, have been shown to be successful in training middle school youths to avoid recreational drugs and to resist peer pressure to use cigarettes and alcohol.[137] The latest survey of evidence-based drug use prevention programs in general shows that they are increasingly being implemented in middle schools across the country.[138] While

AP Images/Brad Doherty

Education programs delivered in schools and communities are a widely used strategy to prevent drug use by children and teens. Here, students at Champion Elementary School in Brownsville, Texas, participate in the 2015 annual Red Ribbon campaign organized by local and national law enforcement agencies. The campaign is designed to educate children about the dangers of drugs.

Drug Abuse Resistance Education (D.A.R.E.)

A landmark study of "Take Charge of Your Life," touted as the new D.A.R.E., found that the new curriculum reduced the use of marijuana among teens who reported using it at the start of the study, but increased the initiation of smoking and drinking among teens. The end result: D.A.R.E. America, the organization that oversees the program, will no longer use the new curriculum.

Over the last 15 years, national evaluations and independent reviews, including a study by the General Accountability Office (GAO), have repeatedly questioned the effectiveness of D.A.R.E., the most popular and widespread school-based substance abuse prevention program, leading many communities to discontinue its use. This was also due to the program not meeting US Department of Education effectiveness standards. To meet these criticisms head-on, D.A.R.E. began testing a new curriculum for middle and high school programs called "Take Charge of Your Life" (TCYL). The program focuses on older students and relies more on having them question their assumptions about drug use than on listening to lectures on the subject. The program works largely on changing social norms, teaching students to question whether they really have to use drugs to fit in with their peers. Emphasis shifted from fifth-grade students to those in the seventh grade, and a booster program was added in ninth grade, when kids are more likely to experiment with drugs. Police officers serve more as coaches than as lecturers, encouraging students to challenge the social norm of drug use in discussion groups. Students also do more role-playing in an effort to learn decision-making skills. There is also an emphasis on the role of media and advertising in shaping behavior.

A large-scale experimental study was launched to test the effectiveness of the program. The study was led by researchers at the University of Akron with $14 million in funding from the Robert Wood Johnson Foundation. Eighty-three school districts in six metropolitan areas from across the country—Detroit, Houston, Los Angeles, Newark, New Orleans, and St. Louis—involving nearly 20,000 seventh-grade students, were randomly assigned to the program (41 school districts) or to a control group that used the schools' existing substance abuse prevention education program (42 school districts). Five years later and two years after the program ended—when students were in 11th grade—researchers once again interviewed the students about their past-month and past-year use of tobacco, alcohol, and marijuana. Study results showed that there was a significant decrease in marijuana use among teens enrolled in the TCYL program compared to those who were not, but this only applied to those who were already using marijuana at the start of the study. The program had no effect on the initiation or onset of marijuana use. More problematic was the finding that 3 to 4 percent more students who took part in the TCYL program, compared to those in the control group, used alcohol and tobacco by the 11th grade.

The main conclusion of the researchers was that the TCYL program should not be implemented in schools as a universal prevention intervention. This was the original designation of the program, and it was to be achieved by altering students' intentions to use drugs—preventing them from trying drugs in the first place. Further analyses suggested that "both the content and intensity of the specific lessons around the targeted messages may not have been powerful enough to affect student substance using behaviors."

CRITICAL THINKING

1. What do these study results mean for the future of D.A.R.E.? Should schools continue to use it? What are the implications of its continued use in schools?

2. Are the reasons for teenage drug use so complex that a single school-based program is doomed to fail?

SOURCES: Zili Sloboda, Richard C. Stephens, Peggy C. Stephens, Scott F. Grey, Brent Teasdale, Richard D. Hawthorne, Joseph Williams, and Jesse F. Marquette, "The Adolescent Substance Abuse Prevention Study: A Randomized Field Trial of a Universal Substance Abuse Prevention Program," *Drug and Alcohol Dependence* 102:1–10 (2009); Peggy C. Stephens, Zili Sloboda, Richard C. Stephens, Brent Teasdale, Scott F. Grey, Richard D. Hawthorne, and Joseph Williams, "Universal School-Based Substance Abuse Prevention Programs: Modeling Targeted Mediators and Outcomes for Adolescent Cigarette, Alcohol and Marijuana Use," *Drug and Alcohol Dependence* 102:19–29 (2009); Brent Teasdale, Peggy C. Stephens, Zili Sloboda, Scott F. Grey, and Richard C. Stephens, "The Influence of Program Mediators on Eleventh Grade Outcomes for Seventh Grade Substance Users and Nonusers," *Drug and Alcohol Dependence* 102:11–18 (2009); University of Akron, "Press Release: Landmark Substance-Abuse Study Completed," March 31, 2009; Carol H. Weiss, Erin Murphy-Graham, and Sarah Birkeland, "An Alternative Route to Policy Influence: How Evaluations Affect D.A.R.E.," *American Journal of Evaluation* 26:12–30 (2005); General Accountability Office, *Youth Illicit Drug Use Prevention: D.A.R.E. Long-Term Evaluations and Federal Efforts to Identify Effective Programs* (Washington, DC: Author, 2003).

not considered to be evidence-based, Drug Abuse Resistance Education (D.A.R.E.) continues to be widely used across the country and has undergone a large-scale evaluation of its new curriculum, "Take Charge of Your Life." Because of its continued widespread use and influence, D.A.R.E. is the subject of the accompanying Focus on Delinquency feature.

Countering the media's influence on adolescents' intentions to use drugs has also been a focus of education strategies.[139] Two large-scale studies demonstrate the effectiveness of antidrug messages targeted at youth. An evaluation of the National Youth Anti-Drug Media Campaign, which features ads showing the dangers of marijuana use, reported that 41 percent of students in grades 7 to 12 "agree a lot" that the ads made them less likely to try or use drugs. Importantly, the study also reported that past-year marijuana use among the students was down 6 percent.[140] The second study, the National Survey on Drug Use and Health, which asked young people ages 12 to 17 about antidrug messages they had heard or seen outside of school hours, reported that past-month drug use by those exposed to

For a web-based **antidrug education campaign**, see the Partnership for Drug-Free Kids at Drugfree.org (http://www.drugfree.org/). You can also go to the official website for **D.A.R.E.** (http://www.dare.org/).

the messages was 18 percent lower than those who had not been exposed to the messages (8.4 percent compared to 10.2 percent).[141] Parental involvement by way of support and monitoring has also been shown to play a role in reducing adolescent drug use.[142] For instance, the National Survey on Drug Use and Health found that the rate of past-month use of any illicit drug was significantly lower for youths who reported that their parents always or sometimes helped them with their homework compared with youths who reported that their parents seldom or never helped (7.3 percent compared to 14.7 percent).[143]

Community Strategies

Another type of drug control effort relies on local community groups. Representatives of local government agencies, churches, civic organizations, and similar institutions are being brought together to create drug-prevention programs. Their activities include drug-free school zones, which encourage police to keep drug dealers away from schools; Neighborhood Watch programs, which are geared to reporting drug dealers; citizen patrols, which frighten dealers away from public-housing projects; and community centers, which provide an alternative to the street culture.

Community-based programs reach out to some of the highest-risk youths, who are often missed by the well-known education programs that take place in schools.[144] These programs try to get youths involved in after-school programs offering counseling, delivering clothing, food, and medical care when needed, and encouraging school achievement. Community programs also sponsor drug-free activities involving the arts, clubs, and athletics. In many respects, evaluations of community programs have shown that they may encourage antidrug attitudes and help insulate participating youths from an environment that encourages drugs.[145]

Treatment Strategies

multisystemic therapy (MST)
Addresses a variety of family, peer, and psychological problems by focusing on problem solving and communication skills training.

In 2013 (most recent data available), 122,000 youths ages 12 to 17 were admitted to drug treatment facilities in the United States.[146] Several approaches are available to treat these users. Some efforts stem from the perspective that users have low self-esteem, and they use various techniques to build up the user's sense of self. Some use psychological counseling, and others, such as the **multisystemic therapy (MST)** technique developed by Scott Henggeler, direct attention to family, peer, and psychological problems by focusing on problem solving and communication skills.[147] Because of its importance and effectiveness as a drug and delinquency treatment strategy, MST is the subject of the accompanying Evidence-Based Juvenile Justice feature.

Another approach is to involve users in outdoor activities, wilderness training, and after-school community programs.[148] More intensive efforts use group therapy, in which leaders try to give users the skills and support to help them reject the social pressure to use drugs. These programs are based on the Alcoholics Anonymous philosophy that users must find the strength to stay clean and that support from those who understand their experiences can be a successful way to achieve a drug-free life. One effective approach is brief alcohol intervention, which incorporates therapeutic components and consists of a small number of sessions (as few as one and as many as five) delivered by medical professionals or psychologists. A recent review found that brief interventions for adolescents and young adults targeted at both alcohol and other illicit drugs were effective in reducing both substances, but brief interventions targeted only on alcohol had no effect on other drugs.[149]

Residential programs are used with more heavily involved drug abusers. Some are detoxification units that use medical procedures to wean patients from the more addicting drugs. Others are therapeutic communities that attempt to deal with the psychological causes of drug use. Hypnosis, aversion therapy (getting users to associate drugs with unpleasant sensations, such as nausea), counseling, biofeedback, and other techniques are often used.

Multisystemic Therapy

MST is an increasingly popular multimodal treatment approach designed for serious juvenile offenders. The particular type of treatment is chosen according to the needs of the young person; therefore, the nature of the treatment is different for each youth. The treatment may include individual, family, peer, school, and community interventions, including parent training and skills training; more often, though, it is referred to as a "family-based treatment."

MST has proven successful in reducing delinquency, substance abuse, and other problematic behaviors in a number of experiments with serious juvenile offenders. Scott Henggeler and his colleagues carried out a long-term follow-up of a randomized experiment to test the efficacy of MST compared to traditional counseling services for 118 substance-abusing juvenile offenders. The average age at treatment was 16 years and the average age at follow-up was 19.5 years. Compared to those who received traditional counseling services (the control group), MST participants had significantly lower yearly conviction rates for aggressive criminal activity (15 percent versus 57 percent), but not for property crimes. Treatment effects on long-term illicit drug use were mixed, with biological measures (e.g., urine analysis) indicating significantly higher rates of marijuana abstinence for MST participants compared to control group participants (55 percent versus 28 percent), but no effect on cocaine use.

In another randomized experiment, Cindy Schaeffer and Charles Borduin carried out an even longer-term follow-up to test the efficacy of MST compared to individualized therapy for 176 serious and violent juvenile offenders. The average age at treatment was 14 years and the average age at follow-up

was about 29 years. Compared to those who received individual therapy, MST participants had significantly lower recidivism rates (50 percent versus 81 percent), including lower rates of rearrest for violent offenses (14 percent versus 30 percent). MST participants also had 54 percent fewer arrests and 57 percent fewer days of confinement in adult detention facilities compared to their control counterparts.

MST has also been shown to be highly cost-effective. According to the Washington State Institute for Public Policy, for every $1 spent on MST, more than $8 are saved in victim costs and juvenile justice and criminal justice costs. This finding has proven particularly influential with policy makers and legislators across the country, who are grappling with how best to keep juvenile crime rates from going up in tough economic times.

CRITICAL THINKING

1. What factors account for MST's success in reducing delinquency, substance abuse, and other problematic behaviors?

2. How does MST compare with other treatment strategies to reduce juvenile drug use? Do you think more communities should use it to address juvenile drug use? If so, what are the most important challenges that the program will need to address?

SOURCES: Stephanie Lee, Steve Aos, Elizabeth K. Drake, Anne Pennucci, Marna G. Miller, and Laurie Anderson, *Return on Investment: Evidence-Based Options to Improve Statewide Outcomes* (Olympia: Washington State Institute for Public Policy, 2012); Brandon C. Welsh and Peter W. Greenwood, "Making It Happen: State Progress in Implementing Evidence-Based Programs for Delinquent Youth," *Youth Violence and Juvenile Justice* 13:243–257 (2015); Cindy M. Schaeffer and Charles M. Borduin, "Long-Term Follow-Up to a Randomized Clinical Trial of Multisystemic Therapy with Serious and Violent Juvenile Offenders," *Journal of Consulting and Clinical Psychology* 73:445–453 (2005); Scott W. Henggeler, W. Glenn Clingempeel, Michael J. Brondino, and Susan G. Pickrel, "Four-Year Follow-Up of Multisystemic Therapy with Substance-Abusing and Substance-Dependent Juvenile Offenders," *Journal of the American Academy of Child and Adolescent Psychiatry* 41:868–874 (2002).

There is little evidence that these residential programs can effectively reduce teenage substance abuse.[150] Many are restricted to families whose health insurance will pay for short-term residential care; when the coverage ends, the children are released. Adolescents do not often enter these programs voluntarily, and most have little motivation to change.[151] A stay can stigmatize residents as "addicts," even though they never used hard drugs; while in treatment, they may be introduced to hardcore users with whom they will associate upon release. One residential program that has been proposed for reducing teenage substance abuse is UCLA's Comprehensive Residential Education, Arts, and Substance Abuse Treatment (CREASAT) program, which integrates "enhanced substance abuse services" (group therapy, education, vocational skills) and visual and performing arts programming.[152]

Harm Reduction

A **harm reduction** approach involves lessening the harms caused to youths by drug use and by some of the more punitive responses to drug use. Harm reduction encapsulates some of the efforts advanced under the community and treatment

harm reduction
Efforts to minimize the harmful effects caused by drug use.

strategies noted above, but maintains as its primary focus efforts to minimize the harmful effects of drug use. This approach includes the following components:

- The availability of drug treatment facilities so that all addicts who wish to do so can overcome their habits and lead drug-free lives

- The use of health professionals to administer drugs to addicts as part of a treatment and detoxification program

- Needle exchange programs that will slow the transmission of HIV and educate drug users about how HIV is contracted and spread

- Special drug courts or pretrial diversion programs that compel drug treatment (juvenile drug courts are discussed in Chapter 13)[153]

Needle exchange programs—providing drug users with clean needles in exchange for used ones—have been shown to maintain the low prevalence of HIV transmission among drug users and lower rates of hepatitis C. Methadone maintenance clinics in which heroin users receive doctor-prescribed methadone (a nonaddictive substance that satisfies the cravings caused by heroin) have been shown to reduce illegal heroin use and criminal activity.[154]

Critics of the harm reduction approach warn that it condones or promotes drug use, "encouraging people either to continue using drugs or to start using drugs, without recognizing the dangers of their addiction."[155] Advocates, on the other hand, refer to harm reduction as an important first step in dealing with drug use: "There are safer ways of using drugs, and harm reduction for patients is a valuable interim measure to help them make informed choices and improve their overall health."[156]

Advocates also call for this approach to replace the War on Drugs, and claim that this change in drug policy will go a long way toward solving two key problems caused by punitive responses. First, it will reduce the number of offenders, both juvenile and adult, being sent to already overcrowded institutionalized settings for what amounts to less serious offenses. Second, it will discourage police crackdowns in minority neighborhoods that result in racial minorities being arrested and formally processed at much higher rates for drug offenses.[157] The War on Drugs has also been a major source of the racial discrimination that occurs in both the adult and juvenile justice systems.[158] (For more on racial discrimination in the juvenile justice system, see Chapters 13, 14, and 15.)

To learn more about the **harm reduction** approach to teenage drug use, check out the Harm Reduction Coalition: http://harmreduction.org/.

What Does the Future Hold?

The United States appears willing to go to great lengths to fight the drug war.[159] The financial cost alone of the 40-year War on Drugs has been considerable. A detailed study by the Associated Press puts the government price tag at $1 trillion.[160] Innovative prevention and treatment programs have been stepped up. Indeed, the National Research Council's scientific panel on the demand for illegal drugs concluded that the short-term effectiveness of many treatment modalities has been "repeatedly and convincingly demonstrated," and called for greater research to investigate the long-term benefits.[161] Yet all drug control strategies are doomed to fail as long as youths want to take drugs and drugs remain widely available and accessible. Prevention, deterrence, and treatment strategies ignore the core reasons for the drug problem: poverty, alienation, and family disruption. As the gap between rich and poor widens and the opportunities for legitimate advancement decrease, it should come as no surprise that adolescent drug use continues.

legalization of drugs
Decriminalizing drug use to reduce the association between drug use and crime.

Some commentators have called for the **legalization of drugs**. This approach can have the short-term effect of reducing the association between drug use and crime (because, presumably, the cost of drugs would decrease), but it may have grave consequences. Drug use would most certainly increase, creating an overflow of unproductive people who must be cared for by the rest of society. The problems

On October 20, 2010, Mexican authorities carried out a controlled burn of 134 tons of marijuana in the border town of Tijuana. The drugs were seized by the Mexican Army after a clash with local drug traffickers. It was the largest confiscation in recent years. Legalization of marijuana in some states could drastically change how the Mexican government enforces its drug laws. Coordination between the countries will be crucial.

Francisco Vega/AFP/Getty Images

of teenage alcoholism should serve as a warning of what can happen when controlled substances are readily available. In the current climate of some states allowing the recreational use of marijuana, further research is needed to examine the direct and indirect effects of partial decriminalization on drug-use rates.

The studies of drug dealing in Philadelphia and Washington, DC, suggest that law enforcement efforts may have little influence on drug abuse rates as long as dealers can earn more than the minimal salaries they might earn in the legitimate world. Only by giving youths legitimate future alternatives can hard-core users be made to forgo drug use willingly.[162]

SUMMARY

1 Identify which drugs are most frequently abused by American youth

- Alcohol is the drug most frequently abused by American teens.

- Other popular drugs include marijuana and prescription drugs.

2 Interpret the extent of the drug problem among American youth today

- Self-report surveys indicate that just under half of all high school seniors have tried drugs.

- Surveys of arrestees indicate that a significant proportion of teenagers are drug users and many are high school dropouts.

- The number of drug users may be even higher than surveys suggest, because surveys of teen abusers may be missing the most delinquent youths.

3 Discuss how teenage drug use in this country has changed over time

- The national survey conducted by PRIDE, the Monitoring the Future survey, and the National Survey on Drug Use and Health report that drug and alcohol use are much lower today than 15 and 20 years ago.

4 Appraise the main explanations for why youths take drugs

- The main explanations for why youths take drugs include growing up in disorganized areas in which there is a high degree of hopelessness, poverty, and despair; peer pressure; parental substance abuse; emotional problems; and suffering from general problem behavior syndrome.

5 **Identify the different behavior patterns of drug-involved youths**

- Some youths are occasional users who might sell to friends.
- Others are seriously involved in both drug abuse and delinquency; many of these are gang members.
- There are also "losers," who filter in and out of the juvenile justice system, and a small percentage of teenage users remain involved with drugs into adulthood.

6 **Examine the relationship between drug use and delinquency**

- It is not certain whether drug abuse causes delinquency.
- Some experts believe there is a common cause for both delinquency and drug abuse—perhaps alienation and rage.

7 **Discuss the major drug control strategies**

- Some try to inhibit the importation of drugs, others to close down major drug rings, and a few to stop street-level dealing.
- There are also attempts to treat users through rehabilitation programs, reduce juvenile use by educational efforts, and implement harm reduction measures.
- These efforts have not been totally successful, although overall use of drugs may have declined somewhat.

8 **Assess the pros and cons of government use of different drug control strategies**

- It is difficult to eradicate drug abuse because there is so much profit to be made from the sale of drugs.
- One suggestion: legalize drugs. But critics warn that such a step may produce greater numbers of substance abusers. Supporters of legalization argue that it would greatly reduce the violence and other criminal activity associated with drug dealing.

KEY TERMS

substance abuse, p. 419
marijuana, p. 419
hashish, p. 419
synthetic marijuana, p. 420
cocaine, p. 421
crack, p. 421
heroin, p. 421
addict, p. 421

alcohol, p. 421
anesthetic drugs, p. 422
inhalants, p. 422
sedatives, p. 422
tranquilizers, p. 422
hallucinogens, p. 422
stimulants, p. 423
anabolic steroids, p. 423

designer drugs, p. 424
addiction-prone personality, p. 430
gateway drug, p. 432
multisystemic therapy (MST), p. 442
harm reduction, p. 443
legalization of drugs, p. 444

QUESTIONS FOR DISCUSSION

1. Discuss the differences among the various categories and types of substances of abuse. Is the term "drugs" too broad to have real meaning?

2. Why do you think youths take drugs? Do you know anyone with an addiction-prone personality?

3. What policy might be the best strategy to reduce teenage drug use: Source control? Reliance on treatment? National education efforts? Community-level enforcement? Harm reduction measures?

4. Under what circumstances, if any, might the legalization or decriminalization of drugs be beneficial to society?

5. Do you consider alcohol a drug? Should greater controls be placed on the sale of alcohol?

6. Do TV shows and films glorify drug usage and encourage youths to enter the drug trade? Should all images of drinking and smoking be banned from TV?

VIEWPOINT

The president has appointed you the new "drug czar." You have $10 billion under your control with which to wage your campaign. You know that drug use is unacceptably high, especially among poor, inner-city kids, that a great deal of criminal behavior is drug-related, and that drug-dealing gangs are expanding around the United States.

At an open hearing, drug control experts express their policy strategies. One group favors putting the money into hiring new law enforcement agents who will patrol borders, target large dealers, and make drug raids here and abroad. They also call for such get-tough measures as the creation of strict drug laws and the mandatory waiver of young drug dealers to the adult court system.

A second group believes the best way to deal with drugs is to spend the money on community treatment programs, expanding the number of beds in drug detoxification units, and funding research on how to reduce drug dependency clinically.

A third group argues that neither punishment nor treatment can restrict teenage drug use and that the best course is to educate at-risk kids about the dangers of substance abuse and then legalize all drugs but control their distribution. This course of action will help reduce crime and violence among drug users and also balance the national debt, because drugs could be heavily taxed.

- Do you believe drugs should be legalized? If so, what might be the negative consequences of legalization?
- Can any law enforcement strategies reduce drug consumption?
- Is treatment an effective drug control technique?

DOING RESEARCH ON THE WEB

The following organizations provide more information on different approaches to reducing teenage drug use. Before you answer the questions above, check out their websites. The Open Society Institute (http://www.opensocietyfoundations.org) has a special interest in alleviating the harms caused by drug use and punitive drug policies. The Centers for Disease Control and Prevention, through its Office on Smoking and Health (http://www.cdc.gov/tobacco/about/osh/), is the lead federal agency for comprehensive tobacco prevention and control. The mission of the National Institute on Drug Abuse (http://www.drugabuse.gov/) is to lead the nation in bringing the power of science to bear on drug abuse and addiction. The National Center on Addiction and Substance Abuse (http://www.centeronaddiction.org/) brings together under one roof all the professional disciplines needed to study and combat abuse of all substances. US Customs and Border Protection (http://www.cbp.gov/) has many components, one of which is enforcing drug laws.

NOTES

All URLs accessed September 2016.

1. Lloyd D. Johnston, Patrick M. O'Malley, Richard A. Miech, Jerald G. Bachman, and John E. Schulenberg, *Monitoring the Future National Results on Drug Use, 1975–2015: Overview, Key Findings on Adolescent Drug Use* (Ann Arbor, MI: Institute for Social Research, University of Michigan, 2016), Table 5.
2. Tamara M. Haegerich and Patrick H. Tolan, "Delinquency and Comorbid Conditions," in Barry C. Feld and Donna M. Bishop, eds., *The Oxford Handbook of Juvenile Crime and Juvenile Justice* (New York: Oxford University Press, 2012).
3. Office of Applied Studies, Substance Abuse and Mental Health Services Administration, "Youth Violence and Illicit Drug Use," *The NSDUH Report 5* (Washington, DC: Author, 2006).
4. Gary M. McClelland, Linda A. Teplin, and Karen M. Abram, *Detection and Prevalence of Substance Use Among Juvenile Detainees* (Washington, DC: Office of Juvenile Justice and Delinquency Prevention, 2006), pp. 4, 6.
5. Jonathan G. Tubman, Andrés G. Gil, and Eric F. Wagner, "Co-Occurring Substance Use and Delinquent Behavior During Early Adolescence: Emerging Relations and Implications for Intervention Strategies," *Criminal Justice and Behavior* 31:463–488 (2004).
6. Dennis Coon, *Introduction to Psychology* (St. Paul, MN: West, 1992), p. 178.
7. Johnston, O'Malley, Miech, Bachman, and Schulenberg, *Monitoring the Future National Results on Drug Use, 1975–2015*, p. 13.
8. Ibid, p. 13.
9. Rosalie L. Pacula, David Powell, Paul Heaton, and Eric L. Sevigny, "Assessing the Effects of Medical Marijuana Laws on Marijuana Use: The Devil Is in the Details," *Journal of Policy Analysis and Management* 34:7–31 (2015).
10. Ibid; Melanie Wall, Ernest Poh, Magdalena Cerdá, Katherine Keyes, Sandro Galea, and Deborah Hasin, "Adolescent Marijuana Use from 2002 to 2008: Higher in States with Medical Marijuana Laws, Cause Still Unclear," *Annals of Epidemiology* 21:714–716 (2011).
11. Deborah S. Hasin, Melanie Wall, Katherine M. Keyes, Magdalena Cerdá, John Schulenberg, Patrick M. O'Malley, Sandro Galea, Rosalie, Pacula, and Tianshu Feng, "Medical Marijuana Laws and Adolescent Marijuana Use in the USA from 1991 to 2014: Results from Annual, Repeated Cross-Sectional Surveys," *Lancet Psychiatry*, published online June 16, 2015.

12. Alan Neaigus, Aylin Atillasoy, Samuel Friedman, Xavier Andrade, Maureen Miller, Gilbert Ildefonso, and Don Des Jarlais, "Trends in the Noninjected Use of Heroin and Factors Associated with the Transition to Injecting," in James Inciardi and Lana Harrison, eds., *Heroin in the Age of Crack-Cocaine* (Thousand Oaks, CA: Sage Publications, 1998), pp. 108–130.

13. Brian P. Schaefer, Anthony G. Vito, Catherine D. Marcum, George E. Higgins, and Melissa L. Ricketts, "Heroin Use Among Adolescents: A Multi-Theoretical Examination," *Deviant Behavior* 36:101–112 (2015).

14. Johnston, O'Malley, Miech, Bachman, and Schulenberg, *Monitoring the Future National Survey Results on Drug Use, 1975–2015*, Tables 5 and 6.

15. Federal Bureau of Investigation, *Crime in the United States, 2014* (Washington, DC: US Government Printing Office, 2015), Tables 29, 38.

16. Centers for Disease Control and Prevention, "Teen Drinking and Driving: A Dangerous Mix," *CDC Vital Signs*, October 2012.

17. Henrick J. Harwood, *Updating Estimates of the Economic Costs of Alcohol Abuse in the United States: Estimates, Update Methods, and Data*, report prepared by the Lewin Group for the National Institute of Alcohol Abuse and Alcoholism (Rockville, MD: US Department of Health and Human Services, 2000), Table 3.

18. D. J. Rohsenow, "Drinking Habits and Expectancies About Alcohol's Effects for Self versus Others," *Journal of Consulting and Clinical Psychology* 51:75–76 (1983).

19. Spencer Rathus, *Psychology*, 4th ed. (New York: Holt, Rinehart & Winston, 1990), p. 161.

20. National Drug Intelligence Center, *Methamphetamine Drug Threat–Assessment* (Johnstown, PA: Author, 2005), p. 10.

21. Mary Tabor, "'Ice' in an Island Paradise," *Boston Globe*, December 8, 1989, p. 3.

22. Johnston, O'Malley, Miech, Bachman, and Schulenberg, *Monitoring the Future National Survey Results on Drug Use, 1975–2015*, Table 2.

23. Dana L. Radatz, Abby L. Vandenberg, and Lisa L. Sample, "Predictors of Methamphetamine Use Among Adolescents: Findings from a Midwestern Sample," *Journal of Drug Issues*. DOI: 10.1177/0022042614559840 (2014).

24. National Drug Intelligence Center, *National Drug Threat Assessment, 2011* (Johnstown, PA: Author, 2011), Table 6, p. 34.

25. Dana Hunt, Sarah Kuck, and Linda Truitt, *Methamphetamine Use: Lessons Learned* (Cambridge, MA: Abt Associates, 2005), pp. iv, v.

26. Fox Butterfield, "Fighting an Illegal Drug Through Its Legal Source," *New York Times*, January 30, 2005, p. A18; Kate Zernike, "Potent Mexican Meth Floods in as States Curb Domestic Variety," *New York Times*, January 23, 2006.

27. Nancy Nicosia, Rosalie Liccardo Pacula, Beau Kilmer, Russell Lundberg, and James Chiesa, *The Economic Cost of Methamphetamine Use in the United States, 2005* (Santa Monica, CA: RAND Corporation, 2009).

28. Paul Goldstein, "Anabolic Steroids: An Ethnographic Approach," unpublished paper (Narcotics and Drug Research, Inc., March 1989).

29. Centers for Disease Control and Prevention, "Use of Cigarettes and Other Tobacco Products Among Students Aged 13–15 Years—Worldwide, 1999–2005," *Morbidity and Mortality Weekly Report* 55:553–556 (2006).

30. Joe Nocera, "If It's Good for Philip Morris, Can It Also Be Good for Public Health?" *New York Times Magazine*, June 18, 2006, pp. 46–53, 70, 76–78.

31. Clete Snell and Laura Bailey, "Operation Storefront: Observations of Tobacco Retailer Advertising Compliance with Tobacco Laws," *Youth Violence and Juvenile Justice* 3:78–90 (2005).

32. Johnston, O'Malley, Miech, Bachman, and Schulenberg, *Monitoring the Future National Results on Drug Use, 1975–2015*, Table 5.

33. Carrie Arnold, "Vaping and Health: What Do We Know About E-Cigarettes?" *Environmental Health Perspectives* 122:A244–249 (2014).

34. Centers for Disease Control and Prevention, "E-Cigarette Use Triples Among Middle and High School Students in Just One Year," press release, April 16, 2015.

35. Johnston, O'Malley, Miech, Bachman, and Schulenberg, *Monitoring the Future National Results on Drug Use, 1975–2015: Overview, Key Findings on Adolescent Drug Use*, Table 6.

36. Marissa D. King, Jennifer Jennings, and Jason M. Fletcher, "Medical Adaptation to Academic Pressure: Schooling, Stimulant Use, and Socioeconomic Status," *American Sociological Review* 79:1039–1066 (2014); Lauren K. Whiteside, Rebecca M. Cunningham, Erin E. Bonar, Frederic Blow, Peter Ehrlich, and Maureen A. Walton, "Nonmedical Prescription Stimulant Use Among Youth in the Emergency Department: Prevalence, Severity and Correlates," *Journal of Substance Abuse Treatment* 48:21–27 (2015).

37. Johnston, O'Malley, Miech, Bachman, and Schulenberg, *Monitoring the Future National Survey Results on Drug Use, 1975–2015*, Tables 2, 6.

38. *Pride Surveys Questionnaire for Grades 6 thru 12 Standard Report: 2013–14 Pride National Summary* (Bowling Green, KY: PRIDE Surveys, September 2014).

39. Substance Abuse and Mental Health Services Administration, *Behavioral Health Barometer: United States, 2014* (Rockville, MD: Substance Abuse and Mental Health Services Administration, 2015).

40. Ibid., p. 3.

41. Substance Abuse and Mental Health Services Administration, *Results from the 2013 National Survey on Drug Use and Health: Summary of National Findings* (Rockville, MD: Substance Abuse and Mental Health Services Administration, 2014).

42. Substance Abuse and Mental Health Services Administration, *Behavioral Health Barometer: United States, 2014*, p. 5.

43. Substance Abuse and Mental Health Services Administration, *Results from the 2013 National Survey on Drug Use and Health: Summary of National Findings*, Figure 2.11.

44. Office of National Drug Control Policy, *Girls and Drugs: A New Analysis: Recent Trends, Risk Factors, and Consequences* (Washington, DC: Office of National Drug Control Policy, Executive Office of the President, 2006), Figure 3.

45. Substance Abuse and Mental Health Services Administration, *Results from the 2013 National Survey on Drug Use and Health: Summary of National Findings*, pp. 25–26.

46. Diana C. Noone, "Drug Use Among Juvenile Detainees," in National Institute of Justice, *Arrestee Drug Abuse Monitoring: 2000 Annual Report* (Washington, DC: National Institute of Justice, 2003), p. 135.

47. McClelland, Teplin, and Abram, *Detection and Prevalence of Substance Use Among Juvenile Detainees*.

48. Julia Yun Soo Kim, Michael Fendrich, and Joseph Wislar, "The Validity of Juvenile Arrestees' Drug Use Reporting: A Gender Comparison," *Journal of Research in Crime and Delinquency* 37:419–432 (2000).

49. Yvonne M. Terry-McElrath, Patrick M. O'Malley, and Lloyd D. Johnston, "Reasons for Drug Use Among American Youth by Consumption Level, Gender, and Race/Ethnicity: 1976–2005," *Journal of Drug Issues* 39:677–714 (2009).

50. Ibid., Figure 1, p. 686.

51. G. E. Vallant, "Parent-Child Disparity and Drug Addiction," *Journal of Nervous and Mental Disease* 142:534–539 (1966).

52. Charles Winick, "Epidemiology of Narcotics Use," in D. Wilner and G. Kassenbaum, eds., *Narcotics* (New York: McGraw-Hill, 1965), pp. 3–18.

53. Justin Hayes-Smith and Rachel Bridges Whaley, "Community Characteristics and Methamphetamine Use: A Social Disorganization Perspective," *Journal of Drug Issues* 39:547–576 (2009); see also Rachel Bridges Whaley, Justin M. Smith, and Rebecca Hayes-Smith, "Teenage Drug and Alcohol Use: Comparing Individual and Contextual Effects," *Deviant Behavior* 32:818–845 (2011).

54. Joan S. Tucker, Michael S. Pollard, Kayla de la Haye, David P. Kennedy, and Harold D. Green, "Neighborhood Characteristics and the Initiation of Marijuana Use and Binge Drinking," *Drug and Alcohol Dependence* 128:83–89 (2013); Allison B. Brenner, José A. Bauermeister, and Marc A. Zimmerman, "Neighborhood Variation in Adolescent Alcohol Use: Examination of Sociological and Social Disorganization Theories," *Journal of Studies on Alcohol and Drug Issues* 72:651–659 (2011).

55. Delbert Elliott, David Huizinga, and Scott Menard, *Multiple Problem Youth: Delinquency, Substance Abuse and Mental Health Problems* (New York: Springer-Verlag, 1989).

56. Emily M. Wright, Abigail A. Fagan, and Gillian M. Pinchevsky, "Penny for Your Thoughts? The Protective Effect of Youths' Attitudes Against Drug Use in High-Risk Communities," *Youth Violence and Juvenile Justice* 14:110–129 (2016).

57. Peter Reuter, Robert MacCoun, and Patrick Murphy, *Money from Crime: A Study of the Economics of Drug Dealing in Washington, D.C.* (Santa Monica, CA: RAND Corporation, 1990).

58. Thomas Dishion, Deborah Capaldi, Kathleen Spracklen, and Fuzhong Li, "Peer Ecology of Male Adolescent Drug Use," *Development and Psychopathology* 7:803–824 (1995).

59. C. Bowden, "Determinants of Initial Use of Opioids," *Comprehensive Psychiatry* 12:136–140 (1971).

60. Traci M. Schwinn and Steven P. Schinke, "Alcohol Use and Related Behaviors Among Late-Adolescent Urban Youths: Peer and Parental

Influences," *Journal of Child and Adolescent Substance Abuse* 23:58–64 (2014); see also Terence Thornberry and Marvin Krohn, "Peers, Drug Use and Delinquency," in David Stoff, James Breiling, and Jack Maser, eds., *Handbook of Antisocial Behavior* (New York: Wiley, 1997), pp. 218–233.

61. Gregory M. Zimmerman and Bob Edward Vásquez, "Decomposing the Peer Effect on Adolescent Substance Use: Mediation, Nonlinearity, and Differential Nonlinearity," *Criminology* 49:1235–1274 (2011).

62. Richard Cloward and Lloyd Ohlin, *Delinquency and Opportunity: A Theory of Delinquent Gangs* (New York: Free Press, 1960).

63. Daniel T. Ragan, "Revisiting 'What They Think': Adolescent Drinking and the Importance of Peer Beliefs," *Criminology* 52:488–513 (2014); Denise Kandel and Mark Davies, "Friendship Networks, Intimacy, and Illicit Drug Use in Young Adulthood: A Comparison of Two Competing Theories," *Criminology* 29:441–471 (1991).

64. Jean Marie McGloin, Christopher J. Sullivan, and Kyle J. Thomas, "Peer Influence and Context: The Interdependence of Friendship Groups, Schoolmates and Network Density in Predicting Substance Use," *Journal of Youth and Adolescence* 43:1436–1452 (2014).

65. Derek A. Kreager and Dana L. Haynie, "Dangerous Liaisons? Dating and Drinking Diffusion in Adolescent Peer Networks," *American Sociological Review* 76:737–763 (2011).

66. James Inciardi, Ruth Horowitz, and Anne Pottieger, *Street Kids, Street Drugs, Street Crime: An Examination of Drug Use and Serious Delinquency in Miami* (Belmont, CA: Wadsworth, 1993), p. 43.

67. D. Baer and J. Corrado, "Heroin Addict Relationships with Parents During Childhood and Early Adolescent Years," *Journal of Genetic Psychology* 124:99–103 (1974).

68. Timothy Ireland and Cathy Spatz Widom, *Childhood Victimization and Risk for Alcohol and Drug Arrests* (Washington, DC: National Institute of Justice, 1995).

69. See S. F. Bucky, "The Relationship Between Background and Extent of Heroin Use," *American Journal of Psychiatry* 130:709–710 (1973); I. Chien, D. L. Gerard, R. Lee, and E. Rosenfield, *The Road to H: Narcotics Delinquency and Social Policy* (New York: Basic Books, 1964).

70. Meeyoung O. Min, Sonia Minnes, Adelaide Lang, Paul Weishampel, Elizabeth J. Short, Susan Yoon, and Lynn T. Singer, "Externalizing Behavior and Substance Use Related Problems at 15 Years in Prenatally Cocaine Exposed Adolescents," *Journal of Adolescence* 37:269–279 (2014); Sonia Minnes, Lynn Singer, Meeyoung O. Min, Miaoping Wu, Adelaide Lang, and Susan Yoon, "Effects of Prenatal Cocaine/Polydrug Exposure on Substance Use by Age 15," *Drug and Alcohol Dependence* 134:201–210 (2014).

71. J. S. Mio, G. Nanjundappa, D. E. Verlur, and M. D. DeRios, "Drug Abuse and the Adolescent Sex Offender: A Preliminary Analysis," *Journal of Psychoactive Drugs* 18:65–72 (1986).

72. G. T. Wilson, "Cognitive Studies in Alcoholism," *Journal of Consulting and Clinical Psychology* 55:325–331 (1987).

73. John Hagedorn, Jose Torres, and Greg Giglio, "Cocaine, Kicks, and Strain: Patterns of Substance Use in Milwaukee Gangs," *Contemporary Drug Problems* 25:113–145 (1998).

74. Abigail A. Fagan, M. Lee Van Horn, Susan Antaramian, and J. David Hawkins, "How Do Families Matter? Age and Gender Differences in Family Influence on Delinquency and Drug Use," *Youth Violence and Juvenile Justice* 9:150–170 (2011).

75. For a comprehensive review of genetics and delinquency in general, see Melissa Peskin, Andrea L. Glenn, Yu Gao, Jianghong Liu, Robert A. Schug, Yaling Yang, and Adrian Raine, "Personal Characteristics of Delinquents: Neurobiology, Genetic Predispositions, Individual Psychosocial Attributes," in Barry C. Feld and Donna M. Bishop, eds., *The Oxford Handbook of Juvenile Crime and Juvenile Justice* (New York: Oxford University Press, 2012), pp. 73–106.

76. D. W. Goodwin, "Alcoholism and Genetics," *Archives of General Psychiatry* 42:171–174 (1985).

77. Ibid.

78. Patricia Dobkin, Richard Tremblay, Louise Masse, and Frank Vitaro, "Individual and Peer Characteristics in Predicting Boys' Early Onset of Substance Abuse: A Seven-Year Longitudinal Study," *Child Development* 66:1198–1214 (1995).

79. Ric Steele, Rex Forehand, Lisa Armistead, and Gene Brody, "Predicting Alcohol and Drug Use in Early Adulthood: The Role of Internalizing and Externalizing Behavior Problems in Early Adolescence," *American Journal of Orthopsychiatry* 65:380–387 (1995).

80. Ibid., pp. 380–381.

81. Jerome Platt and Christina Platt, *Heroin Addiction* (New York: Wiley, 1976), p. 127.

82. Rathus, *Psychology*, p. 158.

83. Eric Strain, "Antisocial Personality Disorder, Misbehavior and Drug Abuse," *Journal of Nervous and Mental Disease* 183:162–165 (1995).

84. Dobkin, Tremblay, Masse, and Vitaro, "Individual and Peer Characteristics in Predicting Boys' Early Onset of Substance Abuse."

85. J. Shedler and J. Block, "Adolescent Drug Use and Psychological Health: A Longitudinal Inquiry," *American Psychologist* 45:612–630 (1990).

86. Greenwood, "Substance Abuse Problems Among High-Risk Youth and Potential Interventions," p. 448.

87. John Wallace and Jerald Bachman, "Explaining Racial/Ethnic Differences in Adolescent Drug Use: The Impact of Background and Lifestyle," *Social Problems* 38:333–357 (1991).

88. Marvin Krohn, Terence Thornberry, Lori Collins-Hall, and Alan Lizotte, "School Dropout, Delinquent Behavior, and Drug Use," in Howard Kaplan, ed., *Drugs, Crime and Other Deviant Adaptations: Longitudinal Studies* (New York: Plenum Press, 1995), pp. 163–183.

89. B. A. Christiansen, G. T. Smith, P. V. Roehling, and M. S. Goldman, "Using Alcohol Expectancies to Predict Adolescent Drinking Behavior After One Year," *Journal of Counseling and Clinical Psychology* 57:93–99 (1989).

90. Sun Joon Jang, Todd W. Ferguson, and Jeremy R. Rhodes, "Does Alcohol or Delinquency Help Adolescents Feel Better Over Time? A Study on the Influence of Heavy Drinking and Violent/Property Offending on Negative Emotions," *International Journal of Offender Therapy and Comparative Criminology* 60:619–639 (2016).

91. See Mark A. Kleiman, Jonathan P. Caulkins, and Angela Hawken, *Drugs and Drug Policy: What Everyone Needs to Know* (New York: Oxford University Press, 2011), pp. 82–83.

92. Inciardi, Horowitz, and Pottieger, *Street Kids, Street Drugs, Street Crime*, p. 135.

93. Ibid., p. 136.

94. Eric R. Kandel and Denise B. Kandel, "A Molecular Basis for Nicotine as a Gateway Drug," *New England Journal of Medicine* 371:932–943 (2014).

95. Mary Ellen Mackesy-Amiti, Michael Fendrich, and Paul Goldstein, "Sequence of Drug Use Among Serious Drug Users: Typical vs. Atypical Progression," *Drug and Alcohol Dependence* 45:185–196 (1997).

96. The following sections lean heavily on Marcia Chaiken and Bruce Johnson, *Characteristics of Different Types of Drug-Involved Youth* (Washington, DC: National Institute of Justice, 1988).

97. Ibid., p. 100.

98. Inciardi, Horowitz, and Pottieger, *Street Kids, Street Drugs, Street Crime.*

99. Patrick M. Seffrin and Bianca I. Domahidi, "The Drugs-Violence Nexus: A Systematic Comparison of Adolescent Drug Dealers and Drug Users," *Journal of Drug Issues* 44:394–413 (2014).

100. Chaiken and Johnson, *Characteristics of Different Types of Drug-Involved Youth*, p. 12.

101. Rick Graves and Ed Allen, *Narcotics and Black Gangs* (Los Angeles: Los Angeles County Sheriff's Department, n.d.).

102. John Hagedorn, "Neighborhoods, Markets, and Gang Drug Organization," *Journal of Research in Crime and Delinquency* 31:264–294 (1994).

103. Chaiken and Johnson, *Characteristics of Different Types of Drug-Involved Youth*, p. 14.

104. For an excellent overview of the drugs–crime relationship, see David A. Boyum, Jonathan P. Caulkins, and Mark A. R. Kleiman, "Drugs, Crime, and Public Policy," in James Q. Wilson and Joan Petersilia, eds., *Crime and Public Policy* (New York: Oxford University Press, 2011), pp. 370–373.

105. Eric Baumer, Janet Lauritsen, Richard Rosenfeld, and Richard Wright, "The Influence of Crack Cocaine on Robbery, Burglary, and Homicide Rates: A Cross-City, Longitudinal Analysis," *Journal of Research in Crime and Delinquency* 35:316–340 (1998).

106. Ibid.

107. James Inciardi, "Heroin Use and Street Crime," *Crime and Delinquency* 25:335–346 (1979); James Inciardi, *The War on Drugs* (Palo Alto, CA: Mayfield, 1986); see also W. McGlothlin, M. Anglin, and B. Wilson, "Narcotic Addiction and Crime," *Criminology* 16:293–311 (1978); George Speckart and M. Douglas Anglin, "Narcotics Use and Crime: An Overview of Recent Research Advances," *Contemporary Drug Problems* 13:741–769 (1986); Charles Faupel and Carl Klockars, "Drugs-Crime Connections: Elaborations from the Life Histories of Hard-Core Heroin Addicts," *Social Problems* 34:54–68 (1987).

108. Eric Baumer, "Poverty, Crack and Crime: A Cross-City Analysis," *Journal of Research in Crime and Delinquency* 31:311–327 (1994).

109. Mildred M. Maldonado-Molina, Jennifer M. Reingle, and Wesley G. Jennings, "Does Alcohol Use Predict Violent Behaviors? The Relationship Between Alcohol Use and Violence in a Nationally Representative Longitudinal Sample," *Youth Violence and Juvenile Justice* 9:99–111 (2011); Kelli A. Komro, Amy L. Tobler, Mildred M. Maldonado-Molina, and Cheryl L. Perry, "Effects of Alcohol Use Initiation Patterns on High-Risk Behaviors Among Urban, Low-Income, Young Adolescents," *Prevention Science* 11:14–23 (2010); Marvin Dawkins, "Drug Use and Violent Crime Among Adolescents," *Adolescence* 32:395–406 (1997); Helene Raskin White and Stephen Hansell, "The Moderating Effects of Gender and Hostility on the Alcohol-Aggression Relationship," *Journal of Research in Crime and Delinquency* 33:450–470 (1996).

110. Fox Butterfield, "Justice Department Ends Testing of Criminals for Drug Use," *New York Times*, January 28, 2004.

111. Arrestee Drug Abuse Monitoring [ADAM] Program, *Preliminary Data on Drug Use and Related Matters Among Adult Arrestees and Juvenile Detainees, 2002* (Washington, DC: National Institute of Justice), Tables 2 and 3.

112. Carl McCurley and Howard Snyder, *Co-occurrence of Substance Use Behaviors in Youth* (Washington, DC: Office of Juvenile Justice and Delinquency Prevention, US Department of Justice, 2008).

113. Boyum, Caulkins, and Kleiman, "Drugs, Crime, and Public Policy," p. 372.

114. B. D. Johnson, E. Wish, J. Schmeidler, and D. Huizinga, "Concentration of Delinquent Offending: Serious Drug Involvement and High Delinquency Rates," *Journal of Drug Issues* 21:205–229 (1991).

115. Inciardi, Horowitz, and Pottieger, *Street Kids, Street Drugs, Street Crime.*

116. Stefano Passini, "The Delinquency-Drug Relationship: The Influence of Social Reputation and Moral Disengagement," *Addictive Behaviors* 37:577–579 (2012); W. David Watts and Lloyd Wright, "The Relationship of Alcohol, Tobacco, Marijuana, and Other Illegal Drug Use to Delinquency Among Mexican-American, Black, and White Adolescent Males," *Adolescence* 25:38–54 (1990).

117. For a general review of this issue, see Helene Raskin White, "The Drug Use–Delinquency Connection in Adolescence," in Ralph Weisheit, ed., *Drugs, Crime and Criminal Justice* (Cincinnati: Anderson, 1990), pp. 215–256; Speckart and Anglin, "Narcotics Use and Crime"; Faupel and Klockars, "Drugs-Crime Connections."

118. Delbert Elliott, David Huizinga, and Suzanne Ageton, *Explaining Delinquency and Drug Abuse* (Beverly Hills: Sage Publications, 1985).

119. David Huizinga, Scott Menard, and Delbert Elliott, "Delinquency and Drug Use: Temporal and Developmental Patterns," *Justice Quarterly* 6:419–455 (1989).

120. Jason A. Ford, "The Connection Between Heavy Drinking and Juvenile Delinquency During Adolescence," *Sociological Spectrum* 25:629–650 (2005).

121. Graham Farrell, "Drugs and Drug Control," in Graeme Newman, ed., *Global Report on Crime and Justice* (New York: Oxford University Press, 1999), p. 177.

122. US Department of State, *1998 International Narcotics Control Strategy Report*, February 1999.

123. Clifford Krauss, "Neighbors Worry About Colombian Aid," *New York Times*, August 25, 2000, p. A3; see also Juan Forero, "Colombia's Coca Survives US Plan to Uproot It," *New York Times*, August 19, 2006.

124. United Nations, *2014 World Drug Report* (Vienna: Office on Drugs and Crime, United Nations, 2014).

125. Carlotta Gall, "Another Year of Drug War, and the Poppy Crop Flourishes," *New York Times*, February 17, 2006.

126. United Nations Office on Drugs and Crime, *Afghanistan Opium Survey 2015: Executive Summary* (Vienna: Author, October 2015), p. 7.

127. Drug Enforcement Administration, *2015 National Drug Threat Assessment Summary* (Washington, DC: Drug Enforcement Administration, US Department of Justice, 2015), p. 27.

128. United Nations, *2014 World Drug Report*.

129. "Operation Webslinger Targets Illegal Internet Trafficking of Date-Rape Drug," *US Customs Today* 38 (2002).

130. Gardiner Harris, "Two Agencies to Fight Online Narcotics Sales," *New York Times*, October 18, 2003.

131. Drug Enforcement Administration, *2015 National Drug Threat Assessment Summary*, p. 49.

132. Fox Butterfield, "Home Drug-Making Laboratories Expose Children to Toxic Fallout," *New York Times*, February 23, 2004.

133. International Centre for Science in Drug Policy, *Effect of Drug Law Enforcement on Drug-Related Violence: Evidence from a Scientific Review* (Vancouver, Canada: Author, 2010).

134. Mark Moore, *Drug Trafficking* (Washington, DC: National Institute of Justice, 1988).

135. Christopher L. Ringwalt, Susan Ennett, Amy Vincus, Judy Thorne, Louise Ann Rohrbach, and Ashley Simons-Rudolph, "The Prevalence of Effective Substance Use Prevention in US Middle Schools," *Prevention Science* 3:257–265.

136. Jane Carlisle Maxwell, Melissa Tackett-Gibson, and James Dyer, "Substance Use in Urban and Rural Texas School Districts," *Drugs: Education, Prevention and Policy* 13:327–339 (2006).

137. Denise C. Gottfredson, David B. Wilson, and Stacy S. Najaka, "School-Based Crime Prevention," in Lawrence W. Sherman, David P. Farrington, Brandon C. Welsh, and Doris Layton-MacKenzie, eds., *Evidence-Based Crime Prevention*, rev. ed. (New York: Routledge, 2006), Table 4.9; see also Phyllis Ellickson, Robert Bell, and K. McGuigan, "Preventing Adolescent Drug Use: Long-Term Results of a Junior High Program," *American Journal of Public Health* 83:856–861 (1993).

138. Christopher Ringwalt, Amy A. Vincus, Sean Hanley, Susan T. Ennett, J. Michael Bowling, and Susan Haws, "The Prevalence of Evidence-Based Drug Use Prevention Curricula in US Middle Schools in 2008," *Prevention Science* 12:63–69 (2011).

139. Tracy M. Scull, Janis B. Kupersmidt, and Jennifer Toller Erausquin, "The Impact of Media-Related Cognitions on Children's Substance Use Outcomes in the Context of Parental and Peer Substance Use," *Journal of Youth and Adolescence* 43:717–728 (2014).

140. *Partnership Attitude Tracking Study: Teens, 2004* (Washington, DC: Office of National Drug Control Policy, 2005), pp. 12, 24.

141. Substance Abuse and Mental Health Services Administration, *Results from the 2013 National Survey on Drug Use and Health: Summary of National Findings*, p. 80.

142. Melissa A. Lippold, Mark T. Greenberg, and Linda M. Collins, "Youths' Substance Use and Changes in Parental Knowledge-Related Behaviors During Middle School: A Person-Oriented Approach," *Journal of Youth and Adolescence* 43:729–744 (2014).

143. Substance Abuse and Mental Health Services Administration, *Results from the 2013 National Survey on Drug Use and Health: Summary of National Findings*, p. 80.

144. Lori K. Holleran, Margaret A. Taylor-Seehafer, Elizabeth C. Pomeroy, and James Alan Neff, "Substance Abuse Prevention for High-Risk Youth: Exploring Culture and Alcohol and Drug Use," *Alcoholism Treatment Quarterly* 23:165–184 (2005).

145. Brandon C. Welsh and Akemi Hoshi, "Communities and Crime Prevention," in Sherman, Farrington, Welsh, and MacKenzie, eds., *Evidence-Based Crime Prevention*, pp. 184–186.

146. Substance Abuse and Mental Health Services Administration, *Results from the 2013 National Survey on Drug Use and Health: Summary of National Findings*, p. 94.

147. Scott W. Henggeler, Sonja K. Schoenwald, Charles M. Borduin, Melisa D. Rowland, and Phillippe B. Cunningham, *Multisystemic Treatment of Antisocial Behavior in Children and Adolescents* (New York: Guilford, 1998).

148. Eli Ginzberg, Howard Berliner, and Miriam Ostrow, *Young People at Risk: Is Prevention Possible?* (Boulder, CO: Westview Press, 1988), p. 99.

149. Emily E. Tanner-Smith, Katarzyna T. Steinka-Fry, Emily A. Hennessy, Mark W. Lipsey, and Ken C. Winters, "Can Brief Alcohol Interventions for Youth also Address Concurrent Illicit Drug Use? Results from a Meta-Analysis," *Journal of Youth and Adolescence* 44:1011–1023 (2015).

150. Laurie Chassin, "Juvenile Justice and Substance Abuse," *The Future of Children* 18:165–183 (2008); James C. Howell, *Preventing and Reducing Juvenile Delinquency: A Comprehensive Framework*, 2nd ed. (Thousand Oaks, CA: Sage, 2009), p. 272.

151. Ginzberg, Berliner, and Ostrow, *Young People at Risk: Is Prevention Possible?*

152. Donnie W. Watson, Lorrie Bisesi, Susie Tanamly, and Noemi Mai, "Comprehensive Residential Education, Arts, and Substance Abuse Treatment (CREASAT): A Model Treatment Program for Juvenile Offenders," *Youth Violence and Juvenile Justice* 1:388–401 (2003).

153. Steven R. Donziger, ed., *The Real War on Crime: The Report of the National Criminal Justice Commission* (New York: HarperPerennial, 1996), pp. 201–202.

154. Charlotte Allan and Nat Wright, "Harm Reduction: The Least Worst Treatment of All; Tackling Drug Addiction Has Few Easy Solutions," *Student British Medical Journal* 12:92–93 (2004), at 92.

155. Ibid.

156. Ibid.; see also Erik K. Laursen and Paul Brasler, "Is Harm Reduction a Viable Choice for Kids Enchanted with Drugs?" *Reclaiming Children and Youth* 11:181–183 (2002).

157. Donziger, *The Real War on Crime*, p. 201.

158. Robert J. MacCoun and Karin D. Martin, "Drugs," in Michael Tonry, ed., *The Oxford Handbook of Crime and Public Policy* (New York: Oxford University Press, 2009), p. 513.

159. Eric L. Jensen, Jurg Gerber, and Clayton Mosher, "Social Consequences of the War on Drugs: The Legacy of Failed Policy," *Criminal Justice Policy Review* 15:100–121 (2004).

160. Associated Press, "AP Impact: US Drug War Has Met None of Its Goals," *New York Times*, May 14, 2010.

161. Peter Reuter, ed., *Understanding the Demand for Illegal Drugs* (Washington, DC: National Research Council, National Academies Press, 2010), p. 103.

162. Reuter, MacCoun, and Murphy, *Money from Crime*, pp. 165–168.

CHAPTER 12

Delinquency Prevention:

Social and Developmental Perspectives

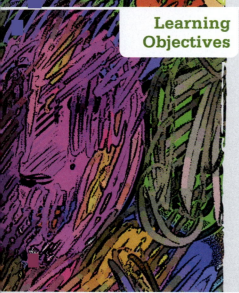

FOR MICHELLE, a British citizen, age 16 and pregnant with her first child, violence came early in life and at the hands of her mother, her unborn child's grandmother. Living in poverty, with no family other than her distant mother, and having already experienced violence by a loved one, Michelle (her last name withheld to protect her identity) was confronted with many of the obstacles in life that put her and her baby at increased risk for a wide range of health and social problems. Some of these problems include abuse of drugs and alcohol, unemployment, and reliance on social services, and for the child, low birth weight, neglect and abuse, behavioral problems, and later involvement in delinquent and criminal activities.

In the late 2000s, the British government set out to help improve the life chances of Michelle and her baby along with hundreds of other similar young mothers and their newborns by providing specially trained nurses to visit them at their homes during the final months of pregnancy and up to the child's second birthday. The nurses visit every week in the beginning and then every other week. Each visit lasts about two hours. During these visits mothers get advice about care of the child, infant development, and the importance of proper nutrition and avoiding smoking and drinking during pregnancy. The home visits also serve to improve the well-being of the mothers, linking them to community resources to help with employment, education, or addiction recovery. In the words of early intervention expert Deanna Gomby and her colleagues, "Home visitors can see the environments in which families live, gain a better understanding of the families' needs, and therefore tailor services to meet those needs. The relationships forged between home visitors and parents can break through loneliness and isolation and serve as the first step in linking families to their communities."[1]

As part of the Nurse-Family Partnership, registered nurse Karla Work visits with Marilu Molina and her 15-month-old son, Damian.

In the United States, this program, known as the Nurse-Family Partnership and developed by David Olds at the University of Colorado, has proven tremendously successful. Through three large-scale trials in Elmira (New York), Memphis, and Denver, it has been found to improve women's prenatal health, increase the spacing between subsequent pregnancies, reduce child abuse, neglect, and injuries, improve children's school readiness, and reduce adolescent crime and substance use. Today, the Nurse-Family Partnership is operating in 581 counties in 43 states across the country, serving almost 33,000 families each year.[2]

It was this success that caught the attention of the British government. (The program has already been implemented in 10 cities and towns across Britain.) For Michelle and hundreds of other teenage mothers like her, the government sees this scientifically proven program as the best chance of saving these children from the cycle of violence, poverty, and despair to which their young mothers fell victim.[3]

Public officials faced with the problem of juvenile delinquency in their cities have many options. For some, it will be a clear choice of getting tough on juvenile delinquency and implementing punitive or justice-oriented measures. For others, it will be a matter of getting tough on the causes of juvenile delinquency and implementing prevention programs to ward off delinquency before it takes place. Still others will combine justice and nonjustice measures to combat the problem. Ideally, decisions about which approach or which combination of measures to use will be based on the needs of the community and the highest-quality available evidence on what works best in preventing juvenile delinquency.

This chapter begins with a discussion of key features of delinquency prevention, which include the differences between prevention and other approaches to tackle delinquent behavior, the financial costs that delinquency imposes on society, and efforts to make sense of the many different types of prevention programs and measures. The history of delinquency prevention in the United States is also discussed. Next, we review the effectiveness of delinquency prevention programs that are provided in the childhood years. Daycare, preschool, and primary school programs are among the different types of prevention programs covered. This is followed by a review of the effectiveness of a wide range of delinquency prevention programs implemented in the teenage years, including school-based, after-school, and job training programs. The chapter concludes with a look at key issues to be faced in the ongoing efforts to prevent delinquency.

The Many Faces of Delinquency Prevention

Preventing juvenile delinquency means many different things to many different people. Programs or policies designed to prevent juvenile delinquency can include the police making an arrest as part of an operation to address gang problems, a juvenile court sanction to a secure correctional facility, or, in the extreme case, a death penalty sentence. These measures are often referred to as **delinquency control** or **delinquency repression**. More often, though, **delinquency prevention** refers to intervening in young people's lives before they engage in delinquency in the first place—that is, preventing the first delinquent act. According to Peter Lejins, "If societal action is motivated by an offense that has already taken place, we are dealing with control; if the offense is only anticipated, we are dealing with prevention."[4] This subscribes to the notion of a "pure prevention," a view that has long existed in the scholarship and practice of criminology in the United States.[5]

Both forms of delinquency prevention have a common goal of trying to prevent the occurrence of a future delinquent act, but what distinguishes delinquency prevention from delinquency control is that prevention typically does not involve the juvenile justice system. Instead, programs or policies designed to prevent delinquency involve daycare providers, nurses, teachers, social workers, recreation staff at the YMCA, counselors at Boys and Girls Clubs of America, other young people in school, and parents. This form of delinquency prevention is sometimes referred to as nonjustice delinquency prevention or alternative delinquency prevention. Exhibit 12.1 lists examples of programs to prevent and control delinquency.

Delinquency prevention programs are not designed with the intention of excluding juvenile justice personnel. Many types of delinquency prevention programs, especially those that focus on adolescents, involve juvenile justice personnel such as police, prosecutors, or juvenile probation officers. In these cases, the juvenile justice personnel work in close collaboration with those from such areas as education, health care, recreation, and social.[6] In this chapter, we focus on delinquency prevention programs that are driven or led by these non–juvenile justice agencies.

delinquency control or delinquency repression
Involves any justice program or policy designed to prevent the occurrence of a future delinquent act.

delinquency prevention
Involves any nonjustice program or policy designed to prevent the occurrence of a future delinquent act.

exhibit 12.1

Delinquency Prevention vs. Control

Prevention	Control
Home visitation	Antigang police task force
Preschool	Boot camps
Child skills training	Wilderness programs
Mentoring	Probation
After-school recreation	Electronic monitoring
Job training	Secure confinement

An important issue facing delinquency prevention is cost: programs cost money to run. Expenses include staff salaries, equipment, and sometimes rent for the facilities in which programs take place. Though prevention programs can be costly, they are beneficial because they save money that would otherwise be spent in the justice system.

Costs of Delinquency: A Justification for Prevention

The impacts of juvenile delinquency on society, which include such things as damaged property, pain and suffering to victims, and the involvement of police and other agencies of the juvenile justice system, can be converted into dollars and cents. The damaged property will need to be repaired or replaced, and it is the victim who will often have to pay for this, as many crime victims do not have insurance. The pain and suffering inflicted on an individual from an assault or robbery can result not only in immediate costs of medical care and lost wages from missing work, but also in reduced quality of life from debilitating injuries or fear of being victimized again, which can result in not being able to go to work, long-term medical care, and counseling.

Here again it is the crime victim and also the victim's family, employer, and many services, such as Medicaid, welfare, and mental health, that incur the dollar costs associated with these services. Victim costs resulting from an aggravated assault are as high as $37,000, and are even higher for rape and arson. The average murder costs around $5 million.[7] Another study puts the total cost of a murder, which includes victim costs plus costs to the justice system, at just under $10 million.[8] Then there is the cost of the involvement of the police, courts, and corrections agencies. While some of the costs incurred by the juvenile justice system go toward addressing the needs of victims, such as follow-up interviews by police and court-based victim assistance programs, the majority of the costs are directed at the processing of offenders. Police arrest, public defender costs, court appearances, serving a sentence—whether it be probation or incarceration—and aftercare programs upon release into the community are all costly steps in the justice system. There are also costs incurred by society in efforts to prevent juvenile delinquency, through different types of prevention programs.

Mark Cohen and Alex Piquero estimate that the typical criminal career over the juvenile and adult years (ages 10 to 26) costs society between $2.6 and $4.6 million.[9] Adding the costs of drug use and dropping out of high school brings the total cost to $3.2 to $5.5 million. A much lower estimate of the cost of a criminal career—for the adult years only—was reported by criminologists Matt DeLisi and Jewel Gatling. Based on a sample of 500 career criminals, the authors found that the average criminal career costs society more than $1.1 million.[10] Another study of 500 urban boys between the ages of 7 and 17—based on the youngest sample of the Pittsburgh Youth Study—estimated that those who were chronic offenders caused as much as eight times higher average costs to victims than other juvenile offenders, with costs approaching $1 million for the chronic offenders.[11]

Studies have also looked at the costs of juvenile delinquency to different states and the nation as a whole.

State Costs Ted Miller and his associates examined the costs of juvenile violence in the state of Pennsylvania.[12] The study was based on the violent offenses of murder, rape, robbery, assault, and physical and sexual abuse. Violence by juveniles was estimated to cost $2.6 billion in victim costs and $46 million in perpetrator costs per year. Juvenile perpetrator costs were made up of costs to the juvenile and adult justice systems, which included costs from probation, detention, juvenile treatment programs, and incarceration in adult prisons. Interestingly, this study also reported on the costs of violence against juveniles that was committed by adults and other juveniles. Compared to the victim costs of violence committed by juveniles, the victim costs of violence committed against juveniles was much higher: $4.5 billion versus $2.6 billion. The main reason for this difference was because juveniles suffered more sexual abuse—a very costly offense—at the hands of adults, but there was very little sexual abuse by juveniles against adults.

National Costs   Some estimates for the total monetary burden of crime per year to the United States reach as high as $3.2 trillion.[13] The only national estimate of the costs of juvenile delinquency focuses on a limited number of violent offenses. Homicides and assault-related injuries perpetrated by juveniles cost the United States $16 billion each year.[14] This estimate includes some of the costs incurred by federal, state, and local governments to assist victims of juvenile violence, such as medical treatment for injuries and services for victims in the form of aid for lost wages. These are tangible, or out-of-pocket, victim costs. Missing from this total are the intangible or indirect costs suffered by victims, including pain, suffering, and reduced quality of life. These costs can be as much as four or five times the tangible costs. Also missing from this $16 billion price tag of juvenile violence are the costs from society's response to juvenile violence, which include early prevention programs, services for juveniles, and the juvenile justice system. These costs are unknown.

Considering these costs, it is not surprising that there has been a long-standing effort to prevent juvenile delinquency.

A Brief History of Delinquency Prevention

The history of the prevention of juvenile delinquency in the United States is closely tied to the history of juvenile justice in this country. From the founding of the House of Refuge, which opened in New York in 1825, to more contemporary events, such as amendments to the federal Juvenile Justice and Delinquency Prevention Act of 1974, child-saving organizations and lawmakers have had an interest in both the prevention and control of delinquency. However, many social scientists have noted that efforts to prevent juveniles from engaging in delinquency in the first place were secondary to and often overlooked in favor of interventions with juveniles who had already committed delinquent acts.[15] This imbalance between prevention and control of juvenile delinquency remains in place to this day.

Chicago Area Project   One of the earliest juvenile delinquency prevention programs was the Chicago Area Project, started in 1933 by Clifford Shaw and Henry McKay.[16] This project was designed to produce social change in communities that suffered from high delinquency rates and gang activity. As part of the project, qualified local leaders coordinated social service centers that promoted community solidarity and counteracted social disorganization. More than 20 different programs were developed, featuring discussion groups, counseling services, hobby groups, school-related activities, and recreation. There is still some question of whether these programs had a positive influence on the delinquency rate. Some evaluations indicated positive results, but others showed that the Chicago Area Project efforts did little to reduce juvenile delinquency.[17]

Cambridge-Somerville Youth Study   Another well-known delinquency prevention program that was implemented around the same time as the Chicago project was the Cambridge-Somerville (Massachusetts) Youth Study.[18] The focus of this program was more on improving individuals than their surroundings. One interesting feature of this program is that it was the first delinquency prevention program to be evaluated using a **randomized experimental design**. Prior to the start of the program, 650 boys (325 matched pairs), which was later reduced to 506 (253 matched pairs), were assigned to receive the program (the **experimental group**) or not receive the program (the **control group**). The experimental group boys received regular friendly attention from counselors for an average of five years and whatever

randomized experimental design
Considered the "gold standard" of evaluation designs to measure the effect of a program on delinquency or other outcomes. Involves randomly assigning subjects either to receive the program (the experimental group) or not receive it (the control group).

experimental group
A group of subjects that receives a prevention program.

control group
A comparison group of subjects that does not receive a prevention program.

medical and educational services were needed. The counselors talked to the boys, took them on trips and to recreational activities, tutored them in reading and arithmetic, played games with them at the project's center, encouraged them to attend church, and visited their families to give advice and general support. The program was to have continued for 10 years, but when America became involved in World War II, many of the adult counselors were drafted.[19] An evaluation of the program 30 years after it ended, when the men were an average age of 45 years, found that those in the experimental group committed more crime than those in the control group.[20] One possible reason for this negative result was that one element of the program was carried out in groups instead of one on one. This was a summer camp that many of the boys attended, and for some over multiple years. The group format was thought to have resulted in minor delinquents being influenced by more involved or serious delinquents, resulting in peer contagion or deviancy training.[21]

Detached Street Workers   In the 1950s, a major focus of delinquency prevention programs was to reach out to youths who were unlikely to use community centers. Instead of having troubled youths come to them, detached street workers were sent into inner-city neighborhoods, creating close relationships with juvenile gangs and groups in their own milieu.[22] The best-known detached street worker program was Boston's Mid-City Project, which dispatched trained social workers to seek out and meet with youth gangs three to four times a week on the gangs' own turf. Their goal was to modify the organization of the gang and allow gang members a chance to engage in more conventional behaviors. The detached street workers tried to help gang members get jobs and educational opportunities. They acted as go-betweens for gang members with agents of the power structure—lawyers, judges, parole officers, and the like. Despite these efforts, an evaluation of the program by Walter Miller failed to show that it resulted in a significant reduction in criminal activity.[23]

Federally Funded Programs   The 1960s ushered in a tremendous interest in the prevention of delinquency. Much of this interest was in programs based on social structure theory. This approach seemed quite compatible with the rehabilitative policies of the Kennedy (New Frontier) and Johnson (Great Society/War on Poverty) administrations. Delinquency prevention programs received a great deal of federal funding. The most ambitious of these was the New York City-based Mobilization for Youth (MOBY). Funded by more than $50 million, MOBY attempted an integrated approach to community development. Based on Cloward and Ohlin's concept of providing opportunities for legitimate success, MOBY created employment opportunities in the community, coordinated social services, and sponsored social action groups such as tenants' committees, legal action services, and voter registration. But MOBY ended for lack of funding amid questions about its utility and use of funds.

Improving the socialization of lower-class youths to reduce their potential for future delinquency was also an important focus of other federally funded programs during the 1960s. The largest and best known of these programs was Head Start, a national program for preschoolers that continues to this day. (See the accompanying Evidence-Based Juvenile Justice feature.)

To read more about **Head Start**, visit its website: http://www.acf.hhs.gov/ohs/.

Contemporary Preventive Approaches   The emphasis on large-scale federally funded programs aimed at the prevention of delinquency continued into the 1970s and 1980s, and these types of programs are still important today. But in recent years the focus of delinquency prevention efforts has shifted from neighborhood reclamation projects of the 1960s to more individualized, family-centered treatments.[24]

Classifying Delinquency Prevention

Just as there are a number of different ways to define delinquency prevention and very little agreement on the best way to do so,[25] the organization or classification

Head Start

Head Start is probably the best-known effort to help lower-class youths achieve proper socialization and, in so doing, reduce their potential for future criminality. Head Start programs were instituted in the 1960s as part of President Lyndon Johnson's War on Poverty. In the beginning, Head Start was a two-month summer program for children who were about to enter a school that was aimed at embracing the "whole child." In embracing the whole child, the school offered comprehensive programming that helped improve physical health, enhance mental processes, and improve social and emotional development, self-image, and interpersonal relationships. Preschoolers were provided with an enriched educational environment to develop their learning and cognitive skills. They were given the opportunity to use pegs and pegboards, puzzles, toy animals, dolls, letters and numbers, and other materials that middle-class children take for granted. These opportunities provided the children a leg up in the educational process.

Today, with annual funding approaching $8.6 billion and an enrollment of close to 1 million children, the Head Start program is administered by the Head Start Bureau, the Administration on Children, Youth, and Families (ACYF), the Administration for Children and Families (ACF), and the Department of Health and Human Services (DHHS). Since 1965, Head Start has served more than 33 million children. Head Start teachers strive to provide a variety of learning experiences appropriate to the child's age and development. These experiences encourage the child to read books, to understand cultural diversity, to express feelings, and to play with and relate to peers in an appropriate fashion. Students are guided in developing gross and fine motor skills and self-confidence. Health care is also an issue, and most children enrolled in the program

Head Start teacher Marcus Tate helps 5-year-olds Almanis Herndon (left), and Kymani Fitzgerald plant a garden at the Z. L. Madden Learning Center in Spartanburg, South Carolina, on May 15, 2013. Tate was named the Head Start Teacher of the Year for the state.

receive comprehensive health screening, physical and dental examinations, and appropriate follow-up. Many programs provide meals, and in so doing help children receive proper nourishment.

Head Start programs now serve parents in addition to their preschoolers. Some programs allow parents to enroll in classes, which cover parenting, literacy, nutrition/weight loss, domestic violence prevention, and other social issues; social services, health, and educational services are also available.

of delinquency prevention is equally diverse, and there is very little agreement on the most effective way to do this.[26]

Public Health Approach   One of the first efforts to classify the many different types of delinquency prevention activities drew upon the public health approach to preventing diseases and injuries.[27] This method divided delinquency prevention activities into three categories: primary prevention, secondary prevention, and

Considerable controversy has surrounded the success of the Head Start program. In 1970, the Westinghouse Learning Corporation issued a definitive evaluation of the Head Start effort and concluded that there was no evidence of lasting cognitive gains on the part of the participating children. Initial gains seemed to fade away during the elementary school years, and by the third grade, the performance of the Head Start children was no different from that of their peers.

While disappointing, this evaluation focused on IQ levels and gave short shrift to improvement in social competence and other survival skills. More recent research has produced dramatically different results. One report found that by age 5, children who experienced the enriched daycare offered by Head Start averaged more than 10 points higher on their IQ scores than their peers who did not participate in the program. Other research that carefully compared Head Start children to similar youngsters who did not attend the program found that the former made significant intellectual gains. Head Start children were less likely to have been retained in a grade or placed in classes for slow learners, they outperformed peers on achievement tests, and they were more likely to graduate from high school.

Head Start kids also made strides in nonacademic areas: They appear to have better health, immunization rates, nutrition, and enhanced emotional characteristics after leaving the program. Research also shows that the Head Start program can have important psychological benefits for the mothers of participants, such as decreasing depression and anxiety and increasing feelings of life satisfaction. While findings in some areas may be tentative, they are all in the same direction: Head Start enhances school readiness and has enduring effects on social competence.

If, as many experts believe, there are close links among school performance, family life, and crime, programs such as Head Start can help some potentially criminal youths avoid coming into conflict with the law. A large-scale study of the long-term effects of Head Start by economists Eliana Garces, Duncan Thomas, and Janet Currie provides some support for this view. Based on a national panel survey of households, the authors found that children who attended Head Start (at ages 3 to 5) were significantly less likely to report being arrested or referred to court for a crime by ages 18 to 30, compared to their siblings who did not attend the program.

Head Start has also been shown to be a worthwhile investment of taxpayer dollars in both the short and long term. This was the conclusion of a review of cost-benefit analyses of Head Start by economists Jens Ludwig and Deborah Phillips. One of the cost-benefit analyses found that the program's short- and medium-term benefits could offset between 40 and 60 percent of its costs, and the addition of a small fraction of long-term benefits (like reductions in juvenile crime) could make it pay for itself.

Despite these views and the research findings, Head Start faces challenges on a number of fronts. Some proposals for change include turning the program over to state control, focusing more narrowly on improving children's literacy, and mandating more qualified teachers but not providing the necessary resources to improve their low pay. Experts and advocates alike argue that these measures threaten to "water down" one of the most successful national programs for children and families in need.

CRITICAL THINKING

1. Head Start reaches almost one-half of all children and families in need. In addition to spending more money, what does the US government need to do to expand Head Start's reach?

2. What changes could be made to Head Start to make it more effective in improving the lives of children and families?

SOURCES: Head Start Bureau, *Head Start Program Facts: Fiscal Year 2015* (Washington, DC: Head Start Bureau, August 24, 2016); Holly S. Schindler and Hirokazu Yoshikawa, "Preventing Crime Through Intervention in the Preschool Years," in Brandon C. Welsh and David P. Farrington, eds., *The Oxford Handbook of Crime Prevention* (New York: Oxford University Press, 2012); Jens Ludwig and Deborah A. Phillips, "Long-Term Effects of Head Start on Low-Income Children," *Annals of the New York Academy of Sciences* 1136:257–268 (2008); Edward Zigler, Walter S. Gilliam, and Stephanie M. Jones, eds., *A Vision for Universal Preschool Education* (New York: Cambridge University Press, 2006); US Department of Health and Human Services, Administration for Children and Families, *Head Start Impact Study: First Year Findings* (Washington, DC: Author, 2005); Carol H. Ripple and Edward Zigler, "Research, Policy, and the Federal Role in Prevention Initiatives for Children," *American Psychologist* 58:482–490 (2003); Eliana Garces, Duncan Thomas, and Janet Currie, "Longer-Term Effects of Head Start," *American Economic Review* 92:999–1012 (2002); Janet Currie, "Early Childhood Education Programs," *Journal of Economic Perspectives* 15:213–238 (2001).

tertiary prevention. Primary prevention focuses on improving the general well-being of individuals through such measures as access to health care services and general prevention education, and modifying conditions in the physical environment that are conducive to delinquency through such measures as removing abandoned vehicles and improving the appearance of buildings. Secondary prevention focuses on intervening with children and young people who are potentially at risk for becoming offenders, as well as the provision of neighborhood programs to deter

CONCEPT SUMMARY 12.1

Developmental Perspective on Delinquency Prevention

- Informed by human development theories and longitudinal studies
- Designed to prevent the development of criminal potential in individuals
- Targeted at risk factors for delinquency and protective factors against delinquency
- Provided to children and families
- Implemented at different stages over the life course: childhood, early school years, adolescence, and transition to work

known delinquent activity. Tertiary prevention focuses on intervening with adjudicated juvenile offenders through such measures as substance abuse treatment and imprisonment. Here, the goal is to reduce repeat offending or recidivism.[28]

Developmental Perspective   Another popular approach to classifying delinquency prevention activities is the developmental perspective. Developmental prevention refers to interventions, especially those targeting **risk factors** and **protective factors** that are designed to prevent the development of criminal potential in individuals.[29] Developmental prevention of juvenile delinquency is informed generally by motivational or human development theories on juvenile delinquency, and specifically by longitudinal studies that follow samples of young persons from their early childhood experiences to the peak of their involvement with delinquency in their teens and crime in their 20s.[30] The developmental perspective claims that delinquency in adolescence (and later criminal offending in adulthood) is influenced by "behavioral and attitudinal patterns that have been learned during an individual's development."[31] There is considerable evidence of behavioral continuity: child antisocial behavior is linked with juvenile crime, juvenile crime with offending in early adulthood, and offending in early adulthood with adult criminality.[32] Concept Summary 12.1 lists key features of the developmental perspective. From this perspective, prevention activities are organized around different stages of the life course. We divide our discussion of developmental prevention of juvenile delinquency into two stages: childhood and adolescence.

For the most part, we have adopted the developmental perspective in discussing the effectiveness of different types of delinquency prevention programs in the rest of this chapter. This approach has several advantages: It allows for assessing the success of programs at different life-course stages; its coverage of the types of delinquency prevention programs that have been implemented is vast; and it is a well-recognized approach that has been used by other social scientists in reviews of the effectiveness of delinquency prevention.[33]

risk factor
A negative prior factor in an individual's life that increases the risk of occurrence of a future delinquent act.

protective factor
A positive prior factor in an individual's life that decreases the risk of occurrence of a future delinquent act.

Early Prevention of Delinquency

In the effort to address juvenile delinquency, early childhood interventions—initiated before delinquency occurs—have received much interest and have come to be seen as an important part of an overall strategy to reduce the harm caused by juvenile delinquency. Recent research shows that the general public is highly supportive of delinquency prevention programs and is even willing to pay more in taxes for these programs compared to more punitive options like military-style boot camps and prison. (This is discussed in the Focus on Delinquency feature entitled "Public Support for Delinquency Prevention.") Early childhood delinquency prevention programs aim at positively influencing the early risk factors or "root causes" of delinquency and criminal offending that may continue into the adult years. These early risk factors are many, some of which include growing up in

Public Support for Delinquency Prevention

Politicians who support "get-tough" responses to juvenile offenders have long claimed to have the full backing of the general public, and that it is indeed the public that demands tougher dispositions (or sentences) such as military-style boot camps and longer terms in institutions to hold them accountable for their transgressions. To be sure, there is public support for get-tough responses to juvenile delinquency, especially violent acts. But this support is not at the levels often claimed and, more importantly, not as high when compared to alternatives such as rehabilitation or treatment for juvenile offenders or early childhood or youth prevention programs. This overestimate of the punitiveness of the general public on the part of politicians and others has become known as the "mythical punitive public."

Some new research provides more evidence to substantiate the mythical punitive public—that is, that citizens are highly supportive of delinquency prevention and are even willing to pay more in taxes to support these programs compared to other responses. In a review of the public opinion literature, criminologist Frank Cullen and his colleagues found that the American public is generally supportive of delinquency prevention programs, especially for at-risk children and youth. They also found that public opinion is no longer a barrier—as it once was perceived to be—to the implementation of delinquency prevention programs in communities across the country.

In a study of public preferences of responses to juvenile offending, criminologist Daniel Nagin and his colleagues found that the public values early prevention and offender rehabilitation or treatment more than increased incarceration. As shown in Table 12.A, households were willing to pay an average of $125.71 in additional taxes on nurse home visitation programs to prevent delinquency compared to $80.97 on longer sentences, a difference of $44.74 per year. Support for paying more in taxes for rehabilitation was also higher than for longer sentences: $98.10 versus $80.97. At the state level, public support for the prevention option translated into $601 million that hypothetically could be used to prevent delinquency compared to $387 million for longer sentences for juvenile offenders.

This study was based on a large sample of residents in Pennsylvania and used a highly rigorous methodology of public opinion polling known as contingent valuation (CV), which has many advantages over conventional polling methods. The contingent valuation approach allows for the "comparison of respondents' willingness to pay for competing policy alternatives." Similar findings were shown in a follow-up study comparing rehabilitation and incarceration of juvenile offenders in Pennsylvania and three other states (Illinois, Louisiana, and Washington).

In another innovative study to gauge the public's preferences for a range of alternative responses to crime, Mark Cohen, Roland Rust, and Sara Steen found the public overwhelmingly supported increased spending of tax dollars on youth prevention programs compared to building more prisons. Public support for spending more taxes on drug treatment for nonviolent offenders as well as police also ranked higher than support for building more prisons, but not as high as for youth prevention programs.

While the mythical punitive public appears to be just that, there is no denying that the general public does see some value in get-tough policies to tackle juvenile crime. But this new crop of public opinion research reveals—even more convincingly than past research—that there is a growing demand for early prevention programs and little demand for increased use of incarceration.

CRITICAL THINKING

1. If you were a politician, would these research findings influence your decision on the policy positions you take on juvenile crime?

2. Public opinion is one important consideration in implementing delinquency prevention programs. What are some other key factors?

SOURCES: Julian V. Roberts and Ross Hastings, "Public Opinion and Crime Prevention: A Review of International Trends," in Brandon C. Welsh and David P. Farrington, eds., *The Oxford Handbook of Crime Prevention* (New York: Oxford University Press, 2012); Alex R. Piquero and Laurence Steinberg, "Public Preferences for Rehabilitation Versus Incarceration of Juvenile Offenders," *Journal of Criminal Justice* 38:1–6 (2010); Francis T. Cullen, Brenda A. Vose, Cheryl N. Lero, and James D. Unnever, "Public Support for Early Intervention: Is Child Saving a 'Habit of the Heart'?" *Victims and Offenders* 2:108–124 (2007); Mark A. Cohen, Roland T. Rust, and Sara Steen, "Prevention, Crime Control or Cash? Public Preferences Toward Criminal Justice Spending Priorities," *Justice Quarterly* 23:317–335 (2006); Daniel S. Nagin, Alex R. Piquero, Elizabeth S. Scott, and Laurence Steinberg, "Public Preferences for Rehabilitation versus Incarceration of Juvenile Offenders: Evidence from a Contingent Valuation Survey," *Criminology and Public Policy* 5:627–652 (2006); Julian V. Roberts, "Public Opinion and Youth Justice," in Michael Tonry and Anthony N. Doob, eds., *Youth Crime and Youth Justice: Comparative and Cross-National Perspectives. Crime and Justice: A Review of Research*, Vol. 31 (Chicago: University of Chicago Press, 2004).

TABLE 12.A: Public Willingness to Pay for Delinquency Prevention vs. Other Measures

Program	Average WTP per Household per Year	Statewide WTP per Year
Longer sentence	$80.97	$387 million
Rehabilitation	$98.10	$468 million
Nurse visitation	$125.71	$601 million

Note: WTP = willingness to pay.

Source: Adapted from Nagin, Piquero, Scott, and Steinberg, "Public Preferences for Rehabilitation versus Incarceration of Juvenile Offenders: Evidence from a Contingent Valuation Survey," Table 2.

poverty, a high level of hyperactivity or impulsiveness, inadequate parental supervision, and harsh or inconsistent discipline. Early childhood interventions are often multidimensional, targeted at more than one risk factor, because they take a variety of different forms, including cognitive development, child skills training, and family support. The following sections examine early childhood delinquency prevention programs that have been implemented in the four most influential settings: home, daycare, preschool, and the school. Most of the programs have been carried out in the United States.

Home-Based Programs

In a supportive and loving home environment, parents care for their children's health and general well-being, help instill in their children positive values such as honesty and respect for others, and nurture prosocial behaviors. One of the most important types of home-based programs to prevent juvenile delinquency involves the provision of support for families. Support for families in their homes can take many different forms. A popular and effective form of family support is home visitation.[34]

Home Visitation   The best-known home visitation program is the Nurse-Family Partnership (formerly Prenatal/Early Infancy Project) that was started in Elmira, New York.[35] This program was designed with three broad objectives:

- To improve the outcomes of pregnancy

- To improve the quality of care that parents provide to their children (and their children's subsequent health and development)

- To improve women's personal life-course development (completing their education, finding work, and planning future pregnancies)[36]

The program targeted first-time mothers-to-be under 19 years of age, unmarried, or poor. In all, 400 women were enrolled in the program. The mothers-to-be received home visits from nurses during pregnancy and during the first two years of the child's life. Each home visit lasted about one and one-quarter hours, and the mothers were visited on average every two weeks. The home visitors gave advice to the mothers about care of the child, infant development, and the importance of proper nutrition and avoiding smoking and drinking during pregnancy. Fifteen years after the program started, children of the mothers who received home visits had half as many arrests as children of mothers who received no home visits (the control group).[37] It was also found that these children, compared to those in the control group, had fewer convictions and violations of probation, were less likely to run away from home, and were less likely to drink alcohol. In addition to the program's success in preventing juvenile crime and other delinquent activities, it also produced a number of improvements in the lives of the mothers, such as lower rates of child abuse and neglect, crime in general, and substance abuse, as well as less reliance on welfare and social services.[38] A RAND study found that the program's desirable effects, for both the children and the mothers, translated into substantial financial benefits for government and taxpayers, and that the total amount of these benefits was more than four times the cost of the program (see Figure 12.1).[39] A more recent analysis of the program's costs and benefits—based on a large number of studies across the country—showed a favorable return of $2.90 for every dollar spent on the program.[40] In the latest follow-up of the program, when the children were 19 years old, girls incurred significantly fewer arrests and convictions compared to their control counterparts, while few program effects were observed for the boys.[41]

Two other experiments of the Nurse-Family Partnership (NFP) program in Memphis, Tennessee, and Denver, Colorado, have produced similar benefits for the mothers and their children, including a reduction in child abuse and neglect.[42] The success of the program has resulted in its use in 581 counties in 43 states across the country, serving almost 33,000 families each year.[43] In Colorado, the program was established in law, and in its first year of operation served almost 1,400 families in 49 of the state's 64 counties.[44] It is also now being replicated throughout England.[45] The use of nurses instead of paraprofessionals, its intensity (a minimum of two years), and its targeted nature (for first-time, disadvantaged mothers only) are critical features that distinguish it from other, less effective home visitation programs such as Hawaii Healthy Start.[46]

To read more about the **Nurse-Family Partnership**, visit their website: http://www.nursefamilypartnership.org/.

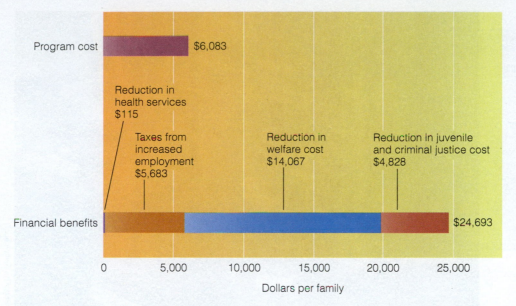

figure 12.1

Costs and Benefits of Home Visits for High-Risk Families

SOURCE: Adapted from Greenwood et al., "Estimating the Costs and Benefits of Early Childhood Interventions: Nurse Home Visits and the Perry Preschool," Table 4.3.

Improving Parenting Skills

Another form of family support that has shown some success in preventing juvenile delinquency is improving parenting skills. Although the main focus of parent training programs is on the parents, many of these programs also involve children with the aim of improving the parent–child bond.

Two reviews capture the broad-scale effectiveness of family-based prevention programs. The first one involved a meta-analysis of the effects of early prevention programs that included parents and children up to age 5.[47] Eleven high-quality studies were included that covered a variety of program modalities, including home visitation, family support services, and parental education (improvement of core parenting skills). Results showed significant effects across a number of important domain outcomes, including educational success, delinquency, cognitive development, involvement in the justice system, and family well-being. Program duration and intensity were associated with larger effects, but not multicomponent programs. This latter finding goes against much past research, including the latest results on the effectiveness of the Fast Track multicomponent, multisite prevention program (see Chapter 6).[48]

The second study involved an updated systematic review and meta-analysis of the effects of early family/parent training programs for children up to age 5 years on antisocial behavior and delinquency.[49] It included 78 randomized controlled experiments and investigated the full range of these programs, including home visits, parent education plus daycare, and parent training. Results indicated that early family/parent training is a highly effective intervention for reducing antisocial behavior and delinquency. These programs also produce a wide range of other important benefits for families, including improved school readiness and school performance on the part of children and greater employment and educational opportunities for parents. Significant differences were not detected across program type, such as traditional parent training versus home visiting.

Oregon Social Learning Center   The most widely cited parenting skills program is one created at the Oregon Social Learning Center (OSLC) by Gerald Patterson and his colleagues.[50] Patterson's research convinced him that poor parenting skills were associated with antisocial behavior in the home and at school. Family disruption and coercive exchanges between parents and children led to increased family tension, poor academic performance, and negative peer relations. The primary cause of the problem seemed to be that parents did not know how to deal effectively with their children. Parents sometimes ignored their children's

Parent training, family support services, and parent education are just a few of the many types of programs directed at improving parenting skills and the parent–child bond to help reduce delinquency. Pictured here is a parenting exercise during a fatherhood development class led by Alphonso Pettis (right) at the Next Door Foundation in Milwaukee. The program is part of President Obama's "My Brother's Keeper" initiative, which is designed to help boys and young men of color improve their life opportunities.

The Washington Post/Getty Images

behavior, but at other times the same actions would trigger explosive rage. Some parents would discipline their children for reasons that had little to do with the children's behavior, instead reflecting their own frustrations.

The children reacted in a regular progression, from learning to be noncompliant to learning to be assaultive. Their "coercive behavior," which included whining, yelling, and temper tantrums, would sometimes be acquired by other family members. Eventually family conflict would flow out of the home and into the school and social environment.

The OSLC program uses behavior modification techniques to help parents acquire proper disciplinary methods. Parents are asked to select several behaviors for change and to count the frequency of their occurrence. OSLC personnel teach social skills to reinforce positive behaviors, and constructive disciplinary methods to discourage negative ones. Incentive programs are initiated in which a child can earn points for desirable behaviors. Points can be exchanged for allowance, prizes, or privileges. Parents are also taught disciplinary techniques that stress firmness and consistency rather than "nattering" (low-intensity behaviors, such as scowling or scolding) or explosive discipline, such as hitting or screaming. One important technique is the "time out," in which the child is removed for brief isolation in a quiet room. Parents are taught the importance of setting rules and sticking to them. A number of evaluation studies carried out by Patterson and his colleagues showed that improving parenting skills can lead to reductions in juvenile delinquency.[51]

To read more about the **OSLC parenting skills program**, visit their website: http://www.oslc.org/.

Many programs have been modeled on this parent training method. The Positive Parenting Program, or Triple P, is one example. Triple P emphasizes the importance of developing parents' resilience and capacity for self-regulation as part of a program that helps them acquire skills to become self-sufficient and self-confident in their parenting.[52] A meta-analysis of Triple P involving 11 studies found that it was effective in reducing children's antisocial behavior.[53]

The parent training method used by the OSLC may be the most cost-effective method of early intervention. A RAND study found that parent training costs about one-twentieth what a home visit program costs and is more effective in preventing serious crimes. The study estimates that 501 serious crimes could be prevented for every million dollars spent on parent training (or $2,000 per crime), a far cheaper solution than long-term incarceration, which would cost about $16,000 to prevent a single crime.[54]

Daycare Programs

Daycare services are available to children as young as 6 weeks old in the United States and other Western countries.[55] In addition to allowing parents to return to work, daycare serves to provide children with a number of benefits, including social interaction with other children and stimulation of their cognitive, sensory, and motor control skills. The effectiveness of early childhood intervention has been studied in two programs described here—one in Syracuse, New York, and one in Houston, Texas.

Among the best known of early childhood intervention programs that provide high-quality daycare services is the Syracuse University Family Development Research Program. This program involved high-risk women during the later stages of their pregnancies. After the women gave birth, paraprofessionals were assigned to work with them, encouraging sound parent–child relationships, providing nutrition information, and helping them establish relationships with social service agencies. In addition, the children received free full-time daycare, designed to develop their intellectual abilities, up to age 5. A 10-year follow-up compared children involved in the program with a control group and found that those who received the intervention were less likely to be referred to the juvenile court for delinquency offenses, more likely to express positive feelings about themselves, and able to take a more active role in dealing with personal problems. Girls seemed especially to benefit, doing better in school; parents were more likely to express prosocial attitudes.[56]

Another high-quality daycare program was that of the Houston Parent-Child Development Center. Like the Syracuse University program, mothers and their children received services. In the first year of the program, the mothers received home visits from social service professionals, for the purpose of informing them about child development and parenting skills and helping them to develop prosocial bonds with their children. In the second year of the program, the mothers and their children attended a child development center four mornings a week. Here, children were provided with daycare services to foster cognitive skills and encourage positive interactions with other children. Mothers participated in classes on family communication and child management. Eight years after the program ended, children who received the program were less involved in fighting and other delinquent activities when compared to a control group.[57]

The success of these programs rests in their targeting of important individual- and family-level risk factors for delinquency, such as low intelligence,

Daycare programs serve largely as an organized form of child care to allow parents to return to work. But they also provide children with a number of important benefits, including social interaction with other children and stimulation of their cognitive, sensory, and motor control skills. Here, two children play at Kids Korner Preschool and Daycare in Idaho Falls.

AP Images/Monte LaOrange

impulsiveness, and inconsistent and poor parenting. Social scientists point to a package of child- and parent-centered interventions targeted at multiple risk factors as a core ingredient of successful delinquency prevention programs.[58]

Preschool

Preschool programs differ from daycare programs in that preschool is geared more toward preparing children for school. Preschool is typically provided to children ages 3 to 5 years. These are the formative years of brain development; more learning takes place during this developmental stage than at any other stage over the life course. Low intelligence and school failure are important risk factors for juvenile delinquency.[59] (See Chapter 6 for why these are risk factors for juvenile delinquency.) For these reasons, highly structured, cognitive-based preschool programs give young children a positive start in life. Some key features of preschool programs include the provision of:

- Developmentally appropriate learning curricula
- A wide array of cognitive-based enriching activities
- Activities for parents, usually of a less intensive nature, so that they may be able to support the school experience at home[60]

A preschool in Michigan, a program in Chicago, and Head Start centers in Washington provide some positive findings on the benefits of early intervention.

Started in the mid-1960s, the Perry Preschool in Ypsilanti, Michigan, provided disadvantaged children with a program of educational enrichment supplemented with weekly home visits. The main hypothesis of the program was that "good preschool programs can help children in poverty make a better start in their transition from home to community and thereby set more of them on paths to becoming economically self-sufficient, socially responsible adults."[61] The main intervention was high-quality, active-learning preschool programming administered by professional teachers for two years. Preschool sessions were half a day long five days a week for the duration of the 30-week school year. The educational approach focused on supporting the development of the children's cognitive and social skills through individualized teaching and learning.

A number of assessments were made of the program at important stages of development. The first assessment of juvenile delinquency, when the participants were age 15, found that those who received the program reported one-third fewer offenses than a control group.[62] By the age of 27, program participants had accumulated half the arrests of the control group. The researchers also found that the preschoolers had achieved many other significant benefits compared to their control group counterparts, including higher monthly earnings, higher percentages of home ownership and second car ownership, a higher level of schooling completed, and a lower percentage receiving welfare benefits.[63] All of these benefits translated into substantial dollar cost savings. It was estimated that for each dollar it cost to run and administer the program, more than $7 was saved to taxpayers, potential crime victims, and program participants.[64] An independent study by RAND also found that Perry Preschool was a very worthwhile investment.[65]

The most recent assessment of the effectiveness of Perry Preschool—when the subjects were age 40—found that it continues to make a difference in the lives of those who were enrolled in the program. Compared to the control group, program group members had achieved many significant benefits:

- Fewer lifetime arrests for violent crimes (32 percent versus 48 percent), property crimes (36 percent versus 58 percent), and drug crimes (14 percent versus 34 percent)
- Higher levels of schooling completed (77 percent versus 60 percent graduated from high school)
- Higher annual earnings (57 percent versus 43 percent had earnings in the top half of the sample)[66]

An assessment of the costs and benefits at age 40 found that for every dollar spent on the program, more than $17 was returned to society—in the form of savings in crime, education, welfare, and increased tax revenue.[67] Re-analyses of these economic findings by economist James Heckman confirmed the overall value of the program but found a lower return, on the order of $7 of benefit per dollar of cost.[68]

The Child-Parent Center (CPC) program in Chicago, like Perry Preschool, provided disadvantaged children ages 3 to 4 years with high-quality, active-learning preschool supplemented with family support. However, unlike Perry, CPC continued to provide the children with the educational enrichment component into elementary school, up to the age of 9 years. Just focusing on the effect of the preschool, it was found that, compared to a control group, those who received the program were less likely to be arrested for nonviolent offenses (17 percent versus 25 percent) and violent offenses (9 percent versus 15 percent) by the time they were 18. Preschool participants, compared to a control group, were also less likely to be arrested more than once (10 percent versus 13 percent). There were other significant benefits realized by the preschool participants compared to the control group:

- A higher rate of high school completion (50 percent versus 39 percent)
- More years of completed education (11 years versus 10)
- A lower rate of dropping out of school (47 percent versus 55 percent)[69]

A more recent evaluation when participants were age 24 found that the experimental group, compared to the control group members, had significantly lower rates of felony arrest (17 percent versus 21 percent) and lower rates of incarceration (21 percent versus 26 percent).[70] Positive results were found for official justice contact in a follow-up at age 28 as well.[71] The success of the CPC program in preventing juvenile delinquency and improving other life-course outcomes produced substantial cost savings. For each dollar spent on the program, $7.14 was saved to taxpayers, potential crime victims, and program participants.[72]

Another early intervention that closely resembles these preschool programs is Head Start. (See the Evidence-Based Juvenile Justice feature earlier in the chapter.) Head Start provides children with, among other things, an enriched educational environment to develop their learning and cognitive skills. One study of Head Start centers in Seattle, Washington, found that very young children who were enrolled in the program were less likely to misbehave than children in the control group.[73] Other studies have shown that Head Start is a worthwhile investment of taxpayer dollars in both the short and long term.[74]

Overall, high-quality, intensive preschool programs show strong support for preventing delinquency and improving the lives of young people.[75] The provision of family support services combined with preschool programming likely adds to the strength of the Perry and CPC programs in preventing delinquency, but it is clear that preschool was the most important element. The intellectual enrichment component of preschool helps prepare children for the academic challenges of elementary and later grades; reducing the chances of school failure is a significant factor in reducing delinquency. Other research emphasizes the noncognitive skills or "grit" that these early intervention programs can inculcate in the participating children.[76] Another notable point about the positive findings of Perry and CPC is that these two programs were implemented many years apart, yet the CPC, as a semi-replication of Perry, demonstrates that preschool programs today can still be effective in preventing delinquency.

School Programs in the Primary Grades

Schools are a critical social context for delinquency prevention efforts, from the early to later grades.[77] (See Chapter 10.) All schools work to produce vibrant and productive members of society. The school's role in preventing delinquency in general, which is the focus of this section, differs from measures taken to make

To read more about **SSDP**, visit their website: http://ssdp-tip.org/SSDP/.

the school a safer place.[78] In this case, a school may adopt a greater security orientation and implement such measures as metal detectors, police in school, and closed-circuit television cameras. A number of experimental programs have attempted to prevent or reduce delinquency by manipulating factors in the learning environment; three are discussed here.

The Seattle Social Development Project (SSDP) used a method in which teachers learn techniques that reward appropriate student behavior and minimize disruptive behavior. The program started in first grade and continued through sixth grade. Students were taught in small groups. Students were also provided with skills training to help them master problem solving, communication, and conflict resolution skills. Family training classes were offered, teaching parents how to reward and encourage desirable behavior and provide negative consequences for undesirable behavior in a consistent fashion. Other parent training focused on improving their children's academic performance while reducing at-risk behaviors such as drug abuse. In short, the program was extremely comprehensive, targeting an array of risk factors for delinquency.

A long-term evaluation of the Seattle program—at age 21—found that children who received the program reported more commitment and attachment to school, better academic achievement, fewer delinquent acts, and fewer instances of selling drugs compared to a control group. Program participants were also less likely than their control counterparts to have received an official court charge in their lifetime.[79] In the latest follow-up, which included 93 percent of the original sample, the investigators found that the full intervention group (compared to the control groups) reported significantly better educational and economic attainment, mental health, and sexual health by age 27, but no effects were found for substance abuse and criminal activity at ages 24 or 27.[80]

In Montreal, child psychologist Richard Tremblay set up an experiment to investigate the effects of an early preventive intervention program for 6-year-old boys who were aggressive and hyperactive and from poor neighborhoods. Known as the Montreal Longitudinal-Experimental Study, the program lasted for two years and had two components: school-based social skills training and home-based parent training. Social skills training for the children focused predominantly on improving social interactions with peers. The parent-training component was based on the social learning principles of Gerald Patterson and involved training parents in how to provide positive reinforcement for desirable behavior, use nonpunitive and consistent discipline practices, and develop family crisis management techniques. The program was successful in reducing delinquency. By age 12, boys in the experimental group compared to those in the control group committed less burglary and theft and were less likely to be involved in fights. At every age from 10 to 15, self-reported delinquency was lower for the boys in the experimental group compared to those in the control group.[81] In the latest follow-ups when the study participants were 24 and 28 years old, it was found that those in the experimental group were still less likely to have a criminal record than their control counterparts, but the effect was not as pronounced as in earlier years.[82]

The final school-based prevention program is the Good Behavior Game (GBG). It uses a universal classroom behavior management strategy that is designed to foster learning by teaching children to regulate their own and their classmates' behavior. Teachers are trained in the curriculum and receive supportive monitoring throughout the school year. In an experimental study in 19 urban elementary schools in Baltimore, Maryland, first-grade students were randomly assigned to groups that included equal numbers of aggressive and disruptive children. While GBG was in progress, teachers monitored the behavior of students in each group. Misbehavior of any student in a group resulted in a check mark being placed on the chalkboard for that group. At the end of the session, groups with fewer than five check marks received a reward. At the beginning of the program, game sessions were announced and tangible rewards such as stickers were given immediately following the session. As the program became more familiar to students, sessions started unannounced and less tangible rewards were given, like extended recess. In addition, the time between the session and the granting of rewards was extended. The program lasted for two years in the first and second grades.

After one year, experimental students were rated as less aggressive and shy than control students by teachers and peers. Positive effects of the program were most evident among students rated as highly aggressive at baseline. Positive effects of the intervention were maintained through sixth grade for boys, with the highest baseline ratings of aggression at first-grade entry.[83] In a long-term follow-up when study participants were between 19 and 21 years old, significant reductions in rates of violent and criminal behavior were observed among males in the highest-risk group compared to their control counterparts (34 percent versus 50 percent). Also, significant reductions in rates of drug abuse/dependence disorders were found among males overall (19 percent versus 38 percent) and in the highest-risk group (29 percent versus 68 percent) compared to their control counterparts.[84]

Schools may not be able to reduce delinquency single-handedly, but a number of viable alternatives to their present operations could aid a communitywide effort to reduce the problem of juvenile crime. A review of school-based programs was conducted by Denise Gottfredson and her colleagues as part of a study to determine the best methods of delinquency prevention. Some of their findings are contained in Exhibit 12.2. The main difference between the programs that work and those that do not is that successful programs target an array of important risk factors. Often it is not enough to improve only the school environment or only the family environment; for example, a youth who has a troubled family life may find it more difficult to do well at school, regardless of the improvements made at school. Some effective early school-based delinquency prevention programs also show that greater gains are made with those who are at the highest risk for future delinquency. An evaluation of Peace-Builders, a school-based violence prevention program for kindergarteners to fifth graders, found that decreases in aggression and improvements in social competence were larger for the highest-risk kids compared to those at medium and low levels of risk.[85] Another important ingredient of successful school-based programs is that they be intensive; two or three sessions a semester often does not cut it.

---

exhibit 12.2

School-Based Delinquency Prevention Programs

What Works?

- Programs aimed at building school capacity to initiate and sustain innovation

- Programs aimed at clarifying and communicating norms about behaviors by establishing school rules, improving the consistency of their enforcement (particularly when they emphasize positive reinforcement of appropriate behavior), or communicating norms through schoolwide campaigns (e.g., antibullying campaigns) or ceremonies

- Comprehensive instructional programs that focus on a range of social competency skills (such as developing self-control and skills in stress management, responsible decision making, social problem solving, and communication) and that are delivered over a long period of time to continually reinforce skills

What Does Not Work?

- Instructional programs that do not focus on social competency skills or do not make use of cognitive-behavioral teaching methods

What Is Promising?

- Programs that group youths into smaller "schools within schools" to create smaller units, more supportive interactions, or greater flexibility in instruction

- Classroom or instructional management

SOURCES: Denise C. Gottfredson, Philip J. Cook, and Chongmin Na, "Schools and Prevention," in Brandon C. Welsh and David P. Farrington, eds., *The Oxford Handbook of Crime Prevention* (New York: Oxford University Press, 2012); Denise C. Gottfredson, David B. Wilson, and Stacy Skroban Najaka, "School-Based Crime Prevention," in Lawrence W. Sherman, David P. Farrington, Brandon C. Welsh, and Doris Layton MacKenzie, eds., *Evidence-Based Crime Prevention.* Copyright © 2006. Reproduced by permission of Taylor and Francis Books, UK.

Prevention of Delinquency in the Teenage Years

Like early childhood interventions, delinquency prevention programs started in the teenage years also play a vital role in an overall strategy to reduce juvenile delinquency. A wide range of non–juvenile justice delinquency prevention programs attempt to address such risk factors as parental conflict and separation, poor housing, dropping out of high school, and antisocial peers. The following sections examine the five main delinquency prevention approaches targeted at teenagers: mentoring, school-based programs, after-school programs, job training, and comprehensive community-based programs.

Mentoring

Mentoring programs usually involve nonprofessional volunteers spending time with young people at risk for delinquency, dropping out of school, school failure, and other social problems. Mentors behave in a supportive, nonjudgmental manner while acting as role models.[86] In recent years, there has been a large increase in the number of mentoring programs, many of which are aimed at preventing delinquency.[87] High-profile cases, such as the story of Westley "Wes" Moore (see the Youth Stories feature), have also drawn attention to the need for mentoring young people.[88]

Federal Mentoring Programs   The Office of Juvenile Justice and Delinquency Prevention (OJJDP) has supported mentoring for many years in all parts of the United States, most notably through the Juvenile Mentoring Program (JUMP), the Mentoring Initiative for System Involved Youth (MISIY), and its latest initiative, a collaboration with MENTOR: The National Mentoring Partnership, which involved the launching of the online National Mentoring Resource Center. Between 2008 and 2014, federal appropriations for mentoring have totaled more than $615 million. Under JUMP, thousands of at-risk youths were provided with mentors.

The most common areas of increased risk for youths, based on a large number of girls and boys enrolled in the program, are school and social/family domains.

Mentoring is one of many types of interventions that have been used with teens considered to be at risk for a range of social problems, including school failure and delinquency. Here, Adriana Maldonado (left), a senior at Atrisco Heritage Academy high school, meets with her mentor, Daisy Astorga, a sophomore at Smith College.

AP Images/Adolphe Pierre-Louis

Wes Moore

Westley "Wes" Moore was born in Baltimore, Maryland, in 1979. He graduated high school from Valley Forge Military School, earned a bachelor's degree from Johns Hopkins University, was awarded a Rhodes scholarship to study at Oxford University in England, was honored as a combat veteran of the war in Afghanistan, and worked as a White House Fellow for Secretary of State Condoleezza Rice during the Bush administration. Many other notable accomplishments have since followed. This was the successful Wes Moore, the one who made it.

Another Wes Moore was also born in Baltimore—just blocks from the other—in the late 1970s. He didn't graduate from high school, let alone go on to university or a successful professional career. Instead, he is serving a life sentence in Jessup Correctional Institution in Maryland for participating in an armed robbery that resulted in the death of Sergeant Bruce Prothero, a 13-year veteran of the Baltimore County police department and father of five children.

Identical names aside, the two men shared similar histories. Both grew up in disadvantaged circumstances on the rough streets of Baltimore. Both lost their fathers at an early age. Each had runs-in with the police and found themselves in difficulty at school at one time or another. As the author Wes Moore states in his book *The Other Wes Moore: One Name, Two Fates*, "The chilling truth is that his story could have been mine. The tragedy is that my story could have been his."

So how did one of them make it? What made the difference in helping one escape a life of delinquency and crime and go on to a successful personal and professional life? These questions are at the heart of Moore's book. He attributes his ability to escape the fate of his namesake—and the tens of thousands of other inner-city kids facing similar circumstances then and today—to no single factor, but rather a number of influences. One of these was caring, strong mentors who were there for him when he needed it most. His mom, grandparents, and commander at military school were crucial. Mentoring is an important delinquency prevention strategy in the United States. Another valuable influence

Andy Kropa/Getty Images Entertainment/Getty Images

in his life was being entrusted with responsibilities, which, in his words, "forced me to get serious about my behavior." Today, Wes Moore works with organizations across the country that invest in youths and support them in making the best choices possible.

CRITICAL THINKING

This is a powerful story. Can it be used to help improve the lives of other children in similar circumstances? What is needed to make this happen?

SOURCE: Wes Moore, *The Other Wes Moore: One Name, Two Fates* (New York: Spiegel and Grau, 2010).

(See Table 12.1.) Mentors work one-on-one with young people.[89] Research has shown that mentoring and other types of delinquency prevention programs offered in group settings, particularly for high-risk youths, may end up causing more harm than good. By participating in these types of programs in groups, young people who are more chronically involved in delinquency may negatively affect those who are marginally involved in delinquency.[90]

Effectiveness of Mentoring The overall effectiveness of mentoring in preventing delinquency is reported in two comprehensive reviews of the literature. In one systematic review and meta-analysis that included 18 mentoring programs, British criminologists Darrick Jolliffe and David Farrington found that

table 12.1

Risk Factors of Young People in the Juvenile Mentoring Program (JUMP)

Risk Domain	Percentage of Enrolled Youth*	
	Male (n = 3,592)	Female (n = 3,807)
School problems	74.6%	63%
School behavior	39.5	23.5
Poor grades	53.6	45.9
Truancy	10.4	9.1
Social/family problems	51.7	56.4
Delinquency	17.5	8.5
Fighting	12.8	6.3
Property crime	2.8	0.5
Gang activity	3	1
Weapons	1.1	0.4
Alcohol use	3.2	1.5
Drug use	4	1.8
Tobacco use	2.3	1.9
Pregnancy/early parenting	0.2	1.5

Source: Laurence C. Novotney, Elizabeth Mertinko, James Lange, and Tara Kelly Baker, *Juvenile Mentoring Program: A Progress Review* (Washington, DC: OJJDP *Juvenile Justice Bulletin*, 2000), p. 5.

* Percentage of total JUMP enrollment for each gender. For 23 youths, no gender was reported in the database.

the average effect across the studies corresponded to a significant 10 percent reduction in delinquency.[91] The authors also found that mentoring was more effective in reducing delinquency when the average duration of each contact between mentor and youth was greater, in smaller-scale studies, and when mentoring was combined with other interventions. A second systematic review and meta-analysis by Patrick Tolan and his colleagues examined the effects of mentoring on a wide range of areas, including delinquency, academic achievement, drug use, and aggression.[92] The review included 39 programs, some of which were included in the Jolliffe and Farrington review. The authors found that mentoring had a positive effect in all four areas, but the largest effects involved reductions in delinquency and aggression.

We have reported on some of the most effective mentoring programs (Chapter 8 also profiles two successful programs). But why do some mentoring programs work and others do not? The biggest issue has to do with what the mentors actually do and how they do it. Mentors should be a source of support and guidance to help young people deal with a broad range of issues that have to do with their family, school, and future career. They work one-on-one with young people, in many cases forming strong bonds. Care is taken in matching the mentor and young person. Other research on effective mentoring relationships between adults and teens points to the need for the mentors to display empathy, pay particular attention to and nurture the strengths of the young person, and treat him or her "as a person of equal worth and value."[93]

To learn more about effective mentoring programs operated by **Big Brothers Big Sisters of America**, visit their website: www.bbbs.org/.

School Programs for Teens

Safety of students takes on a much higher profile in middle schools and high schools than in the early grades because of a larger number of school shootings and other violent incidents. However, the role of schools in the prevention of delinquency in the wider community remains prominent. A wide range of programs to deal with juvenile delinquency in the community have been set up in middle schools and high schools across the United States and in other countries. We review just a couple of the most influential school-based delinquency prevention programs.

Project PATHE   Positive Action Through Holistic Education (PATHE) is a comprehensive program used in secondary schools that reduces school disorder and aims to improve the school environment. The goal is to enhance students' experiences and attitudes about school by increasing their bonds to the school, enhancing their self-esteem, and improving educational and occupational attainment. These improvements will help reduce juvenile delinquency.

PATHE was initially operated in four middle schools and three high schools in South Carolina. It focused on four elements: strengthening students' commitment to school, providing successful school experiences, encouraging attachment to the educational community, and increasing participation in school activities. By increasing students' sense of belonging and usefulness, the project sought to promote a positive school experience. The PATHE program has undergone extensive evaluation by sociologist Denise Gottfredson, who found that the schools in which it was used experienced a moderate reduction in delinquency.[94]

Violence Prevention Curriculum for Adolescents   Violence prevention curricula as part of health education classes is one type of school-based prevention program that has received much attention in recent years in the United States.[95] However, few rigorous evaluations of these programs or other instructional-based violence prevention programs in schools have assessed effects on juvenile violence.[96] One of these evaluations assessed the impact of this type of program on high school students in a number of locations across the country. The curriculum was designed to do five main things in the following order:

1. Provide statistical information on adolescent violence and homicide

2. Present anger as a normal, potentially constructive emotion

3. Create a need in the students for alternatives to fighting by discussing the potential gains and losses from fighting

4. Have students analyze the precursors to a fight and practice avoiding fights using role-play and video

5. Create a classroom ethos that is nonviolent and values violence prevention behavior[97]

The curriculum was administered in 10 sessions. The sessions were very interactive between the teacher and the students, relying on many different techniques, including brainstorming and role-playing. Like many school-based delinquency prevention programs, the violence prevention curriculum was concerned with reducing delinquency, specifically fighting, in schools and in the larger community. An evaluation of the program in four major urban areas showed that fighting had been significantly reduced among the young people who attended the sessions compared to a control group that did not receive the curriculum.[98]

The review of what works in preventing delinquency in schools by Denise Gottfredson and her colleagues (refer to Exhibit 12.2) is not limited to the early grades, but also includes programs in middle schools and high schools. And the conclusion on the effectiveness of school-based delinquency prevention programs in the later grades is the same as for the early grades: some programs work and some programs do not work. But what are the key features of successful school-based delinquency prevention programs? As with the successful school programs in the early grades, successful programs in the later grades are those that target a number of important risk factors. For the two programs described here, this meant a focus on reducing school disorder and improving the school environment. Two additional components of successful school-based delinquency prevention programs in the later grades are improving the family environment by engaging parents in helping the student to learn, and reducing negative peer influences through information about the downsides of gun carrying, drug use, and gang involvement.

After-School Programs

More than two-thirds of all married couples with school-age children (ages 6 to 17) have both parents working outside the home, and the proportion of single parents working outside the home is even higher.[99] This leaves many unsupervised young people in communities during the after-school hours (2:00 PM to 6:00 PM), which is believed to be the main reason for the elevated rates of delinquency during this period of time.[100] After-school programs have become a popular response to this problem in recent years. While recreation is just one form of after-school program—other options include child care centers, tutoring programs at schools, dance groups, and drop-in clubs—it plays an important role in young people's lives, especially for a large number who do not have access to organized sport and other recreational opportunities. State and federal budgets for education, public safety, delinquency prevention, and child care provide some funding for after-school programs.

In a large-scale study of after-school programs in Maryland, Denise Gottfredson and her colleagues found that participation in the programs reduced delinquent behavior among children in middle school but not elementary school. The researchers found that increasing intentions not to use drugs as well as positive peer associations were the key reasons for the favorable effects on delinquency among the older children. Interestingly, decreasing the time spent unsupervised or increasing the involvement in constructive activities was found to play no significant role.[101] In another evaluation of an after-school program—the All Stars program for middle school students—by Denise Gottfredson and her colleagues, no differences were observed in delinquency, substance use, and other problem behaviors among youths who received the program compared to a similar group of youths who did not get the program.[102] The authors identified limited time to achieve full implementation and potential deviance training as key factors for the program's inability to produce positive change. A recent systematic review and meta-analysis of after-school programs largely confirms these findings.[103] Based on 17 after-school programs of three main types (academic, recreation, and skills training/mentoring), there was evidence that the intervention had a small but nonsignificant effect on delinquency.

Boys and Girls Clubs of America One of the most successful after-school programs in preventing delinquency (and substance abuse) is provided by the Boys and Girls Clubs of America. Founded in 1902, the Boys and Girls Clubs of

In addition to providing supervision following school time, after-school programs engage children and teens in learning new skills and building upon existing interests. In some of these programs, the prevention of delinquency remains a primary objective. Shown here are students of Coburg Community Charter School in Coburg, Oregon, participating in an after-school female empowerment program, sponsored by Girls on the Run.

AP Images/Andy Nelson

America is a nonprofit organization with a membership today of more than 4 million boys and girls nationwide. Boys and Girls Clubs (BGCs) provide programs in six main areas:

- Cultural enrichment
- Health and physical education
- Social recreation
- Personal and educational development
- Citizenship and leadership development
- Environmental education[104]

One study examined the effectiveness of BGCs for high-risk youths in public housing developments at five sites across the country. The usual services of BGCs, which include reading classes, sports, and homework assistance, were offered, as well as a program to prevent substance abuse, known as SMART Moves (Self-Management and Resistance Training). This program targets the specific pressures that young people face to try drugs and alcohol. It also provides education to parents and the community at large to assist young people in learning about the dangers of substance abuse and strategies for resisting the pressures to use drugs and alcohol.[105] Evaluation results showed that housing developments with BGCs, with and without SMART Moves, had fewer damaged units and less delinquency in general than housing developments without the clubs. There was also an overall reduction in substance abuse, drug trafficking, and other drug-related delinquency activity.[106]

To learn more about the **Boys and Girls Clubs of America**, visit their website: http://www.bgca.org/.

Participate and Learn Skills   A Canadian program implemented in a public housing development in the nation's capital, Ottawa, recruited low-income young people to participate in after-school activities, such as sports (ice hockey), music, dance, and scouting. Known as Participate and Learn Skills (PALS), the program ran for almost three years and aimed to advance young people toward higher skill levels in the activities they chose and to integrate them into activities in the wider community. PALS was based on the belief that skill development in sports, music, dance, and so on could affect other areas of young people's lives, such as prosocial attitudes and behaviors, which in turn could help them avoid engaging in delinquent activities.

At the end of the program, it was found that those who participated in the after-school activities were much better off than their control counterparts on a range of measures. The strongest impact of the program was found for juvenile delinquency, with an 80 percent reduction in police arrests. This positive effect was diminished somewhat in the 16 months after the program ended. The researchers speculated that the effects of the program may wear off. Substantial gains were also observed in skill acquisition, as measured by the number of levels advanced in an activity, and in integration in the wider community. These benefits translated into impressive cost savings. For every dollar that was spent on the program, more than $2.50 was saved to the juvenile justice system (fewer arrests), the housing development (less need for private security services), and the city government.[107]

Despite the mixed findings on the effectiveness of after-school programs in preventing juvenile delinquency, there is nothing to suggest that they should be discontinued.[108] Instead, researchers and others have called attention to the need to address key concerns with after-school programs, including their ability to provide sufficient and rewarding activities, reach high-risk youths who could benefit the most from the program, and reduce substantially the amount of unsupervised socializing.[109] There is a real need for further evaluation and testing of alternative after-school program models.[110] The fact that some (but not all) types of delinquency are elevated during the after-school hours underscores the importance of high-quality after-school programs.[111]

Job Training

The effects of having an after-school job can be problematic (see Chapter 3). Some research indicates that it may be associated with delinquency and substance abuse. However, helping kids to prepare for the adult workforce is an important aspect of delinquency prevention. Job training programs help improve the chances of youths' obtaining jobs in the legal economy and thereby may reduce delinquency.[112] The developmental stage of transition to work is difficult for many young people.[113] Coming from a disadvantaged background, having poor grades in school or perhaps dropping out of school, and having some involvement in delinquency can all pose difficulties in securing a steady, well-paying job in early adulthood. Programs like the two described here are concerned not only with providing young people with employable skills but also with helping them overcome some of these immediate obstacles.

Job Corps   The best-known and largest job training program in the United States is Job Corps, established in 1964 as a federal training program for disadvantaged, unemployed youths. The designers of the national program, the Department of Labor, were hopeful that spin-off benefits in the form of reduced dependence on social assistance and a reduction in delinquency would result from empowering at-risk youth to achieve stable, long-term employment opportunities. The program is still active today, operating out of 125 centers across the nation, and each year it provides services to more than 60,000 young people at a cost of over $1.5 billion.[114]

The main goal of Job Corps is to improve the employability of participants by offering a comprehensive set of services that largely includes vocational skills training, basic education (the ability to obtain graduate equivalent degrees), and health care. Job Corps is provided to young people between the ages of 16 and 24 years. Most of the young people enrolled in the program are at high risk for delinquency, substance abuse, and social assistance dependency. Almost all of the Job Corps centers require the participants to live at the center while taking the program.

A large-scale evaluation of Job Corps, involving 15,400 young people, found that participation in the program resulted in significant reductions in criminal

Job Corps is a national program serving more than 60,000 at-risk young people each year. It seeks to help them improve their vocational skills and education, find sustainable jobs, serve their communities, and avoid lives of crime. Pictured here are teen Job Corps students removing graffiti from the Tatum Waterway near Biscayne Bay, Florida.

RosalreneBetancourt 9/Alamy Stock Photo

activity, improvements in educational attainment, and greater earnings. Program participants had an average arrest rate of 29 percent compared to 33 percent for their control counterparts. An analysis of tax data showed that earnings gains were sustained for the oldest participants eight years after they had left the program.[115] An earlier evaluation of Job Corps found it to be a worthwhile investment of public resources: for each dollar that was spent on the program, $1.45 was saved to government or taxpayers, crime victims, and program participants.[116] A later analysis of the program's costs and benefits also found it to be a worthwhile investment of public resources, saving society at large $2 for each dollar spent on the program.[117]

To read more about **Job Corps**, visit their website: http://www .jobcorps.gov/.

YouthBuild U.S.A.   Another job training program for disadvantaged, unemployed youths is YouthBuild U.S.A. Started in 1978 by a group of young people in New York City, YouthBuild has become a national program with offices in 46 states, Washington, DC, and the Virgin Islands. Since 1994, it has helped more than 140,000 youths between the ages of 16 and 24 years in 260 urban and rural programs across the country.[118] The program's focus is on building or renovating affordable housing—more than 30,000 units have been built since 1994—and through this, young people learn skills in carpentry and construction. YouthBuild also provides educational services, such as help in achieving a high school diploma or preparing for college, and promotes the development of leadership skills. The program's impact on delinquency varies from site to site, with some sites reporting reductions as high as 40 percent among youths enrolled in the program compared to similar youths who did not receive the program.[119] The latest, most rigorous evaluation of YouthBuild so far, which involved an 18-month follow-up after the completion of the program, reports significant reductions in offending and improvements in educational attainment—graduating from high school or obtaining a GED—for those who graduated from the program compared to those who dropped out.[120] A cost-benefit analysis of the program demonstrated substantial monetary benefits for program participants and the public, with a return of $7 to $21 for every dollar spent on the program.[121]

Comprehensive Community-Based Programs

Experimentation with comprehensive community-based delinquency prevention programs began with Shaw and McKay's Chicago Area Project in the 1930s (see Chapter 4). The Mobilization for Youth program of the 1960s is another example of this type of initiative to prevent juvenile delinquency. Neither of these programs was found to be overly successful in reducing delinquency, but few of these types of programs have been evaluated. Typically implemented in neighborhoods with high delinquency and crime rates, they are made up of a range of different types of interventions and usually involve an equally diverse group of community and government agencies that are concerned with the problem of juvenile delinquency, such as the YMCA/YWCA, Boys and Girls Clubs of America, and social and health services. The CASASTART program and the Communities That Care (CTC) program rely on a systematic approach or comprehensive planning model to develop preventive interventions. This includes analyzing the delinquency problem, identifying available resources in the community, prioritizing the most important delinquency problems, and identifying successful programs in other communities and tailoring them to local conditions and needs.[122] Not all comprehensive community-based prevention programs follow this model, but the evidence suggests that this approach will produce the greatest reductions in juvenile delinquency.[123] One of the main drawbacks to this approach is the difficulty in sustaining the level of resources and the cooperation between agencies that are necessary to lower the rates of juvenile delinquency across a large geographical area such as a city.[124]

CASASTART Another example of a comprehensive community-based delinquency prevention program that has been evaluated is the Children At Risk (CAR) program, which is now undergoing further experimentation and is known as CASASTART, or the Center on Addiction and Substance Abuse's Striving Together to Achieve Rewarding Tomorrows.[125] The program was set up to help improve the lives of young people at high risk for delinquency, gang involvement, substance abuse, and other problem behaviors. It was delivered to a large number of young people in poor and high-crime neighborhoods in five cities across the country. It involved a wide range of preventive measures, including case management and family counseling, family skills training, tutoring, mentoring, after-school activities, and community policing. The program was different in each neighborhood. A study of all five cities showed that one year after the program ended the young people who received the program, compared to a control group, were less likely to have committed violent delinquent acts and to have used or sold drugs. Some of the other beneficial results for those in the program included less association with delinquent peers, less peer pressure to engage in delinquency, and more positive peer support.[126]

Future of Delinquency Prevention

The success of delinquency prevention is shown by evaluations of individual programs (as described throughout this chapter) and larger efforts to assess what works, such as the Blueprints for Healthy Youth Development initiative, discussed in the accompanying Evidence-Based Juvenile Justice feature. Despite the success of many different types of delinquency prevention programs—from preschool to mentoring—these programs receive a fraction of what is spent on the juvenile justice system to deal with young people once they have broken the law.[127] This is also true in the adult criminal justice system.[128] To many juvenile justice officials, policy makers, and politicians, prevention is tantamount to being soft on crime, and delinquency prevention programs are often referred to as "pork," otherwise known as pork barrel, or wasteful, spending.[129] Aside from these views, delinquency prevention programs face a number of very real obstacles:

- *Ethical concerns about early intervention.*[130] Is it right to intervene in the lives of children and young people using methods that may or may not be successful?

- *Labeling and stigmatization associated with programs that target high-risk populations.*[131] Children and families receiving support may be called hurtful names and/or looked down upon by fellow community members.

- *Effects of evidence-based delinquency prevention programs can attenuate or diminish when scaled up for wider public use.*[132] Reductions in delinquency and other problem behaviors observed in small-scale studies are difficult to maintain when these programs are disseminated on a much larger scale—across a city, county, state, or even country. Researchers and policy makers need to understand the key programmatic and implementation factors that make these programs successful and take the necessary steps so effects can be maintained.

- *Long delay before early childhood programs can have an impact on delinquency.*[133] While the saying "pay now, save later" is true for early childhood delinquency prevention programs, the length of time for this benefit to be felt can act as a deterrent. In a society and political system that demand immediate results, the building of a juvenile corrections facility is often seen as a more tangible measure than the building of a preschool.

Blueprints for Healthy Youth Development

In 1996, the Center for the Study and Prevention of Violence (CSPV) at the University of Colorado at Boulder launched the Blueprints for Violence Prevention initiative. Now known as Blueprints for Healthy Youth Development, the main goal of the initiative is to "prevent problem behaviors and promote a healthy course of youth development." The Blueprints project identifies effective programs and helps practitioners implement them in their local communities. For programs to be labeled as effective, they must adhere to a set of strict scientific standards. The key standards include:

- Statistical evidence of effectiveness in reducing problem behaviors, including violence and substance abuse

- Evaluations using the most rigorous designs (e.g., randomized experiments)

- Large sample size to allow for any changes to be detected

- Low attrition of subjects

- Use of reliable and accepted instruments to assess impact on problem behaviors

- Sustained reductions in problem behaviors for at least one year after the end of the program

- Replication: implementation of the program in at least two different sites

More than 1,400 programs have been reviewed so far. There are 14 model programs that have proven to be effective in reducing problem behaviors. Another 53 programs have been designated as promising. Not all of the model or promising programs are designed to prevent violence or drug use before it takes place; some are designed for offenders and involve the juvenile justice system. Some of the model programs include:

- Nurse-Family Partnership: Prenatal and infancy home visitation by nurses

- Promotion of alternative thinking strategies

- Life skills training

- Functional Family Therapy: Brings together families and juvenile offenders to address family problems and unlearn aggressive behavior

- Multisystemic Therapy: Multiple component treatment for chronic and violent juvenile offenders, which may involve individual, family, peer, school, and community interventions

- Multidimensional Treatment Foster Care: An alternative to incarceration that matches juvenile offenders with trained foster families

- Project Towards No Drug Abuse

- Brief Alcohol Screening and Intervention for College Students (BASICS)

These model programs are distributed to communities and serve as a prevention menu, allowing communities to select proven programs that are best suited to their needs. Detailed information on the usage of the full range of these programs has not been collected for some time, but it is known that every state in the country has implemented one or more of the model programs and many of these programs are widely used. The CSPV is engaged in a number of projects to test how well some of the programs are being implemented. Without a high level of implementation quality or fidelity to the model, programs stand little chance to make a difference in delinquency rates in communities.

CRITICAL THINKING

1. What is the value of replicating delinquency prevention programs in multiple sites?

2. How is the Blueprints initiative helpful to communities faced with a delinquency problem?

SOURCES: Abigail A. Fagan and Molly Buchanan, "What Works in Crime Prevention? Comparison and Critical Review of Three Crime Prevention Registries," *Criminology and Public Policy* 6:617–649 (2016); Brandon C. Welsh and Peter W. Greenwood, "Making It Happen: State Progress in Implementing Evidence-Based Programs for Delinquent Youth," *Youth Violence and Juvenile Justice* 13:243–257 (2015); Delbert S. Elliott, "Crime Prevention and Intervention over the Life Course," in Chris Gibson and Marvin Krohn, eds., *Handbook of Life Course Criminology* (New York: Springer, 2013); Peter W. Greenwood, "New Standards for Demonstrating Program Effectiveness," *Criminology and Public Policy* 11:251–257 (2012); Sharon F. Mihalic, Abigail A. Fagan, and Susanne Argamaso, "Implementing the LifeSkills Training Drug Prevention Program: Factors Related to Implementation Fidelity," *Implementation Science* 3(5) (2008).

The future of delinquency prevention programs depends on educating the public and key decision makers about the value of preventing delinquency. One example of this is discussing the success of prevention programs in financial terms.[134] For the handful of programs that have measured costs and benefits, some of which are discussed in this chapter, the savings are substantial.[135] The costs of running prevention programs are low relative to the costly nature of delinquency. Notwithstanding these important issues, the future of delinquency prevention is likely to be bright. With many local efforts, state initiatives, and a growing list of national programs showing positive results, the prevention of delinquency is proving its worth.

SUMMARY

1 Explain the difference between delinquency prevention and delinquency control

- Prevention is distinguished from control or repression in that prevention seeks to reduce the risk factors for delinquency before antisocial behavior or delinquency becomes a problem.
- Delinquency control programs, which involve the juvenile justice system, intervene in the lives of juvenile offenders with the aim of preventing the occurrence of future delinquent acts.

2 Evaluate the magnitude of cost to society caused by juvenile crime and violence

- The costs of juvenile delinquency are considerable.
- These costs include the responses of the juvenile justice system, losses to victims of delinquent acts, and the financial impact on offenders and their families.
- One approach to reducing these costs that has garnered a great deal of attention in recent years is prevention.

3 Identify some of the major historical events that gave rise to the present focus on delinquency prevention

- The history of the prevention of juvenile delinquency in the United States is closely tied to the history of the juvenile justice system in this country.
- A number of key events, including the Chicago Area Project, Cambridge-Somerville Youth Study, and federally funded initiatives, helped shape the development of delinquency prevention today.

4 Compare and contrast the different approaches to classifying delinquency prevention programs

- There are a number of different ways to classify or organize delinquency prevention programs, including the public health approach and the developmental perspective.

5 Discuss the key features of the developmental perspective of delinquency prevention

- Key features of the developmental perspective of delinquency prevention include the targeting of risk factors and the promotion of protective factors, the provision of services to children and families, and programs provided over the life course.

6 Discover the many different types of effective delinquency prevention programs for children and teens

- Some of the most effective delinquency prevention programs for children and teens include home visits for new mothers, parent training, enriched preschool programs, and job programs.
- School-based programs that are intensive, cognitive-oriented, and targeted to high-risk kids have also proven effective.

7 Analyze the key factors of effective programs

- Effective delinquency prevention programs are theory-driven, intensive, target multiple risk factors for delinquency, and have a successful implementation.

8 Identify other benefits produced by delinquency prevention programs

- Delinquency prevention programs have also been shown to lead to improvements in other areas of life, such as educational achievement, health, and employment.
- These benefits often translate into substantial cost savings.

9 Discuss pressing issues facing the future of delinquency prevention

- More attention needs to be paid to understanding what works in preventing delinquency and addressing some of the concerns with prevention programs.
- Intervening in the lives of children, young people, and their families to prevent delinquency before it takes place is a key component of an overall strategy to address the problem of juvenile delinquency.

KEY TERMS

delinquency control or delinquency repression, p. 454

delinquency prevention, p. 454

randomized experimental design, p. 456

experimental group, p. 456

control group, p. 456

risk factor, p. 460

protective factor, p. 460

QUESTIONS FOR DISCUSSION

1. Prevention and control are the two broad-based approaches that can be used to reduce delinquency. How do these approaches differ?

2. The costs of juvenile delinquency are wide ranging and substantial. Do you think these costs justify spending money on delinquency prevention programs?

3. What are some of the benefits of implementing prevention programs in childhood compared to adolescence?

4. In addition to reducing delinquency, many prevention programs also have a positive impact on other social problems. Identify four of these problems, and give an example of a program that was successful in reducing each of them.

5. What are comprehensive community-based delinquency prevention programs?

6. Many programs have been successful in preventing delinquency, but many have not been successful. What are some of the reasons why a program may fail to reduce delinquency?

VIEWPOINT

You are the mayor of a medium-sized city. Juvenile delinquency is on the rise, and there have been disturbing reports of increased gang activity. The police chief informs you that some urban gangs, seeking to migrate to your city, have sent members to recruit local youth. Their appeal appears to be working, and several local chapters of the Crips, Bloods, and Latin Kings have now been formed. Street shootings, thefts of cars, and other serious delinquency problems have risen in recent weeks, and all have been linked to this new gang activity. The police, business groups in the downtown core of the city, and the public are all calling for you to take immediate action to deal with these problems.

When you meet with local community leaders, they inform you that the gangs appeal to many local kids who come from troubled homes and have no real hope of success in the conventional world. Some are doing poorly in school and receive little educational support. Others who have left school have trouble finding jobs. The gangs also appeal to kids with emotional and developmental problems.

The police chief says that you cannot coddle these hoodlums. He tells you to put more police on the streets and hire more police officers. He also argues that you should lobby the governor and legislature to pass new laws making it mandatory that kids involved in gang violence are transferred to the adult court for trial.

In contrast, community advocates ask you to spend more money on disadvantaged families so they have access to child care and health care. They suggest you beef up the educational budget to reduce class sizes, reduce dropout rates, and improve attendance rates.

- Would you spend more money on community-based services for young people, or would you order the chief to crack down on the gangs?

- If you choose to spend money on prevention, which programs would you support?

- When should prevention begin? Should kids be given special help even before they get in trouble with the law?

DOING RESEARCH ON THE WEB

To form your prevention plan, get more information at these organizations that have different approaches to preventing juvenile delinquency: The American Youth Policy Forum (http://www.aypf.org/) provides high-quality information on youth issues and a forum for leaders in government, programming, and research, as well as the youths themselves, to share viewpoints and expertise. Fight Crime: Invest in Kids (https://www.strongnation.org/fightcrime/) is a nonprofit anticrime organization of more than 5,000 police chiefs, sheriffs, prosecutors, attorneys general, and other law enforcement leaders and violence survivors that evaluates prevention strategies and recommends those proven effective. The National Crime Prevention Council (http://www.ncpc.org/) produces tools that communities can use to learn crime prevention strategies, engage community members, and coordinate with local agencies. The Child Welfare League of America (http://www.cwla.org/) is a national leader dedicated to ensuring safety, permanence, and well-being for children, youth, and their families.

NOTES

All URLs accessed September 2016.

1. Deanna S. Gomby, Patti L. Culross, and Richard E. Behrman, "Home Visiting: Recent Program Evaluations—Analysis and Recommendations," *The Future of Children* 9:4–26 (1999).

2. Nurse-Family Partnership, *Nurse-Family Partnership Snapshot* (Denver, CO: NFP National Service Office, May 2016).

3. Helen Rumbelow and Alice Miles, "How to Save This Child from a Life of Poverty, Violence and Despair," *The Times*, June 9, 2007; Gomby, Culross, and Behrman, "Home Visiting: Recent Program Evaluations," p. 5.

4. Peter P. Lejins, "The Field of Prevention," in William E. Amos and Charles F. Wellford, eds., *Delinquency Prevention: Theory and Practice* (Englewood Cliffs, NJ: Prentice Hall, 1967), p. 2.

5. Brandon C. Welsh and Rebecca P. Pfeffer, "Reclaiming Crime Prevention in an Age of Punishment: An American History," *Punishment and Society* 15:534–553 (2013).

6. See, for example, John Paul Wright, Pamela M. McMahon, Claire Daly, and J. Phil Haney, "Getting the Law Involved: A Quasi-Experiment in Early Intervention Involving Collaboration Between Schools and the District Attorney's Office," *Criminology and Public Policy* 11:227–249 (2012).

7. Mark A. Cohen and Alex R. Piquero, "New Evidence on the Monetary Value of Saving a High Risk Youth," *Journal of Quantitative Criminology* 25:25–49 (2009).

8. Mark A. Cohen, Roland T. Rust, Sara Steen, and Simon T. Tidd, "Willingness-to-Pay for Crime Control Programs," *Criminology* 42:89–109 (2004), p. 98, Table 2.

9. Cohen and Piquero, "New Evidence on the Monetary Value of Saving a High Risk Youth."

10. Matt DeLisi and Jewel M. Gatling, "Who Pays for a Life of Crime? An Empirical Assessment of the Assorted Victimization Costs Posed by Career Criminals," *Criminal Justice Studies* 16:283–293 (2003).

11. Brandon C. Welsh, Rolf Loeber, Bradley R. Stevens, Magda Stouthamer-Loeber, Mark A. Cohen, and David P. Farrington, "Costs of Juvenile Crime in Urban Areas: A Longitudinal Perspective," *Youth Violence and Juvenile Justice* 6:3–27 (2008).

12. Ted R. Miller, Deborah A. Fisher, and Mark A. Cohen, "Costs of Juvenile Violence: Policy Implications," *Pediatrics* 107:1–7 (2001), http://pediatrics.aappublications.org; see also Joint State Government Commission, General Assembly of the Commonwealth of Pennsylvania, *The Cost of Juvenile Violence in Pennsylvania*, staff report to the Task Force to Study the Issues Surrounding Violence as a Public Health Concern (Harrisburg, PA: Author, January 1995).

13. David A. Anderson, "The Costs of Crime," *Foundations and Trends in Microeconomics* 7:209–265 (2012); see also Patricio Domínguez and Steven Raphael, "The Role of the Cost-of-Crime Literature in Bridging the Gap Between Social Science Research and Policy Making: Potentials and Limitations," *Criminology and Public Policy* 14:589–632 (2015).

14. Centers for Disease Control and Prevention, *Understanding Youth Violence: Fact Sheet* (2012), http://www.cdc.gov/violenceprevention/pdf/yv-factsheet-a.pdf.

15. Barry Krisberg and James Austin, *The Children of Ishmael: Critical Perspectives on Juvenile Justice* (Palo Alto, CA: Mayfield, 1978), pp. 7–45; Joseph G. Weis and J. David Hawkins, *Preventing Delinquency* (Washington, DC: Office of Juvenile Justice and Delinquency Prevention, 1981), pp. 1–6; Richard J. Lundman, *Prevention and Control of Juvenile Delinquency*, 3rd ed. (New York: Oxford University Press, 2001), pp. 23, 25.

16. Clifford R. Shaw and Henry D. McKay, *Juvenile Delinquency and Urban Areas: A Study of Rates of Delinquents in Relation to Differential Characteristics of Local Communities in American Cities* (Chicago: University of Chicago Press, 1942).

17. For an intensive look at the Chicago Area Project, see Steven Schlossman and Michael Sedlak, "The Chicago Area Project Revisited," *Crime and Delinquency* 29:398–462 (1983).

18. Joan McCord and William McCord, "A Follow-Up Report on the Cambridge-Somerville Youth Study," *Annals of the American Academy of Political and Social Science* 322:89–96 (1959).

19. Richard J. Lundman, *Prevention and Control of Juvenile Delinquency*, 3rd ed. (New York: Oxford University Press, 2001), p. 50.

20. Joan McCord, "A Thirty-Year Follow-Up of Treatment Effects," *American Psychologist* 33:284–289 (1978).

21. Thomas J. Dishion, Joan McCord, and François Poulin, "When Interventions Harm: Peer Groups and Problem Behavior," *American Psychologist* 54:755–764 (1999). See also Joan McCord, "Counterproductive Juvenile Justice," *Australian and New Zealand Journal of Criminology* 35:230–237 (2002); Joan McCord, "Cures that Harm: Unanticipated Outcomes of Crime Prevention Programs," *Annals of the American Academy of Political and Social Science* 587:16–30 (2003).

22. See New York City Youth Board, *Reaching the Fighting Gang* (New York: Author, 1960).

23. Walter Miller, "The Impact of a 'Total Community' Delinquency Control Project," *Social Problems* 10:168–191 (1962).

24. See Karol L. Kumpfer and Rose Alvarado, "Family-Strengthening Approaches for the Prevention of Youth Problem Behaviors," *American Psychologist* 58:457–465 (2003).

25. Brandon C. Welsh and David P. Farrington, "Crime Prevention and Public Policy," in Brandon C. Welsh and David P. Farrington, eds., *The Oxford Handbook of Crime Prevention* (New York: Oxford University Press, 2012); Trevor Bennett, "Crime Prevention," in Michael Tonry, ed., *The Handbook of Crime and Punishment* (New York: Oxford University Press, 1998).

26. D. R. Foxcroft, "Can Prevention Classification Be Improved by Considering the Function of Prevention?" *Prevention Science* 15:818–822 (2014).

27. Paul J. Brantingham and Frederick L. Faust, "A Conceptual Model of Crime Prevention," *Crime and Delinquency* 22:284–296 (1976); see also Steven P. Lab, *Crime Prevention: Approaches, Practices, and Evaluations*, 8th ed. (Waltham, MA: Anderson, 2014).

28. See Brandon C. Welsh, Anthony A. Braga, and Christopher J. Sullivan, "Serious Youth Violence and Innovative Prevention: On the Emerging Link Between Public Health and Criminology," *Justice Quarterly* 31:500–523 (2014).

29. David P. Farrington, "Early Developmental Prevention of Juvenile Delinquency," *Criminal Behavior and Mental Health* 4:209–227 (1994).

30. David P. Farrington, "The Development of Offending and Antisocial Behavior from Childhood: Key Findings from the Cambridge Study in Delinquent Development," *Journal of Child Psychology and Psychiatry* 36:929–964 (1995).

31. Richard E. Tremblay and Wendy M. Craig, "Developmental Crime Prevention," in Michael Tonry and David P. Farrington, eds., *Building a Safer Society: Strategic Approaches to Crime Prevention. Crime and Justice: A Review of Research*, vol. 19 (Chicago: University of Chicago Press, 1995), p. 151.

32. David P. Farrington, "Longitudinal and Experimental Research in Criminology," in Michael Tonry, ed., *Crime and Justice 1975–2025* (Chicago: University of Chicago Press, 2013).

33. See Christopher J. Sullivan, "Enhancing Translational Knowledge on Developmental Crime Prevention: The Utility of Understanding Expert Decision Making," *Criminology and Public Policy* 12:343–351 (2013); Brandon C. Welsh and David P. Farrington, eds., *The Oxford Handbook of Crime Prevention*; Tremblay and Craig, "Developmental Crime Prevention"; Gail A. Wasserman and Laurie S. Miller, "The Prevention of Serious and Violent Juvenile Offending," in Rolf Loeber and David P. Farrington, eds., *Serious and Violent Juvenile Offenders: Risk Factors and Successful Interventions* (Thousand Oaks, CA: Sage Publications, 1998); Joan McCord, Cathy Spatz Widom, and Nancy A. Crowell, eds., *Juvenile Crime, Juvenile Justice*, panel on Juvenile Crime: Prevention, Treatment, and Control (Washington, DC: National Academy Press, 2001); Patrick Tolan, "Crime Prevention: Focus on Youth," in James Q. Wilson and Joan Petersilia, eds., *Crime: Public Policies for Crime Control* (Oakland, CA: Institute for Contemporary Studies, 2002).

34. Gomby, Culross, and Behrman, "Home Visiting."

35. David L. Olds, Charles R. Henderson, Robert Chamberlin, and Robert Tatelbaum, "Preventing Child Abuse and Neglect: A Randomized Trial of Nurse Home Visitation," *Pediatrics* 78:65–78 (1986).

36. David L. Olds, Charles R. Henderson, Charles Phelps, Harriet Kitzman, and Carole Hanks, "Effects of Prenatal and Infancy Nurse Home Visitation on Government Spending," *Medical Care* 31:155–174 (1993).

37. David L. Olds et al., "Long-Term Effects of Nurse Home Visitation on Children's Criminal and Antisocial Behavior: 15-Year Follow-Up of a Randomized Controlled Trial," *Journal of the American Medical Association* 280:1238–1244 (1998).

38. David L. Olds et al., "Long-Term Effects of Home Visitation on Maternal Life Course and Child Abuse and Neglect: Fifteen-Year Follow-Up of a Randomized Trial," *Journal of the American Medical Association* 278:637–643 (1997).

39. Peter W. Greenwood, Lynn A. Karoly, Susan S. Everingham, Jill Houbé, M. Rebecca Kilburn, C. Peter Rydell, Matthew Sanders, and James Chiesa, "Estimating the Costs and Benefits of Early Childhood Interventions: Nurse Home Visits and the Perry Preschool," in Brandon C. Welsh, David P. Farrington, and Lawrence W. Sherman, eds., *Costs and Benefits of Preventing Crime* (Boulder, CO: Westview Press, 2001), p. 133.

40. Ted Miller, *Nurse-Family Partnership Home Visitation: Costs, Outcomes, and Return on Investment* (Beltsville, MD: H.B.S.A., Inc., 2013).

41. John Eckenrode, Mary Campa, Dennis W. Luckey, Charles R. Henderson, Robert Cole, Harriet Kitzman, Elizabeth Anson, Kimberly Sidora-Arcoleo, Jane Powers, and David L. Olds, "Long-Term Effects of Prenatal and Infancy Nurse Home Visitation on the Life Course of Youths: 19-Year Follow-Up of a Randomized Trial," *Archives of Pediatrics and Adolescent Medicine* 164:9–15 (2010).

42. David L. Olds, J. R. Holmberg, N. Donelan-McCall, Dennis W. Luckey, M. D. Knudtson, and J. Robinson, "Effects of Home Visits by Paraprofessionals and by Nurses on Children: Follow-Up of a Randomized Trial at Ages 6 and 9 Years," *JAMA Pediatrics* 168:114–121 (2014); Harriet Kitzman, David L. Olds, Robert E. Cole, C. A. Hanks, Elizabeth A. Anson, Kimberly Sidora-Arcoleo, and J. R. Holmberg, "Enduring Effects of Prenatal and Infancy Home Visiting by Nurses on Children: Follow-Up of a Randomized Trial Among Children at Age 12 Years," *Archives of Pediatrics and Adolescent Medicine* 164:412–418 (2010).

43. Nurse-Family Partnership, *Nurse-Family Partnership Snapshot* (Denver, CO: Nurse-Family Partnership, May 2016).

44. Ned Calonge, "Community Interventions to Prevent Violence: Translation into Public Health Practice," *American Journal of Preventive Medicine* 28:4–5 (2005).

45. Rumbelow and Miles, "How to Save This Child from a Life of Poverty, Violence and Despair."

46. Anne K. Duggan et al., "Evaluation of Hawaii's Healthy Start Program," *The Future of Children* 9:66–90 (1999); Anne K. Duggan, Amy Windham, Elizabeth McFarlane, Loretta Fuddy, Charles Rohde, Sharon Buchbinder, and Calvin Sia, "Hawaii's Healthy Start Program of Home Visiting for At-Risk Families: Evaluation of Family Identification, Family Engagement, and Service Delivery," *Pediatrics* 105:250–259 (2000).

47. Matthew Manning, Ross Homel, and Christine Smith, "A Meta-Analysis of the Effects of Early Developmental Prevention Programs in At-Risk Populations on Non-Health Outcomes in Adolescence," *Children and Youth Services Review* 32:506–519 (2010).

48. Conduct Problems Prevention Research Group, "Fast Track Intervention Effects on Youth Arrests and Delinquency," *Journal of Experimental Criminology* 6:131–157 (2010); see also Richard E. Tremblay and Wendy M. Craig, "Developmental Crime Prevention," in Tonry and Farrington, eds., *Building a Safer Society: Strategic Approaches to Crime Prevention*.

49. Alex R. Piquero, Wesley G. Jennings, Brie Diamon, David P. Farrington, Richard E. Tremblay, Brandon C. Welsh, and Jennifer M. Reingle Gonzalez,, "A Meta-Analysis Update of the Effects of Early/Family Parent Training Programs on Antisocial Behavior and Delinquency," *Journal of Experimental Criminology* 12:229–248 (2016).

50. See Gerald R. Patterson, "Performance Models for Antisocial Boys," *American Psychologist* 41:432–444 (1986); Gerald R. Patterson, *Coercive Family Process* (Eugene, OR: Castalia, 1982).

51. Gerald R. Patterson, Patricia Chamberlain, and John B. Reid, "A Comparative Evaluation of a Parent-Training Program," *Behavior Therapy* 13:638–650 (1982); Gerald R. Patterson, John B. Reid, and Thomas J. Dishion, *Antisocial Boys* (Eugene, OR: Castalia, 1992).

52. Matthew R. Sanders, Carol Markie-Dadds, Lucy A. Tully, and William Bor, "The Triple P-Positive Parenting Program: A Comparison of Enhanced, Standard, and Self-Directed Behavioral Family Intervention for Parents of Children with Early Onset Conduct Problems," *Journal of Consulting and Clinical Psychology* 68:624–640 (2000).

53. Rae Thomas and Melanie J. Zimmer-Gembeck, "Behavioral Outcomes of Parent-Child Interaction Therapy and Triple P-Positive Parenting Program: A Review and Meta-Analysis," *Journal of Abnormal Child Psychology* 35:475–495 (2007).

54. Peter W. Greenwood, Karyn E. Model, C. Peter Rydell, and James Chiesa, *Diverting Children from a Life of Crime: Measuring Costs and Benefits* (Santa Monica, CA: RAND Corporation, 1998).

55. Sonya Michel, *Children's Interests/Mother's Rights: The Shaping of America's Child Care Policy* (New Haven, CT: Yale University Press, 1999).

56. J. Ronald Lally, Peter L. Mangione, and Alice S. Honig, "The Syracuse University Family Development Research Program: Long-Range Impact of an Early Intervention with Low-Income Children and their Families," in D. R. Powell, ed., *Parent Education as Early Childhood Intervention: Emerging Directions in Theory, Research and Practice* (Norwood, NJ: Ablex, 1988).

57. Dale L. Johnson and Todd Walker, "Primary Prevention of Behavior Problems in Mexican-American Children," *American Journal of Community Psychology* 15:375–385 (1987).

58. Tremblay and Craig, "Developmental Crime Prevention."

59. Farrington, "Early Developmental Prevention of Juvenile Delinquency," pp. 216–217.

60. Schindler and Yoshikawa, "Preventing Crime Through Intervention in the Preschool Years"; Greg J. Duncan and Katherine Magnuson, "Individual and Parent-Based Intervention Strategies for Promoting Human Capital and Positive Behavior," in P. Lindsay Chase-Lansdale, Kathleen Kiernan, and Ruth J. Friedman, eds., *Human Development Across Lives and Generations: The Potential for Change* (New York: Cambridge University Press, 2004).

61. Lawrence J. Schweinhart, Helen V. Barnes, and David P. Weikart, *Significant Benefits: The High/Scope Perry Preschool Study Through Age 27* (Ypsilanti, MI: High/Scope Press, 1993), p. 3.

62. Lawrence J. Schweinhart and David P. Weikart, *Young Children Grow Up: The Effects of the Perry Preschool Program Through Age 15* (Ypsilanti, MI: High/Scope Press, 1980).

63. Schweinhart, Barnes, and Weikart, *Significant Benefits: The High/Scope Perry Preschool Study Through Age 27*, p. xv.

64. W. Steven Barnett, *Lives in the Balance: Age 27 Benefit-Cost Analysis of the High/Scope Perry Preschool Program* (Ypsilanti, MI: High/Scope Press, 1996); W. Steven Barnett, "Cost-Benefit Analysis," in Schweinhart, Barnes, and Weikart, eds., *Significant Benefits: The High/Scope Perry Preschool Study Through Age 27*.

65. Greenwood et al., "Estimating the Costs and Benefits of Early Childhood Interventions: Nurse Home Visits and the Perry Preschool."

66. Lawrence J. Schweinhart, "Long-Term Follow-Up of a Preschool Experiment," *Journal of Experimental Criminology* 9:389–409 (2013); Lawrence J. Schweinhart, Jeanne Montie, Xiang Zongping, W. Steven Barnett, Clive R. Belfield, and Milagros Nores, *Lifetime Effects: The High/Scope Perry Preschool Study Through Age 40* (Ypsilanti, MI: High/Scope Press, 2005).

67. Clive R. Belfield, Milagros Nores, W. Steven Barnett, and Lawrence J. Schweinhart, "The High/Scope Perry Preschool Program: Cost-Benefit Analysis Using Data from the Age-40 Follow-Up," *Journal of Human Resources* 41:162–190 (2006).

68. James J. Heckman, Seong Hyeok Moon, Rodrigo Pinto, Peter Savelyev, and Adam Yavitz, "Analyzing Social Experiments as Implemented: A Reexamination of the Evidence from the HighScope Perry Preschool Program," *Quantitative Economics* 1:1–46 (2010); James J. Heckman, Seong Hyeok Moon, Rodrigo Pinto, Peter Savelyev, and Adam Yavitz, "The Rate of Return to the HighScope Perry Preschool Program," *Journal of Public Economics* 94:114–128 (2010).

69. Arthur J. Reynolds, Judy A. Temple, Dylan L. Robertson, and Emily A. Mann, "Long-Term Effects of an Early Childhood Intervention on Educational Achievement and Juvenile Arrest: A 15-Year Follow-Up of Low-Income Children in Public Schools," *Journal of the American Medical Association* 285:2339–2346 (2001).

70. Arthur J. Reynolds, Judy A. Temple, Suh-Ruu Ou, Dylan L. Robertson, Joshua P. Mersky, James W. Topitzes, et al., "Effects of a School-Based, Early Childhood Intervention on Adult Health and Well-Being," *Archives of Pediatrics and Adolescent Medicine* 161:730–739 (2007).

71. Arthur J. Reynolds, Judy A. Temple, Suh-Ruu Ou, Irma A. Arteaga, and Barry White, "School-Based Early Childhood Education and Age-28 Well-Being: Effects by Timing Dosage and Subgroups," *Science* 333:360–364 (2011).

72. Arthur J. Reynolds, Judy A. Temple, and Suh-Ruu Ou, "School-Based Early Intervention and Child Well-Being in the Chicago Longitudinal Study," *Child Welfare* 82:633–656 (2003).

73. Carolyn Webster-Stratton, "Preventing Conduct Problems in Head Start Children: Strengthening Parenting Competencies," *Journal of Consulting and Clinical Psychology* 66:715–730 (1998).

74. Jens Ludwig and Deborah A. Phillips, "Long-Term Effects of Head Start on Low-Income Children," *Annals of the New York Academy of Sciences* 1136:257–268 (2008).

75. Schindler and Yoshikawa, "Preventing Crime Through Intervention in the Preschool Years"; Edward Zigler and Sally J. Styfco, "Extended Childhood Intervention Prepares Children for School and Beyond," *Journal of the American Medical Association* 285:2378–2380 (2001).

76. See Paul Tough, *How Children Succeed: Grit, Curiosity, and the Hidden Power of Character* (Boston: Houghton Mifflin Harcourt, 2012).

77. Delbert S. Elliott, Beatrix Hamburg, and Kirk R. Williams, "Violence in American Schools: An Overview," in Delbert S. Elliott, Beatrix Hamburg, and Kirk R. Williams, eds., *Violence in American Schools: A New Perspective* (New York: Cambridge University Press, 1998), p. 16.

78. Denise C. Gottfredson, Philip J. Cook, and Chongmin Na, "Schools and Prevention," in Welsh and Farrington, eds., *The Oxford Handbook of Crime Prevention*.

79. J. David Hawkins, Brian H. Smith, Karl G. Smith, Rick Kosterman, and Richard F. Catalano, "Promoting Social Development and Preventing Health and Behavior Problems During the Elementary Grades: Results from the Seattle Social Development Project," *Victims and Offenders* 2:161–181 (2007).

80. J. David Hawkins, Rick Kosterman, Richard F. Catalano, Karl G. Hill, and Robert D. Abbott, "Effects of Social Development Intervention in Childhood 15 Years Later," *Archives of Pediatrics and Adolescent Medicine* 162:1133–1141 (2008).

81. Richard E. Tremblay et al., "Parent and Child Training to Prevent Early Onset of Delinquency: The Montréal Longitudinal-Experimental Study," in Joan McCord and Richard E. Tremblay, eds., *Preventing Antisocial Behavior: Interventions from Birth Through Adolescence* (New York: Guilford, 1992); Richard E. Tremblay, Linda Pagani-Kurtz, Louise C. Mâsse, Frank Vitaro, and Robert O. Pihl, "A Bimodal Preventive Intervention for Disruptive Kindergarten Boys: Its Impact Through Mid-Adolescence," *Journal of Consulting and Clinical Psychology* 63:560–568 (1995); Richard E. Tremblay, Louise C. Mâsse, Linda Pagani-Kurtz, and Frank Vitaro, "From Childhood Physical Aggression to Adolescent Maladjustment: The Montreal Prevention Experiment," in R. DeV. Peters and R. J. McMahon, eds., *Preventing Childhood Disorders, Substance Abuse, and Delinquency* (Thousand Oaks, CA: Sage Publications, 1996).

82. Frank Vitaro, Mara Brendgen, Charles-Édouard Giguère, and Richard E. Tremblay, "Early Prevention of Life-Course Personal and Property Violence: A 19-Year Follow-Up of the Montreal Longitudinal-Experimental Study (MLES)," *Journal of Experimental Criminology* 9:411–427 (2013); Rachel Boisjoli, Frank Vitaro, Eric Lacourse, Edward D. Barker, and Richard E. Tremblay, "Impact and Clinical Significance of a Preventive Intervention for Disruptive Boys: 15-Year Follow-Up," *British Journal of Psychiatry* 191:415–419 (2007).

83. Sheppard G. Kellam, George W. Rebok, Nicholas Ialongo, and Lawrence S. Mayer, "The Course and Malleability of Aggressive Behavior from Early First Grade into Middle School: Results of a Developmental Epidemiologically Based Preventive Trial," *Journal of Child Psychology and Psychiatry* 35:259–282 (1994).

84. Sheppard G. Kellam, C. Hendricks Brown, Jeanne M. Poduska, Nicholas S. Ialongo, Wei Wang, Peter Toyinbo, Hanno Petras, Carla Ford, Amy Windham, and Holly C. Wilcox, "Effects of a Universal Classroom Behavior Management Program in First and Second Grades on Young Adult Behavioral, Psychiatric, and Social Outcomes," *Drug and Alcohol Dependence* 95S:5–28 (2008); Hanno Petras, Sheppard G. Kellam, C. Hendricks Brown, Bengt Muthén, Nicholas S. Ialongo, and Jeanne M. Poduska, "Developmental Epidemiological Courses Leading to Antisocial Personality Disorder and Violent and Criminal Behavior: Effects by Young Adulthood of a Universal Preventive Intervention in First- and Second-Grade Classrooms," *Drug and Alcohol Dependence* 95S:45–59 (2008).

85. Alexander T. Vazsonyi, Lara B. Belliston, and Daniel J. Flannery, "Evaluation of a School-Based, Universal Violence Prevention Program: Low-, Medium-, and High-Risk Children," *Youth Violence and Juvenile Justice* 2:185–206 (2004).

86. James C. Howell, ed., *Guide for Implementing the Comprehensive Strategy for Serious, Violent, and Chronic Juvenile Offenders* (Washington, DC: Office of Juvenile Justice and Delinquency Prevention, US Department of Justice, 1995), p. 90.

87. Office of Justice Programs, "Mentoring," *OJP Fact Sheet* (Washington, DC: Office of Justice Programs, US Department of Justice, November 2011).

88. Wes Moore, *The Other Wes Moore: One Name, Two Fates* (New York: Spiegal and Grau, 2010).

89. Office of Justice Programs, "Mentoring."

90. Thomas J. Dishion, Joan McCord, and François Poulin, "When Interventions Harm: Peer Groups and Problem Behavior," *American Psychologist* 54:755–764 (1999).

91. Darrick Jolliffe and David P. Farrington, *The Influence of Mentoring on Reoffending* (Stockholm: National Council for Crime Prevention, 2008).

92. Patrick H. Tolan, David B. Henry, Michael S. Schoeny, Peter Lovegrove, and Emily Nichols, "Mentoring Programs to Affect Delinquency and Associated Outcomes of Youth at Risk: A Comprehensive Meta-Analytic Review," *Journal of Experimental Criminology* 10:179–206 (2014).

93. Renée Spencer, "Understanding the Mentoring Process Between Adolescents and Adults," *Youth and Society* 37:287–315 (2006), at 309–311.

94. Denise C. Gottfredson, "An Empirical Test of School-Based Environmental and Individual Interventions to Reduce the Risk of Delinquent Behavior," *Criminology* 24:705–731 (1986); Denise C. Gottfredson, "Changing School Structures to Benefit High-Risk Youth," in Peter Leone, ed., *Understanding Troubled and Troubling Youth* (Newbury Park, CA: Sage Publications, 1990); Denise C. Gottfredson, *Schools and Delinquency* (New York: Cambridge University Press, 2001).

95. Debra Galant, "Violence Offers Its Own Lessons," *New York Times*, June 15, 2003.

96. Gottfredson et al., "School-Based Crime Prevention."

97. James Larson, "Violence Prevention in the Schools: A Review of Selected Programs and Procedures," *School Psychology Review* 23:151–164 (1994).

98. Ibid., p. 153.

99. Denise C. Gottfredson, Gary D. Gottfredson, and Stephanie A. Weisman, "The Timing of Delinquent Behavior and Its Implications for After-School Programs," *Criminology and Public Policy* 1:61–86 (2001), at 61.

100. Ibid., p. 63.

101. Denise C. Gottfredson, Stephanie A. Gerstenblith, David A. Soulé, Shannon C. Womer, and Shaoli Lu, "Do After School Programs Reduce Delinquency?" *Prevention Science* 5:253–266 (2004), at 263–264.

102. Denise C. Gottfredson, Amanda Cross, Denise Wilson, Melissa Rorie, and Nadine Connell, "An Experimental Evaluation of the All Stars Prevention Curriculum in a Community After School Setting," *Prevention Science* 11:142–154 (2010).

103. Sema A. Taheri and Brandon C. Welsh, "After-School Programs for Delinquency Prevention: A Systematic Review and Meta-Analysis," *Youth Violence and Juvenile Justice* 14:272–290 (2016).

104. Steven P. Schinke, Mario A. Orlandi, and Kristin C. Cole, "Boys and Girls Clubs in Public Housing Developments: Prevention Services for Youth at Risk," *Journal of Community Psychology, Office of Substance Abuse Prevention* Special Issue:118–128 (1992).

105. Ibid., p. 120.

106. Ibid., pp. 125–127.

107. Marshall B. Jones and David R. Offord, "Reduction of Anti-Social Behavior in Poor Children by Nonschool Skill Development," *Journal of Child Psychology and Psychiatry* 30:737–750 (1989).

108. Taheri and Welsh, "After-School Programs for Delinquency Prevention: A Systematic Review and Meta-Analysis."

109. Amanda Brown Cross, Denise C. Gottfredson, Denise M. Wilson, Melissa Rorie, and Nadine Connell, "The Impact of After-School Programs on the Routine Activities of Middle-School Students: Results from a Randomized, Controlled Trial," *Criminology and Public Policy* 8:391–412 (2009).

110. Ibid.; Gottfredson, Gerstenblith, Soulé, Womer, and Lu, "Do After School Programs Reduce Delinquency?"

111. Denise C. Gottfredson and David A. Soulé, "The Timing of Property Crime, Violent Crime, and Substance Abuse Among Juveniles," *Journal of Research in Crime and Delinquency* 42:110–120 (2005).

112. McCord, Widom, and Crowell, eds., *Juvenile Crime, Juvenile Justice*, pp. 150–151.

113. Rolf Loeber and David P. Farrington, eds., *From Juvenile Delinquency to Adult Crime: Criminal Careers, Justice Policy, and Prevention* (New York: Oxford University Press, 2012).

114. Job Corps, US Department of Labor, http://www.jobcorps.gov/centers.aspx.

115. Peter Z. Schochet, John Burghardt, and Sheena McConnell, "Does Job Corps Work? Impact Findings from the National Job Corps Study," *American Economic Review* 98:1864–1886 (2008).

116. David A. Long, Charles D. Mallar, and Craig V. D. Thornton, "Evaluating the Benefits and Costs of the Job Corps," *Journal of Policy Analysis and Management* 1:55–76 (1981).

117. Sheena McConnell and Steven Glazerman, *National Job Corps Study: The Benefits and Costs of Job Corps* (Washington, DC: Employment and Training Administration, US Department of Labor, 2001).

118. YouthBuild U.S.A., "About YouthBuild," http://www.youthbuild .org/about-youthbuild; Tim Cross and Daryl Wright, "What Works with At-Risk Youths," *Corrections Today* 66:64–68 (2004), at 64.

119. Cross and Wright, "What Works with At-Risk Youths," p. 65; see also Wally Abrazaldo, Jo-Ann Adefuin, Jennifer Henderson-Frakes, Charles Lea, Jill Leufgen, Heather Lewis-Charp, Sukey Soukam-neuth, and Andrew Wiegand, *Evaluation of the YouthBuild Youth Offender Grants, Final Report* (Oakland, CA: Social Policy Research Associates, 2009).

120. Mark A. Cohen and Alex R. Piquero, "An Outcome Evaluation of the YouthBuild USA Offender Project," *Youth Violence and Juvenile Justice* 8:373–385 (2009).

121. Mark A. Cohen and Alex R. Piquero, "Benefits and Costs of a Tar-geted Intervention Program for Youthful Offenders: The YouthBuild USA Offender Project," *Journal of Benefit-Cost Analysis* 6:603–627 (2015).

122. Margaret R. Kuklinski, John S. Briney, J. David Hawkins, and Richard F. Catalano, "Cost-Benefit Analysis of Communities That Care Out-comes at Eighth Grade," *Prevention Science* 13:150–161 (2012); see also J. David Hawkins, Richard F. Catalano, and Associates, *Communities That Care: Action for Drug Abuse* (San Francisco: Jossey-Bass, 1992).

123. Dennis P. Rosenbaum and Amie M. Schuck, "Comprehensive Com-munity Partnerships for Preventing Crime," in Welsh and Farrington, eds., *The Oxford Handbook of Crime Prevention*.

124. Abraham Wandersman and Paul Florin, "Community Interventions and Effective Prevention," *American Psychologist* 58:441–448 (2003).

125. Lawrence F. Murray and Steven Belenko, "CASASTART: A Com-munity-Based, School-Centered Intervention for High-Risk Youth," *Substance Use and Misuse* 40:913–933 (2005); National Center on Ad-diction and Substance Abuse, *CASASTART* (New York: Columbia University, 2007).

126. Adele V. Harrell, Shannon E. Cavanagh, and Sanjeev Sridharan, *Eval-uation of the Children At Risk Program: Results 1 Year After the End of the Program* (Washington, DC: NIJ Research in Brief, 1999).

127. Brandon C. Welsh and David P. Farrington, "Science, Politics, and Crime Prevention: Toward a New Crime Policy," *Journal of Criminal Justice* 40:128–133 (2012); see also Bryan J. Vila, "Human Nature and Crime Control: Improving the Feasibility of Nurturant Strategies," *Politics and the Life Sciences* 16:3–21 (1997).

128. Francis T. Cullen and Paula Smith, "Treatment and Rehabilitation," in Michael Tonry, ed., *The Oxford Handbook of Crime and Criminal Justice* (New York: Oxford University Press, 2011).

129. Richard A. Mendel, *Prevention or Pork? A Hard-Headed Look at Youth-Oriented Anti-Crime Programs* (Washington, DC: American Youth Policy Forum, 1995), p. 1.

130. McCord, "Cures that Harm: Unanticipated Outcomes of Crime Prevention Programs." See also Thomas Gabor, "Prevention into the Twenty-First Century: Some Final Remarks," *Canadian Journal of Criminology* 32:197–212 (1990).

131. David R. Offord, Helena Chmura Kraemer, Alan E. Kazdin, Peter S. Jensen, and Richard Harrington, "Lowering the Burden of Suffering from Child Psychiatric Disorder: Trade-Offs Among Clinical, Tar-geted, and Universal Interventions," *Journal of the American Academy of Child and Adolescent Psychiatry* 37:686–694 (1998).

132. David L. Olds, "Improving Standards for Evidence-Based Policy," *Criminology and Public Policy* 15:669–676 (2016); Brandon C. Welsh, Christopher J. Sullivan, and David L. Olds, "When Early Crime Prevention Goes to Scale: A New Look at the Evidence," *Prevention Science* 11:115–125 (2010); Kenneth A. Dodge, "The Science of Youth Violence Prevention: Progressing from Developmental Epidemiology to Efficacy to Effectiveness to Public Policy," *American Journal of Preventive Medicine* 20:63–70 (2001).

133. David P. Farrington and Brandon C. Welsh, *Saving Children from a Life of Crime: Early Risk Factors and Effective Interventions* (New York: Oxford University Press, 2007).

134. Patricio Domínguez and Steven Raphael, "The Role of the Cost-of-Crime Literature in Bridging the Gap Between Social Science Re-search and Policy Making: Potentials and Limitations," *Criminology and Public Policy* 14:589–632 (2015); National Crime Prevention Coun-cil, "Saving Money While Stopping Crime," *Topics in Crime Prevention* (Washington, DC: NCPC, Fall 1999).

135. Brandon C. Welsh, David P. Farrington, and B. Raffan Gowar, "Ben-efit-Cost Analysis of Crime Prevention Programs," *Crime and Justice* 44:447–516 (2015); Stephanie Lee, Steve Aos, Elizabeth K. Drake, Anne Pennucci, Marna G. Miller, and Laurie Anderson, *Return on Investment: Evidence-Based Options to Improve Statewide Outcomes* (Olympia: Washington State Institute for Public Policy, 2012).

part four

The Juvenile Justice System

Since 1900, a separate juvenile justice system has been developed that features its own rules, institutions, laws, and processes. The separation of juvenile and adult offenders reflects society's concern for the plight of children. Ideally, care, protection, and treatment are the bywords of the juvenile justice system. However, because of public fear of violent youth, there have been efforts to "toughen up" the juvenile justice system and treat some delinquents much more like adult offenders. Because of these concerns, the treatment of delinquents has become an American dilemma. Severe punishment seems to have little deterrent effect on teenagers—if anything, it may prepare them for a life of adult criminality. Many incarcerated adult felons report that they were institutionalized as youths. The juvenile justice system is caught between the futility of punishing juveniles and the public's demand that something be done about serious juvenile crime. Yet, the rehabilitative ideal of the juvenile justice system has not been totally lost. Even though the nation seems to be in a punishment cycle, juvenile justice experts continue to press for judicial fairness, rehabilitation, and innovative programs for juvenile offenders.

Part Four provides a general overview of the juvenile justice system, including its process, history, and legal rules. Chapter 13 reviews the history and development of juvenile justice and provides an overview of its major components, processes, goals, and institutions. Chapter 14 deals with police handling of delinquent and status offenders. It contains information on the police role, the organization of police services, legal rights of minors in police custody, and prevention efforts. Chapter 15 is concerned with the juvenile court process. It describes such issues and programs as diversion; the transfer of youths to adult courts; legal rights during trial; the roles of the prosecutor, the juvenile court judge, and the defense attorney; and the sentencing of juvenile offenders. Chapter 16 discusses efforts to treat juveniles who have been found to be delinquent. It reviews the history and practices of probation, community corrections, and juvenile institutions. Finally, Chapter 17 reviews international efforts to treat delinquent offenders. It compares how other nations organize their juvenile justice systems and treat juvenile offenders with methods used in the United States.

CHAPTER 13

Juvenile Justice:
Then and Now

Learning Objectives

1 Illustrate the major social changes leading to the creation of the first modern juvenile court in Chicago in 1899

2 Discuss some of the landmark Supreme Court decisions that have influenced present-day juvenile justice procedures

3 Identify how children are processed by the juvenile justice system, beginning with arrest and concluding with reentry into society

4 Explain the conflicting values in contemporary juvenile justice

5 Compare key similarities and differences between the adult and juvenile justice systems

6 Argue the pros and cons of the juvenile justice system's goal to treat rather than punish and assess if this goal is being met today

7 Evaluate the key elements of a comprehensive juvenile justice strategy to deal with juvenile delinquency

8 Discuss the differences between prevention and intervention efforts to reduce juvenile delinquency

9 Identify and comment on pressing issues in the future of juvenile justice

Chapter Outline

Juvenile Justice in the Nineteenth Century
Urbanization
The Child Saving Movement
House of Refuge
Were They Really Child Savers?
Development of Juvenile Institutions
Children's Aid Society
Society for the Prevention of Cruelty to Children

A Century of Juvenile Justice
The Illinois Juvenile Court Act and Its Legacy
Reforming the System

Juvenile Justice Today
The Juvenile Justice Process
Conflicting Values in Juvenile Justice
Criminal Justice vs. Juvenile Justice

A Comprehensive Juvenile Justice Strategy
Prevention
Intervention
Graduated Sanctions
Institutional Programs
Alternative Courts

Future of Juvenile Justice

Chapter Features

Professional Spotlight: Carla Stalnaker

Focus on Delinquency: Similarities and Differences Between Juvenile and Adult Justice Systems

Evidence-Based Juvenile Justice—Intervention: Teen Courts

Case Profile: Jennifer's Story

Youth Stories: Chrystal Carreras

ACCORDING TO THE MIAMI, FLORIDA, state attorney's office, Michael Hernandez, age 14, acted alone and with premeditation in slashing the throat of his friend and classmate, Jaime Gough, also 14, in a bathroom at the Southwood Middle School. Hernandez then returned to class in his blood-soaked clothes. The knife used in the killing, along with a bloody latex glove, was later found in the accused's book bag.

Hernandez has never disputed these events or his role in the killing, although the motive remains a mystery. Hernandez's taped confession to Miami-Dade police detective Salvatore Garolfalo, taken just hours after the killing, is revealing of his intentions on that day:

> Garolfalo: "Why did you suggest to Jaime to go inside the
>   school today?"
> Hernandez: "I planned to murder him."
> Garolfalo: "Do you know why you were going to do this?"
> Hernandez: "No, I don't."

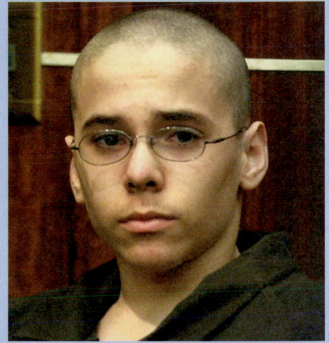

AP Images/Alan Diaz

Michael Hernandez's waiver to adult court was never in question. Nor was his sentence when he was convicted of first-degree murder: life without parole. Until recently, in Florida and in many other states across the country this was a mandatory sentence that the judge had to impose. In 2010, the US Supreme Court, in *Graham v. Florida*, upheld that juveniles who commit crimes in which someone is killed may be sentenced to life in prison without the possibility of parole. The court struck down the practice of sentencing juveniles to life without parole for nonhomicide crimes.[1] In 2012, the Supreme Court revisited this issue in *Miller v. Alabama* and *Jackson v. Hobbs* and ruled that the sentence of life without the possibility of parole for all juvenile offenders, including those convicted of homicide, could not be imposed automatically.[2] (See Chapter 15 for more details on these rulings.) In 2013, on the basis of the Supreme Court ruling and because Hernandez's sentence was under appeal at the time, the third District Court of Appeal ruled that a new sentencing hearing must take place. As a result of these rulings and a new Florida law, the latest sentencing hearing, carried out in 2016, established that the defendant will get a "judicial review" on parole eligibility after serving 25 years of his sentence.

Society has struggled with cases like that of Michael Hernandez ever since the creation of the first modern juvenile court in Chicago in 1899. This chapter begins with a discussion of the major social changes leading up to this milestone event. We then cover the reform efforts of the twentieth century, including the movement to grant children the procedural rights typically given to adult offenders. This discussion includes descriptions of some landmark Supreme Court decisions that have influenced present-day juvenile justice procedures.

The second part of this chapter presents an overview of the contemporary juvenile justice system and the various philosophies, processes, organizations, and legal constraints that dominate its operations. The chapter describes the process that takes a youthful offender through a series of steps, beginning with arrest and concluding with reentry into society. What happens to young people who violate the law? Do they have legal rights? How are they helped? How are they punished? Should juvenile killers be released from custody before their 18th birthday? Should the goal of the system be rehabilitation or punishment?

To help address such questions, we have included a discussion of the similarities and differences between the adult and juvenile justice systems. This discussion draws attention to the principle that children are treated separately. By segregating delinquent children from adult offenders, society has placed greater importance on the delinquent being a child rather than being a criminal. Consequently, rehabilitation rather than punishment has traditionally been the goal. Today, with children committing more serious crimes, the juvenile justice system is having great difficulty handling these offenders.

In the final section, we discuss the need for a comprehensive juvenile justice strategy and the role of the federal government in juvenile justice reform—the key element in funding state juvenile justice and delinquency prevention efforts.

Juvenile Justice in the Nineteenth Century

At the beginning of the nineteenth century, delinquent, neglected, and runaway children in the United States were treated the same as adult criminal offenders.[3] Like children in England, when convicted of crimes they received harsh sentences similar to those imposed on adults. The adult criminal code applied to children, and no juvenile court existed.

During the early nineteenth century, various pieces of legislation were introduced to humanize criminal procedures for children. The concept of probation, introduced in Massachusetts in 1841, was geared toward helping young people avoid imprisonment. Many books and reports written during this time heightened public interest in juvenile care.

Despite this interest, no special facilities existed for the care of youths in trouble with the law, nor were there separate laws or courts to control their behavior. Youths who committed petty crimes, such as stealing or vandalism, were viewed as wayward children or victims of neglect and were placed in community asylums or homes. Youths who were involved in more serious crimes were subject to the same punishments as adults—imprisonment, whipping, or death.

Several events led to reforms and nourished the eventual development of the juvenile justice system: (a) urbanization, (b) the child saving movement and growing interest in the concept of *parens patriae*, and (c) development of institutions for the care of delinquent and neglected children.

Urbanization

Especially during the first half of the nineteenth century, the United States experienced rapid population growth, primarily due to an increased birthrate and expanding immigration. The rural poor and immigrant groups were attracted to urban commercial centers that promised jobs in manufacturing. In 1790, 5 percent of the population lived in cities. By 1850, the share of the urban population had increased to 15 percent; it jumped to 40 percent in 1900, and 51 percent in 1920.[4] New York had nearly quadrupled its population in the 30-year stretch between 1825 and 1855—from 166,000 in 1825 to 630,000 in 1855.[5]

Urbanization gave rise to increased numbers of young people at risk, who overwhelmed the existing system of work and training. To accommodate destitute youths, local jurisdictions developed poorhouses (almshouses) and workhouses. The poor, the insane, the diseased, and vagrant and destitute children were housed there in crowded and unhealthy conditions.

By the late eighteenth century, the family's ability to exert control over children began to be questioned. Villages developed into urban commercial centers, and work began to center around factories, not the home. Children of destitute families left home or were cast loose to make out as best they could; wealthy families could no longer absorb vagrant youth as apprentices or servants.[6] Chronic poverty became an American dilemma. The affluent began to voice concern over the increase in the number of people in what they considered the "dangerous classes"—the poor, single, criminal, mentally ill, and unemployed.

Urbanization and industrialization also generated the belief that certain segments of the population (youths in urban areas, immigrants) were susceptible to the influences of their decaying environment. The children of these classes were considered a group that might be "saved" by a combination of state and community intervention.[7] Intervention in the lives of these so-called dangerous classes became acceptable for wealthy, civic-minded citizens. Such efforts included *settlement houses*, a term used around the turn of the twentieth century to describe shelters or nonsecure residential facilities for vagrant children.

The Child Saving Movement

The problems generated by urban growth sparked interest in the welfare of the "new" Americans, whose arrival fueled this expansion. In 1816, prominent New Yorkers formed the Society for the Prevention of Pauperism. Although they concerned themselves with shutting down taverns, brothels, and gambling parlors, they also were concerned that the moral training of children of the dangerous classes was inadequate. Soon other groups concerned with the plight of poor children began to form. They focused on extending government control over youthful activities (drinking, vagrancy, and delinquency) that had previously been left to private or family control.

These activists became known as *child savers*. Prominent among them were penologist Enoch Wines, Judge Richard Tuthill, Lucy Flowers, of the Chicago Women's Association, Sara Cooper, of the National Conference of Charities and Corrections, and Sophia Minton, of the New York Committee on Children.[8] Poor children could become a financial burden, and the child savers believed these children presented a threat to the moral fabric of society. Child saving organizations influenced state legislatures to enact laws giving courts the power to commit children who were runaways or criminal offenders to specialized institutions. Less well known were the "black child-savers," who fought to overcome the racial discrimination facing African American children who came in conflict with the law. In his historical study of the black child-savers, Geoff Ward documents the struggles and successes of the African American community in early juvenile justice reform.[9]

House of Refuge

The most prominent of the care facilities developed by child savers was the **House of Refuge**.[10] Its creation was effected by prominent Quakers and influential political leaders, such as Cadwallader Colden and Stephen Allen, the founders of the Society for the Prevention of Pauperism.

The first House of Refuge, constructed in New York City, was the product of the society's reform efforts. Though the house was privately managed, the state legislature began providing funds, partly through a head tax on arriving transatlantic passengers and seamen, plus the proceeds from license fees for New York City's taverns, theaters, and circuses. These revenue sources were deemed appropriate, since supporters blamed immigration, intemperance, and commercial entertainment for juvenile crime!

The reformatory opened on January 1, 1825, with only six boys and three girls, but within the first decade of its operation 1,678 inmates were admitted. Most kids were sent because of vagrancy and petty crimes and were sentenced or committed indefinitely until they reached adulthood. Originally, the institution accepted inmates from across the state of New York, but when a Western House of Refuge was opened in Rochester, New York, in 1849, residents came mostly from the New York City environs.

Once a resident, the adolescent's daily schedule was devoted for the most part to supervised labor, which was regarded as beneficial to education and discipline.

House of Refuge
A care facility developed by the child savers to protect potential criminal youths by taking them off the street and providing a family-like environment.

The House of Refuge was one of the earliest juvenile institutions in the United States to offer residents vocational training. Here, boys from the Rochester House of Refuge in Rochester, New York, take a break for a baseball game, circa 1875.

Inmate labor also supported operating expenses for the reformatory. Male inmates worked in shops that produced brushes, cane chairs, brass nails, and shoes. The female inmates sewed uniforms, did laundry, and carried out other domestic work. A badge system was used to segregate inmates according to their behavior. Although students received rudimentary educational skills, greater emphasis was placed on evangelical religious instruction; non-Protestant clergy were excluded. The reformatory had the authority to bind out inmates through indenture agreements to private employers; most males were farm workers and females were domestic laborers.

The Refuge Movement Spreads   When the House of Refuge opened, the majority of children admitted were status offenders placed there because of vagrancy or neglect. Children were placed in the institution by court order, sometimes over parents' objections. Their length of stay depended on need, age, and skill. Critics complained that the institution was run like a prison, with strict discipline and absolute separation of the sexes. Such a harsh program drove many children to run away, and the House of Refuge was forced to take a more lenient approach. Despite criticism, the concept enjoyed expanding popularity. In 1826, the Boston City Council founded the House of Reformation for juvenile offenders.[11] The courts committed children found guilty of criminal violations, or found to be beyond the control of their parents, to these schools. Because the child savers considered parents of delinquent children to be as guilty as convicted offenders, they sought to have the reform schools establish control over the children. Refuge managers believed they were preventing poverty and crime by separating destitute and delinquent children from their parents and placing them in an institution.[12]

The earliest institutions resembled the New York House of Refuge and housed a small number of children in relatively small buildings. But by the 1850s, the number of incarcerated children began to climb, resulting in the construction of larger institutions removed from the urban environment. For example, in New York the number of youthful residents expanded from 9 at the outset to more than 1,000 housed on Randall's Island in the East River in an institution indistinguishable from an adult prison.[13] Despite ongoing criticism and scandal, the Houses of Refuge hung on for more than 100 years. After the Civil War, the urban Refuge began to be replaced by state institutions located in rural areas. In 1935, the institution on Randall's Island closed forever.

Were They Really Child Savers?

Debate continues over the true objectives of the early child savers. Some historians conclude that they were what they seemed—concerned citizens motivated by humanitarian ideals.[14] Modern scholars, however, have reappraised the child saving movement. In *The Child Savers*, Anthony Platt paints a picture of representatives of the ruling class who were galvanized by immigrants and the urban poor to take action to preserve their own way of life.[15] He claims:

> The child savers should not be considered humanists: (1) their reforms did not herald a new system of justice but rather expedited traditional policies which had been informally developed during the nineteenth century; (2) they implicitly assumed the natural dependence of adolescents and created a special court to impose sanctions on premature independence and behavior unbecoming to youth; (3) their attitudes toward delinquent youth were largely paternalistic and romantic but their commands were backed up by force; (4) they promoted correctional programs requiring longer terms of imprisonment, longer hours of labor, and militaristic discipline, and the inculcation of middle class values and lower class skills.[16]

Other critical thinkers followed Platt in finding that child saving was motivated more by self-interest than by benevolence. For example, Randall Shelden and Lynn Osborne traced the child saving movement in Memphis, Tennessee, and found that its leaders were a small group of upper-class citizens who desired to control the behavior and lifestyles of lower-class youth. The outcome was ominous. Most cases petitioned to the juvenile court (which opened in 1910) were for petty crimes and status offenses, yet 25 percent of the youths were committed to some form of incarceration; more than 96 percent of the actions with which females were charged were status offenses.[17]

In summary, these scholars believe that the reformers applied the concept of *parens patriae* for their own purposes, including the continuance of middle- and upper-class values and the furtherance of a child labor system consisting of marginal and lower-class skilled workers. In the course of "saving children" by turning them over to houses of refuge, the basic legal rights of children were violated: children were simply not granted the same constitutional protections as adults.

Development of Juvenile Institutions

State intervention in the lives of children continued well into the twentieth century. The child savers influenced state and local governments to create special institutions, called *reform schools*, which would house delinquent youths who would have otherwise been sent to adult prisons. The first institutions opened in Westborough, Massachusetts, in 1848 and in Rochester, New York, in 1849.[18] Institutional programs began in Ohio in 1850 and in Maine, Rhode Island, and Michigan in 1906. The Houses of Refuge began to be replaced by rural facilities, which used cottages rather than large prisonlike facilities to house residents. In New York, for example, the legislature authorized a State Training School for Boys at Warwick for inmates under 16, and the State Vocational School at Coxsackie for those 16 to 19.[19]

Children spent their days working in the institution, learning a trade where possible, and receiving some basic education. They were racially and sexually segregated, discipline was harsh, and their physical care was poor. Some were labeled as criminal but were in reality abused and neglected. They too were subject to harsh working conditions, strict discipline, and intensive labor.[20] Although some people viewed reform schools as humanitarian answers to poorhouses and prisons, many were opposed to such programs.

Children's Aid Society

As an alternative to secure correctional facilities, New York philanthropist Charles Loring Brace helped develop the **Children's Aid Society** in 1853.[21] Brace's formula for dealing with delinquent youths was to rescue them from the harsh environment of the city and provide them with temporary shelter.

Children's Aid Society
Child saving organization that took children from the streets of large cities and placed them with farm families on the prairie.

orphan trains
The name for trains in which urban youths were sent west by the Children's Aid Society for adoption with local farm couples.

Deciding there were simply too many needy children to care for in New York City, and believing the urban environment was injurious to children, Brace devised what he called his *placing-out plan* to send these children to western farms where they could be cared for and find a home. They were placed on what became known as **orphan trains**, which made preannounced stops in western farming communities. Families wishing to take in children would meet the train, be briefly introduced to the passengers, and leave with one of the children. Brace's plan was activated in 1854 and very soon copied by other child care organizations. Though the majority of the children benefited from the plan and did find a new life, others were less successful, and some were exploited and harmed by the experience. By 1930, political opposition to Brace's plan, coupled with the negative effects of the economic depression, spelled the end of the orphan trains, but not before 150,000 children were placed in rural homesteads.

To read more about **the life of Charles Loring Brace**, you can visit this biographical web page: http://www.trailblazerbooks.com/books/roundup/Roundup-bio.html.

Society for the Prevention of Cruelty to Children

In 1874, the first **Society for the Prevention of Cruelty to Children** (SPCC) was established in New York. Agents of the society were granted power to remove children from their homes and arrest anyone who interfered with their work; they also assisted the court in making placement decisions.[22] By 1890, the society controlled the intake and disposition of an annual average of 15,000 poor and neglected children. By 1900, there were 300 such societies in the United States.[23]

Leaders of the SPCCs were concerned that abused boys would become lower-class criminals and that mistreated young girls might become sexually promiscuous women. A growing crime rate and concern about a rapidly changing population served to swell SPCC membership. In addition, these organizations protected children who had been subjected to cruelty and neglect at home and at school.

SPCC groups influenced state legislatures to pass statutes protecting children from parents who did not provide them with adequate food and clothing or made them beg or work in places where liquor was sold.[24] Criminal penalties were

Society for the Prevention of Cruelty to Children
Established in 1874, these organizations protected children subjected to cruelty and neglect at home or at school.

In 1874, Henry Bugh and Etta Angell Wheeler persuaded a New York court to take a child, Mary Ellen, away from her stepmother on the grounds of child abuse. This is the first recorded case in which a court was used to protect a child. Mary Ellen is shown at age 9 (left) when she appeared in court showing bruises from a whipping and several gashes from a pair of scissors. The second photograph shows her a year later.

Photos provided by the American Humane Association/Visit www.americanhumane.org

The First Juvenile Institutions and Organizations

Reform schools	Devoted to the care of vagrant and delinquent youths
Children's Aid Society	Designed to protect delinquent youths from the city's dangers through the provision of temporary shelter
Orphan trains	The practice of using trains to place delinquent urban youths with families in western farming communities
Society for the Prevention of Cruelty to Children	Designed to protect abused and neglected children by placing them with other families and advocating for criminal penalties for negligent parents

created for negligent parents, and provisions were established for removing children from the home. In some states, agents of the SPCC could actually arrest abusive parents; in others, they would inform the police about suspected abuse cases and accompany officers when they made an arrest.[25]

The organization and control of SPCCs varied widely. The New York City SPCC was a city agency supported by municipal funds. It conducted investigations of delinquent and neglected children for the court. In contrast, the Boston SPCC emphasized delinquency prevention and worked with social welfare groups; the Philadelphia SPCC emphasized family unity and was involved with other charities.[26] Concept Summary 13.1 describes those first juvenile institutions and organizations.

A Century of Juvenile Justice

Although reform groups continued to lobby for government control over children, the committing of children under the doctrine of *parens patriae* without due process of law began to be questioned. Could the state incarcerate children who had not violated the criminal law? Should children be held in the same facilities that housed adults? Serious problems challenged the effectiveness of the existing system. Institutional deficiencies, the absence of due process for poor, ignorant, and noncriminal delinquents, and the treatment of these children by inadequate private organizations all spurred the argument that a juvenile court should be established.

Increasing delinquency rates also hastened the development of a juvenile court. Theodore Ferdinand's analysis of the Boston juvenile court found that in the 1820s and 1830s very few juveniles were charged with serious offenses. By 1850, juvenile delinquency was the fastest growing component of the local crime problem.[27] Ferdinand concluded that the flow of juvenile cases strengthened the argument that juveniles needed their own court.

The Illinois Juvenile Court Act and Its Legacy

The child saving movement culminated in passage of the Illinois Juvenile Court Act of 1899, which established the nation's first independent juvenile court. Interpretations of its intentions differ, but unquestionably the Illinois Juvenile Court Act established juvenile delinquency as a legal concept. For the first time the distinction was made between children who were neglected and those who were delinquent. Delinquent children were those under the age of 16 who violated the law. Most important, the act established a court and a probation program specifically for children. In addition, the legislation allowed children to be committed to institutions and reform programs under the control of the state. The key provisions of the act were these:

- A separate court was established for delinquent and neglected children.
- Special procedures were developed to govern the adjudication of juvenile matters.
- Children were to be separated from adults in courts and in institutional programs.
- Probation programs were to be developed to assist the court in making decisions in the best interests of the state and the child.

Following passage of the Illinois Juvenile Court Act, similar legislation was enacted throughout the nation. The special courts these laws created maintained jurisdiction over predelinquent (neglected and dependent) and delinquent children. Juvenile court jurisdiction was based primarily on a child's noncriminal actions and status, not strictly on a violation of criminal law. The *parens patriae* philosophy predominated, ushering in a form of personalized justice that still did not provide juvenile offenders with the full array of constitutional protections available to adult criminal offenders. The court's process was paternalistic rather than adversarial. Attorneys were not required, and hearsay evidence, inadmissible in criminal trials, was admissible in the adjudication of juvenile offenders. Verdicts were based on a *preponderance of the evidence* instead of the stricter standard used by criminal courts, *beyond a reasonable doubt*, and children were often not granted any right to appeal their convictions.

The principles motivating the Illinois reformers were these:

- Children should not be held as accountable as adult transgressors.
- The objective of the juvenile justice system is to treat and rehabilitate rather than punish.
- Disposition should be predicated on analysis of the youth's special circumstances and needs.
- The system should avoid the trappings of the adult criminal process with all its confusing rules and procedures.

This was a major event in the juvenile justice movement. Its significance was such that by 1917, juvenile courts had been established in all but three states.

The Legacy of Illinois   Just what were the ramifications of passage of the Illinois Juvenile Court Act? The traditional interpretation is that the reformers were genuinely motivated to pass legislation that would serve the best interests of the child. US Supreme Court Justice Abe Fortas took this position in the landmark 1967 *In re Gault* case:

> The early reformers were appalled by adult procedures and penalties and by the fact that children could be given long prison sentences and mixed in jails with hardened criminals. They were profoundly convinced that society's duty to the child could not be confined by the concept of justice alone. . . . The child—essentially good, as they saw it—was to be made to feel that he was the object of the state's care and solicitude, not that he was under arrest or on trial. . . . The idea of crime and punishment was to be abandoned. The child was to be treated and rehabilitated and the procedures from apprehension through institutionalization were to be clinical rather than punitive.[28]

The child savers believed that children were influenced by their environments. Society was to be concerned with what their problems were and how these problems could be handled in the interests of the children and the state.

Nowhere can this procedural informality be seen more fully than in the Denver Juvenile Court presided over by Judge Benjamin Lindsey.[29] He viewed the children who came before him as "his boys" who were fundamentally good human beings led astray by their social and psychological environment. While Lindsey had no specific statutory authority to do so, he adopted a social worker–friend approach to the children who had been petitioned to court. The need for formal adjudication of the charges was unimportant compared to an effort to treat and rehabilitate these wayward youth. He condemned the criminal justice system, which he saw operating as a "medieval torture chamber" that victimized children.[30]

The Early Juvenile Court   The major functions of the juvenile justice system were to prevent juvenile crime and to rehabilitate juvenile offenders. The roles of the judge and the probation staff were to diagnose the child's condition and prescribe programs to alleviate it; judgments about children's actions and consideration for their constitutional rights were secondary.

By the 1920s, noncriminal behavior in the form of incorrigibility and truancy from school was added to the jurisdiction of many juvenile court systems. Of particular interest was the sexual behavior of young girls, and the juvenile court enforced a strict moral code on working-class girls, not hesitating to incarcerate those who were sexually active.[31] Programs of all kinds, including individualized counseling and institutional care, were used to *cure* juvenile criminality.

By 1925, juvenile courts existed in virtually every jurisdiction in every state. Although the juvenile court concept expanded rapidly, it cannot be said that each state implemented it thoroughly. Some jurisdictions established elaborate juvenile court systems, whereas others passed legislation but provided no services. Some courts had trained juvenile court judges; others had nonlawyers sitting in juvenile cases. Some courts had extensive probation departments; others had untrained probation personnel. In 1920, a US Children's Bureau survey found that only 16 percent of these new juvenile courts held separate calendars or hearings for children's cases or had an officially established probation service, and recorded social information about the children coming through the court. In 1926, it was reported that five out of six of these courts in the United States failed to meet the minimum standards of the Children's Bureau.[32]

Great diversity also marked juvenile institutions. Some maintained a lenient orientation, but others relied on harsh punishments, including beatings, straitjacket restraints, immersion in cold water, and solitary confinement with a diet of bread and water.

These conditions were exacerbated by the rapid growth in the juvenile institutional population. Between 1890 and 1920, the number of institutionalized youths jumped 112 percent, a rise that far exceeded the increase in the total number of adolescents in the United States.[33] Although social workers and court personnel deplored the increased institutionalization of youth, the growth was due in part to the successful efforts by reformers to close poorhouses, thereby creating a need for institutions to house their displaced populations. In addition, the lack of a coherent national policy on needy children allowed private entrepreneurs to fill the void.[34] Although the increase in institutionalization seemed contrary to the goal of rehabilitation, such an approach was preferable to the poorhouse and the streets.

Reforming the System

Reform of this system was slow in coming. In 1912, the US Children's Bureau was formed as the first federal child welfare agency. By the 1930s, the bureau began to investigate the state of juvenile institutions and tried to expose some of their more repressive aspects.[35] After World War II, critics such as Paul Tappan and Francis Allen began to identify problems in the juvenile justice system, among which were the neglect of procedural rights and the warehousing of youth in ineffective institutions. Status offenders commonly were housed with delinquents and given sentences that were more punitive than those given to delinquents.[36]

From its origin, the juvenile court system denied children procedural rights normally available to adult offenders. Due process rights, such as representation by counsel, a jury trial, freedom from self-incrimination, and freedom from unreasonable search and seizure, were not considered essential for the juvenile

The **Children's Bureau (CB)** is the oldest federal agency for children and is part of the Administration on Children, Youth and Families, a section of the Administration for Children and Families (ACF) under the Department of Health and Human Services. It is responsible for assisting states in the delivery of child welfare services— services designed to protect children and strengthen families. Visit their website at http://www.acf.hhs .gov/programs/cb/.

court system because its primary purpose was not punishment but rehabilitation. However, the dream of trying to rehabilitate children was not achieved. Individual treatment approaches failed, and delinquency rates soared.

Reform efforts, begun in earnest in the 1960s, changed the face of the juvenile justice system. In 1962, New York passed legislation creating a family court system.[37] The new court assumed responsibility for all matters involving family life, with emphasis on delinquent and neglected children. In addition, the legislation established the person in need of supervision (PINS) classification. This category included individuals involved in such actions as truancy and incorrigibility. By using labels like PINS and children in need of supervision (CHINS) to establish jurisdiction over children, juvenile courts expanded their role as social agencies. Because noncriminal children were now involved in the juvenile court system to a greater degree, many juvenile courts had to improve their social services. Efforts were made to personalize the system of justice for children. These reforms were soon followed by a due process revolution, which ushered in an era of procedural rights for court-adjudicated youth.

In the 1960s and 1970s, the US Supreme Court radically altered the juvenile justice system when it issued a series of decisions that established the right of juveniles to receive due process of law.[38] The Court established that juveniles had the same rights as adults in important areas of trial process, including the right to confront witnesses, notice of charges, and the right to counsel. Exhibit 13.1 illustrates some of the most important legal cases bringing procedural due process to the juvenile justice process.

exhibit 13.1

Leading Constitutional Cases in Juvenile Justice

Kent v. United States (1965) Determined that a child has due process rights, such as having an attorney present at waiver hearings.

In re Gault (1967) Ruled that a minor has basic due process rights, including (a) notice of the charges with respect to their timeliness and specificity, (b) right to counsel, (c) right to confrontation and cross-examination, (d) privilege against self-incrimination, (e) right to a transcript of the trial record, and (f) right to appellate review.

McKeiver v. Pennsylvania (1971) Held that trial by jury in a juvenile court's adjudicative stage is not a constitutional requirement.

Breed v. Jones (1975) Ruled that a child has the protection of the double-jeopardy clause of the Fifth Amendment and cannot be tried twice for the same crime.

Fare v. Michael C. (1979) Held that a child's request to see his probation officer at the time of interrogation did not operate to invoke his Fifth Amendment right to remain silent. According to the Court, the probation officer cannot be expected to offer the type of advice that an accused would expect from an attorney. The landmark *Miranda v. Arizona* case ruled that a request for a lawyer is an immediate revocation of a person's right to silence, but this rule is not applicable for a request to see the probation officer.

Eddings v. Oklahoma (1982) Ruled that a defendant's age should be a mitigating factor in deciding whether to apply the death penalty.

Schall v. Martin (1984) Upheld a statute allowing for the placement of children in preventive detention before their adjudication. The Court concluded that it was not unreasonable to detain juveniles for their own protection.

New Jersey v. T.L.O. (1985) Determined that the Fourth Amendment applies to school searches. The Court adopted a "reasonable suspicion" standard, as opposed to the stricter standard of "probable cause," to evaluate the legality of searches and seizures in a school setting.

Thompson v. Oklahoma (1988) Ruled that imposing capital punishment on a juvenile murderer who was 15 years old at the time of the offense violated the Eighth Amendment's constitutional prohibition against cruel and unusual punishment.

Stanford v. Kentucky and Wilkins v. Missouri (1989) Concluded that the imposition of the death penalty on a juvenile who committed a crime between the ages of 16 and 18 was not unconstitutional and that the Eighth Amendment's cruel and unusual punishment clause did not prohibit capital punishment.

Vernonia School District v. Acton (1995) Held that the Fourth Amendment's guarantee against unreasonable searches is not violated by the suspicionless drug testing of all students choosing to participate in interscholastic athletics. The Supreme Court expanded power of public educators to ensure safe learning environments in schools.

United States v. Lopez (1995) Ruled that Congress exceeded its authority under the Commerce Clause when it passed the Gun-Free School Zone Act, which made it a federal crime to possess a firearm within 1,000 feet of a school.

SOURCES: *Kent v. United States*, 383 U.S. 541, 86 S.Ct. 1045, 16 L.Ed.2d 84 (1966); *In re Gault*, 387 U.S. 1; 87 S.Ct. 1248 (1967); *McKeiver v. Pennsylvania*, 403 U.S. 528, 91 S.Ct.1976 (1971); *Breed v. Jones*, 421 U.S. 519, 95 S.Ct. 1779 (1975); *Fare v. Michael C.*, 442 U.S. 707, 99 S.Ct. 2560 (1979); *Eddings v. Oklahoma*, 455 U.S. 104, 102 S.Ct. 869, 71 L.Ed.2d 1 (1982); *Schall v. Martin*, 467 U.S. 253, 104 S.Ct. 2403 (1984); *New Jersey v. T.L.O.*, 469 U.S. 325, 105 S.Ct. 733 (1985); *Thompson v. Oklahoma*, 487 U.S. 815, 108 S.Ct. 2687, 101 L.Ed.2d 702 (1988); *Stanford v. Kentucky*, 492 U.S. 361, 109 S.Ct. 2969 (1989); *Wilkins v. Missouri*, 492 U.S. 361, 109 S.Ct. 2969 (1989); *Vernonia School District v. Acton*, 515 U.S. 646, 115 S.Ct. 2386, 132 L.Ed.2d 564 (1995); *United States v. Lopez*, 115 S.Ct. 1624 (1995).

Federal Commissions In addition to the legal revolution brought about by the Supreme Court, a series of national commissions sponsored by the federal government helped change the shape of juvenile justice. In 1967, the President's Commission on Law Enforcement and the Administration of Justice, organized by President Lyndon Johnson, suggested that the juvenile justice system must provide underprivileged youths with opportunities for success, including jobs and education, with an even greater focus on delinquency prevention.[39] The commission also recognized the need to develop effective law enforcement procedures to control hard-core offenders, at the same time granting them due process. The commission's report acted as a catalyst for passage of the federal Juvenile Delinquency Prevention and Control (JDP) Act of 1968. This law created a Youth Development and Delinquency Prevention Administration, which concentrated on helping states develop new juvenile justice programs, particularly those involving diversion of youth, decriminalization, and decarceration. In 1968, Congress also passed the Omnibus Safe Streets and Crime Control Act.[40] Title I of this law established the **Law Enforcement Assistance Administration (LEAA)** to provide federal funds for improving the adult and juvenile justice systems. In 1972, Congress amended the JDP Act to allow the LEAA to focus its funding on juvenile justice and delinquency prevention programs. State and local governments were required to develop and adopt comprehensive plans to obtain federal assistance.

Law Enforcement Assistance Administration (LEAA)
Unit in the US Department of Justice established by the Omnibus Crime Control and Safe Streets Act of 1968 to administer grants and provide guidance for crime prevention policy and programs.

Because crime continued to receive much publicity, a second effort called the National Advisory Commission on Criminal Justice Standards and Goals was established in 1973 by the Nixon administration.[41] Its report identified such strategies as (a) preventing delinquent behavior, (b) developing diversion activities, (c) establishing dispositional alternatives, (d) providing due process for all juveniles, and (e) controlling violent and chronic delinquents. This commission's recommendations formed the basis for the Juvenile Justice and Delinquency Prevention Act of 1974.[42] This act eliminated the Youth Development and Delinquency Prevention Administration and replaced it with the Office of Juvenile Justice and Delinquency Prevention (OJJDP) within the LEAA. In 1980, the LEAA was phased out, and the OJJDP became an independent agency in the Department of Justice. Throughout the 1970s, its two most important goals were (1) removing juveniles from detention in adult jails, and (2) eliminating the incarceration together of delinquents and status offenders. During this period, the OJJDP stressed the creation of formal diversion and restitution programs.

To read about the **Juvenile Justice and Delinquency Prevention Act of 1974**, go to this website: https://www.ncjrs.gov/txtfiles/ojjjact.txt.

The latest effort was the Violent Crime Control and Law Enforcement Act of 1994.[43] The largest piece of crime legislation in the history of the United States, it provided 100,000 new police officers and billions of dollars for prisons and prevention programs for both adult and juvenile offenders. A revitalized juvenile justice system would need both a comprehensive strategy to prevent and control delinquency and a consistent program of federal funding.[44]

Juvenile Justice Today

Today the juvenile justice system exercises jurisdiction over two distinct categories of offenders—delinquents and status offenders.[45] *Delinquent children* are those who fall under a jurisdictional age limit, which varies from state to state, and who commit an act in violation of the penal code. *Status offenders* are commonly characterized in state statutes as persons or children in need of supervision (PINS or CHINS). Most states distinguish such behavior from delinquent conduct to reduce the effect of any stigma on children as a result of their involvement with the juvenile court. In addition, juvenile courts generally have jurisdiction over situations involving conduct directed at (rather than committed by) juveniles, such as parental neglect, deprivation, abandonment, and abuse.

The states have also set different maximum ages below which children fall under the jurisdiction of the juvenile court. Most states (and the District of Columbia) include all children under 18, others set the upper limit at 16, and still others only include children age 15 and under (see Table 13.1).

table 13.1

Oldest Age for Juvenile Court Jurisdiction in Delinquency Cases

Age	State (total number)
15	New York, North Carolina (2)
16	Georgia, Louisiana, Michigan, Missouri, New Hampshire, South Carolina, Texas, Wisconsin (8)
17	Alabama, Alaska, Arizona, Arkansas, California, Colorado, Connecticut, Delaware, Florida, Hawaii, Idaho, Illinois, Indiana, Iowa, Kansas, Kentucky, Maine, Maryland, Massachusetts, Minnesota, Mississippi, Montana, Nebraska, Nevada, New Jersey, New Mexico, North Dakota, Ohio, Oklahoma, Oregon, Pennsylvania, Rhode Island, South Dakota, Tennessee, Utah, Vermont, Virginia, Washington, West Virginia, Wyoming (40 and the District of Columbia)

Source: Angel Zang, *U.S. Age Boundaries of Delinquency*, JJGPS StateScan (Pittsburgh: National Center for Juvenile Justice, 2015), p. 2.

Some states exclude certain classes of offenders or offenses from the juvenile justice system. For example, youths who commit serious violent offenses such as rape and/or murder may be automatically excluded from the juvenile justice system and treated as adults, on the premise that they stand little chance of rehabilitation within the confines of the juvenile system. Juvenile court judges may also transfer, or *waive*, repeat offenders whom they deem untreatable by the juvenile authorities.

Today's juvenile justice system exists in all states by statute. Each jurisdiction has a juvenile code and a special court structure to accommodate children in trouble. Nationwide, the juvenile justice system consists of thousands of public and private agencies, with a total budget amounting to hundreds of millions of dollars. Most of the nation's police agencies have juvenile components, and there are more than 3,000 juvenile courts and about an equal number of juvenile correctional facilities.

Figure 13.1 depicts the numbers of juvenile offenders removed at various stages of the juvenile justice process. These data do not take into account the large number of children who are referred to community diversion and mental health programs. There are thousands of these programs throughout the nation. This multitude of agencies and people dealing with juvenile delinquency has led to the development of what professionals view as an incredibly expansive and complex system.

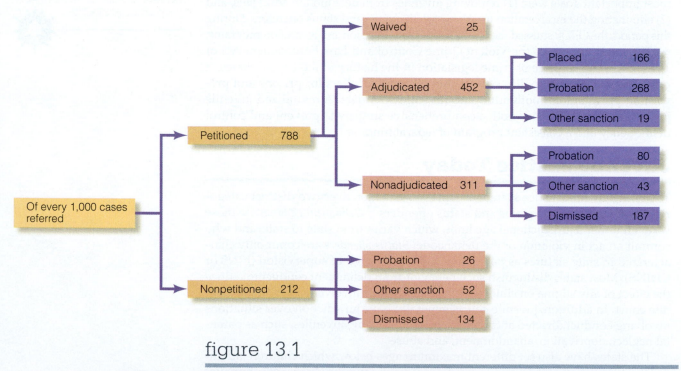

figure 13.1

Case Processing of Typical Violent Crimes in the Juvenile Justice System

Note: Cases are categorized by their most severe or restrictive sanction. Detail may not add to totals because of rounding.

SOURCE: Sarah Hockenberry and Charles Puzzanchera, *Juvenile Court Statistics 2013* (Pittsburgh: National Center for Juvenile Justice, 2015), p. 66.

The Juvenile Justice Process

How are children processed by the juvenile justice system?[46] Most children come into the justice system as a result of contact with a police officer. When a juvenile commits a serious crime, the police are empowered to make an arrest. Less serious offenses may also require police action, but in these instances, instead of being arrested, the child may be warned or a referral may be made to a social service program. Sixty-two percent of all children arrested are referred to the juvenile court.[47] Figure 13.2 outlines the **juvenile justice process**, and a detailed analysis of this process is presented in the next sections.

Police Investigation When youths commit a crime, police have the authority to investigate the incident and decide whether to release the youths or commit them to the juvenile court. This is often a discretionary decision, based not only on the nature of the offense but also on conditions existing at the time of the arrest. Such factors as the seriousness of the offense, the child's past contacts with the police, and whether the child denies committing the crime determine whether a petition is filed. Juveniles in custody have constitutional rights similar to those of adult offenders. Children are protected against unreasonable search and seizure under the Fourth and Fourteenth Amendments of the Constitution. The Fifth Amendment places limitations on police interrogation procedures.

Detention If the police decide to file a petition, the child is referred to juvenile court. The primary decision at this point is whether the child should remain in the community or be placed in a detention facility or in shelter care (temporary foster homes, detention boarding homes, programs of neighborhood supervision). Historically, this has been one of the more controversial stages in the juvenile justice process.[48] In the past, children were routinely held in detention facilities to await court appearances. Normally, a **detention hearing** is held to determine whether to remand the child to a shelter. At this point, the child has a right to counsel and other procedural safeguards. A child who is not detained is usually released to a parent or guardian. Most state juvenile-court acts provide for a child to return home to await further court action, except when it is necessary to protect the child, when the child presents a serious danger to the public, or when it is not certain that the child will return to court. In many cases the police will refer the child to a community service program instead of filing a formal charge.

juvenile justice process
Under the paternal (*parens patriae*) philosophy, juvenile justice procedures are informal and nonadversarial, invoked for the juvenile offender rather than against him or her; a petition instead of a complaint is filed; courts make findings of involvement or adjudication of delinquency instead of convictions; and juvenile offenders receive dispositions instead of sentences.

detention hearing
A hearing by a judicial officer of a juvenile court to determine whether a juvenile is to be detained or released while juvenile proceedings are pending in the case.

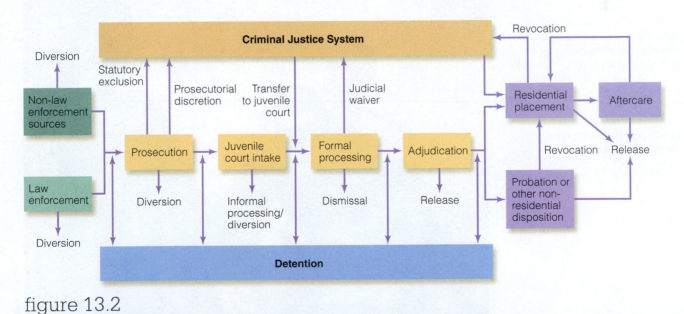

figure 13.2

Case Flow Through the Juvenile Justice Process

SOURCE: Office of Juvenile Justice and Delinquency Prevention, http://ojjdp.gov/ojstatbb/structure_process/case.html (accessed October 2016).

Pretrial Procedures   In most jurisdictions, the adjudication process begins with some sort of hearing. At this hearing, juvenile court rules normally require that juveniles be informed of their right to a trial, that the plea or admission be voluntary, and that they understand the charges and consequences of the plea. The case will often not be further adjudicated if a child admits to the crime at the initial hearing.

In some cases, youths may be detained at this stage pending a trial. Juveniles who are detained are eligible for bail in a handful of jurisdictions. Plea bargaining may also occur at any stage of the proceedings. A plea bargain is an agreement between the prosecution and the defense by which the juvenile agrees to plead guilty for certain considerations, such as a lenient sentence. This issue is explored more thoroughly in Chapter 15, which discusses pretrial procedures.

If the child denies the allegation of delinquency, an **adjudicatory hearing** or trial is scheduled. Under extraordinary circumstances, a juvenile who commits a serious crime may be transferred or waived to an adult court. Today, most jurisdictions have laws providing for such transfers. Whether such a transfer occurs depends on the type of offense, the youth's prior record, the availability of treatment services, and the likelihood that the youth will be rehabilitated in the juvenile court system.[49]

Adjudication   In the trial, or adjudication, stage of the juvenile court process, a hearing is held to determine the facts of the case. The court hears evidence on the allegations in the delinquency petition. This is a trial on the merits (dealing with issues of law and facts), and rules of evidence similar to those of criminal proceedings generally apply. At this stage, the juvenile offender is entitled to many of the procedural guarantees given adult offenders. These include the right to counsel, freedom from self-incrimination, the right to confront and cross-examine witnesses, and, in certain instances, the right to a jury trial. In addition, many states have their own procedures concerning rules of evidence, competence of witnesses, pleadings, and pretrial motions. At the end of the adjudicatory hearing, the court enters a judgment against the juvenile.

adjudicatory hearing
The fact-finding process wherein the juvenile court determines whether there is sufficient evidence to sustain the allegations in a petition.

Also known as the trial stage, adjudication in the juvenile court process involves a hearing to determine the facts of the case. On December 9, 2015, in district court in Albuquerque, New Mexico, Alex Rios is handcuffed after being found guilty of two counts of second-degree murder. As a teenager, he participated in the killing of two homeless Native American men in July 2014.

AP Images/Roberto E. Rosales

The sentencing stage of the juvenile justice process is called disposition. At this point, the court orders treatment for the juvenile. Here, Meagan Grunwald, 18, reacts to the judge's sentencing decision of 25 years to life for her role in a crime spree that resulted in the death of a sheriff's deputy. The sentence was delivered in the Fourth District Court in Provo, Utah, on July 8, 2015. Grunwald will be eligible for parole in 2042.

Disposition   If the adjudication process finds the child guilty, the court must decide what should be done to treat the child. Most juvenile court acts require a dispositional hearing separate from the adjudication. This two-stage decision is often referred to as a **bifurcated process**. The dispositional hearing is less formal than adjudication. Here, the judge imposes a **disposition** on the offender in light of the offense, the youth's prior record, and his or her family background. The judge can prescribe a wide range of dispositions, ranging from a reprimand to probation to institutional commitment. In theory, the judge's decision serves the best interests of the child, the family, and the community.

Treatment   After disposition in juvenile court, delinquent offenders may be placed in some form of correctional treatment. Probation is the most commonly used formal sentence for juvenile offenders, and many states require that a youth fail on probation before being sent to an institution (unless the criminal act is extremely serious). Probation involves placing the child under the supervision of the juvenile probation department for the purpose of community treatment. Because of the importance of probation to the juvenile justice system, we discuss the career of one juvenile probation officer in the accompanying Professional Spotlight feature.

The most severe of the statutory dispositions available to the juvenile court involves commitment of the child to an institution. The committed child may be sent to a state training school or a private residential treatment facility. These are usually minimum-security facilities with small populations and an emphasis on treatment and education. Some states, however, maintain facilities with populations of over 1,000 youths. Currently there are slightly more than 54,000 youths in some form of correctional institution in the United States.[50]

Some jurisdictions allow for a program of juvenile aftercare or parole. A youth can be paroled from an institution and placed under the supervision of a parole officer. This means that he or she will complete the period of confinement in the community and receive assistance from the parole officer in the form of counseling, school referral, and vocational training.[51]

Juveniles who are committed to programs of treatment and control have a legal right to treatment. States are required to provide suitable rehabilitation programs that include counseling, education, and vocational services. Appellate courts have ruled that if such minimum treatment is not provided, individuals must be released from confinement.

bifurcated process
The procedure of separating adjudicatory and dispositionary hearings so different levels of evidence can be heard at each.

disposition
For juvenile offenders, the equivalent of sentencing for adult offenders; however, juvenile dispositions should be more rehabilitative than retributive.

Carla Stalnaker
Juvenile Probation Officer

CARLA STALNAKER is a juvenile probation officer at the Fourth Judicial Circuit Court in Clinton County, Illinois. She chose this career because she has always been interested in working with adolescents in some capacity. Stalnaker believes that adolescents are at a pivotal point in life to make positive life changes. They are old enough to have the cognitive skills necessary for making positive change and they are young enough that their habits are changeable.

Stalnaker prepared for her career by first getting a bachelor's degree in psychology with a specialization in adolescent development. Prior to becoming a juvenile probation officer, she worked for eight years in a long-term residential group home for behavior disordered and developmentally delayed youth. She points to this experience as the key to preparing her to be a juvenile probation officer.

For Stalnaker, the most rewarding part of being a juvenile probation officer is having the ability to help youths who are overlooked or pushed aside by society. Many times these young people are labeled as the "bad kids," so they tend to become lost and hopeless. She feels very strongly that these youths need someone to provide appropriate discipline, support, and reinforcement to help them get on the right path.

What does Stalnaker feel is the biggest challenge in her job? She says it is the lack of sufficient funding. There are many programs and services available to youths that provide much needed treatment and support. However, there is rarely (if ever) funding to be able to access these programs and services. She finds it especially difficult to cope with this issue. Another challenge is the parent component of juvenile probation. While the youth committed the offense, the role of the parents is crucial in both why their son or daughter committed the offense and putting a plan in place to best help them.

Stalnaker finds that there are a number of important misconceptions about a job in juvenile probation. One is that juvenile probation eventually sends all the offenders to jail, boot camp, or tries to scare kids straight. This could not be further from the truth. Another misconception is that youths on probation are all "bad kids." Yet another misconception is that the probation department has unlimited resources. Importantly, it is doing a far better job at targeting resources and connecting youths to the services they need so that they will stay out of trouble once they leave probation.

Conflicting Values in Juvenile Justice

This overview of the juvenile justice process hints at the often-conflicting values at the heart of the system. Efforts to ensure that juveniles are given appropriate treatment are consistent with the doctrine of parens patriae that predominated in the first half of the twentieth century. (See Exhibit 13.2 for a time line of ideologies of juvenile justice during the twentieth century.)

Since the mid-twentieth century, the juvenile court has struggled to provide treatment for juvenile offenders while guaranteeing them constitutional due

---

exhibit 13.2

Time Line of Juvenile Justice Ideology

Prior to 1899 Juveniles treated similarly to adult offenders. No distinction by age or capacity to commit criminal acts.

1899 to 1950s Children treated differently, beginning with the Illinois Juvenile Court Act of 1899. By 1925, juvenile court acts are established in virtually every state.

1950s to 1970s Recognition by experts that the rehabilitation model and the protective nature of *parens patriae* have failed to prevent delinquency.

1960s to 1970s Constitutional due process is introduced into the juvenile justice system. The concept of punishing children or protecting them under *parens patriae* is under attack by the courts.

1970s to 1980s Failure of rehabilitation and due process protections to control delinquency leads to a shift to a crime control and punishment philosophy similar to that of the adult criminal justice system.

Early 1990s Mixed constitutional protections with some treatment. Uncertain goals and programs; the juvenile justice system relies on punishment and deterrence.

Mid-1990s to present Attention given to strategy that focuses on reducing the threat of juvenile crime and expanding options for handling juvenile offenders. Emphasis is placed on "evidence-based" programs and policies and striking a balance between prevention and control programs. Effort is made to use the restorative justice model, which involves balancing the needs of the victim, the community, and the juvenile.

process. But at various points in time the system has been overwhelmed by the increase in violent juvenile crime and family breakdown that some judges and politicians have suggested abolishing the juvenile system.[52] Even those experts who want to retain an independent juvenile court have called for its restructuring. Crime control advocates want to reduce the court's jurisdiction over juveniles charged with serious crimes and liberalize the prosecutor's ability to try them in adult courts. In contrast, child advocates suggest that the court scale back its judicial role and transfer its functions to community groups and social service agencies.[53]

Criminal Justice vs. Juvenile Justice

The components of the adult and juvenile criminal processes are similar. However, the juvenile system has a separate organizational structure. In many communities, juvenile justice is administered by people who bring special skills to the task. Also, more kinds of facilities and services are available to juveniles than to adults.

One concern of the juvenile court reform movement was to make certain that the stigma attached to a convicted offender would not be affixed to young people in juvenile proceedings. Thus, even the language used in the juvenile court differs from that used in the adult criminal court (see Exhibit 13.3). Juveniles are not indicted for a crime; they have a **petition** filed against them. Secure pretrial holding facilities are called *detention centers* rather than jails. Similarly, the criminal trial is called a *hearing* in the juvenile justice system. (See the Focus on Delinquency box entitled "Similarities and Differences Between Juvenile and Adult Justice Systems.")

petition
Document filed in juvenile court alleging that a juvenile is a delinquent, a status offender, or a dependent and asking that the court assume jurisdiction over the juvenile.

exhibit 13.3

Comparison of Terms Used in Adult and Juvenile Justice Systems

	Juvenile Terms	Adult Terms
The person and the act	Delinquent child	Criminal
	Delinquent act	Crime
Preadjudicatory stage	Take into custody	Arrest
	Petition	Indictment
	Agree to a finding	Plead guilty
	Deny the petition	Plead not guilty
	Adjustment	Plea bargain
	Detention facility; child care shelter	Jail
Adjudicatory stage	Substitution	Reduction of charges
	Adjudication or fact-finding hearing	Trial
	Adjudication	Conviction
Postadjudicatory stage	Dispositional hearing	Sentencing hearing
	Disposition	Sentence
	Commitment	Incarceration
	Youth development center; treatment; training school	Prison
	Residential child care facility	Halfway house
	Aftercare	Parole

Similarities and Differences Between Juvenile and Adult Justice Systems

Since its creation, the juvenile justice system has sought to maintain its independence from the adult justice system. Yet there are a number of similarities that characterize the institutions, processes, and law of the two systems.

Similarities

- Police officers, judges, and correctional personnel use discretion in decision making in both the adult and the juvenile systems.

- The right to receive *Miranda* warnings applies to juveniles as well as to adults.

- Juveniles and adults are protected from prejudicial lineups or other identification procedures.

- Similar procedural safeguards protect juveniles and adults when they make an admission of guilt.

- Prosecutors and defense attorneys play equally critical roles in juvenile and adult advocacy.

- Juveniles and adults have the right to counsel at most key stages of the court process.

- Pretrial motions are available in juvenile and criminal court proceedings.

- Negotiations and plea bargaining exist for juvenile and adult offenders.

- Juveniles and adults have a right to a hearing and an appeal.

- The standard of evidence in juvenile delinquency adjudications, as in adult criminal trials, is proof beyond a reasonable doubt.

- Juveniles and adults can be placed on probation by the court.

- Both juveniles and adults can be placed in pretrial detention facilities.

- Juveniles and adults can be kept in detention without bail if they are considered dangerous.

- After trial, both can be placed in community treatment programs.

- Juveniles and adults can be required to undergo drug testing.

- Boot camp correctional facilities are now being used for both juveniles and adults.

A Comprehensive Juvenile Justice Strategy

At a time when much attention is focused on serious juvenile offenders, a comprehensive strategy has been called for to deal with all aspects of juvenile crime. This strategy focuses on delinquency prevention and expanding options for handling juvenile offenders. It addresses the links among crime and poverty, child abuse, drugs, weapons, and school behavior. Programs are based on a continuum of care that begins in early childhood and progresses through late adolescence. The components of this strategy include (a) prevention in early childhood, (b) intervention for at-risk teenage youths, (c) graduated sanctions to hold juvenile offenders accountable for crimes, (d) proper utilization of detention and confinement, and (e) placement of serious juvenile offenders in adult courts.[54] There are many expected benefits from the use of this comprehensive strategy (see Exhibit 13.4).

exhibit 13.4

Benefits of Using the Comprehensive Strategy

- Increased prevention of delinquency (and thus fewer young people enter the juvenile justice system)
- Enhanced responsiveness from the juvenile justice system
- Greater accountability on the part of youth
- Decreased costs of juvenile corrections

- A more responsible juvenile justice system
- More effective juvenile justice programs
- Less delinquency
- Fewer delinquents become serious, violent, and chronic offenders
- Fewer delinquents become adult offenders

SOURCE: James C. Howell, *Preventing and Reducing Juvenile Delinquency: A Comprehensive Framework.* Copyright © 2009 by Sage Publications. Reprinted by permission.

Differences

- The primary purposes of juvenile procedures are protection and treatment. With adults, the aim is to punish the guilty. Age determines the jurisdiction of the juvenile court. The nature of the offense determines jurisdiction in the adult system. Juveniles can be ordered to the criminal court for trial as adults.

- Juveniles can be apprehended for acts that would not be criminal if committed by an adult (status offenses).

- Juvenile proceedings are not considered criminal; adult proceedings are.

- Juvenile court procedures are generally informal and private. Those of adult courts are more formal and are open to the public.

- Courts cannot release identifying information about a juvenile to the press, but they must release information about an adult.

- Parents are highly involved in the juvenile process but not in the adult process.

- The standard of arrest is more stringent for adults than for juveniles.

- Juveniles are released into parental custody. Adults are generally given the opportunity for bail.

- Juveniles have no constitutional right to a jury trial. Adults have this right. Some state statutes provide juveniles with a jury trial.

- Juveniles can be searched in school without probable cause or a warrant.

- A juvenile's record is generally sealed when the age of majority is reached. The record of an adult is permanent.

- A juvenile court cannot sentence juveniles to county jails or state prisons; these are reserved for adults.

CRITICAL THINKING

1. What are some of the key principles of the juvenile justice system that distinguish it from the adult justice system and that have come under increased scrutiny of late?

2. What can be done to ensure that these key principles are protected so that the juvenile justice system remains distinct from the adult system?

Proponents of this strategy have called for an expanded framework that focuses on youth facing a wider range of problem behaviors, including mental health, school, and drug use problems, and a greater integration of services across juvenile justice, child welfare, and other youth-serving agencies.[55]

Additional support for a comprehensive juvenile justice strategy comes from the findings of a large-scale national survey of juvenile justice practitioners.[56] The researchers interviewed 534 practitioners in 282 of the most populated counties, covering 45 states and the District of Columbia. Juvenile court judges, prosecutors, public defenders, and court administrators, including chief probation officers, were asked about their views on a wide range of issues affecting juvenile justice policy, including recent changes to policy and practice. Among the most revealing findings of the survey were the practitioners' views about the most effective juvenile justice policies and practices; these included substance abuse treatment, sex offender treatment, mental health treatment, and reentry services and planning (see Table 13.2). Equally revealing were the practitioners' views about the most ineffective juvenile justice policies and practices: the top five were reduced confidentiality of court records, transfer to criminal or adult court, juvenile curfew laws, parental accountability laws, and statutes and rules setting time limits in court.[57]

Prevention

Research has identified an array of early risk factors that are associated with future delinquency. For young children, some of the most important risk factors include low intelligence and attainment, impulsiveness, poor parental supervision, parental conflict, and living in crime-ridden and deprived neighborhoods.[58] A number of early childhood programs have been shown to be effective in tackling these risk factors and preventing delinquency and later criminal offending, including

table 13.2

Juvenile Justice Practitioner Views of the Best Policies and Practices

	Less Crime	Less Recidivism	Appropriate Punishment	Fair Treatment	Efficiency of Process	Traditional Mission	Total Top-5 Rankings
Substance abuse treatment	J, P, D, C	J, P, D, C	J, P, D, C	J, P, D, C	J, P, D, C	J, P, D, C	24
Sex offender treatment	J, P, D, C	J, P, D, C	J, P, D, C	J, P, D, C	J, P, D, C	J, P, C	23
Mental health treatment	J, P, D, C	J, P, D, C	J, D, C	J, P, D, C	J, P, D, C	J, P, D, C	23
Reentry services and planning	J, P, D, C	J, P, D, C	J, D, C	J, P, D, C	J, P, D, C	J, P, D, C	23
Coordination with social services	J, D, C	J, D, C		J		J, P, D, C	11
Alternatives to detention			D	D	J, D	D	5
Restorative justice programs/policies			J, C				2
Using risk and needs assessments				C	C		2
Prosecuting youth gang members	P	P	P	P	P		5
Victim participation in proceedings			P				1
Transferring juveniles			P				1

Note: The presence of a practitioner code (J, P, D, or C) indicates that for a given outcome dimension, the policy or practice was ranked among the top five for that particular group. J = judges; P = prosecutors; D = defense attorneys; C = court administrators.

Source: Adapted from Daniel P. Mears, Tracey L. Shollenberger, Janeen B. Willison, Colleen E. Owens, and Jeffrey A. Butts, "Practitioner Views of Priorities, Policies, and Practices in Juvenile Justice," *Crime and Delinquency* 56:535–563 (2010), Table 2, p. 548.

preschool intellectual enrichment, child skills training, parent management training, and parent education programs such as home visiting.[59] Some of these programs can pay back program costs and produce substantial monetary benefits for the government and taxpayers.[60] As discussed earlier, recent research also shows that the general public is highly supportive of delinquency prevention programs and is even willing to pay more in taxes for these programs compared to punitive options like military-style boot camps and prison.

There are a number of evidence-based and promising federal early childhood programs. Head Start provides children in poverty with, among other things, an enriched educational environment to develop learning and cognitive skills to be better prepared for the early school years. One study found that children who attended Head Start at ages 3 to 5 were significantly less likely to report being arrested or referred to court for a crime by ages 18 to 30 compared to their siblings who did not attend the program.[61] Another study found that a publicly funded prekindergarten program in Boston—similar to Head Start—produced substantial gains for children's language, literacy, numeracy, and mathematics skills.[62] Smart Start is designed to make sure certain children are healthy before starting school. State-funded home-visiting programs like those in Hawaii and Colorado are especially concerned with reducing child abuse and neglect and bettering the lives of at-risk families and their children.[63] Chapter 12 discusses some of these programs in greater detail.

Intervention

Intervention programs focus on teenage youths considered to be at higher risk for engaging in petty delinquent acts, using drugs or alcohol, or associating with antisocial peers.[64] Interventions at this stage are designed to ward off involvement in more serious delinquency. Many jurisdictions are developing new intervention programs for teenage youths. An example is the Big Brothers Big Sisters program, which matches an adult volunteer with a youngster.[65] Other programs have a therapeutic component and are targeted at the most at-risk youths as well as serious juvenile offenders. Examples include Multisystemic Therapy (discussed in Chapter 11), Functional Family Therapy, and Multidimensional Treatment Foster Care. Functional Family Therapy involves modifying patterns of family interaction—by modeling, prompting, and reinforcement—to encourage clear communication of requests and solutions between family members and to minimize conflict.[66] Multidimensional Treatment Foster Care involves individual-focused therapeutic care (e.g., skill building in problem solving) and parent training.[67] Known as brand name evidence-based programs, these interventions are widely used across the country and have played an important role in juvenile justice reform in a number of states.[68]

Graduated Sanctions

Another solution being explored by states across the country is graduated sanctions. Types of graduated sanctions include immediate sanctions for nonviolent offenders (these consist of community-based diversion and day treatment); intermediate sanctions such as probation and electronic monitoring, which target repeat minor offenders and first-time serious offenders; and secure institutional care, which is reserved for repeat serious offenders and violent offenders. The philosophy behind this approach is to limit the most restrictive sanctions to the most dangerous offenders while increasing restrictions and intensity of treatment services as offenders move from minor to serious offenses.[69]

Institutional Programs

Another key to a comprehensive strategy is improving institutional programs. Many experts believe juvenile incarceration is overused, particularly for nonviolent offenders. That is why the concept of deinstitutionalization—removing as many youths from secure confinement as possible—was established by the Juvenile Justice and Delinquency Prevention Act of 1974. Considerable research supports the fact that warehousing juveniles without proper treatment does little to deter criminal behavior. The most effective secure corrections programs are those that provide individual services for a small number of participants.[70]

Alternative Courts

New venues of juvenile justice that provide special services to youths while helping to alleviate the case flow problems that plague overcrowded juvenile courts are

In teen courts, which are increasingly being used across the country as alternatives to traditional forms of juvenile courts, young people rather than adults determine the disposition of a case. Shown here is a teen court jury prior to hearing cases in La Plata, Maryland.

The Washington Post/Getty Images

Teen Courts

To relieve overcrowding and provide an alternative to traditional forms of juvenile courts, jurisdictions across the country are experimenting with teen courts, also called youth courts. These differ from other juvenile justice programs, because young people rather than adults determine the disposition in a case. Cases handled in these courts typically involve young juveniles (ages 10 to 15) with no prior arrest records who are being charged with minor law violations, such as shoplifting, vandalism, and disorderly conduct. Usually, young offenders are asked to volunteer to have their case heard in a teen court instead of the more formal court of the traditional juvenile justice system.

As in a regular juvenile court, teen court defendants may go through an intake process, a preliminary review of charges, a court hearing, and disposition. In a teen court, however, other young people are responsible for much of the process. Charges may be presented to the court by a 15-year-old "prosecutor." Defendants may be represented by a 16-year-old "defense attorney." Other youths may serve as jurors, court clerks, and bailiffs. In some teen courts, a youth "judge" (or panel of youth judges) may choose the best disposition or sanction for each case. In a few teen courts, teens even determine whether the facts in a case have been proven by the prosecutor (similar to a finding of guilt). Offenders are often ordered to pay restitution or perform community service. Some teen courts require offenders to write formal apologies to their victims; others require offenders to serve on a subsequent teen court jury. Many courts use other innovative dispositions, such as requiring offenders to attend classes designed to improve their decision-making skills, enhance their awareness of victims, and deter them from future delinquent behavior.

Although juveniles make the decisions, adults are also involved in teen courts. They often administer the programs, and they are usually responsible for essential functions, such as budgeting, planning, and personnel. In many programs, adults supervise the courtroom activities, and they often coordinate the community service placements where the young offenders work to fulfill the terms of their dispositions. In some programs, adults act as the judges while teens serve as attorneys and jurors.

Proponents of teen court argue that the process takes advantage of one of the most powerful forces in the life of an adolescent—the desire for peer approval and the reaction to peer pressure. According to this argument, youth respond better to prosocial peers than to adult authority figures. Thus, teen courts are seen as a potentially effective alternative to traditional juvenile courts staffed with paid professionals, such as lawyers, judges, and probation officers. Teen courts advocates also point out that the benefits extend beyond defendants. Teen courts may benefit the volunteer youth attorneys and judges, who probably learn more about the legal system than they could in a classroom. The presence of a teen court may also encourage the entire community to take a more active role in responding to juvenile crime. In sum, teen courts offer at least four potential benefits:

- *Accountability*. Teen courts may help ensure that young offenders are held accountable for their illegal behavior, even when their offenses are relatively minor and would not likely result in sanctions from the traditional juvenile justice system.

- *Timeliness*. An effective teen court can move young offenders from arrest to sanctions within a matter of days rather than the months that may pass with traditional juvenile courts. This rapid response may increase the positive impact of court sanctions, regardless of their severity.

---

teen courts
Courts that make use of peer juries to decide nonserious delinquency cases.

drug courts
Courts whose focus is to provide treatment for youths accused of drug-related acts.

To read more about **juvenile drug courts**, go to this website: http://www.ojjdp.gov/pubs/248406.pdf.

being implemented across the United States. Two of these kinds of courts are **teen courts** and juvenile **drug courts**. Because of their rising popularity and importance to the juvenile justice system, each is the subject of a special feature in this chapter.

Teen Courts   Also called youth courts, teen courts are an alternative to traditional forms of juvenile court that have received increased attention of late in an effort to relieve overcrowding and provide a more effective response to reducing recidivism. The Evidence-Based Juvenile Justice box entitled "Teen Courts" discusses this alternative, and the Case Profile describes a case handled in teen court.

Drug Courts   In a systematic review and meta-analysis of the effects of drug courts, Ojmarrh Mitchell and his colleagues found that drug courts are an effective alternative crime control measure to reduce recidivism rates among

- *Cost savings*. Teen courts usually depend heavily on youth and adult volunteers. If managed properly, they may handle a substantial number of offenders at relatively little cost to the community.

- *Community cohesion*. A well-structured and expansive teen court program may affect the entire community by increasing public appreciation of the legal system, enhancing community-court relationships, encouraging greater respect for the law among youth, and promoting volunteerism among both adults and youth.

The teen court movement is one of the fastest growing delinquency intervention programs in the country. As of February 2016 (latest data available), there were approximately 1,400 teen courts in operation in 49 states and the District of Columbia, serving an estimated 110,000 to 125,000 young offenders each year; another 100,000 youths benefit from their participation as volunteers. Some recent evaluations (but not all) of teen courts have found that they did not "widen the net" of justice by handling cases that in the absence of the teen court would have been subject to a lesser level of processing. Also, the OJJDP Evaluation of Teen Courts Project, which covered four states—Alaska, Arizona, Maryland, and Missouri—and compared 500 first-time offending youths referred to teen court with 500 similar youths handled by the regular juvenile justice system, found that six-month recidivism rates were lower for those who went through the teen court program in three of the four jurisdictions. Importantly, in these three teen courts, the six-month recidivism rates were under 10 percent. Similar findings were reported in a rigorous evaluation of a teen court in Florida and in one for repeat offenders in Washington State. However, other recent evaluations of teen courts in Kentucky, New Mexico, and Delaware indicate that short-term recidivism rates range from 25 to 30 percent. A couple of recent evaluations report no effects or gender differences in effects on delinquency. The conclusions from the OJJDP teen court evaluation may be the best guide for future experimentation with teen courts:

Teen courts and youth courts may be preferable to the normal juvenile justice process in jurisdictions that do not, or cannot, provide meaningful sanctions for all young, first-time juvenile offenders. In jurisdictions that do not provide meaningful sanctions and services for these offenders, youth court may still perform just as well as a more traditional, adult-run program.

CRITICAL THINKING

1. Could teen courts be used to try serious criminal acts, such as burglary and robbery?

2. Is a conflict of interest created when teens judge the behavior of other teens? Does the fact that they themselves may one day become defendants in a teen court influence decision making?

SOURCES: California Association of Youth Courts, "Youth Courts: Fact Sheet," http://calyouthcourts.com/about/about-youth-courts (accessed September 2016); Jeffrey A. Butts, John K. Roman, and Jennifer Lynn-Whaley, "Varieties of Juvenile Court: Nonspecialized Courts, Teen Courts, Drug Courts, and Mental Health Courts," in Barry C. Feld and Donna M. Bishop, eds., *The Oxford Handbook of Juvenile Crime and Juvenile Justice* (New York: Oxford University Press, 2012); Michael Norris, Sarah Twill, and Chigon Kim, "Smells Like Teen Spirit: Evaluating a Midwestern Teen Court," *Crime and Delinquency* 57:199–221 (2011); Denise M. Wilson, Denise C. Gottfredson, and Wendy Povitsky Stickle, "Gender Differences in Effects of Teen Courts on Delinquency: A Theory-Guided Evaluation," *Journal of Criminal Justice* 37:21–27 (2009); Deborah Kirby Forgays and Lisa DeMilio, "Is Teen Court Effective for Repeat Offenders? A Test of the Restorative Justice Approach," *International Journal of Offender Therapy and Comparative Criminology* 49:107–118 (2005); Andrew Rasmussen, "Teen Court Referral, Sentencing, and Subsequent Recidivism: Two Proportional Hazards Models and a Little Speculation," *Crime and Delinquency* 50:615–635 (2004); Jeffrey A. Butts and Janeen Buck, "Teen Courts: A Focus on Research," *Juvenile Justice Bulletin October 2000* (Washington, DC: Office of Juvenile Justice and Delinquency Prevention, 2000); Paige Harrison, James R. Maupin, and G. Larry Mays, "Teen Court: An Examination of Processes and Outcomes," *Crime and Delinquency* 47:243–264 (2001); Anthony P. Logalbo and Charlene M. Callahan, "An Evaluation of a Teen Court as a Juvenile Crime Diversion Program," *Juvenile and Family Court Journal* 52:1–11 (2001).

drug-involved offenders. Of the 154 independent evaluations included in the review, only 34 (22 percent) were of juvenile drug courts.[71] This small number is explained, in part, by the relatively recent interest of juvenile justice agencies in experimenting with drug courts.[72] The findings of the 34 juvenile drug court evaluations show that this is an effective intervention for reducing juvenile recidivism, but the effects are substantially smaller compared to adult drug courts.[73] A long-term follow-up of juveniles who successfully completed drug court in Tennessee found that their involvement in adult crime was lower for felonies but not for misdemeanors.[74] Intriguingly, a nine-site national study of juvenile drug courts by Christopher Sullivan and his colleagues found that they were largely ineffective in reducing recidivism. The research draws attention to the need to distinguish between adult and juvenile drug courts and calls for greater adherence to principles of effective intervention.[75] Drug courts are the topic of the Youth Stories feature, "Chrystal Carreras."

case profile

Jennifer's Story

JENNIFER, a bright young Caucasian female, lived in a fast-paced urban community with her parents and two younger brothers. At 16 years old, she was in trouble. Jennifer went to a party one night and found out that her boyfriend, Sam, whom she had dated for several months and with whom she felt she had a serious relationship, had been cheating on her with a classmate. She was irate. Although Sam was not at the party, the other girl was there. She and Jennifer had words and threw a few punches at each other. Both were asked to leave, but Jennifer refused and the police were called to the party. Jennifer received a ticket for disorderly conduct.

At Jennifer's initial hearing on the matter, she was told about youth court. If she would agree to plead guilty to the charge and attend and cooperate with youth court recommendations, her record would be cleared. Jennifer agreed to the youth court diversion program and the referral was made. Facing a jury of her peers, she explained what happened the night she received the ticket. The youth court encourages family involvement, so Jennifer's mother accompanied her for support. Jennifer explained that she had recently lost a close relative and that she had been under a lot of stress when the fight occurred. She was sorry for her behavior and wanted things to be better.

The jury "sentenced" Jennifer to attend counseling and a drug and alcohol pre-assessment, as well as to write a paper on how to better handle her anger. Defendants in the court are also required to serve on two future juries themselves and given 90 days to comply, or the case is returned to juvenile court for disposition. Jennifer cooperated with the requirements, and her record was cleared. She completed her jury duty and has chosen to continue as a regular volunteer. According to the program director, Jennifer is an "excellent volunteer with great leadership potential." She avoided any further delinquent behavior, graduated from high school, and is now pursuing a degree in computer science.

CRITICAL THINKING

1. Some might argue that Jennifer's referral to youth court was too lenient. Do you think this was an appropriate treatment consistent with *parens patriae*?

2. What types of juvenile delinquent behavior/charges would not be appropriate for a teen court? What are the most appropriate types of cases for this intervention and why?

3. If you were the program director of a teen court, what would you do if the jury was being too punitive with a peer? It is important to respect the jury's decisions, but there are times when an adult may need to step in. What would be the best process for this?

Future of Juvenile Justice

The National Research Council and Institute of Medicine's Panel on Juvenile Crime expressed alarm over an increasingly punitive juvenile justice system and called for a number of changes to uphold the importance of treatment for juveniles. One of their recommendations is particularly noteworthy:

The federal government should assist the states through federal funding and incentives to reduce the use of secure detention and secure confinement, by developing community-based alternatives. The effectiveness of such programs both for the protection of the community and the benefit of the youth in their charge should be monitored.[76]

Although calling for reforms to the juvenile justice system was a key element of the national panel's final report, panel members were equally or more concerned with the need to prevent delinquency before it occurs and intervene with at-risk children and adolescents. Importantly, there is growing public support for prevention and intervention programs designed to reduce delinquency,[77] not to mention

youth STORIES

Chrystal Carreras

As of 2012, there were 451 juvenile drug courts operating in 49 states and the District of Columbia, Guam, and Northern Mariana Islands; another 48 are in the planning process. These special courts have jurisdiction over the burgeoning number of cases involving substance abuse and trafficking. Although juvenile drug courts operate under a number of different frameworks, the aim is to place nonviolent first offenders into intensive treatment programs rather than in a custodial institution.

One of these juvenile drug courts is the Recovery and Progress Court at the Lane County Juvenile Justice Center in Eugene, Oregon. The RAP Court—as it is fondly called—has the distinction of being the first juvenile drug court in the state. The court was established by a number of leading juvenile justice experts and advocates, including Lane County's juvenile court judge Kip Leonard, former youth services director Steve Carmichael, and juvenile public defender Peter Warburg, who were committed to addressing the key causes of illicit drug use by juveniles. The court follows a hybrid treatment-justice model, providing each participant with individual and family counseling, intensive monitoring and treatment, and judicial check-ins on a weekly basis. It is described in this manner: "Together, court workers and family members identify and build up each youth's strengths, reward their progress, and hold them accountable when they stumble."

One of the court's first graduates was Chrystal Carreras, now 31 and shown in the photograph. Chrystal started using drugs at an early age. By 11, she was smoking pot, and by 14, she had moved on to methamphetamine. Her drug use was fueled by problems at home, and it was not long before she came to the attention of police; by 15, she was arrested again and enrolled in the RAP Court. As she recalled in an interview for the local newspaper, the *Register-Guard*:

> I didn't get along with my mom, so I was out on the streets even before I started using meth. I was homeless, in and out of jail. I really believe I would have ended up in a really bad place by now—probably in prison or dead—if it hadn't been for RAP Court.

Chrystal Carreras stands in front of the County Juvenile Justice Center in Eugene, Oregon, where she was one of the first graduates of the juvenile drug court.

How do the different components of the drug court benefit juvenile substance abusers? Some argue that these programs need to be multifaceted to address the different needs of the juveniles. It may be the case that each juvenile who succeeds in the program takes something away that is special to her or his own circumstance. This was certainly the case with Chrystal. She attributes her success in staying away from drugs to the court ordering her to live with her grandmother. She needed that structure and the responsibility that came with it. Also important was the individual-level support that she received from Judge Leonard and her probation officer. Another component of the RAP Court, which is tremendously popular with all of the participants, is that upon successfully completing the program the youths—at their graduation ceremony—get the chance to literally tear up their juvenile "rap sheet"—their official record of delinquent activity. Chrystal is especially grateful for this. It allowed her to start a whole new life.

CRITICAL THINKING

1. Could juvenile drug courts also work with violent offenders? What about repeat offenders? Explain some of the challenges.

SOURCES: Karen McCowan, "The Successful Recovery and Progress Court for Lane County Youth Marks 10 Years," *Register-Guard*, April 15, 2010; "Summary of Drug Court Activity by State and County: Juvenile/Family Drug Courts" (Washington, DC: Bureau of Justice Assistance Drug Court Clearinghouse at American University, November 30, 2012), p. 44; Holly Hills, Jennie L. Shufelt, and Joseph J. Cocozza, *Evidence-Based Practice Recommendations for Juvenile Drug Courts* (Delmar, NY: National Center for Mental Health and Juvenile Justice, 2009); Kathryn E. McCollister, Michael T. French, Ashli J. Sheidow, Scott W. Henggeler, and Colleen A. Halliday-Boykins, "Estimating the Differential Costs of Criminal Activity for Juvenile Drug Court Participants: Challenges and Recommendations," *Journal of Behavioral Health Services and Research* 36:111–126 (2009); Office of Juvenile Justice and Delinquency Prevention, *How OJJDP Is Serving Children, Families, and Communities: 2008 Annual Report* (Washington, DC: US Department of Justice, OJJDP, 2009).

a high level of public disapproval for abolishing the juvenile justice system in favor of a harsher, criminal justice system response.[78] The panel also called attention to the need for more rigorous experimentation with prevention and intervention programs that have demonstrated success in reducing risk factors associated with delinquency.[79] Quite a few states, such as Pennsylvania, Connecticut, Maine, and Washington, have begun to incorporate a research-based approach to guide juvenile justice programming and policy.[80]

It should be noted that there is some, albeit limited, evidence that points to a slowdown of sorts in recent years in this get-tough approach toward juvenile offenders. An analysis of state juvenile transfer laws finds that there has been a considerable reduction in the number of states that have expanded their transfer provisions. At the same time, very few states have reversed their restrictive transfer laws.[81]

Those who support the juvenile justice concept believe that it is too soon to write off the rehabilitative ideal that has always underpinned the separate treatment of juvenile offenders. They note that fears of a juvenile crime wave are misplaced and that the actions of a few violent children should not mask the needs of millions who can benefit from solicitous treatment rather than harsh punishments. And although a get-tough approach may reduce the incidence of some crimes, economic analysis indicates that the costs incurred by placing children in more punitive secure facilities exceeds the benefits accrued in crime reduction.[82]

SUMMARY

1 Illustrate the major social changes leading to the creation of the first modern juvenile court in Chicago in 1899

- Urbanization created a growing number of at-risk youth in the nation's cities.

- Reformers known as child savers sought to create an independent category of delinquent offender and keep their treatment separate from adults.

2 Discuss some of the landmark Supreme Court decisions that have influenced present-day juvenile justice procedures

- Over the past five decades, the US Supreme Court and lower courts have granted procedural safeguards and the protection of due process in juvenile courts.

- Major court decisions have laid down the constitutional requirements for juvenile court proceedings.

- In years past, the protections currently afforded to both adults and children were not available to children.

3 Identify how children are processed by the juvenile justice system, beginning with arrest and concluding with reentry into society

- The juvenile justice process consists of a series of steps: (1) police investigation, (2) intake procedure in the juvenile court, (3) pretrial procedures used for juvenile offenders, and (4) adjudication, disposition, and postdispositional procedures.

4 Explain the conflicting values in contemporary juvenile justice

- Some experts want to get tough with young criminals, while others want to focus on rehabilitation.

- Crime control advocates want to reduce the court's jurisdiction over juveniles charged with serious crimes and liberalize the prosecutor's ability to try them in adult courts.

- Child advocates suggest that the court scale back its judicial role and transfer its functions to community groups and social service agencies.

5 Compare key similarities and differences between the adult and juvenile justice systems

- One similarity is the right to receive *Miranda* warnings; this applies to juveniles as well as adults.

- One difference is that juvenile proceedings are not considered criminal, while adult proceedings are.

6 Argue the pros and cons of the juvenile justice system's goal to treat rather than punish and assess if this goal is being met today

- There has been a movement to toughen the juvenile justice system, and because of this, many view the importance of treatment as having been greatly diminished.

- Proponents of treatment argue that it is best suited to the developmental needs of juveniles.
- Critics contend that treatment simply serves to mollycoddle juveniles and reduces the deterrent value of the juvenile court.

7 Evaluate the key elements of a comprehensive juvenile justice strategy to deal with juvenile delinquency

- A comprehensive juvenile justice strategy has been developed to preserve the need for treatment services for juveniles while using appropriate sanctions to hold juveniles accountable for their actions.
- Elements of this strategy include delinquency prevention, intervention programs, graduated sanctions, improvement of institutional programs, and treating juveniles like adults.
- New courts, such as drug courts and teen courts, are now in place.

8 Discuss the differences between prevention and intervention efforts to reduce juvenile delinquency

- Prevention measures target children and teens in an effort to prevent the onset of delinquency.
- Intervention efforts target children and teens considered at higher risk for delinquency and are designed to ward off involvement in more serious delinquent behavior.

9 Identify and comment on pressing issues in the future of juvenile justice

- The future of the juvenile justice system continues to be debated.
- There are some promising signs, such as juvenile crime rates being lower than in decades past, public support for prevention and intervention programs, and some states beginning to incorporate research-based initiatives to guide juvenile justice programming and policy.

KEY TERMS

House of Refuge, p. 491
Children's Aid Society, p. 493
orphan trains, p. 494
Society for the Prevention of Cruelty to Children, p. 494

Law Enforcement Assistance Administration (LEAA), p. 499
juvenile justice process, p. 501
detention hearing, p. 501
adjudicatory hearing, p. 502

bifurcated process, p. 503
disposition, p. 503
petition, p. 505
teen courts, p. 510
drug courts, p. 510

QUESTIONS FOR DISCUSSION

1. What factors precipitated the development of the Illinois Juvenile Court Act of 1899?

2. One of the most significant reforms in dealing with the juvenile offender was the opening of the New York House of Refuge in 1825. What were the social and judicial consequences of this reform on the juvenile justice system?

3. The child savers have been accused of wanting to control the lives of poor and immigrant children for their own benefit. Are there any parallels to the child saving movement in modern-day America?

4. Should there be a juvenile justice system, or should juveniles who commit serious crimes be treated as adults, and the others handled by social welfare agencies?

5. The Supreme Court has made a number of major decisions in the area of juvenile justice. What are these decisions? What is their impact on the juvenile justice system?

6. What is the meaning of the term *procedural due process of law*? Explain why and how procedural due process has had an impact on juvenile justice.

7. The formal components of the criminal justice system are often considered to be the police, the court, and the correctional agency. How do these components relate to the major areas of the juvenile justice system? Is the operation of justice similar in the juvenile and adult systems?

8. What role has the federal government played in the juvenile justice system over the last 30 years?

VIEWPOINT

Fourteen-year-old Daphne, a product of New York City's best private schools, lives with her wealthy family in a luxury condo in a fashionable neighborhood. Her father is an executive at a local financial services conglomerate and earns close to a million dollars per year. Daphne is always in trouble at school, and teachers report she is impulsive and has poor self-control. At times she can be kind and warm, but on other occasions she is obnoxious, unpredictable, insecure, and demanding of attention. She is overly self-conscious about her body and has a drinking problem.

Despite repeated promises to get her life together, Daphne likes to hang out at night in a local park, drinking with neighborhood kids. On more than one occasion she has gone to the park with her friend and confidant Chris, a quiet boy with his own personal problems. His parents have separated and he is prone to suffer severe anxiety attacks. He has been suspended from school and diagnosed with depression, for which he takes two drugs—an antidepressant and a sedative.

One night, the two met up with Michael, a 44-year-old with a long history of alcoholism. After a night of drinking, a fight broke out and Michael was stabbed, his throat cut, and his body dumped in a pond. Soon after the attack, Daphne called 911, telling police that a friend "jumped in the lake and didn't come out." Police searched the area and found Michael's slashed and stabbed body in the water; the body had been disemboweled in an attempt to sink it. When the authorities traced the call, Daphne was arrested, and she confessed to police that she had helped Chris murder the victim.

During an interview with court psychiatrists, Daphne admitted she participated in the killing but could not articulate what caused her to get involved. She had been drinking and remembers little of the events. She said she was flirting with Michael, and Chris stabbed him in a jealous rage. She spoke in a flat, hollow voice and showed little remorse for her actions. It was a spur-of-the-moment thing, she claimed, and, after all, it was Chris who had the knife and not she. Later, Chris claimed that Daphne instigated the fight, egged him on, taunting him that he was too scared to kill someone. Chris said that Daphne, while drunk, often talked of killing an adult because she hates older people, especially her parents.

If Daphne is tried as a juvenile she can be kept in institutions until she is 17; the sentence could be expanded to age 21, but only if she has behavior problems in custody and demonstrates conclusive need for further secure treatment.

- Should the case of Daphne be dealt with in the juvenile court, even though the maximum possible sentence she can receive is two to six years? If not, over what kind of cases should the juvenile court have jurisdiction?

- How does the concept of *parens patriae* apply in cases such as Daphne's?

- If you believe that the juvenile court is not equipped to handle cases of extremely violent youth, then should it be abolished?

- What reforms must be made in the juvenile justice system to rehabilitate adolescents like Daphne? Or should it even try?

DOING RESEARCH ON THE WEB

Before you answer these questions, you may want to learn more about this topic by checking out the websites of the National Center for Juvenile Justice (http://www.ncjj.org/) and the Urban Institute (http://www.urban.org/), both of which specialize in research and technical assistance related to juvenile justice. The Washington State Institute for Public Policy (http://www.wsipp.wa.gov/) carries out research at legislative direction on juvenile justice and delinquency, among other issues, and ensures that studies answer relevant policy questions.

The Office of Juvenile Justice and Delinquency Prevention (http://www.ojjdp.gov/) has information on prevention and intervention programs in addition to many other aspects of juvenile justice. The Office of the Surgeon General (http://www.surgeongeneral.gov/) is especially concerned with violence prevention.

NOTES

All URLs accessed September 2016.

1. *Graham v. Florida*, 560 U.S. ___ (2010).
2. 567 U.S. ___ (2012).
3. Robert M. Mennel, "Origins of the Juvenile Court: Changing Perspectives on the Legal Rights of Juvenile Delinquents," *Crime and Delinquency* 18:68–78 (1972).
4. Anthony Salerno, "The Child Saving Movement: Altruism or Conspiracy," *Juvenile and Family Court Journal* 42:37 (1991).
5. Frank J. Coppa and Philip C. Dolce, *Cities in Transition: From the Ancient World to Urban America* (Chicago: Nelson Hall, 1974), p. 220.
6. Robert Mennel, "Attitudes and Policies Toward Juvenile Delinquency," *Crime and Justice*, Vol. 5 (Chicago: University of Chicago Press, 1983), p. 198.
7. Anthony M. Platt, *The Child Savers: The Invention of Delinquency* (Chicago: University of Chicago Press, 1969).
8. See Anne Meis Knupfer, *Reform and Resistance: Gender, Delinquency, and America's First Juvenile Court* (London: Routledge, 2001).
9. Geoff K. Ward, *The Black Child-Savers: Racial Democracy and Juvenile Justice* (Chicago: University of Chicago Press, 2012).
10. This section is based on material from the New York State Archives, *The Greatest Reform School in the World: A Guide to the Records of the New York House of Refuge: A Brief History 1824–1857* (Albany, NY, 2001); Sanford J. Fox, "Juvenile Justice Reform: A Historical Perspective," *Stanford Law Review* 22:1187–1229 (1970).
11. Robert S. Pickett, *House of Refuge—Origins of Juvenile Reform in New York State, 1815–1857* (Syracuse, NY: Syracuse University Press, 1969).
12. Mennel, "Origins of the Juvenile Court," pp. 69–70.
13. Sanford Fox, "The Early History of the Court" from *The Future of Children* (Los Altos, CA: David and Lucile Packard Foundation, 1996).
14. Salerno, "The Child Saving Movement," p. 37.
15. Platt, *The Child Savers*.
16. Ibid., p. 116.
17. Randall Shelden and Lynn Osborne, "'For Their Own Good': Class Interests and the Child Saving Movement in Memphis, Tennessee, 1900–1917," *Criminology* 27:747–767 (1989).
18. US Department of Justice Office of Juvenile Justice and Delinquency Prevention, *Two Hundred Years of American Criminal Justice: An LEAA Bicentennial Study* (Washington, DC: LEAA, 1976).
19. New York State Law Ch. 412, Laws of 1929; Ch. 538, Laws of 1932.
20. Beverly Smith, "Female Admissions and Paroles of the Western House of Refuge in the 1880s: An Historical Example of Community Corrections," *Journal of Research in Crime and Delinquency* 26:36–66 (1989).
21. Sanford J. Fox, "Juvenile Justice Reform: A Historical Perspective," *Stanford Law Review* 22:1187–1229 (1970).
22. Fox, "The Early History of the Court."
23. Elizabeth Pleck, "Criminal Approaches to Family Violence, 1640–1980," in Lloyd Ohlin and Michael Tonry, eds., *Family Violence* (Chicago: University of Chicago Press, 1989), pp. 19–58.
24. Elizabeth Pleck, *Domestic Tyranny: The Making of Social Policy Against Family Violence from Colonial Times to the Present* (New York: Oxford University Press, 1987), pp. 28–30.
25. Linda Gordon, *Family Violence and Social Control* (New York: Viking, 1988).
26. Kathleen Block and Donna Hale, "Turf Wars in the Progressive Era of Juvenile Justice: The Relationship of Private and Public Child Care Agencies," *Crime and Delinquency* 37:225–241 (1991).
27. Theodore Ferdinand, "Juvenile Delinquency or Juvenile Justice: Which Came First?" *Criminology* 27:79–106 (1989).
28. *In re Gault*, 387 U.S. 1, 87 S.Ct. 1428, 18 L.Ed.2d 527 (1967).
29. Fox, "The Early History of the Court," p. 4.
30. Ibid.
31. Mary Odem and Steven Schlossman, "Guardians of Virtue: The Juvenile Court and Female Delinquency in Early 20th-Century Los Angeles," *Crime and Delinquency* 37:186–203 (1991).
32. Fox, "The Early History of the Court," p. 4.
33. John Sutton, "Bureaucrats and Entrepreneurs: Institutional Responses to Deviant Children in the United States, 1890–1920," *American Journal of Sociology* 95:1367–1400 (1990).
34. Ibid., p. 1383.
35. Marguerite Rosenthal, "Reforming the Juvenile Correctional Institution: Efforts of the U.S. Children's Bureau in the 1930s," *Journal of Sociology and Social Welfare* 14:47–74 (1987); see also David Steinhart, "Status Offenses," The Center for the Future of Children, The Juvenile Court (Los Altos, CA: David and Lucile Packard Foundation, 1996).
36. For an overview of these developments, see Theodore Ferdinand, "History Overtakes the Juvenile Justice System," *Crime and Delinquency* 37:204–224 (1991).
37. N.Y. Fam.Ct. Act, Art. 7, Sec. 712 (Consol. 1962).
38. *Kent v. United States*, 383 U.S. 541, 86 S.Ct. 1045, 16 L.Ed.2d 84 (1966); *In re Gault*, 387 U.S. 1, 87 S.Ct. 1428, 18 L.Ed.2d 527 (1967): Juveniles have the right to notice, counsel, confrontation, and cross-examination, and to the privileges against self-incrimination in juvenile court proceedings. *In re Winship*, 397 U.S. 358, 90 S.Ct. 1068, 25 L.Ed.2d 368 (1970): Proof beyond a reasonable doubt is necessary for conviction in juvenile proceedings. *Breed v. Jones*, 421 U.S. 519, 95 S.Ct. 1779, 44 L.Ed.2d 346 (1975): Jeopardy attaches in a juvenile court adjudicatory hearing, thus barring subsequent prosecution for the same offense as an adult.
39. Brandon C. Welsh and Rebecca D. Pfeffer, "Reclaiming Crime Prevention in an Age of Punishment: An American History," *Punishment and Society* 15:534–553 (2013).
40. Public Law 90-351, Title I—Omnibus Safe Streets and Crime Control Act of 1968, 90th Congress, June 1968.
41. National Advisory Commission on Criminal Justice Standards and Goals, *A National Strategy to Reduce Crime* (Washington, DC: US Government Printing Office, 1973).
42. Juvenile Justice and Delinquency Prevention Act of 1974, Public Law 93-415 (1974). For a critique of this legislation, see Ira Schwartz, *Justice for Juveniles—Rethinking the Best Interests of the Child* (Lexington, MA: D. C. Heath, 1989), p. 175.
43. For an extensive summary of the Violent Crime Control and Law Enforcement Act of 1994, see *Criminal Law Reporter* 55:2305–2430 (1994).
44. Shay Bilchik, "A Juvenile Justice System for the 21st Century," *Crime and Delinquency* 44:89 (1998).
45. For a comprehensive view of juvenile law, see Craig Hemmens, Benjamin Steiner, and David Mueller, *Criminal Justice Case Briefs: Significant Cases in Juvenile Justice* (New York: Oxford University Press, 2004).
46. For an excellent review of the juvenile process, see Jeffrey Butts and Gregory Halemba, *Waiting for Justice—Moving Young Offenders Through the Juvenile Court Process* (Pittsburgh: National Center for Juvenile Justice, 1996).
47. Federal Bureau of Investigation, *Crime in the United States 2014* (Washington, DC: Government Printing Office, 2015), Table 68.
48. William H. Barton, "Detention," in Barry C. Feld and Donna M. Bishop, eds., *The Oxford Handbook of Juvenile Crime and Juvenile Justice* (New York: Oxford University Press, 2012).
49. K. L. Jordan and David L. Myers, "Juvenile Transfer and Deterrence: Reexamining the Effectiveness of a 'Get Tough' Policy," *Crime and Delinquency* 57:247–270 (2011).
50. Melissa Sickmund, T. J. Sladky, W. Kang, and Charles Puzzanchera, "Easy Access to the Census of Juveniles in Residential Placement: 1997–2013," 2015, http://www.ojjdp.gov/ojstatbb/ezacjrp/.
51. Edward P. Mulvey and Carol A. Schubert, "Youth in Prison and Beyond," in Feld and Bishop, eds., *The Oxford Handbook of Juvenile Crime and Juvenile Justice*.
52. Donna M. Bishop and Barry C. Feld, "Trends in Juvenile Justice Policy and Practice," in Feld and Bishop, eds., *The Oxford Handbook of Juvenile Crime and Juvenile Justice*.
53. Fox Butterfield, "Justice Besieged," *New York Times*, July 21, 1997, p. A16.
54. National Conference of State Legislatures, *A Legislator's Guide to Comprehensive Juvenile Justice, Juvenile Detention, and Corrections* (Denver: National Conference of State Legislators, 1996).
55. James C. Howell, Marion R. Kelly, James Palmer, and Ronald L. Mangum, "Integrating Child Welfare, Juvenile Justice, and Other Agencies in a Continuum of Services," *Child Welfare* 83:143–156 (2004).
56. Daniel P. Mears, Tracey L. Shollenberger, Janeen B. Willison, Colleen E. Owens, and Jeffrey A. Butts, "Practitioner Views of Priorities, Policies, and Practices in Juvenile Justice," *Crime and Delinquency* 56:535–563 (2010).
57. Ibid, p. 557.

58. David P. Farrington and Brandon C. Welsh, *Saving Children from a Life of Crime: Early Risk Factors and Effective Interventions* (New York: Oxford University Press, 2007).

59. Ibid.

60. Brandon C. Welsh, David P. Farrington, and B. Raffan Gowar, "Benefit-Cost Analysis of Crime Prevention Programs," in Michael Tonry, ed., *Crime and Justice: A Review of Research*, Vol. 44 (Chicago: University of Chicago Press, 2015); Stephanie Lee, Steve Aos, Elizabeth K. Drake, Anne Pennucci, Marna G. Miller, and Laurie Anderson, *Return on Investment: Evidence-Based Options to Improve Statewide Outcomes* (Olympia, WA: Washington State Institute for Public Policy, 2012).

61. Eliana Garces, Duncan Thomas, and Janet Currie, "Longer-Term Effects of Head Start," *American Economic Review* 92:999–1012 (2002).

62. Christina Weiland and Hirokazu Yoshikawa, "Impacts of Prekindergarten Program on Children's Mathematics, Language, Literacy, Executive Function, and Emotional Skills," *Child Development* 84:2112–2130 (2013).

63. Ned Calonge, "Community Interventions to Prevent Violence: Translation into Public Health Practice," *American Journal of Preventive Medicine* 28(2S1):4–5 (2005); Anne K. Duggan, Amy Windham, Elizabeth McFarlane, Loretta Fuddy, Charles Rohde, Sharon Buchbinder, and Calvin Sia, "Hawaii's Healthy Start Program of Home Visitation for At-Risk Families: Evaluation of Family Identification, Family Engagement, and Service Delivery," *Pediatrics* 105:250–259 (2000).

64. *Youth Violence: A Report of the Surgeon General* (Rockville, MD: US Department of Health and Human Services, 2001).

65. Jean Baldwin Grossman and Joseph P. Tierney, "Does Mentoring Work? An Impact Study of the Big Brothers Big Sisters Program," *Evaluation Review* 22:403–426 (1998).

66. Thomas L. Sexton and Charles W. Turner, "The Effectiveness of Functional Family Therapy for Youth with Behavioral Problems in a Community Practice Setting," *Journal of Family Psychology* 24:339–348 (2012).

67. Patricia Chamberlain, Leslie D. Leve, and David S. DeGarmo, "Multidimensional Treatment Foster Care for Girls in the Juvenile Justice System: 2-Year Follow-Up of a Randomized Clinical Trial," *Journal of Consulting and Clinical Psychology* 75:187–193 (2007).

68. Brandon C. Welsh and Peter W. Greenwood, "Making It Happen: State Progress in Implementing Evidence-Based Programs for Delinquent Youth," *Youth Violence and Juvenile Justice* 13:243–257 (2015); Peter W. Greenwood and Brandon C. Welsh, "Promoting Evidence-Based Practice in Delinquency Prevention at the State Level: Principles, Progress, and Policy Directions," *Criminology and Public Policy* 11:493–513 (2012).

69. James C. Howell, *Preventing and Reducing Juvenile Delinquency: A Comprehensive Framework*, 2nd ed. (Thousand Oaks, CA: Sage Publications, 2009), p. 220; see also Shelley Zavlek, *Planning Community-Based Facilities for Violent Juvenile Offenders as Part of a System of Graduated Sanctions* (Washington, DC: OJJDP Juvenile Justice Bulletin, 2005).

70. Peter W. Greenwood and Susan Turner, "Juvenile Crime and Juvenile Justice," in James Q. Wilson and Joan Petersilia, eds., *Crime and Public Policy* (New York: Oxford University Press, 2011).

71. Ojmarrh Mitchell, David B. Wilson, Amy Eggers, and Doris Layton MacKenzie, "Assessing the Effectiveness of Drug Courts on Recidivism: A Meta-Analytic Review of Traditional and Non-Traditional Drug Courts," *Journal of Criminal Justice* 40:60–71 (2012).

72. Laurie Chassin, "Juvenile Justice and Substance Abuse," *The Future of Children* 18:165–183 (2008), at 170.

73. Mitchell, Wilson, Eggers, and MacKenzie, "Assessing the Effectiveness of Drug Courts on Recidivism: A Meta-Analytic Review of Traditional and Non-Traditional Drug Courts," Table 3, p. 64.

74. W. Craig Carter and R. Donald Barker, "Does Completion of Juvenile Drug Court Deter Adult Criminality?" *Journal of Social Work Practice in the Addictions* 11:181–193 (2011).

75. Christopher J. Sullivan, Lesli Blair, Edward Latessa, and Carrie Coen Sullivan, "Juvenile Drug Courts and Recidivism: Results from a Multisite Outcome Study," *Justice Quarterly* 33:291–318 (2016); Lesli Blair, Carrie Sullivan, Edward Latessa, and Christopher J. Sullivan, "Juvenile Drug Courts: A Process, Outcome, and Impact Evaluation," *Juvenile Justice Bulletin*, May 2015, Office of Juvenile Justice and Delinquency Prevention.

76. Joan McCord, Cathy Spatz Widom, and Nancy A. Crowell, *Juvenile Crime, Juvenile Justice*, panel on Juvenile Crime: Prevention, Treatment, and Control (Washington, DC: National Academy Press), p. 224.

77. Francis T. Cullen, Brenda A. Vose, Cheryl N. Lero, and James D. Unnever, "Public Support for Early Intervention: Is Child Saving a 'Habit of the Heart'?" *Victims and Offenders* 2:108–124 (2007).

78. Daniel P. Mears, Carter Hay, Marc Gertz, and Christina Mancini, "Public Opinion and the Foundation of the Juvenile Court," *Criminology* 45:223–258 (2007), p. 246.

79. McCord, Spatz Widom, and Crowell, *Juvenile Crime, Juvenile Justice*, p. 152.

80. Brandon C. Welsh and Peter W. Greenwood, "Making It Happen: Progress in Implementing Evidence-Based Programs for Delinquent Youth," *Youth Violence and Juvenile Justice* 13:243–257 (2015).

81. Patrick Griffin, Sean Addie, Benjamin Adams, and Kathy Firestine, *Trying Juveniles as Adults: An Analysis of State Transfer Laws and Reporting* (Washington, DC: Office of Juvenile Justice and Delinquency Prevention, 2011).

82. Lee, Aos, Drake, Pennucci, Miller, and Anderson, *Return on Investment: Evidence-Based Options to Improve Statewide Outcomes*.

CHAPTER 14
Police Work with Juveniles

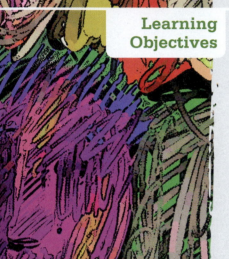

Learning Objectives

1. Identify key historical events that have shaped juvenile policing in America today
2. Discuss the key roles and responsibilities of the police in responding to juvenile offenders
3. Describe the organization and management of police services for juveniles
4. Identify the major court cases that have influenced police practices
5. Discuss key legal aspects of police work, including search and seizure and custodial interrogation, and how they apply to juveniles
6. Describe police use of discretion and factors that influence discretion
7. Articulate the importance of police use of discretion with juveniles and some of the associated problems
8. Appraise the major policing strategies to prevent delinquency
9. Compare the pros and cons of police using different delinquency prevention strategies

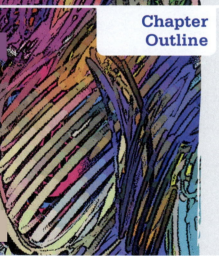

Chapter Outline

History of Juvenile Policing

Community Policing in the New Millennium
    The Community Policing Model

The Police and Juvenile Offenders
    Police Services
    Police Roles
    Police and Violent Juvenile Crime

Police and the Rule of Law
    The Arrest Procedure
    Search and Seizure
    Custodial Interrogation

Discretionary Justice
    Environmental Factors
    Police Policy
    Situational Factors
    Bias and Police Discretion

Police Work and Delinquency Prevention
    Aggressive Law Enforcement
    Police in Schools
    Community-Based Policing Services
    Problem-Oriented Policing

Future of Juvenile Policing

Chapter Features

Focus on Delinquency: Juvenile Views About Police

Cyber Delinquency: Policing Juveniles in Cyberspace

Youth Stories: Latin King Goonies

Focus on Delinquency: Juvenile Race, Gender, and Ethnicity in Police Decision Making

Case Profile: Rico's Story

Evidence-Based Juvenile Justice—Intervention: Pulling Levers Policing

IN THE EARLY EVENING OF March 31, 2006, six gunshots rang out in the Wilson-Haverstick housing project in Trenton, New Jersey. One of these shots—from a .45 caliber handgun—struck 7-year-old Tajahnique Lee as she was riding her bicycle to her grandmother's apartment. The bullet passed in one cheek and out the other, knocking out two molars and clipping the tip of her tongue. Tajahnique was rushed to the emergency room at the local Trenton hospital. She survived.

As shocking as this near-tragedy was, the events that have since transpired have become even more troubling for the police. Trenton police believe that the stray bullet that struck Tajahnique was intended for a gang member affiliated with the Gangsta Killer Bloods who was driving through the housing complex. The police also believe that the bullet, along with the five others that were shot, came from the gun of a member of the local rival gang known as Sex Money Murder, part of the larger Bloods gang. The police interviewed more than 100 residents and rounded up an equal number of suspected gang members in the days following the shooting. This led to the arrest of two members of Sex Money Murder.

Abandoned homes in Trenton, New Jersey, the city where Tajahnique Lee, age 7, was shot.

But this would be as far as the police would get. The one eyewitness to the shooting changed his story; others who had cooperated earlier in the investigation refused to talk further with police, and even the shooting victim's grandmother and other family members were not willing to talk with police. One neighbor—who wished to remain anonymous—said of the little girl who was shot: "What are you going to do, testify so they can come back and get the rest of your family?" Faced with little information and no witness willing to testify in court, prosecutors were forced to release the two suspects three weeks later. The case remains unsolved.

This case, just one of many across the country, is at the center of a growing concern to police that juvenile and criminal violence, particularly by gangs, is increasingly being perpetrated with near immunity because of witness intimidation. Threats of reprisals against witnesses willing to testify in court or come forward to the police with information have significantly hampered police efforts to solve juvenile gang killings and other violent crimes, and, in the words of one reporter, "allowed gangs to tyrannize entire communities."[1] While certainly in the extreme, this case highlights an important obstacle facing police work in juvenile justice today. How the police respond to juvenile offenders is the focus of this chapter.

The chapter first takes a brief look at the history of policing juveniles, from the time of the Norman conquest of England up to today. Community policing in modern times is the focus of the next section. Here the relationship between police and community efforts to prevent crime is explored. We then look at the roles and responsibilities of the police and the organization and management of police–juvenile operations. Legal aspects of police work, including the arrest procedure, search and seizure, and custodial interrogation, are reviewed. We also examine the concept of police discretion in light of the broad authority that police have in dealing with juveniles. The chapter ends with a review of police work and delinquency prevention. A wide range of police techniques in preventing delinquency are discussed, including those that rely on the deterrent powers of police and those that engage schools and the community.

History of Juvenile Policing

Providing specialized police services for juveniles is a relatively recent phenomenon. At one time citizens were responsible for protecting themselves and maintaining order.

The origin of police agencies can be traced to early English society.[2] Before the Norman conquest of England, the **pledge system** assumed that neighbors would protect each other from thieves and warring groups. Individuals were entrusted with policing themselves and resolving minor problems. By the thirteenth century, however, the **watch system** was created to police larger communities. Men were organized in church parishes to patrol areas at night and guard against disturbances and breaches of the peace. This was followed by establishment of the constable, who was responsible for dealing with more serious crimes. By the seventeenth century, the constable, the justice of the peace, and the night watchman formed the nucleus of the police system in England.

When the Industrial Revolution brought thousands of people from the countryside to work in factories, the need for police protection increased. As a result, the first organized police force was established in London in 1829. The British "bobbies" (so called after their founder, Sir Robert Peel) were not successful at stopping crime and were influenced by the wealthy for personal and political gain.[3]

In the American colonies, the local sheriff became the most important police official. By the mid-1800s, city police departments had formed in Boston, New York, and Philadelphia. Officers patrolled on foot, and conflicts often arose between untrained officers and the public.

By this time, children began to be treated as a distinguishable group (see Chapter 1). When children violated the law they were often treated the same as adult offenders. But even at this stage a belief existed that the enforcement of criminal law should be applied differently to children.

During the late nineteenth century and into the twentieth century, the problems associated with growing numbers of unemployed and homeless youths increased. Groups such as the Wickersham Commission of 1931 and the International Association of Chiefs of Police became the leading voices for police reform.[4] Their efforts resulted in creation of specialized police units, known as delinquency control squads.

The most famous police reformer of the 1930s was August Vollmer. As the police chief of Berkeley, California, Vollmer instituted numerous reforms, including university training, modern management techniques, prevention programs, and juvenile aid bureaus.[5] These bureaus were the first organized police services for juvenile offenders.

In the 1960s, policing entered a turbulent period.[6] The US Supreme Court handed down decisions designed to restrict police operations and discretion. Civil unrest produced growing tensions between police and the public. Urban police departments were unable to handle the growing crime rate. Federal funding from the Law Enforcement Assistance Administration (LEAA), an agency set up to fund justice-related programs, was a catalyst for developing hundreds of new police programs and enhancement of police services for children. By the 1980s, most urban police departments recognized that the problem of juvenile delinquency required special attention.

Today, the role of the juvenile police officer—an officer assigned to juvenile work—has taken on added importance. Most of the nation's urban law enforcement agencies now have specialized juvenile police programs. Typically, such programs involve prevention (police athletic leagues, community outreach) and law enforcement work (juvenile court, school policing, gang control). Other concerns of the programs include child abuse, domestic violence, and missing children.

pledge system
Early English system in which neighbors protected each other from thieves and warring groups.

watch system
Replaced the pledge system in England; watchmen patrolled urban areas at night to provide protection from harm.

For a comprehensive history of the **London Metropolitan Police** from 1829 to the present day and descriptions of famous and lesser known events throughout the history of the Met as well as biographies of key figures and details of famous cases, visit their website: http://content.met.police.uk /Site/history.

Community Policing in the New Millennium

In the minds of most citizens, the primary responsibility of the police is to protect the public. While the image depicted in films, books, and TV shows is one of crime fighters who always get their man, since the 1960s the public has become increasingly aware that the reality of police work is substantially different from its fictional glorification. When police departments failed to bring the crime rate down despite massive government subsidies, when citizens complained of civil rights violations, and when tales of police corruption became widespread, it was evident that a crisis was imminent in American policing.

Over the last three decades, a new view of policing has emerged. Discarding the image of crime fighters who track down serious criminals or stop armed robberies in progress, many police departments have adopted the concept that the police role should be to maintain order and be a visible and accessible component of the community. The argument is that police efforts can be successful only when conducted in partnership with concerned citizens. This movement is referred to as community policing.[7]

Interest in community policing does not mean that the crime control model of law enforcement is history. An ongoing effort is being made to improve the crime-fighting capability of police agencies, and there are some indications that the effort is paying off.[8] Some research suggests that police innovation in crime-fighting techniques contributed to the substantial reduction in crime rates during the 1990s, whereas other research suggests that the reduction simply had more to do with cities hiring more police.[9]

Working with juvenile offenders can be especially challenging for police officers because the desire to help young people and to steer them away from crime seems to conflict with the traditional police duties of crime prevention and maintenance of order. In addition, the police are faced with ongoing delinquency problems and renewed gang activity. Although the need to help troubled youths may conflict with traditional police roles, it fits nicely with the emerging community policing models. Improving these relationships is critical, because many juveniles do not have a high regard for the police.[10] Because of its importance, this is discussed in more detail in the accompanying Focus on Delinquency box.

community policing
Police strategy that emphasizes reducing fear, organizing the community, and maintaining order rather than fighting crime.

One of the main functions of the police is to deter juvenile crime. But in the last few decades policing has taken on many new functions, including being a visible and accessible component of the community, working with youths and other community members to address delinquency problems. This has come to be known as community policing.

Karsten Moran/The New York Times/Redux Pictures

FOCUS ON DELINQUENCY

Juvenile Views About Police

In study after study, from Phoenix to Chicago to Philadelphia, police get mixed to less-than-favorable reviews from juveniles, and minority teens are especially critical of police performance in their community. One large-scale study carried out in 11 cities across the country found that African American teens rated the police less favorably than did all other racial groups for all questions asked (e.g., "Are police friendly? Are police courteous?"). The most striking racial differences pertained to the question about police honesty: Only 15 percent of African American youths said the police were honest. In contrast, 57 percent of European Americans, 51 percent of Asians, 31 percent of Hispanics, and 30 percent of Native Americans said they were.

Another study, carried out in Cincinnati, focused exclusively on the attitudes of female juveniles toward the police and found similar results. Of the more than 400 female high school students interviewed, African Americans compared to their European American counterparts were significantly more likely to report having an overall negative attitude toward police. When asked about police honesty ("In general, I trust the police"), the difference was even greater: only 22 percent of African American female juveniles either agreed or strongly agreed with the statement compared to 56 percent of European American female juveniles.

Some studies have looked specifically at the influence of police contact on juvenile perceptions toward the police. Not surprisingly, juveniles who have had prior contact with the police hold less favorable attitudes toward the police compared to their counterparts who have not had any contact. This is a consistent finding across studies. Less well known is what may explain this relationship. In a national study it was found that police contact, with the exception of arrest, did not predict negative attitudes toward the police when involvement in delinquent peer groups and community ties were controlled.

In addition to the importance these results hold for improving police relations with juveniles, especially minorities, in order to prevent crime, the results may also hold special significance for the reporting of crimes to the police to address juvenile victimization. Research shows that juvenile crime victims are much less likely than adult victims to contact the police. This disparity in reporting crimes to the police holds true even after taking account of a number of important factors, such as crime severity, school victimization, and reporting crimes to officials other than police.

CRITICAL THINKING

1. What are the key factors that are driving the poor views of police by minority youths?

2. What might explain the differences between male and female juveniles in their unfavorable views toward the police?

SOURCES: Yuning Wu, Rodney Lake, and Liqun Cao, "Race, Social Bonds, and Juvenile Attitudes Toward the Police," *Justice Quarterly* 32:445–470 (2015); Joanna M. Lee, Laurence Steinberg, and Alex R. Piquero, "Ethnic Identity and Attitudes Toward the Police Among African American Juvenile Offenders," *Journal of Criminal Justice* 38:781–789 (2010); Bradley T. Brick, Terrance J. Taylor, and Finn-Aage Esbensen, "Juvenile Attitudes Towards the Police: The Importance of Subcultural Involvement and Community Ties," *Journal of Criminal Justice* 37:488–495 (2009); Jamie L. Flexon, Arthur J. Lurigio, and Richard G. Greenleaf, "Exploring the Dimensions of Trust in the Police Among Chicago Juveniles," *Journal of Criminal Justice* 37:180–189 (2009); Kenneth Dowler and Raymond Sparks, "Victimization, Contact with Police, and Neighborhood Conditions: Reconsidering African American and Hispanic Attitudes Toward the Police," *Police Practice and Research* 9:395–415 (2008); Yolander G. Hurst, M. Joan McDermott, and Deborah L. Thomas, "The Attitudes of Girls Toward the Police: Differences by Race," *Policing* 28:578–593 (2005), at 585–586; Adam M. Watkins, "Examining the Disparity Between Juvenile and Adult Victims in Notifying the Police: A Study of Mediating Variables," *Journal of Research in Crime and Delinquency* 42:333–353 (2005).

The Community Policing Model

The premise of the community policing model of crime prevention is that the police can carry out their duties more effectively by gaining the trust and assistance of concerned citizens. Under this model, the main police role is to increase feelings of community safety and encourage area residents to cooperate with their local police agencies.[11] Advocates of community policing regard the approach as useful in juvenile justice for a number of reasons:

- Direct engagement with a community gives police more immediate information about problems unique to a neighborhood and better insight into their solutions.

- Freeing officers from the emergency response system permits them to engage more directly in proactive crime prevention.

- Making police operations more visible increases police accountability to the public.

- Decentralizing operations allows officers to develop greater familiarity with the needs of various constituencies in the community and to adapt procedures to accommodate those needs.

- Encouraging officers to view citizens as partners improves relations between police and the public.

- Moving decision making to patrol officers places more authority in the hands of the people who best know the community's problems and expectations.[12]

The community policing model has been translated into a number of policy initiatives. It has encouraged police departments to get officers out of patrol cars, where they were insulated from the community, and into the streets via foot patrol.[13] The official survey of policing in the United States—the Law Enforcement Management and Administrative Statistics (LEMAS) survey—reports that seven out of 10 local police departments include a community policing component.[14] Between 2003 and 2013 (the most recent data available), the percentage of local police departments using community policing officers has increased, sometimes substantially, in all sizes of cities, from rural to large urban, with the largest increase taking place in cities with less than 10,000 residents.[15]

The federal Office of Community Oriented Policing Services (COPS) is involved in a number of initiatives to reduce gun violence by serious juvenile offenders.[16] One of these initiatives is Project Safe Neighborhoods, which brings together federal, state, and local law enforcement, prosecutors, and community leaders to deter and punish gun crime.[17]

Efforts are being made by police departments to involve citizens in delinquency control. Community policing is a philosophy that promotes community, government, and police partnerships that address juvenile crime, as well as adult crime.[18] Although there is not a great deal of evidence that these efforts can lower crime rates,[19] they do seem to be effective methods of improving perceptions of community safety and the quality of community life,[20] and involving citizens in the juvenile justice network. Under the community policing philosophy, prevention programs may become more effective crime control measures. Programs that combine the reintegration of youths into the community after institutionalization with police surveillance and increased communication are vital for improving police effectiveness with juveniles.

The Police and Juvenile Offenders

The increase in serious juvenile crime throughout the 1980s and into the early 1990s made it obvious that the police can no longer neglect youthful antisocial behavior. Departments need to assign resources to the problem and have the proper organization for coping with it. The theory and practice of police organization have undergone many changes, and as a result, police departments are giving greater emphasis to the juvenile function. The organization of juvenile work depends on the size of the police department, the kind of community in which the department is located, and the amount and quality of resources available in the community.

Juvenile officers operate either as specialists in a police department or as part of the department's juvenile unit. Here, Detective Alicia Hernandez (center), a member of the New York City Police Department's Juvenile Robbery Intervention Program, conducts her first visit to a juvenile offender as part of the program.

Todd Heisler/The New York Times/Redux Pictures

Police Services

Police who work with juvenile offenders usually have skills and talents that go beyond those generally associated with regular police work. In large urban police departments, juvenile services are often established through a special unit. Ordinarily this unit is the responsibility of a command-level police officer, who assigns officers to deal with juvenile problems throughout the police department's jurisdiction. Police departments with very few officers have little need for an internal division with special functions. Most small departments make one officer responsible for handling juvenile matters for the entire community. A large proportion of justice agencies have written policy directives for handling juvenile offenders. Figure 14.1 illustrates the major elements of a police department organization dealing with juvenile offenders. However, in both large and small departments, officers assigned to work with juveniles will not necessarily be the only ones involved in handling juvenile offenses. When officers on patrol encounter a youngster committing a crime, they are responsible for dealing with the problem initially; they generally refer the case to the juvenile unit or to a juvenile police officer for follow-up. The emergence of cybercrimes has brought new challenges to police who work with juveniles. The accompanying Cyber Delinquency feature profiles a promising initiative in policing cybercrimes.

Police Roles

juvenile officers
Police officers who specialize in dealing with juvenile offenders; they may operate alone or as part of a juvenile police unit within the department.

Juvenile officers operate either as specialists within a police department or as part of the juvenile unit of a police department. Their role is similar to that of officers working with adult offenders: to intervene if the actions of a citizen produce public danger or disorder. Most juvenile officers are appointed after having had some general patrol experience. A desire to work with juveniles as well as an aptitude for the work are considered essential for the job. Officers must also have a thorough knowledge of the law, especially the constitutional protections available to juveniles. Some officers undergo special training in the handling of aggressive or potentially aggressive juveniles.[21]

Most officers regard the violations of juveniles as nonserious unless they are committed by chronic troublemakers or involve significant damage to persons or property. Police encounters with juveniles are generally the result of reports made by citizens, and the bulk of such encounters pertain to matters of minor legal consequence.[22] Of course, police must also deal with serious juvenile offenders whose criminal acts are similar to those of adults; these are a minority of the offender population. Thus, police who deal with delinquency must concentrate on being peacekeepers and crime preventers.[23]

role conflicts
Conflicts police officers face that revolve around the requirement to perform their primary duty of law enforcement and a desire to aid in rehabilitating youthful offenders.

Handling juvenile offenders can produce major **role conflicts** for police. They may experience a tension between their desire to perform what they consider

Prevention programs

- Community Relations
- Police Athletic League (PAL)
- D.A.R.E. programs (drug prevention)
- Officer Friendly

Juvenile crimes

- Detective Bureau
- Juvenile Court Processing
- School Liaison
- Gang Control Unit

figure 14.1

Typical Urban Police Department Organization with Juvenile Justice Component

Policing Juveniles in Cyberspace

As new crimes emerge or as traditional crimes become more problematic, there is often the need for police to become more specialized and allocate resources to focused units within the police department. Gang, auto theft, and robbery units are a few examples of specialized police units. Some of these units come and go as demand for their services changes; others become permanent fixtures in the departmental structure. The broad nature of crimes that take place online or in cyberspace has also demanded increased specialization on the part of the police. How specialized different police departments have had to become to try to prevent and control cybercrime is not entirely clear. What is clear is that police departments—and sometimes within specialized cybercrime units—across the country have initiated any number of programs to prevent and control cybercrimes committed by or perpetrated against children and adolescents.

One of the more innovative programs designed by law enforcement to address juvenile cybercrime is the public education campaign known as "SafetyNet: Smart Cyber Choices." Established in 2008 by the San Diego Police Foundation in cooperation with the San Diego Internet Crimes Against Children Task Force, and funded by the federal government's Office of Juvenile Justice and Delinquency Prevention and the AT&T Foundation and the Lotus Children's Fund, SafetyNet is designed to educate children and teens about the risks of the Internet, including cyberbullying, phishing, sexting, and sexual predators. Also crucial to the program is the teaching of responsible and ethical use of the Internet.

With a special focus on middle school students, the public education campaign works closely with teachers and school administrators, parents, and students. The program is comprised of two main components:

- *Assemblies.* Middle school students attend assemblies designed to educate them about cyber safety. The message is about risks they need to be aware of as well as harms they can cause to others by engaging in irresponsible or even criminal behavior. Each assembly lasts between 45 and 60 minutes and is led by a San Diego police officer or a trainer from the San Diego Police Foundation.

- *Parent workshops.* Geared to parents of middle school students and other interested adults, these workshops are designed to educate parents about the risks their children face online and strategies parents can take to ensure the safety of their children. One of the key elements of the workshops is to help parents better monitor their children's online activity. The workshops are held in the community—sometimes at schools—and are led by a member of the San Diego law enforcement team.

The campaign also provides parents and educators with access to e-learning guides and new updates on the SafetyNet website.

Since the start of the program, more than 120,000 students in the San Diego metropolitan area have attended assemblies, and thousands of parents have attended workshops. Internal evaluations of the program show some promising results. Participating students report an increased understanding of online risks, and parents report an increased willingness to supervise their children's online activities.

CRITICAL THINKING

1. Cybercrimes by and against juveniles present many challenges to the police. What are some of the challenges facing the SafetyNet program? How can these challenges be overcome?

2. How restrictive should parents be in monitoring their children's online activities?

SOURCES: San Diego Police Foundation, "SafetyNet: Smart Cyber Choices," http://www.smartcyberchoices.org/ (accessed October 2016); Melissa J. Tetzlaff-Bemiller, "Undercover Online: An Extension of Traditional Policing in the United States," *International Journal of Cyber Criminology* 5:813–824 (2011); Catherine D. Marcum, George E. Higgins, Tina L. Freiburger, and Melissa L. Ricketts, "Policing Possession of Child Pornography Online: Investigating the Training and Resources Dedicated to the Investigation of Cyber Crime," *International Journal of Police Science and Management* 12:516–525 (2010).

their primary duty, law enforcement, and the need to aid in the rehabilitation of youthful offenders. Police officers' actions in cases involving adults are usually controlled by the law and their own judgment or discretion. (The concept of discretion is discussed later in this chapter.) In contrast, a case involving a juvenile often demands that the officer consider the "best interests of the child" and how the officer's actions will influence the child's future well-being. However, in recent years police have become more likely to refer juvenile offenders to courts. It is estimated that 62 percent of all juvenile arrests are referred to juvenile court, whereas 28 percent of all juvenile arrests are handled informally within the police department and released or are referred to a community-service agency (see Figure 14.2). These informal dispositions are the result of the police officer's discretionary authority.

Police intervention in situations involving juveniles can be difficult and emotional. The officer often encounters hostile behavior from the juvenile offender, as well as agitated witnesses. Overreaction by the officer can result in a violent incident. Even if the officer succeeds in quieting or dispersing the witnesses, they will probably reappear the next day, often in the same place.[24]

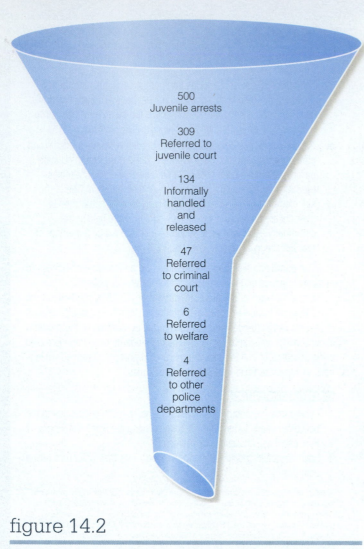

500
Juvenile arrests

309
Referred to
juvenile court

134
Informally
handled
and
released

47
Referred
to criminal
court

6
Referred
to welfare

4
Referred
to other
police
departments

figure 14.2

Police Response to Juvenile Crime

SOURCE: FBI, *Crime in the United States, 2014* (Washington, DC: US Government Printing Office, 2015), Table 68.

Role conflicts are common, because most police–juvenile encounters are brought about by loitering and rowdiness rather than by serious law violations. Public concern has risen about out-of-control youth. Yet, because of legal constraints and family interference, the police are often limited in the ways they can respond to such offenders.[25]

Another role conflict arises in the use of juveniles as police **informants**. Informants are individuals who have access to criminal networks and who, under conditions of anonymity, provide information to authorities in exchange for money or special treatment.[26] Police rely on informants, both adult and juvenile, to obtain evidence to make arrests in serious cases that the police may otherwise not be able to solve, such as gun and drug trafficking. Juvenile informants are also used in less serious cases where age is important to the crime—for example, when retailers sell cigarettes or alcohol to minors. Police must balance the need to obtain evidence and the vulnerabilities of (and extra safeguards that are needed for) juveniles in these cases. As criminologist Mary Dodge notes, there is a need for a higher degree of scrutiny in the use of juvenile police informants, and this practice should not be warranted in all circumstances.[27]

What role should the police play in mediating problems with youths—law enforcer or delinquency prevention worker? The answer may lie somewhere in between. Most police departments operate juvenile programs that combine law enforcement and delinquency prevention roles, and the police work with the juvenile court to determine a role most suitable for their community.[28] Police officers may even act as prosecutors in some rural courts when attorneys are not available. Thus, the police–juvenile role extends from the on-the-street encounter to the station house to the court. For juvenile matters involving minor criminal conduct or incorrigible behavior, the police ordinarily select the least restrictive alternative, which includes such measures as temporary assistance or referral to community agencies. In contrast, violent juvenile crime requires that the police arrest youths while providing constitutional safeguards similar to those available to adult offenders.

informant
A person who has access to criminal networks and shares information with authorities in exchange for money or special treatment under conditions of anonymity.

Police and Violent Juvenile Crime

Violent juvenile offenders are defined as those adjudicated delinquent for crimes of homicide, rape, robbery, aggravated assault, and kidnapping. Juveniles account for one out of every ten violent crime arrests (10 percent).[29] Since the mid-1990s, the juvenile violence rate has declined rather substantially, leveling off in more recent years. Many experts predicted a surge of violence as children of baby boomers entered their "prime crime" years, whereas others predicted that juvenile arrests for violent crime would double by the year 2010.[30] (See Chapter 2 for more on juvenile crime rates.) Despite reductions in violent juvenile offending, there are still countless stories of violent acts perpetrated by juveniles. The accompanying Youth Stories feature looks at one of the more vicious of these events.

youth STORIES

Latin King Goonies

The Latin King Goonies are not believed to be affiliated with the notorious Latin Kings street gang. The New York City police consider them to be a loose-knit gang operating out of the Bronx. In some respects this meant little to the events that unfolded on Sunday, October 3, 2010.

Beginning in the early morning hours, a number of the gang members abducted their first victim, a 17-year-old boy who was known to them because of his aspirations to join the gang. The boy was brought to a Bronx apartment and savagely beaten. According to New York City Police Commissioner Raymond Kelley, the boy was "thrown into a wall, made to strip naked, hit in the head with a beer can, cut with a box cutter, and sodomized with the wooden handle of a plunger." It turned out that the purpose of the beating was to obtain the boy's confession about performing sex acts with a 30-year-old man who was suspected by the gang as being gay.

At around 8:30 in the evening, gang members abducted and beat a second 17-year-old boy. The beating was just as savage. Again, the purpose was to extract a confession about sex acts he performed with the 30-year-old. In the meantime, the man was lured to the apartment under the pretense that a party was taking place. Upon arriving he was subsequently tied up and savagely beaten, sodomized, and forced to drink 10 cans of Four Loko, an alcohol-infused energy drink. This went on for hours, during which he was called antigay slurs. He was eventually robbed and left for dead.

In addition to threatening the younger victims if they went to the police, the attackers even went so far as to clean up

Nelson Falu, one of the Latin King Goonies arrested in connection with savage hate crimes.

the crime scene. Commissioner Kelly quoted one of the detectives as saying, "[It] was the cleanest crime scene I've ever seen." He added, "Lots of bleach and paint were used to cover the blood shed by their tortured prey. They even poured bleach down the drains." Altogether, seven gang members, ranging in age from 16 to 23, were charged in the attacks and six received prison terms, with the leader of the gang sentenced to 14 years in prison.

CRITICAL THINKING

What motivated these youths to carry out such violent crimes? Are hate crimes like this becoming more common?

SOURCES: Kevin Deutsch, "Three Accused Goonies Indicted in Brutal Bronx Gay Bashing," *New York Daily News*, October 29, 2010; Michael Wilson and Al Baker, "Lured into a Trap, then Tortured for Being Gay," *New York Times*, October 8, 2010; James B. Jacobs and Kimberly Potter, *Hate Crimes: Criminal Law and Identity Politics* (New York: Oxford University Press, 2001).

Police and other justice agencies are experimenting with different methods of controlling violent youth. Some of these methods, such as placing more officers on the beat, have existed for decades; others rely on state-of-the-art technology to pinpoint the locations of violent crimes and develop immediate countermeasures. Research shows that there are a number of effective policing practices, including increased directed patrols in street-corner hot spots of crime, proactive arrests of serious repeat offenders, and **problem-oriented policing**.[31] (See Exhibit 14.1 for a complete list of policing practices that work, do not work, or are promising.) These strategies address problems of community disorganization and can be effective deterrents when combined with other laws and policies, such as targeting illegal gun carrying.[32] Although many of these policing strategies are not new, implementing them as one element of an overall police plan may have an impact on preventing juvenile violence.

problem-oriented policing
Law enforcement that focuses on addressing the problems underlying incidents of juvenile delinquency rather than the incidents only.

exhibit 14.1

Policing Programs

What Works

- Increased directed patrols in street-corner hot spots of crime
- Proactive arrests of serious repeat offenders
- Proactive arrests of drunk drivers
- Arrests of employed suspects for domestic assault
- Problem-oriented policing
- Neighborhood watch
- Focused deterrence policing with specific crimes

What Does Not Work

- Arrests of some juveniles for minor offenses
- Arrests of unemployed suspects for domestic assault

- Drug market arrests
- Community policing that is not targeted at risk factors
- Adding extra police to cities with no regard to assignment or activity

What Is Promising

- Police traffic enforcement patrols targeting illegally carried handguns
- Community policing when the community is involved in setting priorities
- Community policing focused on improving police legitimacy
- Warrants for arrest of suspect absent when police respond to domestic violence

SOURCES: Anthony A. Braga and David Weisburd, "The Effects of Focused Deterrence Strategies on Crime: A Systematic Review and Meta-Analysis of the Empirical Evidence," *Journal of Research in Crime and Delinquency* 49:323–358 (2012); Lawrence W. Sherman and John E. Eck, "Policing for Crime Prevention," in Lawrence W. Sherman, David P. Farrington, Brandon C. Welsh, and Doris Layton MacKenzie, eds., *Evidence-Based Crime Prevention*, rev. ed. (New York: Routledge, 2006), pp. 321–322; Trevor H. Bennett, Katy Holloway, and David P. Farrington, "Does Neighborhood Watch Reduce Crime? A Systematic Review and Meta-Analysis," *Journal of Experimental Criminology* 2:437–458 (2006).

Finally, one key component of any innovative police program dealing with violent juvenile crime is improved communications between the police and the community.

Police and the Rule of Law

When police are involved with criminal activity of juvenile offenders, their actions are controlled by statute, constitutional case law, and judicial review. Police methods of investigation and control include (a) the arrest procedure, (b) search and seizure, and (c) custodial interrogation.

The Arrest Procedure

When a juvenile is apprehended, the police must decide whether to release the youngster or make a referral to the juvenile court. Cases involving serious crimes against property or persons are often referred to court. Less serious cases, such as disputes between juveniles, petty shoplifting, runaways, and assaults of minors, are often diverted from court action.

arrest
Taking a person into the custody of the law to restrain the accused until he or she can be held accountable for the offense in court proceedings.

probable cause
Reasonable grounds to believe that an offense was committed and that the accused committed that offense.

Most states require that the law of **arrest** be the same for both adults and juveniles. To make a legal arrest, an officer must have probable cause to believe that an offense took place and that the suspect is the guilty party. **Probable cause** is usually defined as falling somewhere between mere suspicion and absolute certainty. In misdemeanor cases, the police officer must personally observe the crime in order to place a suspect in custody. For a felony, the police officer may make the arrest without having observed the crime if the officer has probable cause to believe the crime occurred and the person being arrested committed it. A felony is a serious offense; a misdemeanor is a minor or petty crime. Crimes such as murder, rape, and robbery are felonies; crimes such as petty larceny and disturbing the peace are misdemeanors.

The main difference between arrests of adult and juvenile offenders is the broader latitude police have to control youthful behavior. Most juvenile codes, for instance, provide broad authority for the police to take juveniles into custody.[33]

exhibit 14.2

Uniform Juvenile Court Act, Section 13 (Taking into Custody)

a. A child may be taken into custody:
1. pursuant to an order of the court under this Act;
2. pursuant to the laws of arrest;
3. by a law enforcement officer (or duly authorized officer of the court) if there are reasonable grounds to believe that the child is suffering from illness or injury or is in immediate danger from his surroundings, and that his removal is necessary; or

4. by a law enforcement officer (or duly authorized officer of the court) if there are reasonable grounds to believe that the child has run away from his parents, guardian, or other custodian.

b. The taking of a child into custody is not an arrest, except for the purpose of determining its validity under the constitution of this State or of the United States.

SOURCE: National Conference of Commissioners on Uniform State Laws, *Uniform Juvenile Court Act.*

Such statutes are designed to give the police the authority to act *in loco parentis* ("in place of the parent"). Accordingly, the broad power granted to police is consistent with the notion that a juvenile is not arrested but taken into custody, which implies a protective rather than a punitive form of detention.[34] Once a juvenile is arrested, however, the constitutional safeguards of the Fourth and Fifth Amendments available to adults apply to the juvenile as well.

Section 13 of the Uniform Juvenile Court Act is an example of the provisions used in state codes regarding juvenile arrest procedures (see Exhibit 14.2). There is currently a trend toward treating juvenile offenders more like adults. Related to this trend are efforts by the police to provide a more legalistic and less informal approach to the arrest process, and a more balanced approach to case disposition.[35]

Search and Seizure

Do juveniles have the same right to be free from unreasonable **search and seizure** as adults? In general, a citizen's privacy is protected by the Fourth Amendment of the Constitution, which states:

> *The right of the people to be secure in their persons, houses, papers, and effects, against unreasonable searches and seizures, shall not be violated, and no warrants shall issue, but upon probable cause, supported by oaths or affirmation, and particularly describing the place to be searched, and the persons or things to be seized.*[36]

Most courts have held that the Fourth Amendment ban against unreasonable search and seizure applies to juveniles and that illegally seized evidence is inadmissible in a juvenile trial. To exclude incriminating evidence, a juvenile's attorney makes a pretrial motion to suppress the evidence, the same procedure that is used in the adult criminal process.

A full discussion of search and seizure is beyond the scope of this book, but it is important to note that the Supreme Court has ruled that police may stop a suspect and search for evidence without a warrant under certain circumstances. In an important 2009 case, *Arizona v. Gant*, the Court limited a police officer's ability to search a vehicle for evidence.[37] After Rodney Gant was arrested for driving with a suspended license, he was handcuffed and locked in the back of a patrol car. A police officer noticed a jacket on the backseat, searched the jacket, and found cocaine. The Court ruled that police may search a vehicle incident to a recent occupant's arrest only if the arrestee is within reaching distance of the passenger compartment at the time of the search or it is reasonable to believe the vehicle contains evidence of the offense of arrest. The search of Gant's jacket was deemed unreasonable since he could not gain access to it, and the cocaine was therefore inadmissible at trial. The *Gant* case is important because controlling a suspect after arrest is critical to police safety. Some officers may now sacrifice safety concerns in order to search suspects or their vehicles.

search and seizure
The US Constitution protects citizens from any search and seizure by police without a lawfully obtained search warrant; such warrants are issued when there is probable cause to believe an offense has been committed.

Arizona v. Gant
This case placed specific limitations on police searches of a suspect's vehicle.

The Supreme Court has ruled that there are many circumstances in which the police can stop a suspect and search for evidence without a warrant, also called a warrantless search. Here, in this July 26, 2012, photo, police in Anaheim, California, search a teen suspected of loitering near a shopping center.

In general, a person may be searched after a legal arrest, but then only in the immediate area of the suspect's control. For example, after an arrest for possession of drugs, the pockets of a suspect's jacket may be searched;[38] an automobile may be searched if there is probable cause to believe a crime has taken place;[39] a suspect's outer garments may be frisked if police are suspicious of his or her activities;[40] and a search may be conducted if a person volunteers for the search.[41] These rules are usually applied to juveniles as well as to adults. Concept Summary 14.1 reviews when warrantless searches are allowed.

Custodial Interrogation

custodial interrogation
Questions posed by the police to a suspect held in custody in the prejudicial stage of the juvenile justice process; juveniles have the same rights against self-incrimination as adults do when being questioned.

Miranda v. Arizona
Police interrogations of suspects in custody are subject to constitutional limitations.

In years past, police often questioned juveniles without their parents or even an attorney present. Any incriminating statements arising from such **custodial interrogation** could be used at trial. However, in the 1966 case *Miranda v. Arizona*, the Supreme Court placed constitutional limitations on police interrogation

CONCEPT SUMMARY 14.1

Warrantless Searches

Action	Scope of Search
Stop-and-frisk	Pat-down of a suspect's outer garments.
Search incident to arrest	Full body search after a legal arrest.
Automobile search	If probable cause exists, full search of car, including driver, passengers, and closed containers found in trunk. Search must be reasonable.
Consent search	Warrantless search of person or place is justified if suspect knowingly and voluntarily consents to search.
Plain view	Suspicious objects seen in plain view can be seized without a warrant.
Electronic surveillance	Material can be seized electronically without a warrant if suspect has no expectation of privacy.
Home entry	A home can be entered without a warrant if there is reason to believe that evidence of a crime is being destroyed.

ZUMA Press, Inc./Alamy Stock Photo

procedures with adult offenders. *Miranda* held that persons in police custody must be told the following:

- They have the right to remain silent.
- Any statements they make can be used against them.
- They have the right to counsel.
- If they cannot afford counsel, it will be furnished at public expense.[42]

The *Miranda* **warning** has been made applicable to juveniles taken into custody. The Supreme Court case of *In re Gault* stated that constitutional privileges against self-incrimination apply in juvenile as well as adult cases. Because *In re Gault* implies that *Miranda* applies to custodial interrogation in criminal procedures, state court jurisdictions apply the requirements of *Miranda* to juvenile proceedings as well. Since the *Gault* decision in 1967, virtually all courts that have ruled on the question of the *Miranda* warning have concluded that the warning does apply to the juvenile process. More recently (in 2011), the Supreme Court, in *J.D.B. v. North Carolina*, ruled that age does matter and that greater care must be taken by the police when questioning children in their custody.[43]

One problem associated with custodial interrogation of juveniles has to do with waiver of *Miranda* rights: Under what circumstances can juveniles knowingly and willingly waive the rights given them by *Miranda v. Arizona*? Does a youngster, acting alone, have sufficient maturity to appreciate the right to remain silent?

Most courts have concluded that parents or attorneys need not be present for juveniles effectively to waive their rights.[44] In a frequently cited California case, *People v. Lara*, the court said that the question of a juvenile's waiver is to be determined by the totality of the circumstances doctrine.[45] This means that the validity of the waiver rests not only on the age of the youth but also on a combination of other factors, including the child's education, the child's knowledge of the charge, whether the child was allowed to consult with family or friends, and the method of interrogation.[46] The general rule is that juveniles can waive their rights to protection from self-incrimination, but that the validity of this waiver is determined by the circumstances of each case.

Research by law professor Barry Feld suggests that older juveniles—16- and 17-year-olds—sufficiently understand their *Miranda* rights, but younger ones do not. He argues that mandating recordings of all police interrogations would go some way toward ensuring that juveniles of all ages do in fact understand their rights and minimize the risk of false confessions, which is especially problematic among younger juveniles.[47]

The waiver of *Miranda* rights by a juvenile is one of the most controversial legal issues addressed in the state courts. It has also been the subject of federal constitutional review. In two cases, *Fare v. Michael C.* and *California v. Prysock*, the Supreme Court has attempted to clarify children's rights when they are interrogated by the police. In *Fare v. Michael C.*, the Court ruled that a child's asking to speak to his probation officer was not the equivalent of asking for an attorney; consequently, statements he made to the police absent legal counsel were admissible in court.[48] In *California v. Prysock*, the Court was asked to rule on the adequacy of a *Miranda* warning given to Randall Prysock, a youthful murder suspect.[49] After reviewing the taped exchange between the police interrogator and the boy, the Court upheld Prysock's conviction when it ruled that even though the *Miranda* warning was given in slightly different language and out of exact context, its meaning was easily understandable, even to a juvenile.

Taken together, *Fare* and *Prysock* make it seem indisputable that juveniles are at least entitled to receive the same *Miranda* rights as adults. *Miranda v. Arizona* is a historic decision that continues to protect the rights of all suspects placed in custody.

Miranda **warning**
Supreme Court decisions require police officers to inform individuals of their constitutional rights when under arrest; warning must also be given when suspicion begins to focus on an individual in the accusatory stage.

For a detailed look at the landmark Supreme Court decision in *Miranda v. Arizona*, visit a website hosted by the Public Broadcasting Service: http://www.pbs.org/wnet/supremecourt/rights/landmark_miranda.html.

Fare v. Michael C. and *California v. Prysock*
These cases make it seem indisputable that juveniles are at least entitled to receive the same *Miranda* rights as adults.

Discretionary Justice

Today, juvenile offenders receive nearly as much procedural protection as adult offenders. However, the police have broader authority in dealing with juveniles than with adults. Granting such discretion to juvenile officers raises some important questions: Under what circumstances should an officer arrest status offenders? Should a summons be used in lieu of arrest? Under what conditions should a juvenile be taken into protective custody?

When police confront a case involving a juvenile offender, they rely on their discretion to choose an appropriate course of action. Police discretion is selective enforcement of the law by authorized police agents. Discretion gives officers a choice among possible courses of action within the limits on their power.[50] It is a prime example of *low-visibility decision making*—a public official making decisions that the public is not in a position to regulate or criticize.[51]

Discretion exists not only in the police function but also in prosecutorial decision making, judicial judgments, and corrections. Discretion results in the law being applied differently in similar situations. For example, two teenagers are caught in a stolen automobile; one is arrested, the other released. Two youths are drunk and disorderly; one is sent home, the other to juvenile court. A group of youngsters is involved in a gang fight; only a few are arrested, the others are released.

Much discretion is exercised in juvenile work because of the informality that has been built into the system in an attempt to individualize justice.[52] Furthermore, officials in the juvenile justice system make decisions that are often without oversight or review. The daily procedures of juvenile personnel are rarely subject to judicial review, except when they clearly violate a youth's constitutional rights. As a result, discretion sometimes deteriorates into discrimination and other abuses on the part of the police.

The real danger in discretion is that it allows the law to discriminate against precisely those elements in the population—the poor, the ignorant, the unpopular—who are least able to draw attention to their plight.[53] The problem of discretion in juvenile justice is one of extremes. Too little discretion provides insufficient flexibility to treat juvenile offenders as individuals. Too much discretion can lead to injustice. Guidelines and controls are needed to structure the use of discretion.

Generally, the first contact a youth has with the juvenile justice system is with the police. Research indicates that most police decisions arising from this initial contact involve discretion.[54] These studies show that many juvenile offenders are never referred to juvenile court.

In a classic 1963 study, Nathan Goldman examined the arrest records of more than 1,000 juveniles from four communities in Pennsylvania.[55] He concluded that more than 64 percent of police contacts with juveniles were handled informally. Subsequent research offered additional evidence of informal disposition of juvenile cases.[56] For example, in the 1970s, Paul Strasburg found that about 50 percent of all children who come in contact with the police do not get past the initial stage of the juvenile justice process.[57]

A study conducted in the early 2000s, analyzed juvenile data collected as part of the Project on Policing Neighborhoods—a comprehensive study of police patrols in Indianapolis, Indiana, and St. Petersburg, Florida. This study indicated that police still use discretion.[58] It found that 13 percent of police encounters with juveniles resulted in arrest.[59]

After arrest, the most current data show a decrease in the number of cases referred to the juvenile court. The Federal Bureau of Investigation (FBI) estimates that 62 percent of juvenile arrests are referred to juvenile court.[60] Despite the variations between the estimates, these studies indicate that the police use significant discretion in their decisions regarding juvenile offenders. Research shows that differential decision making goes on without clear guidance.

If all police officers acted in a fair and just manner, the seriousness of the crime, the situation in which it occurred, and the legal record of the juvenile would be the factors that affect decision making. Research does show that police are much more likely to take formal action if the crime is serious and has been reported by a victim who is a respected member of the community, and if the offender is well known to them.[61] However, there are other factors that are believed to shape police discretion; they are discussed next.

Environmental Factors

How does a police officer decide what to do with a juvenile offender? The norms of the community are a factor in the decision. Some officers work in communities that tolerate a fair amount of personal freedom. In liberal environments, the police may be inclined to release juveniles rather than arrest them. Other officers work in conservative communities that expect a no-nonsense approach to police enforcement. Here, police may be more inclined to arrest a juvenile.

Police officers may be influenced by their perception of community alternatives to police intervention. Some officers may use arrest because they believe nothing else can be done.[62] Others may favor referring juveniles to social service agencies, particularly if they believe a community has a variety of good resources. These referrals save time and effort; records do not have to be filled out, and court appearances can be avoided. The availability of such options allows for greater latitude in police decision making.[63]

Police Policy

The policies and customs of the local police department also influence decisions. Juvenile officers may be pressured to make more arrests or to refrain from making arrests under certain circumstances. Directives instruct officers to be alert to certain types of juvenile violations. The chief of police might initiate policies governing the arrest practices of the juvenile department. For example, if local merchants complain that youths congregating in a shopping center parking lot are inhibiting business, police may be called on to make arrests. Under other circumstances, an informal warning might be given. Similarly, a rash of deaths caused by teenage drunk driving may galvanize the local media to demand police action. The mayor and the police chief, sensitive to possible voter dissatisfaction, may then demand that formal police action be taken in cases of drunk driving.

Another source of influence is pressure from supervisors. Some supervising officers may believe it is important to curtail disorderly conduct or drug use. In addition, officers may be influenced by the discretionary decisions made by their peers.

Justice in Policing A growing body of research shows that by police exercising a greater degree of fairness, or procedural justice, in making arrests and handling offenders after arrest they can better gain offenders' cooperation as well as deter them from further involvement in criminal activity.[64] This holds special relevance in the context of a number of policing styles, including aggressive law enforcement (discussed later in the chapter) and broken windows policing. Yale University legal scholar Tracey Meares questions the trade-off that is so often justified for the use of broken windows policing: short-term and modest reductions in crime at the expense of undermining the fairness of law enforcement in the eyes of community residents.[65] Meares argues that future evaluations of this form of policing need to pay just as much attention to its potential to uphold fairness and legitimacy as its potential to reduce crime.

One of the first studies to assess the effect of police fairness on criminal offending was carried out by criminologist Raymond Paternoster and his colleagues. As part of the Milwaukee domestic assault experiment, they found that men who were arrested for assaulting their female spouses were much less likely—by almost 40 percent—to commit another act of assault against their spouses if they were handled by police in a fair and just manner compared to a similar group of men who were not handled in a fair way.[66]

procedural justice
An evaluation of the fairness of the manner in which an offender's problem or dispute was handled by police.

broken windows policing
Drawing on the broken windows theory developed by Wilson and Kelling, police target disorderly behaviors and conditions in an effort to prevent the onset of more serious crime problems.

Perceptions of police fairness are not limited to the arrest procedure; they include other, less formal contacts with police. In a recent study of procedural justice and order maintenance policing in St. Louis, Missouri, 45 high-risk, young, male adolescents were questioned about their experiences with and perceptions of the police.[67] Thirty-five of them (78 percent) reported that they had been stopped and frisked by the police at least one time in their lives; many reported multiple occasions. Most of them held a negative view of this interaction, which was often accompanied by the police being "discourteous and even verbally abusive." The authors concluded that, in the absence of strict codes of conduct, the growing use of stop-and-frisks by police in inner cities across the country could substantially erode procedural justice and "undermine police legitimacy."[68] This needs to be considered alongside recent evidence from New York City that suggests that stop, question, and frisk practices have a modest deterrent effect on crime.[69] Another study reveals that youths who view the police as legitimate are more willing to assist the police.[70]

There are some indications that this research is leading police departments to implement policies on procedural fairness and train their officers appropriately.[71] Nevertheless, police scholars acknowledge that more needs to be done and have called for more research on the subject to better understand the mechanisms that result in crime control effectiveness.[72]

Situational Factors

In addition to the environment, a variety of situational factors affect a police officer's decisions. Situational factors are those attached to a particular crime, such as specific traits of offenders. Traditionally, it was believed that police officers rely heavily on the demeanor and appearance of the juvenile in making decisions. Some research shows that the decision to arrest is often based on factors such as dress, demeanor, speech, and level of hostility toward the police.[73] Kids who display "attitude" were believed to be the ones more likely to be arrested than those who are respectful and contrite.[74] However, other research has challenged the influence of demeanor on police decision making, suggesting that it is delinquent behavior and actions that occur during police detention that influence the police decision to take formal action.[75] For example, a person who struggles or touches police during a confrontation is a likely candidate for arrest, but those who merely sport a bad attitude or negative demeanor are as likely to suffer an arrest as the polite and contrite.[76] In a recent study that found that juveniles are significantly more likely to be arrested than adults, disrespectful demeanor on the part of juveniles toward police did not increase their likelihood of arrest. Disrespectful adults, on the other hand, were more likely to be arrested.[77]

It is possible that the earlier research reflected a time when police officers demanded absolute respect and were quick to take action when their authority was challenged. The more recent research may indicate that police, through training or experience, are now less sensitive to slights and confrontational behavior and view them as part of the job. Most studies conclude that the following variables are important in the police discretionary process:[78]

- The attitude of the complainant
- The type and seriousness of the offense
- The race, sex, and age of the offender
- The attitude of the offender
- The offender's prior contacts with the police
- The perceived willingness of the parents to assist in solving the problem (in the case of a child)
- The setting or location in which the incident occurs

The 2014 police shooting death of 18-year-old Michael Brown in Ferguson, Missouri, and other events across the country drew greater attention to the view that police are more likely to act formally with African American suspects. Shown here are pictures of Michael Brown alongside his casket at his funeral at the Friendly Temple Missionary Baptist Church in St. Louis, Missouri, on August 25, 2014.

Richard Perry/The New York/Redux Pictures

- Whether the offender denies the actions or insists on a court hearing (in the case of a child)
- The likelihood that a child can be served by an agency in the community

Bias and Police Discretion

Do police allow bias to affect their decisions on whether to arrest youths? Do they routinely use racial profiling when they decide to make an arrest? A great deal of debate has been generated over this issue. Some experts believe that police decision making is deeply influenced by the offender's personal characteristics, whereas others maintain that crime-related variables are more significant.

Racial Bias It has long been charged that police are more likely to act formally with African American suspects and use their discretion to benefit whites.[79] In the context of traffic stops by police, the phrase "driving while black" has been coined to refer to the repeated findings of many studies that African American drivers are disproportionately stopped by police and that race is the primary reason for this practice.[80]

The 2014 police-shooting death of Michael Brown in Ferguson, Missouri, the subsequent riots and protests in Ferguson, and other similar tragic incidents (and protests) across the country have further amplified the view that police are more likely to act formally with African American suspects. Commentators called attention to a number of policing styles and practices—aggressive law enforcement, broken windows policing, stop-and-frisk—that may very well be contributing to this unfair treatment of African Americans by the police.[81] Created in response to the Ferguson events, the President's Task Force on 21st Century Policing released its final report in May 2015. Among the key recommendations:

- Law enforcement needs to adopt procedural justice as the guiding principle for all internal and police–citizen interactions.
- Police agencies need to develop "clear and comprehensive policies" on the use of force.
- Police agencies need to emphasize community policing practices for crime reduction.[82]

table 14.1

African American Representation in Arrest Statistics

Most serious offense	African American juvenile arrests in 2014 (%)
Murder	57
Forcible rape	33
Robbery	71
Aggravated assault	42
Burglary	42
Larceny/theft	36
Motor vehicle theft	47
Weapons	40
Drug abuse violations	23
Curfew and loitering	46

Note: Percentage is of all juvenile arrests.

Source: Federal Bureau of Investigation, *Crime in the United States, 2014* (Washington, DC: US Government Printing Office, 2015), Table 43b.

As Table 14.1 shows, African American youths are arrested at a rate disproportionate to their representation in the population. Research on this issue has yielded mixed conclusions. One view is that although discrimination may have existed in the past, there is no longer a need to worry about racial discrimination because minorities now possess sufficient political status to protect them within the justice system.[83] As Harvard University law professor Randall Kennedy forcefully argues, even if a law enforcement policy exists that disproportionately affects African American suspects, it might be justified as a "public good" because law-abiding African Americans are statistically more often victims of crimes committed by other African Americans.[84]

In contrast to these views, several research efforts do show evidence of police discrimination against African American youths.[85] Donna Bishop and Michael Leiber found that race can have a direct effect on decisions made at several junctures of the juvenile justice process.[86] According to Bishop and Leiber, African Americans are more likely than whites to be recommended for formal processing, referred to court, adjudicated delinquent, and given harsher dispositions for comparable offenses. In the arrest category, specifically, being African American increases the probability of formal police action.[87]

For further information on racial bias in police decisions, see the Focus on Delinquency box. Further research is needed to better understand and document what appears to be findings of disproportional arrests of minority juvenile offenders.[88]

Gender Bias Is there a difference between police treatment of male and female offenders? Some experts favor the *chivalry hypothesis*, which holds that police are likely to act paternally toward young girls and not arrest them. Others believe that police may be more likely to arrest female offenders because their actions violate officers' stereotypes of the female.

There is some research support for various forms of gender bias. The nature of this bias may vary according to the seriousness of the offense and the age of the offender. Studies offer a variety of conclusions, but there seems to be general agreement that police are less likely to process females for delinquent acts and that they discriminate against them by arresting them for status offenses.[89] Kimberly Kempf-Leonard has found that this gender bias is not straightforward from arrest through disposition:

> Available evidence suggests that juvenile justice processing initiates at arrest and referral in a somewhat biased, stereotypical manner, proceeds with more fair and balanced adjudication, and then concludes with differential treatment, which may be especially detrimental for girls who are placed out of home.[90]

Juvenile Race, Gender, and Ethnicity in Police Decision Making

Does police discretion work against the young, males, the poor, and minority group members, or does it favor special interest groups? Research has uncovered information supporting both sides.

Although the police are involved in at least some discrimination against racial minorities who are juveniles, the frequency and scope of such discrimination may be less than anticipated. Some of today's literature shows that the police are likely to interfere with or arrest poor African American youths. The police frequently stop and question youths of color walking down the streets of their neighborhoods or hanging around street corners. If this is the case, then race plays a role in police discretion.

In contrast to these findings, data from other studies indicate that racial bias does not influence the decision to arrest and move a youngster through the juvenile justice system. The attitude of the youth, prior record, seriousness of crime, setting or location of the crime, and other variables control police discretion, not race, ethnicity, or gender. Another problem in determining the impact of race or gender on police discretion is that the victim's race, not the juvenile offender's, may be the key to racial bias. Police officers may take different action when the victim is white rather than when the victim is a minority group member.

Police bias may also be a result of organizational and administrative directions as opposed to bias by an individual officer "on the beat" or in a cruiser. Some police departments have been found to use racial profiles for stopping and questioning suspects.

Obviously, not all officers operate unfairly or with a racial bias. Quite possibly the impact of juvenile race on police discretion varies from jurisdiction to jurisdiction and from one group of juveniles to another. Many African American youngsters, for example, view their gang affiliation as a means of survival. Teenage gang members and their families often feel frustrated about the lack of opportunities and their experiences as being targets of discrimination.

Despite all the research findings, uncertainty about the extent and degree of racial bias continues to plague the juvenile justice system. Unfortunately, minority youths are involved in a disproportionate percentage of all juvenile arrests. This often gives the impression that racial, gender, and ethnic bias exists in urban police departments.

CRITICAL THINKING

What do you think? Do the police take race into account when making decisions to arrest juveniles suspected of violating the law?

SOURCES: Donna M. Bishop and Michael J. Leiber, "Racial and Ethnic Differences in Delinquency and Justice System Responses," in Barry C. Feld and Donna M. Bishop, eds., *The Oxford Handbook of Juvenile Crime and Juvenile Justice* (New York: Oxford University Press, 2012); National Council on Crime and Delinquency, *And Justice for Some: Differential Treatment of Youth of Color in the Justice System* (San Francisco: Author, 2007); Wesley G. Skogan and Kathleen Frydl, eds., *Fairness and Effectiveness in Policing: The Evidence* (Washington, DC: National Academy Press, 2004).

Organizational Bias The policies of some police departments may result in biased practices. Research has found that police departments can be characterized by their professionalism (skills and knowledge) and bureaucratization.[91] Departments that are highly bureaucratized (high emphasis on rules and regulations) and at the same time unprofessional are most likely to be insulated from the communities they serve. Organizational policy may be influenced by the perceptions of police decision makers. A number of experts have found that law enforcement administrators have a stereotyped view of the urban poor as troublemakers who must be kept under control.[92] Consequently, lower-class neighborhoods experience much greater police scrutiny than middle-class areas, and their residents face a proportionately greater chance of arrest. A significant body of literature shows that police are more likely to "hassle" or arrest African American males in poor neighborhoods than white males in middle-class neighborhoods.[93] It is therefore not surprising, as Harvard criminologist Robert Sampson has found, that teenage residents of neighborhoods in low socioeconomic areas have a significantly greater chance of acquiring police records than youths living in higher socioeconomic areas, regardless of the actual crime rates in these areas.[94] Sampson's research indicates that although police officers may not discriminate on an individual level, departmental policy that focuses on lower-class areas may result in class and racial bias in the police processing of delinquent youth.

In summary, the policies, practices, and customs of the local police department influence discretion. Conditions vary from department to department and depend on the judgment of the chief and others in the organizational hierarchy. Because the police retain a large degree of discretionary power, the ideal of nondiscrimination is often difficult to achieve in practice. Discretionary decision making in juvenile police work can be better understood by examining Figure 14.3.

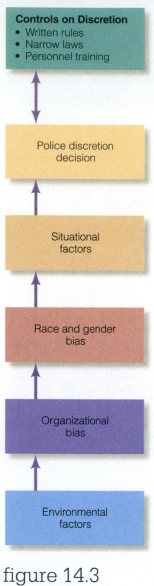

Controls on Discretion
- Written rules
- Narrow laws
- Personnel training

Police discretion
decision

Situational
factors

Race and gender
bias

Organizational
bias

Environmental
factors

figure 14.3

Discretionary Justice with Juveniles

Police Work and Delinquency Prevention

Police have taken the lead in delinquency prevention. They have used a number of strategies: some rely on their deterrent powers;[95] others rely on their relationship with schools, the community, and other juvenile justice agencies; and still others rely on a problem-solving model. Concept Summary 14.2 lists the main police strategies to prevent delinquency.

Aggressive Law Enforcement

One method of contemporary delinquency prevention relies on aggressive patrolling targeted at specific patterns of delinquency. Police departments in Chicago and Los Angeles have at one time used saturation patrols, targeting gang areas and arresting members for any law violations. These tactics have not proven to be effective against gangs. This is a finding of a large-scale review of law enforcement and other responses to the country's gang problems.[96] Conducted by the Justice Policy Institute, the review also found that "heavy-handed suppression efforts" result in increased rather than decreased cohesion among gang members and further exacerbates the sometimes-fragile relations that exist between the police and some communities.[97]

Police in Schools

One of the most important institutions playing a role in delinquency prevention is the school (see Chapter 10). In schools across the country, there are an estimated 13,000 full-time police working as school resource officers. In addition to helping make the school environment safe for students and teachers, school resource officers work closely with staff and administrators in developing delinquency prevention programs.[98] For example, these officers and liaison officers from schools and police departments have played a leadership role in developing recreational programs for juveniles. In some instances, police have actually operated such programs. In others, they have encouraged community support for recreational activities, including Little League baseball, athletic clubs, camping outings, and police athletic and scouting programs, with some schools also showing reductions in arrests for assault and weapons offenses.[99] School resource officers can make a difference in the lives of youths,[100] and this is the subject of the Case Profile entitled "Rico's Story." At the same time, some research points to concerns about the criminalization of behavior by school resource officers that was once handled informally by school officials,[101] and the media is replete with examples of minor infractions turning into arrests and referrals to juvenile court.[102]

The Gang Resistance Education and Training (G.R.E.A.T.) program is one example of a police and school partnership to reduce delinquency. Modeled after

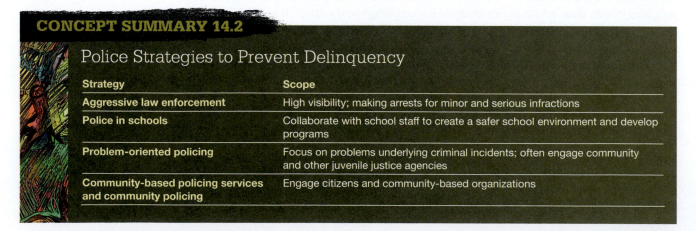

CONCEPT SUMMARY 14.2

Police Strategies to Prevent Delinquency

Strategy	Scope
Aggressive law enforcement	High visibility; making arrests for minor and serious infractions
Police in schools	Collaborate with school staff to create a safer school environment and develop programs
Problem-oriented policing	Focus on problems underlying criminal incidents; often engage community and other juvenile justice agencies
Community-based policing services and community policing	Engage citizens and community-based organizations

case profile

Rico's Story

RICO grew up in Harlem, one of 12 children raised primarily by their mother, a strong and determined African American woman who struggled daily to provide for the basic needs and safety of her family. Rico's father, a man of Puerto Rican descent, was heavily involved in criminal activity and drifted in and out of their lives for brief periods of time.

Rico attended a large New York public high school where there were approximately 8,000 students. Violence and gang activity were common in both his community and the school setting; sexual assaults took place in school stairwells, fights occurred on a daily basis, young drug dealers did business in the hallways, and there had been murders in school. Rico found it difficult to focus on academics with such chaos and fear all around him. The school, like many in the area, enlisted the assistance of the New York City Police Department in an effort to create a safer learning environment. Eight full-time uniformed and armed police officers patrolled the school daily. They had the capability and discretion to arrest on site and to intervene as needed, and they worked in collaboration with the educators and administrators to reduce violence and crime on school grounds. In the lunchroom, halls, and school auditorium, police officers were dressed in full uniform and acted clearly as authority figures. The officers also worked hard to be approachable and friendly to the students. They made efforts to have relationships with the students so that they could be a resource during challenging times.

Rico was a brilliant and gifted young man who, despite being in some trouble during his younger years, aspired to go to college and make a better life for himself. Several of his teachers encouraged him in his studies and although he was thriving academically, he needed a safer environment where he could focus on his education.

During his freshman year, Rico and some other students were playing cards in front of the school during a lunch break when another student threw a glass bottle at Rico's head and threatened his life. Rico went after the young man and a fight ensued. The police at the school intervened to stop the fight and address the young men's behavior. Although both teens could have been arrested for disorderly conduct or battery, Rico explained to them that he was defending himself, and the officers agreed. Knowing he was an excellent student who did not typically engage in this type of conduct, the officers chose to talk with Rico and try to encourage him in a more positive direction, rather than arresting him.

After graduating from high school, Rico attended the University of Cincinnati on a full athletic scholarship for football and track, and he also became a member of the US boxing team. Upon completing his undergraduate degree, Rico attended medical school. Today he is Dr. Richard Larkin, assistant professor at a community college in Illinois. In addition to crediting the New York City Police Department and his teachers for their efforts, he credits his mother's hard work, strict discipline, and tremendous drive for his success.

CRITICAL THINKING

1. In Rico's case, he did not receive any serious consequences for his actions. Do you agree with what the officers did? Why do you think he wasn't charged?

2. Do you agree that police officers should have the right to use their discretion in school settings? What are the benefits of this approach?

D.A.R.E. (Drug Abuse and Resistance Education), G.R.E.A.T. was first developed in 1991 among a number of Arizona police departments in an effort to reduce adolescent involvement in criminal behavior. Today the program is in school curricula in all 50 states and the District of Columbia as well as in a number of Central American countries.[103] The program's primary objective is the prevention of delinquency and gang involvement. Trained police officers administer the program in school classrooms about once a week. The program consists of four components: a 13-week middle school curriculum (see Exhibit 14.3 for its 13 lessons), a six-week elementary school curriculum, a summer program, and family training. Since the start of the program, more than 6 million children have participated in the G.R.E.A.T. curriculum, and more than 13,000 police officers have been trained to deliver it.

Evaluations of G.R.E.A.T. when it was just an eight-week program for middle school students showed mixed results in reducing delinquency and gang involvement. One evaluation found that students who completed the curriculum developed more prosocial attitudes and had lower rates of gang membership and delinquency than those in a comparison group who were not exposed to G.R.E.A.T.[104] Another evaluation of the program, four years after students

The **G.R.E.A.T. (Gang Resistance, Education, and Training) program** (http://www.great-online.org/) is a school-based, law enforcement officer–instructed classroom curriculum. With prevention as its primary objective, the program is intended as an immunization against delinquency, youth violence, and gang membership.

Youth gang and violence problems have given rise to many innovative police-led delinquency prevention programs. One of these is the Gang Resistance Education and Training (G.R.E.A.T.) program, which aims to reduce gang involvement. Partnering with schools across the country, trained police officers and other juvenile justice officials instruct students on conflict resolution, social responsibility, and the dangers of gang life. Pictured here is fifth grader David Vargas addressing fellow graduates of the G.R.E.A.T. program, all fourth and fifth graders from Munroe Elementary School in Denver, Colorado.

Joe Amon/Getty Images

completed the curriculum, did not find any significant differences for gang membership or delinquency compared to a control group. The evaluation did find that those who took the program held more prosocial attitudes than those who were not in the program.[105] These evaluations contributed to the new and more comprehensive program, which was implemented on a national scale in 2003.

In 2006, the National Institute of Justice awarded a five-year grant to the University of Missouri-St. Louis to evaluate the new version of G.R.E.A.T. The evaluation was carried out in seven cities across the country and included 31 public middle schools, 195 classrooms (102 received G.R.E.A.T. and 93 did not receive the program), and approximately 4,000 students. Short-term results—one year after the program ended—were very promising. Compared to the group of students who did not receive the program, G.R.E.A.T. students self-reported lower rates of gang membership and more prosocial attitudes on a range of outcomes related to the program.[106]

Another example of police working in close collaboration with schools is the Community Outreach Through Police in Schools Program. This program brings

exhibit 14.3

Lessons of the Middle School G.R.E.A.T. Program

1. **Welcome to G.R.E.A.T.** Students get acquainted with the program.

2. **What's the Real Deal?** Students learn facts and myths about gangs and violence.

3. **It's About Us.** Students learn about their roles and responsibilities to their community and what they can do about gangs.

4. **Where Do We Go from Here?** Students are taught how to set realistic and achievable goals.

5. **Decisions, Decisions, Decisions.** Students learn the impact of decisions on goals.

6. **Do You Hear What I Am Saying?** Students are taught effective communication skills.

7. **Walk in Someone Else's Shoes.** Students learn about expressing empathy for others.

8. **Say It Like You Mean It.** Students learn about self-expression.

9. **Getting Along Without Going Along.** Students become acquainted with negative influences and peer pressure and how to resist them.

10. **Keeping Your Cool.** Students are taught techniques to control anger.

11. **Keeping It Together.** Students are taught techniques to recognize anger in others and how to diffuse that anger.

12. **Working It Out.** Students learn about resolving interpersonal conflict and where to go for help.

13. **G.R.E.A.T. Days Ahead.** Students review what they have learned and think about how to make their school safe.

SOURCE: Gang Resistance Education and Training, https://www.great-online.org/Home/About/MiddleSchool (accessed October 2016).

together Yale University's Child Study Center and the New Haven Police Department to address the mental health and emotional needs of middle school students who have been exposed to violence in the community. Specifically, the program aims to help these students:

- Better understand the way their feelings affect their behavior
- Develop constructive means of responding to violence and trauma
- Change their attitudes toward police and learn how to seek help in their community[107]

An evaluation of the program found that students benefited from it in a number of ways, including improved emotional and psychological functioning (e.g., feeling less nervous, having fewer thoughts of death), as well as improved attitudes toward and relationships with the police.[108]

Community-Based Policing Services

Some police departments are now replacing more aggressive measures with cooperative community-based efforts. Because police officers are responsible for the care of juveniles taken into custody, it is essential that they work closely with social service groups day by day. In addition, the police are assuming a leadership role in identifying the needs of children in the community and helping the community meet those needs. In helping to develop delinquency prevention programs, the police are working closely with youth service bureaus, schools, recreational facilities, welfare agencies, and employment programs.

Using community services for juveniles has many advantages. Such services allow young people to avoid the stigma of being processed by a police agency. They also improve the community's awareness of the needs of young people and make it possible to restrict court referral to cases involving serious crime. These are some of the goals of Police Working with Youth, a Connecticut program designed to increase positive youth development and positive police interactions with youth. An evaluation of the program found that participating youths with low levels of social and emotional competencies showed a range of improvements in these areas compared to a similar group of youths who did not participate in the program.[109]

Curfews represent another form of community-based policing service. Curfew laws vary with respect to the locale affected, the time frame, and the sanctions. Most restrict minors to their homes or property between the hours of 11:00 PM and 6:00 AM. Sanctions for curfew violations by youths range from fines to being charged with a misdemeanor violation, and may include participation in diversion programs or, in some jurisdictions, jail time for parents.

Curfew enforcement activities are implemented through regular law enforcement and special policing units. High-quality evaluation studies of the impact of juvenile curfew ordinances are limited, but a recent assessment of the empirical evidence, including an evaluation of a curfew law in Charlotte, North Carolina, suggests that on their own, curfews are not effective in managing juveniles or reducing juvenile delinquency.[110] A systematic review of the existing empirical research on juvenile curfew laws reached the same conclusion.[111] The review also found that juvenile curfew laws had no lasting impact on reducing juvenile victimization, an important community justification for these laws. Based on this research and that curfew enforcement is an inefficient use of police resources, Kenneth Adams has called for juvenile curfews to be abolished.[112]

Problem-Oriented Policing

Also referred to as problem-solving policing, problem-oriented policing involves a systematic analysis and response to the problems or conditions underlying criminal incidents rather than the incidents themselves.[113] The theory is that by attending to the underlying problems that cause criminal incidents, the police will have a

Pulling Levers Policing

Closely related to problem-oriented policing, pulling levers policing is about activating or pulling every deterrent "lever" available to reduce the targeted delinquency problem. If it is juvenile gang violence, responses may include shutting down drug markets, serving warrants, enforcing probation restrictions, and making disorder arrests. Also important to this approach is communicating direct and explicit messages to offenders about the responses they can expect if this behavior is not stopped.

In a recent systematic review and meta-analysis of pulling levers policing, Anthony Braga and David Weisburd found that it is an effective approach to reducing a wide range of crime problems, including homicides, gang violence, gun assaults, and illegal drug possession. The review included 11 high-quality studies of programs from across the country, including Los Angeles, Chicago, Indianapolis, and Newark.

One of the most successful examples of this policing strategy is in Boston. Known as Operation Ceasefire, this program aims to reduce youth homicide victimization and youth gun violence. Although it is a police-led program, Operation Ceasefire involves many other juvenile and criminal justice and social agencies, including probation and parole, the Bureau of Alcohol, Tobacco, Firearms, and Explosives (ATF), gang outreach and prevention street workers, and the Drug Enforcement Administration (DEA). (Interagency cooperation is another key component of the pulling levers approach.) This group of agencies has become known as the Ceasefire Working Group.

The program has two main elements:

■ A direct law enforcement focus on illicit gun traffickers who supply youth with guns

■ An attempt to generate a strong deterrent to gang violence

A wide range of measures have been used to reduce the flow of guns to youth, including pooling the resources of local, state, and federal justice authorities to track and seize illegal guns and targeting traffickers of the types of guns most used by gang members. The response to gang violence has been equally comprehensive. The Ceasefire Working Group delivered its message clearly to gang members: "We're ready, we're watching, we're waiting: Who wants to be next?" An example of how the Working Group communicated this message to gang members is shown by the poster shown here, which was displayed throughout known gang areas in the city.

An evaluation from before the program started to the time it ended showed a 63 percent reduction in the mean monthly number of youth homicide victims across the city. The program was also associated with significant decreases in the mean monthly number of gun assaults and overall gang violence across the city. In a comparison with other New England cities and large cities across the United States, most of which also experienced a reduction in youth homicides over the same period, it was found that the significant reduction in youth homicides in Boston was due to Operation Ceasefire.

Maintaining the level of intensity of this program and cooperation of the many agencies involved, which are essential ingredients of its success, has not been easy. In recent years, there have been cutbacks in local policing, fewer federal criminal justice resources made available to the program, and a perception that the deterrence strategy is no longer focused on the most dangerous suspects. Recent research suggests that in order for the program to maintain its success it will also have to adapt to changes in the nature of gang and youth violence across the city.

The **Center for Problem-Oriented Policing** (http://www.popcenter.org/) aims to advance the concept and practice of problem-oriented policing in open and democratic societies. It does so by making readily accessible information about ways in which police can more effectively address specific crime and disorder problems. The center is a nonprofit organization comprising affiliated police practitioners, researchers, and universities dedicated to the advancement of problem-oriented policing.

greater chance of preventing the crimes from reoccurring—the main problem with reactive or "incident-driven policing."[114] However, as noted by Harvard criminologist Mark Moore, "This is not the same as seeking out the root causes of the crime problem in general. It is a much shallower, more situational approach."[115]

The systematic nature of problem-oriented policing is characterized by its adherence to a four-step model, often referred to as S.A.R.A., which stands for Scanning, Analysis, Response, and Assessment. The four steps are as follows:

1. Scanning involves identifying a specific crime problem through various data sources (e.g., victim surveys, 911 calls).

2. Analysis involves carrying out an in-depth analysis of the crime problem and its underlying causes.

3. Response brings together the police and other partners to develop and implement a response to the problem based on the results produced in the analysis stage.

4. Assessment is the stage in which the response to the problem is evaluated.[116]

FREDDIE CARDOZA

Problem:
Violent Gang Member

"Given his extensive criminal record, if there was a Federal law against jaywalking, we'd indict him for that."
—*Don Stern, U.S. Attorney*

Solution:
Armed Career Criminal Conviction

Arrested with one bullet
Sentence: 19 years, 7 months
No possibility of parole

Address:

Otisville Federal Correctional Institute
Maximum Security Facility, New York

The Los Angeles Operation Ceasefire took place in the Hollenbeck area, which suffers from exceptionally high rates of gang-related gun violence. Organized by 19 public and private agencies, it too was designed to send gang members the message that serious consequences would result for all gang members if they used guns. The researchers found that the intervention was most effective in reducing gun crimes during the suppression phase, with slightly smaller effects evidenced in the deterrence phase. As with Boston, the long-term success of the Los Angeles initiative and those in other cities will depend on sufficient resources, continued collaboration among the many participating agencies, and the ability to adapt to changing conditions in gang behavior.

CRITICAL THINKING

1. What is the importance of having a multidisciplinary team as part of the pulling levers strategy?

2. With comprehensive programs it is often difficult to assess the independent effects of the different program elements. In your opinion, what is the most important element of Boston's Operation Ceasefire? Why?

SOURCES: Andrew V. Papachristos and David S. Kirk, "Changing the Street Dynamic: Evaluating Chicago's Group Violence Reduction Strategy," *Criminology and Public Policy* 14:525–558 (2015); Anthony A. Braga, David Hureau, and Andrew V. Papachristos, "Deterring Gang-Involved Gun Violence: Measuring the Impact of Boston's Operation Ceasefire on Street Gang Behavior," *Journal of Quantitative Criminology* 30:113–139 (2014); Anthony A. Braga and David Weisburd, "The Effects of Focused Deterrence Strategies on Crime: A Systematic Review and Meta-Analysis of the Empirical Evidence," *Journal of Research in Crime and Delinquency* 49:323–358 (2012); George E. Tita, K. Jack Riley, Greg Ridgeway, and Peter W. Greenwood, *Reducing Gun Violence: Operation Ceasefire in Los Angeles* (Washington, DC: National Institute of Justice, 2005); Anthony A. Braga, David M. Kennedy, Elin J. Waring, and Anne Morrison Piehl, "Problem-Oriented Policing Deterrence and Youth Violence: An Evaluation of Boston's Operation Ceasefire," *Journal of Research in Crime and Delinquency* 38:195–225 (2001); David M. Kennedy, "Pulling Levers: Chronic Offenders, High-Crime Settings, and a Theory of Prevention," *Valparaiso University Law Review* 31:449–484 (1997).

Like community policing, problem-oriented policing is viewed as a proactive delinquency prevention strategy. Unlike community policing, however, the engagement of the community in problem-oriented policing is not imperative, but more often than not these operations involve close collaborations with the community. Collaborations with other juvenile justice agencies, such as probation, are also common in problem-oriented policing operations.[117]

As you may recall, problem-oriented policing has been shown to be effective in reducing juvenile delinquency in some circumstances.[118] A number of successful practices resulted in the federal COPS office initiating a national Problem-Solving Partnerships (PSP) program with the objective of assisting police agencies to "solve recurrent crime and disorder problems by helping them form community partnerships and engage in problem-solving activities."[119] Various case studies to emerge out of a national evaluation of this program by the Police Executive Research Forum identify a wide range of successful efforts to reduce delinquency.[120] The COPS office also initiated a series of guides to aid police in addressing specific crime problems, with one focusing on underage drinking[121] and another on gun violence among serious young offenders.[122]

Closely related to problem-oriented policing is another strategy commonly referred to as "pulling levers policing." It is described as a highly focused deterrence strategy that involves communicating direct and explicit messages to offenders about the responses they can expect if certain illegal behavior (e.g., gun violence) is not ceased.[123] One of the most successful applications of this policing strategy is Boston's Operation Ceasefire,[124] which is discussed in the Evidence-Based Juvenile Justice feature.

Today, many experts consider delinquency prevention efforts to be crucial to the development of a comprehensive approach to youth crime. Although such efforts cut across the entire juvenile justice system, police programs have become increasingly popular.

Future of Juvenile Policing

Many challenges confront the police response to juvenile offending today and will continue to do so in the years to come. Witness intimidation, charges of racial profiling, poor relations with some communities and groups of young people who are distrustful of the police, and the role of spectators in police–citizen interactions are some of the key challenges.[125] The police are making progress in dealing with many of these and other challenges, and in the years ahead it will be even more important that the police implement greater transparency in their operations, be more accountable to those they serve, especially young people, and exercise a greater degree of fairness or procedural justice in arresting juvenile offenders and handling them after arrest. It is very likely that future success in controlling as well as preventing juvenile offending will come to depend even more on these factors.

The integration of "soft" and "hard" technologies into police work with juveniles will also become more important in the years to come. Soft technology involves information technology (IT) systems to enhance police operational and administrative decision making, such as in analyses of city crime patterns and deployment of resources to the most crime-prone areas.[126] Hard technology involves nonlethal weapons, such as the Taser or stun gun,[127] and other alternative weapons systems used by police.[128] Increasingly, the police are also turning to various forms of surveillance technology, such as closed-circuit television (CCTV) and body-worn cameras, to deter juvenile and other crime in public places. The Bureau of Justice Statistics estimates that almost one-third (32 percent) of local police departments across the country use body-worn cameras.[129] Although evaluations have shown

Police programs that work closely with juveniles in the community are an important component of an overall strategy to reduce delinquency. Pictured here is Officer Mohamed Mohamed of the Mankato (Minnesota) Police Department, talking with a group of young soccer players as part of his community policing duties.

AP Images/Pat Christman

CCTV systems to be rather ineffective in reducing crime, real-time communication links between police and CCTV operators and their use in high-crime areas may improve effectiveness.[130] The latest research on body-worn cameras suggests that they can be effective in reducing citizens' complaints against the police.[131]

As we have seen throughout this chapter, some new approaches to policing juvenile delinquency show promising results in reducing serious offenses, such as gang activity and gun crimes. These include community-based policing services, police in schools, and—one of the most successful approaches—problem-oriented policing. Versions of Operation Ceasefire in Boston, which brought together a broad range of juvenile justice and social agencies and community groups and produced substantial reductions in youth violence, are now being replicated in other cities across the country. With the research evidence demonstrating that targeted problem-solving policing strategies of this type are the most effective in reducing serious urban crime problems,[132] continued use of these strategies holds much promise in maintaining record low rates of juvenile violence.

SUMMARY

1 Identify key historical events that have shaped juvenile policing in America today

- Modern policing developed in England at the beginning of the nineteenth century.

- The Industrial Revolution, recognition of the need to treat children as a distinguishable group, and growing numbers of unemployed and homeless youths were among the key events that helped shape juvenile policing in America.

2 Discuss the key roles and responsibilities of the police in responding to juvenile offenders

- The role of juvenile officers is similar to that of officers working with adult offenders: to intervene if the actions of a citizen produce public danger or disorder.

- Juvenile officers must also have a thorough knowledge of the law, especially the constitutional protections available to juveniles.

3 Describe the organization and management of police services for juveniles

- Juvenile officers operate either as specialists in a police department or as part of the juvenile unit of a police department.

- The organization of juvenile work depends on the size of the police department, the kind of community in which the department is located, and the amount and quality of resources available in the community.

4 Identify the major court cases that have influenced police practices

- Through a number of cases, the US Supreme Court established that police may stop a suspect and search for evidence without a warrant under certain circumstances.

- Through the *Miranda v. Arizona* decision, the Supreme Court established a clearly defined procedure for custodial interrogation.

5 Discuss key legal aspects of police work, including search and seizure and custodial interrogation, and how they apply to juveniles

- Most courts have held that the Fourth Amendment ban against unreasonable search and seizure applies to juveniles and that illegally seized evidence is inadmissible in a juvenile trial.

- Most courts have concluded that parents or attorneys need not be present for children effectively to waive their right to remain silent.

6 Describe police use of discretion and factors that influence discretion

- Discretion is a low-visibility decision made in the administration of adult and juvenile justice.

- Discretionary decisions are often made without guidelines from the police administrator.

- Numerous factors influence the decisions police make about juvenile offenders, including the seriousness of the offense, the harm inflicted on the victim, and the likelihood that the juvenile will break the law again.

7 Articulate the importance of police use of discretion with juveniles and some of the associated problems

- Discretion is essential in providing individualized justice.

- Problems with discretion include discrimination, unfairness, and bias toward particular groups of juveniles.

8 Appraise the major policing strategies to prevent delinquency

- The major policing strategies to prevent delinquency include aggressive law enforcement, police in schools, community-based and community policing, and problem-oriented policing.

9 Compare the pros and cons of police using different delinquency prevention strategies

- Innovation in policing strategies can address the ever-changing nature of juvenile delinquency.

- Tailoring policing activities to local conditions and engaging the community and other stakeholders show promise in reducing delinquency.

- Saturation patrols that include targeting gang areas and arresting members for any law violations have not proven to be effective against gangs.

- Maintaining the level of intensity and cooperation of the many agencies involved in problem-oriented policing strategies, which are essential to their success, is not easy and requires sustainable funding.

KEY TERMS

pledge system, p. 522
watch system, p. 522
community policing, p. 523
juvenile officers, p. 526
role conflicts, p. 526
informant, p. 528

problem-oriented policing, p. 529
arrest, p. 530
probable cause, p. 530
search and seizure, p. 531
Arizona v. Gant, p. 531
custodial interrogation, p. 532

Miranda v. Arizona, p. 532
Miranda warning, p. 533
Fare v. Michael C. and *California v. Prysock*, p. 533
discretion, p. 534
procedural justice, p. 535
broken windows policing, p. 535

QUESTIONS FOR DISCUSSION

1. The term *discretion* is often defined as selective decision making by police and others in the juvenile justice system who are faced with alternative modes of action. Discuss some of the factors affecting the discretion of the police when dealing with juvenile offenders.

2. What role should police organizations play in delinquency prevention and control? Is it feasible to expect police departments to provide social services to children and families? How should police departments be better organized to provide for the control of juvenile delinquency?

3. What qualities should a juvenile police officer have? Should a college education be a requirement?

4. In light of the traditional and protective roles assumed by law enforcement personnel in juvenile justice, is there any reason to have a *Miranda* warning for youths taken into custody?

5. Can the police and community be truly effective in forming a partnership to reduce juvenile delinquency? Discuss the role of the juvenile police officer in preventing and investigating juvenile crime.

6. The experience of Boston's successful Operation Ceasefire program suggests that it may be difficult to sustain the intensity and problem-solving partnerships needed to keep violent juvenile crime under control over the long term. What other innovative problem-oriented policing measures could be employed to achieve this?

VIEWPOINT

You are a newly appointed police officer assigned to a juvenile unit of a medium-sized urban police department. Wayne is an 18-year-old white male who was caught shoplifting with two male friends of the same age. He attempted to leave a large department store with a $25 shirt and was apprehended by a police officer in front of the store.

Wayne seemed quite remorseful about the offense. He said several times that he didn't know why he did it and that he had not planned to do it. He seemed upset and scared, and while admitting the offense, did not want to go to court. Wayne had three previous contacts with the police as a juvenile: one for malicious mischief when he destroyed some property, another involving a minor assault on a boy, and a third involving another shoplifting charge. In all three cases, Wayne promised to refrain from ever committing such acts again and as a result was not required to go to court. The other shoplifting incident involved a baseball worth only $3.

Wayne appeared at the police department with his mother. His parents are divorced. The mother did not seem overly concerned about the case and felt that her son was not really to blame. She argued that he was always getting in trouble and she was not sure how to control him. She blamed most of his troubles with the law on his being in the wrong crowd. Besides, a $25 shirt was "no big deal," and she offered to pay back the store. The store has left matters in the hands of the police and would support any decision you make.

Deciding what to do in a case like Wayne's is a routine activity for most police officers. When dealing with juveniles, they must consider not only the nature of the offense but also the needs of the juvenile. Police officers realize that actions they take can have a long-term effect on an adolescent's future.

- Would you submit Wayne's case for prosecution, release him with a warning, or use some other tactic?
- Should police officers be forced to act as counselors for troubled youth?

DOING RESEARCH ON THE WEB

Before you answer these questions, do some research at these police websites. The International Association of Chiefs of Police (http://www.theiacp.org/) aims to foster cooperation and the exchange of information and experience among police leaders and police organizations.

The Police Foundation's (http://www.policefoundation .org/) goal is to help the police be more effective in doing their job, whether it is in deterring robberies, intervening in potentially injurious family disputes, or working to improve relationships between the police and the communities they serve.

The Police Executive Research Forum (PERF) (http://www.policeforum.org/) is a national membership organization of progressive police executives from the largest city, county, and state law enforcement agencies.

The Office of Community Oriented Policing Services (COPS) (http://www.cops.usdoj.gov/), within the US Department of Justice, advances the practice of community policing in America's state, local, and tribal law enforcement agencies.

NOTES

All URLs accessed September 2016.

1. David Kocieniewski, "A Little Girl Shot, and a Crowd that Didn't See," *New York Times*, July 9, 2007.
2. This section relies on sources such as Malcolm Sparrow, Mark Moore, and David Kennedy, *Beyond 911: A New Era for Policing* (New York: Basic Books, 1990); Daniel Devlin, *Police Procedure, Administration, and Organization* (London: Butterworth, 1966); Robert Fogelson, *Big City Police* (Cambridge, MA: Harvard University Press, 1977); Roger Lane, *Policing the City, Boston 1822–1885* (Cambridge, MA: Harvard University Press, 1967); Roger Lane, "Urban Police and Crime in Nineteenth-Century America," in Norval Morris and Michael Tonry, eds., *Crime and Justice*, Vol. 2 (Chicago: University of Chicago Press, 1980), pp. 1–45; J. J. Tobias, *Crime and Industrial Society in the Nineteenth Century* (New York: Schocken, 1967); Samuel Walker, *A Critical History of Police Reform: The Emergence of Professionalism* (Lexington, MA: Lexington Books, 1977); Samuel Walker, *Popular Justice* (New York: Oxford University Press, 1980); President's Commission on Law Enforcement and the Administration of Justice, *Task Force Report: The Police* (Washington, DC: US Government Printing Office, 1967), pp. 1–9.
3. See Walker, *Popular Justice*, p. 61.
4. Law Enforcement Assistance Administration, *Two Hundred Years of American Criminal Justice* (Washington, DC: US Government Printing Office, 1976).
5. August Vollmer, *The Police and Modern Society* (Berkeley: University of California Press, 1936).
6. O. W. Wilson, *Police Administration*, 2nd ed. (New York: McGraw-Hill, 1963).
7. Wesley G. Skogan, *Police and Community in Chicago: A Tale of Three Cities* (New York: Oxford University Press, 2006); see also Herman Goldstein, "Toward Community-Oriented Policing: Potential Basic Requirements and Threshold Questions," *Crime and Delinquency* 33:630 (1987).
8. See Anthony A. Braga and David Weisburd, *Policing Problem Places: Crime Hot Spots and Effective Prevention* (New York: Oxford University Press, 2010); Wesley G. Skogan and Kathleen Frydl, eds., *Fairness and Effectiveness in Policing: The Evidence* (Washington, DC: The National Academies Press, 2004); David Weisburd and Anthony A. Braga, eds., *Police Innovation: Contrasting Perspectives* (New York: Cambridge University Press, 2006).
9. Franklin E. Zimring, *The City that Became Safe: New York's Lessons for Urban Crime and Its Control* (New York: Oxford University Press, 2011); Skogan and Frydl, *Fairness and Effectiveness in Policing*; Joel Wallman and Alfred Blumstein, "After the Crime Drop," in Alfred Blumstein and Joel Wallman, eds., *The Crime Drop in America*, 2nd ed. (New York: Cambridge University Press, 2006); Lawrence W. Sherman, "Fair and Effective Policing," in James Q. Wilson and Joan Petersilia, eds., *Crime: Public Policies for Crime Control* (Oakland, CA: Institute for Contemporary Studies, 2002); Steven D. Levitt, "Understanding Why Crime Fell in the 1990s: Four Factors that Explain the Decline and Six that Do Not," *Journal of Economic Perspectives* 18:163–190 (2004).
10. Daniel M. Stewart, Robert G. Morris, and Henriikka Weir, "Youth Perceptions of the Police: Identifying Trajectories," *Youth Violence and Juvenile Justice* 12:22–39 (2014); Claudio G. Vera Sanchez and Ericka

B. Adams, "Sacrificed on the Altar of Public Safety: The Policing of Latino and African American Youth," *Journal of Contemporary Criminal Justice* 27:322–341 (2011); Jamie L. Flexon, Arthur J. Lurigio, and Richard G. Greenleaf, "Exploring the Dimensions of Trust in the Police Among Chicago Juveniles," *Journal of Criminal Justice* 37:180–189 (2009); see also Yolander Hurst, James Frank, and Sandra Lee Browning, "The Attitudes of Juveniles Toward the Police: A Comparison of Black and White Youth," *Policing* 23:37–53 (2000).

11. For an analysis of this position, see George Kelling and James Q. Wilson, "Broken Windows: The Police and Neighborhood Safety," *Atlantic Monthly* 249:29–38 (1982).

12. US Department of Justice, "Community Policing," *National Institute of Justice Journal* 225:1–32 (1992).

13. Robert Trojanowicz and Hazel Harden, *The Status of Contemporary Community Policing Programs* (East Lansing, MI: Michigan State University Neighborhood Foot Patrol Center, 1985).

14. Brian A. Reaves, *Local Police Departments, 2013: Personnel, Policies, and Practices* (Washington, DC: Bureau of Justice Statistics, 2015), p. 8.

15. Ibid.

16. See Anthony A. Braga, *Gun Violence Among Serious Young Offenders* (Washington, DC: Office of Community Oriented Policing Services, US Department of Justice, 2004).

17. See Danielle Wallace, Andrew V. Papachristos, Tracey Meares, and Jeffrey Fagan, "Desistance and Legitimacy: The Impact of Offender Notification Meetings on Recidivism Among High Risk Offenders," *Justice Quarterly* (2015), DOI: 10.1080/07418825.2015.1081262; Edmund F. McGarrell, Nicholas Corsaro, Natalie Hipple, and Tim Bynum, "Project Safe Neighborhoods and Violent Crime Trends in U.S. Cities: Assessing Violent Crime Impact," *Journal of Quantitative Criminology* 26:165–190 (2010); Andrew V. Papachristos, Tracey Meares, and Jeffrey Fagan, (2007), "Attention Felons: Evaluating Project Safe Neighborhoods in Chicago," *Journal of Empirical Legal Studies* 4:223–272 (2007).

18. Susan Guarino-Ghezzi, "Reintegrative Police Surveillance of Juvenile Offenders: Forging an Urban Model," *Crime and Delinquency* 40:131–153 (1994).

19. Charlotte Gill, David Weisburd, Cody W. Telep, Zoe Vitter, and Trevor Bennett, "Community-Oriented Policing to Reduce Crime, Disorder and Fear of Crime and Increase Satisfaction and Legitimacy Among Citizens: A Systematic Review," *Journal of Experimental Criminology* 10:399–428 (2014); see also David Weisburd and John E. Eck, "What Can Police Do to Reduce Crime, Disorder, and Fear?" *Annals of the American Academy of Political and Social Science* 593:42–65 (2004), p. 57, Table 1.

20. Gill, Weisburd, Telep, Vitter, and Bennett, "Community-Oriented Policing to Reduce Crime, Disorder and Fear of Crime and Increase Satisfaction and Legitimacy Among Citizens"; Michael D. Reisig and Roger B. Parks, "Community Policing and Quality of Life," in Wesley G. Skogan, ed., *Community Policing: Can It Work?* (Belmont, CA: Wadsworth, 2004).

21. Denise C. Herz, "Improving Police Encounters with Juveniles: Does Training Make a Difference?" *Justice Research and Policy* 3:57–77 (2001).

22. Donald Black and Albert J. Reiss Jr., "Police Control of Juveniles," *American Sociological Review* 35:63 (1970); Richard Lundman, Richard Sykes, and John Clark, "Police Control of Juveniles: A Replication," *Journal of Research on Crime and Delinquency* 15:74 (1978).

23. American Bar Association, *Standards Relating to Police Handling of Juvenile Problems* (Cambridge, MA: Ballinger, 1977), p. 1.

24. Samuel Walker, *The Police of America* (New York: McGraw-Hill, 1983), p. 133.

25. Karen A. Joe, "The Dynamics of Running Away, Deinstitutionalization Policies and the Police," *Juvenile Family Court Journal* 46:43–45 (1995).

26. Mary Dodge, "Juvenile Police Informants: Friendship, Persuasion, and Pretense," *Youth Violence and Juvenile Justice* 4:234–246 (2006), at 234.

27. Ibid., p. 244.

28. Richard J. Lundman, *Prevention and Control of Delinquency*, 3rd ed. (New York: Oxford University Press, 2001), p. 23.

29. FBI, *Crime in the United States, 2014* (Washington, DC: US Government Printing Office, 2015), Table 32.

30. See Franklin E. Zimring, *American Juvenile Justice* (New York: Oxford University Press, 2005), Ch. 8.

31. Anthony A. Braga and David Weisburd, *Policing Problem Places: Crime Hot Spots and Effective Prevention* (New York: Oxford University Press, 2010); David Weisburd, Cody W. Telep, Joshua C. Hinkle, and John E.

Eck, "Is Problem-Oriented Policing Effective in Reducing Crime and Disorder? Findings from a Campbell Systematic Review," *Criminology and Public Policy* 9:139–172 (2010); Lawrence W. Sherman and John E. Eck, "Policing for Crime Prevention," in Lawrence W. Sherman, David P. Farrington, Brandon C. Welsh, and Doris Layton MacKenzie, eds., *Evidence-Based Crime Prevention*, rev. ed. (New York: Routledge, 2006); Wesley G. Skogan and Kathleen Frydl, eds., *Fairness and Effectiveness in Policing: The Evidence* (Washington, DC: National Academy Press, Committee to Review Research on Police Policy and Practices, 2004).

32. Christopher S. Koper and Evan Mayo-Wilson, "Police Crackdowns on Illegal Gun Carrying: A Systematic Review of Their Impact on Gun Crime," *Journal of Experimental Criminology* 2:227–261 (2006).

33. Linda Szymanski, *Summary of Juvenile Code Purpose Clauses* (Pittsburgh: National Center for Juvenile Justice, 1988); see also, for example, GA Code Ann. 15; Iowa Code Ann. 232.2; Mass. Gen. Laws, ch. 119, 56.

34. Samuel M. Davis, *Rights of Juveniles—The Juvenile Justice System* (New York: Clark-Boardmen, rev. June 1989), sec. 3.3.

35. National Council of Juvenile and Family Court Judges, *Juvenile and Family Law Digest* 29:1–2 (1997).

36. See Fourth Amendment, US Constitution.

37. *Arizona v. Gant*, 556 U.S. ___ (2009).

38. *Chimel v. Cal.*, 395 U.S. 752, 89 S.Ct. 2034 (1969).

39. *United States v. Ross*, 456 U.S. 798, 102 S.Ct. 2157 (1982).

40. *Terry v. Ohio*, 392 U.S. 1, 88 S.Ct. 1868 (1968).

41. *Bumper v. North Carolina*, 391 U.S. 543, 88 S.Ct. 1788 (1968).

42. *Miranda v. Arizona*, 384 U.S. 436, 86 S.Ct. 1602 (1966).

43. 564 U.S. ___ (2011).

44. *Commonwealth v. Gaskins*, 471 Pa. 238, 369 A.2d 1285 (1977); *In re E.T.C.*, 141 Vt. 375, 449 A.2d 937 (1982).

45. *People v. Lara*, 67 Cal.2d 365, 62 Cal.Rptr.586, 432 P.2d 202 (1967).

46. *West v. United States*, 399 F.2d 467 (5th Cir. 1968).

47. Barry C. Feld, *Kids, Cops, and Confessions: Inside the Interrogation Room* (New York: New York University Press, 2012); Feld, "Police Interrogation of Juveniles: An Empirical Study of Policy and Practice," *Journal of Criminal Law and Criminology* 97:219–316 (2006); Feld, " Juveniles' Competence to Exercise *Miranda* Rights: An Empirical Study of Policy and Practice," *Minnesota Law Review* 91:26–100 (2006).

48. *Fare v. Michael C.*, 442 U.S. 707, 99 S.Ct. 2560 (1979).

49. *California v. Prysock*, 453 U.S. 355, 101 S.Ct. 2806 (1981).

50. Kenneth C. Davis, *Discretionary Justice: A Preliminary Inquiry* (Baton Rouge: Louisiana State University Press, 1969); H. Ted Rubin, *Juvenile Justice: Police, Practice and Law* (Santa Monica, CA: Goodyear, 1979).

51. Joseph Goldstein, "Police Discretion Not to Invoke the Criminal Process: Low-Visibility Decisions in the Administration of Justice," *Yale Law Journal* 69:544 (1960).

52. Victor Streib, *Juvenile Justice in America* (Port Washington, NY: Kennikat, 1978).

53. Herbert Packer, *The Limits of the Criminal Sanction* (Palo Alto, CA: Stanford University Press, 1968).

54. Black and Reiss, "Police Control of Juveniles"; Richard J. Lundman, "Routine Police Arrest Practices," *Social Problems* 22:127–141 (1974); Robert E. Worden and Stephanie M. Myers, *Police Encounters with Juvenile Suspects* (Albany, NY: Hindelang Criminal Justice Research Center and School of Criminal Justice, University at Albany, SUNY, 2001).

55. Nathan Goldman, *The Differential Selection of Juvenile Offenders for Court Appearance* (Washington, DC: National Council on Crime and Delinquency, 1963).

56. Irving Piliavin and Scott Briar, "Police Encounters with Juveniles," *American Journal of Sociology* 70:206–214 (1964); Theodore Ferdinand and Elmer Luchterhand, "Inner-City Youth, the Police, Juvenile Court, and Justice," *Social Problems* 8:510–526 (1970).

57. Paul Strasburg, *Violent Delinquents: Report to Ford Foundation from Vera Institute of Justice* (New York: Monarch, 1978), p. 11; Robert Terry, "The Screening of Juvenile Offenders," *Journal of Criminal Law, Criminology, and Police Science* 58:173–181 (1967).

58. Joan McCord, Cathy Spatz Widom, and Nancy A. Crowell, eds., *Juvenile Crime, Juvenile Justice*, panel on Juvenile Crime: Prevention, Treatment, and Control (Washington, DC: National Academy Press, 2001), p. 163.

59. Worden and Myers, *Police Encounters with Juvenile Suspects*.

60. FBI, *Crime in the United States, 2014*, Table 68.

61. Douglas Smith and Christy Visher, "Street-Level Justice: Situational Determinants of Police Arrest Decisions," *Social Problems* 29:167–178 (1981).

62. Douglas Smith and Jody Klein, "Police Control of Interpersonal Disputes," *Social Problems* 31:468–481 (1984).

63. Goldman, *The Differential Selection of Juvenile Offenders for Court Appearance*, p. 25; Norman Werner and Charles Willie, "Decisions of Juvenile Officers," *American Journal of Sociology* 77:199–214 (1971).

64. Angela Higginson and Lorraine Mazerolle, "Legitimacy Policing of Places: The Impact on Crime and Disorder," *Journal of Experimental Criminology* 10:429–457 (2014); Skogan and Frydl, *Fairness and Effectiveness in Policing*, pp. 301–303; Sherman, "Fair and Effective Policing," pp. 404–405.

65. Tracey L Meares, "Broken Windows, Neighborhoods, and the Legitimacy of Law Enforcement or Why I Fell In and Out of Love with Zimbardo," *Journal of Research in Crime and Delinquency* 52:609–625 (2015).

66. Raymond Paternoster, Ronet Bachman, Robert Brame, and Lawrence W. Sherman, "Do Fair Procedures Matter? The Effect of Procedural Justice on Spouse Assault," *Law and Society Review* 31:163–204 (1997).

67. Jacinta M. Gau and Rod K. Brunson, "Procedural Justice and Order Maintenance Policing: A Study of Inner-City Young Men's Perceptions of Police Legitimacy," *Justice Quarterly* 27:255–279 (2010).

68. Ibid., p. 273.

69. David Weisburd, Alese Wooditch, Sarit Weisburd, and Sue-Ming Yang, "Do Stop, Question, and Frisk Practices Deter Crime? Evidence at Microunits of Space and Time," *Criminology and Public Policy* 15:31–56 (2016); see also Robert Apel, "On the Deterrent Effect of Stop, Question, and Frisk," *Criminology and Public Policy* 15:57–66 (2016).

70. Lyn Hinds, "Youth, Police Legitimacy and Informal Contact," *Journal of Police and Criminal Psychology* 24:10–21 (2009).

71. Dennis P. Rosenbaum, Daniel S. Lawrence, Susan M. Hartnett, Jack McDevitt, and Chad Posick, "Measuring Procedural Justice and Legitimacy at the Local Level: The Police-Community Interaction Survey," *Journal of Experimental Criminology* 11:335–366 (2015); Wesley G. Skogan, Maarten Van Craen, and Cari Hennessy, "Training Police for Procedural Justice," *Journal of Experimental Criminology* 11:319–334 (2015).

72. Ibid.; Skogan and Frydl, *Fairness and Effectiveness in Policing*, p. 7.

73. Aaron Cicourel, *The Social Organization of Juvenile Justice* (New York: Wiley, 1968).

74. Piliavin and Briar, "Police Encounters with Juveniles," p. 214.

75. David Klinger, "Demeanor or Crime? Why 'Hostile' Citizens Are More Likely to Be Arrested," *Criminology* 32:475–493 (1994).

76. Richard Lundman, "Demeanor or Crime? The Midwest City Police-Citizen Encounters Study," *Criminology* 32:631–653 (1994).

77. Robert A. Brown, Kenneth J. Novak, and James Frank, "Identifying Variation in Police Officer Behavior Between Juveniles and Adults," *Journal of Criminal Justice* 37:200–208 (2009), p. 206.

78. James Fyfe, David Klinger, and Jeanne Flaving, "Differential Police Treatment of Male-on-Female Spousal Violence," *Criminology* 35:455–473 (1997).

79. Rob Tillyer, "Opening the Black Box of Officer Decision-Making: An Examination of Race, Criminal History, and Discretionary Searches," *Justice Quarterly* 31:961–985 (2014); Dale Dannefer and Russell Schutt, "Race and Juvenile Justice Processing in Police and Court Agencies," *American Journal of Sociology* 87:1113–1132 (1982); Smith and Visher, "Street-Level Justice: Situational Determinants of Police Arrest Decisions"; also, Ronald Weitzer, "Racial Discrimination in the Criminal Justice System: Findings and Problems in the Literature," *Journal of Criminal Justice* 24:309–322 (1996); Ronald Weitzer and Steven A. Tuch, "Perceptions of Racial Profiling: Race, Class, and Personal Experience," *Criminology* 40:435–456 (2002).

80. Patricia Warren, Donald Tomaskovic-Devey, William Smith, Matthew Zingraff, and Marcinda Mason, "Driving While Black: Bias Processes and Racial Disparity in Police Stops," *Criminology* 44:709–738 (2006); Richard J. Lundman and Robert L. Kaufman, "Driving While Black: Effects of Race, Ethnicity, and Gender on Citizen Self-Reports of Traffic Stops and Police Actions," *Criminology* 41:195–220 (2003).

81. Derrick Z. Jackson, "'Broken Windows,' Broken Policy," *Boston Globe*, December 29, 2014; Editorial Board, "Broken Windows, Broken Lives," *New York Times*, July 25, 2014, http://www.nytimes.com/2014/07/26/opinion/broken-windows-broken-lives.html.

82. President's Task Force on 21st Century Policing, *Final Report of the President's Task Force on 21st Century Policing* (Washington, DC: Office of Community Oriented Police Services, 2015).

83. Dan M. Kahan and Tracey L. Meares, "The Coming Crisis of Criminal Procedure," *Georgetown Law Journal* 86:1153–1184 (2000).

84. Randall Kennedy, *Race, Crime and the Law* (New York: Vintage, 1998).

85. Donna M. Bishop and Charles E. Frazier, "The Influence of Race in Juvenile Justice Processing," *Journal of Research in Crime and Delinquency* 25:242–261 (1988); Terence Thornberry, "Race, Socioeconomic Status, and Sentencing in the Juvenile Justice System," *Journal of Criminal Law and Criminology* 70:164–171 (1979); Dannefer and Schutt, "Race and Juvenile Justice Processing in Police and Court Agencies"; Jeffrey Fagan, Ellen Slaughter, and Eliot Hartstone, "Blind Justice? The Impact of Race on the Juvenile Justice Process," *Crime and Delinquency* 33:224–258 (1987).

86. Donna M. Bishop and Michael J. Leiber, "Racial and Ethnic Differences in Delinquency and Justice System Responses," in Barry C. Feld and Donna M. Bishop, eds., *The Oxford Handbook of Juvenile Crime and Juvenile Justice* (New York: Oxford University Press, 2012).

87. Ibid.

88. See Samuel Walker, Cassie Spohn, and Miriam DeLone, *The Color of Justice: Race, Ethnicity, and Crime in America* (Belmont, CA: Wadsworth, 1996).

89. Meda Chesney-Lind and Randall G. Shelden, *Girls, Delinquency, and Juvenile Justice*, 3rd ed. (Belmont, CA: Wadsworth, 2004), p. 35.

90. Kimberly Kempf-Leonard, "The Conundrum of Girls and Juvenile Justice Processing," in Feld and Bishop, eds., *The Oxford Handbook of Juvenile Crime and Juvenile Justice*, p. 514.

91. Douglas Smith, "The Organizational Context of Legal Control," *Criminology* 22:19–38 (1984); see also Stephen Mastrofski and Richard Ritti, "Police Training and the Effects of Organization on Drunk Driving Enforcement," *Justice Quarterly* 13:291–320 (1996).

92. Katherine Beckett and Steve Herbert, *Banished: The New Social Control in Urban America* (New York: Oxford University Press, 2010).

93. President's Task Force on 21st Century Policing, *Final Report of the President's Task Force on 21st Century Policing* (Washington, DC: Office of Community Oriented Police Services, 2015).

94. Robert Sampson, "Effects of Socioeconomic Context of Official Reaction to Juvenile Delinquency," *American Sociological Review* 51:876–885 (1986).

95. See Daniel S. Nagin, Robert M. Solow, and Cynthia Lum, "Deterrence, Criminal Opportunities, and Police," *Criminology* 53:74–100 (2015).

96. Judith Greene and Kevin Pranis, *Gang Wars: The Failure of Enforcement Tactics and the Need for Effective Public Safety Strategies* (Washington, DC: Justice Policy Institute, 2007).

97. Ibid., p. 5.

98. Brian A. Reaves, *Local Police Departments, 2013: Personnel, Policies, and Practices* (Washington, DC: Bureau of Justice Statistics, 2015).

99. Edmund F. McGarrell, "Policing Juveniles," in Feld and Bishop, eds., *The Oxford Handbook of Juvenile Crime and Juvenile Justice*, p. 557.

100. Kerrin C. Wolf, "Arrest Decision Making by School Resource Officers," *Youth Violence and Juvenile Justice* 12:137–151 (2014).

101. Chongmin Na and Denise C. Gottfredson, "Police Officers in Schools: Effects on School Crime and the Processing of Offending Behaviors," *Justice Quarterly* 30:619–650 (2013).

102. Donna Lieberman, "Schoolhouse to Courthouse," *New York Times*, December 9, 2012, Sunday Review section, p. 5.

103. Gang Resistance Education and Training, https://www.great-online.org/Home/About/What-Is-GREAT; Finn-Aage Esbensen, Dana Peterson, Terrance J. Taylor, and D. Wayne Osgood, "Results from a Multi-Site Evaluation of the G.R.E.A.T. Program," *Justice Quarterly* 29:125–151 (2012); see also Finn-Aage Esbensen, Dana Peterson, Terrance J. Taylor, and Adrienne Freng, *Youth Violence: Sex and Race Differences in Offending, Victimization, and Gang Membership* (Philadelphia: Temple University Press, 2010).

104. Finn-Aage Esbensen and D. Wayne Osgood, "Gang Resistance Education and Training (G.R.E.A.T.): Results from the National Evaluation," *Journal of Research in Crime and Delinquency* 36:194–225 (1999).

105. Finn-Aage Esbensen, D. Wayne Osgood, Terrance J. Taylor, Dana Peterson, and Adrienne Freng, "How Great Is G.R.E.A.T.? Results from a Longitudinal Quasi-Experimental Design," *Criminology and Public Policy* 1:87–118 (2001).

106. Esbensen, Peterson, Taylor, and Osgood, "Results from a Multi-Site Evaluation of the G.R.E.A.T. Program."

107. Yale University Child Study Center, *Community Outreach Through Police in Schools* (Washington, DC: Office for Victims of Crime Bulletin, 2003), p. 2.

108. Ibid., p. 3.

109. Stephen A. Anderson, Ronald M. Sabatelli, and Jennifer Trachtenberg, "Community Police and Youth Programs as a Context for Positive Youth Development," *Police Quarterly* 10:23–40 (2007).

110. J. David Hirschel, Charles W. Dean, and Doris Dumond, "Juvenile Curfews and Race: A Cautionary Note," *Criminal Justice Policy Review* 12:197–214 (2001), p. 209; see also McCord, Spatz Widom, and Crowell, eds., *Juvenile Crime, Juvenile Justice*, p. 145.

111. Kenneth Adams, "The Effectiveness of Juvenile Curfews at Crime Prevention," *Annals of the American Academy of Political and Social Science* 587:136–159 (2003).

112. Kenneth Adams, "Abolish Juvenile Curfews," *Criminology and Public Policy* 6:663–670 (2007).

113. Mark H. Moore, "Problem-Solving and Community Policing," in Michael Tonry and Norval Morris, eds., *Modern Policing. Crime and Justice: A Review of Research*, Vol. 15 (Chicago: University of Chicago Press, 1992), p. 99.

114. Anthony A. Braga, *Problem-Oriented Policing and Crime Prevention*, 2nd ed. (Monsey, NY: Criminal Justice Press, 2008).

115. Moore, "Problem-Solving and Community Policing," p. 120.

116. Debra Cohen, *Problem-Solving Partnerships: Including the Community for a Change* (Washington, DC: Office of Community Oriented Policing Services, 2001), p. 2.

117. See Leanne F. Alarid, Barbara A. Sims, and James Ruiz, "Juvenile Probation and Police Partnership as Loosely Coupled Systems: A Qualitative Analysis," *Youth Violence and Juvenile Justice* 9:79–95 (2011); John L. Worrall and Larry K. Gaines, "The Effect of Police-Probation Partnerships on Juvenile Arrests," *Journal of Criminal Justice* 34:579–589 (2006).

118. See Weisburd, Telep, Hinkle, and Eck, "Is Problem-Oriented Policing Effective in Reducing Crime and Disorder? Findings from a Campbell Systematic Review."

119. Cohen, *Problem-Solving Partnerships: Including the Community for a Change*, p. 2.

120. Ibid., pp. 5–7.

121. Kelly Dedel Johnson, *Underage Drinking. Problem-Specific Guides Series*, No. 27 (Washington, DC: Office of Community Oriented Policing Services, 2004).

122. Anthony A. Braga, *Gun Violence Among Serious Young Offenders, Problem-Specific Guides Series*, No. 23, rev. ed. (Washington, DC: Office of Community Oriented Policing Services, 2010).

123. Ibid, p. 16.

124. Anthony A. Braga, David M. Kennedy, Elin J. Waring, and Anne Morrison Piehl, "Problem-Oriented Policing Deterrence, and Youth Violence: An Evaluation of Boston's Operation Ceasefire," *Journal of Research in Crime and Delinquency* 38:195–225 (2001).

125. Hans Toch, *Cop Watch: Spectators, Social Media, and Police Reform* (Washington, DC: American Psychological Association, 2012).

126. Christopher J. Harris, "Police and Soft Technology: How Information Technology Contributes to Police Decision Making," in James M. Byrne and Donald J. Rebovich, eds., *The New Technology of Crime, Law and Social Control* (Monsey, NY: Criminal Justice Press, 2007).

127. Robert J. Kane and Michael D. White, "TASER Exposure and Cognitive Impairment: Implications for Valid *Miranda* Waivers and the Timing of Police Custodial Interrogations," *Criminology and Public Policy* 15:79–107 (2016); Michael D. White, Justin T. Ready, Robert J. Kane, and L. M. Dario, "Examining the Effects of the TASER on Cognitive Functioning: Findings from a Pilot Study with Police Recruits," *Journal of Experimental Criminology* 10:267–290 (2014).

128. Don Hummer, "Policing and 'Hard' Technology," in Byrne and Rebovich, eds., *The New Technology of Crime, Law and Social Control*.

129. Brian A. Reaves, *Local Police Departments, 2013: Equipment and Technology* (Washington, DC: US Department of Justice, Bureau of Justice Statistics, 2015).

130. Eric L. Piza, Joel M. Caplan, Leslie W. Kennedy, and Andrew M. Gilchrist, "The Effects of Merging Proactive CCTV Monitoring with Directed Police Patrol: A Randomized Controlled Trial," *Journal of Experimental Criminology* 11:43–69 (2015); Brandon C. Welsh and David P. Farrington, *Making Public Places Safer: Surveillance and Crime Prevention* (New York: Oxford University Press, 2009).

131. Barak Ariel, William A. Farrar, and Alex Sutherland, "The Effect of Police Body-Worn Cameras on Use of Force and Citizens' Complaints Against Police: A Randomized Controlled Trial," *Journal of Quantitative Criminology* 31:509–535 (2015); see also Justin T. Ready and Jacob T. N. Young, "The Impact of On-Officer Video Cameras on Police-Citizen Contacts: Findings from a Controlled Experiment in Mesa, AZ," *Journal of Experimental Criminology* 11:445–458 (2015).

132. David Weisburd and John E. Eck, "What Can Police Do to Reduce Crime, Disorder, and Fear?" *Annals of the American Academy of Political and Social Science* 593:42–65 (2004); Wesley G. Skogan and Kathleen Frydl, eds., *Fairness and Effectiveness in Policing: The Evidence*, Committee to Review Research on Police Policy and Practices (Washington, DC: National Academy Press, 2004).

CHAPTER 15

Juvenile Court Process:
Pretrial, Trial, and Sentencing

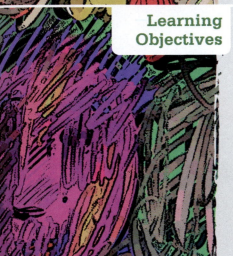

Learning Objectives

1 Discuss the roles and responsibilities of the main players in the juvenile court

2 Identify key issues of the preadjudicatory stage of juvenile justice, including detention, intake, diversion, pretrial release, plea bargaining, and waiver

3 Compare the pros and cons of transferring youths to adult court

4 Explain key issues of the trial stage of juvenile justice, including constitutional rights of youths and disposition

5 Appraise the major US Supreme Court decisions that have influenced the handling of juveniles at the preadjudicatory and trial stages

6 Discuss the most common dispositions for juvenile offenders

7 Compare the pros and cons of confidentiality in juvenile proceedings and privacy of juvenile records

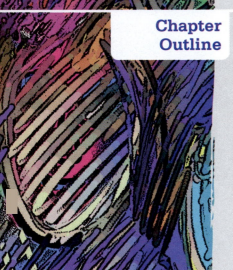

Chapter Outline

Chapter Features

Professional Spotlight: Lamont Christian Berecz

Youth Stories: Hubert Morgan

Evidence-Based Juvenile Justice—Intervention: Transfers to Adult Court Found Ineffective in Reducing Violence

"BUM FIGHTS," a website depicting homeless men and women fighting one another as well as performing dangerous and humiliating acts, and other "bum-rushing" video sites that show people causing harm to homeless people, influenced their decision to do it. This was the response of one of four teens, all of whom were found guilty in the gruesome beating death of Michael Roberts, 53, a frail homeless man who slept in woods not far from downtown Daytona Beach, Florida. The teens also said they did it "for fun" and because they had nothing better to do. The teens stumbled upon Roberts in the woods as they were searching for a place to smoke marijuana.

In three separate attacks over the course of two hours, the four teenagers—a fifth teen later pleaded no contest to a lesser charge of simple battery and received one year of probation—used their fists, feet, sticks, and logs to kill Michael Roberts as he begged for his life. As reported in the *Daytona Beach News-Journal*, Roberts died of "blunt force trauma to the head, suffered broken ribs, and was found covered in a rug with defensive wounds on his arms. But the medical examiner couldn't say for sure which was the fatal blow."

Daytona Beach Circuit Court Judge Joseph Will sentenced the four teens to a total of 120 years in prison: 35 years for both Jeffery Spurgeon, 19, and Christopher Scamahorn, 15; 28 years for Justin Stearns, 18; and 22 years for Warren Messner, 16. The two youngest, Scamahorn and Messner, were placed in a secure juvenile facility where they will remain until they

Warren Messner

turn 18 and then be transferred to an adult prison; the other two were placed in an adult prison. All four will be eligible for release upon serving 85 percent of their sentence and then will remain on supervised probation for life. Before sentencing the juveniles, Judge Will, a veteran of the juvenile and criminal courts, commented that he had never presided over a case involving such a savage murder.

C ases like these draw the ire of many and rekindle the debate over whether the juvenile court should be abolished. Because of the heinous nature of this crime, these juveniles were transferred to adult court. Some argue that this case shows exactly how the juvenile court should operate: reserve punishment for the most serious violent juvenile offenders through transfer to the adult system and provide specialized treatment for the rest. It may be that striking the right balance between treatment and punishment is becoming more important than calling for further get-tough measures.

Because the judicial process is one of the most critical points in the juvenile justice process, it is covered here in some detail. We begin with a discussion of the juvenile court and its jurisdiction. We then turn to issues involving the preadjudicatory stage of juvenile justice: detention, intake, diversion, pretrial release, plea bargaining, and waiver. The trial stage is examined next, looking at the rights of the child at trial—particularly those rights dealing with counsel and trial by jury—through a detailed analysis of US Supreme Court decisions. Procedural rules that govern the adjudicatory and dispositional hearings are also reviewed. We conclude with a discussion of dispositional alternatives and trends in sentencing.

The Juvenile Court and Its Jurisdiction

Today's juvenile delinquency cases are sometimes handled as part of a criminal trial court jurisdiction or even within the probate court. Also called surrogate court in some states, probate court is a court of special jurisdiction that handles wills, administration of estates, and guardianship of minors and incompetents. However, in most jurisdictions juvenile cases are treated in the structure of a family court or an independent juvenile court. The independent juvenile court is a specialized court for children, designed to promote rehabilitation of youths within a framework of procedural due process. It is concerned with acting both in the best interest of the child and in the best interest of public protection, two often-incompatible goals. Family courts, in contrast, have broad jurisdiction over a wide range of personal and household problems, including delinquency, paternity, child support, and custody issues. The major advantages of such a system are that it can serve sparsely populated areas, it permits judicial personnel and others to deal exclusively with children's matters, and it can obtain legislative funding more readily than other court systems.

Court Case Flow

In 2013 (the latest data available), just over 1 million delinquency cases were referred to juvenile court. This represents a 44 percent decrease in court case flow from the peak year in 1997 and a 37 percent decrease in the last decade (2004 to 2013). This recent decline comes after a steady increase or upward trend in court case flow that began in the mid-1980s.[1]

There were distinct gender- and race-based differences in the juvenile court population. In 2013, 72 percent of delinquency cases involved a male and 28 percent a female. However, the number of females processed by juvenile courts has increased from 1985, when 19 percent of the cases involved females. Similarly, 35 percent of the juvenile court population were African American youths, although African Americans make up only 16 percent of the general population.[2]

The Actors in the Juvenile Courtroom

The key players in the juvenile court are defense attorneys, prosecutors, and judges.

Juvenile defense attorneys play an active and important part in virtually all stages of juvenile court proceedings, ranging from representing youths in police custody to filing their final appeals. Shown here are defense attorney Joseph P. Cataldo and his client Michelle Carter, 18, in juvenile court in New Bedford, Massachusetts, August 24, 2015. Carter was charged with involuntary manslaughter for allegedly pressuring her friend, Conrad Roy III, 18, to commit suicide in 2014.

AP Images/Peter Pereira/The New Bedford Standard Times

The Defense Attorney   As a result of a series of Supreme Court decisions, the right of a delinquent youth to have counsel at state trials has become a fundamental part of the juvenile justice system.[3] Today, courts must provide counsel to indigent defendants who face the possibility of incarceration. Over the past three decades, the rules of juvenile justice administration have become extremely complex. Preparation of a case for juvenile court often involves detailed investigation of a crime, knowledge of court procedures, use of rules of evidence, and skills in trial advocacy. The right to counsel is essential if children are to have a fair chance of presenting their cases in court.[4]

In many respects, the role of **juvenile defense attorney** is similar to that in the criminal and civil areas. Defense attorneys representing children in the juvenile court play an active and important part in virtually all stages of the proceedings. The defense attorney helps clarify jurisdictional problems and to decide whether there is sufficient evidence to warrant filing a formal petition. The defense attorney helps outline the child's position regarding detention hearings and bail, and explores the opportunities for informal adjustment of the case. If no adjustment or diversion occurs, the defense attorney represents the child at adjudication, presenting evidence and cross-examining witnesses to see that the child's position is made clear to the court. Defense attorneys also play a critical role in the dispositional hearing. They present evidence bearing on the treatment decision and help the court formulate alternative plans for the child's care. Finally, defense attorneys pursue any appeals from the trial, represent the child in probation revocation proceedings, and generally protect the child's right to treatment.

Important to these roles are the attorney–juvenile relationship and the competence of the attorney. Some studies report that many juvenile offenders do not trust their attorney,[5] but juvenile offenders represented by private attorneys are more trusting in their attorney than those represented by court-appointed attorneys.[6] One possible reason for this difference may be the belief among juveniles that because court-appointed attorneys work for the "system" they might share information with the judge, police, or others.[7] Another dimension of the attorney–juvenile relationship is effective participation of the juvenile as a defendant, which "requires a personally relevant understanding of the lawyer's advocacy role and the confidential nature of the attorney–client relationship."[8] One study investigating effective participation among juvenile and adult defendants concluded that juveniles are in need of extra procedural safeguards, such as training for lawyers on how to be more effective counselors.[9] There may also be a need to improve the competency of juvenile defense attorneys, as well as to overcome some of the time constraints they face in case preparation. In a study of legal representation of juveniles charged with felonies in three juvenile courts in Missouri, it was found that they were more likely to receive an out-of-home placement disposition (instead of a less punitive disposition) if they had an attorney, even after controlling for other legal and individual factors.[10] Two other studies found that youths not represented by an attorney were more likely to have the charges dismissed than similar youth represented by an attorney,[11] and in one of these studies the effect was more pronounced for minorities.[12] Yet another study, the largest to date, which compared the case processing of almost 70,000 juvenile offenders in Minnesota, found that legal representation—next to an extensive prior record—was the strongest predictor of an out-of-home placement disposition.[13] (See the following section for other problems specific to public defenders.)

In some cases, a **guardian *ad litem*** may be appointed by the court.[14] The guardian *ad litem*—ordinarily seen in abuse, neglect, and dependency cases—may be appointed in delinquency cases where there is a question of a need for a particular treatment (such as placement in a mental health center), and offenders and their attorneys resist placement. The guardian *ad litem* may advocate for the commitment on the basis that it is in the child's best interests. This position fulfills many roles, ranging from legal advocate to concerned individual who works with parents and human service professionals in developing a proper treatment plan that best serves the interests of the minor child.[15]

juvenile defense attorney
Represents children in juvenile court and plays an active role at all stages of the proceedings.

guardian *ad litem*
A court-appointed attorney who protects the interests of the child in cases involving the child's welfare.

public defender
An attorney who works in a public agency or under private contractual agreement as defense counsel to indigent defendants.

Court Appointed Special Advocates (CASA)   This organization employs volunteers who advise the juvenile court about child placement. The CASA programs (*casa* is Spanish for "home") have demonstrated that volunteers can investigate the needs of children and provide vital links among the judge, the attorneys, and the child in protecting the juvenile's right to a safe placement.[16]

Public Defender Services for Children   To satisfy the requirement that indigent children be provided with counsel, the federal government and the states have expanded **public defender** services. Three alternatives exist for providing children with legal counsel: an all–public defender program, an appointed private-counsel system, and a combination system of public defenders and appointed private attorneys.

The public defender program is a statewide program established by legislation and funded by the state government to provide counsel to children at public expense. This program allows access to the expertise of lawyers, who spend a considerable amount of time representing juvenile offenders every day. Defender programs generally provide separate office space for juvenile court personnel, as well as support staff, and training programs for new lawyers.

In many rural areas, where individual public defender programs are not available, defense services are offered through appointed private counsel. Private lawyers are assigned to individual juvenile court cases, and they receive compensation for the time and services they provide. When private attorneys are used in large urban areas, they are generally selected from a list established by the court, and they often operate in conjunction with a public defender program. The weaknesses of a system of assigned private counsel include assignment to cases for which the lawyers are unqualified, inadequate compensation, and lack of supportive or supervisory services.

Although efforts have been made to supply juveniles with adequate legal representation, many juveniles still go to court unrepresented or with an overworked lawyer who provides inadequate representation. In a six-state study of access to counsel and quality of legal representation for indigent juveniles, the American Bar Association found a wide range of problems facing public defenders.[17] With juvenile offenders facing the prospect of much longer sentences, mandatory minimum sentences, and time in adult prisons, the need for quality defense attorneys for juveniles has never been greater.

Closely related to the diminishing resources of public defender services is the increasing problem with financial costs that are levied on juvenile offenders. In a recent national survey conducted by the Juvenile Law Center, it was found that juvenile offenders are subject to a range of court costs, fees, and fines in every state, with the impacts being most consequential on families of juvenile offenders who are poor and racial minorities.[18]

juvenile prosecutor
Government attorney responsible for representing the interests of the state and bringing the case against the accused juvenile.

The Prosecutor   The **juvenile prosecutor** is the attorney responsible for bringing the state's case against the accused juvenile. Depending on the level of government and the jurisdiction, the prosecutor can be called a district attorney, a county attorney, a state attorney, or a US attorney. Prosecutors are members of the bar selected for their positions by political appointment or popular election.

Ordinarily, the juvenile prosecutor is a staff member of the prosecuting attorney's office. If the office of the district attorney is of sufficient size, the juvenile prosecutor may work exclusively on juvenile and other family law matters. If the caseload of juvenile offenders is small, the juvenile prosecutor may also have criminal prosecution responsibilities.

For the first 60 years of its existence, the juvenile court did not include a prosecutor, because the concept of an adversary process was seen as inconsistent with the philosophy of treatment. The court followed a social service helping model, and informal proceedings were believed to be in the best interests of the child.

Today, in a more legalistic juvenile court, almost all jurisdictions require by law that a prosecutor be present in the juvenile court.

A number of states have passed legislation giving prosecutors control over intake and waiver decisions. Some have passed concurrent-jurisdiction laws that allow prosecutors to decide in which court to bring serious juvenile cases. In some jurisdictions, it is the prosecutor and not the juvenile court judge who is entrusted with the decision of whether to transfer a case to adult court. Consequently, the role of juvenile court prosecutor is now critical in the juvenile justice process. Including a prosecutor in juvenile court balances the interests of the state, the defense attorney, the child, and the judge, preserving the independence of each party's functions and responsibilities.

The prosecutor has the power either to initiate or to discontinue delinquency or status offense allegations. Like police officers, prosecutors have broad discretion in the exercise of their duties. Because due process rights have been extended to juveniles, the prosecutor's role in the juvenile court has in some ways become similar to the prosecutor's role in the adult court.

Because children are committing more serious crimes today and because the courts have granted juveniles constitutional safeguards, the prosecutor is likely to play an increasingly significant role in the juvenile court system. According to authors James Shine and Dwight Price, the prosecutor's involvement will promote a due process model that should result in a fairer, more just system for all parties. But they also point out that, to meet current and future challenges, prosecutors need more information on such issues as how to identify repeat offenders, how to determine which programs are most effective, how early-childhood experiences relate to delinquency, and what measures can be used in place of secure placements without reducing public safety.[19]

Today, prosecutors are addressing the problems associated with juvenile crime. A balanced approach has been recommended—one that emphasizes enforcement, prosecution, and detention of serious offenders and the use of proven prevention and intervention programs.[20] Prosecutors are also engaged in collaborations with schools and other local social institutions to help prevent juvenile delinquency.[21]

The Juvenile Court Judge   Even with the elevation of the prosecutor's role, the **juvenile court judge** is still the central character in a court of juvenile or family law. The responsibilities of this judge have become far more extensive and complex in recent years. (See Exhibit 15.1 for duties of the juvenile court judge.) Because of the importance of the juvenile court judge in the juvenile justice system, we discuss the career of one of these judges in the accompanying Professional Spotlight feature.

In addition, judges often have extensive influence over other agencies of the court: probation, the court clerk, the law enforcement officer, and the office of the juvenile prosecutor.[22] Juvenile court judges exercise considerable leadership in

juvenile court judge
A judge elected or appointed to preside over juvenile cases and whose decisions can only be reviewed by a judge of a higher court.

---

exhibit 15.1

Duties of the Juvenile Court Judge

- Rule on pretrial motions involving such legal issues as arrest, search and seizure, interrogation, and lineup identification
- Make decisions about the continued detention of children prior to trial
- Make decisions about plea bargaining agreements and the informal adjustment of juvenile cases

- Handle trials, rule on the appropriateness of conduct, settle questions of evidence and procedure, and guide the questioning of witnesses
- Assume responsibility for holding dispositional hearings and deciding on the treatment accorded the child
- Handle waiver proceedings
- Handle appeals where allowed by statute

developing solutions to juvenile justice problems. In this role they must respond to the pressures the community places on juvenile court resources. According to the *parens patriae* philosophy, the juvenile judge must ensure that the necessary community resources are available so that the children and families who come before the court can receive the proper care and help.[23] This may be the most untraditional role for the juvenile court judge, but it may also be the most important.

In some jurisdictions juvenile court judges handle family-related cases exclusively. In others they preside over criminal and civil cases as well. Traditionally, juvenile court judges have been relegated to a lower status than other judges. The National Council of Juvenile and Family Court Judges, as part of a larger effort to improve juvenile courts, took up this issue by recommending that "Juvenile delinquency court judges should have the same status as the highest level of trial court in the state and should have multiple year or permanent assignments."[24] Furthermore, judges assigned to juvenile courts have not ordinarily been chosen from the highest levels of the legal profession. Such groups as the American Judicature Society have noted that the field of juvenile justice has often been shortchanged by the appointment of unqualified judges. In some jurisdictions, particularly major urban areas, juvenile court judges may be of the highest caliber, but many courts continue to function with mediocre judges.

The **National Council of Juvenile and Family Court Judges** (http://www.ncjfcj.org/) is dedicated to serving the nation's children and families by improving the courts of juvenile and family jurisdictions.

professional SPOTLIGHT

© Lamont Christian Berecz

Lamont Christian Berecz
Juvenile Court Judge

LAMONT CHRISTIAN BERECZ is a juvenile court judge assigned to the Ada County Juvenile Court Services in Boise, Idaho. Judge Berecz decided to work in the juvenile justice system because of the vast potential to impact society in a positive way. He often tells people that the juvenile courts are one of the few places in the criminal justice system where you can see hope. He believes that in dealing with adult offenders you also hope for change, but juveniles are at such a vital stage of their lives that if you can reach them now, you can greatly affect their futures.

Judge Berecz prepared for his career as a juvenile court judge by first getting an undergraduate degree and then a law degree. After his first year of law school, he interned in a prosecuting attorney's office over the summer and was assigned to the juvenile division. It was that exposure to juvenile justice that opened his eyes to the possibilities and challenges of working with troubled youth within the legal system.

After law school, he served as a prosecutor for several years before taking the bench as a juvenile court judge. While that study of the law prepared him for the legal aspects of his job, Judge Berecz says that he values his experience working with kids over the years as a vital component to his success as a juvenile court judge.

What does Judge Berecz feel is the most rewarding part of his job? It is seeing kids change for the better. To see a child from a dysfunctional home or abusive past turn the corner and begin to realize their potential is what keeps him going in this line of work. Not all of the juveniles he sees take advantage of the services, programs, and accountability that the juvenile court provides, but the ones who do bring him the most reward and satisfaction.

For Judge Berecz, the biggest challenge he faces is dealing with the emotional toll that comes from daily seeing the heartache, trauma, neglect, and failure that surround so many juvenile offenders. Parents often present quite a challenge as well. He has seen cases where a parent started their child on drugs, abandoned them, or otherwise sabotaged the juvenile's future. On the other end of the spectrum, there are parents who view their child as a victim, who instill a sense of entitlement and resist efforts to hold their child accountable. Nevertheless, Judge Berecz finds that it is imperative that he engages the family and their unique challenges in impacting that child for positive change.

Judge Berecz finds that a common misconception people hold about his job is that there is some sort of power trip or rush that comes from being a judge and having so much authority. Quite to the contrary, he finds it to be a grave responsibility that at times can weigh on him. He says that it is not always easy to have to be the final word. On the other hand, he adds, you have the opportunity to implement great change. Judge Berecz believes that the judges who are successful in juvenile justice are those who view their position as a sacred trust given to them by the people in their community.

Inducing the best-trained individuals to accept juvenile court judgeships is a very important goal. Where the juvenile court is part of the highest general court of trial jurisdiction, the problem of securing qualified personnel is not as great. However, if the juvenile court is of limited or specialized jurisdiction and has the authority to try only minor cases, it may attract only poorly trained personnel. Lawyers and judges who practice in juvenile court receive little respect. The juvenile court has a negative image because even though what it does is of great significance to parents, children, and society in general, it has been placed at the lowest level of the judicial hierarchy.

Juvenile Court Process

Now that we have briefly described the setting of the juvenile court and the major players who control its operations, we turn to a discussion of the procedures that shape the contours of juvenile justice—the pretrial process and the juvenile trial and disposition. Many critical decisions are made at this stage in the juvenile justice system: whether to detain youths or release them to the community; whether to waive youths to the adult court or retain them in the juvenile justice system; whether to treat them in the community or send them to a secure treatment center. Each of these can have a profound influence on the child, with effects lasting throughout the life course. What are these critical stages, and how are decisions made within them?

Release or Detain?

After a child has been taken into custody and a decision is made to treat the case formally (i.e., with a juvenile court hearing), a decision must be made either to release the child into the custody of parents or to detain the child in the temporary care of the state in physically restrictive facilities, pending court disposition or transfer to another agency.

Detention can be a traumatic experience because many facilities are prisonlike, with locked doors and barred windows. Consequently, most experts in juvenile justice advocate that detention be limited to alleged offenders who require secure custody for the protection of themselves and others. However, children who are neglected and dependent, runaways, and those who are homeless may under some circumstances be placed in secure detention facilities along with violent and dangerous youths until more suitable placements can be found.[25] Others have had a trial but have not been sentenced, or are awaiting the imposition of their sentence. Some may have violated probation and are awaiting a hearing while being kept alongside severely mentally ill adolescents for whom no appropriate placement can be found. Another group are adjudicated delinquents awaiting admittance to a correctional training school.[26] Consequently, it is possible for nonviolent status offenders to be housed in the same facility with delinquents who have committed felony-type offenses.

A study of child detention centers in New Jersey found that one out of every four youths in the centers (about 2,500 out of 10,000) were placed there inappropriately and should have instead been placed in hospitals, foster care homes, or other noncustodial settings. Because of the inappropriate placement in detention facilities, many of these youths were preyed upon by violent youth, did not receive much-needed medical or mental care, and resorted to self-harm or suicide attempts as a way to cope or escape from the dangerous and chaotic setting.[27] In another study of detained youth in Cook County's Temporary Juvenile Detention Center in Chicago, 1 in 10 (10.3 percent) considered taking their own life in the past six months and 11 percent attempted suicide at some point in their detention. It was also found that suicide attempts were more prevalent among female detainees.[28]

Detention
Temporary care of a child alleged to be delinquent who requires secure custody in physically restricting facilities pending court disposition or execution of a court order.

To remedy these situations, an ongoing effort has been made to remove status offenders and neglected or abused children from detention facilities that also house juvenile delinquents. In addition, alternatives to detention centers—temporary foster homes, detention boarding homes, and programs of neighborhood supervision—have been developed.[29] These alternatives, referred to as **shelter care**, enable youths to live in a more homelike setting while the courts dispose of their cases.

Project Confirm in New York City is one example of an effort to reduce the detention of foster care youths who have been arrested. Very often these youths who otherwise would have been released are placed in detention facilities because their guardians fail to appear in court, a result of a breakdown in communication between (and within) the child welfare and juvenile justice systems. The project involved two main strategies to overcome this problem: notifying project staff upon a youth's arrest to allow for a search of child welfare databases, and court conferencing among child welfare and juvenile justice authorities. An evaluation of the project found that disparity in detention experienced by foster care youths compared to a similar group of non-foster care youths was reduced among those charged with minor offenses and with no prior detentions but increased among those charged with more serious offenses and prior police contact. The authors speculate that the improved quality of information provided by the project to the court, especially prior detentions, coupled with court officials' preconceived notions of the likelihood of these youths to commit another crime or fail to appear in court, resulted in more serious cases being detained.[30]

National Detention Trends   Despite an ongoing effort to limit detention, juveniles are still being detained in one out of every five delinquency cases (21 percent), with some variation across the major offense categories: violent (26 percent), property (17 percent), drugs (14 percent), and public order (24 percent). While the detention rate for delinquency cases is slightly down from 1990, in which the percentage of cases detained was highest (23 percent), between 1990 and 2013, the total number of juveniles held in short-term detention facilities decreased 27 percent, from 302,800 to 221,600.[31]

The typical delinquent detainee is male, over 16 years of age, and charged with a violent crime.[32] Racial minorities are heavily overrepresented in detention (see Figure 15.1), especially those who are indigent and whose families may be

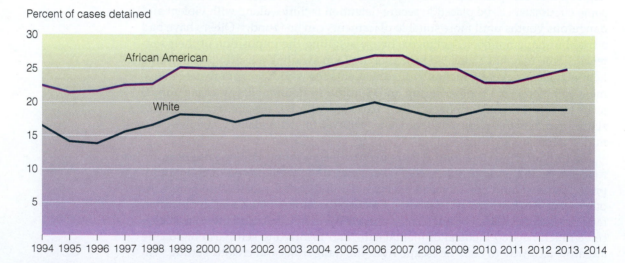

Percent of cases detained

figure 15.1

Cases Involving Detention of African American Juveniles vs. White Juveniles

SOURCE: Melissa Sickmund, Anthony Sladky, and Wei Kang, *Easy Access to Juvenile Court Statistics: 1985–2013* (Pittsburgh: National Center for Juvenile Justice, 2015), http://ojjdp.gov/ojstatbb/ezajcs/ (accessed October 2016).

receiving public assistance. Minority overrepresentation is particularly vexing, considering that detention may increase the risk of a youth being adjudicated and eventually confined.[33]

In a study of the extent of racial discrimination and disparity among male juvenile property offenders in six Missouri counties at four stages of juvenile justice (decision to file a petition, pretrial detention, adjudication, and disposition), it was found that African American youth were more likely than white youth to be detained prior to adjudication (40 percent compared to 22 percent).[34] The study also found that African American youth were more likely to be formally referred, and white youth were more likely to be adjudicated. The authors speculate that a "correction of biases" may be one reason for white youth being more likely than African American youth to be adjudicated—that is, "judges may dismiss black youths because they feel that a detained youth has been punished enough already."[35] In another study, being African American was one of the key factors that predicted longer time spent in detention. Also important were prior mental health service, neglect, physical abuse, personal crime offense, and early age of first delinquency adjudication.[36]

The Decision to Detain   Most children taken into custody by the police are released to their parents or guardians. Some are held overnight until their parents can be notified of the arrest. Police officers normally take a child to a place of detention only after other alternatives have been exhausted. Many juvenile courts in urban areas have staff members, such as intake probation officers, on duty 24 hours a day to screen detention admissions.

Ordinarily, delinquent children are detained if the police believe they are inclined to run away while awaiting trial, or if they are likely to commit an offense dangerous to the parent. There is evidence that some decision makers are more likely to detain minority youth, especially if they live in dangerous, lower-class areas.[37] The use of screening instruments to determine the need for detention has proven useful.[38]

Generally, children should not be held in a detention facility or shelter care unit for more than 24 hours without a formal petition (a written request to the court) being filed to extend the detention period. To detain a juvenile, there must be clear evidence of probable cause that the child has committed the offense and that he or she will flee if not detained. Although the requirements for detention hearings vary, most jurisdictions require that they occur almost immediately after the child's admission to a detention facility and provide the youth with notice and counsel.

New Approaches to Detention   Efforts have been ongoing to improve the process and conditions of detention. Experts maintain that detention facilities should provide youth with education, visitation, private communications, counseling, continuous supervision, medical and health care, nutrition, recreation, and reading. Detention should also include, or provide, a system for clinical observation and diagnosis that complements the wide range of helpful services.[39]

The consensus today is that juvenile detention centers should be reserved for youths who present a clear threat to the community. In some states, nonsecure facilities are being used to service juveniles for a limited period. Alternatives to secure detention include in-home monitoring, home detention, day-center electronic monitoring, high-intensity community supervision, and comprehensive case management programs.

Undoubtedly, juveniles pose special detention problems, but some efforts are being made to improve programs and to reduce pretrial detention use, especially in secure settings. Of all the problems associated with detention, however, none is as critical as the issue of placing youths in adult jails.

Restricting Detention in Adult Jails   A significant problem in juvenile justice is placing youths in adult jails. This is usually done in rural areas where no other facility exists. Almost all experts agree that placing children under the age of 18 in any type of jail facility should be prohibited because youngsters can easily be victimized by other inmates and staff, be forced to live in squalid conditions, and be subject to physical and sexual abuse.

Until a few years ago, placing juveniles in adult facilities was common, but efforts have been made to change this situation. In 1989, the Juvenile Justice and Delinquency Prevention Act (JJDPA) of 1974 was amended to require that the states remove all juveniles from adult jails and lockups. According to federal guidelines, all juveniles in state custody must be separated from adult offenders, or the state could lose federal juvenile justice funds. The OJJDP defines separation as the condition in which juvenile detainees have either totally independent facilities or shared facilities that are designed so that juveniles and adults neither have contact nor share programs or staff.[40]

Much debate has arisen over whether the initiative to remove juveniles from adult jails has succeeded. Most indications are that the number of youths being held in adult facilities has declined significantly from the almost 500,000 a year recorded in 1979.

Removing Status Offenders

Along with removing all juveniles from adult jails, the OJJDP has made deinstitutionalization of status offenders a cornerstone of its policy. The Juvenile Justice and Delinquency Prevention Act of 1974 prohibits the placement of status offenders in secure detention facilities.

Removing status offenders from secure facilities serves two purposes: it reduces interaction with serious offenders, and it insulates status offenders from the stigma associated with being a detainee in a locked facility. Efforts appear to be working, and the number of status offenders being held in some sort of secure confinement has been on a two-decade decline. Nonetheless, the debate over the most effective way to handle juvenile status offenders continues, and some critics have argued that if the juvenile court is unable to take effective action in status offender cases, it should be stripped of jurisdiction over these youths. Most judges would prefer to retain jurisdiction so they can help children and families resolve problems that cause runaways, truancy, and other status offense behaviors.[41]

Bail for Children

bail
Amount of money that must be paid as a condition of pretrial release to ensure that the accused will return for subsequent proceedings. Bail is normally set by the judge at the initial appearance, and if unable to make bail, the accused is detained in jail.

One critical pretrial issue is whether juveniles can be released on **bail**. Adults retain the right, via the Eighth Amendment to the Constitution, to reasonable bail in noncapital cases. Most states, however, refuse juveniles the right to bail. They argue that juvenile proceedings are civil, not criminal, and that detention is rehabilitative, not punitive. In addition, they argue that juveniles do not need a constitutional right to bail because statutory provisions allow children to be released into parental custody.

State juvenile bail statutes fall into three categories: those guaranteeing the right to bail, those that grant the court discretion to give bail, and those that deny a juvenile the right to bail.[42] This disparity may be a function of the lack of legal guidance on the matter. The Supreme Court has never decided the issue of juvenile bail. Some courts have stated that bail provisions do not apply to juveniles. Others rely on the Eighth Amendment against cruel and unusual punishment, or on state constitutional provisions or statutes, and conclude that juveniles do have a right to bail.

preventive detention
Keeping the accused in custody prior to trial because the accused is suspected of being a danger to the community.

Preventive Detention

Although the Supreme Court has not yet decided whether juveniles have a right to traditional money bail, they have concluded that the state has a right to detain dangerous youths until their trial, a practice called **preventive detention**. On June 4, 1984, the Supreme Court dealt with this issue in *Schall v. Martin*, when it upheld the state of New York's preventive detention statute.[43] However, the case also established a due process standard for detention hearings that includes notice and a statement of substantial reasons for the detention. Despite these measures, opponents hold that preventive detention deprives offenders of their freedom because guilt has not been proven. It is also unfair, they claim, to punish people for what judicial authorities believe they may do in the future, as it is impossible to predict who will be a danger to the community. Moreover, because judges use discretion in their detention decisions, an offender could unfairly be deprived of freedom without legal recourse. Today, most states allow "dangerous" youths to be held indefinitely before trial. Because preventive detention may attach a stigma of guilt to a child presumed innocent, the practice remains a highly controversial one, and the efficacy of such laws remains largely unknown.[44]

The Intake Process

The term **intake** refers to the screening of cases by the juvenile court system. The child and his or her family are screened by intake officers to determine whether the services of the juvenile court are needed. Intake officers may (a) send the youth home with no further action, (b) divert the youth to a social agency, (c) petition the youth to the juvenile court, or (d) file a petition and hold the youth in detention. The intake process reduces demands on court resources, screens out cases that are not within the court's jurisdiction, and enables assistance to be obtained from community agencies without court intervention. Juvenile court intake is provided for by statute in almost all of the states.

After reviewing the case, justice system authorities decide whether to dismiss, informally handle, or formally process the case by taking the matter before a judge. Eighteen percent (191,800) of all delinquency cases in 2013 were dismissed at intake, often because they were not legally sufficient. Another 27 percent (283,800) were processed informally, with the juvenile voluntarily agreeing to the recommended disposition (e.g., voluntary treatment).[45]

Intake screening allows juvenile courts to enter into consent decrees with juveniles without filing petitions and without formal adjudication. A **consent decree** is an order of the court that authorizes disposition of the case without a formal label of delinquency. It is based on an agreement between the intake department of the court and the juvenile who is the subject of the complaint.

But intake also suffers from some problems.[46] Although almost all state juvenile court systems provide intake and diversion programs, few formal criteria exist for selecting children for such alternatives. There are also legal problems associated with the intake process. Among them are whether the child has a right to counsel, whether the child is protected against self-incrimination, and to what degree the child needs to consent to nonjudicial disposition as recommended by the intake

intake
Process during which a juvenile referral is received and a decision is made to file a petition in juvenile court to release the juvenile, to place the juvenile under supervision, or to refer the juvenile elsewhere.

consent decree
A court order authorizing disposition of a case without a formal label of delinquency.

The intake process involves the screening of cases by the juvenile court system. Intake officers, who are often probation staff members, determine whether the services of the juvenile court are needed. Here, juvenile offenders beginning the intake process are searched by a correctional officer at the Department of Youth Services Detention Center in Rathbone, Ohio.

AP Images/Will Shilling

officer. Finally, intake dispositions are often determined by the prior record rather than by the seriousness of the offense or the social background of the child. Race has also been shown to influence intake decisions. A study of juvenile males in one county court in Iowa found that African American juveniles were more likely than their Caucasian counterparts to receive a court referral.[47] Race has also been shown to play a role in the decision to make a court referral for status offenders.[48] This is part of the widely documented (but understudied) problem of disproportionate minority contact that extends from first contact with police throughout the entire juvenile justice process.[49]

Diversion

diversion
Official halting or suspending of a formal criminal or juvenile justice proceeding at any legally prescribed processing point after a recorded justice system entry, and referral of that person to a treatment or care program or a recommendation that the person be released.

One of the most important alternatives chosen at intake is nonjudicial disposition or, as it is variously called, nonjudicial adjustment, handling or processing, informal disposition, adjustment, or (most commonly) **diversion**. Juvenile diversion is the process of placing youths suspected of law-violating behavior into treatment-oriented programs prior to formal trial and disposition in order to minimize their penetration into the justice system and thereby avoid stigma and labeling.[50]

Diversion implies more than simply screening out cases for which no additional treatment is needed. Screening involves abandoning efforts to apply coercive measures to a defendant. In contrast, diversion encourages an individual to participate in some specific program or activity to avoid further prosecution.

Most court-based diversion programs employ a particular formula for choosing youths, which is quite similar to police-based diversion programs.[51] Criteria such as being a first offender, a nonviolent offender, or a status offender, or being drug or alcohol dependent, are used to select clients. In some programs, youths will be asked to partake of services voluntarily in lieu of a court appearance. In other programs, prosecutors will agree to defer, and then dismiss, a case once a youth has completed a treatment program. Finally, some programs can be initiated by the juvenile court judge after an initial hearing. Concept Summary 15.1 lists the factors considered in diversion decisions.

In sum, diversion programs have been created to remove nonserious offenders from the justice system, provide them with nonpunitive treatment services, and help them avoid the stigma of a delinquent label.

Issues in Diversion: Widening the Net   Diversion has been viewed as a promising alternative to official procedures, but over the years its basic premises have been questioned.[52] The most damaging criticism has been that diversion programs are involving children in the juvenile justice system who previously would have been released without official notice. This is referred to as **widening the net**. Various studies indicate that police and court personnel are likely to use diversion programs for youths who ordinarily would have been turned loose at the intake or arrest stage.[53] Why does net-widening occur? One explanation is that police and prosecutors find diversion a more attractive alternative than both official processing and outright release—diversion helps them resolve the conflict between doing too much and doing too little.

widening the net
Phenomenon that occurs when programs created to divert youths from the justice system actually involve them more deeply in the official process.

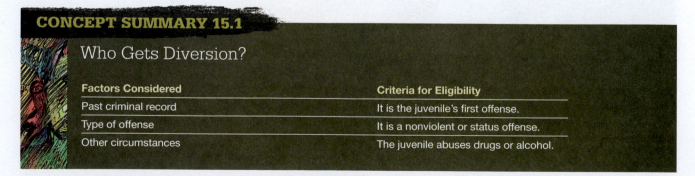

CONCEPT SUMMARY 15.1

Who Gets Diversion?

Factors Considered	Criteria for Eligibility
Past criminal record	It is the juvenile's first offense.
Type of offense	It is a nonviolent or status offense.
Other circumstances	The juvenile abuses drugs or alcohol.

Diversion has also been criticized as ineffective—that is, youths being diverted make no better adjustment in the community than those who go through official channels. However, not all experts are critical of diversion. Some challenge the net-widening concept as naive: How do we know that diverted youths would have had less interface with the justice system if diversion didn't exist?[54] Even if juveniles escaped official labels for their current offense, might they not eventually fall into the hands of the police? The rehabilitative potential of diversion should not be overlooked.[55] There is some evidence that diversion with a treatment component for juveniles suffering from mental health problems can delay or prevent further delinquent activity.[56]

Some experts even argue that diversion has been the centerpiece or at least a core element of the juvenile justice system's success in limiting the growth of juvenile incarceration rates over the last three decades, which were dwarfed by the dramatic increase in incarceration rates among young adult offenders (ages 18 to 24) over the same period of time.[57] In the words of legal scholar Franklin Zimring:

> The angry assaults on juvenile courts throughout the 1990s are a tribute to the efficacy of juvenile justice in protecting delinquents from the incarcerative explosion that had happened everywhere else.[58]

The Petition

A **complaint** is the report made by the police or some other agency to the court to initiate the intake process. Once the agency makes a decision that judicial disposition is required, a petition is filed. Recall from Chapter 13 that the petition is the formal complaint initiating judicial action against a juvenile charged with delinquency or a status offense. The petition includes basic information such as the name, age, and residence of the child; the parents' names; and the facts alleging the child's delinquency. The police officer, a family member, or a social service agency can file a petition.

If after being given the right to counsel, the child admits the allegation in the petition, an initial hearing is scheduled for the child to make the admission before the court, and information is gathered to develop a treatment plan. If the child does not admit to any of the facts in the petition, a date is set for a hearing on the petition. This hearing, whose purpose is to determine the merits of the petition, is similar to the adult trial. Once a hearing date has been set, the probation department is normally asked to prepare a social study report. This predisposition report contains relevant information about the child, along with recommendations for treatment and service.

When a date has been set for the hearing on the petition, parents or guardians and other persons associated with the petition (witnesses, the arresting police officer, and victims) are notified. On occasion, the court may issue a summons—a court order requiring the juvenile or others involved in the case to appear for the hearing. The statutes in a given jurisdiction govern the contents of the petition. Some jurisdictions, for instance, allow for a petition to be filed based on the information of the complainant alone. Others require that the petition be filed under oath or that an affidavit accompany the petition. Some jurisdictions authorize only one official, such as a probation officer or prosecutor, to file the petition. Others allow numerous officials, including family and social service agencies, to set forth facts in the petition.

The Plea and Plea Bargaining

In the adult criminal justice system, the defendant normally enters a plea of guilty or not guilty. Upward of 95 percent of all adult defendants plead guilty. A large proportion of those pleas involve **plea bargaining**, the exchange of prosecutorial and judicial concessions for guilty pleas.[59] Plea bargaining permits a defendant to plead guilty to a less serious charge in exchange for an agreement by the prosecutor to recommend a reduced sentence to the court.[60] In the case of juvenile justice, it involves a discussion between the child's attorney and the prosecutor by which the child agrees to plead guilty to obtain a reduced charge or a lenient sentence.

complaint
Report made by the police or some other agency to the court that initiates the intake process.

plea bargaining
The exchange of prosecutorial and judicial concessions for a guilty plea by the accused; plea bargaining usually results in a reduced charge or a more lenient sentence.

youth STORIES

Hubert Morgan

It was just meant to be a good-natured bout of wrestling—or "horseplay," as it would come to be classified in the official report of the incident—a way for juvenile inmates and correctional officers to let off some steam and pass the time. No one was supposed to get hurt. Although correctional officers were prohibited from engaging in such "inappropriate contact," inmates reported that wrestling was commonplace among guards and inmates. On April 29, 2009, at the Cuyahoga Hills Juvenile Correctional Facility in Cuyahoga County, Ohio, juvenile correctional officer William Hesson, 39, died from being kicked in the chest by Hubert Morgan, 17. According to the official report from the investigation into the incident, Hesson had Morgan in a headlock when Morgan kneed him in the chest. The coroner determined that Hesson died of a "cardiac rhythm disturbance caused by a blow to the abdomen" and ruled his death a homicide.

Like many times before, the two had gone to the laundry room to wrestle, sometimes with other inmates. But the prosecutor did not take this incident lightly, charging Morgan with murder and felonious assault. If convicted, Hubert Morgan faced the prospect of a life sentence without the possibility of parole. In the course of the defendant being charged and awaiting his trial in adult court, Morgan's lawyer set about to negotiate a plea for a lower sentence. A plea bargain was eventually struck between the two parties and accepted by the judge. On January 4, 2010, Hubert Morgan, now age 18, pleaded guilty to voluntary manslaughter, with a maximum sentence of 10 years in prison. On March 1, the defendant was sentenced to 7 years in prison.

The following are some key points in the plea bargaining process:

■ Plea bargaining negotiations generally involve one or more of the following: reduction of a charge, change in

AP Images/Plain Dealer, Marvin Fong

the proceedings from that of delinquency to a status offense, elimination of possible waiver to the criminal court, and agreements regarding dispositional programs for the child.

■ In states where youths are subject to long mandatory sentences, reduction of the charges may have a significant impact on the outcome of the case.

■ In states where youths may be waived to the adult court for committing certain serious crimes, a plea reduction may result in the juvenile courts maintaining jurisdiction.

CRITICAL THINKING

Is this an appropriate case for plea bargaining? Considering the above points, when should plea bargaining be used for juvenile offenders?

SOURCES: Pat Galbincea with Donna J. Miller, "Wakeman Teen Sentenced to Seven Years for Horseplay that Killed Juvenile Detention Center Guard," *Plain Dealer*, March 2, 2010, http://blog.cleveland.com /metro/2010/03/wakeman_teen_sentenced_seven_y.html; "Ohio Guard Dies After Horseplay with Teen," *USA Today*, January 5, 2010, http://usatoday30.usatoday.com/news/nation/2010-01-05-ohio-youth-prison -horseplay-death_N.htm. (URLs accessed October 2016.)

Few juvenile codes require a guilty or not-guilty plea when a petition is filed against a child. In most jurisdictions an initial hearing is held at which the child either submits to a finding of the facts or denies the petition.[61] If the child admits to the facts, the court determines an appropriate disposition. If the child denies the allegations, the case normally proceeds to trial. When a child enters no plea, the court ordinarily imposes a denial of the charges. This may occur where a juvenile doesn't understand the nature of the complaint or isn't represented by an attorney.

A high percentage of juvenile offenders enter guilty pleas—that is, they admit to the facts of the petition. How many of these pleas involve plea bargaining is unknown. In the past it was believed that plea bargaining was unnecessary in the juvenile justice system because there was little incentive to bargain in a system that does not have jury trials or long sentences. In addition, because the court must dispose of cases in the best interests of the child, plea negotiation seemed unnecessary. Consequently, there has long been a debate over the appropriateness of plea bargaining in juvenile justice. The arguments in favor of plea bargaining include lower court costs and efficiency. Counterarguments hold that plea bargaining with juveniles is an unregulated and unethical process. When used, experts believe the process requires the highest standards of good faith by the prosecutor.[62]

There is little clear evidence on how much plea bargaining takes place in the juvenile justice system, but it is apparent that such negotiations do take place and seem to be increasing. Joseph Sanborn found that about 20 percent of the cases processed in Philadelphia resulted in a negotiated plea. Most were for reduced sentences, typically probation in lieu of incarceration. Sanborn found that plea bargaining was a complex process, depending in large measure on the philosophy of the judge and the court staff. In general, he found it to have greater benefit for the defendants than for the court.[63] More recent research conducted by criminologists John Burrow and Patrick Lowery focused on the factors that influence plea bargaining for juvenile offenders. Using a large group of waiver-eligible offenders in a juvenile court in South Carolina, the researchers found that the key factors included type of offense, number of victims, and age and race of the offender.[64]

In summary, the majority of juvenile cases that are not adjudicated seem to be the result of admissions to the facts rather than actual plea bargaining. Plea bargaining is less common in juvenile courts than in adult courts because incentives such as dropping multiple charges or substituting a misdemeanor for a felony are unlikely. Nonetheless, plea bargaining is firmly entrenched in the juvenile process. Any plea bargain, however, must be entered into voluntarily and knowingly; otherwise, the conviction may be overturned on appeal. Because of its importance in the juvenile court process, plea bargaining is the subject of the accompanying Youth Stories feature.

Transfer to the Adult Court

One of the most significant actions that can occur in the early court processing of a juvenile offender is the **transfer process**. Otherwise known as waiver, bindover, or removal, this process involves transferring a juvenile from the juvenile court to the adult criminal court. Virtually all state statutes allow for this kind of transfer.

transfer process
Transfer of a juvenile offender from the jurisdiction of juvenile court to adult criminal court.

Some youths who commit the most serious crimes are routinely waived to adult court. Pictured here is Braiden McCahren, 18, outside the courthouse in Pierre, South Dakota. In September 2013, McCahren was convicted by a jury in adult court for second-degree murder in the December 2012 death of Dalton Williams, 16.

AP Images/Courtesy of KDLT-TV

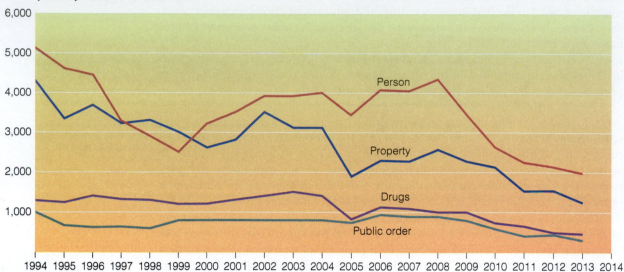

Cases judicially waived to criminal court

figure 15.2

Delinquency Cases Waived to Criminal Court, by Type of Offense

SOURCE: Melissa Sickmund, Anthony Sladky, and Wei Kang, *Easy Access to Juvenile Court Statistics: 1985–2013* (Pittsburgh: National Center for Juvenile Justice, 2015), http://ojjdp.gov/ojstatbb/ezajcs/ (accessed October 2016).

The number of delinquency cases judicially waived to criminal court peaked in 1994 at 13,100 cases, an increase of 82 percent over the number of cases waived in 1985 (7,200). From 1994 to 2013 (the latest data available), however, the number of cases waived to criminal court declined by 69 percent to 4,000 cases, representing 1 percent of the formally processed delinquency caseload.[65] Between 1985 and 2013, person offense cases were the most likely to be waived to criminal court. The only exceptions were 1989 to 1992, when drug offenses were most likely to be judicially waived.[66] Figure 15.2 shows numbers of delinquency cases waived to criminal court from 1994 to 2013.

Waiver Procedures

Today, all states allow juveniles to be tried as adults in criminal courts in one of three ways:

- *Concurrent jurisdiction.* In 14 states and the District of Columbia, the prosecutor has the discretion of filing charges for certain offenses in either juvenile or criminal court.

- *Statutory exclusion policies.* In 29 states, certain offenses are automatically excluded from juvenile court. These offenses can be minor, such as traffic violations, or serious, such as murder or rape. Statutory exclusion accounts for the largest number of juveniles tried as adults.

- *Judicial waiver.* In the waiver (or bindover or removal) of juvenile cases to criminal court, a hearing is held before a juvenile court judge, who then decides whether jurisdiction should be waived and the case transferred to criminal court. Forty-four states and the District of Columbia (not Connecticut, Massachusetts, Montana, Nebraska, New Mexico, or New York) offer provisions for juvenile waivers.[67]

Due Process in Transfer Proceedings

The standards for transfer procedures are set by state statute. Some jurisdictions allow for transfer between the ages of 14 and 17. Others restrict waiver proceedings to mature juveniles and specify particular offenses. In a few jurisdictions, any child can be transferred to the criminal court system, regardless of age.

Those states that have amended their waiver policies with statutory exclusion policies now exclude certain serious offenses from juvenile court jurisdiction. For example, Indiana excludes cases involving 16- and 17-year-olds charged with murder, drug and weapons offenses, and certain felonies and other person offenses. In Illinois, youths ages 13 and older who are charged with murder and youths ages 15 and older who are charged with drug and weapons offenses and certain felonies and other person offenses are automatically sent to criminal court. In Nevada and Pennsylvania, any child accused of murder, regardless of age, is tried before the criminal court.[68] Other jurisdictions use exclusion to remove traffic offenses and public-ordinance violations.

The trend toward excluding serious violent offenses from juvenile court jurisdictions is growing in response to the demand to get tough on crime. In addition, large numbers of youth under age 18 are tried as adults in states where the upper age of juvenile court jurisdiction is 15 or 16.

In a small number of states, statutes allow prosecutors to file particularly serious cases in either the juvenile court or the adult court.[69] Prosecutor discretion may occasionally be a more effective transfer mechanism than the waiver process, because the prosecutor can file a petition in criminal or juvenile court without judicial approval.

Since 1966, the US Supreme Court and other federal and state courts have attempted to ensure fairness in the judicial waiver process by handing down decisions that spell out the need for due process. Two Supreme Court decisions, *Kent v. United States* (1966) and *Breed v. Jones* (1975), are relevant.[70] The *Kent* case declared a District of Columbia transfer statute unconstitutional and attacked the subsequent conviction of the child by granting him the specific due process rights of having an attorney present at the hearing and access to the evidence that would be used in the case.

The *Kent* case was significant because it examined for the first time the substantial degree of discretion associated with a transfer proceeding. Thus, the Supreme Court significantly limited its holding to the statute involved but justified its reference to constitutional principles relating to due process and the assistance of counsel. In addition, it said that the juvenile court waiver hearings need to measure up to the essentials of due process and fair treatment. Furthermore, in an appendix to its opinion, the Court set up the following criteria concerning waiver of the jurisdictions:

- The seriousness of the alleged offense to the community
- Whether the alleged offense was committed in an aggressive, violent, or willful manner
- Whether the alleged offense was committed against persons or against property
- The prosecutive merit of the complaint
- The sophistication and maturity of the juvenile
- The record and previous history of the juvenile
- Prospects for adequate protection of the public and the likelihood of reasonable rehabilitation

In *Breed v. Jones*, the Supreme Court declared that the child was to be granted the protection of the double jeopardy clause of the Fifth Amendment after he was tried as a delinquent in the juvenile court: once found to be a delinquent, the youth can no longer be tried as an adult. The *Breed* case provided answers on several transfer issues: (a) It prohibits trying a child in an adult court when there has been a prior adjudicatory juvenile proceeding; (b) probable cause may exist at a transfer hearing, and this does not violate subsequent jeopardy if the child is transferred to the adult court; and (c) because the same evidence is often used in both the transfer hearing and subsequent trial in either the juvenile or adult court, a different judge is often required for each hearing.

Today, as a result of *Kent* and *Breed*, states that have **transfer hearings** provide a legitimate transfer hearing, sufficient notice to the child's family and defense attorney, the right to counsel, and a statement of the reason for the court order regarding transfer. These procedures recognize that the transfer process is critical in determining the statutory rights of the juvenile offender.

transfer hearings
Preadjudicatory hearing in juvenile court for the purpose of determining whether juvenile court should be retained over a juvenile or waived and the juvenile transferred to adult court for prosecution.

Transfers to Adult Court Found Ineffective in Reducing Violence

In all the debate surrounding transfers of juvenile offenders to adult or criminal court, one of the most important issues—for some it is the bottom line on this matter—concerns whether or not transfers are effective in reducing crime rates. One of the pressing questions is this: are juveniles who are transferred to and convicted in adult court less likely to recidivate than

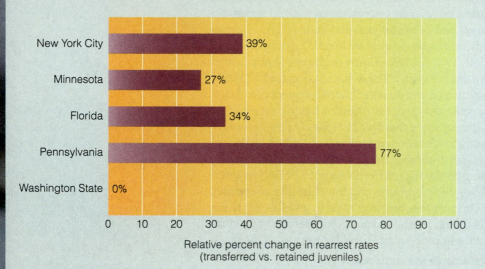

figure 15.A

Effects of Transfer on Rearrests of Transferred Juveniles

SOURCE: Adapted from Angela McGowan et al., "Effects on Violence of Laws and Policies Facilitating the Transfer of Juveniles from the Juvenile Justice System to the Adult Justice System: A Systematic Review," *American Journal of Preventive Medicine* 32(4S): 7–28 (2007).

similar youths who are convicted in juvenile court? This pertains to a specific or individual deterrent effect of transfers. Another key question, which pertains to a general deterrent effect, can be framed as such: do transfers decrease crime

rates in the juvenile population as a whole? This could be for a city or state, for example. In recent years, a number of high-quality studies have investigated the effectiveness of transfers on these two fronts.

The Task Force on Community Preventive Services, an independent group that receives support from the US Department of Health and Human Services and the Centers for Disease Control and Prevention, conducted the first comprehensive, methodologically rigorous review of the literature—known as a systematic review—on the effects of transfer laws and policies on crime rates. The review identified six high-quality evaluation studies (each had experimental and comparable control groups) that measured the specific deterrent effect of transfers on violent crime rates. As shown in Figure 15.A, not one of the studies found that transfers produced lower violent crime rates. In fact, four of the studies found a harmful effect, meaning that juveniles transferred to adult court had higher violent rearrest rates than their counterparts who were retained in juvenile court. For these four studies, rearrest rates for the transferred juveniles were between 27 percent and 77 percent higher than the nontransferred juveniles. The authors of the review also reported that these studies found harmful effects for total crime rates as well. (The sixth study, which also found similar harmful effects for violent crime but favorable effects for

Should Youths Be Transferred to Adult Court?

Most juvenile justice experts oppose waiver because it clashes with the rehabilitative ideal. Basing waiver decisions on type and seriousness of offense rather than on the rehabilitative needs of the child has advanced the *criminalization* of the juvenile court and interfered with its traditional mission of treatment and rehabilitation.[71] And despite this sacrifice, there is little evidence that strict waiver policies can lower crime rates.[72] This issue is the subject of the Evidence-Based Juvenile Justice feature entitled "Transfers to Adult Court Found Ineffective in Reducing Violence."

Some experts also question whether juveniles waived to adult court, particularly younger ones, are competent to be tried as adults. Adjudicative competency property crime, could not be presented in the figure because the review authors could not calculate a comparable effect size.) The Washington State study found that transfers to adult court made no difference: violent crime rearrest rates were neither higher nor lower for transferred juveniles compared to retained juveniles 18 months after release from prison. Another systematic review with several more studies, which included meta-analytic techniques, showed similar results.

On the matter of a general deterrent effect of transfers, less could be said. The review identified three high-quality evaluation studies that measured whether transfer laws deter juveniles in the general population from violent crime. Inconsistent results were found across the studies: one study reported no effect, one reported mixed effects, and one reported harmful effects. Based on these inconsistent results, the task force concluded that there was insufficient evidence at present to make a determination on the effectiveness of transfer laws and policies in reducing juvenile violence generally.

A more recent study on the general deterrent effects of transfer, the largest and perhaps most rigorous one yet to investigate this question, may shed some light on these inconsistent results. (This study was not included in the systematic review because it was outside the review's publication date cutoff.) Criminologists Benjamin Steiner, Craig Hemmens, and Valerie Bell examined 22 states that enacted statutory exclusion or automatic transfer laws after 1979. The study found no reduction in arrest rates for violent juvenile crime in 21 of the 22 states over a period of five years following the introduction of the transfer law. Only Maine experienced a reduction in its juvenile arrest rate for violent crime, a reduction that was both immediate and permanent, and thus could be said to provide support for a general deterrent effect of the transfer law.

Based on the overall findings, the Task Force on Community Preventive Services concluded that transferring juvenile offenders to the adult system is "counter-productive for the purpose of reducing juvenile violence and enhancing public safety." They did not go so far as to recommend that states repeal their transfer laws and discontinue the practice of transfers altogether, possibly because of the inconsistent results found for general deterrent effects. Legal scholar Michael Tonry, in commenting on the report, says it is time that some of these changes take place. He also calls for more individualized treatment for juvenile offenders, noting that, "One-size-fits-all policies inevitably produce anomalies, injustices, and unwanted side effects (including increased violent re-offending)." Research on the perceptions of the public as well as practitioners backs up some of these views, indicating that they want transfers used sparingly and selectively and when there is a balance between effective rehabilitation and punishment.

CRITICAL THINKING

1. Based on this research evidence, what would you recommend to your state legislator? Should the practice of transferring juvenile offenders to adult court be ceased altogether, or should transfers be used only in isolated cases involving extreme violence? Or do you remain unconvinced by this research and feel transfers should continue as is?

2. While the issue of effects of transfers on crime rates is important, what are some other key issues that need to be considered?

SOURCES: Steven N. Zane, Brandon C. Welsh, and Daniel P. Mears, "Juvenile Transfer and the Specific Deterrence Hypothesis: Systematic Review and Meta-Analysis," *Criminology and Public Policy* 15:901–925 (2016); David L. Myers, Daniel Lee, Dennis Giever, and Jay Gilliam, "Practitioner Perceptions of Juvenile Transfer in Pennsylvania," *Youth Violence and Juvenile Justice* 9:222–240 (2011); Brandon K. Applegate, Robin King Davis, and Francis T. Cullen, "Reconsidering Child Saving: The Extent and Correlates of Public Support for Excluding Youths from Juvenile Courts," *Crime and Delinquency* 55:51–77 (2009); Jeffrey Fagan, "Juvenile Crime and Criminal Justice: Resolving Border Disputes," *The Future of Children* 18(2):81–118 (2008); Angela McGowan, Robert Hahn, Akiva Liberman, Alex Crosby, Mindy Fullilove, Robert Johnson, Eve Moscicki, LeShawndra Price, Susan Snyder, Farris Tuma, Jessica Lowy, Peter Briss, Stella Cory, Glenda Stone, and the Task Force on Community Preventive Services, "Effects on Violence of Laws and Policies Facilitating the Transfer of Juveniles from the Juvenile Justice System to the Adult Justice System: A Systematic Review," *American Journal of Preventive Medicine* 32(4S):7–28 (2007); Michael Tonry, "Treating Juveniles as Adult Criminals: An Iatrogenic Violence Prevention Strategy if Ever There Was One," *American Journal of Preventive Medicine* 32(4S):3–4 (2007); Benjamin Steiner, Craig Hemmens, and Valerie Bell, "Legislative Waiver Reconsidered: General Deterrent Effects of Statutory Exclusion Laws Enacted Post-1979," *Justice Quarterly* 23:34–59 (2006).

pertains to the mental capacity or cognitive skills of the youth to understand the nature and object of the proceedings against him or her. Two studies found that the mental competency of youths under the age of 16 to stand trial is far below that of similarly charged adults, with one study comparing the competency of young juvenile offenders to that of severely mentally impaired adults.[73]

Waiver can also create long-term harm. Waived children may be stigmatized by a conviction in the criminal court. Labeling children as adult offenders early in life may seriously impair their future educational, employment, and other opportunities. Youthful offenders convicted in adult courts are more likely to be incarcerated and to receive longer sentences than had they remained in the juvenile court.

This is the conclusion of a growing number of high-quality studies.[74] In one study in New York and New Jersey, juveniles transferred to criminal court were almost three times more likely to receive sentences of incarceration than juvenile court defendants (36 percent versus 14 percent).[75] In another study in Pennsylvania, the average sentence length for juvenile offenders sentenced in adult court was found to be significantly longer than for a similar group of young adult offenders (18 months compared to 6 months).[76] And these children may be incarcerated under conditions so extreme—and in institutions where they may be physically and sexually exploited—that they will become permanently damaged.[77] In a small-scale study of female youths transferred to criminal court and subsequently placed in a prison for adult women, it was found that the prison was severely limited in its ability to care for and provide needed treatment services for these youths compared with the adults.[78]

Waivers do not always support the goal of increased public protection. Because juveniles may only serve a fraction of the prison sentence imposed by the criminal court, the actual treatment of delinquents in adult court is similar to what they might have received had they remained in the custody of juvenile authorities.[79] This has prompted some critics to ask, why bother transferring these children?

Sometimes waiver can add an undue burden to youthful offenders. Studies have found that although transfer to criminal court was intended for the most serious juvenile offenders, many transferred juveniles were not violent offenders but repeat property offenders.[80] Cases involving waiver take significantly longer than comparable juvenile court cases, during which time the waived youth is more likely to be held in a detention center.

Transfer decisions are not always carried out fairly or equitably, and there is evidence that minorities are waived at a rate that is greater than their representation in the population.[81] Forty-five percent of all waived youth are African Americans, even though they represent 35 percent of the juvenile court population.[82] A federal study of juveniles waived to criminal court in the nation's 40 largest counties found that 62 percent of waived youth were African American.[83] Between the peak year of 1994 and 2013, the number of judicially waived cases involving African American youth decreased by 69 percent (from 5,800 to 1,800 cases) compared with a 72 percent decrease for European American youth (from 7,500 to 2,100 cases).[84]

In Support of Waiver   Not all experts challenge the waiver concept. Waiver is attractive to conservatives because it jibes with the get-tough policy currently popular. Some have argued that the increased use of waiver can help get violent offenders off the streets and should be mandatory for juveniles committing serious violent crimes.[85] Others point to studies that show that, for the most part, transfer is reserved for the most serious cases and the most serious juvenile offenders. Kids are most likely to be transferred to criminal court if they have injured someone with a weapon or if they have a long juvenile court record.[86] The most recent federal study of waiver found that 27 percent of juveniles tried in criminal court were sent to prison. This outcome might be expected because those waived to criminal court were more likely (64 percent) than adults (24 percent) to be charged with a violent felony. These juvenile defendants were generally regarded as serious offenders, because 52 percent did not receive pretrial release, 63 percent were convicted of a felony, and 43 percent of those convicted received a prison sentence.[87] In an analysis of a Virginia statute that grants prosecutors the authority to certify a juvenile offender to criminal court at intake, it was found that serious offenders were more likely to be waived to criminal court.[88] Clearly, many waived juveniles might be considered serious offenders.

Franklin Zimring argues that, despite its faults, waiver is superior to alternative methods for handling the most serious juvenile offenders.[89] Some cases involving serious offenses, he argues, require a minimum criminal penalty greater than that available to the juvenile court. It is also possible that some juveniles take advantage of decisions to transfer them to the adult court. Although the charge against a child may be considered serious in the juvenile court, the adult criminal court will not find it so; consequently, a child may have a better chance for dismissal of the charges or acquittal after a jury trial.

In sum, though the use of waiver has been in decline, it is still an important strategy for attacking serious youth crime.[90] Its continued use can be attributed to the get-tough attitude toward the serious juvenile offender.

Juvenile Court Trial

If the case cannot be decided during the pretrial stage, it will be brought forth for a trial in the juvenile court. An adjudication hearing is held to determine the merits of the petition claiming that a child is either a delinquent youth or in need of court supervision. The judge is required to make a finding based on the evidence and arrive at a judgment. Adjudication is comparable to an adult trial. Rules of evidence in adult criminal proceedings are generally applicable in juvenile court, and the standard of proof used—*beyond a reasonable doubt*—is similar to that used in adult trials.

State juvenile codes vary with regard to the basic requirements of due process and fairness. Most juvenile courts have bifurcated hearings—that is, separate hearings for adjudication and disposition (sentencing). At disposition hearings, evidence can be submitted that reflects nonlegal factors, such as the child's home life.

Most state juvenile codes provide specific rules of procedure, which have several purposes: They require that a written petition be submitted to the court, ensure the right of a child to have an attorney, provide that the adjudication proceedings be recorded, allow the petition to be amended, and provide that a child's plea be accepted. Where the child admits to the facts of the petition, the court generally seeks assurance that the plea is voluntary. If plea bargaining is used, prosecutors, defense counsel, and trial judges take steps to ensure the fairness of such negotiations.

At the end of the adjudication hearing, most juvenile court statutes require the judge to make a factual finding on the legal issues and evidence. In the criminal court, this finding is normally a prelude to reaching a verdict. In the juvenile court, however, the finding itself is the verdict—the case is resolved in one of three ways:

- The juvenile court judge makes a finding of fact that the child or juvenile is not delinquent or in need of supervision.

- The juvenile court judge makes a finding of fact that the juvenile is delinquent or in need of supervision.

- The juvenile court judge dismisses the case because of insufficient or faulty evidence.

In some jurisdictions, informal alternatives are used, such as filing the case with no further consequences or continuing the case without a finding for a period of time, such as six months. If the juvenile does not get into further difficulty during that time, the case is dismissed. These alternatives involve no determination of delinquency or noncriminal behavior. Because of the philosophy of the juvenile court that emphasizes rehabilitation over punishment, a delinquency finding is not the same thing as a criminal conviction. The disabilities associated with conviction, such as disqualifications for employment or being barred from military service, do not apply in an adjudication of delinquency.

There are other differences between adult and juvenile proceedings. For instance, while adults are entitled to public trials by a jury of their peers, these rights are not extended to juveniles.[91] Because juvenile courts are treating some defendants similar to adult criminals, an argument can be made that the courts should extend to these youths the Sixth Amendment right to a public jury trial.[92] For the most part, however, state juvenile courts operate without recognizing a juvenile's constitutional right to a jury trial.

The **National Center for State Courts (NCSC)** (http://www.ncsc.org/) is an independent, nonprofit court improvement organization founded at the urging of former Chief Justice of the Supreme Court Warren E. Burger. All of NCSC's services—research, information services, education, consulting—focus on helping courts plan, make decisions, and implement improvements that save time and money, while ensuring judicial administration that supports fair and impartial decision making.

Constitutional Rights at Trial

In addition to mandating state juvenile code requirements, the Supreme Court has mandated the application of constitutional due process standards to the juvenile trial. **Due process**, addressed in the Fifth and Fourteenth Amendments to the US Constitution, refers to the need for rules and procedures that protect individual rights. Having the right to due process means that no person can be deprived of life, liberty, or property without such protections as legal counsel, an open and fair hearing, and an opportunity to confront those making accusations against him or her.

For many years, children were deprived of their due process rights because the *parens patriae* philosophy governed their relationship to the juvenile justice system. Such rights as having counsel and confronting one's accusers were deemed unnecessary. After all, why should children need protection from the state when the state was seen as acting in their interest? As we have seen, this view changed in the 1960s, when the Supreme Court began to grant due process rights and procedures to minors. The key case was that of Gerald Gault; it articulated the basic requirements of due process that must be satisfied in juvenile court proceedings.[93]

The *Gault* decision was significant not only because of the procedural reforms it initiated but also because of its far-reaching impact throughout the entire juvenile justice system. *In re Gault* instilled in juvenile proceedings the development of due process standards at the pretrial, trial, and posttrial stages of the juvenile process. While recognizing the history and development of the juvenile court, it sought to accommodate the motives of rehabilitation and treatment with children's rights. It recognized the principle of fundamental fairness of the law for children as well as for adults. Judged in the context of today's juvenile justice system, *In re Gault* redefined the relationships among juveniles, their parents, and the state. It remains the single most significant constitutional case in the area of juvenile justice.

The Gault decision reshaped the constitutional and philosophical nature of the juvenile court system and, with the addition of legal representation, made it more similar to the adult system.[94] Following the *Gault* case, the Supreme Court decided in *In re Winship* that the amount of proof required in juvenile delinquency adjudications is "beyond a reasonable doubt," a level equal to the requirements in the adult system.[95]

Although the ways in which the juvenile court operates were altered by *In re Gault* and *In re Winship*, the trend toward increased rights for juveniles was somewhat curtailed by the Supreme Court's decision in *McKeiver v. Pennsylvania* (1971), which held that trial by jury in a juvenile court's adjudicative stage is not a constitutional requirement.[96] This decision does not prevent states from giving the juvenile a trial by jury, but in the majority of states a child has no such right.

Once an adjudicatory hearing has been completed, the court is normally required to enter a judgment or finding against the child. This may take the form of declaring the child delinquent, adjudging the child to be a ward of the court, or possibly even suspending judgment so as to avoid the stigma of a juvenile record. After a judgment has been entered, the court can begin its determination of possible dispositions.

Disposition

The sentencing step of the juvenile justice process is called disposition. At this point the court orders treatment for the juvenile. According to prevailing juvenile justice philosophy, dispositions should be in the best interest of the child, which in this context means providing the necessary help to resolve or meet the adolescent's personal needs while at the same time meeting society's needs for protection.

As already mentioned, in most jurisdictions, adjudication and disposition hearings are separated, or bifurcated, so that evidence that could not be

due process
Basic constitutional principle based on the concept of the primacy of the individual and the complementary concept of limitation on governmental power; safeguards the individual from unfair state procedures in judicial or administrative proceedings. Due process rights have been extended to juvenile trials.

Due Process Advocacy, a publication of the Office of Juvenile Justice and Delinquency Prevention, offers a comprehensive review of **due process issues in juvenile justice** (http://www.ncjrs .gov/txtfiles/fs9749.txt).

In re Winship
Proof beyond a reasonable doubt is necessary for conviction in juvenile proceedings.

entered during the juvenile trial can be considered at the dispositional hearing. At the hearing, the defense counsel represents the child, helps the parents understand the court's decision, and influences the direction of the disposition. Others involved at the dispositional stage include representatives of social service agencies, psychologists, social workers, and probation personnel.

The Predisposition Report   After the child has admitted to the allegations, or the allegations have been proved in a trial, the judge normally orders the probation department to complete a predisposition report. The predisposition report, which is similar to the presentence report of the adult justice system, has a number of purposes:

- It helps the judge decide which disposition is best for the child.
- It aids the juvenile probation officer in developing treatment programs if the child is in need of counseling or community supervision.
- It helps the court develop a body of knowledge about the child that can aid others in treating the child.[97]

Sources of dispositional data include family members, school officials, and statements from the juvenile offenders themselves. The results of psychological testing, psychiatric evaluations, and intelligence testing may be relevant. Furthermore, the probation officer might include information about the juvenile's feelings concerning his or her case.

Some state statutes make the predisposition report mandatory. Other jurisdictions require the report only when there is a probability that the child will be institutionalized. Some appellate courts have reversed orders institutionalizing children when the juvenile court did not use a predisposition report in reaching its decision. Access to predisposition reports is an important legal issue.

In the final section of the predisposition report, the probation department recommends a disposition to the presiding judge. This is a critical aspect of the report because it has been estimated that the court follows more than 90 percent of all probation department recommendations.

Juvenile Court Dispositions   Historically, the juvenile court has had broad discretionary power to make dispositional decisions. The major categories of dispositional choices are community release, out-of-home placements, fines or restitution, community service, and institutionalization.[98] A more detailed list of the dispositions open to the juvenile court judge appears in Exhibit 15.2.

Most state statutes allow the juvenile court judge to select whatever disposition seems best suited to the child's needs, including institutionalization. In some states the court determines commitment to a specific institution; in other states the youth corrections agency determines where the child will be placed. In addition to the dispositions in Exhibit 15.2, some states grant the court the power to order parents into treatment or to suspend a youth's driver's license. The Case Profile entitled "Cliff's Story" highlights the need for innovative dispositions to address the multifaceted needs of young people who come in conflict with the law.

Today it is common for juvenile court judges to employ a graduated sanction program for juveniles: (1) immediate sanctions for nonviolent offenders, which consist of community-based diversion and day treatment imposed on first-time, nonviolent offenders; (2) intermediate sanctions, which target repeat minor offenders and first-time serious offenders; and (3) secure care, which is reserved for repeat serious offenders and violent offenders.[99]

In 2013 (the latest data available), juveniles were adjudicated delinquent in 55 percent of the 582,800 cases brought before a judge. Once adjudicated, the majority of these juveniles (64 percent, or 205,300 cases) were placed on formal probation, 24 percent (78,700 cases) were placed in a residential facility, and 12 percent (39,300 cases) were given another disposition, such as referral to an outside agency, community service, or restitution.[100]

exhibit 15.2

Common Juvenile Dispositions

Disposition	Action Taken
Informal consent decree	In minor or first offenses, an informal hearing is held, and the judge will ask the youth and his or her guardian to agree to a treatment program, such as counseling. No formal trial or disposition hearing is held.
Probation	A youth is placed under the control of the county probation department and is required to obey a set of probation rules and participate in a treatment program.
Home detention	A child is restricted to his or her home in lieu of a secure placement. Rules include regular school attendance, curfew observance, avoidance of alcohol and drugs, and notification of parents and the youth worker of the child's whereabouts.
Court-ordered school attendance	If truancy was the problem that brought the youth to court, a judge may order mandatory school attendance. Some courts have established court-operated day schools and court-based tutorial programs staffed by community volunteers.
Financial restitution	A judge can order the juvenile offender to make financial restitution to the victim. In most jurisdictions, restitution is part of probation (see Chapter 16), but in a few states, such as Maryland, restitution can be a sole order.
Fines	Some states allow fines to be levied against juveniles age 16 and over.
Community service	Courts in many jurisdictions require juveniles to spend time in the community working off their debt to society. Community service orders are usually reserved for victimless crimes, such as possession of drugs, or crimes against public order, such as vandalism of school property. Community service orders are usually carried out in schools, hospitals, or nursing homes.
Outpatient psychotherapy	Youths who are diagnosed with psychological disorders may be required to undergo therapy at a local mental health clinic.
Drug and alcohol treatment	Youths with drug- or alcohol-related problems may be allowed to remain in the community if they agree to undergo drug or alcohol therapy.
Commitment to secure treatment	In the most serious cases a judge may order an offender admitted to a long-term treatment center, such as a training school, camp, ranch, or group home. These may be either state-run or privately run institutions, usually located in remote regions. Training schools provide educational, vocational, and rehabilitation programs in a secure environment (see Chapter 16).
Commitment to a residential community program	Youths who commit crimes of a less serious nature but who still need to be removed from their homes can be placed in community-based group homes or halfway houses. They attend school or work during the day and live in a controlled, therapeutic environment at night.
Foster home placement	Foster homes are usually used for dependent or neglected children and status offenders. Judges place delinquents who have insurmountable problems in state-licensed foster care homes.

Although the juvenile court has been under pressure to get tough on youth crime, these figures show that probation is the disposition of choice, even in the most serious cases,[101] and its use has grown in recent years. Between 1985 and 2013, the number of cases in which the court ordered an adjudicated delinquent to be placed on formal probation increased slightly (6 percent, from 193,100 to 205,300), while the number of cases involving placement in a residential facility decreased by a full one-quarter (25 percent, from 104,500 to 78,700).[102] Recent research shows that the age of the offender may play a role in these dispositions. Daniel Mears and his colleagues found that "true" juvenile offenders—defined as those in the "middle of the range of the court's age of jurisdiction"—were substantially more likely to receive a disposition of probation or placement compared to younger and older adjudicated juvenile offenders.[103] Figure 15.3 shows recent changes in juvenile court placement of adjudicated youths for different crime types.

Juvenile Sentencing Structures

For most of the juvenile court's history, disposition was based on the presumed needs of the child. Although critics have challenged the motivations of early reformers in championing rehabilitation, there is little question that the rhetoric of the juvenile court has promoted that ideal.[104] For example, in their classic work *Beyond the Best Interest of the Child*, Joseph Goldstein, Anna Freud, and Albert Solnit say that placement of children should be based on the **least detrimental alternative**

least detrimental alternative
Choice of a program for the child that will best foster the child's growth and development.

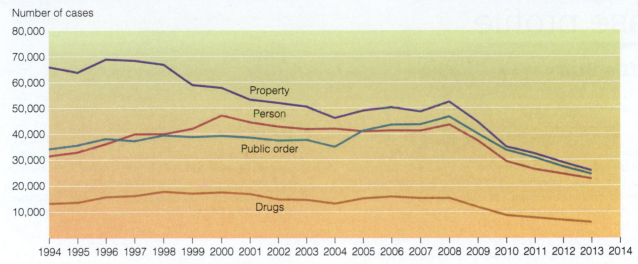

Number of cases

| | Property | Person | Public order | Drugs |

figure 15.3

Juvenile Court Placement of Adjudicated Youths, by Type of Offense

SOURCE: Melissa Sickmund, Anthony Sladky, and Wei Kang, *Easy Access to Juvenile Court Statistics: 1985–2013* (Pittsburgh: National Center for Juvenile Justice, 2015), http://ojjdp.gov/ojstatbb/ezajcs/ (accessed October 2016).

available in order to foster the child's development.[105] Most states have adopted this ideal in their sentencing efforts, and state courts usually insist that the purpose of disposition must be rehabilitation and not punishment.[106] Consequently, it is common for state courts to require judges to justify their sentencing decisions if it means that juveniles are to be incarcerated in a residential treatment center: They must set forth in writing the reasons for the placement, address the danger the child poses to society, and explain why a less-restrictive alternative has not been used.[107]

Traditionally, states have used the **indeterminate sentence** in juvenile court. In about half of the states, this means having the judge place the offender with the state department of juvenile corrections until correctional authorities consider the youth ready to return to society or until the youth reaches legal majority. A preponderance of states consider 18 to be the age of release; others peg the termination age at 19; in a few states, youths can retain minority status until their 21st birthday. In practice, few youths remain in custody for the entire statutory period; juveniles are usually released if their rehabilitation has been judged to have progressed satisfactorily. This practice is referred to as the **individualized treatment model**.

indeterminate sentence
Does not specify the length of time the juvenile must be held; rather, correctional authorities decide when the juvenile is ready to return to society.

individualized treatment model
Each sentence must be tailored to the individual needs of the child.

When making disposition decisions, juvenile court judges may select programs that will enhance life skills and help youths form a positive bond with society. Pictured here is Jhenifer, 19, at the J. DeWeese Carter Center in Chestertown, Maryland. Jhenifer has spent the last four years in residential treatment programs.

Gabriella Demczuk/The New York Times/Redux

case profile

Cliff's Story

CLIFF is a 16-year-old Caucasian youth being raised by his grandparents in a small rural community. He and his younger sisters were removed from their parental home when Cliff was 7 due to domestic violence and parental drug abuse. Although Cliff was well cared for by his grandparents, he engaged in several delinquent behaviors. He was charged with disorderly conduct for breaking windows in the family home and for threatening to physically assault his grandfather. Cliff was doing poorly in school; his grades dropped dramatically, and concerned family members were worried that he was using drugs.

Cliff began dating a girl he met at school, but her parents did not approve and refused to allow her to go out with him. Upset about the situation, Cliff reacted by taking his anger out on his family and by threatening suicide. He was hospitalized for an evaluation and diagnosed with bipolar disorder. He was at risk for being removed from the family home and placed in detention. Fortunately for Cliff, he received juvenile probation and was ordered by the court to receive a mental health assessment and treatment. Cliff also received medications and a referral for the Functional Family Therapy (FFT) intervention.

The FFT program has three phases that target juvenile delinquents and their families. During FFT intervention, other services to the family are stopped in order for the family to focus on the FFT process and plan. During the first phase of the program, attempts are made to engage and motivate all family members to participate in the process. Also during this initial phase, the family therapists focus on redefining the problem (Cliff's problematic behavior and mental health concerns) as a family issue, and encouraging family members to view the issues in a new light. Everyone has a part in the problem and thus in the solution. In the second phase, the therapists work to help the family change their behaviors. They create real and obtainable goals and provide assistance to increase the family's problem-solving skills. This again takes the focus off the adolescent and distributes the responsibility among all family members. In the last phase, the therapists worked with Cliff's family to generalize their new skills to many different situations.

The FFT therapists worked with Cliff's family for 4 months and then did follow-up calls at 6 and 12 months. They saw a reduction in Cliff's problematic behavior and criminal activity, as well as fewer calls to the police over the course of the intervention.

CRITICAL THINKING

1. How do you think this case might have ended if Cliff had initially been placed in detention?

2. How should the juvenile justice system handle cases where adolescents are suffering from significant mental health issues and committing crimes? How might a teen's mental health issues affect his behavior and his ability to understand the consequences of this behavior? Should mental health treatment be court ordered? Should juvenile probation officers be required to have a solid understanding of mental health issues?

3. The Functional Family Therapy (FFT) approach takes the focus of the intervention off the adolescent and places responsibility on the entire family to create solutions. Why do you think it works for many juveniles involved in the justice system? What are your concerns about this approach? Do you think there are some situations where this type of intervention may not be appropriate or successful? Why?

Another form of the indeterminate sentence allows judges to specify a maximum term. Under this form of sentencing, youths may be released if the corrections department considers them to be rehabilitated or they reach the automatic age of termination (usually 18 or 21). In states that stipulate a maximum sentence, the court may extend the sentence, depending on the youth's progress in the institutional facility.

determinate sentence
Specifies a fixed term of detention that must be served.

mandatory sentence
Defined by a statutory requirement that states the penalty to be set for all cases of a specific offense.

A number of states have changed from an indeterminate to a **determinate sentence**. This means sentencing juvenile offenders to a fixed term of incarceration that must be served in its entirety. Other states have passed laws creating **mandatory sentences** for serious juvenile offenders. Juveniles receiving mandatory sentences are usually institutionalized for the full sentence and are not eligible for early parole. The difference between mandatory and determinate sentences is that the mandatory sentence carries a statutory requirement that a certain penalty be set in all cases on conviction for a specified offense.

Blended Sentences State sentencing trends indicate that punishment and accountability, in addition to rehabilitation, have become equally important in juvenile justice policy. As a result, many states have created blended sentencing structures for cases involving serious offenders. Blended sentencing allows the imposition of juvenile and adult sanctions for juvenile offenders adjudicated in juvenile court or convicted in criminal court.[108] In other words, this expanded sentencing authority allows criminal and juvenile courts to impose either a juvenile or an adult sentence, or both, in cases involving juvenile offenders. When both sentences are imposed simultaneously, the court suspends the adult sanction. If the youth follows the conditions of the juvenile sentence and commits no further violation, the adult sentence is revoked. Blended sentences of one type or another exist in 32 states.[109] One study found that a number of factors are related to the decision to invoke the adult portion of the blended sentence, including offense type at commitment, age at commitment, and institutional misconduct.[110]

The Death Penalty for Juveniles

On March 1, 2005, the Supreme Court, in the case of *Roper v. Simmons*, put an end to the practice of the death penalty for juveniles in the United States. At issue was the minimum age that juveniles who were under the age of 18 when they committed their crimes could be eligible for the death penalty.[111] At the time, 16- and 17-year-olds were eligible for the death penalty, and 21 states permitted the death penalty for juveniles,[112] with a total of 72 juvenile offenders on death row.[113] In a 5–4 decision, the Court ruled that the juvenile death penalty was in violation of the Eighth Amendment's ban on cruel and unusual punishment.[114]

Roper v. Simmons
Repealed death penalty sentences for all juveniles in the United States.

The execution of minor children has not been uncommon in our nation's history; at least 366 juvenile offenders have been executed since 1642.[115] This represents about 2 percent of the total of more than 18,000 executions carried out since colonial times. Between the reinstatement of the death penalty in 1976 and the last execution of a juvenile in 2003, 22 juvenile offenders had been executed in seven states. Texas accounted for 13 of these 22 executions. All 22 of the executed juvenile offenders were male, 21 committed their crimes at age 17, and just over half (13 of them) were minorities.[116]

Past Legal Issues In *Thompson v. Oklahoma* (1988), the Supreme Court prohibited the execution of persons under age 16, but left open the age at which execution would be legally appropriate.[117] They then answered this question in two 1989 cases, *Wilkins v. Missouri* and *Stanford v. Kentucky*, in which they ruled that states were free to impose the death penalty for murderers who committed their crimes after they reached age 16 or 17.[118] According to the majority opinion, society at that time had not formed a consensus that the execution of such minors constitutes a cruel and unusual punishment.

Those who oppose the death penalty for children find that it has little deterrent effect on youngsters who are impulsive and do not have a realistic view of the destructiveness of their misdeeds or their consequences. Victor Streib, the leading critic of the death penalty for children, argues that such a practice is cruel and unusual punishment because (a) the condemnation of children makes no measurable contribution to the legitimate goals of punishment; (b) condemning any minor to death violates contemporary standards of decency; (c) the capacity of the young for change, growth, and rehabilitation makes the death penalty particularly harsh and inappropriate; and (d) both legislative attitudes and public opinion reject juvenile executions.[119] Those who oppose the death penalty for children also refer to a growing body of research that shows that the brain continues to develop through the late teen years, as do important mental functions, such as planning, judgment, and emotional control.[120] Opposition to the juvenile death penalty is also backed up by declining public support in the United States (at least for the execution of juveniles) and world opinion.[121] Concerns over the execution of innocents also weigh heavily in this debate.[122] In 2014, a South Carolina judge vacated the 1944 murder conviction of 14-year-old George Stinney, Jr. The media reported that he was the youngest person executed in the United States in the last century.[123] Supporters of the death penalty hold that regardless of their age people can form criminal intent and therefore should be responsible for their actions. If the death penalty is legal for adults, they assert, then it can also be used for children who commit serious crimes.

Life Without Parole for Juveniles

Closely tied to the end of the practice of the death penalty for juveniles is a debate that concerns juveniles sentenced to life without the possibility of parole. In a provocatively titled article, "A Slower Form of Death: Implications of *Roper v. Simmons* for Juveniles Sentenced to Life Without Parole," legal scholar Barry Feld argues that the Supreme Court's diminished responsibility standard—used in their decision to end the juvenile death penalty—should also apply to cases in which juvenile offenders are receiving life sentences without the possibility of parole.[124] The main reasons for this view center on the overly punitive nature of this sentence and the need to differentiate between juvenile and adult culpability.[125] To achieve this end, Feld proposes that "states formally recognize youthfulness as a mitigating factor by applying a 'youth discount' to adult sentence lengths."[126] This could have implications for thousands of juvenile offenders now and in the future. Amnesty International and Human Rights Watch estimate that there are 2,225 prisoners in the United States who "have been sentenced to spend the rest of their lives in prison for the crimes they committed as children." Of this total, 356 (or 16 percent) were between 13 and 15 years old at the time they committed their crimes.[127] A recent survey of 1,579 of these juveniles by the Sentencing Project found that these youths have endured socioeconomic disadvantages, education failure, and abuse. The life sentences were characterized by extreme racial disparities, and state prison policies preclude many from receiving treatment programs.[128]

While sentencing juveniles to life without parole raises any number of legal, moral, and social issues for some, others argue that "death is different" and the standards applied in *Roper v. Simmons* should not apply here.[129] The more controversial matter concerns juveniles who have received this sentence for crimes other than murder.

In 2009, the Supreme Court agreed to take up the matter of juveniles sentenced to life without the possibility of parole. The Court accepted appeals from two individuals, both from Florida, who are serving life sentences for nonhomicide crimes committed when they were juveniles. In the first case, which goes back to 1989, Joe Sullivan, then 13, was convicted of raping a 72-year-old woman. In the other case, Terrance Graham, who was 17 years old, was convicted of a probation violation for a home invasion robbery in 2004. In their briefs to the Court, both petitioners argued that the sentence of life without the possibility of parole violates the Eighth Amendment's prohibition of cruel and unusual punishment. In oral arguments before the Court, the justices did not revisit the question that "juveniles generally are psychologically less mature than adults," but instead focused on "whether the mitigating trait of immaturity justified a categorical exclusion of juveniles from the sentence of life without parole."[130]

Graham v. Florida
Repealed life sentences without the possibility of parole for juveniles convicted of nonhomicide crimes.

On May 17, 2010, the Supreme Court, in the case of *Graham v. Florida*, put an end to the practice of life sentences without the possibility of parole for juveniles convicted of nonhomicide crimes.[131] The Court agreed that this sentence violated the Eighth Amendment's ban on cruel and unusual punishment. The Court did leave in place the prospect that juveniles could continue to receive a life sentence without parole for crimes in which someone is killed. In two separate cases involving 14-year-olds convicted of homicide and sentenced to life without parole, *Miller v. Alabama* and *Jackson v. Hobbs*, the Supreme Court subsequently decided to revisit this issue.[132]

On June 25, 2012, the Court ruled that the sentence of life without the possibility of parole for all juvenile offenders, including those convicted of homicide, could not be imposed automatically. The mandatory nature of the sentence was seen as a violation of the Eighth Amendment's ban on cruel and unusual punishment. While the ruling left open the possibility of this sentence for juvenile offenders convicted of homicide, consideration needed to be given to individual circumstances and mitigating factors.[133] In the intervening years, many states have struggled with how to apply this ruling and if it should apply retroactively. A handful of state supreme courts have ruled in favor of retroactivity (e.g., Massachusetts, Illinois, Iowa, Nebraska, Mississippi), while other state supreme courts have rejected this possibility (e.g., Michigan, Pennsylvania, Minnesota, Louisiana). The Supreme Court agreed to hear a case on this matter, *Montgomery v. Louisiana*, and in January 2016 ruled that juveniles sentenced to life without parole have the right to seek parole.[134] It is estimated that this retroactive judgment is applicable to as many as 2,500 incarcerated individuals.[135]

The Child's Right to Appeal

Regardless of the sentence imposed, juveniles may want to appeal the decision made by the juvenile court judge. Juvenile court statutes normally restrict appeals to cases where the juvenile seeks review of a **final order**, one that ends the litigation between two parties by determining all their rights and disposing of all the issues.[136] The **appellate process** gives the juvenile the opportunity to have the case brought before a reviewing court after it has been heard in the juvenile or family court. Today, the law does not recognize a federal constitutional right of appeal. In other words, the US Constitution does not require any state to furnish an appeal to a juvenile charged and found to be delinquent in a juvenile or family court. Consequently, appellate review of a juvenile case is a matter of statutory right in each jurisdiction. However, the majority of states do provide juveniles with some method of statutory appeal.

The appeal process was not always part of the juvenile law system. In 1965, few states extended the right of appeal to juveniles.[137] Even in the *Gault* case in 1967, the Supreme Court refused to review the Arizona juvenile code, which provided no appellate review in juvenile matters. It further rejected the right of a juvenile to a transcript of the original trial record.[138] Today, however, most jurisdictions that provide a child with some form of appeal also provide for counsel and for securing a record and transcript, which are crucial to the success of any appeal.

Because juvenile appellate review is defined by individual statutes, each jurisdiction determines for itself what method of review will be used. There are two basic methods of appeal: the direct appeal and the collateral attack.

The *direct appeal* normally involves an appellate court review to determine whether, based on the evidence presented at the trial, the rulings of law and the judgment of the court were correct. The second major area of review involves the *collateral attack* of a case. The term *collateral* implies a secondary or indirect method of attacking a final judgment. Instead of appealing the juvenile trial because of errors, prejudice, or lack of evidence, *collateral review* uses extraordinary legal writs to challenge the lower-court position. One such procedural device is the **writ of habeas corpus**. Known as the "Great Writ," this refers to a procedure for determining the validity of a person's custody. In the context of the juvenile court, it is used to challenge the custody of a child in detention or in an institution. This writ is often the method by which the Supreme Court exercises its discretionary authority to hear cases regarding constitutional issues. Even though there is no constitutional right to appeal a juvenile case and each jurisdiction provides for appeals differently, juveniles have a far greater opportunity for appellate review today than in years past.

Confidentiality in Juvenile Proceedings

Along with the rights of juveniles at adjudication and disposition, the issue of **confidentiality** in juvenile proceedings has also received attention in recent years. The debate on confidentiality in the juvenile court deals with two areas: (1) open

final order
Order that ends litigation between two parties by determining all their rights and disposing of all the issues.

appellate process
Allows the juvenile an opportunity to have the case brought before a reviewing court after it has been heard in juvenile or family court.

writ of habeas corpus
Judicial order requesting that a person detaining another person produce the body of the prisoner and give reasons for his or her capture and detention.

confidentiality
Restriction of information in juvenile court proceedings in the interest of protecting the privacy of the juvenile.

versus closed hearings and (2) privacy of juvenile records. Confidentiality has become moot in some respects, as many legislatures have broadened access to juvenile records.

Open vs. Closed Hearings   Generally, juvenile trials are closed to the public and the press, and the names of the offenders are kept secret. The Supreme Court has ruled on the issue of privacy in three important decisions. In *Davis v. Alaska*, the Court concluded that any injury resulting from the disclosure of a juvenile's record is outweighed by the right to completely cross-examine an adverse witness.[139] The *Davis* case involved an effort to obtain testimony from a juvenile probationer who was a witness in a criminal trial. The Supreme Court held that a juvenile's interest in confidentiality was secondary to the constitutional right to confront adverse witnesses.

The decisions in two subsequent cases, *Oklahoma Publishing Co. v. District Court* and *Smith v. Daily Mail Publishing Co.*, sought to balance juvenile privacy with freedom of the press. In the *Oklahoma* case, the Supreme Court ruled that a state court was not allowed to prohibit the publication of information obtained in an open juvenile proceeding.[140] The case involved an 11-year-old boy suspected of homicide, who appeared at a detention hearing where photographs were taken and published in local newspapers. When the local district court prohibited further disclosure, the publishing company claimed that the court order was a restraint in violation of the First Amendment, and the Supreme Court agreed.

The *Smith* case involved the discovery and publication of the identity of a juvenile suspect in violation of a state statute prohibiting publication. The Supreme Court, however, declared the statute unconstitutional because the Court believed the state's interest in protecting the child's identity was not of such a magnitude as to justify the use of such a statute.[141] Therefore, if newspapers lawfully obtain pictures or names of juveniles, they may publish them. Based on these decisions, it appears that the Supreme Court favors the constitutional rights of the press over the right to privacy of the juvenile offender.

None of the decisions, however, give the press or public access to juvenile trials. Some jurisdictions still bar the press from juvenile proceedings unless they show at a hearing that their presence will not harm the youth. However, the trend has been to make it easier for the press and the public to have open access to juvenile trials. Georgia amended its juvenile code to allow public access to juvenile hearings in cases in which a juvenile is charged with certain designated felonies, such as kidnapping and attempted murder. Missouri also passed legislation that "removes the veil of secrecy that once kept juvenile court proceedings private— in the hope that allowing names and photos in newspapers will discourage teen crime and alert school officials." Michigan has granted public access to court proceedings and documents in cases involving delinquents, truants, runaways, and abuse victims. In recent years many jurisdictions have amended their laws to provide for greater openness in juvenile courts.[142]

Privacy of Juvenile Records   For most of the twentieth century, juvenile records were kept confidential.[143] Today, the record itself, or information contained in it, can be opened by court order in many jurisdictions on the basis of statutory exception. The following groups can ordinarily gain access to juvenile records: law enforcement personnel, the child's attorney, the parents or guardians, military personnel, and public agencies such as schools, court-related organizations, and correctional institutions.

Most states recognize the importance of juvenile records in sentencing. Many first-time adult offenders committed numerous crimes as juveniles, and evidence of these crimes may not be available to sentencing for the adult offenses unless states pass statutes allowing access. Knowledge of a defendant's juvenile record may help prosecutors and judges determine appropriate sentencing for offenders ages 18 to 24, the age group most likely to be involved in violent crime.

According to experts such as Ira Schwartz, the need for confidentiality to protect juveniles is far less than the need to open up the courts to public scrutiny.[144] The problem of maintaining confidentiality of juvenile records will become more acute in the future as electronic information storage makes these records both more durable and more accessible.

In conclusion, virtually every state provides prosecutors and judges with access to the juvenile records of adult offenders. There is great diversity, however, regarding provisions for the collection and retention of juvenile records.[145]

Future of the Juvenile Court

The future of the juvenile court is subject to wide-ranging and sometimes contentious debate. Some experts, including legal scholar Barry Feld, believe that over the years the juvenile justice system has taken on more of the characteristics of the adult courts, which Feld refers to as the "criminalizing" of the juvenile court,[146] or in a more stern admonition: "Despite juvenile courts' persisting rehabilitative rhetoric, the reality of *treating* juveniles closely resembles *punishing* adult criminals."[147] Robert Dawson suggests that because the legal differences between the juvenile and criminal systems are narrower than they ever have been, it may be time to abolish the juvenile court.[148]

Other juvenile justice experts, such as Peter Greenwood, contend that, despite these and other limitations, the treatment programs that the modern juvenile court currently provides play a central role in society's response to the most serious delinquents.[149] Greenwood argues that this comes with a number of specific responsibilities that juvenile courts must take on so as to ensure that these programs are indeed effective, including awareness of the most up-to-date scientific evidence on the effectiveness of court-based programs, diversion of cases that can be handled informally outside of the system, disposition of cases to appropriate programs, and quality control.[150]

Part of the answer to making this happen and overcoming the often default position of getting tough on juvenile offenders,[151] argue criminologists Daniel Mears, Carter Hay, Marc Gertz, and Christina Mancini, is that the juvenile court and the juvenile justice system in general need to be guided by a core set of rational and science-based principles such as "systematic assessments of culpability and treatment needs and a consistent balancing of punishment and treatment."[152] These become the overriding considerations in how the juvenile court can best serve society, a course of action that the public finds much more appealing than the wholesale criminalization of children.[153]

SUMMARY

1 Discuss the roles and responsibilities of the main players in the juvenile court

- Prosecutors, judges, and defense attorneys are the key players in the juvenile court. The juvenile prosecutor is the attorney responsible for bringing the state's case against the accused juvenile.

- The juvenile judge must ensure that the children and families who come before the court receive the proper help.

- Defense attorneys representing children in the juvenile court play an active and important part in virtually all stages of the proceedings.

2 Identify key issues of the preadjudicatory stage of juvenile justice, including detention, intake, diversion, pretrial release, plea bargaining, and waiver

- Many decisions about what happens to a child may occur prior to adjudication.

- Due to personnel limitations, the juvenile justice system is not able to try every child accused of a crime or status offense. Therefore, diversion programs seem to hold greater hope for the control of delinquency.

- As a result, such subsystems as statutory intake proceedings, plea bargaining, and other informal adjustments are essential ingredients in the administration of the juvenile justice system.

3 Compare the pros and cons of transferring youths to adult court

- Each year, thousands of youths are transferred to adult courts because of the seriousness of their crimes. This process, known as waiver, is an effort to remove serious offenders from the juvenile process and into the more punitive adult system.

- Most juvenile experts oppose waiver because it clashes with the rehabilitative ideal.

- Supporters argue that its increased use can help get violent juvenile offenders off the street, and they point to studies showing for the most part that transfer is reserved for the most serious cases and the most serious juvenile offenders.

4 Explain key issues of the trial stage of juvenile justice, including constitutional rights of youths and disposition

- Most jurisdictions have a bifurcated juvenile code system that separates the adjudication hearing from the dispositional hearing.

- Juveniles alleged to be delinquent have virtually all the constitutional rights given a criminal defendant at trial—except possibly the right to a trial by jury.

- Juvenile proceedings are generally closed to the public.

5 Appraise the major US Supreme Court decisions that have influenced the handling of juveniles at the preadjudicatory and trial stages

- *In re Gault* is the key legal case that set out the basic requirements of due process that must be satisfied in juvenile court proceedings.

- In *Roper v. Simmons*, the Supreme Court ruled that the death penalty for juveniles is prohibited, because it constitutes cruel and unusual punishment.

- In *Montgomery v. Louisiana*, the Supreme Court ruled that all juveniles sentenced to life without parole have the right to seek parole.

6 Discuss the most common dispositions for juvenile offenders

- The major categories of dispositional choice in juvenile cases include probation, community release, out-of-home placements, and institutionalization.

- Although the traditional notion of rehabilitation and treatment as the proper goals for disposition is being questioned, many juvenile codes do require that the court consider the least-restrictive alternative.

7 Compare the pros and cons of confidentiality in juvenile proceedings and privacy of juvenile records

- Many state statutes require that juvenile hearings be closed and that the privacy of juvenile records be maintained.

- This is done to protect the child from public scrutiny and to provide a greater opportunity for rehabilitation.

- This approach may be inconsistent with the public's interest in taking a closer look at the juvenile justice system.

KEY TERMS

juvenile defense attorney, p. 557

guardian *ad litem*, p. 557

public defender, p. 558

juvenile prosecutor, p. 558

juvenile court judge, p. 559

detention, p. 561

shelter care, p. 562

bail, p. 564

preventive detention, p. 564

intake, p. 565

consent decree, p. 565

diversion, p. 566

widening the net, p. 566

complaint, p. 567

plea bargaining, p. 567

transfer process, p. 569

transfer hearing, p. 571

due process, p. 576

In re Winship, p. 576

least detrimental alternative, p. 578

indeterminate sentence, p. 579

individualized treatment model, p. 579

determinate sentence, p. 580

mandatory sentence, p. 580

Roper v. Simmons, p. 581

Graham v. Florida, p. 582

final order, p. 583

appellate process, p. 583

writ of habeas corpus, p. 583

confidentiality, p. 583

Davis v. Alaska, p. 584

Oklahoma Publishing Co. v. District Court and *Smith v. Daily Mail Publishing Co.*, p. 584

QUESTIONS FOR DISCUSSION

1. Discuss and identify the major participants in the juvenile adjudication process. What are each person's roles and responsibilities in the course of a juvenile trial?

2. The criminal justice system in the United States is based on the adversarial process. Does the same adversary principle apply in the juvenile justice system?

3. Children have certain constitutional rights at adjudication, such as the right to an attorney and the right to confront and cross-examine witnesses. But they do not have the right to a trial by jury. Should juvenile offenders have a constitutional right to a jury trial? Should each state make that determination? Discuss the legal decision that addresses this issue.

4. What is the point of obtaining a predisposition report in the juvenile court? Is it of any value in cases where the child is released to the community? Does it have a significant value in serious juvenile crime cases?

5. The standard of proof in juvenile adjudication is to show that the child is guilty beyond a reasonable doubt. Explain the meaning of this standard of proof in the US judicial system.

6. Should states adopt get-tough sentences in juvenile justice or adhere to the individualized treatment model?

7. What are blended sentences?

8. Do you agree with the Supreme Court's 2005 ruling that prohibits the death penalty for juvenile offenders?

VIEWPOINT

As an experienced family court judge, you often face difficult decisions, but few are more difficult than the case of John, arrested at age 14 for robbery and rape. His victim, a young neighborhood girl, was badly injured in the attack and needed extensive hospitalization; she is now in counseling. Even though the charges are serious, because of his age John can still be subject to the jurisdiction of the juvenile division of the state family court. However, the prosecutor has filed a petition to waive jurisdiction to the adult court. Under existing state law, a hearing must be held to determine whether there is sufficient evidence that John cannot be successfully treated in the juvenile justice system and therefore warrants transfer to the adult system; the final decision on the matter is yours alone.

At the waiver hearing, you discover that John is the oldest of three siblings living in a single-parent home. He has had no contact with his father for more than 10 years. His psychological evaluation showed hostility, anger toward females, and great feelings of frustration. His intelligence is below average, and his behavioral and academic records are poor. In addition, he seems to be involved with a local youth gang, although he denies any association with them. This is his first formal involvement with the juvenile court. Previous contact was limited to a complaint for disorderly conduct at age 13, which was dismissed by the court's intake department.

During the hearing, John verbalizes what you interpret to be superficial remorse for his offenses.

To the prosecutor, John seems to be a youth with poor controls who is likely to commit future crimes. The defense attorney argues that there are effective treatment opportunities within the juvenile justice system that can meet John's needs. Her views are supported by an evaluation of the case conducted by the court's probation staff, which concludes that the case can be dealt with in the confines of juvenile corrections.

If the case remains in the juvenile court, John can be kept in custody in a juvenile facility until age 18; if transferred to felony court, he could be sentenced to up to 20 years in a maximum-security prison. As the judge, you recognize the seriousness of the crimes committed by John and realize that it is very difficult to predict or assess his future behavior and potential dangerousness.

- Would you authorize a waiver to adult court or keep the case in the juvenile justice system?
- Can 14-year-olds truly understand the seriousness of their behavior?
- Should a juvenile court judge consider the victim in making a disposition decision?

DOING RESEARCH ON THE WEB

Some websites that can help you make your decision are listed here. The American Bar Association's Juvenile Justice Committee (http://apps.americanbar.org/dch /committee.cfm?com=CR200000) is the focal point of research on and advocacy for juvenile justice issues. The OJJDP Statistical Briefing Book (SBB) (http://www.ojjdp .gov/ojstatbb/) enables users to access online information to learn more about juvenile crime and victimization and about youth involved in the juvenile justice system. The American Youth Policy Forum's (http://www .aypf.org/) mission is to broaden the awareness and

understanding of policy makers and to strengthen the youth policy-making process by bridging policy, practice, and research.

The Children's Research Center (CRC) (http://www .nccdglobal.org/what-we-do/major-projects/children -s-research-center) was established to help federal, state, and local child welfare agencies reduce child abuse and neglect by developing case management systems and conducting research that improves service delivery to children and families.

NOTES

All URLs accessed October 2016.

1. Sarah Hockenberry and Charles Puzzanchera, *Juvenile Court Statistics 2013* (Pittsburgh: National Center for Juvenile Justice, 2015), pp. 6–7.
2. Ibid., pp. 12, 19.
3. *Powell v. Alabama*, 287 U.S. 45, 53 S.Ct. 55, 77, L.Ed.2d 158 (1932); *Gideon v. Wainwright*, 372 U.S. 335, 83 S.Ct. 792, 9 L.Ed.2d 799 (1963); *Argersinger v. Hamlin*, 407 U.S. 25, 92 S.Ct. 2006, 32 L.Ed.2d 530 (1972).
4. See Judith B. Jones, *Access to Counsel* (Washington, DC: Office of Juvenile Justice and Delinquency Prevention, 2004).
5. For a review of these studies, see T. Grisso, "The Competence of Adolescents as Trial Defendants," *Psychology, Public Policy, and Law* 3:3–32 (1997).
6. Christine Schnyder Pierce and Stanley L. Brodsky, "Trust and Understanding in the Attorney-Juvenile Relationship," *Behavioral Sciences and the Law* 20:89–107 (2002), at 102.
7. Ibid.
8. Melinda G. Schmidt, N. Dickon Reppucci, and Jennifer L. Woolard, "Effectiveness of Participation as a Defendant: The Attorney-Juvenile Client Relationship," *Behavioral Sciences and the Law* 21:175–198 (2003), at 177.
9. Ibid., p. 193.
10. George W. Burruss Jr. and Kimberly Kempf-Leonard, "The Questionable Advantage of Defense Counsel in Juvenile Court," *Justice Quarterly* 19:37–67 (2002), at 60–61.
11. Loris Guevara, Denise Herz, and Cassia Spohn, "Race, Gender, and Legal Counsel: Differential Outcomes in Two Juvenile Courts," *Youth Violence and Juvenile Justice* 6:83–104 (2008), at 98.
12. Lori Guevara, Cassia Spohn, and Denise Herz, "Race, Legal Representation, and Juvenile Justice: Issues and Concerns," *Crime and Delinquency* 50:344–371 (2004), at 362–364.
13. Barry C. Feld and Shelly Schaefer, "The Right to Counsel in Juvenile Court: The Conundrum of Attorneys as an Aggravating Factor at Disposition," *Justice Quarterly* 27:713–741 (2010); Barry C. Feld and Shelly Schaefer, "The Right to Counsel in Juvenile Court: Law Reform to Deliver Legal Services and Reduce Justice by Geography," *Criminology and Public Policy* 9:327–356 (2010).
14. Howard Davidson, "The Guardian *ad Litem*: An Important Approach to the Protection of Children," *Children Today* 10:23 (1981); Daniel Golden, "Who Guards the Children?" *Boston Globe Magazine*, December 27, 1992, p. 12.
15. Chester Harhut, "An Expanded Role for the Guardian *ad Litem*," *Juvenile and Family Court Journal* 51:31–35 (2000).
16. Steve Riddell, "CASA, Child's Voice in Court," *Juvenile and Family Justice Today* 7:13–14 (1998).
17. American Bar Association, "News Release: ABA President Says New Report Shows 'Conveyor Belt Justice' Hurting Children and Undermining Public Safety," Washington, DC, October 21, 2003.
18. Jessica Feierman, *Debtors' Prison for Kids? The High Cost of Fines in the Juvenile Justice System* (Philadelphia: Juvenile Law Center, 2016).
19. James Shine and Dwight Price, "Prosecutor and Juvenile Justice: New Roles and Perspectives," in Ira Schwartz, ed., *Juvenile Justice and Public Policy* (New York: Lexington Books, 1992), pp. 101–133.
20. James Backstrom and Gary Walker, "A Balanced Approach to Juvenile Justice: The Work of the Juvenile Justice Advisory Committee," *The Prosecutor* 32:37–39 (1988); see also *Prosecutors' Policy Recommendations on Serious, Violent, and Habitual Youthful Offenders* (Alexandria, VA: American Prosecutors' Institute, 1997).
21. John Paul Wright, Pamela M. McMahon, Claire Daly, and J. Phil Haney, "Getting the Law Involved: A Quasi-Experiment in Early Intervention Involving Collaboration Between Schools and the District Attorney's Office," *Criminology and Public Policy* 11:227–249 (2012).
22. Erica Goode, "Judge in Maryland Locks Up Youths and Rules their Lives," *New York Times*, December 19, 2014.
23. Leonard P. Edwards, "The Juvenile Court and the Role of the Juvenile Court Judge," *Juvenile and Family Court Journal* 43:3–45 (1992); Lois Haight, "Why I Choose to Be a Juvenile Court Judge," *Juvenile and Family Justice Today* 7:7 (1998).
24. National Council of Juvenile and Family Court Judges, *Juvenile Delinquency Guidelines: Improving Court Practice in Juvenile Delinquency Cases* (Reno, NV: Author, 2005), p. 24.
25. Madeline Wordes and Sharon Jones, "Trends in Juvenile Detention and Steps Toward Reform," *Crime and Delinquency* 44:544–560 (1998).
26. Robert Shepard, *Juvenile Justice Standards Annotated: A Balanced Approach* (Chicago: ABA, 1997).
27. Leslie Kaufman, "Child Detention Centers Criticized in New Jersey," *New York Times*, November 23, 2004.
28. Karen M. Abram, Jeanne Y. Choe, Jason J. Washburn, Linda A. Teplin, Devon C. King, Mina K. Dulcan, and Elana D. Bassett, *Suicidal Thoughts and Behaviors Among Detained Youth* (Washington, DC: Office of Juvenile Justice and Delinquency Prevention, US Department of Justice, 2014), p. 1.
29. William H. Barton, "Detention," in Barry C. Feld and Donna M. Bishop, eds., *The Oxford Handbook of Juvenile Crime and Juvenile Justice* (New York: Oxford University Press, 2012), p. 654.
30. Dylan Conger and Timothy Ross, "Project Confirm: An Outcome Evaluation of a Program for Children in the Child Welfare and Juvenile Justice Systems," *Youth Violence and Juvenile Justice* 4:97–115 (2006).
31. Hockenberry and Puzzanchera, *Juvenile Court Statistics 2013*, p. 32.
32. Ibid., pp. 32, 34.
33. Donna Bishop, Michael Leiber, and Joseph Johnson, "Contexts of Decision Making in the Juvenile Justice System: An Organizational Approach to Understanding Minority Overrepresentation," *Youth*

Violence and Juvenile Justice 8:213–233 (2010); Nancy Rodriguez, "The Cumulative Effect of Race and Ethnicity in Juvenile Court Outcomes and Why Preadjudication Detention Matters," *Journal of Research in Crime and Delinquency* 47:391–413 (2010).

34. Katherine E. Brown and Leanne Fiftal Alarid, "Examining Racial Disparity of Male Property Offenders in the Missouri Juvenile Justice System," *Youth Violence and Juvenile Justice* 2:107–128 (2004), at 116.

35. Ibid., p. 119; Nancy Rodriguez, "Juvenile Court Context and Detention Decisions: Reconsidering the Role of Race, Ethnicity, and Community Characteristics in Juvenile Court Processes," *Justice Quarterly* 24:629–656 (2007), at 649.

36. Christopher A. Mallett, Patricia Stoddard-Dare, and Mamadou M. Seck, "Explicating Correlates of Juvenile Offender Detention Length: The Impact of Race, Mental Health Difficulties, Maltreatment, Offense Type, and Court Dispositions," *Youth Justice* 11:134–149 (2011).

37. James Maupin and Lis Bond-Maupin, "Detention Decision-Making in a Predominantly Hispanic Region: Rural and Non-Rural Differences," *Juvenile and Family Court Journal* 50:11–21 (1999).

38. Edward P. Mulvey and Anne-Marie R. Iselin, "Improving Professional Judgments of Risk and Amenability in Juvenile Justice," *The Future of Children* 18(2):35–57 (2008), at 47–48.

39. Earl Dunlap and David Roush, "Juvenile Detention as Process and Place," *Juvenile and Family Court Journal* 46:1–16 (1995).

40. "OJJDP Helps States Remove Juveniles from Jails," *Juvenile Justice Bulletin* (Washington, DC: US Department of Justice, 1990).

41. David Steinhart, "Status Offenders," *The Future of Children: The Juvenile Court*, Vol. 6 (Los Altos, CA: David and Lucile Packard Foundation, 1996), pp. 86–96.

42. Mark Soler, James Bell, Elizabeth Jameson, Carole Shauffer, Alice Shotton, and Loren Warboys, *Representing the Child Client* (New York: Matthew Bender, 1989), sec. 5.03b.

43. *Schall v. Martin*, 467 U.S. 253 (1984).

44. Jeffrey Fagan and Martin Guggenheim, "Preventive Detention for Juveniles: A Natural Experiment," *Journal of Criminal Law and Criminology* 86:415–428 (1996).

45. Hockenberry and Puzzanchera, *Juvenile Court Statistics 2013*, p. 52.

46. See Daniel P. Mears, "The Front End of the Juvenile Court: Intake and Informal Versus Formal Processing," in Feld and Bishop, eds., *The Oxford Handbook of Juvenile Crime and Juvenile Justice*, pp. 582–583.

47. Michael J. Leiber and Joseph D. Johnson, "Being Young and Black: What Are Their Effects on Juvenile Justice Decision Making?" *Crime and Delinquency* 54:560–581 (2008).

48. Jennifer H. Peck, Michael J. Leiber, and Sara Jane Brubaker, "Gender, Race, and Juvenile Court Outcomes: An Examination of Status Offenders," *Youth Violence and Juvenile Justice* 12:250–267 (2014).

49. Alex R. Piquero, "Disproportionate Minority Contact," *The Future of Children* 18(2):59–79 (2008); Kimberly Kempf-Leonard, "Minority Youths and Juvenile Justice: Disproportionate Minority Contact After Nearly 20 Years of Reform Efforts," *Youth Violence and Juvenile Justice* 5:71–87 (2007).

50. See David P. Farrington and Joseph Murray, eds., *Labeling Theory: Empirical Tests* (New Brunswick, NJ: Transaction Publishers, 2014).

51. Daniel P. Mears, Joshua J. Kuch, Andrea M. Lindsey, Sonja E. Siennick, George B. Pesta, Mark A. Greenwald, and Thomas G. Blomberg, "Juvenile Court and Contemporary Diversion: Helpful, Harmful, or Both?" *Criminology and Public Policy* 15:953–981 (2016); Jamie J. Fader, Brian Lockwood, Victoria L. Schall, and Benjamin Stokes, "A Promising Approach to Narrowing the School-to-Prison Pipeline: The WISE Arrest Diversion Program," *Youth Violence and Juvenile Justice* 13:123–142 (2015).

52. Deborah A. Chapin and Patricia A. Griffin, "Juvenile Diversion," in Kirk Heilbrun, Naomi E. Sevin Goldstein, and Richard E. Redding, eds., *Juvenile Delinquency: Prevention, Assessment, and Intervention* (New York: Oxford University Press, 2005); see also Edwin E. Lemert, "Diversion in Juvenile Justice: What Hath Been Wrought?" *Journal of Research in Crime and Delinquency* 18:34–46 (1981).

53. Don C. Gibbons and Gerald F. Blake, "Evaluating the Impact of Juvenile Diversion Programs," *Crime and Delinquency Journal* 22:411–419 (1976); Richard J. Lundman, "Will Diversion Reduce Recidivism?" *Crime and Delinquency Journal* 22:428–437 (1976); B. Bullington, J. Sprowls, D. Katkin, and M. Phillips, "A Critique of Diversionary Juvenile Justice," *Crime and Delinquency* 24:59–71 (1978); Thomas Blomberg, "Diversion and Accelerated Social Control," *Journal of Criminal Law and Criminology* 68:274–282 (1977); Sharla Rausch and Charles Logan, "Diversion from Juvenile Court: Panacea or Pandora's Box," in J. Klugel, ed., *Evaluating Juvenile Justice* (Beverly Hills: Sage Publications, 1983), pp. 19–30.

54. Arnold Binder and Gilbert Geis, "Ad Populum Argumentation in Criminology: Juvenile Diversion as Rhetoric," *Criminology* 30:309–333 (1984).

55. Christopher J. Sullivan and Edward Latessa, "The Coproduction of Outcomes: An Integrated Assessment of Youth and Program Effects on Recidivism," *Youth Violence and Juvenile Justice* 9:191–206 (2011).

56. Alison Evans Cuellar, Larkin S. McReynolds, and Gail A. Wasserman, "A Cure for Crime: Can Mental Health Treatment Diversion Reduce Crime Among Youth?" *Journal of Policy Analysis and Management* 25:197–214 (2006).

57. Peter W. Greenwood, *Changing Lives: Delinquency Prevention as Crime-Control Policy* (Chicago: University of Chicago Press, 2006), Ch. 8; Franklin E. Zimring, *American Juvenile Justice* (New York: Oxford University Press, 2005), Ch. 4.

58. Zimring, *American Juvenile Justice*, p. 47.

59. Michael Tonry, "Crime and Criminal Justice," in Michael Tonry, ed., *The Oxford Handbook of Crime and Criminal Justice* (New York: Oxford University Press, 2011), p. 15.

60. Shawn D. Bushway, Allison D. Redlich, and Robert J. Norris, "An Explicit Test of Plea Bargaining in the Shadow of the Trial," *Criminology* 52:723–754 (2014).

61. Sanford Fox, *Juvenile Courts in a Nutshell* (St. Paul, MN: West, 1985), pp. 154–156.

62. See Darlene Ewing, "Juvenile Plea Bargaining: A Case Study," *American Journal of Criminal Law* 6:167 (1978); Adrienne Volenik, *Checklists for Use in Juvenile Delinquency Proceedings* (Chicago: American Bar Association, 1985); Bruce Green, "Package Plea Bargaining and the Prosecutor's Duty of Good Faith," *Criminal Law Bulletin* 25:507–550 (1989).

63. Joseph Sanborn, "Philosophical, Legal, and Systematic Aspects of Juvenile Court Plea Bargaining," *Crime and Delinquency* 39:509–527 (1993).

64. John D. Burrow and Patrick G. Lowery, "A Preliminary Assessment of the Impact of Plea Bargaining Among a Sample of Waiver-Eligible Offenders," *Youth Violence and Juvenile Justice* 13:211–227 (2015).

65. Hockenberry and Puzzanchera, *Juvenile Court Statistics 2013*, p. 52.

66. Ibid, p. 39.

67. Patrick Griffin, Sean Addie, Benjamin Adams, and Kathy Firestine, *Trying Juveniles as Adults: An Analysis of State Transfer Laws and Reporting* (Washington, DC: Office of Juvenile Justice and Delinquency Prevention, 2011), p. 3.

68. Ibid.

69. Ibid.

70. *Kent v. United States*, 383 U.S. 541, 86 S.Ct. 1045, 16 L.Ed.2d 84 (1966); *Breed v. Jones*, 421 U.S. 519, 95 S.Ct. 1179, 44 L.Ed.2d 346 (1975).

71. Barry Feld, "The Juvenile Court Meets the Principle of the Offense: Legislative Changes in Juvenile Waiver Statutes," *Journal of Criminal Law and Criminology* 78:471–534 (1987); Paul Marcotte, "Criminal Kids," *American Bar Association Journal* 76:60–66 (1990); Dale Parent et al., *Transferring Serious Juvenile Offenders to Adult Courts* (Washington, DC: US Department of Justice, National Institute of Justice, 1997).

72. See Elizabeth Drake, *The Effectiveness of Declining Juvenile Court Jurisdiction of Youthful Offenders* (Olympia: Washington State Institute for Public Policy, 2013); Kareem L. Jordan and David L. Myers, "Juvenile Transfer and Deterrence: Reexamining the Effectiveness of a 'Get-Tough' Policy," *Crime and Delinquency* 57:247–270 (2011); Richard E. Redding, *Juvenile Transfer Laws: An Effective Deterrent to Delinquency?* (Washington, DC: Office of Juvenile Justice and Delinquency Prevention, 2010); Craig A. Mason, Derek A. Chapman, Chang Shau, and Julie Simons, "Impacting Re-Arrest Rates Among Youth Sentenced in Adult Court: An Epidemiology Examination of the Juvenile Sentencing Advocacy Project," *Journal of Clinical Child and Adolescent Psychology* 32:205–214 (2003); David L. Myers, "The Recidivism of Violent Youths in Juvenile and Adult Court: A Consideration of Selection Bias," *Youth Violence and Juvenile Justice* 1:79–101 (2003); Richard Redding, "Juvenile Offenders in Criminal Court and Adult Prison: Legal, Psychological and Behavioral Outcomes," *Juvenile and Family Court Journal* 50:1–15 (1999).

73. Thomas Grisso, Laurence Steinberg, Jennifer Woolard, Elizabeth Cauffman, Elizabeth Scott, Sandra Graham, Fran Lexcon, N. Dickon Reppucci, and Robert Schwartz, "Juveniles' Competence to Stand Trial: A Comparison of Adolescents' and Adults' Capacities as Trial Defendants," *Law and Human Behavior* 27:333–363 (2003); Darla M. Burnett, Charles D. Noblin, and Vicki Prosser, "Adjudicative Competency in a Juvenile Population," *Criminal Justice and Behavior* 31:438–462 (2004).

74. Megan C. Kurlychek and Brian D. Johnson, "Juvenility and Punishment: Sentencing Juveniles in Adult Criminal Court," *Criminology* 48:725–758 (2010).

75. Aaron Kupchik, "The Decision to Incarcerate in Juvenile and Criminal Courts," *Criminal Justice Review* 31:309–336 (2006), at 321–322.

76. Megan C. Kurlychek and Brian D. Johnson, "The Juvenile Penalty: A Comparison of Juvenile and Young Adult Sentencing Outcomes in Criminal Court," *Criminology* 42:485–517 (2004), at 498.

77. Redding, "Juvenile Offenders in Criminal Court and Adult Prison: Legal, Psychological and Behavioral Outcomes," p. 11; see also Richard E. Redding, "The Effects of Adjudicating and Sentencing Juveniles as Adults: Research and Policy Implications," *Youth Violence and Juvenile Justice* 1:128–155 (2003).

78. Emily Gaarder and Joanne Belknap, "Tenuous Borders: Girls Transferred to Adult Court," *Criminology* 40:481–518 (2002), at 508.

79. Redding, "Juvenile Offenders in Criminal Court and Adult Prison."

80. Benjamin Adams and Sean Addie, *Delinquency Cases Waived to Criminal Court, 2005* (Washington, DC: US Department of Justice, Office of Juvenile Justice and Delinquency Prevention, OJJDP Fact Sheet, 2009), p. 2.

81. Jeffrey Fagan, "Juvenile Crime and Criminal Justice: Resolving Border Disputes," *The Future of Children* 18(2):81–118 (2008).

82. Hockenberry and Puzzanchera, *Juvenile Court Statistics 2013*, pp. 58, 59.

83. Gerard Rainville and Steven K. Smith, *Juvenile Felony Defendants in Criminal Courts: Survey of 40 Counties, 1998* (Washington, DC: US Department of Justice, Office of Juvenile Justice and Delinquency Prevention, 2003).

84. Hockenberry and Puzzanchera, *Juvenile Court Statistics 2013*, p. 58.

85. Barry Feld, "Delinquent Careers and Criminal Policy," *Criminology* 21:195–212 (1983).

86. Howard N. Snyder, Melissa Sickmund, and Eileen Poe-Yamagata, *Juvenile Transfers to Criminal Court in the 1990s: Lessons Learned from Four Studies* (Washington, DC: Office of Juvenile Justice and Delinquency Prevention, 2000).

87. Rainville and Smith, *Juvenile Felony Defendants in Criminal Courts.*

88. Sanjeev Sridharan, Lynette Greenfield, and Baron Blakley, "A Study of Prosecutorial Certification Practice in Virginia," *Criminology and Public Policy* 3:605–632 (2004).

89. Franklin E. Zimring, "Treatment of Hard Cases in American Juvenile Justice: In Defense of the Discretionary Waiver," *Notre Dame Journal of Law, Ethics and Policy* 5:267–280 (1991); Lawrence Winner, Lonn Kaduce, Donna Bishop, and Charles Frazier, "The Transfer of Juveniles to Criminal Courts: Reexamining Recidivism over the Long Term," *Crime and Delinquency* 43:548–564 (1997).

90. Rainville and Smith, *Juvenile Felony Defendants in Criminal Courts.*

91. Institute of Judicial Administration, American Bar Association Joint Commission on Juvenile Justice Standards, *Standards Relating to Adjudication* (Cambridge, MA: Ballinger, 1980).

92. Joseph B. Sanborn Jr., "The Right to a Public Jury Trial—A Need for Today's Juvenile Court," *Judicature* 76:230–238 (1993). In the context of delinquency convictions to enhance criminal sentences, see Barry C. Feld, "The Constitutional Tension Between *Apprendi* and *McKeiver*: Sentence Enhancement Based on Delinquency Convictions and the Quality of Justice in Juvenile Courts," *Wake Forest Law Review* 38:1111–1224 (2003).

93. *In re Gault*, 387 U.S. 1, 87 S.Ct. 1248 (1967); see David S. Tanenhaus, *The Constitutional Rights of Children: In re Gault and Juvenile Justice* (Lawrence, KS: University Press of Kansas, 2011).

94. Linda Szymanski, *Juvenile Delinquents' Right to Counsel* (Pittsburgh: National Center for Juvenile Justice, 1988).

95. *In re Winship*, 397 U.S. 358, 90 S.Ct. 1068 (1970).

96. *McKeiver v. Pennsylvania*, 403 U.S. 528, 91 S.Ct. 1976 (1971).

97. Fox, *Juvenile Courts in a Nutshell*, p. 221.

98. Stacy Hoskins Haynes, Alison C. Cares, and R. Barry Ruback, "Juvenile Economic Sanctions: An Analysis of Their Imposition, Payment, and Effect on Recidivism," *Criminology and Public Policy* 13:31–60 (2014).

99. James C. Howell, *Preventing and Reducing Juvenile Delinquency: A Comprehensive Framework*, 2nd ed. (Thousand Oaks, CA: Sage, 2009).

100. Hockenberry and Puzzanchera, *Juvenile Court Statistics 2013*, p. 52.

101. Ibid.

102. Ibid.

103. Daniel P. Mears, Joshua C. Cochran, Brian J. Stults, Sara J. Greenman, Avinash S. Bhati, and Mark A. Greenwald, "The 'True' Juvenile Offender: Age Effects and Juvenile Court Sanctioning," *Criminology* 52:169–194 (2014), pp. 169, 186.

104. Anthony Platt, *The Child Savers: The Invention of Delinquency* (Chicago: University of Chicago Press, 1969); David Rothman, *Conscience and Convenience: The Asylum and the Alternative in Progressive America* (Boston: Little, Brown, 1980).

105. Joseph Goldstein, Anna Freud, and Albert Solnit, *Beyond the Best Interests of the Child* (New York: Free Press, 1973).

106. See, for example, *in Interest on M.P.* 697 N.E.2d 1153 (Il. App. 1998); *Matter of Welfare of CAW* 579 N.W.2d 494 (MN. App. 1998).

107. See, for example, *Matter of Willis Alvin M.* 479 S.E.2d. 871 (WV 1996).

108. Barry C. Feld and Donna M. Bishop, "Transfer of Juveniles to Criminal Court," in Feld and Bishop, eds., *The Oxford Handbook of Juvenile Crime and Juvenile Justice.*

109. Griffin, Addie, Adams, and Firestine, *Trying Juveniles as Adults: An Analysis of State Transfer Laws and Reporting*, p. 3.

110. Chad R. Trulson, Jonathan W. Caudill, Scott H. Belshaw, and Matt DeLisi, "A Problem of Fit: Extreme Delinquents, Blended Sentencing, and the Determinants of Continued Adult Sanctions," *Criminal Justice Policy Review* 22:263–284 (2011).

111. *Roper v. Simmons*, 125 S.Ct. 1183 (2005).

112. Erica Goode, "Young Killer: Bad Seed or Work in Progress?" *New York Times*, November 25, 2003.

113. Adam Liptak, "Court Takes Another Step in Reshaping Capital Punishment," *New York Times*, March 2, 2005.

114. *Roper v. Simmons*, 125 S.Ct. 1183 (2005).

115. Victor L. Streib, *The Juvenile Death Penalty Today: Death Sentences and Executions for Juvenile Crimes, January 1, 1973–September 30, 2003* (Ada, OH: The Claude W. Pettit College of Law, Ohio Northern University, October 6, 2003), p. 3.

116. Ibid.

117. Steven Gerstein, "The Constitutionality of Executing Juvenile Offenders, *Thompson v. Oklahoma*," *Criminal Law Bulletin* 24:91–98 (1988); *Thompson v. Oklahoma*, 108 S.Ct. 2687 (1988).

118. 109 S.Ct. 2969 (1989); for a recent analysis of the *Wilkins* and *Stanford* cases, see the note in "*Stanford v. Kentucky* and *Wilkins v. Missouri*: Juveniles, Capital Crime, and Death Penalty," *Criminal Justice Journal* 11:240–266 (1989).

119. Victor Streib, "Excluding Juveniles from New York's Impendent Death Penalty," *Albany Law Review* 54:625–679 (1990).

120. Goode, "Young Killer: Bad Seed or Work in Progress?"

121. Peter J. Benekos and Alida V. Merlo, "Juvenile Offenders and the Death Penalty: How Far Have Standards of Decency Evolved?" *Youth Violence and Juvenile Justice* 3:316–333 (2006), at 324.

122. Bryan Stevenson, *Just Mercy: A Story of Justice and Redemption* (New York: Spiegel and Grau, 2014).

123. Campbell Robertson, "South Carolina Judges Vacates Conviction of George Stinney in 1944 Execution," *New York Times*, December 17, 2014.

124. Barry C. Feld, "A Slower Form of Death: Implications of *Roper v. Simmons* for Juveniles Sentenced to Life Without Parole," *Notre Dame Journal of Law, Ethics and Public Policy* 22:9–65 (2008).

125. See Barry C. Feld, "Procedural Rights in Juvenile Courts: Competence and Consequences," in Feld and Bishop, eds., *The Oxford Handbook of Juvenile Crime and Juvenile Justice*; Peter J. Benekos and Alida V. Merlo, "Juvenile Justice: The Legacy of Punitive Policy," *Youth Violence and Juvenile Justice* 6:28–46 (2008); Laurence Steinberg and Ron Haskins, "Keeping Adolescents Out of Prison," *The Future of Children* 18(2):1–7 (2008).

126. Feld, "A Slower Form of Death," p. 10.

127. Amnesty International and Human Rights Watch, *The Rest of Their Lives: Life Without Parole for Children Offenders in the United States* (New York: Human Rights Watch, 2005), p. 1.

128. Ashley Nellis, *The Lives of Juvenile Lifers: Findings from a National Survey* (Washington, DC: The Sentencing Project, 2012).

129. See Elizabeth S. Scott and Laurence Steinberg, "The Young and the Reckless," *New York Times*, November 14, 2009.

130. Ibid.

131. *Graham v. Florida*, 130 S.Ct. 2011 (2010).

132. Adam Liptak, "Supreme Court Revisits Issue of Harsh Sentences for Juveniles," *New York Times*, March 21, 2012, A15.

133. 567 U.S. __ (2012); Erik Eckholm, "Juveniles Facing Lifelong Terms Despite Rulings," *New York Times*, January 19, 2014.

134. 577 U.S. ___ (2016).

135. The Campaign for the Fair Sentencing of Youth, http://fairsentencingofyouth.org/.

136. Paul Piersma, Jeanette Ganousis, Adrienne E. Volenik, Harry F. Swanger, and Patricia Connell, *Law and Tactics in Juvenile Cases*

(Philadelphia: American Law Institute, American Bar Association, Committee on Continuing Education, 1977), p. 397.

137. J. Addison Bowman, "Appeals from Juvenile Courts," *Crime and Delinquency Journal* 11:63–77 (1965).

138. *In re Gault*, 387 U.S. 1 (1967); 87 S.Ct. 1428.

139. *Davis v. Alaska*, 415 U.S. 308 (1974); 94 S.Ct. 1105.

140. *Oklahoma Publishing Co. v. District Court*, 430 U.S. 97 (1977); 97 S.Ct. 1045.

141. *Smith v. Daily Mail Publishing Co.*, 443 U.S. 97, 99 S.Ct. 2667, 61 L.Ed.2d 399 (1979).

142. Thomas Hughes, "Opening the Doors to Juvenile Court: Is There an Emerging Right of Public Access?" *Communications and the Law* 19:1–50 (1997).

143. Linda Szymanski, *Confidentiality of Juvenile Court Records* (Pittsburgh: National Center for Juvenile Justice, 1989).

144. Ira M. Schwartz, *Justice for Juveniles: Rethinking the Best Interests of the Child* (Lexington, MA: D. C. Heath, 1989), p. 172.

145. Richard E. Redding, "Use of Juvenile Records in Criminal Court," *Juvenile Justice Fact Sheet* (Charlottesville, VA: Institute of Law, Psychiatry, and Public Policy, University of Virginia, 2000).

146. Barry Feld, "Criminology and the Juvenile Court: A Research Agenda for the 1990s," in Ira M. Schwartz, ed., *Juvenile Justice and Public Policy— Toward a National Agenda* (New York: Lexington Books, 1992), p. 59.

147. Barry C. Feld, "Juvenile and Criminal Justice Systems' Responses to Youth Violence," in Michael Tonry and Mark H. Moore, eds., *Youth Violence: Crime and Justice: A Review of Research*, vol. 24 (Chicago: University of Chicago Press, 1998), p. 222.

148. Robert O. Dawson, "The Future of Juvenile Justice: Is It Time to Abolish the System?" *Journal of Criminal Law and Criminology* 81:136–155 (1990); see also Leonard P. Edwards, "The Future of the Juvenile Court: Promising New Directions," *The Future of Children: The Juvenile Court* (Los Altos, CA: David and Lucile Packard Foundation, 1996).

149. Peter W. Greenwood, *Changing Lives: Delinquency Prevention as Crime Control Policy* (Chicago: University of Chicago Press, 2006), p. 183; see also Daniel P. Mears, Joshua C. Cochran, Sarah J. Greenman, Avinash S. Bhati, and Mark A. Greenwald, "Evidence on the Effectiveness of Juvenile Court Sanctions," *Journal of Criminal Justice* 39:509–520 (2011).

150. Greenwood, *Changing Lives: Delinquency Prevention as Crime Control Policy*, pp. 193–194.

151. Peter J. Benekos and Alida V. Merlo, "Juvenile Justice: The Legacy of Punitive Policy," *Youth Violence and Juvenile Justice* 6:28–46 (2008).

152. Daniel P. Mears, Carter Hay, Marc Gertz, and Christina Mancini, "Public Opinion and the Foundation of the Juvenile Court," *Criminology* 45:223–258 (2007), p. 250.

153. Ibid., p. 246; see also Daniel P. Mears, Justin T. Picket, and Christina Mancini, "Support for Balanced Juvenile Justice: Assessing Views About Youth, Rehabilitation, and Punishment," *Journal of Quantitative Criminology* 31:459–479 (2015); Brandon K. Applegate, Robin King Davis, and Francis T. Cullen, "Reconsidering Child Saving: The Extent and Correlates of Public Support for Excluding Youths from Juvenile Courts," *Crime and Delinquency* 55:51–77 (2009).

CHAPTER 16

Juvenile Corrections:
Probation, Community Treatment, and Institutionalization

Learning Objectives

1 Contrast community treatment and institutional treatment for juvenile offenders

2 Explain the disposition of probation, including how it is administered and by whom and recent trends in its use

3 Discuss new approaches for providing probation services to juvenile offenders and comment on their effectiveness in reducing recidivism

4 Illustrate key historical developments of secure juvenile corrections in this country, including the principle of *least restrictive alternative*

5 Discuss recent trends in the use of juvenile institutions for juvenile offenders and how their use differs across states

6 Identify key issues facing the institutionalized juvenile offender

7 Appraise the effectiveness of various juvenile correctional treatment approaches in use today

8 Discuss juvenile offenders' legal right to treatment

9 Explain the nature of aftercare for juvenile offenders and comment on recent innovations in juvenile aftercare and reentry programs

Chapter Outline

Juvenile Probation
Historical Development
Expanding Community Treatment
Contemporary Juvenile Probation
Duties of Juvenile Probation Officers

Probation Innovations
Intensive Supervision
Electronic Monitoring
Restorative Justice
Balanced Probation
Restitution
Residential Community Treatment
Nonresidential Community Treatment

Secure Corrections
History of Juvenile Institutions

Juvenile Institutions Today: Public and Private
Population Trends
Physical Conditions

The Institutionalized Juvenile
Male Inmates
Female Inmates

Correctional Treatment for Juveniles
Individual Treatment Techniques: Past and Present
Group Treatment Techniques
Educational, Vocational, and Recreational Programs
Wilderness Programs
Juvenile Boot Camps

The Legal Right to Treatment
The Struggle for Basic Civil Rights

Juvenile Aftercare and Reentry
Supervision
Aftercare Revocation Procedures

Future of Juvenile Corrections

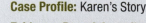

Chapter Features

Case Profile: Karen's Story

Evidence-Based Juvenile Justice— Treatment: Multidimensional Treatment Foster Care (MTFC)

Focus on Delinquency: Mental Health Needs of Juvenile Inmates

Professional Spotlight: Kristi Swanson

Youth Stories: "New Chef" Michael

NOT LONG AFTER HE HAD arrived at the N. A. Chaderjian Youth Correctional Facility, also known as "Chad," in Stockton, California, Joseph Daniel Maldonado, age 18, was found dead in his cell. He had committed suicide. Corrections officers found his limp body on the lower bunk with sheets wrapped around his neck and tied to the upper bunk. The officers were alerted to a potential problem upon discovering that the inmate's cell window was covered with paper, preventing anyone from seeing into the cell. A medical team was dispatched, but they were unable to revive Joseph. He was pronounced dead one hour later.

This was not an isolated event. Joseph's suicide was one of five suicide deaths inside the California juvenile correctional system over a period of 18 months. The other four inmates who committed suicide were Dyron Brewer, 24; Deon Whitfield, 17; Durrell Feaster, 18; and Roberto Lombana, 18.

Some of the circumstances leading up to Joseph's suicide are still in dispute. The Maldonado family claims that Joseph asked for psychological counseling on four separate occasions and it was denied each time. Joseph had sought counseling because he was depressed and troubled over his recent transfer to Chad, considered by many to be the "worst of the worst" of California's juvenile correctional institutions. Not in dispute, however, are other events that contributed to Joseph's death. Chief among them was the inability of his family to visit or get in touch with him for a lengthy period of time. When Joseph was transferred to Chad, his visitors' list (a list of family members and others who can offer support) was not sent with him. An eight-week lockdown of Pajaro Hall, the ward Joseph resided in, due to gang violence further blocked any contact with family members. In its official report on the suicide, the California Inspector General ruled that Joseph Maldonado's death may have been entirely preventable.

Out of these tragedies has come some good. In October 2007, the Family Connection and Young Offender Rehabilitation Act was signed into law. The act mandates that the California Department of Corrections and Rehabilitation's Division of Juvenile Justice ensure that inmates are able to "communicate with family members, clergy, and others, and to participate in programs that will

Jennell Happy, 42, outside of the Los Angeles County Hall of Administration, April 28, 2004, calling for action in the death of her nephew Durrell Feaster, 18, in a California Youth Authority prison.

facilitate his or her education, rehabilitation, and accountability to victims." The act also requires that a number of practical steps be taken to improve contact between family members and inmates, such as establishing a toll-free number for families to confirm visiting times, as well as taking into consideration the proximity of family when placing a juvenile offender in an institution.[1] In 2012, a settlement was reached in a wrongful-death suit filed by the family against state correctional authorities.[2]

T his case highlights the importance of correctional treatment for juvenile offenders. There is a wide choice of correctional treatments available for juveniles, which can be subdivided into two major categories: community treatment and institutional treatment. **Community treatment** refers to efforts to provide care, protection, and treatment for juveniles in need. These efforts include probation, treatment services (such as individual and group counseling), restitution, and other programs. Community treatment also refers to the use of privately

community treatment
Using nonsecure and noninstitutional residences, counseling services, victim restitution programs, and other community services to treat juveniles in their own communities.

593

maintained residences, such as foster homes, small-group homes, and boarding schools, which are located in the community. Nonresidential programs, where youths remain in their own homes but are required to receive counseling, vocational training, and other services, also fall under the rubric of community treatment.

Institutional treatment facilities are correctional centers operated by federal, state, and county governments; these facilities restrict the movement of residents through staff monitoring, locked exits, and interior fence controls. A variety of functions within juvenile corrections are served by these facilities, including (a) reception centers that screen juveniles and assign them to an appropriate facility, (b) specialized facilities that provide specific types of care, such as drug treatment, (c) training schools or reformatories for youths needing a long-term secure setting, (d) ranch or forestry camps that provide long-term residential care, and (e) boot camps, which seek to rehabilitate youths through the application of rigorous physical training.

Choosing the proper mode of juvenile corrections can be difficult. Some experts believe that any hope for rehabilitating juvenile offenders and resolving the problems of juvenile crime lies in community treatment programs.[3] Such programs are smaller than secure facilities for juveniles, operate in a community setting, and offer creative approaches to treating the offender. In contrast, institutionalizing young offenders may do more harm than good. It exposes them to prisonlike conditions and to more-experienced delinquents without giving them the benefit of constructive treatment programs.[4]

Those who favor secure treatment are concerned about the threat that violent young offenders present to the community and believe that a stay in a juvenile institution may have a long-term deterrent effect. They point to the findings of Charles Murray and Louis B. Cox, who uncovered what they call a **suppression effect**—a reduction in the number of arrests per year following release from a secure facility—which is not achieved when juveniles are placed in less-punitive programs.[5] Murray and Cox concluded that the justice system must choose which outcome its programs are aimed at achieving: prevention of delinquency, or the care and protection of needy youths. If the former is a proper goal, institutionalization or the threat of institutionalization is desirable.

We begin this chapter with a detailed discussion of community treatment, examining both traditional probation and new approaches for providing probation services to juvenile offenders. Next, we trace the development of alternatives to incarceration, including community-based, nonsecure treatment programs and graduated sanctions (programs that provide community-based options while reserving secure care for violent offenders). The current state of secure juvenile corrections is then reviewed, beginning with some historical background, followed by a discussion of life in institutions, treatment issues, legal rights, and aftercare and reentry programs.

Juvenile Probation

Probation and other forms of community treatment generally refer to nonpunitive legal dispositions for delinquent youths, emphasizing treatment without incarceration. Probation is the primary form of community treatment used by the juvenile justice system. A juvenile who is on probation is maintained in the community under the supervision of an officer of the court. Probation also encompasses a set of rules and conditions that must be met for the offender to remain in the community. Juveniles on probation may be placed in a wide variety of community-based treatment programs that provide services ranging from group counseling to drug treatment.

Community treatment is based on the idea that the juvenile offender is not a danger to the community and has a better chance of being rehabilitated within the community. It provides offenders with the opportunity to be supervised by trained personnel who can help them reestablish forms of acceptable behavior in a community setting. When applied correctly, community treatment (a) maximizes the liberty of the individual while vindicating the authority of the law and protecting the public, (b) promotes rehabilitation by maintaining normal community contacts, (c) avoids the negative effects of confinement, which often severely complicate the reintegration of the offender into the community, and (d) greatly reduces the financial cost to the public.[6]

Historical Development

Although the major developments in community treatment have occurred in the twentieth century, its roots go back much farther. In England, specialized procedures for dealing with youthful offenders were recorded as early as 1820, when the magistrates of the Warwickshire quarter sessions (periodic court hearings held in a county, or shire, of England) adopted the practice of sentencing youthful criminals to prison terms of one day, then releasing them conditionally under the supervision of their parents or masters.[7]

In the United States, juvenile probation developed as part of the wave of social reform characterizing the latter half of the nineteenth century. Massachusetts took the first step. Under an act passed in 1869, an agent of the state board of charities was authorized to appear in criminal trials involving juveniles, to find them suitable homes, and to visit them periodically. These services were soon broadened, so that by 1890 probation had become a mandatory part of the court structure.[8]

Probation was a cornerstone in the development of the juvenile court system. In fact, in some states, supporters of the juvenile court movement viewed probation as the first step toward achieving the benefits that the new court was intended to provide. The rapid spread of juvenile courts during the first decades of the twentieth century encouraged the further development of probation. The two were closely related, and to a large degree, both sprang from the conviction that the young could be rehabilitated and that the public was responsible for protecting them.

Expanding Community Treatment

By the mid-1960s, juvenile probation had become a complex institution that touched the lives of an enormous number of children. Many experts considered that institutionalization of even the most serious delinquent youths was a mistake. Reformers believed that confinement in a high-security institution could not solve the problems that brought a youth into a delinquent way of life, and that the experience could actually help amplify delinquency once the youth returned to the community.[9] Surveys indicating that 30 to 40 percent of adult prison inmates had prior experience with the juvenile court, and that many had been institutionalized as youths, gave little support to the argument that an institutional experience can be beneficial or reduce recidivism.[10]

The Massachusetts Experience The expansion of community programs was energized by correctional reform in the Commonwealth of Massachusetts. Since the early 1970s, Massachusetts has led the movement to keep juvenile offenders in the community. After decades of documenting the failures of the youth correctional system, Massachusetts, led by its juvenile correctional commissioner Jerome Miller, closed most of its secure juvenile facilities.[11] Today, 40 years later, the Massachusetts Department of Youth Services still operates a community-based correctional system. The majority of youths are serviced in nonsecure community settings, and only a few dangerous or unmanageable youths are placed in some type of secure facilities.

Many of the early programs suffered from residential isolation and limited services. Over time, however, many of the group homes and unlocked structured residential settings were relocated in residential community environments and became highly successful in addressing the needs of juveniles, while presenting little or no security risk to themselves or others.

Though the efforts to turn juvenile corrections into a purely community-based system has not been adopted elsewhere, the Massachusetts model encouraged development of nonpunitive programs, which have proliferated across the nation. The concept of probation has been expanded, and new programs have been created.

Contemporary Juvenile Probation

Traditional probation is still the backbone of community-based corrections. As Figure 16.1 shows, some 205,300 juveniles were placed on formal probation in 2013 (the latest data available), which amounts to 64 percent of all juvenile dispositions. The use of probation has decreased by 43 percent since 2004, when around 359,900 adjudicated youths were placed on probation.[12] These figures show that regardless of public sentiment, probation continues to be a popular dispositional alternative for judges. Here are the arguments in favor of probation:

- For youths who can be supervised in the community, probation represents an appropriate disposition.

- Probation allows the court to tailor a program to each juvenile offender, including those involved in person-oriented offenses. Recent research, however, raises questions about the adequacy of the present system to attend to the specific needs of female youths on probation.[13]

- The justice system continues to have confidence in rehabilitation, while accommodating demands for legal controls and public protection, even when caseloads may include many more serious offenders than in the past.

- Probation is often the disposition of choice, particularly for status offenders.[14]

The Nature of Probation   In most jurisdictions, probation is a direct judicial order that allows a youth who is found to be a delinquent or status offender to remain in the community under court-ordered supervision. A probation sentence implies a contract between the court and the juvenile. The court promises to hold a period of institutionalization in abeyance; the juvenile promises to adhere to a set of rules mandated by the court. If the rules are violated—and especially if the juvenile

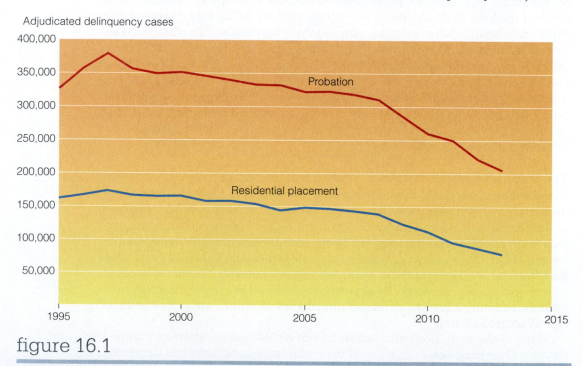

figure 16.1

Probation and Correctional Population Trends

SOURCE: Melissa Sickmund, Anthony Sladky, and Wei Kang, *Easy Access to Juvenile Court Statistics: 1985–2013* (Pittsburgh: National Center for Juvenile Justice, 2015), http://ojjdp.gov/ojstatbb/ezajcs/ (accessed October 2016).

commits another offense—the probation may be revoked. In that case, the contract is terminated and the original commitment order may be enforced. The rules of probation vary, but they typically involve conditions such as attending school or work, keeping regular hours, remaining in the jurisdiction, and staying out of trouble.

In the juvenile court, probation is often ordered for an indefinite period. Depending on the statutes of the jurisdiction, the seriousness of the offense, and the juvenile's adjustment on probation, youths can remain under supervision until the court no longer has jurisdiction over them (when they reach the age of majority). State statutes determine whether a judge can specify how long a juvenile may be placed under an order of probation. In most jurisdictions, the status of probation is reviewed regularly to ensure that a juvenile is not kept on probation needlessly. Generally, discretion lies with the probation officer to discharge youths who are adjusting to the treatment plan.

Conditions of Probation   Rules mandating that a juvenile on probation behave in a particular way are the **conditions of probation**. They can include restitution or reparation, intensive supervision, intensive counseling, participation in a therapeutic program, or participation in an educational or vocational training program. In addition to these specific conditions, state statutes generally allow courts to insist that probationers lead law-abiding lives, maintain a residence in a family setting, refrain from associating with certain types of people, and remain in a particular area unless they have permission to leave. (See Figure 16.2 for different probation options.)

Although probation conditions vary, they are never supposed to be capricious, cruel, or beyond the capacity of the juvenile to satisfy. Furthermore, conditions of probation should relate to the crime that was committed and to the conduct of the youth. Courts have invalidated probation conditions that were harmful or that violated the juvenile's due process rights. Restricting a young person's movement, insisting on a mandatory program of treatment, ordering indefinite terms of probation, and demanding financial reparation where this is impossible are all grounds for appellate court review. For example, it would not be appropriate for a probation order to bar a youth from visiting his girlfriend (unless he had threatened or harmed her) merely because her parents objected to the relationship.[15] However, courts have ruled that it is permissible to bar juveniles from such sources of danger as a "known gang area" in order to protect them from harm.[16]

conditions of probation
The rules and regulations mandating that a juvenile on probation behave in a particular way.

figure 16.2

Conditions of Probation

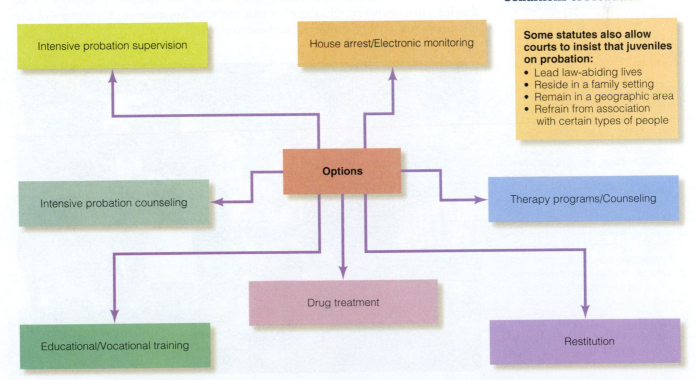

Some statutes also allow courts to insist that juveniles on probation:
- Lead law-abiding lives
- Reside in a family setting
- Remain in a geographic area
- Refrain from association with certain types of people

Intensive probation supervision

House arrest/Electronic monitoring

Intensive probation counseling

Options

Therapy programs/Counseling

Educational/Vocational training

Drug treatment

Restitution

If a youth violates the conditions of probation—and especially if the juvenile commits another offense—the court can revoke probation. In this case, the contract is terminated and the original commitment order may be enforced. The juvenile court ordinarily handles a decision to revoke probation upon recommendation of the probation officer. Today, as a result of Supreme Court decisions dealing with the rights of adult probationers, a juvenile is normally entitled to legal representation and a hearing when a violation of probation occurs.[17]

Duties of Juvenile Probation Officers

juvenile probation officer
Officer of the court involved in all four stages of the court process—intake, predisposition, postadjudication, and postdisposition—who assists the court and supervises juveniles placed on probation.

The **juvenile probation officer** plays an important role in the justice process, beginning with intake and continuing throughout the period in which a juvenile is under court supervision. Their role is so important and influence so great that much research has been generated over the years on how juvenile probation officers perform their duties, including their approach to treatment and punishment.[18] Probation officers are involved at four stages of the court process. At *intake*, they screen complaints by deciding to adjust the matter, refer the juvenile to an agency for service, or refer the case to the court for judicial action. During the *predisposition* stage, they participate in release or detention decisions. At the *postadjudication* stage, they assist the court in reaching its dispositional decision. During *postdisposition*, they supervise juveniles placed on probation.

At intake, the probation staff has preliminary discussions with the juvenile and the family to determine whether court intervention is necessary or whether the matter can be better resolved by some form of social service. If the juvenile is placed in a detention facility, the probation officer helps the court decide whether the juvenile should continue to be held or released pending the adjudication and disposition of the case.

social investigation report or predisposition report
Developed by the juvenile probation officer, this report consists of a clinical diagnosis of the juvenile and his or her need for court assistance, relevant environmental and personality factors, and any other information that would assist the court in developing a treatment plan for the juvenile.

The probation officer exercises tremendous influence over the youth and the family by developing a **social investigation report** (also called a **predisposition report**) and submitting it to the court. This report is a clinical diagnosis of the youth's problems and of the need for court assistance based on an evaluation of social functioning, personality, and environmental issues. The report includes an analysis of the child's feelings about the violations and his or her capacity for change. It also examines the influence of family members, peers, and other environmental influences in producing and possibly resolving the problems. All of this information is brought together in a complex but meaningful picture of the offender's personality, problems, and environment.[19]

Juvenile probation officers provide supervision and treatment in the community. The treatment plan is a product of the intake, diagnostic, and investigative aspects of probation. Treatment plans vary in terms of approach and structure. Some juveniles simply report to the probation officer and follow the conditions of probation. In other cases, juvenile probation officers will supervise young people more intensely, monitor their daily activities, and work with them in directed treatment programs. Here, a juvenile probation officer and police officer talk with Crips gang members in California.

A. Ramey/Photo Edit

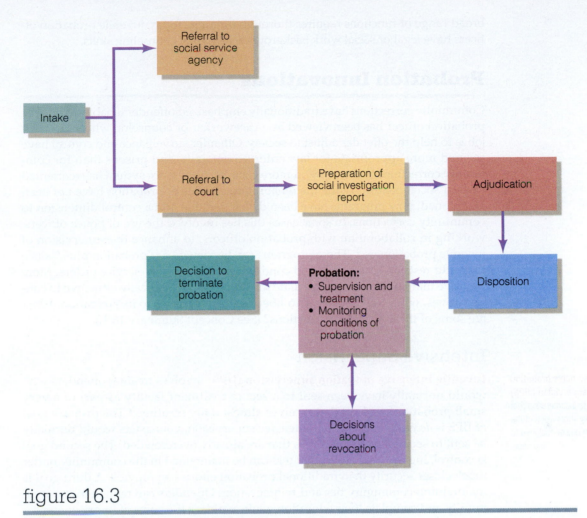

figure 16.3

The Juvenile Probation Officer's Influence

Juvenile probation officers also provide the youth with supervision and treatment in the community. Treatment plans vary in terms of approach and structure. Some juveniles simply report to the probation officer and follow the conditions of probation. In other cases, the probation officer may need to provide extensive counseling to the youth and family or, more typically, refer them to other social service agencies, such as a drug treatment center. In Florida, juvenile probation officers are guided by a disposition matrix in making recommendations to the juvenile court.[20] Figure 16.3 provides an overview of the juvenile probation officer's sphere of influence. Exhibit 16.1 summarizes the probation officer's role. Performance of such a

---

exhibit 16.1

Duties of the Juvenile Probation Officer

- Provide direct counseling and casework services
- Interview and collect social service data
- Make diagnostic recommendations
- Maintain working relationships with law enforcement agencies
- Use community resources and services
- Direct volunteer case aides

- Write predisposition or social investigation reports
- Work with families of children under supervision
- Provide specialized services, such as group therapy
- Supervise specialized caseloads involving children with special problems
- Make decisions about the revocation of probation and its termination

broad range of functions requires thorough training. Today, juvenile probation officers have legal or social work backgrounds or special counseling skills.

Probation Innovations

Community corrections have traditionally emphasized offender rehabilitation. The probation officer has been viewed as a caseworker or counselor, whose primary job is to help the offender adjust to society. Offender surveillance and control have seemed more appropriate for law enforcement, jails, and prisons than for community corrections.[21] Since 1980, a more conservative justice system has reoriented toward social control. While the rehabilitative ideals of probation have not been abandoned, new programs have been developed that add a control dimension to community corrections. In some cases this has involved the use of police officers, working in collaboration with probation officers, to enhance the supervision of juvenile probationers.[22] These programs can be viewed as "probation plus," since they add restrictive penalties and conditions to community-service orders. More punitive than probation, intermediate sanctions can be politically attractive to conservatives, while still appealing to liberals as alternatives to incarceration. What are some of these alternative sanctions? (See Concept Summary 16.1.)

Intensive Supervision

juvenile intensive probation supervision (JIPS)
A true alternative to incarceration that involves almost daily supervision of the juvenile by the probation officer assigned to the case.

Juvenile intensive probation supervision (JIPS) involves treating offenders who would normally have been sent to a secure treatment facility as part of a very small probation caseload that receives almost daily scrutiny.[23] The primary goal of JIPS is *decarceration*; without intensive supervision, youngsters would normally be sent to secure juvenile facilities that are already overcrowded. The second goal is control; high-risk juvenile offenders can be maintained in the community under much closer security than traditional probation efforts can provide. A third goal is maintaining community ties and reintegration. Offenders can remain in the community and complete their education while avoiding the pains of imprisonment.

Intensive probation programs get mixed reviews. Some jurisdictions find that they are more successful than traditional probation supervision and come at a much cheaper cost than incarceration.[24] However, some studies indicate that the failure rate

CONCEPT SUMMARY 16.1

Community-Based Corrections

Although correctional treatment in the community generally refers to nonpunitive legal dispositions, in most cases there are still restrictions designed to protect the public and hold juvenile offenders accountable for their actions.

Type	Main Restrictions
Probation	Regular supervision by a probation officer; youth must adhere to conditions such as attend school or work, stay out of trouble
Intensive supervision	Almost daily supervision by a probation officer; adhere to similar conditions as regular probation
House arrest	Remain at home during specified periods; often there is monitoring through random phone calls, visits, or electronic devices
Restorative justice	Restrictions may be prescribed by community members to help repair harm done to victim
Balanced probation	Restrictions tailored to the risk the juvenile offender presents to the community
Restitution	None.
Residential programs	Placement in a residential, nonsecure facility such as group home or foster home; adhere to conditions; close monitoring
Nonresidential programs	Remain in own home; comply with treatment regime

is high and that younger offenders who commit petty crimes are the most likely to fail when placed in intensive supervision programs.[25] It is not surprising that intensive probation clients fail more often because, after all, they are more serious offenders who might otherwise have been incarcerated and are now being watched and supervised more closely than other probationers. In one experimental study of intensive probation supervision plus a coordinated team approach for high-risk juveniles, known as the Los Angeles County Repeat Offender Prevention Program (ROPP), mixed results were found for those who received the program compared to a similar group of youths who received regular probation only. Recidivism was reduced in the short term but not over the long term, school performance was increased, and there was no difference in probation technical violations.[26] In another California experiment of juvenile intensive probation supervision, no significant differences were observed in recidivism rates among those youths who received intensive probation compared to a similar group of youths who received regular probation.[27] Further analyses of this program revealed no effects on key family and peer relationship measures.[28]

An innovative experiment in three Mississippi counties examined the differential effects on juvenile justice costs for intensive supervision and monitoring, regular probation, and cognitive behavioral treatment, which involved sessions on problem solving, social skills, negotiation skills, the management of emotion, and values enhancement, to improve the thinking and reasoning ability of juvenile offenders. After one year of the program the intensive supervision treatment was found to be less cost effective than the other two treatments, with the cognitive behavioral treatment imposing the fewest costs on the juvenile justice system.[29]

Despite its poor showing in a number of evaluations, juvenile intensive probation supervision continues to be used across the country. When used in combination with other probation innovations and tailored to the needs of the juvenile, it can produce promising results. The Case Profile entitled "Karen's Story" highlights one such success.

Electronic Monitoring

Another program that has been used with adult offenders and is finding its way into the juvenile justice system is **house arrest**, which is often coupled with **electronic monitoring**. This program allows offenders sentenced to probation to remain in the community on condition that they stay at home during specific

house arrest
An offender is required to stay at home during specified periods of time; monitoring is done by random phone calls and visits or by electronic devices.

electronic monitoring
Active monitoring systems consist of a radio transmitter worn by the offender that sends a continuous signal to the probation department computer, alerting officials if the offender leaves his or her place of confinement. Passive systems employ computer-generated random phone calls that must be answered in a certain period of time from a particular phone or other device.

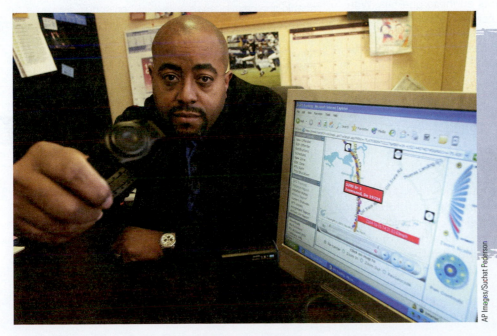

A number of probation innovations have been experimented with to keep juvenile offenders from being sent to secure juvenile facilities. One of these is electronic monitoring, which, in addition to requiring juveniles to follow regular conditions of probation, monitors their movements to keep them confined to specified areas such as home, work, or school. Pictured here is Steven Wesley, regional manager for Delaware Juvenile Probation and Aftercare, holding a GPS transmitter that is used to track the movements of juvenile delinquents placed on house arrest. The transmitter can be worn on the wrist or ankle.

AP Images/Suchat Pederson

case profile

Karen's Story

KAREN GILLIGAN, 16, was the oldest of four children living with their parents in a small rural community. Her mother worked two jobs, her father was unemployed, and both parents drank heavily. Karen's high school attendance was sporadic. She had started to experiment with alcohol and vandalized local businesses. After being arrested in a stolen car on several occasions, Karen was referred to juvenile court and was put on community supervision and probation. An initial assessment was provided by her probation officer, and formal dispositional recommendations were made to the court. She was to remain at home on house arrest for 60 days, attend school regularly and maintain at least a C average, follow an alcohol and drug assessment program, and participate in weekly family therapy with her parents. Karen was also ordered to cooperate with the juvenile restitution program, pay her restitution in full within six months, and participate in the Community Adolescent Intensive Supervision Program, as arranged by her probation officer.

Not used to being accountable to anyone, Karen struggled in the beginning with all the new rules and expectations. She missed some of her initial appointments and skipped some classes at school. Karen's probation officer began making unannounced visits to her at school, trying to help her understand the consequences of her behavior. Through the intensive supervision program, every day after school Karen was required to attend a local community center where she received tutoring, group counseling with other offenders, and the guidance of many counselors. The group sessions focused on changing negative thinking, offering alternatives to aggression, and avoiding criminal behavior, gang involvement, and drugs and alcohol.

It was clear to her probation officer that Karen possessed many strengths and positive attributes. She enjoyed dancing and singing, and even liked school at times. The team of professionals encouraged her to focus on these qualities. With help, Karen began to understand her destructive behavior and seek ways to turn her life around. She spoke with her probation officer about creating life goals and making plans for achieving them.

In addition to Karen's individual counseling, her family participated in weekly family therapy to talk about their issues and to address how to best support the children. Initially, the sessions were very challenging and stressful for the entire family. They blamed each other for their difficulties, and Karen seemed to be the target of much of the anger expressed by her parents. The therapist worked with them to reduce the conflict and help them establish goals for their therapy that could improve their family life.

During the many months of intensive supervision, treatment, and family therapy, Karen was able to stop her delinquent behavior, pay her restitution, attend school regularly, and improve her communication with her parents. Through therapy, Karen's mother also acknowledged that she needed some assistance with her drinking and entered treatment. Karen's probation officer provided the court with regular monthly progress reports showing significant improvement in her behavior and lifestyle choices. Karen has proven her success and continues to live with her parents and siblings. She plans to attend a local college after graduation to prepare for a career in the medical field.

CRITICAL THINKING

1. Do you agree or disagree with the probation officer's recommendations to the court? What would you have done differently? Can you think of additional programs or services that would have been helpful in this situation?

2. Initially, Karen struggled with rules and expectations. Her probation officer worked with her to help her accomplish the goals. What could you say to a juvenile who is in this situation? How would you try to motivate a teen in trouble with the law?

3. Do you think it was a good idea to put Karen on house arrest in her parental home? What problems could have come of this? If Karen had continued to break the law, should she have been removed? When should a juvenile delinquent be removed from her parents' home due to her criminal behavior? What crimes do you think would justify an automatic removal and what would need to be accomplished for the child to return?

periods (e.g., after school or work, on weekends, and in the evenings). Offenders may be monitored through random phone calls, visits, or, in some jurisdictions, electronic devices.

Two types of electronic systems are used: active and passive. *Active systems* monitor the offender by continuously sending a signal back to the central office. If an offender leaves home at an unauthorized time, the signal is broken and the failure recorded. In some cases, the control officer is automatically notified through a beeper. In contrast, *passive systems* usually involve random phone calls generated by computers to which the juvenile offender must respond within a particular time (e.g., 30 seconds). Some passive systems require the offender to place the monitoring device in a verifier box that sends a signal back to the control computer; another approach is to have the arrestee repeat words that are analyzed by a voice verifier and compared with tapes of the juvenile's voice.

Most systems employ radio transmitters that receive a signal from a device worn by the offender and relay it back to the computer via telephone lines. Probationers are fitted with an unremovable monitoring device that alerts the probation department's computers if they leave their place of confinement.[30]

Joseph B. Vaughn conducted one of the first surveys of juvenile electronic monitoring in 1989, examining eight programs in five different probation departments.[31] Vaughn found that all the programs adopted electronic monitoring to reduce institutional overcrowding and that most agencies reported success in reducing the number of days juveniles spent in detention. In addition, the programs allowed the youths, who would otherwise be detained, to remain in the home and participate in counseling, educational, or vocational activities. Of particular benefit to pretrial detainees was the opportunity to remain in a home environment with supervision. This experience provided the court with a much clearer picture of how the juvenile would eventually reintegrate into society. However, Vaughn found that none of the benefits of the treatment objective in the programs had been empirically validated.

There is widespread belief that electronic monitoring can be effective, with some evaluations showing that recidivism rates are no higher than in traditional programs, costs are lower, and institutional overcrowding is reduced. Some studies also reveal that electronic monitoring seems to work better with some individuals than others: serious felony offenders, substance abusers, repeat offenders, and people serving the longest sentences are the most likely to fail.[32] However, in a review on the effects of electronic monitoring on recidivism, criminologists Marc Renzema and Evan Mayo-Wilson found that the results do not support the claim that it works at the present time. This conclusion was largely based on there being too few high-quality studies available and a difficulty in isolating the independent effects of programs that combine electronic monitoring with other interventions. The researchers do not call for an end to the use of electronic monitoring, but call for new and better experiments.[33]

Restorative Justice

Restorative justice is a nonpunitive strategy for delinquency control that attempts to address the issues that produce conflict between two parties (offender and victim) and, hence, reconcile the parties. Restoration rather than retribution or punishment is at the heart of the restorative justice approach. Seven core values characterize restorative justice:

- Crime is an offense against human relationships.
- Victims and the community are central to justice processes.
- The first priority of justice processes is to assist victims.
- The second priority of justice processes is to restore the community, to the degree possible.
- The offender has a personal responsibility to victims and to the community for crimes committed.
- The offender will develop improved competency and understanding as a result of the restorative justice experience.
- Stakeholders share responsibilities for restorative justice through partnerships for action.[34]

Criminologists Heather Strang and Lawrence Sherman carried out a systematic review and meta-analysis of the effects of restorative justice on juvenile reoffending and victim satisfaction. The review involved two studies from Australia, one from the United Kingdom, and one from the United States that evaluated the restorative justice practice of face-to-face conferences. (The main reason for the small number of studies is that the authors used only those studies that employed the highest-quality evaluation design— randomized controlled experiments—to assess program effects.) The conferences proceeded as follows:

> *Any victims (or their representatives) present have the opportunity to describe the full extent of the harm a crime has caused, offenders are required to listen to the victims and to understand the consequences of their own actions, and all participants are invited to deliberate about what actions the offender could take to repair them. The precondition of such a conference is that the offender does not dispute the fact that he is responsible for the harm caused, and the conference cannot and will not become a trial to determine what happened.*[35]

The review found evidence that this form of restorative justice can be an effective strategy in reducing repeat offending by juveniles.[36] The review also found that the strategy was more effective for adult offenders than juvenile offenders, at least for violent crime.[37] An earlier version of the review found that face-to-face conferences can be effective in preventing victims from committing crimes of retaliation against their perpetrators. Perhaps not surprisingly, across all studies victim satisfaction levels strongly favored restorative justice compared to traditional juvenile justice proceedings.[38]

In a larger scale review—involving twelve experiments of this form of restorative justice (four in Australia and eight in the United Kingdom)— Sherman, Strang, and their colleagues found both short- and long-term benefits for both crime victims and their offenders. For example, the programs were most effective with the most serious and frequent offenders.[39] Successful results have also been demonstrated in other restorative justice programs for juvenile offenders.[40]

Balanced Probation

Some jurisdictions have turned to a **balanced probation** approach in an effort to enhance the success of probation.[41] Balanced probation systems integrate community protection, the accountability of the juvenile offender, and individualized attention to the offender (see Figure 16.4). These programs are based on the view that juveniles are responsible for their actions and have an obligation to society whenever they commit an offense; they are the product of an overall effort to bring greater balance to the juvenile justice system.[42] The probation officer establishes a program tailored to the offender while helping the offender accept responsibility for his or her actions. The balanced approach is promising because it specifies a distinctive role for the juvenile probation system.[43]

Restitution

Victim restitution is another widely used method of community treatment. In most jurisdictions, restitution is part of a probationary sentence and is administered by the county probation staff. In many jurisdictions, independent restitution programs have been set up by local governments; in others, restitution is administered by a private nonprofit organization.[44]

Restitution can take several forms. A juvenile can reimburse the victim of the crime or donate money to a charity or public cause; this is referred to as **monetary restitution** and is one type of an economic sanction. In other instances, a juvenile may be required to provide some service directly to the

The **Reintegrative Shaming Experiments project** (http://aic.gov.au /criminal_justice_system/rjustice/rise .html) has been running in the Australian Capital Territory since 1995. It examines conferencing in Canberra, which is based on the "Wagga model" of police-run conferences. The study is being conducted by the Centre for Restorative Justice at the Australian National University.

balanced probation
Programs that integrate community protection, accountability of the juvenile offender, competency, and individualized attention to the juvenile offender; based on the principle that juvenile offenders must accept responsibility for their behavior.

monetary restitution
A requirement that juvenile offenders compensate crime victims for out-of-pocket losses caused by the crime, including property damage, lost wages, and medical expenses.

figure 16.4

Balanced Approach Mission

SOURCE: Gordon Bazemore and Mark Umbreit, *Balanced and Restorative Justice for Juveniles—A Framework for Juvenile Justice in the 21st Century* (Washington, DC: Office of Juvenile Justice and Delinquency Prevention, 1997), p. 14.

victim (**victim service restitution**) or to assist a community organization (**community service restitution**).

Requiring youths to reimburse the victims of their crimes is the most widely used method of restitution in the United States. Less widely used (but more common in Europe) is restitution to a charity. In the past few years, numerous programs have been set up for the juvenile offender to provide service to the victim or to participate in community programs—for example, working in schools for children with developmental delays. In some cases, juveniles are required to contribute both money and community service. Other programs emphasize employment.[45]

Restitution programs can be employed at various stages of the juvenile justice process. They can be part of a diversion program prior to conviction, a method of informal adjustment at intake, or a condition of probation. Restitution has a number of advantages: It provides alternative sentencing options; it offers monetary compensation or service to crime victims; it allows the juvenile the opportunity to compensate the victim and take a step toward becoming a productive member of society; it helps relieve overcrowded juvenile courts, probation caseloads, and detention facilities.[46] Finally, like other alternatives to incarceration, restitution has the potential for allowing vast savings in the operation of the juvenile justice system. Monetary restitution programs in particular may improve the public's attitude toward juvenile justice by offering equity to the victims of crime and ensuring that offenders take responsibility for their actions.

Despite its many advantages, some believe restitution supports retribution rather than rehabilitation because it emphasizes justice for the victim and criminal responsibility for illegal acts. There is some concern that restitution creates penalties for juvenile offenders where none existed before.[47]

The use of restitution is increasing. In 1977, there were fewer than 15 formal restitution programs around the United States. By 1985, formal programs existed in 400 jurisdictions, and 35 states had statutory provisions that gave courts the authority to order juvenile restitution.[48] Today, all 50 states, as well as the District of Columbia, have statutory restitution programs.

Does Restitution Work?   How successful is restitution as a treatment alternative? Most evaluations have shown that it is reasonably effective and should be expanded.[49] In an analysis of restitution programs across the country, Peter Schneider and Matthew Finkelstein found that between 73 and 74 percent of youths who received restitution as a condition of probation successfully completed their orders. The researchers also found that juvenile restitution programs that reported a reduction in recidivism rates were the ones with high successful completion rates.[50] More recently, in an analysis of more than 900 juvenile cases in five Pennsylvania counties, criminologists Stacy Haynes, Alison Cares, and Barry Ruback found that restitution was imposed in one-third (33 percent) of eligible cases, while fees (to cover justice administration costs) were imposed in the remaining two-thirds of the eligible cases.[51] The authors also found that payment of economic sanctions in general, which included restitution, was related to lower rates of recidivism—that is, those juvenile offenders who paid a greater percentage of their economic sanctions were less likely to recidivate.

Restitution programs may be difficult to implement in some circumstances. Offenders may find it difficult to make monetary restitution without securing new employment, which can be difficult during periods of high unemployment. Problems also arise when offenders who need jobs suffer from drug abuse or emotional problems. Public and private agencies are likely sites for community service restitution, but their directors are sometimes reluctant to allow delinquent youths access to their organizations. Beyond these problems, some juvenile probation officers view restitution programs as a threat to their authority and to the autonomy of their organizations.

victim service restitution
The juvenile offender is required to provide some service directly to the crime victim.

community service restitution
The juvenile offender is required to assist some worthwhile community organization for a period of time.

Another criticism of restitution programs is that they foster involuntary servitude. Indigent clients may be unfairly punished when they are unable to make restitution payments or face probation violations. To avoid such bias, probation officers should first determine why payment has stopped and then suggest appropriate action, rather than simply treating nonpayment as a matter for law enforcement.

Finally, restitution orders are subject to the same abuses as traditional sentencing methods. Restitution orders given to one delinquent offender may be quite different from those given another in a comparable case. To remedy this situation, a number of jurisdictions have been using guidelines to encourage standardization of orders.

Residential Community Treatment

As noted earlier, many experts believe that institutionalization of even the most serious delinquent youths is a mistake. Confinement in a high-security institution usually cannot solve the problems that brought a youth into a delinquent way of life, and the experience may actually amplify delinquency once the youth returns to the community. Many agree that warehousing juveniles without attention to their treatment needs does little to prevent their return to criminal behavior. Research has shown that the most effective secure-corrections programs provided individualized services for a small number of participants. Large training schools have not proved to be effective.[52] This realization has produced a wide variety of residential community treatment programs to service youths who need a more secure environment than can be provided by probation services, but who do not require placement in a state-run juvenile correctional facility.

How are community corrections implemented? In some cases, youths are placed under probation supervision, and the probation department maintains a residential treatment facility. Placement can also be made to the department of social services or juvenile corrections with the direction that the youth be placed in a residential facility. **Residential programs** are typically divided into four major categories: (1) group homes, including boarding schools and apartment-type settings, (2) foster homes, (3) family group homes, and (4) rural programs.

Group homes are nonsecure residences that provide counseling, education, job training, and family living. They are staffed by a small number of qualified persons and generally house 12 to 15 youngsters. The institutional quality of the environment is minimized, and youths are given the opportunity to build a close relationship with the staff. Youths reside in the home, attend public schools, and participate in community activities in the area.

Foster care programs offer support and shelter for juvenile offenders who have lost their parents or whose parents cannot care for them. The foster parents provide a stable environment and the nurturance and guidance to help juveniles make a successful return to the community. In recent years one foster care program—the Multidimensional Treatment Foster Care (MTFC) program—has been especially effective in reducing juvenile offending. Because of its importance it is the subject of the accompanying Evidence-Based Juvenile Justice feature.

Family group homes combine elements of foster care and group home placements. Juveniles are placed in a group home that is run by a family rather than by a professional staff. Troubled youths have an opportunity to learn to get along in a family-like situation, and at the same time the state avoids the startup costs and neighborhood opposition often associated with establishing a public institution.

Rural programs include forestry camps, ranches, and farms that provide recreational activities or work for juveniles. Programs typically handle from 30 to 50 youths. Such programs have the disadvantage of isolating juveniles from the community, but reintegration can be achieved if the youth's stay is short and if family and friends are allowed to visit.

residential programs
Placement of a juvenile offender in a residential, nonsecure facility such as a group home, foster home, family group home, or rural home where the juvenile can be closely monitored and develop close relationships with staff.

group homes
Nonsecured, structured residences that provide counseling, education, job training, and family living.

foster care programs
Juveniles who are orphans or whose parents cannot care for them are placed with families who provide the attention, guidance, and care they did not receive at home.

family group homes
A combination of foster care and a group home in which a juvenile is placed in a private group home run by a single family rather than by professional staff.

rural programs
Specific recreational and work opportunities provided for juveniles in a rural setting, such as a forestry camp, a farm, or a ranch.

Multidimensional Treatment Foster Care (MTFC)

Foster care programs involve one or two juveniles who live with a family—usually a husband and wife who serve as surrogate parents. The juveniles enter into a close relationship with the foster parents and receive the attention and care they did not receive at home. The quality of the foster home experience depends on the foster parents. Foster care for adjudicated juvenile offenders has not been extensive in the United States. Welfare departments generally handle foster placements, and funding of this treatment option has been a problem for the juvenile justice system. However, foster home services have expanded as a community treatment approach.

One example of an effective foster care model is the Multidimensional Treatment Foster Care (MTFC) program, developed by social scientists at the Oregon Social Learning Center. Designed for the most serious and chronic young offenders, this program combines individual therapy such as skill building in problem solving for the youths and family therapy for the biological or adoptive parents. The foster care families receive training by program staff so they can provide the young people with close supervision, fair and consistent limits and consequences, and a supportive relationship with an adult. Foster care families also receive close supervision and are consulted regularly on the progress of the youths by program staff.

An experiment of MTFC, which included 79 adolescent males under the control of the juvenile justice system, found that one year after the completion of the program, youths who received MTFC were significantly less likely to be arrested than their control counterparts who received services-as-usual group home care. A two-year follow-up of this experiment, when the youths were between 16 and 19 years old, showed that the benefits persisted. MTFC was significantly more effective than group home care, as measured by referrals for violent offending and self-reports of violent behavior. Twenty-four percent of the group home care condition had two or more criminal referrals for violent offenses compared to only 5 percent in the MTFC condition. Rates of self-reported violent offending were four to nine times higher among group home care participants compared to those who received MTFC.

In another experiment, Patricia Chamberlain and her colleagues examined the effects of MTFC with group care for 81 serious and chronic female juvenile offenders between the age of 13 and 17 years. Follow-up took place when the youths were 15 to 19 years old. Analyses showed that MTFC was more effective than group care, as measured by days in locked settings, number of criminal referrals, and self-reported delinquency. Further analyses revealed that older MTFC participants exhibited less delinquency relative to younger participants in both conditions. Systematic reviews and meta-analyses have also shown that MTFC is effective as well as cost-effective in reducing juvenile offending.

CRITICAL THINKING

1. MTFC involves a number of important components that contribute to its effectiveness. Do you think one of the components is more effective than the others?

2. MTFC's effectiveness with some of the most serious and chronic juvenile offenders shows that it is never too late to intervene. What does this mean for how society uses treatment and punishment to address juvenile offending?

SOURCES: William Turner and Geraldine MacDonald, "Treatment Foster Care for Improving Outcomes in Children and Young People: A Systematic Review," *Research on Social Work Practice* 21:501–527 (2011); Patricia Chamberlain, Leslie D. Leve, and David S. DeGarmo, "Multidimensional Treatment Foster Care for Girls in the Juvenile Justice System: 2-Year Follow-up of a Randomized Clinical Trial," *Journal of Consulting and Clinical Psychology* 75:187–193 (2007); J. Mark Eddy, Rachel Bridges Whaley, and Patricia Chamberlain, "The Prevention of Violent Behavior by Chronic and Serious Male Juvenile Offenders: A 2-Year Follow-up of a Randomized Clinical Trial," *Journal of Emotional and Behavioral Disorders* 12:2–8 (2004); Patricia Chamberlain and John B. Reid, "Comparison of Two Community Alternatives to Incarceration," *Journal of Consulting and Clinical Psychology* 66:624–633 (1998).

Most residential programs use group counseling as the major treatment tool. Although group facilities have been used less often than institutional placements, there is a trend toward developing community-based residential facilities.

Nonresidential Community Treatment

In **nonresidential programs** youths remain in their homes and receive counseling, education, employment, diagnostic, and casework services. A counselor or probation officer gives innovative and intensive support to help the youth remain at home. Family therapy, educational tutoring, and job placement may all be part of the program. Nonresidential programs are often modeled on the Provo experiment, begun in 1959 in Utah, and on the Essexfields Rehabilitation Project, started

nonresidential programs
Juveniles remain in their own homes but receive counseling, education, employment, diagnostic, and casework services through an intensive support system.

Nonresidential community treatment provides juvenile offenders with the opportunity to live at home while receiving various programs that focus on counseling, education, and employment. Pictured here are Philip Graceffa and his mom, Cynthia, at her home in Rockford, Illinois. Philip just completed the Redeploy Illinois program, a nonresidential program for juveniles offered throughout the state.

AP Images/Sophia Tareen

in the early 1960s in Essex County, New Jersey.[53] (See Chapter 11 for a discussion of one of the best-known approaches—multisystemic therapy [MST].)

Secure Corrections

When the court determines that community treatment cannot meet the special needs of a delinquent youth, a judge may refer the juvenile to a secure treatment program. Today, correctional institutions operated by federal, state, and county governments are generally classified as either secure or open facilities. Secure facilities restrict the movement of residents through staff monitoring, locked exits, and interior fence controls. Open institutions generally do not restrict the movement of the residents and allow much greater freedom of access to the facility.[54] In the following sections, we analyze the state of secure juvenile corrections, beginning with some historical background. This is followed by a discussion of life in institutions, the juvenile client, treatment issues, legal rights, and aftercare and reentry programs.

History of Juvenile Institutions

Until the early 1800s, juvenile offenders, as well as neglected and dependent children, were confined in adult prisons. The inhumane conditions in these institutions were among the factors that led social reformers to create a separate children's court system in 1899.[55] Early juvenile institutions were industrial schools modeled after adult prisons but designed to protect children from the evil influences in adult facilities. The first was the New York House of Refuge, established in 1825. Not long after this, states began to establish **reform schools** for juveniles. Massachusetts was the first, opening the Lyman School for Boys in Westborough in 1846. New York opened the State Agricultural and Industrial School in 1849, and Maine opened the Maine Boys' Training School in 1853. By 1900, 36 states had reform schools.[56] Although it is difficult to determine exact populations of these institutions, by 1880 there were approximately 11,000 youths in correctional facilities, a number that more than quadrupled by 1980.[57] Early reform schools were generally punitive in nature and were based on the concept of rehabilitation (or reform) through hard work and discipline.

reform schools

Institutions in which educational and psychological services are used in an effort to improve the conduct of juveniles who are forcibly detained.

In the second half of the nineteenth century, emphasis shifted to the **cottage system**. Juvenile offenders were housed in compounds of cottages, each of which could accommodate 20 to 40 children. A set of parents ran each cottage, creating a homelike atmosphere. This setup was believed to be more conducive to rehabilitation.

The first cottage system was established in Massachusetts in 1855, the second in Ohio in 1858.[58] The system was held to be a great improvement over training schools. The belief was that by moving away from punishment and toward rehabilitation, not only could offenders be rehabilitated, but also crime among unruly children could be prevented.[59]

Twentieth-Century Developments   The early twentieth century witnessed important changes in juvenile corrections. Because of the influence of World War I, reform schools began to adopt a militaristic style. Living units became barracks; cottage groups became companies; house fathers became captains; and superintendents became majors or colonels. Military-style uniforms were standard wear. In addition, the establishment of the first juvenile court in 1899 reflected the expanded use of confinement for delinquent children. As the number of juvenile offenders increased, the forms of juvenile institutions varied to include forestry camps, ranches, and vocational schools. Beginning in the 1930s, camps modeled after those run by the Civilian Conservation Corps became a part of the juvenile correctional system. These camps centered on conservation activities and work as a means of rehabilitation.

Los Angeles County was the first to use camps during this period.[60] Southern California was experiencing problems with transient youths who came to California with no money and then got into trouble with the law. Rather than filling up the jails, the county placed these offenders in conservation camps, paid them low wages, and released them when they had earned enough money to return home. The camps proved more rehabilitative than training schools, and by 1935 California had established a network of forestry camps for delinquent boys. The idea soon spread to other states.[61]

Also during the 1930s, the US Children's Bureau sought to reform juvenile corrections. The bureau conducted studies to determine the effectiveness of the training school concept. Little was learned from these programs because of limited funding and bureaucratic ineptitude, and the Children's Bureau failed to achieve any significant change. But such efforts recognized the important role of positive institutional care.[62]

Another innovation came in the 1940s with passage of the American Law Institute's Model Youth Correction Authority Act. This act emphasized reception/classification centers. California was the first to try this idea, opening the Northern Reception Center and Clinic in Sacramento in 1947. Today, many such centers are scattered around the United States.

Since the 1970s, a major change in institutionalization has been the effort to remove status offenders from institutions housing juvenile delinquents. This includes removing status offenders from detention centers and removing all juveniles from contact with adults in jails. This *decarceration* policy mandates that courts use the **least restrictive alternative** in providing services for status offenders. A noncriminal youth should not be put in a secure facility if a community-based program is available. In addition, the federal government prohibits states from placing status offenders in separate facilities that are similar in form and function to those used for delinquent offenders. This is to prevent states from merely shifting their institutionalized population around so that one training school houses all delinquents and another houses all status offenders, but actual conditions remain the same.

Throughout the 1980s and into the 1990s, admissions to juvenile correctional facilities grew substantially.[63] Capacities of juvenile facilities also increased, but not enough to avoid overcrowding. Training schools became seriously overcrowded in

cottage system
Housing juveniles in a compound containing a series of cottages, each of which accommodates 20 to 40 children and is run by a set of cottage parents who create a homelike atmosphere.

least restrictive alternative
Choosing a program with the least restrictive or secure setting that will best benefit the child.

some states, causing private facilities to play an increased role in juvenile corrections. Reliance on incarceration became costly to states: inflation-controlled juvenile corrections expenditures for public facilities grew to more than $2 billion in 1995, an increase of 20 percent from 1982.[64] A 1994 report issued by the OJJDP said that crowding, inadequate health care, lack of security, and poor control of suicidal behavior were widespread in juvenile corrections facilities. Despite new construction, crowding persisted in more than half the states.[65] Citing a number of these and other problems facing juvenile offenders in secure facilities, in January 2016 President Barack Obama issued a ban on the use of solitary confinement of juvenile offenders held in federal prisons.[66]

Juvenile Institutions Today: Public and Private

Most juveniles are housed in public institutions administered by state agencies: child and youth services, health and social services, corrections, or child welfare.[67] In some states these institutions fall under a centralized system that covers adults as well as juveniles. Recently, a number of states have removed juvenile corrections from an existing adult corrections department or mental health agency. However, the majority of states still place responsibility for the administration of juvenile corrections within social service departments.

Supplementing publicly funded institutions are private facilities that are maintained and operated by private agencies funded or chartered by state authorities. The majority of today's private institutions are relatively small facilities holding fewer than 30 youths. Many have a specific mission or focus (e.g., treating females who display serious emotional problems). Although about 80 percent of public institutions can be characterized as secure, only 20 percent of private institutions are high-security facilities.

Population Trends

Although most delinquents are held in public facilities, most status offenders are held in private facilities. At last count (2013), there were 54,148 juvenile offenders being held in public (68 percent) and private (32 percent) facilities in the United States. The number of juveniles held in custody reached its peak in 2000 and has decreased by 50 percent through 2013.[68] According to a report by the Annie E. Casey Foundation, the 2010 census figures (70,792 juvenile offenders in residential facilities) marked a 35-year low in youth incarceration. The more than decade-long decline in youth incarceration has not led to an increase in youth crime; juvenile crime has actually been falling during this period of time (see Chapter 1).[69]

The juvenile custody rate varies widely across the country: the District of Columbia makes the greatest use of custodial treatment, incarcerating 560 delinquents in juvenile facilities per 100,000 juveniles in the population, whereas Vermont has the lowest juvenile custody rate at 46. The District of Columbia's juvenile custody rate is more than three times the national average (see Table 16.1).[70] Some states rely heavily on privately run facilities, whereas others place many youths in out-of-state facilities.

This wide variation in state-level juvenile custody rates has been the subject of much speculation but little empirical research. In an important study, criminologist Daniel Mears found three main explanations for why some states incarcerate juveniles at a much higher rate than others: (1) they have high rates of juvenile property crime and adult violent crime; (2) they have higher adult custody rates; and (3) there is a "cultural acceptance of punitive policies" in some parts of the country. Interestingly, Mears found that western and midwestern states were more likely to have higher juvenile incarceration rates than southern states, thus calling into question the widely held view that the South is disproportionately punitive.[71]

Although the number of institutionalized youths appears to have stabilized in the last few years, the data may reveal only the tip of the iceberg. The data do not

table 16.1

State Comparison of Numbers and Rates of Juvenile Offenders in Custody, 2013

State of Offense	Number	Rate	State of Offense	Number	Rate
US Total	54,148	173	Missouri	1,053	191
Alabama	933	184	Montana	150	151
Alaska	195	241	Nebraska	411	204
Arizona	882	122	Nevada	591	201
Arkansas	681	215	New Hampshire	78	68
California	8,094	197	New Jersey	888	95
Colorado	1,077	197	New Mexico	402	179
Connecticut	279	74	New York	1,650	116
Delaware	159	176	North Carolina	543	70
District of Columbia	228	560	North Dakota	171	253
Florida	2,802	152	Ohio	2,283	186
Georgia	1,557	159	Oklahoma	519	125
Hawaii	78	60	Oregon	1,086	281
Idaho	450	236	Pennsylvania	2,781	222
Illinois	1,617	134	Rhode Island	159	158
Indiana	1,581	219	South Carolina	672	159
Iowa	735	227	South Dakota	333	376
Kansas	885	278	Tennessee	666	99
Kentucky	774	170	Texas	4,383	161
Louisiana	774	180	Utah	612	160
Maine	162	130	Vermont	27	46
Maryland	771	127	Virginia	1,563	188
Massachusetts	393	60	Washington	1,014	144
Michigan	1,683	183	West Virginia	510	294
Minnesota	939	165	Wisconsin	816	156
Mississippi	243	74	Wyoming	165	279

Note: The rate is the number of juvenile offenders in residential placement in 2013 per 100,000 juveniles in the population.

Source: Melissa Sickmund, Anthony J. Sladky, Wei Kang, and Charles Puzzanchera, "Easy Access to the Census of Juveniles in Residential Placement" (2015), http://www.ojjdp.gov/ojstatbb/ezacjrp/ (accessed October 2016).

include many minors who are incarcerated after they are waived to adult courts or who have been tried as adults because of exclusion statutes. Most states place underage juveniles convicted of adult charges in youth centers until they reach the age of majority, whereupon they are transferred to an adult facility. In addition, there may be a hidden, or subterranean, correctional system that places wayward youths in private mental hospitals and substance abuse clinics for behaviors that might otherwise have brought them a stay in a correctional facility or community-based program.[72] These data suggest that the number of institutionalized children may be far greater than reported in the official statistics.[73] Studies also show that large numbers of youths are improperly incarcerated because of a lack of appropriate facilities. A nationwide survey carried out by congressional investigators as part of the House Committee on Government Reform found that 15,000 children with psychiatric disorders who were awaiting mental health services were improperly incarcerated in secure juvenile detention facilities.[74] In New Jersey, investigations into the state's child welfare system found that large numbers of teenage foster children were being held in secure juvenile detention facilities. Other states resort to similar practices, citing a lack of appropriate noncorrectional facilities.[75]

Physical Conditions

The physical plants of juvenile institutions vary in size and quality. Many older training schools still place all offenders in a single building, regardless of the offense. More acceptable structures include a reception unit with an infirmary, a security unit, and dormitory units or cottages. Planners have concluded that the most effective design for training schools is to have facilities located around a community square. The facilities generally include a dining hall and kitchen area, a storage warehouse, academic and vocational training rooms, a library, an auditorium, a gymnasium, an administration building, and other basic facilities.

The individual living areas also vary, depending on the type of facility and the progressiveness of its administration. Most traditional training school conditions were appalling. Today, however, most institutions provide toilet and bath facilities, beds, desks, lamps, and tables. New facilities usually try to provide a single room for each individual. However, the Juvenile Residential Facility Census, which collects information about the facilities in which juvenile offenders are held, found that 21 percent of the 1,985 facilities that reported information were either at capacity or overcrowded, with the latter defined as having more residents than available standard beds.[76]

The physical conditions of secure facilities for juveniles have come a long way from the training schools of the turn of the century. However, many administrators realize that more modernization is necessary to comply with national standards for juvenile institutions.[77] Although some improvements have been made, there are still enormous problems to overcome.[78]

The Institutionalized Juvenile

The typical resident of a juvenile facility is a 15- or 16-year-old male from a racial or ethnic minority group. Most incarcerated youths are property or drug offenders.[79]

Minority youths are incarcerated at a rate two to four times that of white youths. The difference is greatest for African American youths, with a custody rate of 464 per 100,000 juveniles; for white youths the rate is 100.[80] In a number of states, such as California, Colorado, Massachusetts, Nebraska, New Jersey, New York, Pennsylvania, and Wisconsin, the difference in custody rates between African Americans and white youths is considerably greater (see Table 16.2). Research has found that this overrepresentation is not a result of differentials in arrest rates, but often stems from disparity at early stages of case processing.[81] Of equal importance, minorities are more likely to be confined in secure public facilities rather than in open private facilities that might provide more costly and effective treatment, and among minority groups African American youths are more likely to receive punitive treatment—throughout the juvenile justice system—compared with others.[82]

Minority youths accused of delinquent acts are less likely than white youths to be diverted from the court system into informal sanctions and are more likely to receive sentences involving incarceration.[83] It has also been reported that minority youths are less likely to receive rehabilitative interventions than their white counterparts.[84] Today, more than 7 in 10 juveniles in custody belong to racial or ethnic minorities.[85] Racial disparity in juvenile disposition is a growing problem that demands immediate public scrutiny.[86] In response, many jurisdictions have initiated studies of racial disproportion in their juvenile justice systems, along with federal requirements to reduce disproportionate minority confinement, now referred to as disproportionate minority contact (DMC), as contained in the Juvenile Justice and Delinquency Prevention Act of 2002.[87] A report on state compliance to reduce DMC demonstrates that some progress has been made but that many challenges remain, including the need for full- or part-time staff to coordinate DMC initiatives, incomplete and inconsistent data systems, and the need for ongoing evaluation of focused interventions and systemwide efforts to reduce DMC.[88] Some promising practices in reducing DMC, such as cultural competency training and increasing community-based detention alternatives, are beginning to emerge.[89]

The **Center for the Promotion of Mental Health in Juvenile Justice** (http://www.promotementalhealth.org/) is dedicated to providing expert guidance to juvenile justice settings regarding best practices for mental health assessment and referral.

table 16.2

State Comparison of Custody Rates Between European American and African American Juvenile Offenders, 2013

State of Offense	White	Black	State of Offense	White	Black
United States	*100*	*464*	Missouri	128	519
Alabama	110	355	Montana	116	681
Alaska	150	413	Nebraska	116	837
Arizona	94	293	Nevada	148	597
Arkansas	109	586	New Hampshire	29	1,052
California	91	748	New Jersey	17	439
Colorado	135	923	New Mexico	132	422
Connecticut	17	306	New York	58	344
Delaware	65	504	North Carolina	29	166
District of Columbia	144	671	North Dakota	160	727
Florida	100	365	Ohio	109	550
Georgia	67	321	Oklahoma	75	468
Hawaii	12	77	Oregon	229	913
Idaho	217	628	Pennsylvania	99	803
Illinois	65	388	Rhode Island	67	721
Indiana	164	545	South Carolina	88	218
Iowa	160	973	South Dakota	211	713
Kansas	176	1,079	Tennessee	48	274
Kentucky	122	495	Texas	100	434
Louisiana	65	362	Utah	84	2,162
Maine	108	825	Vermont	38	195
Maryland	43	280	Virginia	93	506
Massachusetts	25	206	Washington	105	427
Michigan	94	559	West Virginia	255	712
Minnesota	89	705	Wisconsin	59	946
Mississippi	23	142	Wyoming	225	276

Note: The rate is the number of juvenile offenders in residential placement in 2013 per 100,000 juveniles in the population.

Source: Melissa Sickmund, Anthony J. Sladky, Wei Kang, and Charles Puzzanchera, "Easy Access to the Census of Juveniles in Residential Placement" (2015), http://www.ojjdp.gov/ojstatbb/ezacjrp/ (accessed October 2016).

Across all races and ethnicities, mental health needs are particularly acute among institutionalized juveniles.[90] Because of the importance of this topic, it is featured in the accompanying Focus on Delinquency box.

For more than two decades, shocking exposés, sometimes resulting from investigations by the US Department of Justice's civil rights division, continue to focus public attention on the problems of juvenile corrections.[91] For example, allegations of sexual victimization of juveniles reported by juvenile correctional administrators show a rather large increase in both state and local/private facilities. Between 2005 and 2012, the rate of allegations in state facilities more than doubled, from 19 to 47 per 1,000 youth. Between 2010 and 2012, the rate of allegations in local/private facilities increased from 7 to 14 per 1,000 youths.[92] While rates of sexual victimization among incarcerated juveniles remain a serious problem, the latest national survey of prison inmates by the Department of Justice shows that juvenile inmates are at no greater risk for sexual abuse than adult inmates.[93]

Today, more so than in past years, some critics believe public scrutiny has improved conditions in training schools. There is greater professionalism among the staff, and staff brutality seems to have diminished. Status offenders and delinquents are, for the most part, held in separate facilities. Confinement length is shorter, and rehabilitative programming has increased. However, there are significant differences in the experiences of male and female delinquents within the institution.

Mental Health Needs of Juvenile Inmates

Research suggests that as many as two out of every three (65 percent) juvenile offenders in juvenile correctional facilities suffer from mental health problems, and a large proportion of these youths enter the system without previously having been diagnosed or receiving treatment. Incarcerated youths suffering from mental health problems may find it harder to adjust to their new environment, which may in turn lead to acting-out behaviors, disciplinary problems, and problems in participating in treatment programs. All of these problems increase the risk of recidivism upon release to the community.

These findings are cause for concern on their own, but have become more pressing as many states, in an effort to trim their budgets, are cutting back on funding for community- and school-based mental health programs. In a survey of state mental health offices, at least 32 states reported funding cuts—by an average of 5 percent—to these programs in the current fiscal year. These same states are planning to double these reductions in funding in the years to come. According to Joseph Penn, a child psychologist at the Texas Youth Commission, "We're seeing more and more mentally ill kids who couldn't find community programs that were intensive enough to treat them. Jails and juvenile justice facilities are the new asylums."

Even with a diagnosis, treatment services can be scarce in juvenile correctional facilities. One study found that only one out of four juvenile offenders (23 percent) diagnosed with a mental disorder received any treatment.

Another study found that 85 percent of this population reported at least one perceived barrier to accessing mental health services. Contributing to the problem is that there is little information on what treatment works best for these juveniles. Columbia University's Center for the Promotion of Mental Health in Juvenile Justice and the National Center for Mental Health and Juvenile Justice are leading a national push for improved treatment as well as improved mental health assessments beginning as early as intake.

CRITICAL THINKING

1. What are some short-term measures that can be taken to help address the mental health needs of incarcerated juveniles? Is treatment in the community a realistic option?

2. What should states be doing to plan for the long-term needs of this population?

SOURCES: Linda A. Teplin, Karen M. Abram, Jason J. Washburn, Leah J. Welty, Jennifer A. Hershfield, and Mina K. Dulcan, *The Northwestern Juvenile Project: Overview* (Washington, DC: Office of Juvenile Justice and Delinquency Prevention, 2013); Lisa Rapp-Paglicci, Chris Stewart, William Rowe, and J. Mitchell Miller, "Addressing the Hispanic Delinquency and Mental Health Relationship Through Cultural Arts Programming: A Research Note," *Journal of Contemporary Criminal Justice* 27:110–121 (2011); Solomon Moore, "Mentally Ill Offenders Strain Juvenile System," *New York Times*, August 10, 2009; Thomas Grisso, "Adolescent Offenders with Mental Disorders," *The Future of Children* 18(2):143–164 (2008); Kathleen R. Skowyra and Joseph J. Cocozza, *Blueprint for Change: A Comprehensive Model for the Identification and Treatment of Youth with Mental Health Needs in Contact with the Juvenile Justice System* (Delmar, NY: National Center for Mental Health and Juvenile Justice, 2007); Deborah Shelton, "Patterns of Treatment Services and Costs for Young Offenders with Mental Disorders," *Journal of Child and Adolescent Psychiatric Nursing* 18:103–112 (2005).

Male Inmates

Males make up the great bulk of institutionalized youth, accounting for almost seven out of every eight (or 86 percent) juvenile offenders in residential placement,[94] and most programs are directed toward their needs. In many ways their experiences mirror those of adult offenders. In an important paper, Clemens Bartollas and his associates identified an inmate value system that they believed was common in juvenile institutions:

- Exploit whomever you can.
- Don't play up to staff.
- Don't rat on your peers.
- Don't give in to others.[95]

In addition to these general rules, the researchers found that there were separate norms for African American inmates ("exploit whites; no forcing sex on blacks; defend your brother") and for whites ("don't trust anyone; everybody for himself").

Other research efforts confirm the notion that residents do in fact form cohesive groups and adhere to an informal inmate culture.[96] The more serious the youth's record and the more secure the institution, the greater the adherence to the inmate social code. Male delinquents are more likely to form allegiances with members of their own racial group and to attempt to exploit those outside the group. They also scheme to manipulate staff and take advantage of weaker peers. However, in institutions that are treatment oriented, and where staff–inmate relationships are more intimate, residents are less likely to adhere to a negativistic inmate code.

Female Inmates

Between 1991 and the peak year of 2001, the number of female juvenile offenders in custody increased by 57 percent, from 9,600 to 15,100. In the last 13 years, from 2001 to 2013, the number of female juvenile offenders in custody decreased by almost half (49 percent, from 15,100 to 7,700). Over this same period, the proportion of female juvenile offenders of the total number of offenders in custody stayed fairly constant at 14 percent. Up until this period of time, the proportion of female juvenile offenders in custody had been increasing.[97]

The growing involvement of female youths in criminal behavior and the influence of the feminist movement have drawn more attention to the female juvenile offender, revealing a double standard of justice. For example, girls are more likely than boys to be incarcerated for status offenses. Institutions for girls are generally more restrictive than those for boys, and they have fewer educational and vocational programs and fewer services. Institutions for girls also do a less-than-adequate job of rehabilitation.[98] It has been suggested that this double standard operates because of a male-dominated justice system that seeks to "protect" young girls from their own sexuality.[99]

Over the years, the number of females held in public institutions has declined, albeit less so in the past few years. This represents the continuation of a long-term trend to remove girls, many of whom are nonserious offenders, from closed institutions and place them in private or community-based facilities. It is estimated that 37 percent of all female youths in residential placement are held in private facilities; for male youths it is 31 percent.[100]

The same double standard that brings a girl into an institution continues to exist once she is in custody. For example, institutional programs for girls tend to be oriented toward reinforcing traditional roles for women. Most of these programs also fail to account for the different needs of African American and Caucasian females, as in the case of coping with past abuse.[101] How well these programs rehabilitate girls is questionable. The one exception to this double standard is that female youths are incarcerated for similar terms as male youths.[102]

Many characteristics of juvenile female offenders are similar to those of their male counterparts, including poor social skills and low self-esteem. Other problems are more specific to the female juvenile offender (sexual abuse issues, victimization histories, lack of placement options).[103] Female juvenile offenders also have higher rates of mental health problems than their male counterparts.[104] In addition, there have been numerous allegations of emotional and sexual abuse by correctional workers, who either exploit vulnerable young women or callously disregard their emotional needs. An interview survey conducted by the National Council on Crime and Delinquency uncovered numerous incidents of abuse and bitter resentment by the young women over the brutality of their custodial treatment.[105]

Although there are more coed institutions for juveniles than in the past, most girls remain incarcerated in single-sex institutions that are isolated in rural areas and rarely offer adequate rehabilitative services. Several factors account for the different treatment of girls. One is sexual stereotyping by administrators, who believe that teaching girls "appropriate" sex roles will help them function effectively in society. These beliefs are often held by the staff as well, many of whom hold highly sexist ideas of what is appropriate behavior for adolescent girls. Another factor that accounts for the different treatment of girls is that staff members often are not adequately trained to understand and address the unique needs of this population.[106] Girls' institutions tend to be smaller than boys' institutions and lack the resources to offer as many programs and services as do the larger male institutions.[107]

It appears that although society is more concerned about protecting girls who act out, it is less concerned about rehabilitating them because the crimes they commit are not serious. These attitudes translate into fewer staff, older facilities, and poorer educational and recreational programs than those found in boys' institutions.[108] To help address these and other problems facing female juveniles in institutions, the American Bar Association and the National Bar Association recommend a number of important changes, including these:

- Identify, promote, and support effective gender-specific, developmentally sound, culturally sensitive practices with girls.
- Promote an integrated system of care for at-risk and delinquent girls and their families based on their competencies and needs.
- Assess the adequacy of services to meet the needs of at-risk or delinquent girls and address gaps in service.
- Collect and review state and local practices to assess the gender impact of decision making and system structure.[109]

Some of these recommendations are starting to garner serious attention—notably, with the emergence of a growing body of evidence of effective programs for female juveniles in institutions and at other stages in the juvenile justice system.[110] Also, building on these and other recommendations, in 2014 the Office of Juvenile Justice and Delinquency Prevention established the National Girls Initiative with one aim to "develop programs that will result in systemic improvement and lasting change on behalf of girls and young women in—or at risk for entering—the juvenile justice system."[111]

Correctional Treatment for Juveniles

Nearly all juvenile institutions implement some form of treatment program: counseling, vocational and educational training, recreational programs, or religious counseling. In addition, most institutions provide medical programs as well as occasional legal service programs. Generally, the larger the institution, the greater the number of programs and services offered.

The purpose of these programs is to rehabilitate youths to become well-adjusted individuals and send them back into the community to be productive citizens. Despite good intentions, however, the goal of rehabilitation is rarely attained, due in large part to poor implementation of the programs.[112] A significant number of juvenile offenders commit more crimes after release,[113] and some experts believe that correctional treatment has little effect on recidivism.[114] However, a large-scale empirical review of institutional treatment programs found that serious juvenile offenders who receive treatment have recidivism rates about 10 percent lower than similar untreated juveniles, and that the best programs reduced recidivism by as much as 40 percent.[115] The most successful of these institutional treatment programs provide training to improve interpersonal skills and family-style teaching to improve behavioral skills (see Exhibit 16.2). Also important is the need to foster healthy, supportive relationships between incarcerated youth and juvenile care workers.[116]

What are the drawbacks to correctional rehabilitation? One of the most common problems in efforts to rehabilitate juveniles is a lack of well-trained staff. Budgetary limitations are a primary concern. It costs a substantial amount of money per year to keep a child in an institution, which explains why institutions generally do not employ large professional staffs.

However, some correctional programs are highly cost efficient, producing monetary benefits that outweigh the costs of running the program.[117] In a study with the provocative title, "Are Violent Delinquents Worth Treating?" researchers Michael Caldwell, Michael Vitacco, and Gregory Van Rybroek found that an institutional treatment program for violent juvenile offenders that was effective in reducing recidivism rates produced cost savings to taxpayers that were seven times greater than what it cost to run the program. These findings can be particularly influential on policy makers and government funding agencies.[118]

"Beyond the Walls: Improving Conditions of Confinement for Youth in Custody" (https://www.ncjrs.gov/pdffiles/164727.pdf), published by the Office of Juvenile Justice and Delinquency Prevention, is the leading resource on the **legal and regulatory guidelines for the humane treatment of juvenile offenders in correctional institutions.**

exhibit 16.2

Effectiveness of Institutional Treatment Programs for Serious Juvenile Offenders

Positive Effects, Consistent Evidence

- Interpersonal skills
- Family-style group home

Positive Effects, Less Consistent Evidence

- Behavioral programs
- Community residential
- Multiple services

Mixed but Generally Positive Effects, Inconsistent Evidence

- Individual counseling
- Guided group
- Group counseling

Weak or No Effects, Inconsistent Evidence

- Employment related
- Drug abstinence
- Wilderness/challenge

Weak or No Effects, Consistent Evidence

- Milieu therapy

SOURCE: Adapted from Mark W. Lipsey and David B. Wilson, "Effective Intervention for Serious Juvenile Offenders: A Synthesis of Research," in Rolf Loeber and David P. Farrington, eds., *Serious and Violent Juvenile Offenders: Risk Factors and Successful Interventions* (Thousand Oaks, CA: Sage, 1998).

The most glaring problem with treatment programs is that they are not administered as intended. Although the official goals of many institutions may be treatment and rehabilitation, the actual programs may center around security and punishment. The next sections describe some treatment approaches that aim to rehabilitate offenders.

Individual Treatment Techniques: Past and Present

In general, effective individual treatment programs are built around combinations of psychotherapy, reality therapy, and behavior modification. **Individual counseling** is one of the most common treatment approaches, and virtually all juvenile institutions use it to some extent. This is not surprising, as psychological problems such as depression are prevalent in juvenile institutions.[119] Individual counseling does not attempt to change a youth's personality. Rather, it attempts to help individuals understand and solve their current adjustment problems. Some institutions employ counselors who are not professionally qualified, which subjects offenders to a superficial form of counseling.

Professional counseling may be based on **psychotherapy**, which requires extensive analysis of the individual's childhood experiences. A skilled therapist attempts to help the individual make a more positive adjustment to society by altering negative behavior patterns learned in childhood. Another frequently used treatment is **reality therapy**.[120] This approach, developed by William Glasser during the 1970s, emphasizes current, rather than past, behavior by stressing that offenders are completely responsible for their own actions. The object of reality therapy is to make individuals more responsible people. This is accomplished by giving youths confidence through developing their ability to follow a set of expectations as closely as possible. The success of reality therapy depends greatly on the warmth and concern of the counselor.

Behavior modification is used in many institutions.[121] It is based on the theory that all behavior is learned and that current behavior can be shaped through rewards and punishments. This type of program is easily used in an institutional setting that offers privileges as rewards for behaviors such as work, study, or the development of skills. It is reasonably effective, especially when a contract is formed with the youth to modify certain behaviors. When youths know what is

individual counseling
Counselors help juveniles understand and solve their current adjustment problems

psychotherapy
Highly structured counseling in which a skilled therapist helps a juvenile solve conflicts and make a more positive adjustment to society.

reality therapy
A form of counseling that emphasizes current behavior and that requires the individual to accept responsibility for all of his or her actions.

The William Glasser Institute (http://www .wglasser.com/) monitors all training leading to **Choice Theory/Reality Therapy Certification** and the achievement of faculty status. The institute also maintains the records of those who complete various stages of the process worldwide.

behavior modification
A technique for shaping desired behaviors through a system of rewards and punishments.

expected of them, they plan their actions to meet these expectations and then experience the anticipated consequences. In this way, youths can be motivated to change.

Group Treatment Techniques

Group therapy is more economical than individual therapy because one therapist can counsel more than one individual at a time. Also, the support of the group is often valuable to individuals in the group, and individuals derive hope from other members of the group who have survived similar experiences. Another advantage of group therapy is that a group can often solve a problem more effectively than an individual.

One disadvantage of group therapy is that it provides little individual attention. Everyone is different, and some group members may need more individualized treatment. Others may be afraid to speak up in the group and thus fail to receive the benefits of the group experience. Conversely, some individuals may dominate group interaction, making it difficult for the leader to conduct an effective session. In addition, group condemnation may seriously hurt a participant. Finally, there is also the concern that by providing therapy in a group format, those who are more chronically involved in delinquency may negatively affect those who are marginally involved.[122] This can also happen with delinquency prevention programs that operate outside of the juvenile justice system (see Chapter 12).

Guided group interaction (GGI) is a fairly common method of group treatment. It is based on the theory that through group interactions, a delinquent can acknowledge and solve personal problems. A leader facilitates interaction, and a group culture develops. Individual members can be mutually supportive and can reinforce acceptable behavior. In the 1980s, a version of GGI called **positive peer culture (PPC)** became popular. These programs use groups in which peer leaders encourage other youths to conform to conventional behaviors. The rationale is that if negative peer influence can encourage youths to engage in delinquent behavior, then positive peer influence can help them conform.[123] Though research results are inconclusive, there is evidence that PPC may facilitate communication ability for incarcerated youth.[124]

Another common group treatment approach, **milieu therapy**, seeks to make all aspects of the inmates' environment part of their treatment and to minimize differences between custodial staff and treatment personnel. Based on psychoanalytic theory, milieu therapy was developed during the late 1940s and early 1950s by Bruno Bettelheim.[125] This therapy attempted to create a conscience, or superego, in delinquent youths by getting them to depend on their therapists to a great extent and then threatening them with loss of the caring relationship if they failed to control their behavior. Today, milieu therapy more often makes use of peer interactions and attempts to create an environment that encourages meaningful change, growth, and satisfactory adjustment. This is often accomplished through peer pressure to conform to group norms.

Educational, Vocational, and Recreational Programs

Because educational programs are an important part of social development and have therapeutic as well as instructional value, they are an essential part of most treatment programs. What takes place through education is related to all other aspects of the institutional program—work activities, cottage life, recreation, and clinical services.

Educational programs are probably the best-staffed programs in training schools, but even at their best, most are inadequate. Training programs must contend with myriad problems. Many of the youths coming into these institutions are mentally challenged, have learning disabilities, and are far behind their grade levels in basic academics. Most have become frustrated with the educational experience, dislike school, and become bored with any type of educational program. Their sense of frustration often leads to disciplinary problems.

Ideally, institutions should allow the inmates to attend a school in the community or offer programs that lead to a high school diploma or GED certificate. In recent years, a growing number of residential facilities have begun offering these types of programs. Almost 9 out of every 10 (87 percent) juvenile residential facilities provide high school-level education; 8 of every 10 (81 percent) residential facilities provide middle school-level education, and 70 percent provided GED preparation.[126] Secure institutions, because of their large size, are more likely than group homes or day treatment centers to offer programs such as remedial reading, physical education, and tutoring. Some offer computer-based learning and programmed learning modules. The Professional Spotlight discusses the career of one teacher who works in a juvenile correctional facility.

Vocational programs also play a vital role in the treatment of juvenile offenders in secure institutions. Because of their importance, they are the subject of the accompanying Youth Stories feature. Recreational activity is also an important way to help relieve adolescent aggression, as evidenced by the many programs that focus on recreation as the primary treatment technique.

professional SPOTLIGHT

KRISTI SWANSON is a teacher in the juvenile unit of an Idaho prison that is run by the Ada County Juvenile Court Services. The program she works for specializes in helping juvenile offenders obtain their high school education. The program serves juveniles who are neither good candidates for traditional school nor any longer allowed in traditional school because of suspension, expulsion, or safety issues.

Swanson started her career in an educational program for adolescents in the neuro-psych unit of a hospital. Although she enjoyed the position, she has always been drawn to working with young people in trouble with the law and in a nontraditional school environment. Her philosophy regarding kids who have broken the law has always been that kids are not bad. They make choices, and some of those choices are not always productive.

Swanson prepared for being a teacher by obtaining a bachelor's degree in education. She earned her degree in English, secondary education. She found her experience working at a hospital for a year to be extremely beneficial. This is because mental health issues play such a large part when considering the proper course of action to take regarding students in a juvenile correctional facility.

What does Kristi Swanson feel is the most rewarding part of her job? It is found in the stories where a student was able to turn his or her life around and be successful. These kids often have any number of barriers to their education, including substance abuse, parental substance abuse, physical and/or mental abuse, incarcerated parents, coming from disadvantaged homes, and pregnancy. Many times these kids are referred to Swanson and her colleagues with very little expectation that they will be able to help them where others have failed. That challenge, combined with the capability of each of the young people, keeps the job very interesting.

As a teacher, Swanson's greatest challenge involves dealing with students who continually make poor choices despite the best efforts of staff. Eventually, the time comes when one has to decide how much more energy should be directed toward those students, sometimes to the detriment of others.

The school day at the juvenile unit is divided into three blocks, one hour and 45 minutes apiece. Swanson spends time helping the teens with math, science, English, history, government, economics, and other subjects. Her daily routine also involves responding to inquiries from probation officers, writing letters that accompany students to court, and grading assignments. Notes are needed on each student every day. The notes are sent to the probation department at the end of each week. There are also numerous meetings with parents and probation officers regarding school progress. She is also trained to intervene to deescalate problems and help keep the school a safe place for the students. Sometimes that means providing a listening ear, a shoulder to cry on, or a trip to the social worker's office.

© Kristi Swanson

Kristi Swanson
Teacher, Idaho Prison
Juvenile Unit

"New Chef" Michael

Pesto tortes, bacon-wrapped dates, goat cheese–stuffed mushrooms, and chocolate mousse were on the menu. These were just some of the tasty dishes prepared by juvenile inmates for Los Angeles County supervisors and other county officials. The catered event took place on a patio atop the Los Angeles County building on a beautiful spring day. It was billed as an event to showcase the cooking talents of the latest group of "new chefs" enrolled in the culinary arts class at Camp Gonzalez, a juvenile detention center in Calabasas, California.

For the last several years, Alexis Higgins, a chef from Los Angeles Mission College, has run the culinary program at Camp Gonzalez. The program enrolls about 50 juvenile probationers who have been sentenced to a period of institutional confinement or have violated the conditions of their probation order and are now serving their sentence at the detention center. The juvenile inmates—all males—come from some of the toughest neighborhoods in Los Angeles. The goal of the program is to introduce the juveniles to something creative and provide them with the opportunity to develop skills for a job or further study upon return to the community. According to Higgins, "Learning cooking skills offers a path to a better life. Cooking jobs are plentiful and well paid."

For Michael, a 15-year-old from Palmdale, it is all about the new experience and the prospect of finding work upon release. (Los Angeles County Juvenile Court Judge Michael Nash, who oversees the program, allowed the youths to speak about their experiences so long as their last names were not disclosed.) The program is challenging, and the inmates must endure some of the usual chiding from their fellow inmates about burning the food—they sometimes cook for the full detention center—and that cooking is not a man's job. Michael takes these comments in stride. He noted, "Sometimes you get frustrated, but you have to not give up." Other inmates in the cooking program echoed this sentiment.

Vocational training has long been used as a treatment technique for juveniles. Early institutions were even referred

Probation officer C. Yepez and Michael, 15, at Camp Gonzalez, a juvenile detention center in Calabasas, California, which offers culinary arts classes.

© Spencer Weiner/Los Angeles Times

to as "industrial schools." Today, vocational programs in institutions include auto repair, printing, woodworking, mechanical drawing, food service, cosmetology, secretarial training, and data processing. A common drawback of vocational training programs is sex-typing. The recent trend has been to allow equal access to all programs offered in institutions that house both girls and boys. Sex-typing (e.g., when girls are only offered cosmetology or food service and boys are only offered auto repair or woodwork) is more difficult to avoid in single-sex institutions, because funds are not usually available for all types of training.

CRITICAL THINKING

How important are vocational programs for juvenile offenders who are serving time in an institutional setting? Do we need more of these programs? What are some of their drawbacks?

SOURCES: Molly Hennessy-Fiske, "Recipe for a New Life—with a Dash of Hope," *Los Angeles Times*, May 4, 2009; Sarah Livsey, Melissa Sickmund, and Anthony Sladky, *Juvenile Residential Facility Census, 2004: Selected Findings* (Washington, DC: US Department of Justice, Office of Juvenile Justice and Delinquency Prevention, National Report Series, 2009).

Treatment programs that seem to be most effective for rehabilitating juvenile offenders use a combination of techniques. Programs that are comprehensive, build on a juvenile's strengths, and adopt a socially grounded position have a much greater chance for success. Successful programs address issues relating to school, peers, work, and community.

Wilderness Programs

Wilderness probation programs involve troubled youths in outdoor activities as a mechanism to improve their social skills, self-concept, and self-control. Typically, wilderness programs maintain exposure to a wholesome environment; where the concepts of education and the work ethic are taught and embodied in adult role models, troubled youth can regain a measure of self-worth.

A number of wilderness programs for juvenile offenders have been evaluated for their effects on recidivism. In a detailed review of the effects of wilderness programs—those emphasizing physical activity over more therapeutic goals—on recidivism, Doris MacKenzie concludes that these programs do not work.[127] Although some of the programs show success, such as the Spectrum Wilderness Program in Illinois,[128] others had negative effects—that is, the group that received the program had higher arrest rates than the comparison group that did not receive the program. Taken together, the programs suffered from:

- Poor implementation
- Weak evaluation designs or problems with too few subjects or large dropout rates
- Failure to adhere to principles of successful rehabilitation, such as targeting high-risk youths and lasting for a moderate period of time[129]

Wilderness programs that include a therapeutic component, in contrast, have been shown to be effective in reducing juvenile offending. Sandra Wilson and Mark Lipsey found that, on average, these programs produced a 20 percent reduction in recidivism rates, with the most successful ones offering more intensive physical activity or therapeutic services.[130]

wilderness probation
Programs involving outdoor expeditions that provide opportunities for juveniles to confront the difficulties of their lives while achieving positive personal satisfaction.

Juvenile Boot Camps

Correctional **boot camps** were designed with the idea of combining the get-tough elements of adult programs with education, substance abuse treatment, and social skills training. In theory, a successful boot camp program should rehabilitate juvenile offenders, reduce the number of beds needed in secure institutional programs, and thus reduce the overall cost of care. The Alabama boot camp program for youthful offenders estimated savings of $1 million annually when compared with traditional institutional sentences.[131] However, no one seems convinced that participants in these programs have lower recidivism rates than those who serve normal sentences.

The bottom line for juvenile boot camps, like other correctional sanctions, is whether or not they reduce recidivism. A meta-analysis of the effects of juvenile boot camps on recidivism found this to be an ineffective correctional approach to reducing it; from the 17 different program samples, the control groups had, on average, lower recidivism rates than the treatment groups (boot camps).[132] Interestingly, when compared with the effects of 26 program samples of boot camps for adults, the juvenile boot camps had a higher average recidivism rate, although the difference was not significant.[133]

Why do boot camps for juveniles fail to reduce future offending? The main reason is that they provide little in the way of therapy or treatment to correct offending behavior.[134] Also, few are linked to services to help juvenile offenders transition back to the community. One juvenile boot camp program in Quehanna, Pennsylvania, which included a mandatory residential aftercare component,

boot camps
Juvenile programs that combine get-tough elements from adult programs with education, substance abuse treatment, and social skills training.

showed a reduction in recidivism rates two years postrelease.[135] Experts have also suggested that part of the reason for not finding differences in recidivism between boot camps and other correctional alternatives (the control groups) may be due to juveniles in the control groups receiving enhanced treatment, whereas juveniles in the boot camps are spending more time on physical activities.[136]

The general ineffectiveness of boot camps to reduce reoffending in the community by juvenile offenders (and adult offenders) appears to have resulted in this approach falling into disfavor with some correctional administrators. At the height of its popularity in the mid-1990s, more than 75 state-run boot camps were in operation in more than 30 states across the country.[137]

The Legal Right to Treatment

The primary goal of placing juveniles in institutions is to help them reenter the community successfully. Therefore, lawyers claim that children in state-run institutions have a legal right to treatment.

right to treatment
Philosophy espoused by many courts that juvenile offenders have a statutory right to treatment while under the jurisdiction of the courts.

The concept of a **right to treatment** was introduced to the mental health field in 1960 by Morton Birnbaum, who argued that individuals deprived of their liberty because of a mental illness are entitled to treatment to correct that condition.[138] The right to treatment has expanded to include the juvenile justice system, an expansion bolstered by court rulings that mandate that rehabilitation and not punishment or retribution be the basis of juvenile court dispositions.[139] It stands to reason, then, that if incarcerated, juveniles are entitled to the appropriate social services that will promote their rehabilitation.

One of the first cases to highlight this issue was *Inmates of the Boys' Training School v. Affleck* in 1972.[140] In its decision, a federal court argued that rehabilitation is the true purpose of the juvenile court and that without that goal, due process guarantees are violated. It condemned such devices as solitary confinement, strip cells, and lack of educational opportunities, and held that juveniles have a statutory right to treatment. The court also established the following minimum standards for all juveniles confined in training schools:

- A room equipped with lighting sufficient for an inmate to read until 10:00 PM
- Sufficient clothing to meet seasonal needs
- Bedding, including blankets, sheets, pillows, pillowcases, and mattresses, to be changed once a week
- Personal hygiene supplies, including soap, toothpaste, towels, toilet paper, and toothbrush
- A change of undergarments and socks every day
- Minimum writing materials: pen, pencil, paper, and envelopes
- Prescription eyeglasses, if needed
- Equal access to all books, periodicals, and other reading materials located in the training school
- Daily showers
- Daily access to medical facilities, including provision of a 24-hour nursing service
- General correspondence privileges[141]

In 1974, in the case of *Nelson v. Heyne*, the First Federal Appellate Court affirmed that juveniles have a right to treatment and condemned the use of corporal punishment in juvenile institutions.[142] In *Morales v. Turman*, the court held that all juveniles confined in training schools in Texas have a right to treatment, including development of education skills, delivery of vocational education, medical and psychiatric treatment, and adequate living conditions.[143] In another case, *Pena v. New York State Division for Youth*, the court held that the use of isolation, hand restraints, and tranquilizing drugs at Goshen Annex Center violated the Fourteenth Amendment right to due process and the Eighth Amendment right to protection against cruel and unusual punishment.[144]

The right to treatment has also been limited. For example, in *Ralston v. Robinson*, the Supreme Court rejected a youth's claim that he should continue to be given treatment after he was sentenced to a consecutive term in an adult prison for crimes committed while in a juvenile institution.[145] In the *Ralston* case, the offender's proven dangerousness outweighed the possible effects of rehabilitation. Similarly, in *Santana v. Callazo*, the US First Circuit Court of Appeals rejected a suit brought by residents at the Maricao Juvenile Camp in Puerto Rico on the grounds that the administration had failed to provide them with an individualized rehabilitation plan or adequate treatment. The circuit court concluded that it was a legitimate exercise of state authority to incarcerate juveniles solely to protect society if they are dangerous.

Ralston v. Robinson
This case placed limits on the right to treatment for juvenile offenders.

The Struggle for Basic Civil Rights

Several court cases have led federal, state, and private groups, including the American Bar Association, the American Correctional Association, and the National Council on Crime and Delinquency, to develop standards for the juvenile justice system. These standards provide guidelines for conditions and practices in juvenile institutions and call on administrators to maintain a safe and healthy environment for incarcerated youths.

For the most part, state-sponsored brutality has been outlawed, although the use of restraints, solitary confinement, and even medication for unruly residents has not been eliminated. The courts have ruled that corporal punishment in any form violates standards of decency and human dignity.

There are a number of mechanisms for enforcing these standards. For example, the federal government's Civil Rights of Institutionalized Persons Act (CRIPA) gives the Civil Rights Division of the US Department of Justice (DOJ) the power to bring actions against state or local governments for violating the civil rights of persons institutionalized in publicly operated facilities.[146] CRIPA does not create any new substantive rights; it simply confers power on the US attorney general to bring action to enforce previously established constitutional or statutory rights of institutionalized persons; about 25 percent of cases involve juvenile detention and correctional facilities. There are many examples in which CRIPA-based litigation has helped ensure that incarcerated adolescents obtain their basic civil rights.

What provisions does the juvenile justice system make to help institutionalized offenders return to society? The remainder of this chapter is devoted to this topic.

Juvenile Aftercare and Reentry

Aftercare in the juvenile justice system is the equivalent of parole in the adult criminal justice system. When juveniles are released from an institution, they may be placed in an aftercare program of some kind, so that those who have been institutionalized are not simply returned to the community without some transitional assistance. Whether individuals who are in aftercare as part of an indeterminate sentence remain in the community or return to the institution for further rehabilitation depends on their actions during the aftercare period. Aftercare is an extremely important stage in the juvenile justice process because few juveniles age out of custody.[147]

Reentry involves aftercare services, but includes preparation for release from confinement, also called prerelease planning.[148] Reentry is further distinguished from aftercare in that reentry is seen as the whole process and experience of the

aftercare
Transitional assistance to juveniles, equivalent to adult parole, to help youths adjust to community life.

reentry
The process and experience of returning to society upon release from a custody facility postadjudication.

Aftercare—the juvenile equivalent of parole in the adult criminal justice system—includes a range of services designed to help juveniles adjust to community life upon release from an institution. The Silver Oak Academy, shown here, is a privately run facility in Keymar, Maryland, which provides achievement-based programs to aid juvenile offenders in their transition to the community.

The website for the Serious and Violent Offender Reentry Initiative (SVORI) Multisite Evaluation provides detailed information regarding the **evaluation activities associated with the Serious and Violent Offender Reentry Initiative** (http://www.crimesolutions.gov /ProgramDetails.aspx?ID=167). RTI International and the Urban Institute are conducting the comprehensive implementation, impact, and economic evaluations.

transition of juveniles from "juvenile and adult correctional settings back into schools, families, communities, and society at large."[149] The concept of reentry, which is also the term given to it in the adult criminal justice system, is by no means new.[150] Recently, however, it has come to characterize the larger numbers of juvenile and adult offenders returning to communities each year and the increased needs these offenders exhibit with respect to employment, education, and mental health and substance abuse problems.[151] For juvenile offenders, reentry goes beyond the all-too-common practice of juveniles being placed in aftercare programs that are the same as adult parole programs, which "fail to take account of their unique needs and the challenges they face."[152] (See Exhibit 16.3 for a profile of juvenile offenders returning to the community.) Through the Serious and Violent Offender Reentry Initiative (SVORI), the federal government has invested $150 million on reentry programs for adult and juvenile offenders in all 50 states, the District of Columbia, and the Virgin Islands.[153] A multisite evaluation of SVORI, which included 337 juvenile male offenders, found that those who received the program, compared to their control group counterparts, were: (a) more likely to still be in school 3 months and 15 months after release from confinement and (b) more likely to have a job with benefits. No differences were found between SVORI participants and the control group in substance abuse, physical health, mental health, and recidivism outcomes.[154] Another federal government initiative, titled the Juvenile Re-Entry Assistance Program and spearheaded by the Departments of Justice and Housing and Urban Development, aims to provide reentry services for juveniles facing challenges with housing and employment. The program works closely with public housing authorities and legal assistance organizations.[155] Some promising results have been shown with other juvenile reentry programs across the country.[156]

Supervision

One purpose of aftercare and reentry is to provide support during the readjustment period following release. First, individuals whose activities have been regimented for some time may not find it easy to make independent decisions. Second, offenders may perceive themselves as scapegoats, cast out by society. Finally, the community may view the returning minor with a good deal of prejudice; adjustment problems may reinforce a preexisting need to engage in deviant behavior.

A Profile of Juvenile Reentry

It is estimated that about 100,000 juvenile offenders each year are released from custody facilities following adjudication (or conviction in the adult system) and return to the communities from which they came. Reentry services play an important role in their successful reintegration to society. A profile of these juveniles shows that:

- 86 percent are male.

- 12 percent are age 14 or younger, and 44 percent are age 17 or older.

- 40 percent are white, 38 percent are black, and 18 percent are Hispanic.

- 34 percent are committed for a violent offense, 32 percent for a property offense, 10 percent for a drug offense, 10 percent for a public order offense, 10 percent for a technical violation of probation or parole, and 5 percent for a status offense.

SOURCE: Howard N. Snyder and Melissa Sickmund, *Juvenile Offenders and Victims: 2006 National Report* (Pittsburgh: National Center for Juvenile Justice, 2006).

Juveniles in aftercare programs are supervised by parole caseworkers or counselors whose job is to maintain contact with the juvenile, make sure that a corrections plan is followed, and show interest and caring. The counselor also keeps the youth informed of services that may assist in reintegration and counsels the youth and his or her family. Unfortunately, aftercare caseworkers, like probation officers, often carry such large caseloads that their jobs are next to impossible to do adequately. One recent study highlights the importance of the perceived quality of the relationship between juvenile female offenders and their parole caseworkers and the benefits this holds for reducing violent recidivism.[157]

The Intensive Aftercare Program (IAP) Model   New models of aftercare and reentry have been aimed at the chronic and/or violent offender. The **Intensive Aftercare Program (IAP)** model, developed by David Altschuler and Troy Armstrong, offers a continuum of intervention for serious juvenile offenders returning to the community following placement.[158] The IAP model begins by drawing attention to five basic principles, which collectively establish a set of fundamental operational goals:

Intensive Aftercare Program (IAP)
A balanced, highly structured, comprehensive continuum of intervention for serious and violent juvenile offenders returning to the community.

- Preparing youth for progressively increased responsibility and freedom in the community

- Facilitating youth-community interaction and involvement

- Working with both the offender and targeted community support systems (families, peers, schools, employers) on qualities needed for constructive interaction and the youth's successful community adjustment

- Developing new resources and supports where needed

- Monitoring and testing the youth and the community on their ability to deal with each other productively

These basic goals are then translated into practice, which incorporates individual case planning with a family and community perspective. The program stresses a mix of intensive surveillance and services, and a balance of incentives and graduated consequences coupled with the imposition of realistic, enforceable conditions. There is also "service brokerage," in which community resources are used and linkage with social networks established.[159]

The IAP initiative was designed to help correctional agencies implement effective aftercare programs for chronic and serious juvenile offenders. After many years of testing, the program is now being aimed at determining how juveniles are prepared for reentry into their communities, how the transition is handled, and how the aftercare in the community is provided.[160]

Aftercare Revocation Procedures

Juvenile parolees are required to meet established standards of behavior, which generally include but are not limited to the following:

- Adhere to a reasonable curfew set by youth worker or parent.
- Refrain from associating with persons whose influence would be detrimental.
- Attend school in accordance with the law.
- Abstain from drugs and alcohol.
- Report to the youth worker when required.
- Refrain from acts that would be crimes if committed by an adult.
- Refrain from operating an automobile without permission of the youth worker or parent.
- Refrain from being habitually disobedient and beyond the lawful control of parent or other legal authority.
- Refrain from running away from the lawful custody of parent or other lawful authority.

If these rules are violated, the juvenile may have his parole revoked and be returned to the institution. Most states have extended the same legal rights enjoyed by adults at parole revocation hearings to juveniles who are in danger of losing their aftercare privileges, as follows:

- Juveniles must be informed of the conditions of parole and receive notice of any obligations.
- Juveniles have the right to legal counsel at state expense if necessary.
- They maintain the right to confront and cross-examine witnesses against them.
- They have the right to introduce documentary evidence and witnesses.
- They have the right to a hearing before an officer who shall be an attorney but not an employee of the revoking agency.[161]

Future of Juvenile Corrections

There exists much debate about the effectiveness of community versus institutional treatment. Considerable research shows that warehousing juveniles without proper treatment does little to prevent future delinquent activities.[162] The most effective secure corrections programs are those that provide individual services for a small number of participants.[163] Evaluations of community treatment provide evidence of a number of successful ways to respond to delinquency without jeopardizing the safety of community residents, and members of the public continue to express their support for more treatment over punishment.[164]

There is also a long-standing debate about the effectiveness of correctional treatments compared with other delinquency prevention measures. In their assessment of the full range of interventions to prevent serious and violent juvenile offending, Rolf Loeber and David Farrington found that it is never too early and never too late to make a difference.[165] Though some critics believe that juveniles are being coddled, in the future it is likely that innovative treatment methods will be applied continually within the juvenile justice system.

On another front, deinstitutionalization has become an important goal of the juvenile justice system. The Office of Juvenile Justice and Delinquency Prevention provided funds to encourage this process. In the early 1980s, the deinstitutionalization movement seemed to be partially successful. Admissions to public juvenile correctional facilities declined in the late 1970s and early 1980s. In addition, the number of status offenders being held within the juvenile justice system was reduced. Following a substantial increase in the number of institutionalized children in the 1990s and early 2000s, numbers have decreased of late. During these years, the majority of states achieved compliance with the Deinstitutionalizing Status Offenders (DSO) mandate. Because juvenile crime is a high priority, the challenge to the states will be to retain a focus on treatment despite political—certainly not public[166]—assertions of the need for more punitive approaches. If that can be achieved, deinstitutionalization will remain a central theme in the juvenile justice system.

A more pressing problem is that a disproportionate number of minority youths continue to be incarcerated in youth facilities. The difference is greatest for African American youths, with the incarceration rate being almost four times greater than that for Caucasian youths. Of equal importance, minorities are more likely to be placed in secure public facilities rather than in open private facilities that might provide more effective treatment. The OJJDP is committed to ensuring that the country address situations where there is disproportionate confinement of minority offenders in the nation's juvenile justice system. In the future, it is expected that this initiative will result in a more fair and balanced juvenile justice system.

Aftercare and reentry services represent crucial elements of a juvenile offender's successful transition back to the community. Correctional authorities recognize that juvenile offenders who are released from confinement are at heightened risk for returning to a life of crime without assistance in overcoming barriers with employment, education, and housing and dealing with mental health, substance abuse, and other problems.[167] Many jurisdictions are experiencing success with halfway houses, reintegration centers, and other reentry programs, and the federal government's substantial investment in reentry programs through the Serious and Violent Offender Reentry Initiative is promising.

SUMMARY

1 Contrast community treatment and institutional treatment for juvenile offenders

- Community treatment encompasses efforts to keep offenders in the community and spare them the stigma of incarceration. The primary purpose is to provide a nonrestrictive or home setting, employing educational, vocational, counseling, and employment services.

- Institutional treatment encompasses provision of these services but in more restrictive and sometimes secure facilities.

2 Explain the disposition of probation, including how it is administered and by whom and recent trends in its use

- Probation is the most widely used method of community treatment. Youths on probation must obey rules given to them by the court and participate in some form of treatment program. If rules are violated, youths may have their probation revoked.

- Behavior is monitored by probation officers.

- Formal probation accounts for 64 percent of all juvenile dispositions, and its use has decreased somewhat in the last decade.

3 Discuss new approaches for providing probation services to juvenile offenders and comment on their effectiveness in reducing recidivism

- It is now common to enhance probation with more restrictive forms of treatment, such as intensive supervision and house arrest with electronic monitoring.

- Residential community treatment programs allow youths to live at home while receiving treatment in a nonpunitive, community-based center.

- Some of these probation innovations, such as intensive supervision, get mixed reviews on their effectiveness in reducing recidivism, while others, such as restitution and restorative justice, show success.

4 Illustrate key historical developments of secure juvenile corrections in this country, including the principle of least restrictive alternative

- The secure juvenile institution was developed in the mid-nineteenth century as an alternative to placing youths in adult prisons.

- Youth institutions evolved from large, closed institutions to cottage-based education- and rehabilitation-oriented institutions.
- The concept of least restrictive alternative is applicable in decisions on placing juvenile offenders to institutions to ensure that the setting benefits the juvenile's treatment needs.

5 Discuss recent trends in the use of juvenile institutions for juvenile offenders and how their use differs across states

- The juvenile institutional population has decreased in recent years.
- A large number of youths continue to be "hidden" in private medical centers and drug treatment clinics.
- There are wide variations in juvenile custody rates across states.

6 Identify key issues facing the institutionalized juvenile offender

- A disproportionate number of minorities are incarcerated in more secure, state-run youth facilities.
- Compared to males, female juvenile inmates are faced with many hardships.

7 Appraise the effectiveness of various juvenile correctional treatment approaches in use today

- Most juvenile institutions maintain intensive treatment programs featuring individual or group therapy.
- Rehabilitation remains an important goal of juvenile practitioners.

8 Discuss juvenile offenders' legal right to treatment

- The right to treatment is an important issue in juvenile justice.
- Legal decisions have mandated that a juvenile cannot simply be warehoused in a correctional center but must receive proper care and treatment to aid rehabilitation.
- What constitutes proper care is still being debated.

9 Explain the nature of aftercare for juvenile offenders and comment on recent innovations in juvenile aftercare and reentry programs

- Juveniles released from institutions are often placed on parole or in aftercare.
- Many jurisdictions are experiencing success with halfway houses, reintegration centers, and other reentry programs.

KEY TERMS

community treatment, p. 593

suppression effect, p. 594

probation, p. 594

conditions of probation, p. 597

juvenile probation officer, p. 598

social investigation report, or predisposition report, p. 598

juvenile intensive probation supervision (JIPS), p. 600

house arrest, p. 601

electronic monitoring, p. 601

balanced probation, p. 604

monetary restitution, p. 604

victim service restitution, p. 605

community service restitution, p. 605

residential programs, p. 606

group homes, p. 606

foster care programs, p. 606

family group homes, p. 606

rural programs, p. 606

nonresidential programs, p. 607

reform schools, p. 608

cottage system, p. 609

least restrictive alternative, p. 609

individual counseling, p. 617

psychotherapy, p. 617

reality therapy, p. 617

behavior modification, p. 617

group therapy, p. 618

positive peer culture (PPC), p. 618

milieu therapy, p. 618

wilderness probation, p. 621

boot camps, p. 621

right to treatment, p. 622

Ralston v. Robinson, p. 623

aftercare, p. 623

reentry, p. 623

Intensive Aftercare Program (IAP), p. 625

QUESTIONS FOR DISCUSSION

1. Would you want a community treatment program in your neighborhood? Why or why not?

2. Is widening the net a real danger, or are treatment-oriented programs simply a method of helping troubled youths?

3. If youths violate the rules of probation, should they be placed in a secure institution?

4. Is juvenile restitution fair? Should a poor child have to pay back a wealthy victim?

5. What are the most important advantages to community treatment for juvenile offenders?

6. What is the purpose of juvenile probation? Identify some conditions of probation and discuss the responsibilities of the juvenile probation officer.

7. Has community treatment generally proven successful?

8. Why have juvenile boot camps not been effective in reducing recidivism?

VIEWPOINT

As a local juvenile court judge, you have been assigned the case of Jim Butler, a 13-year-old juvenile so short he can barely see over the bench. On trial for armed robbery, the boy has been accused of threatening a woman with a knife and stealing her purse. Barely a teenager, he has already had a long history of involvement with the law. At age 11 he was arrested for drug possession and placed on probation; soon after, he stole a car. At age 12 he was arrested for shoplifting. Jim is accompanied by his legal guardian, his maternal grandmother. His parents are unavailable because his father abandoned the family years ago and his mother is currently undergoing inpatient treatment at a local drug clinic. After talking with his court-appointed attorney, Jim decides to admit to the armed robbery. At a dispositional hearing, his attorney tells you of the tough life Jim has been forced to endure. His grandmother states that, although she loves the boy, her advanced age makes it impossible for her to provide the care he needs to stay out of trouble. She says that Jim is a good boy who has developed a set of bad companions; his current scrape was precipitated by his friends. A representative of the school system testifies that Jim has above-average intelligence and is respectful of teachers. He has potential, but his life circumstances have short-circuited his academic success. Jim himself shows remorse and appears to be a sensitive youngster who is easily led astray by older youths.

You must now make a decision. You can place Jim on probation and allow him to live with his grandmother while being monitored by county probation staff. You can place him in a secure incarceration facility for up to three years. You can also put him into an intermediate program such as a community-based facility, which would allow him to attend school during the day while residing in a halfway house and receiving group treatment in the evenings. Although Jim appears to be a possibility for rehabilitation, his crime was serious and involved the use of a weapon. If he remains in the community he may offend again; if he is sent to a correctional facility he will interact with older, tougher kids. What mode of correctional treatment would you choose?

- Would you place Jim on probation and allow him to live with his grandmother while being monitored?
- Would you send him to a secure incarceration facility for up to three years?
- Would you put him into an intermediate program such as a community-based facility?

DOING RESEARCH ON THE WEB

To help with your decision, do some research at these websites. California's Division of Juvenile Justice (http://www.cdcr.ca.gov/Juvenile_Justice/) receives its youthful offender population from both juvenile and superior court referrals. Those youths are sent to the DJJ to receive various training and treatment services. The Center for the Study and Prevention of Violence (CSPV) (http://www.colorado.edu/cspv/) is a research program of the Institute of Behavioral Science (IBS) at the University of Colorado at Boulder that works from a multidisciplinary platform on the subject of violence and facilitates the building of bridges between the research community and practitioners and policy makers.

The Washington State Institute for Public Policy (http://www.wsipp.wa.gov/) and the Urban Institute (http://www.urban.org/) both focus on juvenile justice research. The Children's Research Center (CRC) (http://www.nccdglobal.org/what-we-do/children-s-research-center) conducts research that improves service delivery to children and families.

NOTES

All URLs accessed October 2016.

1. Josh Richman, "Juvenile Prison Bill Inspired by Ward's Suicide Advances," *Inside Bay Area*, August 31, 2007; Kim McGill, "New Name, Same Pain—Another Young Person Dies Behind Bars in California," *Pacific News Service*, September 20, 2005.

2. *Prison Legal News*, "$350,000 Settlement Reached in Negligence Suit Over California Youth Prison Suicide," *Prison Legal News*, February 15, 2012, https://www.prisonlegalnews.org/news/2012/feb/15/350000 -settlement-reached-in-negligence-suit-over-california-youth-prison -suicide/.

3. See Christina Stahlkopf, Mike Males, and Daniel Macallair, "Testing Incapacitation Theory: Youth Crime and Incarceration in California," *Crime and Delinquency* 56:253–268 (2010).

4. See Matt DeLisi, Alan J. Drury, Anna E. Kosloski, Jonathan W. Caudill, Peter J. Conis, Craig A. Anderson, Michael G. Vaughn, and Kevin M. Beaver, "The Cycle of Violence Behind Bars: Traumatization and Institutional Misconduct Among Juvenile Delinquents in Confinement," *Youth Violence and Juvenile Justice* 8:107–121 (2010).

5. Charles Murray and Louis B. Cox, *Beyond Probation* (Beverly Hills: Sage Publications, 1979).

6. Robert Shepard Jr., ed., *Juvenile Justice Standards: A Balanced Approach* (Chicago: ABA, 1996).

7. George Killinger, Hazel Kerper, and Paul F. Cromwell Jr., *Probation and Parole in the Criminal Justice System* (St. Paul, MN: West, 1976), p. 45; National Advisory Commission on Criminal Justice Standards and Goals, *Corrections* (Washington, DC: US Government Printing Office, 1983), p. 75.

8. Ibid.

9. Jerome Miller, *Last One over the Wall: The Massachusetts Experiment in Closing Reform Schools* (Columbus: Ohio State University Press, 1998).

10. Bureau of Justice Statistics, *Report to the Nation on Crime and Justice* (Washington, DC: US Government Printing Office, 1988), pp. 44–45; Peter Greenwood, "What Works with Juvenile Offenders: A Synthesis of the Literature and Experience," *Federal Probation* 58:63–67 (1994).

11. Robert Coates, Alden Miller, and Lloyd Ohlin, *Diversity in a Youth Correctional System* (Cambridge, MA: Ballinger, 1978); Barry Krisberg, James Austin, and Patricia Steele, *Unlocking Juvenile Corrections* (San Francisco: National Council on Crime and Delinquency, 1989).

12. Sarah Hockenberry and Charles Puzzanchera, *Juvenile Court Statistics 2013* (Pittsburgh: National Center for Juvenile Justice, 2015), p. 50.

13. Emily Gaarder, Nancy Rodriguez, and Marjorie S. Zatz, "Criers, Liars, and Manipulators: Probation Officers' Views of Girls," *Justice Quarterly* 21:547–578 (2004).

14. Hockenberry and Puzzanchera, *Juvenile Court Statistics 2013*, p. 83.

15. *In re J.G.*, 692 N.E.2d 1226 (Ill. App. 1998).

16. *In re Michael D.*, 264 CA Rptr 476 (Cal. App. 1989).

17. *Morrissey v. Brewer*, 408 U.S. 471, 92 S.Ct. 2593, 33 L.Ed.2d 484 (1972); *Gagnon v. Scarpelli*, 411 U.S. 778, 93 S.Ct. 1756, 36 L.Ed.2d 655 (1973).

18. See Michael Leiber, Jennifer H. Peck, and Maud Beaudry-Cyr, "When Does Race and Gender Matter? The Interrelationships Between the Gender of Probation Officers and Juvenile Court Detention and Intake Outcomes," *Justice Quarterly* 33:614–641 (2016); Geoff Ward and Aaron Kupchik, "What Drives Juvenile Probation Officers? Relating Organizational Contexts, Status Characteristics, and Personal Convictions to Treatment and Punishment Orientations," *Crime and Delinquency* 56:35–69 (2010).

19. See Gina M. Vincent, Melissa L. Paiva-Salisbury, Nathan E. Cook, Laura S. Guy, and Rachael T. Perrault, "Impact of Risk/Needs Assessment on Juvenile Probation Officers' Decision Making: Importance of Implementation," *Psychology, Public Policy, and Law* 18:549–576 (2012).

20. Michael T. Baglivio, Mark A. Greenwald, and Mark Russell, "Assessing the Implications of a Structured Decision-Making Tool for Recidivism in a Statewide Analysis: Disposition Matrix for Court Recommendations Made by Juvenile Probations Officers," *Criminology and Public Policy* 14:5–49 (2015).

21. Richard Lawrence, "Reexamining Community Corrections Models," *Crime and Delinquency* 37:449–464 (1991).

22. See Matthew J. Giblin, "Using Police Officers to Enhance the Supervision of Juvenile Probationers: An Evaluation of the Anchorage CAN Program," *Crime and Delinquency* 48:116–137 (2002).

23. See Richard G. Wiebush, "Juvenile Intensive Supervision: The Impact on Felony Offenders Diverted from Institutional Placement," *Crime and Delinquency* 39:68–89 (1993).

24. For a review of these programs, see James Austin, Kelly Dedel Johnson, and Ronald Weitzer, *Alternatives to the Secure Detention and Confinement of Juvenile Offenders* (Washington, DC: OJJDP Bulletin, 2005), pp. 18–19.

25. Peter W. Greenwood and Susan Turner, "Probation and Other Noninstitutional Treatment: The Evidence Is In," in Barry C. Feld and Donna M. Bishop, eds., *The Oxford Handbook of Juvenile Crime and Juvenile Justice* (New York: Oxford University Press, 2012), Table 29.1.

26. Sheldon X. Zhang and Lening Zhang, "An Experimental Study of the Los Angeles County Repeat Offender Prevention Program: Its Implementation and Evaluation," *Criminology and Public Policy* 4:205–236 (2005).

27. Jodi Lane, Susan Turner, Terry Fain, and Amber Sehgal, "Evaluating an Experimental Intensive Juvenile Probation Program: Supervision and Official Outcomes," *Crime and Delinquency* 51:26–52 (2005).

28. Eve Brank, Jodi Lane, Susan Turner, Terry Fain, and Amber Sehgal, "An Experimental Juvenile Probation Program: Effects on Parent and Peer Relationships," *Crime and Delinquency* 54:193–224 (2008).

29. Angela A. Robertson, Paul W. Grimes, and Kevin E. Rogers, "A Short-Run Cost-Benefit Analysis of Community-Based Interventions for Juvenile Offenders," *Crime and Delinquency* 47:265–284 (2001).

30. Richard Ball and J. Robert Lilly, "A Theoretical Examination of Home Incarceration," *Federal Probation* 50:17–25 (1986); Joan Petersilia, "Exploring the Option of House Arrest," *Federal Probation* 50:50–56 (1986); Annesley Schmidt, "Electronic Monitors," *Federal Probation* 50:56–60 (1986); Michael Charles, "The Development of a Juvenile Electronic Monitoring Program," *Federal Probation* 53:3–12 (1989).

31. Joseph B. Vaughn, "A Survey of Juvenile Electronic Monitoring and Home Confinement Programs," *Juvenile and Family Court Journal* 40:1–36 (1989).

32. Sudipto Roy, "Five Years of Electronic Monitoring of Adults and Juveniles in Lake County, Indiana: A Comparative Study on Factors Related to Failure," *Journal of Crime and Justice* 20:141–160 (1997).

33. Marc Renzema and Evan Mayo-Wilson, "Can Electronic Monitoring Reduce Crime for Moderate- to High-Risk Offenders?" *Journal of Experimental Criminology* 1:215–237 (2005).

34. Anne Seymour and Trudy Gregorie, "Restorative Justice for Young Offenders and Their Victims," *Corrections Today* 64:90–92 (2002), at 90.

35. Lawrence W. Sherman and Heather Strang, *Restorative Justice: The Evidence* (London: The Smith Institute, 2007); Heather Strang and Lawrence W. Sherman, "Restorative Justice to Reduce Victimization," in Brandon C. Welsh and David P. Farrington, eds., *Preventing Crime: What Works for Children, Offenders, Victims, and Places* (New York: Springer, 2006), p. 148; see also Lawrence W. Sherman, Heather Strang, Caroline Angel, Daniel Woods, Geoffrey C. Barnes, Sarah Bennett, and Nova Inkpen, "Effects of Face-to-Face Restorative Justice on Victims of Crime in Four Randomized, Controlled Trials," *Journal of Experimental Criminology* 1:367–395 (2005).

36. Lawrence W. Sherman, Heather Strang, Evan Mayo-Wilson, Daniel J. Woods, and Barak Ariel, "Are Restorative Justice Conferences Effective in Reducing Repeat Offending? Findings from a Campbell Systematic Review," *Journal of Quantitative Criminology* 31:1–24 (2015), p. 13.

37. Ibid.

38. Strang and Sherman, "Restorative Justice to Reduce Victimization," pp. 152–156.

39. Lawrence W. Sherman, Heather Strang, Geoffrey Barnes, Daniel J. Woods, Sarah Bennett, Nova Inkpen, Dorothy Newbury-Birch, Meredith Rossner, Caroline Angel, Malcolm Maearns, and Molly Slothower, "Twelve Experiments in Restorative Justice: The Jerry Lee Program of Randomized Trials of Restorative Justice Conferences," *Journal of Experimental Criminology* 11:501–540 (2015).

40. Edmund F. McGarrell and Natalie Kroovand Hipple, "Family Group Conferencing and Re-Offending among First-Time Juvenile Offenders: The Indianapolis Experiment," *Justice Quarterly* 24:221–246 (2007); Kathleen J. Bergseth and Jeffrey A. Bouffard, "The Long-Term Impact of Restorative Justice Programming for Juvenile Offenders," *Journal of Criminal Justice* 35:433–451 (2007); Nancy Rodriguez, "Restorative Justice, Communities, and Delinquency: Whom Do We Reintegrate?" *Criminology and Public Policy* 4:103–130 (2005).

41. Andrew J. DeAngelo, "Evolution of Juvenile Justice: Community-Based Partnerships Through Balanced and Restorative Justice," *Corrections Today* 67(5):105–106 (2005); Dennis Mahoney, Dennis Romig, and Troy Armstrong, "Juvenile Probation: The Balanced Approach," *Juvenile and Family Court Journal* 39:1–59 (1988).

42. Daniel P. Mears, Justin T. Pickett, and Christina Mancini, "Support for Balanced Juvenile Justice: Assessing Views About Youth, Rehabilitation, and Punishment," *Journal of Quantitative Criminology* 31:459–479 (2015).

43. Gordon Bazemore, "On Mission Statements and Reform in Juvenile Justice: The Case of the Balanced Approach," *Federal Probation* 61:64–70 (1992); Gordon Bazemore and Mark Umbreit, *Balanced and Restorative Justice* (Washington, DC: Office of Juvenile Justice and Delinquency Prevention, 1994).

44. Peter R. Schneider and Matthew C. Finkelstein, eds., *RESTTA National Directory of Restitution and Community Service Programs* (Washington, DC: Office of Juvenile Justice and Delinquency Prevention, US Department of Justice, 1998).

45. Gordon Bazemore, "New Concepts and Alternative Practice in Community Supervision of Juvenile Offenders: Rediscovering Work Experience and Competency Development," *Journal of Crime and Justice* 14:27–45 (1991).

46. Stacy Hoskins Haynes, Alison C. Cares, and R. Barry Ruback, "Juvenile Economic Sanctions: An Analysis of Their Imposition, Payment, and Effect on Recidivism," *Criminology and Public Policy* 13:31–60 (2014).

47. See Jessica Feierman, *Debtors' Prison for Kids? The High Cost of Fines in the Juvenile Justice System* (Philadelphia: Juvenile Law Center, 2016).

48. Anne Schneider, "Restitution and Recidivism Rates of Juvenile Offenders: Results from Four Experimental Studies," *Criminology* 24:533–552 (1986).

49. Shay Bilchik, *A Juvenile Justice System for the 21st Century* (Washington, DC: Office of Juvenile Justice and Delinquency Prevention, 1998).

50. Schneider and Finkelstein, *RESTTA National Directory of Restitution and Community Service Programs*, Tables 12, 15.

51. Haynes, Cares, and Ruback, "Juvenile Economic Sanctions: An Analysis of Their Imposition, Payment, and Effect on Recidivism," pp. 49–50.

52. See Peter W. Greenwood and Susan Turner, "Juvenile Crime and Juvenile Justice," in James Q. Wilson and Joan Petersilia, eds., *Crime and Public Policy* (New York: Oxford University Press, 2011); Shelley Zavlek, *Planning Community-Based Facilities for Violent Juvenile Offenders as Part of a System of Graduated Sanctions* (Washington, DC: OJJDP Bulletin, 2005), p. 5.

53. Lamar T. Empey and Maynard Erickson, *The Provo Experiment* (Lexington, MA: D. C. Heath, 1972); Paul Pilnick, Albert Elias, and Neale Clapp, "The Essexfields Concept: A New Approach to the Social Treatment of Juvenile Delinquents," *Journal of Applied Behavioral Sciences* 2:109–121 (1966); Yitzhak Bakal, "Reflections: A Quarter Century of Reform in Massachusetts Youth Corrections," *Crime and Delinquency* 40:110–117 (1998).

54. US Department of Justice, *Children in Custody 1975–85: Census of Public and Private Juvenile Detention, Correctional, and Shelter Facilities* (Washington, DC: US Department of Justice, 1989), p. 4.

55. For a detailed description of juvenile delinquency in the 1800s, see J. Hawes, *Children in Urban Society: Juvenile Delinquency in Nineteenth Century America* (New York: Oxford University Press, 1971).

56. Dwight C. Jarvis, Institutional *Treatment of the Offender* (New York: McGraw-Hill, 1978), p. 101.

57. Margaret Werner Cahalan, *Historical Corrections Statistics in the United States, 1850–1984* (Washington, DC: US Department of Justice, 1986), pp. 104–105.

58. Clemens Bartollas, Stuart J. Miller, and Simon Dinitz, *Juvenile Victimization: The Institutional Paradox* (New York: Wiley, 1976), p. 6.

59. LaMar T. Empey, *American Delinquency—Its Meaning and Construction* (Homewood, IL: Dorsey, 1978), p. 515.

60. Edward Eldefonso and Walter Hartinger, *Control, Treatment, and Rehabilitation of Juvenile Offenders* (Beverly Hills: Glencoe, 1976), p. 151.

61. Ibid., p. 152.

62. M. Rosenthal, "Reforming the Justice Correctional Institution: Efforts of U.S. Children's Bureau in the 1930s," *Journal of Sociology and Social Welfare* 14:47–73 (1987).

63. Peter W. Greenwood, *Changing Lives: Delinquency Prevention as Crime-Control Policy* (Chicago: University of Chicago Press, 2006), Ch. 8; Franklin E. Zimring, *American Juvenile Justice* (New York: Oxford University Press, 2005), Ch. 4.

64. National Conference of State Legislatures, *A Legislator's Guide to Comprehensive Juvenile Justice, Juvenile Detention and Corrections* (Denver: National Conference of State Legislators, 1996).

65. Ibid.

66. Michael D. Shear, "Obama Bans Solitary Confinement of Juveniles in Federal Prisons," *New York Times*, January 25, 2016.

67. Melissa Sickmund, Anthony J. Sladky, Wei Kang, and Charles Puzzanchera, "Easy Access to the Census of Juveniles in Residential Placement: 1997–2013," 2015, http://www.ojjdp.gov/ojstatbb/ezacjrp/.

68. Ibid.

69. Annie E. Casey Foundation, *Reducing Youth Incarceration in the United States* (New York: Annie E. Casey Foundation, 2013).

70. Sickmund, Sladky, Kang, and Puzzanchera, "Easy Access to the Census of Juveniles in Residential Placement: 1997–2013."

71. Daniel P. Mears, "Exploring State-Level Variation in Juvenile Incarceration Rates: Symbolic Threats and Competing Explanations," *Prison Journal* 86:470–490 (2006).

72. Barry Krisberg, "Juvenile Corrections: An Overview," in Feld and Bishop, eds., *The Oxford Handbook of Juvenile Crime and Juvenile Justice*.

73. Ibid.

74. Robert Pear, "Many Youths Reported Held Awaiting Mental Help," *New York Times*, July 8, 2004.

75. Richard Lezin Jones and Leslie Kaufman, "New Jersey Youths Out of Foster Homes End Up in Detention," *New York Times*, May 31, 2003.

76. Sarah Hockenberry, Melissa Sickmund, and Anthony Sladky, *Juvenile Residential Facility Census, 2012: Selected Findings* (Washington, DC: Office of Juvenile Justice and Delinquency Prevention, 2015), p. 6.

77. John M. Broder, "Dismal California Prisons Hold Juvenile Offenders: Reports Document Long List of Maltreatment," *New York Times*, February 15, 2004, p. 12.

78. Shawn C. Marsh and William P. Evans, "Youth Perspectives on Their Relationships with Staff in Juvenile Correction Settings and Perceived Likelihood of Success on Release," *Youth Violence and Juvenile Justice* 7:46–67 (2009); Attapol Kuanliang, Jon R. Sorensen, and Mark D. Cunningham, "Juvenile Inmates in an Adult Prison System: Rates of Disciplinary Misconduct and Violence," *Criminal Justice and Behavior* 35:1186–1201 (2008).

79. Krisberg, "Juvenile Corrections: An Overview," p. 758.

80. Sickmund, Sladky, Kang, and Puzzanchera, "Easy Access to the Census of Juveniles in Residential Placement."

81. Donna M. Bishop and Michael J. Leiber, "Racial and Ethnic Differences in Delinquency and Justice System Responses," in Feld and Bishop, *The Oxford Handbook of Juvenile Crime and Juvenile Justice*; Alex R. Piquero, "Disproportionate Minority Contact," *The Future of Children* 18(2):59–79 (2008); Michael J. Leiber and Kristan C. Fox, "Race and the Impact of Detention on Juvenile Justice Decision Making," *Crime and Delinquency* 51:470–497 (2005).

82. Krisberg, "Juvenile Corrections: An Overview," p. 759; Rodney L. Engen, Sara Steen, and George S. Bridges, "Racial Disparities in the Punishment of Youth: A Theoretical and Empirical Assessment of the Literature," *Social Problems* 49:194–220 (2002).

83. See Scott R. Maggard, "Assessing the Impact of the Juvenile Detention Alternatives Initiative (JDAI): Predictors of Secure Detention and Length of Stay Before and After JDAI," *Justice Quarterly* 32:571–597 (2015); Tina L. Freiburger and Alison S. Burke, "Status Offenders in the Juvenile Court: The Effects of Gender, Race, and Ethnicity on the Adjudication Decision," *Youth Violence and Juvenile Justice* 9:352–365 (2011).

84. Joshua C. Cochran and Daniel P. Mears, "Race, Ethnic, and Gender Divides in Juvenile Court Sanctioning and Rehabilitative Intervention," *Journal of Research in Crime and Delinquency* 52:181–212 (2015).

85. Sickmund, Sladky, Kang, and Puzzanchera, "Easy Access to the Census of Juveniles in Residential Placement"; see also National Council on Crime and Delinquency, *And Justice for Some: Differential Treatment of Youth of Color in the Justice System* (San Francisco: Author, 2007).

86. John F. Chapman, Rani A. Desai, Paul R. Falzer, and Randy Borum, "Violence Risk and Race in a Sample of Youth in Juvenile Detention: The Potential to Reduce Disproportionate Minority Confinement," *Youth Violence and Juvenile Justice* 4:170–184 (2006).

87. Heidi M. Hsia, George S. Bridges, and Rosalie McHale, *Disproportionate Minority Confinement: 2002 Update: Summary* (Washington, DC: Office of Juvenile Justice and Delinquency Prevention, 2004).

88. Office of Juvenile Justice and Delinquency Prevention, "Disproportionate Minority Contact," *In Focus* (Washington, DC: Office of Juvenile Justice and Delinquency Prevention, November 2012), p. 3.

89. Ashley Nellis and Brad Richardson, "Getting Beyond Failure: Promising Approaches for Reducing DMC," *Youth Violence and Juvenile Justice* 8:266–276 (2010); Emily R. Cabaniss, James M. Frabutt, Mary H. Kendrick, and Margaret B. Arbuckle, "Reducing Disproportionate Minority Contact in the Juvenile Justice System: Promising Practices," *Aggression and Violent Behavior* 12:393–401 (2007).

90. Helene R. White, Jing Shi, Paul Hirschfield, Eun Young Mun, and Rolf Loeber, "Effects of Institutional Confinement for Delinquency on Levels of Depression and Anxiety Among Male Adolescents," *Youth Violence and Juvenile Justice* 8:295–313 (2010).

91. See David M. Halbfinger, "Care of Juvenile Offenders in Mississippi Is Faulted," *New York Times*, September 1, 2003.

92. Bureau of Justice Statistics, *Sexual Victimization Reported by Juvenile Correctional Authorities, 2007–12* (Washington, DC: Bureau of Justice Statistics, 2016).

93. Allen J. Beck, Marcus Berzofsky, Rachel Caspar, and Christopher Krebs, *Sexual Victimization in Prisons and Jails, Reported by Inmates, 2011–12: National Inmate Survey, 2011–12* (Washington, DC: US Department of Justice, Bureau of Justice Statistics, 2013).

94. Sickmund, Sladky, Kang, and Puzzanchera, "Easy Access to the Census of Juveniles in Residential Placement."

95. Bartollas, Miller, and Dinitz, *Juvenile Victimization*.

96. Christopher Sieverdes and Clemens Bartollas, "Security Level and Adjustment Patterns in Juvenile Institutions," *Journal of Criminal Justice* 14:135–145 (1986).

97. Sickmund, Sladky, Kang, and Puzzanchera, "Easy Access to the Census of Juveniles in Residential Placement."

98. Krisberg, "Juvenile Corrections: An Overview," p. 760.

99. Several authors have written of this sexual double standard. See Meda Chesney-Lind and Randall G. Shelden, *Girls, Delinquency, and the Juvenile Justice System*, 3rd ed. (Belmont, CA: Wadsworth, 2004); E. A. Anderson, "The Chivalrous Treatment of the Female Offender in the Arms of the Criminal Justice System: A Review of the Literature," *Social Problems* 23:350–357 (1976); G. Armstrong, "Females Under the Law: Protected but Unequal," *Crime and Delinquency*

23:109–120 (1977); M. Chesney-Lind, "Judicial Enforcement of the Female Sex Role: The Family Court and the Female Delinquent," *Issues in Criminology* 8:51–59 (1973); M. Chesney-Lind, "Juvenile Delinquency: The Sexualization of Female Crime," *Psychology Today* 19:43–46 (1974); Allan Conway and Carol Bogdan, "Sexual Delinquency: The Persistence of a Double Standard," *Crime and Delinquency* 23:13–35 (1977).

100. Sickmund, Sladky, Kang, and Puzzanchera, "Easy Access to the Census of Juveniles in Residential Placement."

101. Kristi Holsinger and Alexander M. Holsinger, "Differential Pathways to Violence and Self-Injurious Behavior: African American and White Girls in the Juvenile Justice System," *Journal of Research in Crime and Delinquency* 42:211–242 (2005).

102. Paul E. Tracy, Kimberly Kempf-Leonard, and Stephanie Abramoske-James, "Gender Differences in Delinquency and Juvenile Justice Processing: Evidence from National Data," *Crime and Delinquency* 55:171–215 (2009).

103. Sara Goodkind, Irene Ng, and Rosemary C. Sarri, "The Impact of Sexual Abuse in the Lives of Young Women Involved or at Risk of Involvement with the Juvenile Justice System," *Violence Against Women* 12:465–477 (2006); see also Emily Gaarder and Joanne Belknap, "Tenuous Borders: Girls Transferred to Adult Court," *Criminology* 40:481–518 (2002).

104. Elizabeth Cauffman, "Understanding the Female Offender," *The Future of Children* 18(2):119–142 (2008), at 124.

105. Leslie Acoca, "Outside/Inside: The Violation of American Girls at Home, on the Streets, and in the Juvenile Justice System," *Crime and Delinquency* 44:561–589 (1998).

106. Barbara Bloom, Barbara Owen, Elizabeth Piper Deschenes, and Jill Rosenbaum, "Improving Juvenile Justice for Females: A Statewide Assessment in California," *Crime and Delinquency* 48:526–552 (2002), at 548.

107. For a historical analysis of a girls' reformatory, see Barbara Brenzel, *Daughters of the State* (Cambridge, MA: MIT Press, 1983).

108. Ilene R. Bergsmann, "The Forgotten Few Juvenile Female Offenders," *Federal Probation* 53:73–79 (1989).

109. *Justice by Gender: The Lack of Appropriate Prevention, Diversion and Treatment Alternatives for Girls in the Justice System: A Report* (Chicago: American Bar Association and National Bar Association, 2001), pp. 27–29.

110. Jacob C. Day, Margaret A. Zahn, and Lisa P. Tichavsky, "What Works for Whom? The Effects of Gender Responsive Programming on Boys and Girls in Secure Detention," *Journal of Research in Crime and Delinquency* 52:93–129 (2015); Angela M. Wolf, Juliette Graziano, and Christopher Hartney, "The Provision and Completion of Gender-Specific Services for Girls on Probation: Variation by Race and Ethnicity," *Crime and Delinquency* 55:294–312 (2009); Margaret A. Zahn, Jacob C. Day, Sharon F. Mihalic, and Lisa Tichavsky, "Determining What Works for Girls in the Juvenile Justice System: A Summary of Evaluation Evidence," *Crime and Delinquency* 55:266–293 (2009).

111. Office of Juvenile Justice and Delinquency Prevention, *Girls and the Juvenile Justice System: Policy Guidance* (Washington, DC: Office of Juvenile Justice and Delinquency Prevention, October 2015); see also Francine T. Sherman and Annie Black, *Gender Injustice: System-Level Juvenile Justice Reforms for Girls* (Washington, DC: National Crittenton Foundation, 2015).

112. Doris Layton MacKenzie, "Preventing Future Criminal Activities of Delinquents and Offenders," in Brandon C. Welsh and David P. Farrington, eds., *The Oxford Handbook of Crime Prevention* (New York: Oxford University Press, 2014); Doris Layton MacKenzie, "Reducing the Criminal Activities of Known Offenders and Delinquents: Crime Prevention in the Courts and Corrections," in Lawrence W. Sherman, David P. Farrington, Brandon C. Welsh, and Doris Layton MacKenzie, eds., *Evidence-Based Crime Prevention*, rev. ed. (New York: Routledge, 2006), p. 352.

113. Patrick A. Langan and David J. Levin, *Recidivism of Prisoners Released in 1994* (Washington, DC: Bureau of Justice Statistics, 2002).

114. David Farabee, *Rethinking Rehabilitation: Why Can't We Reform Our Criminals?* (Washington, DC: American Enterprise Institute, 2005); for a rebuttal of this view, see James M. Byrne and Faye S. Taxman, "Crime (Control) Is a Choice: Divergent Perspectives on the Role of Treatment in the Adult Corrections System," *Criminology and Public Policy* 4:291–310 (2005).

115. Mark W. Lipsey and David B. Wilson, "Effective Intervention for Serious Juvenile Offenders: A Synthesis of Research," in Rolf Loeber and David P. Farrington, eds., *Serious and Violent Juvenile Offenders: Risk Factors and Successful Interventions* (Thousand Oaks, CA: Sage, 1998).

116. Shawn C. Marsh, William P. Evans, and Michael J. Williams, "Social Support and Sense of Program Belonging Discriminate Between Youth-Staff Relationship Types in Juvenile Correction Settings," *Child Youth Care Forum* 39:481–494 (2010).

117. Steve Aos and Elizabeth K. Drake, *Prison, Police, and Programs: Evidence-Based Options that Reduce Crime and Save Money* (Olympia: Washington State Institute for Public Policy, 2013).

118. Michael F. Caldwell, Michael Vitacco, and Gregory J. Van Rybroek, "Are Violent Delinquents Worth Treating: A Cost-Benefit Analysis," *Journal of Research in Crime and Delinquency* 43:148–168 (2006).

119. Thomas Grisso, "Adolescent Offenders with Mental Disorders," *The Future of Children* 18(2):143–164 (2008).

120. See, generally, William Glasser, "Reality Therapy: A Realistic Approach to the Young Offender," in Robert Schaste and Jo Wallach, eds., *Readings in Delinquency and Treatment* (Los Angeles: Delinquency Prevention Training Project, Youth Studies Center, University of Southern California, 1965); see also Richard Rachin, "Reality Therapy: Helping People Help Themselves," *Crime and Delinquency* 16:143 (1974).

121. Helen A. Klein, "Toward More Effective Behavior Programs for Juvenile Offenders," *Federal Probation* 41:45–50 (1977); Albert Bandura, *Principles of Behavior Modification* (New York: Holt, Rinehart & Winston, 1969); H. A. Klein, "Behavior Modification as Therapeutic Paradox," *American Journal of Orthopsychiatry* 44:353 (1974).

122. Steven N. Zane, Brandon C. Welsh, and Gregory M. Zimmerman, "Examining the Iatrogenic Effects of the Cambridge-Somerville Youth Study: Existing Explanations and New Appraisals," *British Journal of Criminology* 56:141–160 (2016); Joan McCord, "Cures that Harm: Unanticipated Outcomes of Crime Prevention Programs," *Annals of the American Academy of Political and Social Science* 587:16–30 (2003); Thomas J. Dishion, Joan McCord, and François Poulin, "When Interventions Harm: Peer Groups and Problem Behavior," *American Psychologist* 54:755–764 (1999).

123. Larry Brendtero and Arlin Ness, "Perspectives on Peer Group Treatment: The Use and Abuses of Guided Group Interaction/Positive Peer Culture," *Child and Youth Services Review* 4:307–324 (1982).

124. Elaine Traynelis-Yurek and George A. Giacobbe, "Communication Rehabilitation Regime for Incarcerated Youth: Positive Peer Culture," *Journal of Offender Rehabilitation* 26:157–167 (1998).

125. Bruno Bettelheim, The *Empty Fortress* (New York: Free Press, 1967).

126. Sarah Livsey, Melissa Sickmund, and Anthony Sladky, *Juvenile Residential Facility Census, 2004: Selected Findings* (Washington, DC: Office of Juvenile Justice and Delinquency Prevention, 2009), p. 10.

127. Doris Layton MacKenzie, "Evidence-Based Corrections: Identifying What Works," *Crime and Delinquency* 46:457–471 (2000), at 466; MacKenzie, "Reducing the Criminal Activities of Known Offenders and Delinquents," p. 355.

128. Thomas Castellano and Irina Soderstrom, "Therapeutic Wilderness Programs and Juvenile Recidivism: A Program Evaluation," *Journal of Offender Rehabilitation* 17:19–46 (1992).

129. MacKenzie, "Reducing the Criminal Activities of Known Offenders and Delinquents," p. 355.

130. Sandra Jo Wilson and Mark W. Lipsey, "Wilderness Challenge Programs for Delinquent Youth: A Meta-Analysis of Outcome Evaluations," *Evaluation and Program Planning* 23:1–12 (2003).

131. Jerald Burns and Gennaro Vito, "An Impact Analysis of the Alabama Boot Camp Program," *Federal Probation* 59:63–67 (1995).

132. David B. Wilson and Doris Layton MacKenzie, "Boot Camps," in Brandon C. Welsh and David P. Farrington, eds., *Preventing Crime: What Works for Children, Offenders, Victims, and Places?* (New York, Springer, 2006), p. 80, Table 2.

133. Ibid., p. 80.

134. Ibid.; Doris Layton MacKenzie, *What Works in Corrections: Reducing the Criminal Activities of Offenders and Delinquents* (New York: Cambridge University Press, 2006), p. 294.

135. Megan Kurlychek and Cynthia Kempinen, "Beyond Boot Camp: The Impact of Aftercare on Offender Reentry," *Criminology and Public Policy* 5:363–388 (2006).

136. MacKenzie, "Reducing the Criminal Activities of Known Offenders and Delinquents," p. 348.

137. Dale G. Parent, *Correctional Boot Camps: Lessons Learned from a Decade of Research* (Washington, DC: National Institute of Justice, 2003); see also Livsey, Sickmund, and Sladky, *Juvenile Residential Facility Census, 2004*, p. 4.

138. Morton Birnbaum, "The Right to Treatment," *American Bar Association Journal* 46:499 (1960).

139. See, for example, *Matter of Welfare of CAW*, 579 N.W.2d 494 (MN App. 1998).

140. *Inmates of the Boys' Training School v. Affleck*, 346 F. Supp. 1354 (D.R.I. 1972).

141. Ibid., p. 1343.

142. *Nelson v. Heyne*, 491 F.2d 353 (1974).

143. *Morales v. Turman*, 383 F. Supp. 53 (E.D. Texas 1974).

144. *Pena v. New York State Division for Youth*, 419 F. Supp. 203 (S.D.N.Y. 1976).

145. *Ralston v. Robinson*, 102 S.Ct. 233 (1981).

146. Patricia Puritz and Mary Ann Scali, *Beyond the Walls: Improving Conditions of Confinement for Youth in Custody* (Washington, DC: Office of Juvenile Justice and Delinquency Prevention, 1998).

147. Doris Layton MacKenzie and Rachel Freeland, "Examining the Effectiveness of Juvenile Residential Programs," in Feld and Bishop, eds., *The Oxford Handbook of Juvenile Crime and Juvenile Justice*, p. 792.

148. David M. Altschuler and Rachel Brash, "Adolescent and Teenage Offenders Confronting the Challenges and Opportunities of Reentry," *Youth Violence and Juvenile Justice* 2:72–87 (2004), at 72.

149. Daniel P. Mears and Jeremy Travis, "Youth Development and Reentry," *Youth Violence and Juvenile Justice* 2:3–20 (2004), at 3.

150. Edward J. Latessa, "Homelessness and Reincarceration: Editorial Introduction," *Criminology and Public Policy* 3:137–138 (2004).

151. Joan Petersilia, *When Offenders Come Home: Parole and Prisoner Reentry*, revised ed. (New York: Oxford University Press, 2009).

152. Margaret Beale Spencer and Cheryl Jones-Walker, "Intervention and Services Offered to Former Juvenile Offenders Reentering Their Communities: An Analysis of Program Effectiveness," *Youth Violence and Juvenile Justice* 2:88–97 (2004), at 91.

153. Pamela K. Lattimore, "Reentry, Reintegration, Rehabilitation, Recidivism, and Redemption," *The Criminologist* 31:1, 3–6 (2006), at 1; see also Laura Winterfield, Christine Lindquist, and Susan Brumbaugh, *Sustaining Juvenile Reentry Programming After SVORI* (Washington, DC: Urban Institute, 2007).

154. Stephanie R. Hawkins, Pamela K. Lattimore, Debbie Dawes, and Christy A. Visher, *Reentry Experiences of Confined Juvenile Offenders: Characteristics, Service Receipt, and Outcomes of Juvenile Male Participants in the SVORI Multi-site Evaluation* (Washington, DC: National Criminal Justice Reference Service, US Department of Justice, 2009), pp. 6–7.

155. Office of Public Affairs, US Department of Justice, "The Justice Department and U.S. Department of Housing and Urban Development Announce New Juvenile Re-Entry Assistance Program," November 2, 2015, https://www.justice.gov/opa/pr/justice-department-and-us-department-housing-and-urban-development-announce-new-juvenile-re.

156. Jeffrey A. Bouffard and Kathleen J. Bergseth, "The Impact of Reentry Services on Juvenile Offenders' Recidivism," *Youth Violence and Juvenile Justice* 6:295–318 (2008); He Len Chung, Carol A. Schubert, and Edward P. Mulvey, "An Empirical Portrait of Community Reentry Among Serious Juvenile Offenders in Two Metropolitan Cities," *Criminal Justice and Behavior* 34:1402–1426 (2007).

157. Sarah Vidal, Barbara A. Oudekerk, N. Dickon Reppucci, and Jennifer Woolard, "Examining the Link Between Perceptions of Relationship Quality with Parole Officers and Recidivism Among Female Youth Parolees," *Youth Violence and Juvenile Justice* 31:60–76 (2015).

158. David M. Altschuler and Troy L. Armstrong, "Juvenile Corrections and Continuity of Care in a Community Context—The Evidence and Promising Directions," *Federal Probation* 66:72–77 (2002).

159. David M. Altschuler and Troy L. Armstrong, "Intensive Aftercare for High-Risk Juveniles: A Community Care Model" (Washington, DC: Office of Juvenile Justice and Delinquency Prevention, 1994).

160. David M. Altschuler, "Juvenile Reentry and Aftercare," *Georgetown Journal on Poverty Law and Policy* 16:655–667 (2009).

161. See *Morrissey v. Brewer*, 408 U.S. 471, 92 S.Ct. 2593, 33 L.Ed.2d 484 (1972).

162. Thomas A. Loughran, Edward P. Mulvey, Carol A. Schubert, Jeffrey Fagan, Alex R. Piquero, and Sandra H. Losoya, "Estimating a Dose-Response Relationship Between Length of Stay and Future Recidivism in Serious Juvenile Offenders," *Criminology* 47:699–740 (2009); Kristin Parsons Winokur, Alisa Smith, Stephanie R. Bontrager, and Julia L. Blankenship, "Juvenile Recidivism and Length of Stay," *Journal of Criminal Justice* 36:126–137 (2008).

163. Greenwood and Turner, "Juvenile Crime and Juvenile Justice."

164. Alex R. Piquero, Francis T. Cullen, James D. Unnever, Nicole L. Piquero, and Jill A. Gordan, "Never Too Late: Public Optimism About Juvenile Rehabilitation," *Punishment and Society* 12:187–207 (2010); Alex R. Piquero and Laurence Steinberg, "Public Preferences for Rehabilitation versus Incarceration of Juvenile Offenders," *Journal of Criminal Justice* 38:1–6 (2010).

165. Rolf Loeber and David P. Farrington, "Never Too Early, Never Too Late: Risk Factors and Successful Interventions for Serious and Violent Juvenile Offenders," *Studies on Crime and Crime Prevention* 7:7–30 (1998).

166. See Piquero, Cullen, Unnever, Piquero, and Gordan, "Never Too Late"; Piquero and Steinberg, "Public Preferences for Rehabilitation versus Incarceration of Juvenile Offenders."

167. Stephanie Hartwell, Robert McMackin, Robert Tansi, and Nozomi Bartlett, "'I Grew Up Too Fast for My Age': Postdischarge Issues and Experiences of Male Juvenile Offenders," *Journal of Offender Rehabilitation* 49:495–515 (2010).

CHAPTER 17
Delinquency and Juvenile Justice Abroad

Chapter Features

Focus on Delinquency: Youth Violence in Japan

Cyber Delinquency: Youth and Cybercrime in Europe and Asia

Evidence-Based Juvenile Justice—Treatment: Precourt Diversion Programs Around the World

Focus on Delinquency: The Changing Nature of Youth Justice in Canada

Youth Stories: Keeping Incarcerated Juveniles Safe

TOXIC PET FOOD, lead paint in toys, faulty automobile tires, and dangerous chemicals in specialty foods have led to widespread consumer safety alerts and large-scale recalls by companies in the United States and caused many local problems in China, where these goods are manufactured. These events are not the result of delinquent acts perpetrated by Chinese youths. But they do signal the changing times in China, and the changing times also appear to be behind a growing problem with crime and juvenile delinquency in that country.

These events, shaped by globalization, a rapidly expanding Chinese economy, and a fiercely competitive manufacturing sector, follow on the heels of one of the worst individual atrocities committed in China in recent memory. Dubbed the "Kindergarten Killer" by the Chinese media, Fu Hegong, age 31, was recently convicted and sentenced to death for the brutal murder of a teacher and a 5-year-old boy. Fu had broken into a Beijing kindergarten to rob it. Discovered by the teacher, he killed her by smothering her with a quilt. He then took the life of the young student who was with the teacher at the time. Beijing's No. 2 Intermediate Court also found the "Kindergarten Killer" guilty of three other, unrelated murders, one of a security guard in a botched robbery.

Although rare, it is atrocities like these that have brought further national and international attention to China's growing problem with crime and delinquency of late, and prompted the Chinese government to take a number of steps to improve school security

Security guards at a primary school in Beijing, China.

as well as community safety. The rise in crime and delinquency in China has been linked to the country's ongoing social and economic upheaval that began in 1979 when the country first adopted its reform policies and embraced the outside world. Though the rapid economic growth has transformed society, rapid change has strained traditional norms, values, and ethics.

China is not alone in experiencing some of these social and economic shifts and the associated problems. Many nations around the world are experiencing an upsurge in juvenile problem behavior, including gang violence, prostitution, and drug abuse. In response to the growing number of delinquent acts, some nations are now in the process of revamping their juvenile justice systems in an effort to increase their effectiveness and efficiency. This chapter addresses these issues by looking at international perspectives on delinquency and juvenile justice systems. We begin by providing a snapshot of juvenile delinquency around the world. We discuss the challenges and benefits of making comparisons across nations and examine trends in delinquency rates in different countries compared with the United States. Next we provide a review of juvenile justice systems in **developed countries**, organized around important issues facing juvenile justice today, such as minimum age of criminal responsibility, transfers to adult court, and maximum length of sentence for incarcerated juveniles. The chapter concludes with a profile of the juvenile justice system in England, examining the many different stages that juveniles may face as they go through the system.

developed countries
Recognized by the United Nations as the richest countries in the world.

Delinquency Around the World

Juvenile delinquency is problematic in many parts of the world. Where has this occurred, and what has been the cause?

Europe

Juvenile violence and property crime are difficult to characterize in Europe, with some countries reporting low levels of involvement on the part of teens and other countries reporting much higher levels.[1] One of the most alarming developments has been the involvement of children in the international sex trade.[2] Russia is plagued with Internet sex rings that involve youths in pornographic pictures. In Moscow, more than 800 tapes and videos were seized during Operation Blue Orchid, a joint operation conducted by Russian police and US Customs agents.[3] Operation Blue Orchid led to criminal investigations against people who ordered child pornography in more than 20 nations. Equally disturbing has been the involvement of European youths in global prostitution rings.[4] Desperate young girls and boys in war-torn areas such as the former Yugoslavia and in impoverished areas such as Eastern Europe have become involved with gangs that ship them around the world. In one case, an organized crime group involved in wildlife smuggling of tiger bones and skins to Asian markets began a sideline of supplying sex clubs with young Russian women.[5] In another case, as a result of a 12-nation crackdown on the trafficking of women for sex commerce, the Southeast European Cooperative Initiative in Bucharest, Romania, identified 696 victims of trafficking and 831 suspected traffickers.[6]

Western Europe has also experienced some alarming acts of teen violence. In Erfurt, Germany, a 19-year-old male, armed with a pump-action shotgun and a handgun, entered his high school and shot dead 14 teachers, two students, and a police officer; he then took his own life. The youth had just been expelled from the school. It was the worst mass killing in Germany since World War II.[7]

Germany has also been plagued with skinhead violence since reunification in 1989. Most German skinheads are social misfits, with minimal education and few employment opportunities. Because unemployment is high, they feel helpless and hopeless regarding their future, and many resort to physical violence in reaction to their plight.[8] Most of the increase in German youth violence has been encountered in what was communist East Germany before the reunification. Youth violence in the east is considerably higher than in the west, a factor linked to the exposure of eastern youth to greater poverty and unemployment than their West German peers.[9]

France too has experienced problems with violent hate crimes, as well as (to a lesser extent) street crime in Paris.[10] In 2005, riots erupted in the suburbs of Paris and quickly spread to other regions of the country. The immediate cause of the riots was the death of two teenage boys of African descent who were believed to have been chased by police and were electrocuted upon entering a power substation in the suburb of Clichy-sous-Bois. The larger cause was escalating tension between the government and immigrant populations who charge that the government is to blame for their communities' high rates of unemployment because of long-standing discrimination against them and their French-born children.[11] The rioting lasted for three weeks and caused immense property damage: 10,000 vehicles, 255 schools, and 233 government buildings were burned, and 51 post office and 140 public transportation vehicles were damaged by stone throwing. Of the 498 juveniles who were apprehended by the police and referred to youth court, 108 were held in police custody to await trial.[12]

What has fueled these acts of teen violence? Although each nation is quite different, all share an explosive mix of racial tension, poverty, envy, drug abuse, broken families, unemployment, and alienation. Some of the areas hardest hit have been undergoing rapid social and economic change—the fall of communism, the end of the Cold War, the effects of the global economy, an influx of multinational immigration—as they move toward increased economic integration, privatization, and diminished social services. In Europe, the main reason for an increase in teen violence is believed to be the tremendous growth in immigrant youth populations.[13] This is not because immigrants are more prone to violence, but rather because of the relative poverty and social disintegration they face upon arriving in very homogenous countries such as Sweden, the Netherlands, and Germany.[14] This view has also been advanced as one of the main reasons for the growth in rates of total violent crime (adult plus juvenile) in Europe during the early 1990s to early 2000s.[15] The result of these rapid changes has been the development of personal alienation in an anomic environment. (See Chapter 4 for more on the effect of anomie.) Kids become susceptible to violence when institutional and interpersonal sources of stability, such as schools and parents, are weak and/or absent.[16]

The Americas

Shocking stories of teen violence are also not uncommon in North America and South America. In Canada, there has been a rash of school shootings in the last two decades. Many have resulted in death and serious injury of other students and teachers. School shootings in Canada increased substantially immediately following the massacre at Columbine High School in the United States in 1999, prompting some Canadian social scientists to speculate that these were copycat crimes. But other research points to the growing number of students who have access to guns and carry them to school as well as an increase in school violence in general.[17]

In Mexico, violent crime is one of the biggest problems facing the country. In one case in Mexico City, a 15-year-old male was arrested and convicted in the beheading of four rival drug gang members. The juvenile was a hired killer for a drug cartel working in the city. His sentence was three years in prison.[18]

A wave of violence raging between Mexican drug lords for control of lucrative drug markets and the federal police and military has claimed as many as 185,000 lives in the past decade.[19] Many thousands of these victims have been innocent civilians, including some American tourists and those living near the United States–Mexico border.[20]

South America has a long history of violent uprisings, police abuse, and political unrest. Some countries are more violent than others. In Brazil, violence is the second leading cause of death behind heart disease; there are more deaths each year by murder than by cancer. Young people are responsible for a disproportionate number of these homicides. Drug trafficking gangs are largely responsible for the violence. Some of this violence has been fueled by an increasing appetite for illegal drugs, including ecstasy and other designer drugs, among the country's young people.[21] In Rio de Janeiro, the country's showcase city, these heavily armed gangs, referred to as "organized terrorist groups" by the head police authority, have taken to bombing government buildings, shopping centers, and tourist attractions. This is being done to cause the government to ease up on its long-standing campaign against these criminal groups.[22] Rio de Janeiro was also the site of the country's worst school shooting. In April 2011, 12 students, ages 12 to 14, were killed in the Tasso da Silveria school in Realengo, a working-class neighborhood just west of the city; another 10 students were hospitalized for gunshot wounds.[23]

Other atrocities in South America include a government cover-up of killings of juvenile and other gang members in a prison in El Porvenir, Honduras, and in Guatemala.[24] The killing of street children continues to take place in many South American cities. These are children who leave home at a very young age because of abuse, neglect, or the loss of their parents, and earn their living largely by committing petty delinquent acts, begging, and selling garbage. In Rio de Janeiro, killings of street children are commonplace. Death squads, drug lords, juvenile gangs, and sometimes the police are behind these killings.

death squads
Common to South America, organized government or criminal groups that selectively kill members of opposing groups and incite fear in those groups and among their supporters.

Drug trafficking gangs are responsible for a large share of violence in several South American countries. Shown here are armed teenage boys who operate as security guards, lookouts, and distributors for local drug lords in Rio de Janeiro, Brazil.

Australia and New Zealand

Although not normally associated with high crime and delinquency rates, these island nations have had their share of youth crime. In New Zealand, weapon carrying in schools is especially problematic. Seventeen percent of high school students reported bringing a weapon of some type—usually a knife or pocket knife—to school in the last 12 months; one-quarter (24 percent) reported carrying a weapon outside of school. Oftentimes, weapon carrying was for self-protection.[25]

Australia has also experienced juvenile violence, with some notable changes in recent years. According to the latest data (2012), juveniles are the offenders in 3 percent of all the homicides occurring in Australia (down from 5 percent in 2010), while juveniles account for 13 percent of all of the homicide victims (up from 9 percent in 2010).[26]

Asia

In Japan, juvenile crime and violence in particular have been on the decline for almost a full decade, with the data suggesting a trend back to some level of normalization. Between 2002 and 2013 (latest data available), juvenile crime rates have fallen by approximately 50 percent.[27] This comes after a rather trying period during the 1990s, with overall crime rates reaching a post–World War II peak in 2002.[28] According to the National Police Agency in Japan, juvenile crime and foreign criminal gangs were the "twin causes" of the rising crime rates during this period of time.[29] This was an especially trying time in Japan. Over the span of a decade, juvenile arrests for violent crime increased 60 percent, and the number of arrests for homicide by juveniles increased by one-quarter (24 percent, from 75 to 93).[30] Police in the Fukushima Prefecture, located north of Tokyo, arrested a 15-year-old boy for killing his father. The 15-year-old punched his 61-year-old father in the face and stomped on his stomach until he was dead. The incident was especially shocking because it occurred one day after a 13-year-old was arrested for beating his mother to death because he objected to the meal she had cooked![31] The term *hikikomori* (those who isolate themselves) has been coined to describe troubled youth who commit crimes and engage in other antisocial acts.[32] The overall increase in teen violence and particularly heinous crimes like these were behind the Japanese government's get-tough measures introduced to the Juvenile Act (*Shônen-hô*), the first revisions to the act in 50 years.[33] The Japanese experience with delinquency and youth violence is the topic of the accompanying Focus on Delinquency feature.

Youth Violence in Japan

Japan has long been considered a low-crime country. Despite its industrial might and highly urbanized population—trademarks of high-crime countries in the developed world—Japan has maintained extremely low delinquency and crime rates in the post–World War II era. This continues today, but it was not so long ago that this trend was interrupted with a dramatic upsurge in violence among young people. As shown in Figure 17-A, police arrests of 15- to 19-year-olds for violent offenses started to climb in 1996, following years of stability. (Although these figures are not expressed as rates per juvenile population, the increase in arrests between 1996 and 2005 far surpasses any increase in the juvenile population.) In 2003, the peak year, 1,896 arrests were made for juvenile murder and robbery. Arrests for violent crimes have declined in more recent years.

During the upsurge in juvenile violence, shocking events, rarely experienced before in Japan, became more common. Japanese youth gangs carried out what they call "uncle hunting," whereby four or five gang members single out a lone businessman walking home, rob him, and beat him to the ground. Victim reports claim that gangs were not only doing this for the money but also for the thrill of inflicting pain on others. Other events included a 13-year-old boy murdering his female schoolteacher and a 16-year-old boy stabbing his girlfriend when she tried to end the relationship.

So what is the explanation for this sudden rise in youth violence in Japan? Japanese social scientists, politicians, leaders of business, and the public all weighed in on the debate. One of the more controversial views was that the increase in juvenile violence and crime in general was being fueled by an increase in the number of multinational immigrants (for the most part other Asians) who came to find work in Japan. As in Europe, it is not that these new populations are more prone to violence, but rather that they are less well off financially, due in part to work being scarce, and are disconnected from familial and social groups.

Other views pointed to a decline in cultural values and societal norms, which are widely regarded as being fundamental to the economic success and crime-free lifestyle that Japan has long enjoyed. Conformity, sense of community, belonging to a group, honor or "face," and respect for authority are all believed to have declined during this time period, especially among young people. Economic stagnation also played a role in the rise in youth violence. A higher unemployment rate and fewer opportunities left many young people feeling marginalized and frustrated. It was also estimated that 45 percent of all crimes in Japan were committed by people under age 20, about double what it is in the United States. This figure remains about the same today, but juvenile crime and violence is much lower. Explanations for the drop and stability in juvenile crime and violence in Japan are not well known, with some pointing to more effective policing and delinquency prevention strategies.

CRITICAL THINKING

1. What are some other possible reasons for Japan's increase in youth violence during the mid-1990s to mid-2000s?

2. Compared to the United States, can Japan today still be considered a low-crime country?

SOURCES: National Police Agency, *White Paper on Crime 2014* (Tokyo: National Police Agency, 2015), http://hakusyo1.moj.go.jp/en/nendo_nfm.html (accessed October 2016); Chris Lewis, Graham Brooks, Thomas Ellis, and Koichi Hamai, "Comparing Japanese and English Juvenile Justice: Reflections on Change in the Twenty-First Century," *Crime Prevention and Community Safety* 11(2):75–89 (2009); Trevor Ryan, "Creating 'Problem Kids': Juvenile Crime in Japan and Revisions to the Juvenile Act," *Journal of Japanese Law* 10:153–188 (2005); Aki Roberts and Gary LaFree, "Explaining Japan's Postwar Violent Crime Trends," *Criminology* 42:179–209 (2004); Nobuo Komiya, "A Cultural Study of the Low Crime Rate in Japan," *British Journal of Criminology* 39:369–390 (1999); Freda Adler, *Nations Not Obsessed with Crime* (Littleton, CO: Rothman, 1983).

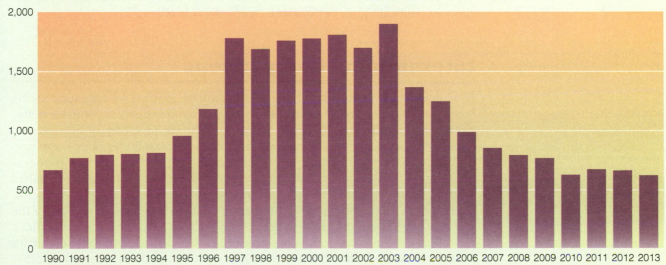

Number of arrests

figure 17-A

Juvenile Arrests for Violent Offenses

Note: Arrests are for murder and robbery.

SOURCE: National Police Agency, *White Paper on Crime 2014* (Tokyo: National Police Agency, 2015), http://hakusyo1.moj.go.jp/en/nendo_nfm.html (accessed October 2016).

Japan is not the only Asian nation to have experienced shocking juvenile crimes. Killings of schoolchildren by middle-aged men have prompted serious concern in Beijing and other major Chinese cities. In a span of just three months in 2010 (March to May), five separate mass killings were perpetrated against schoolchildren. In one incident, seven children, their kindergarten teacher, and a mother of one of the children were killed by a knife-wielding man. At the time, because Chinese families who lived in cities were only allowed one child (this policy has since changed), children were elevated to an almost godlike status. In commenting on why the attackers targeted children, Beijing sociologist Tang Jun said, "They choose children because it'll have the largest negative impact on society."[34] Despite the change in policy, these attacks against children have continued in China. In one incident in 2012, 22 schoolchildren, ages 6 to 11, and a teacher were stabbed in the village of Chengping in Henan Province.[35]

During this period of time, Chinese authorities report that juvenile delinquency had been on the increase for several years, with violence being a major component of juvenile crime.[36] The rise in delinquency has been linked to China's ongoing social and economic upheaval that began in 1979 when the country first adopted its reform policies and embraced the outside world.[37] Though the rapid economic growth has transformed society, rapid change has strained traditional norms, values, and ethics. Although China is often known for its ruthless suppression of crime and liberal use of the death penalty, the government has adopted a more humane approach to treating delinquents. The aim is to act as a wise and concerned pseudo-parent, emphasizing prevention and education rather than punishment and repression.

Africa

Juvenile crime and gang violence also flare up in many African countries. Abject poverty, ethnic tensions, and an ever-growing gap between the haves and have-nots underlie much of the violence throughout Africa. In some African countries like Mauritius, Seychelles, Botswana, Cape Verde, and South Africa, which have experienced economic gains in recent years, benefits are often undermined by declines in political rights, personal safety, and the rule of law.[38]

International Comparisons

How does youth crime around the world compare to what we are experiencing here in the United States? There have been numerous efforts to compare delinquency across different countries.[39] Social scientists have carried out international comparisons for many reasons, including to test theories of delinquency; to compare delinquency and punishment over long periods of time; to investigate the effects of government policies on delinquency, such as gun control or child welfare benefits; to examine why some countries have very low delinquency rates; or just for general interest.[40] (Concept Summary 17.1 reviews the key reasons for making cross-national comparisons.) Advocacy organizations as well as governments sometimes point to events or trends in other countries to show how the United States is doing better or sometimes worse than other countries.

Problems of Cross-National Research

Unlike comparisons of delinquency in different cities or parts of the same country, international comparisons involving two or more countries demand that researchers pay a great deal more attention to what is being compared, what countries are

Key Reasons for Cross-National Comparisons

Focus	Scope
Delinquency	To assess which countries have high and low delinquency rates
Theories of delinquency	To determine if similar theories can be used to explain delinquency in different countries
Juvenile justice system	To compare differences in juvenile justice philosophy and administration
Treatment and prevention	To compare different responses to juvenile delinquency and evaluate their effectiveness across countries

being compared, and so on.[41] Comparing delinquency rates across countries can be difficult because of three main problems:

■ The legal definitions of juvenile crime vary from country to country.[42]

■ The measurement of juvenile crime varies across countries. In the United States, arrests are used to measure juvenile crime, while in many European countries, the number of cases solved by the police measures crime.[43]

■ The age group defined as "juvenile" is not always the same.[44]

Despite these problems, valid comparisons of delinquency across different countries can still be made. The key is to acquire valid data and then make comparisons between nations that use similar methods of measuring youth crime. The best data sources are listed in Table 17.1.[45]

The United Nations Survey of Crime Trends and Operations of Criminal Justice Systems (UNCJS) provides data on juvenile delinquency and adult crime, as well as data on juvenile justice and criminal justice systems. Conducted every five years since 1977, the UNCJS survey makes it possible to look at changes over time and for a very large number of countries around the world. However, because the data are a collection of statistics sent to the United Nations by individual countries, they are really no better than using official data provided by individual countries.

table 17.1

International Sources of Delinquency Data

Data Source	Type of Delinquency Data Collected	Organization in Charge of Data Collection	Number of Countries Represented	Frequency of Data Collection
UNCJS	Police statistics	United Nations	103	Every five years (since 1977)
INTERPOL	Police statistics	International Criminal Police Organization	179	Annually
WHO	Medically certified homicides	World Health Organization	191	Annually
European Sourcebook of Crime and Criminal Justice Statistics	Police statistics	Consortium of government agencies	36	Annually
International Self-Report Delinquency Study	Self-reports	Netherlands Ministry of Justice	31	1991–92 and 2006–07

Sources: Marcelo F. Aebi et al., *European Sourcebook of Crime and Criminal Justice Statistics, 2014* (Helsinki, Finland: European Institute for Crime Prevention and Control, 2014); Josine Junger-Tas, Ineke H. Marshall, Dirk Enzmann, Martin Killias, Majone Steketee, and Beata Gruszczynska, eds., *Juvenile Delinquency in Europe and Beyond: Results of the Second International Self-Report Delinquency Study* (New York: Springer, 2010); Graeme Newman and Gregory J. Howard, "Introduction: Data Sources and Their Use," in Graeme Newman, ed., *Global Report on Crime and Justice* (New York: Oxford University Press, 1999), pp. 3–12.

The *European Sourcebook of Crime and Criminal Justice Statistics*, an initiative of the Council of Europe, is very similar to the UNCJS, but is limited to official statistics from Europe. Where the two data sources differ is that the Council of Europe is trying to develop a uniform system in the way official statistics on delinquency and crime are collected and reported.[46]

The International Criminal Police Organization (INTERPOL) and the World Health Organization (WHO) are two other sources of official statistics on delinquency and crime at the international level. The two sources differ in a number of ways. INTERPOL compiles police crime statistics (completions and attempts) received from countries that are members of the organization. WHO, on the other hand, compiles homicide statistics (completions only) based on medical records received from countries that are affiliated with the organization. WHO's measure of homicide, which is based on the "classification of causes of death worldwide" and determined by medical practitioners,[47] is considered the most accurate source of homicide statistics[48] and is used in many international studies of homicide.[49] The main reason for WHO being the most accurate source of homicide data is that medical doctors and coroners are trained to determine cause of death.

The International Self-Report Delinquency (ISRD) study, which was first carried out in 12 developed countries in the early 1990s and repeated with 31 developed countries in the mid-2000s, was the first attempt to measure self-reported delinquency at an international level using a standard questionnaire.[50] Because the same questionnaire is used for all subjects, delinquency rates can be compared in a more valid way across countries or clusters of countries. A third and even larger ISRD study is planned for future years.[51]

Benefits of Cross-National Research

Are juvenile offenders in the United States more violent than those in Japan? Are delinquents in Western Europe more likely to steal cars? How does Australia's juvenile justice system differ from that of the United States? Knowledge of the nature of juvenile delinquency and how juvenile justice systems operate in other countries is not only beneficial for the concerned citizen but also important to social scientists and government policy makers. Investigating whether juvenile offenders in the United States are more violent than, say, juveniles in Canada may lead to important discoveries to help explain any differences that exist. These discoveries may in turn be useful to policy makers and lead to action, such as more funding for problem-solving policing tactics to reduce gun violence by juveniles.[52] (See Chapter 14 for examples of police efforts to reduce juvenile gun violence.)

Another value served by cross-national comparisons, whether it is delinquency rates or the treatment of incarcerated juvenile offenders, is to let a country know how well or how poorly it is doing relative to other countries. On the one hand, a poor international rating for the United States on juvenile homicides by an international agency, such as the United Nations, may prompt the US government to take action to address this problem. On the other hand, a good international rating on, say, the legal rights afforded to detained juveniles demonstrates that the United States is on the right track. This could lead to other countries making changes to follow the US example.

Other benefits from cross-national comparisons can come from studying low-crime countries.[53] Examining these countries to find out how they maintain low delinquency rates may yield important insights for countries with higher delinquency rates. According to criminologists Harry Dammer and Jay Albanese, another good reason to make cross-national comparisons is the need to address transnational and international crime problems.[54] **Transnational crimes** are those activities that extend into two or more countries and violate the laws of those countries, such as illegal migration, trafficking in body

To read more about the **United Nations**, visit their website: http://www.un.org/en/.

To read more about **INTERPOL**, visit their website: http://www.interpol.int/.

transnational crime
Crime that is carried out across the borders of two or more countries and violates the laws of those countries.

parts, trafficking in illegal drugs and weapons, and theft and trafficking in automobiles.[55]

International crimes are those that are recognized by international law, such as war crimes.[56] Criminal activities that take place across borders have grown considerably in the last two decades. One researcher describes some of the contributing factors this way:

> The end of the Cold War, the collapse of state authority in some countries and regions, and the process of globalization—of trade, finance, communications and information—have all provided an environment in which many criminal organizations find it more profitable and preferable to operate across national borders than confine their activities to one country.[57]

international crime
Crime that is punishable under international law.

This phenomenon has become known as the globalization of delinquency and crime.[58]

The best method for comparing the level of delinquency across countries is to use data that have been collected in a uniform way, such as using a standard questionnaire that asks young people in different countries the same questions about their involvement in delinquency. Despite its limitations, the best source of delinquency rates is police statistics available from individual countries.

German social scientist Christian Pfeiffer examined trends in juvenile crime and violence in 10 European countries and the United States.[59] The European countries were England, Sweden, Germany, the Netherlands, Italy, Austria, France, Denmark, Switzerland, and Poland. A follow-up study conducted by the European Crime Prevention Network (ECPN) examined trends in juvenile violence in countries that are members of the European Union.[60] Delinquency data were available from police statistics from the mid-1980s to the early 2000s. Three main findings emerged from the Pfeiffer study:

- Juvenile violence, especially robbery and offenses involving serious bodily harm, increased substantially over this period in almost all of the countries.

- Total juvenile crime, which includes burglary, motor vehicle theft, larceny, and vandalism, increased very little over this period of time, with some countries showing no increase or an actual decrease.

- Crimes of violence committed by young adults (18–20) or by adults in general have increased far less rapidly since the mid-1980s than have those committed by juveniles, and in some countries they have not increased at all.[61]

The main finding to emerge from the ECPN study was that the upward trend in juvenile violence in Europe continued into the early 2000s. As previously noted, this increase in teen violence is evident in both the absolute rate of offending and the proportion of total offenses committed.[62] While cross-national data are not yet available on cybercrimes committed by youths, the Cyber Delinquency box profiles some experiences in Europe and Asia.

In the next sections, we will look at what these international data tell us about the differences in delinquency trends between the United States and similar nations. First, it is important to note that the availability of reliable, up-to-date, and comparable data on juvenile offending continues to present serious limitations for cross-national comparisons. Even the *European Sourcebook of Crime and Criminal Justice Statistics*—the major source of crime data on the continent—is limited by what the individual countries collect and make available.[63]

Juvenile Violence

The increase in juvenile violence between the mid-1980s and mid-1990s was greater in European countries than it was in the United States. However, while juvenile violence continued to increase in many European countries throughout the rest of the 1990s and into the early 2000s, teen violence in the United States dropped precipitously. Between the peak year of 1994 and 2012 (the latest data available), the American juvenile arrest rate for violent crime decreased by almost two-thirds (63 percent).[64] (See Chapter 2 for more details on trends in juvenile violence in the United States.)

Youth and Cybercrime in Europe and Asia

The problem of cyber delinquency and its growth in the United States is well documented in the media, and research is providing a better understanding of its nature, extent, and relationship to other social problems. Delinquent acts committed in cyberspace are wide-ranging, from bullying to computer hacking to inciting violence. (See other chapters for more details on examples of some of these crimes by American youths.)

Less well known—at least on this side of the Atlantic—is the nature and extent of cybercrimes by youths in Europe and Asia, not to mention how these crimes may be contributing to changes in juvenile crime rates overall. In a recent study of crime rates (adult and juvenile) in Western Europe between 1998 and 2007, European criminologists Marcelo Aebi and Antonia Linde report that the increase in violent crime appears to be related to changes in lifestyle and demographics of younger European generations. One of the main lifestyle changes concerns the Internet and its influence on youths' free time. The authors conclude:

Youths who have unlimited access to the Internet spend more time at home—and are more exposed to the risk of engaging in computer related offences, which have been increasing constantly—while those who have a limited access to the Web spend more time in the streets and are differentially exposed to the risk of engaging in conventional delinquency.

Ongoing research efforts in a number of foreign countries offer to shed more light on cyber delinquency in Europe as well as Asia. What follows are some examples of computer-related offenses committed by youths in European and Asian countries:

- A study of the content of cyberbullying in Web forums among middle and high school students in China found that the majority of incidents involved "denigration, outing, and flaming." It was also common for cyberbullying incidents to include disparaging, violent, and obscene language.

- A study of digital image bullying—a more specific form of cyberbullying—among high school and university students in Belgium found that 10 percent had been victims and 9 percent had been bullies.

- In Singapore, Taiwan, a 17-year-old male was convicted of hacking into several computer servers in a number of foreign countries. His sole defense was that he was just doing it out of curiosity.

CRITICAL THINKING

1. Do you think the Internet—and its influence on youths' free time—has had an effect on juvenile crime rates in the United States?

2. Should we expect there to be differences in the nature of cyber-crimes perpetrated by youths in Europe and the United States? How is your thinking shaped by the global reach of the Internet?

SOURCES: Hee Jhee Jiow, "Cyber Crime in Singapore: An Analysis of Regulation Based on Lessig's Four Modalities of Constraint," *International Journal of Cyber Criminology* 7:18–27 (2013); Lieve Lembrechts, "Digital Image Bullying Among School Students in Belgium: An Exploration of the Characteristics of Bullies and Their Victims," *International Journal of Cyber Criminology* 6:968–983 (2012); Marcelo F. Aebi and Antonia Linde, "Is There a Crime Drop in Western Europe?" *European Journal of Criminal Policy and Research* 16:251–277 (2010); Chang Su and Thomas J. Holt, "Cyber Bullying in Chinese Web Forums: An Examination of Nature and Extent," *International Journal of Cyber Criminology* 4:672–684 (2010).

Juvenile violence raises serious concerns in all parts of the world. Here, community members in La Loche, Saskatchewan, in Western Canada, hold a prayer vigil on January 24, 2016. The vigil was in response to a mass shooting at a local school and home perpetrated by a 17-year-old boy from the community.

AP Images/Jason Franson/The Canadian Press

table 17.2

Juvenile Homicides in Europe and the United States

Country	Total Homicide Rate (per 100,000 pop.)	Percentage of Juveniles Involved	Age of Juveniles (Years)
Austria	2.2	7.1	14–18
Belgium	7.0	4.8	16–18
France	3.4	8.1	10–17
Germany	3.5	7.3	14–17
Hungary	2.7	5.6	14–17
Italy	0.5	30.5	14–17
Netherlands	19.5	6.5	12–17
United States	3.3	6.7	10–17

Note: All European data are from 2010; US data are from 2014.

Sources: Marcelo F. Aebi et al., *European Sourcebook of Crime and Criminal Justice Statistics, 2014*, 5th ed. (Helsinki, Finland: European Institute for Crime Prevention and Crime Control, 2014), p. 80; FBI, *Crime in the United States, 2014* (Washington, DC: US Government Printing Office, 2015), Tables 30, 32.

With the exception of homicide, rates of violent crime (juvenile and adult) continued to increase in Western European countries into the late 2000s.[65]

Canada, the other North American country for which data were available to add to this comparison, showed a somewhat similar pattern to the United States: a substantial increase in juvenile violence between the mid-1980s and mid-1990s followed by a much smaller decline up to 2015 (the latest data available on youths charged).[66] During the upward trend period (1986 to 1995), rates of all categories of juvenile violence in Canada showed a marked increase: homicide up 50 percent, assault up 150 percent, sexual assault up 40 percent, and robbery up 160 percent.[67]

The most recent and best available comparative data from Europe focuses on the percentage of juveniles involved in different types of violent crime, including homicide. As shown in Table 17.2, Italian youth were heavily overrepresented in the commission of homicides—accounting for almost one-third (30.5 percent)— with Italy having the lowest overall homicide rate. France (8.1 percent) and Germany (7.3 percent) had the next highest involvement of juveniles in the commission of homicide. At 6.7 percent, the US involvement of juveniles in homicide was slightly higher than in the Netherlands (6.5 percent) and slightly lower than in Austria (7.1 percent).

Juvenile Property Crime

Juvenile property crime rates (including burglary, motor vehicle theft, larceny, and vandalism) increased very little in Europe and North America from the mid-1980s to the mid-1990s. On the other hand, like juvenile violence, property crime rates increased substantially in two countries during this period of time: Germany with a 75 percent increase and Italy with a 140 percent increase. It is not altogether clear why juvenile property crime rates in these two countries increased as much as this. Perhaps the factors that were driving the increases in juvenile violence in these countries were also having an effect on less serious forms of delinquency, such as theft, burglary, and motor vehicle theft.

More recent data on juvenile property crime in Canada show that the slight increase in rates during the mid-1980s to mid-1990s changed to more than a 50 percent decrease between 1995 and 2014.[68] This reversal was also found in the United States, whereby juvenile property crime rates decreased by almost two-thirds (65 percent) between the peak years of 1994 and 2012.[69] European Union countries also experienced a drop (albeit much smaller than in Canada and the United States) in juvenile property crime from the mid-1990s into the late 2000s.[70] This is in sharp contrast to the increase in juvenile violence that most European countries experienced over the same period.

table 17.3

Juvenile Burglaries in Europe and the United States

Country	Total Burglary Rate (per 100,000 pop.)	Percentage of Juveniles Involved	Age of Juveniles (Years)
Austria	157	28.9	14–18
Belgium	111	22.5	16–18
France	67	31.8	10–17
Germany	31	22.2	14–17
Hungary	49	19.1	14–17
Italy	14	10	14–17
United States	75	16.2	10–17

Note: All European data are from 2010; US data are from 2014.

Sources: Marcelo F. Aebi et al., *European Sourcebook of Crime and Criminal Justice Statistics, 2014*, 5th ed. (Helsinki, Finland: European Institute for Crime Prevention and Crime Control, 2014), p. 80; FBI, *Crime in the United States, 2014* (Washington, DC: US Government Printing Office, 2015), Tables 30, 32.

As with juvenile violence, the most recent and best available comparative data from Europe focuses on the percentage of juveniles involved in different types of property crime, including burglary. As shown in Table 17.3, the percentage of juveniles involved in burglaries was highest in France (31.8 percent) and lowest in Italy (10 percent). At 16.2 percent, the United States had the next lowest involvement of juveniles in burglaries.

Juvenile Drug Use

The latest comparative study of teenage drug use in Europe found that just under one in five students (18 percent) had used illicit drugs over their lifetime.[71] This compares with 35 percent of American students who have used illicit drugs over their lifetime, based on the same sample and reporting period in the Monitoring the Future (MTF) survey.[72] (See Chapter 11 for more details on the MTF survey.) Comparisons across European countries of the percentage of students who have ever used illicit drugs are just as striking, ranging from a low of 6 percent in the Faroe Islands and the Republic of Moldova to a high of 37 percent in the Czech Republic (see Figure 17.1). Carried out by a consortium of agencies, the European School Survey Project on Alcohol and other Drugs (ESPAD) surveyed just over 96,000 10th-grade students in 35 European countries.

Although American students are more likely to use marijuana and other illicit drugs over their lifetime, European students are more likely to smoke cigarettes and use alcohol over their lifetime. In the United States, 47 percent of 10th-grade students report any alcohol use, while in the Czech Republic, Greece, and Hungary, the three countries with the highest rates, 96, 94, and 93 percent of students, respectively, report any alcohol use. Of the 35 European countries, Iceland was the only one that had a lower rate of teenage alcohol use (35 percent) than the United States.[73]

In some of these European countries alcohol consumption is associated with teen violence. Using a past ESPAD study, which included 30 European countries, researchers found that drinking has a strong effect on teen violence in the Nordic and Eastern European countries

The latest comparative study of teenage drug use found that slightly less than one in five European students (18 percent) had used illicit drugs over their lifetime. Pictured here are a group of teenagers partying at a campsite in Wales.

Keith Morris/Alamy Stock Photo

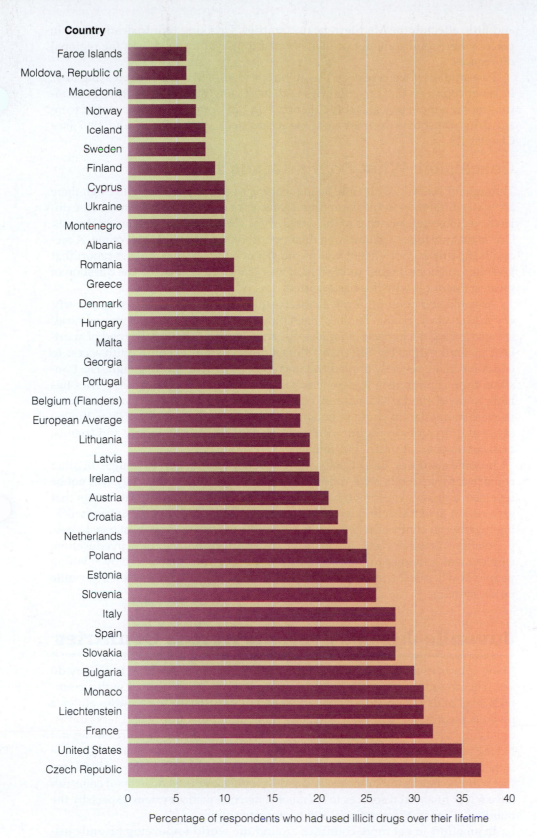

figure 17.1

Lifetime Teenage Illicit Drug Use in Europe and the United States

SOURCE: Ludwig Kraus et al., *The 2015 ESPAD Report: Results from the European School Survey Project on Alcohol and Other Drugs* (Lisbon, Portugal: European Monitoring Centre for Drugs and Drug Addiction, 2016), Table 7a.

and little effect in the Mediterranean countries. Drinking to intoxication and in places where adults are not present seemed to play a major role in the regional differences.[74]

Past studies of teenage drug use in Europe (2007–2011) show decreasing rates in fewer countries (7) than countries with increasing rates (11); another 14 countries report a more or less stable situation.[75] In the United States, the rate of teenage drug use shows declines from the recent peak years of 1996 and 1997 (see Chapter 11).

Conclusion: What Do the Trends Tell Us?

Throughout the world, juvenile delinquency is a serious problem. Although there are many differences in the nature and character of juvenile delinquency in the different regions and countries of the world, there are a number of common threads. One is that juveniles account for a disproportionate amount of total crime. A second is the presence of violent youth gangs. Some European countries report that juvenile violence is higher today than it was 15 and 20 years ago. The question of greatest interest is why this has occurred.

As noted above, all countries share an explosive mix of racial tension, poverty, envy, drug abuse, broken families, unemployment, and alienation. Some countries are also feeling the impacts of rapid social and economic change. The end of apartheid in South Africa has left many broken promises for its youth, with access to education being severely limited and unemployment at an all-time high. The transition from communism to democracy in many Eastern European countries has had profound effects. Neighboring countries have had to cope with a tremendous increase in immigrant youth populations in search of jobs and better lives, but because of difficulties in finding jobs and social isolation from family and friends, many of these youths turn to delinquency.[76]

In some countries, these trends in delinquency have begun to change. In other countries, these trends have continued, and it is very likely that they will not be reversed unless governments are willing to tackle the many causal factors that give rise to juvenile delinquency. In some cases, this will mean countries working together to control the flow of immigration and providing assistance to new populations. In other cases, it will mean investing greater resources in education, employment training programs, and assistance programs for unemployed young people. It will also be important for countries to have effective and fair juvenile justice systems.

To read more about delinquency across countries and what is being done to prevent it, visit the **International Centre for the Prevention of Crime**: http://www.crime-prevention-intl.org/.

Juvenile Justice Systems Across Countries

Many countries in the world have formal juvenile justice systems, but many do not. The presence of juvenile justice systems is strongly associated with a country's level of development; that is, developed or industrialized countries all have juvenile justice systems, while a smaller number of **developing** and **least developed countries** have juvenile justice systems. Part of the reason for countries not having separate justice systems to deal with juvenile delinquency and adult crime is the lack of importance placed on the special needs of juveniles who come in conflict with the law. Another reason is that developing and least developed countries have fewer financial resources to spend on a juvenile justice system, especially the building of separate correctional and treatment facilities.

In an effort to get more countries around the world to develop juvenile justice systems and improve the administration of juvenile justice, in 1985 the United Nations adopted the "Standard Minimum Rules for the Administration of Juvenile Justice" (see Exhibit 17.1). Also known as the "Beijing Rules" of juvenile justice because they were developed at a meeting in Beijing, these rules set out minimum standards for countries to follow in the administration of juvenile justice.[77]

developing countries
Recognized by the United Nations as countries that are showing signs of improved economic growth and are making the transition from low income to high income.

least developed countries
Recognized by the United Nations as being the poorest countries in the world and suffering from long-term barriers to economic growth.

Few African nations have the resources to expend on Western-style treatment programs for juvenile offenders. Here, youths perform farming duties in the juvenile facility in Wau, South Sudan.

Kate Holt/eyevine/Redux

exhibit 17.1

Highlights of the "Standard Minimum Rules for the Administration of Juvenile Justice"

These rules were adopted by the UN General Assembly on November 29, 1985, on the recommendation of the Seventh UN Congress on the Prevention of Crime and the Treatment of Offenders (resolution 40/33).

Part 1: General Principles

- Member states shall seek to further the well-being of juveniles and their families.

- Member states shall try to develop conditions to ensure meaningful lives in the community for juveniles.

- Sufficient attention should be given to positive measures involving mobilization of resources, such as the family, volunteers and community groups, to promote the well-being of juveniles.

- Juvenile justice shall be an integral part of the national development process of each country.

- In legal systems recognizing the concept of an age of criminal responsibility for juveniles, such an age level shall not be fixed too low, bearing in mind emotional, mental, and physical maturity.

- Any reaction by the juvenile justice system to juvenile offenders shall be in proportion to both the offenders and the offense.

- Appropriate scope for the exercise of discretionary powers shall be allowed at all stages of legal processing affecting juveniles.

- Efforts shall be made to ensure sufficient accountability at all stages in the exercise of such discretion.

- Basic procedural safeguards, such as the presumption of innocence, the right to be notified of charges, the right to remain silent, the right to counsel, the right to the presence of a parent or guardian, the right to confront and cross-examine witnesses

and the right to appeal, shall be guaranteed at all stages of proceedings.

- The juvenile's right to privacy shall be respected at all stages.

Part 2: Investigation and Prosecution

- Upon the apprehension of a juvenile, parents or guardians shall be notified as soon as possible.

- Consideration shall be given to dealing with juvenile offenders without resort to trial, and any diversion to appropriate community or other services shall require consent of the juvenile or parents.

Part 3: Adjudication and Disposition

- The placement of a juvenile in an institution shall always be a disposition of last resort and for the minimum necessary period.

Part 4: Non-Institutional Treatment

- Efforts shall be made to provide necessary assistance, such as lodging, education, vocational training and employment, to facilitate the rehabilitation process.

Part 5: Institutional Treatment

- Juveniles in institutions shall be kept separate from adults, and special attention shall be used to the greatest extent possible.

Part 6: Aftercare

- Efforts shall be made to provide semi-institutional arrangements, such as halfway houses, educational homes, and daytime training centers, to assist juveniles in their reintegration into society.

SOURCE: Abridged from United Nations, *The United Nations and Crime Prevention: Seeking Security and Justice for All* (1996).

There are many features of juvenile justice that are of interest to compare across countries. This section looks at the key features of juvenile justice systems in a number of developed countries: specialized police services for juveniles, age of criminal responsibility, presence of juvenile court, transfers to adult court, sentencing, treatment of incarcerated juveniles, and aftercare services.

Juvenile Policing

Specialized policing services for juveniles is an important but relatively recent addition to the repertoire of services offered by juvenile justice systems in many developed countries. The number of police officers assigned to juvenile work has increased in recent years. The International Association of Chiefs of Police found that of the 1,400 departments surveyed in 1960, approximately 500 had juvenile units. By 1970, the number of police departments with a juvenile specialist doubled.[78] Still, few developing or least developed countries have police officers trained specifically to deal with juvenile offenders.

In the United States, juvenile officers operate either as specialists within a police department or as part of the juvenile unit of a police department. Their role is similar to that of officers working with adult offenders: to intervene if the actions of a citizen produce public danger or disorder. (See Chapter 14 for more information on juvenile policing in the United States.) In Australia and New Zealand, police departments have established specialized youth aid sections, and in New Zealand it is reported that this national unit is responsible for diverting more than half of all juvenile offenders out of the juvenile justice system.[79]

Canada has developed special juvenile gang units as part of police departments. Juvenile gang units exist in all of the police departments of the biggest Canadian cities, such as Montreal, Toronto, Vancouver, and Halifax, as well as in many medium-sized and smaller cities and towns.[80] Overcoming discriminatory policing is of special concern to help reduce disproportionate minority contact in some Canadian cities and towns.[81]

In Japan, the police response to juvenile delinquency is based on a welfare approach. This includes emphasizing punishment as a last resort; promoting a treatment, care, and social work ethic; and working with local agencies responsible for education and job training.[82] Also important in Japan are police boxes (*koban*) in urban areas and police houses (*chuzaisho*) in rural areas that have special officers who deal with juvenile delinquency. Because of the sheer number of these police stations in the country—about 6,600 *koban* and 8,100 *chuzaisho*—the police have a very good understanding of conditions that might give rise to juvenile delinquency and violence problems in the community. This knowledge assists them in intervening before problems get out of control. In addition to juvenile police officers, there is a police-established system of volunteers to aid the police in dealing with juvenile delinquency. There are three types of voluntary systems:

- Guidance volunteers

- Police helpers for juveniles

- Instructors for juveniles

Guidance volunteers work with the police in providing advice to young people about the dangers of being involved in gangs or using drugs; they also provide some counseling services to young people in trouble with the law. Police helpers are mostly retired police officers in charge of dispersing large groups of juvenile delinquents, such as gangs. They are not a riot squad, but simply assist the police in dealing with large groups of young people who may be looking for trouble or are involved in delinquent acts. Instructors are authorized by the 1985 Law on Regulation of Business Affecting Public Morals to protect juveniles from unsafe

The **International Association of Chiefs of Police** is the world's oldest and largest nonprofit membership organization of police executives, with over 18,000 members in over 100 different countries. Visit their website at http://www.theiacp.org/.

environments—that is, where young people are being abused or neglected.[83] In many ways, these individuals act as child or juvenile protection agents.

Age of Criminal Responsibility: Minimum and Maximum

Across the world there is a great deal of variation in the minimum age a person can be held responsible for his or her criminal actions, ranging from a low of 6 years in Sri Lanka to a high of under 21 years in Indonesia. In the majority of countries around the world, full adult criminal responsibility begins at age 18 years or older.[84] This general pattern is the same for the developed countries listed in Table 17.4. Australia, England, and Switzerland have the lowest minimum age of criminal responsibility at 10 years, and Belgium has the highest at 16 to 18 years. Interestingly, in the United States, 36 states have no set minimum age that a young person can be held criminally responsible. By common law, states may use 7 years as the minimum, but in practice children under the age of 10 are rarely brought before a juvenile court.

In those countries in which the minimum age is quite high, such as Belgium (16 to 18 years), Denmark (15 years), or Sweden (15 years), what happens to young people below the minimum age who commit delinquent acts? Doing nothing is not an option in any of the developed countries. Instead, these young people are dealt with under various forms of child or social welfare or child protection legislation. Under these laws young people may be placed in state-run homes, undergo counseling, or report to a social worker on a regular basis.

In some countries the minimum age can be lowered. This is typically done when the offense is very serious. In New Zealand, the minimum age is 14, but if the offense is murder or manslaughter, the minimum age becomes 10. In Romania, the minimum age can be dropped from 16 to 14 if the young person is capable of understanding right from wrong.[85]

Presence of Juvenile Court

The majority of the developed countries have courts specifically for juveniles (see Table 17.4), and they operate pretrial diversion programs. Many of these pretrial diversion programs are effective in reducing juvenile recidivism. (See the Evidence-Based Juvenile Justice feature entitled "Precourt Diversion Programs Around the World.") Only Denmark, Russia, and Sweden do not have juvenile courts. In Denmark and Sweden, it is the child welfare system that is responsible for juvenile offenders.[86] In Russia, juveniles appear before regular adult criminal courts. In Denmark, the Administration of Justice Act provides special rights for juveniles who appear in adult court—for example, closing the proceedings to the public and press.[87] Swedish adult courts also try to protect the identity of juvenile offenders if the court believes that publicity may be harmful to the juvenile.[88] In Russia too there are some protections afforded the juvenile: Age must be taken into account as a mitigating factor, the juvenile's living conditions must be considered, and whether or not the offense was committed with an adult.[89]

Transfers to Adult Court

Transfers of juvenile offenders to adult court are a widely accepted practice in developed countries (see Table 17.4). In all of the countries in which transfers are allowed, the main criterion is that the offense was of a very serious or violent nature. Other criteria can include the youth's record of delinquency and the use of weapons. But in these cases, the evidence must be particularly strong for a transfer to take place.

table 17.4

International Comparisons of Juvenile Justice Systems

Country	Minimum Age of Criminal Responsibility	Age of Adult Criminal Responsibility	Court that Handles Juveniles	Transfer to Adult Court Allowable?	Maximum Length of Sentence for a Juvenile	Separation of Incarcerated Juveniles from Adults
Australia	10*	16–17**	Children's courts	Yes, for serious felonies	2–7 years	Not mandatory, generally separated in practice
Austria	14	19	Special sections in local and regional courts; youth courts	No	Half of adult sentence	Yes
Belgium	16–18	18	Special juvenile courts	Yes	No juvenile incarcerations in juvenile court	Not mandatory, generally separated in practice
Canada	12	18	Youth courts	Yes	10 years	Yes
Denmark	15	15	No juvenile court	N/A	8 years	Yes
England	10	18	Youth courts	Yes	2 years	Yes
France	13	18	Children's tribunals; youth courts of assizes	No	Half of adult sentence	Yes
Germany	14	18	Single-sitting judge; juvenile court; juvenile chamber	Yes	10 years	Yes
Hungary	14	18	Special sections of regular court	No	15 years	Yes
Italy	14	18	Separate juvenile courts	No	One-third of adult sentence	Yes
Japan	14	20	Family courts	Yes	Lifetime sentence	Yes
The Netherlands	12	18	Special juvenile courts	Yes	Lifetime sentence	Yes
New Zealand	14; 10 for murder and manslaughter	18	Youth courts	Yes	No juvenile incarcerations in youth court	No (some exceptions)
Russia	16; 14 for certain crimes	18	No juvenile court	N/A	10 years	Yes
Sweden	15	18	No juvenile court	N/A	No lifetime sentence	Yes
Switzerland	10	15	Special juvenile courts and/ or juvenile prosecutors	No	1 year	Yes
United States	6–10 for 14 states; 36 other states have no set minimum but may use age 7	15 for 2 states; 16 for 10 states; 17 for 38 states	Juvenile courts	Yes	Lifetime sentence	Yes

*The lower age limit is 7 in Tasmania.

**Age of full criminal responsibility differs by state.

N/A = not available.

Sources: Adapted from Marcelo F. Aebi et al., *European Sourcebook of Crime and Criminal Justice Statistics, 2014* (Helsinki, Finland: European Institute for Crime Prevention and Control, 2014); Michael Tonry and Colleen Chambers, "Juvenile Justice Cross-Nationally Considered," in Barry C. Feld and Donna M. Bishop, eds., *The Oxford Handbook of Juvenile Crime and Juvenile Justice* (New York: Oxford University Press, 2012), pp. 871–879; Joan McCord, Cathy Spatz Widom, and Nancy Crowell, eds., *Juvenile Crime, Juvenile Justice*, Panel on Juvenile Crime: Prevention, Treatment, and Control (Washington, DC: National Academy Press, 2001), pp. 18–20, Table 1-1.

Precourt Diversion Programs Around the World

Keeping youths who have become involved in minor delinquent acts from being formally processed through the juvenile justice system is a top priority of many countries around the world. This is because they recognize the need to protect young people against the stigma and labeling that can occur from being "processed" through a juvenile court. In many ways, entering the juvenile justice system is viewed as a last resort to dealing with juvenile delinquency. Informal processing or precourt diversion programs, which vary from country to country, also represent a cost savings from the expense of paying for juvenile court judges, prosecutors, public defenders, and other justice personnel and administrative costs. These alternative approaches are more often used in European, particularly Western European, countries than in the United States. These programs are also very popular in Australia and New Zealand. Part of the reason for the greater use of these programs outside of the United States is that these countries are less punitive toward juvenile offenders than the United States. What follows are profiles of the use of precourt diversion programs in the Netherlands, France, and Australia.

Netherlands

In response to a sharp rise in juvenile vandalism and its associated costs, the government of the Netherlands implemented a precourt diversion program called *Het Alternatief* (the alternative) or HALT. Begun in the 1970s in the city of Rotterdam, the program quickly spread throughout the country and is now a national program in 65 locations. Accountability and assistance are at the center of the program. Young people ages 12 to 18 years caught for the first or second time committing an act of vandalism (the program is now used for other offenses as well) are offered the chance to avoid formal prosecution by participating in the program. Juveniles who go through the program must repair the vandalism damage they have caused, and counselors work with the young people to assist them with employment, housing, and education issues. If the program is successfully completed, police charges are dropped and the case is dismissed, and in those cases that are not successful, an official report is sent to the prosecutor. An evaluation of the program in three cities (Rotterdam, Eindoven, and Dordrecht) found the program to be very effective in reducing future acts of vandalism. Juvenile offenders in the treatment group were 63 percent less likely to be rearrested versus a comparison group that were 25 percent less likely to be rearrested.

France

Maisons de justice, or community justice centers, are one of the most well-known pretrial diversion programs for juvenile offenders in France. Set up by the Ministry of Justice and community associations across the country, the centers address minor offenses and other legal problems through alternative justice approaches. One of these alternative approaches is victim–offender mediation, whereby a trained staff member works with the offender, the victim, and sometimes the victim's family to settle a dispute without the need for formal justice proceedings. An apology or an order of restitution or compensation is commonly reached as part of victim–offender mediation. Although there has been no formal evaluation of community justice centers, they are widely credited as helping to relieve some of the backlog in the courts and to settle cases much faster than traditional means.

Australia

Precourt diversion programs have gone through extensive changes in Australia in recent years. Up to the early 1990s, there were two types of juvenile diversion programs: police cautions, which involve the police more or less warning offenders that the next time they are caught, formal action will be taken; and children's panels, made up of police and social workers who admonish a young person for his or her delinquent behavior. Today, precourt diversion programs for juvenile offenders include an expanded use of police cautions and the addition of restorative justice-based programs known as family group conferences (FGCs). These conferences bring together the juvenile offender and his or her family, the victim, and a professional coordinator to discuss the problem caused by the juvenile offender and to agree on a mutually acceptable resolution that will benefit all parties and the wider community. FGCs attempt to provide the victim with restoration and restitution and the offender with rehabilitation and reintegration. An evaluation of an FGC program in Queensland showed that reoffending rates were reduced by 44 percent three to five years postconference, and 82 percent of the conference participants, victims included, were satisfied with the agreed outcomes.

CRITICAL THINKING

1. What are some of the problems with precourt diversion programs?

2. Should these programs also be used for serious and violent juvenile offenders?

SOURCES: Michael O'Connell and Elizabeth O'Connell, "Youth Justice and Youth Crime in Australia," in John A. Winterdyk, ed., *Juvenile Justice: International Perspectives, Models and Trends* (Boca Raton, FL: CRC Press, 2014); Kathleen Daly, Brigitte Bouhours, Roderic Broadhurst, and Nini Loh, "Youth Sex Offending: Recidivism and Restorative Justice: Comparing Court and Conference Cases," *Australian and New Zealand Journal of Criminology* 46:241–267 (2013); T. Wing Lo, Gabrielle M. Maxwell, and Dennis S. W. Wong, "Diversion from Youth Courts in Five Asia Pacific Jurisdictions: Welfare or Restorative Solutions," *International Journal of Offender Therapy and Comparative Criminology* 50:5–20 (2006); Josine Junger-Tas, "Youth Justice in the Netherlands," in Michael Tonry and Anthony N. Doob, eds., *Youth Crime and Youth Justice: Comparative and Cross-National Perspectives. Crime and Justice: A Review of Research*, Vol. 31 (Chicago: University of Chicago Press, 2004).

In the developed countries of Austria, France, Hungary, Italy, and Switzerland, transfers of juveniles to adult court are not permissible. Typically, this is because youths can receive an adult sentence while still under the authority of the juvenile court. This is also the case in Canada, where, until recently, transfers of juveniles to adult court were allowed. Under the Youth Criminal Justice Act there is a procedure that allows a juvenile to stay in youth court and be dealt with as a juvenile, and in the case of serious offenses the juvenile can receive an adult sentence.[90]

Sentencing Policies

The maximum sentence length for juvenile offenders varies considerably across developed countries. In Belgium and New Zealand, there can be no sentence of incarceration for youths who appear before juvenile court; instead, youths must be transferred to adult court to receive custodial sentences. Some countries, such as Austria, France, and Italy, specify that sentences can only be for one-half or one-third of what an adult would receive for a similar offense. In Italy, juveniles who are sentenced to custody can receive up to one-third of the same sentence for adults but, unlike adults, can be conditionally released at any stage of the sentence regardless of the amount of time spent in custody.[91]

The countries with the harshest sentence for juvenile offenders are the United States, Japan, and the Netherlands, where juvenile offenders can receive lifetime sentences. In Japan, a life sentence may mean spending between 10 and 15 years in a correctional facility with or without forced labor, while in the Netherlands, a life sentence may mean serving as much as 20 years.[92] In the United States, juveniles who are convicted of homicide and receive a lifetime sentence can now receive parole at some point in their sentence.. This is a result of a 2016 decision of the US Supreme Court, in the case of *Montgomery v. Louisiana*, which ruled that juveniles sentenced to life without parole (the formal name of the sentence) have the right to seek parole.[93] (See Chapter 15 for more details on this important case.)

In Russia, the maximum sentence length for juveniles is 10 years, and Russia has made extensive use of incarceration (or commitment), with 50 to 60 percent of all adjudicated juvenile offenders receiving some form of this disposition.[94] Switzerland, on the other hand, is the most lenient country: one year is the longest period of time that a juvenile offender can be sentenced to custody, and transfers to adult court are not allowed.

Some least developed and developing countries, which are known for their harsh sentences for juvenile offenders, have begun to reassess some of their sentencing policies. For example, Iran declared a judicial ban on executing offenders who committed criminal acts under the age of 18. Human Rights Watch claimed that this could save the lives of more than 130 juvenile offenders who were on death row at the time.[95]

Finding an appropriate balance between punishment (in the form of secure commitment) and treatment for juvenile offenders is more difficult for some countries than others. This is the subject of the Focus on Delinquency feature entitled "The Changing Nature of Youth Justice in Canada."

Incarcerated Juveniles

In Scandinavian countries (Denmark, Finland, Norway, and Sweden), youths may be held in a prison or secure social institution. The prison focuses on security, and the institution focuses on treatment, addressing the individual needs of juvenile offenders through social skills training, counseling, and education. Wherever possible the treatment option is used throughout Scandinavia.[96] This is not the case in some European countries that once placed a special emphasis on treatment over security, as well as on the minimal use of incarceration for

The Changing Nature of Youth Justice in Canada

Canada, a welfare state with an extensive social safety network that includes (among other benefits) universal health care coverage and yearlong maternity leave, is well known for its liberal views on social issues. Some of these include efforts to limit the use of prisons for offenders, the implementation of tough gun control laws, partial legalization of marijuana use, and support for same-sex marriage. But this liberal view may be changing somewhat with respect to the government's response to juvenile delinquency.

In 1984, the Young Offenders Act (YOA) replaced the Juvenile Delinquents Act (JDA), which had been the legislative framework for youth justice in Canada since 1908. In addition to numerous legal and procedural changes, the movement from the JDA to the YOA marked a change in principles of youth justice, from a welfare orientation to a more legalistic orientation. (Like the United States, Canada adheres to the *parens patriae* treatment philosophy. This did not change under the new law and continues to this day.) Some of the YOA's important provisions include:

- A minimum age of criminal responsibility of 12 years (it was 7 years) and a uniform age of adult criminal responsibility of 18 years.

- Youthful offenders are entitled to child care/youth care experts as well as lawyers for counsel.

- The primary purpose of intervention is a balance between penalizing delinquent behavior and providing appropriate treatment.

Over the years, academics and juvenile justice practitioners alike criticized the YOA for not providing clear legislative direction to guide appropriate implementation in several key areas, such as transfers to adult court. This lack of clear legislative direction was thought to be an important factor contributing to problems and deficiencies in Canada's youth justice system. Furthermore, as Canadian criminologists Anthony Doob and Jane Sprott point out:

There are two substantial problems with the YOA on which almost all policy and academic observers agreed: the youth justice system is being overused for minor offenses, and too many youths are going to custody, especially for relatively minor offenses.

These concerns were at the heart of the federal government's youth justice law, the Youth Criminal Justice Act (YCJA), which was proclaimed into force in April 2003. Also important to this law was a get-tough approach, or at least the appearance of this. Some of these

get-tough measures included a greater focus on holding youths accountable for their actions, making it easier to impose adult sanctions on the most serious and violent juvenile offenders, and publishing the offender's identity, again in the most serious cases. Interestingly, the law also established specific guidelines for police use of discretion in dealing with juvenile offenders.

The YCJA also greatly expanded aftercare programs for juvenile offenders. For example, it is now mandatory that all periods of time spent in an institution be followed by a period of intensive supervision in the community. The length of time of supervision is also stipulated in the law: It must be no less than half the time spent in custody. Thus, a juvenile offender who spends 12 months in an institution must then spend 6 months in intensive supervision while in the community. Under the previous law, there were no requirements for supervision following a custodial sentence.

Another important change to the juvenile aftercare system introduced by this law is a number of conditions, both mandatory and optional, that the judge can impose on the youth as part of supervision orders. Mandatory conditions include keeping the peace and reporting to authorities. Optional conditions include attending school, getting a job, adhering to a curfew, abstaining from alcohol and drugs, and not associating with gang members. Experts report that some of these changes have vastly improved Canada's youth justice system and, importantly, reduced the use of custodial sentences without increasing youth crime.

CRITICAL THINKING

1. How would you characterize the changes in Canada's youth justice laws over the last century?

2. Could juvenile justice in the United States benefit from incorporating some of the recent changes to Canada's youth justice laws?

SOURCES: John A. Winterdyk and Anne Miller, "Juvenile Justice and Young Offenders: A Canadian Overview," in John A. Winterdyk, ed., *Juvenile Justice: International Perspectives, Models and Trends* (Boca Raton, FL: CRC Press, 2014); Nicholas Bala, Peter J. Carrington, and Julian V. Roberts, "Youth Justice Reform in Canada: Reducing Use of Courts and Custody Without Increasing Youth Crime," in David J. Smith, ed., *A New Response to Youth Crime* (Cullompton, Devon, UK: Willan Publishing, 2010); Jane B. Sprott and Carolyn Greene, "Trust and Confidence in the Courts: Does the Quality of Treatment Young Offenders Receive Affect Their Views of the Courts?" *Crime and Delinquency* 56:269–289 (2010); Jennifer L. Schulenberg, "Police Culture and Young Offenders: The Effect of Legislative Change on Definitions of Crime and Delinquency," *Police Quarterly* 9:423–447 (2006); Anthony N. Doob and Jane B. Sprott, "Youth Justice in Canada," in Michael Tonry and Anthony N. Doob, eds., *Youth Crime and Youth Justice: Comparative and Cross-National Perspectives, Crime and Justice: A Review of Research*, Vol. 31 (Chicago: University of Chicago Press, 2004), pp. 224–225.

juvenile offenders. The Netherlands is one example. Between the early 1990s and mid-2000s, institutional placements of juvenile offenders grew from 700 to 2,400.[97] American criminologist Alfred Blumstein notes that this is part of a larger movement throughout Europe that has embraced more punitive policies similar to those used in the United States.[98] How effective this practice is has been the subject of much research in a number of developed countries.[99] The incarceration of juveniles also draws attention to the importance of keeping juvenile and adult

Keeping Incarcerated Juveniles Safe

The separation of juveniles from adults in correctional facilities is an important rule under the UN's "Standard Minimum Rules for the Administration of Juvenile Justice" because juveniles are susceptible to negative influences of more seasoned and crime-prone adult offenders. In many ways, juvenile offenders become the apprentices of adult offenders, learning about new techniques to commit delinquent and criminal acts. Another reason for separating adults and juveniles in correctional institutions is for the physical safety of juveniles. With the average juvenile offender having less physical strength than the average adult offender, adults often prey upon juveniles. Many juvenile inmates are harmed or killed by adult prisoners.

Child and teenage prisoners in Navotas City Jail in Manila, Philippines.

Martin Sasse/laif/Redux

Pictured here are child and teenage prisoners, some as young as 8 years old, in Navotas City Jail in Manila, the capital of the Philippines. In this one cell, 17 minors are housed with 28 adult prisoners. The cell is only 14 square meters. This is the way it is throughout all of the city's jails. Disease, maltreatment, and violence—especially toward the youngest inmates—are commonplace in the overcrowded, mixed jails. Little is known about the care of juvenile inmates in these jails and the conditions they must endure. Even more troubling is that less is known about incarcerated juveniles in many other developing and least developed countries.

In almost all developed countries, incarcerated juveniles are kept separate from incarcerated adults. In Australia and Belgium, for example, separate incarceration is not mandatory, but in practice this is generally done. (See Table 17.4 for all of the included developed countries.) In New Zealand, the practice differs from all of the other countries. Incarcerated juveniles are not separated from incarcerated adults. But there are a few exceptions. For example, a juvenile offender who has been transferred to adult court and sentenced to a term of imprisonment may be held at the discretion of the Director General of Social Welfare and the Secretary for Justice in a social welfare facility until age 17.

CRITICAL THINKING

What are the policies for incarcerating juvenile offenders in developed countries? What is needed to get poorer nations to adopt some of these policies to help make juvenile prisoners safer?

SOURCES: Michael Tonry and Colleen Chambers, "Juvenile Justice Cross-Nationally Considered," in Barry C. Feld and Donna M. Bishop, eds., *The Oxford Handbook of Juvenile Crime and Juvenile Justice* (New York: Oxford University Press, 2012), pp. 871–879; Trevor Bradley, Juan Tauri, and Reece Walters, "Demythologising Youth Justice in Aotearoa/New Zealand," in John Muncie and Barry Goldson, eds., *Comparative Youth Justice: Critical Issues* (Thousand Oaks, CA: Sage, 2006), p. 80.

To read more about **juvenile justice in Australia**, go to the Australian Institute of Criminology: http://www.aic.gov.au/.

inmates separate from one another. This is the subject of the Youth Stories feature entitled "Keeping Incarcerated Juveniles Safe."

Aftercare

When juveniles are released from an institution, they may be placed in an aftercare program of some kind, rather than simply returned to the community without transitional assistance. This transitional assistance can take the form of halfway houses, educational homes, or daytime training centers. The UN's "Standard Minimum Rules for the Administration of Juvenile Justice" recommend that all countries implement aftercare programs to help juveniles prepare for their return to the community.

All developed countries provide juveniles with a wide range of aftercare programs. In Hong Kong, part of the People's Republic of China, supervision orders are the most commonly used aftercare program to help juvenile offenders make a successful transition from the correctional institution to their community. Juveniles are first granted early release from a correctional facility, with the provision that they must abide by a number of conditions. These conditions differ according to the nature of the delinquent act they committed, but almost always involve regular visits with their parole officer. Some juveniles have to attend drug addiction treatment centers.[100]

In many developed countries, juvenile offenders are eligible for early release or parole much earlier than adult offenders sentenced to the same amount of time in institutions. In Germany, for example, a juvenile may be released to the community upon serving one-third of his or her sentence, while an adult must serve at least half of the sentence before being paroled.[101]

The next section profiles the juvenile justice system in England. It looks at the many different stages that juveniles may face as they go through the system, from arrest through sentencing. Comparisons are made with the US juvenile justice system. One reason for making England the subject of this profile is that, like the United States, it is a highly developed industrialized country, and so comparisons are more meaningful. Another reason is the long-standing shared history between the two countries: much of US common law is derived from English law.

A Profile of Juvenile Justice in England

In 1908, England passed legislation that established for the first time that young offenders were to be treated separately from adult offenders; the law was known as the Children Act. Like the United States, England adheres to the *parens patriae* treatment philosophy, which recognizes that youth are in need of special consideration and assistance. The Children Act was founded on three main principles:

- Juvenile offenders should be kept separate from adult criminals and should receive treatment differentiated to suit their special needs.
- Parents should be made more responsible for the wrongdoing of their children.
- The imprisonment of juveniles should be abolished.[102]

Many changes have since taken place in juvenile justice in England. The following discussion of the different stages that juveniles may face as they go through the system reflects the way things are today. (See Figure 17.2.)

Apprehension and Charge

The process of juvenile justice begins when police apprehend and charge a young person suspected of committing a delinquent act. The police are not the only ones involved at this stage. Parents or guardians of the young person are contacted and requested to attend the police station. If they cannot attend, social workers may offer assistance to the juvenile once an arrest has been made. The role of social workers at this stage is to act as an "appropriate adult" to help safeguard the legal rights of the juvenile. Alternatively, the juvenile may be represented by a defense attorney. The right to have legal representation exists throughout all stages of the juvenile justice system.[103] This is the same as in the US juvenile justice system.

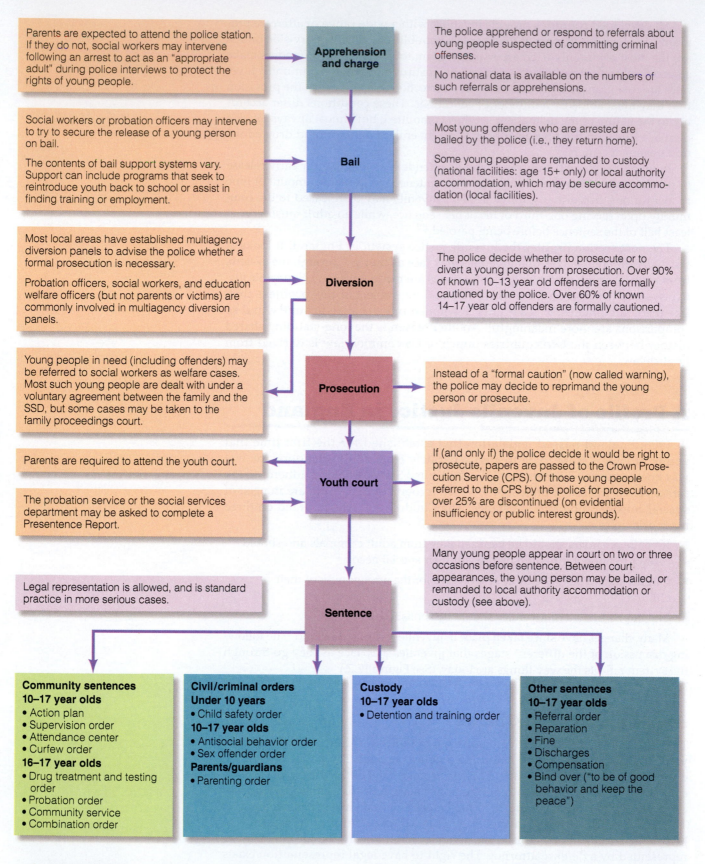

Parents are expected to attend the police station. If they do not, social workers may intervene following an arrest to act as an "appropriate adult" during police interviews to protect the rights of young people.

Apprehension and charge

The police apprehend or respond to referrals about young people suspected of committing criminal offenses.

No national data is available on the numbers of such referrals or apprehensions.

Social workers or probation officers may intervene to try to secure the release of a young person on bail.

The contents of bail support systems vary. Support can include programs that seek to reintroduce youth back to school or assist in finding training or employment.

Bail

Most young offenders who are arrested are bailed by the police (i.e., they return home).

Some young people are remanded to custody (national facilities: age 15+ only) or local authority accommodation, which may be secure accommodation (local facilities).

Most local areas have established multiagency diversion panels to advise the police whether a formal prosecution is necessary.

Probation officers, social workers, and education welfare officers (but not parents or victims) are commonly involved in multiagency diversion panels.

Diversion

The police decide whether to prosecute or to divert a young person from prosecution. Over 90% of known 10–13 year old offenders are formally cautioned by the police. Over 60% of known 14–17 year old offenders are formally cautioned.

Young people in need (including offenders) may be referred to social workers as welfare cases. Most such young people are dealt with under a voluntary agreement between the family and the SSD, but some cases may be taken to the family proceedings court.

Prosecution

Instead of a "formal caution" (now called warning), the police may decide to reprimand the young person or prosecute.

Parents are required to attend the youth court.

The probation service or the social services department may be asked to complete a Presentence Report.

Youth court

If (and only if) the police decide it would be right to prosecute, papers are passed to the Crown Prosecution Service (CPS). Of those young people referred to the CPS by the police for prosecution, over 25% are discontinued (on evidential insufficiency or public interest grounds).

Legal representation is allowed, and is standard practice in more serious cases.

Sentence

Many young people appear in court on two or three occasions before sentence. Between court appearances, the young person may be bailed, or remanded to local authority accommodation or custody (see above).

Community sentences
10–17 year olds
• Action plan
• Supervision order
• Attendance center
• Curfew order
16–17 year olds
• Drug treatment and testing order
• Probation order
• Community service
• Combination order

Civil/criminal orders
Under 10 years
• Child safety order
10–17 year olds
• Antisocial behavior order
• Sex offender order
Parents/guardians
• Parenting order

Custody
10–17 year olds
• Detention and training order

Other sentences
10–17 year olds
• Referral order
• Reparation
• Fine
• Discharges
• Compensation
• Bind over ("to be of good behavior and keep the peace")

figure 17.2

The Juvenile Justice System in England

SOURCE: Adapted from Loraine Gelsthorpe and Vicky Kemp, "Juvenile Justice: England and Wales," in John A. Winterdyk, ed., *Juvenile Justice: International Perspectives, Models and Trends*, (Boca Raton, FL: CRC Press, 2014).

Bail

Once a decision has been made by the police to charge the juvenile, a bail hearing must take place to determine whether the juvenile can go home or be remanded to custody. This differs from the practice in the United States, where relatively few juveniles hold the right to be released on bail; in fact, most states refuse juveniles the right to bail. This is because detention is seen as rehabilitative, not punitive, and statutory provisions allow juveniles to be released into the custody of their parents. (See Chapter 15 for more information on bail for juveniles in the United States.)

In England, most juvenile offenders who are arrested are granted bail. For those who are denied bail, there are two options for where they will be held. National custody facilities can be used for juveniles 15 years and older or local authority (local government) facilities may be used. For juveniles without legal representation, social workers or probation officers may assist the juvenile to be released on bail.

Precourt Diversion

Police "cautions"—the police issuing a warning to a young person involved or suspected of being involved in a delinquent act—is by far the most widely used and important precourt diversion measure in England. Begun in the 1970s, police cautions quickly became an essential component of the juvenile justice system. Although important administratively, so as to avoid the youth courts from becoming backlogged, police cautions were designed first and foremost with the best interests of the young person in mind:

> Prosecution should not occur unless it was "absolutely necessary" or as "a last resort" and that the prosecution of first-time offenders where the offence was not serious was unlikely to be "justifiable" unless there were "exceptional circumstances." Prosecution was to be regarded as a "severe step."[104]

Instead of a formal caution (now called a warning under the "final warning scheme"), the police may either issue a "reprimand" to a suspected juvenile delinquent, or they may prosecute. Reprimands involve the police making a verbal admonition. They may go something like this: "I want you to behave properly from now on and do not get yourself involved in anything that requires us to bring you down to the station." These are not recorded by police and, therefore, cannot be used in court.

In the United States, police do not use a system of formal or other cautions per se; instead, they must rely on their discretionary authority. (See Chapter 14 for more details.) Upon the arrest of a juvenile, the police have the following options: refer to juvenile court, handle informally and release, refer to criminal court, refer to welfare, or refer to another police department. It is estimated that 28 percent of all juvenile arrests are handled informally within the police department or are referred to a community service agency.[105]

Prosecution

In England, the prosecution of a juvenile offender is the mandate of the **Crown Prosecution Service**. The CPS is a national agency established by statute in 1985. It is headed by the director of public prosecutions, who is accountable to the attorney general.[106] In the United States, each jurisdiction has its own prosecuting attorney who oversees public prosecutions; with England having a central government system (there are no states), the reporting structure is somewhat different.

Importantly, in England a prosecution can only take place once the police have recommended to the CPS that it be done. This differs slightly from the practice in the United States in that the prosecutor has the power either to initiate or discontinue allegations against a juvenile. In England the prosecutor does, however, have the right to dismiss a case (allegation), and this is done in more than 25 percent of the cases

Crown Prosecution Service
The national agency in England that is in charge of all criminal prosecutions of juveniles and adults.

that the police recommend to the CPS. A prosecutor may dismiss a case for two reasons: (1) there is insufficient evidence, or (2) it is not in the public interest. The latter is done when it is felt that the harm to the offender that comes from prosecuting him or her will outweigh any benefit to society from doing so. In the event that the prosecution dismisses a case because it is not in the public interest, the prosecution may recommend to the police that they issue a formal caution.[107]

Youth Court

Like the United States and most other developed countries, England has a special court that handles juveniles; it is called a youth court. Even before the commencement of trial a juvenile may have already had a number of hearings before youth court, such as a bail hearing or a hearing on transfer to adult court. In most instances, trials of juveniles are presided over by a three-member panel of youth court lay magistrates or judges. In urban areas it is common for a trial to be presided over by a single professional or more qualified judge. Juries are not used in English youth courts. The lay or nonprofessional youth court judges are elected to a three-year term by and from the court district in which they presently serve. These judges receive special training in the juvenile offender laws. During trials they are often assisted by a legally trained court clerk.[108]

In the United States, only one juvenile court judge presides over a trial in the juvenile courtroom. Judges are assisted by court clerks, but unlike in England, court clerks in the United States rarely have law degrees and do not advise judges on legal matters. In the United States, juvenile court judges are either elected or appointed to that position, but when they are elected, it is by the public, not their fellow judges, as in England. In the United States, trial by jury in a juvenile court is seldom used; the majority of states do not allow for it.

Social workers and probation officers are other important actors in the English juvenile courtroom. Once a finding of guilt has been rendered, either party may be asked by the court to prepare a presentence report to assist the judge in sentencing. This is similar to a predisposition report in the US juvenile justice system. As in the United States, plea bargaining is allowed for juveniles in England and is used extensively.

As in the United States, juveniles in England can be transferred to adult court—what is referred to as **Crown Court**. A juvenile can be transferred to Crown Court for two main reasons: (1) the juvenile is charged with a heinous crime, such as murder, or (2) the juvenile is charged with a serious crime in conjunction with an adult.[109]

Crown Court
In England, the criminal court that deals with adult offenders or juveniles who have been transferred from youth court.

Sentencing

Once the juvenile has been convicted, the youth court judge passes sentence, either immediately following conviction or at a special hearing a short time later. As in the United States, sentences (dispositions) for juvenile offenders are much more punitive in England today than they were 20 or 30 years ago.[110] In the early 1980s, England changed its approach to the sentencing of juvenile offenders dramatically, moving away from a focus on institutional placements toward community-based sanctions. The murder of James Bulger by two 10-year-olds and an upsurge of juvenile violence in the country led to the passage of the Criminal Justice and Public Order Act in 1994. This made incarceration of juvenile offenders the preferred choice once again; it also increased the maximum sentence length and made it easier for very young juvenile offenders to be placed in correctional facilities. This punitive approach to dealing with juvenile offending, especially serious and violent juvenile offending, was continued with the passage of the Crime and Disorder Act in 1998 and the Youth Justice and Criminal Evidence Act in 1999.

As shown in Figure 17.2, a wide range of sentencing options is available to the youth court judge, including custodial sentences, community sentences, civil/criminal orders, and a general category of other sentences, which includes fines and compensation. Interestingly, juvenile boot camps modeled on the US experience have received some interest in England, with two being introduced on a demonstration basis. One offered a high-intensity treatment regime coupled with work or training placement on release, while the other offered more of a military-style regime. The former program showed more favorable recidivism results and was more cost effective,[111] but public support for boot camps proved unfavorable, and the programs were shut down.

England's punitive approach to juvenile offending is somewhat tempered by the availability of a wide range of community sentences like probation and after-care services, and the new youth rehabilitation order, which took effect with the passage of the Criminal Justice and Immigration Act in 2008.[112] For example, attendance center orders require juvenile offenders to report to a specified place in the community once a week for a range of activities, including recreation, social skills training, and vocational skills training. There are also community punishment orders, which require juvenile offenders to perform various work-related activities in the community, and community punishment and rehabilitation orders that combine community service with increased supervision.[113] Some of these options and reforms are believed to be behind a recent decline in the number of incarcerated juvenile offenders.[114]

Future of International Juvenile Justice

Harry Dammer, Erika Fairchild, and Jay Albanese noted that three issues are at the heart of the future of juvenile justice around the world: visibility, community, and anticipating trends.[115] Visibility has to do with the openness of the juvenile justice system, from hearings being open to the public to the need for greater oversight to safeguard juvenile offenders who are in institutions. In the case of the second issue, the authors argue that it is crucial that the "future of juvenile justice be guided by the recognition that communities are essential to producing delinquency, and they are essential in its prevention and in the reintegration of delinquents in society."[116] This second part of this view takes us back to Chapters 12 and 13, which highlighted the benefits of community-based prevention in the early and teen years and the need for a comprehensive juvenile justice strategy. Restorative justice and victim–offender mediation, both of which have received increased support over the last 20 years in many Western nations, are also crucial to this cause.[117]

On the matter of the key issue of anticipating trends that will impact juvenile justice, the authors contend that more needs to be done by national governments to be better informed about future potential problems and the best courses of action. This calls for more timely and high-quality research on the causes and correlates of juvenile offending. A great deal can be learned about studying past and current events that may help ameliorate looming social problems. Comparative research among similar nations may also go some way toward informing governments of shared future problems, whether it is new forms of delinquency or crises facing the juvenile justice system, such as overcrowding or declining resources for treatment services.

This knowledge-based approach is applicable to current events in many countries around the world. Some developed countries have taken measures to get tough on juvenile offending. In some cases, this is being done because of a real increase in delinquency, particularly violence. In other cases, this is being done because of a perceived increase in delinquency coupled with a political response to a "punitive public" (at least for violent juvenile offenders).[118] And while a more punitive juvenile justice system seems to be the future for many countries, a number are also making concerted efforts to reserve punitive sanctions for only the most serious and violent juvenile offenders and to provide more effective treatment, reentry, and aftercare services.

SUMMARY

1 Outline some of the different delinquency problems facing the regions of the world

- Juvenile delinquency poses a serious problem to all regions of the world. Violent hate crimes plague many European countries.
- Gang violence is prevalent in the Americas and remains a concern in parts of Africa.

2 Identify the main challenges of conducting international comparisons of delinquency

- There is a long history of comparing delinquency and juvenile justice systems across different countries, but important issues need to be considered when making international comparisons. Differences in legal systems, culture, language, and other factors demand that close attention be paid to what is being compared and what countries are being compared.
- Comparing delinquency rates across countries has three main challenges: Legal definitions of juvenile crime vary from country to country, measurement of juvenile crime varies across countries, and the age group defined as "juvenile" is not always the same.

3 Discuss the benefits of international comparative research

- Knowledge of the nature of juvenile delinquency and how juvenile justice systems operate in other countries can be useful for concerned citizens, social scientists, and policy makers.
- Comparative research can provide information on how well or how poorly one country is doing relative to other countries.
- Comparative research can lead to important discoveries that lead to action, such as more funding for problem-solving policing tactics to reduce juvenile gun violence.

4 Compare trends in juvenile violence, property crime, and drug use in Europe and North America

- From the mid-1990s to the late 2000s, the upward trend in juvenile violence in Europe continued, while this trend was reversed in North America, with rates continuing to drop or stabilize into the mid-2010s.
- During the first time period, juvenile property crime increased very little, with some countries showing no increase or a small decrease, followed by a downward trend in juvenile property crime across Europe (up to late 2000s) and North America (into the early 2010s).
- Recent figures for teenage drug use reveal that American students are more likely to use marijuana and other illicit drugs over their lifetime, while European students are more likely to smoke cigarettes and use alcohol.

5 Appraise key explanations for changes in these types of delinquency in Europe and North America

- Key explanations for the increase in teen violence include an explosive mix of racial tension, poverty, envy, drug abuse, broken families, unemployment, and alienation.

6 Interpret the work of the United Nations to help countries improve their juvenile justice systems

- Many countries in the world have formal juvenile justice systems, but many do not.
- In an effort to get more countries around the world to develop juvenile justice systems and improve the administration of juvenile justice, in 1985 the United Nations adopted the "Standard Minimum Rules for the Administration of Juvenile Justice."

7 Identify differences and similarities on key issues of juvenile justice around the world

- Juvenile justice systems in developed countries have many commonalities but also differ in many respects.
- Some of the key issues include juvenile policing, age of criminal responsibility, presence of juvenile court, transfers to adult court, sentencing, treatment of incarcerated juveniles, and aftercare programs.

8 Outline the key stages of juvenile justice in England

- The juvenile justice system in England was developed at the beginning of the twentieth century.
- The key stages of juvenile justice in England include apprehension and charge, bail, precourt diversion, prosecution, youth court, and sentencing.

9 Explain the differences and similarities in juvenile justice in the United States and England

- Like the United States, England adheres to the treatment philosophy known as *parens patriae*, which recognizes that youth are in need of special consideration and assistance.
- There are many other similarities between the British and US juvenile justice systems, such as the use of bail hearings, plea bargaining, and the ability to transfer youths to adult court.
- There are also a number of important differences in juvenile justice between the two countries. For example, in England police use a system of formal or other cautions to divert juveniles from youth court, while in the United States police rely on their discretionary authority. In England, trials of juveniles in youth court are presided over by a three-member panel of youth court judges. In the United States, only one juvenile court judge presides over a trial in the juvenile courtroom.

KEY TERMS

QUESTIONS FOR DISCUSSION

1. International comparisons of delinquency and juvenile justice systems are best done "like-with-like." What are some of the things that need to be considered in order to produce valid comparisons across countries?

2. What are some of the benefits and challenges in making international comparisons of delinquency?

3. Across the world there is a great deal of variation in the minimum age a person can be held responsible for his or her criminal actions. What are the advantages and disadvantages of having a low minimum age?

4. Which developed countries appear to be the most lenient in their treatment of juvenile offenders, and which appear to be the most punitive?

5. What are some of the differences between juvenile justice systems in the United States and England? Identify two or three key differences and discuss how these differences could benefit the other country.

VIEWPOINT

As the recently elected prime minister of the United Kingdom, you are faced with having to deal with national and international implications arising from the following case, which still resonates today. In August 2001, two British teenagers, Jon Venables and Robert Thompson, were granted parole after serving eight years for the brutal murder of 2-year-old James Bulger. On February 12, 1993, these two boys, then 10 years old, abducted James from a mall just outside Liverpool. James's mother had stopped to look at a display window of one of the stores, letting go of James's hand for a few seconds. When she turned around James was gone. The whole event was caught on the mall's surveillance system. The horrifying video showed the two boys walking up to James and calmly leading him out of the mall. The 2-year-old's badly beaten body was found a short time later near railway tracks, a short distance from the mall. Because of the video, the two child killers were quickly apprehended and taken into custody. Throughout England there was a kind of collective agony for the death of the boy and the mother's loss of her young son.

The capture and subsequent trial of these two boys sparked debate throughout the country and the world. Immediately, England and other countries began to reconsider the minimum age at which children can be held responsible for their delinquent or criminal actions. Fortunately for this case, in England the minimum age was 10 years. But in other countries, such as Canada, Italy, Japan, and Russia, the minimum age is much higher.

Like the capture and trial of these child killers, their release and events leading up to it caused national and international debate over the administration of juvenile justice. In January 1994, it was learned that the decision of Lord Justice Morland to detain the boys "at Her Majesty's pleasure"—the equivalent of a life sentence—had been recommended to be no higher than eight years. As a discretionary sentence, this was legal, but was it too lenient for the crime? England and other countries were soon contemplating mandatory minimum sentences for juvenile offenders, and in England the then Home Secretary, Michael Howard, tried unsuccessfully to have the boys serve a minimum of 15 years. Then, in the early months of 2001, the public learned that the two boys were to be paroled sometime in the summer. In addition, their identities were to be changed to protect them from reprisal from the public, and there were rumors about them being sent to another country.

These events put England's juvenile offender laws and juvenile justice system to an extreme test in trying to balance the rights of the offender with the rights of the community and the moral and public outrage caused by this violent act. The international implications of these events were wide reaching, causing some countries to reexamine their juvenile offender laws and how they deal with violent juvenile offenders. As prime minister, how would you answer these questions from the media?

- Did the English juvenile justice system fail the victim's family and society as a whole?

- Should England have done more to keep these juveniles locked up for a longer time, or was the sentence appropriate?

- What can the English government do to try to prevent this from happening again? Should they change their juvenile offender laws and policies?

DOING RESEARCH ON THE WEB

For ways to think about this issue, go to the Campbell Collaboration Crime and Justice Coordinating Group (CCJG) (https://www.campbellcollaboration.org /crime-and-justice/explore/crime-and-justice-2), an international network of researchers that prepares and disseminates systematic reviews of high-quality research on methods to reduce crime and delinquency and improve the quality of justice. The European Institute for Crime Prevention and Control (http://www.heuni.fi/), affiliated with the United Nations and based in Helsinki, promotes the international exchange of information on crime prevention and control among European countries.

The World Health Organization (WHO) (http://www.who.int/) is the directing and coordinating authority for health within the UN system. It is responsible for providing leadership on global health matters, and injuries and violence prevention are a major component of its mandate. Another UN agency, the United Nations Office on Drugs and Crime (UNODC) (http://www.unodc.org/) is a global leader in the fight against illicit drugs and international crime.

The mission of the Organisation for Economic Co-operation and Development (OECD) (http://www.oecd.org/) is to promote policies that will improve the economic and social well-being of people around the world. A major component of its mandate is the prevention of juvenile delinquency.

NOTES

All URLs accessed October 2016.

1. Marcelo F. Aebi et al., *European Sourcebook of Crime and Criminal Justice, 2014* (Helsinki, Finland: European Institute for Crime Prevention and Control, 2014); Marian FitzGerald, Alex Stevens, and Chris Hale, *A Review of the Knowledge on Juvenile Violence: Trends, Policies and Responses in the EU Member States* (Brussels: European Crime Prevention Network, European-Commission, 2004), p. 51.

2. Richard Wortley, "Child Pornography," in Mangai Natarajan, ed., *International Crime and Justice* (New York: Cambridge University Press, 2011).

3. Pornography Cartel Broken," *Crime and Justice International* 17:13 (2001).

4. Alexis A. Aronowitz, "Understanding Trafficking in Human Beings: A Human Rights, Public Health, and Criminal Justice Issue," in Natarajan, ed., *International Crime and Justice.*

5. Sarah Shannon, "The Global Sex Trade: Humans as the Ultimate Commodity," *Crime and Justice International* 17:5–7 (2001).

6. David Binder, "12 Nations in Southeast Europe Pursue Traffickers in Sex Trade," *New York Times,* October 19, 2003, p. 6.

7. Reuters, "18 Dead in Shooting at High School in Eastern Germany," *New York Times,* April 26, 2002; Edmund L. Andrews, "Deep Shock in Germany, Where Guns Are Rare," *New York Times,* April 28, 2002, p. 15.

8. Stephan Lhotzky, "Will Kai Become a Skinhead? Cultures of Hate— Germany the New Europe," *Reclaiming Children and Youth* 10:86–91 (2001).

9. Christian Pfeiffer, "The Impoverishment of the Lower Classes Is Increasing Juvenile Aggressivity," *European Education* 32:95–100 (2000).

10. John Tagliabue, "Synagogue in Paris Firebombed; Raids Go On," *New York Times,* April 5, 2002, p. 5; John Tagliabue, "Paris Takes Aim at Its Crime Rate," *New York Times,* August 24, 2003, p. 3, section 5.

11. Associated Press, "As Anniversary of Riots Nears, Suburban Youths March on Paris," *New York Times,* October 26, 2006.

12. Gendrot, "France: The Politicization of Youth Justice," p. 59.

13. Roberta Belli, Joshua D. Freilich, and Graeme R. Newman, "Migration and Crime," in Natarajan, ed., *International Crime and Justice.*

14. Richard Bernstein, "Crimes Most Outlandish, but Why in Germany?" *New York Times,* February 11, 2004; Christian Pfeiffer, "Juvenile Crime and Violence in Europe," in Michael Tonry, ed., *Crime and Justice: A Review of Research,* Vol. 23 (Chicago: University of Chicago Press, 1998), p. 300.

15. FitzGerald, Stevens, and Hale, *A Review of the Knowledge on Juvenile Violence;* Martin Killias and Marcelo F. Aebi, "Crime Trends in Europe from 1990 to 1996: How Europe Illustrates the Limits of the American Experience," *European Journal on Criminal Policy and Research* 8:43–63 (2000).

16. John Hagan, Hans Merkens, and Klaus Boehnke, "Delinquency and Disdain: Social Capital and the Control of Right-Wing Extremism Among East and West Berlin Youth," *American Journal of Sociology* 100:1028–1053 (1995).

17. John A. Winterdyk and Anne Miller, "Juvenile Justice and Young Offenders: A Canadian Overview of Canada," in John A. Winterdyk, ed., *Juvenile Justice: International Perspectives, Models and Trends,* (Boca Raton, FL: CRC Press, 2014).

18. Randal C. Archibold, "Killer, 15, Is Sentenced in Drug Case in Mexico," *New York Times,* July 26, 2011.

19. Mario Berlanga, "Want to Make Ethical Purchases? Stop Buying Illegal Drugs," *New York Times*, September 27, 2016.

20. Associated Press, "Official: Student Killed in Mexico Was US Citizen," *New York Times*, November 5, 2010.

21. Alexei Barrionuevo, "Ecstasy Ensnares a New Class of Teenage Users in Brazil," *New York Times*, February 15, 2009.

22. Larry Rohter, "Rio's Drug Wars Begin to Take Toll on Tourism," *New York Times*, April 27, 2003, p. 3, section 5; Larry Rohter, "As Crime and Politics Collide in Rio, City Cowers in Fear," *New York Times*, May 8, 2003.

23. Alexei Barrionuevo, "Brazil Mourns Children Gunned Down at School," *New York Times*, April 10, 2011, p. 15.

24. Tim Weiner, "Cover-Up Found in Honduras Prison Killings," *New York Times*, May 20, 2003; Ginger Thompson, "Guatemala Bleeds in Vise of Gangs and Vengeance," *New York Times*, January 1, 2006, p. 4.

25. Louise Marsh, Rob McGee, and Sheila Williams, "Why Do New Zealand High School Students Carry Weapons?" *Australian and New Zealand Journal of Criminology* 44:425–439 (2011).

26. Australian Institute of Criminology, *Homicide in Australia: 2010–11 to 2011–12 National Homicide Monitoring Program Annual Report* (Canberra: Australian Institute of Criminology, 2015), Tables 11 and 15.

27. National Police Agency, *White Paper on Crime 2014* (Tokyo: National Police Agency, 2015). Available at http://hakusyo1.moj.go.jp/en /nendo_nfm.html.

28. Reuters, "Stabbing Spree on Japanese Buses Leaves 13 Injured," *New York Times*, December 17, 2010.

29. Norimitsu Onishi, "Crime Rattles Japanese Calm, Attracting Politician's Notice," *New York Times*, September 6, 2003.

30. Shinpei Nawa, "Postwar Fourth Wave of Juvenile Delinquency and Tasks of Juvenile Police," in *Current Juvenile Police Policy in Japan* (Tokyo: Police Policy Research Center, National Police Academy of Japan, 2006), Table 1.

31. "Japan Again Hit by Incidents of Violent Teen Crime," *Crime and Justice International* 17:15 (2001).

32. Horace Lyons, "Hikikomori and Youth Crime," *Crime and Justice International* 17:9–10 (2001).

33. Trevor Ryan, "Creating 'Problem Kids': Juvenile Crime in Japan and Revisions to the Juvenile Act," *Journal of Japanese Law* 10:153–188 (2005), at 153.

34. Edward Wong, "Fifth Deadly Attack on School Haunts China," *New York Times*, May 12, 2010.

35. Associated Press, "Man Stabs 22 Children in China," *New York Times*, December 14, 2012.

36. Brett Finn, "World in Brief," *Crime and Justice International* 23(101):42 (2007); Dawei Wang, "The Study of Juvenile Delinquency and Juvenile Protection in the People's Republic of China," *Crime and Justice International* 22(94):4–13 (2006), at 5.

37. Jianming Mei and Mu Wang, "Social Change, Crime, and Criminology in China," *Crime and Justice International* 23(97):14–21 (2007); Liling Yue, "Youth Injustice in China," in Winterdyk, ed., *Juvenile Justice Systems: International Perspectives*, 2nd ed.

38. Reuters, "Africans See Economic Gains, Democracy Losses—Index," *New York Times*, October 4, 2010.

39. For a general overview, see James Lynch and William Alex Pridemore, "Crime in International Perspective," in James Q. Wilson and Joan Petersilia, eds., *Crime and Public Policy* (New York: Oxford University Press, 2011); Piers Beirne, "Cultural Relativism and Comparative Criminology," *Contemporary Crises* 7:371–391 (1983).

40. John Henry Sloan et al., "Handgun Regulation, Crime, Assaults, and Homicide: A Tale of Two Cities," *New England Journal of Medicine* 319:1256–1262 (1988); Martin Killias, John van Kesteren, and Martin Rindlisbacher, "Guns, Violent Crime, and Suicide in 21 Countries," *Canadian Journal of Criminology* 43:429–448 (2001); Richard R. Bennett, "Constructing Cross-Cultural Theories in Criminology," *Criminology* 18:252–268 (1980); David Shichor, "Crime Patterns and Socioeconomic Development: A Cross-National Analysis," *Criminal Justice Review* 15:64–77 (1990); David P. Farrington, Patrick A. Langan, and Per-Olof H. Wikström, "Changes in Crime and Punishment in America, England and Sweden Between the 1980s and the 1990s," *Studies on Crime and Crime Prevention* 3:104–131 (1994); Patrick A. Langan and David P. Farrington, *Crime and Justice in the United States and in England and Wales, 1981–96* (Washington, DC: Bureau of Justice Statistics, 1998); Joanne Savage and Bryan Vila, "Lagged Effects of Nurturance on Crime: A Cross-National Comparison," *Studies on Crime and Crime Prevention* 6:101–120 (1997); Marshall B. Clinard, *Cities with Little Crime: The Case of Switzerland* (New York: Cambridge University Press, 1978); Freda Adler, *Nations Not Obsessed with Crime* (Littleton,

CO: Rothman, 1983); Manuel Eisner, "Crime, Problem Drinking, and Drug Use: Patterns of Problem Behavior in Cross-National Perspective," *Annals of the American Academy of Political and Social Science* 580:201–225 (2002).

41. Gregory J. Howard, Martin Gottschalk, and Graeme R. Newman, "Criminology, Method, and Qualitative Comparative Analysis," in Natarajan, ed., *International Crime and Justice*; Lynch and Pridemore, "Crime in International Perspective"; Graeme R. Newman and Gregory J. Howard, "Introduction: Data Sources and Their Use," in Graeme R. Newman, ed., *Global Report on Crime and Justice* (New York: Oxford University Press, 1999), p. 18.

42. Jan van Dijk and Kristiina Kangaspunta, "Piecing Together the Cross-National Crime Puzzle," *National Institute of Justice Journal* 242:34–41 (2000).

43. Joan McCord, Cathy Spatz Widom, and Nancy Crowell, eds., *Juvenile Crime, Juvenile Justice*, Panel on Juvenile Crime: Prevention, Treatment, and Control (Washington, DC: National Academy Press, 2001), p. 17.

44. Pfeiffer, "Juvenile Crime and Violence in Europe," p. 261.

45. For more detail on the different international sources, see Natarajan, ed., *International Crime and Justice*; Lynch and Pridemore, "Crime in International Perspective"; Gregory J. Howard, Graeme Newman, and William Alex Pridemore, "Theory, Method, and Data in Comparative Criminology," in David Duffee, ed., *Measurement and Analysis of Crime and Justice: Volume 4. Criminal Justice 2000* (Washington, DC: National Institute of Justice, 2000).

46. Marcelo F. Aebi et al., *European Sourcebook of Crime and Criminal Justice Statistics, 2014*, 5th ed. (Helsinki, Finland: European Institute for Crime Prevention and Control, 2014).

47. Newman and Howard, "Introduction: Data Sources and Their Use."

48. Gary LaFree, *Losing Legitimacy: Street Crime and the Decline of Social Institutions in America* (Boulder, CO: Westview Press, 1997), p. 29.

49. See, for example, Franklin E. Zimring and Gordon Hawkins, *Crime Is Not the Problem: Lethal Violence in America* (New York: Oxford University Press, 1997).

50. Josine Junger-Tas, Ineke H. Marshall, Dirk Enzmann, Martin Killias, Majone Steketee, and Beata Gruszczynska, eds., *Juvenile Delinquency in Europe and Beyond: Results of the Second International Self-Report Delinquency Study* (New York: Springer, 2010); Josine Junger-Tas, Gert-Jan Terlouw, and Malcolm W. Klein, eds., *Delinquent Behavior Among Young People in the Western World: First Results of the International Self-Report Delinquency Study* (New York: Kugler Publications, 1994).

51. Ni He and Ineke H. Marshall, "The International Self-Report Delinquency Study (ISRD)," in Natarajan, ed., *International Crime and Justice*.

52. See also Philip L. Reichel, *Comparative Criminal Justice Systems: A Topical Approach*, 3rd ed. (Upper Saddle River, NJ: Prentice Hall, 2002), pp. 4–5.

53. See, for example, Clinard, *Cities with Little Crime: The Case of Switzerland*; Adler, *Nations Not Obsessed with Crime*.

54. Harry R. Dammer and Jay S. Albanese, *Comparative Criminal Justice Systems*, 5th ed. (Belmont, CA: Wadsworth, 2014).

55. Phil Williams, "Emerging Issues: Transnational Crime and Its Control," in Newman, ed., *Global Report on Crime and Justice*, p. 222.

56. Williams, "Emerging Issues: Transnational Crime and Its Control," p. 222.

57. Ibid., p. 221.

58. Mark Findlay, *The Globalisation of Crime: Understanding Transnational Relationships in Context* (Cambridge: Cambridge University Press, 1999).

59. Pfeiffer, "Juvenile Crime and Violence in Europe."

60. Fitzgerald, Stevens, and Hale, *A Review of the Knowledge on Juvenile Violence: Trends, Policies and Responses in the EU Member States*.

61. Pfeiffer, "Juvenile Crime and Violence in Europe," p. 256.

62. Fitzgerald, Stevens, and Hale, *A Review of the Knowledge on Juvenile Violence: Trends, Policies and Responses in the EU Member States*, p. 51.

63. Aebi et al., *European Sourcebook of Crime and Criminal Justice Statistics—2014*.

64. Charles Puzzanchera and Wei Kang, "Easy Access to FBI Arrest Statistics 1994–2012," 2014, http://www.ojjdp.gov/ojstatbb/ezaucr/.

65. Marcelo F. Aebi and Antonia Linde, "Is There a Crime Drop in Western Europe?" *European Journal of Criminal Policy and Research* 16:251–277 (2010).

66. Mary K. Allen, *Police-Reported Crime Statistics in Canada, 2015* (Ottawa: Canadian Centre for Justice Statistics, 2016), Chart 16.

67. Marnie Wallace, *Police-Reported Crime Statistics in Canada, 2008* (Ottawa: Canadian Centre for Justice Statistics, 2009), Chart 13a;

Rebecca Kong, *Canadian Crime Statistics, 1996* (Ottawa: Canadian Centre for Justice Statistics, 1997), p. 17, Table 4.

68. Mary K. Allen and Tamy Superle, *Youth Crime in Canada, 2014* (Ottawa: Canadian Centre for Justice Statistics, 2015), Chart 2; Wallace, *Police-Reported Crime Statistics in Canada, 2008*, Chart 13a.

69. Puzzanchera and Kang, "Easy Access to FBI Arrest Statistics 1994–2012."

70. Aebi and Linde, "Is There a Crime Drop in Western Europe?"; Fitzgerald, Stevens, and Hale, *A Review of the Knowledge on Juvenile Violence: Trends, Policies and Responses in the EU Member States*, p. 49.

71. Ludwig Kraus et al., *The 2015 ESPAD Report: Results from the European School Survey Project on Alcohol and Other Drugs* (Lisbon, Portugal: European Monitoring Centre for Drugs and Drug Addiction, 2016).

72. Lloyd D. Johnston, Patrick M. O'Malley, Richard A. Miech, Jerald G. Bachman, and John E. Schulenberg, *Monitoring the Future National Results on Drug Use, 1975–2015: Overview, Key Findings on Adolescent Drug Use* (Ann Arbor: Institute for Social Research, University of Michigan, 2016), Table 5.

73. Kraus et al., *The 2015 ESPAD Report: Results from the European School Survey Project on Alcohol and Other Drugs*, Table 6.

74. Björn Hibell et al., *The 2011 ESPAD Report: Substance Use Among Students in 36 European Countries* (Stockholm: The Swedish Council for Information on Alcohol and Other Drugs, Council of Europe, and Pompidou Group, 2012), p. 136.

75. Richard B. Felson, Jukka Savolainen, Thoroddur Bjarnason, Amy L. Anderson, and I. Tusty Zohra, "The Cultural Context of Adolescent Drinking and Violence in 30 European Countries," *Criminology* 49:699–728 (2011).

76. Aebi and Linde, "Is There a Crime Drop in Western Europe?"

77. Elmar G. M. Weitekamp, Hans-Juergen Kerner, and Gernot Trueg, *International Comparison of Juvenile Justice Systems: Report to the National Academy of Sciences Commission on Behavioral and Social Sciences and Education* (Tuebingen, Germany: Institute of Criminology, University of Tuebingen, July 1999), p. 13.

78. National Advisory Commission on Criminal Justice Standards and Goals, *Task Force Report on Juvenile Justice and Delinquency Prevention* (Washington, DC: Law Enforcement Assistance Administration, 1976), p. 258.

79. Dammer and Albanese, *Comparative Criminal Justice Systems*.

80. John A. Winterdyk, "Juvenile Justice and Young Offenders: An Overview of Canada," in Winterdyk, ed., *Juvenile Justice Systems: International Perspectives*, 2nd ed., p. 91.

81. Robin T. Fitzgerald and Peter J. Carrington, "Disproportionate Minority Contact in Canada: Police and Visible Minority Youth," *Canadian Journal of Criminology and Criminal Justice* 53:449–486 (2011).

82. Chris Lewis, Graham Brooks, Thomas Ellis, and Koichi Hamai, "Comparing Japanese and English Juvenile Justice: Reflections on Change in the Twenty-First Century," *Crime Prevention and Community Safety* 11(2):75–89 (2009).

83. Minoru Yokoyama, "Juvenile Justice and Juvenile Crime: An Overview of Japan," in Winterdyk, ed., *Juvenile Justice Systems: International Perspectives*, 2nd ed., pp. 337–338.

84. Michael Tonry and Colleen Chambers, "Juvenile Justice Cross-Nationally Considered," in Barry C. Feld and Donna M. Bishop, eds., *The Oxford Handbook of Juvenile Crime and Juvenile Justice* (New York: Oxford University Press, 2012), p. 879; Satyanshu Mukherjee and Philip Reichel, "Bringing to Justice," in Newman, ed., *Global Report on Crime and Justice*, p. 79.

85. Winterdyk, ed., *Juvenile Justice Systems: International Perspectives*, p. xviii.

86. Tonry and Chambers, "Juvenile Justice Cross-Nationally Considered," p. 871.

87. Weitekamp, Kerner, and Trueg, *International Comparison of Juvenile Justice Systems*, p. 83.

88. Ibid., p. 268.

89. Ibid., p. 253.

90. Doob and Sprott, "Youth Justice in Canada," p. 232.

91. Uberto Gatti and Alfredo Verde, "Comparative Juvenile Justice: An Overview of Italy," in Winterdyk, ed., *Juvenile Justice Systems: International Perspectives*, 2nd ed., p. 305.

92. Weitekamp, Kerner, and Trueg, *International Comparison of Juvenile Justice Systems*, pp. 208, 223.

93. 577 U.S. ___ (2016).

94. James L. Williams and Daniel G. Rodeheaver, "Punishing Juvenile Offenders in Russia," *International Criminal Justice Review* 12:93–110 (2002), at 104.

95. Reuters, "Rights Groups Welcome Iran Ban on Youth Executions," *New York Times*, October 18, 2008.

96. Anette Storgaard, "Juvenile Justice in Scandinavia," *Journal of Scandinavian Studies in Criminology and Crime Prevention* 5:188–204 (2004), at 198–199; see also Tonry and Chambers, "Juvenile Justice Cross-Nationally Considered," pp. 882–883.

97. John Muncie and Barry Goldson, "States of Transition: Convergence and Diversity in International Youth Justice," in Muncie and Goldson, eds., *Comparative Youth Justice: Critical Issues*, p. 206.

98. Alfred Blumstein, "Crossnational Measures of Punitiveness," in Natarajan, ed., *International Crime and Justice*; Alfred Blumstein, "The Roots of Punitiveness in a Democracy," *Journal of Scandinavian Studies in Criminology and Crime Prevention* 8:2–16 (2007).

99. See Rolf Loeber, Machteld Hoeve, N. Wim Slot, and Peter van der Laan, eds., *Persisters and Desisters in Crime from Adolescence into Adulthood: Explanation, Prevention and Punishment* (Surrey, UK: Ashgate, 2012); Martin Killias, Santiago Redondo, and Jerzy Sarnecki, "European Perspectives," in *From Juvenile Delinquency to Adult Crime: Criminal Careers, Justice Policy, and Prevention*, eds., Rolf Loeber and David P. Farrington (New York: Oxford University Press, 2012); Andrew McGrath, "The Effect of Custodial Penalties on Juvenile Reoffending," *Australian and New Zealand Journal of Criminology* 45:26–44 (2012).

100. Harold Traver, "Juvenile Delinquency in Hong Kong," in Winterdyk, ed., *Juvenile Justice Systems: International Perspectives*, 2nd ed., p. 211.

101. Hans-Jörg Albrecht, "Youth Justice in Germany," in Tonry and Doob, eds., *Youth Crime and Youth Justice: Comparative and Cross-National Perspectives. Crime and Justice: A Review of Research*, Vol. 31, p. 473.

102. Loraine Gelsthorpe and Vicky Kemp, "Juvenile Justice: England and Wales," in Winterdyk, ed., *Juvenile Justice: International Perspectives, Models and Trends*.

103. Weitekamp, Kerner, and Trueg, *International Comparison of Juvenile Justice Systems*, p. 90.

104. Loraine Gelsthorpe and Vicky Kemp, "Comparative Juvenile Justice: England and Wales," in Winterdyk, ed., *Juvenile Justice Systems: International Perspectives*, 2nd ed., p. 138.

105. Federal Bureau of Investigation, *Crime in the United States, 2014* (Washington, DC: US Government Printing Office, 2015), Table 68.

106. Weitekamp, Kerner, and Trueg, *International Comparison of Juvenile Justice Systems*, p. 90.

107. Ibid., p. 103.

108. Ibid., p. 100.

109. Ibid., p. 90.

110. Tonry and Chambers, "Juvenile Justice Cross-Nationally Considered," p. 881.

111. David P. Farrington, John Ditchfield, Gareth Hancock, Philip Howard, Darrick Jolliffe, Mark S. Livingston, and Kate A. Painter, *Evaluation of Two Intensive Regimes for Young Offenders*, Home Office Research Study No. 239 (London: Home Office, 2002).

112. John Graham, "Responding to Youth Crime," in David J. Smith, ed., *A New Response to Youth Crime* (Cullompton, Devon, UK: Willan Publishing, 2010), p. 119.

113. Gelsthorpe and Kemp, "Juvenile Justice: England and Wales."

114. Graham, "Responding to Youth Crime," p. 127.

115. Harry R. Dammer and Erika Fairchild, with Jay S. Albanese, *Comparative Criminal Justice Systems*, 3rd ed. (Belmont, CA: Wadsworth, 2006), p. 349.

116. Ibid., pp. 349–350.

117. Muncie and Goldson, "States of Transition: Convergence and Diversity in International Youth Justice," p. 209.

118. Julian V. Roberts, "Public Opinion and Youth Justice," in Tonry and Doob, eds., *Youth Crime and Youth Justice: Comparative and Cross-National Perspectives. Crime and Justice: A Review of Research*, Vol. 31, pp. 509–510; see also Julian V. Roberts and Ross Hastings, "Public Opinion and Crime Prevention: A Review of International Trends," in Brandon C. Welsh and David P. Farrington, eds., *The Oxford Handbook of Crime Prevention* (New York: Oxford University Press, 2012).

Glossary

abandonment Parents physically leave their children with the intention of completely severing the parent–child relationship.

active speech A form of expression that involves speaking or taking some other physical action such as parading with a banner.

addict A person with an overpowering physical or psychological need to continue taking a particular substance or drug.

addiction-prone personality A personality that has a compulsion for mood-altering drugs, believed by some to be the cause of substance abuse.

adjudicatory hearing The fact-finding process wherein the juvenile court determines whether there is sufficient evidence to sustain the allegations in a petition.

adolescent-limited offenders Kids who get into minor scrapes as youths but whose misbehavior ends when they enter adulthood.

advisement hearing A preliminary protective or temporary custody hearing in which the court will review the facts, determine whether removal of the child is justified, and notify parents of the charges against them.

aftercare Transitional assistance to juveniles, equivalent to adult parole, to help youths adjust to community life.

age of onset Age at which youths begin their delinquent careers; early onset is believed to be linked with chronic offending patterns.

aging-out process (also known as desistance or spontaneous remission) The tendency for youths to reduce the frequency of their offending behavior as they age; aging-out is thought to occur among all groups of offenders.

alcohol Fermented or distilled liquids containing ethanol, an intoxicating substance.

alexithymia A deficit in emotional cognition that prevents people from being aware of their feelings or being able to understand or talk about their thoughts and emotions; sufferers seem robotic and emotionally dead.

anabolic steroids Drugs used by athletes and bodybuilders to gain muscle bulk and strength.

anesthetic drugs Central nervous system depressants.

anomie Normlessness produced by rapidly shifting moral values; according to Merton, anomie occurs when personal goals cannot be achieved using available means.

antisocial personality disorder (ASPD) A person lacking in warmth and affection, exhibiting inappropriate behavior responses, and unable to learn from experience.

appellate process Allows the juvenile an opportunity to have the case brought before a reviewing court after it has been heard in juvenile or family court.

Arizona v. Gant This case placed specific limitations on police searches of a suspect's vehicle.

arousal theorists Delinquency experts who believe that aggression is a function of the level of an individual's need for stimulation or arousal from the environment. Those who require more stimulation may act in an aggressive manner to meet their needs.

arrest Taking a person into the custody of the law to restrain the accused until he or she can be held accountable for the offense in court proceedings.

at-risk youth Young people who are extremely vulnerable to the negative consequences of school failure, substance abuse, and early sexuality.

attachment theory A form of psychodynamic tradition that holds that the ability to form attachments—emotional bonds to another person—has important lasting psychological implications that follow adolescents across the life span.

attention deficit hyperactivity disorder (ADHD) A disorder in which a child shows a developmentally inappropriate lack of attention, impulsivity, and hyperactivity.

authority conflict pathway Pathway to delinquent deviance that begins at an early age with stubborn behavior and leads to defiance and then to authority avoidance.

bail Amount of money that must be paid as a condition of pretrial release to ensure that the accused will return for subsequent proceedings. Bail is normally set by the judge at the initial appearance, and if unable to make bail, the accused is detained in jail.

balanced probation Programs that integrate community protection, accountability of the juvenile offender, competency, and individualized attention to the juvenile offender; based on the principle that juvenile offenders must accept responsibility for their behavior.

balancing-of-the-interests approach Efforts of the courts to balance the parents' natural right to raise a child with the child's right to grow into adulthood free from physical abuse or emotional harm.

barrio A Spanish word meaning "neighborhood."

battered child syndrome Nonaccidental physical injury of children by their parents or guardians.

behaviorism Branch of psychology concerned with the study of observable behavior rather than unconscious processes; focuses on particular stimuli and responses to them.

behavior modification A technique for shaping desired behaviors through a system of rewards and punishments.

best interests of the child A philosophical viewpoint that encourages the state to take control of wayward children and provide care, custody, and treatment to remedy delinquent behavior.

Bethel School District No. 403 v. Fraser A school has the right to control lewd and offensive speech that undermines the educational mission.

bifurcated process The procedure of separating adjudicatory and dispositionary hearings so different levels of evidence can be heard at each.

biosocial theory A theory of delinquency causation that integrates biologically determined traits and environmental stimuli.

blended families Nuclear families that are the product of divorce and remarriage, blending one parent from each of two families and their combined children into one family unit.

Board of Education of Independent School District No. 92 of Pottawatomie County et al. v. Earls et al. Drug testing of students by school officials, if done in a reasonable fashion, is a legitimate exercise of school authority.

boot camps Juvenile programs that combine get-tough elements from adult programs with education, substance abuse treatment, and social skills training.

broken home Home in which one or both parents are absent due to divorce or separation; children in such an environment may be prone to antisocial behavior.

broken windows policing Drawing on the broken windows theory developed by Wilson and Kelling, police target disorderly behaviors and conditions in an effort to prevent the onset of more serious crime problems.

bullying Repeated, negative acts committed by one or more children against another; the acts may be physical or verbal.

callous and unemotional traits (CU) A persistent pattern of behavior that reflects a disregard for others, and also a lack of empathy and generally deficient affect.

chancery courts Court proceedings created in fifteenth-century England to oversee the lives of highborn minors who were orphaned or otherwise could not care for themselves.

child abuse Any physical, emotional, or sexual trauma to a child, including neglecting to give proper care and attention, for which no reasonable explanation can be found.

Children's Aid Society Child saving organization that took children from the streets of large cities and placed them with farm families on the prairie.

child savers Nineteenth-century reformers who developed programs for troubled youth and influenced legislation creating the juvenile justice system; today some critics view them as being more concerned with control of the poor than with their welfare.

chivalry hypothesis (also known as paternalism hypothesis) The view that low female crime and delinquency rates are a reflection of the leniency with which police treat female offenders.

choice theory Holds that youths will engage in delinquent and criminal behavior after weighing the consequences and benefits of their actions; delinquent behavior is a rational choice made by a motivated offender who perceives that the chances of gain outweigh any possible punishment or loss.

chronic delinquent offenders (also known as chronic juvenile offenders, chronic delinquents, or chronic recidivists) Youths who have been arrested four or more times during their minority and perpetuate a striking majority of serious criminal acts. This small group is believed to engage in a significant portion of all delinquent behavior; these youths do not age out of crime but continue their criminal behavior into adulthood.

classical criminology Holds that decisions to violate the law are weighed against possible punishments, and to deter crime, the pain of punishment must outweigh the benefit of illegal gain; led to graduated punishments based on seriousness of the crime (let the punishment fit the crime).

cliques Small groups of friends who share intimate knowledge and confidences.

cocaine A powerful natural stimulant derived from the coca plant.

cognitive theory The branch of psychology that studies the perception of reality and the mental processes required to understand the world we live in.

collective efficacy The ability of communities to regulate the behavior of their residents through the influence of community institutions, such as the family and school. Residents in these communities share mutual trust and a willingness to intervene in the supervision of children and the maintenance of public order.

community policing Police strategy that emphasizes reducing fear, organizing the community, and maintaining order rather than fighting crime.

community service restitution The juvenile offender is required to assist some worthwhile community organization for a period of time.

community treatment Using nonsecure and noninstitutional residences, counseling services, victim restitution programs, and other community services to treat juveniles in their own communities.

complaint Report made by the police or some other agency to the court that initiates the intake process.

conditions of probation The rules and regulations mandating that a juvenile on probation behave in a particular way.

conduct disorder (CD) A disorder of childhood and adolescence that involves chronic behavior problems, such as defiant, impulsive, or antisocial behavior and substance abuse.

confidentiality Restriction of information in juvenile court proceedings in the interest of protecting the privacy of the juvenile.

consent decree A court order authorizing disposition of a case without a formal label of delinquency.

contagion effect Delinquency spreads when kids copy the behavior of peers and siblings.

continuity of crime The idea that chronic juvenile offenders are likely to continue violating the law as adults.

control group A comparison group of subjects that does not receive a prevention program.

cottage system Housing juveniles in a compound containing a series of cottages, each of which accommodates 20 to 40 children and is run by a set of cottage parents who create a homelike atmosphere.

covert pathway Pathway to a delinquent career that begins with minor underhanded behavior, leads to property damage, and eventually escalates to more serious forms of theft and fraud.

crack A highly addictive crystalline form of cocaine containing remnants of hydrochloride and sodium bicarbonate, which emits a crackling sound when smoked.

criminal atavism The idea that delinquents manifest physical anomalies that make them biologically and physiologically similar to our primitive ancestors, savage throwbacks to an earlier stage of human evolution.

critical feminism Holds that gender inequality stems from the unequal power of men and women and the subsequent exploitation of women by men; the cause of female delinquency originates with the onset of male supremacy and the efforts of males to control females' sexuality.

crowds Loosely organized groups who share interests and activities.

Crown Court In England, the criminal court that deals with adult offenders or juveniles who have been transferred from youth court.

Crown Prosecution Service The national agency in England that is in charge of all criminal prosecutions of juveniles and adults.

cultural deviance theory A unique lower-class culture develops in disorganized neighborhoods whose set of values and beliefs puts residents in conflict with conventional social norms.

culture of poverty View that lower-class people form a separate culture with their own values and norms, which are sometimes in conflict with conventional society.

cultural transmission Cultural norms and values are passed down from one generation to the next.

cumulative disadvantage The tendency of prior social problems to produce future ones that accumulate and undermine success.

custodial interrogation Questions posed by the police to a suspect held in custody in the prejudicial stage of the juvenile justice process; juveniles have the same rights against self-incrimination as adults do when being questioned.

cyberbullying Willful and repeated harm inflicted through Internet social media sites or electronic communication methods such as Twitter.

Davis v. Alaska This case put further limits on the juvenile's right to privacy in court proceedings.

death squads Common to South America, organized government or criminal groups that selectively kill members of opposing groups and incite fear in those groups and among their supporters.

degradation ceremony Going to court, being scolded by a judge, or being found delinquent after a trial are examples of public ceremonies that can transform youthful offenders by degrading their self-image.

deinstitutionalization Removing juveniles from adult jails and placing them in community-based programs to avoid the stigma attached to these facilities.

delinquency control or delinquency repression Involves any justice program or policy designed to prevent the occurrence of a future delinquent act.

delinquency prevention Involves any nonjustice program or policy designed to prevent the occurrence of a future delinquent act.

designer drugs Lab-made drugs designed to avoid existing drug laws.

detached street workers Social workers who go out into the community and establish close relationships with juvenile gangs with the goal of modifying gang behavior to conform to conventional behaviors and help gang members get jobs and educational opportunities.

detention Temporary care of a child alleged to be delinquent who requires secure custody in physically restricting facilities pending court disposition or execution of a court order.

detention hearing A hearing by a judicial officer of a juvenile court to determine whether a juvenile is to be detained or released while juvenile proceedings are pending in the case.

determinate sentence Specifies a fixed term of detention that must be served.

developed countries Recognized by the United Nations as the richest countries in the world.

developing countries Recognized by the United Nations as countries that are showing signs of improved economic growth and are making the transition from low income to high income.

developmental theory The view that delinquency is a dynamic process influenced by social experiences as well as individual characteristics.

deviancy training A process in which close friends reinforce deviant behavior choices through talk and interaction.

differential association theory Asserts that criminal behavior is learned primarily within interpersonal groups and that youths will become delinquent if definitions they have learned favorable to violating the law exceed definitions favorable to obeying the law within that group.

differential opportunity The view that lower-class youths, whose legitimate opportunities are limited, join gangs and pursue criminal careers as alternative means to achieve universal success goals.

differential susceptibility model The view that some people are predisposed to environmental influences.

diffusion of benefits An effect that occurs when efforts to prevent one type of delinquent act may actually prevent another.

disaggregated Analyzing the relationship between two or more independent variables (such as murder convictions and death sentence) while controlling for the influence of a dependent variable (such as race).

discretion Use of personal decision making and choice in carrying out operations in the criminal justice system, such as deciding whether to make an arrest or when to accept a plea bargain.

disorganized neighborhood Inner-city areas of extreme poverty where the critical social control mechanisms have broken down.

displacement A program that helps lower crime rates at specific locations or neighborhoods may be redirecting offenders to alternative targets.

disposition For juvenile offenders, the equivalent of sentencing for adult offenders; however, juvenile dispositions should be more rehabilitative than retributive.

disposition hearing A court hearing during which the social service agency presents its case plan and recommendations for care of the child and treatment of the parents, including incarceration and counseling or other treatment.

disruptive behavior disorder (DBD) A consistent pattern of behaviors that continually breaks normal social rules and is extremely oppositional and defiant of authority.

diversion Official halting or suspending of a formal criminal or juvenile justice proceeding at any legally prescribed processing point after a recorded justice system entry, and referral of that person to a treatment or care program or a recommendation that the person be released.

dramatization of evil The process of social typing that transforms an offender's identity from a doer of evil to an evil person.

drift Idea that youths move in and out of delinquency and that their lifestyles can embrace both conventional and deviant values.

dropout factory High schools in which the number of seniors is 60 percent (or less) of the number of ninth-graders.

dropping out Leaving school before completing the required program of education.

drug courts Courts whose focus is to provide treatment for youths accused of drug-related acts.

due process Basic constitutional principle based on the concept of the primacy of the individual and the complementary concept of limitation on governmental power; safeguards the individual from unfair state procedures in judicial or administrative proceedings. Due process rights have been extended to juvenile trials.

egalitarian families Husband and wife share power at home; daughters gain a kind of freedom similar to that of sons, and their law-violating behaviors mirror those of their brothers.

ego identity According to Erik Erikson, ego identity is formed when youths develop a full sense of the self, combining how they see themselves and how they fit in with others.

electronic monitoring Active monitoring systems consist of a radio transmitter worn by the offender that sends a continuous signal to the probation department computer, alerting officials if the offender leaves his or her place of confinement. Passive systems employ computer-generated random phone calls that must be answered in a certain period of time from a particular phone or other device.

enculturated The process by which an established culture teaches an individual its norms and values, so that the individual can become an accepted member of the society. Through enculturation, the individual learns what is accepted behavior within that society and his or her particular status within the culture.

evolutionary theory Explaining the existence of aggression and violent behavior as positive adaptive behaviors in human evolution; these traits allowed their bearers to reproduce disproportionately, which has had an effect on the human gene pool.

experimental group A group of subjects that receives a prevention program.

expressive crimes Crimes that have no purpose except to accomplish the behavior at hand, such as shooting someone.

extravert A person who behaves impulsively and doesn't have the ability to examine motives and behavior.

familicide Mass murders in which a spouse and one or more children are slain.

family group homes A combination of foster care and a group home in which a juvenile is placed in a private group home run by a single family rather than by professional staff.

Fare v. Michael C.* and *California v. Prysock These cases make it seem indisputable that juveniles are at least entitled to receive the same *Miranda* rights as adults.

Federal Bureau of Investigation (FBI) Arm of the US Department of Justice that investigates violations of federal law, gathers crime statistics, runs a comprehensive crime laboratory, and helps train local law enforcement officers.

final order Order that ends litigation between two parties by determining all their rights and disposing of all the issues.

focal concerns The value orientation of lower-class culture that is characterized by a need for excitement, trouble, smartness, fate, and personal autonomy.

focused deterrence A policy that relies on pulling every deterrent "lever" available to reduce crime in the targeted problem.

foster care Placing a child in the temporary care of a family other than its own as a result of state intervention into problems within the birth family; can be used as a temporary shelter while a permanent adoption effort is being completed.

foster care programs Juveniles who are orphans or whose parents cannot care for them are placed with families who provide the attention, guidance, and care they did not receive at home.

free will View that people are in charge of their own destinies and are free to make personal behavior choices unencumbered by environmental factors.

gang Group of youths who collectively engage in delinquent behaviors.

gang sweep A method of enforcement in which police, armed with arrest and search warrants, enter a neighborhood in force in an operation to make as many arrests as possible.

gateway drug A substance that leads to use of more serious drugs; alcohol use has long been thought to lead to more serious drug abuse.

gender policing Pressure to conform to gender expectations.

gender-schema theory A theory of development that holds that children internalize gender scripts reflecting the gender-related social practices of the culture. Once internalized, these gender scripts predispose the kids to construct a self-identity that is consistent with the scripts.

gender similarities hypothesis The belief that gender differences in personality, cognition, intelligence, etc., are much smaller than previously believed.

general deterrence Crime control policies that depend on the fear of criminal penalties, such as long prison sentences for violent crimes; the aim is to convince law violators that the pain outweighs the benefit of criminal activity.

General Strain Theory (GST) According to Agnew, the view that multiple sources of strain interact with an individual's emotional traits and responses to produce criminality.

General Theory of Crime (GTC) A developmental theory that modifies social control theory by integrating concepts from biosocial, psychological, routine activities, and rational choice theories.

globalization The process of creating a global economy through transnational markets and political and legal systems.

graffiti Inscriptions or drawings made on a wall or structure and used by delinquents for gang messages and turf definition.

Graham v. Florida Repealed life sentences without the possibility of parole for juveniles convicted of nonhomicide crimes.

group homes Nonsecured, structured residences that provide counseling, education, job training, and family living.

group therapy Counseling several individuals together in a group session; individuals can obtain support from other group members as they work through similar problems.

guardian *ad litem* A court-appointed attorney who protects the interests of the child in cases involving the child's welfare.

hallucinogens Natural or synthetic substances that produce vivid distortions of the senses without greatly disturbing consciousness.

harm reduction Efforts to minimize the harmful effects caused by drug use.

hashish A concentrated form of cannabis made from unadulterated resin from the female cannabis plant.

Hazelwood School District v. Kuhlmeier School officials have the right to censor "active speech"—for example, controlling the content of articles in a student publication.

hearsay Out-of-court statements made by one person and recounted in court by another; such statements are generally not allowed as evidence except in child abuse cases in which a child's statements to social workers, teachers, or police may be admissible.

heroin A narcotic made from opium and then cut with sugar or some other neutral substance until it is only 1 to 4 percent pure.

house arrest An offender is required to stay at home during specified periods of time; monitoring is done by random phone calls and visits or by electronic devices.

House of Refuge A care facility developed by the child savers to protect potential criminal youths by taking them off the street and providing a family-like environment.

identity crisis Psychological state, identified by Erikson, in which youth face inner turmoil and uncertainty about life roles.

income inequality The unequal distribution of household or individual income across the various participants in an economy.

indeterminate sentence Does not specify the length of time the juvenile must be held; rather, correctional authorities decide when the juvenile is ready to return to society.

individual counseling Counselors help juveniles understand and solve their current adjustment problems

individualized treatment model Each sentence must be tailored to the individual needs of the child.

informant A person who has access to criminal networks and shares information with authorities in exchange for money or special treatment under conditions of anonymity.

Ingraham v. Wright Corporal punishment in schools is legally permissible.

inhalants Volatile liquids that give off a vapor, which is inhaled, producing short-term excitement and euphoria followed by a period of disorientation.

in loco parentis Latin for "in place of parents" or "instead of a parent." Used to signify that parents have given a person or institution all the rights to behave, act, and be and act as a parent.

In re Winship Proof beyond a reasonable doubt is necessary for conviction in juvenile proceedings.

instrumental crimes Offenses designed to improve the financial or social position of the criminal.

intake Process during which a juvenile referral is received and a decision is made to file a petition in juvenile court to release the juvenile, to place the juvenile under supervision, or to refer the juvenile elsewhere.

integrated theories Theories that incorporate social, personal, and developmental factors into complex explanations of human behavior.

Intensive Aftercare Program (IAP) A balanced, highly structured, comprehensive continuum of intervention for serious and violent juvenile offenders returning to the community.

international crime Crime that is punishable under international law.

interstitial group Delinquent group that fills a crack in the social fabric and maintains standard group practices, such as setting goals, recruiting new members, developing status, and assigning roles.

intrafamily violence An environment of discord and conflict within the family; children who grow up in dysfunctional homes often exhibit delinquent behaviors, having learned at a young age that aggression pays off.

J.D.B. v. North Carolina A suspect's age must be considered in determining whether a confession was freely given and whether they believed they were in custody.

juvenile court judge A judge elected or appointed to preside over juvenile cases and whose decisions can only be reviewed by a judge of a higher court.

juvenile defense attorney Represents children in juvenile court and plays an active role at all stages of the proceedings.

juvenile delinquency Participation in illegal behavior by a minor who falls under a statutory age limit.

juvenile intensive probation supervision (JIPS) A true alternative to incarceration that involves almost daily supervision of the juvenile by the probation officer assigned to the case.

juvenile justice process Under the paternal (*parens patriae*) philosophy, juvenile justice procedures are informal and nonadversarial, invoked for the juvenile offender rather than against him or her; a petition instead of a complaint is filed; courts make findings of involvement or adjudication of delinquency instead of convictions; and juvenile offenders receive dispositions instead of sentences.

juvenile justice system The segment of the justice system, including law enforcement officers, the courts, and correctional agencies, designed to treat youthful offenders.

juvenile officers Police officers who specialize in dealing with juvenile offenders; they may operate alone or as part of a juvenile police unit within the department.

juvenile probation officer Officer of the court involved in all four stages of the court process—intake, predisposition, postadjudication, and postdisposition—who assists the court and supervises juveniles placed on probation.

juvenile prosecutor Government attorney responsible for representing the interests of the state and bringing the case against the accused juvenile.

klikas Subgroups of same-aged youths in Hispanic gangs that remain together and have separate names and a unique identity in the gang.

latent delinquents Youths whose troubled family life leads them to seek immediate gratification without consideration of right and wrong or the feelings of others.

latent trait A stable feature, characteristic, property, or condition, such as defective intelligence or impulsive personality, that makes some people delinquency prone over the life course.

Law Enforcement Assistance Administration (LEAA) Unit in the US Department of Justice established by the Omnibus Crime Control and Safe Streets Act of 1968 to administer grants and provide guidance for crime prevention policy and programs.

learning disability (LD) Neurological dysfunction that prevents an individual from learning to his or her potential.

least detrimental alternative Choice of a program for the child that will best foster the child's growth and development.

least developed countries Recognized by the United Nations as being the poorest countries in the world and suffering from long-term barriers to economic growth.

least restrictive alternative Choosing a program with the least restrictive or secure setting that will best benefit the child.

legalization of drugs Decriminalizing drug use to reduce the association between drug use and crime.

liberal feminism Asserts that females are less delinquent than males because their social roles provide them with fewer opportunities to commit crimes; as the roles of girls and women become more similar to those of boys and men, so too will their crime patterns.

life-course persisters Delinquents who begin their offending career at a very early age and continue to offend well into adulthood.

life-course theory Focuses on changes in criminality over the life course; developmental theory.

major depressive episode (MDE) A period of at least two weeks when a person experienced a depressed mood or loss of interest or pleasure in daily activities plus at least four additional symptoms of depression (such as problems with sleep, eating, energy, concentration, and feelings of self-worth).

mandatory sentence Defined by a statutory requirement that states the penalty to be set for all cases of a specific offense.

marijuana The dried leaves of the cannabis plant.

Maryland v. Craig A state statute that allows closed-circuit television (CCTV) testimony in child abuse cases is legal because it requires a determination that the child will suffer distress if forced to testify in court. CCTV can serve as the equivalent of in-court testimony and does not interfere with the defendant's right to confront witnesses.

masculinity hypothesis View that women who commit crimes have biological and psychological traits similar to those of men.

middle-class measuring rods Standards by which teachers and other representatives of state authority evaluate students' behavior; when lower-class youths cannot meet these standards they are subject to failure, which brings on frustration and anger at conventional society.

milieu therapy All aspects of the environment are part of the treatment, and meaningful change, increased growth, and satisfactory adjustment are encouraged; this is often accomplished through peer pressure to conform to the group norms.

Miller v. Alabama In this case, the Supreme Court held that mandatory life sentences, without the possibility of parole, are unconstitutional for juvenile offenders.

minimal brain dysfunction (MBD) Damage to the brain itself that causes antisocial behavior injurious to the individual's lifestyle and social adjustment.

Miranda v. Arizona Police interrogations of suspects in custody are subject to constitutional limitations.

Miranda **warning** Supreme Court decisions require police officers to inform individuals of their constitutional rights when under arrest; warning must also be given when suspicion begins to focus on an individual in the accusatory stage.

monetary restitution A requirement that juvenile offenders compensate crime victims for out-of-pocket losses caused by the crime, including property damage, lost wages, and medical expenses.

mood disorder A condition in which the prevailing emotional mood is distorted or inappropriate to the circumstances.

Morse v. Frederick School officials can control student speech at off-campus events.

multisystemic therapy (MST) Addresses a variety of family, peer, and psychological problems by focusing on problem solving and communication skills training.

National Crime Victimization Survey (NCVS) The ongoing victimization study conducted jointly by the Justice Department and the US Census Bureau that surveys victims about their experiences with law violation.

National Incident-Based Reporting System (NIBRS) Program that collects data on each reported crime incident and requires local police to provide at least a brief account of each incident and arrest.

nature theory Holds that low intelligence is genetically determined and inherited.

near-groups Clusters of youth who, outwardly, seem unified but actually have limited cohesion, impermanence, minimal consensus of norms, and shifting membership.

negative affective states Anger, depression, disappointment, fear, and other adverse emotions that derive from strain.

neglect Passive neglect by a parent or guardian, depriving children of food, shelter, health care, and love.

neurological Pertaining to the brain and nervous system structure.

neuroticism A personality trait marked by unfounded anxiety, tension, and emotional instability.

neutralization techniques A set of attitudes or beliefs that allow would-be delinquents to negate any moral apprehension they may have about committing crime so that they may freely engage in antisocial behavior without regret.

New Jersey v. T.L.O. The Fourth Amendment controls on search and seizure apply to school officials as well as police.

nonresidential programs Juveniles remain in their own homes but receive counseling, education, employment, diagnostic, and casework services through an intensive support system.

nuclear family A family unit composed of parents and their children; this smaller family structure is subject to great stress due to the intense, close contact between parents and children.

nurture theory Holds that intelligence is partly biological but mostly sociological; negative environmental factors encourage delinquent behavior and depress intelligence scores for many youths.

Office of Juvenile Justice and Delinquency Prevention (OJJDP) Branch of the US Justice Department charged with shaping national juvenile justice policy through disbursement of federal aid and research funds.

Oklahoma Publishing Co. v. District Court and *Smith v. Daily Mail Publishing Co.* These cases set out to produce a greater balance between individual privacy and freedom of the press in juvenile court proceedings.

orphan trains The name for trains in which urban youths were sent west by the Children's Aid Society for adoption with local farm couples.

overt pathway Pathway to a delinquent career that begins with minor aggression, leads to physical fighting, and eventually escalates to violent delinquency.

parens patriae Power of the state to act on behalf of the child and provide care and protection equivalent to that of a parent.

parental efficacy Families in which parents integrate their children into the household unit while helping them assert their individuality and regulate their own behavior.

Part I crimes Offenses including homicide and non-negligent manslaughter, forcible rape, robbery, aggravated assault, burglary, larceny, arson, and motor vehicle theft. Recorded by local law enforcement officers, these crimes are tallied quarterly and sent to the FBI for inclusion in the UCR.

Part II crimes All crimes other than Part I crimes; recorded by local law enforcement officers, arrests for these crimes are tallied quarterly and sent to the FBI for inclusion in the UCR.

passive speech A form of expression protected by the First Amendment but not associated with actually speaking words; examples include wearing symbols or protest messages on buttons or signs.

paternalistic family A family style wherein the father is the final authority on all family matters and exercises complete control over his wife and children.

patriarchal A social system in which men are dominant in family, government, and business matters.

persistence The process by which juvenile offenders persist in their delinquent careers rather than aging out of crime.

petition Document filed in juvenile court alleging that a juvenile is a delinquent, a status offender, or a dependent and asking that the court assume jurisdiction over the juvenile.

plea bargaining The exchange of prosecutorial and judicial concessions for a guilty plea by the accused; plea bargaining usually results in a reduced charge or a more lenient sentence.

pledge system Early English system in which neighbors protected each other from thieves and warring groups.

Poor Laws English statutes that allowed the courts to appoint overseers over destitute and neglected children, allowing placement of these children as servants in the homes of the affluent.

positive peer culture (PPC) Counseling program in which peer leaders encourage other group members to modify their behavior, and peers help reinforce acceptable behaviors.

posting A system of positions, facial expressions, and body language used by gang members to convey a message.

power-control theory Holds that gender differences in the delinquency rate are a function of class differences and economic conditions that influence the structure of family life.

precocious sexuality Sexual experimentation in early adolescence.

predatory crime Violent crimes against people, and crimes in which an offender attempts to steal an object directly from its holder.

prestige crimes Stealing or assaulting someone to gain prestige in the neighborhood; often part of gang initiation rites.

pretrial conference The attorney for the social services agency presents an overview of the case, and a plea bargain or negotiated settlement can be agreed to in a consent decree.

preventive detention Keeping the accused in custody prior to trial because the accused is suspected of being a danger to the community.

primary deviance Norm violations that have very little influence on the actor and can be quickly forgotten and/or overlooked.

primogeniture During the Middle Ages, the right of firstborn sons to inherit lands and titles, leaving their brothers the option of a military or religious career.

probable cause Reasonable grounds to believe that an offense was committed and that the accused committed that offense.

probation Nonpunitive, legal disposition for juveniles emphasizing community treatment in which the juvenile is closely supervised by an officer of the court and must adhere to a strict set of rules to avoid incarceration.

problem behavior syndrome (PBS) A cluster of antisocial behaviors that may include family dysfunction, substance abuse, smoking, precocious sexuality and early pregnancy, educational underachievement, suicide attempts, sensation seeking, and unemployment, as well as delinquency.

problem-oriented policing Law enforcement that focuses on addressing the problems underlying incidents of juvenile delinquency rather than the incidents only.

procedural justice An evaluation of the fairness of the manner in which an offender's problem or dispute was handled by police.

propensity An innate inclination, preference, or tendency to act in a specific way.

protective factor A positive prior factor in an individual's life that decreases the risk of occurrence of a future delinquent act.

psychodynamic theory Branch of psychology that holds that the human personality is controlled by unconscious mental processes developed early in childhood.

psychotherapy Highly structured counseling in which a skilled therapist helps a juvenile solve conflicts and make a more positive adjustment to society.

public defender An attorney who works in a public agency or under private contractual agreement as defense counsel to indigent defendants.

racial profiling Police practice of routinely searching, questioning, and detaining all African American males in an area, especially after a crime has been committed involving a black suspect.

racial threat theory As the size of the black population increases, the perceived threat to the white population increases, resulting in a greater amount of social control imposed against African Americans by police.

Ralston v. Robinson This case placed limits on the right to treatment for juvenile offenders.

randomized experimental design Considered the "gold standard" of evaluation designs to measure the effect of a program on delinquency or other outcomes. Involves randomly assigning subjects either to receive the program (the experimental group) or not receive it (the control group).

reaction formation A psychological reaction that occurs when a person does or says something that is the opposite of what he or she really wants or what is socially expected and appropriate.

reality therapy A form of counseling that emphasizes current behavior and that requires the individual to accept responsibility for all of his or her actions.

reentry The process and experience of returning to society upon release from a custody facility postadjudication.

reflected appraisal The process in which a person's awareness of how other people see them becomes the basis for self-perception.

reform schools Institutions in which educational and psychological services are used in an effort to improve the conduct of juveniles who are forcibly detained.

reintegrative shaming Techniques used to allow offenders to understand and recognize their wrongdoing and shame themselves. To be reintegrative, shaming must be brief and controlled and then followed by ceremonies of forgiveness, apology, and repentance.

representing Tossing or flashing gang signs in the presence of rivals, often escalating into a verbal or physical confrontation.

residential programs Placement of a juvenile offender in a residential, nonsecure facility such as a group home, foster home, family group home, or rural home where the juvenile can be closely monitored and develop close relationships with staff.

resource dilution A condition that occurs when parents have such large families that their resources, such as time and money, are spread too thin, causing lack of familial support and control.

restorative justice Using humanistic, nonpunitive strategies to right wrongs and restore social harmony.

retrospective reading An attempt to explain present misbehavior with behavior from the past.

review hearings Periodic meetings to determine whether the conditions of the case plan for an abused child are being met by the parents or guardians of the child.

right to treatment Philosophy espoused by many courts that juvenile offenders have a statutory right to treatment while under the jurisdiction of the courts.

risk factor A negative prior factor in an individual's life that increases the risk of occurrence of a future delinquent act.

role conflicts Conflicts police officers face that revolve around the requirement to perform their primary duty of law enforcement and a desire to aid in rehabilitating youthful offenders.

role diffusion According to Erik Erikson, role diffusion occurs when people spread themselves too thin, experience personal uncertainty, and place themselves at the mercy of people who promise to give them a sense of identity they cannot develop for themselves.

Roper v. Simmons Repealed death penalty sentences for all juveniles in the United States.

routine activities theory View that crime is a "normal" function of the routine activities of modern living; offenses can be expected if there is a motivated offender and a suitable target that is not protected by capable guardians.

rural programs Specific recreational and work opportunities provided for juveniles in a rural setting, such as a forestry camp, a farm, or a ranch.

Safford Unified School District v. Redding School searches must be reasonable and, considering the circumstances of the case, not overly intrusive.

Santa Fe Independent School District, Petitioner v. Jane Doe Student-led prayers at a school football game are inappropriate and are in violation of the First Amendment separation of church and state.

Santosky v. Kramer The US Supreme Court recognized the child's right to be free from parental abuse and set down guidelines for a termination-of-custody hearing, including the right to legal representation.

secondary deviance Deviant acts that define the actor and create a new identity.

sedatives Drugs of the barbiturate family that depress the central nervous system into a sleeplike condition.

self-control theory The theory of delinquency that holds that antisocial behavior is caused by a lack of self-control stemming from an impulsive personality.

self-fulfilling prophecy Deviant behavior patterns that are a response to an earlier labeling experience; youths act out these social roles even if they were falsely bestowed.

self-report survey Questionnaire or survey technique that asks subjects to reveal their own participation in delinquent or criminal acts.

sentencing circle A peacemaking technique in which offenders, victims, and other community members are brought together in an effort to formulate a sanction that addresses the needs of all.

shame The feeling we get when we don't meet the standards we have set for ourselves or that significant others have set for us.

shelter care A place for temporary care of children in physically unrestricting facilities.

siege mentality Residents become so suspicious of authority that they consider the outside world to be the enemy out to destroy the neighborhood.

situational crime prevention Crime prevention method that relies on reducing the opportunity to commit criminal acts by (a) making them more difficult to perform, (b) reducing their reward, and (c) increasing their risks.

skinhead Member of a white supremacist gang, identified by a shaved skull and Nazi or Ku Klux Klan markings.

social bond Ties a person to the institutions and processes of society; elements of the bond include attachment, commitment, involvement, and belief.

social capital Positive relations with individuals and institutions, as in a successful marriage or a successful career, that support conventional behavior and inhibit deviant behavior.

social conflict theory (also called conflict theory) Asserts that society is in a state of constant internal conflict, and focuses on the role of social and governmental institutions as mechanisms for social control.

social control Ability of social institutions to influence human behavior; the justice system is the primary agency of formal social control.

social control theory Posits that delinquency results from a weakened commitment to the major social institutions (family, peers, and school); lack of such commitment allows youths to exercise antisocial behavioral choices.

social disorganization theory The inability of a community to exert social control allows youths the freedom to engage in illegal behavior.

social ecologists Theorists who focus attention on the influence social institutions have on individual behavior and who suggest that law-violating behavior is a response to social rather than individual forces operating in an urban environment.

social investigation report or predisposition report Developed by the juvenile probation officer, this report consists of a clinical diagnosis of the juvenile and his or her need for court assistance, relevant environmental and personality factors, and any other information that would assist the court in developing a treatment plan for the juvenile.

socialization The process by which human beings learn to adopt the behavior patterns of the community in which they live, which requires them to develop the skills and knowledge necessary to function within their culture and environment.

social learning theory (psychological) The view that behavior is modeled through observation, either directly through intimate contact with others or indirectly through media; interactions that are rewarded are copied, whereas those that are punished are avoided.

social learning theory Hypothesizes that delinquency is learned through close relationships with others; asserts that children are born good and learn to be bad from others.

social reaction theory (also called labeling theory) Posits that society creates deviance through a system of social control agencies that designate (or label) certain individuals as delinquent, thereby stigmatizing youths and encouraging them to accept this negative personal identity.

social structure theories Explain delinquency using socioeconomic conditions and cultural values.

Society for the Prevention of Cruelty to Children Established in 1874, these organizations protected children subjected to cruelty and neglect at home or at school.

specific deterrence Sending convicted offenders to secure incarceration facilities so that punishment is severe enough to convince offenders not to repeat their criminal activity.

state dependence The propensity to commit crime profoundly and permanently disrupts normal socialization over the life course.

status dropout rate The percentage of an age group that is not enrolled in school and has not earned a high school diploma or equivalent.

status frustration A form of culture conflict experienced by lower-class youths because social conditions prevent them from achieving success as defined by the larger society.

status offense Conduct that is illegal only because the child is underage.

status symbol Something, such as a possession, rank, or activity, by which one's social or economic prestige is measured.

stigmatize To mark someone with disgrace or reproach; to characterize or brand someone as disgraceful or disreputable.

stimulants Synthetic substances that produce an intense physical reaction by stimulating the central nervous system.

strain theory Links delinquency to the strain of being locked out of the economic mainstream, which creates the anger and frustration that lead to delinquent acts.

stratified society Grouping society into classes based on the unequal distribution of scarce resources.

street efficacy Using one's wits to avoid violent confrontations and to feel safe.

substance abuse Using drugs or alcohol in such a way as to cause physical, emotional, and/or psychological harm to yourself.

subterranean values The ability of youthful law violators to repress social norms.

suppression effect A reduction in the number of arrests per year for youths who have been incarcerated or otherwise punished.

swaddling The practice during the Middle Ages of completely wrapping newborns in long bandage-like cloths in order to restrict their movements and make them easier to manage.

symbolic interaction Holds that people communicate via symbols—gestures, signs, words, or images—that stand for or represent something else.

synthetic marijuana A mixture of chemicals derived from the cannibinoid family.

target-hardening technique Crime prevention technique that makes it more difficult for a would-be delinquent to carry out the illegal act—for example, by installing a security device in a home.

teen courts Courts that make use of peer juries to decide nonserious delinquency cases.

Tinker v. Des Moines Independent Community School District Students have freedom of speech unless it disrupts the operation of the school.

tracking Dividing students into groups according to their ability and achievement levels.

trait theory Holds that youths engage in delinquent or criminal behavior due to aberrant physical or psychological traits that govern behavioral choices; delinquent actions are impulsive or instinctual rather than rational choices.

trajectory theory The view that there are multiple independent paths to a delinquent career and that there are different types and classes of offenders.

tranquilizers Drugs that reduce anxiety and promote relaxation.

transfer hearing Preadjudicatory hearing in juvenile court for the purpose of determining whether juvenile court should be retained over a juvenile or waived and the juvenile transferred to adult court for prosecution.

transfer process Transfer of a juvenile offender from the jurisdiction of juvenile court to adult criminal court.

transitional neighborhood Area undergoing a shift in population and structure, usually from middle-class residential to lower-class mixed use.

transnational crime Crime that is carried out across the borders of two or more countries and violates the laws of those countries.

Troxel v. Granville The Supreme Court ruled that the due process clause of the Constitution protects against government interference with certain fundamental rights and liberty interests, including parents' fundamental right to make decisions concerning the care, custody, and control of their children.

truant Being out of school without permission.

turning points Positive life experiences, such as gaining employment, getting married, or joining the military, which create informal social control mechanisms that limit delinquent behavior opportunities.

underclass Group of urban poor whose members have little chance of upward mobility or improvement.

Uniform Crime Report (UCR) Compiled by the FBI, the UCR is the most widely used source of national crime and delinquency statistics.

victim service restitution The juvenile offender is required to provide some service directly to the crime victim.

vulnerability model Assumes there is a direct link between traits and crime; some people are vulnerable to crime from birth.

waiver (also known as bindover or removal) Transferring legal jurisdiction over the most serious and experienced juvenile offenders to the adult court for criminal prosecution.

watch system Replaced the pledge system in England; watchmen patrolled urban areas at night to provide protection from harm.

wayward minors Early legal designation of youths who violate the law because of their minority status; now referred to as status offenders.

White v. Illinois The Supreme Court ruled that the state's attorney is not required to produce young victims at trial or to demonstrate the reason why they were unavailable to serve as witnesses.

widening the net Phenomenon that occurs when programs created to divert youths from the justice system actually involve them more deeply in the official process.

wilderness probation Programs involving outdoor expeditions that provide opportunities for juveniles to confront the difficulties of their lives while achieving positive personal satisfaction.

writ of habeas corpus Judicial order requesting that a person detaining another person produce the body of the prisoner and give reasons for his or her capture and detention.

zero tolerance policy Mandating that action be taken for the slightest infraction of a school or criminal code violation.

Case Index

Name Index

In this index n indicates note, nn indicates notes, f indicates figure, t indicates table, and e indicates exhibit.

A

Aaberg, Tammy, *394*
Aaron, Lauren, 325*n*93
Abbott, Robert, 250*n*177, 377*n*125
Ablow, Jennifer, 131*n*199
Abrahamsen, David, 132*n*231
Abram, Karen M., 447*n*4, 448*n*47, 588*n*28, 614
Abramoske-James, Stephanie, 632*n*102
Abrazaldo, Wally, 485*n*119
Ackerman, Jeff, 283*n*47
Acoca, Leslie, 632*n*105
Adam, Michele, 237, 250*n*155
Adams, Benjamin, 518*n*81, 589*nn*67–69, 590*n*80, 590*n*109
Adams, Ericka B., 549–550*n*10
Adams, Kenneth, 40*n*97, 543, 552*nn*111–112
Adams, Mike, 211*n*50, 211*n*59, 211*nn*12–13
Adams, William, 284*n*107
Adamson, Christopher, 375*n*43
Addie, Sean, 518*n*81, 589*nn*67–69, 590*n*80, 590*n*109
Addington, Lynn A., 128*n*36, 176*n*29
Adefuin, Jo-Ann, 485*n*119
Adler, Freda, 272, 285*nn*131–132, 665*n*40, 665*n*53
Adler, Nancy, 177*n*83
Aebi, Marcelo, 644, 645*t*, 646*t*, 652*t*, 664*n*1, 664*n*15, 665*n*46, 665*n*63, 665*n*65, 666*n*70, 666*n*76
Agerbo, E., 131*n*188
Ageton, Suzanne, 211*n*40, 450*n*118
Aggleton, John, 131*n*182
Agnew, Robert, 75*n*67, 132*n*251, 147, 150, 155, 178*n*104, 178*n*115, 178*n*117, 178*n*121, 178*n*123, 178*n*128, 178*n*132, 180*n*209, 283*n*40, 283*n*66, 283*nn*29–30, 325*n*76
Agrawal, Arpana, 375*n*19
Ahmed, Eliza, 212*n*96, 212*n*97
Ahonen, Lia, 74*n*45, 270, 285*n*129
Ahsan, Habibul, 129*n*124
Aichorn, August, 109, 132*n*230
Aiken, Leona, 179*n*160, 324*n*49
Ainsworth-Darnell, James, 176*n*20, 176*n*28
Akers, Ronald, 74*n*43, 249*n*119
Akse, Joyce, 133*n*257
Alarid, Leanne Fiftal, 283*n*20, 552*n*117, 589*nn*34–35
Albanese, Jay, 642, 661, 665*n*54, 666*n*79, 666*nn*115–116
Alberts-Corush, Jody, 132*n*209
Albrecht, Hans-Jörg, 666*n*101
Aldao, Amelia, 283*n*28
Aleva, Liesbeth, 284*n*90
Ali, Muhammad, *240*
Allan, Charlotte, 451*nn*154–156
Allemand, J. Mathias, 283*n*22
Allen, Andrea, 416*n*77
Allen, Ed, 449*n*101
Allen, Francis, 497
Allen, Jeff, 131*n*168
Allen, Mary K., 665*n*66, 666*n*68
Allen, Stephen, 491
Allen, Thomas, 416*n*77
Allhusen, Virginia, 129*n*119
Allison, Carlie, 283*n*27
Almovist, Frederik, 324*n*27
Altheimer, Irshad, 75*n*69, 176*n*18
Altschuler, Andrea, 177*n*83
Altschuler, David, 625, 633*n*148, 633*nn*158–160
Altshuler, Sandra, 325*n*101
Alvarado, Rose, 179*n*167, 482*n*24
Amarasiriwardena, Chitra J., 130*n*133
Amato, Paul, 324*n*52
Ambrosini, Gina, 130*n*138
Amos, William E., 482*n*4

B

Bachman, Jerald, 53, 74*n*18, 74*n*33, 248*n*85, 283*n*48, 284*n*111, 425, 426*f*, 447*n*1, 447*nn*7–8, 448*n*14, 448*n*22, 448*n*32, 448*n*35, 448*n*37, 449*n*87, 666*n*72
Bachman, Ronet, 551*n*66
Backstorm, Teresa Vigil, 377*n*179

Andenaes, Johannes, 128*n*48
Anderson, Amy, 179*n*174, 180*n*235, 666*n*75
Anderson, Craig, 53, 74*n*37, 115, 629*n*4
Anderson, David A., 482*n*13
Anderson, E. A., 631*n*99
Anderson, Elijah, 155
Anderson, Laurie, 443, 485*n*135, 518*n*60, 518*n*82
Anderson, Linda, 128*n*65
Anderson, Stephen A., 552*n*109
Andiloro, Nancy, 248*n*71
Andrade, Xavier, 448*n*12
Andrews, D. A., 133*n*291, 248*n*77
Andrews, Edmund L., 664*n*7
Andrews, Howard, 130*n*126
Angel, Caroline, 630*n*35, 630*n*39
Anglin, Deirdre, 377*n*145
Anglin, M. Douglas, 449*n*107, 450*n*117
Anson, Elizabeth, 483*n*41, 483*n*42
Antaramian, Susan, 323*n*2, 449*n*74
Anthony, J. C., 177*n*66
Anwar, Shamena, 129*n*77, 129*n*78
Aos, Steve, 443, 485*n*135, 518*n*60, 518*n*82, 632*n*117
Apel, Robert, 127*n*26, 127*n*28, 128*n*52, 128*n*56, 551*n*69
Applegate, Brandon K., 573, 591*n*153
Arbuckle, Margaret B., 631*n*89
Archer, John, 283*n*39
Archibold, Randal C., 664*n*18
Arciaga, Michelle, 347*e*
Argamaso, Susanne, 479
Ariel, Barak, 552*n*131, 630*n*36
Aries, Philippe, 16, 39*n*39, 39*n*41
Armistead, Lisa, 449*nn*79–80
Armstrong, David, 247*n*41
Armstrong, G., 631*n*99
Armstrong, Todd A., 177*n*80
Armstrong, Troy, 625, 630*n*41, 633*nn*158–159
Arneklev, Bruce, 134*n*330, 249*n*111, 249*n*113
Arnold, Carrie, 448*n*33
Arnold, Tim, 40*n*83
Arnulf, Isabelle, 129*n*120, 129*n*121
Aronowitz, Alexis A., 664*n*4
Arseneault, Louise, 131*n*199
Arteaga, Irma A., 483*n*71
Arter, Michael, 74*n*24
Arthur, Lindsay, 40*n*91
Arthur, Michael, 282*n*11
Arum, Richard, 75*n*60, 415*n*6
Arvanites, Thomas, 212*n*90
Asberg, Kia, 285*n*139
Äsberg, Marie, 130*n*141
Ascani, Nathaniel, 212*n*73
Asendorf, J. B., 399
Astor, Ron Avi, 416*n*78
Astorga, Daisy, *470*
Atillasoy, Aylin, 448*n*12
Atkisson, Curtis, 180*n*208
August, Gerald, 179*n*196
Augustyn, Megan Bears, 284*n*112
Austin, James, 212*n*79, 482*n*15, 630*n*11, 630*n*24
Austin, Roy, 285*n*135
Austin, Stephen, 40*n*67
Austin, W. Timothy, 129*n*104
Auty, Katherine, 247*n*37

Backstrom, James, 588*n*20
Bacon, Sarah, 237, 248*n*56, 249*n*96, 250*n*152
Badeau, Sue, 326*n*159
Baer, Daniel, 449*n*67
Baer, Douglas, 324*n*53
Baer, Judith, 133*n*284
Baghurst, Peter, 130*n*130
Baglivio, Michael T., 630*n*20
Baier, Colin, 179*n*177
Bailey, Carol, 211*n*51, 211*nn*48–49
Bailey, Laura, 448*n*31
Bakal, Yitzhak, 631*n*53
Baker, Al, 529
Baker, Laura, 131*n*200, 325*n*100
Baker, Tara Kelly, 472*t*
Bala, Nicholas, 655
Baldry, Anna, 399
Balfour, Gillian, 285*n*144
Balingit, Moriah, 415*n*1
Ball, Richard, 630*n*30
Ball, Robert A., 180*n*207
Balter, Mitchell, 247*n*46
Bandura, Albert, 115, 133*n*271, 133*n*274, 632*n*121
Banich, Marie T., 130*n*151
Bao, Wan-Ning, 178*n*129
Bard, Barbara, 130*n*156
Barendregt, Marko, 133*n*252, 133*n*253
Barfield-Cottledge, Tiffiney, 180*n*218
Barkan, Steven E., 248*n*84, 324*n*30
Barker, Edward D., 283*n*67, 375*n*33, 484*n*82
Barker, Gareth, 130*n*150
Barker, Gordon, 284*n*107
Barker, R. Donald, 518*n*74
Barkley, Russell, 131*n*169
Barnard, John, 39*n*49
Barnes, Geoffrey C., 630*n*35, 630*n*39
Barnes, Grace, 128*n*38, 283*n*33
Barnes, Helen V., 483*n*61, 483*n*63, 483*n*64
Barnes, J. C., 129*n*110, 129*n*112, 132*n*216, 249*n*108, 250*n*157, 250*n*168, 250*n*169, 375*n*13, 375*n*27
Barnett, Arnold, 76*n*89
Barnett, W. Steven, 483*n*64, 483*n*66, 483*n*67
Baron, Stephen, 178*n*116, 375*n*32
Barr, Ashley B., 222*e*, 248*n*83, 248*n*84
Barr, Dana B., 130*n*126
Barrett, David, 282*n*4
Barrionuevo, Alexei, 665*n*21, 665*n*23
Barrueco, Sandra, 247*n*47
Bartels, Jared, 134*n*324
Bartlett, Nozomi, 633*n*167
Bartollas, Clemens, 614, 631*n*58, 631*nn*95–96
Barton, William H., 517*n*48, 588*n*29
Bartusch, Dawn Jeglum, 248*n*49
Barzee, Wanda, 68
Bassett, Elena D., 588*n*28
Bates, John, 177*n*86, 179*n*165, 284*n*73, 325*n*78, 327*n*172
Bates, Leigh, 128*n*52
Battin, Sara, 377*n*125
Baucom, D. H., 284*n*81
Bauer, Erin, 416*n*52
Bauermeister, José A., 448*n*54
Baum, Melissa, 68
Baumeister, Roy, 128*n*67
Baumer, Eric P., 74*n*14, 449*n*108, 449*nn*105–106
Bauserman, Robert, 327*n*180
Bayh, Birch, 417*n*101
Bazemore, Gordon, 205, 212*n*106, 212*n*107, 604*f*, 630*n*43, 630*n*45
Beach, Steven, 129*n*115, 131*n*183
Beaton, Susan, 416*n*84, 416*n*97

Glueck, Sheldon, 119, 133*n*292, 216, 246*n*6, 246*nn*7–8, 283*n*62, 324*n*33
Goddard, Henry, 120, 134*n*312
Gold, Martin, 74*n*32, 415*n*35
Golden, Daniel, 588*n*14
Golding, Jean, 129*n*119
Goldkamp, John, 128*n*62
Goldman, Abigail, 376*n*104
Goldman, M. S., 449*n*89
Goldman, Nathan, 534, 550*n*55, 551*n*63
Goldman, Russell, 69
Goldschmidt, Lidush, 325*n*102
Goldson, Barry, 656, 666*n*97, 666*n*117
Goldstein, Herman, 549*n*7
Goldstein, Joseph, 550*n*51, 578, 590*n*105
Goldstein, Naomi E. Sevin, 589*n*52
Goldstein, Paul, 448*n*28, 449*n*95
Goldweber, Asha, 284*n*71, 284*n*114
Golinelli, Daniela, 40*n*62
Gomby, Deanna S., 482*n*1, 482*n*34
Gonzales, Nancy, 179*n*160, 324*n*49
Gonzalez, Jennifer M. Reingle, 483*n*49
Gonzalez, Victor, 374*n*1
Goode, Erica, 588*n*22, 590*n*112, 590*n*120
Goodkind, Sara, 283*n*48, 632*n*103
Goodman, John, 132*n*209
Goodman, Robert, 133*n*255
Goodstein, Laurie, 210*n*8
Goodwin, D. W., 449*nn*76–77
Gordan, Jill A., 633*n*164, 633*n*166
Gordon, Leslie C., 324*n*31
Gordon, Linda, 326*n*155, 517*n*25
Gordon, Rachel, 377*n*141
Gordon, Robert, 180*n*207, 212*n*85
Gottesman, Irving, 131*n*181
Gottfredson, Denise, 128*n*44, 283*n*66, 283*nn*49–50, 327*n*189, 416*n*50, 416*n*52, 416*n*83, 416*n*94, 416*n*96, 450*n*137, 469, 469e, 473, 474, 484*n*78, 484*n*94, 484*n*96, 484*n*101, 484*n*102, 484*n*110, 484*n*111, 484*n*99–100, 484*nn*109–110, 511, 551*n*101
Gottfredson, Gary, 416*n*50, 416*n*83, 416*n*94, 416*n*96, 484*n*99–100
Gottfredson, Michael, 75*n*73, 75*n*75, 230–236, 249*n*97, 249*n*109, 249*n*128, 249*nn*98–99, 249*nn*102–103, 250*n*140, 415*n*37
Gottfredson, Nisha, 416*n*50
Gottschalk, Martin, 665*n*41
Gough, Kirsty, 323*n*5
Gould, Leroy, 74*n*43
Gould, Roger, 39*n*5
Gowar, B. Raffan, 485*n*135, 518*n*60
Gowen, L. Kris, 40*n*69, 284*n*68
Graceffa, Philip, 608
Grady, Melissa D., 132*n*239
Graham, John, 666*n*112, 666*n*114
Graham, Phillip, 268, 285*n*123
Graham, Sandra, 589*n*73
Graham, Terrance, 582
Graif, Corina, 176*n*53
Grandjean, P., 129*n*120
Granic, Isabela, 179*n*175
Grasmick, Harold, 176*n*38, 177*n*95, 249*n*111, 249*n*113, 249*n*126, 249*n*133
Graves, Rick, 449*n*101
Gray-Ray, Phyllis, 211*n*50, 211*n*59, 211*nn*12–13
Graziano, Joseph, 129*n*124, 130*n*130, 130*n*131
Graziano, Juliette, 632*n*110
Green, Bruce, 589*n*62
Green, Donald, 128*n*65
Green, Harold D., 448*n*54
Green, Kerry, 284*nn*98–99
Green, Lorraine, 129*n*98
Greenberg, Mark T., 450*n*142
Greenberg, Stephanie, 177*n*62
Greene, Carolyn, 655
Greene, Edie, 40*n*105, 40*n*107
Greene, Jack, 416*n*82, 416*n*86
Greene, Judith, 378*n*207, 551*nn*96–97
Greene, Tom, 130*n*130
Greenfield, Lynette, 590*n*88
Greening, Leilani, 133*n*289
Greenleaf, Richard G., 524, 550*n*10
Greenman, Sara J., 590*n*103, 591*n*149
Greenwald, Mark A., 589*n*51, 590*n*103, 591*n*149, 630*n*20
Greenwood, Peter W., 76*n*101, 443, 449*n*86, 479, 483*n*39, 483*n*54, 483*n*65, 518*n*68, 518*n*70, 518*n*80,

545, 585, 589*n*57, 591*nn*149–150, 630*n*10, 630*n*25, 631*n*52, 631*n*63, 633*n*163
Gregorie, Trudy, 630*n*34
Gregory, Alice, 132*n*214
Grey, Scott F., 441
Griffin, Patricia A., 589*n*52
Griffin, Patrick, 518*n*81, 589*nn*67–69, 590*n*109
Griffiths, Curt Taylor, 212*n*106
Grigor, Joanne, 285*n*161
Grimes, Paul W., 630*n*29
Grimm, Gavin, 381
Grisso, Thomas, 588*n*5, 589*n*73, 614, 632*n*119
Griswold, Manzer, 284*n*106
Groff, Elizabeth, 129*n*101
Gross, Harriet, 134*n*306
Grossman, Elyse, 40*n*96
Grossman, Jean Bladwin, 518*n*65
Grotzinger, Andrew, 375*n*22
Grubstein, Lori, 76*n*96
Gruenewald, Paul, 177*n*73
Grunwald, Meagan, *503*
Grus, Catherine, 326*n*121
Gruszczynska, Beata, 641t, 665*n*50
Guarino, Richard, 40*n*99
Guarino-Ghezzi, Susan, 550*n*18
Guarneri, Christine E., 39*n*3
Gudjonsson, Gisli, 133*n*302
Guevara, Loris, 588*nn*11–12
Guggenheim, Martin, 589*n*44
Guijarro, Margarita, 247*n*28
Gulley, Bill, 131*n*196, 325*n*96
Gundry, Gwen, 325*n*106
Gunter, Tracy, 131*n*168
Guy, Laura S., 630*n*19

H

Haack, D., 130*n*139
Haapanen, Rudy, 129*n*79, 129*n*88, 132*n*250, 250*n*147
Haas, Ain, 178*n*129
Haberman, Cory, 129*n*101
Habermann, Niels, 130*n*155
Hadders-Algra, Mijna, 130*n*135
Haegerich, Tamara M., 447*n*2
Hafen, Christopher, 375*n*9
Hagan, John, 247*n*23, 277, 278, 285*n*156, 285*n*157, 664*n*16
Hagedorn, John, 376*n*67, 376*n*68, 376*n*78, 377*n*160, 378*n*206, 449*n*73, 449*n*102
Hahm, Hyeouk Chris, 284*n*116
Hahn, Robert, 573
Halbfinger, David M., 631*n*91
Hale, Bill, 133*n*257
Hale, Chris, 664*n*1, 664*n*15, 665*n*60, 665*n*62, 666*n*70
Hale, Donna, 517*n*26
Halemba, Gregory, 517*n*46
Halldorsson, Thorhallur I., 130*n*135
Halleck, Seymour, 132*n*233, 132*n*242
Hallet, Amanda, 247*n*28
Hallett, Michael, 75*n*55
Halliday-Boykins, Colleen A., 513
Halpern, Diane, 283*n*14
Haltigan, John, 285*n*162
Hamai, Koichi, 639, 666*n*82
Hamburg, Beatrix, 484*n*77
Hamby, Sherry, 76*n*105, 76*n*106, 285*n*117
Hamparian, Donna, 75*n*77, 76*n*92
Han, Yoonsun, 180*n*222
Hancock, Gareth, 666*n*111
Hancock, James Austin, *231*
Haney, J. Phil, 482*n*6, 588*n*21
Hanks, C. A., 483*n*42
Hanks, Carole, 482*n*36
Hanley, Sean, 450*n*138
Hannon, Lance, 176*n*7
Hansell, Stephen, 450*n*109
Hansen, David, 39*n*30
Hapy, Jennell, *593*
Harden, Hazel, 550*n*13
Harden, Paige, 375*n*22
Harden, Philip, 130*n*154, 325*n*103
Hardin, Rusty, *301*
Harding, Courtney, 415*n*25
Harding, Karen, 131*n*173
Hardt, Robert, 74*n*16
Hareven, Tamara K., 39*n*49
Harhut, Chester, 588*n*15

Harlow, Caroline Wolf, 415*n*33
Harper, Shaun, 385
Harper-Chang, Lisa, 377*n*131
Harrell, Adele V., 485*n*126
Harrington, Kathy, 247*n*34
Harrington, Richard, 485*n*131
Harris, Angela P., 285*n*149
Harris, Christopher J., 552*n*126
Harris, Eric, 395, 396e
Harris, Gardiner, 450*n*130
Harris, Judith Rich, 375*n*15, 375*nn*11–12
Harris, Keith, 176*n*45
Harris, Mark, 176*n*44
Harris, Meena, 39*n*35, 175*n*2, 375*nn*56–57
Harris, Nathan, 212*n*96
Harris, Philip, 76*n*96
Harris-McKoy, DeAnna, 179*n*161, 324*n*55
Harrison, Hannah Moore, 374*n*6
Harrison, Lana, 448*n*12
Harrison, Paige, 511
Hart, C., 133*n*267
Hart, Elizabeth, 131*n*170
Hart, Timothy, 74*n*39
Hartinger, Walter, 631*nn*60–61
Hartnett, Susan M., 551*n*71
Hartney, Christopher, 632*n*110
Hartstone, Eliot, 551*n*85
Hartwell, Stephanie, 633*n*167
Hartwig, Holly, 285*n*164
Harvey, Shane, 118
Harwin, Alex, 417*n*129
Harwood, Henrick J., 448*n*17
Hasin, Deborah, 447*n*10, 447*n*11
Haskett, Mary, 326*n*121
Haskins, Ron, 590*n*125
Hastings, Ross, 461, 666*n*118
Haviland, Amelia, 127*n*28
Hawes, J., 631*n*55
Hawk, Shila René, 177*n*75
Hawk, Skyler, 283*n*21
Hawken, Angela, 449*n*91
Hawkins, Gordon, 665*n*49
Hawkins, J., 282*n*11
Hawkins, J. David, 76*n*102, 222e, 247*n*48, 248*n*51, 249*n*129, 250*n*149, 250*n*151, 250*n*177, 323*n*2, 377*n*125, 449*n*74, 482*n*15, 484*n*79, 484*n*80, 485*n*122
Hawkins, Stephanie, 268, 285*n*123, 633*n*154
Haws, Susan, 450*n*138
Hawthorne, Richard D., 441
Hawton, Keith, 247*n*31
Hay, Carter, 75*n*69, 176*n*18, 178*n*127, 179*n*167, 211*n*18, 211*n*33, 212*n*98, 249*n*106, 324*n*62, 518*n*78, 585, 591*nn*152–153
Hay, Dale, 133*n*285, 282*n*6, 282*n*12
Hayes-Smith, Justin, 448*n*53
Hayes-Smith, Rebecca, 448*n*53
Haynes, Stacy, 590*n*98, 605, 631*n*51
Haynie, Dana, 127*n*25, 131*n*197, 177*n*58, 179*n*185, 179*n*198, 249*n*130, 262, 284*n*70, 284*n*75, 285*n*137, 323*n*4, 375*n*23, 375*n*31, 449*n*65
Hayslett-McCall, Karen L., 132*n*238
He, J., 129*n*123
He, Ni, 665*n*51
Healy, Deirdre, 247*n*19
Healy, William, 121, 134*n*313, 261, 283*nn*56–57
Heath, Andrew, 375*n*19
Heaton, Joan, 229
Heaton, Paul, 447*nn*9–10
Heaton, Tim B., 323*n*20
Heckert, Alex, 165, 180*n*206, 212*n*74
Heckert, Druann, 165, 180*n*206, 212*n*74
Heckman, James, 467, 483*n*68
Heflinger, Craig Anne, 375*n*16
Hegong, Fu, 635
Heilbrun, Kirk, 589*n*52
Heimer, Karen, 133*n*264, 133*n*265, 176*n*42, 211*n*46, 283*n*37
Heinrich, Danny, 67
Heinzow, Birger, 130*n*125
Hektner, Joel, 179*n*196
Helenius, Hans, 324*n*27
Helfer, Ray, 326*n*139
Hellman, Daryl, 416*n*84, 416*n*97
Hellum, Frank, 40*n*89
Hemmens, Craig, 40*n*100, 517*n*45, 573
Henderson, Charles, Jr., 130*n*130, 482*n*35, 482*n*36, 483*n*41

McCord, Joan, 247n20, 323n7, 482n18, 482n20, 482n21, 482n33, 484n81, 484n90, 484n112, 485n130, 518n76, 518n79, 550n58, 552n110, 632n122, 652t, 665n43
McCord, William, 482n18
McCowan, Karen, 513
McCrary, Gregg, 229
McCurley, Carl, 435, 436t, 450n112
McDermott, Joan, 524
McDevitt, Jack, 376n113, 551n71
McDonald, Lance, 327n186
McDonough, Meghan, 375n26
McDougal, Jim, 378n187, 378n190
McDowall, David, 40n93
McDuff, Pierre, 376n120
McFall, Richard, 134n320
McFarland, Christine, 130n129
McFarland, Joel, 387f, 415n12
McFarlane, Elizabeth, 483n46, 518n63
McGarrell, Edmund, 207, 550n17, 551n99, 630n40
McGee, Jocelyn, 282n13, 283n15
McGee, Rob, 133n295, 665n25
McGill, Kim, 629n1
McGloin, Jean Marie, 133n282, 134n327, 247n42, 247n43, 247n44, 249n114, 284n112, 375n16, 449n64
McGlothlin, W., 449n107
McGowan, Angela, 572f, 573
McGrath, Andrew, 666n99
McGue, Matt, 132n203
McGuffin, Peter, 132n203
McGuigan, K., 450n137
McHale, Rosalie, 631n87
McHugh, Suzanne, 131n197
McKay, Henry, 141, 142, 176n36, 176n40, 324n36, 456, 482n16
McLanahan, Sara, 323n11, 324n45
McLaughlin, Joseph, 415n15
McLeod, Geraldine, 324n29
McMackin, Robert, 633n167
McMahon, Pamela M., 482n6, 588n21
McMahon, R. J., 484n81
McManus, Terry, 417n117
McMillan, Richard, 176n39
McMorris, Barbara J., 248n79
McNulty, Thomas, 75n63, 134n326, 415n36
McPherson, Susan, 327n186
McReynolds, Larkin S., 589n56
Mdzinarishvili, A., 129n123
Mead, George Herbert, 210n3
Meadows, Sarah, 282n9, 323n9
Mealey, Linda, 133n300
Meares, Tracey, 535, 550n17, 551n65, 551n83
Mears, Daniel, 248n73, 283n19, 508t, 517nn56–57, 518n78, 573, 578, 585, 589n46, 589n51, 590n103, 591n149, 591nn152–153, 610, 630n42, 631n71, 631n84, 633n149
Measelle, Jeffrey, 131n199
Medaris, Michael, 417nn111–112
Medina, Justin, 177n81
Mednick, Birgitte, 130n152
Mednick, Sarnoff, 75n81, 130n137, 130n152, 131n179, 132n210
Meesters, Cor, 131n169
Meeus, Wim, 133n257, 283n21
Mehlkop, Guido, 128n45
Mei, Jianming, 665n37
Meier, Megan, 11
Meier, Robert, 176n35
Meisner, Jason, 199
Melde, Chris, 178n138, 247n15, 356, 377n130
Meldrum, Ryan, 179n195, 249n106, 375n27
Mellingen, Kjetil, 130n137
Melnick, Merrill, 283n33
Meltzer, Howard, 133n255
Menard, Scott, 248n87, 249n129, 250n156, 437, 448n55, 450n119
Mendel, Richard A., 485n129
Mendenhall, Ruby, 177n76
Menlove, Frances, 132n271
Mennel, Robert M., 39n49, 517n3, 517n6, 517n12
Merkens, Hans, 664n16
Merlo, Alida V., 590n121, 591n151
Mersky, Joshua, 179n164, 483n70
Mertinko, Elizabeth, 472t
Merton, Robert, 148, 148t, 149, 178n108
Meseck-Bushey, Sylvia, 131n196, 325n96
Messer, Julie, 133n255

Messerschmidt, James, 276, 283n16, 285n148
Messerschmidt, Pamela, 416n75
Messersmith, Emily, 53
Messner, Steven, 74n8, 75n68, 127n15, 150, 175n3, 176n10, 176n39, 178nn112–113
Messner, Warren, 555, 555
Metsger, Linda, 128n73
Michaelsen, Kim Fleischer, 130n135
Michel, Sonya, 483n55
Mick, Eric, 131n171
Midgley, Erin Kathleen, 284n108, 325n91
Miech, Richard A., 74n18, 247n32, 425, 426f, 447n1, 447nn7–8, 448n14, 448n22, 448n32, 448n35, 448n37, 666n72
Miethe, Terance, 74n39
Mihalic, Sharon F., 479, 632n110
Mikulich-Gilbertson, Susan K., 130n151
Milan, Stephanie, 247n14
Miles, Alice, 482n3, 483n45
Miller, Alden, 630n11
Miller, Anne, 655, 664n17
Miller, Brenda, 325n115, 326n133
Miller, Darcy, 282n5
Miller, Donna J., 568
Miller, J. Mitchell, 247n30, 284n69, 614
Miller, Jerome, 595, 630n9
Miller, Jody, 248n52, 268, 276, 283nn49–50, 285n122, 285n150, 376nn85–86, 377nn177–178, 401, 416n87
Miller, Kathleen, 283n33
Miller, Laurie S., 482n33
Miller, Lisa, 178n102
Miller, Marna G., 443, 485n135, 518n60, 518n82
Miller, Maureen, 448n12
Miller, Nancy, 40n96
Miller, Shari, 283n66, 285n130
Miller, Stuart J., 631n58, 631n95
Miller, Ted, 455, 482n12, 483n40
Miller, Todd, 247n28
Miller, Walter, 153, 154e, 178nn140–141, 179n179, 335e, 375n49, 375nn38–39, 375nn51–52, 457, 482n23
Miller-Johnson, Shair, 375n10
Milner, Trudie, 128n68
Min, Meeyoung O., 449n70
Miner, Michael, 326n135
Minnes, Sonia, 449n70
Minor, M. William, 180n207
Minter, Mallory, 248n60
Minton, Sophia, 491
Minton, Todd D., 40n62
Minugh, Allison, 416n77
Mio, J. S., 449n71
Miodovnik, Amir, 130n127
Mirowsky, John, 177n70
Mischel, Walter, 115, 133n290
Mitchell, Brian David, 68
Mitchell, Derek, 134n310
Mitchell, Kimberly, 39n26
Mitchell, Nick, 212n72, 212n78
Mitchell, Ojmarrh, 211n22, 249n132, 510, 518n71, 518n73
Mitchell, S. David, 416n89
Mitchell, Sadie, 43
Mitri, Lysee, 113
Mocan, Naci, 128n40
Moch, Annie, 39n17
Model, Karyn E., 483n54
Modrowski, Crosby, 377n165
Modzeleski, William, 416n62
Moffitt, Terrie, 75n81, 76n97, 131n166, 131n199, 132n205, 132n206, 133n295, 134n320, 237–239, 247n29, 247n32, 248n49, 248n58, 248n60, 250n143, 250n145, 250n154, 250n160, 250n166, 250n167, 250n171, 250nn174–175, 270, 284n72, 324n43, 415n35
Mohamed, Ahmed, 183
Mohamed, Mohamed, 546
Moilanen, Irma, 324n27
Molina, Marilu, 453
Monaghan, Rachel, 39n23, 416n65
Monahan, Susanne, 75n47
Monahan, Thomas, 324n35
Monge, Peter, 375n34
Montie, Jeanne, 483n66
Monuteaux, Michael, 131n171
Moon, Byongook, 178n134, 283n25
Moon, Seong Hyeok, 483n68

Moore, Elizabeth, 249n118
Moore, Joan, 269, 285nn125–126, 345, 375n54, 376n83, 376n90
Moore, Kristin, 180n228
Moore, Mark, 378n202, 450n134, 544, 549n2, 552n113, 552n115, 591n147
Moore, Melanie, 179n169
Moore, Solomon, 614
Moore, Westley "Wes," 471, 484n88
Moran, P., 133n267
Morash, Merry, 178n134, 283n25, 283nn49–50, 285n159, 285n166
Morenoff, Jeffrey, 176n49, 176n54
Morgan, Hubert, 568
Morgan, Rachel E., 57
Morris, Allison, 282n8
Morris, Miranda, 283n17
Morris, Norval, 75n73, 324n22, 549n2, 552n113
Morris, Robert, 180n208, 211n62, 249n132, 250n162, 375n13, 549n10
Morris, Ruth, 266, 284n100, 284n102, 324n34
Morse, Edward, 247n29
Morse, Stephen J., 40n57
Morselli, Carlo, 127n12, 179nn187–188
Mortensen, P. B., 131n188
Morton, Lindsay, 283n27
Mosciki, Eve, 573
Mossakowski, Krysia, 247n29
Moule, Richard, Jr., 155, 377n184
Mouren, Marie-Christine, 129n120, 129n121
Mowen, Thomas, 415n3
Mueller, David, 378n198, 517n45
Muftic, Lisa, 178n114
Muhleman, Donn, 284n77
Mukherjhee, Satyanshu, 666n84
Mullen, Paul, 133n268
Mullins, Christopher, 211n37
Mulvey, Edward, 74n24, 75n79, 128n55, 517n51, 589n38, 633n156, 633n162
Mun, Eun Young, 631n90
Muncie, John, 656, 666n97, 666n117
Murata, K., 129n120
Murcheson, C., 134n311
Muris, Peter, 131n169
Murphy, Brian, 145
Murphy, Fred, 74n16
Murphy, Patrick, 448n57, 451n162
Murphy-Graham, Erin, 441
Murray, Charles, 130n160, 194, 212n68, 594, 629n5
Murray, Ellen, 180n215
Murray, Joseph, 248n72, 325n85, 325n90, 325n92, 589n50
Murray, Lawrence F., 485n125
Murray, R. M., 131n188
Murry, Velma McBride, 132n239
Musci, Rashelle, 169
Musk, Elon, 150
Musu-Gillette, Lauren, 387f, 415n12, 415n17
Mutchnick, Robert, 129n104
Muthan, Hoda, 199
Muthén, Bengt, 484n84
Myers, David, 40n61, 517n49, 573, 589n72
Myers, Jane, 285n164
Myers, Stephanie M., 550n54, 550n59

N
Na, Chongmin, 484n78, 551n101
Nagin, Daniel, 127n28, 128n45, 128n46, 128n49, 128n51, 128n53, 128n61, 128n65, 128n74, 128n75, 220, 248n50, 248n65, 248n68, 249n114, 249n117, 250n150, 250n151, 461, 461t, 551n95
Najaka, Stacy Skroban, 450n137, 469e
Najdowski, Cynthia, 127n30
Najman, Jake, 131n195, 323n15, 325n95
Nanjundappa, G., 449n71
Nash, Michael, 620
Natarajan, Mangai, 664n2, 664n4
Nation, Maury, 375n16
Natsuaki, Misaki, 75n71, 75n76
Nawa, Shinpei, 665n30
Neaigus, Alan, 448n12
Neal, David, 74n17
Neal, Stephen, 284n79
Nedelec, Joseph L., 132n216, 134n308
Needleman, Herbert, 130n129, 130n130
Neff, James Alan, 450n144
Nellis, Ashley, 590n128, 631n89

Neppl, Tricia K., 323n20
Ness, Arlin, 632n123
Ness, Roberta, 130n129
Newbury-Birch, Dorothy, 630n39
Newman, Graeme, 40n56, 641t, 664n13, 665n41, 665n45, 665n47
Newman, Tony, 128n63
Ng, Christina, 249n92
Ng, Irene, 632n103
Nguyen, Holly, 333e
Nicewander, W. Alan, 228, 249n93
Nichols, Emily, 484n92
Nicosia, Nancy, 448n27
Niederhoffer, Arthur, 358, 377nn148–149
Nielsen, Mark, 115
Niemelä, Solja, 324n27
Nieuwbeerta, Paul, 246n5, 247n38, 325n85
Nilsonne, Äsa, 130n141
Nilsson, Anders, 75n65
Nilsson, L.-L., 133n265
Nixon, Jay, 425, 425
Nixon, K., 129n123
No, Unkyung, 115
Noblin, Charles D., 589n73
Nocera, Joe, 448n30
Nofziger, Stacey, 176n8, 249n105, 249n106
Noone, Diana C., 448n46
Nordström, Anna-Lena, 130n141
Nordström, Peter, 130n141
Nordström, Tanja, 131n172
Nores, Milagros, 483n66, 483n67
Noriega, Manuel, 439
Normore, Anthony, 275
Norris, Michael, 511
Norris, Robert J., 589n60
Novak, Kenneth, 75n49, 551n77
Novotney, Laurence C., 472t
Nowotny, Kathryn, 377n164
Nurco, David, 247n46
Nutton, Jennifer, 132n240
Nuutila, Art-Matti, 324n27
Nye, F. Ivan, 74n32, 295, 297, 324n48, 325n73

O

Oakes, Jeannie, 391, 415n43, 415n45
Obama, Barack, 464, 610
Obradovic, Jelena, 249n131
O'Brien, Natalie, 415n39
O'Connell, Elizabeth, 653
O'Connell, Michael, 653
Oddy, Wendy, 130n138
Odem, Mary, 517n31
O'Donovan, Michael, 131n182
Offord, David R., 484n107, 485n131
Oghia, Michael, 324n44
Oglivie, James, 99, 130n148
Ogloff, James, 133n268
Ohlin, Lloyd, 39n50, 156, 179nn153–158, 359, 449n62, 457, 630n11
Oken, Emily, 130n133, 130n135
Olds, David L., 482n35, 482n36, 482n37, 483n38, 483n41, 483n42, 485n132
Olsen, Sjurdur F., 130n135
Olweus, Dan, 398, 399
O'Malley, Patrick, 74n18, 74n33, 283n48, 284n111, 425, 426f, 447n1, 447n11, 447nn7–8, 448n14, 448n22, 448n32, 448n35, 448n37, 448nn49–50, 666n72
O'Neal, Eryn Nicolle, 377n184
O'Neal, Shaquille, 240
Onge, Jarron Saint, 377n164
Onishi, Norimitsu, 665n29
Opler, Mark, 130n131
Orlandi, Mario A., 484nn104–106
Orme, Nicholas, 16, 39n40
Ormrod, Richard, 76n106
Orosco, Carlena, 375n8
Orsi, Rebecca, 248n87
Ortman, Jennifer M., 39n3
Osborn, Denise, 128n35, 133n267
Osborne, Lynn, 493, 517n17
Osgood, Aurea, 324n44
Osgood, D. Wayne, 53, 228, 248n85, 249n93, 284n80, 284n111, 323n4, 375n31, 551nn103–106
Oshima, Karen Matta, 323n6
Osterdal, Marie Louise, 130n135
Ostrow, Miriam, 450n148, 450n151

O'Sullivan, Therese, 130n138
O'Toole, Mary Ellen, 416n62
Ou, Suh-Ruu, 483n70, 483n71, 483n72
Oudekerk, Barbara A., 57, 633n157
Ouimet, Marc, 249n111, 249n113
Ouimette, Paige Crosby, 132n243
Ousey, Graham, 53, 177n57, 177n58, 250n173
Owen, Barbara, 632n106
Owen, Michael, 131n182
Owens, Colleen E., 508t, 517nn56–57
Owens, Elizabeth, 131n174
Owens, Jennifer Gatewood, 250n158
Özbay, Özden, 180n222
Özcan, Yusuf Ziya, 180n222
Ozonoff, Al, 284n116

P

Pacheco, Daniel, 250n162
Packer, Herbert, 550n53
Pacula, Rosalie L., 447n11, 447nn9–10, 448n27
Padilla, Felix, 361, 375n53, 377n172
Pagani-Kurtz, Linda, 484n81
Paik, Anthony, 283n37
Painter, Kate A., 666n111
Paiva-Salisbury, Melissa L., 630n19
Pajer, Kathleen, 263, 282n3, 284n79
Pallone, Nathaniel, 324n68
Palma, Sheila, 415n15
Palmer, Emma, 323n5
Palmer, James, 517n55
Palmer, Julie, 176n7
Pan, En-Ling, 324n32
Pandit, Eesha, 69
Papachristos, Andrew, 128n70, 129n99, 357, 377n142, 550n17
Papachristos, Andrew V., 545
Papillo, Angela Romano, 180n228
Paradis, Emily, 326n136
Parcel, Toby, 415n48
Pardini, Dustin, 248n72, 249n131, 325n90
Parent, Dale, 589n71, 632n137
Park, Yoonhwan, 176n51, 176n55
Parker, Akeema, 30
Parker, Karen, 75n52, 176n30
Parker, M. Michaux, 376n66
Parks, Roger B., 550n20
Parrott, Caroline, 132n241
Parrott, Scott, 132n241
Parsons, Deborah, 212n105
Parsons, Patrick J., 130n130
Parsons, Thomas, 282n13, 283n15
Parvez, Faruque, 129n124
Paschall, Mallie, 75n59
Pasko, Lisa, 279, 285n138, 285n167
Passini, Stefano, 450n116
Patchin, Justin, 11, 13, 39n24, 39n27, 39n29, 176n9, 397, 416n68
Patel, Sadiq, 132n248
Paterno, Joe, 306
Paternoster, Raymond, 74n42, 127n26, 127n28, 128n65, 128n76, 211n26, 212n71, 237, 246n11, 248n56, 248n65, 248n68, 248n84, 249n96, 250n152, 250n170, 324n30, 415n13, 415n24, 535, 551n66
Patterson, Charlotte, 324n59, 324n65
Patterson, Gerald, 247n24, 247n33, 248n57, 463, 464, 483n50, 483n51
Patterson, Megan, 375n22
Patton, Jonnetta, 240
Pauwels, Lieven, 128n66
Payne, Allison Ann, 180n225, 211n27, 247n16, 283n66, 283nn49–50, 416n50, 416n94, 416n96
Payne, Danielle, 179n173, 374n5
Payne, Gary, 178n125, 180n234
Pear, Robert, 631n74
Peck, Jennifer H., 589n48, 630n18
Pedersen, Sara, 375n33
Pedroza, Juan, 375n8
Peel, Robert, 522
Peete, Thomas, 128n68
Peguero, Anthony, 393, 416n56
Pelham, Molina, Jr., 131n169
Pelham, William, 130n157
Peng, Samuel, 416n76, 416n85
Penke, Lars, 283n22
Penn, Joseph, 614
Pennucci, Anne, 443, 485n135, 518n60, 518n82

Pepler, D. J., 283n18
Perel, James, 284n79
Perera, Frederica, 130n126
Perez, Cynthia, 246n12, 247n32
Perkins, Molly, 247n18, 248n70
Perlmutter, M., 133n280
Perrault, Rachael T., 630n19
Perron, Brian, 130n145
Perrone, Paul, 374n2
Perry, Cheryl L., 450n109
Perry, David, 133n272
Perry, Louise, 133n272
Perusse, Daniel, 132n204
Peskin, Melissa, 449n75
Pesta, George B., 589n51
Petechuk, David, 66e
Peters, R. DeV., 484n81
Petersilia, Joan, 211n29, 482n33, 549n9, 631n52, 633n151, 665n39
Peterson, Adrian, 301
Peterson, Dana, 551n103, 551nn105–106
Peterson, John, 40n89
Peterson, Ruth, 176n29, 176n31, 176n44
Peterson, Zoë, 127n13
Petras, Hanno, 246n5, 247n47, 484n84
Petrocelli, Matthew, 212n81
Petrosino, Anthony, 212n95
Petrosino, Carolyn, 212n95
Pettis, Alphonso, 464
Pettit, Gregory, 177n86, 179n165, 284n73, 325n78, 327n172
Petts, Richard, 159, 179n178
Pfeffer, Rebecca P., 482n5, 517n39
Pfeiffer, Christian, 643, 664n9, 664n14, 665n44, 665n59, 665n61
Phelps, Charles, 482n36
Philibert, Robert, 129n115, 131n183
Phillips, Deborah, 459, 483n74
Phillips, Julie, 74n36, 75n61, 75n64
Phillips, Llad, 323n13
Phillips, M., 589n53
Phillips, Richard Todd, 215
Phillips, Tim, 177n70
Pi, Yijun, 178n129
Piaget, Jean, 116, 133n275
Pickett, Justin, 211n25, 591n153, 630n42
Pickett, Robert S., 517n11
Pickrel, Susan G., 443
Piehl, Anne Morrison, 545, 552n124
Pierce, Christine Schnyder, 588nn6–7
Pierce, Glenn, 376n113
Piersma, Paul, 590n136
Piha, Jorma, 324n27
Pihl, Robert, 130n154, 325n103, 484n81
Piliavin, Irving, 167, 180n210, 180n213, 550n56, 551n74
Pilnick, Paul, 631n53
Pinchevsky, Gillian M., 448n56
Pincus, Jonathan, 130n156
Pinderhughes, Ellen, 247n14
Pinto, Rodrigo, 483n68
Piquero, Alex, 15, 74n22, 128n55, 130n142, 133n259, 134n322, 134n323, 178n125, 178n126, 178n131, 178n139, 211n62, 212n81, 221, 235, 246n5, 246n10, 246n11, 247n37, 247n38, 247n42, 247n44, 247n45, 248n86, 249n100, 249n112, 249n114, 249n122, 249n132, 250n139, 250n145, 250n147, 250n160, 250n165, 250n170, 262, 284n75, 284n91, 375n35, 415n27, 415n34, 455, 461, 461t, 482n7, 482n9, 483n49, 485n120, 485n121, 524, 589n49, 631n81, 633n162, 633n164, 633n166
Piquero, Alex R., 39n36
Piquero, Nicole Leeper, 178n131, 248n58, 250n143, 633n164, 633n166
Pittaro, Michael, 275
Piza, Eric L., 552n130
Platt, Anthony, 39n48, 198, 212n87, 493, 517n7, 517nn15–16, 590n104
Platt, Christina, 449n81
Platt, Jerome, 449n81
Pleck, Elizabeth, 39n50, 39n53, 40n55, 517n23, 517n24
Ploeger, Matthew, 127n27, 179n189, 179n196, 283n19
Plomin, Robert, 132n206, 132n214
Plushnick-Masti, Ramit, 160, 179n180
Poduska, Jeanne M., 484n84
Poe-Yamagata, Eileen, 590n86

Rubin, H. Ted, 550*n*50
Rubin, Joel, 40*n*103
Rubin, K. H., 399
Rubin, Robert, 284*n*79
Rubio, Alexandra, *314*
Rubio, Angel and Sandra, *314*
Ruchkin, Vladislav, 324*n*60
Rudo-Hutt, Anna, 131*n*177
Rudolph, Jennifer, 178*n*133, 247*n*22
Ruggiero, Kenneth, 416*n*75
Ruiter, Stijn, 127*n*14
Ruiz, James, 552*n*117
Rumbelow, Helen, 482*n*3, 483*n*45
Rush, Haley, 113
Russell, Mark, 630*n*20
Rust, Roland, 461, 482*n*8
Rutter, Michael, 132*n*205
Ryan, Joseph, 134*n*324
Ryan, Trevor, 639, 665*n*33
Rydell, C. Peter, 483*n*39, 483*n*54
Ryer, Charles, 327*n*186

S

Saar, Saada, 279
Sabatelli, Ronald M., 552*n*109
Sabo, Don, 283*n*33
Sabol, William, 129*n*87
Sack, William, 326*n*141
Sagatun, Inger, 327*n*185
Sakamoto, Wayne, 347e
Saldana, Lisa, 285*n*160
Salekin, Randall, 283*n*67
Salerno, Anthony, 517*n*4, 517*n*14
Saltzman, Jonathan, 40*n*102
Sami, Nilofar, 131*n*174
Sample, Lisa, 285*n*162, 448*n*23
Sampson, Robert, 145, 176*n*49, 176*n*54, 177*n*62,
    177*n*78, 177*n*94, 177*n*96, 211*n*41, 211*n*43, 223–228,
    236, 247*n*25, 248*n*62, 248*n*66, 248*n*81, 250*n*141, 294,
    324*n*37, 325*n*104, 539, 551*n*94
Sanborn, Joseph, 589*n*63, 590*n*92
Sanchagrin, Kenneth, 283*n*37
Sanders, Matthew, 483*n*39, 483*n*52
Sanders, Wiley B., 39*n*45
Sandusky, Gerald Arthur "Jerry," 306, *306*
Sansone, Lori, 326*n*133
Sansone, Randy, 326*n*133
Santiago, Nixzaliz, 300
Sarkar, N. N., 326*n*132
Sarkar, Rina, 326*n*132
Sarri, Rosemary C., 632*n*103
Saunders, Benjamin, 416*n*75
Saunders, Frank, 284*n*105
Savage, Joanne, 665*n*40
Savelyev, Peter, 483*n*68
Savitz, L., 324*n*37
Savolainen, Jukka, 131*n*172, 248*n*91, 666*n*75
Scali, Mary Ann, 633*n*146
Scamahorn, Christopher, 555
Scarpitti, Frank, 180*n*215
Schaefer, Brian, 448*n*13
Schaefer, Catherine, 130*n*131
Schaefer, David R., 57
Schaefer, Diane, 212*n*103
Schaefer, Shelly, 588*n*13
Schaeffer, Cindy, 247*n*47, 443
Schafer, Joseph, 177*n*59
Schafer, Stephen, 74*n*13
Schafer, Walter, 415*n*5
Schaible, Lonnie, 75*n*69, 176*n*18
Schall, Victoria L., 589*n*51
Scharf, P., 133*n*277
Schaste, Robert, 632*n*120
Schicor, David, 335e
Schiff, Mara, 212*n*107
Schindler, Holly S., 459, 483*n*60, 484*n*75
Schinke, Steven P., 448*n*60, 484*nn*104–106
Schlesinger, Raci, 75*n*53
Schlossman, Steven, 482*n*17, 517*n*31
Schmeidler, J., 450*n*114
Schmidt, Annesley, 630*n*30
Schmidt, Eberhard, 130*n*125
Schmidt, Janell, 180*n*211
Schmidt, M. H., 130*n*139
Schmidt, Melinda G., 250*n*178, 588*nn*8–9
Schmidt, Nicole, 211*n*36, 211*n*38
Schnaas, Lourdes, 130*n*130

Schnebly, Stephen M., 177*n*80
Schneider, Anne, 630*n*48
Schneider, Jacqueline, 247*n*40
Schneider, Peter, 605, 630*n*44, 631*n*50
Schochet, Peter Z., 484*n*115
Schoenwald, Sonja K., 450*n*147
Schoeny, Michael S., 484*n*92
Schofield, Thomas J., 323*n*20
Schrag, Clarence, 178*n*148
Schreck, Christopher, 249*n*104, 284*n*69
Schroeder, Ryan, 226, 248*n*90, 324*n*44
Schubert, Carol, 74*n*22, 517*n*51, 633*n*156, 633*n*162
Schuck, Amie M., 485*n*123
Schug, Robert A., 449*n*75
Schulenberg, Jennifer, 333e, 655
Schulenberg, John, 53, 74*n*18, 248*n*85, 425, 426f,
    447*n*1, 447*n*11, 447*nn*7–8, 448*n*14, 448*n*22, 448*n*32,
    448*n*35, 448*n*37, 666*n*72
Schur, Edwin, 134*n*333, 210*n*2
Schuster, Richard, 75*n*77, 76*n*92
Schutt, Russell, 74*n*44, 551*n*79, 551*n*85
Schwartz, Ira, 585, 591*n*144, 591*n*146
Schwartz, Jennifer, 283*n*47
Schwartz, Joseph A., 132*n*216, 134*n*308
Schwartz, Martin, 283*n*36, 285*n*152
Schwartz, Robert, 589*n*73
Schweinhart, Lawrence J., 483*n*61, 483*n*62, 483*n*63,
    483*n*64, 483*n*66, 483*n*67
Schweit, Katherine, 127*n*5
Schwendinger, Herman, 285*n*140
Schwendinger, Julia, 285*n*140
Schwinn, Traci M., 448*n*60
Schworm, Peter, 186
Scott, Elizabeth S., 461, 461t, 589*n*73, 590*nn*129–130
Scourfield, Jane, 132*n*203
Scull, Tracy M., 450*n*139
Sealock, Miriam, 285*n*165
Seck, Mamadou M., 589*n*36
Seddig, Daniel, 179*n*168, 415*n*4
Sedlak, Michael, 482*n*17
Seeley, John R., 133*n*256
Seeley, Ken, 399, 416*n*72
Seffrin, Patrick, 180*n*236, 449*n*99
Segady, Thomas, 40*n*67
Segal, Nancy, 131*n*201
Seguin, Jean, 130*n*154
Sehgal, Amber, 630*nn*27–28
Selk, Avi, 210*n*1
Selke, William, 212*n*80
Sellers, Christine S., 180*n*201
Sellers, Courtenay, 133*n*269
Sellin, Thorsten, 64, 75*n*77, 76*n*90, 127*n*8, 129*n*108,
    246*n*9, 415*nn*31–32
Sen, Bisakha, 323*n*8
Sevigny, Eric L., 447*nn*9–10
Sexton, Thomas L., 518*n*66
Seymour, Anne, 204e, 630*n*34
Shakib, Sohaila, 416*n*55
Shane, Jon, 133*n*269
Shannon, Lyle W., 76*n*92, 415*n*30
Shannon, Sarah, 664*n*5
Shantz, David, 129*n*103
Shapira, Nathan, 247*n*35
Sharkey, Patrick, 145, 177*n*78, 178*nn*99–100
Sharman, Leah, 39*n*6
Sharrock, Katy, *359*
Shattuck, Anne, 76*n*105
Shau, Chang, 589*n*72
Shauffer, Carole, 589*n*42
Shaver, Debra, 130*n*161
Shaw, Clifford, 141, 142, 157, 176*n*36, 176*n*40, 324*n*36,
    456, 482*n*16
Shaw, Daniel, 325*n*86
Shaw, Mary, 323*n*15
Shaw-Smith, Unique, 248*n*75
Shear, Michael D., 631*n*66
Shedler, J., 449*n*85
Sheidow, Ashli J., 513
Shelden, Randall, 40*n*88, 285*n*163, 493, 517*n*17,
    551*n*89, 631*n*99
Shelley-Tremblay, John, 415*n*39
Shelton, Deborah, 614
Shepard, Robert, 588*n*26, 630*n*6
Shepherd, Jonathan, 247*n*37
Sherman, Francine T., 632*n*111
Sherman, Lawrence W., 180*n*211, 327*n*189, 450*n*137,
    469e, 483*n*39, 530e, 549*n*9, 550*n*31, 551*n*64, 551*n*66,
    604, 630*nn*35–39, 632*n*112

Shi, Jing, 631*n*90
Shichor, David, 665*n*40
Shields, Ian, 180*n*207
Shifley, Rick, 212*n*100
Shihadeh, Edward, 176*n*52
Shine, James, 559, 588*n*19
Shirley, Mary, 74*n*16
Shoenberger, Nicole, 165, 180*n*206
Shoesmith, Gary L., 53
Shollenberger, Tracey L., 508t, 517*nn*56–57
Shook, Jeffrey, 115, 283*n*48
Short, Elizabeth J., 449*n*70
Short, James, 74*n*32, 180*n*207, 335e
Short, Tamsin B. R., 133*n*268
Shotton, Alice, 589*n*42
Shover, Neal, 75*n*87
Shrout, Patrick, 211*n*9
Shufelt, Jennie L., 513
Shulman, Elizabeth, 377*n*165
Shum, David, 130*n*148
Shutt, J. Eagle, 249*n*108
Sia, Calvin, 483*n*46, 518*n*63
Sickmund, Melissa, 517*n*50, 570f, 579f, 590*n*86, 596f,
    611t, 613t, 620, 625e, 631*n*70, 631*n*76, 631*n*80,
    631*n*85, 631*n*94, 631*n*97, 631*nn*67–68, 632*n*100,
    632*n*126, 632*n*137
Sidora-Arcoleo, Kimberly, 483*n*41, 483*n*42
Siegel, Jane, 326*n*134
Siegel, Larry, 74*n*13
Sieleni, Bruce, 131*n*168
Siennick, Sonja, 133*n*266, 248*n*73, 248*n*85, 296,
    589*n*51
Sieverdes, Christopher, 631*n*96
Sigurdsson, Jon Fridrik, 133*n*302
Silbereisen, Ranier, 250*n*159
Silberman, Matthew, 128*n*65
Silburn, Sven, 130*n*138
Sillanmäki, Lauri, 324*n*27
Silva, Julie, 131*n*171, 248*n*80
Silva, Manori, 130*n*127
Silva, Phil, 76*n*97, 131*n*166, 134*n*320, 247*n*32, 248*n*49,
    250*nn*174–175, 284*n*72
Silver, Clayton, 324*n*60, 415*n*2
Silver, Eric, 133*nn*261–262, 178*n*102
Silver, H. K., 325*n*111
Silverman, Eli B., 74*n*11
Silverman, F. N., 325*n*111
Silverman, Jenna, 324*n*60
Silverman, Melissa, 132*n*250
Simi, Pete, 130*n*161
Simmons, Jay, 203
Simmons, Sara, 248*n*87
Simon, Leonore, 74*n*19, 131*n*165, 248*n*76, 325*n*99
Simon, Patricia, 247*n*29
Simon, Rae, 324*n*28
Simon, Rita James, 272, 285*nn*133–134
Simon, Ronald, 161
Simons, Julie, 589*n*72
Simons, Leslie Gordon, 132*n*239, 133*n*263, 323*n*3,
    324*n*61
Simons, Ronald, 104, 129*n*115, 132*n*215, 132*n*239,
    133*n*263, 155, 178*n*121, 179*n*181, 211*n*19, 222e,
    248*n*83, 248*n*84, 250*n*134, 323*n*3, 324*n*31
Simons, Ronald L., 131*n*183
Simons-Rudolph, Ashley, 450*n*135
Simpson, Donville, 43
Simpson, John, 285*n*156, 285*n*157
Simpson, Sally, 285*n*165
Sims, Barbara A., 552*n*117
Sinai, Cave, 130*n*141
Singer, Lynn T., 449*n*70
Skardhamar, Torbjorn, 248*n*91
Skinner, B. F., 114
Skinner, William, 179*n*196
Skogan, Wesley, 177*n*67, 549*n*7, 549*n*8, 550*n*20,
    550*n*31, 551*n*64, 551*n*71, 551*n*72, 552*n*132
Skogan, Wesley G., 539
Skowyra, Kathleen R., 614
Slade, Eric, 324*n*69
Sladky, Anthony, 570f, 579f, 596f, 611t, 613t, 620,
    631*n*70, 631*n*76, 631*n*80, 631*n*85, 631*n*94, 631*n*97,
    631*nn*67–68, 632*n*100, 632*n*126, 632*n*137
Sladky, T. J., 517*n*50
Slater, E., 283*n*63, 284*n*101
Slaughter, Ellen, 551*n*85
Slavkovich, Vesna, 129*n*124
Slawson, John, 121, 134*n*317
Sloan, John Henry, 665*n*40

Sloan, John J., 128n50
Sloboda, Zili, 441
Slocum, Lee Ann, 211n63, 250n158
Slot, N. Wim, 666n99
Slothower, Molly, 630n39
Small, John, 284n104
Smallbone, Stephen, 128n31
Smallish, Lori, 131n169
Smart, Elizabeth, 68, *68*
Smith, Alisa, 633n162
Smith, Beverly, 517n20
Smith, Brian H., 484n79
Smith, Carolyn, 40n86, 131n193, 179n170, 179n192, 247n28, 283n65, 285n137, 324n40, 325n77, 325n89, 327nn183–184, 377n128, 377n132, 377n156
Smith, Christine, 483n47
Smith, Dana, 285n160
Smith, David J., 655
Smith, Douglas, 180n211, 211n41, 551n79, 551n91, 551nn61–62
Smith, Edward, 385
Smith, G. T., 449n89
Smith, Hayden, 247n36
Smith, Joseph, *260*
Smith, Justin M., 448n53
Smith, Karl G., 484n79
Smith, Michael, 212n81
Smith, Paula, 485n128
Smith, Philip, 177n70
Smith, Steven K., 590n83, 590n87, 590n90
Smith, Timothy, 247n28
Smith, William, 128n41, 551n80
Smith-Adcock, Sondra, 285n128
Snell, Clete, 448n31
Snowden, Edward, 196
Snyder, Howard, 76n92, 435, 436t, 450n112, 590n86, 625e
Snyder, Lindsey, 131n171
Snyder, Phyllis, 40n90, 40n92
Snyder, Susan, 573
Socia, Kelly, 177n79
Soderstrom, Irina, 632n128
Soler, Mark, 589n42
Soller, Marie, 132n250
Solnit, Albert, 578, 590n105
Solomon, Amy, 211n39, 248n67
Solórzano, Borromeo Enrique Henriquez, *340*
Solow, Robert M., 551n95
Somerville, Dora, 266, 284n103
Somkin, Carol, 177n83
Sonnenberg, Sherrie, 285n162
Sorenson, Ann Marie, 249n111, 249n113, 376n122, 377n159
Sorenson, Jon R., 631n78
Sorenson, Susan, 282n7
Sorg, Evan, 129n101
Soto, Danielle, 211n37
Soukamneuth, Sukey, 485n119
Soulé, David, 128n44, 416n52, 484n101, 484n110, 484n111
Sourander, Andre, 324n27
South, Scott, 176n50
Soyfer, Liana, 131n177
Spano, Richard, 356, 377n133
Sparks, Justin, *438*
Sparks, Raymond, 524
Sparks, Sarah D., 417n129
Sparrow, Malcolm, 549n2
Spatz Widom, Cathy, 326n131, 327n179, 327n181, 449n68, 482n33, 484n112, 518n76, 518n79, 550n58, 552n110, 652t, 665n43
Speckart, George, 450n117
Spelman, William, 176n47
Spence, Karen, 415n48
Spencer, Margaret Beale, 633n152
Spencer, Renée, 484n93
Spencer, Thomas, 131n171
Spergel, Irving, 177n63, 335e, 359, 361, 369, 375n48, 375nn41–42, 376n99, 377n154, 377n171, 377n176, 377nn161–162, 378n205
Spielvogel, Jackson, 39n38
Spilseth, Donald, 205
Spivak, Andrew L., 285n155
Spohn, Cassia, 75n58, 551n88, 588nn11–12
Spohn, Ryan, 323n12
Spracklen, Kathleen, 375n28, 448n58

Sprott, Jane, 415n48, 655, 666n90
Sprowls, J., 589n53
Spurgeon, Jeffrey, 555
Squires, Gregory, 176n57
Sridharan, Sanjeev, 485n126, 590n88
Stack, Susan, 75n81
Staff, Jeremy, 53, 248n85, 415n38
Stahlkopf, Christina, 629n3
Stairsm Jayne, 75n57
Stalnaker, Carla, 504
Stamatel, Janet, 177n79
Stancl, Anthony, 12, *12*
Stanley, Fiona, 130n138
Starling, Jean, 284n115
Stattin, Hakin, 375n9
Stearns, Justin, 555
Steele, Brandt F., 325n111, 326n139, 326n140
Steele, Patricia, 630n11
Steele, Ric, 449nn79–80
Steen, Sara, 75n51, 75n56, 461, 482n8, 631n82
Steenbeek, Wouter, 178n98
Steer, Colin, 129n119
Steffensmeier, Darrell, 75n57, 177n58, 283n47, 283nn49–50, 285n137
Stein, Judith, 180n223
Stein, Nancy, 285n151
Steinberg, Laurence, 325n74, 377n165, 434, 461, 461t, 524, 589n73, 590n125, 590nn129–130, 633n164, 633n166
Steiner, Benjamin, 40n100, 517n45, 573
Steiner, Hans, 132n250, 133n259, 284n91
Steingürber, Hans-J., 130n125
Steinhart, David, 517n35, 589n41
Steinharthe, David J., 40n70, 40n76
Steinka-Fry, Katarzyna T., 450n149
Steinke, Camela M., 40n87
Steinmentz, Suzanne, 326n123
Steketee, Majone, 284n93, 284n113, 641t, 665n50
Stemen, Don, 75n47
Stephens, Gene, 212n99
Stephens, Peggy C., 441
Stephens, Richard C., 441
Stepp, Stephanie D., 74n45
Sterk, Claire, 247n18, 248n70
Stermac, Lana, 326n136
Stetson, Barbara, 179n186
Stevens, Alex, 664n1, 664n15, 665n60, 665n62, 666n70
Stevens, Bradley R., 482n11
Stevens, H., 131n188
Stevens, Tia, 278, 285n166
Stevens, Tomika, 416n75
Stevenson, Bryan, 590n122
Stevenson, Margaret, 127n30
Stewart, Anna, 130n148
Stewart, Chris, 614
Stewart, Claire, 133n286
Stewart, Daniel M., 549n10
Stewart, Eric, 155, 178n121, 211n25, 222e, 249n104, 284n69
Stewart, Eric A., 131n183
Stice, Eric, 296
Stickle, Wendy Povitsky, 511
Stinney, George, Jr., 581
Stockdale, Laura, 115
Stoddard, Cody, 40n100
Stoddard-Dare, Patricia, 589n36
Stoff, David, 449n60
Stogner, John, 178n122, 247n30, 284n69
Stokes, Benjamin, 589n51
Stokes, Robert, 416n82, 416n86
Stolzenberg, Lisa, 57, 75n52, 75n57, 170, 180n233, 324n42
Stone, Glenda, 573
Stone, Lawrence, 39n37, 39n43
Storgaard, Anette, 666n96
Storr, C. L., 177n66
Stouthamer-Loeber, Madga, 247n26, 247n29, 247n31, 250n164, 250n171, 323n22, 324n40, 324n67, 377n141, 482n11
Stowell, Jacob, 75n70
Strachman, Amy, 39n6
Strain, Eric, 449n83
Strang, Emily, 127n13
Strang, Heather, 604, 630nn35–39
Strasburg, Paul, 534, 550n57
Stratton, Howard, 250n180

Straus, Murray, 297, 304, 325n70, 325nn71–72, 326n123, 326n124, 326n125, 326n126
Streib, Victor, 550n52, 590n119, 590nn115–116
Streuning, Elmer, 211n9
Strodtbeck, Fred, 180n207, 335e
Strom, Marin, 130n135
Stuart, Hunter, 160, 179n180
Stuart, Jaimee, 375n26
Stults, Brian, 75n52, 590n103
Sturges, Susan, 415n2
Su, Chang, 644
Subramanian, S. V., 176n7
Subrick, Stephen, 130n138
Sullivan, Carrie Coen, 518n75
Sullivan, Christopher, 133n269, 247n42, 247n43, 247n44, 249n112, 249n114, 323n21, 449n64, 482n28, 482n33, 485n132, 511, 518n75, 589n55
Sullivan, Joe, 582
Sullivan, Mercer, 361, 377n170
Sum, Andrew, 415n15
Superle, Tamy, 666n68
Susser, Ezra S., 130n131
Sutherland, Alex, 552n131
Sutherland, Edwin, 121, 134n318, 161–163, 179n182, 179n183, 179n184
Sutton, John R., 39n52, 517nn33–34
Sutton, Tara, 132n239
Svensson, Robert, 128n66
Swahn, Monica, 416n74
Swanger, Harry F., 590n136
Swanson, Kristi, 619
Swartz, James A., 128n72
Swartz, Kristin, 177n75
Sweeten, Gary, 151, 178n120, 178n139, 211n20, 248n86, 250n134, 388, 415n24
Swisher, Raymond, 248n74, 248n75, 325n91
Swords, Daniel, *314*
Sykes, Gini, 357, 377n144
Sykes, Gresham, 180n202, 180n204
Sykes, Richard, 550n22
Szymanski, Linda, 550n33, 590n94, 591n143

T

Taanila, Anja, 131n172
Tabor, Mary, 448n21
Tackett, Jennifer, 375n22
Tackett-Gibson, Melissa, 450n136
Tagliabue, John, 664n10
Taheri, Sema, 128n58, 417n104, 484n103, 484n108
Tamminen, Tuulk, 324n27
Tanamly, Susie, 450n152
Tancredi, Laurence, 130n143
Tang, Deliang, 130n126
Tannenbaum, Frank, 192, 211n56, 211n61
Tanner, Julian, 212n75
Tanner-Smith, Emily E., 450n149
Tansi, Robert, 633n167
Tapia, Mike, 378n192, 378n204
Tappan, Paul, 497
Tatchell, Renny, 250n179
Tatchell, Thomas, 250n179
Tate, Marcus, *458*
Tatelbaum, Robert, 482n35
Taub, Richard, 212n89
Tauri, Juan, 656
Taussig, Cara, 327n188, 327n190
Taussig, Heather, 327n174
Taxman, Faye S., 632n114
Taylor, Alan, 131n199, 132n205, 324n43
Taylor, Bruce, 129n100
Taylor, Jeanette, 132n203
Taylor, Qiuordai, 137
Taylor, Ralph, 176n46, 177n87
Taylor, Terrance J., 524, 551n103, 551nn105–106
Taylor, Wendy, 129n89
Taylor-Seehafer, Margaret A., 450n144
Tear, Morgan, 115
Teasdale, Brent, 441
Tekin, Erdal, 317, 327n178
Telep, Cody, 53, 550n31, 550nn19–20, 552n118
Temple, Judy A., 483n69, 483n70, 483n71, 483n72
Teo, Mackenzie, *312*
Teplin, Linda A., 447n4, 448n47, 588n28, 614
ter Laak, Jan, 284n90
Terloux, Gert-Jan, 665n50
Terman, L. M., 134n311

Subject Index

In this index *t* indicates table, *f* indicates figure, and *e* indicates exhibit.

Missouri (*continued*)
    parental responsibility laws, 35
    public access to juvenile hearings, 584
    racial discrimination in court process, 563
MISTY. *See* Mentoring Initiative for System Involved
    Youth (MISTY)
Mobilization for Youth (MOBY), 457, 477
MOBY. *See* Mobilization for Youth (MOBY)
Model Youth Correction Authority Act, 609
Monetary policy, 200
Monetary restitution, 604, 605
Monitoring the Future (MTF) study, 47, 53–55,
    424–426
Monozygotic (MZ) twins, 105, 106
Mood disorder, 111
Moral beliefs, 168
Moral entrepreneurs, 185
Mother's employment, 298
MPD. *See* Multiple personality disorder (MPD)
MS-13 gang, 329, *340*, 351
MST. *See* Multisystemic therapy (MST)
MTF. *See* Monitoring the Future (MTF) study
MTFC. *See* Multidimensional treatment foster care
    (MTFC)
MTV generation, 4e
Multidimensional treatment foster care (MTFC), 509,
    606, 607
Multiple personality disorder (MPD), 302
Multisystemic therapy (MST), 442, 443
My Brother's Keeper, *464*
MZ twins, Monozygotic (MZ) twins

N

National Advisory Commission on Criminal Justice
    Standards and Goals, 31, 499
National Advisory Committee on Handicapped
    Children, 100
National Bar Association, 616
National Center for Children in Poverty, 175
National Center for Education Statistics (NCES), 383,
    384, 387, 390
National Center for Juvenile Justice, 516
National Center for Learning Disabilities, 102
National Center for Mental Health and Juvenile
    Justice, 614
National Center for State Courts (NCSC), 575
National Center on Addiction and Substance Abuse,
    447
National Council of Juvenile and Family Court
    Judges, 560
National Council on Alcoholism and Drug
    Dependence, 422
National Council on Crime and Delinquency, 615,
    623
National Crime Prevention Council, 481
National Crime Victimization Survey (NCVS)
    defined, 49
    methodological problems, 49
    modifications, 49
    relationship between victims and offenders, 70
National detention trends, 562–563, 562f
National Drug Intelligence Center, 423
National Gang Center (NGC), 335e, 355, 366, 374
National Gang Intelligence Center (NGIC), 351, 363
National Gang Report, 338
National Girls Initiative, 616
National health care policy, 7
National Incident-Based Reporting System
    (NIBRS), 46
National Institute of Justice, 542
National Institute on Drug Abuse, 447
National Juvenile Justice Standards Project, 31
National Library of Medicine, 323
National Longitudinal Study of Adolescent Health,
    101
National Longitudinal Survey of Youth, 436
National Mentoring Resource Center, 470
National Scholastic Press Association journalism
    website, 282
National Survey of Children's Exposure to Violence
    (NatSCEV), 69
National Survey on Drug Use and Health (NSDUH),
    427, 441, 442
National Youth Anti-Drug Media Campaign, 441
National Youth Gang Survey (NYGS), 338
National Youth Survey, 437
National Youth Tobacco Survey, 424

Native Americans, Pine Ridge reservation, *151*
NatSCEV. *See* National Survey of Children's
    Exposure to Violence (NatSCEV)
Nature theory, 120–121
Nature versus nurture, 120–121. *See also* Genetic
    factors
NCES. *See* National Center for Education Statistics
    (NCES)
NCLB. *See* No Child Left Behind (NCLB)
NCSC. *See* National Center for State Courts (NCSC)
Near-groups, 342
Nebraska, life without parole, 583
Needle exchange programs, 444
Negative affective states, 151–152
Negative experiences, 152
Negative life events, 218–219
Neglect, 302. *See also* Abuse and neglect
Neighborhood decay, 143
Neighborhood supervision, 562
Neighborhood Watch, 442
Neighborhood watch program, 91
Nepal, 274
Netherlands, 652t, 653, 655
Network of affiliates, 163. *See also* Peers
Neurological, 98
Neurological dysfunction, 98–103
Neuroticism, 119
Neutralization techniques, 164
Neutralization theory, 163–166, 171
Nevada, statutory exclusion policies, 570–571
Nevil family murders, 295
New Hampshire
    age of juvenile jurisdiction, 23
    "Romeo and Juliet" law, 186
New Jersey
    child detention centers, 561
    Essexfields Rehabilitation Project, 607–608
    foster children in secure detention, 611
    reporting abuse, 309
    transfer to adult court, 574
"New Kid Ruse," 70
New York City
    Brownsville, *198*
    child savers, 21
    crack gangs, 435
    drug-related homicides, 435
    gang-control efforts, 370
    MOBY, 457
    Pan Am Shelter, *5*
    police presence in schools, 403
    Project Confirm, 562
    stop, question, and frisk practices, 536
New York House of Refuge, 608. *See also* House of
    Refuge
New York State
    age of juvenile jurisdiction, 23
    Nixzmary's law, 301
    oldest age for juvenile court jurisdiction, 500t
    Southwest Key Programs, 29
    State Agricultural and Industrial School, 608
    status offenders, 32
    transfer to adult court, 574
New Zealand, 206–207, 638
Next Door Foundation, *464*
NGC. *See* National Gang Center (NGC)
NGIC. *See* National Gang Intelligence Center (NGIC)
NIBRS. *See* National Incident-Based Reporting
    System (NIBRS)
Nixzmary's law, 301
No Child Left Behind (NCLB), 404
Nonintervention, 195
Nonjudicial adjustment, 566
Nonjudicial disposition, 566
Nonjustice delinquency prevention, 454. *See also*
    Delinquency prevention
Nonresidential programs, 607–608
Nonsecure facilities, 563
Nonstarters, 237
North Carolina
    age of juvenile jurisdiction, 23
    notifying court of suspected abuse, 310
    oldest age for juvenile court jurisdiction, 500t
Northern Reception Center and Clinic, 609
NSDUH. *See* National Survey on Drug Use and
    Health (NSDUH)
Nuclear family, 287
Nurse-Family Partnership (NFP), 453, 462
Nurture theory, 121

NYGS. *See* National Youth Gang Survey (NYGS)
NYPD School Safety Division, 403

O

Obamacare, 7
Observational and interview research, 50e
ODD. *See* Oppositional defiant disorder (ODD)
OECD. *See* Organisation for Economic Cooperation
    and Development (OECD)
Off-campus speech, 408–409
Offense specialization/generalization, 220
Office of Community Oriented Policing Services
    (COPS), 525, 545, 549
Office of Juvenile Justice and Delinquency
    Prevention (OJJDP)
    "Beyond the Walls: Improving Conditions of
        Confinement for Youth in Custody," 616
    correctional facilities, 610
    defined, 28
    deinstitutionalization, 626
    disproportionate confinement of minority
        offenders, 627
    Due Process Advocacy, 576
    Evaluation of Teen Courts Project, 511
    Gang Reduction Program, 369
    goals, 499
    Homebuilders, 319
    National Girls Initiative, 616
    SafetyNet: Smart Cyber Choices, 527
    secure lockups, 28
    separation of juvenile detainees, 564
    Statistical Briefing Book (SBB), 588
    website, 516
Office of National Drug Control Policy, 439
Office of the Surgeon General, 516
Office on Smoking and Health, 447
Official labeling, 187, 190
O.H. Close Youth Correctional Facility, *120*
Ohio, cottage system, 609
OJJDP. *See* Office of Juvenile Justice and Delinquency
    Prevention (OJJDP)
OJJDP Evaluation of Teen Courts Project, 511
OJJDP Statistical Briefing Book (SBB), 588
Oklahoma
    banning over-the-counter cold medicine, 423
    parental responsibility laws, 35
Olweus Program, 398
Omega-6 fats, 97
107 Hoover Crips, 351
Open institutions, 608
Open Society Institute, 447
Open vs. closed hearings, 584
Operation Blue Orchid, 636
Operation Ceasefire, 88, 367, 544–545, 547
Operation Gray Lord, 439
Operation Innocence Lost program, 275
Operation Night Light, 367
Operation Peacekeeper, 369
Operation Webslinger, 439
Oppositional defiant disorder (ODD), 111
Oregon, legalization of marijuana, 420
Oregon Social Learning Center (OSLC), 463–464
Organisation for Economic Cooperation and
    Development (OECD), 664
Organizational bias, 539
Organized crime and youth gangs, 358
Organized gang, 341
Oriana House, 367
Orphan trains, 494
Orphan's court, 20
OSLC. *See* Oregon Social Learning Center (OSLC)
Other Wes Moore: One Name, Two Fates, The (Moore),
    471
Outpatient psychotherapy, 578e
Overachieving students, 165–166
Overt pathway, 238, 238f
Overview. *See* Concept summary
Oxycontin, 426

P

"p/v," 346
Pacatal, 422
PACE. *See* Practical Academic Cultural Educational
    (PACE) Center
PALS. *See* Participate and Learn Skills (PALS)
Pan Am Shelter, *5*
Panel on Juvenile Crime, 512